AA HOTELS AND RESTAURANTS IN BRITAIN

Editor: Patricia Kelly

Consultant Editor: I M Tyers

Designer: Richard Brown Associates

Maps by: Cartographic Department

Compiled by: Publications Research Unit

Advertising by: Peter Whitworth
Tel Basingstoke 20123

WARNING:
The majority of establishments in this guide quote prices inclusive of VAT at 8%
This must be taken into account.

CONTENTS

The contents of this publication are believed correct at the time of printing, but the current position may be checked through the AA. While every effort is made to ensure that information appearing in advertisements is correct, no responsibility can be accepted by the AA for any inaccuracies.

Produced by the Publications Division of the Automobile Association, Fanum House, Basingstoke, Hampshire RG21 2EA.

ISBN 0 86145 006 X 55835

CONTENTS

Town plans in this book are based on the Ordnance Survey Map with the sanction of the Controller, HMSO.
Photographs by courtesy of Malcolm Reid and Colin Long, the Roux Brothers, Pierre Koffman and the BTA.

Phototypeset by Vantage Photosetting Co Ltd, Southampton.
Printed and bound in Great Britain by William Clowes (Beccles) Ltd.
Colour printing by Camgate Litho Ltd, London.

Symbols and abbreviations

Explanations of criteria used in classification and of various symbols may be found in *About this guide* on page 22.

- ✱ 1979 prices
- Telephone
- Private bathroom/shower with own toilet
- Four-poster beds
- Night porter
- Air conditioning throughout
- Room(s) set aside for non-smokers
- Central heating throughout
- No dogs allowed overnight in hotel bedrooms
- P Open parking for cars
- Garage or covered space
- No parking on premises
- No coach parties accepted
- Garden over ½ acre
- Indoor swimming pool
- Outdoor swimming pool
- 9-hole golf course
- 18-hole golf course
- Tennis court(s)
- Fishing
- Riding stables on premises
- Special facilities for children (see *About this guide* page 23)
- Type of cooking. If this symbol is not shown, the type of cooking is English, Scottish or Welsh according to the part of Britain in which the hotel is situated
- Afternoon tea
- Morning coffee
- The hotel can accommodate disabled persons (see *About this guide* page 24)
- S% Service charge levied and included in prices
- This symbol shows that the hotel offers cheaper off-season weekends

alc	*à la carte*
sB&B	Single room including breakfast per person per night
sB&B	Single room with private bath/shower and toilet and breakfast per person per night
dB&B	Double room (2 persons) including breakfast
dB&B	Double room (2 persons) with private bath/shower and toilet and breakfast
CTV	Colour television (see *About this guide* page 30)
Etr	Easter
fr	from
Map	National grid reference
mdnt	midnight
Plan	Number gives location of hotel or restaurant on town plan
rm	Letting bedrooms in main building
RS	Restricted service (see *About this guide* page 30)
TV	Monochrome television (see *About this guide* page 30)
Wine	Minimum price of full bottle of wine *(eg 70cl)*
xmas	Special Christmas 1979 programme for residents

Prices

Prices should always be checked before booking as they are likely to fluctuate significantly during the currency of this guide. The effect of inflation, possible variation in the rate of VAT and indeed many other factors, may influence prices in the coming year. Published prices, which have been provided by hoteliers and restaurateurs in good faith, must therefore be accepted as indications rather than firm estimates.

Credit cards

The numbered boxes below indicate the credit cards which the hotels and restaurants accept.

1	Access	4	Carte Blanche
2	American Express	5	Diners
3	Barclays Visa	6	Euro

Symboles et abréviations

Les explications des critères utilisés pour le classement et des divers symboles se trouvent dans *About this guide*, page 22.

- ✱ prix 1979
- téléphone
- salle de bain/douche particulière avec WC particuliers
- Lits à quatre montants
- Concierge de nuit
- Conditionnement d'air intégral
- Chambre(s) réservée(s) aux non-fumeurs
- Chauffage central intégral
- Défense de garder des chiens pendant la nuit dans les chambres
- P Stationnement pour voitures
- Garage à ciel ouvert ou à espaces couverts
- Pas de stationnement sur place
- Les groupes en car ne seront pas admis
- Jardin de plus de 0,20 ha.
- Piscine à l'intérieur
- Piscine à l'exterieur
- Terrain de golf à 9 trous
- Terrain de golf à 18 trous
- Court(s) de tennis
- Pêche
- Ecuries d'équitation sur les lieux
- Facilités spéciales pour enfants (page 23)
- Catégorie de cuisine. Si ce symbole ne figure pas, la cuisine est anglaise, écossaise ou galloise, selon la région de la Grande-Bretagne où l'hôtel se trouve
- Thé l'après-midi
- Café le matin
- L'hôtel peut recevoir des invalides
- S% Le service est compris dans les prix
- Ce symbole indique que l'hôtel offre des week-ends à prix réduit hors saison

alc	*à la carte*
sB&B	Chambre à un lit et petit déjeuner par personne et par nuit
sB&B	Chambre à un lit avec bain/douche et WC particuliers, et petit déjeuner par personne et par nuit
dB&B	Chambre à deux lits (2 personnes) avec petit déjeuner
dB&B	Chambre à deux lits (2 personnes) avec bain/douche, et WC particuliers, et petit déjeuner par personne et par nuit
CTV	TV en couleurs (page 30)
Etr	Pâques
fr	à partir de
Map	Repère du quadrillage de carte national
mdnt	minuit
Plan	Le numéro indique l'emplacement de l'hôtel ou du restaurant sur le plan de la ville
rm	Location de chambres dans le bâtiment principal
RS	Service limité
TV	TV en noir et blanc (page 30)
Wine	Prix minimum d'une bouteille de vin (70cl)
xmas	Programme spécial de Noël 1979 pour les clients

Prix

Il conviendra dans tous les cas de vérifier les prix avant de réserver car ils peuvent subir des fluctuations considérables au cours de la disponibilité du présent guide. Les effets de l'inflation, toutes modifications de la TVA et en fait de nombreux autres facteurs pourraient influer sur les prix pendant l'année. Les prix publiés, qui ont été indiqués par les hôtels et les restaurants en toute bonne foi, devront en conséquence s'entendre comme indication plutôt qu'un tarif ferme.

Cartes de crédit

Les numéros ci-dessous indiquent les cartes de crédit acceptées par les hôtels et les restaurants.

1	Access	4	Carte Blanche
2	American Express	5	Diners
3	Barclays Visa	6	Euro

Zeichenerklärung

Erklärungen über die Klassifizierung und die Zeichen sind auf Seite 22 aufgeführt.

- * 1979 Preise
- ☎ Telefon
- Zimmer mit Privatbad/Dusche und WC
- Himmelbett
- Nachtportier
- Klimaanlage durchaus
- Sonderzimmer für Nichtraucher
- Fernheizung durchaus
- Hundeverbot im Zimmer während der Nacht
- P Parken im Freien
- Garagen bzw. Überdachtes Parken
- Parken an Ort und Stelle
- Reisebusgesellschaften nicht aufgenommen
- Garten grösser als einen halben Acre
- Hallenbad
- Freibad
- 9 Golfplatz mit 9 Holes
- 18 Golfplatz mit 18 Holes
- Tennisplatz (Plätze)
- Angeln
- Reitstall an Ort und Stelle
- Sonderdienstleistungen für Kinder (seite 23)
- Küche. Wenn dieses Zeichen nicht aufgeführt wird, ist die Küche englisch, schottisch oder walisisch je nach der Gegend, wo das Hotel sich befindet
- Nachmittagstee
- Kaffee vormittags
- ♿ Für Körperbehinderte geeignet
- S% Bedienungsgeld erhoben und Preise sind einschl. Bedienungsgeld
- Betrieb gibt Wochenendermässigungen für Vor- und Nachsaison
- alc *à la carte*
- sB&B Übernachtung in einem Einzelzimmer mit Frühstück pro Person
- sB&B Übernachtung in einem Einzelzimmer mit Bad/Dusche und WC mit Frühstück pro Person
- dB&B Doppelzimmer (2 Personen) mit Frühstück
- dB&B Doppelzimmer (2 Personen) mit Privatbad/Dusche und WC mit Frühstück
- CTV Farbfernsehen (seite 30)
- Etr Ostern
- fr Von
- Map Planquadratangabe
- mdnt Mitternacht
- Plan Nummer gibt die Lage des Hotels am Stadtplan an
- rm Zimmeranzahl im Hauptgebäude
- RS Beschränkte Dienstleistungen
- TV Schwarzweissfernsehen (seite 30)
- Wine Mindestpreis für eine Flasche Wein (dh 70cl)
- *xmas* Sonderweihnachtsprogramm für Gäste in 1979

Verklaring der tekens

Verklaring der tekens en classificatie kunnen op pagina 22 gevonden worden.

- * 1979 prijzen
- ☎ Telefoon
- privé badkamer/douche met toilet
- hemelbedden
- nachtportier
- overal air conditioning
- kamer(s) gereserveerd voor niet-rokers
- overal centrale verwarming
- 's nachts geen honden toegelaten op kamers
- P open parkeerplaats
- garage of overdekte parkeerruimte
- Verboden op het terrein te parkeren
- geen busreisgezelschappen toegelaten
- tuin groter dan 0,2ha
- overdekt zwembad
- openlucht zwembad
- 9 9-hole golfbaan
- 18 18-hole golfbaan
- tennisba(a)n(en)
- visplaats
- manege op terrein
- speciale voorzieningen voor kinderen (pagina 23)
- keuken. Wanneer dit symbool niet wordt aangegeven, dan is de keuken Engels, Schots of Wales afhankelijk van waar het hotel is gelegen
- middag thee
- ochtend koffie
- ♿ het hotel kan invaliden opnemen
- S% bedieningsgeld geheven en bij prijs inbegrepen
- hotel biedt weekendkortingen aan in voor – en naseizoen
- alc *à la carte*
- sB&B éénpersoonskamer inclusief ontbijt per persoon per nacht
- sB&B éénpersoonskamer met badkamer/douche en toilet, inclusief ontbijt per persoon per nacht
- dB&B tweepersoonskamer inclusief ontbijt
- dB&B tweepersoonskamer met badkamer/douche en toilet, inclusief ontbijt
- CTV Kleurentelevisie (pagina 30)
- Etr Pasen
- fr van af
- Map coördinaten referentie
- mdnt middernacht
- Plan nummer geeft lokatie van hotel op plattegrond aan
- rm aantal kamers in hoofdgebouw
- RS beperkte service
- TV Zwart/wit televisie (pagina 30)
- Wine minimum prijs voor fles wijn (70cl)
- *xmas* speciaal Kerstmisprogramma voor hotelgasten in 1979

Preise

Preise sollten vor der Reservierung nachgeprüft werden, weil wesentliche Änderungen während der Gültigkeit des Reiseführers zustandekommen könnten. Die Inflation, eventuelle MWSt – Änderungen könnten die Preise im Laufe des Jahres beeinflussen. Die veröffentlichten Preise, die von Hotel – und Restaurant Besitzern in gutem Glauben zur Verfügung gestellt werden, müssen deshalb eher als Grobpreise und nicht als Festpreise angesehen werden.

Kreditkarten

Die untenaufgeführten Zahlen bezeichen die von Hotels und Restaurants angenommenen Kreditkarten:–

1 Access
2 American Express
3 Barclays Visa
4 Carte Blanche
5 Diners
6 Euro

Prijzen

Kontroleer altijd de prijzen voordat u boekt, aangezien aanzienlijke veranderingen kunnen plaatsvinden tijdens de geldigheidsduur van deze gids. Inflatie, mogelijke variatie in de BTW percentages kunnen de prijzen in het komende jaar beïnvloeden. Gepubliceerde prijzen, die door de hotel – en restauranteigenaars in goed vertrouwen ter beschikking zijn gesteld, moeten daarom gezien worden als globale prijzen en niet als vaststaande prijzen.

Kredietkaarten

De hierna vermelde Getallen geven de kredietkaarten aan, die door hotels en restaurants worden geaccepteerd.

1 Access
2 American Express
3 Barclays Visa
4 Carte Blanche
5 Diners
6 Euro

NEVER MIND THE QUALITY...

Ian Tyers,
Consultant Editor

What is value for money? Like beauty, it is largely in the eye of the beholder – difficult to describe, but you know when you have experienced it.

To be fair, if you choose to stay in a Park Lane hotel in London, you must expect to pay high prices for the benefit of enjoying the services provided in an establishment built on one of the most expensive pieces of real estate in England (with all that it means in terms of fixed overheads). So do not compare the costs with its provincial equivalent. But when our inspectors report from hotels in different parts of the country that newspapers are charged at double their price plus VAT, telephone calls attract mark-ups of well over 100%, coffees and afternoon teas are offered at outrageous prices, (presumably positively to discourage custom) there must be serious doubts whether or not these establishments want to provide value for money in their overall pricing structure.

A discerning customer can use a simple rule of thumb to assess value for money. Having patronised a hotel or restaurant, he can ask himself two questions. 'Did I enjoy myself'? and 'will I return'? If the answer is yes to both, the hotelier or restaurateur has few problems.

Standards in restaurants show a steady improvement, but there are still a number of niggling practices which continue to offend. A glaring example is the exorbitant cover charge: up to 75p in many places without anything to show for it except a roll, butter and condiments. It is either due to greed on the part of the caterer, or a miscalculation of fair food costings to cover overheads.

Another example is the price of vegetables. It has been encouraging to note the improvement in the provision and preparation of fresh vegetables but with prices as high as £1.25 in certain establishments in central London and 60–75p, outside, one wonders what has happened to people's sense of value. Together, cover charge, potatoes, and green vegetables and coffee can amount to around a third of the total food bill! And all this before service charge and VAT.

Thankfully, our inspectors report a country-wide improvement in accommodation standards. Hotels are offering more attractive décor, greater comfort, and significantly more private bathrooms. But however luxurious a hotel may be, however excellent the food offered, a visit can be made or marred by the service. Hoteliers often complain that it is difficult to attract and retain the right staff. But employers who care about the welfare of their staff can overcome these problems. A newcomer with the right personality is an asset to any business. With encouragement and a guiding hand he will soon learn and, even if his inexperience still shows, his cheerful and friendly approach to customers will be worth more than the grudging correctness of his trained, though unmotivated counterpart.

That it is possible to give a warm welcome, and achieve high standards in hospitality, facilities and service, while still running a profitable business, is shown by the number of hotels and establishments which this year have won our approval. Red stars, for hotels, and rosettes for food and service in restaurants, are used by the AA to highlight those establishments that our inspectors have recommended as being of special merit.

To show you in detail the qualities necessary to win these awards, the Chief Hotel Inspector describes four such establishments in his article on pages 9–19.

Of 3,840 hotels classified by the AA in this guide, 42 have been awarded red stars. Of 1,136 restaurants, five hold the triple rosette for excellent cuisine, twelve the double rosette and 156 the single rosette. There is, of course, still scope for improvement.

These awards achieve two aims. First, they inform AA members and travellers from home and abroad of hotels and restaurants which are the best of their kind, however elaborate or however simple. Second, they encourage hoteliers and restaurateurs in Great Britain to strive for higher standards, not only by providing better amenities, facilities, food and service, but also by offering that extra touch of welcome and hospitality which, though intangible and indefinable, can be recognised by the guest at once, and which he will remember long after he has left.

In the past we have been criticised for the strong views we have expressed on many facets of the catering industry. We make no apology; it has been, and continues to be, our objective to give praise where we feel praise is due, and to censure where this is considered appropriate and necessary.

For 1980 we make a special plea to Managers. Show yourselves! A hotel is as good as its manager. He should be seen by his guests and, within reason, hold himself readily available to them. His regular presence at the point of sale would do wonders to quality control and act as an inspiration and example to his staff. This can only serve to benefit the customer.

It is, of course, for the customer and the potential customer that this book has been prepared. We are grateful to readers whose comments have helped us to improve its presentation, and to hoteliers and restaurateurs who have co-operated so willingly in providing the information on which it is based.

If it helps visitors to find a hotel or restaurant to suit their requirements, and at the same time encourages further improvement of standards in British hotels and restaurants, it will have achieved its aim.

FOUR MORE OF THE BEST

Geoffrey Lerway, the AA's Chief Hotels Inspector

Last year we reported the influence of gifted amateurs in the hotel and restaurant industry. This year – for no particular reason – three out of my four choices are, on the contrary, well-trained professionals.
Bur firstly, I revert to the **Box Tree at Ilkley**, arguably the best restaurant outside of London and Bray, whose owners Malcolm Reid and Colin Long started 18 years ago from other walks of life.

Malcolm Reid and Colin Long

❀❀❀XXXBox Tree, Ilkley, West Yorkshire

Both men were born in Leeds and eventually met at a tennis club in 1956. They discovered a mutual enjoyment of food, both having been brought up in homes where food was considered important. (I am increasingly aware and impressed by the influence good home cooking has had on everyone I meet in the food world, whether professional or not.) They used to save up for weeks in order to spend a weekend in London at a good hotel like the Savoy or Dorchester. They also visited the Continent and discovered French food, that which was to play so important a part in their careers.

Then their paths separated – Malcolm Reid bought a snack bar and Colin Long went to sea on P & O liners. On one of his leaves they met again and discussed their future. They decided to enter the restaurant business. Colin had to return to sea while Malcolm looked for suitable premises. He found a café for sale in Ilkley and went to see it but was diverted by an attractive little cottage that was also for sale. After a talk with his father who pointed out that although he was thinking about the café, all he in fact talked about was the cottage, he realised that he truly liked it. So, after borrowing the money from his parents he bought Box Tree Cottage. He cabled Colin who was at the other end of the world and he came back six weeks later.

The 300-years-old cottage was originally a farmhouse with attractive features but had been neglected. There was much to be done. Finally they were able to open in September 1962 when they served afternoon teas only. They were a success and an encouragement to the young owners, and gave them the confidence to serve lunches. From that moment on, they learned as they went along, continuing to visit other restaurants and reproducing dishes that took their fancy. From these small beginnings, they went on to serve dinners, after obtaining a license, and have never looked back. Right from the start, they had decided that they would serve nothing but the best, fresh, wholesome food so that, although the menus were simply English, the food was of good quality, decently cooked and therefore enjoyable.

As the business grew and became more prosperous, they felt able to spend more on the Box Tree's décor. Initially they had bought some reproduction paintings to brighten up the place. One day they were chagrined to hear one of their customers – a duchess with a piercing voice, exclaim, – 'It's very nice, but, of course, it's all reproduction'. They ruefully decided that they would never again buy anything but the genuine article. Nor have they! Over the last ten years the restaurant has been extended until it now seats about 50 and is beautifully decorated with antiques, objets d'art, pictures, prints, lithographs, porcelain and bric à brac, together with flowers informally arranged in attractive vessels.

It is rare in my experience for two men to teach themselves to cook with such classic skill and with such a sense of gastronomic art. Their not-too-long menus present an adequate choice of dishes that will not preclude anyone, whatever their taste, from selecting a well-balanced meal. They long ago dropped teas and lunches so that they could concentrate on the grand cuisine. The menu is of four courses and priced from £10.50 to £12.75 according to the main course chosen.

To begin with, you may choose a dariole de champignons et truffles; a mould is lined with a quenelle mixture of chicken, filled with chopped mushrooms and truffles, cooked and served with an exquisitely delicate Madeira sauce. Another choice could be the mousse de sole reputation – it was as light and as flavoursome as one could wish for. Amongst the main courses praised have been the saddle of hare with two purées, of chestnut and mushrooms, with a game sauce; medallions of beef with peppercorns in a Brouilly sauce, and sweetbreads Perigourdine. That increasingly popular pudding, marquise de chocolat au cognac – with plenty of cognac – seems to be a favourite among the desserts but they have all been praised, particularly the coupe de truffes pralin and meringue Alicia Markova.

Box Tree can boast a wine list of 200, some dating back to 1937. There are other rarities which can be expensive in terms of money but not in value – some, I suspect, could hardly be replaced at the price at which they are sold here. In any case, there are lots of good wines at moderate prices as well as a fair selection of half bottles that can make life more interesting for the enthusiast who wants a comparative tasting.

Colin and Malcolm have earned the loyalty of their staff who have been trained to look after you attentively. If I have a criticism, it is more directed to the hierarchy in the restaurant whose knowledge of food and wine does not match the skills in the kitchen. But perhaps this is carping. I am of the opinion that food lovers in Britain owe them a debt of gratitude for their pioneering efforts. They speak lightheartedly of their early difficulties but I know that they must have had a hard time. They stuck to their guns and eventually helped to convert the public to their type of food.

Colin and Malcolm tell the story of one Sunday lunchtime, when they had inadvertently sent a sauce boat of chocolate sauce instead of gravy to a customer for his roast beef. Too late to correct it they waited for the waitress to return and told her to try and save the situation. She went to the customer and asked how his beef was, by now covered with the sauce. He replied, 'Eeh, it's luvely, Luv'. Well, I suppose it is possible that they might still get the odd customer like that today. What is most unlikely is that such an error would occur, because Malcolm Reid and Colin Long, years ago completely untutored in the art of cooking, are now, as the brass plate outside proclaims, 'Restaurateurs'.

❀❀❀XXXLe Gavroche, London SW1

The Roux Brothers

When watching high-class competitive events such as the Olympic Games I have always been impressed by the margin by which the winner seems to exceed his world-class competitors. And so it is with the cooking at Le Gavroche! To me it stands head and shoulders above the rest of the competition in Britain.

The reasons are not hard to find. When one knows the Roux brothers, the owners of the restaurant, one understands the dedication to perfection which motivates them. Born in Charolles near Lyon, an area famous for its cuisine, they come from three generations of charcutiers and pâtissiers. They both went to Paris for their apprenticeship in Pâtisserie and this they firmly believe to be the best foundation for all cookery. When one has learnt the delicacy and balance necessary for pastry cooking the art can be translated to produce better-quality savoury cooking. This is indicated by the fact that the younger brother, Michel, is one of the few men to have become a Meilleur Oeuvrier de France in pastry and cookery.

Another great influence on their skills has been the people they have worked for. Though trained in the highest of classical principles the Roux brothers have never worked for commercial interests but for embassies and private families where the personal taste of their employers has had its influence in altering classical dishes to produce a cuisine that is delicate and soignée.

Albert has worked for the British and the French Embassies, Lady Astor, Mr Charles Clore and Mr & Mrs Cazelet, the well-known race horse trainers. Michel has worked for the British Embassy in Paris and also for the Rothschild family. He went there as a sous-chef before his National Service and afterwards at the age of 25 he returned as chef de cuisine.

Having always wanted to run a restaurant, in the mid '60s they turned their minds to setting up on their own. Naturally they first thought of opening somewhere in France but they realised they could operate a restaurant in London at half the price. With the support of Mr & Mrs Cazelet and some of their friends, they were able to do this in 1967. They quickly overcame their teething troubles and the restaurant was such an instant success they were able to repay their debts within two years. Unable to resist a challenge they went on to open Le Poulbot, Le Gamin, a simpler brasserie-type restaurant – both in the city and, finally, the Waterside at Bray. They also have a charcuterie in Lower Sloane Street.

Their particular brand of cooking is naturally based on tip-top quality raw materials prepared with delicacy and skill and slavish attention to fresh and natural flavours. Certain of their mousselines and sorbets have such intense flavours that they seem to taste like the concentrated essences of the main ingredients.

I particularly remember a dish I had earlier this year, aiguillettes de becasse au Chambertin; this was the breast of a woodcock, cooked nicely underdone, garnished with mousseline of the rest of the meat and served with a most delicate and limpid wine sauce made from the woodcock stock and, without resorting to flour, reduced to a glaze. Served with a delicious puree of spinach it was perfect for even the most jaded palate. I know of no other restaurant in Britain that can maintain such consistently high standards.

Le Gavroche is not large, it seats only 50, but it is a comfortable and elegant room with air conditioning. Most of the seating is banquette so that few parties have to be accommodated in the middle of the room. There is a bar but it is too small for anything other than a waiting area. After a welcoming greeting one's order is helpfully taken, and as a further aid in helping to choose, a series of beautifully presented cold dishes are brought to your table (indeed, one has not to let one's eyes rule one's stomach).

The menu changes periodically but there are a number of favourites which are usually to be found. Some examples are crême de cresson, rillettes de canard, mousselines de brochet Chloë, papillotte de saumon fume Claudine, le gratin de crabe au Jurançon and Coquilles St Jacques aux truffes among the first courses; sole Bacule, the famous caneton Gavroche, rognons de veau aux trois moutardes and tournedos Huguette; among the puddings are the famous charlotte aux poires J Millet, tarte des demoiselles Tatin and the sablé aux fraises but, as I have suggested, the sorbets are always acceptable, doubly so if one has chosen too rich a meal. Coffee and the petits fours secs, amongst the best I have ever tasted, particularly the miniature macaroons, follow, and complete a perfect meal.

There is a large list of over 200 wines, containing some rarities, for example, a Chateaux Lafite 1945 at £245! I wonder how many people can afford that? It is possible to select wines at more reasonable prices but they are never really cheap. And how can they be? It is a long list and the Roux brothers have a lot of money tied up in large stocks for the future. Moreover, unlike some less scrupulous restaurateurs, they do not put wines on their list before they are ready for drinking.

In conclusion, although it is such an expensive restaurant, I like it very much. I would rather eat here twice a year than almost anywhere else in Britain every month.

❀❀XX Tante Claire, London SW3

In September 1977 a new restaurant was opened in London by 30-year-old Pierre Koffman and his attractive wife Annie. After the slump in 1974 little had happened on the London restaurant scene so I suppose that it is understandable that a new venture of this quality would quickly get off the ground and be a success. And a success it has certainly been.

Tante Claire is run in the well-tried tradition of French restaurants where the proprietor does the cooking while his wife looks after the front of the house. It is also fashionable in being small – it seats only 35 – which is good because of the practicality of supervising a small place with comparative ease. The restaurant itself is a long and narrow room with luxuriously comfortable banquette seating, which has been designed by Michael Inchbeald, and Klimt prints on the walls. With the good table appointments, the whole makes for a quiet elegance that provides the right sort of atmosphere for eating out.

Pierre Koffman comes from Tarbes in south west France – an area known for its fine regional food – and he claims that the foundation of his fondness for good food and cooking is to be found in the region and in his family. His mother was a professional cook, but more particularly, he claims that his grandmother was his

Pierre Koffman, owner of Tante Claire

chief inspiration. With the best of raw materials at her disposal and with her innate cooking skills, she taught him about 'quality' and developed his liking for good food to the extent that he decided to make cooking his career.
After the usual gruelling course habitual at French cookery schools, he worked for various restaurants at Strasbourg, Juan les Pins, La Soutard and Lausanne. As he says, 'Nowhere very famous, but all good restaurants of repute with that serious French approach to food'.

In 1970 he came to Britain and joined the Roux brothers as chef de partie at Le Gavroche. He did well there and opened the Brasserie Benoits as chef de cuisine, the position which he later took at the Waterside at Bray. It was during his time in Britain that he met and married Annie. She, too, had attended a catering college and she joined him as manageress at the Waterside. In 1974 they returned to France but two years later came back again. Like most chefs, he wanted a restaurant of his own, and by now, had saved enough to start one with a manageable loan.

While he freely acknowledges the influence of the Roux brothers on his work, he is his own man and has evolved his own style of cuisine which he practices at the Tante Claire. He is modest and quiet and claims no great innovatory ability; he merely adapts classical dishes; nevertheless, many of his dishes do have individuality.

What raises Pierre Koffman's food to the heights it has achieved are not only the raw materials he uses – he naturally buys the best available even when it necessitates going to France for foie gras, truffles and primeurs, the wonderful chickens from Bresse and the Bordeaux pigeons – but his subtle and refined cooking, and, most especially, his gastronomic taste. One of his tours de force is andouillettes de la mer au vinaigre de cassis; this is a slice of turbot stuffed with a mousse mixture of fish with pieces of turbot and strips of smoked salmon, poached and served with a piquant sauce made from fish fumet, butter, vinegar and just the right amount of blackcurrants.

More simply, yet perhaps more subtle is the salade de homard aux fines herbes; lobster meat with just a little sliced chicken dressed on a salad of lettuce, watercress, enlivened with a touch of fresh mango and beautifully dressed with the herbs. More complicated but just as delicious is the pied de cochon farcie au ris de veau where a pig's foot is cooked, the bones removed and replaced with a delicate mousse of sweetbreads and braised, then served with a Madeira sauce. In some ways it reminds me of Chinese food in its use of texture; the gelatinous quality of the skin combines so well with and even enhances the sauce. It must be twenty years since I last had this dish and I was delighted to meet it again.

There are lots of other delicious things, the fine selection of puddings for instance, which include soufflé glace aux framboises and the light sorbets freshly made from whatever fruits are in season. But I could go on for ever!
The menu is à la carte and changes seasonally. At lunch there is an attractive table d'hôte at £27.00. On one side is the standard menu with about two choices for each course and, on the other, a cuisine minceur menu both representing excellent value.

As I have said, Mrs Koffman supervises out front with the help of Raymond Langlois as head waiter. He has come from Barrier's at Tours and is unfailing in his solicitous service with the aid of the rest of the French staff.
On talking to Pierre and Annie Koffman, they seem quite content. I asked them about their ambitions for the future and all they seemed to want was, not a bigger, but a better restaurant. Apparently they feel that their customers could be more comfortable so they would like a small bar area where the clientèle could gather while waiting for friends or for a table. At present there is no room for them to expand, so eventually they hope to be able to afford other premises more to their liking. Well I hope so; they have achieved success quite quickly. They must be the youngest restaurateurs to be awarded two rosettes, and I feel that they still have far to go; so far, in fact, that theirs might well turn out to be one of the really great British restaurants!

❀❀❀ XXXXX Connaught Hotel, London W1

In 1896 Auguste Scorrier bought the Coburg Hotel, which had been previously owned by the Grosvenor Estate, and set about re-building it with these prophetic words, 'the cuisine and the cellar will alike be sans reproche, and the Coburg Hotel will be found in every possible detail to justify its association with a part of London which has for generations, and is likely always to be, instinctively identified with all that is aristocratic, refined and luxurious in a metropolitan society'.

During the First World War, because of anti-German feeling, it was found necessary to change the name of the hotel to that of the King's brother-in-law, the Duke of Connaught. It has been known as the Connaught ever since. After the War it was run more as a private hotel with tables reserved for mostly permanent guests. Until Mr Rudolph Richard became the General Manager in 1935, that is. He was a well-qualified Swiss hotel-keeper and was determined to raise the standards to those of a well-kept private house with impeccable house-keeping, kitchen and wine cellar. Quietly and discreetly he began his self-imposed task, imperceptably achieving his improvements – notably the foundation of the fine wine cellar – until the outbreak of the last War. There were difficulties but the proximity of the American Embassy and the fact that General de Gaulle chose the Connaught as his wartime headquarters saved the hotel from going the way of the majority of hotels at that time. With peace, came the opportunity for Mr Richard to carry on his quest and the hotel established its reputation for providing the best of foods and wine.

Another milestone in the Hotel's history came with the appointment of Mr Daniel Dunas in 1965 as chef de cuisine. It was his time as chef with the Duke of Marlborough that encouraged his feeling for our English cooking which he translated so successfully to the Connaught. Unfortunately Mr Dunas was enticed back to Ottawa to work for the Governor General of Canada. Sadly the '70s turned out to be a period of great change, and when in 1973 Mr Pallo Zago took over the management of the hotel, he had grave doubts. However, he had a good background; born in Treviso in Italy, his first contact with the hotel trade was by helping his uncle, a wine merchant, to build a 25-roomed hotel – it grew into a 150-roomed hotel! He stayed on to help run it, decided that he liked the administrative side and set about a systematic training. Eventually he reached the Gritti Palace Hotel in Venice as Asst General Manager under the famous Raffaele Masprone. After seven years he took a similar position at the Excelsior Palace at the Lido, where he played a prominent part in restoring the hotel to its former glory. In 1971 he was invited by Sir Hugh Wontner to become Mr Fornara's assistant at the new Berkeley. Again he was concerned with the building and early organisation of the hotel.

Like Auguste Scorrier and Rudolph Richard he intended to maintain and reinforce the standards of the Connaught. His first test came with the departure of Chef Dunas. He was lucky to find Mr Michel Bourdin who was sous-chef at Maxims in Paris, working under the famous Alex Hubert; and before that at Le Doyen in Paris. So, appearing just the man, he was appointed chef de cuisine. In quick succession, Mr Chevalier was appointed Restaurant Manager and Mr Bovo, Grill Manager. With Mr Perez in charge of the private dining rooms, and the other old heads of departments and long-serving staff, the Connaught was set on course for another historic period. Now, six years later, Mr Zago and his team have every reason to be pleased with the progress they have made. The Connaught is often likened to a private house. I quite agree. It is easy to imagine oneself living there. The staff, too, contribute to this feeling. During my very first visit to the Hotel, when, late at night, I ordered early morning tea, on mentioning my room number the reply came very quickly, 'Oh, yes Mr Lerway, you like China tea, don't you? At what time would you like it?' The day waiter had passed on my preferences to the night waiter. There are many other incidents of this caring attitude.

If all this wasn't rare enough, the Connaught can also boast a fine, indeed, superb cuisine which must be unique in Britain. The surroundings, the service and the cuisine are eminently classical and to achieve such standards today is becoming increasingly rare. The strength of Michel Bourdin's cooking lies in its wonderful specialities. These exercise the highest skills and such items as quenelles de saumon fumé braisées au Champagne rose and contrefilet de boeuf farci Bressoise compôte de legumes frai indicate this. Apart from these dishes which appear daily, there is a small selection of permanent specialities which require ordering in advance. They feature items such as the zephyr de sole tout Paris; noisettes d'agneau Edward VII, or the caneton du Norfolk poêlé au citron, which is cooked under cover on the top of the stove and served with a delicious, refreshing lemon sauce.

Of course, such excellence does not come cheaply but I, at any rate, find the Connaught value for money. In fact, the residential side is much cheaper than at many more pretentious hotels in London. There are few places where you can find so complete an hotel – beautiful public rooms and bedrooms with every comfort, efficient and considerate staff *and* one of Britain's best restaurants.

CONNAUGHT TRIFLE

1 SPONGE CAKE
Sherry and Rum (6 tablespoons Sherry, 2 tablespoons Rum)
Blackberry jam
Sauce Anglaise
Whipped, sweetened cream
Almonds, cherries, angelica and redcurrant jelly

*****

Method:
Slice the sponge and spread with blackberry jam, then cut into small cubes, Soak each in the sherry and rum and pile up in a dish. Leave to soak for 1 to 2 hours. Make the Sauce Anglaise and, while hot, pour over the soaked sponge. Leave until well chilled, then pile with cream and decorate with split almonds, cherries, angelica and make a design with the redcurrant jelly.

Sauce Anglaise:
pt milk
3 egg yolks
2oz sugar

Method:
Boil milk. Beat yolks and sugar together. Add the boiling milk.
Return to pan and cook to thicken but do not boil.

KEY TO HOTEL AND RESTAURANT CLASSIFICATIONS

All listed hotels have bedrooms with hot and cold water, adequate bath and lavatory arrangements, service of all meals to residents and of most meals to non-residents. Details of the principal requirements for each classification are printed in the leaflet *Hotels and the Automobile Association* available from Hotels Department, AA Regional Headquarters, (addresses in *Members' Handbook*). It is emphasised that hotels often satisfy some of the requirements for higher classifications than those awarded. The basic requirements for the recommendation of any restaurant are a high standard of cuisine, prompt and courteous service, pleasant atmosphere, and value for money.

Hotels

★ Good hotels and inns generally of small scale and with modest facilities and furnishings, frequently run by the proprietor himself. All bedrooms with hot and cold water; adequate bath and lavatory arrangements; main meals with a choice of dishes served to residents; menus for residents and meal facilities for non-residents may be limited for lunch, and especially at weekends.

★★ Hotels offering a higher standard of accommodation; more baths and perhaps a few private bathrooms/showers; lavatories on all floors; wider choice of meals.

★★★ Well-appointed hotels with more spacious accommodation and at least 40% of the bedrooms with private bathrooms/showers; full meal facilities for residents every day of the week but at weekends service to non-residents may be restricted.

★★★★ Exceptionally well-appointed hotels offering a high standard of comfort and cuisine with 80% of the bedrooms providing private bathrooms/showers. At weekends meal service to non-residents may be restricted.

★★★★★ Luxury hotels, offering very high standards of accommodation, service and comfort. All bedrooms with private bathrooms/showers.

(RP) Recommended hotels which do not conform to the minimum classification requirements in respect of porterage, reception facilities and choice of dishes; facilities for non-residents often limited.

★ Signifies the classification of the great majority of AA-recommended hotels offering traditional hospitality and service in traditional accommodation.

☆ Denotes purpose-built hotels, some motels, motor hotels, motor inns, posthouses and similar establishments which conform to the major requirements for black star classification. In some cases, porterage, room service, and lounge accommodation may be rather restricted; this is offset by the provision of purpose-built bedrooms all with either private bath and/or shower, more parking space, and extended meal hours. It is emphasised that white stars are an indication of a type of hotel only. Leaflet HH30 listing white star hotels is available from Regional Offices, Hotels Department.

★ Denotes hotels which are considered to be of outstanding merit within their normal star ratings.

Hotels which display many of the characteristics of a traditional country house, and are set in rural surroundings. Reception and service facilities may differ from those at hotels of similar classification.

○ Newly opened hotels or larger hotels which are expected to open during the currency of this publication. At the time of going to press, no inspection would have been made.

Restaurants

X Modest but good restaurant
XX Restaurant offering a higher standard of comfort than above
XXX Well-appointed restaurant
XXXX Exceptionally well-appointed restaurant
XXXXX Luxury restaurant

Cuisine

❀ Hotel or restaurant where the cuisine can be especially recommended.

❀❀ Hotel or restaurant offering very much above average food irrespective of the classification, together with a high standard of service within the classification.

❀❀❀ Hotel or restaurant offering outstanding food, irrespective of classification, together with a high standard of service within the classification.

ABOUT THIS GUIDE

The aim of this guide is to provide, in a form easily understood by the reader, as much up-to-date information as possible about selected hotels and restaurants. The use of symbols and abbreviations, keys to which are set out on pages 4–5, helps to make this possible within a compact gazetteer section. Explanations of the AA classification and recommendation system and notes on the gazetteer are set out below.

Our classification system

The award of 'stars' to hotels, and 'crossed knife and fork' ratings to restaurants, is based on the degree of comfort, the range of facilities and the standard of service provided. The classification indicates the type of hotel or restaurant a visitor may expect to find. Classifications are decided on a purely objective basis, as distinct from accolades such as red stars and rosettes, which reflect personal opinions. The AA system of appointing hotels and restaurants began in 1908. Over the years, standards have been adapted to take into account both current trends in hotel construction and operation, and the changing requirements of members visiting hotels. Details of the individual classification requirements for our appointed hotels may be found in the AA booklet *Hotels and the Automobile Association* available from the Hotels Department of AA regional headquarters.

Hotels

Application for recognition and appointment is made to the AA by the proprietors. An inspector then visits the hotel unannounced, stays overnight and takes every opportunity of testing as many services as possible. Having settled his bill in the morning, he introduces himself and makes a thorough inspection of the entire premises. At subsequent discussions with the management he will draw attention to any points which may affect the classification.

Once granted recognition and given a rating, hotels are subject to annual inspection to ensure that standards are maintained. If the hotel changes hands, it is automatically deleted until the new proprietor applies for recognition and the hotel has been reassessed.

Current applications, and possible reclassifications or deletions, are considered monthly by the Appointment Committee. This Committee also keeps the Association's general policy of classification under review.

Restaurants

Restaurant classifications are made rather differently. For the most part, the approach is made by the Association rather than the proprietor. AA inspectors seek out new restaurants and visit them anonymously. Subsequently they report to the Classification Committee who, if the restaurant is considered to be of a high enough standard, award 'crossed knives and forks' to denote the physical amenities. Each hotel restaurant of particular merit in London is classified independently of its parent hotel.

Rosettes

It was in 1955 that the Association introduced its first subjective award system. It was felt that an accolade should be awarded to hotels and restaurants where our inspectors considered the food was of a particularly high standard. With this in mind, the award of rosettes for cuisine was instituted. An explanation of the basis on which these awards are made may be found on page 20.

The Inspectors

Much of the inspectors' work consists of routine examination of premises, furniture, equipment and facilities. Life for them is by no means one long round of food, wine and luxury living.

Inspectors are drawn from hotel and catering industries and from experienced staff within the Association. This creates a balance, between the qualified men and women with specialised knowledge of the industries, on the one hand, and those with an expert appreciation of members' needs, on the other. Regular courses serve to keep their knowledge abreast of the times, and consultants are available in each region, to assist the inspectors in providing informed and unbiased reports upon which the Appointment Committee can base its decisions. Additional information from members – who themselves form a nation-wide inspectorate – is also greatly valued.

GENERAL INFORMATION

Annexes

The number of bedrooms available in an annexe is shown in the gazetteer entry, but only provided they are of the same standard as those in the rest of the hotel. Facilities may not be the same as in the main building, however, and it is advisable to check the nature of the accommodation and the tariff before making a reservation.

Central heating

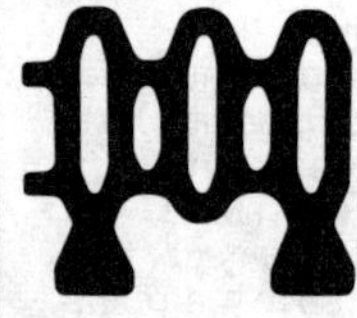

The central heating symbol in a hotel's entry does not mean that this facility is available all year round. Some hotels only operate their central heating during the winter months, and then at their own discretion.

Children

Hotels listed accommodate children of all ages unless a minimum age is given but it does not necessarily follow that it is able to provide special facilities. If you have very young children, enquire into the arrangements such as cots and highchairs, and whether reductions are made for children before reserving accommodation. Establishments which do have special facilities for children are indicated by the symbol . All the following amenities will be found at these establishments: baby-sitting service or baby intercom system, playroom or playground, laundry facilities, drying and ironing facilities, cots and high chairs, and special meals.

Coaches

Some of the gazetteer entries include a no-coaches symbol. This information has been compiled and published in good faith from the details supplied to the AA by the establishment concerned. If, however, the establishment is an inn in law, it has certain well-defined obligations to travellers. This would be a matter for the customer to take up with either the proprietor or the licensing authorities of the area.

Company-owned hotels

In some entries, the name of the group operating the hotel follows the address. A key to the abbreviations used may be found on page 65.
A company must own at least six hotels or a hotel must be affiliated to the following marketing consortia: Best Western, Inter-Hotels and Prestige before its name is shown in the guide.

Complaints

Members who wish to complain about food, services or facilities are urged to do so promptly, on the spot, since this should provide an opportunity for the hotelier or restaurateur to correct matters. If a personal approach fails, members should inform the AA regional office nearest to the establishment concerned.

Deposits

Some hotels, particularly in large towns and holiday centres, find it necessary to ask for a deposit – especially from chance callers who are staying for only one night. It is therefore advisable to effect insurance cover against a possible cancellation – eg *AA Travelsure*.

Disabled persons

If the wheelchair symbol ♿ is shown in a hotel's entry it means that the disabled person can be accommodated. This information has been supplied to the AA by the hotel proprietor, but it is advisable to check with the hotel concerned before making reservations. Details more relevant to disabled persons may be obtained from the *AA Guide for the Disabled* available from AA offices, free to members. Members with any form of disability should notify proprietors so that appropriate arrangements can be made to minimise difficulties, particularly in the event of an emergency.

Dogs

Hotels that do not allow dogs into bedrooms are indicated by a symbol but other establishments may impose restrictions as to the size of dogs permitted, and the rooms into which they may be taken. The conditions under which pets are accepted should be confirmed with the management when bookings are being made.

Dress

Some hotels and restaurants do not permit guests to enter the dining-room or restaurant in informal or unconventional dress.

Fire precautions

So far as we can discover every hotel in Great Britain listed in this publication has applied for and not been refused a fire certificate. Remember that the Fire Precautions Act (1971) does not apply to the Channel Islands, or the Isle of Man, which exercise their own rules with regard to fire precautions for hotels.

Gazetteer entry

Red Star establishments are included in a special colour section; see pages 33 to 64. However, there are also cross-references under individual locations.
The London section is now gazetteered in alphabetical sequence within the England section; see pages 226 to 267.
In the restaurant entry, the '*bedrooms available*' phrase is for information only, and does not infer they have been appointed by the AA.
Establishment names shown in *italics* indicate that particulars have not been confirmed by the management.
The order is red stars, then black in descending star rating and alphabetical listing within each classification. Hotels preceed restaurants.

Licence to sell alcohol

All hotels and restaurants listed are licensed for the sale and consumption of intoxicating liquor unless otherwise stated.

Licences

Note that at hotels which have registered clubs, club membership cannot take effect – nor can a drink be bought – until forty-eight hours after joining.

DON'T DRINK

AND DRIVE

Facts and Figures

Hotels

There are 4113 AA-appointed hotels in Great Britain and Ireland of which 3868 are within the United Kingdom, Channel Islands and Isle of Man and 245 are in the Republic of Ireland.

Classifications

Classification		Number
★★★★★	(including red)	23
★★★★	(including red)	160
☆☆☆☆		63
★★★	(including red)	922
☆☆☆		174
★★	(including red)	1899
☆☆		59
★	(including red)	735
☆		2
ⓟ		76
	TOTAL	**4113**

Restaurants

There are 1197 AA-classified restaurants in Great Britain and Ireland of which 1136 are in the United Kingdom, Channel Islands and Isle of Man and 61 are in the Republic of Ireland.

Classifications

Classification	Number
XXXXX	15
XXXX	23
XXX	151
XX	515
X	493
TOTAL	**1197**

A Note on Hotel Prices

The following chart gives **average** minimum and maximum prices in each category. Bed and full English breakfast prices for 5, 4 and 3-star hotels are per night without bath.

London prices were not taken into account when the chart was compiled as tariffs can be up to 25% more expensive than those in the provinces.

Prices quoted are inclusive of service and VAT. **The selection of hotel tariffs was made when the VAT rate was 8%. This should be taken into consideration when using this chart.**

Classification	Single Bed & Breakfast		Double Bed & Breakfast		Dinner	
	Min	*Max*	*Min*	*Max*	*Min*	*Max*
★★★★★	£26	£29	£46	£48	£8	£9
★★★★	£22	£23	£33	£34	£6	£6
★★★	£15	£16	£24	£27	£5	£5.50
★★	£9	£10	£17	£18.50	£4	£5
★	£8	£9	£14.50	£16	£3.50	£4.50
ⓟ	£6.50	£7.50	£12	£14	£3.50	£4

Licensing hours

The general licensing hours, subject to modification by the Justices, permitted in public houses are as follows:

England 11.00–15.00hrs and 17.30–22.30hrs on weekdays (23.00hrs in London and certain other places), 12.00–14.00hrs and 19.00–22.30hrs on Sundays, Christmas Day, and Good Friday.

Wales As above except that there is no Sunday opening in the following 'dry' districts (June 1978): Meirionnydd; Ceredigion (old administrative county of Cardiganshire); Ynys Mon (Anglesey); Carmarthen (large part of former county of Carmarthenshire); Arfon (virtually old county of Caernarfonshire); Dwyfor (part of old county of Caernarfonshire).

Scotland 11.00–14.30hrs & 17.00–23.00 on seven days a week; some still close at 22.00hrs or 22.30hrs on Mondays to Thursdays. Many do not open on Sundays depending on the area.

Channel Islands, Isle of Man & Isles of Scilly Licensing hours in these areas are complex and details may be obtained from leaflet HH20 *The Law about Licensing Hours & Children/Young Persons on Licensed Premises* available from AA offices.

Licensed hotels and restaurants The general position is as follows: separate rules apply to these premises. However, with exceptions, the permitted hours are as above with extensions in certain circumstances. Hotel residents may be served intoxicating liquor at any time but special rules govern their guests.

Children and young persons on licensed premises

England Children under 14 are not allowed in bars (including any place exclusively or mainly used for the sale and consumption of intoxicating liquor) during permitted hours (unless they are children of the licence-holder, or are resident but not employed in the premises or are passing through the bar to or from some other part of the building which is not a bar and to or from which there is no other convenient access. When a bar is usually set apart for the service of table meals and is not used for the sale of intoxicating liquor except for consumption by persons having table meals there is an ancillary to the meal this prohibition does not apply. In licensed premises, alcoholic drinks may not be sold to, or purchased by, persons under the age of 18; neither may such persons consume intoxicating liquor in a bar. 16–18-year-olds may purchase beer, porter, cider or perry for consumption with a meal in a part of the premises (not a bar) usually set apart for the service of meals.

Basically similar laws apply in Wales and Scotland but more details, together with information pertaining in the Channel Islands, Isle of Man and Isles of Scilly, may be found in the leaflet, HH20, mentioned above.

NB *Contents of the above two main sections have been compiled by the AA on the information available to it, as part of its service to members and the contents are believed correct as at 23 January 1978. However it should be noted that laws can change.*

Meals

The terms quoted are for full English breakfast unless otherwise stated.
All four- and five-star hotels serve *morning coffee*. Many one- and two-star hotels now provide more limited lunch facilities than in the past, especially to non-residents. In awarding stars, the Association has taken each such case on its merits. Some hotels also find it uneconomical to serve *afternoon tea*, but this is normally available at all four- and five-star hotels, and at most three-star hotels. In some parts of the country, it is usual to serve *high tea* instead of *dinner*, which may however, be available on request. The last time at which high tea or dinner may be ordered on weekdays is shown, but some latitude may be allowed at weekends. So far as Sunday is concerned, some hotels serve the main meal at midday, and provide a *cold supper* only in the evening. Staff shortages, and other difficulties may oblige a hotel to serve meals between stated hours only.

Night porter

All four- and five-star hotels have night porters on duty. Other hotels employing a night porter are indicated in the gazetteer by means of a crescent moon symbol ☽.

Prices

Prices should be checked before booking as they are likely to fluctuate during the currency of this guide. The effects of inflation, possible variations in the rate of VAT and, indeed, many other factors, may influence prices in the coming year. Published prices have been provided by hoteliers and restaurateurs in good faith but must be accepted as indications rather than firm estimates. Where proprietors have not provided information about 1980 prices, members are requested to make enquiries direct. Bed and breakfast terms (which include a full English breakfast unless otherwise stated) are quoted in the guide. These show minimum and maximum prices for one and two persons, but charges may vary according to the time of year. In some hotels only Continental breakfast is offered and this is highlighted in the gazetteer. Prices are inclusive of VAT and service where applicable. Some hotels charge for bed, breakfast and dinner whether dinner is taken or not. Most hotels will accept cheques in payment of accounts only if notice is given and some form of identification (preferably a banker's card) produced. Travellers' cheques issued by the lending banks and agencies are accepted by many hotels, but not all. If a hotel accepts credit cards, this is indicated in the relevant gazetteer entry.
Minimum and maximum table d'hôte prices are given for main meals served in hotel dining-rooms and restaurants. Where an à la carte menu is available, the average price of a three-course dinner and lunch is shown. In cases where establishments offer both types of menu, table d'hôte prices are the only ones given, but with an indication that à la carte is also available. All prices should include cover charge. The price of wine quoted is that of the cheapest full bottle (*ie 70cl*).

Reservations

Book as early as possible, particularly if accommodation is required during a holiday period. If you have to change your plans, for any reason, inform the hotel as soon as you are able. Failure to do so may result in your being held responsible for part of the cost of the accommodation. Many hotels, particularly in short-season holiday areas, accept period bookings only at full-board rate, while some will not accept reservations from midweek, and many do not take advance bookings for bed and breakfast.
(see also 'Deposits' paragraph.)

Restricted service

Some hotels operate a restricted service during the less busy months. This is indicated by the prefix RS. RS Nov–Mar, for example, indicates that a restricted service is operated from November to March. This may take the form of a reduction on meals served, accommodation available or in some cases both services may be restricted. The gazetteer entry will indicate at which hotels restrictions operate.

Telephone calls

Many hotels impose a surcharge for calls made through the switchboard. Always ascertain full details before making the call.

Telephone numbers

Unless otherwise stated, the **telephone exchange name** given in the gazetteer is that of the town under which the establishment is listed. Where the exchange for a particular establishment is not that of the town under which it appears, the name of the exchange is given after the telephone symbol ☎ and before the number.
In some areas telephone numbers are likely to be changed by the Post Office during the currency of this publication. If any difficulty is found when making a reservation it is advisable to check with the operator.

Television

If the gazetteer entry shows 'CTV' or 'TV' this indicates that either colour or monochrome television is available in a lounge. The entry may also show whether colour or monochrome television is available in guests' bedrooms. This can be in the form of televisions permanently fixed or available on demand from the hotel management. *'TV available in bedrooms'* also means that there could be either colour or monochrome television depending on the room occupied. In all cases these points should be checked on making a reservation.

Value Added Tax

In the United Kingdom and the Isle of Man, VAT is payable on both basic prices and any service. The symbol S% in the gazetteer indicates that the inclusive prices shown reflect any separate accounting for service made by the establishment. VAT does not apply in the Channel Islands. With this exception, prices quoted in the gazetteer are inclusive of VAT.

Example of a Gazetteer entry

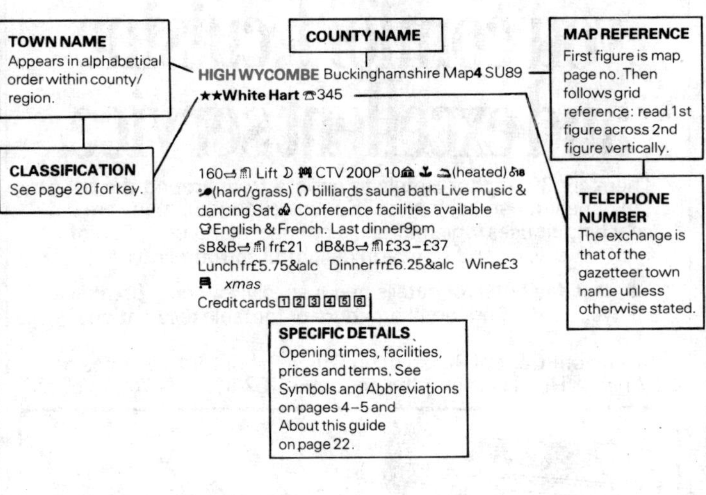

Additional information

After each placename of the county, or region, is given. Remember that this is the administrative county, or region, and not necessarily a part of the correct postal address. With Scottish regions or islands, the old county name follows in italics.

There may well be a few map or town plan entries unsupported by text. This is because these have to be completed before the final amendments due date for gazetteer copy.

For details of guesthouses, farmhouses and inns, see Guesthouses, Farmhouses and Inns in Britain, *available from all AA offices.*

Key to town plans

RED STAR LINE-UP

Red stars were introduced in 1975 and are awarded only after a great deal of consideration. They indicate the hotels our inspectors have recommended as the very best of their kind. When a hotel changes hands, they are automatically withdrawn. Change of management, too, is likely to result in the award being carefully reviewed.
In each of the establishments highlighted in this colour feature, we believe you will find a warm welcome and a high standard of hospitality.
Indeed, this is a red star line-up to be proud of!

★★★ Elms Hotel, Abberley
☎Great Witley666
Set in glorious Worcestershire countryside and built in the reign of Queen Anne is the Elms, one of the Midlands' most beautiful hotels. There are some 12 acres of parkland with formal gardens, croquet and putting lawns, tennis courts and a herb garden which reputedly is the largest in a British hotel.

The garden also has a kitchen plot which provides the fresh produce used in the kitchen. As one might expect, good use is made of other fine raw materials and menus have interesting dishes representing good value.

Although the casual visitor can see many of the good points of the Elms, it is the resident guest who gets the full picture, for it is to the bedrooms that Donald Crossthwaite, the proprietor, has devoted his greatest attention. The original ground floor rooms should be mentioned because of their exquisite proportions. Mr Crossthwaite's latest improvements have been to the private bathrooms which have been luxuriously appointed with bidets, double handbasins and other expensive furnishings.

(on A443) (Prestige)
20⇾⋒ 1 ☽ CTV CTV in bedrooms 60P 20
(hard) English & Continental.
Last dinner 9.30pm S%
*sB&B⇾⋒£17.60 dB&B⇾⋒£25.60
Continental breakfast Lunch£4.65&alc
Tea60p High Tea£2.75 Dinner£7.70–£9.10
Wine£2.40 *xmas* Credit cards 1 2 3 5 6

❀★★★The Bell Inn, Aston Clinton

☎Aylesbury630252

The Bell Inn was a coaching house many years ago, once belonging to the Duke of Buckingham and used by him as a staging post between Stowe and the present day Buckingham Palace. The Bell continues to provide rest and refreshment for travellers today, just as it did in 1650.

When we first awarded rosettes for cuisine in 1955, The Bell received one and is unique in being the only establishment to have held it consistently since. Mr Michael Harris and his charming wife are totally involved in the running of this establishment, and, together with the staff, have worked hard to improve standards. It is one of our better rosetted restaurants and on occasions comes near to deserving an extra rosette.

The Bell Inn has also become noted as a hotel, and a most individual one at that. While there are some charming rooms in the hotel, it is the conversion of the stables and malthouse around the cobbled yard across the road that is especially appealing. The genuine old brick houses with their exterior staircases and French blue enamelled house numbers are most distinctive.

21⇨⋒ 1▭ ⋈ CTV in bedrooms 150P ⚓
Last dinner9.45pm ✋ S%
✳sB&B⇨⋒£18.50–£22
dB&B⇨⋒£27.50–£40 Continental breakfast
Lunch£11alc Dinner£12alc Wine£3
Credit cards 1 3

★★♣Downrew House, Barnstaple

☎2497

A nice old house of the Queen Anne period, situated in twelve acres of grounds on the lower slope of Codden Hill with delightful views of undulating Devon countryside, owned and personally run by Desmond and Aleta Ainsworth, who have constantly strived to improve it during their 15 years' ownership. The most recent adjunct is the conversion of the old stone barn near the main house to a wing of five double bedrooms with bathrooms en suite with its own TV room and games room.

We have referred to the Ainsworths' efforts, but not to their attention to detail. No stone is left unturned to please – personal welcome, personal service and the provision of everything to satisfy guests' needs. There is even a choice of packed lunches, permanently available.

Only light lunches are served, so that attractive Aleta Ainsworth's culinary prowess can be concentrated on the set dinner – a four-course meal with no choice. Another menu is available in the bar, but a half-hour's notice is required.

(off unclass road 1½m SE of Bishops Tawton: (A377))
Closed Nov – mid Mar; 7rm(4⇨⋒) Annexe: 7rm(6⇨⋒) ⋈ CTV CTV available in bedrooms ✈ 12P ⛟ ⚓ ⇨(heated) ↗(hard) ♀English & French. Last dinner9pm sB&B£19–£23.60 sB&B⇨⋒£19–£23.60 dB&B£38–£47.20 dB&B⇨⋒£38–£47.20
Dinner£7.31–£8.56&alc Wine£3 ♜ *xmas*

Stay and eat with your friend.

"I can take you to thousands of hotels and restaurants all over the UK. Fill your car with petrol, top up your oil, take care of breakdowns at thousands of garages. Even pay for your AA subscription. All because I'm flexible. And your friend."

Access. Your flexible friend.

A SERVICE OF LLOYDS, MIDLAND, NATIONAL WESTMINSTER, WILLIAMS & GLYN'S AND CLYDESDALE BANKS, THE ROYAL BANK OF SCOTLAND, NORTHERN AND ULSTER BANKS.

For further details, call in at any bank displaying the Access sign or write to:
Access, Joint Credit Card Company, Southend-on-Sea X, SS99 0BR.

★★★The Cavendish Hotel, Baslow

☎2311

One of England's most beautiful shires, Derbyshire has more than its fair share of attractions with peaks, dales and stately homes, and The Cavendish is certainly one of the best centres from which to tour the county.

Like most of the buildings in the village, the hotel is built of mellow stone and the original Georgian façade presents a most dignified frontage. Please don't think you will be kept awake by traffic noise, because, due to improvements, the bedrooms now all face to the rear with fine views along the valley to Chatsworth Park.

The restaurant is called the Paxton Room, after the designer of the Crystal Palace, and antique prints showing exhibits from that period cover the walls. There is an enterprising menu which contains items specially chosen for the English Tourist Board's 'A Taste of England' campaign. Generally our members have thought the set menus provided the best value. As can be expected in an area that abounds with game, various sorts figure prominently in season.

13 CTV in bedrooms 40P Last dinner 10pm sB&B £24.30 dB&B £32.40 Lunch £4–£5&alc Tea £1.50alc Dinner £4–£5&alc Wine £2.95 Credit cards 2 3

❀★★★Priory Hotel, Bath ☎21887

It has not been our policy to award red stars to an hotel under new ownership, but reports that we have received from our members and inspectors indicate that since some early teething troubles, the Priory has become better and better. Add to this the obvious professionalism of John Donnithorne, the proprietor, and we are able to recommend the hotel with confidence again this year.

Built in 1830, in Victorian Gothic style, and about 20 minutes' from the city centre, the Priory is set in its own peaceful gardens where one can take afternoon tea. There is also a swimming pool.

The interior has been beautifully designed by Thea Dupays, the previous owner, and the lounge is particularly delightful to relax in.

The menu is chosen from a well-selected changing list of dishes made from excellent raw materials. Some of them are cooked with real skill and delicacy and one of our inspectors on a 2 and 3-rosette tour enjoyed his meal here better than any other. He particularly mentioned the mousse of scallops with white butter sauce. Rosette has been awarded for dinner only.

Weston Rd Plan **10**
Closed 24Dec–1Jan; 15 2 CTV in bedrooms 20P (heated) Children under 10yrs not accommodated French. Last dinner 10pm sB&B £18–£22 dB&B £32.50–£42.50 Continental breakfast Lunch fr £3&alc Tea fr 80p Dinner fr £8&alc Wine £3.25

★★Highbury, Bembridge ☎2838
Conspicuous by the orange canopies and cheerful window boxes, the Highbury is situated a few minutes from the beach in this unspoiled village. An Edwardian villa converted over the years from a guesthouse, it is a small hotel, whose owners, Tony and Frances Cobb, virtually started from scratch, and have devoted much of their time and energy into effecting its transformation. Apart from the refurbishing of the bedrooms, a new extension has been built and a heated swimming pool installed in the pleasant garden.

The bedrooms are simple, but gracious and comfortably furnished, mostly in individual style, demonstrating feminine touches. The dining room is decorated with copper bric à brac and is romantically candle-lit at night. The food, from an extensive and varied à la carte menu, is good and the local fish and shellfish can be highly recommended. Fresh vegetables are used when available and the rolls are all home made.

While all these factors are most desirable, the most important one at the Highbury is the presence of the Cobbs. Their personalities, and welcomed attention to one's needs lift this hotel quite out of the ordinary.

Lane End
Closed 24–28Dec; 9rm(6⇌ 🚿) 1 ⊟ 🎮 TV in bedrooms 12P ⛟ ⚓ ⛱(heated) sauna bath
Last dinner10pm S% sB&B£13
sB&B⇌ 🚿 £18 dB&B£24 dB&B⇌ 🚿 £26
Lunch fr£3.50 Dinner£4–£7 Wine£3
Credit cards 1 2 3 5

★★★★Lodore Swiss, Borrowdale
☎285
The Lodore Swiss Hotel, a gabled, stone building with modern frontage, is owned and managed by the England family, who are Swiss and who have brought with them Swiss traditions of hospitality and hotelmanship to this corner of English Lakeland.

The hotel is equipped to provide every sort of indoor entertainment. When the weather fails, facilities now include a hotel shop, tennis court, solarium, sauna baths, indoor and outdoor heated swimming pools, hairdressing salons, ballroom and, most importantly, a nursery for very young children. In fact, family holidays are very much a feature of the Lodore Swiss and facilities for children are exceptional.

Each bedroom has its own private facilities, appointed to a very high standard. Many rooms overlook the Lake and even those which do not, still portray the meticulous thought associated with all aspects of the hotel.

Truly a hotel where personal service reigns supreme. It is little wonder that guests come from all parts of the world to sample the hospitality of Tony England and his family.

Telex no64305
Closed 5Nov–19Mar; 72⇌ 🚿 Lift ☽ 🎮 CTV in bedrooms ⊘ 80P 24🏠 ⛟ ⚓ ⊡ ⛱(heated) (hard) sauna bath Live music & dancing Sat International. Last dinner9pm
sB&B⇌ 🚿 fr£19 dB&B⇌ 🚿 fr£38
Lunch fr£4.50&alc Tea£1alc
Dinner fr£6.50&alc Wine£2.95

❀★★ Farlam Hall, Brampton
☎Hallbankgate234

Farlam Hall was a 17th-C farmhouse which, in 1830, became a manor and boasts of having given hospitality to John Wesley and George Stephenson. It stands in five acres of grounds close to Hadrian's Wall, and in a convenient spot for a number of interesting trips, giving magnificent views over gardens and the hills beyond.

The hotel is run by the Quinion family; Mr & Mrs Quinion attending to the general management. They are most anxious to please without being intrusive. Their son exercises his culinary skills in the kitchen and produces good food that has gained considerable reputation locally. The dishes are uncomplicated and reflect not only some regional influences, but also the good raw materials used. Many of the vegetables are garden fresh. Bread and all the puddings are home baked. A rosette has been awarded for dinner only.

Their daughter, too, is most active at Farlam Hall. In fact, much of the hotel's success stems from the way everyone works as a team.

Hallbankgate (2¾m SE A689)
Closed Xmas & Feb; RS Nov–Jan; 11rm(4⇌ ⋒)
CTV 35P Last dinner8pm
sB&B£10.50 sB&B⇌ ⋒£12 dB&B£21
dB&B⇌ ⋒£24 Lunch£5alc
Dinner£6.95–£7.25 Wine£3 Credit card 1

★★★★ Lygon Arms, Broadway ☎2255

In the centre of one of the most famous Cotswold villages, the Lygon Arms has provided shelter and refreshment for visitors for around 400 years. Both Oliver Cromwell and Charles I are believed to have stayed here. No doubt they were well looked after but certainly they could not have had the welcome that awaits present-day visitors who are drawn from all points of the globe.

The gabled, mellow-stone frontage gives little impression of the extensive improvements that have gone on behind it, but all in perfect harmony with such a lovely old building and designed to give its guests the utmost comfort.

There is a permanent programme of improvement and since our last visit, a wing of bedrooms, once housing chauffeurs and staff, has been luxuriously modernised and had private bathrooms added. The Orchard Wing, built in 1968, is currently undergoing a complete refurnishing as part of the owner's constant plan to keep ahead of guests' needs.

67rm(64⇌ ⋒) 3 CTV CTV in bedrooms
100P 2 (hard) Conference facilities
available Last dinner9.15pm S%
sB&B⇌ ⋒£27.50 dB&B⇌ ⋒ fr£47.50
Continental breakfast Lunch£4.75&alc
Tea60p–£1.50 Dinner£7.50&alc Wine£3.85
xmas Credit cards 1 2 3 4 5 6
Telex no338260

★**Winter's Tale, Burford** ☎3176

Although a converted house, this Cotswold-stone building on the main Oxford Road has all the trappings of a traditional inn. The open-plan ground floor contains the reception area and restaurant but is dominated by the horse-shoe character bar which enjoys a diverse trade of locals, residents and passers-by. In the basement, slightly claustrophobic according to some, cosy to others, is the residents' lounge with TV.

The restaurant is also attractively decorated and furnished with modest country antiques. There is an original menu, mostly of English dishes, making full use of fresh, raw materials – much of it local and reflecting the interest shown by Mrs Stirling and her son, Richard.

Colonel Stirling with his wife and son, provide a cheerful, homely atmosphere for their guests. We have only three one-red star hotels and think it a sad commentary on British innkeepers, people who generally do have control of their own businesses, that this is so, when the scope for family hospitality is so great.

Closed Xmas; 6rm(5 ⇌ ⋒) TV available in bedrooms 75P Live music & dancing mthly Children under 10yrs not accommodated Last dinner 8.30pm ✻sB&B£9.50 dB&B ⇌ ⋒ £17–£18 Continental breakfast Lunch£3.20alc Dinner£5alc Wine£2.50 Credit cards 3 5

★★★★**Grosvenor Hotel, Chester** ☎24024

The Grosvenor Hotel is a fine, traditional hotel, situated in the centre of the City, amongst the unique Rows with shops at street level as well as on top of them at a higher level. The hotel was built in 1865 and although now completely modernised, still retains some of the dignity and charm of that period, reflected in its beautiful oak staircase and exquisite chandeliers.

Boasting a tradition of fine food, service and comfort, English or international dishes, enhanced by an excellent wine list, are served in the elegant restaurant. At lunch time, The Causerie, provides a selection of cold meats or fish dishes in the famed Scandinavian smørgasbord. Downstairs, the Grosvenor bar is a popular rendezvous for shoppers and businessmen.

Each individually decorated bedroom has its own private bathroom, colour television, radio, telephone and refrigerated mini-bar. There are several private suites, attractively and comfortably furnished, in which guests can relax after exploring historical Chester and enjoy the lavish services provided for them by General Manager, Richard Edwards and his staff.

Eastgate St (Prestige) Telex no 61240 100 ⇌ ⋒ Lift CTV in bedrooms Guide dogs only Conference facilities available French. Last dinner 10pm sB&B ⇌ ⋒ £28 dB&B ⇌ ⋒ £46 Lunch fr£5.50&alc Tea fr£2 High Tea fr£3 Dinner fr£8&alc Wine£4.50 Credit cards 1 2 3 5

★★ Kennel Holt, Cranbrook

☎712032

Ideally placed in the Weald of Kent, overlooking wooded valley and set amid rolling orchards and hop gardens, Kennel Holt is an attractive Elizabethan manor house personally supervised by the proprietors, Mr & Mrs Fletcher, who totally believe in the importance of traditional English courtesy.

Cooking is English with fresh vegetables from the garden in season and even out of season Mrs Fletcher has put aside a large stock in her freezer. There is no choice of main dishes at dinner, but anyone with a positive dislike would be offered some sort of alternative.

The lounges are delightful, with antiques and pleasing soft furnishings, and really evoke the spirit of a welcoming country house, particularly so in winter when log fires are ablaze.

7rm(4⇌ ⋒) CTV 20P
Last dinner 7.30pm S% sB&B£11.50
dB&B£23 dB&B⇌ ⋒£28 Wine£3

❀★★★ Maison Talbooth, Dedham

☎Colchester 322367

This lovely country house has many assets – spacious bedrooms, all individually decorated and furnished – exotic, well-equipped adjoining bathrooms – a delightful lounge in which to relax and, not the least of which, the owner himself, Gerald Milson and his kindly staff who do so much.

But perhaps the chief reason for its wide appeal is the absence of a formal reception desk, that makes the visitor forget 'hotel' and which is the mark of Maison Talbooth.

There is no restaurant on the premises but one is situated nearly a mile away, located by a river in an ideal 'Constable' setting. Transport can be arranged.

We have found that the new chef has managed a vast improvement in the food and this is reflected in the rosette awarded this year. The cooking is serious and we hope it will go from strength to strength.

Stratford Rd
Rosette awarded to XXX Le Talbooth Restaurant, see page 154.
Closed 25–30Dec; 10⇌ ⋒ CTV in bedrooms
20P English & Continental.
Last dinner 9pm dB&B⇌ ⋒£33–£49.50
Continental breakfast Tea£1.30alc
Credit cards 1 2 3 5 6

❀★★★ Gravetye Manor, East Grinstead ☎Sharpthorne810567
This hotel is not easy to find but is well worth the trouble when one discovers the lovely creeper-clad Elizabethan manor, set in 1,000 acres of plantations and thirty acres of gardens with a trout-stocked lake.

It is difficult to believe that in this beautiful and tranquil setting, you are only 30 miles from London. The gardens deserve a special mention because the house was owned from 1884 to 1935 by William Robertson, one of the great gardeners. Here, he pioneered the English natural garden that is the envy of the world.

Peter Herbert is the present owner of the hotel-cum-country club – residents automatically become members – and he has combined the tasteful country house ambience with the amenities of a modern hotel with complete success. Polished wood floors, oak panelling, lovely antiques and comfortable chairs and sofas, all in perfect harmony.

Karl Loderer, the chef, has left to run his own restaurant, and his successor is Michael Quinn. Naturally, his style is quite different, and more refined say some, when comparing him to Karl Loderer.

(3m SW off unclass road joining B2110 & B2028)
Gatwick plan **10**
14⇌ 1 CTV in bedrooms 30P 4
Children under 7yrs not accommodated
English & French. Last dinner 9.30pm
sB&B⇌ fr£33 (room only) dB&B⇌ fr£42 (room only) Wine £4.50

★★★★Cavendish, Eastbourne

☎27401

A large, Victorian sea-front hotel which continues to provide efficient and friendly service. A great many of the staff have long service to their credit and it is mainly due to them that stays here are so enjoyable. But credit must also be given to the interior designers who have achieved almost a feeling of intimacy with their décor and furnishings. An open fire is lit in the main lounge on all but the warmest days.

The Cavendish is very comfortable and can offer facilities for wet days. Many of the bedrooms are traditionally decorated and have balconies overlooking the sea. All are air conditioned.

We think this is probably one of the nicest seaside hotels in Britain, as well as being a good centre from which to explore the surrounding Sussex district.

Grand Pde (De Vere) Telex no87579 Plan **2**
115 Lift CTV CTV in bedrooms 35P
Conference facilities available English & Continental. Last dinner9.30pm S%
sB&B £20 dB&B £38
Lunch fr£6.25&alc Tea fr£1.30&alc
Dinner fr£7.25&alc Wine£3.75 *xmas*
Credit cards 1 2 3 5 6

❀★White Moss House, Grasmere

☎295

For perfect peace and relaxation, away from life's daily pressures, one could not do better than choose to stay at White Moss House in the heart of English Lakeland. Owned and personally run by Jean and Arthur Butterworth, the house stands in a slightly elevated position overlooking Rydal Water with the imposing fells and mountains beyond.

Mrs Butterworth is in full charge of the kitchen and does all the cooking. And Mr Butterworth supervises the dining room, serving wines and ensuring continuity throughout the entire proceedings. Rosette has been awarded for dinner only.

Bedrooms are all comfortably furnished and tastefully decorated. Books, magazines, sewing kits, hairdryers and good quality soaps are provided.

Although there are only five bedrooms in White Moss House, a converted cottage (Brookstone), set on the fells above, and reached either by car (5 minutes) or an energetic 10-minute walk, additionally offers two bedrooms, a bathroom, lounge, dining room and kitchenette, all incorporating the same high standards as in White Moss itself, and in an ideal setting for honeymooners or those seeking peaceful isolation.

Closed Nov–Mar; RS Wed; (Dinner not served);
5rm(3) Annexe: 2 TV available in bedrooms 8P Children under 15yrs not accommodated Last dinner7.30pm S%
*dB&B£25–£29 (incl dinner)
dB&B £29–£37 (incl dinner) Dinner£8.50
Wine£3

★★♣Buckland-Tout-Saints, Kingsbridge ☎2586

A gracious and well-proportioned house, personally run by the owners, Mr & Mrs V E Shepherd, who offer friendly, welcoming and attentive service. They are helped by their son, David, and Caroline, his wife, who concentrate on the front office, dining room and kitchen. The site is mentioned in the Doomsday Book but the pleasant building is 18th-century and stands in 27 acres of parkland with delightful views of the surrounding countryside, affording peace and tranquillity.

The public rooms are attractive and uncluttered. The lounges feature lots of old china and pictures, and there is some interesting pine panelling in the dining room, while the main lounge has a fine, moulded plaster ceiling and oak panelling.

Fixed price menus are served in the dining room. It is advisable to choose the simple dishes where the good quality of the raw materials is most evident.

(2½m NE on unclass road) (Best Western) Telex no45562
Closed Nov–Mar; 14 CTV CTV available in bedrooms 20P English, French & Italian. Last dinner 9pm S%
*sB&B £19–£23 dB&B £28–£36
Bar lunch £1.50–£5.10 Tea £1–£2
High Tea £2.50–£5 Dinner £8 Wine £3
Credit cards 1 2 3 4 6

❀★★♣Mallory Court, Leamington Spa ☎30214

'Small is beautiful' could well have been coined at this country house set in fine Warwickshire countryside. Mallory Court was built in 1918 by Sir John Black of Standard Motors and the present owners, Alan Holland and Jeremy Mort, have deliberately retained some of the fittings of that period, as well as later additions of the inter-war years. Both perfectionists, the owners have only added newer furnishings which are complementary.

Most visitors will be drawn here for the food, as the hotel is fast obtaining the reputation of being one of the best in the Midlands. The dining room has lovely oak panelling and the table appointments of restful pale green tablecloths and napkins, crystal glassware and gold-banded white china help to arouse one's expectations.

The menu is sensibly small but offers a sufficient range of dishes. Our inspectors have all commented on the excellent classic sauces. We look forward to a continued improvement over the next year or so that might gain Mallory Court a further rosette.

Harbury Ln, Bishops Tachbrook (2m S off A452)
Closed last 2wks Feb; 5rm(2) 1 CTV in bedrooms 50P 6 squash Children under 14yrs not accommodated French.
Last dinner 10pm S% sB&B £15
sB&B £17 dB&B £28 dB&B £32
Continental breakfast Dinner £10 Wine £4
Credit cards 1 2 3 5

❀★★★★★Berkeley, London SW1
☎01–235 6000

Inspectors and members agree that the Berkeley is perhaps *the* best five-star hotel in London. Mr Charles Fornara, the General Manager, has inspired his staff to provide the traditional type of service long associated with the Savoy Group as a whole and with the old Berkeley in particular. Nearly all the staff take the trouble to know guests' names and to refer to them by name throughout their stay.

The décor throughout the hotel, and especially on the ground floor, is quite lovely and highlights some pieces that were happily saved from the old Berkeley. They help to create an atmosphere that would be virtually impossible in a completely new hotel – more reminiscent, in fact, of a well-kept private house.

As one would expect, the bedrooms are of a good size, individually designed by a team of interior decorators (a programme of redecoration is still going on) and are furnished in discreet good taste.

Catering in the restaurant is classically French while Le Perroquet offers hot and cold buffets at lunchtime, while during the evening a full à la carte menu is provided, amid a sophisticated atmosphere with dancing.

Wilton Pl, Knightsbridge, SW1 Telex no 919252
Plan 5: **2** B2
152 ⇐ ⋒ Lift ☽ ⊞ ⋒ CTV in bedrooms ⊗ ⋒ ⋕
▭ (heated) sauna bath ⊕ international.
Credit cards 1 2 3 4 6

❀❀❀★★★★★Connaught, London W1
☎01–499 7070

See 'Four more of the Best' pages 18–19 where the Connaught has been specially highlighted by our Chief Hotels Inspector.

Carlos Pl, W1 Plan 1: **15** D1
89 ⇐ ⋒ Lift ☽ ⋒ CTV in bedrooms ⊗ 2 ⋒ ⋕ ♿
⊕ English & French. Last dinner 10.30pm ⊕
⊕ Wine £3.75 Credit cards 1 6

★★★★★Claridge's, London, W1
☎01-629 8860
In a world where traditional modes of service seem to be on the wane, discreet expertise continues to be seen at Claridges. Spaciously built and with a dignity and calm, this hotel is widely associated with visiting foreign royalty and other discerning guests. But there is more to Claridges than that – whether you arrive in grand style, or by rather more modest means, you are assured the same polite and extremely correct treatment.

The public rooms are most elegant with some nice pieces of furniture and lots of wonderful flower arrangements. Catering is looked after in the restaurant by Mr Kruder and Chef Roland offers the usual classic menu. For less formal dining, the Causerie, under the direction of Mr P Maud, continues to be a popular eating place with its Scandinavian-style cold buffet, introduced by Danish General Manager Mr Lund Hansen, and in operation now for many years. Mr Hansen deserves the greatest credit for the way in which he has maintained the high standard.

Brook St, W1 Telex no 21872 Plan 1 : **13** D2
255 Lift CTV in bedrooms P
International. Credit cards 1 3 6

★★★★★Dorchester, London W1
☎01-629 8888
The Dorchester went through a difficult period following the departure of Peter Stafford, the Managing Director, but after yet another change of management, it now seems to have settled down under the direction of Mr Jean Ruault. He has announced his intentions for the hotel – including the installation of air conditioning – and we trust that the hotel will now maintain the international standards to which we are accustomed.

By and large, the Dorchester retains its thoroughly English environment and nowhere is this more obvious than during the afternoons when tea is served in the lounge, a noted rendezvous in central London.

All the public rooms are luxurious, including the intimate bar and the elegant Terrace Room restaurant. There is also the Spanish-style Grill Room, now smaller with its own kitchen more conveniently placed, both restaurants under the direction of Chef Mossiman who has introduced a set 'surprise' menu.

Services in all respects, particularly room service and valeting, are well up to expectations and the friendly staff seem delighted to serve. Truly, one of the great hotels.

Park Ln, W1 Telex no 887704 Plan 1 : **19** E1
286 Lift CTV in bedrooms P Live music & dancing Mon – Fri Conference facilities available International. Last dinner mdnt S% *Lunch £6.50&alc Tea £2.50 – £3.15 Dinner £11.50&alc Wine £6 Credit cards 1 2 3 4 5 6

❀★★★★★Savoy, London WC2

☎01–836 4343

Very much the 'grande dame' of London's hotels, the Savoy, while showing signs of its age, is growing old gracefully. The impressive façade and lobby still provide a special thrill when one enters. Not just because of the physical aspects, but also because of the hotel's sense of history that somehow one immediately becomes aware of. Many of the delights of good living have been created here since the days of Ritz and Escoffier.

There are two restaurants, the main one, although recently redecorated, still conveying old-style charm. This provides table d'hôte menus both for lunch and for dinner with cabaret and dancing. It remains superlative value. But it is the Grill Room which we believe has the better food. The menu is comparatively short, so they are able to concentrate all their efforts into the dishes. Now that the newness is wearing off, the Grill Room is developing an aura all of its own. Mr Fiorantina, the Maitre d'hôtel, supervises his staff with the greatest attention to detail.

Strand, WC2 Plan2: **35** C5
400 Lift CTV in bedrooms 450
Live music & dancing 6 nights wkly
Conference facilities available English & French. Last dinner mdnt Credit cards 1 2 3

❀★★★★Capital, London SW3

☎01–589 5171

A small quality hotel situated just to the south of Knightsbridge and close to Harrods, unique in being started and owned by one man, Mr David Levin, who realised his life's ambition in opening the Capital.

Naturally, in the context of modern building costs, not all the rooms are spacious, but they have excellent amenities and their en suite bathrooms are equipped with all that one might need.

Taking the view that guests in London hotels do not spend much time in them, Mr Levin has dispensed with a lounge and has concentrated on the smart bar which has become a famous meeting place as well as serving the small modern restaurant.

The standard of food in the restaurant remains high, although not reaching the gastronomic heights experienced in previous years. However, it still very much deserves its rosette and guests will not be disappointed with the good French food. The wine list is extensive and well chosen with many wines at most reasonable prices.

Basil St, SW3 Telex no 919042 Plan4: **14** B6
60 Lift CTV in bedrooms 6P 10

French. Last dinner 10.30pm
sB&B fr£43.50 dB&B fr£62
Lunch £9.50alc Dinner £9.50alc Wine £4.25
Credit cards 1 2 3 4 5 6

★★★★Goring, London, SW1

☎01-834 8211

There are few luxury hotels left in Britain which are privately owned, let alone one that has been actively run by three generations of the same family, but this is such an hotel. Taking the family name, Goring, it was built in 1910 and was the first hotel to be built with private bathrooms and central heating. Obviously a forerunner, the Goring has ever since kept up with the times.

The comfortable, sensitively-decorated bedrooms are now air-conditioned and equipped with self-dial telephones as well as colour televisions, and those bedrooms at the front of the building are double glazed to ensure quiet nights' sleep.

But, as with all our red star hotels, it is the service element that distinguishes it from the rest. Under the inspiration of Mr George Goring and led by his manager, Mr William Cowpe, the staff go out of their way to provide personal and meticulous service.

Beeston Pl, Grosvenor Gdns, London SW1
Telex no 919166 Plan 5: **9** C3
100🛁🚿 Lift ☽ ▦ CTV in bedrooms 🚫🐕 🅿 🌬
🍽English & French. Last dinner 9.30pm ☕ 🫖
S% sB&B🛁🚿£37.50 dB&B🛁🚿£50
Lunch £5–£6.50&alc Tea £1.25
Dinner £6–£7.50&alc Wine £4.50
Credit cards 1 2 3 5 6

★★★★Selfridge, London, W1

☎01-408 2080

There are not many hotels which leave you with a lasting impression, but Selfridges is such an hotel. Mr Christopher Cole opened it for his own company in 1973 and it is largely due to his personal high standards and motivation that the hotel has reached the heights it has.

All the public rooms are on the first floor and they have been decorated with great finesse. The lounge deserves special attention – it has really comfortable armchairs and most efficient service. There is the Stove Bar with surprisingly period rustic décor, which has gained a great following locally.

Fletcher's restaurant, across the way, shares the rest of the hotel's modern design and has a menu that should satisfy most people's appetites. First-class materials are used and are soundly cooked. For those not wanting a formal meal, the Coffee Shop has proved a great success.

Orchard St, W1 (EMI) Telex no 22361 Plan 1: **65** C1
298🛁🚿 Lift ☽ ▦ CTV in bedrooms 🚫🐕 P
Conference facilities available 🍽International.
Last dinner 10.30pm ☕ 🫖 S%
*sB&B🛁🚿£44.50 dB&B🛁🚿£59
Continental breakfast Lunch £6.20&alc
Tea £1alc Dinner £5.50alc Wine £3.55
Credit cards 1 2 3 4 5 6

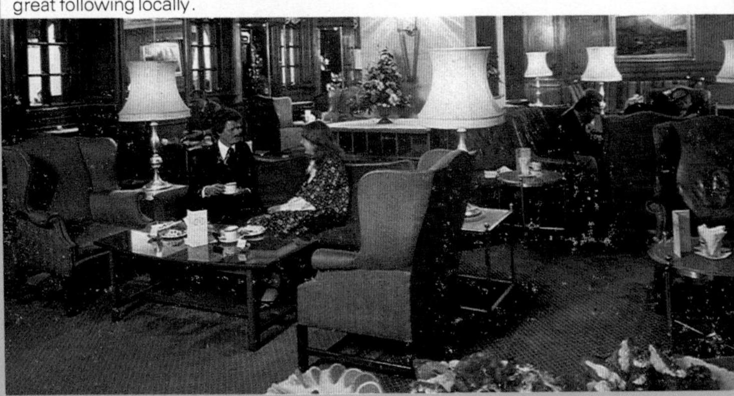

★★★Basil Street, London SW3
☎01–581 3311
First built as the Sloane Gate Hotel in 1910, the Basil Street is a small, dignified hotel that recognises the importance of personal service. From the time one is escorted to the Porter's Lodge and introduced to the concierge, one is treated more as a privileged member of an exclusive London club, than just as a guest.

Reminders of the Edwardian era are apparent in the space and solidity of structure, the paintings and antiques. Rising from the lobby is the original mahogany staircase which leads to the rest of the public rooms on the first floor. The lounge is a lovely, panelled room with 18th-C furniture – plush armchairs and sofas nicely arranged in cosy groups. Nearby is a drawing room equally well furnished and with a bar where polite waiters serve drinks.

The traditional dining room serves lunch only but the hotel does have 'The Downstairs', a wine and food bar, and 'The Upstairs' for dining by candlelight and very handy for pre-theatre dinners.

Basil St, Knightsbridge, SW3 Telex no28379
Plan4: **10** B6
113rm(65⇨ ⑪) Lift ☽ ₦ CTV CTV available in bedrooms ₱ ⌂ ⇔ Conference facilities available ☋International. Last dinner9.45pm
♁ ☑ S% sB&B£19–£20
sB&B⇨ ⑪£32–£35 dB&B£30–£32
dB&B⇨ ⑪£43–£46 Continental breakfast
Lunch fr£4.75&alc Tea fr£1.75
Dinner fr£5.75&alc Wine£3.30 ⊟ *xmas*
Credit cards 1 2 3 5 6

★★★Lowndes, London SW1
☎01–235 6020
Situated in the heart of Belgravia, convenient for Knightsbridge, the elegant interior belies the faceless façade created in the recent development of this part of Lowndes Street. One enters into an impressive marble-floored lobby, with a smallish but adequate lounge area with crystal chandeliers. Leading off is the bar in Chinese Chippendale style with an amiable and efficient bartender in residence.

In fact, all the staff are friendly and obliging and it is mainly due to their efforts that this hotel has warranted red stars. Indeed, many aspects of Lowndes are of four-star rating.

A new menu, à la carte, has been brought in by the chef, James Rhodes, and the food is up to standard. These are early days, but perhaps next year we shall see the award of a rosette or restaurant classification.

A word must be said about Mr N L O'Neill, the manager. His enthusiasm and enterprise contribute greatly to the successful running of the hotel; these essential qualities he imparts to his staff and to the ultimate benefit of his guests.

We are pleased to add the Lowndes Hotel to our select list of red star establishments.

19 Lowndes St, SW1 (Thistle) Telex no919065
Plan5: **15** C1
80⇨ ⑪ Lift ☽ ⊞ ₦ CTV CTV in bedrooms ⊗ ⇔
☋French. Last dinner9pm ♁ ☑ S%
✱sB&B⇨ ⑪£44.90 dB&B⇨ ⑪£59.80
Lunch£10alc Dinner£15alc Wine£5
Credit cards 1 2 3 4 5 6

★Ebury Court, London SW1
☎01–730 8147
It is fitting that the efforts made by the owners, Mr & Mrs Topham since they bought the Ebury Court before the War, have been successful enough to deserve our red star accolade. The only one-star hotel we so recommend in London.

The Ebury Court was first opened as a small club, which still exists and affords temporary membership to hotel residents wishing to use the bar and its adjoining garden room. It was expanded year by year through purchasing neighbouring houses as they became available. Like all such structures, there is not the space to do what one would like and some of the bedrooms are small. But they are cosy and prettily decorated with many feminine touches.

As one would expect from a personally-run hotel, the long-serving staff are most helpful. The receptionists are a mine of information and will be able to tell you when to see the troops pass the Hotel on their way for the Changing of the Guard.

26 Ebury St, SW1 Plan5: **5** C3
37rm(11 ⇌ ⋒) 3 ⊟ Lift ☽ CTV TV available in bedrooms P ⇔ Last dinner 9pm S%
✱sB&B fr£13.50 dB&B fr£22.50
dB&B ⇌ ⋒ fr£30 Lunch £5.50alc
Dinner £5.25alc Wine £2.25 ⊓

❀★★★ Hunstrete House, Marksbury
☎Compton Dando 578
We featured this Hotel in our 'Six of the best' article last year. Since then the Dupays have sold the Priory at Bath (see page 36) so that they can concentrate all their energies into Hunstrete House.

There were some early teething troubles but they were quickly sorted out and we have received nothing but praise since last autumn.

This fine Georgian house is set in 90 acres of gardens and grounds and, in addition to a croquet lawn, a hard tennis court and heated swimming pool were installed earlier in 1979. The interior is most impressive – stunning décor enhanced by some lovely furniture and furnishings. There are a number of lounges which all provide a variety of decorative schemes.

As can be seen, we have awarded Hunstrete House a rosette for cuisine and it is well deserved. Table d'hôte meals are provided, priced according to the main dish chosen. The restaurant enjoys a good local reputation so there is a largish chance trade. The service is solicitous and friendly in this oasis for people who want the convenience of the city combined with the peace of the country.

(2m W off A368)
Closed 23Dec–4Jan; 13 ⇌ ⋒ 1 ⊟ CTV in bedrooms ⊗ 30P ⇔ ⚓ ⇌(heated) (hard)
Children under 9yrs not accommodated
English & French. Last dinner 9.30pm
sB&B ⇌ ⋒ £24.75–£27
dB&B ⇌ ⋒ £38.50–£50.60
Continental breakfast Lunch fr£4.50
Tea fr80p Dinner £8alc Wine £3 ⊓
Credit card 2

★★★ Meudon, Mawnan Smith

☎250541

Just a few miles from Falmouth, this hotel lies in one of the more sheltered corners of south Cornwall, between the Fal and Helford rivers.

Some of the bedrooms, and all of the public rooms, are situated in the old, Cornish granite-built mansion, but a wing of modern rooms with private bathrooms has been added. There are several lounges, the main one giving excellent views. Situated below is the dining room where local seafood – including oysters from the Duchy of Cornwall's oyster farm – is a worthy feature of the menu.

But the greatest trait of the Meudon, and one that the architect has made full use of, is the lush garden, consisting of 8½ acres of combe running down to a private beach. Around about are more formal gardens, becoming wilder and wilder with semi-tropical vegetation and rock pools, as one descends. Some of the more delicate plants have succumbed to the hard winter, but a profusion of such exotics as eucalyptus, banana, flame trees, giant ferns and mimosa still flourish.

Altogether a most agreeable hotel for stays in or out of season.

(1½m E unclass road) (Prestige)
Closed Jan; 38rm(30) TV in bedrooms
50P English & French.
Last dinner 9pm S% sB&B£10–£15
sB&B £15–£26 dB&B£28–£50
dB&B £28–£50 Lunch fr£3.75
Dinner fr£5.50 Wine£3.75 *xmas*
Credit cards 1 2 3 5 6

★★ Fifehead Manor, Middle Wallop

☎Wallop566

An elegant, small manor house, part of which dates back to the 11th century, with ample, prettily furnished bedrooms, set amid picturesque countryside.

A recent addition of a nearby barn converted to single rooms presents an attractive feature. There is a pleasant lounge, well furnished with some antiques, and the open plan bar (which sells tasty bar food) provides a lively meeting place for residents and fishermen from the River Test close by.

Margaret Leigh-Taylor, the Dutch owner of Fifehead Manor, brings her talent to bear in the kitchen where good raw materials are used imaginatively. The service is courteous and our members generally have a high opinion of the catering, and of the hotel as a whole.

Closed 23Dec–6Jan; 7 Annexe: 5
TV in bedrooms 50P 4 International.
Last dinner 9.30pm S%
*sB&B £17 dB&B £28 Lunch£7alc
Tea£1.50alc Dinner£8alc Wine£2.80
Credit cards 1 2 3 5

❀★★★★ Chewton Glen, New Milton ☎Highcliffe5341
On the edge of the New Forest and standing in 30 acres of grounds and gardens with terraces, swimming pool, tennis court and croquet lawn, this fine hotel receives so many awards and accolades – and deservedly so.

Martin Skan and his charming wife have dedicated themselves to converting the old building into the luxurious hotel it is today by achieving and maintaining standards of excellence that would be hard to equal anywhere.

The bedrooms vary in size but all are comfortably and exquisitely decorated with Boussac, Warner and Sanderson fabrics, often with matching curtains and bedspreads. One wing was built only a few years ago and now the old coach house has been converted to provide two-storey suites – and quite lovely they are, too.

Not only has the hotel bettered its reputation year by year, but so has the restaurant. The new chef, Christian Deteil, has improved the food enormously and this year even more so. Under the leadership of the head waiter, Toni Ferrario, the service equals the cooking ability, so that the diner can expect a complete experience.

Christchurch Rd Telex no 41456
40 CTV in bedrooms 100P (heated) (hard) Conference facilities available Children under 7yrs not accommodated French. Last dinner 9.30pm S% sB&B fr£28 dB&B fr£56 Continental breakfast Lunch fr£7 Tea fr£2 Dinner fr£11.50 Wine£4.50 *xmas* Credit cards 1 2 3 5 6

★★★ Tresanton, St Mawes ☎544
Under the long ownership of Mrs Farquharson-Oliver and managed by Miss McAndrew, the Tresanton comprises three buildings in two acres of sub-tropical gardens terraced on a hillside overlooking a delightful bay. On the other side of the narrow road is the private beach from which one can swim and there are also moorings for yachts.

Car parking can be difficult but, on arrival, the porter quickly welcomes you and is happy to park your car, after escorting you to the charming receptionist. She, in turn, escorts you to your bedroom showing the facilities as you go.

The catering is good whether you partake of the buffet-style tea with Indian or China tea, the copious and traditional breakfast or main meals, served in the dining room which gives fine views of the Roseland Peninsula.

Most of our inspectors, as well as many of our members, consider the Tresanton to be one of their favourite hotels, even among our red star selection.

Closed 15Nov–18Feb; 22rm(20) Annexe: 8rm(4) CTV CTV available in bedrooms Children under 12yrs not accommodated English & French. Last dinner 8.45pm S% sB&B£20.79–£26.14 (incl dinner) sB&B £22.57–£27.92 (incl dinner) dB&B£49.90–£54.65 (incl dinner) dB&B £49.90–£71.28 (incl dinner) Lunch£7.13&alc Dinner£10.10&alc Wine£3.50

❀❀★★★ Sharrow Bay, Pooley Bridge ☎301

After a pleasant drive skirting Ullswater, one arrives at the gates of the Sharrow Bay Hotel. The house stands on the extreme edge of the Lake on a wooded promontory backed by Barton Fells and beyond can be seen the Helvellyn Range across the sky-line.

On entering the hotel, the immediate impression is of grandeur, the high standard of décor and decorative antique bric à brac combine to create this atmosphere. The bedrooms follow the same high standard and attention to detail is shown by the presence of home-made biscuits, a flask of iced water, bowls of pot pourri and a card of welcome alongside a glass of sherry. This care and thought is to be found in every department of the Hotel.

Special mention must be made of the beautifully appointed Bank House, a converted Georgian farmhouse, situated on a hillside about a mile along the lane from Sharrow, in which the bedrooms have been designed and furnished to a most luxurious standard.

To sample Sharrow Bay's cuisine is itself a memorable experience. Mr Coulson's dedication and skills ensure the ultimate in perfection and even if he is not there his equally dedicated young kitchen staff portray the same style and flair which has now become a hallmark of Sharrow Bay. Mr Sack, with unobtrusive thoroughness, makes sure that guests are looked after in the dining room.

The comprehensive Wine List contains many fine clarets including a Chateau Latour Pauillac 1966 and a Chateau Haut Brion of the same vintage. White wines are also well represented.

Sharrow Bay (1¾m S unclass road)
Closed Dec–Feb; 12rm(7)
Annexe: 17rm(14) CTV in bedrooms
20P 4 Children under 13yrs not accommodated English & French.
Last dinner 8.30pm S%
sB&B fr£32.40(incl dinner) sB&B fr£35.64 (incl dinner) dB&B fr£29.16 (incl dinner)
dB&B fr£35.64 (incl dinner) Lunch £9.18
Tea £2.70 Dinner £11.34 ✱Wine £3.78

❀★★Rising Sun, St Mawes ☎233
Owned and run by Mrs Campbell-Marshall for over 40 years, the Rising Sun is ideally situated overlooking the harbour and sea-wall of this characteristic Cornish village.

Not pretentious in any way, the Hotel provides simple, cheerful accommodation. The bedrooms have floral wallpapers and toning soft furnishings, giving a cottagey effect, whilst downstairs highly polished antique furniture, old maps and model ships can be seen. The lounge is comfortable and has a colour TV, but it is the bar which enjoys the patronage of locals as well as residents and forms the focal point of the Hotel.

Guests and visitors alike appreciate the restaurant for its excellent food, particularly the seafood dishes. It is run by Harry Law who is in his 27th year at the Rising Sun. Of inestimable help to residents, he always remembers the personal wishes of his customers.

Some people still miss the table d'hôte menu which was considered exceptional value, but the à la carte is extensive and the cooking, with Chef Jeffrey West in charge, exceeds the everyday standards for this type of hotel.

Closed 15Nov–28Dec; 14rm(9⇌ ⋒) Annexe: 6⇌ ⋒ ⊞ CTV 6P Children under 10 yrs not accommodated Last dinner 8.45pm sB&B£15 sB&B⇌ ⋒£15 dB&B£30 dB&B⇌ ⋒£35 Lunch£6alc Tea50palc Dinner£8alc Wine£2.70

★★★★Marine, Salcombe ☎2251
Once the home of Lord Kinsale, the Marine has been in existence for nearly 100 years. However, constant improvements and alterations have transformed it into a sophisticated modern hotel with well-appointed public rooms and comfortable bedrooms.

Situated at one end of the town on one of Devon's finest, sheltered estuaries, the Hotel has well-kept terraced, sub-tropical gardens, reached by a novel tiny cliff railway. At the water's edge, there are private landing stages for yachtsmen and facilities exist for fishing or water-sports.

The Marine has good amenities which include heated indoor and outdoor swimming pools – the latter being of good size – a games room and a hairdressing salon. There is also dancing three nights a week in season.

A well balanced table d'hôte menu as well as an à la carte menu are provided in the restaurant. Services throughout are good.

Cliff Rd (Prestige) Telex no 45185 Closed Dec–Feb; 51⇌ ⋒ Lift ☽ ⊞ CTV CTV in bedrooms 60P (heated) Live music & dancing 3 nights wkly Children under 7yrs not accommodated English & French. Last dinner 9.30pm S% *sB&B⇌ ⋒£17.25–£22.25 dB&B⇌ ⋒£34.50–£51.50 Lunch fr£5 Tea£1.50alc Dinner fr£8.20&alc Wine£3 Credit cards 1 2 3 5 6

❀★★Close, Tetbury ☎52272
This handsome Cotswold-stone building was built in the 16th century by a prosperous wool merchant and Mr Lauzier, the owner, has clearly made use of the local antique country furniture to furnish some of the lovely oak-beamed bedrooms, a few with four-poster beds. Most are roomy and well fitted out, and have many thoughtful extras. At the rear of the Close is a walled garden with a small pool and paved terrace that is most welcome during warm weather.

The chic restaurant in Adam style is an inviting, well-appointed room overlooking the garden. It is well patronised locally so residents may feel a bit overwhelmed, particularly at lunchtimes.

At the moment – there is doubt about the future – we understand that a restricted menu is served so that they can concentrate on the ambitious French menu. (Rosette has been awarded for dinner only.)

Their set menus, however, are well composed, often of interesting dishes, and the extras like the crudités to start, home-made rolls and petit fours to finish, always please.

8 Long St (Prestige)
12⇌ ⋒ 2▭ CTV in bedrooms
French. Last dinner 9.30pm S%
sB&B⇌⋒£12–£18 dB&B⇌⋒£19–£34.50
Continental breakfast Lunch fr£6 Dinner fr£9
Wine£4.50 *xmas* Credit cards 1 2 3 4 5 6

★★Winterbourne, Ventnor
☎852535
Charles Dickens wrote *David Copperfield* here when the Winterbourne was a private house, and declared it as, 'Most delightful and beautiful . . . the prettiest place I ever saw in my life, at home or abroad'. Hardly relevant today, you might think, but in fact the statement still holds true.

It is a fine, stone-built house set in lovely gardens with marvellous sea views. A footpath leads down to the usually quiet beach below. There is a 9-hole putting green and croquet lawn in the grounds.

Winterbourne is owned and run by Roger Henderson whose taste is clearly demonstrated in the decoration of the bedrooms and public rooms. They are a feast to the eye. Also an old coach house has been converted to an annexe of bedrooms, each with its own bathroom en suite.

Inspired by the owners, who are most active themselves, the service is welcoming and friendly.

Bonchurch (1m E)
Closed 11Nov–17Jan; 13rm(11⇌⋒)
Annexe:6⇌⋒ CTV in bedrooms 21P
Children under 7yrs not accommodated
English & French. Last dinner 9pm
SB&B£15.40–£16.95
sB&B⇌⋒£17.60–£19.40
dB&B£30.80–£33.90
dB&B⇌⋒£35.20–£38.80 Lunch£3.96
Tea55p Dinner£7 Wine£3
Credit cards 1 2 5

★★★ Bishopstrow House, Warminster ☎212312

Situated about one mile to the east of Warminster, and approached by a narrow drive, this stone-built house has gracious lines and stands in 25 acres of its grounds. Built in 1817 for the Temple family, it is a fine example of a gentleman's residence of the time.

Mr & Mrs Schiller bought Bishopstrow a few years ago and have taken great pains in its restoration. One room with a four-poster has been furnished with 16th-C oak furniture; another features a small four-poster that once belonged to Admiral Lord Nelson. There is also a coach house and the ancient well-appointed stables are worth seeing.

There are few staff about, but as it's a private house, just ring a bell and one's needs are immediately attended to, usually by the Schillers themselves – nothing seems too much trouble for them.

Mr Schiller supervises the service in the dining room and attends to the wines. The à la carte menu is sensibly short and represents good value. Good raw materials are used and are soundly cooked.

Boreham Rd (2m SE A36)
Closed mid Dec – mid Jan; 9 3 CTV CTV in bedrooms 20P 2 (hard)
Children under 9yrs not accommodated
English & French. Last dinner 9pm
*sB&B fr£19.44 dB&B fr£23.76
Continental breakfast Lunch£7.50–£9&alc
Tea£2&alc Dinner£7.50–£9&alc Wine£4.50
Credit cards 1 3

★★★ Bear, Woodstock ☎811511

Just eight miles from the hustle and bustle of Oxford lies the picturesque village of Woodstock. In its cobbled square is this equally picturesque inn, reputedly dating from 1232, with vistas of nearby Blenheim Park. It has been beautifully restored by the present owners who have retained as much as possible of the old features of the hotel, including the huge inglenook and other fireplaces (log fires blaze in winter), beamed ceilings and 16th-C staircase. It all adds to the authentic atmosphere of a time-honoured British inn, and creates a mecca for tourists of all nationalities.

The bedrooms, too, have been elegantly converted and equipped with every modern amenity: colour TVs, phones, trouser presses etc, as well as more personal items such as shower caps, shampoo, sewing kits and bathrobes.

Befitting the Bear's international clientèle, the restaurant offers a good choice of food and wine. However, it can get fairly busy, and on such occasions, one can take refuge in the more sedate first floor lounge, where service can easily be obtained.

Park St
31rm(25) Annexe: 6 CTV CTV available in bedrooms 40P 6 English & French. Last dinner 10.30pm
sB&B£14.50–£15.50 sB&B £19–£21
dB&B£29–£32 dB&B £39–£42
Lunch£4.25–£4.75&alc
Dinner£4.95–£5.95&alc Wine£3.50 *xmas*
Credit cards 1 2 3 5

❀❀★★Miller Howe, Windermere
☎2536

So much has been written about John Tovey's small, luxurious Hotel that it is difficult, indeed almost impossible, not to repeat what has already been said. Nevertheless, some changes have been made, and regular visitors will be pleased to learn that several bedrooms have been stylishly re-decorated, with one now incorporating two single, four-poster beds, and that both the ladies' and gentlemen's non-residents' toilets have been luxuriously modernised.

The restaurant extension has been completely covered with a fresco of an Italian Mediterranean scene and, outside, landscaping has been commenced on previously barren meadowland, sloping gently towards the Lake, which will, when completed, greatly enhance the gardens.

For those unfamiliar with Miller Howe, it can best be described as an elegant, luxurious country house hotel, offering a very high standard of comfort, British hospitality and service at its best and with a superb cuisine. In fact, in a previous edition we said that Miller Howe personifies quiet, good taste, thoughtfulness and fastidious care, but, above all, it is John Tovey, a prince among hoteliers. We have no reason to change our views.

Rayrigg Rd Plan**17**
Closed 2Jan–28Mar; 13⇨ ⋒ 1▭ ✗ ⋒TV available in bedrooms P ⋒ ⚓ Children under 12yrs not accommodated Last dinner8.30pm ⋒ ⋒ dB&B⇨⋒£25–£44 (incl dinner) Tea fr£1.50 Dinner fr£10.25 Wine£4.75 *xmas* Credit cards 2 5

★★★★ Longueville Manor, St Saviour, Jersey ☎Jersey25501
This old Norman-style building, with parks dating from the 12th and 17th centuries, is a luxurious treat from the trippers' haven of St Helier a mile and a half away.

Bought by the Lewis family after the War, it was converted to an hotel and opened as such in 1949, and offers 34 comfortable bedrooms to which a great deal of effort has been given.

On the ground floor is a smart cocktail bar, attractive lounges and a dining room with well-polished oak panelling. All is bright and clean with lots of fresh flowers. The atmosphere is cheerful and warming.

Of course, it is the staff that plays so important a role. Led by Mr & Mrs Lewis and their daughter and son-in-law, Mr & Mrs Dufty, the young, and mostly local, staff contribute greatly to one's feeling of well-being. Those in the dining room were extremely charming according to many of our reports.

(off St Helier/Grouville road A3)
Telex no4192306
34 CTV in bedrooms 40P (heated) Children under 7yrs not accommodated International.
Last dinner 8.45pm S%
sB&B £21–£24 dB&B £40–£46
Lunch fr£5&alc Dinner fr£7.25&alc
Wine£2.75 Credit cards 1 2 3 4 5 6

★★★★★ Gleneagles, Auchterarder ☎2231
Built on the lines of a French château, this Hotel, set in 700 acres within view of the Perthshire Hills, seems to represent a world of its own. The interior lives up to its outside promise. Broad, marble staircases, high-ceilinged lounges and the rich-looking bar all contributing to the opulence of this grand hotel.

Functions can sometimes intrude but generally the services are efficient and room service is extremely prompt. The valets, especially,are most helpful and so is George Seaman, the head barman for many years now. Naturally with its large American trade, he is quite a whiz with cocktails. Not only that, he runs his bar wonderfully – we think that it must be one of the best-run bars outside London.

The restaurant is expensive and the cooking is classical, the table d'hôte menus probably representing the best value. At such a hotel as this, jackets and ties are mandatory during the evenings, but Turtle neck sweaters are acceptable. If one intends to dance, black ties are preferred on Saturdays.

(British Transport) Telex no76105
Closed end Oct – mid Apr; 189 Lift CTV in bedrooms P (heated) 18 squash sauna bath Live music & dancing twice wkly
Conference facilities available English & French. Last dinner 10pm S%
sB&B fr£41 dB&B fr£74 Lunch fr£9
Dinner fr£10.80 Wine£3.60
Credit cards 1 2 3 4 5 6

❀❀❀★★★★ Inverlochy Castle, Fort William ☎2177

In 1873 Queen Victoria stayed at Inverlochy Castle for a week and wrote, 'I never saw a lovelier or more romantic spot'. Guests have been repeating her remark ever since. Set in fifty acres of wooded grounds, against a magnificent backdrop of Ben Nevis, it is surrounded by a stunning panorama of hills, woodlands and lochs.

Its gracious rooms are beautifully furnished with Eastern carpets, antique furniture and objets d'art. Fine decorative points of interest have been retained, like the frescoed ceiling of the Great Hall.

But the physical attributes are nothing compared to the overall 'feel' provided by Mrs Greta Hobbs, with her manager and staff. There is no obvious sign that the castle is an hotel and one quickly learns to look upon it as a private house; anything you require, you ring for and someone appears like a genie to attend to your needs. There is even someone on duty all night. From the moment you arrive, you instinctively know that this is somewhere special.

Immaculate young waiters serve your meal in the dining room. Soups are first class – Bortsch, for instance, with the most superb piroshkies; and there are fine dishes like the simple Dublin Bay Prawns, salmon mousse or pickled salmon in the Scandinavian style. This is what plain, but exquisitely cooked British food is all about. Rosettes awarded for dinner only.

(3m NE A82)
Closed mid Nov – Mar; 13 CTV in bedrooms P 2 (hard) billiards International. Last dinner 8.30pm
sB&B £50 dB&B £72 Dinner £17
Wine £5 Credit cards 2 3

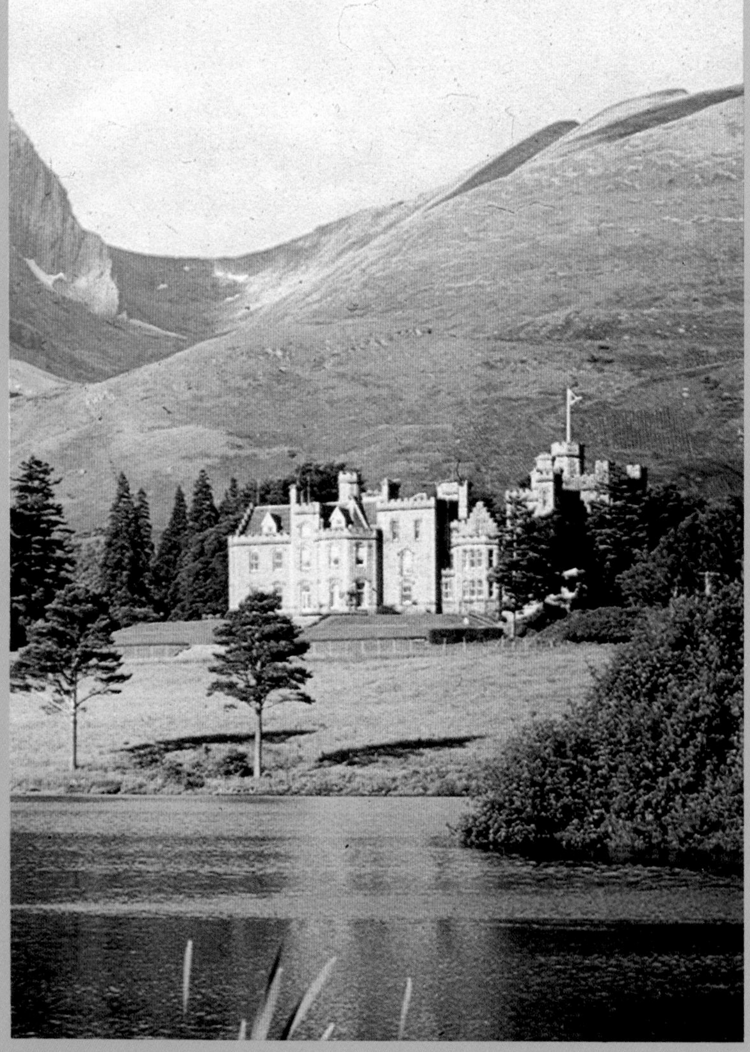

★★★♣Greywalls, Gullane ☎842144
Designed by Sir Edward Lutyens for the Hon Alfred Lyttleton and erected in 1901, Greywalls is an absolutely charming building of pleasing lines, and built in the local Rattlebag stone.

The present owner's grandfather, Lt Col Sir James Horlick, bought it in 1924 and it has remained in the family ever since, being turned into an hotel in 1947. The present family name is Weaver and the hotel is managed by Mr Ford.

The public rooms reflect the private house nature of the building with attractive lounges furnished with easy chairs, deep sofas and lots of nice, old pieces of furniture. In one of the sitting rooms there is a collection of books, many of them owned by the family and portraying the tastes of the inter-war years.

Meals are of good quality and are pleasantly served by charming young girls under the supervision of the smart young head waiter, Ian McDevitt.

Duncur Rd
Closed 12Oct–16Apr; 20rm(17⇌ ⋒) ☽ ⚑ CTV 60P ⊞ ⚘ ↗(hard) ♀French.
Last dinner9.30pm sB&B£22–£24
sB&B⇌ ⋒£24–£26 dB&B£44–£48
dB&B⇌ ⋒£48–£52 Lunch£4.50–£5.50
Dinner£8.50–£9.50&alc Wine£3.75
Credit cards 1 2 3 5

❀★★♣Dunain Park, Inverness
☎30512
Beautifully restored six years ago by Judith and Michael Bulger, this peaceful country house is situated with views of the Caledonian Canal. There are two comfortable lounges, with fires in winter, where one can unwind among the antiques and enjoy an aperitif before meals. There are plenty of magazines around and games like Monopoly, chess and Scrabble to keep one amused. In the gardens there is a croquet lawn and, as an added attraction to children, some farm pets – the Bulgers advise in their brochure that they cannot commend the manners of the goat or of the geese!

But as befits the holder of one of our rosettes (for dinner only), and our last year's regional winner of the 'Pick of the Crop' competition, their great strength lies in the restaurant which has deservedly gained a good name locally. The menu is simple and sensibly short enabling Judith Bulger to lavish her considerable talents on the cooking. Most of the vegetables are provided from the garden and other local produce is used to good advantage. There is enough quantity to satisfy the most robust appetite.

Run like a country house, the Bulgers have succeeded in making the sort of atmosphere that guests are anxious to return to again and again.

Plan**6**
Closed mid Nov–mid Mar; 6rm(4⇌ ⋒) 1⊟ ⚑ TV 30P 1⌂ ⊞ ⚘ ♀International. Last dinner9pm
✿ ⊈ S% ✱dB&B£22.56–£30.88
dB&B⇌ ⋒£26.12–£36.64 Dinner£8.31
Wine£2.61

★★★ Isle of Eriska, Ledaig ☎205
We wrote at great length about this Hotel in our 'Four of the Best' feature two years ago, when we pointed out the unique qualities of this impressive, baronial-type house of granite and sandstone. Its setting with views over the Firth of Lorne to the mountains of Mull is quite splendid.

Since the hotel was opened by the Rev Robin Buchanan-Smith and his charming wife Sheena seven years ago, Isle of Eriska has acquired a nationwide acclaim for both surroundings and cuisine. The Buchanan-Smiths run it more on the lines of an Edwardian home of some substance, but one cannot say that it is completely like a private house. The owners take their work very seriously and their total professional approach comes very much to the fore.

A small farm provides most of the produce for meals. There is only a buffet for lunch and Sunday supper but on other nights a six-course set dinner is served. Items like cream, preserves, bread and even some cheeses are all produced at Ledaig.

Closed Nov–Mar; 24 P (hard) Last dinner8.30pm S%
sB&B £28–£31 (incl dinner)
dB&B £56–£70 (incl dinner) Lunch£4.25
High Tea£5 Dinner£10 Wine£3.10
Credit card 2

★★ Cringletie House, Peebles
☎Eddleston233
A red sandstone, baronial-style house built in 1861, and situated well back from the main road in 28 acres of grounds. It was formerly the home of the Wolfe Murray family and it was Lt Col Alexander Murray from Cringletie who accepted the surrender of Quebec after General Wolfe was killed.

The grounds afford scope for relaxation with the additional amenities of putting and croquet as well as a hard tennis court. The gardens are well maintained and there is a wall section with yew hedging and an extensive kitchen garden whose produce is put to good effect in the dining room.

The house offers many interesting facets in the lounges, cocktail bar and dining room although better quality furniture would be more in keeping. Mr Maquire, the proprietor, greets you on arrival and carries your bags to the bedrooms and thereafter is the true mine host for the rest of your stay, while his wife looks after the kitchen. The wine list offers a good selection and there is also a fine choice of malt whisky for a comparative tasting, for those who want to sample the local products.

Closed mid Nov–mid Mar; 16rm(9) Lift CTV
40P (hard) International.
Last dinner8.30pm sB&B£12.50
dB&B £27 Lunch£4.25 Tea£1.25
Dinner£7.50 Wine£2.85

★★★ Banchory Lodge, Banchory
☎2625

On the 2,000-year-old site of early settlers, this fine, white-painted Georgian house is built virtually on the confluence of the Dee and Water of Feugh.

The Jaffrays, Dugald and Maggie, opted out of farming thirteen years ago and opened Banchory Lodge, having had to restore it from dereliction. It has clearly been a labour of love as can be seen by the care that has gone into every aspect of the hotel. There is an indefinable something that, more than anything else, makes it so welcoming. And that is where the Jaffrays and their staff shine. They have created an ambience that is formal and homely.

In the dining room you will be looked after by Peter Selby and his staff. The menu is well composed so you are assured an enjoyable dinner. Breakfast, too, is not without its delights with well-cooked traditional dishes nicely served.

Banchory Lodge is a fishermen's hotel to some extent, so it is not surprising to see them well catered for in respect of drying rooms etc. In the hall there is an oilcloth-covered table with a set of scales for the successful ones to weigh and exhibit their catch. But there is much to do for the non-fisherman; several golf courses nearby, plenty of walking and, when the conditions are right, ski-ing at Glenshee.

Closed Dec & Jan; 27rm(22 ⇌ ⥣) 3 CTV TV available in bedrooms 50P 2 sauna bath English & French. Last dinner 9.30pm S%
sB&B fr£12.60 sB&B⇌⥣ fr£12.60
dB&B fr£25.20 dB&B⇌⥣ fr£25.20
Lunch fr£3.50 Tea fr£1.25 Dinner fr£7.50
Wine £2.80 Credit cards 2 3

❀★ Bridge of Cally, Bridge of Cally
☎231

Situated apparently in the middle of nowhere, it is, in fact, not far from Blairgowrie at the junction of the A93 and the A924 to Pitlochry, where there are many entertainments, including the Festival Theatre.

Overlooking the River Ardle, the hotel, the dominant building in the hamlet, has fishing rights and there is also a stretch of the Ericht and a small loch available to guests. Surrounded by woodland and the Perthshire Hills, shooting can be arranged and also golf is available.

The hotel is owned by Mr & Mrs Tom Campbell, both outgoing personalities, and aided by Jim and Maggie Boulton, do their best to ensure that you receive the best treatment.

We awarded the hotel a rosette for its dinners and it is well justified. There is a choice of a three or four-course meal from the table d'hôte menu at appropriate prices. For a one-star hotel, this is a remarkable place and we wish many hotels would follow its example. It reminded one of our crew of a small French country hotel providing genuine hospitality and good quality food at reasonable prices.

10rm(4⇌⥣) CTV 30P
Last dinner 8pm S%
*sB&B £7.50–£8.50 dB&B £14.50–£16
dB&B⇌⥣ £16.50–£18.50 Bar lunch 50p
Tea 65p Dinner £4.75–£5.30 Wine £2.80
Credit card 1

AMERICAN EXPRESS

Cards

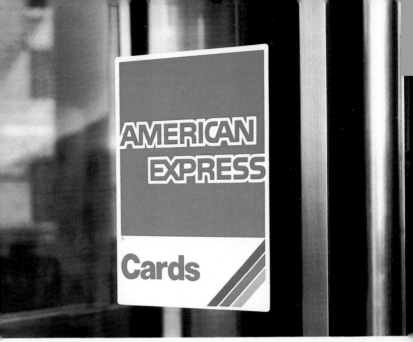

This sign says more about where you stay and dine.

Next time you are looking for somewhere particularly good to stay and dine, you have two useful aids.

The first is *AA Hotels and Restaurants in Britain 1980*, with its wide selection of fine hotels and restaurants all over England, Scotland and Wales.

The second is the American Express sign.

This sign on the door tells you a lot about the quality of service to be found inside. Not just in hotels and restaurants either, but in shops, stores, theatres, car-hire companies and the thousands of other establishments in Britain and around the world which proudly display the sign. Remember, too, that the Card is a truly international currency, and is as valid and welcome in Birmingham and Bristol as it is in Biarritz, Bombay or Boston. Apart from taking care of the day-to-day travel and entertainment bills, simply and in style, it is ready to help you in almost any financial emergency.

If you are not yet enjoying the benefits of carrying the Card, pick up an application form at any establishment displaying the sign, branches of Lloyds Banks or American Express Travel Service Offices; or apply to Brighton direct on 0273-693555.

The American Express Card. Don't leave home without it.

American Express Company – incorporated with limited liability in the U.S.A.
J. S. Quartley, Resident Vice President – United Kingdom and Ireland.

★★♣Polmaily House, Drumnadrochit ☎343

Not far from Loch Ness in the countryside of Glenurquhart, this Edwardian gentleman's house is a pleasant building set in 20 acres of tree-studded land and gardens. There are a swimming pool, hard tennis court and putting green in the grounds and clay pigeon shooting and fishing nearby.

Owned and run by the Misses Brown and Innes, Polmaily House is a simple, but nevertheless, centrally heated hotel. The bedrooms are nicely furnished, one containing a Hepplewhite-style four-poster. A collection of musical instruments including a piano and spinet, are displayed in the lounge, but it is the bar showing armaments and equestrian accoutrements that is the hive of activity – especially so before dinner when guests exchange their day's experiences.

Closed Nov–Mar; 9rm(5⇌ ⋒) 1 ⊟ 25P (hard) International.
Last dinner 8.30pm sB&B£12–£14
dB&B£24–£28 dB&B⇌ ⋒£26–£30
Bar lunch £1–£3 Tea 85p–£1.50
Dinner £7.50–£8.50 Wine £2.50
Credit cards 1 2 3 4

★★★♣Dunkeld House, Dunkeld ☎243

In this ancient town, once the capital of Scotland, the 7th Duke of Atholl built his new home in 1900 right on the bank of the river Tay – Dunkeld House. Part of General Wade's military road runs through the wooded grounds which include a croquet lawn as well as pitch and putt and a tennis court. But with the hotel's own $1\frac{1}{2}$-mile fishing beat, it is a 'must' for the salmon fisherman.

The twenty-seven bedrooms are large and comfortably furnished with good quality old furniture, some of it antique. There is a classic drawing room with balcony on the first floor, but most people seem to prefer one of the three lounges on the ground floor.

Run by Peggy, the dining room overlooks the river and gardens. Decorated in Wedgwood style, it has good table appointments and is spotlessly clean. There are table d'hôte menus at fair prices and a French-inspired à la carte.

Dunkeld House has many attractions – not the least of which are its peaceful setting and discreet service by hostesses Mrs Miller and Mrs Chadwick.

Closed Nov–13Jan; 27rm(22⇌ ⋒) CTV in bedrooms 50P 7 (hard) Live music & dancing Sat English & French.
Last dinner 9pm sB&B£11–£11.50
sB&B⇌ ⋒£12.65–£16.90 dB&B£22–£23
dB&B⇌ ⋒£25.30–£41 Lunch £4.50&alc
Tea 85p Dinner £7&alc Wine £4.30

Hotel Groups

Key to abbreviations and central reservation telephone numbers (where applicable)

*Bookings for companies so marked should be made via AA Travel Agencies shown below.

Company	Abbreviations	Telephone No.
Allied Hotels (Scotland) Ltd	Allied Scotland	
Anchor Hotels & Taverns Ltd	Anchor	Farnborough 517517
Ansells Brewery Co Ltd	Ansells	
*Berni Inns Ltd	Berni	
Best Western	Best Western	01–940 9766
Percy R Brend (Hoteliers) Ltd	Percy R Brend	
*British Transport Hotels Ltd	British Transport	01–278 4211
*Centre Hotels Co Ltd	Centre	01–401 0404
*Clansmans Inns	Clansmans	Sunderland 77424
*Commonwealth Holiday Inns of Canada Ltd	Commonwealth	01–722 7755
*Crest Hotels (Europe) Ltd	Crest	01–903 6422
		Coventry 611813
		Preston 677147
		041–812 0123
De Vere Hotels Ltd	De Vere	01–493 2114
Eldridge Pope and Company (Huntsman Hotels)	Eldridge Pope	
Embassy Hotels	Embassy	01–584 8222
*EMI Hotels	EMI	01–388 5055
Frederic Robinson Ltd	Frederic Robinson	
*Grand Metropolitan Hotels Ltd	Grand Met	01–629 6618
Greenall Whitley & Co Ltd	Greenall Whitley	
Henekey Inns Division Catering Ltd	Henekey	
Hotel Representative Inc *(for Berkeley, Claridge's, Connaught, Savoy – London; Lygon Arms, Broadway; Grosvenor, Chester; Chewton Glen, New Milton)*		01–405 5438
Imperial Hotels Ltd	Imperial	01–278 7871
*Inter Hotels	Inter Hotels	01–373 3241
Kingsmead Hotels Ltd	Kingsmead	Reading 302925
Ladbroke Hotels Ltd	Ladbroke	Watford 44400
*Mercury Motor Inns	Ladbroke	051–236 1864
Mount Charlotte Hotels Ltd	Mount Charlotte	
Myddleton Hotels Ltd	Myddleton	
Nicholsons (London) Catering Ltd	Nicholsons	
*Norfolk Capital Hotels Ltd	Norfolk Capital	01–589 7000
MF North Ltd	North	01–589 1212
Open House Inns (Scottish & Newcastle)	Open House	Newcastle-upon-Tyne 21133
*Osprey Hotels	Osprey	041–552 7788
Prestige	Prestige	01–568 6841
Queens Moat Houses	Queens	
*Rank Hotels Ltd	Rank	01–262 2893
*Reo Stakis Organisation Ltd	Reo Stakis	01–930 0342
		041–221 4343
Scottish Highland Hotels	Scottish Highland	041–332 6538
Scottish & Newcastle Inns Ltd	Scottish & Newcastle	Newcastle-upon-Tyne 21073
*Swallow Hotels Ltd	Swallow	Sunderland 77424
Thistle Hotels (Scottish & Newcastle)	Thistle	Newcastle-upon-Tyne 21073
Travco Hotels Ltd	Travco	
Trophy Taverns Ltd	Trophy Taverns	
*Trusthouse Forte Ltd	Trusthouse Forte	01–567 3444
Chef & Brewer	Wessex Taverns	
Whitbread Ltd	Whitbread	
Wolverhampton & Dudley Breweries Ltd	Wolverhampton & Dudley	Wolverhampton 772411

Automobile Association

Bookings for hotels belonging to groups marked * can be made through AA Travel Agencies. The telephone numbers of the principal ones are given below. For a full list of AA Travel Agencies consult the *AA Members' Handbook* or PO Yellow Pages.

Birmingham	021–643 3378
Bristol	Bristol 290991
Cheadle	061–485 8551
Glasgow	041–204 0911
London (City)	01–623 4152
London (West End)	01–930 2462

Hours Mon–Fri 9am–5pm; Sat 9am–12.30pm. Closed Sun. No charges.

ENGLAND

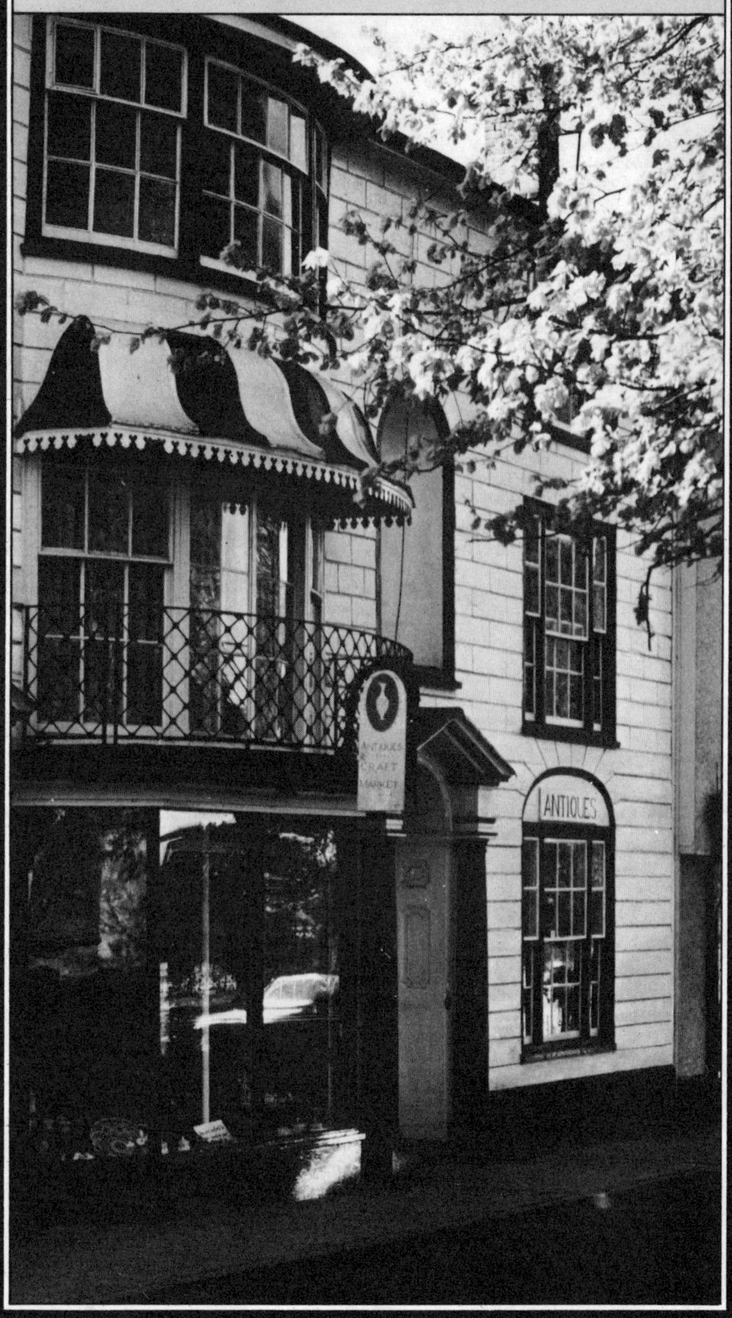

A

ABBERLEY Hereford & Worcester Map**7** SO76
★★★**Elms** (on A443) (Prestige) ☎Great Witley666
See page 33 for details.

ABBOTS SALFORD Warwickshire Map**4** SP05
★★★**Salford Hall** ☎Evesham870561
10rm(5⇌⋒) CTV 100P Last dinner10pm S% ✱sB&B fr£11 sB&B⇌⋒fr£12 dB&B fr£18 dB&B⇌⋒fr£20 Bar lunch65p–£3 Tea65p Dinner£6alc Wine£3.25 *xmas*
Credit cards 1 2 3 4 5 6

ABINGDON Oxfordshire Map**4** SU49
★★**Upper Reaches** Thames St (Trusthouse Forte) ☎22311
Converted Abbey cornmill in country surroundings.
21⇌⋒ TV in bedrooms 90P Last dinner10pm S% sB&B⇌⋒£15.50 dB&B⇌⋒£22 *xmas*
Credit cards 1 2 3 4 5 6

ABRIDGE Essex Map**5** TQ49
✕✕✕**Roding** Market Pl ☎Theydon Bois3030
Closed Sun, Xmas & Public Hols 90seats 10P French. S% ✱Lunch£10alc Dinner£10alc Wine£3 Credit cards 1 2 3 5

ADDINGTON Greater London Map**5** TQ36
✕**Pastori Farmhouse** 86 Selsdon Park Rd ☎01-657 2576
Closed Sun, Mon & 3wks Aug; 35seats 15P English & French. Last dinner10pm Lunch£10alc Dinner£10alc Wine£3.50 Credit cards 1 2 3 5

AFFCOT Salop Map**7** SO48
★***Travellers Rest*** ☎Marshbrook275
10rm(4⇌⋒) TV 15P 1 English, French & German. Last dinner10pm

ALBRIGHT HUSSEY Salop Map**7** SJ51
✕✕***Albright Hussey*** ☎Bomere Heath290523
The battle of Shrewsbury (1406) was fought on the site of this restaurant. The house was used as a garrison during the Civil War.
Closed Mon; Dinner not served Sun; 60seats 200P English & French. Last dinner10pm
Credit cards 1 2 3 5

ALBRIGHTON (nr Wolverhampton) Salop Map**7** SJ80
✕✕✕***Lea Manor*** Holyhead Rd ☎3266
60seats P Live music & dancing Thu–Sun Cabaret Sat English & French. Last dinner10pm.
Credit card 3

ALCESTER Warwickshire Map**4** SP05
☆☆***Cherrytrees Garden Motel*** Stratford Rd ☎2505
Opened in 1965, this modern rustic-built motel off main road has cedarwood chalets in two acres behind.
RS Xmas; Annexe:22⇌⋒ TV 30P Live music & dancing Sat Last dinner9pm

✕✕✕**Arrow Mill** ☎2419
A large water wheel is enclosed in the building which is adjacent to restaurant and bars. The River Arrow runs beneath the buildings.
Closed Mon; Dinner not served Sun; 100seats 200P English & French. Last dinner10.30pm ✱Lunch£7alc Dinner£8.50alc Wine£2.85
Credit cards 1 2 3

ALDBOROUGH Norfolk Map**9** TG13
✕✕**Old Red Lion** ☎Hanworth451
Closed Mon (except Public Hols); 40seats 15P Last dinner9.30pm ✱Lunch£4.32–£4.86&alc Dinner£5.40&alc Wine£2.95

ALDBROUGH (nr Hull) Humberside Map**8** TA23
✕✕***George & Dragon*** ☎230
Closed Mon; Dinner not served Sun; 52seats 20P bedrooms available English & French.
Last dinner9.30pm Credit cards 1 3

ALDEBURGH Suffolk Map**5** TM45
★★★**Brudenell** The Parade (Trusthouse Forte) ☎2071
47⇌⋒ Lift CTV TV in bedrooms 14P 6 Last dinner9pm S% sB&B⇌⋒£16 dB&B⇌⋒£26 *xmas* Credit cards 1 2 3 4 5 6

★★★**Wentworth** Sea Front ☎2312
Closed Jan; 33rm(16⇌⋒) CTV 16P English & French. Last dinner9pm S% sB&B£12.10–£12.65 sB&B⇌⋒£13.75–£14.85 dB&B£23.70–£24.20 dB&B⇌⋒£27.50–£29.70 Lunch£3.50 Tea60p Dinner£5.50–£6 Wine£2.60 Credit card 5

★★★**White Lion** Market Cross Pl ☎2720
32rm(17⇌⋒) CTV 12P Last dinner8.45pm S% sB&B fr£12.70 sB&B⇌⋒fr£15.50 dB&B fr£23 dB&B⇌⋒fr£28.75 Lunch fr£4 Tea fr55p Dinner fr£6.30 Wine£3.10 *xmas*
Credit cards 1 2 3 5 6

★★**Uplands** Victoria Rd ☎2420
Former private house dating back to the 18th century, where Elizabeth Garret Anderson spent most of her childhood.
Closed 1–22Feb & Xmas; 11rm Annexe:8⇌⋒ CTV TV available in bedrooms 25P Last dinner9pm S% sB&B£8–£11.30 sb&B⇌⋒£11.30–£14.20 dB&B£16–£17.40 dB&B⇌⋒£17.40–£20 Lunch£3.50 Dinner£4.50alc Wine£2

ALDERLEY EDGE Cheshire Map**7** SJ87
★★★**De Trafford Arms** London Rd (Greenall Whitley) ☎583881
33rm(22⇌⋒) Lift CTV TV in bedrooms 60P billiards English & French. Last dinner10pm S% sB&B£13–£14 sB&B⇌⋒£15.50–£16.50 dB&B£18–£19 dB&B⇌⋒£20.50–£21.50 Lunch£3.50–£5 Tea35p–£1 Dinner£3.50–£5&alc Wine£3.20
Credit cards 1 2 3 5 6

✕✕***Caprice*** 47 London Rd ☎583942
Closed Mon; 75seats 8P Continental.
Last dinner10.30pm Credit cards 1 2 3 5

✕✕**Le Rabelais** 75 London Rd ☎584848
Closed Sun & 17Aug–14Sep; Lunch not served Sat & Public Hols; 40seats French.
Last dinner11pm ✱Lunch£8.30alc Dinner£8.30alc Wine£2.80 Credit cards 1 5

ALDERNEY Channel Islands
Details follow England

ALFOLD Surrey Map**4** TQ03
✕✕**Chez Jean** Alfold Crossways (On A281) ☎Loxwood752357
Closed Mon; Dinner not served Sun; 65seats French. Last dinner10.15pm Dinner£8.50alc

ALFRISTON East Sussex Map**5** TQ50
★★**Deans Place** ☎870248
Ivy clad 17th-C two-storey mansion set in quiet grounds bounded by River Cuckmere.
Closed Jan; 45rm(25⇌⋒) CTV 50P (heated) (hard) billiards Last dinner8.30pm S% sB&B fr£7.15 sB&B⇌⋒fr£7.90 dB&B fr£13.20 dB&B⇌⋒fr£14.60 Continental breakfast Lunch fr£2.85 Tea fr35p Dinner fr£3.40 Wine£2.20 *xmas*

★★**Star Inn** (Trusthouse Forte) ☎870495
A 13th-C building reputedly built by the Abbots of Battle for the Pilgrims of Bethlehem. Modern extension and car park at rear.

A

34⇌ ⋒ ♯ TV in bedrooms 36P Last dinner9.30pm ♢ S% sB&B⇌⋒£16 dB&B⇌⋒£25.50 ⊟ *xmas* Credit cards 1 2 3 4 5 6

×*Moonraker's* High St ☎870472
Closed 2wks May & Nov & 24Dec–2Jan; Lunch not served; 25seats ♉ English & Continental. Last dinner9.15pm

ALLENDALE Northumberland Map**12** NY85
★★♧Ashleigh ☎351
14rm ♯ CTV ⊘ P ⚓ ♉ Continental. Last dinner10pm ♢ ♔ S% sB&B£10 dB&B£17 Lunch£3.50 Tea£1.30 Dinner£3.80 Credit card 3

★★♧*Riding* ☎237
Local stone building (part 18th century) on outskirts of town. Set in five acres of woodland bordering the East Allen River.
Closed Nov–Feb; 9rm ♯ CTV 20P ⊕ ⚓ ↳ ♉ English & French. Last dinner8pm ♢

ALLENHEADS Northumberland Map**12** NY84
★Allenheads Inn ☎200
RS 20Dec–8Jan (no accommodation); 8rm(1⇌⋒) ♯ TV 25P ↳ Last dinner7pm ♢ ♔ sB&B fr£7.60 sB&B⇌⋒fr£13.25 dB&B fr£12.60 dB&B⇌⋒fr£17.25 Lunch fr£2.60 Tea fr£1 Dinner fr£3.20 Wine£3 ⊟ Credit cards 1 3

ALNMOUTH Northumberland Map**12** NU21
★★Schooner Northumberland St ☎216
RS Nov–Feb; 22rm CTV 40P ⚓ squash Last dinner9.30pm ♢ ✱sB&B£6.50–£8 dB&B£12.50–£16 Lunch£1.25–£4&alc High Tea£1–£2 Dinner£2.50–£6&alc Wine£2.50 ⊟ Credit cards 1 2 3 5

★Osborne House 24–25 Northumberland St ☎476
8rm ♯ CTV 2P ⊕ Last dinner9pm ♢ ♔ sB&B£7–£9 dB&B£14–£18 Lunch£1–£2.50 Dinner£5alc Wine£2.40 ⊟ Credit cards 1 3 5

ALNWICK Northumberland Map**12** NU11
★★★White Swan Bondgate Within (Swallow) ☎2109 Telex no 53168
41rm(40⇌⋒) ☽ ♯ CTV TV in bedrooms 50P ⚓ Last dinner8.45pm ♢ ♔ S% sB&B⇌⋒£12.65–£16.60 dB&B£15.40–£23.60 dB&B⇌⋒£19.25–£26.62 ⊟ *xmas* Credit cards 1 2 3 5

★★*Hotspur* Bondgate Without ☎2924
21rm(14⇌⋒) ♯ CTV 24P 2⌂ Last dinner9pm ♢

ALRESFORD Hampshire Map**4** SU53
★★Bell West St ☎2429
A picturesque Georgian coaching inn.
6rm ♯ CTV ⊘ 4P 2⌂ ⊕ ♉ International. Last dinner8.45pm ♢ sB&B£9.50–£10.50 dB&B£18.50–£22.50 Lunch£2.75–£4&alc High Tea£2.75–£4&alc Dinner£2.75–£5&alc Wine£2.50 ⊟ Credit cards 1 2 3 5

⊛×O'Rorkes 34 Pound Hill ☎2293
Closed Sun, Xmas & last wk Jul–1st wk Aug; Lunch not served; 36seats 20P ♉ Continental. Specialities: Pike Quennelles, Salmon Sauce Messine, Duck with ginger, sherry & orange. Last dinner9.30pm Dinner£9–£11 Wine£3 Credit cards 1 3

ALSTON Cumbria Map**12** NY74
★★Lowbyer Manor ☎230
An old manor house, built during the 17th century, now converted into an hotel.
Closed Nov–Apr; 8rm(4⇌⋒) Annexe: 4⇌⋒ ♯ CTV ⊘ 14P ⊕ ⚓ Children under 6yrs not accommodated ♉ English & French. Last dinner8.30pm sB&B⇌⋒£10.50 dB&B£17.50 dB&B⇌⋒£19.50 Dinner£7alc Wine£3.50

★Hillcrest ☎251
A small hotel of grey stone set in a prominent position with views across a green valley.
11rm CTV 20P 3⌂ ⚓ Last dinner8pm ♢ ♔ ✱sB&B fr£7 dB&B fr£12.50 Lunch£3 Tea£1 Dinner£4 Wine£2.75 Credit card 3

ALTON **Hampshire** Map**4** SU73
★★Alton House Normandy St ☎82369
24rm(9⇌⋒) ♯ CTV 70P ⚓ ⊇(heated) ⟋(hard) ♉ English & French. Last dinner8.30pm ♢ ♔ S% sB&B£9–£9.50 sB&B⇌⋒£11–£12 dB&B£15–£17 dB&B⇌⋒£17–£19 Lunch£2.60–£3 Tea85p–£1 High Tea£2 Dinner£3–£3.50 Wine£2.75 ⊟

★★Swan High St (Anchor) ☎83777 Telex no 858875
Attractive 16th-C former coaching inn, historically linked to the time of the Great Battle during the Civil War.
23⇌⋒ ♯ CTV in bedrooms 100P Last dinner8.45pm ♢ ♔ S% ✱sB&B⇌⋒fr£15.50 dB&B⇌⋒fr£22 Lunch fr£3.25&alc Tea fr40p Dinner fr£3.55&alc Wine£2.65 ⊟ *xmas* Credit cards 1 2 3 4 5 6

ALTON **Staffordshire** Map**7** SK04
××Wild Duck Inn New Rd ☎Oakamoor 702218
Closed Mon (except Public Hols); Dinner not served Sun; 82seats 60P bedrooms available ♉ English & French. Last dinner9.30pm S% Lunch£4.30 Dinner£6alc Wine£3.15 Credit cards 2 3 5

ALTRINCHAM Gt Manchester Map**7** SJ78
☆☆☆Ashley Ashley Rd, Hale (Greenall Whitley) ☎061–928 3794
49⇌⋒ Lift ☽ ♯ CTV in bedrooms 100P Conference

facilities available ☋English & French. Last dinner9.45pm ♔ ♖ sB&B⇌⋒£16.50 dB&B⇌⋒£22 Lunch£3.30&alc Tea45p–£1 Dinner£4.40&alc Wine£2.90 ⊓ Credit cards 1 2 3 4 5 6

★★★***Bowdon*** Langham Rd, Bowdon ☎061–9287121 41rm(38⇌⋒) ☽ ⋒ CTV CTV in bedrooms 150P Live music & dancing Sat ☋English & French. Last dinner10pm ♔ S%

☆☆☆**Cresta Court** Church St (Best Western) ☎061–9288017 Telex no667242 134⇌⋒ Lift ☽ ⋒ CTV in bedrooms 200P Conference facilities available Last dinner11.30pm ♔ ♖ S% sB&B⇌⋒£15 dB&B⇌⋒£23 Lunch£2–£5&alc Dinner£2–£5&alc Wine£2.75 ⊓ Credit cards 1 2 3 5 6

★★★**Woodlands** Wellington Rd, Timperley ☎061–9288631 Telex no667986 35rm(20⇌⋒) ☽ ⋒ CTV CTV available in bedrooms 100P Disco nightly ♧ ☋European. Last dinner11pm ♔ ♖ sB&B£9–£13 sB&B⇌⋒£12–£16 dB&B£14.50–£20.80 dB&B⇌⋒£17–£23 Lunch£2.50–£6&alc Tea30p–£1 High Tea£1–£2.50 Dinner£2.50–£6&alc Wine£2.50 ⊓ *xmas* Credit cards 1 2 3 5

★★**George & Dragon** Manchester Rd (Greenall Whitley) ☎061–9289933 47rm(28⇌⋒) Lift ☽ ⋒ TV TV in bedrooms 60P ♿ ☋French. Last dinner9.45pm ♔ ♖ S% sB&B£13–£14 sB&B⇌⋒£16–£17 dB&B£18.50–£19.50 dB&B⇌⋒£21–£22.50 Lunch£5.50alc Tea40palc Dinner£5.50alc ⊓ Credit cards 1 2 3 4 5 6

☆☆**Pelican** Manchester Rd (Greenall Whitley) ☎061–9627414 50⇌⋒ ☽ ⋒ CTV in bedrooms 150P Last dinner9pm ♔ S% sB&B⇌⋒£16–£17 dB&B⇌⋒£22–£23 Bar lunch£1.95alc Dinner£3.75–£5&alc Wine£2.95 ⊓ Credit cards 1 2 3 5

✕✕**Hilal** 351 Stockport Rd, Timperley (2m E A560) ☎061–9804090 Closed 25Dec; 70seats 20P ☋Indian. Last dinner11.30pm ✻Lunch£2–£2.20&alc Dinner£3.50–£4.50&alc Wine£2.30

✕***Akash*** 336 Manchester Main Rd ☎061–9730697 Closed Xmas Day; 84seats 30P ☋English, Continental & Indian. Last dinner12.30am Credit cards 1 2 3 6

At **Bucklow Hill** (4m SW on A556)
☆☆☆**Swan** (Greenall Whitley) ☎830295 74⇌⋒ 200P

ALVELEY Salop Map**7** SO78
✕✕**Mill** ☎Quatt780437 Dinner not served Sun; 85seats 95P ☋English & French. Last dinner9.30pm Lunch fr£3.50&alc Dinner£7alc Wine£4.10 Credit card 3

ALVESTON Avon Map**3** ST68
☆☆☆**Post House** Thornbury Rd (Trusthouse Forte) ☎Thornbury412521 75⇌⋒ ☽ ⋒ CTV in bedrooms 200P ⚓ ⛆(heated) ♿ Last dinner10.15pm ♔ ♖ S% sB&B⇌⋒£19.75 dB&B⇌⋒£28.50 ⊓ *xmas* Credit cards 1 2 3 4 5 6

★★**Alveston House** ☎Thornbury415050 Telex no444369
Detached Georgian house with new wing extension. Attractive well-kept secluded garden.
14⇌⋒ ⋒ CTV in bedrooms ⊘ 35P Live music & dancing New Year's Eve ☋English & Continental. Last dinner9.30pm ♔

A

sB&B⇌⋒£14.85–£15.95 dB&B⇌⋒£24.75–£25.85 Lunch£3.90–£4.50&alc Dinner£4.50–£5&alc Wine£2.70 Credit cards 1 2 3 4 5 6

AMBERGATE Derbyshire Map**8** SK35
★Hurt Arms ☎2006
6rm CTV 100P Last dinner8pm S% sB&B£7–£8 dB&B£14–£16 Lunch£3 Dinner£4&alc Wine£3.40

AMBERLEY Gloucestershire Map**3** SO80
★★*Amberley Inn* (Best Western) ☎2565
Cotswold-stone inn at roadside next to Minchinhampton Golf course, with delightful views over National Trust land.
11rm(5⇌⋒) Annexe:5rm CTV 25P English & French. Last dinner9.30pm

AMBLESIDE Cumbria Map**7** NY30 See also **Elterwater** and **Langdale, Great**
★★★Rothay Manor Rothay Br ☎3605
Telex no65294
An elegant Regency house scheduled as a building of architectural interest, surrounded by magnificent trees. It lies at the head of Lake Windermere, flanked by the fells of Wansfell and Loughrigg and is within walking distance of Ambleside.
Closed Jan–Feb; 11⇌⋒ CTV in bedrooms 30P English & French. Last dinner9pm sB&B⇌⋒£21–£24 dB&B⇌⋒£35–£37 Lunch£2.50–£3.50 Tea80p–£1.70 Dinner£9.50–£10 Wine£3.30 *xmas* Credit cards 2 5

★★★Waterhead Lake Rd (Best Western) ☎2566
Occupies a fine position overlooking the lake and mountains at Waterhead Bay.
30⇌⋒ CTV 50P Live music & dancing Sat English & French. Last dinner8.45pm S% sB&B⇌⋒£10.80–£14.80 dB&B⇌⋒£21.60–£29.60 Lunch£4 Tea60p–£1 Dinner£6&alc Wine£2.50 *xmas* Credit cards 1 2 3 5

★★Glen Rothay Rydal ☎2524
The Glen Rothay dates from the early 17th century and retains its original oak-panelled lounge with log fires. It is set in lovely grounds, close to the shores of Rydal Water and adjoining Rydal Mount, once the home of the poet Wordsworth.
Closed Jan & Feb; RS Mar; 11⇌⋒ CTV CTV available in bedrooms 25P Last dinner7.30pm S% sB&B⇌⋒£11.50 dB&B⇌⋒£23 Lunch£2.50&alc Tea50p&alc High Tea£1&alc Dinner£5.50–£6.95&alc Wine£2.45 *xmas*

★★Kirkstone Foot Country House ☎2232
Closed 3Nov–27Mar; 12⇌⋒ CTV TV available in bedrooms 30P Last dinner7.45pm

S% sB&B⇌⋒£9–£10 dB&B⇌⋒£18–£20 Lunch£3 High Tea£1.75–£2 Dinner£5.50–£6.50 Wine£2.50 Credit cards 1 2 3 4 5 6

★★Salutation Lake Rd (Open House) ☎2244
The Salutation dates from 1656, but has a modernised interior. Situated in the centre of Ambleside, which is in the heart of the National Park.
29rm(1⇌⋒) CTV 70P Disco Fri & Sat Live music & dancing Tue & Sat Last dinner8.45pm S% sB&B£10.50 dB&B£16.75 dB&B⇌⋒£17.75 Bar lunch60p–£1.90 Dinner£4.20&alc Wine£2.75 *xmas* Credit cards 1 2 3 5 6

★★Skelwith Bridge Skelwith Bridge (2½m W A593) ☎2115
The Skelwith Bridge was originally a 17th-C inn. It lies in a woodland setting at the gateway to the Langdale Valley.
Closed Jan; RS Dec & Feb; 20rm(5⇌⋒) CTV 40P English & French. Last dinner8.30pm S% sB&B£10.75–£12 dB&B£21.50–£24 dB&B⇌⋒£24–£26 Lunch£3.65–£4.25 Tea35–50p Dinner£5.50–£6 Wine£2.50 *xmas* Credit card 1

★★Vale View Lake Rd ☎3192
An established hotel of many years, now in the process of being modernised, but still retaining its essential character.
Closed 4Nov–14Mar; 18rm(6⇌⋒) CTV 10P Last dinner8pm S% sB&B£7.50–£8 sB&B⇌⋒£9.50–£10.75 dB&B£13.50–£15 dB&B⇌⋒£15.50–£17.50 Lunch£3.30 Dinner£4.20 Wine£2.50 Credit card 1

★★*Wateredge* ☎2332
Originally two 17th-C cottages with later additions, and lawns extending to the edge of the lake.
Closed 14Nov–8Dec, 24–27Dec & 30Jan to 2Mar; 16rm(4⇌⋒) CTV 30P Children not accommodated Last dinner8pm

★White Lion ☎3140
A 17th-C country inn situated in the centre of the village.
Closed 2wks Xmas; 14rm CTV 20P 8 Children under 4yrs not accommodated Last dinner7.30pm sB&B£8.75 dB&B£17 Lunch fr£3 Tea fr75p Dinner fr£4.50 Wine£3.25

Romney Waterhead (1m S A591) ☎2219
A modern hotel, situated in an elevated position overlooking Waterhead Bay and promenade, with mountains and fell in the distance. It lies in its own grounds and has a marvellous flower garden.
Closed Nov–Mar; 19rm CTV 20P Last dinner7pm *sB&B£7.59 dB&B£16.44 Tea fr95p Dinner fr£4.45 Wine£2.35

AMERSHAM Buckinghamshire Map**4** SU99
★★**Crown** High St (Trusthouse Forte) ☎21541
Pleasant old coaching inn with beams; courtyard and small garden to rear.
17rm(4⇌ ⋒) TV in bedrooms 51P
Last dinner10pm S% sB&B£13
dB&B£19 dB&B⇌⋒£21.50 *xmas*
Credit cards 1 2 3 4 5 6

★**Ken House** Long Park (off A416) ☎6368
Secluded house set in wooded surroundings.
RS Xmas (no restaurant or bar facilities); 24rm(4⇌⋒) CTV 24P 4 Children under 18mths not accommodated Last dinner8.30pm *sB&B£9.50 sB&B⇌⋒£11.12 dB&B£15.12 dB&B⇌⋒£17.28 Lunch£3.62&alc Tea30p Dinner£3.62&alc Wine£2.80

✕**Kings Arms** High St ☎6333
14th-C coaching inn with beamed ceilings.
Closed Mon, Tue after Public Hols; Dinner not served Sun; 30seats 25P English & French.
Last dinner10pm Lunch£5.50alc Dinner£5.50alc
Wine£2.80 Credit cards 1 2 3 5

✕**John's Chinese** 131 Station Rd ☎5505
40seats Chinese. Last dinner11.30pm
*Lunch£2&alc Dinner£3&alc Wine£3.30
Credit cards 2 5

AMESBURY Wiltshire Map**4** SU14
★★***Antrobus Arms*** Church St ☎3163
19rm(11⇌⋒) CTV English & French.
Last dinner8.45pm
Credit cards 1 2 3 4 5 6

AMPFIELD Hampshire Map**4** SU32
☆☆☆**Potters Heron** (Whitbread)
☎Chandlers Ford66611
42⇌⋒ CTV in bedrooms 120P Conference facilities available English & French.
Last dinner10pm sB&B⇌⋒£18
dB&B⇌⋒£27.50 Lunch£3.50alc
Dinner£5.50&alc Wine£3 Credit cards 1 3 5

AMPNEY CRUCIS Gloucestershire Map**4** SP00
✕**Crown of Crucis** ☎Poulton403
Closed Wed; 60seats 150P English & French.
Last dinner9pm *Lunch£4–£6&alc Dinner£6alc
Wine£2.95

AMPTHILL Bedfordshire Map**4** TL03
✕**Kings Arms** Kings Arms Yard (off Church St)
☎404303
Pleasant 17th-C building with low-beamed first floor dining room situated in small courtyard.
Closed Mon; Lunch not served Sat; Dinner not served Sun; 45seats 12P French.
Last dinner10pm S% Lunch fr£3.65&alc
Dinner£5.50alc Wine£2.85 Credit cards 1 2 3 5

ANDOVER Hampshire Map**4** SU34
★★**Star & Garter** High St ☎3332
18rm(6⇌⋒) CTV TV in bedrooms 40P 4 Disco Wed & Fri English & French. Last dinner10pm
S% sB&B fr£9.75 sB&B⇌⋒fr£14
dB&B fr£17.80 dB&B⇌⋒fr£18.70
Lunch fr£3.30&alc Tea40–60p
Dinner fr£3.30&alc Wine£3.50
Credit cards 1 2 3 4 5 6

★★**White Hart** Bridge St (Anchor) ☎2266
Telex no858875
Historical, 16th-C former coaching inn situated near prehistoric sites and ancient crossroads.
22rm(12⇌⋒) CTV in bedrooms 20P
Last dinner9.30pm S% *sB&B fr£11
sB&B⇌⋒fr£15.50 dB&B fr£18.50
dB&B⇌⋒fr£22 Lunch fr£3.50 Dinner fr£4
Wine£2.65 *xmas* Credit cards 1 2 3 4 5 6

ANGMERING-ON-SEA West Sussex Map**4** TQ00
★★**South Strand** South Strand ☎Rustington5086
12rm(3⇌⋒) CTV 25P Last dinner8pm
S% sB&B£9–£9.50 sB&B⇌⋒£12–£12.50
sB&B£16.50–£17.50 dB&B⇌⋒£19.50–£20.50
Lunch£5–£5.25 Tea30–35p High Tea40–50p
Dinner£5–£5.25 Wine£2.75 *xmas*

ANNFIELD PLAIN Co Durham Map**12** NZ15
✕***Ye Olde Earl Grey Inn*** Kyo Rd ☎Stanley34187
Small, white-faced building with old beams around windows and doors.
64seats English, Scottish, French & Italian.
Last dinner10pm

APPLEBY Cumbria Map**12** NY62
★★★***Appleby Manor*** Roman Rd ☎51571
A pink sandstone Victorian country house of 1877, standing in three acres of its own grounds, with lawns and orchards.
13rm(6⇌⋒) CTV 40P 7 English & German.
Last dinner10pm Credit cards 1 3 4 5

★★***Royal Oak Inn*** Bongate ☎51463
14th-C coaching inn in the Eden Valley.
8rm CTV 9P 3 Mainly grills. Last dinner9pm

★★**Tufton Arms** Market Sq, Boroughgate ☎51593
A 19th-C coaching inn with modern interior, but retaining its original cobbled yard, and is centrally situated in the Market Square. Facilities include exclusive rights to an 11-mile stretch of the River Eden.
28rm(15⇌⋒) CTV 20P 6 Last dinner9pm
S% sB&B£10 dB&B⇌⋒£11
dB&B£18.50 dB&B⇌⋒£20 Lunch£3.75–£4.50
Tea50p Dinner£5–£5.75&alc Wine£2.75
Credit cards 1 2 3 5

★**Courtfield** Bongate ☎51394
Small homely establishment occupying Victorian building, formerly a Vicarage. Set in three acres of gardens and is situated on the outskirts of the town.
8rm Annexe: 6rm CTV CTV available in bedrooms 30P 2 Last dinner8pm S% sB&B£7–£8
dB&B£14–£16 Dinner£6–£7 Wine£2.60
Credit cards 1 3

★**Glen** Boroughgate ☎51598
This small, modernised hotel dates from the early 18th century, but still retains its old world charm.
RS Jan–Feb (no accommodation; no dinner Mon–Fri); 8rm CTV 4P Last dinner8pm
sB&B£6.50 dB&B£13 Lunch£3alc
Dinner£4.20alc Wine£2.10

✕**Bongate** Bongate ☎51498
Closed Wed (winter only); 40seats 40P bedrooms available Last dinner9pm *Lunch£5alc
Dinner£5alc Wine£2 Credit card 3

APPLEDORE Devon Map**2** SS43
★★**Seagate** The Quay ☎Bideford2589
Closed 6Oct–25Apr; 10rm CTV 6P 2
Last dinner9.30pm S% sB&B£9 dB&B£16
Bar lunch40p–£2.15 Dinner£5–£5.75 Wine£2.50

ARDINGLY West Sussex Map**4** TQ32
✕***Camelot*** High St ☎892503
Closed Mon except Bank Hols; Dinner not served Sun; 40 seats English & French. Last dinner9pm
Credit cards 1 2 3 5 6

ARMATHWAITE Cumbria Map**12** NY54
★***Duke Head Inn*** ☎226
An old-world village inn, situated in the centre of the village close to the River Eden, with large garden, aviaries and a fish pool.
8rm TV Last dinner8pm

A

★**Red Lion** ☎204
An 18th-C coaching inn situated by the bridge over the River Eden. The now-converted old stables house the Stable Bar, attractively furnished with antiques, horse brasses, harnesses etc.
Closed 24–26 Dec 11rm ₩ CTV 40P 1🏠 ↳ Last dinner8.30 ♆ sB&B£7 dB&B£13.50 Lunch£3 Dinner£4 Wine£2.50 ▤

ARMITAGE (nr Rugeley) Staffordshire Map**7** SK01
✕✕**Old Farmhouse** ☎490353
Closed Sat, Sun, Public Hols, 22–26 Dec, 26–30 May, 28 Jul–8 Aug & 6–7 Oct; Lunch not served Mon; 100seats 40P Last dinner9.30pm
✱Lunch£2.95–£5.35 Dinner£5.50–£7.50 Wine£2.95 Credit cards 1 6

ARUNDEL West Sussex Map**4** TQ00
★★★**Norfolk Arms** High St ☎882101
18th-C coaching inn with central arch and ornate staircase. Situated in the centre of Arundel within the shadow of the castle.
22rm(13⇌ ⋒) 5▭ CTV in bedrooms 20P Last dinner10pm ♆ sB&B£11–£15 sB&B⇌ ⋒£13.50–£17 dB&B£20–£24 dB&B⇌ ⋒£22.50–£26.50 Lunch£2.95–£3.75 Dinner£4.35–£4.75&alc Wine£2.95 ▤ Xmas Credit Cards 1 2 3 5

✕✕***St Mary's Gate Inn*** London Rd ☎883145
17th-C inn with small dining room, situated next to the Cathedral.
Dinner not served Sun; 60seats P bedrooms available Last dinner9.30pm

ASCOT Berkshire Map**4** SU96
★★★**Berystede** Bagshot Rd, Sunninghill (Trusthouse Forte) ☎23311 Telex no847707
A pleasant mansion built originally as a private house in the late 19th century, situated in own wooded grounds, with lawns and rosebeds.
96⇌ ⋒ Lift ☽ ₩ CTV in bedrooms 176P 6🏠 ⚓ ⇁(heated) Conference facilities available Last dinner10pm ♆ ⚲ S% sB&B⇌ ⋒£23.50 dB&B⇌ ⋒£32 ▤ *xmas* Credit cards 1 2 3 4 5 6

★★**Royal Foresters** London Rd ☎Winkfield Row4747
15⇌ ⋒ Annexe:20⇌ ⋒ CTV in bedrooms 100P ♉Mainly grills. Last dinner10pm ♆ ⚲ S% ✱sB&B⇌ ⋒ fr£18 dB&B⇌ ⋒ fr£25.60 Lunch£3–£5 Tea fr70p Dinner£3–£5 Wine£3.50 Credit cards 1 2 3 4 5 6

ASHBOURNE Derbyshire Map**7** SK14
★★**Green Man** St John Street (Greenall Whitley) ☎3861
Inn dating from Queen Anne period, that was previously an 18th-C magistrate's meeting place.
RS Xmas & New Year 17rm(9⇌ ⋒) CTV 25P Last dinner9.45pm ♆ sB&B£11–£12 sB£B⇌ ⋒£13–£14 dB&B£17–£18 dB&B⇌ ⋒£19–£20 Lunch£2.90&alc Dinner£7alc ▤ Credit cards 1 2 3 4 5 6

ASHBURTON Devon Map**3** SX77
☆☆**Dartmoor Motel** (A38/B3357) ☎52232
Closed Xmas Day; RS 2wks Xmas; 6⇌ ⋒ Annexe:14⇌ ⋒ ✗ ₩ CTV TV available in bedrooms 50P 2🏠 ♿ Last dinner10pm ♆ ⚲ sB&B⇌ ⋒£10.50 dB&B⇌ ⋒£16–£18 Lunch fr£2.40 Tea fr60p High Tea fr80p Dinner£5alc ▤ Credit cards 2 3 5

★★♔**Holne Chase** ☎Poundsgate280
Beautifully situated on edge of Dartmoor, in nine acres of grounds.
12rm(8⇌ ⋒) ₩ CTV 20P 5🏠 ⚘ ⚓ ↳ ♿ Last dinner9pm ♆ ⚲ sB&B£7.95–£10.75 sB&B⇌ ⋒£12.79–£13.45 dB&B£20.50 dB&B⇌ ⋒£25.50 Lunch£3.80 Tea75p Dinner£4.80–£5.50 Wine£2.20 ▤ *xmas* Credit cards 1 2 3 5 6

ASHBY DE LA ZOUCH Leicestershire Map**8** SK31
★★**Royal** Station Rd (Crest) ☎2833
30rm(8⇌ ⋒) ☽ CTV available in bedrooms 150P ⚓ ♉English & French. Last dinner9pm ♆ S% ✱sB&B£10.36 sB&B⇌ ⋒£16.20 dB&B£17.28 dB&B⇌ ⋒£23.76 ▤ Credit cards 1 2 3 4 5 6

✕**La Zouch** Kilwardby St ☎2536
Closed Mon; Dinner not served Sun; 48seats ₱ ♉Continental. Last dinner10pm Lunch fr£3.25&alc Dinner£6.50alc Wine£3 Credit cards 1 2 3 5 6

ASHFORD Kent Map**5** TR04
★★**County** High St ☎20047
17rm ₩ CTV in bedrooms 4P 2🏠 ♉European. Last dinner10pm ♆ ⚲ sB&B£12.50 dB&B£16 Lunch£2–£7 Tea fr75p Dinner£2.50–£7 Wine£2.30 ▤ Credit cards 1 2 3 5

★★**George** High St ☎25512
13rm(1⇌ ⋒) ₩ CTV 4P 4🏠 ♉European. Last dinner10pm ♆ ⚲ S% sB&B£12 dB&B£15 Lunch fr£2.25&alc Dinner fr£2.50&alc ▤ Credit cards 1 2 3 5

★★**Spearpoint** Canterbury Rd, Kennington ☎21833
The triangle of land adjacent to hotel was formerly used for local hangings.
25rm(20⇌ ⋒) ☽ ₩ CTV in bedrooms ⊘ 40P ⚘ ⚓ Live music & dancing Sat ♉French. Last dinner9.45pm ♆ S% sB&B£11.50 sB&B⇌ ⋒£15.50 dB&B£20.50 dB&B⇌ ⋒£24.50 Lunch£5.50alc Dinner£7.50alc Wine£3.25 ▤ Credit cards 1 2 3 5 6

A

×Old Cottage 20 North St ☎20347
Closed Mon & last 2wks Aug; Dinner not served Sun; 38seats P French Last dinner9.30pm Lunch£2.70–£3.70&alc Dinner£7alc Wine£2.90 Credit cards 1 2 3 5

ASHINGTON West Sussex Map**4** TQ11
★★Mill House Mill Ln ☎892426
7rm(2) CTV in bedrooms 10P Children under 5yrs not accommodated Last dinner9.30pm dB&B£18.50 dB&B£21.50 Lunch£6alc Dinner£7alc Credit cards 2 3

ASHLEY HEATH Dorset Map**4** SU10
★★Struan Horton Rd ☎Ringwood3553
10rm(2) CTV 110P Last dinner9.45pm S% sB&B£8.50 sB&B£8.75 dB&B£13 dB&B£14.50 Lunch£2.50&alc Dinner£6alc Wine£2.80 Credit cards 1 2 5

ASHTON-UNDER-LYNE Gt Manchester Map**7** SJ99
★★York House York Pl, off Richmond St ☎061–330 5899
Large, detached house with Victorian-style restaurant, close to town centre.
RS Xmas Day; 17rm(4) CTV CTV in bedrooms 26P Live music & dancing wkly Cabaret wkly English & French. Last dinner9.30pm S% sB&B£9.20–£12.47 sB&B fr£12.47 dB&B fr£16.04 dB&B fr£18.41 Lunch fr£2.95&alc Dinner£5alc Wine£2.90 Credit card 5

ASHURST Hampshire Map**4** SU31
××Happy Cheese 189 Lyndhurst Rd ☎3232
Closed Sun, 25–26Dec & Public Hols; Lunch not served Sat; 50seats 20P English & French. Last dinner10pm (Sats 10.45pm) Lunch£7alc Dinner£7alc Wine£2.75 Credit cards 1 2

ASKHAM Cumbria Map**12** NY52
★★*Queens Head* ☎Hackthorpe225
An 18th-C coaching inn on the Earl of Lonsdale's estate. Original beams can be seen in the lounge.
RS End Oct–Etr; 8rm CTV 30P 4 Last dinner7.30pm

ASTON CLINTON Buckinghamshire Map**4** SP81
★★★ Bell Inn ☎Aylesbury630252
See page 34 for details.

ASTON ROWANT Oxfordshire Map**4** SU79
★★Lambert Arms ☎Kingston Blount51496
17th-C half-timbered coaching inn on A40 with modern motel block at rear. Traditional beamed interior and extensive views of Beacon Hill and surrounding countryside.
5rm(1) Annexe: 7 CTV in bedrooms 100P 5 Disco Thu Live music & dancing Fri English & French. Last dinner5pm S% Lunch£3–£5&alc Tea£1.50–£2.50 High Tea£1.50–£2.50 Dinner£3–£5&alc Wine£2.50 Credit cards 1 2 3 5

ASTWOOD BANK Hereford & Worcester Map**4** SP06
×Nevill Arms ☎2603
Closed Mon; Dinner not served Sun; 40seats 50P English & French. Last dinner9.30pm S% Lunch fr£3.50 Dinner£5.50alc Wine£3.50

ATCHAM Salop Map**7** SJ50
★★*Mytton & Mermaid* ☎Cross Houses220
8rm(3) CTV 80P Last dinner9.30pm Credit cards 1 3

ATHERSTONE Warwickshire Map**4** SP39
★Old Red Lion ☎3156
17th-C former coaching inn in centre of village.
RS Xmas; 10rm CTV 25P 4 Last dinner10pm S% sB&B£8.50 dB&B£14 Lunch£4alc Tea60p alc Dinner£5.50alc Wine£2.50 Credit cards 1 2 3 6

AUDENSHAW Gt Manchester Map**7** SJ99
★*Trough House* 103 Manchester Rd ☎061–370 1574
Closed Bank Hols; 14rm Annexe: 14rm(1) CTV 100P Last dinner8.30pm

AUDLEM Cheshire Map**7** SJ64
★Crown ☎811233
17th-C former coaching house at A529/A525 junction.
6rm CTV 30P Disco 4 nights wkly Cabaret wkly Last dinner8pm S% sB&B£6.50 dB&B£12 Bar lunch£1.50alc Dinner£4alc Wine£2.50

AXBRIDGE Somerset Map**3** ST45
××Oak House The Square ☎732444
Small olde-world restaurant in quiet country town.
Closed 26Dec–5Jan; 120seats P bedrooms available Last dinner9.30pm Lunch£1.30–£3 Dinner£5alc Wine£2.95 Credit cards 2 5

AXMINSTER Devon Map**3** SY29
★★Woodbury Park Woodbury Cross ☎33010
10rm(3) CTV 50P (heated) sauna bath International. Last dinner9.30pm sB&B£10.50–£12.50 sB&B£11–£13 dB&B£19.50–£23 dB&B£23–£26 Lunch£2.50–£4&alc Tea30–75p&alc Dinner£4–£5.50&alc Wine£2.20 *xmas* Credit cards 1 2 3 5 6

★*Cedar* Silver St ☎32304
Converted 18th-C house near town centre.
19rm(2) CTV 20P English & Continental. Last dinner8pm

B

AYLESBURY Buckinghamshire Map**4** SP81
★★**Bell** Market Sq (Trusthouse Forte) ☎82141
Old coaching house situated in centre of old market town.
22rm(8⇌⋒) TV in bedrooms ⊮ Last dinner9.30pm ✿ S% sB&B£12 sB&B⇌⋒£15 dB&B£17.50 dB&B⇌⋒£20.50 ⊟ Credit cards ①②③④⑤⑥

★★**Kings Head** Market Sq (Crest) ☎5158
One of the most perfect examples of Tudor architecture in Britain. Frequented by Henry VIII and Oliver Cromwell.
15rm CTV available in bedrooms 15P ⊗ ♡English & French. Last dinner9pm ✿ ⊻ S% ✱sB&B£10.36 dB&B£16.41 ⊟ *xmas*
Credit cards ①②③④⑤⑥

AYNHO Northamptonshire Map**4** SP53
✕✕***Cartwright*** ☎Croughton218
70seats 30P Last dinner10.30pm
Credit cards ①②③④⑤⑥

AYTON, GREAT North Yorkshire Map**8** NZ51
★***Royal Oak*** High Green ☎2361
8rm(1⇌⋒) CTV ⊘ 6P Last dinner9pm ✿ ⊻ S%
Credit cards ①②④

BABBACOMBE Devon Map**3** SX96 **See under Torquay**

BACKFORD CROSS Cheshire Map**7** SJ37
☆☆☆**Wirral Ladbroke Mercury Motor Inn** Backford Cross Roundabout, A41/A5117 (Ladbroke)
☎Great Mollington851551 Telex no61552
122⇌⋒ ☽ ♛ CTV in bedrooms 122P ⚓ ↳ ⌂
Conference facilities available Last dinner10.30pm
✿ sB&B⇌⋒£21–£22
dB&B⇌⋒£27.50–£28.50 Lunch£4.50&alc
Dinner£5.50&alc Wine£3.20 ⊟
Credit cards ①②③④⑤⑥

BAGINTON Warwickshire Map**4** SP37
✕✕**Old Mill** ☎Coventry303588
Lunch not served Sat; Dinner not served Sun; 100seats 500P ♡English & Continental.
Last dinner10pm ✱Lunch fr£3.50&alc
Dinner£7.50alc Wine£2.75
Credit cards ①②③④⑤⑥

BAGSHOT Surrey Map**4** SU96
★★★★ **Pennyhill Park** College Ride ☎71774
16⇌⋒ ☽ ⊞ ♛ CTV in bedrooms 250P ⚓ ⌓(heated) ♂9 ↗(hard/grass) ↳ ∩ sauna bath Live music & dancing Sat ⌂ ♿ ♡International.
Last dinner10.30pm ✿ ⊻ ✱sB&B⇌⋒fr£22.65 dB&B⇌⋒fr£32 Lunch fr£5.50&alc Tea fr50p&alc High Tea fr£2&alc Dinner fr£5.95&alc Wine£4.10 ⊟ *xmas* Credit cards ①②③⑤

★★**Cricketers'** London Rd (Trusthouse Forte)
☎73196
Popular inn with cricket ground to rear.
26rm(12⇌⋒) ♛ TV in bedrooms 50P ⚓
Last dinner10pm ✿ ⊻ S% sB&B£12
sB&B⇌⋒£15 dB&B£17.50 dB&B⇌⋒£22 ⊟
xmas Credit cards ①②③④⑤⑥

BAINBRIDGE North Yorkshire Map**7** SD99
★★**Rose & Crown** Village Green
☎Wensleydale50225
Original 15th-C inn with open fireplace and old beams.
Closed Dec–Feb (except Xmas); 12rm ♛ CTV 60P
Last dinner8.30pm ✿ sB&B£9.50 dB&B£19
Bar lunch fr75p Dinner£5.50 Wine£3.10 ⊟
xmas Credit cards ①②③

BAKEWELL Derbyshire Map**8** SK26
★★**Rutland Arms** The Square ☎2812
22⇌⋒ Annexe: 11⇌⋒ ♛ CTV in bedrooms ⊘ 60P ↳ ♡English & French. Last dinner10pm ✿ ⊻ S% ✱sB&B⇌⋒£15.10 dB&B⇌⋒£22.50
Lunch£4.95&alc Tea25p Dinner fr£4.95&alc
Wine£3.20 *xmas* Credit cards ①②③⑤

⊕**Milford House** Mill St ☎2130
Three-storey 19th-C house containing some interesting clocks.
Closed 25Dec–Jan; 10rm(4⇌⋒) ♛ CTV ⊘ 10P 7⌂ ⊗ Children under 10yrs not accommodated
Last dinner7pm ✱sB&B£8.10 dB&B£15.10
dB&B⇌⋒£17.28 Lunch£2.97 Dinner£3.51
Wine£2.50

BALSALL COMMON West Midlands Map**4** SP27
✕✕**Ye Old Saracen's Head** ☎Berkswell33862
70seats 250P Live music & dancing Thu ♡English, French & Italian. Last dinner10pm S%
Lunch£5alc Dinner£5alc Wine£2.74
Credit cards ①②⑤

BAMBURGH Northumberland Map**12** NU13
★★**Lord Crewe Arms** Front St ☎243
Closed Nov–Mar; 26rm(12⇌⋒) CTV 34P ⊗ Children under 5yrs not accommodated ♡English & French.
Last dinner8.30pm S% sB&B£10–£12
dB&B£18–£20 dB&B⇌⋒£21–£23
Lunch fr£2.20 Dinner fr£5.75 Wine£2.40 ⊟

★**Sunningdale** ☎334
18rm(6⇌⋒) ♛ CTV 16P ⊗ Last dinner7pm ✿
sB&B£5.40–£7.56 sB&B⇌⋒£6.48–£9.72
dB&B£10.80–£15.12 dB&B⇌⋒£12.96–£19.44
Lunch£3–£3.25&alc Dinner£3.90–£5&alc
Wine£3.20 ⊟

B

B

BAMPTON Devon Map**3** SS92
★**White Horse** ☎245
Former 14th-C coaching house in town square.
11rm CTV 10P 🐕 ⌁ Lastdinner8.15pm ♉ S%
sB&B£6.53–£7.72 dB&B£13.06–£15.44
Barlunch20–50p Teafr45p Dinner£2.40–£4.20
Wine£1.73

BANBURY Oxfordshire Map**4** SP44
★★★★**Whately Hall** Horse Fair (Trusthouse Forte)
☎3451 Telex837149
17th-C stone building with modern wing set in two acres of gardens; stone-vaulted ceiling in cocktail bar.
78rm(70⇌ ⋒) Lift ☽ ⋈ TV in bedrooms 80P ♿
Conference facilities available Lastdinner9.30pm
♉ ♈ S% sB&B£12 sB&B⇌⋒£17 dB&B£19
dB&B⇌⋒£28.50 ⊓ *xmas*
Creditcards 1 2 3 4 5 6
★★★***Manor*** 27–29 Oxford Rd ☎59361
Telex no837450
30⇌⋒ ☽ ⋈ CTV & TV available in bedrooms ⊘ 30P
🐕 Live music & dancing Sat ♡English & French.
Lastdinner10pm Creditcards 1 2 3 5

BARBON Cumbria Map**7** SD68
★★**Barbon Inn** ☎233
17th-C inn situated in the centre of the unspoilt village in the Lune Valley.
9rm 1⊟ CTV CTV available in bedrooms 10P 3⌂ 🐕 ⚓
Children under 12yrs not accommodated ♡English & French. Lastdinner9.30pm ♉ ♈ ✱sB&B£8.75
dB&B£17.50 Lunch£4alc Tea£1.10alc
Dinner£6.50alc ⊓ Creditcards 2 5

BARDFIELD, GREAT Essex Map**5** TL63
✕***Corn Dolly*** High St ☎Gt Dunmow810554
Closed Mon & Tue; Dinner not served Sun; 30seats
♡English & French.

BARDON MILL Northumberland Map**12** NY76
★**Bowes** ☎237
6rm CTV 10P Lastdinner9.30pm ♉ ♈ S%
✱sB&B£5.40 dB&B£10.80
Lunch£1.60–£2.10&alc Teafr£1 High Tea fr£1
Dinner£2.10–£2.90&alc Wine£2.54

BARDSEY North Yorkshire Map**8** SE34
✕✕***Bingley Arms*** Church Ln ☎Collingham Bridge2462
One of England's oldest inns; mentioned in the Domesday Book.
Closed Sun; 70seats 200P ♡English & French.
Lastdinner9.30pm S% Creditcards 1 2 3 5 6

BARFORD Warwickshire Map**4** SP26
★★**Glebe** Church St ☎624218
Georgian country inn situated in one acre of gardens.
12rm(9⇌⋒) CTV ⊘ 30P ⚓ Lastdinner10pm ♉
sB&B£11.50 sB&B⇌⋒£12.50 dB&B£20
dB&B⇌⋒£21.40 Barlunch£2alc Dinner£4.50alc
Wine£4 Creditcards 1 2 3 5

BARFORD ST MARTIN Wiltshire Map**4** SU03
✕✕**Chez Maurice** ☎Wilton (Wilts)2240
Closed Sun & Boxing Day; Dinner not served Xmas Day; 40seats 20P ♡French. Lastdinner9.30pm
Lunch£3.50–£4.75&alc Dinner£6.75–£7.50&alc
Wine£3 Creditcards 3 5

BAR HILL Cambridgeshire Map**5** TL36
☆☆☆***Cambridgeshire*** ☎Crafts Hill80555
Telex no817141
100⇌⋒ ☽ ⋈ CTV in bedrooms 200P ⚓ ⊡(heated)
⛳18 ♪(hard) squash sauna bath Live music & dancing wkly ♡English & Continental. Lastdinner10.30pm
♉ ♈ ⊓ Creditcards 1 2 3 5 6

BARLBOROUGH Derbyshire Map**8** SK47
XXRoyal Oak ☎Chesterfield810425
Dinner not served Sun; 70seats 50P English & French. Last dinner10pm S% Lunch£3–£4&alc Dinner£4–£5&alc Wine£3 Credit cards 1 5

BARLEY Lancashire Map**7** SD84
XXBarley Mow ☎Nelson64293
Closed Mon; Lunch not served Tue & Sat; 36seats 12P Last dinner10pm Lunch fr£3.75&alc Dinner£7alc

BARNARD CASTLE Co Durham Map**12** NZ01
★Kings Head 12–14 Market Place
☎Teesdale38356
RS Nov–Mar; 14rm(8⇌⋒) CTV 30P 2 Last dinner8.30pm S% *sB&B£9 sB&B⇌⋒£10.50 dB&B£16 dB&B⇌⋒£19 Lunch£4alc High Tea£2.50alc Dinner£4.50alc Wine£2.25 Credit cards 1 3 5

BARNBY MOOR Nottinghamshire Map**8** SK68
★★★Ye Olde Bell (Trusthouse Forte)
☎Retford705121 Telex no56446
An original 17th-C posting house. Queen Victoria and her mother the Duchess of Kent stayed here, and Queen Maud of Norway had a permanent suite of rooms at the hotel.
57rm(45⇌⋒) TV in bedrooms 250P Conference facilities available Last dinner9.30pm S% sB&B£13.50 sB&B⇌⋒£15.50 dB&B£20 dB&B⇌⋒£22 *xmas* Credit cards 1 2 3 4 5 6

BARNSDALE BAR South Yorkshire Map**8** SE51
☆☆☆TraveLodge (Trusthouse Forte)
☎Wentbridge711 Telex no557457
Restaurant facilities in adjacent service area.
71⇌⋒ CTV in bedrooms 60P Mainly grills. S% sB&B⇌⋒£14 dB&B⇌⋒£17.50 Continental breakfast Credit cards 1 2 3 4 5 6

BARNSLEY South Yorkshire Map**8** SE30
★★Queen's Regent St (Anchor) ☎84192
Telex no858875
36⇌⋒ CTV in bedrooms Last dinner9.30pm S% *sB&B⇌⋒£14 dB&B⇌⋒£20 Lunch fr£2.20&alc Dinner fr£3.20&alc Wine£2.85 Credit cards 1 2 3 4 5 6

★Royal Church St (Anchor) ☎203658
Telex no858875
17rm(1⇌⋒) Lift CTV CTV in bedrooms 2P Last dinner9.15pm S% *sB&B fr£10.25 sB&B⇌⋒ fr£14 dB&B fr£17.50 dB&B⇌⋒ fr£20 Lunch fr£3.50 Dinner fr£4 Wine£2.85 *xmas* Credit cards 1 2 3 4 5 6

BARNSTAPLE Devon Map**2** SS53
☆☆☆Barnstaple Motel Braunton Rd ☎76221
60⇌⋒ CTV 150P 34 (heated) English & French. Last dinner10pm S% sB&B⇌⋒£12 dB&B⇌⋒£22 Lunch£3.50&alc Tea£1 Dinner£5&alc Credit cards 1 2 3 5

★★★Imperial Taw Vale Pde (Trusthouse Forte)
☎5861
56⇌⋒ Lift TV in bedrooms 80P Last dinner9pm S% sB&B⇌⋒£16 dB&B⇌⋒£26 *xmas* Credit cards 1 2 3 4 5 6

☆☆☆North Devon Motel Taw Vale (Percy R. Brend)
☎72166
26⇌⋒ CTV CTV in bedrooms 70P Live music & dancing Sat English & French. Last dinner9.30pm *sB&B⇌⋒£12.47 dB&B⇌⋒£21.38 Lunch£3.80&alc Dinner£4.20&alc Wine£3.10 Credit cards 1 2 3

B

★★ **Downrew House** Bishops Tawton (off unclass road 1½m SE of Bishops Tawton: A377) ☎2497
See page 34 for details

★★ ***Roborough House*** ☎72354
White, stucco two-storey building in fourteen acres of grounds just outside town centre.
11⇌ CTV 40P Disco Sat International. Last dinner9.30pm
Credit cards 1 2 3 5 6

★★**Royal & Fortesque** Boutport St (Percy R. Brend) ☎2289
Named after King Edward VII, then Prince of Wales, who was a visitor.
64rm(16⇌) Lift ☽ CTV TV available in bedrooms 20P 6 Live music & dancing 3 nights wkly English & French. Last dinner9pm ✻sB&B£9.50 sB&B⇌£10.67 dB&B£17.23 dB&B⇌£19.02 Lunch£1.89 Dinner£4.05&alc Wine£2.60 *xmas*
Credit cards 1 2 3

✕✕✕**Lynwood House** Fortesque Rd ☎3695
Closed 1st wk Jan & 2wks mid Nov; Lunch not served Sat; Dinner not served Sun; 50seats 35P English & Continental. Last dinner9.30pm Lunch£5.50alc Dinner£9alc Wine£3.95
Credit cards 1 2 3 5

BARNT GREEN Hereford & Worcester Map**7** SP07
✕✕**Barnt Green Inn** ☎021-445 4949
Lunch not served Sat; Dinner not served Sun; 100seats 200P Live music & dancing Sat English & French. Last dinner9.45pm Lunch£3.85&alc Dinner£4.95–£5.95&alc Wine£3.45
Credit cards 1 2 5

BARR, GREAT West Midlands Map**7** SP09
☆☆☆**Post House** Chapel Ln (6m NW junc M6/A34) (Trusthouse Forte) ☎021-357 7444 Telex no338497
204⇌ ☽ CTV in bedrooms 280P (heated)
Conference facilities available Last dinner10.30pm S% sB&B⇌£19.75 dB&B⇌£28.50 Credit cards 1 2 3 4 5 6

★★**Barr** Pear Tree Dr, off Newton Rd (1m W of junc A34/A4041) (Greenall Whitley) ☎021-357 1141
Telex no336406
111⇌ ☽ CTV in bedrooms 250P Live music & dancing Sat English & Continental.
Last dinner10pm S%
sB&B⇌£15.50–£17.50 dB&B⇌£20–£23
Lunch£3.50–£4&alc Dinner£4.25–£5&alc
Wine£3 Credit cards 1 2 3 5 6

BARRASFORD Northumberland Map**12** NY97
Barrasford Arms Main Rd ☎Humshaugh237
5rm CTV 12P Children under 10yrs not accommodated Last dinner8.30pm
✻sB&B£10 dB&B£14 Lunch£3 High Tea £3 Dinner fr£5 Wine£2 Credit card 3

BARROW-IN-FURNESS Cumbria Map**7** SD16
★★**White House** Abbey Rd ☎27303
Large public house on main road.
28rm(2⇌) ☽ CTV in bedrooms 100P 6
Last dinner9.30pm sB&B fr£8.41
sB&B⇌£9.57–£11.38 dB&B fr£15.67
dB&B⇌£18.15–£20.24 Lunch fr£2.20&alc
Dinner£4.84alc Wine£2.35

BARTON Lancashire Map**7** SD53
★★***Barton Grange*** Garstang Rd ☎Broughton (Preston)862551
Large detached house with extensions.
60rm(58⇌) ☽ CTV 80P (heated) (hard)
Live music & dancing Sat Last dinner9pm

BARTON-ON-SEA Hampshire Map**4** SZ29
★★★**Red House** Barton Court Av (Best Western)
☎New Milton610119
26rm(18⇌⋒) Annexe: 19rm(10⇌⋒) ☽ 𝍖 CTV 80P
3🏠 Live music & dancing Sat ♿ ♉ English & French.
Lastdinner9.30pm ♁ S% sB&B£10.90–£11.80
sB&B⇌⋒£12–£13.25 dB&B£17.50–£19
dB&B⇌⋒£19.50–£21.50 Lunch£3.25
Dinner£4.50&alc Wine£3 ⊟ *xmas*
Credit cards 1 2 3 5

BASILDON Essex Map**5** TQ78
★★★**Essex Centre** Cranes Farm Rd (Centre) ☎3955
Telex no995141
120⇌⋒ Lift ☽ 𝍖 CTV in bedrooms ⊘ 110P
Conference facilities available Lastdinner10pm ♁
♁ S% ✱sB&B⇌⋒£16 dB&B⇌⋒£21
Continental breakfast Lunch£3.55 Dinner£3.55
Wine£3.40 ⊟ Credit cards 1 2 3 4 5 6

BASINGSTOKE Hampshire Map**4** SU65
★★★**Hampshire Moat House** Grove Rd (Queens)
☎68181
85⇌⋒ ☽ 𝍖 CTV in bedrooms 140P ♿ Conference
facilities available ♉ French. Lastdinner10.30pm
♁ ⊈ S% sB&B⇌⋒£19.50 dB&B⇌⋒£25.50
Lunch£4.50–£4.75&alc Tea£1–£2
Dinner£4.50–£4.75&alc Wine£3.50 ⊟
Credit cards 1 2 3 5 6

☆☆☆**Ladbroke Mercury Motor Inn** Aldermaston
Roundabout, Ringway North (A339) (Ladbroke)
☎20212 Telex no858223
82⇌⋒ ☽ 𝍖 CTV in bedrooms 150P Conference
facilities available Lastdinner10.30pm ♁
sB&B⇌⋒£21–£22 dB&B⇌⋒£28–£29
Lunch fr£4.50&alc Dinner fr£5.50&alc Wine£3.20
⊟ Credit cards 1 2 3 4 5 6

★★**Red Lion** 24 London St (Anchor) ☎28525
Telex no 858875
Early 19th-C three-storey inn with beamed interior, and modern extension.
43rm(30⇌ ⋒) ⋈ CTV in bedrooms 50P ♔ ♖ S%
✻sB&B fr£12 sB&B⇌ ⋒ fr£15.50 dB&B fr£19.50
dB&B⇌ ⋒ fr£22 Wine£2.65 ▣ *xmas*
Credit cards 1 2 3 4 5 6

BASLOW Derbyshire Map**8** SK27
★★★ **Cavendish** ☎2311
See page 34 for details

BASSENTHWAITE Cumbria Map**11** NY23
★★★ **Armathwaite Hall**
☎Bassenthwaite Lake 551
37⇌ ⋒ Lift ☽ ⋈ CTV in bedrooms 100P 10 ⛫ ⚓ (hard) squash billiards Live music & dancing Sat
English, French & Italian. Last dinner 9.15pm ♔
♖ ✻sB&B⇌ ⋒ £14 dB&B⇌ ⋒ £34 Lunch£3.50
Tea£1.10 Dinner£6&alc Wine£2.50 ▣ *xmas*
Credit cards 1 2 3 5 6

★★★***Castle Inn*** ☎Bassenthwaite Lake 401
Two storey building dating from 1720, situated at crossroads on A591.
Closed Nov & Xmas; 21⇌ ⋒ ⋈ CTV ⊘ 100P ⚓
(heated) (grass) Live music & dancing Fri & Sat (in winter) Children under 7yrs not accommodated
Last dinner 8.30pm ♔ ♖ Credit cards 1 2 3 6

★★ **Overwater** Ireby (2m N)
☎Bassenthwaite Lake 566
Designated as a building of architectural and historical interest, once occupied by the Cumbrian family of Gilbanks as far back as 1780.
Closed Jan–2Mar; 13rm(9⇌ ⋒) 1▭ ⋈ CTV 25P 1⛫
⚓ Last dinner 8.30pm ♔ ♖ sB&B£11
sB&B⇌ ⋒ £12.50 dB&B£15 dB&B⇌ ⋒ £18
Lunch£2.75–£3.50 Tea40–80p
High Tea50p–£1.20 Dinner£4–£5.75&alc
Wine£2.80 ▣ *xmas* Credit cards 1 2 3 5

★★***Pheasant Inn*** ☎Bassenthwaite Lake 234
Black and white old coaching inn of character off A66 at north end of Bassenthwaite Lake. Peacefully situated below Thornthwaite Forest.
Closed Xmas Day; 17rm(10☎ ⋒) Annexe: 3rm(1⇌ ⋒)
⋈ 80P ⚓ Last dinner 8.30pm ♔ ♖

Ravenstone ☎Bassenthwaite Lake 240
Gabled stone Victorian country-house style building in two acres of gardens.
Closed Nov–Mar; 12rm ⋈ TV ⊘ 12P ⚓ billiards
Last dinner 6.30pm ♔ ♖ sB&B£8.85
dB&B£17.70 Lunch£1.40 Tea60p Dinner£3.90
Wine£2

BATH Avon Map**3** ST76 **See plan**
☆☆☆☆**Beaufort** Walcot St (Myddleton) ☎63411
Telex no 449519 Plan**1**
123⇌ ⋒ Lift ☽ ⋈ CTV in bedrooms ⊘ ⛫ Conference facilities available Last dinner 9.45pm ♔ ♖ S%
✻sB&B⇌ ⋒ £17.55–£21 dB&B☎ ⋒ £25–£29
Continental breakfast Lunch£3.50–£4&alc
Tea£1–£1.50 Dinner£5&alc Wine£2.90 ▣
Credit cards 1 2 3 5

★★★★**Francis** Queen Sq (Trusthouse Forte)
☎24257 Telex no 449162 Plan**3**
Rebuilt in Georgian style following wartime destruction, this hotel is situated in the city centre.
66⇌ ⋒ Lift ☽ ⋈ CTV in bedrooms 60P ♿
Last dinner 9.30pm ♔ ♖ S% sB&B⇌ ⋒ £22
dB&B⇌ ⋒ £31 ▣ *xmas* Credit cards 1 2 3 4 5 6

★★★★**Royal Crescent** 16 Royal Cres ☎319090
Telex no 444251 Plan**12**
29rm(27⇌ ⋒) 2▭ Lift ☽ ⋈ CTV in bedrooms ⊘ 8P

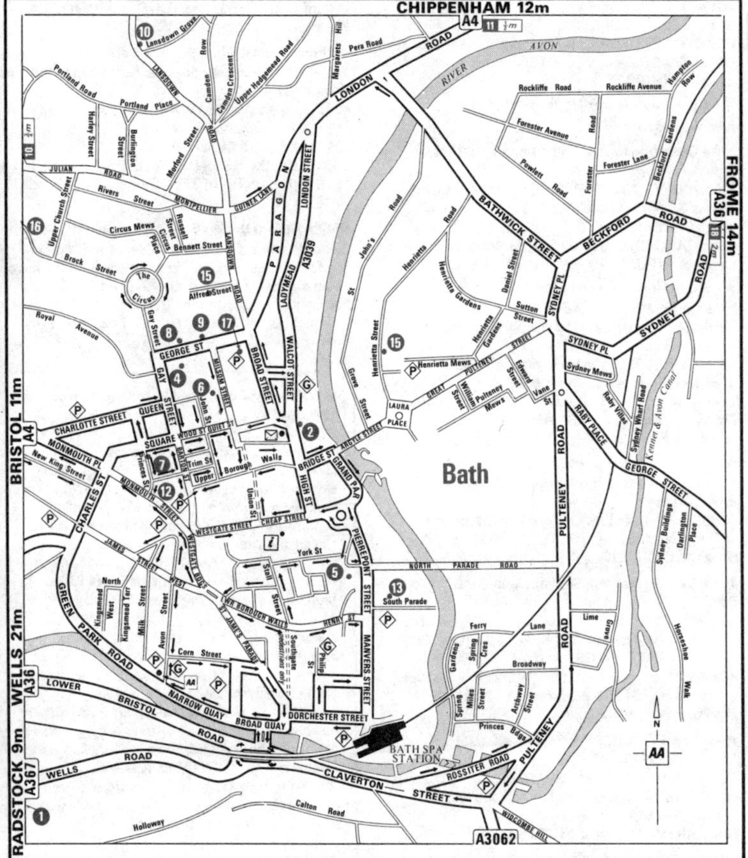

1 Beaufort ☆☆☆☆
2 Fernley ★★
3 Francis ★★★★
4 Hole in the Wall ❀✕✕✕
5 Laden Table ❀✕
6 Lansdown Grove ★★★
7 Old Mill Hotel ✕✕
8 Popjoys ❀❀✕✕✕
9 Pratts ★★★
10 Priory ❀★★★
11 Redcar ★★★
12 Royal Crescent ★★★★
13 Royal York ★★★
14 Scanda ✕
15 Wood's ✕✕

4🏠 ⛳ ⚓ 🍷International. Lastdinner10.30pm 🍸 S% ✱sB&B⇌🚿 fr£23.50 dB&B⇌🚿£37.50–£73.50 Lunch£6 Tea£2 Dinner£7–£10&alc Wine£3.70 *xmas* Credit cards ① ② ③

B

✱★★★ Priory Weston Rd ☎21887 Plan**10**
see page 36 for details

★★★Gainsborough Weston Ln ☎311380 Not on plan
Closed Xmas; 13⇌🚿 🍽 CTV CTV in bedrooms 🐕 14P ⛳ ⚓ Lastdinner9.30pm ✿ ✱sB&B⇌🚿£13.50 dB&B⇌🚿£22.50–£25 Lunch£4.50 Dinner£5.90–£7.25 Wine£2.70 🅱 Credit cards ① ② ③ ⑥

★★★Lansdown Grove Lansdown Rd (Best Western) ☎315891 Plan**6**
Georgian mansion set in own grounds on the slopes of Lansdown.
46⇌🚿 Lift ☽ 🍽 CTV in bedrooms 20P 8🏠 ⚓ 🍷English & French. Lastdinner9.30pm ✿ S% sB&B⇌🚿 fr£21 dB&B⇌🚿 fr£36 Lunch fr£4&alc Dinner fr£6&alc Wine£3 🅱 *xmas* Credit cards ① ② ③ ⑤

★★★*Pratts* South Pde ☎60441 Plan**9**
Built in 1743–48, and an example of John Wood's architecture.
50rm(28⇌🚿) Lift ☽ 🍽 CTV & CTV in bedrooms 🍷European. Lastdinner8.30pm ✿ 🍸 ♿ 🅱 Credit cards ① ② ③ ⑥

★★★Redcar Henrietta St (Kingsmead) ☎60231 Plan**11**
35rm(16⇌🚿) ☽ 🍽 CTV in bedrooms 20P ♪ Cabaret 3 nights wkly 🍷English & French. Lastdinner10pm ✿ 🍸 sB&B£14 sB&B⇌🚿£18 dB&B£23 dB&B⇌🚿£27 Lunch£3.50–£4.25&alc Tea50p Dinner£3.50–£4.25&alc Wine£2.95 🅱 *xmas* Credit cards ① ② ③ ⑤ ⑥

★★★Royal York (Norfolk Capital) ☎61541 Telex no23241 Plan**13**
Built of stone in 1760 and popular during the coaching era. Visited by Queen Victoria when she was Princess in 1830.
56rm(30⇌🚿) 1🛏 Lift ☽ 🍽 CTV 6🏠 🍷English & French. Lastdinner9.30pm ✿ 🍸 S% sB&B£13.75 sB&B⇌🚿£18.15 dB&B£22.25 dB&B⇌🚿£29.25 Lunch fr£3.25&alc Tea fr£1.25 Dinner fr£4.25&alc Wine£4 🅱 *xmas* Credit cards ① ② ③ ⑤ ⑥

★★🏰Combe Grove Monkton Combe (3m S on unclass road linking A36 & A367) ☎834644 Not on plan
7rm(2⇌🚿) 🍽 CTV in bedrooms 🐕 50P 5🏠 ⛳ ⚓ 🍷French. Lastdinner10pm ✿ 🍸 S% ✱sB&B£15–£20 sB&B⇌🚿£15–£20 dB&B£30–£36 dB&B⇌🚿£40–£50 Lunch£4.95–£5.95 Tea50p–£1.50 Wine£3.40 🅱 *xmas* Credit cards ① ③ ⑤

★★Fernley North Pde ☎61603 Plan**2**
19th-C stone and brick building in city centre opposite Parade Gardens.
47rm(27⇌🚿) Lift 🍽 CTV 🐕 🅿 Live music nightly 🍷English & French. Lastdinner9.30pm ✿ 🍸 S% sB&B fr£13.68 sB&B⇌🚿 fr£16.10 dB&B fr£26.35 dB&B⇌🚿 fr£28.75 Lunch fr£4 Tea fr50p High Tea fr£2.50 Dinner fr£5 Wine£3 🅱

✱XXXHole in the Wall 16 George St ☎25242 Plan**4**
Closed Sun & 24Dec–3Jan; 56seats 🅿 🍷French. Specialities: Escalope of Pork Chandelle. Best end of Lamb roasted with herbs. Calves Liver Campagnarde. Lastdinner10.30pm Lunch£6.50alc Dinner£10alc Wine£2.60 Credit cards ① ② ③ ⑤

✱✱XXXPopjoys Beau Nash House, Sawclose ☎60494 Plan**8**
Beau Nash House, a Georgian building with a fine carved entrance, was once the home of Richard (Beau) Nash and his mistress, Juliana Popjoy, and it has achieved its name in the 20th century as a small restaurant of high quality.
In partnership with Kenneth Bell of Thornbury Castle, this restaurant is run by Stephen Ross and his wife who make every effort to set high standards of cuisine with imaginative dishes prepared from good raw materials according to season.
A selection of starters may include various terrines and mousses and amongst the items our inspectors have praised is a hot avocado purée in a light pastry case served with hollandaise sauce; a delicious fish soup and fillet de sole farci with a sauce safran. Amongst the main courses was a portion of brill cooked in the cuisine minceur style which was simply done with finely diced vegetables; served with natural fish and vegetable juices, a purity of taste was maintained. The fillet de boeuf grillé au poivre vert was also praised.
The wine list is extensive and includes many château and domaine bottled wines with a burgundy from good negociants.
It is pleasant to find the wines nicely served, the red in particular being decanted upon ordering.
Closed Sun & 24Dec–24Jan; Lunch not served Mon & Sep–Mar; 50seats 🅿 🍷English & French. Specialities: Terrine de Poisson. Paupiette de Veau. Walnut Tart. Lastdinner10.30pm S% ✱Lunch£8alc Dinner£10alc Wine£4.05 Credit cards ① ② ⑥

××Old Mill Hotel Restaurant Tollbridge Rd Batheaston (3m NE on A4 Chippenham road) ☎858476 Plan**7**
85seats 40P bedrooms available Last dinner9.30pm Lunch fr£3.75 Dinner£8.50alc Wine£4 Credit cards 1 2 3

××Wood's 9 Alfred St ☎314812 Plan**15**
Closed Sun & Mon; 80seats P English & French. Last dinner10pm Lunch£3.25 Dinner£6–£8.50 Wine£2.75 Credit cards 1 2 3 5

❀×Laden Table 7 Edgar Buildings, George St ☎64356 Plan**5**
Closed Sun, Mon & Xmas; 20seats P French. Last dinner9pm ✻Dinner£6.75–£7.25 Wine£3.50 Credit cards 1 3

×Scanda Bathampton ☎62539 Plan**14**
Self-service Norwegian restaurant.
Closed 26 Dec; Dinner not served 25 Dec; 320seats 300P bedrooms available Disco Wed–Sat English & Norwegian. Last dinner10.30pm Lunch£3.51 Dinner£7.79 Wine£3.10 Credit cards 1 3 5 6

BATTLE East Sussex Map**5** TQ71
★George High St (Trusthouse Forte) ☎2844
Coaching inn from which the traditional Good Friday marble race to Battle Abbey begins.
15rm(2⇌ ⋒) CTV 20P Last dinner9pm S% sB&B£11 dB&B£17 dB&B⇌⋒£20.50 *xmas* Credit cards 1 2 3 4 5 6

BAUGHTON Hereford & Worcester Map**3** SO84
×*Gay Dog Inn* ☎Upton-on-Severn2706
Closed Sun, Xmas & 2wks end Sep & Oct; Dinner not served Mon; 28seats P English & Italian. Last dinner9.30pm

BAWTRY South Yorkshire Map**8** SK69
★★★Crown High St (Anchor) ☎Doncaster710341 Telex no858875
18th-C posting house.
58⇌ ⋒ CTV in bedrooms 58P sauna bath English & French. Last dinner9.45pm S% ✻sB&B⇌⋒£17 dB&B⇌⋒£24.25 Lunch fr£3.50 Tea fr95p Dinner fr£4.50 Wine£2.65 *xmas* Credit cards 1 2 3 4 5 6

×××Dower House Market Pl ☎Doncaster710497
Closed Sun, Xmas & 2wks Feb; 66seats 20P English & French. Last dinner9.45pm ✻Lunch£2.70–£6.50 dinner£5.65–£8.30 Wine£2 Credit cards 2 5

BAYCLIFF Cumbria Map**7** SD27
★★*Fishermans Arms* ☎Bardsea387
On coast road between Ulverston and Barrow-in-Furness in a good position for exploring the Cumbrian Coast and Lake District.
12rm CTV 60P Last dinner9.15pm Credit cards 2 3 6

BAY HORSE Lancashire Map**7** SD45
★Foxholes ☎Forton791237
RS Tue (no lunch); 10rm(1⇌ ⋒) 50P Last dinner9pm S% sB&B fr£7.50 dB&B fr£14.50 dB&B⇌⋒ fr£17 Lunch fr£3 Dinner£6.05alc Wine£2.50 Credit cards 1 3

BEACHLEY Gloucestershire Map**3** ST59
★★Old Ferry ☎Chepstow2474
16rm(3⇌ ⋒) CTV TV available in bedrooms 100P Last dinner9pm sB&B fr£9.18 sB&B⇌⋒ fr£10.80 dB&B fr£16.74 dB&B⇌⋒ fr£18.90 Lunch£3.50alc Dinner£4.50alc Wine£3.50 Credit cards 1 2 3 5 6

BEACONSFIELD Buckinghamshire Map**4** SU99
☆☆☆☆**Bellhouse** (2m E A40) (De Vere) ☎Gerrards Cross87211 Telex no22121
Newly-built around the old shell and surrounded by pleasant countryside.
120⇌ ⋒ Lift TV in bedrooms 750P Conference facilities available Last dinner9.45pm S% sB&B⇌⋒£24 dB&B⇌⋒£32 Lunch fr£5.75&alc Tea fr£1.20 Dinner fr£6.25&alc Wine£3.50 *xmas* Credit cards 1 2 3 5 6

☆☆**Beaconsfield Crest** Aylesbury End (Crest) ☎71211
41rm Annexe: 28⇌ ⋒ CTV available in bedrooms 100P Last dinner9.30pm S% ✻sB&B£12.47 sB&B⇌⋒£16.25 dB&B£17.92 dB&B⇌⋒£22.78 Continental breakfast Credit cards 1 2 3 4 5 6

×China Diner 7 The Highway, Station Rd ☎3345
Closed 25 & 26Dec; 58seats P Pekinese & Szechuan. Last dinner11.30pm Lunch£2.50–£5.50&alc Dinner£3.50–£6&alc Wine£2.95 Credit cards 1 2 3 5 6

×Jasmine 15A Penn Rd ☎5335
Closed Xmas; 102seats 50P Chinese. Last dinner11.30pm Lunch£1.50–£2.00 Dinner£3.00–£5.00 Wine£3.00 Credit cards 1 2 3 5

BEAMINSTER Dorset Map**3** ST40
★★*White Hart* Hogshill St ☎862779
Old coaching inn in centre of small country town.
7rm TV 10P Last dinner10pm Credit cards 1 3 5

××Pickwicks The Square ☎862094
Closed Sun; Lunch not served; 36seats 20P International. Last dinner9.30pm S% Dinner fr£7.50 Wine£3 Credit cards 1 3

BEAULIEU Hampshire Map**4** SU30
★★★Montagu Arms ☎612324
Gabled and creeper-clad inn built of mellow local brick.

B

26⇌⋔ 6▭ ☽ ₩ CTV in bedrooms 150P 10⌂ ♣ ⚓ ↺ ♀English & French. Last dinner 10pm ♈ ⚱ S% sB&B⇌⋔£14–£17 dB&B⇌⋔£22–£30 Lunch£3.85&alc Tea£1.25 High Tea£2 Dinner£5.25&alc Wine£4.25 ⊓ *xmas* Credit cards ① ② ③ ⑤

BECCLES Suffolk Map**5** TM49
★★**Waveney House** Puddingmoor ☎712270
15rm(13⇌⋔) 1▭ ₩ CTV in bedrooms 40P ♣ ⚓ ↺ ⚘ ♀English & French. Last dinner 9.45pm ♈ ⚱ S% sB&B£13.50 sB&B⇌⋔£15.70 dB&B£22 dB&B⇌⋔£25.85 Lunch£3.25–£3.50&alc Tea£1 Dinner£4–£4.50&alc Wine£3.50 ⊓ Credit cards ① ② ③ ⑤ ⑥

BECKERMET Cumbria Map**11** NY00
★★**Blackbeck** ☎352
Converted Georgian farmhouse with 1½ acres of paddock.
24rm(15⇌⋔) ₩ CTV CTV available in bedrooms 100P ♀Mainly grills. Last dinner 9.30pm ♈ S% sB&B fr£10 sB&B⇌⋔ fr£18 dB&B fr£15 dB&B⇌⋔ fr£22 Lunch fr£2.50 Dinner fr£3.50 Wine£2.80 ⊓ Credit cards ① ② ③ ⑥

BEDFORD Bedfordshire Map**4** TL04
★★★**Bedford Moat House** St Mary's Street (Queens) ☎55131 Telex no 825243
Modern hotel on banks of River Ouse, overlooking the old town and a fine Georgian bridge.
80rm(76⇌⋔) Lift ☽ ₩ CTV TV in bedrooms ⊘ 20P 16⌂ Live music & dancing Sat Conference facilities available ♀English & French. Last dinner 9.45pm ♈ ⚱ S% sB&B£15–£17 sB&B⇌⋔£16–£18 dB&B⇌⋔£21–£24 Lunch£3.75–£4.50&alc Tea45p Dinner£4.75–£5.50&alc Wine£3.75 ⊓ Credit cards ① ② ③ ⑤

★★★**Woodlands Manor** Clapham (2m N A6) ☎63281
18⇌⋔ ☽ ₩ CTV in bedrooms ⊘ 100P ♣ ⚓ ⌓ Live music & dancing Sat Conference facilities available ♀French. Last dinner 10pm ♈ ⚱ ✻sB&B⇌⋔£16.20 dB&B⇌⋔£25.40 Lunch£3.50–£3.75&alc Dinner£4.75–£6.25&alc Wine£2.80 Credit cards ① ② ③ ⑤

★★**Bedford Swan** The Embankment ☎46565
Late 18th-C hotel, with new extension, in attractive riverside position.
103rm(78⇌⋔) 2▭ ☽ ₩ CTV 70P ♀English & French. Last dinner 9.30pm ♈ ⚱ S% ✻sB&B£9.99 sB&B⇌⋔£13.99 dB&B£14.85 dB&B⇌⋔£19.98 Lunch fr£3.51 Dinner fr£3.89 Wine£2.95 Credit cards ① ② ③ ⑤

★★**De Parys** De Parys Av ☎52121 Telex no 826386
The hotel is said to have been built on the site of the hospital and rectory of St John, founded in 1118 by Robert de Parys.
Closed Xmas wk; 33rm(12⇌⋔)
Annexe: 16rm(4⇌⋔) ₩ CTV ⚓ ♿ ♀English & French. Last dinner 8pm ♈ ⚱ ✻sB&B fr£8.50 sB&B⇌⋔ fr£12 dB&B fr£15.85 dB&B⇌⋔ fr£17.60 Lunch£3.80&alc Tea25p Dinner£3.80&alc Wine£2.70 ⊓ Credit cards ① ⑥

BEELEY Derbyshire Map**8** SK26
XX***Devonshire Arms*** ☎Darley Dale 3259
Stone-built, beamed village inn with attractive modern restaurant extension.
Closed Mon; Dinner not served Sun; 60seats 60P ♀English & Continental. Last dinner 10pm

BEER Devon Map**3** SY28
★★**Dolphin** Fore St ☎Seaton 20068
Closed Nov–21 Mar; 23rm CTV 24P ⚘

Lastdinner7.45pm S% sB&B£8.25 dB&B£16.50 Barlunch40p–£1.50 Dinner£4.75&alc Wine£2.40

BEESTON Cheshire Map**7** SJ55
☆☆☆**Wild Boar Motor Inn** ☎Bunbury260309 Telexno61455
Closed 25&26Dec; Annexe:30 CTV CTV in bedrooms 100P French. Lastdinner10pm *sB&B £16.40 dB&B £27.80 Lunch£4.95&alc Dinner£10alc Wine£5.30 Creditcards 1 2 3 5

BEETHAM Cumbria Map**7** SD47
★**Wheatsheaf** ☎Milnthorpe2123
A small, but attractive hotel, pleasantly situated in the old world village of Beetham just off the A6 and only 4 miles from the M6 (junc 35).
8rm(2) CTV 50P 8 Lastdinner8.30pm sB&B£8–£9 sB&B £9–£10 dB&B£16–£17 dB&B £18–£19 Lunch£4 Tea£1.25 Dinner£6 Wine£3.50

BELBROUGHTON Hereford & Worcester Map**7** SO97
XX***Bell Inn*** Bell End ☎730232
Closed Mon; Lunch not served Sat; Dinner not served Sun; 78seats 140P English & French. Lastdinner10.15pm Creditcards 1 2 3 5

XX***Four Winds*** Hollies Hill ☎730332
Closed Mon; Lunch not served Sat; Dinner not served Sun; 68seats Lastdinner9.30pm

XX***Talbot Inn*** ☎730249
Small village inn with simple, beamed restaurant.
Closed Mon & last wk Aug–mid Sep; Dinner not served Sun; 70seats 60P Lastdinner9.30pm

BELFORD Northumberland Map**12** NU13
★★**Blue Bell** (Swallow) ☎543 Telexno53168
Creeper-clad inn with restaurant overlooking garden.
13rm(4) CTV 24P Lastdinner9pm S% sB&B£11.55–£12.50 sB&B £12.65–£15.35 dB&B£16.50–£22.10 dB&B £19.80–£25.75 *xmas* Creditcards 1 2 3 5

★***Black Swan*** ☎266
8rm(1) CTV 20P Lastdinner9pm

BELSTONE Devon Map**2** SX69
★★**Skaigh House** ☎Sticklepath243
Victorian building with terrace, lawns and grounds, above the River Taw.
Closed Nov–Mar; 10rm(1) CTV 16P Lastdinner8.30pm sB&B£10.75 dB&B£21.50–£24 dB&B £26 Dinner£5 Wine£2.20

BEMBRIDGE Isle of Wight Map**4** SZ68
★★**Highbury** Lane End ☎2838
See page 37 for details

★★**Elm Country** ☎2248
Closed 20Oct–Feb; 13rm(10) TV available in bedrooms 60P International. Lastdinner9.30pm sB&B£8 sB&B £9 dB&B£16 dB&B £18 Lunch fr£3.50&alc Tea fr£1 High Tea£1.50 Dinner fr£3.50&alc Wine£1.80

BERKELEY Gloucestershire Map**3** ST69
★★**Berkeley Arms** ☎291
18th-C red-brick building with central, wide arched entrance.
14rm(6) CTV 30P 6 English & French. Lastdinner8.30pm *sB&B£7.50–£8 sB&B £8.25–£8.75 dB&B£12.50–£13 dB&B £13.50–£15 Lunch£3–£4 Tea£1.25 Dinner fr£4&alc Wine£2.20 *xmas* Creditcards 1 3

BERKELEY ROAD Gloucestershire Map**3** ST70
★***Prince of Wales*** Bristol Rd ☎Berkeley474
8rm CTV 40P 2 Live music & dancing Sat Cabaret Sat Mainly grills. Lastdinner8pm

BERKHAMSTED Hertfordshire Map**4** SP90
★**Swan** High St ☎71451
Closed Xmas; 14rm(2) 1 CTV TV in bedrooms 12P 1 sauna bath Lastdinner10pm sB&B fr£12 sB&B fr£16 dB&B fr£20 dB&B fr£22 Lunch fr£5&alc Dinner fr£5&alc Wine£3.50 Creditcard 3

X***La Fiorentina*** Lower Kings Rd ☎3003
Closed Sun & Mon; 65seats Italian. Lastdinner9.30pm Creditcards 1 2 3 5

BERKSWELL West Midlands Map**4** SP27
XX**Bear Inn** ☎33202
The Bear Inn dates from the 15th century.
Closed Sun; English & Continental. Lastdinner10pm Lunch£7.40alc Dinner£7.40alc Wine£3.20 Creditcards 1 2 4 5 6

BERRY POMEROY Devon Map**3** SX86
★**Loventor Manor** ☎Paignton557713
Originally an 11th-C manor, rebuilt in the Georgian period; peacefully situated in unspoilt countryside.
Closed Dec–Feb except Xmas; 12rm(2) 1 CTV 50P Lastdinner7pm sB&B£5.50–£8.50 sB&B £6.30–£9.40 dB&B£11–£17 dB&B £12.60–£18.60 Barlunch£1–£1.50 Tea80p–£1 Dinner£3.50–£4.50 Wine£3 *xmas*

B

BERWICK-UPON-TWEED Northumberland Map**12** NT95
★★★**Turret House** Etal Rd ☎7344
Closed Feb; 11rm(6⇌ ⋒) CTV in bedrooms 100P Children under 5yrs not accommodated French & Italian. Last dinner 8.30pm sB&B£15.50 sB&B☎⋒£15.50 dB&B£24 dB&B⇌⋒£28 Lunch£2.50 Dinner£7.10 Wine£2.90 Credit cards 2 3 5

★★**Castle** Castle Gate ☎6471
Terraced hotel on main route through the town.
15rm CTV TV in bedrooms Last dinner 9pm S% sB&B£8.50–£10 dB&B£17–£20 Lunch£3–£4 Dinner£4.50–£5.50 Wine£2.75 Credit cards 1 3 5 6

★★**King's Arms** Hide Hill (Best Western) ☎7454
Impressive stone built hotel, commanding greater part of terrace on Hide Hill.
37rm(20⇌ ⋒) CTV in bedrooms 20P French. Last dinner 10pm S% sB&B£13.65–£15.50 sB&B⇌⋒£17.25 dB&B£26 dB&B☎⋒ fr£30 Lunch£4.50 Dinner fr£6.50 Wine£2.45 *xmas* Credit cards 1 2 3 5

★★**Ravensholme** 32–36 Ravensdowne ☎7170
A cement rendered building situated in quiet side street near the town centre.
14rm(6☎⋒) CTV TV available in bedrooms P International. Last dinner 10pm sB&B£8–£8.50 sB&B⇌⋒£9 dB&B£17 dB&B⇌⋒£18 Lunch£3.25–£4.50&alc Tea£1.50&alc High Tea£2.25&alc Dinner£5–£8&alc Wine£3 Credit cards 1 2 3

★***Queens Head*** Sandgate ☎7852
6rm CTV Mainly grills. Last dinner 9.30pm Credit cards 1 3 6

BEVERLEY Humberside Map**8** TA03
★★★**Beverley Arms** North Bar Within (Trusthouse Forte) ☎Hull 885241
An elegant Georgian building, with a modern extension, said to have had associations with Dick Turpin.
61⇌⋒ Lift TV in bedrooms 70P Last dinner 10pm S% sB&B⇌⋒£15.50 dB&B⇌⋒£22 *xmas* Credit cards 1 2 3 4 5 6

★★***Lairgate*** 30–34 Lairgate ☎Hull 882141
30rm(5⇌⋒) CTV 20P English & Continental. Last dinner 9pm Credit cards 1 6

★***Kings Head*** ☎Hull 883103
Georgian inn in Market Place.
9rm CTV 20P Last dinner 9.30pm

BEWDLEY Hereford & Worcester Map**7** SO77
★★**Black Boy** Kidderminster Rd ☎402119
17th-C country inn near banks of River Severn.
Closed Xmas Day; 17rm(3⇌⋒) Annexe: 8rm(2⇌⋒) CTV 20P S% ✱sB&B£10.45 sB&B⇌⋒£12.95 dB&B£17.20 dB&B⇌⋒£19.50 Lunch fr£3.25&alc Dinner fr£4.25&alc Wine£2.37 Credit cards 1 3 6

✕✕**Bailiff's House** 68 High St ☎402691
Closed Mon; Dinner not served Sun; 40 seats English & French. Lunch£4 Dinner£8.50alc Wine£3.30 Credit cards 1 3

BEXHILL-ON-SEA East Sussex Map**5** TQ70
★**Southlands Court** Hastings Rd ☎210628
28rm(17⇌⋒) CTV 12P 5 Last dinner 7.30pm S% sB&B£6.48 sB&B⇌⋒£7.56 dB&B£11.88 dB&B⇌⋒£14.04 Lunch£2–£2.25&alc Tea 50palc High Tea£2alc Dinner£2.25–£2.50&alc Wine£2.75

BIBURY Gloucestershire Map**4** SP10
★★★**Swan** ☎204
Creeper-clad Cotswold-stone inn with Queen Anne-style doorway; standing by bridge, with delightful riverside gardens opposite.
24⇌⋒ CTV CTV in bedrooms 24P Last dinner 8.30pm ✱sB&B⇌⋒£13.50 dB&B⇌⋒£25 Lunch£4.75 Tea£1.25 Dinner£6.25 Wine£4 *xmas* Credit cards 1 3

BICESTER Oxfordshire Map**4** SP52
★★**King's Arms** Market St (Embassy) ☎2015
14rm CTV 30P Last dinner 9pm S% sB&B£10.50 dB&B£15 Lunch£4.50&alc Dinner£5&alc Wine£4 Credit cards 1 2 3 4 5 6

BICKLEIGH (nr Tiverton) Devon Map**3** SS90
★★**Fisherman's Cot** ☎237
Picturesque thatched building on the river bank.
13rm(8⇌⋒) CTV in bedrooms 200P Disco twice wkly English, French & Italian. Last dinner 9.30pm ✱sB&B£7.50 sB&B⇌⋒£10–£12 dB&B£17 dB&B⇌⋒£19–£20 Lunch fr£4 Dinner£5.75alc Credit cards 1 2 3 5 6

BICKLEY Gt London Map**5** TQ46
★★**Bickley Manor** Thornet Wood Rd ☎01-467 3851 Telex no 898156
40⇌⋒ 1 CTV CTV in bedrooms 100P (hard) Live music & dancing Fri & Sat International. Last dinner mdnt S% ✱sB&B⇌⋒ fr£22.50 dB&B⇌⋒ fr£30 Tea fr£1.50 Dinner fr£6.50 Wine£5 *xmas* Credit cards 1 2 3 4 5 6

BIDDENDEN Kent Map**5** TQ83
✕**Ye Maydes** ☎291306
Black and white medieval house with historic connections with the Flemish weavers and the

famous Maydes of Biddenden.
Closed Mon; Dinner not served Sun; 54seats
English & French. Specialities: Canneton Montmorency, Supreme de Volaille Chimay, Truite aux Amandes. Lastdinner9.30pm
✱Lunch£2.35–£4&alc Dinner£7alc Wine£3.25
Creditcard 1

BIDEFORD Devon Map**2** SS42
★★★**Durrant House** ☎2361
58⇌fl CTV CTV in bedrooms 250P ⚓ (heated) saunabath Discowkly Live music & dancing wkly Conference facilities available French & Italian. Lastdinner9.45pm
sB&B⇌fl£15.50–£19 dB&B⇌fl£24–£29 Bar lunchfr£2 Teafr35p Dinnerfr£5.50 Wine£2
Creditcards 1 2 3 5 6

★★**Royal** Barnstaple St (Percy R. Brend) ☎2005
On edge of town overlooking River Torridge.
34rm(9⇌fl) CTV TV available in bedrooms 30P 4 live music & dancing 3 nights wkly
Lastdinner8.30pm S% ✱sB&B£9.26 sB&B⇌fl£11 dB&B£14.85 dB&B⇌fl£16.04 Lunch£2 Tea40p Dinner£4 *xmas*
Creditcards 1 2 3

★★**Yeoldon House** Durrant Ln, Northam (Best Western) ☎4400
Stone-built house in own grounds with fine views of river and countryside.
Closed Xmas; RS Feb; 10rm(7⇌fl) TV available in bedrooms 20P ⚓ French.
Lastdinner9pm S% sB&B£9.25–£13.75 sB&B⇌fl£10.25–£15.50 dB&B£18.50–£27.50 dB&B⇌fl£20.50–£31 Barlunch£2 Tea50p Dinner£5.50&alc Wine£2.75
Creditcards 1 2 3 4 5 6

B

★🏨**Rosskery** Orchard Hill ☎2872
Set in spacious two-acres of gardens, overlooking the River Torridge.
10rm(4⇌ 🚿) 🚫 CTV ⊘ 20P 🚗 ⚓ ⊽English & French. Last dinner8.30pm ♣ ⊉ S%
sB&B£7.25–£8.75 sB&B⇌🚿£10.25–£11.25
dB&B£15.50–£17.50 dB&B⇌🚿£18–£20
Lunch£3–£4 Tea£1–£2 HighTea£2–£3
Dinner£4–£5&alc Wine£4

BIDFORD-ON-AVON Warwickshire Map**4** SP05
★★**White Lion** ☎3309
13rm(7⇌🚿) 🚫 CTV ⊘ 50P 🚗 ⊽English & French. Last dinner9.30pm ♣ ⊉ ✱sB&B£9.50
sB&B🚿£10 dB&B£14 dB&B⇌🚿£16
Continental breakfast Bar lunch£1 Tea50p
Dinner£6alc Wine£2.65 ⛿ *xmas*
Credit cards 1 3

BIGBURY-ON-SEA Devon Map**3** SX64
★**Henley** ☎240
Small country-house in own grounds with views of Bigbury Bay. Terraced gardens with sub-tropical plants and access to beach.
Closed 27Sep–Etr; 9rm 8P 🚗 ⚓ Children under 3yrs not accommodated Last dinner7pm ♣ ⊉
sB&B£10–£12 dB&B£20–£24 Lunch£2
Tea75p Dinner£3.50 Wine£2.50

BIGGLESWADE Bedfordshire Map**4** TL14
★**Crown** High St ☎312228
Small hotel in town centre.
15rm(4⇌🚿) 🚫 CTV 20P Last dinner8.30pm ♣
sB&B fr£9 sB&B⇌🚿fr£10 dB&B fr£13.40
dB&B⇌🚿fr£14.40 Lunch£2 Dinner£4–£4.50
Wine£2

BILLESLEY Warwickshire Map**4** SP15
★★★🏨***Billesley Manor Country Club***
☎Alcester3737
14⇌🚿 ☽ 🚫 TV in bedrooms ⊘ 100P 🚗 ⚓

BILLINGSHURST West Sussex Map**4** TQ02
✕***15th-Century*** 42 High St ☎2652
A small, white-painted, 15th-C cottage restaurant with latticed windows.
Closed Sun, Mon & Xmas; Lunch not served; 52seats ⊽Continental. Last dinner10pm
Credit card 2

BINGLEY West Yorkshire Map**7** SE13
★★★**Bankfield** Bradford Rd (Embassy) ☎7123
Originally a 19th-C Tudor farmhouse with traditional oak-panelled hall.
74rm(58⇌🚿) ☽ 🚫 CTV TV available in bedrooms 250P ⚓ Conference facilities available
Last dinner9pm ♣ S% sB&B£14
sB&B⇌🚿£16 dB&B£18.50 dB&B⇌🚿£22
Lunch£4.50&alc Dinner£5&alc Wine£4 ⛿
Credit cards 1 2 3 4 5 6

BIRCHINGTON Kent Map**5** TR36
★★**Bungalow** Lyell Rd (Trusthouse Forte)
☎Thanet41276
26rm(4⇌🚿) CTV TV in bedrooms 40P 8🏠 ⚓ ⛾(heated) Last dinner8.45pm ♣ S% sB&B£11
dB&B£17 dB&B⇌🚿£20 ⛿ *xmas*
Credit cards 1 2 3 4 5 6

BIRDLIP Gloucestershire Map**3** SO91
✕✕***Royal George*** ☎Witcombe2506
53seats 50P bedrooms available ⊽English & French.
Last dinner10.30pm

BIRKENHEAD Merseyside Map**7** SJ38
★★★**Bowler Hat** 2 Talbot Rd, Oxton
☎051–652 4931
RS Sat & Sun; 29⇌🚿 ☽ 🚫 CTV in bedrooms 50P 🚗 ⚓ ⊽English, French & Italian. Last dinner10.30pm
✱sB&B⇌🚿£14.85 dB&B⇌🚿£20.75
Continental breakfast Lunch fr£3.55&alc
Dinner fr£4&alc Wine£3.30 ⛿
Credit cards 1 2 3 5

★★★**Central** Clifton Cres (Embassy)
☎051–647 6347
34rm(13⇌🚿) Lift ☽ 🚫 CTV TV available in bedrooms
𝐏 🚗 Last dinner9pm S% sB&B£11
sB&B⇌🚿£14 dB&B£17 dB&B⇌🚿£18
Lunch£4.50&alc Dinner£5&alc Wine£4
Credit cards 1 2 3 4 5 6

★★**Woodside** Woodside (Whitbread)
☎051–647 4121
27rm(11⇌🚿) ☽ 🚫 CTV ⊘ 25P Last dinner8.15pm
S% ✱sB&B£9.90 sB&B⇌🚿£11.55
dB&B£19.35 dB&B⇌🚿£20.35 Lunch£2.50
Dinner£2.80 Wine£2.35

★**Riverhill** Talbot Rd, Oxton ☎051–652 4847
A red-gabled building in own grounds situated in quiet residential district.
9rm(3⇌🚿) CTV 14P 🚗 ⚓ ♿ Last dinner8pm ♣
S% sB&B£9.50–£11 sB&B⇌🚿£11–£12.50
dB&B£14.50–£16 dB&B⇌🚿£16.50–£18.50
Lunch£2 Dinner£3 Wine£3 ⛿

BIRMINGHAM W Midlands Map**7** SP08 **See plan**

★★★★**Albany** Smallbrook Queensway (Trusthouse Forte) ☎021–643 8171 Telex no337031 Plan**1**
Impressive thirteen-storey building dating from 1962, with extensive views over the city.
257⇌⋒ Lift ☽ ₩ CTV in bedrooms ⁋ ⊡(heated) Conference facilities available Last dinner 11pm ♆ ♆ S% sB&B⇌⋒£28 dB&B⇌⋒£36.50 ⊓ Credit cards 1 2 3 4 5 6

★★★★**Grand** Colmore Row (Grand Met) ☎021–236 7951 Telex no338174 Plan**7**
176rm(135⇌⋒) Lift ☽ ₩ CTV in bedrooms ⁋ ⁋ Conference facilities available ♿ Last dinner 10.50pm ♆ ♆ S% ✱sB&B£18.50 sB&B⇌⋒£18.50 dB&B£24.50–£35 dB&B⇌⋒£24.50–£35 ⊓ Credit cards 1 2 3 4 5 6

☆☆☆☆***Holiday Inn*** Broad St (Commonwealth) ☎021–643 2766 Telex no337272 Plan**9**
304⇌⋒ Lift ☽ ⊞ ₩ CTV in bedrooms 500⌂ ⊡(heated) sauna bath Conference facilities available ♀International. Last dinner 11pm ♆ ♆ ⊓ Credit cards 1 2 3 4 5 6

★★★★**Midland** New St (Inter Hotel) ☎021–643 2601 Telex no338419 Plan**14**
113rm(107⇌⋒) Lift ☽ ₩ CTV CTV in bedrooms ⁋ Live music & dancing Sat Oct–May Conference facilities available ♿ Last dinner 10.30pm ♆ ♆ S% sB&B£17.50 sB&B⇌⋒£23.40 dB&B£25.30 dB&B⇌⋒£30.36 Lunch£4.50 Tea£1 High Tea£2.50&alc Dinner£5.50 Wine£3.20 ⊓ Credit cards 1 2 3 5 6

★★★★**Plough & Harrow** Hagley Rd, Edgbaston (Crest) ☎021–454 4111 Telex no338074 Not on plan
44⇌⋒ Lift ☽ CTV in bedrooms 120P ⁋ ⚓ Conference facilities available ♀French. Last dinner 10.15pm ♆ S% ✱sB&B⇌⋒£29.50 dB&B⇌⋒£38.55 Continental breakfast Credit cards 1 2 3 4 5 6

☆☆☆☆**Strathallan** 225 Hagley Rd, Edgbaston (Thistle) ☎021–455 9777 Telex no336680 Not on plan

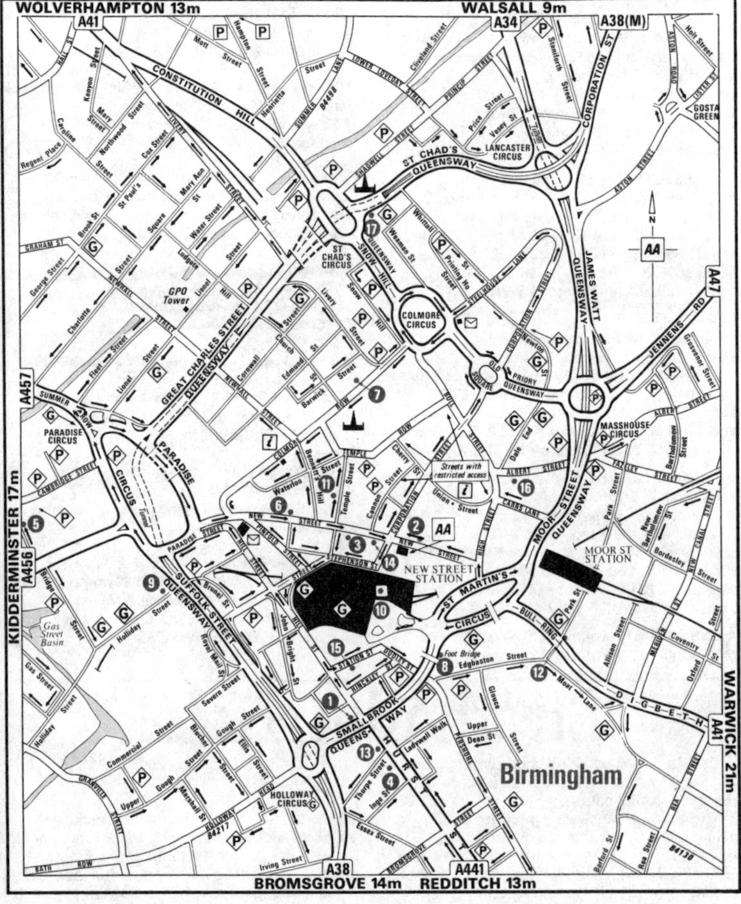

1 Albany ★★★★
2 Birmingham Centre ★★★
3 Burlington ✕✕
4 La Cappanna ✕✕
5 Celebrity ✕✕
6 Gaylord ✕✕
7 Grand ★★★★
8 Heaven Bridge ✕✕
9 Holiday Inn ☆☆☆☆
10 House of Callistephus ✕
11 Imperial Centre ★★
12 Lorenzo's ✕✕
13 Maharaja ✕
14 Midland ★★★★
15 New Happy Gathering ✕✕
16 Rajdoot ❀✕✕
17 Royal Angus ★★★

B

171⇌⋒ Lift ☽ ▦ ₩ CTV in bedrooms 110P 90⌂ Conference facilities available ♡ English and French. Last dinner 10pm ✿ ♨ S% sB&B⇌⋒ £23–£24.40 dB&B⇌⋒ £32–£34.80 Lunch £3.80&alc Dinner £5.40&alc Wine £3.15 ♜ Credit cards 1 2 3 4 5

☆☆☆**Apollo Motor** 243–247 Hagley Rd, Edgbaston ☎021–455 0271 Not on plan
Closed Xmas; 70⇌⋒ Annexe: 20rm ☽ ₩ CTV CTV available in bedrooms 80P Last dinner 10pm ✿ S% sB&B £13.50 sB&B⇌⋒ £20.50 dB&B £20.50 dB&B⇌⋒ £27.50 Lunch £3.75–£4&alc Dinner £4–£4.50&alc Wine £2.85 ♜ Credit cards 1 2 3 5 6

★★★**Birmingham Centre** New St (Centre) ☎021–643 2747 Telex no 338331 Plan **2**
200⇌⋒ Lift ☽ ₩ TV in bedrooms ✇ Conference facilities available Last dinner 9.45pm ✿ ♨ S% ✱sB&B⇌⋒ £15.75 dB&B⇌⋒ £20.25 Continental breakfast Lunch £3.75 Dinner £3.75 Wine £3.40 ♜ Credit cards 1 2 3 4 5 6

★★★**Royal Angus** St Chads, Queensway (EMI) ☎01–236 4211 Telex no 336889 Plan **17**
140⇌⋒ Lift ☽ ₩ CTV in bedrooms ✇ Live music & dancing Sat (Oct–Apr) Conference facilities available ♡ International. Last dinner 10.30pm S% ✱sB&B⇌⋒ £20.25 dB&B⇌⋒ £26.50 Continental breakfast Lunch £4.25&alc Tea 75p alc Dinner £4.25&alc Wine £2.85 ♜ Credit cards 1 2 3 4 5 6

★★**Cobden** 166 Hagley Rd, Edgbaston ☎021–454 6621 Telex no 339715 Not on plan
Unlicensed; 140rm (72⇌⋒) Lift ☽ ₩ CTV TV available in bedrooms 130P ⚓ Last dinner 7.45pm ✿ ♨ S% sB&B fr £9.18 sB&B⇌⋒ fr £14.58 dB&B fr £16.20 dB&B⇌⋒ fr £21.60 Lunch fr £2.50&alc Dinner fr £4.32&alc ♜ Credit cards 1 3

★★**Imperial Centre** Temple St (Centre) ☎021–643 6751 Telex no 338844 Plan **11**
100rm (9⇌⋒) Lift ☽ ₩ CTV Live music Wed & Sun Last dinner 9pm ✿ ♨ S% ✱sB&B fr £8.91 sB&B⇌⋒ fr £10.50 dB&B fr £14.31 dB&B⇌⋒ fr £15.93 Lunch £1–£2.50 Tea fr 35p Dinner £2.75–£3.50 Credit cards 1 2 3 5 6

★★**Norfolk** Hagley Rd, Edgbaston ☎021–454 8071 Telex no 339715 Not on plan
Unlicensed; 191rm (64⇌⋒) Annexe: 21rm Lift ☽ ₩ CTV TV available in bedrooms 130P ⚓ ♿ Last dinner 7.45pm ✿ ♨ S% sB&B fr £9.18 sB&B⇌⋒ fr £14.58 dB&B fr £16.20 dB&B⇌⋒ fr £21.60 Lunch fr £2.50&alc Dinner fr £4.32&alc ♜ Credit cards 1 3

★★**Wheatsheaf** Coventry Rd, Sheldon (Ansells) ☎021–743 2021 Not on plan
100rm (84⇌⋒) ☽ ₩ CTV ✇ 120P ⛟ Last dinner 10pm ✿ S% sB&B £13.53 sB&B⇌⋒ £17.60 dB&B⇌⋒ £21.60 Lunch £3.48&alc Dinner £4.12&alc Wine £3.20 ♜ Credit cards 1 2

XX**Burlington** Burlington Arcade, New St ☎021–643 3081 Plan **3**
Closed Sun; 140seats ₽ ♡ English & French. Last dinner 10.30pm Lunch £2.50&alc Dinner £4.20alc Wine £2.70 Credit cards 1 2 3 5

XX***La Cappanna*** Hurst St ☎021–622 2287 Plan **4**
Closed Sun; 60seats 15P ♡ English, French & Italian. Last dinner 11pm Credit cards 2 5

XX**Celebrity** King Alfred's Place ☎021–643 8969 Plan **5**
Closed Sun & Public Hols; Lunch not served Mon & Sat; ₽ Cabaret Mon–Sat ♡ French. Last dinner 11.15pm ✱Lunch £3.95&alc Dinner £8alc Wine £3.40 Credit cards 1 2 3 4 5 6

XX**Gaylord** 61 New St ☎021–632 4500 Plan **6**
150seats ♡ Indian. Last dinner 11.30pm ✱Lunch £3.50–£5.50&alc Tea £1alc Dinner £3.80–£4.60&alc Credit cards 1 2 3 5

XX***Heaven Bridge*** 308 Bull Ring Centre, Smallbrook Ringway ☎021–643 0033 Plan **8**
100seats ♡ Cantonese. Last dinner 11pm Credit cards 1 2 3

XX**Lorenzo's** Park St ☎021–643 0541 Plan **12**
Closed Sun; Lunch Sat; 60seats ₽ ♡ Italian. Last dinner 11pm Lunch £3.30alc Dinner £8alc Wine £3 Credit cards 1 2 3 5 6

XX***New Happy Gathering*** 43–45 Station St ☎021–643 5247 Plan **15**
115seats ♡ Cantonese. Last dinner mdnt Credit cards 2 5

❁XX**Rajdoot** 12–22 Albert St ☎021–643 8805 Plan **16**
Lunch Sun; 80seats ₽ ♡ North Indian. Last dinner mdnt S% Lunch fr £3 Dinner £6 Wine £3.20 Credit cards 1 2 3 4 5 6

XX***Le Village*** 176 High St, Harborne (4m W off A456) ☎021–426 2481 Not on plan
Closed Sun; 45seats ♡ French. Last dinner 11pm Credit cards 1 2 3 5

X**La Copper Kettle** 151 Milcote Rd, Bearwood (3½m W off A4123) ☎021–429 7920 Not on plan
Closed Sun, Mon & Aug 38seats ₽ ♡ French. Last dinner 10pm S% Lunch £1.50–£5&alc Dinner £4.50–£6&alc Wine £3.60 Credit cards 1 2 3

×**Giovanni's** 27 Poplar Rd, Kings Heath ☎021-443 2391 Not on plan
Closed Mon, Public Hols, Xmas, mid 2wks Feb & Aug; Dinner not served Sun; 43seats ♕English & Italian. Last dinner10.30pm S%
Lunch fr£3.20&alc Dinner£6&alc Wine£2.95
Credit cards 1 3 5

×***House of Callistephus*** 32 West Court, New Shopping Centre ☎021-643 0029 Plan**10**
34seats ♕Cantonese. Last dinner11pm
Credit cards 1 2 3 4 5

×**Maharaja** 23-25 Hurst St ☎021-622 2641 Plan**13**
Closed Sun; 65seats **P** ♕North Indian. Last dinner11.50pm ✱Lunch£2.50alc Dinner£3.50alc Wine£2.95
Credit cards 1 2 3 5 6

×**Michelle** 182-184 High St, Harborne (4m W off A456) ☎021-426 4133 Not on plan
Closed Sun; 40seats **P** ♕French. Last dinner10pm
✱Lunch£2-£5&alc Dinner£4-£7.50&alc
Wine£2.80

×**Pinnocchio's** 8 Chad Sq, Edgbaston ☎021-454 8672 Not on plan
Closed Sun; 45seats 30P ♕Italian. Last dinner10pm
Lunch£2.25-£2.50&alc Dinner£7.50alc

×**Le Provençal** 1 Albany Rd, Harborne (4m W off A456) ☎021-426 2444 Not on plan
Closed, Sun, Public Hols & 1wk after Xmas; Lunch not served Mon & Sat; 46seats **P** ♕French.
Last dinner10pm Lunch£1.60-£2.40&alc Dinner£7alc Wine£3.24 Credit cards 1 3 5

×**Valentino's** High St, Harborne (4m W off A456) ☎021-427 2560 Not on plan
Dinner not served Sun; 50seats 50P ♕English, French & Italian. Last dinner10.30pm
✱Lunch fr£2.50&alc Dinner£5&alc
Credit cards 1 2 3 5

×**La Villa Bianca** 1036 Stratford Rd, Monkspath, Shirley (6m S A34) ☎021-744 7232 Not on plan
Closed Mon; Lunch not served Sat; 50seats 30P ♕Italian. Last dinner10.30pm Lunch£3£alc Dinner£5alc Wine£3.50 Credit cards 1 2 3 5

At **Barr (Great)** (6m NW junc M6/A34)
☆☆☆**Post House** Chapel Ln (Trusthouse Forte) ☎021-357 7444 Not on plan
204⇌⋒ 280P

★★***Barr*** Pear Tree Dv, off Newton Rd (1m W of junc A34/A4041) (Greenall Whitley) ☎021-357 1141 Not on plan
111⇌⋒ 250P

BIRMINGHAM AIRPORT W Midlands Map**7** SP18
★★★★**Excelsior** Coventry Rd, Elmdon (Trusthouse Forte) ☎021-743 8141 Telex no338005
This luxurious building is conveniently situated at the entrance to Birmingham Airport.
141⇌⋒ ☽ ♛ TV in bedrooms 200P Conference facilities available Last dinner10.15pm ✿ S%
sB&B⇌⋒£22.25 dB&B⇌⋒£32.50 ⊟
Credit cards 1 2 3 4 5 6

BIRMINGHAM (National Exhibition Centre) West Midlands Map**7** SP18
★★**Arden Motel** Coventry Rd, Bickenhill Village (A45) ☎Hampden-in-Arden2912
24⇌⋒ ♛ CTV in bedrooms 150P ⛟ Live music & dancing Thu-Sat Last dinner11pm ✿ S%
sB&B⇌⋒£15.50-£19.50 dB&B⇌⋒£21.50
Lunch£3.50-£5&alc Dinner£5-£7&alc
Wine£1.50 Credit cards 1 2 3 5 6

BIRTLE Gt Manchester Map**7** SD81
××***Normandie*** ☎061-764 3869
Lunch not served Sat; Dinner not served Sun; 70seats 60P bedrooms available ♕French. Last dinner10pm Credit cards 1 2 5 6

BISHOP AUCKLAND Co Durham Map**8** NZ22
★★**Binchester Hall** Binchester ☎4646
18rm(10⇌⋒) ♛ CTV 200P ♪ Disco twice wkly
Last dinner10pm ✿ S% sB&B£7 sB&B⇌⋒£9 dB&B£14 dB&B⇌⋒£18 *xmas*

★★**Kings Arms** 36 Market Pl ☎61296
Telex no58136
18⇌⋒ ♛ CTV in bedrooms ⊘ 10P ⛟ ♕English & Continental. Last dinner9.30pm ✿ ☐ S%
sB&B⇌⋒£13.50-£15 dB&B⇌⋒£22-£26
Continental breakfast Lunch£2.50-£3.50&alc
Tea£1.25-£1.50&alc Dinner£4-£5&alc Wine£4
⊟ Credit cards 1 2 3 4 5 6

BISHOP'S CLEEVE Gloucestershire Map**3** SO92
❁×××**Cleeveway House** ☎2585
Pleasant stone-built country house restaurant standing in well kept grounds on the edge of village.
Closed Sun, Mon & 3wks Sep; 40seats 30P 3bedrooms available ♕French. Specialities: Iced Cucumber Soup with Mint & cream, Chicken Breasts with Pernod & cream, Sole in Prawn & Cheese Sauce. Last dinner9.45pm ✱Lunch£6alc Dinner£6alc Wine£2.80 Credit cards 1 2 5

BISHOP'S LYDEARD Somerset Map**3** ST12
×**Rose Cottage Inn** ☎432394
Closed Sun, Mon & 2 weeks from 24Dec; 30seats 20P ♕English & French. Last dinner9.30pm
Dinner£7alc Wine£3

BISHOP'S STORTFORD Hertfordshire Map**5** TL42
★★★**Foxley** Foxley Dr, Stanstead Rd ☎53977
Pleasant country style house situated in private residential area on outskirts of town.
10⇌⋒ ♛ CTV TV available in bedrooms ⊘ 70P ⚓ ♕French. Last dinner9pm ✿ ☐
sB&B⇌⋒£15.50 dB&B⇌⋒£22.50
Lunch£3.50-£7 Tea55p-£1 Dinner£3.50-£7
Wine£3

B

★★**Dane House** Hadham Rd ☎52289
Well converted 20th-C house in own spacious grounds of lawns and rosebeds.
Closed 1–10Jan; 12rm(4⇌ ⋔) TV 80P English & French. Last dinner9.30pm sB&B fr£10.50 sB&B⇌⋔ fr£13.50 dB&B fr£15.50 dB&B⇌⋔ fr£19.50 Lunch fr£3.25&alc Dinner fr£4&alc Wine£2.20 Credit cards 2 5

★★**Thorley Place** Thorley Ln, Thorley ☎54012
Old country house, approximately 3 miles from Bishops Stortford, set in eight acres of grounds.
Closed Xmas; 14rm(7⇌⋔) CTV 30P Last dinner9pm S% *sB&B£10–£11 sB&B⇌⋔£10.50–£12 dB&B£14–£16 dB&B⇌⋔£16–£18 Continental breakfast Lunch fr£3.50 Dinner£3.50&alc Wine£3 Credit cards 1 6

Brook House Northgate End ☎57892
Pleasant Georgian house near town centre.
20rm(5⇌⋔) CTV CTV available in bedrooms 25P Last dinner8pm sB&B£8.64 sB&B⇌⋔£12.96 dB&B£13.50 dB&B⇌⋔£16.20 Lunch£3alc Tea£1.25alc Dinner£4alc Wine£2

BLACKBURN Lancashire Map**7** SD62
★★★**Saxon Inn** Preston New Rd ☎64441
Telex no 63271
100⇌⋔ Lift CTV in bedrooms 200P Live music & dancing Sat Conference facilities available English & French. Last dinner10.30pm S% sB&B⇌⋔£17.02 dB&B⇌⋔£21.34 Lunch£3.30&alc Tea80p Dinner£3.80&alc Wine£3.50 Credit cards 1 2 3 5

BLACKMOOR Hants Map**4** SU73
✕***Silver Birch*** Petersfield Rd ☎262
Closed Mar; Dinner not served Sun; 30seats 50P bedrooms available Last dinner9.30pm Credit card 5

BLACKPOOL Lancashire Map**7** SD33
★★★**Clifton** Talbot Sq ☎21481
A large, four-storey building on the promenade, overlooking the North Pier.
90rm(43⇌⋔) Lift CTV TV available in bedrooms Disco 5 nights wkly Live music & dancing twice wkly Cabaret wkly (summer) Last dinner9.30pm S% *sB&B£12 sB&B⇌⋔£13 dB&B£22 dB&B⇌⋔£24 Lunch£2.75&alc Tea90p High Tea£2.25–£3 Dinner£3.95&alc Wine£2.20 *xmas* credit cards 1 2 3 5 6

★★★**Savoy** North Shore, Queens Prom ☎52561
140rm(62⇌⋔) Lift CTV TV available in bedrooms 50P billiards Live music & dancing Sat Conference facilities available English and French. Last dinner9pm S% sB&B£10.50–£12.50 sB&B⇌⋔£11.50–£13.50 dB&B£20–£22 dB&B⇌⋔£22–£24 Lunch£2.15–£2.50&alc Dinner fr£3.70&alc Wine£2.60 *xmas* Credit cards 1 3 6

★★**Carlton** North Promenade (Crest) ☎28966
Sea front hotel and gabled roof and modern frontage.
56rm(13⇌⋔) Lift CTV TV available in bedrooms 50P Last dinner8pm S% *sB&B£10.80 sB&B⇌⋔£15.12 dB&B£18.09 dB&B⇌⋔£23.76 Credit cards 1 2 3 4 5 6

★★**Claremont** 270 North Prom ☎29122
150rm(100⇌⋔) Lift CTV in bedrooms 100P Disco 5 nights wkly Live music & dancing 2 nights wkly Cabaret 5 nights wkly Conference facilities available Last dinner8.30pm S% sB&B£10.25 sB&B⇌⋔£13.25 dB&B£14.50 dB&B⇌⋔£17.50 Lunch£2–£3.50 Tea85p alc High Tea£1.50–£3 Dinner£3.75–£4.75 Wine£3.50 *xmas*

★★***Headlands*** New South Prom ☎41179
Closed last 2wks Nov; 54rm Lift CTV 30P 8 Last dinner7.30pm

★**Kimberley** New South Promenade ☎41184
Closed 28Dec–15Jan; 54rm(25⇌⋔) Lift CTV 20P Last dinner7pm sB&B£8.10–£8.95 sB&B⇌⋔£9.10–£9.85 dB&B£16.20–£17.90 dB&B⇌⋔£18.20–£19.70 Lunch£2.25–£2.40 Tea29–35p Dinner£2.50–£2.65 Wine£2.10 *xmas* Credit cards 2 6

★**Revill's** North Prom ☎25768
Tall sea front hotel close to town centre.
Closed 12–30Nov; 53rm(3⇌⋔) Lift CTV 14P billiards Last dinner7.30pm sB&B£6–£6.50 sB&B⇌⋔£7–£7.50 dB&B£12–£13 dB&B⇌⋔£13–£14 Bar lunch50p–£1.50 Tea50–75p Dinner£3.50–£4 Wine£3 *xmas*

BLAGDON Avon Map**3** ST55
★★★***Mendip*** ☎62688
Modern, split-level building on hill overlooking the lake.
40⇌⋔ CTV & TV available in bedrooms 250P Conference facilities available English & Scottish. Last dinner10pm Credit cards 3 5

BLAKENEY Norfolk Map**9** TG04
★★★**Blakeney** Quayside ☎Cley 740797
40rm(22⇌⋔) Annexe: 13⇌⋔ CTV CTV available in bedrooms 100P (heated) sauna bath Last dinner9pm *sB&B£8.91–£10.69 sB&B⇌⋔£10.40–£13.66 dB&B£17.82–£21.78 dB&B⇌⋔£20.80–£27.32 Lunch fr£3.50 Dinner fr£4.75 Wine£3 *xmas* Credit cards 1 2 3 5

★★Manor ☎Cley740376
Closed 2wks mid Nov & Xmas; 12rm(8⇌⋒)
Annexe: 10⇌⋒ ⋈ CTV 60P ⇔ ⚓ ⊌English & Continental. Last dinner8.45pm ⊕ ⊈
✻sB&B£9.72 sB&B⇌⋒£11.83 dB&B£19.60
dB&B⇌⋒£22.57–£26.14 Lunch£3.56 Tea90p
High Tea£1.19 Dinner£4.75 Wine£2.20 ⊟

BLANCHLAND Northumberland Map**12** NY95
★★Lord Crewe Arms (Swallow) ☎251
Telex no53168
Once part of a medieval monastery dissolved by Henry VIII.
14rm(5⇌⋒) CTV ⊁ ⚓ Last dinner8.45pm ⊕ ⊈
S% sB&B£9.90–£13.25 dB&B£15.40–£22.50
dB&B⇌⋒£18.15–£25.80 ⊟ *xmas*
Credit cards 1 2 3 5

BLANDFORD FORUM Dorset Map**3** ST80
★★★Crown 1 West St ☎52366
26rm(11⇌⋒) ⋈ CTV ⊘ 100P 4⌂ ⚓ ⌂
Last dinner9pm ⊕ ⊈ sB&B fr£9
sB&B⇌⋒ fr£14 dB&B fr£28 Lunch£3.50–£4
Tea40p–£1 Dinner£4–£5 Wine£2.90 *xmas*
Credit card 1

★★Anvil Pimperne (2m NE A354) ☎53431
7rm(6⇌⋒) ⋈ CTV 26P ⚓ ⌓(heated) ⌂
Last dinner6.30pm ⊕ ⊈ Credit cards 1 2 3

BLEADON Avon Map**3** ST35
✕La Casita Bridgwater Rd ☎812326
Closed Tue; Lunch not served Mon & during winter;
40seats 25P Last dinner10.30pm Dinner£10alc
Credit cards 2 5

BLETSOE Bedfordshire Map**4** TL05
✕✕Falcon Inn ☎Bedford781222
Old country inn on main A6, with pleasant bar, and wood panelled dining room.
Lunch Sat; Dinner not served Sun; 62seats 50P
⊌English & Continental. Last dinner9.45pm S%
✻Lunch£6alc Dinner£6alc Wine£2.75
Credit cards 1 5

BLICKLING Norfolk Map**9** TG12
✕Buckinghamshire Arms Hotel ☎Aylsham2133
Country inn adjoining Blickling Hall.
Closed Mon, 1wk-end Mar & Oct; Lunch not served Tue–Sat; Dinner not served Sun; 48seats 70P bedrooms available ⊌English & French.
Last dinner9.15pm Lunch fr£4.25
Dinner fr£5.60&alc Wine£2.60
Credit cards 1 2 3 5

BLOCKLEY Gloucestershire Map**4** SP13
❁★★Lower Brook House ☎286
Closed 25 Dec–24 Jan; 7rm(5⇌⋒) ⋈ CTV TV available in bedrooms ⊘ ⇔ 10P ⚓ Children under 5yrs not accommodated Last dinner9pm ⊕ ⊈
sB&B£10.25 dB&B£20.50
dB&B⇌⋒£23.50–£25.50 Lunch£3.50alc
Tea fr65p Dinner£5&alc Wine£3.95 ⊟
Credit card 1

BLOFIELD Norfolk Map**5** TG30
✕✕La Locanda Fox Ln ☎Norwich713787
Closed Sun; Lunch not served Sat; 40seats 20P
⊌Italian. Last dinner10.30pm ✻Lunch fr£2.45&alc
Wine£2.95 Credit cards 1 2 3

BLUE ANCHOR Somerset Map**3** ST04
★Langbury ☎Dunster375
Neat, white walled house with own garden in country setting overlooking bay.
Closed Xmas; 10rm ⋈ CTV 10P ⚓ ⌓(heated)
Last dinner7.30pm ⊕ ⊈ S%
sB&B£5.50–£6.50 dB&B£11–£13 Bar lunch
£1–£2 Tea75p–£1.50 Dinner£4 Wine£1.75 ⊟

BLUNDELLSANDS Merseyside Map**7** SJ39
★★**Blundellsands** Serpentine (Whitbread)
☎051–924 6515 Liverpool plan**4**
44rm(28⇌🚿) Lift ☽ 📺 CTV CTV in bedrooms 200P
🚗 Last dinner9pm ♨ 🍸 ✱sB&B£11.85
sB&B⇌🚿£13.35 dB&B£23.70 dB&B⇌🚿£26.70
Lunch£4.10&alc Dinner£4.65&alc Wine£2.35
Credit cards [1] [2] [3] [5]

BLYTH Nottinghamshire Map**8** SK68
★★**Fourways** ☎235
9rm 📺 CTV TV available in bedroom 60P 2🏠 ⚓
Last dinner9.30pm ♨ 🍸 sB&B fr£12
dB&B fr£16 Lunch£2.60–£5.60&alc Tea80p
High Tea£1.35–£5&alc Dinner£5.35alc *xmas*
Credit cards [2] [3]

BODIAM East Sussex Map**5** TQ72
❁✕**Curlew** ☎Hurst Green272
Closed Mon; Dinner not served Sun; 20seats 25P
🍷English & French. Last dinner9pm
Credit cards [1] [2] [3] [4] [5] [6]

BODINNICK Cornwall Map**2** SX15
★**Old Ferry Inn** ☎Polruan237
400-year old inn at edge of Fowey estuary.
RS Oct–Mar (no dinner); 12rm(5⇌🚿) 1🛏 CTV 9P
4🏠 🚗 Last dinner7.30pm ♨ ✱sB&B£7.50
dB&B£15 dB&B⇌🚿£17 Bar lunch35p–75p
Dinner£4.95 Wine£2.65

BODMIN Cornwall Map**2** SX06
★★**Castle Hill House** Castle Hill ☎3009
9rm(3⇌🚿) 1🛏 📺 CTV TV available in bedrooms 50P
⚓ billiards ♣ Last dinner9pm ♨ 🍸 S%
sB&B£8.25–£10 sB&B⇌🚿£9–£11
dB&B£16.50–£18.50 dB&B⇌🚿£20–£26
Lunch£3.75–£4.25&alc Tea£1–£1.50
Dinner£4–£4.50&alc Wine£2.50 🍽
★★***Westberry*** Rhind St ☎2772
18rm(4⇌🚿) 📺 CTV 18P Live music & dancing Fri & Sat 🍷English & French. Last dinner8pm ♨ 🍸

BOGNOR REGIS West Sussex Map**4** SZ99
★★★★**Royal Norfolk** The Esplanade ☎26222
49rm(28⇌🚿) Lift ☽ 📺 CTV CTV available in bedrooms 150P 6🏠 ⚓ ⛱(heated) Live music & dancing Sat 🍷French. Last dinner9.45pm ♨ 🍸
sB&B fr£10 sB&B⇌🚿 fr£15 dB&B fr£30.50
dB&B⇌🚿 fr£54.50 Lunch fr£4.25&alc
Dinner fr£5.25&alc Wine£3.50 🍽 *xmas*
Credit cards [1] [2] [3] [5] [6]
★★**Clarehaven** Wessex Av ☎23265
Well proportioned, three-storey brick building with balconies.
28rm(6⇌🚿) Annexe:6rm 📺 CTV 12P Disco wkly
Live music & dancing wkly ♣ Last dinner8pm ♨
🍸 S% sB&B£9.60–£13.30
dB&B£19.20–£26.60 dB&B⇌🚿£21.60–£29
Lunch£3–£3.75&alc Tea50p–£1.20
Dinner£3.60–£4.50&alc Wine£2.80 *xmas*
★★***Royal*** The Esplanade ☎4665
Three-storey building overlooking the sea.
37rm(11⇌🚿) ☽ 📺 CTV ⊘ 18P 🚗 Live music & dancing Sat 🍷International. Last dinner10pm ♨
🍸 Credit cards [2] [3] [5] [6]
★**Black Mill House** Princess Av ☎21945
A quiet family hotel in an avenue leading to the Marine Gardens and the sea.
20rm(3⇌🚿) Annexe:4rm 📺 CTV 10P 🚗 ♣
Last dinner7.45pm ♨ 🍸 S%
sB&B£8.85–£11.20 dB&B£17.70–£22.40
dB&B⇌🚿£20.10–£24.80 Lunch£2.65–£3.20
Tea30–85p Dinner£3.20–£3.75 Wine£2.60 🍽
xmas

Victoria Aldwick Rd ☎22335
hree-storey building, late 19th-C with gardens, just ff the seafront.
2rm CTV 15P ⚓ Last dinner9pm ✿ S%
B&B£8.35 dB&B⇌⋒£14.30 Lunch£2.38
inner£5alc Wine£2.10 Credit card 3

OLBERRY DOWN Devon Map**3** SX63
Port Light ☎Galmpton384
losed Mon & Tue; 24seats 30P bedrooms available
astdinner8.30pm Lunch£2.25–£3.60
ea27–85p Dinner£3.50–£4.75&alc Wine£2.85

OLLINGTON Cheshire Map**7** SJ97
★★Belgrade ☎73246 Telex no667217
tone-built with a modern extension, this hotel tands in its own grounds, close to the village and ffording good views.
0⇌⋒ ☽ ⋔ CTV in bedrooms ⊘ 60P Live music & ancing Sat Conference facilities available ♉English, rench & Italian. Lastdinner9.45pm ✿ ⊥ S%
*sB&B⇌⋒£16.20 dB&B⇌⋒£21.60
unch fr£2.75 Tea fr£1.29 Dinner fr£3.95&alc
Vine£2.92 Credit cards 1 2 3 4 5 6

OLTON Gt Manchester Map**7** SD70
ee also Egerton
☆☆Bolton Crest Motel Beaumont Rd (Crest)
☎651511
00⇌⋒ Lift ☽ ⋔ CTV in bedrooms 153P ⚓ ⌂
astdinner9.45pm ✿ ⊥ S%
*sB&B⇌⋒£16.79 dB&B⇌⋒£21.60
ontinental breakfast ⊨ Credit cards 1 2 3 4 5 6

★★Pack Horse Bradshawgate, Nelson Sq
Greenall Whitley) ☎27261
0rm(61⇌⋒) Lift ☽ ⋔ CTV CTV in bedrooms ⊨
auna bath Conference facilities available ♿

Lastdinner9pm ✿ S% sB&B£15–£15.50
sB&B⇌⋒£17–£18 dB&B£20–£21
dB&B⇌⋒£24–£25 Lunch£3.75–£4&alc
Dinner£4.50–£5.50&alc Wine£3 ⊨
Credit cards 1 2 3 5 6

BOREHAM STREET East Sussex Map**5** TQ61
★★★White Friars (Best Western)
☎Herstmonceux2355
Ivy-clad, early-Georgian house in four acres of gardens.
Closed Jan; 18rm(9⇌⋒) ⋔ CTV TV available in bedrooms 70P ⚘ ⚓ Lastdinner8.30pm ✿ S%
sB&B fr£11 sB&B⇌⋒ fr£13.50 dB&B fr£22
dB&B⇌⋒ fr£27 Lunch fr£3.75&alc
Dinner fr£4.75&alc Wine£3.90 ⊨
Credit cards 1 3 5

XXSmugglers Wheel ☎Herstmonceux2293
Closed Mon & Feb; Dinner not served Sun; 65seats 20P Live music & dancing last Fri mthly ♉French.
Lastdinner10.30pm Lunch fr£3.50&alc
Dinner£6alc Wine£4 Credit cards 1 2 3 5 6

BOREHAM WOOD Hertfordshire Map**4** TQ19
☆☆☆Thatched Barn Barnet Bypass (Queens)
☎01–953 1622
Pleasant thatched roof hotel.
60⇌⋒ ☽ ⋔ CTV in bedrooms 400P ⚓ ⌓(heated)
Live music & dancing Sat ⌂ ♉English & French.
Lastdinner9.45pm ✿ ⊥ S% sB&B⇌⋒£20
dB&B⇌⋒£26 Lunch fr£4&alc Tea50p
Dinner fr£5.25&alc ⊨ Credit cards 1 2 3 4 5 6

★Grosvenor 148 Shenley Rd ☎01–953 3175
19rm ⋔ CTV ⊘ 10P 3⌂ ⚘ ♉English & French.
Lastdinner10pm ✿ S% sB&B£10 dB&B£17
Lunch fr£3&alc Dinner fr£5&alc Wine£2.50 *xmas*
Credit cards 3 5

BOROUGHBRIDGE N Yorkshire Map**8** SE36
★★★**Three Arrows** Horsefair (Embassy) ☎2245
Late-Victorian country house in 24 acres of secluded grounds.
19rm(10⇌ ⋒) ☽ ⋈ CTV TV available in bedrooms 100P ⚓ Last dinner9.15pm ✿ S% sB&B£10 dB&B£16 dB&B⇌ ⋒£18 Lunch£4.50&alc Dinner£5&alc Wine£4 ▣ Credit cards①②③④⑤⑥

BORROWDALE Cumbria Map**11** NY21 **See also Grange (in-Borrowdale), Rosthwaite and Keswick**
★★★★ **Lodore Swiss** ☎285 Telex no64305
See page 37 for details

★★★**Mary Mount** ☎223 Telex no64305
Closed mid Nov–mid Dec; 9⇌ ⋒ Annexe:6⇌ ⋒ ⋈ CTV CTV in bedrooms ⊘ 30P ⚘ ⚓ ♉English & Continental. Last dinner8.30pm ✿ ⊥ sB&B⇌ ⋒£17 dB&B£26 Bar lunch£2.25alc Tea75palc Dinner£5.50 Wine£2.90 ▣

★★**Borrowdale** ☎224
Creeper-hung, local-stone building set in mountainous surroundings on B5289.
Closed Jan; 37rm(35⇌ ⋒) ⋈ CTV 100P ⚘ ⚓ ♉International. Last dinner8.15pm ✿ ⊥ S% ✱sB&B fr£9.50 sB&B⇌ ⋒ fr£10.10 dB&B⇌ ⋒ fr£20.20 Lunch fr£3.30 Tea fr25p Dinner fr£5.40 Wine£2.59 *xmas*

BOSCASTLE Cornwall Map**2** SX09
★★**Bottreaux House** ☎231
RS mid Nov–Feb; 11rm(2⇌ ⋒) ⋈ CTV TV available in bedrooms 10P ⚘ Children under 8yrs not accommodated ♉English & French. Last dinner9pm S% sB&B£7–£7.50 dB&B£14–£15 dB&B⇌ ⋒£16–£17 Lunch£2.50–£3.50&alc Dinner£4&alc Wine£2.40 ▣ *xmas* Credit cards①③

★★**Valency House** ☎288
Closed mid Nov–Feb; 7rm ⋈ TV ⊘ 7P ⚘ ⚓ ⌂ Last dinner9pm ✿ ⊥ S% sB&B£7–£8 dB&B£14 Lunch£1–£2.50 Tea35–75p Dinner£4&alc Wine£1.75 ▣ Credit cards①③

BOSHAM West Sussex Map**4** SU80
★★**Millstream** Bosham Ln (Best Western) ☎573234
Pleasant one-storey building with part flint, stone & brick façade and wrought-iron balcony.
16rm(12⇌ ⋒) ⋈ CTV CTV available in bedrooms 45P ⚘ ⚓ Children under 12yrs not accommodated ♿ ♉French. Last dinner9.30pm S% sB&B£11 dB&B£22 dB&B⇌ ⋒£26 Lunch£5.50 Dinner£7.50 Wine£2.75 ▣ *xmas* Credit cards①②③⑤

BOSTON Lincolnshire Map**8** TF34
★★**New England** Wide Bargate (Anchor) ☎65255 Telex no858875
11rm(5⇌ ⋒) ⋈ CTV CTV in bedrooms ⚑ Last dinner9.30pm ✿ S% ✱sB&B fr£11 sB&B⇌ ⋒ fr£14.50 dB&B fr£17.50 dB&B⇌ ⋒ fr£21 Lunch fr£3.50 Dinner fr£4 Wine£2.65 ▣ Credit cards①②③④⑤⑥

BOTALLACK Cornwall Map**2** SW33
✕✕**Count House** ☎Penzance788588
Closed Mon & Tue; Lunch not served Wed–Sat; Dinner not served Sun; 36seats 25P Last dinner9.45pm ✱Lunch£3&alc Dinner£7alc Wine£2.95 Credit cards①②③④⑤⑥

BOTLEY Hampshire Map**4** SU51
★★★***Botleigh Grange*** ☎2212
52rm(10⇌ ⋒) ⋈ CTV 180P 6⌂ ⚘ ⚓ ↳ ∩ Last dinner9.30pm

✕**Cobbet's** 13 The Square ☎2068
Closed Sun; Lunch not served Mon; 40seats ♉English & French. Last dinner9.30pm Lunch£9alc Dinner£10alc Wine£2.60

BOTTOM HOUSE Staffordshire Map**7** SK05
✕**Forge** Ashbourne Rd ☎Onecote249
Dinner not served Sun & Mon; 50seats 250P ♉English & French. Last dinner10pm ✱Lunch£1–£1.30&alc Dinner£4.50alc Wine£3.20

BOURNE HEATH Hereford & Worcester Map**7** SO97
✕***Nailers Arms*** Doctors Hill ☎Bromsgrove73045
Closed Mon; Dinner not served Sun; 80seats 90P Last dinner10pm

BOURNEMOUTH & BOSCOMBE Dorset Map**4** SZ09 *Telephone exchange 'Bournemouth'* **See Central & District plans** For additional hotels see **Christchurch & Poole**
★★★★★***Carlton*** East Cliff (Prestige) ☎22011 Telex no41244 Central plan**8**
Large, rambling, honey-coloured building on clifftop, near to funicular and beach; with views of Swanage and the Isle of Wight.
121⇌ ⋒ Lift ☽ ✗ ⋈ CTV in bedrooms 200P 110⌂ ⚓ ⌓(heated) billiards Disco 4 nights wkly Live music 4 nights wkly Live music & dancing twice wkly Conference facilities available ♿ ♉English & Continental. Last dinner11.30pm ✿ ⊥ ▣ Credit cards①②③④⑤⑥

★★★★★**Royal Bath** Bath Rd (De Vere) ☎25555 Telex no41375 Central plan**41**
Pleasing white building near cliff top, with grand interior with magnificent pillared lounge and restaurant. Three acres of lovely gardens with sun terrace.
125⇌ ⋒ Lift ☽ ⋈ CTV in bedrooms 120⌂ ⚓ ⌓(heated) sauna bath ⌂ ♉International.

Last dinner10.30pm ♔ 🍸 S% sB&B⇌⋒£25 dB&B⇌⋒£50 Lunch fr£7.50&alc Tea fr£1.75 Dinner fr£8&alc Wine£4 🅁 *xmas* Credit cards 1 2 3 5 6

★★★★East Cliff Court East Overcliffe Dr ☎24545 Central plan**20**
Imposing building situated on cliff top.
68⇌⋒ Lift ☽ 🍽 CTV in bedrooms 100P 🚗 ⚓ ⛱(heated) Live music & dancing twice wkly in season Cabaret wkly Conference facilities available ♀English & French. Last dinner9.30pm ♔ 🍸 S% ✻sB&B⇌⋒£14.50–£22.50 dB&B⇌⋒£27–£45 Lunch fr£4.50&alc Tea fr£3 Dinner£6–£8&alc Wine£3.10 🅁 *xmas* Credit cards 1 2 3 4 5 6

★★★★Highcliff West Cliff, St Michael's Rd (Best Western) ☎27702 Telex no417153 Central plan**26**
Imposing four-storey building on cliff top with uninterrupted sea views.
97rm(92⇌⋒) Lift ☽ 🍽 CTV in bedrooms 85P 10🏠 ⚓ ⛱(heated) 🎾(hard) sauna bath Disco wkly Live music & dancing 4 nights wkly Conference facilities available ♿ ♿ Last dinner8.45pm ♔ 🍸 S% sB&B fr£13 sB&B⇌⋒£13.50–£18.50 dB&B£25–£32 dB&B⇌⋒£26–£36 Lunch£4.25–£4.75&alc Tea70p–£1 High Tea£3.50–£4 Dinner£5.25–£5.50&alc Wine£2.75 🅁 *xmas* Credit cards 1 2 3 5 6

★★★★Marsham Court Russell Cotes Rd, East Cliff (De Vere) ☎22111 Telex no22121 Central plan**30**
On East Cliff, overlooking the sea.
89rm(80⇌⋒) Lift ☽ 🍽 CTV CTV in bedrooms 🚫 40P 36🏠 ⚓ ⛱(heated) Conference facilities available ♿ ♀English & French. Last dinner9.30pm ♔ 🍸

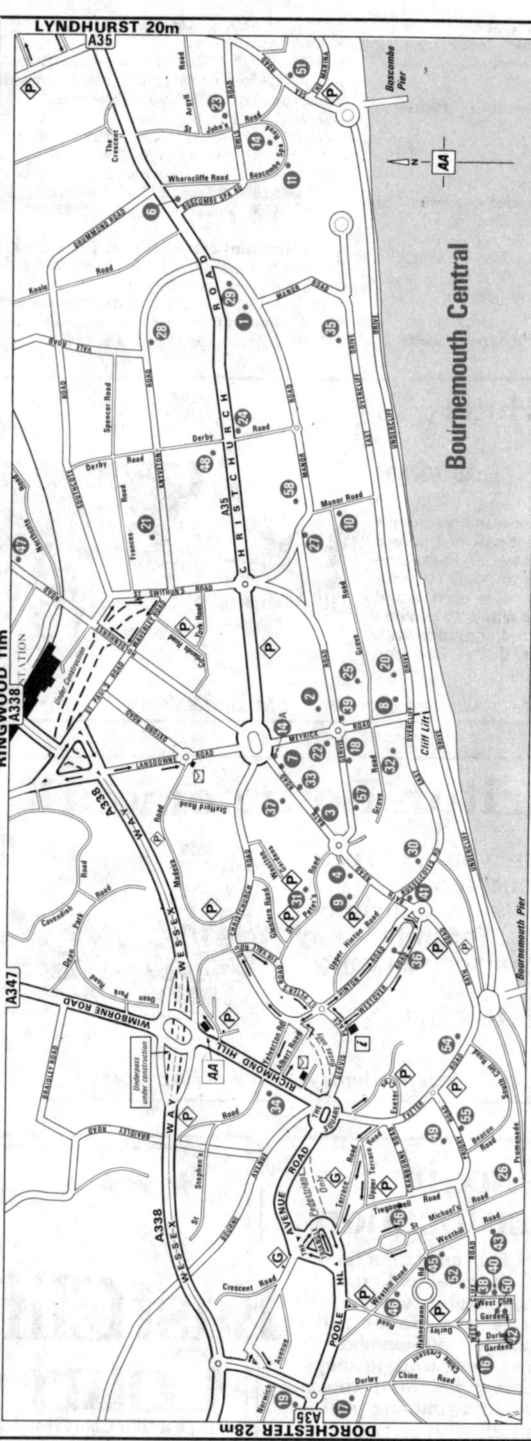

1 Adelphi ★★★
2 Anglo-Swiss ★★★
3 Angus ★★★
4 Belvedere ★★
28 Bournemouth Moat House ★★★
5 Broughty Ferry Children's Hotel ★★
6 Brummels Touring ★★
7 Burley Court ★★★
8 Carlton ★★★★★
9 Hotel Cecil ★★★
10 Chesterwood ★★★
11 Chine ★★★
12 Cliff End ★★★
13 County ★★
14 Hotel Courtlands ★★★
14A Crest Motor ☆☆☆
15 Crust ✕
16 Durley Dean ★★
17 Durley Hall ★★
18 Durlston Court ★★★
19 East Anglia ★★★
20 Eastcliffe Court ★★★★
21 Elstead ★★
22 Embassy ★★★
23 Fircroft ★★
24 Hazelwood ★★★
25 Heathlands ★★★
26 Highcliff ★★★★
27 Hinton Firs ★★
29 Manor House ★
30 Marsham Court ★★★★
31 Melford Hall ★★★
32 Miramar ★★★
33 New Somerset ★★
34 Norfolk ★★★
35 Normandie International ★★★
36 Palace Court ★★★★ La Taverna ✕✕
37 Pavilion ★★★
38 Pinehurst ★★
39 Queens ★★★
40 Hotel Riviera ★
41 Royal Bath ★★★★★
42 St George ★★
43 Savoy ★★★
44 South Western Hotel ✕✕
45 Sun Court ★★
46 Tralee ★★
47 Trattoria San Marco ✕
48 Tree Tops ★
49 Trouville ★★★
50 Ullswater ★
51 Waters Edge ★★
52 Wessex ★★★
53 Whitehall ★★
54 White Hermitage ★★★
55 Winterbourne ★★
56 Winter Gardens ★★
57 Woodcroft Tower ★★
58 Wood Lodge ★

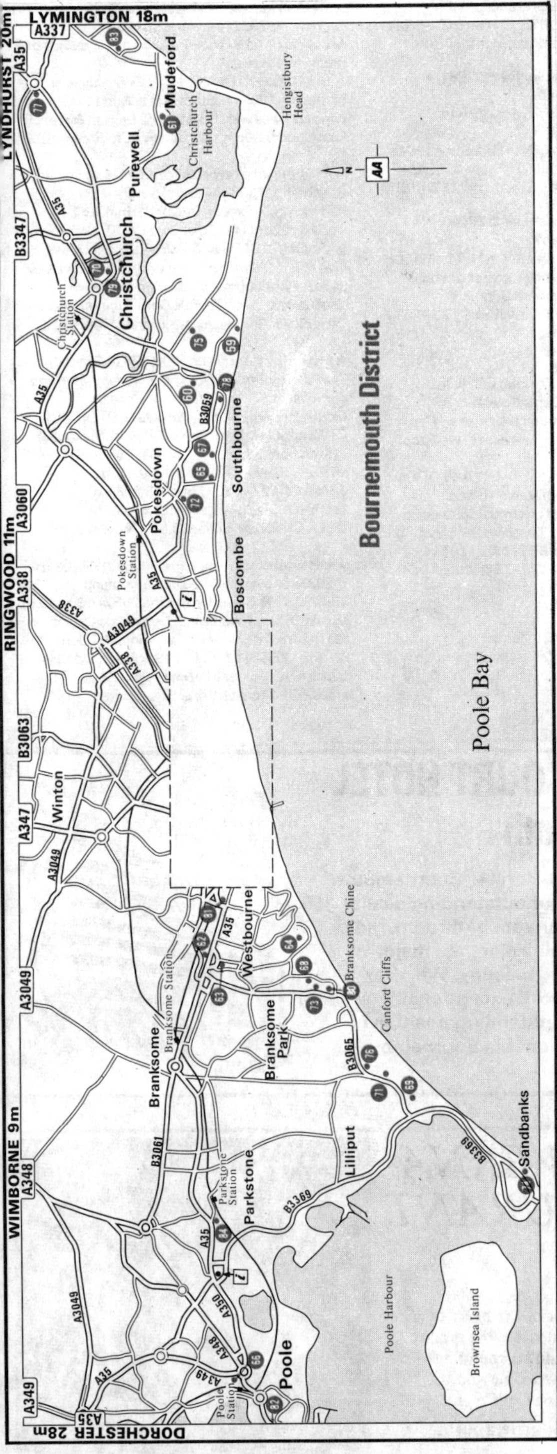

59 Albany ★★
60 Avonmore ★★
61 Avonmouth ★★★ *(see under Christchurch)*
62 Cadogan ★★
63 La Cappa ✕✕
64 Chinehurst ★★
65 Commodore ★★
66 Dolphin ★★★ *(see under Poole)*
67 Grange ★
68 Grovefield Hotel ✕✕ *(see under Poole)*
69 Harbour Heights ★★★ *(see under Poole)*
70 Kings Arms ★★★ *(see under Christchurch)*
71 Norfolk Lodge ⊕ *(see under Poole)*
72 Opus One ✕✕
73 Riviera ⊕
74 Sandbanks ★★★ *(see under Poole)*
75 Saxon King ★★
76 Sea Witch *(see under Poole)*
77 Somerford ⊕ *(see under Christchurch)*
78 Southwood Lodge ★★
79 Splinters ●✕ *(see under Christchurch)*
80 Studland Dene ★★
81 Topo Gigio ✕
82 Warehouse ✕✕ *(see under Poole)*
83 Waterford Lodge ★★ *(see under Christchurch)*
84 Isobels ✕ *(see under Poole)*

B

S% sB&B⇌⋔£20 dB&B⇌⋔£40 Lunch fr£5.25&alc Tea fr£1.25 Dinner fr£5.75&alc Wine£3.75 ⊟ *xmas* Credit cards ① ② ③ ⑤ ⑥

★★★★*Palace Court* Westover Rd ☎27681 Telex no 41141 Central plan **36**
Nine-storey building (dating from 1935) with balconies overlooking the sea.
108⇌⋔ Lift ☽ ✗ ⚿ CTV & CTV in bedrooms 250⌂ Conference facilities available ♉ English & French. Last dinner 9pm ✿ ⚐ ⊟ Credit cards ① ② ③ ⑤ ⑥

★★★Adelphi Manor Rd, East Cliff ☎26546 Telex no 418368 Central plan **1**
54⇌⋔ Lift ☽ ⚿ CTV CTV available in bedrooms 30P ⚓ Live music & dancing wknds Cabaret wknds ♿ ♉ English & French. Last dinner 8.30pm ✿ ⚐ S% sB&B⇌⋔£10–£14.50 dB&B⇌⋔£20–£29 Lunch £3.75 Tea 75p Dinner £4.50 Wine £2 ⊟ *xmas* Credit cards ① ② ③ ⑤

★★★Anglo-Swiss Gervis Rd, East Cliff (Lanz) ☎24794 Telex no 418261 Central plan **2**
Four-storey building with green tiled roof and wrought-iron balconies, with one acre of well-kept gardens.
64rm(44⇌⋔) Annexe: 6rm(1⇌⋔) Lift ☽ ⚿ CTV in bedrooms 60P ⚓ ⛱(heated) squash billiards sauna bath Disco Wed & Sat Live music & dancing Sun, Mon & Fri ♧ ♉ French. Last dinner 8.30pm ✿ ⚐ S% sB&B£10–£12 sB&B⇌⋔£12–£14 dB&B£18–£22 dB&B⇌⋔£22–£26 Lunch fr£4 Dinner fr£5 Wine£2.20 ⊟ *xmas* Credit cards ① ② ③ ⑥

★★★*Angus* Bath Rd ☎26420 Central plan **3**
50rm(27⇌⋔) Lift ☽ ⚿ CTV available in bedrooms 50P ⇐ ♉ International. Last dinner 8.30pm ✿ ⚐ ⊟ Credit card ①

★★★*Bournemouth Moat House* 31 Knyveton Rd (Queens) ☎292244 Central plan **28**
Modernised hotel standing in its own grounds of nearly two acres.
129rm(100⇌⋔) Lift ☽ ⚿ CTV TV available in bedrooms 100P ⚓ ⛱(heated) billiards Live music & dancing twice wkly in season ♉ English & French. Last dinner 8.30pm ✿ ⚐ ⊟ Credit cards ① ② ③

★★★Broughty Ferry Children's Hotel Sea Rd, Boscombe ☎35333 Central plan **5**
RS Nov–Feb (Except Xmas); 68rm(47⇌⋔) Annexe: 22rm(14⇌⋔) ☽ ✗ CTV CTV available in bedrooms ⊘ 60P 4⌂ ⚓ ⛱(heated) Disco twice wkly Live music & dancing twice wkly Cabaret wkly ♧ ♿ Last dinner 8.30pm ✿ ⚐ Lunch £3&alc Tea 60p &alc High Tea 60p &alc Dinner £4&alc Wine£2.75 ⊟ *xmas* Credit cards ① ② ③ ⑤ ⑥

★★★Burley Court Bath Rd ☎22824 Central plan **7**
Two-storey white building overlooking lawn and gardens.
Closed 31 Dec–14 Jan; 45rm(29⇌⋔) Lift ☽ ⚿ CTV CTV available in bedrooms 40P ⇐ ⛱(heated) ♧ Last dinner 8.30pm ✿ ⚐ S% sB&B£10–£15 sB&B⇌⋔£11–£17 dB&B£20–£28 dB&B⇌⋔£22–£32 Lunch £3.80&alc Tea 35–70p &alc High Tea £1.20alc Dinner £4.50&alc Wine£3.50 ⊟ *xmas*

★★★Hotel Cecil Parsonage Rd, Bath Hill (Lanz) ☎293336 Telex no 418261 Central plan **9**
28⇌⋔ Lift ⚿ CTV in bedrooms 25P ⇐ ⛱(heated) squash billiards sauna bath Live music & dancing Fri & Sat Cabaret Fri ♉ French. Last dinner 9.30pm ✿ ⚐ S% sB&B⇌⋔£11–£13 dB&B⇌⋔£22–£26 Lunch fr£4 Dinner fr£5&alc Wine£2.20 ⊟ *xmas* Credit cards ① ② ③ ⑥

★★★**Chesterwood** East Overcliff Dr ☎28057 Central plan **10**
56rm(23⇌⋒) Lift ☽ ⛆ CTV 30P 8🏠 ⚓ ⛱(heated) Live music & dancing 3 nights wkly Cabaret wkly ♧ Last dinner 8pm ♡ ☮ S% ✻sB&B£10 sB&B⇌⋒£11 dB&B£20 dB&B⇌⋒£21 Lunch£3 Tea 20–50p Dinner£4 Wine£2.60 ⚑ *xmas* Credit card 1

★★★**Chine** Boscombe Spa Rd, Boscombe ☎36234 Central plan **11**
Victorian gable and tile building with modern extension; good views over bay and wooded grounds with terraced lawns.
90rm(59⇌⋒) Lift ☽ ⛆ CTV ⊘ 30P 12🏠 ⚓ ⛱(heated) Disco 3 nights wkly Live music & dancing wkly ♧ ♡ English & Continental. Last dinner 8.30pm ♡ ☮ ✻sB&B£9.23–£12.47 sB&B⇌⋒£10.31–£13.55 dB&B£16.84–£23.33 dB&B⇌⋒£19–£25.49 Lunch fr£4 Dinner fr£5 Wine£3 ⚑ *xmas*

★★★**Cliff End** Manor Rd, East Cliff ☎39711 Central plan **12**
Converted residence with new wing, secluded gardens with direct access to Boscombe Chine.
40⇌⋒ Lift ☽ ⛆ CTV in bedrooms 40P ⚓ ⛱(heated) ●(hard) Disco twice wkly in season Live music & dancing twice wkly in season ♧ ♡ English & Continental. Last dinner 8.30pm ♡ ☮ sB&B⇌⋒£11 dB&B⇌⋒£22 Lunch£3 Tea 50p Dinner£4 Wine£3.25 ⚑ *xmas*

★★★**Hotel Courtlands** 16 Boscombe Spa Rd, East Cliff ☎33070 Central plan **14**
Large Victorian building with one acre of lawns and gardens with views of the sea.
50rm(35⇌⋒) Lift ☽ ⛆ CTV CTV in bedrooms 60P ⚓ ⛱(heated) Disco twice wkly in season Live music & dancing twice wkly in season ♿ ♡ English & Continental. Last dinner 8.30pm ♡ S% sB&B£9.55–£12.45 sB&B⇌⋒£11–£13.90 dB&B£19.10–£24.90 dB&B⇌⋒£22–£27.80 Lunch£3.65 Dinner£4.85 Wine£3.30 ⚑ *xmas* Credit cards 1 2 3 5

☆☆☆**Crest Motor** Lansdowne (Crest) ☎23262 Telex no 41232 Central plan **14A**
Modern purpose-built motor hotel of interesting circular design.
102⇌⋒ Lift ☽ ⊞ CTV in bedrooms 150P ♡ ☮ S% ✻sB&B⇌⋒£14.09 dB&B⇌⋒£23.32 Continental breakfast ⚑ Credit cards 1 2 3 4 5 6

★★★**Durlston Court** Gervis Rd, East Cliff (Lanz) ☎291488 Telex no 418261 Central plan **18**
63rm(35⇌⋒) Lift ☽ ⛆ CTV CTV in bedrooms 40P ⛱(heated) squash billiards sauna bath Disco Tue & Fri Live music & dancing Mon, Wed & Sun ♧ ♡ French. Last dinner 8.30pm ♡ ☮ S% sB&B£10–£12 sB&B⇌⋒£12–£14 dB&B£18–£22 dB&B⇌⋒£22–£26 Lunch fr£4 Dinner fr£5 Wine£2.20 ⚑ *xmas* Credit cards 1 2 3 6

★★★**East Anglia** 6 Poole Rd ☎765163 Central plan **19**
49rm(41⇌⋒) Annexe: 20rm(14⇌⋒) Lift ☽ ⛆ CTV in bedrooms ⊘ 80P ⛟ ⛱(heated) sauna bath Live music & dancing twice wkly in season Last dinner 8.30pm ♡ ☮ S% sB&B£10–£20 sB&B⇌⋒£12–£24 dB&B£15–£30 dB&B⇌⋒£16–£34 Lunch fr£3 Dinner fr£4.50 Wine£3 ⚑ *xmas* Credit cards 1 2 3 6

★★★***Embassy*** Meyrick Rd ☎20751 Central plan **22**
45rm(21⇌⋒) Annexe: 15rm Lift ☽ ⛆ CTV 50P 3🏠 ⛟ Live music & dancing Mon & Fri Last dinner 8.30pm ☮

B

★★★**Hazelwood** Christchurch Rd, East Cliff ☎21367 Central plan**24**
58rm(41⇌ ⋒) Lift ☽ 🕅 CTV 40P ⛟ ⚓ ⛆(heated) Live music & dancing twice wkly Cabaret wkly ♡English & French. Last dinner8.30pm ♡ ⚲
Lunch fr£3.25 Tea fr75p Dinner fr£4.50
Wine£2.75 ⊟ *xmas* Credit cards 1 2 3 5

★★★**Heathlands** Grove Rd, East Cliff (Lanz & Inter-Hotel) ☎23336 Telex no418261 Central plan**25**
Fine four-storey building with well-kept lawns and gardens. Elegant modern interior.
120rm (105⇌ ⋒) Lift ☽ 🕅 CTV in bedrooms 80P ⛆(heated) squash billiards sauna bath Disco Mon Live music & dancing Sun, Thu & Fri Cabaret Tue ⛪ ♿ Conference facilities available ♡French. Last dinner8.30pm ♡ ⚲ S% sB&B£10–£12 sB&B⇌ ⋒£12–£14 dB&B£18–£22 dB&B⇌ ⋒£22–£26 Lunch fr£4 Dinner fr£5
Wine£2.20 ⊟ *xmas* Credit cards 1 2 3 5 6

★★★**Melford Hall** St Peters Rd ☎21516 Central plan**31**
Large white building with sundeck, set back from road in 1½ acres of gardens.
68rm(31⇌ ⋒) Lift ☽ CTV CTV available in bedrooms 50P ⚓ Live music & dancing 3 nights wkly Last dinner8pm ♡ ⚲ Wine£3.56 ⊟ *xmas*

★★★**Miramar** Grove Rd ☎26581 Central plan**32**
42rm(36⇌ ⋒) Lift ☽ 🕅 CTV CTV in bedrooms 40P 6⌂ ⛟ ⚓ ⛪ ♿ Last dinner8pm ♡ ⚲
sB&B£13.80–£17.83 sB&B⇌ ⋒£15.53–£19.55
dB&B£27.60–£35.65 dB&B⇌ ⋒£29.90–£39.10
Lunch£4.60–£4.90 Tea46p Dinner£5.20
Wine£3.45 ⊟ *xmas*

★★★**Norfolk** Richmond Hill ☎21521 Central plan**34**
64rm(35⇌ ⋒) Lift ☽ 🕅 CTV ⊘ 50P ⚓ Live music & dancing wkly ♡International. Last dinner8.30pm ♡ ⚲ ✻sB&B£9.82–£12.42
sB&B⇌ ⋒£10.90–£13.50 dB&B£19.66–£24.84
dB&B⇌ ⋒£21.86–£27 Lunch fr£4 Dinner fr£5
Wine£3 ⊟ *xmas* Credit cards 1 3 5 6

★★★**Normandie International** East Overcliff Dr ☎22246 Central plan**35**
Closed Jan; 70rm(65⇌ ⋒) Lift ☽ ✗ 🕅 CTV CTV in bedrooms ⊘ 40P ⚓ Live music & dancing twice wkly Conference facilities available Last dinner9pm ♡ ⚲ S% sB&B£12–£16 sB&B⇌ ⋒£14–£21
dB&B£24–£38 dB&B⇌ ⋒£28–£42
Lunch£3.50–£6.50 Tea40–50p Dinner£4.50–£7
⊟

★★★**Pavilion** Bath Rd (Best Western) ☎291266 Central plan**37**
Comfortable building with modern lounge overlooking front lawns, putting green and gardens.
49rm(37⇌ ⋒) Lift ☽ ⊞ CTV CTV in bedrooms 30P ⛟ ⚓ ⛪ Last dinner8.30pm ♡ ⚲ S%
✻sB&B£14–£16 sB&B⇌ ⋒£15–£17
dB&B£28–£32 dB&B⇌ ⋒£30–£34
Lunch£3.50–£4.50&alc Dinner£4.60–£5.50&alc
⊟ Credit cards 1 2 3 4 5 6

★★★**Queens** Meyrick Rd, East Cliff (North) ☎24415 Telex no262180 Central plan**39**
Comfortable holiday and residential hotel situated near cliff top.
Unlicensed; 116rm(81⇌ ⋒) Lift ☽ 🕅 CTV CTV available in bedrooms 50P 17⌂ ⚓ Conference facilities available Last dinner8.30pm ♡ ⚲ S%
sB&B fr£10.50 sB&B⇌ ⋒ fr£11.50
dB&B fr£19.15 dB&B⇌ ⋒ fr£23 Lunch fr£3.75
Tea fr75p Dinner fr£4.25 ⊟ *xmas*
Credit cards 1 2 3 6

★★★**Savoy** West Hill Rd, West Cliff (Myddleton) ☎294241 Telex no418220 Central plan**43**
On cliff top, honey-coloured brick building with balconies, spacious sun terrace and lounge overlooking the sea.

2rm(80⇌ ⋒) Lift ☽ ⋈ CTV in bedrooms 50P ⚓ (heated) ⌂ ☺English & French. astdinner8.30pm ✿ ☐ S% 3&B£11.50–£15 sB&B⇌ ⋒£12.50–£17.75 3&B£23–£30 dB&B⇌ ⋒£25–£35.50 unch£4.50&alc Tea85p Dinner£6.50&alc /ine£3.25 ⊟ *xmas* Credit cards 1 2 3 4 5 6

★★Trouville Priory Rd ☎22262 Central plan**49** osed Jan & Feb; 80rm(71⇌ ⋒) Lift ☽ ⋈ CTV in edrooms 70P 5⌂ ⇌ Live music & dancing twice kly in season Last dinner8pm ✿ ☐ S% 3&B£13–£18 dB&B⇌ ⋒£26–£36 unch£4&alc Tea50p Dinner£5&alc Wine£3 *mas*

★★Wessex West Cliff Rd (Travco) ☎21911 entral plan**52**

Rambling, four storey Victorian building. 101rm(55⇌ ⋒) Lift ☽ CTV in bedrooms 250P ⇌(heated) billiards sauna bath Live music nightly in season ⌂ Last dinner8.30pm ✿ ☐ sB&B£10.50–£12.50 sB&B⇌ ⋒£12–£14 dB&B£21–£25 dB&B⇌ ⋒£25.50–£29.50 Lunch fr£3.30 Dinner fr£4.40 Wine£2.25 ⊟ *xmas* Credit cards 1 2 3 5 6

★★★White Hermitage Exeter Rd (North) ☎27363 Telex no262180 Central Plan**54** *Building with sun terrace and gardens situated near sea-front facing pier.* Unlicensed; 85rm(36⇌ ⋒) Lift ☽ ✕ ⋈ CTV 60P ⚓ Last dinner8.30pm ✿ ☐ S% sB&B fr£10.25 sB&B⇌ ⋒ fr£11.25 dB&B fr£18.75 dB&B⇌ ⋒ fr£20.75 Lunch fr£3.75 Tea fr75p Dinner fr£4.25 ⊟ *xmas* Credit cards 1 2 3 6

★★***Albany*** Warren Edge Rd, Southbourne ☎428151 District plan**59**
19⇌⋒ Lift CTV 20P Children under 6yrs not accommodated Last dinner8pm
Credit cards 1 2 3 4 5 6

★★**Avonmore** Foxholes Rd, Southbourne ☎428639 District plan**60**
RS Nov–Mar; Unlicensed; 15rm(4⇌⋒) CTV TV available in bedrooms 10P Last dinner7.30pm *sB&B£5.95–£7.02 sB&B⇌⋒£8.25 dB&B£11.88–£14.05 dB&B⇌⋒£14.05–£16.20 Dinner fr£2.97 Credit cards 1 3

★★**Belvedere** Bath Rd ☎21080 Central plan**4**
20rm(2⇌⋒) CTV 30P Live music & dancing wkly Cabaret wkly Last dinner7.50pm sB&B&7.26–£9.35 sB&B⇌⋒£8.08–£10.17 dB&B£14.52–£18.70 dB&B⇌⋒£16.16–£20.34 Bar lunch£1–£2 Dinner£5 Wine£3 *xmas*

★★**Brummells Touring** 2 Boscombe Spa Rd/Christchurch Rd ☎33252 Central plan**6**
Closed Oct–25 May; 23rm(9⇌⋒) CTV 22P billiards Disco twice wkly Live music & dancing twice wkly Cabaret wkly Mainly grills. Last dinner7pm S% sB&B£7–£11 dB&B£13–£20 dB&B⇌⋒£15–£24 Bar lunch£1–£2.50 Dinner£1.50–£3.50&alc Wine£2.80 *xmas*

★★***Cadogan*** 8 Poole Rd ☎763006 District plan**62**
42rm(11⇌⋒) Lift CTV 40P English, French & Italian. Last dinner8pm *xmas*
Credit cards 1 3

★★**Chinehurst** Studland Rd, Westbourne ☎764583 District plan**64**
Closed mid Oct–Mar; Unlicensed; 27rm(12⇌⋒) CTV 22P Children under 3yrs not accommodated Last dinner8pm S% sB&B£6–£8 sB&B⇌⋒£7–£9 dB&B£12–£16 dB&B⇌⋒£14–£18 Lunch£2.85 Tea70p Dinner£5.20

★★**Commodore** Overcliff Dr, Southbourne (Whitbread) ☎423150 District plan**65**
19rm Lift CTV 12P Last dinner8.30pm sB&B£7.75 dB&B£15.50 Lunch fr£2.35 Dinner fr£3.50&alc Wine£2.75
Credit cards 1 3

★★**County** Westover Rd ☎22385 Central plan**13**
58rm(21⇌⋒) Lift CTV 14 Live music & dancing wkly English & French. Last dinner7.30pm sB&B£7.50–£11 dB&B£13–£20 dB&B⇌⋒£15–£22 Lunch£2.25 Tea25p Dinner£3.75 Wine£2.10 *xmas*

★★**Durley Dean** West Cliff Rd ☎27711 Central plan**16**
Situated at the top of Durley Chine within 100 yards of the pine-covered cliffs.
104rm(55⇌⋒) Lift CTV 35P (heated) billiards Live music & dancing 6 nights wkly International. Last dinner8pm sB&B£7.30–£11.30 sB&B⇌⋒£8.80–£12.80 dB&B£14–£22 dB&B⇌⋒£17–£25 Lunch£3.50&alc Tea30p Dinner£4.25&alc Wine£2.80 *xmas*

★★**Durley Hall** Durley Chine Rd ☎766886 Central plan**17**
78rm(50⇌⋒) Annexe:(3☎⋒) Lift CTV in bedrooms 100P Last dinner8.30pm sB&B£10–£13.50 sB&B⇌⋒£13–£15.50 dB&B£16–£23 dB&B⇌⋒£20–£27 Lunch fr£3.50 Dinner fr£4.75 Wine£3.55 *xmas* Credit cards 1 2 3 5 6

★★**Elstead** Knyveton Rd ☎22829 Central plan**21**
61rm(22⇌⋒) Lift CTV CTV available in bedrooms 40P 6 Live music & dancing 3 nights wkly Last dinner8pm sB&B£8–£11 sB&B⇌⋒£9–£12 dB&B£16–£22 dB&B⇌⋒£18–£24 Lunch£2–£3 Dinner£3–£4&alc Wine£2.55 *xmas*

★★**Fircroft** Owls Rd ☎39771 Central plan**23**
Large Victorian building with modern extensions standing in own grounds.
46rm(18⇌⋒) CTV CTV available in bedrooms 50P squash Disco wkly Live music & dancing twice wkly Last dinner8pm S% *sB&B£8–£10.50 sB&B⇌⋒£9–£11.50 dB&B£16–£21 dB&B⇌⋒£18–£23 Bar lunch£1–£3 Tea fr40p Dinner fr£3.25 Wine£2.95 *xmas*

★★**Hinton Firs** Manor Rd ☎25409 Central plan**27**
52rm(22⇌⋒) Annexe:6⇌⋒ Lift CTV 40P (heated) Live music & dancing twice wkly Last dinner8pm S% sB&B£11.30–£12.45 sB&B⇌⋒£13.25–£14.25 dB&B£22.60–£24.90 dB&B⇌⋒£26.50–£28.50 Lunch fr£2.50 Tea fr50p Dinner fr£3 *xmas*

★★**New Somerset** Bath Rd ☎21983 Central plan**33**
38rm(8⇌⋒) Lift CTV TV available in bedrooms 30P Last dinner8pm *sB&B£8–£9 sB&B⇌⋒£9–£10 dB&B£16–£18 dB&B⇌⋒£18–£20 Lunch£2–£3 Tea35p Dinner£3.50–£5.50 Wine£2.95 *xmas*

★★**Pinehurst** West Cliff Gdns ☎26218 Central plan**38**
85rm(11⇌) Lift CTV 38P Disco 3 nights wkly Live music & dancing wkly Last dinner8.30pm S% sB&B£8.25–£11 dB&B£16–£21.50 dB&B⇌£19–£24.50 Lunch fr£3 Tea fr20p Dinner fr£4 Wine£2.40 *xmas*
Credit cards 1 3 6

★★**St George** West Cliff Gdns ☎26038 Central plan**42**
Closed Nov–Mar; 23rm(14⇌⋒) CTV 5P Children under 5yrs not accommodated English & French. Last dinner8pm S% sB&B£6.90–£12.65 dB&B£16.10–£25.30 dB&B⇌⋒£18.40–£32.20 Lunch£2.64 Tea40p Dinner£5 Wine£4.80 Credit cards 1 3 4

★★***Saxon King*** Hengistbury Head, Southbourne ☎423478 District plan**75**
Closed 24–26Dec; 10rm CTV 50P Children under 3yrs not accommodated Last dinner8.45pm

★★**Southwood Lodge** 36 Southwood Av, Southbourne ☎422213 District plan**78**
RS Oct–Mar; 32rm CTV 24P Children under 5yrs not accommodated Last dinner7pm S% sB&B£6–£8.50 dB&B£12–£17 Lunch£2–£2.50 Tea50–75p Dinner£2.50–£3.50 Wine£2.46
Credit cards 1 3

★★***Studland Dene*** Studland Rd, Alum Chine ☎765445 District plan**80**
Overlooking sea; situated on pine-clad slopes of Alum Chine.
Closed 6Nov–Feb; 30rm(6⇌⋒) CTV 30P English & French. Last dinner7.15pm

★★**Sun Court** West Hill Rd ☎21343 Central plan**45**
36rm(27⇌⋒) Lift CTV in bedrooms 26P Last dinner7.30pm sB&B£9.50–£12 sB&B⇌⋒£11–£13.50 dB&B£15–£20 dB&B⇌⋒£18–£23 Lunch fr£3 Tea25–80p High Tea£1.50–£2 Dinner£4.25 Wine£3.30 *xmas* Credit card 2

★★**Tralee** West Hill Rd, West Cliff ☎26246 Central plan**46**
86rm(25⇌⋒) Lift CTV CTV available in bedrooms 40P (heated) billiards sauna bath Disco Thu Live music & dancing 5 nights wkly Cabaret wkly Last dinner7.45pm S%

B

sB&B£8.64–£14.90 sB&B⇌⫴£11.12–£17.78 dB&B£17.78–£29.80 dB&B⇌⫴£22.24–£34.56 Lunch fr£4.32 Tea fr50p High Tea fr£2.50 Dinner fr£4.86 ⊓ *xmas* Credit cards 1 2 3 4 5 6

★★***Water's Edge*** Sea Rd ☎36267 Central plan**51**
40rm(31⇌⫴) Lift ⋈ CTV TV available in bedrooms 33P ⊇(heated) sauna bath Disco twice wkly Live music & dancing 5 nights wkly Last dinner 7.15pm ✿ ⊈

★★**Whitehall** Exeter Park Rd ☎24682 Central plan**53**
50rm(12⇌⫴) Lift ☽ ⋈ CTV 25P ♡English & French. Last dinner 8pm ✿ ⊈ S% sB&B£7.50–£15.50 sB&B⇌⫴£9–£17 dB&B£15–£31 dB&B⇌⫴£18–£34 Lunch£2.75 Tea30p–£1 Dinner£3.50 Wine£2.50 ⊓ *xmas*

★★**Winterbourne** Priory Rd ☎24927 Central plan**55**
44rm(22⇌⫴) Lift ⋈ CTV 22P 6⌂ ⇼ ⚓ ⊇(heated) Disco twice wkly in season Last dinner 8pm ✿ ⊈ S% sB&B£6–£8.50 sB&B⇌⫴£7.50–£10 dB&B£11–£19 dB&B⇌⫴£11–£19 Lunch fr£3 Tea fr25p Dinner fr£4 Wine£2.20 ⊓ *xmas* Credit cards 1 3 6

★★**Winter Gardens** 32 Tregonwell Rd, West Cliff ☎25769 Central plan**56**
Early 19th-C building, once home of Captain Tregonwell's daughter. Public rooms overlook one acre of well-kept gardens.
Unlicensed; 44rm(9⇌⫴) Lift ☽ ⚔ ⋈ CTV CTV available in bedrooms 30P 4⌂ ⚓ Last dinner 7.30pm ✿ ⊈ ✱sB&B£6–£12 sB&B⇌⫴£9 dB&B£12–£24 dB&B⇌⫴£16.50–£30 Lunch£3–£4 Tea60p–£1 Dinner£3.50–£4.50 ⊓

★★**Woodcroft Tower** Gervis Rd, East Cliff ☎28202 Central plan**57**
40rm(12⇌⫴) Lift ☽ CTV 30P 6⌂ ⚓ Live music & dancing wkly (seasonal) Last dinner 8pm ✿ ⊈ sB&B£8.63–£12.08 sB&B⇌⫴£10.35–£13.80 dB&B£17.25–£24.15 dB&B⇌⫴£20.70–£27.60 Lunch£3.20 Tea40p Dinner£3.75 Wine£2.55 ⊓ *xmas*

★★**Yenton** 3–7 Gervis Rd, East Cliff ☎22752 Telex no 418261 Not on plan
Closed Jan; 22rm(13⇌⫴) Annexe: 10rm(7⇌⫴) ⋈ CTV 30P ⚓ ⊡(heated) squash billiards sauna bath Live music & dancing Thu ♿ ♡French. Last dinner 8pm ✿ ⊈ S% sB&B£8.50–£10.50 sB&B⇌⫴£10–£12 dB&B£17–£21 dB&B⇌⫴£20–£24 Lunch fr£3.50 Dinner fr£4.50 Wine£2.20 ⊓ *xmas* Credit cards 1 2 3

★**Grange** Overcliff Dr, Southbourne ☎424228 District plan**67**
33rm(11⇌⫴) Lift CTV TV available in bedrooms 50P ⚓ ♿ Last dinner 7.30pm ✿ ⊈ S% sB&B£4.50–£8 sB&B⇌⫴£5.50–£9.50 dB&B£9–£15 dB&B⇌⫴£10.50–£17 Bar lunch 70p–£2.50 Tea35p–80p Dinner£3&alc Wine£2.05 ⊓

★***Manor House*** Manor Rd, East Cliff ☎36669 Central plan**29**
Closed Nov–Mar; 25rm(5⇌⫴) ⋈ CTV 25P Children under 3yrs not accommodated ✿ ⊈

★**Hotel Riviera, Westcliff Gdns** ☎22845 Central plan**40**
Closed 3 Nov–Mar; 36rm(8⇌⫴) Lift ☽ CTV TV available in bedrooms 24P ⇼ Last dinner 7pm ✿ ⊈ S% sB&B£7–£9 dB£B£14–£18 dB&B⇌⫴£16–£20 Lunch fr£2.50 Dinner fr£3.50 Wine£2 ⊓

★**Tree Tops** 50–52 Christchurch Rd ☎23157 Central plan**48**

B

CADOGAN HOTEL

OPEN ALL THE YEAR AA ★★

An extremely comfortable, modern family Hotel near shops, Entertainment and sea (Durley Chine).

• 50 Bedrooms (half with baths en suite); most centrally heated • Excellent cusine and licensed

• Sun lounges, TV lounge, 2 Cocktail Bars • Large free car park • Baby listening • WEEKLY DANCE DURING SEASON (live music)

Send/phone for COLOUR BROCHURE

8 POOLE ROAD, BOURNEMOUTH Tel: (0202) 763006

DURLEY DEAN HOTEL

WESTCLIFF RD, BOURNEMOUTH BH2 5HE Tel: 27711

100 rooms
Lift
Night Porter
Car Park
Games room
Billiards room
Indoor heated swimming pool
Fully licensed
Grill Bar
Dancing

★★ A Gourmet Choice

Elstead Hotel ★★

Knyveton Road, Bournemouth, BH1 3QP
Tel: Bournemouth 22829 Management. 20112 Visitors.

Exceptional value. Licensed restaurant. Lift to all floors. Suites with private bathroom. Television. Night porter. Efficient central heating throughout. Razor points. Large free car park. Garages. Accommodation 150 guests. Dancing. Games room. Buffet bar. Xmas programme. Children welcome. Baby-sitting service. Reasonable terms for full weekly board which includes table d'hôte. A la carte menu available if desired. Special terms for winter residents.

Coloured brochure on application to the proprietors: Mr and Mrs D F Adcock.

B

58rm(8⇌) Lift 🍴 CTV TV available in bedrooms 60P ⚓ 🏠 Last dinner 7pm ✿ ⚕ S% sB&B£6.50–£7.75 sB&B⇌£9.50–£10.75 dB&B£13–£15.50 dB&B⇌£16–£18.50 Barlunch75p–£1.25 Tea25–50p HighTea75p–£1.25 Dinner£3.50 Wine£2.20 ⛟ *xmas*

★Ullswater West Cliff Gdns ☎25181 Central plan**50** 46rm(6⇌ 🚿) Lift ☽ 🍴 CTV CTV available in bedrooms 20P 🚗 billiards ♀ English & French. Last dinner 8pm ✿ ⚕ sB&B£10.25–£14.60 sB&B⇌🚿£11.50–£15.50 dB&B£20.50–£29.20 dB&B⇌🚿£23–£31 Lunch£2.75–£3.50 Tea80p Dinner fr£4.75 Wine£3.24 ⛟ *xmas*

★Wood Lodge 10 Manor Rd, East Cliff ☎20891 Central plan**58**
Closed mid Oct–Mar; 15rm(8⇌🚿) 🍴 CTV 12P 🚗 ⚓ Last dinner 7pm S% sB&B£7.56–£10 sB&B⇌🚿£9–£11.50 dB&B£15–£20 dB&B⇌🚿£9–£11.50 dB&B£15–£20 dB&B⇌🚿£18–£23 Dinner£3 Wine£2.35

⊕Riviera, Burnaby Rd, Alum Chine ☎763653 District plan**73**
65rm(39⇌🚿) Lift 🍴 CTV 80P ⚓ ⛱ sauna bath Disco twice wkly Live music & dancing 5 nights wkly Last dinner 7.45pm ⛟ *xmas*

XX*La Cappa* 127 Poole Rd ☎761317 District plan**63**
Closed Mon & Sun 15Oct–Mar; Lunch not served; 44seats 20P ♀ English, French & Italian. Last dinner 11.30pm Credit cards 1 2 3 5

XXOpus One 31 Southbourne Gv ☎421240 District plan**72**
Closed Sun, Xmas, 1wk Sep & 1wk Spring; 24seats

P ♀International. Last dinner Mon – Fri 9.30pm Sat 10.30pm Dinner £4.50 – £4.75 £7alc Wine £2.95 Credit cards 1 2 3 5

XXSouth Western Hotel Restaurant Central Station, Holdenhurst Rd ☎21801 Central plan **44** 100seats 30P bedrooms available ♀French. Last dinner 10.30pm ✱Lunch £6alc Dinner £6alc Wine £2.45 Credit cards 1 2 3 5

XX*La Taverna* Westover Rd ☎27681 Central plan **36** Closed Sun; 44seats ♀Italian. Last dinner 11pm Credit cards 1 2 3 5 6

XCrust The Square ☎21430 Central plan **15** Closed 2nd & 3rd wks Jan; 60seats 6P ♀International. Last dinner 11.30pm S% Lunch £5alc Dinner £6.50alc Wine £2.60 Credit cards 1 2 3 5 6

XTopo Gigio 374 Poole Rd ☎761478 District plan **81** 60seats 12P ♀English & Italian. Last dinner 11pm Lunch £3.50alc Dinner £4alc Wine £3.20 Credit cards 1 2 3 5

X*Tratoria San Marco* 148 Holdenhurst Rd ☎21132 Central plan **47** Closed Mon & Xmas; 65seats ♀International. Last dinner 11.30pm Credit cards 1 2 3 5

B

B

BOURTON-ON-THE-WATER Gloucestershire
Map**4** SP12
★★★Old Manse ☎20642
Attractive 18th-C Cotswold-stone house near River Windrush.
9rm(8⇌🚿) CTV 16P Children under 12yrs not accommodated English & French. Lastdinner8.30pm dB&B£15.40–£17.05 dB&B⇌🚿£19.25–£20.90 Continental breakfast Lunchfr£3.50&alc Dinnerfr£4.50&alc Wine£2.70 Creditcard 1

★★Old New Inn High St ☎20467
Part 18th-C building of Cotswold stone with model village in garden.
17rm Annexe:7rm(1⇌🚿) CTV 30P 8 Lastdinner8.15pm S% sB&B£9.90 sB&B⇌🚿£9.90 dB&B£19.80 dB&B⇌🚿£19.80 Lunchfr£4 Dinnerfr£5 Wine£2.80

★Chester House Hotel & Motel ☎20286
Closed Jan & Feb; 8rm(1⇌🚿) Annexe:10⇌🚿 CTV TVavailable in bedrooms 25P Mainly grills. Lastdinner10pm ✻sB&B£10–£12 sB&B⇌🚿£12–£15 dB&B£15 dB&B⇌🚿£17 Lunchfr£4&alc Dinnerfr£4&alc Wine£3.27 *xmas* Creditcards 1 2 3

✕*Rose Tree* Riverside ☎20635
Closed Mon & 2wks Feb; Dinner not served Sun; 30seats bedrooms available English & French. Lastdinner10pm Creditcard 1

BOVEY TRACEY Devon Map**3** SX87
★★Blenheim Brimley Rd ☎832422
Early 20th-C building, in two acres of gardens and orchards.
9rm(1⇌🚿) CTV 8P English, Brazilian & Portuguese Lastdinner8.30pm sB&B£7–£8 sB&B⇌🚿£7.50–£8.50 dB&B£14–£16 dB&B⇌🚿£15–£17 Lunch£2.50–£2.85&alc Tea55–65p Dinner£3.85–£4.50&alc Wine£2.20 *xmas*

★★Coombe Cross Coombe Cross (Inter-Hotel) ☎832476 Telex no 45388
Closed 23Dec–18Feb; 14rm(5⇌🚿) Annexe:6rm CTV 20P 1 Lastdinner8pm S% sB&B£8–£8.80 sB&B⇌🚿£9.25–£10.10 dB&B£16–£17.60 dB&B⇌🚿£18.50–£2.20 Lunch£2.25–£2.75 Tea60p–£1 Dinner£4–£5 Wine£3 Creditcard 2

★★*Dartmoor* Dolphin Sq ☎832211
A three-storey, white-painted building, with Tudor-style façade.
8rm CTV 30P Mainly grills. Lastdinner9.30pm

★★Dolphin Dolphin Sq ☎832413
An original coaching inn with green stucco extensions.
9⇌🚿 CTV 100P 5 International. Lastdinner10.30pm sB&B⇌🚿£8.95–£11.95 dB&B⇌🚿£17.90–£18.90 Lunch£1.15–£3.50 Tea65p Dinner£7.50&alc Wine£2.35 *xmas* Creditcard 1

★★Edgemoor Haytor Rd ☎832466
Built some 100 years ago of Cornish stone and local granite; in own grounds.
14rm(6⇌🚿) CTV 50P 2 English & Continental. Lastdinner9pm sB&B£9.65–£11.50 dB&B£18.15–£21 dB&B⇌🚿£20.40–£24 Lunchfr£3 Teafr60p High Teafr£2 Dinnerfr£5&alc Wine£3.25 *xmas* Creditcards 1 3 5 6

★★Prestbury Brimley Ln ☎833246
Spacious country house with mullioned windows in two acres of secluded grounds in Dartmoor National Park.

Closed Nov–Feb; 10rm(5⇨ 🛁) ✗ 🍽 CTV 12P 4 🏠 ⛟ ⚓ 🎣 Last dinner7.30pm S% sB&B£8.50–£11 sB&B⇨ 🛁£11.50–£14 dB&B£16.50–£21 dB&B⇨ 🛁£19.50–£24 Lunch£1.85–£2.50&alc Tea60p–£1&alc High Tea£1.30–£1.75&alc Dinner£4.25–£5 Wine£2.75 ⊟

★**Redacre** Challabrook Ln ☎833289
7rm CTV CTV available in bedrooms 8P ⛟ ⚓ 🎣 Last dinner8.15pm ✿ ☕ S% sB&B£6.50 dB&B£13 Lunch£3.25–£4 Tea fr30p Dinner£3.75 ⊟ *xmas*

BOWES Co Durham Map**12** NY91
★★**Bowes Moor** Bowes Moor ☎Teesdale28331
Closed Feb; 10rm 🍽 ⊘ 100P ⚓ ↳ 🍷English & French. Last dinner10pm ✿ ☕ S% sB&B£9–£10 dB&B£18–£20 Lunch£4alc Tea30palc High Tea£3.50alc Dinner£8alc Wine£2.20 ⊟ Credit card ③

BOWNESS-ON-WINDERMERE Cumbria Map**7** SD49
Hotels are listed under Windermere

BRACKLEY HATCH Northamptonshire Map**4** SP64
★**Green Man Inn** ☎Syresham209
Country inn with white façade; small garden and traditional interior including oak beams.
Closed Xmas Day; 7rm(2⇨ 🛁) ⊘ P 🏠 ⛟ ⚓ 🍷English & French. Last dinner8.45pm ✿ sB&B£10 sB&B⇨ 🛁£11 dB&B£14.50 dB&B⇨ 🛁£16.50 Lunch£6alc Dinner£6alc Wine£3 Credit cards ③ ⑤

BRADFORD W Yorkshire Map**7** SE13
☆☆☆☆***Norfolk Gardens*** (Reo Stakis) ☎34733
125⇨ 🛁 Lift ☽ 🍽 CTV TV available in bedrooms Disco twice wkly Live music & dancing wkly 🍷English, Scottish & Continental. Last dinner10.15pm ✿ ☕ ⊟ Credit cards ① ② ③ ⑤ ⑥

☆☆☆**Novotel Bradford** Merrydale Rd (3m S on M606) ☎683683 Telex no517312
136⇨ 🛁 Lift ⊞ TV in bedrooms 180P ⚓ ⛱ (heated) Disco Fri & Sat Live music & dancing Fri & Sat Conference facilities available 🍷Continental. Last dinner mdnt ✿ ☕ S% sB&B⇨ 🛁£18–£20 dB&B⇨ 🛁£22.50–£24.50 Lunch£4–£5&alc Tea£2–£2.50&alc High Tea£3–£4&alc Dinner£4–£5&alc Wine£4.20 ⊟ Credit cards ① ② ③ ⑤ ⑥

★★★**Victoria** Bridge St (Trusthouse Forte) ☎28706
67rm(45⇨ 🛁) Lift ☽ 🍽 TV in bedrooms 40P Conference facilities available 🍷Mainly grills. Last dinner10pm ✿ ☕ S% sB&B£15 sB&B⇨ 🛁£17 dB&B£20 dB&B⇨ 🛁£22 ⊟ Credit cards ① ② ③ ④ ⑤ ⑥

BRADFORD-ON-AVON Wiltshire Map**3** ST86
★★***Swan*** Church St ☎2224
18th-C inn with historical associations.
15rm(4⇨ 🛁) TV 25P 6🏠 ⛟ Children under 5yrs not accommodated Last dinner8.15pm

BRADWORTHY Devon Map**2** SS31
★★**Lake Villa** ☎342
Built during 19th-C, this part converted farmhouse and Victorian house is situated on edge of Bradworthy Moor, ½m from the village.
Closed Dec & Jan; 10rm(6⇨ 🛁) 3▭ 🍽 CTV TV available in bedrooms ⊘ 10P 2🏠 ⛟ ⚓ 🎾(hard) billiards Children under 10yrs not accommodated 🍷International. Last dinner9pm ✱Wine£3.25 ⊟

BRAINTREE Essex Map**5** TL72
★★★**White Hart** Bocking End (Trusthouse Forte) ☎21401

An ancient inn with modern interior but retaining 16th-C ceiling beams and wall timbers.
34rm(27⇌🚿) ☽ TV in bedrooms 54P
Last dinner 10pm S% sB&B£13
sB&B⇌🚿£15.50 dB&B⇌🚿£20.50 *xmas*
Credit cards 1 2 3 4 5 6

★★**Old Court** Bradford St ☎21444
10rm CTV 20P Last dinner 9pm
sB&B£8 dB&B£13 Lunch fr£3.25alc
Dinner fr£5&alc Wine£2.25

BRAITHWAITE Cumbria Map**11** NY22
★★**Braithwaite Motor Inn** ☎444
Situated midway between Lake Bassenthwaite and Derwentwater on the A66 at the foot of the Pass of Whinlatter.
35⇌🚿 CTV in bedrooms 40P English & French. Last dinner 9.15pm S%
sB&B⇌🚿£17.50 dB&B⇌🚿£22.50 Lunch£2.75
Dinner£5&alc Wine£3 Credit cards 1 2 3 5 6

★★**Ivy House** ☎338
A 17th-C house with a Georgian wing added in 1790, quietly situated in the centre of the village.
12rm(7⇌🚿) 1 CTV 12P English & French. Last dinner 8pm sB&B£10
dB&B£18 dB&B⇌🚿£20–£22 Lunch£9–£10
Tea£3–£4 Dinner£10 Wine£4.10 *xmas*

★★***Middle Ruddings*** ☎436
Closed New Year's Day; 14rm(5⇌🚿) CTV 25P English & Continental. Last dinner 8.15pm

BRAMBER West Sussex Map**4** TQ11
XXX***Old Tollgate*** The Street ☎Steyning813362
Closed Mon & Jan; Dinner not served Sun; 70seats 30P English & French. Last dinner 9.30pm
Credit cards 2 5

BRAMHALL Gt Manchester Map**7** SJ88
★★★**Pownall Arms** Bramhall Lane South
☎061–439 8116 Telex no 666691
40⇌🚿 Lift ☽ CTV 132P Conference facilities available French. Last dinner 10.15pm S%
sB&B⇌🚿£17.25–£19 dB&B⇌🚿£26.45–£28.75
Lunch£2.60–£3 Dinner£4.50–£5 Wine£2.90
Credit cards 1 2 3 5 6

BRAMHOPE W Yorkshire Map**8** SE24
☆☆☆**Post House** Leeds Rd (Trusthouse Forte)
☎Leeds842911 Telex no 556367
120⇌🚿 Lift ☽ CTV 220P ♿ Conference facilities available Last dinner 10.15pm S%
sB&B⇌🚿£20.75 dB&B⇌🚿£30 *xmas*
Credit cards 1 2 3 4 5 6

BRAMPTON Cambridgeshire Map**4** TL27
☆☆☆**Brampton** (junc A1/A604) (Kingsmead)
☎Huntingdon810434
17⇌🚿 ☽ CTV in bedrooms 250P Live music & dancing Fri Last dinner 10pm S%
*sB&B⇌🚿£17 dB&B⇌🚿 fr£22
Lunch£3.50–£3.75&alc Tea50p
Dinner£3.50–£4.25&alc Wine£2.95 *xmas*
Credit cards 1 2 3 5 6

BRAMPTON Cumbria Map**12** NY56
★★ **Farlam Hall** Hallbankgate (2½m SE A689)
☎Hallbankgate234
See page 38 for details

★★**New Bridge** Lanercost (2½m NE on unclass road)
☎2224
Closed 2wks Nov; 5rm(1⇌🚿) Annexe:7rm(2⇌🚿) CTV 30P Last dinner 8pm S%
sB&B£7.75–£9.50 dB&B£15–£18
dB&B⇌🚿£16.50–£20 Bar lunch 40p–£2.50
Tea40p Dinner£4alc Wine£2.50

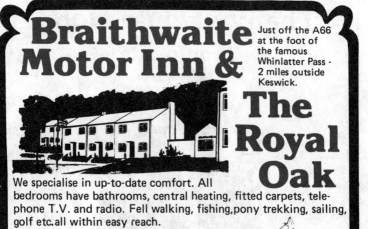

B

●★★**Tarn End** Talkin Tarn (2½m S off B6413) ☎2340
The hotel is situated in a country park and the lawns run down to the Tarn.
Closed Oct & Xmas Day; 6rm TV 100P Children under 15yrs not accommodated English & French. Specialities: Confit d'Oie, Fresh Crab Beignets, Feuillete de Fruits de Mer.
Lastdinner9pm sB&B fr£12 (incl dinner)
Lunch fr£3.50&alc Dinner fr£5&alc Wine£3.85

★**White Lion** High Cross St ☎2338
An old coaching inn dating from before 1690, in one of England's most ancient market towns.
7rm CTV 6P 2 Mainly grills.
Lastdinner8.30pm sB&B£6 dB&B£12
Lunch£2.20–£2.60 Dinner£3.50–£4 Wine£2.20

BRAMSHAW Hampshire Map**4** SU21
★★**Bramble Hill** ☎Cadnam3165
Closed Nov–Mar; 16rm CTV 50P 3
Lastdinner8.15pm sB&B£9.50–£12
dB&B£19–£24 Dinner£4–£4.60 Wine£2.80

BRANDON **Suffolk** Map**5** TL78
★**Great Eastern** ☎Thetford810229
RS Sun (meals); 10rm CTV TV available in bedrooms 16P 8 Lastdinner8pm S%
*sB&B fr£8.21 dB&B fr£13.72
Lunch£2.50–£4.50&alc Dinner£2.50–£4.50&alc
Wine£2.45

BRANDON **Warwickshire** Map**4** SP47
★★★**Brandon Hall** Main St (Trusthouse Forte)
☎Wolston2571 Telex no 31472
Rambling two-storey building in own grounds with stables and outbuildings.
67rm(44⇌ ⋒) TV in bedrooms 250P squash
Conference facilities available Lastdinner9.30pm
S% sB&B£16 sB&B⇌⋒£18.50
dB&B£22 dB&B⇌⋒£24.50 *xmas*
Credit cards 1 2 3 4 5 6

BRANKSOME Dorset See **Poole**

BRANSCOMBE Devon Map**3** SY18
X**Masons Arms** ☎300
Lunch served Sun only; 50seats 35P bedrooms available English & French. Lastdinner9pm
Lunch£3.50 Tea70p Dinner£6–£6.80 Wine£2.40

BRANSTON Lincolnshire Map**8** TF06
★★**Moor Lodge** ☎Lincoln791366
Early 20th-C house with numerous additions including Spanish and Swiss bars.
31rm(8⇌ ⋒) CTV CTV available in bedrooms 120P
Lastdinner9.15pm S% sB&B£12
sB&B⇌⋒£15 dB&B£20 dB&B⇌⋒£25
Lunch fr£3.50&alc Dinner fr£4.50&alc Wine£3
Credit cards 1 2 5

BRAY Berkshire Map**4** SU97
●●●XXXX**Waterside** Ferry Rd
☎Maidenhead20691
Featured in the 1978 Guide as one of the Chief Hotels Inspector's 'Four of the Best', this idyllically-set Thames-side restaurant remains the best out-of-town restaurant near London. While it is ideal for summer days out, the renewed décor provides nearly as attractive a setting in winter, one which brings a certain French freshness to an otherwise dull day. Service is attentive and considerate. Praise continues to be lavished on nearly all the dishes reported to us. Most people seem to visit in the summer when such dishes as feuilleté d'asperges, truite saumonée à la

Champagne, côte d'agneau Germain and sable aux poires are clearly popular but favourite specialities like oeuf froid Albert, mousseline de volaille au Roquefort, soufflé Eléonora, tournedos Arlette and caneton Juliette as well as delicious game dishes are always well received. One inspector reported the soufflé chaud framboise as being the highlight of his meal.
There is also a table d'hôte menu at lunchtime and this has been highly praised both for its quality and value for money. As one would expect from the Roux brothers, the menu is always changing and we sometimes suspect that it is a proving ground for their newly invented dishes. Wines of the highest order make up the list of 150; most are expensive.
Closed Mon & 26Dec–23Jan; 70seats 20P bedrooms available French. Last dinner10pm *Lunch fr£11.50&alc Dinner£18alc Credit cards 1 2 3 5

XX***Hind's Head*** Maidenhead26151
100seats 100P Last dinner10pm
Credit cards 1 2 3 5

BRENDON Devon Map**3** SS74
★**Stag Hunters Inn** 222
On the edge of the Doone Valley with pleasant views of woods, rivers and moors.
Closed Jan–Mar; 23rm TV 50P English & French. Last dinner8.15pm S% *sB&B£7.50–£8.50 dB&B£15–£17 Lunch60p–£1.50 Tea35p High Tea£1 Dinner£4.60–£7 Wine£3.20 *xmas* Credit card 1

BRENTFORD Gt London Map**4** TQ17
XXX**Camellia** Syon Park 01-568 0778
94seats 40P Live music & dancing Sat French. Last dinner10.30pm Lunch£9.85alc Dinner£9.85alc Wine£3.40
Credit cards 1 2 3 4 5

BRENTWOOD Essex Map**5** TQ59
★★★★**Brentwood Moat House** (Queens) 225252
Telex no995182
Dates back to 1520. Home of Catherine of Aragon.
5rm Annexe:17 2 CTV in bedrooms 100P English & French. Last dinner10.15pm S% sB&B£16.75 sB&B £21.75 dB&B£25.50 dB&B £32.50 Lunch£6.50alc Tea£1.50alc High Tea£1.50alc Dinner£6.50alc Wine£3.40 Credit cards 1 2 3 5 6

☆☆☆**Post House** Brook St (Trusthouse Forte) 210888 Telex no995379
120 Lift CTV in bedrooms 148P (heated) Conference facilities available Last dinner10pm S% sB&B £19.75 dB&B £28.50 *xmas* Credit cards 1 2 3 4 5 6

BRIDESTOWE Devon Map**2** SX58
X**White Hart Inn** 318
Reservations only at lunchtime.
20seats 20P bedrooms available English, Austrian & French. Last dinner9pm S% Lunch£3.70 Dinner£7alc Wine£4 Credit cards 1 3 5

BRIDGNORTH Salop Map**7** SO79
★★**Falcon** St John St, Low Town 3134
14rm(2) CTV TV available in bedrooms 200P 4 English & French. Last dinner 9.30pm S% sB&B fr£9.50 sB&B fr£15 dB&B £18 dB&B fr£20 Lunch£2.50–£4.50&alc Tea60p–£1.20 High Tea£1–£2 Dinner£4.50–£6&alc Wine£3.80 *xmas* Credit cards 1 2 3 4 5 6

★★**Parlors Hall** Mill St, Low Town 2604
13rm(1) 1 TV in bedrooms 50P Last dinner9.45pm S% sB&B£10.75 dB&B £15.25 dB&B £16.25 Lunch fr£3.75&alc Tea fr£1 Dinner fr£4&alc Wine£3.50 Credit cards 1 2

XXX**Rib Room** 84–85 High St, North Gate 3640
Closed Sun & Public Hols; 86seats Continental. Last dinner10.30pm *Lunch£2.50&alc Dinner£5.50&alc Wine£3.25 Credit cards 1 2 3 6

BRIDGWATER Somerset Map**3** ST33
XX**Watergate** 2 Castle St, West Quay 3847
Closed Sun, 25–30Dec & Public Hols; Lunch not served Sat; Dinner not served Mon; 56seats 10P French. Last dinner10pm *Lunch£4–£5.50&alc Dinner£4.25&alc Wine£3.40 Credit card 3

BRIDLINGTON Humberside Map**8** TA16
★★★**Expanse** North Marine Dr 75347
46rm(24) Lift CTV TV available in bedrooms 20P 15 Last dinner8.30pm S% sB&B£9–£11.75 sB&B £9.75–£12.50 dB&B£16–£21.30 dB&B £17.50–£22.80 Lunch£3.50 Tea75p Dinner£4.50 Wine£2.50 *xmas* Credit cards 1 2 3

★★**Monarch** South Marine Dr 744447
42rm(16) Lift CTV 10P 6 Last dinner8.30pm S% sB&B£9.60–£11 sB&B £11.25–£12.65 dB&B£18–£20 dB&B £19.65–£21.65 Lunch£3.20 Dinner£4.20 Credit cards 1 3

Ferns Farm Main St, Carnaby (2m W A166) 78961
Originally a farmhouse, built in the 1800s but renovated and converted into a hotel in 1972.
12rm CTV 70P 3 Last dinner8pm

X**Ye Olde Star Inn** Westgate 76039
Closed Mon; 120seats 300P Last dinner8.45pm *Lunch£2.60–£6.25 Dinner£4.25–£7.75 Wine£2.28 Credit cards 1 3

BRIDPORT Dorset Map**3** SY49
★★Eype's Mouth Eype (2m SW) ☎23300
Quiet location in rural valley with views across meadow towards sea.
21rm(10⇌⋒) ꟷ CTV 60P Live music & dancing Sat Lastdinner8.30pm ✿ ⊈ S% sB&B fr£8.95 dB&B fr£17.90 dB&B⇌⋒£20.86 ⊓ *xmas* Credit cards 2 3 5

★★*Greyhound* East St ☎22944
19rm CTV 10🏠 ♕English & French. Lastdinner9.30pm ✿

★★Haddon House West Bay (2m S off B3157 Weymouth road) ☎23626
10rm(8⇌⋒) ꟷ CTV TV in bedrooms 50P ♿ Lastdinner9pm ✿ S% sB&B fr£9.50 sB&B fr£9.50 dB&B fr£19 dB&B⇌⋒ fr£19 Lunch fr£2.95 Dinner£3.95–£5.25 Wine£3.25 Credit card 3

★★West Mead West Rd ☎22609
Mellow-stone manor house standing in own grounds off main road leading out of Bridport.
14rm(7⇌⋒) ☽ ꟷ CTV 100P ⚓ ⚬(hard) Live music & dancing Sat & Sun Lastdinner10pm ✿ ⊈ sB&B fr£7.58 sB&B⇌⋒ fr£9.46 dB&B fr£14.53 dB&B⇌⋒ fr£15.79 Lunch£2–£2.45&alc Tea30–85p High Tea£1.20–£1.50 Dinner£3–£3.30&alc ⊓ *xmas* Credit cards 1 5

★*Bridport Arms* West Bay (2m S off B3157 Weymouth road) ☎22994
14rm Annexe: 5rm ꟷ TV available in bedrooms 15P 6🏠 ✿ ⊈

★⌂Little Wych Burton Rd (2m S B3157 Weymouth road) ☎23490
6rm ꟷ CTV TV available in bedroom 8P ✿ ⚓ ♕English & French. Lastdinner9pm ⊈

sB&B£7.75–£10.60 dB&B£15.50–£17.20 Tea40p Dinner£3.45–£3.80&alc Wine£2.50

✕Bistro Lautrec 53 East St ☎56549
Closed Sun; Lunch not served Sat 44seats ⚑ ♕English & French. Lastdinner10pm Lunch£2.25alc Dinner£4.50alc Wine£2.40

BRIGG Humberside Map**8** TA00
★★Angel Market Pl ☎53118
Black and white, half-timbered building dating back to the 14th-C, when it was a coaching inn.
Closed Xmas Day; 12rm ꟷ CTV ⊘ 100P 8🏠 ⚓ Disco mthly ♕Continental. Lastdinner9.30pm ✿ ✻sB&B£7.35–£8.05 dB&B£12.05–£12.85 Continental breakfast Lunch£2.60 Dinner£5alc Wine£2.15 Credit card 1

BRIGHTLINGSEA Essex Map**5** TM01
★★Brightlingsea Hall Church Rd ☎3900
8rm(1⇌⋒) 1⊟ ꟷ CTV CTV available in bedrooms 50P ⚓ ♕International. Lastdinner9.30pm ✿ S% sB&B£9 dB&B£16.50 dB&B⇌⋒£22 Lunch fr£3&alc Dinner fr£4.25&alc Wine£3 ⊓ Credit cards 1 2 3 5

BRIGHTON East Sussex Map**4** TQ30
See plan
See also **Hove**
★★★★Grand Kings Rd (De Vere) ☎26301
Telex no 877410 Plan**6**
A fine, spacious, eight-storey hotel (built 1864) with delicate wrought-iron balconies and colonnaded entrance.
165⇌⋒ 1⊟ Lift ☽ ꟷ CTV in bedrooms ⚑ Conference facilities available ♕English & French. Lastdinner9.30pm ✿ ⊈ S% sB&B⇌⋒£24 dB&B⇌⋒£40 Lunch fr£6&alc Tea fr£1.25 Dinner fr£7.25&alc Wine£3.75 ⊓ *xmas* Credit cards 1 2 3 5 6

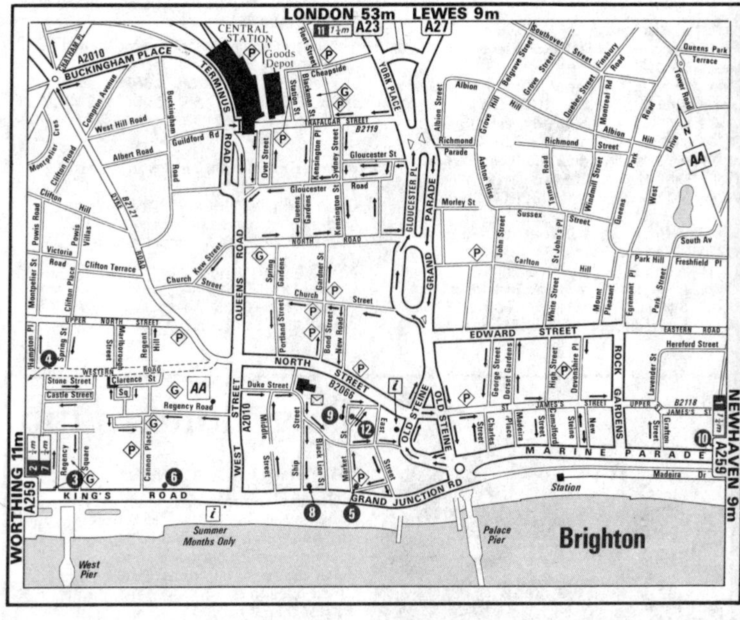

1 Bannisters ✕
2 Christopher's ✕
3 Hotel Curzon ★★
4 Dolçe Vito ✕
5 French Connection ✕✕
6 Grand ★★★★
7 Le Grandgousier ✕
8 Old Ship ★★★
9 Pump House ✕✕
10 Royal Crescent ★★★★
11 Touring ★★
12 Wheeler's ✕✕

B

The Royal Crescent Hotel ★★★★

MARINE PARADE, BRIGHTON
TEL: 606311/5

Quietly located on Marine Parade, facing the sea, above the immediate bustle of busy Brighton town — offers an excellent standard of cuisine, comfort and personal service in an atmosphere of elegance and charm. A 'home from home' in the old tradition, rather than an hotel.

Courtlands Hotel Hove ★★★

Situated in the Drive, Hove, 400 yds from the sea with 65 Bedrooms — 55 with bath or shower, all with Colour TV. Lift, central heating, own free car park and garden. Courtlands is run by the independent family firm of Forfars Local Restaurateurs — Bakers and Outside Catering.

Directors: J S, C A and T C Cutress.

For details write or phone G Messina, Manager, Courtlands Hotel, 19/27 The Drive, Hove, BN3 3JE (0273) 731055. Telex: 87323 F.S.I. Courtlands.

B

★★★★**Royal Crescent** 100 Marine Pde ☎606311 Plan**10**
Elegant, five-storey, Regency building with balconies facing sea. Built on site of house belonging to George Canning.
66⇌⋒ Lift ☽ ⅏ CTV in bedrooms 8⌂ ✠ ♉ English & French. Last dinner 9.45pm ✿ ⊥ S%
✻sB&B⇌⋒ fr£14.50 dB&B⇌⋒ fr£23.80
Lunch£4.50&alc Tea£1.50 Dinner£5.25&alc
Wine£2.35 *xmas* Credit cards 1 2 3 5 6

★★★**Old Ship** King's Rd (Best Western) ☎29001
Telex no 877101 Plan**8**
Hotel's history can be traced back to 1559.
156rm(127⇌⋒) 1▭ Lift ☽ ⅏ CTV in bedrooms ✠
80⌂ Conference facilities available ♉ English & Continental. Last dinner 10pm ✿ ⊥ S%
✻sB&B£14 sB&B⇌⋒£17.50 dB&B£23
dB&B⇌⋒£29.50 Lunch fr£4.50&alc Tea fr£1.10
Dinner fr£5&alc Wine£3.40 ⊟ *xmas*
Credit cards 1 2 3 5 6

★★**Hotel Curzon** Cavendish Pl (Trusthouse Forte)
☎25788 Plan**3**
44rm(12⇌⋒) Lift ☽ ⅏ TV in bedrooms 16P
Last dinner 8.45pm ✿ S% sB&B£13.50
sB&B⇌⋒£15 dB&B£20 dB&B⇌⋒£22 ⊟
xmas Credit cards 1 2 3 4 5 6

★★***Touring*** 216 Preston Rd ☎507853 Plan**11**
25rm(8⇌⋒) ⅏ CTV ✠ 50P ✠ ♉ Mainly grills.
Last dinner 8.45pm ✿ ⊥

✕✕**French Connection** 11 Little East St ☎24454
Plan**5**
Closed Sun, Xmas & Public Hols; 24seats ℙ
♉ English & French. Last dinner 10.30pm
✻Dinner£8alc Wine£3.75 Credit cards 1 2

✕✕**Pump House** 46 Market St ☎26864 Plan**9**
Closed Sun; 60seats ℙ ♉ English & French.
Last dinner 9.45pm Lunch£3.25–£3.50&alc
Dinner£4.25–£5.75&alc Wine£2.75
Credit cards 1 2 3 5 6

✕✕**Wheeler's** 17 Market St ☎25135 Plan**12**
94seats ℙ ♉ French. Last dinner 10.45pm S%
✻Lunch£10alc Dinner£10alc Wine£3.20
Credit cards 1 2 3 4 5 6

✕**Bannisters** 77 St George's Rd, Kemptown
☎687382 Plan**1**
Closed Sun, Mon, last wk Jan & 1st wk Feb; Lunch not served; 24seats ℙ ♉ French. Last dinner 11pm
Dinner£7.95alc Wine£2.85 Credit card 2

✕**Christopher's** 24 Western St ☎775048 Plan**2**
Closed Wed, Xmas, last 2wks Mar & last 2wks Oct;
Lunch not served; 24seats ℙ ♉ French.
Last dinner 10.45pm Dinner£6alc Wine£2.90
Credit cards 1 2 6

✕**Dolce Vito** 106A Western Rd ☎737200 Plan**4**
Closed Tue; 45seats ℙ ♉ Italian.
Last dinner 11.30pm ✻Lunch£5.50alc
Dinner£10alc Wine£3.80
Credit cards 1 2 3 4 5 6

✕***Le Grandgousier*** 15 Western St ☎772005 Plan**7**
Closed Sun; Lunch not served Sat; 34seats
♉ French. Last dinner 9.30pm Credit cards 1 2 3

BRISTOL Avon Map**3** ST57 **See plan**
☆☆☆☆**Bristol EuroCrest** Filton Rd, Hambrook (6m NE off A4174) (Crest) ☎564242 Telex no 449376
Plan**3**
156⇌⋒ Lift ☽ CTV CTV in bedrooms 250P ⚓
Conference facilities available ♉ International.
Last dinner 10pm ✿ ⊥ S% ✻sB&B⇌⋒£18.68
dB&B⇌⋒£25.48 Continental breakfast ⊟
Credit cards 1 2 3 4 5 6

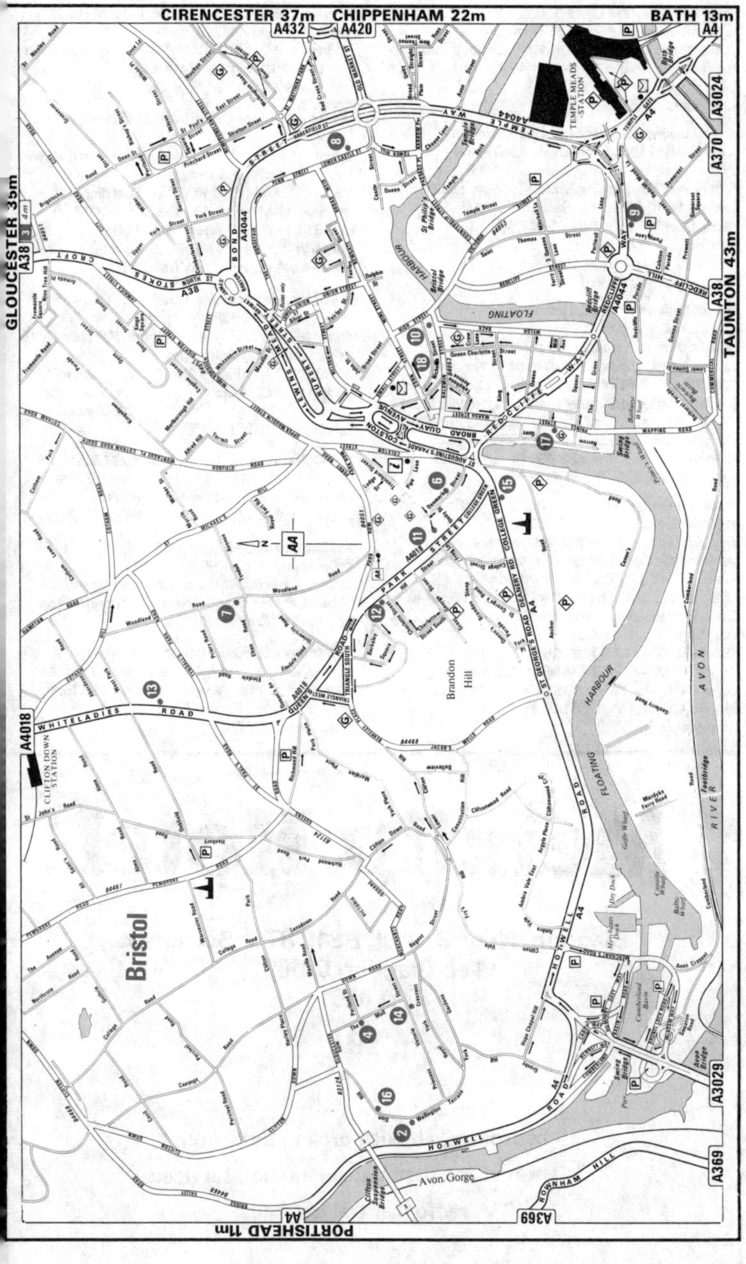

2 Avon Gorge ★★
3 Bristol EuroCrest ☆☆☆☆
4 Cauldron ✕✕
6 Harveys ✕✕✕✕
7 Hawthorns ★★
8 Holiday Inn ☆☆☆☆
9 Ladbroke Dragonara ☆☆☆☆
10 Marco's ✕✕
11 Maxwell Plum ✕
12 Rajdoot ✕✕
13 Restaurant du Gourmet ✕✕
14 Rossi's Ristorante ✕
15 Royal ★★
16 St Vincent's Rocks ★★
17 Unicorn ☆☆☆☆
18 Villa Philipo ✕✕

B

☆☆☆☆***Holiday Inn*** Lower Castle St (Commonwealth) ☎294281 Plan**8**
300⇌⋒ Lift ☽ ▦ ♛ CTV ▭ & ⌐(heated) Conference facilities available ♿ ♡International.
Last dinner10.30pm ♱ ♖ ⊟
Credit cards 1 2 3 5 6

☆☆☆☆**Ladbroke Dragonara** Redcliffe Way (Ladbroke) ☎20044 Telex no449240 Plan**9**
210⇌⋒ Lift ☽ ♛ CTV in bedrooms 150P Live music & dancing Thu–Sat Conference facilities available ♿
Last dinner10.30pm (Sun9.45pm) ♱ ♖ S%
✱sB&B⇌⋒£33 dB&B⇌⋒£44.40
Lunch£3.50–£4.75&alc Tea85p–£1.10
Dinner£3.50–£7.50&alc Wine£3.30 ⊟
Credit cards 1 2 3 5 6

☆☆☆☆**Unicorn** Prince St (Rank) ☎28055 Telex no44315 Plan**17**
Modern hotel situated in city centre, overlooking narrow quay. Access from car park to all floors.
189⇌⋒ Lift ☽ ♛ TV in bedrooms 400⌂ Conference facilities available ♡International. Last dinner10pm
♱ ♖ S% sB&B⇌⋒£17.30 dB&B⇌⋒£27.65
Continental breakfast Lunch£5.35&alc
Dinner£5.35&alc Wine£3.45 ⊟ *xmas*
Credit cards 1 2 3 4 5 6

★★**Avon Gorge** Sion Hill, Clifton (Mount Charlotte) ☎38955 Telex no444237 Plan**2**
Dignified Victorian building, with terrace and fine views of the Clifton Gorge and suspension bridge.
80rm(77⇌⋒) Lift ☽ CTV CTV in bedrooms 25P ⚓
Live music & dancing Fri & Sat Cabaret Fri & Sat ⌂
Conference facilities available ♡French.
Last dinner10pm ♱ ♖ S%
sB&B£12.50–£13.50 sB&B⇌⋒£16–£17
dB&B£18.50–£19.50 dB&B⇌⋒£24–£26
Lunch£4.75alc Tea£1.50alc High Tea£2alc
Dinner£6.50alc Wine£3.50 ⊟
Credit cards 1 2 3 6

★★***Hawthorn's*** Woodland Rd, Clifton (Berni) ☎38432 Telex no44220 Plan**7**
163rm(60⇌⋒) Lift ☽ CTV TV available in bedrooms 60P Live music nightly ♡Mainly grills.
Last dinner11pm ♱ ⊟ Credit cards 1 2 5

★★**Royal** College Green (Norfolk Capital) ☎23591 Telex no23241 Plan**15**
Large brick and stone building adjacent to Cathedral and facing College Green.
130rm(37⇌⋒) Lift ☽ ♛ CTV ₱ Last dinner9pm ♱
♖ S% sB&B fr£13.50 sB&B⇌⋒ fr£17.30
dB&B fr£19.60 dB&B⇌⋒ fr£24.60
Lunch fr£3.25&alc Tea fr£1.25 Dinner fr£4.25&alc
Wine£4 ⊟ Credit cards 1 2 3 5 6

★★**St Vincent's Rocks** Sion Hill, Clifton (Anchor) ☎39251 Telex no858875 Plan**16**
48rm(28⇌⋒) ☽ CTV in bedrooms 24P ♡English & Continental. Last dinner9pm ♱ ♖ S%
✱sB&B fr£12 sB&B⇌⋒ fr£15.50 dB&B fr£19.50
dB&B⇌⋒ fr£22 Lunch fr£3.50&alc Tea fr35p
Dinner fr£3.75&alc Wine£2.65 ⊟ *xmas*
Credit cards 1 2 3 4 5 6

XXXX**Harveys** 12 Denmark St ☎277665 Plan**6**
Closed Sun & Public Hols; Lunch Sat; 120seats ₱
Live music & dancing Sat ♡English & French.
Last dinner11.15pm Credit cards 1 2 3 4 5 6

XX**Cauldron** 19–21 The Mall, Clifton ☎Bristol312522 Plan**4**
Closed Sun & Public Hols; Lunch not served Sat; 50seats ₱ ♡English & French. Last dinner11pm
Wine£3.25 Credit cards 1 2 3 5

XX**Marco's** 59 Baldwin St ☎24869 Plan**10**
Closed Sun & Public Hols; Lunch not served Sat; 70seats ₱ ♡International. Last dinner11.15pm
✱Lunch£10alc Dinner£10alc Wine£2.95
Credit cards 1 2 3 5

✕✕**Rajdoot** 83 Park St ☎28034 Plan**12**
Closed Xmas; Lunch not served Sun & Public Hols; 60seats P ♀Indian. ✱Lunch£2.40–£6.25&alc Dinnerfr£3.50 Wine£3.20
Credit cards 1 2 3 4 5 6

✕✕**Restaurant du Gourmet** 43 Whiteladies Rd ☎36230 Plan**13**
Closed Xmas & Public Hols; Lunch not served; 85seats ♀French. Last dinner mdnt
✱Dinner£10alc Credit cards 1 2 3 5

✕✕**Villa Phillippo** 31 Baldwin St ☎24922 Plan**18**
Closed Sun; Lunch not served Sat; 50seats P ♀French & Italian. Last dinner11.15pm
✱Lunch£8.50alc Dinner£8.50alc Wine£3
Credit cards 1 2 3

✕***Maxwell Plum*** 1 Frogmore St ☎291413 Plan**11**
Closed Sun; 56seats Last dinner11.15pm

✕***Rossi's Ristoranti*** 35 Princess Victoria St ☎30049 Plan**14**
Closed Sun & Bank Hols; Lunch not served Sat; 42seats ♀International. Last dinner11.30pm
Credit cards 1 2 3 5 6

B

BRIXHAM Devon Map**3** SX95
★★**Quayside** King St (Inter-Hotel) ☎3051
Carefully and comfortably modernised old quayside inn above harbour.
32rm(25⇌ ⋒) 1▭ ₦CTV in bedrooms 39P
Cabaret 5 nights wkly ♀English & French.
Last dinner9.30pm ✆ S% sB&B£10.10–£13.10
sB&B⇌⋒£11.05–£14.55 dB&B£17.70–£23.84
dB&B⇌⋒£19.59–£29.74 Lunch£2.50&alc
High Tea£1–£2 Dinner£4&alc Wine£3
xmas Credit cards 1 2 3 4 5 6

★Smuggler's Haunt ☎3050
Stone inn, over 400 years old, with flagstone floor and old fireplaces.
14rm(4⇌⋔) TV Last dinner9.30pm S%
✱sB&B£7.72 sB&B⇌⋔£8.91 dB&B£12.48
dB&B⇌⋔£15.45 Lunch£3.75alc
Dinner£2.35–£5.80&alc Wine£2.85

BROADSTAIRS Kent Map**5** TR36

★★★Castle Keep (Inter-Hotel) ☎Thanet65222
Telex no896570
30rm(27⇌⋔) CTV CTV available in bedrooms
50P (heated) Live music & dancing twice wkly Cabaret wkly English & French.
Last dinner10pm S% sB&B£12.50
sB&B⇌⋔£19.50 dB&B£16.50
dB&B⇌⋔£22.50–£28.50
Lunch£3.50–£4.50&alc Tea50p Dinner£5&alc
Wine£1.80 *xmas* Credit cards 1 2 3 5

★★Castlemere Western Esp ☎Thanet61566
RS Nov–Apr (no lunches) 38rm(22⇌⋔)
Annexe: 4rm(2⇌⋔) CTV CTV available in bedrooms 25P 2 English & French.
Last dinner7.30pm S%
sB&B£8.65–£12.60 sB&B⇌⋔£10.90–£13.25
dB&B£17.30–£25.20 dB&B⇌⋔£21.80–£26.50
Lunch£4.25 Tea60p Dinner£5 Wine£2.65
xmas

★★Fayreness Marine Dr, Kings Gate ☎Thanet61103
8rm(5⇌⋔) TV in bedrooms 40P Children under 6yrs not accommodated Last dinner9.30pm
sB&B£9–£10 sB&B⇌⋔£9.50–£10.50
dB&B£17–£18 dB&B⇌⋔£18–£22
Lunch£3.75–£4.75 Dinner£6alc Wine£3.50
Credit cards 1 2 3 5 6

★★Royal Albion Albion St ☎Thanet68071
Four-storey building on promenade, with a garden verandah and sun lounge giving extensive views of the sea. Dickens was a frequent visitor and wrote part of 'Nicholas Nickleby' here.
22rm(5⇌⋔) CTV TV in bedrooms 8P 6 Live music & dancing Fri Cabaret Sat Last dinner9pm
S% ✱sB&B£8–£9.50
sB&B⇌⋔£10.50–£11.50 dB&B£12.50–£15.50
dB&B⇌⋔£14.50–£17.50 Lunch£2.95&alc
Tea40p Dinner£3.75&alc Wine£3.40 *xmas*
Credit cards 1 2 3 5

Ⓜ Curzon 26 Granville Rd ☎Thanet63227
16rm CTV 12P 6 Children under 2yrs not accommodated Last dinner7.30pm S%
sB&B£6.25 dB&B£12.50 Lunch£2.50–£2.75
Dinner£3.50–£4 Wine£3 Credit card 3

Ⓜ Warwick 16 Granville Rd ☎Thanet62246
13rm CTV 10P English & French. Last dinner8pm
sB&B£7 dB&B£14 Bar lunch50p–£1.20
Tea30p–50p Dinner£3.75 *xmas*
Credit card 1

BROADWAY Hereford & Worcester Map**4** SP03

★★★★ Lygon Arms ☎2255 (Prestige)
See page 38 for details

★★★Broadway The Green ☎2401
13rm(11⇌⋔) Annexe: 11rm(7⇌⋔) CTV 30P
English & French. Last dinner9pm
✱sB&B£10–£12 sB&B⇌⋔£11.50–£14
dB&B£18–£22 dB&B⇌⋔£21–£26
Lunch£4.15alc Tea35–70p Dinner£5.75–£7.25
Wine£3 *xmas* Credit cards 1 2 3 5 6

★★★Dormy House Willersey Hill (2m E off A44)
☎2711
15⇌⋔ Annexe: 21⇌⋔ 1 CTV in bedrooms 60P
French. Last dinner10.30pm
✱sB&B⇌⋔£15 dB&B⇌⋔£29.50
Continental breakfast Lunch£3.50alc Tea40palc

B

The Lygon Arms

Broadway, Worcester

★★★★

'There cannot be a cleaner, civiler Inn than this' — Lord Torrington's Diary 1787

England's most famous Inn built in 1520. The situation close to the Shakespeare country and beside the Cotswold hills provides a perfect centre for the traveller to see many places of interest and to enjoy the tranquility of the countryside.

67 bedrooms all with private bathroom. 4 suites. Modern air-conditioned conference suite. Reduced winter terms (November to March) for stays of two days or longer.

For brochure please write to Douglas Barrington, Managing Director.
The Lygon Arms, Broadway, Worcs. Tel: (038 681) 2255. Telex: 338260
Member of Prestige Hotels, Relais de Campagne, Hotels Representative Inc

DORMY HOUSE

Dine by candlelight in the three star restaurant at Dormy House, high on Willersey Hill, overlooking the Vale of Evesham.
You'll find a welcome which combines traditional Cotswold comfort with the finest of European cuisine prepared from the pick of local produce and prime markets.
All 38 bedrooms are centrally heated, each with colour television and telephone and bathrooms en suite. The eighteen hole Broadway Golf Course, all but surrounds the hotel.
This charming Hotel and Restaurant are under the personal supervision of the Owners, Philip and Ingrid Sorensen and the General Manager Peter Pugson.

DORMY HOUSE ★★★
WILLERSEY HILL, BROADWAY, WORCESTERSHIRE.
Reservations: Broadway (038681) 2711 Telex: 338571

B

Dinner£5alc Wine£3.50 xmas
Credit cards 1 2 4 5 6

★★Collin House Collin Ln 8354
Closed Jan; 6 CTV CTV in bedrooms 20P Children under 10yrs not accommodated English & French. Last dinner 9pm dB&B £25 Lunch£4.95–£5.95 Tea40–80p Dinner£6–£8.50 Wine£2.50 Credit cards 1 2

XXXHunters Lodge Hotel High St 3247
Closed Mon & 2–23 Jan; Dinner not served Sun; 56seats 20P English & French. Last dinner 10pm Lunch£4alc Dinner£7.50alc Wine£3.25
Credit cards 1 2 3 5 6

BROCKDISH Norfolk Map**5** TM27
XXSherriff House Hoxne316
Closed Wed; 16seats P no children under 14yrs Last dinner by arrangement S% *Lunch£10–£12 Dinner£10–£12 Wine£3.24

BROCKENHURST Hampshire Map**4** SU20
★★★Balmer Lawn Lyndhurst Rd (Myddleton) 3116
Impressive Georgian-style mansion of brick and white stucco with balconies and creepers.
Closed 28Dec–7Jan; 60rm(54) Lift CTV in bedrooms 70P 6 (heated) (hard) squash Conference facilities available French. Last dinner 8.55pm S% sB&B£10.75–£14.25 sB&B £12–£18.50 dB&B£21.50–£26 dB&B £24–£33.50 Lunch£4.25–£4.60&alc Tea45p–£1 Dinner£5.25–£5.75&alc Wine£2.80 xmas
Credit cards 1 2 3 5

★★★Brockenhurst Rhinefield Rd 2557
Closed Nov–Mar; 14rm(10) CTV TV available in bedrooms 15P Children under 5yrs not accommodated English & French. Last dinner 8.30pm sB&B£11.25–£13.25 sB&B £12.55–£14.55 dB&B£22.50–£26.50 dB&B £25.10–£29.10 Lunch£5.25–£5.75 Tea£1.25–£1.50 Dinner£5.85–£6.45 Wine£3
Credit cards 1 2 3 5 6

★★★Carey's Manor Motor Lyndhurst Rd 3551
Telex no 47442
Gothic-style building with turret and gables, in secluded grounds of five acres.
57 CTV in bedrooms 100P Live music & dancing Fri & Sat English & French. Last dinner 10pm sB&B £15.75–£17.75 dB&B £23.90–£27.90 Lunch£3.95&alc Dinner£6.95&alc Wine£3.90 xmas
Credit cards 1 2 3 4 5 6

★★★Forest Park Rhinefield Rd 2095
Telex no 47674
Half-timbered, early 20th-C building (once vicarage) with three acres of lawn and grounds overlooking the forest.
40rm(25) CTV in bedrooms 50P (heated) (hard) sauna bath Live music & dancing Sat Last dinner 10pm sB&B£10.75–£14 sB&B £13.75–£15.50 dB&B£18.50–£23.50 dB&B £21.50–£26 Lunch fr£2.75 Dinner£4.45–£5.75&alc Wine£2.95 xmas
Credit cards 1 2 3 5

★★Cloud Meerut Rd 2165
Uninterrupted views of the New Forest.
Closed Nov & first two wks Jan; 20rm CTV 18P 2 Last dinner 7.45pm sB&B£8.96–£12.42 dB&B£17.92–£24.84 Lunch£4–£5 Tea30–60p high Tea£2–£3 Dinner£4–£6 Wine£3.50 xmas

★★*Rose & Crown* Lyndhurst Rd 2225
Creeper-clad coaching inn set in lovely gardens with

errace. Beamed dining room overlooks courtyard gardens.
rm 100P Lastdinner10pm

★★Watersplash The Rise ☎2344
Large, gabled house with two acres of well-kept lawns and gardens in quiet residential area.
8rm(10) CTV 30P 4 (heated) Lastdinner7.45pm S% sB&B£9–£13 sB&B £10.50–£14.50 dB&B£18–£26 dB&B £21–£29 Wine£2.95 xmas Credit cards 1 3

BROCKHAMPTON Hereford & Worcester Map**3** SO63
★★ **Brockhampton Court** ☎How Caple239
Isolated, red-sandstone mansion in five acres of grounds.
Closed 6 Oct–Mar; 32rm(10) CTV 100P 4 Lastdinner8.30pm S% sB&B£10.50–£11.75 dB&B£21–£22.50 dB&B £24.75–£26.25 Lunch£4 Tea70p–£1.30 Dinner£5.25–£5.75 Wine£2.95 xmas

BROME Suffolk Map**5** TM17
★★**Grange Motel** (On A140) ☎Eye456
rm(1) Annexe:22 CTV available in bedrooms 100P Lastdinner9.45pm S% *sB&B £12.50 dB&B £18.50 Lunch£3.50 Tea fr65p Dinner£4.50&alc Wine£2.40 xmas Credit cards 1 2 3 5 6

BROMLEY Gt London Map**5** TQ46
★★★**Bromley Court** Bromley Hill ☎01–464 5011 Telex no896310
130 Lift CTV in bedrooms 120P Disco Sat Live music & dancing Sat Conference facilities available English & French. Lastdinner9.45pm S% sB&B fr£18 dB&B fr£25 Lunch£4.50–£6.50 Dinner£5.50–£7.50 Wine£3.50 xmas Credit cards 1 2 3 4 5 6

×**Capisano's** 9 Simpsons Rd ☎01–464 8036
Closed Sun; Lunch not served Mon; 60seats Italian. Lastdinner11pm Lunch£4alc Dinner£7alc Credit cards 1 2 3 5

BROMLEY CROSS Gt Manchester Map**7** SD71
★★★**Last Drop** Hospital Rd ☎Bolton591131 Telex no635322
Closed Boxing Day; 32 Annexe:37 2 Lift CTV CTV in bedrooms 400P Live music & dancing Sat Conference facilities available International. Lastdinner10pm S% *sB&B fr£18.50 dB&B fr£26.50 Lunch fr£4.50&alc Dinner£10alc Credit cards 1 2 3 4 5 6

BROMPTON-BY-SAWDON N Yorkshire Map**8** SE98
×**Brompton Forge** ☎Scarborough85409
Lunch not served Tue & Sat; Dinner not served Sun; 50seats French.

BROMSGROVE Hereford & Worcester Map**7** SO97
★★★**Perry Hall** Kidderminster Rd (Embassy) ☎31976
A 17th-C house in lawned gardens, once the home of A E Housman.
50 CTV TV available in bedrooms 200P Conference facilities available Lastdinner9.15pm S% sB&B £16 dB&B £20 Lunch£4.50&alc Dinner£5.50&alc Wine£4 Credit cards 1 2 3 4 5 6

BROMYARD Hereford & Worcester Map**3** SO65
★**Hop Pole** The Square ☎2449
10rm 1 CTV 4P

B

✕Old Penny High St ☎3227
Closed Tue; Dinner not served Sun; 34seats
Lastdinner9pm Lunch£2.30–£2.80
Dinner£4.30–£5.20 Wine£2.50 Creditcard 1

BROOK (nr Cadnam) Hampshire Map**4** SU21
★★Bell Inn ☎Cadnam2214
Originally old drover's halt.
11rm(7⇌ ⋒) CTV 150P Lastdinner9.30pm
sB&B£10–£12.96 dB&B£19–£23
dB&B⇌ ⋒£21–£25 Lunch£3.50&alc
Dinner£5.75&alc Wine£2.75

BROUGHTON-IN-FURNESS Cumbria Map**7** SD28
★★*Eccle Riggs* Foxfield Rd ☎398
13rm (4⇌ ⋒) CTV 50P Lastdinner9pm

★Old King's Head Station Rd ☎293
Old white-washed village inn with oak beams, old prints and horse brasses.
Closed 24Dec–2Jan; 9rm CTV 20P 4
Lastdinner7pm S% sB&B£6–£7
dB&B£12–£14 Lunch£2–£3.50
Dinner£3.50–£5 Wine£2.70

BROWN HILLS West Midlands Map**7** SK01
★★Rising Sun Chester Road North (junc A5/A452)
☎5687
9⇌ ⋒ CTV 50P Lastdinner10pm S%
sB&B⇌ ⋒ fr£9.72 dB&B⇌ ⋒ fr£15.12
Dinner£3–£4&alc Wine£2.80

BUCKDEN Cambridgeshire Map**4** TL16
★★*George* High St ☎Huntingdon810304
Former coaching inn dating from 16th-C with small garden situated on old A1.
12rm(2⇌ ⋒) CTV 30P 4 Lastdinner11pm
Creditcards 1 2 3 5

★Lion Great North Rd (Trusthouse Forte)
☎Huntingdon810313
Picturesque former coaching inn, thought to have been a guesthouse associated with see of Lincoln. Fine moulded beams meet in a central boss in the lounge.
11rm TV in bedrooms 22P 4 Lastdinner9.30pm
S% sB&B£12 dB&B£15.50
Creditcards 1 2 3 4 5 6

BUCKDEN North Yorkshire Map**7** SD97
★Buck Inn ☎Kettlewell227
10rm CTV TV in bedrooms 40P sauna bath
Lastdinner9pm S% ✻sB&B£9.50
dB&B£18.50 Lunch£3.50–£3.95 Tea90p–£1
Dinner£4.95 Wine£2.65 *xmas*
Creditcards 1 2 3 5

BUCKFASTLEIGH Devon Map**3** SX76
★Bossell House Plymouth Rd ☎3294
11rm(1⇌ ⋒) Annexe:6rm(1⇌ ⋒) CTV 30P (hard)
Lastdinner10pm sB&B£5.94–£8.10
dB&B£11.88–£16.20 dB&B⇌ ⋒£14.04–£18.36
Dinner fr£3.60&alc Wine£2.15 *xmas*

✕Country Fare 54 Fore St ☎2383
Closed Wed; 40seats International.
Lastdinner9.30pm Lunch£3.25alc
Dinner£5.25alc Wine£2.50
Creditcards 1 2 3 5 6

BUCKHURST HILL Essex Map**5** TQ49
★★Roebuck High Rd (Trusthouse Forte)
☎01–505 4636
Large, brick, steep gabled building with distinctive windows; located at highest point in Epping Forest.
26rm(11⇌ ⋒) TV in bedrooms 40P
Lastdinner10pm S% sB&B£14.50
sB&B⇌ ⋒£16.50 dB&B£19 dB&B⇌ ⋒£21.50
xmas Creditcards 1 2 3 4 5 6

BUCKINGHAM Buckinghamshire Map**4** SP63
★★White Hart Market Sq (Trusthouse Forte) ☎213
21rm(6⇌ ⋒) TV in bedrooms 30P
Lastdinner9.30pm S% sB&B£12
sB&B⇌ ⋒£14.50 dB&B£17 dB&B⇌ ⋒£20.50
Creditcards 1 2 3 4 5 6

★Swan & Castle Castle St ☎3082
17th-C coaching inn in town centre.
RS 25–26Dec (no accommodation); 7rm CTV 20P
S% sB&B£9 dB&B£16.50 Lunch fr£3.25
Dinner£5alc Wine£3.50 Creditcards 1 2 3 5 6

BUCKLAND IN THE MOOR Devon Map**3** SX77
★★Buckland Hall ☎Ashburton52679
Closed mid Oct–Mar; 6rm(4⇌ ⋒) CTV 20P
Children under 8yrs not accommodated
Lastdinner8pm sB&B£10–£12
sB&B⇌ ⋒£11–£13 dB&B£20–£24
dB&B⇌ ⋒£22–£26 Lunch£2–£3&alc
Tea£1–£1.50&alc HighTea£1.50–£2.50&alc
Dinner£4.50–£5.50&alc Wine£2.80

BUCKLERS HARD Hampshire Map**4** SU40
★★Master Builders House ☎253
Overlooking the Beaulieu River and countryside, this was once the home of Henry Adams, 18th-C shipbuilder.
4rm Annexe:23rm(17⇌ ⋒) CTV TV in bedrooms
60P Lastdinner10pm S% sB&B fr£14
sB&B⇌ ⋒ fr£14 dB&B fr£24 dB&B⇌ ⋒ fr£24
Lunch£6alc Tea£1.25–£1.70 Dinner£6alc
Wine£3.50 *xmas* Creditcards 1 2 3 4 5 6

BUCKLOW HILL Cheshire Map**7** SJ78
☆☆☆Swan (Greenall Whitley) ☎830295
Telex no666911
Once a monastery providing sanctuary during the Civil War.
RS Xmas (service & breakfast); 74⇌ ⋒ 4 CTV

edrooms 200P ♀French. Last dinner9.45pm
6 sB&B⇌⋔£20–£21.50
&B⇌⋔£25–£26.50 Lunch£3.75&alc
nner£7alc ⊟ Credit cards 1 2 3 5 6

DE Cornwall Map**2** SS20
★Falcon Abbey Rd ☎2005
ll, white, Victorian building with central tower erlooking Bude canal.
Nov–Mar; 48rm(28⇌⋔) ☽ CTV 50P 4⌂ ⚓ Live usic & dancing twice wkly ♀English & French.
st dinner9.30pm ♁ ⊻ S%
&B£7.36–£11.65 sB&B⇌⋔£9.43–£13.41
&B£14.72–£23.30 dB&B⇌⋔£18.86–£26.82
ntinental breakfast Lunch£2.20alc Tea75p
nner£4.65&alc Wine£2.28 ⊟
edit cards 2 3 5 6

★Grenville Belle Vue (Mount Charlotte) ☎2121
ll, castle like building set back in own grounds, with wers and modern extensions.
osed Oct–Apr; 73rm Lift ☽ CTV 70P 3⌂ (heated) Disco wkly Live music & dancing wkly baret 3 nights wkly Conference facilities available ♿ Last dinner9pm ♁ ⊻ S% sB&B£8–£14 &B£16–£28 Lunch fr£3.75&alc Tea fr90p nner fr£4&alc Wine£3.50 Credit cards 1 2 3

★Hartland Hartland Ter ☎2509
osed Nov–Mar; 30rm(25⇌⋔) Lift ₩ TV in drooms 30P ⛆(heated) Last dinner9pm

★*Strand* The Strand (Trusthouse Forte) ☎3222
⇌⋔ Lift ☽ ₩ CTV TV available in bedrooms ⊘ 0P ♀International. Last dinner9pm ♁ ⊻ ⊟
edit cards 1 2 3

★Burn Court Burn View ☎2872
mfortable, modern hotel occupying unique sition on edge of golf course.
rm(22⇌⋔) CTV ⊘ 12P Disco wkly Live music & dancing wkly Children under 8yrs not accommodated Last dinner8pm sB&B£9.50–£10 sB&B⇌⋔£11–£11.50 dB&B£20–£21 dB&B⇌⋔£22–£30 Lunch£3.25–£4&alc Dinner£4.75–£5.50&alc Wine£2.50

★★*Chough* Widemouth Rd, Upton ☎2386
Farmhouse-style hotel, situated on cliffs overlooking Widemouth Bay, four minutes' walk from beach.
Closed Oct–Etr; 12rm(2⇌⋔) CTV 20P ⛟ ⚓ billiards Last dinner7.30pm

★★Grosvenor Summerleaze Cres ☎2062
Small, comfortable hotel situated facing south and west overlooking sea.
Closed Nov–Feb; 14rm(6⇌⋔) CTV 5P 3⌂ ⛟ Children under 5yrs not accommodated Last dinner7.30pm ♁ S% sB&B£6–£7.50 dB&B£12–£15 dB&B⇌⋔£14–£17 Lunch£2–£3.50 Tea85p–£1 Dinner£3.25–£4.50 Wine£2.40 ⊟ *xmas*

★★St Margaret's Killerton Rd ☎2252
Closed Xmas Day & Boxing Day; 9rm ₩ CTV ⊘ 9P ⛟ ⚓ Children under 3yrs not accommodated Last dinner9.30pm ♁ ⊻ S% sB&B£7.30–£7.85 dB&B£14.60–£15.50 Lunch£2.50–£3.25&alc Tea fr60p Dinner£2.80–£3.50&alc Wine£2.30 Credit cards 1 3

★Camelot Downs View ☎2361
Closed Oct–Mar; 13rm(5⇌⋔) ₩ CTV ⊘ 12P ⚓ Last dinner7pm sB&B£8–£9.20 dB&B£16–£18.40 dB&B⇌⋔£17–£19.40 Lunch£2.50 Tea£1.05 High Tea£1.55 Dinner£3.75 Credit cards 1 3

★Florida 17–18 Summerleaze Cres ☎2451
Terraced stone built holiday hotel, overlooking bay and harbour, close to beach.

B

Closed Sep–Mar; 20rm(5⇨⋒) CTV 10P ♀English & Continental. Last dinner7.45pm ✧ S% sB&B£6.32–£7.83 sB&B⇨⋒£7.40–£8.91 dB&B£12.64–£15.66 dB&B⇨⋒£14.80–£17.82 Dinner£3.67 Wine£3 ♜

★***Maer Lodge*** Crooklets Beach ☎3306
Detached, family holiday hotel.
Closed Oct–mid Apr; 24rm(3⇨⋒) CTV TV available in bedrooms 30P ⚓ Live music twice wkly Live music & dancing wkly Last dinner7.15pm ✧ ☑ ♜

★**Meva Gwin** Upton, Bede Haven ☎2347
Closed Xmas; 19rm(4⇨⋒) ♛ CTV ⊘ 45P Children under 3yrs not accommodated Last dinner7.30pm ✧ ☑ sB&B£5.50–£7.75 dB&B£10.75–£15.75 dB&B⇨⋒£11.75–£18 Lunch£1.60–£2.50 Tea50p–£1.25 Dinner£2–£3.50 Wine£2.20 ♜

★**Penarvor** Crooklets Beach ☎2036
Closed Nov–Mar; 16rm CTV 20P ⚘ ⚓ ✧ ☑ S% ✱sB&B£5.40–£6.48 dB&B£10.80–£12.96 Lunch£2.50 Tea50p High Tea£1.50 Dinner£3.50 Wine£2.50

★***Penwethers*** Killerton Rd ☎2504
Closed Xmas; 8rm CTV ⊘ 8P ⚘ Last dinner10pm ✧ ☑

★***Summerleaze Beach*** Summerleaze Cres ☎2502
31rm CTV 12P Live music & dancing 3 nights wkly Last dinner8pm ✧ ☑ *xmas* Credit card 1

⊛**Flexbury Lodge** Ocean View Rd ☎2344
Closed 6Oct–5May 22rm ♛ CTV 20P ⚓ sauna bath Disco wkly Live music & dancing 3 nights wkly Cabaret wkly Last dinner7.30pm ✧ S% sB&B£3.50–£5 dB&B£7–£10 Lunch£1.50–£1.70 Tea70p Dinner£2 Wine£2 *xmas*

BUDLEIGH SALTERTON Devon Map**3** SY08
★★★***Rosemullion*** Cliff Rd ☎2288
Modernised, gabled building with new extension in quiet location near cliff top.
RS Nov–Apr; 35⇨⋒ Lift ♛ CTV 50P ⚘ Last dinner9.30pm ✧ ☑ Credit card 2

★★***Long Range*** Vales Rd ☎3321
Closed mid Oct–mid Mar; Unlicensed; 10rm(1⇨⋒) CTV ⊘ 8P 2⌂ Children under 4yrs not accommodated Last dinner8pm ✧ S%

★**Nattore Lodge** Westhill ☎2736
Closed Oct–Mar; Unlicensed; 9rm(5⇨⋒) ♛ CTV 12P 1⌂ ⚘ ⚓ Last dinner8pm sB&B fr£8.10 dB&B fr£18.80 Lunch fr£2.50 Tea fr75p Dinner fr£3.30

BULKINGTON (nr Bedworth) Warwickshire Map**4** SP38
★★**Weston Hall** Weston Ln (Trophy Taverns) ☎Bedworth315475
32⇨⋒ ☽ ♛ CTV 250P ⚓ Disco Sat & Sun Live mu & dancing Thu & Fri Cabaret Thu & Fri ♀French & Indian. Last dinner10pm S% ✱sB&B⇨⋒£11 dB&B⇨⋒£16 Lunch£3–£3.50&alc Dinner£3.25–£3.75&alc Wine£2.75 Credit cards 1 3

BULPHAN Essex Map**5** TQ68
★★**Ye Olde Plough House** Brentwood Rd ☎Grays Thurrock891592
Modern chalets contrast with central building, a 14 C Essex yeoman's house.
60⇨⋒ ☽ ♛ CTV TV in bedrooms 150P ⚘ ⚓ ⛆(heated) ⚲(hard) Live music & dancing Sat ♀English & French. ✧ ☑ sB&B⇨⋒ fr£10 dB&B⇨⋒ fr£16 ♜ *xmas* Credit cards 1 2 3 5

BUNWELL Norfolk Map**5** TM19
★★♚**Bunwell Manor** ☎317
Former manor house in three acres of grounds, the main part of which is timber framed and dates back 16th century.
Closed Jan; 10rm(4⇨⋒) ♛ CTV 30P ⚘ ⚓ Children under 8yrs not accommodated ♀English & French Last dinner9pm ✧ ☑ dB&B£9–£10 sB&B⇨⋒£10 dB&B£18–£20 dB&B⇨⋒£20 Lunch£3–£3.50 Tea50p–£1.50 Dinner£3.50–£4&alc Wine£2.40 ♜ Credit cards 1 3

BURFORD Oxfordshire Map**4** SP21
★★**Bull** High St (Nicholsons) ☎2220
Medieval inn with brick and stone façade dating fro the mid 17th century.
12rm(8⇨⋒) 4▭ ♛ CTV 6P 3⌂ Last dinner9.30pm S% sB&B£7.85–£8.75 sB&B⇨⋒£8.35–£9.35 dB&B£15–£16.50 dB&B⇨⇨£15.50–£17 Lunch£2.75&alc Dinner£4&alc ♜ *xmas* Credit cards 1 2 3 5

★★**Cotswold Gateway** ☎2148
Closed Xmas night; 12rm(2⇨⋒) CTV 60P Last dinner10pm ✧ S% Lunch£3.25&alc Dinner£4.75&alc Credit cards 1 2 3 5

★★**Golden Ball** High St ☎3223
11⇨⋒ 2▭ ♛ CTV CTV in bedrooms 16P ♀English Continental. Last dinner9.45pm ✧ ☑ ✱sB&B⇨⋒£12–£18 dB&B⇨⋒£18–£28 Lunch£3.50–£5.60 Tea75p–£1.50 High Tea75p–£2 Dinner£5.60–£8.50 Wine£3.2(♜ Credit cards 1 2 3 5 6

★**Winter's Tale** ☎3176
See page 39 for details

BURGH HEATH Surrey Map**4** TQ25
☆☆**Pickard Motor** Brighton Rd (Best Western) ☎57222 Telex no929908
Annexe:32⇨⋒ ♛ CTV in bedrooms 142P ⚓

ve music & dancing Sat (Oct–Jun) Mainly grills. astdinner10.30pm
B&B £17.50–£19 dB&B £25–£27
unch£3 Tea60palc HighTea£1.50alc
inner£3.50alc Wine£2.75
redit cards 1 2 3 5 6

URHAM Kent Map5 TQ76
XToastmaster's Inn Church St Medway61299
losed Sun, Mon, 25Dec–1Jan & 2wks Sep;
0seats 20P French. Specialities: le Poulet de resse truffee au persil, Salmon in Pastry with Herb auce, Carré d'agneau aux aromantes.
astdinner10pm Lunch£9alc Dinner£9alc
Vine£3.45 Credit card 3

URLEY Hampshire Map4 SU20
★★★Burley Manor 3314 Telexno47674
Country manor house situated in lawns, gardens and parkland.
3rm(17) 1 CTV in bedrooms 50P 1
(heated) Live music & dancing Sat
astdinner10pm sB&B£10.75–£14
sB&B £13.75–£15.50 dB&B£18.50–£23.50
dB&B £21.50–£26 Lunch£4.25
Dinner£4.75–£6.25&alc Wine£2.95 *xmas*
Credit cards 1 2 3 5

★★Moorhill House 3285
Victorian country house in three acres of lawns and wooded grounds.
25rm(13) CTV CTV available in bedrooms 50P
Lastdinner8.30pm
sB&B£11.50–£14 sB&B £13–£15.50
dB&B£20–£25 dB&B £23–£28
Lunch£4.50–£5.50 Tea55p–£1 Dinner£5–£6.50
Wine£2.70 *xmas* Credit cards 1 2 3 5

BURN BRIDGE (nr Harrogate) N Yorks Map8 SE35
XXRoman Court Harrogate879933
Closed Sun; Lunch not served; 70seats 20P
French & Italian. Lastdinner10.30pm
Dinner£7.25–£12.50 Wine£4

BURNHAM Buckinghamshire Map4 SU98
XX*Grovefield* Taplow Common Rd 3131
Three-storey, late Victorian building with traditional half-panelled restaurant overlooking the garden.
Dinner not served Sun; 40seats 75P bedrooms available French. Lastdinner9.30pm
Credit cards 1 2 3 5

BURNHAM MARKET Norfolk Map5 TF84
XFishes Market Pl 588
Closed Mon; Lunch not served Tue; Dinner not served Sun; 36seats

BURNHAM-ON-CROUCH Essex Map5 TQ99
★Ye Olde White Harte The Quay Maldon782106
Old coaching inn once associated with smuggling; overlooks River Crouch estuary.
11rm(1) Annexe: 4rm CTV 14P
Lastdinner9pm sB&B£7.20 dB&B£12.50
dB&B £15.50 Lunch£2.90–£3.10&alc
Dinner£3.20–£3.40&alc Wine£2.40

XX*Contented Sole* High St Maldon782139
Closed Mon & 22Dec–Jan; Dinner not served Sun; 70seats English & French. Lastdinner9.30pm

BURNHAM-ON-SEA Somerset Map3 ST34
★★Dunstan House Love Ln 784343
Detached, Georgian-style two storey house in own gardens.
Closed Xmas; 10rm(4) CTV CTV available in bedrooms 18P 2 Lastdinner10pm S%
sB&B£7.13 sB&B £8.32 dB&B£14.26
dB&B £16.63 Lunch£2.50alc Dinner£5alc
Wine£2.35 Credit cards 1 2 3 5

★★Royal Clarence The Esplanade 783138
14rm CTV CTV available in bedrooms 20P
Lastdinner8.30pm S%
*sB&B£5.50–£7.50 dB&B£11–£14
Lunch£1.75–£2.20&alc Tea£1–£1.50
Dinner£2–£2.50&alc Wine£1.55 *xmas*
Credit cards 1 3 6

★Richmond Hotel 32 Berrow Rd 782984
Victorian-style building with modern extension and simple, traditional furnishings.
12rm(6) CTV CTV available in bedrooms 8P
Children under 5yrs not accommodated
Lastdinner8pm sB&B£6–£7 sB&B £8–£9
dB&B fr£12 dB&B £13.70–£15.40
Lunch£2.50–£2.75 Tea30p Dinner£3.50–£4
Wine£2.50 Credit cards 1 3

BURNLEY Lancashire Map7 SD83
☆☆☆Burnley Crest Motel Keirby Walk (Crest)
27611
Ultra-modern, seven-storey block with glass façade.
48 Lift CTV in bedrooms 50P 16 Conference facilities available Lastdinner9.45pm S%
*sB&B £15.71 dB&B £22.24
Continental breakfast Credit cards 1 2 3 4 5 6

★★Sparrow Hawk 1–3 Grimshaw St 21551
34rm(12) CTV CTV available in bedrooms 25P English & French. Lastdinner8.30pm
*sB&B£12 sB&B £15.25 dB&B£17.50
dB&B £23.50 Lunch fr£4&alc
Dinner fr£4.50&alc

BURNSALL N Yorkshire Map7 SE06
★★Fell 209
12rm CTV 60P Lastdinner9pm S%
sB&B£6–£7.50 dB&B£12–£15 Lunch£3alc
Tea£1.20alc HighTea£1.50alc Dinner£4alc
Wine£2.80 *xmas*

★★Red Lion ☎204
8rm 🍽 CTV 40P ↬ Last dinner 10pm sB&B£6.50
Lunch fr£2.75 Dinner fr£4.25 Wine£2.70 ⊟

B

BURRINGTON Devon Map**2** SS61
★★★⚜Northcote Manor ☎High Bickington 501
13⇌ 🚿 🍽 CTV CTV in bedrooms ⊘ 100P ⚘ ⚓ Live music & dancing Sat Last dinner 10.30pm ✿ ⚐
S% sB&B⇌🚿£14.75–£16.50
dB&B⇌🚿£24–£29 Lunch fr£3&alc
Dinner fr£5.25&alc ⊟ Credit cards 1 2 5

BURSLEDON Hampshire Map**4** SU40
☆☆☆***Solent*** Hamble Ln ☎Bursledon 2151
Southampton plan **14**
52⇌ ☽ TV 250P ⊡ Dancing twice wkly Cabaret twice wkly Conference facilities available ☋ English & French. Last dinner 10.30pm ✿ ⚐
Credit cards 1 2 3 5

BURTON BRADSTOCK Dorset Map**3** SY48
★★*Bay View* ☎205
RS Oct–Mar; 11rm(3⇌🚿) 🍽 CTV 50P ⚓ Live music & dancing nightly (summer only) Last dinner 9.30pm
✿ ⊟

BURTON UPON TRENT Staffordshire Map**8** SK22
★★★Riverside Warren Ln, Branston ☎63117
22⇌🚿 ☽ 🍽 CTV CTV in bedrooms ⊘ 200P ⚓ ↬ Live music & dancing Wed & Fri Last dinner 10.30pm ✿
S% sB&B⇌🚿£12 dB&B⇌🚿£18
Lunch£3–£5&alc Dinner£4–£6&alc Wine£3.50

★★*Midland* Station St ☎68723
14rm(2⇌🚿) 🍽 CTV 40P 2🏠 Last dinner 9pm
Credit cards 1 3

BURY Gt Manchester Map**7** SD81
★*Woolfield House* Wash Lane ☎061–764 3446
13rm 🍽 CTV TV available in bedrooms 60P ☋ English & French. Last dinner 9pm ✿ ⚐
Credit cards 2 4 6

BURY ST EDMUNDS Suffolk Map**5** TL86
★★★Angel Angel Hill ☎3926 Telex no 81630
44rm(34⇌🚿) 4⊟ ☽ 🍽 CTV in bedrooms 10P Live music & dancing mthly Last dinner 10.30pm ✿ ⚐
sB&B£16 sB&B⇌🚿£20 dB&B£23
dB&B⇌🚿£28 Lunch£5.50alc Tea£1alc
Dinner£7.50alc Wine£4.40 ⊟ *xmas*
Credit cards 1 2 3 5 6

★★Everards Cornhill ☎5384
Modernised Georgian inn.
14rm(3⇌🚿) 🍽 CTV 14P 3🏠 ⚘ Last dinner 8.45pm
✿ ✻sB&B fr£8 sB&B⇌🚿 fr£10.25
dB&B fr£14.25 dB&B⇌🚿 fr£15.50 Lunch£3&alc
Dinner£3&alc Credit card 1

★★Suffolk 36 The Butter Market (Trusthouse Forte)
☎3995
41rm(13⇌🚿) ☽ 🍽 TV in bedrooms 16🏠
Last dinner 10pm ✿ S% sB&B£13.50
sB&B⇌🚿£17 dB&B£19 dB&B⇌🚿£21.50 ⊟
Credit cards 1 2 3 4 5 6

BUSHEY Hertfordshire Map**4** TQ19
☆☆☆Watford Ladbroke Mercury Motor Inn Elton Way, Watford Bypass (A41) (Ladbroke)
☎Watford 35881 Telex 923422
188⇌🚿 ☽ 🍽 CTV in bedrooms 200P ♿
Last dinner 10.30pm ✿ sB&B⇌🚿 fr£22.50
dB&B⇌🚿 fr£30 Lunch fr£4.50&alc
Dinner fr£5&alc Wine£3.20 ⊟
Credit cards 1 2 3 4 5 6

BUTTERMERE Cumbria Map**11** NY11
★★Bridge ☎252
Closed Nov–Mar; 24rm(4⇌🚿) ✗ 🍽 30P ⚘
☋ English & French. Last dinner 7.30pm ✿
sB&B£11.50 dB&B£21.20 dB&B⇌🚿£24.20
Bar lunch£1.20–£2.80 Dinner fr£6 Wine£3

BUXTON Derbyshire Map**7** SK07
★★Grove Grove Pde (Frederic Robinson) ☎3804
22rm CTV ⚑ Last dinner 8.30pm ✿ ⚐
✻sB&B£7.25 dB&B£14 Lunch£2.50–£3
Tea40p Dinner£3.50–£5 Wine£2.80 ⊟ *xmas*

★★Lee Wood 13 Manchester Rd (A5002) (Inter-Hotel) ☎3002
In own grounds with uninterrupted views of surrounding countryside.
40⇌🚿 Lift ☽ 🍽 CTV 40P ⚓ ⛳ Last dinner 8.30pm
✿ S% sB&B⇌🚿£12.50–£14
dB&B⇌🚿£22.50–£25.50 Lunch£3–£5&alc
Tea35p–£1 High Tea£2–£4
Dinner£6.70–£5.50&alc Wine£2.50 ⊟
Credit cards 1 2 5 6

★★Sandringham Broad Walk ☎3430
39rm(10⇌🚿) CTV CTV available in bedrooms 8P
Last dinner 8.30pm S% sB&B£8.10–£9.15
dB&B£15.50–£17.50 dB&B⇌🚿£18.50–£21
Lunch£3–£4 Dinner£4.50–£5.50 Wine£2.70 ⊟
Credit cards 1 3

★*Buckingham* 1 Burlington Rd ☎3439
35rm(2⇌🚿) Lift 🍽 CTV 20P ⚓ billiards
Last dinner 8pm ✿ ⚐ ⊟ *xmas*

★Hartingdon Broad Walk ☎2638
Closed 24Dec–3Jan; RS Nov–Apr; 14rm(2⇌🚿)
CTV ⊘ 15P 1🏠 Last dinner 8pm S% sB&B£8
sB&B⇌🚿£10 dB&B£13–£14
dB&B⇌🚿£15–£17 Bar lunch fr50p High tea fr£3
Dinner£4.50–£4.80 ⊟

CADNAM Hampshire Map**4** SU21
✕✕Le Chantecleirc Romsey Rd ☎3271
Closed Sun, Mon, 2wks Jan & 2wks Aug; Lunch Sat;
50seats 24P ☋ French. Last dinner 9.50pm
Lunch£7alc Dinner£7alc Wine£2.90
Credit cards 1 3

C

AISTOR ST EDMUND Norfolk Map**5** TG20
ee also Norwich
) ♔ ***Caistor Hall*** ☎ Framington Earl 2245
eorgian residence, built 1745, in 33 acres of rounds. Situated 3½m from centre of Norwich.
3rm(4⇌⋒) CTV 60P 10⌂ ⚓ ⚔(hard)
astdinner8pm

ALDBECK Cumbria Map**11** NY33
Parkend Parkend (1m W of village) ☎442
losed Mon & Jan & Feb; Lunch not served Nov & ec (except Suns); 32seats 16P Lastdinner8.45pm
% Lunch£4alc Dinner£7&alc Wine£3
redit card 1

ALNE Wiltshire Map**3** ST97
★***Lansdowne Arms*** The Strand ☎812488
wo-storey coaching inn, with cobbled yard.
0rm TV 16P Lastdinner9pm
redit cards 1 3 6

ALVERHALL Salop Map**7** SJ63
Old Jack Inn ☎235
losed Sun; 60seats 30P Lastdinner9.30pm
inner£6alc Wine£2.95

AMBERLEY Surrey Map**4** SU86
★★★**Frimley Hall** Portsmouth Rd (Trusthouse Forte)
☎28321 Telex no 858846
arge ivy-covered mansion in secluded grounds just ff the A325.
7rm(68⇌⋒) CTV CTV in bedrooms 200P ⚓
astdinner9.45pm S% sB&B£16
B&B⇌⋒£19.50 dB&B⇌⋒£25.50 *xmas*
redit cards 1 2 3 4 5 6

AMBORNE Cornwall Map**2** SW64
★★**Tyacks** ☎712628
losed 25 & 26Dec; 11rm(5⇌⋒) CTV 70P 5⌂
isco three nights wkly Live music & dancing wkly
astdinner10pm *sB&B£7.50
B&B⇌⋒£8.50 dB&B£15 dB&B⇌⋒£17
unch£3alc Tea50palc Dinner£5alc Wine£2.50
redit cards 1 3

AMBRIDGE Cambridgeshire Map**5** TL45
★★★★**Garden House** Granta Pl, off Mill Ln
Prestige) ☎63421 Telex no 81463
Modern hotel set in three acres of riverside gardens, lose to city centre.
losed 25–31Dec; 55⇌⋒ Lift CTV in bedrooms 160P ⚓ Live music & dancing Sat Conference facilities available International.
astdinner9.30pm sB&B⇌⋒£24–£27
dB&B⇌⋒£34–£38 Continental breakfast
unch£4.50–£5.50&alc Tea£1
inner£4.75–£5.75&alc Wine£4.50
redit cards 1 2 3 4 5 6

University Arms Regent St (Inter-Hotel) ☎51241
Telex no 817311
Modern extension to well-established Victorian coaching inn. Quietly situated close to city, shopping and colleges.
120rm(100⇌⋒) Lift CTV in bedrooms 75⌂ Live music & dancing Sat Conference facilities available
Lastdinner9.45pm S% sB&B£13.25
sB&B⇌⋒£17.50 dB&B£22 dB&B⇌⋒£26.50
Lunch fr£4.10&alc Tea fr£1.15 Dinner fr£4.70&alc
Wine£2.60 Credit cards 1 2 3 5 6

★★★**Gonville** Gonville Pl (Best Western) ☎66611
Closed 4 days Xmas; 62⇌⋒ Lift CTV CTV available in bedrooms 100P Conference facilities available French. Lastdinner9.30pm
*sB&B⇌⋒ fr£15 dB&B⇌⋒ fr£23
Lunch£3.45–£3.70&alc Tea fr25p
Dinner£3.65–£3.95&alc Wine£3.25
Credit cards 1 2 3 6

★★**Arundell House** 53 Chesterton Rd ☎67701
59rm(33⇌⋒) CTV in bedrooms 35P English & French. Lastdinner9.30pm
*sB&B£8.14–£11.06 sB&B⋒£11.06–£14.37
dB&B£16.75–£19.54 dB&B⇌⋒£19.85–£21.79
Continental breakfast Lunch£4.70&alc Tea55p
Dinner£4.70&alc Wine£2.05 Credit cards 1 3

★★♔**Blue Boar** Trinity St (Trusthouse Forte)
☎63121
48rm(11⇌⋒) TV in bedrooms
Lastdinner10pm S% sB&B£13.50
dB&B£20.50 dB&B⋒£23 *xmas*
Credit cards 1 2 3 4 5 6

XX***Oyster Tavern*** 21 Northampton St ☎53110
Closed Sun; 46seats Lastdinner11pm

X**Peking** 21 Burleigh St ☎54755
Closed Mon & Public Hols; 64seats Pekinese.
Lastdinner10.45pm *Lunch90p–£1.30&alc
Dinner£5alc Wine£2.80

At **Bar Hill** (6m W on A604)
☆☆☆**Cambridgeshire** ☎Crafts Hill 80555
100⇌⋒ 200P

CAMELFORD Cornwall Map**2** SX18
★★**Lanteglos Farmhouse** Lanteglos ☎3551
Closed Oct–Mar; 12rm(10⇌⋒) CTV TV available in bedrooms 26P ⚓ (heated) (hard) squash Disco wkly Live music & dancing wkly Cabaret wkly English & Continental. Lastdinner9.30pm
S% sB&B£10–£12 sB&B⋒£10–£12
dB&B£20–£24 dB&B⇌⋒£20–£24
Bar lunch£1.20–£3.20 Dinner£4.50&alc
Wine£2.85 Credit cards 1 3 5

★**Highermead** College Rd ☎3325
10rm CTV 30P ⚓ billiards Disco
Lastdinner10pm S% sB&B£4.56–£7.56

dB&B£9.12–£15.12 dB&B⇨⋒£10.12–£16.12 Lunch£1.85–£3&alc Tea50p–£1&alc Dinner£3–£4&alc Wine£2.31 ⊟ *xmas* Credit cards ① ③

CANNOCK Staffordshire Map**7** SJ91
★★**Hollies** Hollies Av ☎3151
RS Dec; 6rm ⋔ CTV ⊘ 80P 6⌂ ⚓ Disco mthly Live music & dancing mthly Cabaret mthly Children under 5yrs not accommodated ♀English & French. Last dinner9.30pm ✿ sB&B fr£12 dB&B fr£18 Lunch fr£3.50 Dinner fr£4.50 Wine£3 Credit cards ② ③ ⑤

CANTERBURY Kent Map**5** TR15
★★★**Chaucer** Ivy Ln (Trusthouse Forte) ☎64427
51rm(32⇨⋒) ☽ ⋔ TV in bedrooms 42P Last dinner9.30pm ✿ S% sB&B£14.50 sB&B⇨⋒£17 dB&B£20 dB&B☎⋒£23 ⊟ *xmas* Credit cards ① ② ③ ④ ⑤ ⑥

★★★**County** High St (Inter-Hotel) ☎66266 Telex no965076
An inn stood on this site since 1485; it was once the site of a Roman forum.
74⇨⋒ Lift ☽ ⋔ CTV in bedrooms ⊘ 100P 50⌂ Live music & dancing twice wkly Conference facilities available ♿ Last dinner10pm ✿ ☐ sB&B☎⋒£19 dB&B⇨⋒£30 Lunch£5.50alc Tea65palc Dinner£7.50alc Wine£3.90 *xmas* Credit cards ① ② ③ ④ ⑤ ⑥

★★★**Slatters** St Margarets Street (Grand Met) ☎63271
Situated next to Marlowe Theatre, on site of Roman amphitheatre.

0rm(23⇌⋒) Lift ☽ 🍴 TV available in bedrooms 30P
⛟ Last dinner9.15pm ✿ ⊻ S%
✻sB&B⇌⋒£12 dB&B⇌⋒£20 ⛿
Credit cards 1 2 3 4 5 6

★★**Falstaff** St Dunstans Street (Whitbread) ☎62138
An old beamed building, almost beside the imposing West Gate.
0rm Annexe: 6rm 1⇌ 🍴 CTV TV in bedrooms 20P
Children under 5yrs not accommodated
☺ Mainly grills. Last dinner9pm ✿ S%
✻sB&B fr£9.50 dB&B£19–£22 Lunch fr£3
Dinner£4.50alc Wine£2.45 ⛿
Credit cards 1 2 3 4 5

CARBIS BAY Cornwall Map**2** SW53
See St Ives, Cornwall

CARLISLE Cumbria Map**11** NY35
☆☆☆**Carlisle Crest Motel** Greymoorhill (junc 44 M6) (Crest) ☎31201
A modern building situated adjacent to the motorway.
108⇌⋒☽ CTV in bedrooms 200P ⚓
Last dinner10pm ✿ ⊻ S% ✻sB&B⇌⋒£16.25
dB&B⇌⋒£21.70 Continental breakfast ⛿
Credit cards 1 2 3 4 5 6

★★★**Crown & Mitre** English St (Best Western)
☎25491 Telex no 64183
Conveniently situated close to both the cathedral and castle.
75⇌⋒ Annexe: 18⇌⋒ Lift ☽ 🍴 CTV TV in bedrooms 25P 25🏠 Conference facilities available
Last dinner10pm ✿ ⊻ S%
sB&B⇌⋒£7.02–£18.10
dB&B⇌⋒£16.20–£26.70 Continental breakfast
Lunch fr£2.85&alc Tea30–90p High Tea fr£2.80
Dinner£6.50alc Wine£3.78 ⛿
Credit cards 1 2 3 5 6

★★★**Cumbrian** Court St (Thistle) ☎31951
A well modernised hotel built in 1859 and situated opposite the station. Facilities include a restaurant decorated in the style of the 1890's and Consort Suite.
70⇌⋒ 2⇌ Lift ☽ 🍴 CTV CTV in bedrooms 50P 5🏠
Disco three nights wkly Live music & dancing wkly
☺ International. Last dinner9.30pm ✿ ⊻ S%
sB&B⇌⋒£16–£20 dB&B⇌⋒£25–£30
Lunch£3.50–£4&alc Tea50p
High Tea£2.50–£3.50&alc
Dinner£4.50–£5.25&alc Wine£3.25 ⛿
Credit cards 1 2 3 4 5 6

★★★**Hilltop Motor** London Rd ☎29255
Telex no 64242
A modern hotel, built on a hill known as Gallows Hill, which was the site for public hanging during the Jacobite rebellion.
124rm(102⇌⋒) Lift ☽ 🍴 CTV CTV available in bedrooms 350P Live music & dancing Sat
Conference facilities available ☺ French.
Last dinner9.30pm ✿ ⊻ S% ✻sB&B£10.20
sB&B⇌⋒£14.50–£16.35 dB&B£16.20
dB&B⇌⋒£21.70–£24.20 Lunch fr£3.50&alc
Tea40p–£1.50 Dinner fr£4.32&alc Wine£2.50
⛿ *xmas* Credit cards 1 2 3 5 6

★★**Central** Victoria Viaduct (Greenall Whitley)
☎20256
Stands on old city walls.
84rm(20⇌⋒) Lift ☽ CTV in bedrooms 25🏠
Last dinner9pm ✿ ⊻ ✻sB&B£7.50
sB&B⇌⋒£9 dB&B£12.50 dB&B⇌⋒£14
Lunch fr£2.50 Tea fr£1.20 High Tea fr£2
Dinner fr£3.75 Wine£2.50 Credit cards 1 2 3

★***Vallum House*** Burgh Rd ☎21860
The hotel is at the west side of the city, leading to the Solway coast.
11rm 🍴 CTV 10P Last dinner9pm ✿ ⊻

Ⓟ**Pinegrove** 262 London Rd ☎24828
Closed Xmas & New Year; 9rm(2⇌⋒) CTV 30P 4🏠
⛟ ⚓ Last dinner8pm S% sB&B fr£5.40
sB&B⇌⋒ fr£6.20 dB&B fr£10.80
dB&B⇌⋒ fr£12.40 Bar lunch fr60p
Dinner fr£2.50 Wine£2.50 Credit card 2

Ⓟ**Royal** Lowther St ☎22103
A family and commercial hotel close to railway and bus stations.
Closed Xmas; Unlicensed; 24rm 🍴 CTV P Last High Tea7pm ✿ S% sB&B£6.50 dB&B£12
Lunch fr£1.25 High Tea£1.50–£2.50 ⛿

CARNFORTH Lancashire Map**7** SD47
★★***Royal Station*** ☎2033
9rm CTV 6P 6🏠 Live music Mon Last dinner9.30pm
✿ ⊻

CARTMEL Cumbria Map**7** SD37
★**Priory** The Square ☎267
Early Georgian, creeper-clad house in the centre of village.
Closed Nov–Mar; 9rm(1⇌⋒) 🍴 CTV 8P ⛟
☺ English & French. Last dinner8pm ✿ ⊻ S%
sB&B£6.50–£7.50 dB&B£13–£15
dB&B⇌⋒£15–£17 Lunch£3.25–£3.75
Tea30p–£1.20 Dinner£5–£6 Wine£2.30 ⛿

CASTERTON Cumbria Map**7** SD67
★**Pheasant Inn** ☎Kirkby Lonsdale 71230
Closed Xmas Day; 6rm 🍴 CTV TV available in bedrooms 60P ⚓ Last dinner9.15pm ✿ ⊻
sB&B£7 dB&B£14 Lunch fr£3.25&alc
Tea fr£1.25 High Tea fr£3.25 Dinner fr£5.50&alc
Wine£2.75 ⛿ Credit cards 1 2 3 4 5 6

CASTLE ASHBY Northamptonshire Map**4** SP85
✕✕**Falcon** ☎Yardley Hastings 200
Dinner not served Sun; 70seats 30P

C

bedrooms available ♀ English, French & Italian. Last dinner 9.30pm *Lunch £6.50alc Dinner £6.50alc Wine £2.90 Credit cards 1 2 3 5

CASTLE CARY Somerset Map **3** ST63
★★George ☎50761
Busy former coaching inn, dating from 13th century, in the centre of stone built village.
13rm(5⇌ 🚿) Annexe: 5⇌ 🚿 1🛏 CTV TV available in bedrooms 12P ♿ ♀ English & French. Last dinner 10.30pm S% *sB&B fr£12.50 sB&B⇌ 🚿 fr£14 dB&B fr£20 dB&B fr£23 Lunch £5.50alc Tea £1alc Dinner £9alc Wine £3.50 *xmas* Credit cards 1 2 3 4 5

★Northfield House ☎50697
Mature stone built two storey hotel in High Street.
7rm CTV 10P Last dinner 7.30pm S% sB&B £7–£7.50 dB&B £14–£15 Lunch £3–£3.50 Tea 60–80p Dinner £3–£3.50 Wine £2.50

CASTLE COMBE Wiltshire Map **3** ST87
★★★Manor House ☎782206 Telex no 44220
Originally a 14th-C baron's manor. The 26 acre grounds include parkland, lawns and Italian gardens.
14rm(12⇌ 🚿) Annexe: 20⇌ 🚿 2🛏 CTV in bedrooms 100P (heated) (hard) ♀ French. Last dinner 9.30pm *sB&B fr£11.25 sB&B⇌ 🚿 £16.50 dB&B £24 dB&B⇌ 🚿 £34–£36.50 Lunch £7alc Tea 50p alc Dinner £9.50alc Wine £2.95 *xmas* Credit cards 1 3 4 5

★Castle ☎782233
13th-C inn of Cotswold stone with mellow oak beams.
6rm(⇌ 🚿) TV ♀ English & French. Last dinner 9.30pm

CASTLE DONINGTON Leicestershire Map **8** SK42
★★Donington Manor ☎Derby 810253
Closed 27–30 Dec; 34rm(32⇌ 🚿) Annexe: 3rm(1⇌ 🚿) 2🛏 CTV CTV available in bedrooms 55p Live music & dancing Sat ♀ French Last dinner 9.15pm S% *sB&B⇌ 🚿 £12.50 dB&B £16.75 dB&B⇌ 🚿 £18.90 Credit cards 1 2 3 5

XXPriest House Inn Kings Mills ☎Derby 810649
80 seats 150P bedrooms available Disco Mon Live music & dancing Sat ♀ English & Continental. Last dinner 10pm S% *Lunch £3.30–£3.60 Dinner £5.50alc Wine £2.35 Credit cards 1 2 3 5

CASTLETON **Derbyshire** Map **7** SK18
★★Ye Olde Nag's Head ☎Hope Valley 20248
Formerly a 17th century coaching house, contains fine collection of period furniture.
10rm 1🛏 12P Last dinner 9pm Credit cards 1 2 5

CASTLETON North Yorkshire Map **8** NZ60
★Moorlands ☎206
Closed Nov–Mar; 9rm(6⇌ 🚿) CTV 9P Last dinner 8.30pm S% sB&B £7.25 dB&B⇌ 🚿 £14.50 Lunch £2.85&alc Dinner £4–£4.50&alc Wine £2.95

CAT & FIDDLE (MACCLESFIELD) Cheshire Map **7** SK07
XCat & Fiddle Inn ☎Buxton 3364
40 seats 100P ♀ English & French. Last dinner 10pm Credit cards 1 2 3

CATTERICK N Yorkshire Map **8** SE29
★★Bridge House Catterick Bridge (Embassy) ☎Richmond 818331
19rm(3⇌ 🚿) CTV TV available in bedrooms 50P

Last dinner9pm ♔ S% sB&B£10 dB&B£16 dB&B⇌⋒£18 Lunch£4.50&alc Dinner£4.50&alc Wine£4.50 ⊟ Credit cards ① ② ③ ④ ⑤ ⑥

ATWORTH Cambridgeshire Map**4** TL07
✕*Racehorse* ☎Bythorn262
0seats 70P Live music & dancing Mon–Sat English & French. Last dinner11pm

AULDON LOWE Staffordshire Map**8** SK04
✕✕Jean Pierre ☎Waterhouses338
Closed Sun & 25Dec–Feb; Lunch not served Sat; 5seats P French. Specialities: Coquilles St Jacques au gratin, Sot-l'y-laisses au Calvados, Coupe glacé au Grand Marnier. Last dinner9.15pm S% Lunch£4.50alc Dinner£8.50alc

AVENDISH Suffolk Map**5** TL84
✕✕*Alfonso* ☎Glemsford280372
Lunch not served Mon; Dinner not served Sun; 0seats 50P English, French, Italian, Russian & Swiss. Credit card ⑤

AWSAND Cornwall Map**2** SX45
★Criterion ☎Plymouth822244
Small hotel situated in heart of village, and commanding views of southern coastline.
Closed Nov–Mar; 8rm(2⇌⋒) CTV P Last dinner7.30pm ♔ ☕ ✻sB&B£8–£8.60 dB&B£15–£16 dB&B⇌⋒£17–£18.40 Bar lunch75p–£2.50 Tea25p–£1 Dinner£5 Wine£2.85

CHADLINGTON Oxfordshire Map**4** SP32
★Chadlington House ☎437
A gabled residence standing in its own grounds with views of the Even Lode Valley.
Closed Jan; 10rm(2⇌⋒) 1 CTV 20P 3 Last dinner8.30pm ♔ ☕ sB&B£7–£10 dB&B£13–£18 dB&B⇌⋒£16–£20 Lunch£1.50–£4 Tea90p Dinner£4–£6&alc Wine£2.60 ⊟ *xmas* Credit card ③

CHAGFORD Devon Map**3** SX78
★★★Great Tree Sandy Park (2m N on A382) ☎2491
19th century hunting lodge in 20 acres of grounds. Views of Dartmoor tors.
15⇌⋒ 25P Last dinner10pm ♔ ☕ sB&B⇌⋒£15–£20 (incl dinner) dB&B⇌⋒£30–£38.50 (incl dinner) Lunch£4 Tea25p–£1 Dinner£5.50&alc Wine£2.50 ⊟ *xmas* Credit cards ① ② ③ ⑤ ⑥

★★★Mill End Sandy Park (2m N on A382) ☎2282
Converted water mill with river running through grounds.
Closed Xmas wk; RS Nov–Mar (no lunch); 18rm(11⇌⋒) CTV 16P 4 Last dinner8.30pm ♔ ☕ S% sB£B£13 sB&B⇌⋒£15.50 dB&B£23.50 DB&B⇌⋒£30 Lunch£4.25 Tea£1.25 Dinner£6.75 Wine£3.50 ⊟ Credit cards ① ③

★★Greenacres ☎3471
12rm(4⇌⋒) CTV 16P Children under 6yrs not accommodated English & Continental. Last dinner8.45pm ♔ ☕ ✻sB&B£6.50–£7.80 dB&B£13–£15.60 dB&B⇌⋒£15–£18 Lunch£2.25–£30 Tea50–85p Dinner£3.75&alc Wine£2.25 ⊟ *xmas* Credit cards ① ③ ⑤

★★Moor Park Lower St ☎2202
A fine, stone built, two-storey house incorporating converted cottages, three acres of grounds.
18rm(4⇌⋒) CTV 40P English & French. Last dinner9pm ♔ ☕ S% sB&B£8.50–£9.50 dB&B£15–£17 dB&B⇌⋒£21–£23 Bar lunch65p–£3.50 Tea20–30p Dinner£4&alc Wine£2 ⊟ *xmas* Credit cards ① ⑥

★★**Three Crowns** ☎3444
13th century two-storey stone building, with mullioned windows and thatched roof.
10rm(2⇌⋒) 2▭ 🎹 CTV 6P Last dinner9pm ♉ ☖
✱sB&B£8.91 dB&B£17.82 dB&B⇌⋒£21.98
Lunch fr£3.50 Tea fr85p Dinner fr£4.50&alc
xmas Credit cards 1 2 3 5

★🏰**Easton Court** Easton Cross (1½m NE A382)
☎3469
A thatched 15th-C house, in rural setting.
8rm(5⇌⋒) 🎹 10P ♣ ⚓ Children under 12yrs not accommodated ♉ English & French.
Last dinner8.30pm sB&B£8.50–£13
sB&B⇌⋒£10–£14 dB&B£17–£26
dB&B⇌⋒£20–£28 Dinner£5–£6.50 Wine£3
♖ Credit card 2

❀✗✗**Gidleigh Park Hotel** ☎2225
Tudor style mansion set in its own grounds.
Lunch not served; 30seats 25P bedrooms available ♉ French. Last dinner9.30pm S% ✱Dinner£8
Wine£3.50

CHALFONT ST GILES Buckinghamshire Map**4** SU99
✗✗***Le Relais*** London Rd ☎2590
Closed Mon; Dinner not served Sun; 45seats
♉ French. Last dinner10.15pm

CHANDLER'S FORD Hampshire Map**4** SU41
✗✗***Kings Court*** 83 Winchester Rd ☎2232
Small cottage restaurant completely modernised with attractive but simple décor.
Closed Sun, Mon & New Year; 35seats 35P
♉ English & French. Last dinner9.30pm
Credit card 3

✗✗***Stairway*** Fryern Arcade ☎61444
Closed Sun & Mon; 45seats 80P ♉ French & Italian.
Last dinner10.30pm Credit cards 1 6

CHANNEL ISLANDS Details follow **England**

CHAPEL CLEEVE Somerset Map**3** ST04
★★★**Chapel Cleeve Manor** ☎Washford202
13rm(11⇌⋒) 🎹 CTV CTV in bedrooms 150P ♣ ⚓
🎾(hard) billiards Children under 5yrs not accommodated ♉ English & French.
Last dinner9.30pm ♉ ✱sB&B£11.29
sB&B⇌⋒£13.07 dB&B£20.20 dB&B⇌⋒£23.76
Lunch£3&alc Dinner£7alc Wine£3 ♖ *xmas*
Credit cards 1 2 3 5

CHARD Somerset Map**3** ST30
★★**George** Fore St ☎3413
Coaching inn dating from 16th century.
21rm(3⇌⋒) CTV TV available in bedrooms 100P
♉ English & French. Last dinner9pm ♉ S%
sB&B£8.50 sB&B£12 dB&B£12.50
dB&B⇌⋒£16 Lunch£2.50–£3.50&alc
Dinner fr£3.50&alc Wine£3 Credit cards 1 2 3

CHARING Kent Map**5** TQ94
✗✗**Ristorante Luigi** Charing Hill ☎2286
Closed Sun & Public Hols; 100seats 40P Live music & dancing Fri & Sat ♉ English, French & Italian.
Last dinner10.30pm ✱Lunch fr£3.25&alc
Dinner£6.25alc Wine£2.50 Credit cards 1 6

CHARLBURY Oxfordshire Map**4** SP31
★★***Bell*** Church St ☎278
14rm (6⇌⋒) 🎹 CTV ⊘ 30P ♣ ⚓ Children under 5yrs not accommodated ♉ English & French.
Last dinner9pm ♉ ☖

CHARLWOOD Surrey Map**4** TQ24
Hotels are listed under Gatwick Airport

CHARMOUTH Dorset Map**3** SY39
★★**Charmouth House** ☎60319 Telex no42839
Closed Oct–Mar; 12rm(2⇌⋒) CTV ⊘ 25P
⛱(heated) sauna bath Live music Sat
Last dinner8pm ♉ S% sB&B£9.35–£10.30
dB&B£18.70–£20.60 dB&B⇌⋒£20.30–£22.95
Bar lunch£1.05–£2.90 High Tea40p–£1
Dinner£4.40–£4.95&alc Wine£2 Credit cards 3 6

★★**Fernhill** ☎60492
Large house in 13 acres of grounds, adjacent to golf course and overlooking English Channel.
Closed Dec–Feb; 15rm(6⇌⋒) 🎹 CTV 50P ♣ ⚓
⛱(heated) squash ♧ Last dinner9pm ♉
sB&B£9.50–£13.50 sB&B⇌⋒£11–£15
dB&B£19–£27 dB&B⇌⋒£22–£30
Continental breakfast Bar lunch£1.60–£2
High Tea£2.15 Dinner£4.80–£5.20&alc
Wine£3.20 ♖

★★**Queen's Armes** The Street ☎60339
The hotel has relics and mementoes of historical interest, and has had such guests as Catherine of Aragon, Charles II and Edward VII.
Closed Nov–mid Mar; 14rm(3⇌⋒) 1▭ CTV 15P ♣
⚓ Last dinner8pm ♉ S% ✱sB&B£8.10–£9.20
dB&B£16.20–£18.40 dB&B⇌⋒£19.45–£21.65
Lunch£1.75alc Dinner£4.25 Wine£2.65

★**Sea Horse** Higher Sea Ln ☎60414
18th-C house standing in one acre, with secluded wall garden and views of sea and hills.
Closed Nov–Mar; 10rm Annexe:6rm 🎹 CTV 17P ♣
⚓ ♧ Last dinner7.45pm ♉ ☖ S%
sB&B£6.50–£7.50 dB&B£13–£15 Bar lunch fr60p
Tea fr45p Dinner£3.50 Wine£2.20 ♖

CHARNOCK RICHARD (M6 Motorway Service Area)
Lancashire Map**7** SD51
☆☆☆**TraveLodge** Mill Ln (Trusthouse Forte)
☎Coppull791746
Restaurant situated in adjacent service area (mainly grills).
108⇌⋒ ☽ 🎹 CTV in bedrooms 120P ♣ ♿ S%
sB&B⇌⋒£14 dB&B⇌⋒£17.50
Continental breakfast ♖ Credit cards 1 2 3 4 5 6

CHEADLE HULME Gt Manchester Map**7** SJ88
✗**Cheshire Tandoori** 9 The Precinct
☎061–485 4942
Closed Sun; 45seats P ♉ Indian. Last dinner11pm
✱Lunch£4.80alc Dinner£4.80alc Wine£3.45
Credit cards 1 2 3 5

CHEAM Gt London Map**4** TQ26
✗**Trattoria i Faraglioni** 33/37 Malden Rd
☎01–644 7873
Closed Sun & Xmas; 60seats 10P ♉ Italian.
Last dinner11pm ✱Lunch£6alc Dinner£6alc
Wine£3 Credit cards 2 3 5

CHELMSFORD Essex Map**5** TL70
★★**County** Rainsford Rd ☎66911 Telex no995430
32rm(24⇌⋒) Annexe:18rm ☽ 🎹 CTV 70P ♉ English & French. Last dinner8.15pm ♉ ☖ S%
sB&B£9.25 sB&B⇌⋒£13 dB&B£18
dB&B⇌⋒£20 Continental breakfast
Lunch£3.90&alc Dinner£4.50&alc Wine£3.20
Credit cards 1 2 3 6

★★**South Lodge** 196 New London Rd ☎64564
Telex no99452
17⇌⋒ Annexe:16⇌⋒ ☽ 🎹 CTV in bedrooms 45P
♉ English & French. Last dinner9.30pm ♉ ☖
S% ✱sB&B⇌⋒£21.21 dB&B⇌⋒£29.78
Lunch£4.25–£4.60&alc Tea75p–£1.50
Dinner£4.60&alc Wine£2.80
Credit cards 1 2 3 4 5 6

✗**Sole Mio** 11–15 Baddow Rd ☎50759
Closed Sun & Public Hols; 50seats 6P ♉ English & Italian. Last dinner9.30pm ✱Lunch£3.10&alc
Dinner£6alc Wine£2.75 1 2 3 5 6

CHELTENHAM Gloucestershire Map**3** SO92
See also Cleeve Hill
☆☆☆☆**Golden Valley** Gloucester Rd (Thistle)
☎32691 Telex no43410
103⇌⋒ Lift ☽ 🎹 CTV in bedrooms 300P ⚓ Live

Sole Mio Italian Restaurant

Chelmsford's West End Restaurant

11 Baddow Road, Chelmsford
Tel: (0245) 50759

Situated in the centre of Chelmsford, the Sole Mio has been owned and managed by Signor Amerigo Soldani, who by his insistence on quality and value for money has given the restaurant a fine reputation for the best Italian food. In fact it has brought West End cuisine to the country town. Both à la carte and table d'hôte menus are available and the business lunch is especially recommended.
Seating about 100 persons, the dining room of the restaurant is bright and gay. The Sole Mio has a supper licence, and its wine list includes some of the finest Italian wines available. The restaurant is closed on Sundays and Bank Holidays. Music and dancing.

South Lodge Hotel

Chelmsford's Premier Hotel

196 New London Road
Chelmsford CM2 0AR Essex.
Tel: Chelmsford (STD 0245) 64564
Telex: Lodge Chelmsford 99452

South Lodge enjoys an ideal location mid way between the business centre of Chelmsford and the main A12 London-East Coast route, thus it suits the visiting business man and the family en route.
Accommodation includes double, single and family rooms all with bathrooms en suite. All rooms have telephone and TV. The fully-licensed restaurant which has an international-style menu has a sun lounge annexe opening on to the patio and lawn thus providing the perfect setting for weddings. Conference facilities are available with ample car parking.

C

C

music & dancing wkly in winter Conference facilities available English & French. Last dinner10pm S% sB&B £23.90 dB&B £33.80 Lunch£4.30&alc Dinner£5.40&alc Wine£3 *xmas* Credit cards 1 2 3 4 5

★★★★Queen's The Promenade (Trusthouse Forte) 514724 Telex no43381
76 Lift CTV in bedrooms 32P Conference facilities available Last dinner10.30pm S% sB&B £22.50 dB&B £36 *xmas* Credit cards 1 2 3 4 5 6

★★★De La Bere Southam (3m NE A46) 37771
22 5 CTV in bedrooms P (heated) squash sauna bath Disco Thu & Sat Live music & dancing Fri & Sat English & French. Last dinner9.45pm S% sB&B £14–£20 sB&B £28–£36 Lunch£3.75–£4 Dinner£7alc Wine£3.50 *xmas* Credit cards 1 2 3 4 5 6

★★★Carlton Parabola Rd 514453
49 Lift CTV in bedrooms 17P Live music & dancing Sat in winter Conference facilities available English & French. Last dinner9pm S% *sB&B fr£16.20 dB&B £25.92 Lunch fr£4.35 Dinner fr£5.40 Wine£3 *xmas* Credit cards 1 3

★★★Lilley Brook Cirencester Rd, Charlton Kings 25861
Former 19th-C mansion standing in nine acres of parkland.
30 CTV TV available in bedrooms 200P 4 18 Live music & dancing Sun & Wed Last dinner9.30pm S% *sB&B £17 sB&B £25 Lunch£4–£4.50&alc Tea50p–£1.50 Dinner£5.50–£6.50&alc Wine£3.50 *xmas* Credit cards 1 2 3 5

★★★Wyastone Parabola Rd 45549
6 CTV in bedrooms 6P French. Last dinner10pm S% sB&B £18 dB&B £26 Lunch£3–£4&alc Tea£1.50&alc Dinner£4–£5&alc Wine£3 *xmas* Credit cards 1 2 3 5

★★★Savoy Bayshill Rd (Best Western) 27788
Regency building with a façade and entrance porch of Corinthian columns, situated in a corner site on a quiet street.
57rm(29) Lift CTV TV available in bedrooms 20P 2 sauna bath Mainly grills. Last dinner9pm S% sB&B fr£14.50 sB&B fr£16 dB&B fr£22 dB&B fr£25 Lunch fr£4 Dinner fr£6.50 Wine£3.50 *xmas* Credit cards 1 2 3 4 5 6

★★George St George's Rd (Trusthouse Forte) 35751
42rm(7) CTV TV in bedrooms 12P Last dinner9.15pm S% sB&B£12 sB&B £15.50 dB&B£19.50 dB&B £22 *xmas* Credit cards 1 2 3 4 5 6

★★Greenway Shurdington Rd 862352
13 1 CTV CTV in bedrooms 50P 4 English & French. Last dinner9.30pm S% *sB&B £16.20–£18.36 dB&B £25.92–£28.08 Lunch£3.50&alc Tea50p Dinner£4.50&alc Wine£3.50 *xmas* Credit card 3

★★Lansdown Lansdown Rd (Wessex Taverns) 22700
Regency building occupying corner position on main road.
13rm(1) CTV 40P Mainly grills. Last dinner9pm Credit cards 1 2 3 4 5 6

★★Park Place Park Place 25353
48rm(4) Lift CTV CTV available in bedrooms 40P Last dinner9.30pm sB&B£8.80 sB&B £10.45 dB&B£12.10 dB&B £13.75 Lunch£2.75 Tea75p High Tea fr£1.50 Dinner fr£3.50 Wine£2.05 *xmas* Credit cards 1 2 3 5

★★Prestbury House The Burbage, Prestbury (2m NE A46) 29533
Quietly situated converted Georgian manor.
RS Sun eve; 10rm(8) CTV 20P Last dinner9pm *sB&B fr£10 Lunch fr£4.50 Dinner fr£4.75&alc Wine£3.75

★Overton St George's Rd 23371
Closed Xmas; 15rm(2) CTV 21P 2 Disco Wed–Fri Live music Mon English, French & Italian. Last dinner8pm

★Royal Ascot Western Rd 513640
10rm(1) CTV 25P English & Italian. Last dinner8.30pm S% sB&B£6.65–£7 dB&B£13.30–£14 dB&B £14.90–£15.65 Lunch£2.50–£2.90 Dinner£3–£3.25&alc Wine£2.30 Credit card 3

XXBlack Tulip 99 Promenade 41234
Dinner not served Sun; 50seats 6P English & Continental. Last dinner11pm S% Credit cards 1 2 3 5 6

XFood for Thought 10 Grosvenor St 29836
Closed Sun, Mon, 1wk Xmas & 2wks late Sep; 20seats English & French. Last dinner 9pm Dinner fr£8.10 Wine£3.78

CHENIES Buckinghamshire Map**4** TQ99

★★★Bedford Arms (Thistle) Chorleywood3301
Pleasant old inn in small village.
10 1 CTV CTV available in bedrooms 60P International. Last dinner10pm S% sB&B £22.50–£23.90 dB&B £32–£34.80 Lunch£5–£10 Dinner£10–£20 Wine£3.80 Credit cards 1 2 3 4 5 6

CHERTSEY Surrey Map**4** TQ06
★**Bridge** Bridge Rd ☎63175
rm CTV 60P Disco wkly French.
Last dinner10pm S% ✻sB&B£12.15
dB&B£14.58 Lunch£5alc Dinner£5alc
Wine£1.45 Credit cards 3 5

CHESTER Cheshire Map**7** SJ46
★★★★**Grosvenor** Eastgate St (Prestige) ☎24024
See page 39 for details
☆☆☆**Abbots Well Motor Inn** Whitchurch Rd, Christleton ☎32121 Telex no61561
140⇌ ⫙ CTV in bedrooms 200P
Conference facilities available English & French.
Last dinner10pm S% ✻sB&B⇌£19.40
dB&B⇌£31.30 Lunch fr£4.95&alc
Dinner£10alc Wine£5.20 Credit cards 1 2 3 5
★★★**Blossoms** St John Street ☎23186
Telex no67415
78rm(56⇌) Lift CTV CTV in bedrooms
Conference facilities available Last dinner9.30pm
sB&B£13–£18 sB&B⇌£16–£21
dB&B£25–£33 dB&B⇌£28–£36
Lunch£3.50 £4.50 Dinner£5–£6 Wine£2.50
Credit cards 1 2 3 5
★★★**Mollington Banastre** Parkgate Rd (A540) (Best Western) ☎Great Mollington851471
Mid-Victorian mansion in 8½ acres of grounds.
52rm(45⇌) 3 Lift CTV TV in bedrooms
200P sauna bath Conference facilities available
English & French. Last dinner9.30pm
S% ✻sB&B£19.60 sB&B⇌£19.60
dB&B£27.50 dB&B⇌£28.50 Lunch£7alc
Tea£1alc Dinner£8alc Wine£4.25
Credit cards 1 2 5
☆☆☆**Post House** Wrexham Rd (Trusthouse Forte)
☎674111 Telex no61450
56⇌ CTV in bedrooms 200P Conference facilities available Last dinner9.45pm S%
sB&B⇌£19.25 dB&B⇌£27
xmas Credit cards 1 2 3 4 5 6
★★★**Queen** City Rd (Trusthouse Forte) ☎28341
Telex no617101
A mid-Victorian building adjacent to railway station and near town centre.
91⇌ Lift TV in bedrooms 130P
Last dinner9.15pm S% sB&B⇌£18.50
dB&B⇌£26.50 *xmas*
Credit cards 1 2 3 4 5 6
★★**Oaklands** Hoole Rd (Scottish & Newcastle)
☎22156
20rm(3⇌) CTV 50P English & French.
Last dinner9.30pm S% sB&B£9
sB&B⇌£10.50 dB&B£15.50 dB&B⇌£16
Lunch£2.75&alc Dinner£2.75&alc Wine£2.80
Credit cards 1 2 3 4 5 6
★**Dene** Hoole Rd ☎21165
40rm CTV 75P Last dinner8pm
sB&B£7.02–£8.10 dB&B£13.50–£14.58
Lunch fr£2.50 Dinner fr£2.50 Wine£2.80
★**Ye Olde Kings Head** 48–50 Lower Bridge St (Greenall Whitley) ☎24855
11rm CTV TV available in bedrooms 9
Last dinner8.45pm ✻sB&B£11.75 dB&B£16
Lunch fr£2.75&alc Dinner fr£3.75&alc Wine£2.25
Credit cards 1 2 3 5
✕✕**Courtyard** St Werburgh Street ☎21447
Closed Sun & Public Hols; 120seats English & French. Last dinner10pm ✻Lunch£1–£2&alc
Dinner£4.50£alc Wine£3.50
Credit cards 1 2 3 5 6

At **Backford Cross** (5m W on A41)
☆☆☆**Wirral Ladbroke Mercury Motor Inn**
Roundabout A41/A5117 (Ladbroke)
☎Great Mollington851551
122⇌ 122P

CHESTERFIELD Derbyshire Map**8** SK37
★★★***Station*** Corporation St ☎71141
67rm(52⇌) Lift CTV 50P 10
Last dinner10pm Wine£2.25 Credit card 1
★★**Portland** West Bars (Anchor) ☎34502
Telex no858875
Closed 26Dec; RS 24 & 25Dec (no accommodation)
22rm(11⇌) CTV in bedrooms 29P Mainly grills. Last dinner9pm S% ✻sB&B fr£10.85
sB&B⇌ fr£14.50 dB&B fr£17.50 dB&B fr£20
Lunch fr£2.50&alc Dinner fr£3&alc Wine£2.65
Credit cards 1 2 3 4 5 6

CHESTER-LE-STREET Co Durham Map**12** NZ25
★★★**Lumley Castle** Lumley Castle ☎885326
50⇌ 4 CTV in bedrooms 200P
(heated) sauna bath French. Last dinner10pm
S% sB&B⇌£14.50–£37
dB&B⇌£22–£45 Lunch£2.95–£4&alc Tea£2
Dinner£4.50–£5&alc Wine£2.70 *xmas*
Credit cards 1 2 3 5 6
★★***Lambton Arms*** Front St (Scottish & Newcastle)
☎883265
10rm CTV 40P Live music Sun Last dinner9pm
Credit cards 1 2 3 5

CHESTERTON Oxfordshire Map**4** SP52
✕**Kinchs** ☎Bicester41444
(Rosette awarded for dinner only)
Closed Mon & 1–8Jan; Lunch served Sun only; Dinner not served Sun; 40seats 25P International.
Last dinner9.45pm ✻Lunch£5.75 Dinner£7.20
Wine£3.30 Credit cards 1 2 3 5

CHICHESTER West Sussex Map**4** SU80
★★★**Chichester Lodge** Westhampnett ☎786351
Wood faced, two storey motel (built 1964), linked to stone-faced White Swan Inn by covered walk.

34⇌ ⋒ ☽ ⋒ CTV in bedrooms 100P 10⋒ ⚓ Disco twice wkly ♡French. Last dinner9.30pm ♡ ♡ S% ✱sB&B⇌⋒£15.75 dB&B⇌⋒£21.50 Lunch fr£3.75 Tea£1.25alc Dinner fr£4.50 Wine£2.75 ⋒ *xmas* Credit cards ① ② ③ ⑥

★★★**Dolphin & Anchor** West St (Trusthouse Forte) ☎785121
Building combining two ancient inns, standing opposite the Cathedral and the 15th-C market cross.
54⇌ ⋒ ☽ ⋒ TV in bedrooms 16⋒ Conference facilities available Last dinner10.30pm ♡ ♡ S% sB&B£14.50 sB&B⇌⋒£16 dB&B⇌⋒£22 ⋒ *xmas* Credit cards ① ② ③ ④ ⑤ ⑥

✕✕**Christopher's** 149 St Pancras ☎788724
Closed Sun; Lunch not served Mon; Dinner not served Mon (Sep–May); 39seats P ♡English & French. Last dinner10pm S% ✱Lunch£3–£4&alc Dinner£6.50–£8&alc Wine£2.50
Credit cards ① ② ③ ⑤

CHIDDINGFOLD Surrey Map**4** SU93
✕✕✕**Crown Inn** ☎Wormley2255
Built in 1285, this restaurant is a well-preserved half timbered building. Edward VI is said to have slept here in 1552.
Closed Mon & Tue except Public Hols; 40seats 15P bedrooms available ♡English & Continental. Last dinner9.30pm S% ✱Lunch£7.50alc Dinner£9alc Wine£3.60 Credit cards ② ⑤

CHIDDINGSTONE Kent Map**5** TQ44
✕***Castle Inn*** ☎Penshurst247
Tile-hung building in National Trust village.
Closed Tue & Jan; Lunch not served Wed; 35seats Last dinner9.30pm Credit cards ① ② ⑤

CHIDEOCK Dorset Map**3** SY49
★**Clock House** ☎423
3rm Annexe:3rm(1⇌⋒) CTV 40P ⋒ ⚓ squash Last dinner9.30pm ♡ S% sB&B£6.50–£7.50 sB&B⇌⋒£7–£8 dB&B£13–£15 dB&B⇌⋒£15–£17 Lunch£2–£4 Dinner£4.50–£11&alc Wine£2.10
Credit cards ① ③

CHILGROVE West Sussex Map**4** SU81
❀✕✕**White Horse Inn** ☎East Marden219
A comfortable old country inn, famous for its wine list of 1,500–2,000 wines.
Closed Sun, Mon & Feb; 50seats 200P ♡English & French. Specialities: prawns-cheval blanc, woodcock in cognac, home made ice creams.
Last dinner9.15pm ✱Lunch£3.95&alc Dinner£7.50alc Wine£3.65
Credit cards ① ② ③ ⑤ ⑥

CHILHAM Kent Map**5** TR05
✕***Woolpack Inn*** Main St ☎208
15th-C inn situated in attractive village.
Closed Mon; Dinner not served Sun; 40seats 12P Last dinner8.30pm

CHILLINGTON Devon Map**3** SX74
★**Oddicombe House** ☎Frogmore234
Standing in three acres of grounds with views of the surrounding countryside.
12rm(8⇌⋒) ⋒ CTV 25P ⋒ ⚓ Last dinner9.30pm ♡ ♡ S% sB&B£7.50–£9 sB&B⇌⋒£8.50–£10 dB&B£14.50–£17 dB&B⇌⋒£16–£18.50 Bar lunch£2.25alc Tea80p Dinner£6.50alc Wine£2.40 ⋒
Credit cards ① ③ ⑥

CHIPPENHAM Wiltshire Map**3** ST97
★★**Angel** Market Place (Norfolk Capital) ☎2615 Telex no23241
Modern motel units with wood façade behind 18th-C hotel building.
10rm Annexe:41⇌⋒ ☽ ⋒ TV available in bedrooms 60P Last dinner9.45pm S% sB&B£10.85 sB&B⇌⋒£14.65 dB&B£18.45 dB&B⇌⋒£22.25 Lunch£3.50alc Dinner£4alc Wine£4 ⋒
Credit cards ① ② ③ ⑤ ⑥

★★**Bear** 11 Market Place ☎3272
9rm(2⇌⋒) CTV 12P 5⋒ Last dinner9pm ♡ sB&B£9 sB&B⇌⋒£11 dB&B£18 Lunch£3.50–£5 Dinner£6alc Wine£4
Credit cards ① ③

CHIPPING CAMPDEN Gloucestershire Map**4** SP13
★★**Cotswold House** The Square ☎Evesham840330
18rm(11⇌⋒) Annexe:7rm ⋒ CTV TV available in bedrooms 15P 6⋒ ⋒ ⚓ Children under 6yrs not accommodated ♡English & French.
Last dinner8.30pm ♡ ♡ S%
sB&B£12.20–£13.40 sB&B⇌⋒£15.60–£25.40 dB&B£23.20–£25.50 dB&B⇌⋒£27.50–£30.25 Continental breakfast Lunch£5.45–£6 Tea45p–£1 Dinner£5.70–£6.30 Wine£3.20 ⋒ *xmas* Credit cards ① ⑥

❀★★**King's Arms** The Square ☎Evesham840256
(*Rosette awarded for dinner only*)
Closed Sun eve to Tue eve Nov–Mar; 14rm(2⇌⋒) TV available in bedrooms 6P ♡French. Specialities: assiette crudités, chicken livers in orange & brandy, rack of lamb. Last dinner9.30pm ♡ sB&B£8–£12 dB&B£16–£26 dB&B⇌⋒£20–£30 Bar lunch£3.60alc Tea30–60p Dinner£6–£7 Wine£2.40 ⋒ *xmas* Credit cards ① ② ③ ⑤

★★**Noel Arms** ☎Evesham840317
14th-C inn with open courtyard and bowling green.
21rm(8⇌⋒) 2⋒ ⋒ CTV ⋒ 30P 6⋒ Last dinner9pm ♡ sB&B£11.34 sB&B⇌⋒£12.96 dB&B£21.06

dB&B⇌ fl £24.84 Lunch£3.50 Dinner£4.50 Wine£3 ⊟ *xmas*

CHIPPING NORTON Oxfordshire Map**4** SP32
★★**Crown & Cushion** High St ☎2533
12rm(6⇌ fl) CTV TV available in bedrooms 20P 5 Children under 14yrs not accommodated English & French. Last dinner9pm S% *sB&B£8.50 sB&B⇌ fl £12.50 dB&B£17 dB&B⇌ fl £25 Bar lunch£2.50alc Dinner£6–£8alc Wine£3.70 *xmas* Credit cards 2 6

★★**White Hart** High St (Trusthouse Forte) ☎2572
The 18th-C façade of this inn belies its 14th-C origins.
22rm(6⇌ fl) 1 CTV TV in bedrooms 16P Last dinner9.15pm S% sB&B£11 sB&B⇌ fl £14.50 dB&B£16.50 dB&B⇌ fl £20.50 ⊟ Credit cards 1 2 3 4 5 6

CHIPPING SODBURY Avon Map**3** ST78
✕***Le Cordon Bleu*** 66 Rounceval St ☎318041
Closed Sun; 90seats 25P English, French & Italian. Last dinner11pm Credit cards 3 5

CHOBHAM Surrey Map**4** SU96
✕**Four Seasons** 14–22 High St ☎7238
80seats 10P French, Italian & Spanish. Last dinner10pm Lunch£10alc Dinner£10alc Wine£2.60 Credit cards 1 2 3 5

CHOLLERFORD Northumberland Map**12** NY97
★★★**George** Humshaugh (Swallow) ☎Humshaugh205 Telex no53168
54⇌ fl CTV TV in bedrooms 100P Last dinner10.30pm S% sB&B⇌ fl £12.65–£17.30 dB&B⇌ fl £20.35–£26.60 ⊟ *xmas* Credit cards 1 2 3 5

CHRISTCHURCH Dorset Map**4** SZ19
For hotel locations and additional hotels see **Bournemouth**
★★★**Avonmouth** Mudeford (2m E off B3059) (Trusthouse Forte) ☎483434 Bournemouth district plan**61**
34rm(23⇌ fl) Annexe: 14⇌ fl TV in bedrooms 66P (heated) Last dinner8.45pm S% sB&B£15 sB&B⇌ fl £17 dB&B£23 dB&B⇌ fl £29.50 ⊟ *xmas* Credit cards 1 2 3 4 5 6

★★★**King's Arms** Castle St (Crest) ☎484117 Bournemouth district plan**70**
34rm(24⇌ fl) Lift CTV in bedrooms 80P Last dinner10pm S% *sB&B£10.80 sB&B⇌ fl £15.12 dB&B£19.98 dB&B⇌ fl £25.92 ⊟ *xmas* Credit cards 1 2 3 4 5 6

★★**Waterford Lodge** Friars Cliff, Mudeford (2m E off B3059) ☎Highcliffe72948 Bournemouth district plan**83**
Closed 19Oct–9May; Unlicensed; 18rm(4⇌ fl) CTV 20P Children under 7yrs not accommodated Last dinner7.15pm *sB&B£9.25 sB&B⇌ fl £10.25 dB&B£18.50 dB&B⇌ fl £20.50 Lunch£2.50 Tea70p Dinner£4

Somerford Somerford ☎485376 Bournemouth district plan**77**
7rm 1 CTV TV available in bedrooms 100P Last dinner9.30pm Credit cards 1 2 3 4 5 6

✕**Splinters** 12 Church St ☎483454 Bournemouth district plan**79**
Closed Sun; 36seats French. Specialities: sole barfleur, filet de porc basquaise, tournedos perigourdine. Last dinner10.30pm *Dinner£5alc Wine£3.30

CHUDLEIGH Decon Map**3** SX87
✕***Highwayman's Haunt*** Old Exeter Rd ☎853250
50seats Last dinner9.30pm

C

CHURCH STRETTON Salop Map**7** SO49
During the currency of this publication Church Stretton numbers are liable to change.

★★★Long Mynd Cunnery Rd ☎2244
Four-storey building with stone terraces; 24 acres of high, wooded grounds.
50rm(20⇌ ⋔) CTV TV available in bedrooms 100P 4 (heated) sauna bath English & French. Last dinner9.30pm
✱sB&B fr£9.68 sB&B⇌ ⋔ fr£11.64 dB&B fr£14.85 dB&B⇌ ⋔ fr£17.23 Lunch fr£2.50&alc Tea fr£1 Dinner fr£3.50&alc Wine£3.35 xmas Credit cards ① ② ③ ⑤

★★Stretton Hall All Stretton ☎3224
12rm(5⇌ ⋔) CTV 60P (heated) International. Last dinner9pm
sB&B£17.25 sB&B⇌ ⋔ £24 sB&B£28.80 dB&B⇌ ⋔ £35.95 Lunch£5.35–£7.20&alc Tea£1.55–£2 High Tea£2.40–£3.50&alc Dinner£8.25–£10.25&alc xmas Credit cards ③ ⑤

★Sandford Watling Street South ☎2131
25rm(2⇌ ⋔) CTV CTV available in bedrooms 40P Last dinner8pm sB&B£7–£10 dB&B£12–£16 dB&B⇌ ⋔ £14–£20 Lunch fr£2.50 Tea75p–£1.25 Dinner£3.25–£3.75 Wine£2

CHURSTON FERRERS Devon Map**3** SX95
★★★*Broadsands Links* Bascombe Rd ☎Churston842360
Quietly situated, close to golf course, with views of Torbay.
24⇌ ⋔ CTV 35P (hard) Last dinner8.30pm Credit cards ① ② ③ ⑤ ⑥

CHURT Surrey Map**4** SU83
★★★Frensham Pond (Best Western) ☎Frensham3175 Telex no858610

Two storey building off A287 overlooking the historic Great Pond between Fanham and Hindhead.
7⇌ Annexe: 12⇌ CTV in bedrooms 150P Live music & dancing Sat English & Continental. Last dinner 9.45pm S% sB&B⇌£18.36 dB&B⇌£29.65 Lunch£4.50&alc Dinner£9.18alc *xmas* Credit cards 1 2 3 5

★★Pride of the Valley Inn (Trusthouse Forte) Hindhead 5799
11rm(5⇌) TV in bedrooms 50P Last dinner 10pm S% sB&B£11 dB&B£17.50 dB&B⇌£20.50 *xmas* Credit cards 1 2 3 4 5 6

CIRENCESTER Gloucestershire Map **4** SP00

★★★★King's Head Market Pl (Best Western) 3322 Telex no 43470
14th-C coaching inn with elegant 18th-C frontage, with interesting prints and tapestry-hung interior. Traditional restaurant with original paintings.
73rm(66⇌) 2 Lift CTV in bedrooms 35P Live music & dancing Sat (winter) Conference facilities available Last dinner 10pm sB&B£14.75–£16.50 sB&B⇌£17.75–£19.25 dB&B£28.50 dB&B⇌£32 Lunch fr£5&alc Dinner fr£6.50&alc Wine£4.50 *xmas* Credit cards 1 2 3 4 5 6

★★★Stratton House Gloucester Rd (A417) 61761
31rm(18⇌) CTV CTV available in bedrooms 100P 2 English & French. Last dinner 9.45pm S% sB&B£11.50 sB&B⇌£13 dB&B£23 dB&B⇌£26 Lunch£4.50–£4.75&alc Tea fr70p Dinner£5.50–£6.50&alc Wine£3.25 *xmas* Credit cards 1 2 3 5 6

★★Corinium Court Gloucester St 4499
Closed Xmas; 9rm(5⇌ CTV 50P Last dinner 9.45pm S% *sB&B fr£8.50 sB&B fr£11 dB&B fr£15 dB&B⇌fr£20 Bar lunch £1.50alc Dinner£6alc Wine£3.50 Credit cards 1 2 3 5

★★Fleece Market Pl (Trusthouse Forte) 2680
23rm(6⇌) TV in bedrooms 35P 5 Last dinner 10pm S% sB&B£12 sB&B⇌£14.50 dB&B£18.50 dB&B⇌£21 *xmas* Credit cards 1 2 3 4 5 6

CLACTON-ON-SEA Essex Map **5** TM11

★★Kings Cliff King's Parade, Holland-on-Sea 812343
13rm(1⇌) CTV 100P Last dinner 8pm sB&B£7.50 dB&B£15 dB&B⇌£18 Lunch£2.50–£3&alc Dinner£2.70–£3&alc Wine£2.50

★★*Royal* Marine Pde 21215
Victorian building with modern interior, overlooking sea.
47rm(9⇌) Lift CTV 20P 20 English & French. Last dinner 9pm

CLANFIELD Oxfordshire Map **4** SP20

★★Plough 222
Gabled, three-storey, 16th-C stone building, originally a sub manor house of Clanfield.
6rm(1⇌) 1 CTV 40P Children under 7yrs not accommodated English & Continental. Last dinner 10pm *sB&B fr£15 dB&B⇌fr£17 dB&B fr£25 dB&B⇌fr£27 Lunch fr£5.50 Dinner fr£8.50&alc Wine£3.75 Credit card 2

CLAPHAM North Yorkshire Map **7** SD76

X*Goat Gap* Ingleton 41230
Closed Mon; 30 seats 12P Last dinner 9.45pm Credit card 3

CLARE Suffolk Map **5** TL74

★★Bell 7741
Formerly a coaching inn dating from 16th-C with oak beams. Situated in centre of village.
21rm(13⇌ 4 CTV TV available in bedrooms

16P Lastdinner9.30pm sB&B£14 sB&B⇌ £16.50 dB&B£20 dB&B⇌ £25 Lunchfr£4 Tea£1.50alc Dinner£5&alc Wine£3.80 Creditcards 1 2 3 5

C

CLAUGHTON Lancashire Map**7** SD56
XXOld Rectory (A683) ☎Hornby21455
Closed 1wk Spring, Summer & Autumn Dinner not served Sun & Mon 38seats 25P bedrooms available Lastdinner9pm Lunch£4 Dinner£5–£8 Wine£2.60

CLAVERLEY Salop Map**7** SO79
XRafters ☎346
Closed Sun Lunch not served 60seats 40P Mainly grills Lastdinner9.30pm *Dinner£5.50–£7&alc Wine£2.60 Creditcards 1 3

CLAWTON Devon Map**2** SX39
★★Court Barn ☎North Tamerton219
Early Victorian country house standing in its own grounds.
Closed Nov–28Mar 8rm(3⇌) CTV 10P Lastdinner7.30pm S% dB&B£26–£30 dB&B⇌ £32–£36 Barlunch£2 Dinner£7.50–£9 Wine£3

CLAYTON-LE-WOODS Lancashire Map**7** SD52
★★Pines ☎Preston (Lancs)38551
Closed Xmas 20rm(16⇌) CTV CTV in bedrooms 120P squash Disco Fri English & French. Lastdinner9.30pm sB&Bfr£10.98 sB&B⇌ £12.17–£21.38 dB&Bfr£18.41 dB&B⇌ £20.79–£28.81 Continental breakfast Lunchfr£3.26&alc Dinner£4.87–£6.54&alc Wine£2.55 Creditcards 1 2 3 5

CLEARWELL Gloucestershire Map**3** SO50
XWyndham Arms ☎Coleford3666
Closed Mon 50 seats 30P bedrooms available International Lastdinner10pm S% Lunch£2.25&alc Dinner£8alc Wine£2.60 Creditcards 1 2 6

CLEETHORPES Humberside Map**8** TA30
★★★Kingsway Promenade ☎62836
58rm(45⇌) Lift CTV in bedrooms 30P 20 English & French. Lastdinner9pm S% sB&B£15.50 sB&B⇌ £18.50 dB&B£23.50 dB&B⇌ £27 Lunch£5 Dinner£7 Wine£2.95 *xmas* Creditcards 1 2 3 5

CLEEVE HILL Gloucestershire Map**3** SO92
XXXMalvern View ☎Bishops Cleeve2017
Small hotel set on hillside above Cheltenham. Overlooks Severn Vale and Malvern Hills.
Closed Sun & 3wks Xmas Lunch not served 45seats 20P bedrooms available English & French. Specialities: smoked trout paté, carre d'agneau en croute, quails with black cherries. Lastdinner9.30pm S% Dinner£7.50&alc Wine£4.50 Creditcard 2

CLEOBURY MORTIMER Salop Map**7** SO67
★★Old Lion Inn ☎395
8rm(2⇌) CTV CTV available in bedroom 30P 2 English & French. Lastdinner9.30pm S% sB&B£9.25–£10 sB&B⇌ £12.25–£13 dB&B£16–£16.50 dB&B⇌ £19–23 Barlunch£1–£1.50 Teafr75p Dinnerfr£4.50 Wine£2.80 Creditcards 2 3 5

CLEVEDON Avon Map**3** ST47
★★★Walton Park Wellington Ter ☎874253
Stands in four acres of cliffside gardens overlooking the Bristol Channel.
36rm(16⇌) Lift CTV CTV available in bedrooms 50P 30 Lastdinner8.30pm *sB&Bfr£11.20 sB&B⇌ fr£12.80

B&B fr£19.20 dB&B⇌ fr£21.30 Lunch fr£3.10 ea fr45p Dinner fr£4.95 Wine£2.45 *xmas* redit cards 1 3

★*Highcliffe* Wellington Ter ☎873250
quiet residential area with good views across evern estuary.
9rm(9⇌) CTV 20P English & Continental. ast dinner9pm *xmas* Credit cards 1 3

CLIFTONVILLE Kent see **MARGATE**

CLIMPING West Sussex Map**4** TQ00
★★★ **Bailiffscourt** ☎Littlehampton3952
udor style building reconstructed in the 1930s, with othic archways and courtyards.
Closed Jan–Mar; 23⇌ Annexe:8⇌ 7 CTV in bedrooms P 4 (heated) (hard) Live music & dancing Sat Last dinner9.30pm Credit cards 1 2 3 5 6

CLITHEROE Lancashire Map**7** SD74
★★*Roefield* Edisford Bridge ☎22010
22⇌ 4 CTV 40P sauna bath
Last dinner9pm Credit cards 1 2 3 5

CLOVELLY Devon Map**2** SS32
★**New Inn** ☎303
4rm Annexe: 10rm(3⇌) CTV 12P
Last dinner8.15pm S% ✱sB&B£6.50 dB&B£13 dB&B⇌£15 Lunch£2.50 Tea95p Dinner£4alc Wine£2.50 Credit cards 1 3

★**Red Lion** ☎237
RS Nov–Mar; 10rm TV 20 Last dinner8pm S% sB&B£6.25 dB&B£12.50 Lunch£1.50 Tea90p Dinner£3.60 Credit cards 1 3

C

CLUMBER PARK Nottinghamshire Map**8** SK67
××**Normanton Inn** ☎Worksop5769 (due to change to 475767 during 1980)
Roadhouse inn with rustic brickwork, thought to be a converted manor house. Adjacent to Clumber Park on A614.
60seats 100P ♡English & French. Last dinner8.45pm S% Lunch£3.50&alc Dinner£4&alc Wine£3.10 Credit cards ① ③

COBHAM Surrey Map**4** TQ16
☆☆☆**Seven Hills Motel** (Ladbroke) ☎4471 Telex no929196
Situated in twenty-three acres of parkland with pine trees and rhododendrons.
97rm(94⇌⫛) Lift ☽ ꟷCTV in bedrooms 300P ⚓ ⊇(heated) squash billiards sauna bath Live music & dancing Fri & Sat Conference facilities available ♡Continental. Last dinner10.30pm S% ✱sB&B fr£13 sB&B⇌⫛ fr£15 dB&B⇌⫛ fr£22 Lunch fr£3.95&alc Dinner fr£5.50&alc Wine£2.75 ⫷ Credit cards ① ② ③ ⑤ ⑥

××**San Domenico** Portsmouth Rd ☎3006
Dinner not served Sun; 120seats 65P ♡Italian. Last dinner10.45pm Lunch£8alc Dinner£8alc Wine£2.90 Credit cards ① ② ③ ⑤

COCKERMOUTH Cumbria Map**11** NY13
★★★**Broughton Craggs** Great Broughton ☎824400
Closed Jan; 10⇌⫛ ꟷCTV in bedrooms ⊘ 60P ✿ ⚓ ♡English & French. Last dinner9.30pm ✪ sB&B⇌⫛£14 dB&B⇌⫛£21 Lunch£3.75&alc Dinner£5.20&alc Wine£3 ⫷ *xmas* Credit cards ① ② ③ ⑤ ⑥

★★**Globe** Main St ☎822126
Close to lakes and an ideal touring base.
32rm(4⇌⫛) ꟷ CTV 20⌂ ♡International. Last dinner9.30pm ✪ sB&B fr£9 sB&B⇌⫛ fr£10 dB&B fr£15 dB&B⇌⫛ fr£17 Lunch fr£3 Dinner fr£5.25 ⫷ Credit cards ① ③

★★**Trout** Crown St ☎823591
Modernised but retaining its 18th-C character, the Trout has lawned gardens and a private frontage to the River Derwent, with private fishing rights (spinning or fly).
17rm(4⇌⫛) ☽ ꟷTV in bedrooms 75P ↬ ♡English, French, Italian & Spanish. Last dinner9.30pm ✪ S% sB&B£9.80 sB&B⇌⫛£11.30 dB&B£17.60 dB&B⇌⫛£20.60 Lunch£3.50&alc Dinner£6.50&alc Wine£3

★★**Wordsworth** Main St ☎822757
Formerly a coaching inn dating back to the early 17th century, beside the River Cocker.
18rm(4⇌⫛) 2▭ ꟷ CTV TV available in bedrooms 20P 6⌂ Last dinner9.15pm ✪ sB&B£7.50–£10 sB&B⇌⫛£12–£16 dB&B£15–£20 dB&B⇌⫛£18–£22 Lunch£2–£3 Dinner£4.50–£5&alc Wine£2.25 ⫷

×**Old Court House** Main St ☎823871
Closed Sun & 24–26Dec 30seats ₱ ♡German. Last dinner9.30pm S% ✱Dinner£6 Wine£2.80

At **Moota** (4½m NE on A595)
☆☆**Moota** ☎Aspatria20681
16⇌⫛ 57P

CODICOTE Hertfordshire Map**4** TL21
××**George & Dragon** ☎Stevenage820452
Pleasant old building in small village.
65 seats 35P ♡English & French. Last dinner10pm Lunch fr£5.25&alc Dinner£10alc Wine£3.45 Credit cards ① ② ③ ④ ⑤ ⑥

CODSALL Staffordshire Map**7** SJ80
××***Franco's*** The Square ☎4642
Old cottage, on the corner of the village square, with a black and white half-timbered façade.
Closed Sun & Mon; 72 seats P ♡English, French & Italian. Last dinner10.30pm

COLCHESTER Essex Map**5** TM02
★★**George** 116 High St (Grand Met.) ☎78494
56⇌⋔ Lift ☽ 🍴 CTV 24P ♡ English, French & Scottish. Last dinner10pm ♔ ♖ S%
✱sB&B⇌⋔£12.50 dB&B⇌⋔£19 ⚑
Credit cards 1 2 3 4 5 6

★★**Kings Ford Park** Layer de la Haye (2½ S B1026)
☎Layer de la Haye 301
15rm(6⇌⋔) 1⊟ 🍴 CTV CTV available in bedrooms 100P ⚓ Live music & dancing Sat ♣ ♡ English, French & Italian. Last dinner9.30pm ♔
✱sB&B fr£7.50 sB&B⇌⋔ fr£9 dB&B fr£14 dB&B⇌⋔ fr£16 Lunch fr£3.25&alc Dinner fr£3.50&alc Wine£3 ⚑ *xmas*
Credit cards 1 2 3 5

★★**Red Lion** High St (Trusthouse Forte) ☎77986
Large, Tudor-fronted coaching inn with covered centre courtyard.
19rm ☽ 🍴 CTV ⚑ ♡ Mainly grills.
Last dinner11.30pm ♔ S% sB&B£10.50
dB&B£17 ⚑ *xmas* Credit cards 1 2 3 4 5 6

★★**Rose & Crown** ☎76677
The oldest section of this posting house is the bar which dates from the 15th century.
13rm(4⇌⋔) Annexe: 15⇌⋔ 1⊟ ☽ 🍴 CTV TV available in bedrooms 80P Last dinner9pm ♔ ♖
✱sB&B fr£7.25 sB&B⇌⋔ fr£13 dB&B fr£13.50 dB&B⇌⋔ fr£19.50 Lunch fr£4.25&alc Tea fr50p Dinner£6alc Wine£2.75 Credit cards 1 2 3 5

✕✕**Wm Scragg's** 2 North Hill ☎41111
Closed Sun; 50seats ⚑ Last dinner10.30pm
Lunch£6.20–£9.50 Dinner£6.20–£9.50
Credit cards 1 2 3

At **Marks Tey** (5½ SW on A12)
☆☆☆**Marks Tey** ☎210001
106⇌⋔ 160P

COLEFORD Devon Map**3** SS70
★★♔**Coombe House Country** ☎Copplestone487
8rm(6⇌⋔) CTV TV available in bedrooms ✈ 60P ♣ ⚓ ⊡(heated) Last dinner9.30pm ♔ S%
sB&B£9–£10 sB&B⇌⋔£9.50–£10.50
dB&B£18–£19 dB&B⇌⋔£19–£20
Lunch£3.65–£4 Dinner fr£4 Wine£2.25 ⚑
Credit cards 1 3

COLEFORD Gloucestershire Map**3** SO51
★★**Bells Club** Lords Hill ☎2583
Closed 25 Dec; 25⇌⋔ 🍴 CTV ✈ 250P ⚓ ⊃ ⊘(hard) Disco wkly Live music & dancing wkly ♿
Last dinner9.30pm ♔ S% sB&B⇌⋔£7
dB&B⇌⋔£12 Continental breakfast
Lunch£3&alc Dinner£4–£6&alc Wine£2
Credit cards 1 3

★★**Speech House** Forest of Dean (Trusthouse Forte) ☎Cinderford22607
Contains the original Court Room of the Verderers of the Forest of Dean.
14rm(3⇌⋔) 3⊟ TV in bedrooms 49P
Last dinner9.30pm ♔ ♖ S% sB&B£12
dB&B£19 dB&B⇌⋔£21 ⚑ *xmas*
Credit cards 1 2 3 4 5 6

★♔**Lambsquay** ☎3127 (changing to Dean33127)
A tastefully refurbished Georgian house peacefully situated in the Royal Forest of Dean.
10rm 1⊟ 🍴 TV in bedrooms 30P ♣ ⚓ Children under 10yrs not accommodated ♡ International
Last dinner7.30pm ✱sB&B£9–£10
dB&B£17–£19 dB&B⇌⋔£33–£40
Lunch£4–£4.50&alc Dinner£5–£5.50&alc
Wine£3.50 ⚑ *xmas*

COLERNE Wiltshire Map**3** ST87
✕**Vineyard** ☎Box742491
Ivy-clad stone building. Slopes of earlier vineyard at rear, now forming part of a walled garden.
Dinner not served Sun 68seats 25P ♡ English & French. Last dinner9.30pm Lunch£4.50&alc
Dinner£4.50&alc Wine£2.30
Credit cards 1 2 3 5 6

COLESHILL Warwickshire Map**4** SP28
★★**Swan** High St (Ansells) ☎62212
34rm(25⇌⋔) 🍴 CTV TV in bedrooms ✈ 120P ♣
Last dinner10pm ♔ ♖ S% sB&B£12.55
dB&B£16.95 Lunch£3.50&alc Dinner£3.75£alc
Wine£3.20 ⚑ Credit cards 1 2

COLYTON Devon Map**3** SY29
✕✕**Old Bakehouse** ☎52518
Closed Sun & Nov–Feb; Lunch not served 29seats 10P Bedrooms available ✗ ♡ French.
Last dinner9pm S% Dinner£9alc Wine£3.75

COMBEINTEIGNHEAD Devon Map**3** SX97
★★♔**Netherton House** ☎Shaldon3251
Closed Jan & Feb; RS Nov & Dec; 11rm(7⇌⋔) 🍴 CTV ✈ 30P ♣ ⚓ ⊃(heated) Children under 8yrs not accommodated Last dinner8.30pm ♔ ♖ S%
sB&B£12.50–£13.50 dB&B£22–£28
dB&B⇌⋔£24–£30 Bar lunch£1.50–£2.50
Tea50p–£1 Dinner£6–£7.50 Wine£3.75 ⚑
xmas

COMBE MARTIN Devon Map**2** SS54
★★♔**Higher Leigh** ☎2486
Converted manor house in own grounds.
14rm(3⇌⋔) 🍴 CTV available in bedrooms 35P ♣ ⚓ ↳ billiards sauna bath ♣ ♡ English & Continental.
Last dinner11pm ♔ ♖ S% sB&B£9–£10
dB&B£20–£24 dB&B⇌⋔£20–£24 Lunch£1.80
Tea80p Dinner£2.50–£8 Wine£1.90 ⚑ *xmas*

C

★Delve's ☎3428
Situated on the main Ilfracombe to Minehead road, a Victorian-style hotel.
14rm CTV 20P Last dinner8pm S% sB&B£6.48–£7.02 dB&B£12.96–£14.04 Barlunch50p–£2 Dinner£3.87–£4.50 *xmas*

XXLa Gallerie Victoria St ☎2566
60seats 13P bedrooms available English & French. Last dinner10.30pm ✱Dinner fr£4.50&alc Wine£2.40 Credit cards 1 2 3 5

COMPTON Devon Map**3** SX86
XXCastle Barton Main St ☎Kingskerswell3314
Closed Tue, Nov, Jan & Feb; 24seats 50P bedrooms available Last dinner6pm Lunch90p–£2.90 Tea35–85p High Tea40p–£1.80 Dinner£2.70–£4&alc Wine£2.80

COMPTON (nr Guildford) **Surrey** Map**4** SU94
XWithies Inn ☎Godalming21158
Charming old inn with panelled, candle-lit dining room.
Dinner not served Sun; 35seats Last dinner9pm ✱Lunch£12alc Dinner£12alc Wine£3.50 Credit cards 1 2 3 5

CONGLETON Cheshire Map**7** SJ86
XXLorenzo's at Moody Hall Moody St ☎77364
Closed Mon; Lunch not served Sat; Dinner not served Sun; 80seats 40P English, French & Italian. Last dinner10.30pm ✱Lunch fr£3 Dinner£10alc Wine£3.50 Credit cards 1 2 3 5

CONISTON Cumbria Map**7** SD39
★★*Sun* ☎248
Situated amidst magnificent mountain scenery within easy reach of village.
Closed Nov–Feb; 9rm CTV 20P 3 English & French. Last dinner8pm

★Black Bull Yewdale Rd ☎335
6rm CTV 12P 2 Last dinner8pm S% ✱sB&B fr£6.50 dB&B fr£13 Barlunch fr£1.30&alc High Tea fr£3.50&alc Dinner fr£4.75&alc Wine£3

CONSTANTINE BAY Cornwall Map**2** SW87
★★★Treglos ☎St Meryan520727
Closed 15Nov–11Mar; 41 CTV CTV available in bedrooms 50P 10 (heated) English & French. Last dinner9.30pm sB&B £12.50–£16.50 dB&B £25–£33 Lunch£4–£4.50&alc Tea75p–£1.25 Dinner£5–£5.50&alc Wine£2.75

COODEN BEACH East Sussex Map**5** TQ70
★★★Cooden Beach (Prestige) ☎Cooden2281
Built in 1931, with gardens leading to beach.
37rm(34) CTV TV in bedrooms 50P 12 (heated) French. Last dinner10pm S% sB&B£13.50 sB&B £14.50 dB&B£27 dB&B£29 Lunch£3.50–£3.75&alc Tea£1 Dinner£5.50&alc Wine£3.50 *xmas* Credit cards 1 2 3 5 6

COOKHAM Berkshire Map**4** SU88
XXX*Bel & Dragon* High St ☎Bourne End21263
Pleasant 16th-C inn situated in small village. Spacious restaurant overlooking gardens.
125seats 6P English & Continental. Last dinner10.30pm Credit cards 2 4 6

COPTHORNE West Sussex Map**4** TQ33
Hotels are listed under Gatwick Airport

CORBRIDGE Northumberland Map**12** NY96
★★Angel Inn Main St (Scottish & Newcastle) ☎211
Situated on the main street with an attractive vine-covered façade.
7rm CTV 30P English & French. Last dinner9pm ✱sB&B£9 dB&B£13.50 Lunch£3.50–£3.90 Tea£1.25 High Tea£2.50–£3 Dinner£4–£7.50&alc Wine£2.20 Credit cards 1 2 3 5

XXRamblers of Corbridge Front St ☎2424
Closed Sun, Mon & 2wks Oct; Lunch not served; 55seats International. Last dinner10pm Dinner£10&alc Wine£2.40 Credit cards 1 3

CORNHILL-ON-TWEED Northumberland Map**12** NT83
★★★Tillmouth Park ☎Coldstream2255
County house built in 1882 on banks of River Till.
Closed Dec–Jan; 15rm(6) 1 CTV 50P 1 English & French. Last dinner8.45pm sB&B£12 dB&B£26 dB&B £29–£32 Lunch£4&alc Tea50p High Tea£2 Dinner£5&alc Wine£3.20 Credit cards 1 2 3 5

★★Collingwood Arms (Swallow)
☎Coldstream2424 Telex no53168
16rm(4) CTV 100P Last dinner8.30pm S% sB&B£9.90–£12.50 dB&B£15.40–£22.10 dB&B £19.25–£25.75 *xmas* Credit cards 1 2 3 5

CORSE LAWN Hereford & Worcester Map**3** SO83
XXXCorse Lawn House ☎Tirley479
Closed Mon, 1st 2wks Sep & 1st 2wks Jan; Dinner not served Sun; 70seats 50P English & French. Last dinner10pm Credit cards 1 2 3 5

CORSHAM Wiltshire Map**3** ST86
★★*Methuen Arms* High St ☎12239
Takes its name from Lord Methuen, whose country seat is nearby. Well-known art collector.
17rm(2) CTV 100P 6 English & Continental. Last dinner9.45pm Credit cards 1 3 5

☆☆Stagecoach Motel Park Ln, Pickwick ☎713162

21⇌🛁 ☽ 🍽 CTV CTV in bedrooms 40P ⚓ ♀ English & French. Last dinner9.30pm ♔ ⚿ S% sB&B⇌🛁£11.50–£12.75 dB&B⇌🛁£16.75–£21.50 Lunch£3–£4&alc Tea£1–£1.25&alc High Tea£2–£2.75&alc Dinner£3.50–£4.25&alc Wine£2 🅿 *xmas* Credit card 1

COSSINGTON Leicestershire Map**8** SK61
XXCossington Mill ☎Sileby2205
Closed Sun; Lunch not served Sat; 60seats 60P ♀English & French. Last dinner10pm S% Lunch£3.25–£3.75&alc Dinner£3.25–£3.95&alc Wine£2.25

COTTINGHAM Northamptonshire Map**4** SP89
XX*Hunting Lodge* ☎East Carlton370
Closed Sun & Mon; 50seats 200P Live music & dancing Sat ♀English & Continental. Last dinner10.30pm Credit cards 2 3 5

COVENHAM Lincolnshire Map**8** TF39
XXMill House ☎Fulstow652
Closed Jan; Lunch served Sun only 40 seats 30P ♀English & French. Last dinner10.30pm S% *Lunch£4alc Dinner£8alc Wine£3 Credit cards 1 2 3 5

COVENTRY West Midlands Map**4** SP37
☆☆☆☆**Coventry EuroCrest** Hinckley Rd, Walsgrave (Junc 2 M6) (Crest) ☎613261 Telex no311292
161⇌🛁 Lift ☽ ⊞ 🍽 CTV in bedrooms 250P ⚓ Cabaret Sat Conference facilities available ♀English & French. Last dinner10pm ♔ ⚿ S% *sB&B⇌🛁£17.60 dB&B⇌🛁£26.13 Continental breakfast 🅿 Credit cards 1 2 3 4 5 6

★★★★**De Vere** Cathedral Sq (De Vere) ☎51851 (Telex31380)
A modern building in city centre.
215⇌ 🛁Lift ☽ 🍽 TV in bedrooms ⚑ Conference facilities available ♀English & Continental. Last dinner10.30pm ♔ S% sB&B⇌🛁£26 dB&B⇌🛁£36.50 Lunch£10alc Dinner£10alc Wine£3.75 🅿 *xmas* Credit cards 1 2 3 5 6

★★★★**Hotel Leofric** Broadgate (Embassy ☎21371 Telex no311193
90⇌🛁 Lift ☽ 🍽 CTV TV in bedrooms ⚑ Conference facilities available ♀French Last dinner9.30pm ♔ ⚿ S% sB&B⇌🛁£18 dB&B⇌🛁£26 Continental breakfast Lunch£5&alc Dinner£5.50&alc Wine£5 🅿 Credit cards 1 2 3 4 5 6

★★★***Allesley*** Allesley Village ☎403272
31rm(13⇌🛁) ☽ 🍽 CTV 250P Live music & dancing Tue–Sat ♀English & French. Last dinner10.30pm ♔ ⚿ Credit cards 2 4 5

★★★**Coventry Crest Motel** London Rd, Willenhall (Crest) ☎303398
72rm(53⇌🛁) ☽ CTV in bedrooms 150P ⚓ Last dinner9.45pm ♔ S% *sB&B£12.47 sB&B⇌🛁£15.71 dB&B£19 dB&B⇌🛁£22.24 Continental breakfast 🅿 Credit cards 1 2 3 4 5 6

☆☆☆**Novotel Coventry** Wilstons Ln (junc A444/M6 junc 3) ☎88833 Telex no31545
101⇌🛁 Lift ⊞ 🍽 TV in bedrooms 150P ⚓ ⊡(heated) squash sauna bath Disco Fri & Sat Live music & dancing Sat (Dec) Conference facilities available ♔ ♀English & French. Last dinner11.30pm ♔ ⚿ S% sB&B⇌🛁£17.40 dB&B⇌🛁£20.80 Lunch£4–£6 Dinner£4–£6 Wine£3.35 🅿 *xmas* Credit cards 1 2 3 5

☆☆☆**Post House** Rye Hill, Allesley (Trusthouse Forte) ☎402151 Telex no31427
196⇌🛁 Lift ☽ 🍽 CTV in bedrooms 297P Last dinner10pm ♔ ⚿ S% sB&B⇌🛁£19.75 dB&B⇌🛁£28.50 🅿 Credit cards 1 2 3 4 5 6

C

★★★**Royal Court** Tamworth Rd, Keresley (3m NW on A423) ☎Keresley4171
Closed Xmas Day; 19rm(10⇌ ⋒) ☽ ⋈ CTV CTV in bedrooms ⊘ 350P ⚓ ⁘ Live music & dancing 5 nights wkly ♡ English & French.
Last dinner10.30pm ✿ sB&B£12.50 sB&B⇌ ⋒£16.50 dB&B£16.50 dB&B⇌ ⋒£20 Lunch£4.15–£5&alc Dinner£5–£5.50&alc Wine£3.50 Credit cards 1 2 5

★★**Beechwood** Sandpits Ln, Keresley (3m NW on A423) ☎Keresley4243
28rm ☽ ⋈ CTV in bedrooms 60P ⚓ ♡ English, French & Italian. Last dinner10pm ✿ ♫ sB&B£9 sB&B⇌ ⋒£10 dB&B£16 dB&B⇌ ⋒£18 Lunch£3–£3.50&alc Tea£1–£2.50 Dinner£3–£5&alc Credit cards 1 2 3

XX**Grandstand** Coventry City FC, King Richard St, Highfield ☎27053
Closed Sat & Sun; Dinner not served 130seats 200P ♡ English & French. S% ✱Lunch£4.75&alc Wine£4.50 Credit cards 1 2 3 5

COVERACK Cornwall Map**2** SW71
★★**Coverack Headland** ☎St Keverne243
Stands in twenty-five acres of grounds overlooking its own headland and private beach.
Closed Nov–Mar; 35rm(9⇌ ⋒) ☽ ⋈ CTV P ⚓ ⁘grass Last dinner8.30pm ✿ ♫ sB&B£7.50–£9.75 sB&B⇌ ⋒£8–£10.25 dB&B£13–£17.50 dB&B⇌ ⋒£16–£20.50 Bar lunch80p–£1.60 Tea60–90p Dinner£5&alc Wine£2.80 ⊓ Credit card 5

COWES Isle of Wight Map**4** SZ49
See also Whippingham
★★★**Holmwood** Egypt Point ☎292508
Superbly situated hotel overlooking the Solent.

18rm(8⇄⋒) ⋈ CTV 15P ⋈ Live music & dancing Sat ♿ ⋒French. Last dinner10pm ⋒ ⋒ ✱sB&B£10 dB&B£17 dB&B⇄⋒£19.50 Lunch fr£5.50 Tea fr50p Dinner fr£5.50 Wine£2.75 ⋒ Credit cards 1 2 3 5 6

COWFOLD West Sussex Map**4** TQ22
✕**St Peter Cottage** ☎324
Closed Mon(summer), Mon & Tue (winter) & last 2 wks of Jan & Jun. 60seats ⋒ Last High Tea5.15pm ✱Lunch£2.40–£2.60 Tea90–95p&alc High Tea£1.25alc Credit cards 1 3 6

COXWOLD North Yorkshire Map**8** SE57
✕✕***Fauconberg Arms*** ☎214
Closed Mon 1st 3 wks Oct & 1st wk Feb; 60 seats 15P bedrooms available Last dinner9.30pm

CRACKINGTON HAVEN Cornwall Map**2** SX19
★★**Coombe Barton** ☎St Gennys345
Closed Jan & Feb; 10rm ⋈ CTV 40P Children under 5yrs not accommodated Last dinner9.30pm ⋒ S% sB&B£8.80 dB&B£17.60 Bar lunch£2 Dinner£4.95&alc Wine£2.50 *xmas*

CRAFTHOLE Cornwall Map**2** SX35
⋒ **Whitsand Bay** Portwrinkle ☎St Germans (Cornwall)276
Three-storey, stone-built house with mullioned windows, in own grounds overlooking the sea.
Closed Dec; 38rm(30⇄⋒) CTV 100P ⋒ ⋒18 sauna bath ⋒ Last dinner8.15pm ⋒ ⋒ ✱sB&B£5.50–£7.50 sB&B⇄⋒£6.50–£7.50 dB&B£11–£15 dB&B⇄⋒£13–£15 Lunch£2.50 Tea35p High Tea£1.25 Dinner£3.50 Wine£2 ⋒

CRANBROOK Kent Map**5** TQ73
★★ ⋒**Kennel Holt** ☎712032
See page 40 for details

★★**Willesley** ☎3555
Brick country house, part 14th and 17th-century, standing in four acres of ground.
Closed 1st wk Feb; 16rm(14⇄⋒) ⋈ CTV CTV in bedrooms 50P ⋒ ⋒English & French. Last dinner9.30pm ⋒ S% sB&B£14.37–£16.51 sB&B⇄⋒£16.98–£18.31 dB&B£23–£26.46 dB&B⇄⋒£25.30–£29.07 Lunch£3.73–£4.37&alc Dinner£6.33–£7.24&alc Wine£3.15 ⋒ *xmas* Credit cards 1 2 3 4 5 6

CRANHAM Gloucestershire Map**3** SO81
✕**Royal William** Cranham Wood ☎Painswick813650
63seats 125P Last dinner11.30pm S% Lunch£1.95–£4.35 Dinner£1.95–£4.35 Wine£2.31 Credit cards 1 3

CRANTOCK Cornwall Map**2** SW76
During the currency of this guide Crantock numbers are liable to change.

★★***Crantock Bay*** West Pentire ☎229
Detached residence in own grounds, with views over cliffs and coastline.
Closed end Sep–mid Apr; 35rm (12⇄⋒) ⋈ CTV 35P ⋒ ⋒ Live music & dancing twice wkly Last dinner8pm ⋒ ⋒ ⋒ Credit card 3

★***Fairbank*** West Pentire Rd ☎424
Closed Nov–Mar; 9rm ⋈ TV in bedrooms 30P

★**Glynn Heath** 21 West Pentire Rd ☎373
Residence with commanding sea views, situated in semi-rural area.
Closed Nov–Mar; 11rm CTV 10P ⋒ ⋒ Children not accommodated Last dinner6.30pm ⋒ ⋒ S% sB&B£8–£10 dB&B£15–£19 Lunch£2 Tea£1 Dinner£2.50 Wine£1 ⋒ Credit cards 1 3

CRAVEN ARMS Salop Map**7** SO48
★★***Craven Arms*** ☎3331
Closed Xmas; 9rm 150P 3⋒ Live music & dancing Sat Last dinner9pm ⋒ Credit cards 1 2 5 6

CRAWLEY **Hampshire** Map**4** SU43
✕***Fox & Hounds*** ☎Sparsholt285
Closed Mon & Xmas; Dinner not served Sun; 30seats 34P

CRAWLEY **West Sussex** Map**4** TQ23
Hotels are listed under Gatwick Airport

CREDITON Devon Map**3** SS80
✕**Dartmoor Railway Inn** Station Rd ☎2489
80seats 25P ⋒Mainly grills. Last dinner10pm S% Lunch£2.20–£5.50&alc Dinner£2.50–£5.50&alc Credit cards 1 2 3 5

CRESSAGE Salop Map**7** SJ50
✕**Old Hall** ☎298
Closed Mon; Dinner not served Sun; 90seats 50P bedrooms available ⋒English & French. Last dinner9.30pm ✱Lunch fr£4 Tea£1 Dinner£7alc Wine£3.20 Credit cards 1 2 5

CREWE Cheshire Map**7** SJ75
★★**Crewe Arms** Nantwich Rd (Embassy) ☎2304
35⇄⋒ ☽ ⋈ CTV TV in bedrooms 100P Last dinner9pm ⋒ S% sB&B⇄⋒£15 dB&B⇄⋒£18 Lunch£4.50&alc Dinner£5&alc Wine£4.50 ⋒ Credit cards 1 2 3 4 5 6

★★**Royal** Nantwich Rd (Embassy) ☎57398
37rm(1⇄⋒) ☽ CTV 25P 15⋒ Last dinner9pm ⋒ S% sB&B£10 dB&B£14 dB&B⇄⋒£16 Lunch£4.50&alc Dinner£5&alc Wine£4 Credit cards 1 2 3 4 5 6

CREWKERNE Somerset Map**3** ST40
★**George** Market Sq ☎73650
17th-C coaching inn in town square, furnished in traditional style.

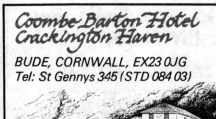

C

16rm TV 30P Mainly grills. Last dinner 9.30pm sB&B£6 dB&B£11 Lunch£2.50–£4&alc Dinner£3–£4.50&alc Wine£2

CRICK Northamptonshire Map**4** SP57

☆☆☆☆**Rugby Post House** (Trusthouse Forte) ☎822101 Telex no 311107
96⇌fl CTV in bedrooms 150P Conference facilities available Last dinner 10.30pm S% sB&B⇌fl£21.25 dB&B⇌fl£30 *xmas*
Credit cards 1 2 3 4 5 6

CRICKLADE Wiltshire Map**4** SU19

★★**White Hart** High St ☎Swindon 750206
Gabled, Victorian hotel of mellow stone, situated in centre of town.
RS 25Dec–2Jan & Pub Hols; 16rm CTV TV in bedrooms 15P 6 Live music & dancing twice wkly Last dinner 8.45pm sB&B£10 dB&B£17 Lunch fr£4&alc Dinner fr£4&alc
Credit cards 1 2 3 5 6

★**Vale Inn** High St ☎Swindon 750223
6rm(1⇌fl) CTV 50P S% *sB&B£6.75 dB&B£11 dB&B⇌fl£11 Bar lunch 60p–£1.50 Dinner£4alc Wine£2.60

CROCKERNWELL Devon Map**3** SX79

★**Bay Tree Motel** ☎Drewsteignton 267
Closed 25 & 26Dec; 8rm(3⇌fl) CTV TV available in bedrooms 30P Last dinner 10pm S% *sB&B£4.50 sB&B⇌fl£5 dB&B£9 dB&B⇌fl£10 Lunch£2.25–£2.50&alc Tea 60–75p High Tea£1.10–£1.40&alc Dinner£2.50–£2.75&alc Wine£2

CROMER Norfolk Map**9** TG24

★★★**Colne House** (Mount Charlotte) ☎512013
Originally the home of Lord Buxton, now extended and providing various facilities for young children. Stands in 5½ acres of grounds.
37rm(19⇌fl) CTV 50P (heated) (hard) Disco wkly Live music & dancing twice wkly Last dinner 8.45pm S% sB&B fr£9.50 sB&B⇌fl fr£12 dB&B fr£19 dB&B⇌fl fr£24 Lunch fr£3.50 Tea fr75p Dinner fr£4.50
xmas Credit cards 1 2 3 4 6

★★***Cliff House*** Overstrand Rd ☎512445
Once the Norfolk home of the Samuel Hoare family. Fine stone-faced residence, set in lawned garden.
27rm(3⇌fl) 2 CTV 25P 15

★★***Cliftonville*** Runton Rd (Inter-Hotel) ☎512543
Imposing Victorian building, overlooking sea. Spacious lounges with carved panelling, stained glass windows, and Minstrels' gallery.
49rm(5⇌fl) Lift CTV 20P 6 billiards Music 2 nights wkly Dancing wkly Last dinner 9pm
Credit cards 1 2 3 5 6

★**West Parade** Runton Rd ☎512443
Late Victorian four storey hotel overlooking sea.
30⇌fl CTV 25P Last dinner 8pm S% *sB&B£8.31–£9.50 dB&B£16.62–£19 Lunch£2 Tea 25–30p Dinner£3 Wine£2.20
xmas

CROOKLANDS Cumbria Map**7** SD58

★★★**Crooklands** ☎432
A 400yr old inn with twisted oak beams in the Banquet room. The Barn Grill and Restaurant are housed in the converted barn.
15rm(12⇌fl) CTV TV available in bedrooms 200P Disco Sat Swiss. Last dinner 10pm S% *sB&B£9.95 sB&B⇌fl£17.45 dB&B£17.30 dB&B⇌fl£23.40 Lunch£3.75–£7.50&alc Tea 60p–£1 Dinner£3.75–£4.25&alc Wine£3.25
Credit cards 1 2 3 5 6

CROSBY-ON-EDEN Cumbria Map **12** NY45
★★**Newby Grange** ☎73645
11rm(4⇌ ⋒) CTV TV available in bedrooms 200P Disco twice wkly Live music & dancing wkly Cabaret wkly English & French. Last dinner9.30pm S% *sB&B£8 sB&B⇌⋒£9 dB&B£14 dB&B⇌⋒£16 Lunch£1.75–£3.50&alc Dinner£2.50–£3.50&alc Wine£3.25 *xmas* Credit cards 1 6

CROWBOROUGH East Sussex Map **5** TQ53
★★★**Crest** Beacon Rd ☎2772
Closed Xmas; 31rm(12⇌⋒) Lift CTV 75P Live music & dancing Fri & Sat Cabaret Fri & Sat English & French. Last dinner8.45pm S% sB&B£11.55 sB&B⇌⋒£14.85 dB&B£18.20 dB&B⇌⋒£22 Lunch£3.90&alc Dinner£4.85&alc Wine£3.50 Credit cards 1 2 3 5 6

CROYDON Greater London Map **4** TQ36
See also Sanderstead
★★★**Aerodrome** Purley Way (Anchor) ☎01-688 5185 Telex no858875
The world's first airport hotel.
RS 24–26Dec (no accommodation); 62rm(47⇌⋒) CTV in bedrooms 80P Last dinner9.15pm S% *sB&B fr£13.75 sB&B⇌⋒ fr£17.50 dB&B fr£21 dB&B⇌⋒ fr£24 Lunch fr£3.50 Tea fr50p Dinner fr£4 Wine£2.65 Credit cards 1 2 3 4 5 6

Briarley 8 Outram Rd ☎01-654 1000
19rm(11⇌⋒) 1 CTV CTV in bedrooms 9P Last dinner8pm S% sB&B£14 dB&B⇌⋒£17.50 dB&B£19.50 dB&B⇌⋒£22.50 Lunch£4 Tea£1 Dinner£5 Wine£2.30 Credit card 1

CRUDWELL Wiltshire Map **3** ST99
Mayfield House ☎409
Located in a quiet Cotswold village, this stone-built building has secluded lawns and garden.
20rm(1⇌⋒) CTV 40P Last dinner9.30pm

CUCKFIELD West Sussex Map **4** TQ32
★★**Hilton Park** ☎Haywards Heath54555
Country house, set in three acres of grounds, laid to lawns and rosebeds, overlooking the South Downs.
14rm(7⇌⋒) CTV TV available in bedrooms 50P 2 English & French. Last dinner8pm S% sB&B fr£12 sB&B⇌⋒ fr£15 dB&B fr£22 dB&B⇌⋒£25 Dinner fr£5 Wine£4 Credit cards 1 2 3 5

CULLINGWORTH West Yorkshire Map **7** SE03
XXX**Five Flags** (Bacchus Room) Manywells Height (nr junc A629/B6429) ☎Bradford834188
Closed Mon; Lunch not served Sat; Dinner not served Sun; 100seats 200P Disco wkly Last dinner10.15pm S% Lunch£3.50alc Dinner£5.95alc Wine£4.45 Credit cards 1 2 3

CUMNOR Oxfordshire Map **4** SP40
XX**Bear & Ragged Staff** ☎2329
Closed Mon; Dinner not served Sun; 20seats 60P English & French. Last dinner10pm *£6&alc Dinner£6&alc Wine£2.90 Credit cards 1 2 5

DARESBURY Cheshire Map **7** SJ58
★★★**Lord Daresbury** Chester Rd (Greenall Whitley) ☎Warrington67331 Telex no629330
108⇌⋒ Lift CTV in bedrooms 450P Conference facilities available English & French. Last dinner9.45pm S% sB&B⇌⋒£21–£22 dB&B⇌⋒£26–£27.50 Lunch£3.50–£4.25&alc Tea40p Dinner fr£4.50&alc Wine£3.30 Credit cards 1 2 3 5 6

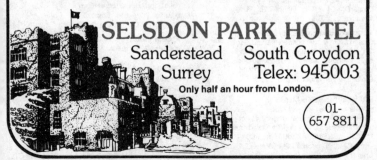

DARLINGTON Co Durham Map**8** NZ21
★★★★**Europa Lodge** Blackwell Grange (Grand Met) ☎60111 Telex no587272
96⇌⋒ Lift ☽ ⚭ TV available in bedrooms 180P 6🏠 ⚓ ⛳18 Conference facilities available ♿ ♡English & French. Last dinner9.45pm ♧ ☕ S% ✱sB&B⇌⋒£15.50 dB&B⇌⋒£22.50 ⊓ *xmas* Credit cards 1 2 3 4 5 6

★★***North Eastern*** Victoria Rd (Whitbread) ☎64373
25⇌⋒ ☽ ⚭ CTV TV available in bedrooms 100P 6🏠 Last dinner8.30pm ♧ ⊓ Credit cards 1 3 5

DARRINGTON West Yorkshire Map**8** SE41
✕✕***Darrington Hotel*** Great North Rd ☎Pontefract71458
Closed Sun; 90seats 120P bedrooms available Last dinner9.30pm Credit cards 1 3

DARTFORD Kent Map**5** TQ57
★★**Royal Victoria and Bull** 1 High St ☎23104
34rm CTV CTV in bedrooms 36P ♡English & French. Last dinner9.45pm ♧ S% sB&B£13.90 dB&B£22 Lunch fr£3.85&alc Dinner fr&3.85&alc Wine£3.20 Credit cards 1 3 4 5

DARTMOUTH Devon Map**3** SX85
★★★**Dart Marina** Sand Quay (Trusthouse Forte) ☎2580
Quiet, comfortable hotel with fine views of the Dart.
33rm(16⇌⋒) ⚭ TV in bedrooms 100P ⛟ Last dinner9pm ♧ S% sB&B£13.50 dB&B£19.50 dB&B⇌⋒£24.50 ⊓ *xmas* Credit cards 1 2 3 4 5 6

★★**Royal Castle** 11 The Quay (Anchor) ☎2397 Telex no858875
Built in 1639 and originally a coaching inn; the hotel stands on the quayside.
20rm(9⇌⋒) 2▭ CTV CTV in bedrooms ⚑ Last dinner 9pm ♧ ☕ S% ✱sB&B fr£11 sB&B⇌⋒ fr£14.50 dB&B fr£18.50 dB&B⇌⋒ fr£22 Lunch fr£2.50 Dinner fr£4.50 Wine£2.65 ⊓ *xmas* Credit cards 1 2 3 4 5 6

★**Kagal House** 10 Foss St ☎3950
Closed Xmas; RSNov–Apr 11rm(10⇌⋒) Lift ⚭ CTV TV available in bedrooms ⚑ ⛟ ♡Mainly grills. Last dinner9pm ♧ ☕ ✱sB&B⇌⋒£8.50–£9.50 dB&B⇌⋒£15–£17 Lunch£1.95 Tea fr65p Dinner£3.50–£5 Credit cards 1 3

★**Royle House** Mount Boone ☎3649
Closed Dec–Feb 9rm(4⇌⋒) CTV 15P ⛟ ⚓ Children under 12yrs not accommodated ♡English & French. Last dinner9pm ♧ ☕ S% ✱sB&B£11–£12 sB&B⇌⋒£14.50–£15.50 dB&B£18–£20 dB&B⇌⋒£20–£22 Bar lunch£1.25–£2 Tea£1–£2 High Tea£1.70–£3 Dinner£7alc Wine£4.10 Credit cards 1 2 3 5

★**Victoria** Victoria Rd ☎2572
RS 25 & 26 Dec; 8rm ⚭ CTV ⚑ ♡English & French. Last dinner10pm ♧ sB&B£7–£7.50 dB&B£14–£15 Bar lunch£1.75–£4 Dinner£4–£4.75&alc Wine£2.75 ⊓ Credit cards 1 3 6

❁✕✕**Carved Angel** 2 South Embankment ☎2465
Closed Mon; Dinner not served Sun 50seats ⚑ ♡European. Specialities: provencal fish soup, salmon in pastry, St Emilion au Chocolat. Last dinner10.30pm S% Lunch£12alc Dinner£12alc Wine£5

DARWEN Lancashire Map**7** SD62
★**Millstone** The Circus ☎72588
9rm CTV ⊘ ⚑ ⛟ Children under 4yrs not accommodated ♡Mainly grills. Last dinner7.15pm ♧ S% sB&B fr£7.42 dB&B fr£14.84 Lunch£2.20 Dinner£3.20alc Wine£2.20 Credit card 3

✕**Le Biftec Bistro** 1 Belgrave Cottage ☎76927
Closed Mon; 30 seats ⚑ Last dinner10pm ✱Lunch£5alc Dinner£8alc Wine£3.45

DATCHET Berkshire Map**4** SU97
★★***Manor*** The Green ☎Slough43442
Pleasant old hotel mentioned in Jerome K Jerome's book 'Three Men in a Boat'.
20rm(3⇌⋒) ⚭ TV in bedrooms ⊘ 20P 2🏠 ♡English & French. Last dinner10pm ♧ ⊓ Credit cards 1 2 3 5

DAWLISH Devon Map**3** SX97
★★★**Langstone Cliff** Dawlish Warren (½m NE off A379 Exeter road) ☎865155
RS Nov–Mar; 69rm(49⇌⋒) Lift ☽ ⚭ CTV ⊘ 200P ⚓ ⛱(heated) ⚲(hard) billiards Disco wkly Live music & dancing three nights wkly ⚘ Conference facilities available Last dinner8pm ♧ ☕ S% sB&B£8–£10 sB&B⇌⋒£9–£13 dB&B£16–£22 dB&B⇌⋒£18–£24 Lunch£3–£3.50 Tea50p Dinner£4–£5 Wine£2.80 ⊓ *xmas* Credit card 1

★★**Charlton House** Exeter Rd ☎863260
Attractive hotel in own grounds facing sea.
Closed Feb; RS Nov–Jan (B&B & evening meal only); 23rm(10⇌⋒) ✗ ⚭ CTV TV available in bedrooms 40P ⛟ ⚓ ⛱(heated) Disco Live music & dancing wkly ⚘ ♿ ♡English & French. Last dinner8.30pm ♧ S% ✱sB&B£7–£7.60 sB&B⇌⋒£8.80–£9.40 dB&B£13.50–£14.70 dB&B⇌⋒£16–£18 Lunch£2.75–£3.50&alc Dinner£4.10–£4.50&alc Wine£2.20 ⊓ *xmas* Credit cards 1 2 3 6

★**Holcombe Head** Windward Ln, Holcombe (1m S A379) ☎862130
closed Dec–Mar; 15rm(1⇌⋒) ⚭ CTV ⊘ 20P ⚓ ⛱ ⚲(hard) ♿ ♡English & Continental. Last dinner7.15pm ♧ ☕ S% sB&B£8.30 sB&B⇌⋒£10.70 sB&B£16.60 dB&B⇌⋒£21.40 Bar lunch32–75p Tea30–60p Dinner£4.40 Wine£2.09 ⊓ *xmas*

DEDHAM Essex Map**5** TM03
★★★ ♛**Maison Talbooth** Stratford Rd ☎Colchester322367
See page 40 for details

★★♛**Dedham Vale** ☎Colchester322273
Victorian country house in 3½ acres of terraced lawns.
RS 1st wk Jan (B&B only); 9rm(5⇌⋒) Annexe: 3rm ⚭ CTV CTV available in bedroom ⊘ 40P ⛟ ⚓ ♡English & French. Last dinner9pm S% ✱sB&B fr£9.50 sB&B⇌⋒ fr£14.30 dB&B fr£19.01 dB&B⇌⋒ fr£23.75 Lunch fr£3.87&alc Dinner fr£5.95&alc Wine£3.30 Credit card 1

❁✕✕✕**Le Talbooth** ☎Colchester323150
Flemish weaver's 16th-C timbered cottage (later toll house) in delightful setting on banks of River Stour.
Closed Xmas wk; 80seats 50P ♡English & French. Specialities: Souffle Talbooth, Dover sole belle Gabrielle. Last dinner9pm ✱Lunch£6.30–£14 Dinner£6.30–£14 Wine£3.15 Credit cards 1 3 6

✕✕***Sun Hotel*** ☎Colchester322179
80seats 12P Last dinner9.45pm Credit card 3

DEFFORD Hereford & Worcester Map**7** SO94
✕✕**Railway Inn – Da Guido** ☎Evesham750309
Closed Mon; Dinner not served Sun; 60seats P ♡French & Italian. ✱Lunch£3.50–£5 Dinner£4.50–£7.50 Credit cards 2 3

DENTON Gt Manchester Map**7** SJ99
★★★**Old Rectory** Meadow Ln, Haughton Green ☎061–336 7516 Telex no668615
RS Sun & Public Hols (no restaurant); 26⇌⋒ ⚭ CTV

CTV in bedrooms ⊘ 60P ⛟ ⚓ ♀ International. Last dinner8.45pm S% sB&B⇌⋒£15.50 dB&B⇌⋒£21–£27.50 Lunch£5alc Dinner£6alc Wine£3.25

DERBY Derbyshire Map**8** SK33

★★★**Midland** Midland Rd (British Transport) ☎45894
33rm(26⇌⋒) ☽ ⋈ CTV TV available in bedrooms 24P ♀ English & French. Last dinner9pm ♧ ♫ S% ✱sB&B⇌⋒ fr£20 dB&B⇌⋒ fr£26.40 Wine£2.95 ⊓ Credit cards 1 2 3 4 5 6

★★★**Pennine** Macklin St (Greenall Whitley) ☎41741
A five-storey block opened in 1967, with views over city centre.
100⇌⋒ Lift ☽ ⋈ CTV in bedrooms P Conference facilities available ♀ International. Last dinner9.45pm ♧ ♫ S% sB&B⇌⋒£18.75–£19.75 dB&B⇌⋒£23.50–£24.50 Barlunch70p–£2.50 Dinner fr£4.50&alc Wine£2.90 ⊓ Credit cards 1 2 3 5

★★**Clarendon** Midland Rd ☎44466
14rm ☽ ⋈ CTV 50P Last dinner9pm ♧ ♫ S% ✱sB&B fr£8.25 dB&B fr£12.50 Lunch fr£2.25 Tea fr50p Dinner fr£3.50 Wine£2.85 ⊓ Credit cards 1 2 3 5

★★**Derby Crest Motel** Pasture Hill, Littleover (Crest) ☎514933
40rm(26⇌⋒) ☽ CTV in bedrooms 200P ⚓ Conference facilities available Last dinner9.15pm ♧ S% ✱sB&B£12.47 sB&B⇌⋒£15.71 dB&B£19 dB&B⇌⋒£22.24 Continental breakfast ⊓ Credit cards 1 2 3 4 5 6

★★**Gables** 119 London Rd ☎40633
Closed 22–31 Dec; 60rm(17⇌⋒) ☽ ⋈ CTV 60P ⛟ Last dinner9.45pm ♧ sB&B£7.13 sB&B⇌⋒£8.91 dB&B£11.28 dB&B⇌⋒£13.07 Lunch£3.50alc Dinner£3.50alc Wine£2.50

★★**International** 288 Burton Rd ☎31939
29rm(18⇌⋒) ☽ ⋈ CTV TV in bedrooms 45P Disco twice wkly ♀ French. Last dinner10pm ♧ ♫ sB&B fr£11 sB&B⇌⋒ fr£17 dB&B⇌⋒ fr£23.50 Lunch fr£4&alc High Tea£2alc Dinner fr£5&alc Wine£3.50 Credit card 2

★★**Kedleston** Kedleston, Quarndon (3m N) ☎56507
13rm(6⇌⋒) ⋈ CTV ⊘ 70P ⛟ ♀ English & French. Last dinner9.30pm ♧ ♫ sB&B£9.50 sB&B⇌⋒£10.50 dB&B£14 dB&B⇌⋒£16 Lunch£2.50–£3&alc Tea£1 Dinner£4.50–£5.50&alc Wine£3 Credit cards 1 2 3 5

★★**Mackworth** Ashbourne Rd, Mackworth (3m NW A52) ☎Kirk Langley324
13rm(5⇌⋒) ⋈ CTV CTV available in bedrooms ⊘ 100P ⚓ Last dinner9.30pm ♧ ♫ sB&B£11.30 sB&B⇌⋒£13.10 dB&B£19.60 dB&B⇌⋒£22 Lunch fr£3 Tea fr30p Dinner fr£3 Wine£3.25 ⊓ Credit cards 1 2 3 5

★★**York** Midland Rd (Embassy) ☎42716
39rm(4⇌⋒) ☽ ⋈ CTV TV available in bedrooms 25P Last dinner9pm ♧ S% sB&B£8.50 dB&B£14 dB&B⇌⋒£18 Lunch£4.50&alc Dinner£5&alc Wine£4 Credit cards 1 2 3 4 5 6

★**Howard** Friar Gate ☎43455
20rm(2⇌⋒) ⋈ CTV 60P ⛟ Disco six nights wkly ♀ French. Last dinner10.30pm ♧ ✱sB&B£7–£8 dB&B£9.50–£10 dB&B⇌⋒£11.50 Lunch£4alc Dinner£4alc Wine£2.40

✕✕**Golden Pheasant** Shelton Lock ☎700112
Dinner not served Sun 100seats 40P Live music & dancing Tue, Thu & Sat ♀ French. Last dinner10pm

*Lunch fr£3&alc Dinner£4–£4.75&alc Wine£2.50 Credit cards 1 2 3 5

✕San Remo 5 Sadler Gate ☎41752
Bright Italian-style restaurant on first floor.
Closed Sun & last wk Jul & first 2 wks Aug; Dinner not served Mon 47seats P English & Italian. Last dinner10pm *Lunch£2.16&alc Dinner£6.48alc Wine£3 Credit card 5

DEREHAM (EAST) Norfolk Map**9** TF91
★★★Phoenix Church St (Trusthouse Forte) ☎2276
28rm(18⇌⋒) TV in bedrooms 30P Last dinner10pm S% sB&B£13 sB&B⇌⋒£15.50 dB&B⇌⋒£21.50 *xmas* Credit cards 1 2 3 4 5 6

★★King's Head Norwich St ☎3842
Small 17th-C modernised inn with walled garden.
10rm(6⇌⋒) CTV CTV in bedrooms 30P 4 English & French. Last dinner9.30pm sB&B£9.90 sB&B⇌⋒£11.50 dB&B£15.50 dB&B⇌⋒£17.50 Lunch£2.75–£3&alc Dinner fr£3.75&alc Wine£2.65 Credit cards 1 3 6

DERSINGHAM Norfolk Map**9** TF62
★Feathers ☎40207
Victorian building in three acres grounds on edge of Sandringham estate.
6rm CTV 50P Children under 14yrs not accommodated Last dinner9pm sB&B£8 dB&B£12 Lunch£2.70&alc Dinner£2.70&alc Wine£2.31

DEVIZES Wiltshire Map**4** SU06
★★Bear Market Pl ☎2444
16th-C coaching house with canopied entrance at side of Market Square.
26rm(14⇌⋒) CTV TV in bedrooms 50P 10 Disco 6 nights wkly Last dinner10pm S% sB&B fr£12.96 sB&B⇌⋒ fr£15.12 dB&B fr£19.44 dB&B⇌⋒ fr£21.60 Lunch fr£3&alc Tea fr50p Dinner fr£3.50 Wine£2.50 Credit cards 1 3 4 5 6

DISLEY Cheshire Map**7** SJ98
✕✕*Copperfield* 49 Buxton Old Rd ☎4333
Lunch not served; 70 seats Last dinner10pm

DISS Norfolk Map**5** TM18
★★*Park* 29 Denmark St ☎2244
9rm CTV 80P Last dinner8.45pm Credit card 3

DITTON PRIORS Salop Map**7** SO68
✕✕Howard Arms ☎200
Closed Mon & 2 wks Sep; Lunch not served Tue–Sat; Dinner not served Sun; 30seats 30P English & French. Last dinner9.30pm Lunch£3.90–£4.70 Dinner£7.15–£8.10

DODDISCOMBSLEIGH Devon Map**3** SX88
✕Nobody Inn ☎Christow52394
Closed Xmas Day; Lunch not served; Dinner not served Sun & Mon; 50seats 50P bedrooms available French. Last dinner9.30pm *Dinner£4alc Wine£1.80

DONCASTER South Yorkshire Map**8** SE50
★★★Danum High St (Embassy) ☎62261
70rm(31⇌⋒) Lift CTV TV in bedrooms 8 Last dinner9.15pm S% sB&B£12 sB&B⇌⋒£14 dB&B£16 dB&B⇌⋒£18 Lunch£4.50&alc Dinner£5&alc Wine£4.50 Credit cards 1 2 3 4 5 6

★★★Earl of Doncaster Bennetthorpe (Anchor) ☎61371 Telex no858875
52⇌⋒ Lift CTV in bedrooms 100P Conference facilities available Last dinner10pm S% *sB&B⇌⋒ fr£15.50 dB&B⇌⋒ fr£21 Lunch£3.50–£4.50 Tea fr60p Dinner£3.50–£4.50 Wine£2.65 Credit cards 1 2 3 4 5 6

★★★Punch's Bawtry Rd (Embassy) ☎55235
Built in 1939 in shape of Punch's head.
26rm(15⇌⋒) CTV TV in bedrooms 50P Last dinner9.15pm S% sB&B£12 sB&B⇌⋒£14 dB&B£16 dB&B⇌⋒£19 Lunch£5&alc Dinner£5.50&alc Wine£4.50 Credit cards 1 2 3 4 5 6

✕Indus 24 Silver St ☎23366
Closed Xmas Day; Lunch not served Sun; 78seats 15P English, Indian & Pakistani. Lunch£2.30–£3.50&alc Dinner£2.30–£3.50&alc Wine£2.20 Credit cards 1 2 3 5

DONNINGTON Salop Map**7** SJ71
See under Telford

DONYATT Somerset Map**3** ST31
✕✕*Thatchers Pond* ☎Ilminster3210
Closed Mon & 24Dec–Jan; 26seats P Last dinner9pm

DORCHESTER Dorset Map**3** SY69
★★★King's Arms ☎5353
18th-C inn with bow windows over porch, with pillars. Has associations with Thomas Hardy.
27rm(16⇌⋒) CTV CTV available in bedrooms 35P Last dinner9.30pm S% sB&B£12 sB&B⇌⋒£15 dB&B£22 dB&B⇌⋒£26 Lunch£3.45 Dinner£6.20&alc Wine£2.60

★★Antelope South St, Cornhill ☎3001
16th-C coaching inn containing court room of 'Bloody Assize' trial held by Judge Jeffries.
21rm(2⇌⋒) CTV 10P 4 Disco 3 nights wkly

English & French. Lastdinner9pm ☆ S%
*sB&B£8.50 sB&B⇌⋒£8.50 dB&B£14.50
dB&B⇌⋒£14.50 Lunch£2.50&alc
Dinner£2.75&alc Wine£2.75 ⊓
Creditcards 1 2 3 5

★★Junction (Eldridge Pope) ☎3094
10rm TV 6P Lastdinner8.45pm ☆ Creditcard 1

DORCHESTER-ON-THAMES Oxfordshire Map**4**
SU59
★★White Hart High St ☎Oxford340074
15rm(14⇌⋒) 2▭ ⊞ ♔ CTV CTV in bedrooms 24P
Lastdinner9.45pm ☆ S% *sB&B fr£15
sB&B⇌⋒ fr£15 dB&B⇌⋒£20–£35
Lunch fr£4.25&alc Dinner fr£4.25&alc Wine£3
Creditcards 1 2 3 5

DORKING Surrey Map**4** TQ14
★★★★Burford Bridge Burford Bridge, Box Hill (2m N A24) (Trusthouse Forte) ☎4561 Telexno859507
30⇌⋒ ☽ ♔ CTV in bedrooms 80P ⚓ ⊐(heated)
sauna bath Lastdinner9.30pm ☆ ⊈ S%
sB&B⇌⋒£22.50 sB&B⇌⋒£30.50 ⊓ *xmas*
Creditcards 1 2 3 4 5 6

☆☆☆Punch Bowl Motor Reigate Rd (Anchor)
☎81935 Telexno858875
Annexe: 29⇌⋒ ☽ ♔ CTV available in bedrooms
80P ⚓ Lastdinner9.15pm ☆ ⊈S%
*sB&B⇌⋒£15 dB&B⇌⋒£22
Lunch£3.30–£3.90 Dinner£3.30–£3.90
Wine£2.65 ⊓ Creditcards 1 2 3 4 5 6

★★★White Horse High St (Trusthouse Forte)
☎81138
This building dates from 1500 and has been an inn since 1750. The cellar is cut from solid sandstone.
69⇌⋒ ☽ ♔ TV in bedrooms 73P
Lastdinner9.20pm ☆ ⊈ S% sB&B⇌⋒£17
dB&B⇌⋒£23 ⊓ *xmas* Creditcards 1 2 3 4 5 6

DORRIDGE West Midlands Map**7** SP17
★★*Forest* Station Approach ☎Knowle2120
11⇌⋒ ♔ CTV 35P Lastdinner9.45pm ☆
Creditcards 1 2 5

DORRINGTON Salop Map**7** SJ40
XXOlde Hall ☎465
Closed Mon; Dinner not served Sun; 65seats 50P
English, French & Italian. Lastdinner10.30pm
*Lunch£2.40–£3&alc Dinner£4.20alc
Wine£3.10 Creditcards 1 3 5

DOVER Kent Map**5** TR34
☆☆☆☆*Holiday Inn* Townwall St (Commonwealth)
☎203270 Telexno96458
83⇌⋒ Lift ☽ ⊞ ♔ CTV in bedrooms ⊐(heated) ♿
International. Lastdinner11pm ☆ ⊈
Creditcards 1 2 3 4 5 6

☆☆☆Dover Motel Whitfield (3m NW junc A2/A256)
☎821222 Telexno965866
58⇌⋒ ☽ ♔ CTV available in bedrooms 60P ⚓
French. Lastdinner10.30pm ☆ ⊈ S%
sB&B⇌⋒£17.50–£22.25 dB&B⇌⋒£25–£31.50
Lunch£3.50–£4 Tea75p–£1.50 HighTea65p–£3
Dinner£4.50alc Wine£3.15 Creditcards 1 2 3 5

★★★White Cliffs Esplanade ☎203633
Telexno965422
63rm(27⇌⋒) Lift ☽ ♔ CTV TV available in bedrooms
25⌂ English & French. Lastdinner9.30pm ☆
⊈ S% *sB&B£10.75–£11.25
sB&B⇌⋒£12.25–£12.75 dB&B£18–£18.50
dB&B⇌⋒£20–£20.50 Lunch fr£4.50&alc
Tea fr45p Dinner fr£4.30&alc Wine£3.85
Creditcards 1 2 3 5 6

★★Dover Stage Marine Pde (Grand Met) ☎201001
Modern buildings overlooking gardens and harbour.
35rm(11⇌⋒) ☽ ♔ TV available in bedrooms 50P
Live music & dancing Sat English & French.
Lastdinner9.30pm ☆ ⊈ S%
*sB&B⇌⋒£8.75–£10 dB&B⇌⋒£11–£16 ⊓
Creditcards 1 2 3 4 5 6

★★*Granham Webb* 163–165 Folkestone Rd
☎201897
Converted Victorian carriage house. Restaurant overlooks gardens which are floodlit at night.
32rm(17⇌⋒) ♔ CTV TV available in bedrooms 80P
⚓ Live music Sat English & French.
Lastdinner10pm ☆ ⊈ ⊓ Creditcards 1 2 3 5

★★*St James* Harold St ☎204579
Converted Victorian rectory in ornamental grounds.
20rm(7⇌⋒) ☽ ♔ CTV TV available in bedrooms 6P
⚓ Live music & dancing Sat English & French.
Lastdinner9.30pm ⊓ Creditcards 1 2 5 6

DOVERDALE Hereford & Worcester Map**7** SO86
XXRipperidge ☎Cutnall Green620
Dinner not served Sun; 120seats 60P Live music & dancing Wed (in winter) English & Italian.
Lastdinner10pm *Lunch£2.53–£4&alc
Dinner£5.37alc Wine£2.75

DOWNDERRY Cornwall Map**2** SX35
★★Wide Sea ☎240
Stands in its own grounds overlooking the sea.
Closed Oct–Feb except Xmas; 34rm(4⇌⋒) ☽ ♔
CTV 32P 8⌂ billiards Lastdinner8.30pm ☆ ⊈
sB&B£6.50 sB&B⇌⋒£7 dB&B£13
dB&B⇌⋒£14 Lunch£2.75–£3&alc
Tea50p–£1&alc Dinner£3.50–£4.50&alc
Wine£1.50 *xmas* Creditcard 3

DOWNHAM MARKET Norfolk Map**5** TF60
★Crown Bridge St ☎2322
17th–C coaching inn with Jacobean staircase. The

small function room was once the village schoolroom.
9rm(2⇌ ⋒) ⋈ CTV TV available in bedrooms ⊘ 50P 2⌂ ⊘ Children under 18yrs not accommodated
Lastdinner9.30pm S% sB&B£9
sB&B⇌ ⋒ fr£10 dB&B fr£16 dB&B⇌ ⋒ fr£18
Lunch£3alc Dinner£5alc Wine£2.85 ⊓
Credit cards 3 5

DOWNTON Wiltshire Map**4** SU12
★***Bull*** ☎20374
300-year-old coaching inn, with fishing rights on the Avon.
Annexe9rm(5⇌ ⋒) TV 40P ⌂ ⚓ Live music Thu
Lastdinner8.45pm Credit cards 1 2 4 5 6

DRAKES BROUGHTON Hereford & Worcester Map**3** SO94
XXX**Plough & Harrow** ☎Worcester840259
Half timbered inn located in the Vale of Evesham.
Closed 26 & 27 Dec; Dinner not served Sun; 60seats 100P International. Lastdinner9.30pm
Lunch£8alc Dinner£8alc Wine£2.95
Credit cards 1 2 3 5

DRIFFIELD, GREAT Humberside Map**8** TA05
★★***Bell*** 46 Market Pl ☎43342
An old coaching inn in the centre of the town.
13⇌ ⋒ ⋈ CTV ⊘ 40P 3⌂ squash billiards Disco Fri & Sat Children under 10yrs not accommodated
Lastdinner9.30pm

★★**Wold House** Nafferton (3m E A166) ☎84242
12rm(5⇌ ⋒) ☽ CTV ⊘ 40P 3⌂ ⚓ (heated)
Lastdinner8.30pm S% sB&B£9.50
sB&B⇌ ⋒ £10.68 dB&B£19 dB&B⇌ ⋒ £21.36
Lunch£3.25 Tea£1.25 High Tea£2.50
Dinner£4.75–£6 Wine£2.50 ⊓

DROITWICH Hereford & Worcester Map**3** SO86
★★★★**Château Impney** (Queens) ☎4411
67⇌ ⋒ 1 Lift ☽ ⋈ CTV CTV in bedrooms 600P ⚓ (hard) Live music & dancing Sat; Conference facilities available English & French.
Lastdinner10.30pm S%
sB&B⇌ ⋒ fr£33.85 dB&B⇌ ⋒ fr£42.85
Lunch£4.99&alc Tea£1.25 Dinner£5.99&alc
Wine£4.25 ⊓ Credit cards 1 2 3 5 6

★★★★**Raven** St Andrews Rd (Inter-Hotel) ☎2224
Telex no339907
16th-C manor house in town centre, originally the old manor house of Wyche.
55⇌ ⋒ Lift ☽ ⋈ CTV in bedrooms ⊘ 150P ⚓ Live music & dancing Sat ♿ Lastdinner9.30pm S%
sB&B⇌ ⋒ £17.50 dB&B⇌ ⋒ £28
Lunch£3.50–£5&alc Dinner£6–£7.50&alc
Wine£3.20 ⊓ *xmas* Credit cards 1 2 3 5 6

★★★**Worcestershire** (Best Western) ☎2371
Telex no338309
Late Victorian building in two acres of gardens.
76⇌ ⋒ Lift ☽ ⋈ CTV in bedrooms 80P ⚓ squash Live music & dancing Sat ♿ Conference facilities available European. Lastdinner9pm S%
sB&B⇌ ⋒ £13–£15 dB&B⇌ ⋒ £18–£20
Continental breakfast Lunch£3.50&alc Tea£1
Dinner£4.50&alc Wine£3.50 ⊓ *xmas*
Credit cards 1 2 3 5

⊛**St Andrew's House** Worcester Rd ☎3202
29rm(4⇌ ⋒) ⋈ CTV CTV available in bedrooms 50P ⚓ ♿ Lastdinner8.30pm S% sB&B fr£11
sB&B⇌ ⋒ fr£12.50 dB&B fr£18 dB&B⇌ ⋒ fr£20
Lunch£2.50–£3.50 Tea£1–£1.50
High Tea£1.50–£2 Dinner£4.75–£6&alc Wine£3
Credit cards 2 3

DRONFIELD Derbyshire Map**8** SK37
★★**Manor** 10 High St ☎413971

S Sun & Mon; 10 CTV CTV in bedrooms 29P
Disco Fri Live music & dancing mthly English &
rench. Last dinner 10pm S%
B&B £15.50 dB&B £22 Lunch £3
inner £5.95&alc Wine £3.95
redit cards 1 5 6

ROXFORD Hampshire Map **4** SU61
White Horse Inn 490
losed Mon; Lunch not served; Dinner not served
un; 28seats 20P bedrooms available
ast dinner 9.30pm

UDLEY West Midlands Map **7** SO99
★**Station** Birmingham Rd (Wolverhampton &
udley) 53418
9rm(11) Lift CTV CTV in bedrooms
00P English & Italian. Last dinner 9pm
% *sB&B £12.20 sB&B £13.80 dB&B £19
B&B £21.20 Lunch £2.95 Dinner £3.35
Vine £2.60 Credit cards 1 3

Ward Arms Birmingham Rd (Wolverhampton &
udley) 52723
3rm CTV 100P Last dinner 8pm S%
sB&B £9.30–£11 dB&B £20.20 Lunch £3
inner £3.65 Wine £2.60 Credit cards 1 3

ULVERTON Somerset Map **3** SS92
★★★**Carnarvon Arms** Brushford (2m S on B3222)
23302
ictorian building in 1½ acres of lawns and shrubs, ituated outside the village.
losed Xmas; 27rm(15) CTV P (heated)
(hard) billiards Last dinner 8.30pm
B&B fr £10 sB&B fr £11 dB&B fr £20
B&B fr £22 Lunch fr £3.25 Tea fr 50p
inner fr £5 Wine £2.45 Credit card 2

★★**Three Acres** Brushford (2m S on B3222)
23426
tands in a fine garden with views of the valleys of he Bark and Exe below.
Closed Nov–Apr; 7rm(1) CTV 10P
Children under 9yrs not accommodated English &
French. Last dinner 7pm sB&B £7.50
dB&B £15 dB&B £15.60 Lunch £2–£3
Tea 35p Dinner fr £5 Wine £2.20

DUNCHURCH Warwickshire Map **4** SP47
X**Old Thatched Cottage** Southam Rd
Rugby 810417
108seats English & French.
Last dinner 10.30pm Lunch £3.40&alc
Dinner £5alc Wine £3.15 Credit cards 1 2 3 5 6

D

DUNHOLME Lincolnshire Map **8** TF07
☆☆**Four Seasons** Scothern Ln Welton 60108
12 TV TV in bedrooms 150P Live music
& dancing 3 nights wkly Cabaret 3 nights wkly
Last dinner 10.30pm S% *sB&B £12.50
dB&B £17 Lunch £2.25&alc Dinner £5alc
Wine £2.95

DUNMOW, GREAT Essex Map **5** TL62
★★**Saracen's Head** High St (Trusthouse Forte)
3901
18th-C inn with traces of previous 17th-C building facing Market Square. Base for smuggling and highway robbery in 18th-C.
14rm (3) TV in bedrooms 22P
Last dinner 10pm S% sB&B £12
sB&B £15 dB&B £17 dB&B £20
xmas Credit cards 1 2 3 4 5 6

DUNSTABLE Bedfordshire Map **4** TL02
★★★***Old Palace Lodge*** Church St 62201
Part of the original Dunstable Palace. Henry VIII is reputed to have stayed here while awaiting his divorce from Catherine of Aragon.
Closed Boxing Day; RS 24, 25 & 27 Dec; 16 2
CTV 50P International.
Last dinner 9.45pm Credit cards 1 2 3 5

★★Highwayman London Rd ☎61999
Closed Xmas Day; RS Sat, Sun & Public Hols (no lunches); 26⇌ ⋒ ☽ ⋈ CTV TV in bedrooms 50P
Last dinner 9.30pm ✿ ⊈ ✱sB&B⇌ ⋒ fr£11.50 dB&B⇌ ⋒ fr£18.40 Lunch fr£3.25 Tea fr50p Dinner fr£3.25&alc Wine£2.50 Credit cards 1 3

DUNSTER Somerset Map **3** SS94
★★★Luttrell Arms 36 High St (Trusthouse Forte) ☎555
15th-C Gothic Hall with hammer-beam roof and carved oak windows, now divided into lounge and bar.
21rm(10⇌ ⋒) 1⊟ TV in bedrooms 2⌂ ⚓
Last dinner 8.30pm ✿ ⊈ S% sB&B£13.50 sB&B⇌ ⋒ £15.50 dB&B£20.50 dB&B⇌ ⋒ £26.50 ⊓ *xmas* Credit cards 1 2 3 4 5 6

★★Osborne House 31 High St (Best Western) ☎475
Closed Nov–Feb; 8rm(1⇌ ⋒) CTV in bedrooms ⚑
Last dinner 8.30pm ✿ ⊈ S%
sB&B£9.50–£10.50 sB&B⇌ ⋒ £12–£15 dB&B£18–£20 dB&B⇌ ⋒ £19–£24
Lunch£4.50–£6 Tea50p–£1.50 Dinner£6–£7.50 Wine£3 ⊓ Credit cards 1 2

★Exmoor House West St ☎268
Closed Jan; RS Feb; 6rm(1⇌ ⋒) ⋈ CTV TV available in bedroom ✱ ☋ English & French.
Last dinner 8pm ✿ ⊈ sB&B£8–£8.75 sB&B⇌ ⋒ £8.75–£9.50 dB&B£13–£14.50 dB&B⇌ ⋒ £14.50–£16 Lunch£1.25–£3.95&alc Tea70p–£1 High Tea£1–£1.50 Dinner£4.50–£6.50&alc Wine£2.95 ⊓ *xmas* Credit card 2

★Foresters Arms ☎313
10rm ⋈ CTV ⚑ Last dinner 7pm ✿ ✱sB&B£8.50 dB&B£17 Bar lunch 70p–£2.60 Dinner£4–£5 Wine£2.90 ⊓ *xmas*

DUNTON GREEN Kent Map **5** TQ55
☆☆Emma London Rd ☎681
50⇌ ⋒ ⊞ ⋈ CTV CTV in bedrooms ✱ 140P ⚓ Disco Mon–Fri Conference facilities available
Last dinner 10pm ✿ ⊈ S%
sB&B⇌ ⋒ £14–£16 dB&B⇌ ⋒ £22–£26
Lunch£4.50–£5.50&alc Tea75p–£1.50&alc Dinner£5–£6&alc Wine£3.25 ⊓ *xmas* Credit cards 1 2 3 5

DURHAM Co Durham Map **12** NZ24
★★★★Royal County Old Elvet (Swallow) ☎66821
Telex no 53168
122rm(105⇌ ⋒) Lift ☽ ⊞ ⋈ CTV in bedrooms 120P sauna bath Conference facilities available ♿
Last dinner 10pm ✿ ⊈ S% sB&B£14 sB&B⇌ ⋒ £19.50 dB&B£22.60 dB&B⇌ ⋒ £26.90 ⊓ *xmas* Credit cards 1 2 3 5

★★★Bowburn Hall Bowburn (3m SE junc A177/A1(M)) ☎770311
20⇌ ⋒ ⊞ ⋈ CTV CTV in bedrooms 50P ⚓ ☋
Last dinner 9.30pm ✿ ✱sB&B⇌ ⋒ £14.58 dB&B⇌ ⋒ £18.36 Lunch£3.80–£6.50 Dinner£5–£6.60 Wine£3.72 ⊓
Credit cards 1 2 3 5 6

☆☆☆Durham Crest Motel Croxdale (2½ S off A167) (Crest) ☎780524
33rm(27⇌ ⋒) CTV in bedrooms 150P ⚓
Last dinner 9.45pm ✿ ⊈ S% ✱sB&B£12.47 sB&B⇌ ⋒ £15.71 dB&B£19 dB&B⇌ ⋒ £22.24 Continental breakfast ⊓ Credit cards 1 2 3 4 5 6

★★★Ramside Hall Belmont (3m NE A690) ☎65282
Gothic-style early 19th-C house standing in 85 acres of parkland.
11rm(10⇌ ⋒) ⋈ CTV CTV in bedrooms 500P ⚓ Live music & dancing Sat ☋ English & French.
Last dinner 10pm ✿ ⊈ ✱sB&B£10.50 sB&B⇌ ⋒ £13.25 dB&B£19 dB&B⇌ ⋒ £20 Lunch fr£4&alc Tea fr£1.25 High Tea fr£3 Dinner fr£5.50&alc Wine£2 ⊓ *xmas* Credit cards 1 2 3 5 6

★★Three Tuns New Elvet (Swallow) ☎64326
Telex no 53168
51⇌ ⋒ ☽ ⋈ CTV CTV in bedrooms 45P
Last dinner 10.15pm ✿ ⊈ S% sB&B£13.90 sB&B⇌ ⋒ £16.80 dB&B£21.40 dB&B⇌ ⋒ £25 ⊓ *xmas* Credit cards 1 2 3 5

❀✕Travellers Rest 72 Claypath ☎65370
Rosette awarded for dinner only.
Closed Sat & Sun; 45 seats ⚑ ☋ French.
Last dinner 9.30pm ✱Lunch£9.25alc Wine£3.90 Credit cards 1 3

DYKE Lincolnshire Map **8** TF12
★Wishing Well ☎Bourne 2970
6rm(2⇌ ⋒) ☽ ⋈ CTV ✱ 50P ⚓ Last dinner 10.30pm ✿ ⊈ S% sB&B£7–£8 sB&B⇌ ⋒ £8–£9 dB&B£13–£14 dB&B⇌ ⋒ £14–£15 Lunch£1.60–£2.90 Tea20–80p Dinner£1.60–£2.90 Wine£2.46 *xmas*

EARLS COLNE Essex Map **5** TL82
✕Drapers House High St ☎2484
Closed Sun, Mon & Public Hols; Lunch not served Sat; 80 seats 20P ☋ English & Continental.
Last dinner 9pm Lunch£2.50–£3&alc Dinner£7.50alc Wine£2.55 Credit cards 1 2 3 5

EASINGWOLD North Yorkshire Map **8** SE56
★★George ☎21698
A former coaching inn.
Closed 25 Dec; 11⇌ ⋒ ⋈ CTV in bedrooms 10P ☋ Mainly grills. Last dinner 9.45pm ✿ sB&B⇌ ⋒ £9 dB&B⇌ ⋒ £16 Lunch£3.50alc Dinner£4alc Wine£3.40 ⊓

EASTBOURNE East Sussex Map **5** TV69 **See plan**
★★★★★Grand King Edward's Pde (De Vere) ☎22611 Telex no 87332 Plan **6**
Large and impressive Victorian sea-front hotel, with lofty entrance hall and two wings enclosing residents' garden.
164⇌ ⋒ Lift ☽ ⋈ CTV in bedrooms 80P ⚓ ⊐(heated) billiards Conference facilities available ☋ ♿ ☋ English & Continental. Last dinner 9.30pm ✿ ⊈ S% sB&B⇌ ⋒ £28 dB&B⇌ ⋒ £56 Lunch fr£7&alc Tea fr£1.75 Dinner fr£8&alc Wine£3.75 ⊓ *xmas* Credit cards 1 2 3 5 6

★★★★Cavendish Grand Pde (De Vere) ☎27401 Plan **2**
See page 42 for details

★★★★Queen's Marine Pde (De Vere) ☎22822
Telex no 877736 Plan **14**
Imposing, late-Victorian, six-storey building, with dormer windows, central tower, and balconies; situated on an island site facing sea.
108⇌ ⋒ Lift ☽ ⋈ CTV in bedrooms 80P billiards Conference facilities available ☋ ☋ English & French
Last dinner 9.30pm ✿ ⊈ S% sB&B⇌ ⋒ £17 dB&B⇌ ⋒ £34 Lunch fr£5.25&alc Tea fr£1.25 Dinner fr£6&alc Wine£3.75 ⊓ *xmas* Credit cards 1 2 3 5 6

★★★Burlington Grand Pde (Myddleton) ☎22724
Telex no 87591 Plan **1**
Five-storey building, with central pillars, modern canopied entrance, and sun verandahs. Close to pier, overlooking gardens and sea.
124rm(78⇌ ⋒) Lift ☽ ⋈ CTV CTV in bedrooms 30⌂ Conference facilities available ☋ ☋ English & French.
Last dinner 8.30pm ✿ ⊈ S%
✱sB&B£7.50–£12.50 sB&B⇌ ⋒ £8.50–£14 dB&B£18–£24 dB&B⇌ ⋒ £26 Lunch£2.75&alc Tea60p Dinner£3.75&alc Wine£3 ⊓ *xmas* Credit cards 1 2 3 5 6

★★★Chatsworth Grand Pde ☎30327 Plan **3**
Four-storey early 20th-C building with sun terrace overlooking sea. Situated between pier and bandstand.
Closed 2 Jan–1 Mar; 46rm(42⇌ ⋒) Lift ☽ CTV

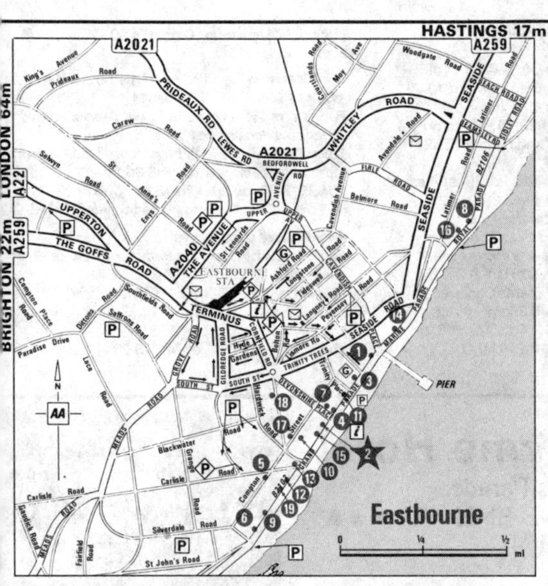

1 Burlington ★★★
2 Cavendish ★★★★
3 Chatsworth ★★★
4 Cumberland ★★★
5 Farrar's ★★
6 Grand ★★★★★
7 Imperial ★★★
8 Langham ★★
9 Lansdowne ★★★
10 Latham House ★
11 Mansion ★★★
12 Oban ★
13 Princes ★★★
14 Queen's ★★★★
15 Sandhurst ★★★
16 San Remo ★
17 Summer Palace XX
18 Sussex ★★
19 Wish Tower ★★★

E

Last dinner 8pm S% sB&B fr£10.80 sB&B fr£11.69 dB&B fr£21.60 dB&B fr£23.42 Lunch fr£4 Tea fr45p Dinner fr£4.70 Wine £2.45 *xmas*

★★★**Cumberland** Grand Pde ☎30342 Plan **4** 70rm(45 Lift CTV TV available in bedrooms Children under 1yr not accommodated French. Last dinner 8pm sB&B £10–£11 sB&B £11–£12.50 dB&B £19.50–£21.50 dB&B £21.50–£25 Lunch £3.25–£5.50&alc Tea 35p–£1.50&alc Dinner £5–£6.50&alc Wine £3 *xmas*

★★★**Imperial** Devonshire Pl (North) ☎20525 Telexno262180 Plan**7**
Unlicensed; 121rm(59⇌ ⋒) Lift ☽ ⋈ CTV 10P Lastdinner8.30pm ♉ ☑ S% sB&B fr£10.25 sB&B⇌ ⋒ fr£11.25 dB&B fr£18.75 dB&B⇌ ⋒ fr£20.75 Lunch fr£3.75 Tea fr75p Dinner fr£4.25 ⊟ *xmas* Credit cards 1 2 3 6

★★★**Lansdowne** King Edward's Pde (Best Western) ☎25174 Plan**9**
Well-appointed seafront hotel close to entertainments complex and shops. Spacious lounges overlook Western lawns and the sea.
Closed 1–13Jan; 141rm(58⇌ ⋒) Lift ☽ CTV TV available in bedrooms 20⌂ billiards Conference facilities available Lastdinner8.30pm ♉ ☑ S% sB&B£8.25–£15.25 sB&B⇌ ⋒£9.75–£16.25 dB&B£16.50–£28 dB&B⇌ ⋒£19.50–£31 Lunch£3.75 Tea50p Dinner£4.50 Wine£3 ⊟ *xmas*

★★★**Mansion** Grand Parade (Trusthouse Forte) ☎27411 Telexno877288 Plan**11**
Four-storey Victorian building, with enclosed sun terrace overlooking sea.
103rm(52⇌ ⋒) Lift ☽ TV in bedrooms ⚑ Conference facilities available Lastdinner8.30pm ♉ ☑ S% sB&B£13.50 sB&B⇌ ⋒£15.50 dB&B£22 dB&B⇌ ⋒£26 ⊟ *xmas* Credit cards 1 2 3 4 5 6

★★★**Princes** Lascelles Ter ☎22056 Plan**13**
Four-storey, late Victorian terraced building just off sea-front.
Closed Dec–Feb; 50rm(24⇌ ⋒) Lift ☽ ⋈ CTV Live music & dancing wkly Jun–Sep ♡ European. Lastdinner8.30pm ♉ ☑ S% sB&B£9.60–£10.50 dB&B£19.20–£24

3&B⇌⋒£24–£27.50 Lunch£3.25–£3.50 ea35p–£1 Dinner£4.20–£4.50 Wine£3.50 ⊟ *nas*

★★Sandhurst Grand Pde ☎27868 Plan**15** rm(30⇌⋒ Lift ☽ CTV TV available in bedrooms ⊟ International. Last dinner8.30pm ✿ ℒ sB&B£8.50–£11.50 sB&B⇌⋒£9–£12.50 dB&B£17–£23 dB&B⇌⋒£18–£25 Lunch fr£4 Tea fr50p Dinner fr£4.50 Wine£2.75 ⊟ *xmas* Credit card②

★★Wish Tower King Edward's Pde (Trusthouse Forte) ☎22676 Telex no877288 Plan**19** rm(40⇌⋒) Lift ☽ CTV TV in bedrooms 3 Last dinner8.30pm ✿ ℒ S% sB&B£13.50 sB&B⇌⋒£15.50 dB&B£22 dB&B⇌⋒£26 ⊟ *xmas* Credit cards①②③④⑤⑥

★★Farrar's 3–5 Wilmington Gdns ☎23737 Plan**5** *White, five-storey, late Victorian building with modern entrance, off sea front. Views of distant Downs.* 44rm(14⇌⋒) Lift ☽ CTV 24P Children under 3yrs not accommodated Last dinner8pm ✿ ℒ sB&B£8.50–£10.50 sB&B⇌⋒£9.50–£11.50 dB&B£17–£21 dB&B⇌⋒£19–£23 Lunch fr£3 Tea fr30p Dinner fr£4.25 Wine£2.80 ⊟ Credit cards①②③

★★Langham Royal Pde ☎31451 Plan**8** *Three-storey, Victorian terraced building, with uninterrupted views of sea.* Closed mid Oct–Mar; 86rm(27⇌⋒) Lift ☽ CTV 3 Disco Wed (high season) Live music & dancing Mon & Fri (high season) Cabaret Fri (high season)

E

☺English & French. Lastdinner7.30pm ♆ ♈ S% sB&B£9.50–£11.50 sB&B⇌⋒£11–£13.50 dB&B£19–£23 dB&B⇌⋒£22–£27 Lunch fr£3.45 Tea fr40p High Tea fr£2 Dinner fr£4.75 Wine£2.75

★★*Sussex* Cornfield Ter (Centre) ☎27681 Plan**18** 35rm Lift ☽ ⋔ CTV Live music Sat ☺International. Lastdinner8.30pm ♆ ⊟ Credit cards 1 2 3

★Latham House Howard Sq ☎20985 Plan**10** Unlicensed; 39rm CTV ⊘ 6P Lastdinner7pm ♆ ♈ S% sB&B£8.50–£9.50 dB&B£17–£19 Lunch fr£2.25 Tea fr35p Dinner fr£2.75 ⊟ *xmas*

★*Oban* King Edward's Pde ☎31581 Plan**12** Closed mid Oct–mid Apr except Xmas; 28rm(10⇌⋒) Lift ☽ CTV Lastdinner7pm ♆ ♈

★San Remo Royal Pde ☎21831 Plan**16** Closed end Oct–Mar; 60rm(3⇌⋒) Lift ☽ ⋔ CTV Live music & dancing 3 nights wkly Cabaret 3 nights wkly Lastdinner6.30pm S% ✻sB&B£7.50–£9.50 sB&B⇌⋒£8.50–£10.50 dB&B£16–£19 dB&B⇌⋒£16–£21 Lunch£2 Dinner£2.50&alc Wine£3

❁✕✕Summer Palace 'Park Gates' Chiswick Pl ☎33056 Plan**17** Closed Xmas; 130seats 20P ☺Pekinese. Lastdinner11.15pm Credit cards 2 3 5

EAST GRINSTEAD West Sussex Map**5** TQ33
❁★★★ ⚘Gravetye Manor (3m SW off unclass road joining B2110 & B2028) ☎Sharpthorne810567 Gatwick plan**10**
See page 41 for details

★★★Ye Olde Felbridge London Rd ☎24424 Telex no95156 Gatwick plan**17** 47⇌⋒ ☽ ⋔ CTV in bedrooms 800P ⚓ ⊐(heated) Disco Thu & Sun Live music & dancing Sat Cabaret Sat Conference facilities available ☺English & French. Lastdinner10.30pm ♆ ♈ S% sB&B⇌⋒£19.50 dB&B⇌⋒£31.50 Lunch£5&alc Tea75palc Dinner£6.50alc Wine£3.25 ⊟ *xmas* Credit cards 1 2 3 4 5 6

EAST HADDON Northamptonshire Map**4** SP66
✕✕Buckby Lion ☎393
Closed Mon; Dinner not served Sun; 70seats 100P Disco Fri ☺English & French. Lastdinner10pm Lunch£3.90 Dinner£5.45 Wine£3 Credit cards 1 2 3

EAST HORSLEY Surrey Map**4** TQ05
✕*Tudor Rose* 15 Bishopsmead Pde ☎4484
Closed Mon & last 2wks Aug; Dinner not served Sun 26seats Lastdinner10pm Credit cards 1 2 3 5

EAST MOLESEY Surrey Map**4** TQ16
✕*Le Chien qui Fume* 107 Walton Rd ☎01–979715
Closed Sun; 50seats ☺French. Lastdinner11pm Credit cards 1 3 5 6

❁✕Lantern 20 Bridge Rd ☎01–9791531
Attractive, cosy restaurant, close to Hampton Bridge
Closed Xmas & Public Hols; Lunch not served; 45seats ⚑ ☺French. Specialities: carré d'agneau, entrecôte au poivre, bourrine provençale. Lastdinner11pm Dinner£8.10alc Wine£3.50 Credit cards 1 2 3 5

✕Vecchia Roma 57 Bridge Rd ☎01–9795490
Small attractive Italian restaurant.
Closed Monday; 70seats ⚑ ☺French & Italian. Lastdinner11pm Lunch£2.95–£3.25&alc Dinner£6.50alc Wine£2.95 Credit cards 1 2 3 5

EAST PORTLEMOUTH Devon Map**3** SX73
★★Gara Rock ☎Salcombe2342
Closed Nov–Mar; RS Etr–mid May; 44rm(31⇌⋒) ⋔ CTV TV available in bedrooms 100P ⚘ ⚓ ⊐(heated)

●(hard) ↬ Disco wkly ♧ ♈English & French. Last dinner8.30pm ✪ ⚐ S% sB&B£10–£18 sB&B⇌🛁£12.50–£20 dB&B£20–£36 dB&B⇌🛁£25–£40 Barlunch£1–£5 Tea£1–£2 Dinner£5–£8.50 Wine£2.50 ⛿ Credit cards 1 2 3

EAST PRESTON West Sussex Map**4** TQ00
XXOld Forge The Street ☎Rustington2040
Victorian water-colour artist E Hardy lived at the Old Forge at the turn of the century. Famous for many local paintings including the murals in Climping Church which can be seen today.
Closed Mon; Dinner not served Sun; 55seats 20P ♈English & French. Last dinner10pm S% Lunch£3.20&alc Dinner£7.50alc Wine£2.95 Credit cards 1 2 3 5 6

EAST SUTTON Kent Map**5** TQ84
★★Shant ☎Sutton Valance2235
11⇌🛁 ☽ 🍴 CTV CTV in bedrooms 50P ⛐ ⚓ ⊃(heated) sauna bath Last dinner10pm ✪ ⚐ S% ✻sB&B⇌🛁£14.85 dB&B⇌🛁£22.75 Lunch£.375&alc Tea fr£1.50 Dinner£6alc Wine£2.52 *xmas* Credit cards 1 2 3 5

EASTWOOD Nottinghamshire Map**8** SK44
★Sun Inn ☎Langley Mill2940
16rm CTV ⊘ 50P ⚓ ♈Italian. Last dinner8pm ✪ ⚐ S% sB&B fr£6.75 dB&B fr£13.50 Lunch95p–£2.95 Dinner£1.80–£2.95 Wine£2.50

EDENHALL Cumbria Map**12** NY53
★★Edenhall ☎Langwathby454
The dining room, with its large expanse of windows, offers fine views of the garden.
22⇌🛁 Annexe:6⇌🛁 🍴 CTV TV available in bedrooms 30P 6🏠 ⛐ ⚓ ↬ ♿ Last dinner8.15pm ✪ ⚐ ✻sB&B⇌🛁£5.50 dB&B⇌🛁£11 Lunch£2.50&alc Tea50–85p High Tea£2.50 Dinner£3&alc Wine£1.75 *xmas* Credit cards 1 2 3 5 6

EGERTON Gt Manchester Map**7** SD71
★★★Egerton House ☎Bolton57171
Closed 1Jan; RS 22–31Dec; 18⇌🛁 🍴 TV in bedrooms 36P 1🏠 ⛐ ⚓ ♈International. Last dinner9.30pm ✪ S% sB&B⇌🛁 fr£20.79 dB&B⇌🛁 fr£25.92 Lunch£3.20&alc Dinner£6.50alc Wine£3.50 Credit cards 1 2 5

EGGESFORD Devon Map**3** SS61
★★ Fox & Hounds ☎Chulmleigh345
Red-brick, detached, building situated in own grounds off Barnstaple/Crediton road.
Closed Xmas; RS Oct–Mar; 10rm(4⇌🛁) Annexe:4⇌🛁 🍴 CTV 100P 6🏠 ⛐ ⚓ ↬ Children under 10yrs not accommodated Last dinner9pm ✪ ⚐ S% sB&B£8–£9 dB&B£16–£18 dB&B⇌🛁£18–£20 Barlunch55p–£3.80&alc Tea30p–£1 Dinner£.450&alc Wine£3

EGHAM Surrey Map**4** TQ07
★★★★Great Fosters Stroude Rd ☎33822
A magnificent mellow brick, Tudor royal hunting lodge, with fine gardens rich topiary work.
23rm(22⇌🛁) 3▭ ☽ 🍴 CTV TV available in bedrooms ⊘ 200P ⚓ ⊃(heated) ●(hard) Live music & dancing Sat ♈English & French. Last dinner9.30pm ✪ ⚐ S% ✻sB&B£17.85–£19 sB&B⇌🛁 fr£17.85 dB&B£31–£44.10 dB&B⇌🛁£31–£44 Lunch£5.75&alc Tea£2.30 Dinner£6.60&alc Wine£3.73 *xmas* Credit cards 1 2 3 5

☆☆☆☆Runnymede (Prestige) ☎6171
Telex no934900
Situated in ten acres of landscaped gardens on the south bank of the Thames, on the spot where the Magna Carta was signed.
90⇌🛁 Lift ☽ 🍴 CTV in bedrooms 250P ⚓ ⛳ ● ↬ squash sauna bath Disco 4 nights wkly Live music & dancing wkly Conference facilities available ♈English & French. Last dinner10pm ✪ ⚐ S% sB&B⇌🛁£23 dB&B⇌🛁£33 Lunch£5&alc Tea50p Dinner£5&alc Wine£4 ⛿ *xmas* Credit cards 1 2 3 5

EGTON BRIDGE North Yorkshire Map**8** NZ80
★*Horse Shoe* ☎Grosmont245
Two-storey stone inn with garden, on island of River Esk.
7rm TV 20P ⚓ Last dinner8pm ✪

ELCOT Berkshire Map**4** SU36
★★Elcot Park (1m N of A4) (Inter-Hotel) ☎Kintbury276 Telex no8951994
Closed Xmas; 24rm(4⇌🛁) 2▭ 🍴 CTV in bedrooms 200P 2🏠 ⚓ ●(hard) ♧ ♈English & French. Last dinner8.45pm ✪ ⚐ S% ✻sB&B£9.72 sB&B⇌🛁£16.20 dB&B£19.44 dB&B⇌🛁£22.68–£32.40 Lunch fr£3.78 Dinner fr£4.59 Wine£2.95 Credit cards 1 2 3 6

ELLESMERE Salop Map**7** SJ33
★Black Lion Scotland St ☎2418
6rm CTV ⊘ 20P 4🏠 Last dinner9.45pm ✪ S% sB&B£5.75 dB&B£11.50 Barlunch50p–£2&alc Dinner£1.75–£4&alc Wine£2.17 Credit card 1

ELSTEAD Surrey Map**4** SU94
XEmmerich's Thurley Rd ☎2323
Closed Mon; Dinner not served Sun; 30seats 8P ♈Austrian. Last dinner9.30pm Lunch£2.50–£3.50&alc Dinner£7.50alc Wine£4.22 Credit cards 3 5

ELTERWATER Cumbria Map**7** NY30
⊛ *Eltermere* (on unclass road between A593 & B5343) ☎Langdale207
Charming old mansion house in own grounds

overlooking one of the smaller lakes.
Closed Nov–Etr; 16rm 20P 4 Children under 5yrs not accommodated Last dinner7.30pm

ELY Cambridgeshire Map**5** TL58
XOld Fire Engine House 25 St Mary's Street 2582
Ely's horse drawn fire engine was kept here until 1912, and is still on view in the garden.
Closed Sun & 24 Dec–4 Jan; 30seats 10P
Specialities: steak & kidney pie, turkey breast in cream sauce, pork chop in cider. Last dinner9pm
Lunch£3.80alc Tea£1alc Dinner£4.80alc

EMBLETON Northumberland Map**12** NU22
★★Dunstanburgh Castle 203
RS Nov–Mar; 19rm(5) CTV 20P 3
Last dinner7.30pm *sB&B£7.83
sB&B£8.94 dB&B£15.66 dB&B£17.82
Lunch£2.75–£3.20 Tea45p–£1.20
High Tea£2.50–£3.50 Dinner fr£4.30 *xmas*

EMBOROUGH Somerset Map**3** ST65
★★Court Stratton-on-Fosse232237
Stone-built detached hotel with pleasant mature gardens.
9rm(4) CTV TV in bedrooms 25P
English & Continental. Last dinner9pm
sB&B£10 sB&B£11.50 dB&B£13.50
dB&B£15.50 Dinner£5alc Wine£3

EMSWORTH Hampshire Map**4** SU70
★★*Brookfield* Havant Rd 3363
16 CTV TV available in bedrooms 50P
French. Last dinner9.30pm

ENFIELD Greater London Map**14** TQ39
★★★Royal Chace The Ridgeway 01-366 6500
50 6 CTV in bedrooms 300P
(heated) (hard) Conference facilities available
French. Last dinner10pm sB&B fr£16.75
dB&B fr£26 Continental breakfast Lunch£5alc
High Tea£3alc Dinner£10alc Wine£3.75
Credit cards 1 2 3 5

★★*Enfield* Rowantree Rd 01–366 3511
35rm(12) CTV 11P 3
Last dinner10.30pm

★★Holtwhites Chase Side 01–363 0124
Telex no 299670
29rm(24) CTV CTV in bedrooms 10P
10 Children under 4 yrs not accommodated
Last dinner9pm sB&B£16–£18
sB&B£20–£25 dB&B£26–£30
dB&B£28–£32 Lunch£4alc Tea£1.75alc
High Tea£3.50 Dinner£8alc Wine£3.50
Credit cards 1 2 3 5 6

XXNorfolk 80 London Rd 01–363 0979
Closed Sun; Dinner not served Mon; English & Continental. Last dinner9.30pm Lunch£8alc
Dinner£8alc Wine£4 Credit cards 1 3 5

ENGLEFIELD GREEN Surrey Map**4** SU97
XXXBailiwick Egham2223
100seats International. Last dinner10pm
*Lunch£7alc Dinner£7alc Wine£3.50
Credit cards 3 5

EPPING Essex Map**5** TL40
☆☆☆Epping Forest Motel High Rd(Grand Met) 73135
42rm Lift TV 25P European. Last dinner9pm
S% *sB&B£12.50
dB&B£17.50 Credit cards 1 2 3 4 5 6

☆☆☆Post House High Rd, Bell Common (Trusthouse Forte) 73137
60 CTV in bedrooms 95P
Last dinner10.15pm S%
sB&B£19.75 dB&B£28.50 *xmas*
Credit cards 1 2 3 4 5 6

EPSOM Surrey Map**4** TQ26
★★Drift Bridge Reigate Rd (Crest)
Burgh Heath52163
29rm(14) CTV available in bedrooms 120P
S% *sB&B£12.96 sB&B£17.28
dB&B£20.52 dB&B£25.92
Credit cards 1 2 3 4 5 6

At **Burgh Heath** (3m SE on A217)

☆☆Pickard Motor Brighton Rd (Best Western)
Burgh Heath57222
32 142P

ERMINGTON Devon Map**2** SX65
★★*Ermewood House* Modbury321
12 CTV TV in bedrooms 25P
Last dinner10pm Credit cards 1 2 3

ESHER Surrey Map**4** TQ16
★Haven Portsmouth Rd (1m NE of Scilly Isles rbt on A307) 01–398 0023
17rm(2) Annexe: 4rm(1) CTV CTV available in bedrooms 20P 1 English & International. Last dinner8pm S%
sB&B fr£10.50 sB&B fr£13 dB&B fr£16.25
dB&B fr£19.25 Dinner£3.50–£5.05 Wine£3
Credit cards 1 2 3 5 6

ETON Berkshire Map**4** SU97
XX*Antico* 42 High St Windsor63977
Closed Sun; 65seats Italian. Credit cards 1 2 3 5

ETTINGTON Warwickshire Map**4** SP24
★★*Chase* Stratford-on-Avon740000
Closed Xmas; 12rm(10) CTV in bedrooms
50P Last dinner9.15pm
Credit cards 2 3

EVERCREECH Somerset Map**3** ST63
★★Glen Queens Rd 830369
Large country house built in 1900 standing in nine acres of private grounds; ¼ mile from village.
13rm(4) Annexe: 4rm CTV 45P
Last dinner9pm S% *sB&B£8.50
sB&B£11.50 dB&B£15.50 dB&B£17.50
Lunch£3.50&alc Tea30–75p High Tea£3.50
Dinner£3.50&alc Wine£2.30 Credit cards 1 2 3

EVERSLEY Hampshire Map**4** SU76
XXNew Mill New Mill Ln (off A327) 732277
Closed Sun; Lunch not served Mon; 80seats 40P
English & French. Last dinner10pm
*Lunch£6alc Dinner£6alc Wine£3.50
Credit cards 1 2 3 5

EVESHAM Hereford & Worcester Map**4** SP04
★★★Evesham Coopers Ln 6344 Telex no 339342
Built on site of Roman Camp – part Tudor, part Georgian. Lebanon Cedar tree planted in 1809, and six Mulberry trees planted by monks in 1500 in the garden.
18rm(17) CTV CTV in bedrooms 60P
International. Last dinner9.30pm S%
sB&B£13 sB&B£17 dB&B£25
dB&B£30 Lunch fr£3.25 Tea fr35p
Dinner£6alc Wine£3.40 *xmas*
Credit cards 1 2 3 5 6

★★Northwick Arms Waterside 6109
The house dates from the 17th-C and was once a Quaker meeting house.
Closed 25–28Dec; 21rm(3) Annexe: 1 CTV
100P Last dinner9.30pm S%
sB&B£9.50–£11 sB&B£12–£14
dB&B£12.50–£14 dB&B£18–£20
Lunch£1.50alc Dinner£4.50alc Wine£2.50
Credit cards 1 3

Park View Waterside ☎2639
losed Xmas; 29rm CTV 50P Lastdinner6pm ♔
% sB&B£6.80–£8.25 dB&B£13.50–£16.50
inner£3.25–£3.50 Wine£2.40
redit cards 1 6

VEN (nr Cirencester) Gloucestershire Map**4** SU09
★★**Wild Duck Inn** ☎Kemble310
⇌ ⋒ 🍴 CTV in bedrooms 50P 1🏠 🚗 Live music
vice wkly ♡English & Continental.
astdinner9.50pm ♔ ♖ sB&B⇌⋒£23.49
B&B⇌⋒£25.63 Continental breakfast
unch£4.75&alc Teafr50p High Tea fr£1.20
inner£4.85&alc Wine£5.50 ▀ *xmas*
redit cards 1 5

EXETER Devon Map**3** SX99 **See plan**
★★★**Buckerell Lodge** Topsham Rd (Crest) ☎52451
Plan**1**
A house dating from the 12th century now converted to a hotel.
19rm(9⇌⋒) ☽ CTV in bedrooms 150P 🚗 ⚓
♡English & French. Lastdinner10pm ♔ S%
✱sB&B£12.15 sB&B⇌⋒£16.20 dB&B£19.17
dB&B⇌⋒£24.30 ▀ Credit cards 1 2 3 4 5 6

☆☆☆**Countess Wear Lodge** Topsham Rd (Grand Met) ☎Topsham5441 Plan**2**
44⇌⋒ ☽ 🍴 TV available in bedrooms 200P ⚓ Live music & dancing Fri–Sun Conference facilities available ♡English & French. Lastdinner10pm S%
✱sB&B⇌⋒£11.50–£13 dB&B⇌⋒£17–£18.50
▀ Credit cards 1 2 3 4 5 6

E

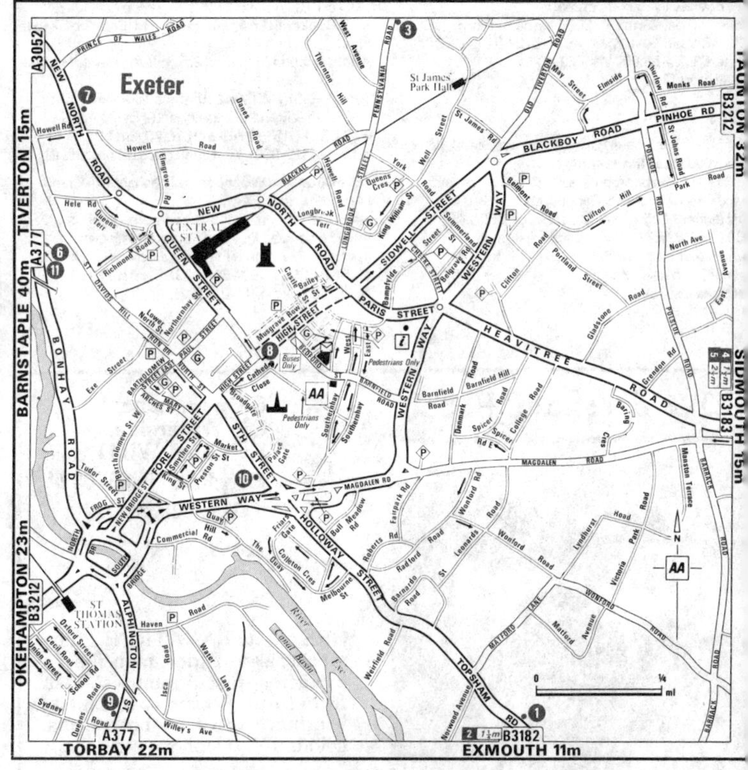

1 Buckerell Lodge ★★★
2 Countess Wear Lodge ☆☆☆
3 Edgerton Park ★★★
4 Exeter Crest Motel ☆☆
5 Gipsy Hill ★★★
6 Great Western ★★
7 Imperial ★★★
8 Royal Clarence ★★★
9 St Andrews ★★
10 White Hart ★★★
11 Hotel Windsor ★★

☆☆☆**Devon Motel** Exeter Bypass, Matford (Percy R. Brend) ☎59268 Not on plan
42⇌⋒ ☽ ℿ CTV TV in bedrooms 100P ⚓ Live music & dancing Sat Cabaret Sun Last dinner 10pm ✿
✻sB&B⇌⋒£11.61 dB&B⇌⋒£17.28
Lunch £2.75 Dinner £3.50&alc Wine £2.75 ⊟
xmas Credit cards 1 2 3

★★★***Edgerton Park*** Pennsylvania Rd ☎74029 Plan **3**
17⇌⋒ ℿ CTV 60P ⁂ ♀ English & French.
Last dinner 9.15pm ✿ ⊻ ⊟
Credit cards 1 2 3 5

★★★**Gypsy Hill** Pinhoe (3m E on B3181) ☎65252 Plan **5**
An old country house, standing in its own grounds with views of the sea and the estuary of the River Exe.
Closed Xmas & New Year; RS 27Dec&1Jan; 21⇌⋒ Annexe: 9⇌⋒ ⊞ ℿ TV in bedrooms 80P ⁂ ⚓
Last dinner 8.45pm ✿ ⊻ S%
sB&B⇌⋒ fr£14.50 dB&B⇌⋒ fr£23
Lunch fr£3.25&alc Dinner fr£4.25&alc ⊟
Credit cards 1 3 6

★★★**Imperial** St David's ☎72750 Plan **7**
Built as a mansion during Queen Anne period; situated in five acres of spacious sheltered grounds.
30rm(19⇌⋒) ☽ ℿ CTV ⊘ 70P 12⌂ ⁂ ⚓
Last dinner 8.30pm S% sB&B fr£13
sB&B⇌⋒ fr£15 dB&B fr£24 dB&B⇌⋒ fr£28
Lunch fr£3.20 Tea fr£1 Dinner fr£4.20
Wine £2.50 ⊟ Credit cards 1 2 3 6

★★★**Royal Clarence** Cathedral Yard (Norfolk Capital) ☎58464 Telex no 23241 Plan **8**
Four-storey, white 18th-C building with bay windows facing Cathedral.
63⇌⋒ Lift ☽ ℿ CTV in bedrooms ℙ ♀ English & Continental. Last dinner 10pm ✿ ⊻ S%
sB&B⇌⋒£18.15 dB&B⇌⋒£28.10
Lunch fr£3.75&alc Tea fr£1.75 High Tea fr£1.75
Dinner fr£4.50&alc Wine £4 ⊟
Credit cards 1 2 3 5 6

★★★**White Hart** 65 South St ☎79897 Plan **10**
Comfortably appointed hotel of character and charm.
Closed 25 & 26Dec; 65rm(51⇌⋒) Lift ☽ ℿ CTV CTV available in bedrooms P ⁂ Last dinner 10pm ✿
sB&B fr£10.70 sB&B⇌⋒£14.50–£16
dB&B£18–£19 dB&B⇌⋒£23–£25 Lunch £3.50
Dinner £5.25&alc Wine £2.60 ⊟
Credit cards 1 2 3 5

☆☆**Exeter Crest Motel** Rydon Ln, Middlemoor (Crest) ☎35353 Plan **4**
57rm(41⇌⋒) ☽ CTV CTV in bedrooms 250P ⚓
Last dinner 9.30pm ✿ S% ✻sB&B£11.39
dB&B⇌⋒£15.17 dB&B£19 dB&B⇌⋒£21.70
Continental breakfast ⊟ Credit cards 1 2 3 4 5 6

★★**Great Western** St David's Station Approach (Trusthouse Forte) ☎74039 Plan**6**
44rm(8⇌⋒) ☽ ⊞ TV in bedrooms ⚑
Last dinner8.45pm ✿ ♀ S% sB&B£12
dB&B⇌⋒£14.50 dB&B£20 dB&B⇌⋒£22.50
⊟ Credit cards 1 2 3 4 5 6

★★**St Andrews** 28 Alphington Rd ☎76784 Plan**9**
Closed Xmas; 20rm ⊞ CTV 20P ⊕ Last dinner8pm
S% sB&B£9.72–£10.26 dB&B£16.20–£16.74
Bar lunch70p–£2 Dinner£4–£5&alc Wine£2.50
⊟ Credit cards 1 3

★★⚘**Trood Country House** Little Silver Ln, Matford (3m S off Exeter Bypass) ☎75839 Not on plan
8rm(2⇌⋒) 1⊟ ✕ CTV available in bedrooms 60P 2⌂
⊕ ⚓ Children under 7yrs not accommodated
Last dinner9.30pm ✿ ♀ S% sB&B£7.50
sB&B⇌⋒£10 dB&B£15–£22
sB&B⇌⋒£17–£22 Continental breakfast
Lunch£3 Tea50p–£1.50 High Tea£2–£3.50
Dinner£3.50–£10&alc Wine£2.90 ⊟
Credit cards 1 3

★★**Hotel Windsor** Bonhay Rd ☎73883 Plan**11**
Closed Xmas; 34rm(9⇌⋒) ☽ ⊞ CTV 20P 6⌂
Last dinner8.15pm ✿ ♀ S% sB&B£7.56
sB&B⇌⋒£9.50 dB&B£14.58 dB&B⇌⋒£16.74
Lunch£2.16 Tea50–75p Dinner£2.97–£3.60
Wine£2.75 Credit card 3

At **Kennford** (6m SW on A38)

☆☆☆**Exeter Ladbroke Mercury Motor Inn** (Ladbroke) ☎Kennford832121 Not on plan
61⇌⋒ 200P

★★**Fairwinds** ☎Kennford832911 Not on plan
7rm(2⇌⋒) 9p

EXFORD Somerset Map**3** SS83

★★★**Crown** ☎243
Closed Jan & Feb; 18⇌⋒ ⊞ CTV CTV in bedrooms 30P 2⌂ ⊕ ⚓ ∩ Children under 8yrs not accommodated ♀French. Last dinner9.30pm ✿
♀ S% sB&B⇌⋒£12–£14 dB&B⇌⋒£24–£28
Lunch fr£4 Tea75p alc Dinner fr£6 Wine£2.30
⊟ *xmas*

★★**White Horse** ☎229
Tudor-style building with half-timbered upper storey 900 feet above sea-level in Exmoor National Park.
Closed 23Oct–26Mar; 21rm(4⇌⋒) ⊞ CTV 20P ⊕
Last dinner8.30pm ✿ ♀ S%
✳sB&B£7.13–£9.50 dB&B£14.26–£19
dB&B⇌⋒£17.58–£22.32 Bar lunch£1.60–£1.90
Tea70p Dinner£3.75–£4.50 Wine£2.50

EXMOUTH Devon Map**3** SY08

★★★**Devoncourt** Douglas Av ☎72277
In four acres of sub-tropical grounds; overlooking sea with direct access to beach.
68⇌⋒ Lift ☽ ⊞ CTV 60P 10⌂ ⊕ ⚓ ⊐(heated)
⚘(hard) ♧ ♿ ♀English & French.
Last dinner8.30pm ✿ ♀ sB&B⇌⋒£12–£13.50
dB&B⇌⋒£24–£27 Lunch fr£2.50&alc Tea fr55p
High Tea fr£1.50 Dinner fr£3.50&alc Wine£2.35
⊟ *xmas*

★★★**Imperial** The Esplanade (Trusthouse Forte) ☎74761
37⇌⋒ Lift ☽ ⊞ TV in bedrooms 40P ⊕ ⚓ ⊐(heated)
Last dinner9pm ✿ ♀ S% sB&B⇌⋒£17.50
dB&B⇌⋒£30.50 ⊟ *xmas*
Credit cards 1 2 3 4 5 6

★★★**Royal Beacon** The Beacon ☎4886
Originally a Georgian posting house, with a Regency style dining room.
35rm(20⇌⋒) Lift ⊞ CTV CTV in bedrooms 30P 10⌂
♧ Last dinner9pm ✿ ♀ S% ✳sB&B£9.75
sB&B⇌⋒£14 dB&B£20 dB&B⇌⋒£28
Lunch fr£3.25&alc Tea fr75p High Tea fr£1.75

inner fr£4.25&alc Wine£2.95
redit cards 1 2 3 4 5 6

★Balcombe House 7 Stevenstone Rd ☎6349
losed Nov–Mar; 12⇌⋒ CTV 12P
ast dinner 5pm S%
B&B⇌⋒£7.75–£9.75
B&B⇌⋒£15.50–£19.50 Bar lunch £1–£2.50
ea £1–£2 High Tea £1.50–£2.50
inner £4.25–£5.25 Wine £2.20

★★Barn Foxholes Hill ☎74411
0rm(9⇌⋒) CTV 30P 3 (grass)
ast dinner 7pm sB&B£12.50 (incl dinner)
B&B£12.50 (incl dinner) dB&B£24.50 (incl dinner)
B&B⇌⋒£24.50 (incl dinner) Lunch £5alc
ea £1.50alc Dinner £5alc Wine £3.25 *xmas*

★★Cavendish 11 Morton Cres, The Esplanade
☎72528
losed Dec–Feb; 64rm(26⇌⋒) Lift CTV 24P Live
usic & dancing 4 nights wkly Last dinner 7.45pm
% ✱sB&B£5.40–£7.02
B&B⇌⋒£5.94–£7.56 dB&B£10.80–£14.04
B&B⇌⋒£11.88–£15.12 Lunch £1.50–£2.50
ea 15–20p Dinner £2–£3 Wine £2.25 *xmas*
redit card 3

★★*Grand* Morton Cres, The Esplanade ☎3278
5rm(25⇌⋒) Lift TV available in bedrooms 70P
auna bath Live music & dancing 3 nights wkly

★★Manor The Beacon ☎72549
7rm(11⇌⋒) Lift CTV 12P 3 Live music &
ancing twice wkly Last dinner 8pm S%
B&B£7.50–£8.50 sB&B⇌⋒£9.50–£10.50
B&B£15–£17 dB&B⇌⋒£19–£21
unch £3–£3.75 Tea 25–30p
igh Tea £1.75–£2.25 Dinner £3.50–£4
Vine £2.50 *xmas*

★Carlton Lodge 15 Carlton Hill ☎3314
rm(1⇌⋒) CTV 8P Last dinner 7pm S%
B&B£6.75–£7.50 sB&B⇌⋒£8–£9
B&B£13.50–£15 dB&B⇌⋒£16–£18
ar lunch £1–£1.50&alc Dinner £2.50–£3.50
Vine £2.40

★Isca House Isca Rd, off Douglas Av ☎3747
losed Nov–Mar; 12rm(2⇌⋒) CTV 12P
Children under 7yrs not accommodated
ast dinner 6.30pm S% sB&B£7.20–£7.50
B&B£14.40–£15 dB&B⇌⋒£16.40–£17
unch £1.50 Dinner £3.50 Wine £2.20

FADMOOR North Yorkshire Map **8** SE68
✕Plough Inn ☎Kirkbymoorside 31515
Closed 1wk Feb, May & Oct; Lunch not served;
Dinner not served Sun & Mon; 28seats P French.
Last dinner 8.30pm S% ✱Wine £2.25

FAIRFORD Gloucestershire Map **4** SP10
★★Bull Market Pl ☎712535
RS Xmas wk; 16rm(6⇌⋒) Annexe: 3rm CTV 50P 3
Last dinner 9pm
sB&B£10–£11.50 sB&B⇌⋒£14 dB&B£19–£21
dB&B⇌⋒£20–£23 Lunch £4alc Tea 40palc
High Tea £1.20alc Dinner £4.50alc Wine £2
Credit cards 1 2

★Hyperion London St ☎712349
21rm(15⇌⋒) CTV TV available in bedrooms 30P
2 Children under 5yrs not accommodated
English & French. Last dinner 7.45pm
sB&B£6.50 sB&B⇌⋒£8.15 dB&B£13
dB&B⇌⋒£16.30 Lunch fr£1.30 Tea fr28p
Dinner fr£5 Wine £2.75 *xmas*
Credit cards 1 2 3 6

✕✕*Pinks* London Rd ☎712355
Cotswold stone restaurant, with pinewood panelling interior.
Closed Xmas; Lunch not served Mon & Sun (winter);
Dinner not served Sun; 50seats 20P English &
Continental. Last dinner 9.45pm Credit cards 1 6

FAIRY CROSS Devon Map **2** SS42
★★★Portledge (off A39) ☎Horns Cross 262
Set in 60 acres of parkland, a fine 17th-C manor house, parts of which date back to 1234. Superbly furnished with many portraits; guns, fine panelling and a 17th-C plastered ceiling in dining room. Armada courtyard, with pillars made from Spanish galleon timbers. Private bathing beach with fine coastal views.
Closed Nov–Mar; 35rm(22⇌⋒) Lift CTV P 4
(heated) (hard) Children under 5yrs not
accommodated English & French.
Last dinner 9pm sB&B£10.75–£12.50
sB&B⇌⋒£11.50–£14.50 dB&B£21.50–£25
dB&B⇌⋒£23–£29 Lunch £2.75–£3.85&alc
Tea 85p&alc Dinner £7.50&alc Wine £3.95

FAKENHAM Norfolk Map **9** TF92
★Crown ☎2010
15th-C coaching inn.
12rm CTV TV available in bedrooms 30P
Last dinner 10pm S% sB&B£8
dB&B£15 Lunch £2.75&alc Tea 30p
Dinner £2.75&alc Wine £2.40
Credit cards 1 2 3

FALFIELD Avon Map **3** ST69
★★Park ☎550 (due to change to 260550 during 1980)
RS Sun; 10rm(6⇌⋒) CTV in bedrooms 100P
French & Italian. Last dinner 10pm S%
sB&B fr£15.50 sB&B⇌⋒ fr£17.50 dB&B fr£20
dB&B⇌⋒ fr£22 Lunch fr£5.50 Dinner fr£7
Wine £3.50 Credit cards 1 2 3 5

FALMOUTH Cornwall Map **2** SW83
★★★Bay Cliff Rd ☎312094 Telex no 45617
Closed Xmas; 39rm(25⇌⋒) Lift CTV CTV
available in bedrooms 40P 4 English &
French. Last dinner 8.30pm S%
✱sB&B£7.20–£12 sB&B⇌⋒£8.20–£13.75
dB&B£14.40–£24 dB&B⇌⋒£16.40–£27.50
Lunch fr£3.50 Tea fr35p High Tea fr£2
Dinner fr£4.50&alc Wine £2.70
Credit cards 1 2 3

★★★Falmouth ☎312671 Telex no 45639
Comfortable, modernised hotel. In own gardens on sea front.
73rm(30⇌⋒) Lift CTV TV available in bedrooms
60P 32 (heated) Live music & dancing
twice wkly Last dinner 8.30pm S%
sB&B£11–£13.50 sB&B⇌⋒£15–£18
dB&B£19–£25.50 dB&B⇌⋒£28–£36
Lunch £4–£4.50&alc Tea £1–£1.20
Dinner £5–£5.70&alc Wine £2.90
Credit cards 1 2 3 6

★★★Green Bank Green Bank Ter ☎312440
A comfortable, traditional, 18th-C inn on the harbour side, with its own pier and landing stage. Letters from Kenneth Grahame to his son, written here 1907, formed basis of Wind in the Willows.
46rm(29⇌⋒) Lift CTV 80P 20 English &
French. Last dinner 9pm S%
sB&B£10.50–£15.50 sB&B⇌⋒£11.50–£16.50
dB&B£22–£32 dB&B⇌⋒£24–£34
Lunch £3.50&alc Tea 80p
Dinner £4.50–£5.50&alc Wine £2.50 *xmas*
Credit cards 1 3 5 6

★★★Green Lawns Western Ter ☎312734
Built 1910 in style of French château; with 1½ acres of terraced lawns.
29rm(21⇌⋒) Annexe: 5rm(2⇌⋒) CTV in
bedrooms 60P English & French.
Last dinner 10pm sB&B£10.53–£17.82
sB&B⇌⋒£13.50–£17.82 dB&B£23.22–£24.30
dB&B⇌⋒£28.08–£35.10 Lunch £3.50&alc
Tea 50p High Tea £1–£4.50 Dinner £4–£4.50&alc
Wine £3 Credit cards 1 2 3 4 5 6

F

★★★**Gyllyngdune** Melvill Rd ☎312978 35⇌⋒ 3▭ ☽ ⊞ ⋈ CTV CTV in bedrooms 40P 4⌂ ⚓ ▭(heated) Last dinner8.30pm ✿ ♔ S% ✱sB&B⇌⋒£11.88–£15.12 sB&B⇌⋒£23.76–£30.24 Lunch£3.50–£5.50&alc Tea£1–£2.50&alc Dinner£5.50–£9&alc Wine£3.20 ⊓

★★★**Royal Duchy** (Percy R Brend) ☎313042 38rm(19⇌⋒) Lift ☽ CTV CTV available in bedrooms 60P ⚓ Live music & dancing Sat ♡ English & French. Last dinner8.30pm ✿ ♔ S% ✱sB&B£9.20 sB&B⇌⋒£10.20 dB&B£18.40 dB&B⇌⋒£20.50 Lunch fr£2.85&alc Tea30–70p Dinner fr£3.85&alc Wine£2.85 ⊓ Credit cards ① ② ③

★★★**St Michaels** Cliff Rd ☎312707 Telex no45617 55rm(48⇌⋒) ☽ ✗ ⋈ CTV CTV in bedrooms 65P ⚓ ♔ Last dinner9pm ✿ ♔ S% sB&B£11 sB&B⇌⋒£14 dB&B£22 dB&B⇌⋒£25 Lunch£3.50&alc Tea£1 Dinner£5–£6&alc Wine£3.80 ⊓ *xmas* Credit cards ① ② ③

★★**Gwendra** Sea Front ☎312178 Closed Nov–Mar; 47rm(9⇌⋒) ⋈ CTV 10P 10⌂ Last dinner8.30pm ✿ ♔ S% sB&B£8.64–£10.80 sB&B⇌⋒£10.80 dB&B£15.12–£19.44 dB&B⇌⋒£19.44 Lunch£2.70 Dinner£3.78 Wine£2.50

★★**Madeira** Sea Front ☎313531 Closed 23 Dec–1 Jan; 49⇌⋒ Lift ☽ ⋈ CTV CTV in bedrooms 20P ⚓ Last dinner8.30pm ✿ S% sB&B⇌⋒£9.99–£17.28 dB&B⇌⋒£18.90–£32.40 Lunch£3.50 Dinner£6.50 Wine£2.75 ⊓ Credit cards ① ② ③

F

★★**Palm Beach** Gyllyngvase ☎313812
Closed Nov–Mar; 18rm(9⇌ ⋒) CTV ⊘ P Disco wkly Live music & dancing wkly Last dinner7.55pm ✿ ☡ ✻sB&B£8–£10 sB&B⇌⋒£9–£11 dB&B£16–£20 dB&B⇌⋒£18–£22 Lunch£3–£4.50 Tea50–80p HighTea£1.50–£2.50 Dinner£4–£6.50 Credit card ③

★★ **Pendower** Sea View Rd ☎312108
Detached family holiday hotel in own small grounds.
Closed Nov–Mar; 29rm(18⇌ ⋒) ⩩ CTV 20P ⚓ ▭ sauna bath Last dinner8pm ✿ ☡ S% ✻sB&B fr£10.35 sB&B⇌⋒ fr£11.55 dB&B fr£19.30 dB&B⇌⋒ fr£21.76 Lunch fr£3.75 Dinner fr£5 Wine£3.30 *xmas*

★★ **Penmere Manor** Mongleath Rd (Best Western) ☎311356
Closed Nov & Dec; RS Jan & Feb (by prior arrangement); 27rm(26⇌ ⋒) ⩩ CTV in bedrooms 40P ⚓ ▭(heated) Live music & dancing Fri Last dinner8pm ✿ S% ✻sB&B£8.50 dB&B£17 dB&B⇌⋒£20.50 Barlunch40p–£1.75 Dinner£4.50 Wine£2.75 Credit cards ① ② ③ ⑥

★★**Rosslyn** Kimberley Park Rd ☎312699
Detached hotel in an acre of grounds and garden, on elevated position overlooking Falmouth.
Closed 15 Oct–20 Apr; 28rm(10⇌ ⋒) CTV 30P ⚓ Disco wkly Last dinner7.15pm ✿ sB&B£8 dB&B£16 dB&B⇌⋒£18 Lunch£3 Dinner£4 Wine£2.50

★★**Somerdale** Sea View Rd ☎312566
In elevated position overlooking coast.
Closed 25 Oct–Feb; 18rm(7⇌ ⋒) Annexe: 1⇌ ⋒ CTV 13P ⚓ Disco twice wkly Last dinner6.30pm ✿ ☡ sB&B£7.75–£9.50 dB&B£14–£18 dB&B⇌⋒£15.50–£19.50 Lunch£1.75–£2.50

F

Tea60–75p Dinner£4.50 Wine£2.90 ⊟
Credit cards 1 3

★***Carthion*** Cliff Rd ☎313669
Closed Nov–Feb; 14rm(10⇌ ⋒) Annexe: 7rm(3⇌ ⋒) 18P ⚓ ✿ ⊥

★**Crill House** Golden Bank ☎312994
Detached residence situated in rural surroundings.
Closed Nov–Mar; 10⇌ ⋒ ⋈ CTV CTV available in bedrooms 20P 2⌂ ⇎ ⚓ ⊐(heated) ♀English & Continental Last dinner7pm ✿ ⊥ S%
sB&B⇌ ⋒£9–£12 dB&B⇌ ⋒£18–£24
Bar lunch£1–£2 Dinner£4.50 Wine£2.50 ⊟

★***Lerryn*** De Pass Rd ☎312489
Closed 7 Sep–27 Apr; Unlicensed; 17rm(9⇌ ⋒) CTV ⊘ 11P ⇎ Children under 10yrs not accommodated

★***Melville*** Sea View Rd ☎312134
Detached three-storey holiday hotel in elevated position with commanding views of Falmouth coast.
Closed Oct–mid Apr; Unlicensed; 21rm CTV 20P 10⌂ ⇎ ⚓ Last dinner8pm

★**Suncourt** Boscowen Rd ☎312886
Closed Nov–Feb 14rm(3⇌ ⋒) CTV 14P ⇎
Last dinner7.30pm S% sB&B£6.48–£7.56
dB&B£12.96–£15.12 dB&B£17.28–£19.44
Lunch£3.24 Dinner£3.78 Wine£3.30

✕**Continental** 29 High St ☎313003
Closed Sun, 25, 26 Dec & 2wks Nov; Lunch not served; 30seats ♀French. Last dinner9.45pm
Dinner£5.50alc Wine£3.25 Credit card 5

FAREHAM Hampshire Map**4** SU50
★★**Red Lion** East St (Whitbread) ☎234113
Bow-windowed former coaching inn.
23rm ♛ CTV ⊘ 100P Last dinner10pm ✿ ☕
✱sB&B£11 dB&B£17.32
Lunch£3.38–£4.77&alc Tea55p
Dinner£4.14–£4.77&alc Wine£2.85 ⊓
Credit cards 1 3 6

FARINGDON Oxfordshire Map**4** SU29
★★**Bell** Market Pl ☎20534
10rm(1⇌⋒) ♛ CTV TV available in bedrooms 16P
5⌂ Last dinner9.30pm S% ✱sB&B£10.25
dB&B£20.50 dB&B⇌⋒£25.50 Lunch£3.50alc
Dinner£5.50alc Credit cards 1 2 3 5

★**Salutation** Market Pl ☎20536
Built mid 19th-C on site of palace of Alfred the Great.
7rm(1⇌⋒) ♛ CTV 4P 2⌂ ♡ English & French.
Last dinner8.45pm ✿ S% sB&B fr£6.48
sB&B⇌⋒ fr£7.56 dB&B fr£12.96
dB&B⇌⋒ fr£14.04 Lunch fr£2 Dinner fr£2.50
Wine£2.80 ⊓ Credit cards 1 3

FARNBOROUGH Hampshire Map**4** SU85
★★★**Queen's** Lynchford Rd (Anchor) ☎45051
Telex no858875
83⇌⋒ ☽ ♛ CTV in bedrooms 100P Disco or Live music & dancing Sat Conference facilities available
Last dinner9pm ✿ ☕ S% ✱sB&B⇌⋒ fr£16
dB&B⇌⋒ fr£23 Lunch fr£3.50&alc Tea fr50p
Dinner fr£3.75&alc Wine£2.65 ⊓
Credit cards 1 2 3 4 5 6

FARNCOMBE Surrey Map**4** SU94
★**Manor Inn** ☎Godalming22195
Tile-hung building with modern extension.
9rm(1⇌⋒) ♛ CTV TV in bedrooms 200P ⛟
Disco wkly Last dinner9.30pm ✿ ☕ S%
✱sB&B£11.50–£13.50 sB&B⇌⋒£11.50–£13.50
dB&B£17–£21 dB&B⇌⋒£17–£21
Lunch fr£4&alc Tea45p–£1 High Tea70p–£1.30
Dinner fr£4&alc Wine£2.75 *xmas*
Credit cards 1 2 3 5

FARNHAM Surrey Map**4** SU84
★★★**Bush** The Borough (Anchor) ☎715237
Telex no858875
An ancient coaching inn, with modern wing.
51rm(32⇌⋒) 1⊟ ☽ ♛ CTV in bedrooms 50P ⚘ Live music & dancing Sat Last dinner10pm ✿ ☕ S%
✱sB&B fr£11.50 sB&B⇌⋒ fr£16 dB&B fr£19.50
dB&B⇌⋒ fr£24.50 Lunch fr£3.50&alc Tea fr£1
Dinner fr£3.50&alc Wine£2.65 ⊓ *xmas*
Credit cards 1 2 3 4 5 6

✕✕**Latour** 69 Castle St ☎721133
Closed Sun, Mon & Aug; 50seats ⊁ ♡ French.
Last dinner10.30pm ✱Lunch£6.25
Dinner£8.53–£12.33 Wine£2.50
Credit cards 1 2 3 5

FARNSFIELD Nottinghamshire Map**8** SK65
✕✕***White Post Inn*** ☎Mansfield882215
120seats 100P Live music & dancing Fri & Sat;
Last dinner9.30pm Credit cards 1 2 3

FARRINGTON GURNEY Avon Map**3** ST55
✕✕**Old Parsonage** Main St ☎Temple Cloud52211
Closed Mon; Dinner not served Sun; 28seats 100P
bedrooms available ♡ French. Last dinner10pm
✱Lunch£10alc Tea£1.25alc Dinner£10alc
Wine£2.95

FAUGH Cumbria Map**11** NY55
★★**String of Horses Inn** ☎Hayton297
13⇌⋒ 2⊟ ☽ ♛ CTV CTV in bedrooms 50P ⛟ ⛆
♡ English & French. Last dinner10.30pm ✿

sB&B⇌fl£14.50–£16.50 dB&B⇌fl£19.50–£28 Lunch£3.50alc Dinner£6alc Wine£2.75 ⊟ Creditcards 1 2 3 5 6

FAWLEY Hampshire Map**4** SU40
★**Falcon** ☎Southampton891005
Modernised Victorian public house in centre of village.
7rm ⅏ TV 70P 3⌂ Lastdinner7.30pm ✿ S% sB&B£6.50–£7 dB&B£13–£14 Lunch£3.50alc Dinner£4.50alc Wine£1.75

FELIXSTOWE Suffolk Map**5** TM33
★★★★**Orwell Moat House** Hamilton Rd (Queens) ☎5511
64rm(52⇌fl) Lift ☽ ⊞ ⅏ CTV in bedrooms 150P ⚓ Disco Sat Conference facilities available ☋French. Lastdinner10pm ✿ ⊻ S% ✻sB&B fr£12.50 sB&B⇌fl fr£16.50 dB&B fr£20.50 dB&B⇌fl fr£25.50 Lunch fr£4&alc Dinner fr£4.25&alc Wine£2.95 ⊟ Creditcards 1 2 3 4 5 6

★★***Cavendish*** Sea Front ☎2696
Three-storey, purpose-built, family-run hotel at southern end of promenade, with public rooms overlooking the sea.
Closed Xmas; 14rm Lift CTV 150P ⛟ Lastdinner8pm ✿ ⊻

★★**North Sea** Sea Front ☎2103
27rm(12⇌fl) ☽ ⅏ CTV TV in bedrooms 15P Lastdinner9.45pm ✿ S% sB&B£14 sB&B⇌fl£15 dB&B£18 dB&B⇌fl£19 Lunch fr£4.25&alc Dinner fr£5&alc Wine£2.50 Creditcards 1 3 6

FELSTED Essex Map**5** TL62
XX***Boote House*** ☎Great Dunmow820279
Closed Sun, Mon, Jan & 1st 2wks Aug; Lunch not served; 50seats ☋English & French. Lastdinner9.30pm ✻ Creditcards 2 5

FENNY BRIDGES Devon Map**3** SY19
★**Fenny Bridges** ☎Honiton850218
6rm ⅏ CTV 75P 1⌂ ⚓ ↳ ☋English & French. Lastdinner9.30pm ✿ S% ✻sB&B£7 dB&B£13 Lunch£2alc Dinner£4alc Wine£1.30 Creditcard 3

FERNDOWN Dorset Map**4** SU00
★★★★**Dormy** New Rd (DeVere) ☎872121 Telexno22121
White, rambling building in style of hacienda, with individual bungalow units.
63⇌fl Annexe:27⇌fl Lift ☽ ⅏ CTV in bedrooms 150P ⚓ ⊃(heated) ⦿(grass) ⌂ Conference facilities available ♿ ☋English & Continental. Lastdinner9.30pm ✿ ⊻ S% sB&B⇌fl£22 dB&B⇌fl£44 Lunch fr£5.25&alc Tea fr£1.25 Dinner fr£6&alc Wine£3.75 ⊟ *xmas* Creditcards 1 2 3 5 6

☆☆**Coach House Motel** Tricketts Cross (junc A31/A348) ☎871222
32⇌fl ⅏ CTV in bedrooms 250P 35⌂ ⚓ ↳ Live music 2 nights wkly ☋English & French. Lastdinner9.45pm ✿ S% sB&B⇌fl fr£14.66 dB&B⇌fl fr£18.98 Lunch£2.45–£2.95 Dinner£3.85–£4.40&alc Wine£2.50 Creditcards 1 2 3 5 6

FERRING West Sussex Map**4** TQ00
★**Greystoke Manor** ☎Worthing42077
Early 18th-C gabled building with a Sussex flint façade.
11rm(3⇌fl) ⅏ CTV 40P 2⌂ ⛟ ⚓ Lastdinner8pm ✿ ⊻ sB&B fr£8.50 sB&B⇌fl fr£9.50 dB&B fr£16.50 dB&B⇌fl fr£18.50 Lunch fr£2.50 Tea fr50p Dinner fr£3.50 Wine£2.75 Creditcards 1 2 3 5 6

F

FILEY North Yorkshire Map**8** TA18
★★★**White Lodge** The Crescent
☎Scarborough512268
23rm(15⇌⫙) Lift ⊞ ⩩ CTV 8P Last dinner9pm ♔
☕ sB&B£8–£10 sB&B⇌⫙£10–£12
dB&B£16–£20 dB&B⇌⫙£20–£24
Lunch£3–£3.50&alc Dinner£5.25–£10&alc
Wine£3.50 ⊟ *xmas* Credit cards 1 3

★★**Hylands** The Crescent ☎Scarborough512091
45rm(9⇌⫙) Lift ☽ CTV Live music & dancing Sat
Last dinner8pm ♔ ☕ ✻sB&B£8.50 dB&B£17
dB&B⇌⫙£19 Lunch£2.80 Dinner£3.50
Wine£2.40 ⊟ *xmas*

FINDON West Sussex Map**4** TQ10
★***Village House*** Horsham Rd ☎3350
10rm(1⇌⫙) ⩩ CTV TV available in bedrooms 16P ⩩
⚓ ♡English & French. Last dinner9pm ♔ ☕
Credit cards 1 2 3 5

❀✕✕**Findon Manor** ☎2269
Closed Sun & Mon; Lunch served Sun only; 35seats
30P bedrooms available ♡French. Specialities: La brioche aux poissons fumées, La bisque de crabe, Le caneton à la façon du patron. Last dinner9pm
Tea fr£1 Dinner£8.50alc Wine£3.50

✕***Darlings Bistro*** The Square ☎3817
Closed Sun; Lunch not served Mon; 45seats
♡English & French. Last dinner11pm

FISHER'S POND Hampshire Map**4** SU42
✕✕**Fisher's Pond** ☎Fair Oak 2209
Closed Mon; Dinner not served Sun; 70seats 60P
♡English & French. Last dinner10pm
✻Lunch£5.50alc Dinner£5.50alc Wine£2.60
Credit cards 1 3 6

FITTLEWORTH West Sussex Map**4** TQ01
★★**Swan** ☎429
13th-C coaching inn with oak beams and unique collection of painted panels in dining room. Situated close to Goodwood, Cowdrey Park and West Sussex Golf Course.
8rm(1⇌⫙) CTV 20P ⩩ ⚓ ♡English & French.
Last dinner8.45pm ♔ ☕ S% sB&B£9.50
dB&B£20 dB&B⇌⫙£22 Lunch£2.75–£6&alc
Dinner£5.50alc *xmas* Credit cards 1 3 5

FLEET Dorset Map **3** SY68
★★**Moonfleet Manor** ☎Weymouth786948
Unique country location with grounds sweeping down to sea-shore. Associated with smuggling novel Moonfleet.
40rm(22⇌⫙) CTV CTV avilable in bedrooms 200P ⚓
(heated) (hard) squash Disco twice wkly
♡English & French. Last dinner9pm ♔ ☕
sB&B fr£8.10 sB&B⇌⫙ fr£11.34 dB&B fr£16.20
dB&B⇌⫙ fr£19.44 Bar lunch£1.50alc
Dinner£4.50–£5.50&alc Wine£2.97 ⊟ *xmas*
Credit cards 2 5

FLEET Hampshire Map**4** SU85
★★★**Lismoyne** Church Rd ☎28555
42rm(27⇌⫙) ☽ ⩩ CTV in bedrooms 80P ⚓
Last dinner9.30pm ♔ ☕ S% ✻sB&B£10.80
sB&B⇌⫙£14.04 dB&B£16.20 dB&B⇌⫙£19.98
Lunch fr£3.02&alc Tea fr27p&alc
High Tea fr£2.70&alc Dinner fr£3.89 *xmas*
Credit cards 3 5

FLEETWOOD Lancashire Map**7** SD34
★★***North Euston*** The Esplanade ☎6525
Mid-Victorian crescent-shaped building erected by Sir Peter Hesketh – founder of the town.
65rm(24⇌⫙)Lift ☽ ⩩ CTV TV available in bedrooms
50P 12 billiards ♿ Last dinner9pm ♔ ☕

FLITTON Bedfordshire Map**4** TL03
✕**White Hart Inn** ☎Silsoe60403
Closed Sun; 50seats 30P ♡English & French.
Last dinner9.45pm Lunch£3.75&alc
Dinner£3.75&alc Wine£3.50

FOLKESTONE Kent Map**5** TR23
★★★★**Burlington** Earls Av (Best Western) ☎55301
Telex no96215
Large, late Victorian, red-brick building with bay windows and Dutch gables. Overlooking Leas and sea.
56⇌⫙ Lift ☽ ⊞ ⩩ CTV CTV in bedrooms 15P ⩩ ⚓
♡Continental. Last dinner9.30pm ♔ ☕ S%
sB&B⇌⫙£14.50–£15.50 dB&B⇌⫙£25–£26
⊟ *xmas* Credit cards 1 2 3 5 6

★★★**Clifton** The Leas (Trusthouse Forte) ☎41231
62rm(36⇌⫙) Lift ☽ ⩩ CTV TV in rooms
Last dinner9pm ♔ ☕ S% sB&B£13
sB&B⇌⫙£16 dB&B£19 dB&B⇌⫙£22.50 ⊟
xmas Credit cards 1 2 3 4 5 6

★★**Windsor** Langhorne Gdns ☎51348
Closed Xmas wk; 30rm(4⇌⫙) Lift ⩩ CTV ⩩
Children under 3yrs not accommodated
Last dinner7.30pm ♔ ☕ S%
sB&B£8.63–£9.22 sB&B⇌⫙£9.86–£10.78
dB&B£17.26–£18.44 dB&B⇌⫙£19.72–£21.56
Lunch£3.08 Tea55p Dinner£3.80&alc ⊟
Credit cards 1 6

★**Westbourne** 7–8 Westbourne Gdns ☎55045
21rm(1⇌⫙) ⩩ CTV ⚓ Live music & dancing wkly
Last dinner7.15pm ♔ ☕ S% sB&B£7–£10
dB&B£12–£18 dB&B⇌⫙£14–£20
Lunch1.25–£3 Tea30p–£1.50
Dinner£2.50–£3.75 Wine£2 ⊟ *xmas*

Greystones Clifton Cres ☎54090
Closed 9 Oct–17 May; 35rm Lift CTV 1 ⚓
Last dinner7.30pm ♔ ☕

✕✕***Hop Kweng*** Majestic House, Sandgate Rd
☎56532
100seats P ♡Chinese. Last dinner11.45pm
Credit cards 2 4 6

XLa Tavernetta Leaside Court ☎54955
A well-appointed lower ground floor restaurant overlooking gardens near sea front.
Closed Sun & 1st 2wks Feb; 55seats 10P
Continental. Last dinner10.30pm
*Lunch£2.80&alc Dinner£6alc Wine£2.85
Credit cards 1 3 4 5 6

XEmilio's Portofino 124A Sandgate Rd ☎55866
Simple restaurant with false ceiling of trellis work.
Closed Mon; 55seats Italian. Last dinner10.30pm
Lunch£2.50&alc Dinner£5alc
Credit cards 1 2 3 5

XNicola's l'Escargot 3 Trinity Cres ☎53864
Closed Sun; 35seats French & Italian.
Last dinner11pm *Lunch£3–£4&alc
Dinner£3–£4&alc Wine£2.75
Credit cards 1 2 3 5 6

FORDINGBRIDGE Hampshire Map**4** SU11
★★Albany Bridge St ☎52237
10rm(1) CTV 14P Last dinner9pm
S% *sB&B£8.31 sB&B£9.50 dB&B£16.63
dB&B£19 Lunch£4.60alc Dinner£4.60alc
Wine£2.85

★★Ashburn ☎52060
26rm(11) Annexe:8 CTV 70P
(heated) English & Continental.
Last dinner8pm sB&B£7.90
sB&B£9.35 dB&B£15.80 dB&B£18.70
Lunch£3.45 Tea£1 Dinner£4.75 Wine£3.10

FORDWICH Kent Map**5** TR15
★★George & Dragon (Whitbread)
☎Canterbury710661
Ancient riverside inn.
Closed Xmas; 9rm(6) Annexe:4rm CTV TV available in bedrooms 50P English & French.
Last dinner9pm S% sB&B£8.95
dB&B£16.75 dB&B£19.80 Lunch£3.45alc
Dinner£5.50alc Wine£2.50
Credit cards 1 2 3 4 5 6

FOREST ROW East Sussex Map**5** TQ43
★★★Roebuck Wych Cross (2m S A22) (Nicholsons)
☎3811 Telex no957088
Early Georgian country inn, with four acres of gardens and views over Ashdown Forest.
36 CTV in bedrooms 200P English & French. last dinner10pm S%
sB&B£18–£20 dB&B£28–£30
Lunch£4&alc Dinner£7.50alc
Credit cards 1 2 3 5 6

FOSSEBRIDGE Gloucestershire Map**4** SP01
★★Fossebridge Inn ☎310
Creeper-clad Cotswold inn next to bridge, with pleasant gardens beside river.
RS Xmas wk (no accommodation); 10rm(2)
Annexe:4) CTV P Children under 10yrs not accommodated Last dinner9.30pm
*sB&B£7.50–£10 dB&B£11.25–£15
dB&B£16.50–£19.50 Lunch£2alc
Dinner£3alc Wine£2.45

FOSTER'S BOOTH Northamptonshire Map**4** SP65
X*Peggotty's* ☎Pattishall391
Dinner not served Sun; 65seats 60P English & French. Last dinner9.30pm Credit cards 1 2 3 5 6

FOWEY Cornwall Map**2** SX15
★★★Fowey ☎2551 Telex45640
33rm(24) 1 Lift CTV 40P Live music & dancing twice wkly Cabaret wkly Conference facilities available Last dinner8.45pm
S% sB&B£14–£17 dB&B£26–£30
dB&B£41–£47 Lunch£4.25–£5.75

Tea fr25p High Tea fr£1 Dinner£5.75–£6.75 Wine£2.46 xmas Credit cards 1 2 3 5 6

★★***Marina*** Esplanade ☎3315
A small hotel of historical and architectural interest.
Closed Xmas; 14rm(4⇌ ⋒) CTV 1P Last dinner9pm Credit card 3

★★***Old Quay*** Fore St ☎3302
In old terrace at waterside, overlooking estuary.
Closed Dec–mid Apr; 14rm(8⇌ ⋒) CTV Last dinner8pm

★★**Penlee** The Esplanade ☎3220
Closed Dec & Jan; RS Nov, Feb & Mar; 12rm(8⇌ ⋒) 1 CTV CTV available in bedrooms 10P Last dinner8pm sB&B£7.50–£8.50 dB&B£15–£17 dB&B⇌ ⋒£18–£25.50 Bar lunch£2.50 Dinner£4.50–£5.50 Wine£2.30 Credit cards 1 2 3

F

★★**Riverside** ☎2275
Comfortable, well situated hotel with fine views.
Closed mid Nov–Mar; RS Oct–mid Nov (B&B only); 14rm(4⇌ ⋒) CTV TV available in bedroom 5P 5 English & French. Last dinner9pm sB&B£7–£8 dB&B£14–£16 dB&B⇌ ⋒£20–£22 Bar lunch50p–£1.50 Dinner£5.50–£7.50&alc Wine£2.40

★★***Square Rig*** North St ☎2328
Closed 8Nov–4Dec; 7rm(6⇌ ⋒) Annexe: 4rm(1⇌ ⋒) TV available in bedrooms Last dinner9.30pm

✕***Le Nautique*** Fore St ☎3594
Closed Oct–mid Apr; 65seats Last dinner11pm

FOWLMERE Cambridgeshire Map**5** TL44
✕✕**Chequers Inn** ☎369
Closed Xmas Day; 36seats English & French. Last dinner10pm S% ✱Lunch£1.50alc Dinner£7alc Wine£3.90 Credit cards 1 2 3 5

FOWNHOPE Hereford & Worcester Map**3** SO53
✕**Green Man Inn** ☎243
Lunch not served; Dinner not served Sun; 75seats 55P bedrooms available Live music & dancing Sat (in winter) English & French. Last dinner9.30pm Dinner£6.40alc Wine£2.90

FRADLEY Staffordshire Map**7** SK11
✕✕***Fradley Arms*** ☎Burton-on-Trent790186
32seats P Last dinner9.45pm Credit card 2

FRAMFIELD East Sussex Map**5** TQ42
✕**Coach House** ☎636
Closed Mon, 1st wk May, last 2wks Oct; Dinner not served Sun; 42seats 15P French. Last dinner9pm Lunch£3.25–£3.50&alc Dinner£6.50alc Wine£3.50

FRAMLINGHAM Suffolk Map**5** TM26
★★**Crown** Market Hill (Trusthouse Forte) ☎723521
Fine modernised coaching inn, situated in town centre.
14rm(4⇌ ⋒) TV in bedrooms 15P Last dinner9.15pm S% sB&B£12 sB&B⇌ ⋒£14.50 dB&B£19 dB&B⇌ ⋒£21 *xmas* Credit cards 1 2 3 4 5 6

FRAMPTON ON SEVERN Gloucestershire Map**3** SO70
★**Old Vicarage Country** Church End ☎Gloucester740562
16rm(7⇌ ⋒) CTV 30P Last dinner7.30pm S% sB&B£6.50–£8 sB&B⇌ ⋒£8.50–£10 dB&B£13–£16 dB&B⇌ ⋒£15–£20 Dinner fr£4 Wine£2.75 *xmas* Credit card 2

FRESHWATER Isle of Wight Map**4** SZ38
★★★**Albion** ☎3631
Facing the Bay with fine sea views.
Closed Oct–Mar; 43rm(37⇌ ⋒) CTV CTV available in bedrooms 75P English & French. Last dinner8.15pm S% ✱sB&B£7–£9 sB&B⇌ ⋒£7–£9 dB&B£14–£18 dB&B⇌ ⋒£14–£18 Lunch£3 Dinner£5 Wine£3.30

★★★**Farringford** Bedbury Ln ☎2500
16⇌ ⋒ Annexe: 24⇌ ⋒ CTV CTV available in bedrooms 150P (heated) (hard) billiards Live music & dancing 3 nights wkly (5 in season) Last dinner9.45pm sB&B⇌ ⋒£12–£16 dB&B⇌ ⋒£24–£36 Lunch£4 Tea£1–£1.20 High Tea£2 Dinner£5–£7 Wine£3.25 *xmas* Credit cards 1 2 3 4 5 6

FRESSINGFIELD Suffolk Map**5** TM27
✕***Fox & Goose*** ☎247
Closed Tue & 21–28Dec; 27seats 25P English & French. Specialities: Truite aux amandes, Poulet a la créme, Rum chocolate truffle. Last dinner8.45pm Lunch£12alc Dinner£12alc Wine£3

FRILFORD Oxfordshire Map**4** SU49
✕✕✕**Noah's Ark** (3½m S on A338 Wantage road) ☎Frilford Heath391470
17th-C building with pleasant modern interior.
Closed Mon; Dinner not served Sun; 65seats 100P French & Italian. Last dinner11pm Lunch fr£3.80&alc Credit cards 2 5

FRILFORD HEATH Oxfordshire Map**4** SU49
★★**The Dog House** ☎390830
8rm CTV 30P ✱sB&B£10–£12 dB&B£16–£18 Lunch fr£3.45&alc Dinner fr£4.25&alc Wine£1.90 Credit cards 1 2 3 5 6

FRIMLEY BRIDGES Hampshire Map**4** SU85
XX***Auctioneer*** ☎Camberley23559
Closed Sun & Bank Hols; Lunch not served Sat; 50 seats 25P English & Continental. Lastdinner10.30pm Creditcards 1 2 3 5

FRINTON-ON-SEA Essex Map**5** TM21
★★★**Frinton Lodge** 32 The Esplanade ☎4391
26rm(18⇌) Lift CTV CTV in bedrooms 15P 5 International. Lastdinner9.30pm sB&B£15–£18 sB&B⇌£16–£20 dB&B£21.50–£24 dB&B⇌£23–£28 Lunch£2.50–£4&alc Tea£1–£1.50 Dinner£5–£5.75&alc Wine£3.50 *xmas* Creditcards 1 2 3 5 6

★★**Maplin** Esplanade ☎3832
Adjacent to golf course, distinctive two-storey, bow-windowed building overlooking the sea.
12rm(10⇌) CTV TV in bedrooms 15P 2 (heated) Children under 10yrs not accommodated Lastdinner9.30pm S% sB&B£11–£11.50 sB&B⇌£12.50–£13 dB&B⇌£26–£27 Lunch£4.75&alc Dinner£6.25&alc Wine£3.90 *xmas* Creditcards 2 5

★**Linnets** Kirby Cross ☎4910 4rm(3⇌) Annexe: 11rm(1⇌) CTV 16P International. Lastdinner9pm S% *sB&B£7.25–£8.75 sB&B⇌£8.25–£8.75 dB&B£14.50–£17.50 dB&B⇌£16.50–£17.50 Barlunch50p–£3&alc Tea50p–£1 Dinner£4&alc Wine£2.50 *xmas*

★**Rock** 1 Third Av ☎5173
9rm CTV TV available in bedrooms 12P 1 Lastdinner10pm S% *sB&B£9.50–£10.50 dB&B£18–£20 Lunch£3.95&alc Tea40p HighTea60p Dinner£3.95–£4.50&alc Wine£2.50 *xmas* Creditcards 1 3 6

FROME Somerset Map**3** ST74
During the currency of this guide Frome telephone numbers are liable to change.
☆☆☆**Mendip Lodge** Bath Rd ☎3223
An established, wood faced building with a motel block.
40⇌ CTV in bedrooms 60P Conference facilities available International. Lastdinner9.45pm *xmas* Creditcards 1 2 3 5

★★★***Portway*** ☎3508
White Regency building with columned portico surrounded by lawns, gardens and trees.
23rm 8⇌) TV 30P 5 English & French. Lastdinner9.15pm Creditcards 2 3 5

★★**George** 4 Market Pl ☎2584
16rm(4⇌) TV available in bedrooms 20 French. Lastdinner9.30pm S% sB&B£9.25 sB&B⇌£10.75 dB&B£15.50 dB&B⇌£17 Lunch£3&alc Tea£1alc Dinner£3.50&alc Wine£2.85 Creditcards 1 2 3 5

FROYLE (nr Alton) Hampshire Map**4** SU74
X**Hen & Chicken Inn** ☎Bentley2115
Dinner not served Sun; 45seats 40P English & Continental. Lastdinner10pm S% Lunch£4.50alc Dinner£7alc Wine£3.20 Creditcards 1 2 3 5

GARFORTH West Yorkshire Map**8** SE43
☆☆☆**Leeds Ladbroke Mercury Motor Inn** (Junc A63/A642) Garforth Roundabout (Ladbroke) ☎Leeds866556 Telexno556324
156⇌ CTV in bedrooms 180P Conference facilities available Lastdinner10.30pm sB&B⇌£22.50 dB&B⇌£30 Lunch£4.50&alc Dinner£5&alc Wine£3.20 Creditcards 1 2 3 4 5 6

GARGRAVE North Yorkshire Map**7** SD95
★★**Anchor Inn** ☎666
RS Nov–Mar (B & B only); 6⇌ CTV CTV in bedrooms P Lastdinner9pm *sB&B⇌£10.70 dB&B⇌£17.10 Creditcards 1 2 3 5 6

GATESHEAD Tyne & Wear Map**12** NZ26
☆☆☆☆**Five Bridges** High West St (Swallow) ☎771105 Telexno53534
Seven-storey, glass-fronted building opened in 1967.
107⇌ Lift CTV CTV in bedrooms 200P Conference facilities available Lastdinner9.45pm S% sB&B⇌ fr£21.35 dB&B⇌ fr£28.50 Creditcards 1 2 3 5

★★★**Springfield** Durham Rd (Embassy) ☎774121
32rm(26⇌) CTV TV available in bedrooms 100P Lastdinner9pm S% sB&B£12 sB&B⇌£15 dB&B£38 dB&B⇌£20 Lunch£4.50&alc Dinner£5&alc Wine£4 Creditcards 1 2 3 4 5 6

GATWICK AIRPORT (London) West Sussex Map**4** TQ24 **See plan**
☆☆☆☆**Copthorne** Copthorne Rd, Copthorne (5m E off B2037) (Prestige) ☎Copthorne714971 Telexno95500 Plan**4**
230⇌ CTV in bedrooms 300P Conference facilities available English & French. Lastdinner10.30pm *sB&B⇌£26.74 dB&B⇌£41.41 Lunch fr£5.25&alc Tea£2–£2.50&alc Dinner£8alc Wine£3.50 Creditcards 1 2 3 4 5 6

☆☆☆☆**Gatwick Park** Povey Cross Rd, Horley ☎Horley5533 Telexno87440 Plan**7A**
Modern hotel opened in 1978.

1 Ladbroke Mercury Motor Inn (formerly Bridge House) ☆☆☆ *(see under Reigate)*
2 Centre Airport ★★★
3 Chequers ☆☆☆
4 Copthorne ☆☆☆☆
5 Europa Lodge ☆☆☆
6 Gatwick Hickmet ☆☆☆
7 Gatwick Manor ☆☆☆
7A Gatwick Park ☆☆☆☆
8 George ★★★
9 Goffs Park ★★
10 Gravetye Manor ❁ ★★★ *(see under East Grinstead)*
11 Hoskins ★★ *(see under Oxted)*
12 Ifield Court ★★
13 Lakers ★★ *(see under Redhill)*
14 Mill House ★
15 Post House ☆☆☆
16 Wonham House ★ *(see under South Godstone)*
17 Ye Olde Felbridge ★★★ *(see under East Grinstead)*

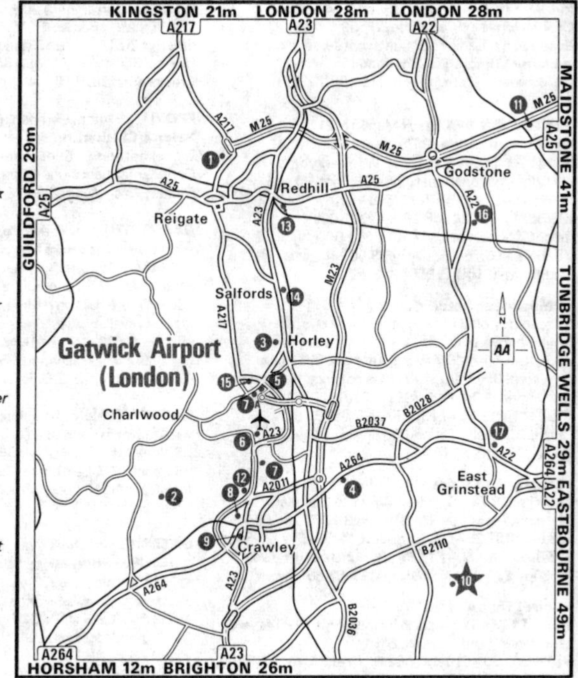

260⇌ ⋒ Lift ☽ ⊞ ₩ CTV in bedrooms 400P ⛟ ⚓ Conference facilities available Last dinner 11.15pm ✿ ⚲ S% ✻sB&B⇌ ⋒ fr£27.59 dB&B⇌ ⋒ fr£36.82 Lunch£4.85&alc Tea£1.50alc Dinner£6.95&alc Wine£3.85 Credit cards 1 2 3 4 5

★★★**Centre Airport** Tushmore Roundabout, Langley Dr. Crawley (Centre) ☎Crawley29991 Telex no877311 Plan**2**
230⇌ ⋒ Lift ☽ ₩ CTV in bedrooms ⊘ 300P Last dinner 10pm ✿ ⚲ S% ✻sB&B⇌ ⋒ £17 dB&B⇌ ⋒ £23 Continental breakfast Lunch£4.75 Dinner£4.75 Wine£3.40 ⊟ Credit cards 1 2 3 4 5 6

☆☆☆**Chequers** Brighton Rd, Horley (Thistle) ☎Horley6992 Plan**3**
Originally a Tudor coaching house, now extended to form a modern hotel.
RS Xmas; 78⇌ ⋒ ☽ ⊞ ₩ CTV in bedrooms 120P ♡English & French. Last dinner 9.45pm ✿ S% ✻sB&B⇌ ⋒ fr£20.40 dB&B⇌ ⋒ fr£27.40 Lunch fr£3.50 Dinner fr£4.90 Wine£2.85 ⊟ *xmas* Credit cards 1 2 3 4 5 6

☆☆☆**Europa Lodge** Longbridge Roundabout, Horley (Grand Met) ☎Horley5599 Telex no877138 Plan**5**
124⇌ ⋒ Lift ☽ ⊞ ₩ CTV CTV available in bedrooms 150⌂ Last dinner 10pm ✿ ⚲ S% ✻sB&B⇌ ⋒ £17.50 dB&B⇌ ⋒ £26 ⊟ Credit cards 1 2 3 4 5 6

☆☆☆**Gatwick Hickmet** Lowfield Heath, Crawley ☎Crawley33441 Telex no87287 Plan**6**
Modern, fully sound proofed hotel situated to the side of the airport.
96⇌ ⋒ Lift ☽ ⊞ ₩ CTV in bedrooms ⊘ 150P Conference facilities available ♡Continental. Last dinner 10.30pm ✿ ⚲ sB&B⇌ ⋒ £20 dB&B⇌ ⋒ £28 Lunch£3–£7&alc Tea75p–£1.25&alc High Tea£1.75–£3&alc Dinner£4.50–£8.50&alc Wine£3.50 *xmas* Credit cards 1 2 3 4 5 6

☆☆☆**Gatwick Manor** London Rd, Crawley (Berni) ☎Crawley26301 Telexno87529 Plan**7**
30⇄ ⋔ ☽ ⋈ TV available in bedrooms ⊘ 400P ⚓ ♿ ♉ Mainly grills Last dinner11pm
sB&B⇄⋔£16–£17 dB&B⇄⋔£25–£27.50
Lunch£2.75–£4.75&alc Dinner£2.75–£4.75
Wine£2.75 ⊨ Credit cards ① ② ③ ⑤ ⑥

★★★**George** High St, Crawley (Trusthouse Forte) ☎Crawley24215 Telexno87385 Plan**8**
Half-timbered and tile-hung 15th-C inn with extension. Gallows sign outside and 17th-C stone mantelpiece inside. Frequented by Prince Regent, and referred to by Conan Doyle in Rodney Stone.
75⇄⋔ ☽ ⋈ TV in bedrooms 120P Conference facilities available Last dinner10pm ✿ ⊥ S%
sB&B⇄⋔£18.75 dB&B⇄⋔£27.50 ⊨ *xmas*
Credit cards ① ② ③ ④ ⑤ ⑥

☆☆☆**Post House** Povey Cross Rd, Horley (Trusthouse Forte) ☎Horley71621 Telexno877351 Plan**15**
149⇄⋔ Lift ☽ ⋈ CTV in bedrooms 350P ⌒(heated)
Last dinner10.15pm ✿ ⊥ S%
sB&B⇄⋔£22.75 dB&B⇄⋔£32.50 ⊨ *xmas*
Credit cards ① ② ③ ④ ⑤ ⑥

★★**Goffs Park** 45 Goffs Park Rd, Crawley ☎Crawley 35447 Plan**9**
40rm(32⇄⋔) ⋈ CTV in bedrooms 80P ⚓ Live music & dancing Sat ♉ English & Continental.
Last dinner9.30pm ✿ ⊥ S% sB&B£13.50
sB&B⇄⋔£13.50 dB&B£18 dB&B⇄⋔£22
Lunch£1.90–£2.40&alc Tea65p
Dinner£3.10&alc Wine£2.80

★★**Ifield Court** Ifield Av, Crawley ☎Crawley34807 Plan**12**
Old Victorian manor house with ivy-clad exterior set in 4½ acres of grounds. Off A23 Brighton Rd 4½ miles from airport.
19⇄⋔ ☽ ⋈ TV available in bedrooms 100P ⚓
Last dinner9.30pm ✿ ⊥ ✻sB&B⇄⋔£16
dB&B⇄⋔£22.50 Bar lunch£1–£1.50 Tea40p
Dinner£1.95–£9.45 Credit cards ① ③

★***Mill House*** Salfords (3½m N A23) ☎Redhill67277 Plan**14**
Annexe: 40rm(13⇄⋔) ☽ ⋈ CTV 100P Live music & dancing Fri & Sat Last dinner10pm ✿
Credit cards ① ② ③ ⑤

GAUNTS EARTHCOTT Avon Map**3** ST68
✕**Manor House** ☎Winterbourne772225
(Reservations essential. Patrons must telephone first to make reservation and to hear instruction how to locate establishment as there is no sign. Own alcohol must be brought.)
Closed Wed & 1st wk autumn; Unlicensed; corkage charge; 20seats 10P Last dinner10.30pm
✻Lunch£7alc Dinner£7alc

GERRARDS CROSS Buckinghamshire Map**4** TQ08
★★★**Bull** (De Vere) ☎85995 Telexno2212
Converted coaching inn, dating from 1688, in own grounds. Situated on A40 Oxford road close to station.
38⇄⋔ 1▭ ☽ ⋈ TV in bedrooms 135P ⚓ ♉ English & French. Last dinner9.30pm ✿ ⊥ S%
sB&B⇄⋔£24 dB&B⇄⋔£32 Lunch£5.75&alc
Tea£1.20&alc Dinner£6.25&alc Wine£3.75 ⊨
xmas Credit cards ① ② ③ ⑤ ⑥

GILLAN Cornwall Map**2** SW72
★**Tregildry** ☎Manaccan378
Overlooking Gillan Cove, with private footpath across fields leading to beach.
Closed 12Oct–Mar; 20rm ⋈ CTV 20P ⇎ ⚓ ⌂
Last dinner7.30pm ✿ ⊥ Wine£2.50
Credit cards ① ② ③ ④ ⑤ ⑥

GILLINGHAM Kent Map**5** TQ76
★**Park** Nelson Rd ☎Medway51546
8rm ⋈ CTV 8⌂ Last dinner7.30pm ✿ ⊥ S%
sB&B£7.75 dB&B£13.50 Lunch fr£1.75
Tea fr75p High Tea fr£1.75 Dinner fr£3.25
Wine£2 Credit card ③

GILSLAND Northumberland Map**12** NY66
★***Station*** ☎206
6rm TV 50P Last dinner8.30pm ✿ ⊥
Credit card ③

GISBURN Lancashire Map**7** SD84
★★★**Stirk House** ☎581
38⇄⋔ ☽ ⋈ CTV CTV in bedrooms 70P ⌒(heated)
♉ English & French. Last dinner9.30pm ✿
sB&B⇄⋔£15.44 dB&B⇄⋔£23.76
Lunch£3.75–£4.25 Dinner£5.50–£6&alc
Wine£2.95 ⊨ *xmas* Credit cards ① ② ③ ⑤

GITTISHAM Devon Map**3** SY19
★★⚜**Combe House** ☎Honiton2756
Closed Jan & Feb; 13rm(11⇄⋔) ⋈ CTV in bedrooms 50P 3⌂ ⇎ ⚓ ↳ ♉ English & French.
Last dinner9.30pm ✿ ⊥ sB&B£16.82
sB&B⇄⋔£19.41–£41.40 dB&B£33.64
dB&B⇄⋔£38.81–£43.99 Lunch fr£6.70
Tea59p–£1.30 Dinner£10.50alc Wine£5.20
Credit cards ② ③ ⑤

GLANTON Northumberland Map**12** NU01
★★**Red Lion** ☎Powburn216
6rm ⋈ CTV 40P Last dinner10pm ✿ ⊥
sB&B fr£6.65 dB&B fr£13.30 Bar lunch£1.50alc
Tea85p Dinner£2.66–£31.6&alc Wine£2.43 ⊨

GLASTONBURY Somerset Map**3** ST53
✕✕**No.3** Magdalene St ☎32129
Closed Mon, May & Nov; Dinner not served Sun; 20seats 8P Last dinner10pm Lunch£8–£10
Dinner£8–£10

✕**Becketts Inn** 43 High St ☎32928
Closed 25 & 26Dec; Lunch not served; 22seats 20P bedrooms available ♉ Mainly grills.
Last dinner9.30pm S% Dinner£5alc Wine£3.25
Credit cards ① ② ③ ⑤

GLENRIDDING Cumbria Map**11** NY31
★★★**Ullswater** ☎444 Telexno64537
48⇄⋔ Lift ▦ ⋈ CTV CTV available in bedrooms 300P ⚓ ⛳ ↳ Live music & dancing Sat
♉ Continental. Last dinner9pm ✿ ⊥
sB&B⇄⋔£9–£13.50 dB&B⇄⋔£18–£32
Lunch£4.50–£5.50 Tea90p–£1.20
Dinner£4.50–£6.50&alc Wine£2 ⊨ *xmas*
Credit cards ① ② ③ ⑤

★★**Glenridding** ☎228
Occupies an unrivalled position at the head of Ullswater.
Closed 4–24Jan; 33rm(18⇄⋔) ✗ ⋈ CTV 40P
Last dinner8.30pm ✿ ⊥ S% sB&B£9–£10
sB&B⇄⋔£10–£11 dB&B£16–£18
dB&B⇄⋔£18–£20 Tea fr65p Dinner fr£4.50
Wine£3 ⊨ *xmas* Credit cards ① ② ③ ⑤ ⑥

GLOUCESTER Gloucestershire Map**3** SO81
★★★**Tara** Upton Hill, Upton St Leonards (3m SE B4073) ☎67412
Fine old Cotswold-stone house with modern extensions. Its elevated position offers panoramic views of the Severn Valley.
22rm(13⇄⋔) ⋈ CTV in bedrooms ⊘ 60P ⚓ ⌒(heated) ⌂ Last dinner9.45pm ✿ ⊥
sB&B£11.50 sB&B⇄⋔£13.50 dB&B£18
dB&B⇄⋔£22 Lunch£6.50alc Tea£1.50alc
Dinner£7alc Wine£3 Credit cards ① ② ③ ⑤ ⑥

★★**Fleece** Westgate St ☎22762
Half timbered 18th-C inn with covered courtyard.
44rm ☽ CTV 8P 24⌂ Last dinner9.15pm ✿ ⊥
S% sB&B£7.50–£8.50 dB&B£14–£16
Lunch£1.40–£2.50 Tea75p–£1.25

G

High Tea£2.40–£2.50 Dinner£2.40–£4&alc Wine£2.75
★★New County Southgate St (Norfolk Capital) ☎24977 Telex no23241
18th-C inn with modern entrance.
39rm(4⇄ ⫙) ☽ CTV Last dinner9.15pm S% sB&B£10.10 sB&B⇄⫙£13.25 dB&B&17.95 dB&B⇄⫙£21.65 Lunch fr£3.25&alc Tea fr£1.25 Dinner fr£4.25&alc Wine£4 Credit cards 1 2 3 5 6
★★New Wellington Bruton Way ☎20022
23rm(4⇄⫙) TV in bedrooms Mainly grills. Last dinner9.45pm S% ✱sB&B£7.80 sB&B⇄⫙£9 dB&B£15 dB&B⇄⫙£16.50 Lunch£1.95 Dinner£3.50alc Wine£3 Credit card 1
★Longford Inn Longford (1½m N A38) ☎23519
6rm Annexe: 1rm CTV 100P 4 Last dinner7.30pm sB&B£6.53 dB&B£13.06 Lunch£2.25–£2.75 Tea60–75p Dinner£2.65–£3.25
XXDon Pasquale 19 Worcester St ☎25636
Closed Sun, Mon & First 3 wks Jul; 28 seats International. Last dinner9.45pm ✱Lunch£5.50alc Dinner£6alc Wine£2.75 Credit cards 1 2 3 5

GOATHLAND North Yorkshire Map**8** NZ80
★★*Goathland Hydro* ☎Whitby86296
Closed mid Oct–Etr; 33rm(9⇄⫙) CTV 25P Last dinner7.45pm

GOLANT Cornwall Map**2** SX15
★★Cormorant ☎Fowey3426
11rm(10⇄⫙) CTV TV available in bedrooms 25P (heated) International. Last dinner9pm ✱sB&B£9.50–£11 sB&B⇄⫙£9.50–£11 dB&B£19–£22 dB&B⇄⫙£19–£22 Lunch fr£3&alc Tea30p–£1 Dinner£3.95
xmas

GOODRICH Hereford & Worcester Map**3** SO51
★★Ye Hostelrie ☎Symonds Yat890241
Closed Xmas; 8rm(4⇄⫙) CTV 18P Last dinner8.30pm S% sB&B£10 sB&B⇄⫙£12 dB&B£14.50 dB&B⇄⫙£17.50 Bar lunch£1–£1.50&alc Dinner£4–£4.50&alc Wine£3.50

GOODRINGTON Devon see **PAIGNTON**

GOODWOOD West Sussex
see **Waterbeach**

GOOSNARGH Lancashire Map**7** SD53
XYe Horns ☎230
Closed Mon; 100seats 50P Last dinner9pm Lunch£3.75 Dinner£5.50 Wine£2.35 Credit card 5

GORLESTON-ON-SEA Norfolk
See **Yarmouth (Great)**

GOSPORT Hampshire Map**4** SZ69
★Anglesey Crescent Rd, Alverstoke (1m S) ☎82157
Regency building listed as being of historical interest.
15rm CTV Last dinner10.30pm ✱sB&B£8.50 dB&B£14.50 Wine£2.40

GOUDHURST Kent Map**5** TQ73
★★Star & Eagle (Whitbread) ☎211512
14th-C building, originally a monastery. Stands next to church, with delightful views over hop gardens and orchards.
Closed Xmas Day; 6rm CTV 18P 2 Last dinner9pm S% sB&B fr£9.57 dB&B fr£14.30 Lunch fr£3.05 Dinner fr£3 Wine£2.45 Credit cards 1 2 3 5
★Goudhurst (1m W of village on A262) ☎211200
Country inn on main road.
6rm TV TV available in bedrooms 25P Last dinner9.30pm sB&B£8–£9 dB&B£15–£17 Lunch£4alc Dinner£5alc Wine£3.15

GRANGE (in-Borrowdale) Cumbria Map**11** NY21
See also Borrowdale and Rosthwaite
★★**Borrowdale Gates** ☎Borrowdale204
An old manor house occupying a secluded position, offering splendid views, and set in its own wooded grounds on the edge of the village.
Closed 5Nov–Mar; 12rm(3⇌ 🛁) CTV available in bedrooms 25P Last dinner8pm

GRANGE-OVER-SANDS Cumbria Map**7** SD47
★★***Grange*** Lindale Rd (Best Western) ☎3666
Telex no65192
A Victorian hotel situated in a sheltered position within easy reach of the M6.
RS Nov–Mar; 32rm(7⇌ 🛁) CTV 30P
Last dinner8.30pm Credit cards 1 2 3 5

★★***Graythwaite Manor*** Fernhill Rd ☎2001
A large country-house-style hotel, occupying a secluded site above the estuary of Morecambe Bay amidst attractively landscaped gardens.
24rm(11⇌ 🛁) CTV 18P 14 (hard)
Last dinner7.30pm

★★**Netherwood** Lindale Rd ☎2552
A Victorian building of baronial proportions, embellished throughout with oak panelling and carving.
23rm(10⇌ 🛁) CTV 60P 8
Last dinner8pm S% sB&B£8–£9
sB&B⇌ 🛁£10.50–£11.50 dB&B£16–£18
dB&B⇌ 🛁£21–£23 Lunch£2.50–£3 Tea£1
High Tea£2.50–£3 Dinner£4–£4.50 Wine£2.85

★**Commodore** Main St ☎2381
All rooms and in particular the dining room, give views over Morecambe Bay and the Pennine Range.
12rm CTV 12P English & French. Last dinner8pm
sB&B£7–£8 dB&B£14–£16
Bar lunch50p–£4 Tea£1–£2 High Tea£2–£3.50
Dinner£3.75–£5 Wine£2.35 *xmas*

★**Methven** Kents Bank Rd ☎2031
Three-storey Victorian house with modern interior; stands in ¾ acre of gardens, with fine views.
Closed 2Nov–28Mar; 14rm(3⇌ 🛁) CTV 14P
Children under 3yrs not accommodated
Last dinner7pm sB&B£6.50–£7
dB&B£13–£14 dB&B⇌ 🛁£16–£17 Lunch£1.75
Tea90p Dinner£3 Wine£2

GRANTHAM Lincolnshire Map**8** SK93
★★★**George** High St ☎3286
Part of hotel was once home of Sir Isaac Newton.
Closed Xmas Day; 40rm(22⇌ 🛁) CTV CTV in bedrooms 100P 4 Live music & dancing Sat (in winter) International. Last dinner9.30pm
S% sB&B£12 sB&B⇌ 🛁£14.50 dB&B£18
dB&B⇌ 🛁£22 Lunch fr£3.75&alc Tea50p–£1.50
Dinner fr£4.95&alc Wine£2.30
Credit cards 1 2 3 5

★★**Kings** North Pde ☎5881
15rm(5⇌ 🛁) CTV in bedrooms 70P 2
French. Last dinner9.30pm S%
sB&B fr£9.90 sB&B⇌ 🛁 fr£12.10 dB&B fr£16.10
dB&B⇌ 🛁 fr£18.50 Lunch£2.85&alc
Dinner£3.60&alc Wine£2.75 Credit cards 1 2 3

GRASMERE Cumbria Map**11** NY30
★★★**Gold Rill Country House** ☎486
An early 19th-C house of local stone. It was named by William Wordsworth.
RS Nov–Mar; 23rm(12⇌ 🛁) CTV 30P
(heated) Children under 5yrs not accommodated
Last dinner8.30pm S% sB&B fr£17 (incl dinner) sB&B⇌ 🛁 fr£19.80 (incl dinner)
dB&B fr£34 (incl dinner) dB&B⇌ 🛁 fr£37.60 (incl dinner) Lunch fr£4.75 Tea fr£1.20 Dinner fr£7.50
Wine£3.10

★★★**Grasmere Red Lion** ☎456
200-year-old coaching inn with modern entrance and interior, opposite the village green.
Closed Dec–Feb; 38rm(28⇌ 🛁) Lift CTV CTV available in bedrooms 40P English & French.
Last dinner9pm Credit cards 1 2 3 5

★★★**Prince of Wales** (Mount Charlotte) ☎344
A large hotel standing by the lakeside in nine acres.
43⇌ 🛁 1 CTV CTV available in bedrooms 50P
English & French. Last dinner8.45pm
sB&B£10 sB&B⇌ 🛁£10–£12.50 dB&B£19
dB&B⇌ 🛁£18–£25 Lunch£3.50&alc Tea75p
High Tea£2 Dinner£4.50&alc
Credit cards 1 2 3

★★★**Swan** (Trusthouse Forte) ☎551
A 17th-C hotel, with later additions, once visited by Sir Walter Scott and Wordsworth.
31rm(15⇌ 🛁) CTV 40P Last dinner8.45pm
S% sB&B£14.50 sB&B⇌ 🛁£17
dB&B£23 dB&B⇌ 🛁£26.50 *xmas*
Credit cards 1 2 3 4 5 6

★**White Moss House** Rydal Water ☎295
See page 42 for details

★**Oak Bank** ☎217
Closed Nov–Mar; 13rm(7⇌ 🛁) CTV 12P
Children under 5yrs not accommodated
Last dinner7.30pm S% sB&B fr£8
sB&B⇌ 🛁 fr£9 dB&B fr£16 dB&B⇌ 🛁 fr£18
Bar lunch fr£1.50 Dinner fr£5 Wine£2.50
Credit cards 1 2 3 5

★**Ravenswood** ☎277
Closed Dec–Feb; 13rm(1⇌ 🛁) CTV 14P
Last dinner7pm S% sB&B£7–£8
dB&B£14–£16 dB&B⇌ 🛁£15–£18
Bar lunch fr45p Tea fr40p High Tea fr£2
Dinner fr£5.50 Wine£2.80

Moss Grove ☎251
RS Dec–Mar; 16rm TV 10P 1
Last dinner7.30pm

GRASSINGTON North Yorkshire Map**7** SE06
★★★**Wilson Arms** ☎752666
23rm(19⇌ 🛁) CTV CTV available in bedroom
60P 6 Live music & dancing Sat (in winter)
English & French. Last dinner9pm S%
sB&B⇌ 🛁£11–£19 dB&B£15–£23
dB&B⇌ 🛁£18–£30 Lunch£3.75–£4.50 Tea£1
Dinner£6.85–£7&alc Wine£3.10 *xmas*

Grassington House ☎752406
Converted early 18th-C manor house.
Closed Nov–Feb; 10rm(4⇌ 🛁) CTV 24P
Last dinner7pm S% sB&B£8–£9
dB&B£14.50–£16.50 dB&B⇌ 🛁£16.50–£18.50
Lunch£2.75–£2.95 Tea£1–£1.20
High Tea£2.25–£2.50 Dinner£3.50–£3.75

GRAVESEND Kent Map**5** TQ67
★★***Clarendon Royal*** Royal Pier Rd (Berni) ☎63151
Closed Xmas Day; 28rm(1⇌ 🛁) TV in bedrooms
70P Mainly grills. Last dinner11pm
Credit cards 1 2 5 6

☆☆**Europa Lodge** Watling St (Grand Met) ☎52768
Telex no966227
Annexe: 114⇌ 🛁 Lift TV 200P Live music & dancing Sat (in winter) Last dinner9.30pm
S% *sB&B⇌ 🛁£12 dB&B⇌ 🛁£18
Credit cards 1 2 3 4 5 6

At **Shorne** (4m SE A2)
☆☆☆**Inn on the Lake** Watling St ☎Shorne333
78⇌ 🛁 250P

GRAYS Essex Map**5** TQ67

At **North Stifford** (2m N on A13)
☆☆☆**Europa Lodge** (Grand Met) ☎Grays Thurrock71451
64⇌ 🛁 80P

G

GRAYSWOOD (nr Haslemere) Surrey Map**4** SU93
XXWheatsheaf Inn ☎Haslemere4440
Closed Mon & Xmas Day; Dinner not served Sun; 50seats 40P English & French. Last dinner9.30pm *Lunch£3–£6&alc Dinner£10alc Wine£4 Credit cards 1 2 3 5

GREASBY Merseyside Map**7** SJ28
XXX*Manor Farm* Greasby Rd ☎051–677 7034
Closed Sun; 120seats 50P English, French & Italian. Last dinner10.30pm

GREAT Places incorporating the word 'Great'–eg Great Malvern, Great Yarmouth–are given under Malvern, Yarmouth, etc.

GRETA BRIDGE Co Durham Map**12** NZ01
★★Morritt Arms ☎Whorlton232
24rm(13⇌🛁) 2▭ CTV 100P 12 Last dinner9pm S% sB&B£14 sB&B⇌🛁£16 dB&B£22 dB&B⇌🛁£25 Lunch£4.25 Tea£1.75 Dinner£5.50 Wine£3 Credit cards 1 5

GRIMSBY Humberside Map**8** TA20
☆☆☆☆Humber Royal Littlecoates Rd (Crest) ☎50295
54rm(49⇌🛁) Lift CTV CTV in bedrooms 250P Conference facilities available English & French. Last dinner10pm S% *sB&B⇌🛁£17.60 dB&B⇌🛁£26.13 Continental breakfast 1 2 3 4 5 6

☆☆☆Grimsby Crest Motel St James's Sq (Crest) ☎59771
132⇌🛁 Lift CTV in bedrooms 90P Last dinner10.30pm S% *sB&B⇌🛁£16.25 dB&B⇌🛁£22.78 Continental breakfast Credit cards 1 2 3 4 5 6

GRIMSTHORPE Lincolnshire Map**8** TF02
XBlack Horse Inn ☎Edenham247
Closed Sun & Xmas Day; 70seats 40P bedrooms available Last dinner9pm (10pm Sat) Lunch£7.50alc Dinner£8.50alc Wine£2.95

GRINDLEFORD Derbyshire Map**8** SK27
★★*Maynard Arms* Main Rd ☎Hope Valley30321
13rm(6⇌🛁) CTV 60P Last dinner9.45pm Credit cards 1 2 3 5

GROBY Leicestershire Map**4** SK50
★★Brant Inn ☎Leicester872703
Closed Public Hols; 9rm(8⇌🛁) TV in bedrooms 130P French Last dinner9.15pm *sB&B fr£10 sB&B⇌🛁 fr£11 dB&B fr£17 dB&B⇌🛁£17 Lunch fr£2&alc Dinner fr£2.50&alc Wine£2.75 Credit cards 1 2 3 5

GUERNSEY
Details for Channel Islands follow England.

GUILDFORD Surrey Map**7** SU94
★★★Angel High St (Trusthouse Forte) ☎64555
Three storey coaching inn with courtyard and 13th-C crypt Interior has 16th-C and 17th-C oak panelling and clock dating from 1688.
24⇌🛁 TV in bedrooms Last dinner9.30pm S% sB&B⇌🛁£16 dB&B⇌🛁£23 *xmas* Credit cards 1 2 3 4 5 6

X*Mad Hatter* 5–6 Sydenham Rd ☎63011
36seats International. Last dinner11pm Credit cards 1 2 3 4 5 6

GULWORTHY Devon Map**2** SX47
XXXHorn of Plenty ☎Gunnislake832528
Closed Thu; Lunch not served Fri; 35seats English & French. Last dinner9.30pm

GUNNISLAKE Cornwall Map**2** SX47
★★Cornish Inn ☎832475
A small country inn situated in the glorious Tamar Valley.
8rm(4⇌) CTV 20P Last dinner9.30pm S% sB&B£6.80–£7.50 sB&B⇌£8.20–£9 dB&B£10.80–£12.20 dB&B⇌£13.80–£15 Lunch£3 Dinner fr£2.20&alc Wine£2.50 Credit cards 1 3 6

HADLEIGH Suffolk Map**5** TM04
X*White Lion* High St ☎3256
White-painted coaching inn with newly converted, beamed restaurant.
Closed Sun; Dinner not served Mon & Tue; 40seats 20P Last dinner9.30pm Credit cards 1 2 3 5

HADLEY WOOD Greater London Map**4** TQ29
★★★★West Lodge Park Cockfosters Rd (Prestige) ☎01–440 8311
On the site of a hunting lodge of Queen Elizabeth I, the present building is late Georgian and stands in quiet parkland and farmland.
53rm(50⇌🛁) 2▭ Lift CTV in bedrooms 75P 3 International. Last dinner9.30pm S% *sB&B⇌🛁£20.50 dB&B£23 dB&B⇌🛁£31.50 Lunch£6.50alc Tea80p Dinner£7.50alc Wine£3.25 Credit cards 1 2 3 5

HAGLEY Hereford & Worcester Map**7** SO98
XXLyttleton Arms ☎882213
Lunch not served Sat; Dinner not served Sun; 120seats 200P French. Last dinner9.50pm Lunch£4.25&alc Dinner£6alc Wine£2.90 Credit cards 1 2

HALE BARNS Greater Manchester Map**7** SJ78
X*Borsalino* 14 The Square ☎061–980 5331

losed Sun, Mon, Xmas & Public Hols; Lunch not erved; 50seats 100P ♉French. astdinner10.30pm Creditcards [1] [2] [3] [5]

ALIFAX West Yorkshire Map**7** SE02
★★Holdsworth House Holdsworth Ln, Holmfield m NW off A629 Keighley road) ☎244270
losed Xmas, New Year & Etr; 30⇌⋒ 🏨 CTV CTV vailable in bedrooms 50P ⛟ ⚓ Disco Sat ♉French. ast dinner10pm ♔ ♖
B&B⇌⋒£16.63–£23.76
B&B⇌⋒£28.51–£35.64 Lunch£6.50–£9&alc inner£6.50–£9&alc Wine£3.50 ⛿
redit cards [1] [2] [3] [5] [6]

White Swan Princess St (Trusthouse Forte) ☎54227
hree storey, store building with windows in classical tyle.
0rm(14⇌⋒) Lift ☽ 🏨 CTV TV in bedrooms 8P astdinner9.45pm ♔ S% sB&B£13.50 B&B⇌⋒£15.50 dB&B£17.50 dB&B⇌⋒£21 ⛿ Creditcards [1] [2] [3] [4] [5] [6]

ALLAND East Sussex Map**5** TQ41
☆Halland Motel ☎456
losed 25&26Dec; 12⇌⋒ 🏨 TV in bedrooms ⊘ 70P 🏛 ⛟ ⚓ Children under 5yrs not accommodated astdinner8.45pm ✱sB&B⇌⋒£11.95 B&B⇌⋒£21.40 Lunch£5alc Dinner£7alc Vine£3.05 Creditcards [2] [5]

ALSETOWN Cornwall Map**2** SW53
✕Chef's Kitchen ☎ Penzance 796218
losed Sun; Lunch not served; 32seats 6P ♉French. astdinner10.30pm

ALSTEAD Essex Map**5** TL83
✕*Fernando's* 26 High St ☎2001
Closed Sun; 45seats 150P ♉International. Creditcards [1] [2] [3] [5] [6]

HAMPOLE South Yorkshire Map**8** SE51
✕✕Hampole Priory ☎Doncaster723740
Dinner not served Sun & Mon; 24seats 20P ♉English & French. Lastdinner9.30pm S% ✱Dinner£7.05alc Wine£2.75 Creditcards [1] [6]

HAMPTON COURT Greater London Map**4** TQ16
★★Greyhound Hampton Court Rd (Henekey) ☎01–977 8121
10rm(6⇌⋒) Annexe:19rm(8⇌⋒) 🏨 TV in bedrooms 30P ♉Mainly grills. Lastdinner9pm ♔ S% sB&B£12 sB&B⇌⋒£15 dB&B£19.50 dB&B⇌⋒£21.50 ⛿ *xmas*
Creditcards [1] [2] [3] [4] [5] [6]

✕✕*Bastians* Hampton Court Rd ☎01–977 6074
Closed Sun & Bank Hols; Lunch not served Sat; 75seats ♉French. Lastdinner11pm
Creditcards [1] [2] [3] [5] [6]

HAMSTEAD MARSHALL Berkshire Map**4** SU46
✕✕*White Hart Inn* ☎Kintbury201
Small country inn, with pleasant restaurant.
RS Sun & Mon; 54seats 30P ♉English & French. Lastdinner10pm

HANDFORTH Cheshire Map**7** SJ88
❀★★★★Belfry Stanley Rd (Inter-Hotel)
☎437 0511 Telexno666358
96⇌⋒ Lift ☽ 🏨 CTV in bedrooms ⊘ 150P ⛟ ⚓ Live music & dancing 5 nights wkly Conference facilities available ♉International. Specialities: Escalope of veal with tarragon, Filet of beef en croute, Roast duckling with honey and almonds. Lastdinner10pm

H

♔ ♔ S% sB&B⇌⋒ fr£20.29 dB&B⇌⋒ fr£31.40 Lunch fr£5.50&alc Tea fr£1.65 Dinner fr£6.50&alc Wine£3.78 Credit cards 1 2 3 5 6

HARBERTONFORD Devon Map**3** SX75
✕***Hungry Horse*** ☎441
Closed Sun, Mon, Feb & 1st 2wks Oct; Lunch not served; 40seats 8P ♀International. Credit card 2

HARLESTON Norfolk Map**5** TM28
★★**Swan** The Thoroughfare ☎852221
13rm(7⇌⋒) 1 CTV TV available in bedrooms 70P ♀English & Italian. Last dinner9.30pm ♔ S% sB&B£9.50–£12.50 sB&B⇌⋒£10.50–£12.50 dB&B£14.50–£15.50 dB&B⇌⋒£15.50–£17.50 Lunch£3–£3.50&alc Dinner£3.50–£5.50&alc Wine£2.30 ⊞ *xmas* Credit cards 1 2 3 5

HARLOW Essex Map**5** TL41
★★★**Saxon Motor Inn** Southern Way ☎22441
Telex no81658
120⇌⋒ ☽ CTV in bedrooms 200P Live music & dancing Sat Conference facilities available ♿ ♀English & French. Last dinner10.30pm ♔ ♔ S% sB&B⇌⋒£17.02 dB&B⇌⋒£21.34 Lunch£3.30&alc Tea80p Dinner£3.80&alc Wine£3.50 Credit cards 1 2 3 5

HARLYN BAY Cornwall Map**2** SW87
★**Polmark** (off B3276) ☎St Merryn520206
Closed Nov–Mar; 6rm Annexe: 11rm CTV 20P (heated) Last dinner8.30pm ♔ ♔ S% sB&B£10.50–£12.50 (incl dinner) Dinner£4.25 Wine£2.50

HAROME North Yorkshire Map**8** SE68
✕**Star Inn** ☎Helmsley397
Closed Sun & Mon; 50seats 40P Last dinner9.30pm S% Lunch50palc Dinner£6.25alc Wine£3 Credit cards 1 2 3 5

HARPENDEN Hertfordshire Map**4** TL11
★★★★**Harpenden Moat House** 18 Southern Rd (Queens) ☎64111
Georgian period house once known as St Dominic's Convent, is of historical interest.
18⇌⋒ Annexe: 17⇌⋒ 1 ☽ CTV CTV in bedrooms 100P ♿ ♀English, French & Italian. Last dinner10.15pm ♔ ♔ S% *sB&B⇌⋒£16–£17.50 dB&B⇌⋒ fr£23 Lunch fr£3.25&alc Dinner£9alc Wine£4 ⊞ Credit cards 1 2 3 4 5 6

★★★**Glen Eagle** 1 Luton Rd ☎60271
Telex no925859
Pleasant hotel with country-house atmosphere.
52rm(43⇌⋒) Lift ☽ CTV available in bedrooms 100P Last dinner10pm ♔ ♔ sB&B fr£14.88 sB&B⇌⋒£22.44–£24.60 sB&B fr£23.28 sB&B⇌⋒£33–£38.40 Lunch£7alc Tea£2alc Dinner£7alc Wine£3 ⊞ Credit cards 1 2 3 5 6

HARROGATE North Yorkshire Map**8** SE35
★★★★**Crown** Crown Pl (Trusthouse Forte) ☎6775
Telex no56752
18th-C stone building near Valley Gardens and Royal Baths.
120⇌⋒ Lift ☽ CTV in bedrooms 50P ♿ Last dinner9.30pm ♔ ♔ S% sB&B⇌⋒£18 dB&B⇌⋒£31 ⊞ *xmas* Credit cards 1 2 3 4 5 6

★★★★**Majestic** Ripon Rd (Trusthouse Forte) ☎68972 Telex no57918
160rm(150⇌⋒) Lift ☽ CTV in bedrooms 200P (heated (hard) Conference facilities available ♿ Last dinner9.15pm ♔ ♔ S% sB&B£18 sB&B⇌⋒£21.50 dB&B£27.50 dB&B⇌⋒£30.50 ⊞ *xmas* Credit cards 1 2 3 4 5 6

★★★★**Old Swan** Swan Rd (Prestige) ☎504051
Telex no57922
147⇌⋒ Lift ☽ CTV CTV available in bedrooms P (hard) Conference facilities available Last dinner10pm ♔ ♔ S% sB&B⇌⋒£22–£25 dB&B⇌⋒£40–£45 Lunch fr£5.50&alc Tea fr£1.50 Dinner fr£6.50&alc Wine£5 ⊞ *xmas* Credit cards 1 2 3 4 5 6

★★★**Cairn** Ripon Rd ☎504005 Telex no57992
Large, stone, three-storey building with balustrade and turret embellishment, standing in own grounds.
137rm(75⇌⋒) Lift ☽ CTV 200P (hard) Conference facilities available ♀English & French. Last dinner9.15pm ♔ ♔ S% *sB&B£15 sB&B⇌⋒£18 dB&B£26 dB&B⇌⋒£29 Lunch£3.75 Tea£1.50 Dinner£4.50 ⊞ *xmas* Credit cards 1 2 3 5 6

★★★**Hotel St George** 1 Ripon Rd (Best Western) ☎61431 Telex no57995
81rm(71⇌⋒) Lift ☽ CTV in bedrooms 21P 20 ♀English & Continental. Last dinner9pm ♔ ♔ S% *sB&B£13–£14.60 sB&B⇌⋒£13–£16.65 dB&B£26–£26.50 dB&B⇌⋒£26–£31.90 Lunch fr£2.70 Tea fr£1.25 Dinner fr£5.40 ⊞ *xmas* Credit cards 1 2 3 5

★★★**Studley** Swan Rd ☎60425
27rm(19⇌⋒) Lift ☽ CTV CTV in bedrooms 10P Children under 7yrs not accommodated ♀French. Last dinner10.30pm *sB&B£13.75–£15.40 sB&B⇌⋒£18.15–£19.80 dB&B£24.75–£26.40 dB&B⇌⋒£29.15–£30.80 Lunch£2.50–£3 Dinner£3.50–£4.55 Wine£2.95 Credit cards 1 2 3 5

★★**Green Park** Valley Dr ☎504681
49rm(15⇌⋒) CTV TV available in bedrooms 16P ♀English & Continental. Last dinner9pm ♔ ♔ sB&B£9.72 sB&B⇌⋒£11.72 dB&B£19.54

B&B⇌ ⋒£22.54 Lunch fr£3.50 Tea fr£1.50
High Tea fr£3.50 Dinner fr£5 Wine£4 xmas
Credit cards 1 3 6

★★Knapping Rise 53 King's Rd ☎67404
7rm CTV 17P 2 English & Italian.
Last dinner9.30pm ✱sB&B£8.50
sB&B⇌⋒£9 dB&B£14 dB&B⇌⋒£17
Lunch£3.50 Tea80p–£1.50
High Tea£1.20–£1.50 Dinner£4.50 Wine£3.20
Credit card 2

★*Caesars* 51 Valley Dr ☎65818
11rm⇌⋒ CTV TV available in bedrooms 1P 1
Last dinner9.30pm

✕✕Number Six 6 Ripon Rd ☎502908
Closed Mon, Last wk Jul & 1st 2wks Aug; 58seats
8P French. Specialities: hot creamed Morecambe shrimps, poussin roti au champagne, delice de sole au Noilly Prat. Last dinner10pm
✱Dinner£6.95–£11.95 Wine£2.95

✕✕Oliver 24 King's Rd ☎68600
Closed Sun & Public Hols; Lunch not served; 80seats
English & French. Last dinner10pm
Dinner£7–£9 Wine£3.40 Credit cards 1 2

✕Roman 23 Cheltenham Cres ☎68568
Closed Sun; 50 seats French & Italian.
Last dinner11pm Dinner£5alc Wine£3.20
Credit cards 1 2 3 6

HARROW Greater London Map**4** TQ18
★★Cumberland 1 St Johns Rd ☎01-8634111
71rm(52⇌⋒) CTV TV in bedrooms 55P
Last dinner9pm S% ✱sB&B£11.88
sB&B⇌⋒£16.20 dB&B£18.90 dB&B⇌⋒£20.52
Lunch£2.11–£2.65&alc Dinner£3.72–£4.45&alc
Wine£2.60

HARROW WEALD Greater London Map**4** TQ19
★★★Grims Dyke Country Old Redding
☎01-9547666
Once the home of W S Gilbert of Gilbert & Sullivan fame.
Closed Xmas Night; RS 23–28 Dec; 12⇌⋒ 1
CTV in bedrooms 60P Live music & dancing Sat
Continental. Last dinner10pm S%
sB&B⇌⋒£19.50 dB&B⇌⋒£27 Lunch£4&alc
Dinner£5&alc Wine£3.20 Credit cards 1 2 3 5

HARTFIELD East Sussex Map**5** TQ43
✕✕Hay Waggon Inn ☎252
Closed Tue & 2wks Nov; Dinner not served Sun;
45seats 36P International. Last dinner9.30pm
✱Lunch£4.50–£6.50 Dinner£8.50alc
Credit cards 1 2 3

HARTINGTON Derbyshire Map**7** SK16
★Charles Cotton ☎229
17th-C inn with grounds bordering River Dene.
8rm CTV 45P Last dinner8pm
sB&B£6.60–£7.80 dB&B£12.80–£14.80
Lunch£2.25–£3.25 Tea85p–£1.25
High Tea£1.50–£2.50 Dinner£3.25–£4.50
Wine£2.20

HARTLAND Devon Map**2** SS22
★★Hartland Quay Hartland Quay ☎218
A stone-built coastguard station, in own grounds at foot of rock cliffs.
Closed Nov–Mar; 16rm(4⇌⋒) CTV 100P 16
Last dinner9pm S% sB&B£7.50–£8
dB&B£15–£16 dB&B⇌⋒£16–£17 Lunch£2alc
Tea fr75p Dinner£3.50–£4&alc Wine£1.50

★West Country Inn Bursdon Moor ☎475
Closed late Oct–Mar; 10rm CTV 60P 2
Last dinner9.30pm sB&B£7 dB&B£14
Bar lunch£1.50alc Dinner£5alc Wine£2

H

HARTLEPOOL Cleveland Map**8** NZ53
★★★**Grand** Swainson St (British Transport) ☎66345
49rm(21⇌⋒) Lift ☽ ₩ TV in bedrooms ♿ ♡English & French. Last dinner9.15pm ♡ ⊥ S%
✱sB&B⇌⋒ fr£19.65 dB&B⇌⋒ fr£26.95
Lunch fr£5.25 Dinner fr£5.60 Wine£2.95 ♜
Credit cards 1 2 3 4 5 6

★★★**Staincliffe** Seaton Carew (Swallow) ☎64301
Telex no53168
23rm(16⇌⋒) ☽ ₩ CTV in bedrooms 70P
Last dinner9.15pm ♡ S% sB&B£14.35
sB&B⇌⋒£18 dB&B£21.95 dB&B⇌⋒£24.65
♜ *xmas* Credit cards 1 2 3 5

HARTLEY WITNEY Hampshire Map**4** SU75
✕**Stilton Dish** Phoenix Green ☎2107
35seats 15P ♡French. Last dinner10pm
✱Dinner£7alc Wine£2.70 Credit cards 1 2 3

HARTOFT END North Yorkshire Map**8** SE79
★★***Blacksmith's Arms*** ☎Lastingham331
12rm(4⇌⋒) ₩ CTV ⛟ ⚓ Children under 16yrs not accommodated Last dinner8pm ♡

HARWICH Essex Map**5** TM23
★★**Cliff** Marine Pde, Dovercourt ☎3345
Telex no987372
34rm(20⇌⋒) ☽ ₩ CTV CTV available in bedrooms 60P ⚓ Last dinner9pm ♡ ⊥ sB&B£10.50
sB&B⇌⋒£12.02 dB&B£21 dB&B⇌⋒£24.04
Lunch£3&alc Tea70p High Tea£1.50
Dinner£3.50&alc Wine£2.80 Credit cards 1 2 3 5

★**Samuel Pepys** 31 Church St ☎3857
7rm ₩ CTV ♡

✕✕**Pier** The Quay ☎3363
Closed Xmas; 134seats 20P ♡English & French.
Last dinner10pm Lunch£7alc Dinner£8.50alc
Wine£3

HASLEMERE Surrey Map**4** SU93
★★★**Georgian** High St ☎51555
Three-storey, 18th-C inn built by Sir James Edward Oglethorpe who founded the state of Georgia USA.
19rm(10⇌⋒) Annexe:3⇌⋒ ₩ CTV 30P ⚓ squash sauna bath ♡English & French. Last dinner9.15pm
♡ ⊥ S% sB&B£10.50 sB&B⇌⋒£11.85
dB&B£18.75 dB&B⇌⋒£21.50
Lunch£3.50–£4&alc Tea75p High Tea£1.50
Dinner£4.50–£5.50&alc Wine£3.50 ♜ *xmas*
Credit cards 1 2 3 5 6

★★★**Lythe Hill** Petworth Rd (1¼m E B2131) (Prestige) ☎51251 Telex no858402
Main building set in three acres of attractive grounds. Annexe rooms, situated above L'Auberge de France restaurant, still retain much of the 14th-C style.
34rm(32⇌⋒) 1▭ ☽ ₩ TV in bedrooms 200P ⚓
⚘(hard) sauna bath Live music & dancing Sat
♡International. Last dinner9.15pm ♡ ⊥ S%
✱sB&B£9.50–£15.50 sB&B⇌⋒£15.50–£25.50
sB&B£18–£20 dB&B⇌⋒£26–£36
Continental breakfast Lunch£4–£5&alc
Tea80p–£1.50 dinner£5.50–£6.50&alc Wine£3
♜ *xmas* Credit cards 1 2 3 5 6

✕✕✕**L'Auberge de France** (Lythe Hill Hotel)
Petworth Rd (1¼m E B2131) ☎51251
14th-C farmhouse of brick and timber; set in extensive grounds. The restaurant is part traditional and part modern with delightful views over wooded hills.
Closed Mon & 25Dec–22Feb; Lunch not served Tue; 50seats 200P bedrooms available ♡French.
Last dinner9.15pm S% Lunch£9alc Dinner£9alc
Wine£3 Credit cards 1 2 3 5 6

HASTINGS & ST LEONARDS East Sussex Map**5** TQ80
★★★ ⚘**Beauport Park** (3m N off A2100) (Inter-Hotel)
☎51222

pacious country house set in 33 acres of garden and arkland.
rm(15⇌⋒) CTV in bedrooms 50P 4 (heated) (grass) squash International.
astdinner8.30pm S% sB&B£11.50 B&B⇌⋒£13.50 dB&B£20 dB&B⇌⋒£24 unch£3.50&alc Tea35p Dinner£4.50&alc Vine£3.20 xmas Credit cards 1 2 3 5

Yelton White Rock ☎422240
0rm Lift CTV 20P Last dinner8pm % sB&B fr£7.50 dB&B fr£14 Lunch fr£2.25 ea fr50p High Tea fr£1.50 Dinner fr£3 Wine£2 xmas Credit cards 1 2

XMitre 56 High St ☎427000
losed Mon, 2wks Nov & 2wks Feb; Lunch not erved Tue–Sat; Dinner not served Sun; 26seats French. Specialities: terrine, steak au poivre, neringue Chantilly. Last dinner10pm Dinner£5.40alc

ATCH BEAUCHAMP Somerset Map**3** ST32
XFarthings ☎480664
losed Sun, Mon & 2wks Jan/Feb; Lunch not erved; 40seats 30P bedrooms available English & rench. Last dinner9.30pm S% Dinner£8alc Vine£3.30 Credit cards 1 2 3 6

ATFIELD Hertfordshire Map**4** TL20
★★★Comet (junc A1/A414) (Embassy) ☎65411
The hotel is situated beside a roundabout, and is named after the De Haviland Comet racer. There is a model of the same in forecourt.
5rm(35⇌⋒) CTV TV in bedrooms 150P ast dinner9.15pm S% sB&B£11.50 B&B⇌⋒£15 dB&B⇌⋒£21 Lunch£4.75&alc Dinner£5.75&alc Wine£4.50 Credit cards 1 2 3 4 5 6

XXSalisbury Old Hatfield ☎62220
Closed 25Dec & Public Hols; Dinner not served Sun; 70seats 20P English & Continental. ast dinner9.45pm S% Lunch£7.50alc Dinner£7.50alc Credit cards 1 2 3 5

ATHERLEIGH Devon Map**2** SS50
★George ☎454
15th-C coaching inn with thatched roof and cobbled courtyard. Situated in village square.
13rm(7⇌⋒) 3 CTV 60P ast dinner9.30pm S% ✱sB&B£7.50 B&B⇌⋒£10–£11.50 dB&B£15 dB&B⇌⋒£17–£19 Lunch£3.50–£3.95&alc Tea25–85p Dinner£4.50–£5&alc Wine£2.60 xmas Credit card 5

★Havelock Arms Market St ☎270
16th-C inn in centre of market town.
6rm CTV 8P Last dinner9pm S% sB&B£4.50–£6 dB&B£9–£12

Lunch£1.50–£2.50 Dinner£3–£3.50 Wine£2.80

HATHERSAGE Derbyshire Map**8** SK28
★★*George* (Whitbread) ☎Hope Valley50436
10rm(5⇌⋒) CTV 40P Last dinner9pm Credit cards 1 3 5

★★Hathersage Inn Main St (Best Western) ☎Hope Valley50259
Closed Xmas wk; 5rm(2⇌⋒) Annexe: 5rm CTV in bedrooms 20P Last dinner10pm S% sB&B fr£9.75 sB&B⇌⋒ fr£11.50 dB&B fr£16.50 dB&B⇌⋒ fr£19.50 Lunch fr£4 Dinner fr£4 Wine£2.20 Credit cards 1 2 3

HATTON Warwickshire Map**4** SP26
XX*New Inn* ☎Warwick42154
Closed Mon; Dinner not served Sun; 55seats 100P English & French. Last dinner10pm

HAVANT Hampshire Map**4** SU70
★★★Bear East St (Whitbread) ☎486501
35rm(17⇌⋒) Lift CTV CTV in bedrooms 100P English & French. Last dinner10.15pm ✱sB&B£10.90 sB&B⇌⋒£14.85 dB&B£17.60 dB&B⇌⋒£22 Lunch£4&alc Dinner£5.28&alc Wine£3 Credit cards 1 2 3 5

H

HAWES North Yorkshire Map**7** SD88
★★Fountain Market Pl ☎206
12⇌⋒ Lift CTV Last dinner8.45pm ✱sB&B⇌⋒£10.20 dB&B⇌⋒£17.20 Lunch£2.75 Dinner fr£3.75&alc Credit cards 1 3 5

HAWESWATER Cumbria Map**12** NY41
★★Haweswater ☎Bampton (Penrith)235
Offers good views of the lake and surrounding countryside.
16rm TV 20P 10 Last dinner7.45pm ✱sB&B fr£7.80 sB&B⇌⋒ fr£8.80 dB&B fr£15.60 dB&B⇌⋒ fr£16.60 xmas Credit cards 1 3 5

HAWKCHURCH Devon Map**3** ST30
★★★Fairwater Head ☎349
Closed Nov–mid Mar; 14⇌⋒ CTV CTV available in bedrooms 25P Last dinner9.30pm S% sB&B⇌⋒£13.80–£15.50 dB&B⇌⋒£24.50–£27.50 Lunch fr£4.25 Dinner£5–£5.50&alc Wine£2.80

HAWKHURST Kent Map**5** TQ73
★★Royal Oak Highgate ☎2184
12rm TV 40P 6 Disco wknds (winter) Live music & dancing wknds (winter) Last dinner9.30pm sB&B£7.50 dB&B£14 Lunch£2.25–£3&alc Dinner£3–£4.50&alc Wine£1.98 Credit cards 2 3 5

★★**Tudor Arms** ☎2312
Part 17th-C inn, in two acres of gardens half a mile outside village. Associated with Hawkhurst gang of smugglers.
RS Sun evenings; 14rm(6⇌⋒) CTV CTV available in bedrooms 40P 3⌂ ♣ ♣ ♀French & Italian. Lastdinner9.15pm S% sB&B£9 sB&B⇌⋒£11 dB&B£18 dB&B⇌⋒£23 Continental breakfast Lunch£2.90&alc Dinner fr£4&alc ⊟ Credit cards ①②③⑤⑥

HAWKSHEAD (nr Ambleside) Cumbria Map**7** SD39
★★★♛ ***Tarn Hows*** Hawkshead Hill ☎330
A beautifully situated country-house hotel in 30 acres of garden and parkland.
Closed 4 Nov–Feb; 24rm (17⇌⋒) Annexe: 4⇌⋒ ♛ CTV TV available in bedrooms 30P ♣ ♣ ⌓(heated) ➶(grass) ∩ ♀English & Continental. Lastdinner8.30pm ✿ ♀ Credit cards ①②③⑥

★**Red Lion** ☎213
15th-C coaching inn which is a prominent feature of the village. The 18th-C dining room boasts a ceiling that is a fine example of Italian craftsmanship.
8rm Annexe: 2⇌⋒ ♛ CTV 12P ♣ ♣ Lastdinner9pm ✿ S% ✱sB&B£7 dB&B£12 Bar lunch£1.50alc High Tea£1.50alc Dinner£2.50alc Wine£2.75 *xmas*

HAWORTH West Yorkshire Map**7** SE03
★**Old White Lion** 6 West Ln ☎42313
Closed Xmas & New Year; 12rm(5⇌⋒) ♛ CTV 4P Live music & dancing twice mthly Lastdinner10pm ♀ ✱sB&B£8.32 sB&B⇌⋒£9.50–£10.69 dB&B£14.26 dB&B⇌⋒£16.59–£19.06 Lunch£2.75–£3.25 Tea30–50p High Tea75p–£1.50 Dinner£3.75alc Wine£3 ⊟ Credit card ③

HAYDON BRIDGE Northumberland Map**12** NY86
★**Anchor** John Martin St ☎227
9rm(2⇌⋒) ♛ CTV 20P ➘ Disco twice wkly Live music & dancing wkly Lastdinner9pm ✿ S% sB&B£7–£8 dB&B£12–£14 dB&B⇌⋒£14–£16 Lunch£3.50alc Dinner£3.50alc Wine£2.50 *xmas*

HAYLE Cornwall Map**2** SW53
★**Penellen** Riviere Towans, Phillack ☎753777
Detached property in own grounds overlooking cliffs and views of St Ives.
Closed Nov–Mar; 12rm(3⋒) CTV ✗ 16P Children under 2yrs not accommodated Lastdinner12pm ✿ ♀ S% sB&B£6.50–£8.50 sB&B⇌⋒£7.50–£9.50 dB&B£11–£15 dB&B⇌⋒£13–£17 Continental breakfast Bar lunch70p–£3 Dinner£4.95–£5.95&alc Wine£2.95 ⊟

HAYLING ISLAND Hampshire Map**4** SU70
☆☆☆☆**Post House** Northney Rd (Trusthouse Forte) ☎5011 Telex no86620
Annexe: 96⇌⋒ ☽ ♛ CTV CTV in bedrooms 150P ♣ ⌓(heated) Conference facilities available Lastdinner10.30pm ✿ S% sB&B⇌⋒£21.25 dB&B⇌⋒£31 ⊟ *xmas* Credit cards ①②③④⑤⑥

★★**Newton House** Manor Rd ☎66131
Closed Xmas & New Year; 30rm(16⇌⋒) ☽ ♛ CTV in bedrooms ✗ 45P ♣ ♣ ⌓(heated) ➶(hard) Children under 1yr not accommodated ♀English & French. Lastdinner9pm ✿ ♀ sB&B£11.80–£12 sB&B⇌⋒£13.80–£14.50 dB&B£22.36–£24.60 dB&B⇌⋒£23–£26 Lunch£3.25–£4 Tea20–30p High Tea60–80p Dinner£3.50–£4&alc Wine£3.30 Credit cards ③⑤

HAYTOR Devon Map**3** SX77
★★♛ **Bel Alp** ☎217
Early 20th-C country house in eight acres of grounds.
Closed Jan; 11rm(5⇌⋒) Lift ♛ CTV 20P ♣ ♣ ➶(hard) billiards ♿ Lastdinner8pm ✿ ♀ S% sB&B£9–£12 sB&B⇌⋒£11.25–£14.75 dB&B£18–£24 dB&B⇌⋒£22.50–£29.50 Lunch£2.75–£3 Tea25–75p High Tea75p–£1.50 Dinner£2.75–£3&alc Wine£3.25 *xmas* Credit cards ①②③

HAYWARDS HEATH West Sussex Map**4** TQ32
★★**Hayworthe Arms** Station Rd ☎412808
18rm(2⇌⋒) ♛ CTV 50P billiards ♀English & French Lastdinner10pm ✿ S% sB&B fr£9.75 sB&B⇌⋒ fr£14 dB&B fr£17.80 dB&B⇌⋒ fr£18.70 Lunch fr£3.50&alc Dinner fr£3.50&alc Wine£3.50 Credit cards ①②③④⑤⑥

HAYWOOD, GREAT Staffordshire Map**7** SJ92
☆☆**Coach & Horses Motel** Pasturefields (on A51) ☎Weston270324
RS pub hols (no restaurant); 37⇌⋒ ☽ ♛ CTV TV available in bedrooms 200P ♣ Conference facilities available ♧ ♀English, French & Italian. Lastdinner9.45pm ✿ S% ✱sB&B⇌⋒£9–£11.50 dB&B⇌⋒£13–£15.50 Lunch fr£2.50 Dinner fr£3.25&alc Wine£2.50 ⊟ Credit cards ①②③④⑤⑥

HEALD GREEN Greater Manchester Map**7** SJ88
✕**La Bonne Auberge** ☎061–437 5701
Closed Sun; Dinner not served Mon; 65seats 100P ♀French. Lastdinner9.45pm ✱Lunch fr£2.20 Dinner£6alc Wine£2.90 Credit cards ②⑤

HEATHROW AIRPORT (London) Greater London Map**4** TQ07 **See plan**
☆☆☆☆**Ariel** Bath Rd, Hayes (Trusthouse Forte) ☎01–759 2552 Telex no21777 Plan**1**
179⇌⋒ Lift ☽ ⊞ ♛ CTV in bedrooms 100P Conference facilities available Lastdinner10.30pm ✿ ♀ S% sB&B⇌⋒£25.25 dB&B⇌⋒£36 Credit cards ①②③④⑤⑥

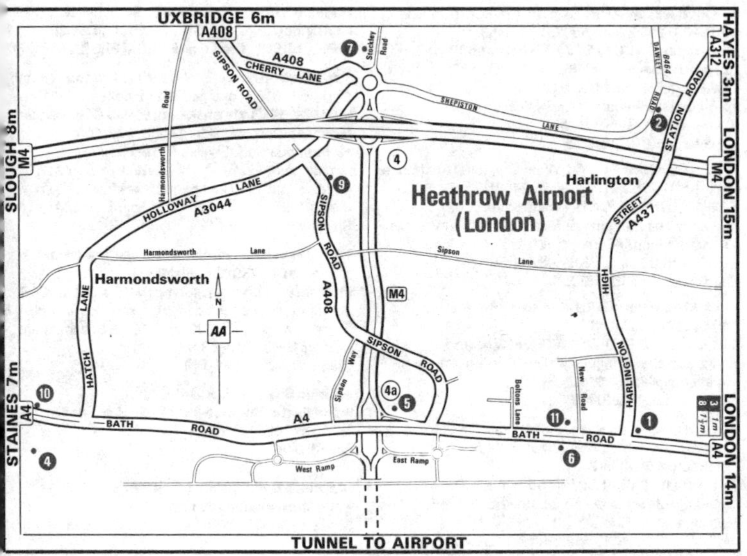

1 Ariel ☆☆☆☆
2 Arlington ☆☆
3 Berkeley Arms ★★★★
4 Centre Airport ★★★
5 Excelsior ☆☆☆☆
Excelsior Hotel Restaurant (Draitone Manor) XXXX
6 Heathrow ★★★★
7 Holiday Inn ☆☆☆☆
8 Master Robert Motel ☆☆☆ *(see under Hounslow)*
9 Post House ☆☆☆
10 Sheraton ☆☆☆☆
11 Skyway ★★★

H

★★★★**Berkeley Arms** Bath Rd, Cranford (Embassy) ☎01–897 2121 Telex no 935728 Plan **3**
42⇌ fl Lift ☽ ♯ CTV CTV in bedrooms 50P ⚓ ♕French. Last dinner 9.45pm ♦ ☕ S% sB&B⇌ fl £21 dB&B⇌ fl £28 Continental breakfast Lunch £5&alc Dinner £6&alc Wine £5 ⊟ Credit cards 1 2 3 4 5 6

☆☆☆☆**Excelsior** Bath Rd, West Drayton (Trusthouse Forte) ☎01–759 6611 Telex no 24525 Plan **5**
662⇌ fl Lift ☽ ⊞ ♯ CTV in bedrooms 500P ⊐(heated) sauna bath Conference facilities available ♿ Last dinner 10.45pm ♦ ☕ S% sB&B⇌ fl £30.50 dB&B⇌ fl £41.50 Credit cards 1 2 3 4 5 6

★★★★***Heathrow*** Bath Rd, West Drayton ☎01–897 6363 Plan **6**
684⇌ fl Lift ☽ ⊞ ♯ CTV 700P ⊐(heated) sauna bath Disco 6 nights wkly ♿ Conference facilities available ♦ ☕ ⊟ Credit cards 1 2 3 4 5 6

☆☆☆☆**Holiday Inn** Stockley Rd, West Drayton (Commonwealth) ☎West Drayton 45555 Telex no 934518 Plan **7**
281⇌ fl Lift ☽ ⊞ ♯ CTV in bedrooms 300P ⚓ ⊐(heated) ♂ (hard) sauna bath ♿ ♕French. Last dinner 11.45pm ♦ ☕ S% ✱sB&B⇌ fl fr £28.38 dB&B⇌ fl fr £38.40 Lunch fr £4.20&alc Dinner fr £4.70&alc Wine £4.30 ⊟ *xmas* Credit cards 1 2 3 4 5 6

☆☆☆☆**Sheraton** Colnbrook Bypass, West Drayton ☎01–759 2424 Telex no 934331 Plan **10**
440⇌ fl Lift ☽ ⊞ ♯ CTV in bedrooms 350P ⚓ ⊐ sauna bath Conference facilities available ♕Continental. Last dinner 10.30pm ♦ ✱sB&B⇌ fl £27.30–£31.08 dB&B⇌ fl £36.78–£40.02 Lunch £3.85–£4.95&alc Dinner £9alc Credit cards 1 2 3 4 5 6

★★★**Centre Airport** Bath Rd, Longford (Centre) ☎01–759 2400 Telex no 934093 Plan **4**
360⇌ fl Lift ☽ ♯ CTV ✈ 800P Conference facilities available Last dinner 10.15pm ♦ ☕ S% ✱sB&B⇌ fl £18.50 dB&B⇌ fl £23.50 Continental breakfast Lunch £4.25 Dinner £4.25 Wine £3.40 ⊟ Credit cards 1 2 3 4 5 6

☆☆☆☆**Post House** Sipson Rd, West Drayton (Trusthouse Forte) ☎01–759 2323 Telex no 934280 Plan **9**
594⇌ fl Lift ☽ ⊞ ♯ CTV in bedrooms 400P Last dinner 11pm ♦ ☕ S% sB&B⇌ fl £24 dB&B⇌ fl £33.50 ⊟ Credit cards 1 2 3 4 5 6

★★★**Skyway** Bath Rd, Hayes (Trusthouse Forte) ☎01–759 6311 Telex no 23935 Plan **11**
455⇌ fl Lift ☽ ⊞ ♯ CTV in bedrooms 230P ⊐(heated) Conference facilities available ♿ Last dinner 10pm ♦ S% sB&B⇌ fl £24.25 dB&B⇌ fl £34 Credit cards 1 2 3 4 5 6

☆☆**Arlington** Shepiston Ln, Hayes (Norfolk Capital) ☎01–573 6162 Telex no 23241 Plan **2**
80⇌ fl ☽ ♯ CTV in bedrooms 80P ⚓ Conference facilities available Children under 12yrs not accommodated ♕English & French. Last dinner 9.45pm ♦ S% sB&B⇌ fl fr £21.10 dB&B⇌ fl fr £27 Continental breakfast Lunch £3.25&alc Dinner £4.25&alc Wine £4 ⊟ Credit cards 1 2 3 5 6

XXXX**Excelsior Hotel Restaurant** (Draitone Manor) ☎01–759 6611 Plan **5**
Closed Sun; Lunch not served Sat; 100 seats 400P bedrooms available Live music Mon–Sat ♕English & French. Last dinner 10.30pm S% ✱Lunch £10alc Dinner £10alc Wine £3.95 Credit cards 1 2 3 4 5 6

At **Hounslow** (3m E on A4)
☆☆☆**Master Robert Motel** Great West Road ☎01–570 6261 Plan **8**
64⇌ fl 64P

HECKFIELD Hampshire Map **4** SU76
XXX***Andwells*** (on A33) ☎202
35 seats 30P ♕French. Last dinner 10.30pm

HEDDON'S MOUTH Devon Map **2** SS64
★★♛**Heddon's Gate** ☎Parracombe 313
Former hunting lodge dating from 1890 in ten acres of woodland.
Closed Nov–Mar; 15rm(7⇌ fl) Annexe: 4⇌ fl 1▭ CTV CTV available in bedrooms 20P ⚓ Children under 5yrs not accommodated Last dinner 7.45pm ♦ ☕ sB&B £7.50 dB&B £15 dB&B⇌ fl £18.50 Bar lunch £1–£2 Tea 60p Dinner £6–£6.50 Wine £2.50 ⊟

HELFORD Cornwall Map **2** SW72
❀XX**Riverside** ☎Manaccan 443
Closed Mon; Lunch served Sun only; Dinner not served Sun; 30 seats ♕International. Last dinner 7.30pm

HELLANDBRIDGE Cornwall Map **2** SX07
XXX**Tredethy Country Hotel** (off B3266) ☎St Mabyn 262
35 seats 30P bedrooms available ♕English & French. Last dinner 9.30pm Dinner £5&alc Wine £1.90 Credit card 5

HELMSLEY North Yorkshire Map **8** SE68
★★★**Black Swan** Market Pl (Trusthouse Forte) ☎466
16th-C stone built house, with oak ceiling timbers, and Jacobean hall panelling.

3⇌⋒ ☽ ⅏ CTV TV in bedrooms 36P 2⌂ ⚓
ast dinner9.15pm ♁ ☎ S% sB&B⇌⋒£17.50
B&B⇌⋒£25 ▀ *xmas* Credit cards1 2 3 4 5 6

·★**Crown** Market Sq ☎297
4rm(5⇌⋒) ⅏ CTV 12P 3⌂ ⇶ Last dinner7.30pm
? ☎ sB&B£8.70 dB&B£17.40
B&B⇌⋒£19.40 Lunch£2.80–£3.20
ea60p–£1 High Tea£1–£2.20 Dinner£4–£5
Vine£2.50 ▀

·★**Feversham Arms** 1 High St (Best Western)
766
)ates from 1855 and stands in the old market town.
)n the edge of the Yorkshire moors.
losed Xmas; 15⇌⋒ ⅏ CTV in bedrooms 30P ⇶ ⚓
• ☋ English, French & Spanish. Last dinner9.30pm
♁ ☎ sB&B⇌⋒£14 dB&B⇌⋒£22
unch£4&alc Tea£2&alc Dinner£6&alc Wine£3
▀

·★**Feathers** Market Pl ☎275
.ocal stone house, partly 14th century and partly 17th
entury with Georgian modifications.
Closed 23Dec–7Jan; 18rm(8⇌⋒) ⅏ CTV TV
available in bedrooms 12P ⚓ Last dinner8.30pm
♁ sB&B£7.72 dB&B£15.44 dB&B⇌⋒£19
unch£3.50 Dinner£5 ▀ Credit cards1 2 3 5 6

IELSTON Cornwall Map**2** SW62
★★**Angel** Coinage Hall St ☎2701
'6th-C coaching inn scheduled as a building of
architectural merit.
21rm CTV 15P ⇶ Last dinner9.30pm ♁ ☎ S%
sB&B£11–£11.50 dB&B£21–£22
unch£2.50–£5 Tea80–90p Dinner£4.95–£6
Vine£2.30 ▀ Credit cards1 2 3 5

HEMEL HEMPSTEAD Hertfordshire Map**4** TL00
☆☆☆**Post House** Breakspear Way (Trusthouse Forte) ☎51122
Annexe:91⇌⋒ Lift ☽ ⅏ CTV in bedrooms 140P
Last dinner9.45pm ♁ ☎ S% sB&B⇌⋒£19.75
dB&B⇌⋒£28.50 ▀ *xmas*
Credit cards1 2 3 4 5 6

☆☆☆**Watermill** London Rd, Bourne End ☎Berkhamsted71241
Hotel built on bank of River Ballbourne with working watermill.
Annexe:40⇌⋒ ☽ ⅏ CTV in bedrooms 100P ⚓ ♿
conference facilities available Last dinner10pm
S% sB&B⇌⋒£18.45 dB&B⇌⋒£25.40
Lunch£3.85&alc Dinner£5.35&alc Wine£2.95
▀ *xmas* Credit cards1 2 3 5

✕**Spinning Wheel** 80 High St ☎64309
Closed Xmas; 55 seats P ☋ Continental.
Last dinner10.30pm S% Lunch£5–£6&alc
Dinner£5.25–£6.25&alc Wine£3.10
Credit cards1 2 3 5 6

✕***White Hart Inn*** High St ☎42458
17th-C inn with low-beamed ceilings situated in old part of Hemel Hempstead.
Closed 3day Xmas & Bank Hols; Dinner not served; 34seats 16P Credit card2

At **Redbourn**
☆☆☆**Aubrey Park** (Best Western) ☎Redbourn2105
57⇌⋒ 100P

HENLEY-IN-ARDEN Warwickshire Map**7** SP16
❀✕✕✕**Beaudesert** ☎2675
Closed Mon & Aug; Lunch not served Tue–Sat; Dinner not served Sun; 50seats 34P ☋ International

Specialities: "Sir Charles' favourite", roast duckling a la Chinoise, smoked pork chop devereux. Last dinner 10.30pm S% Lunch fr£4.40 Dinner £8alc Wine £3.50 Credit cards 1 2 3 5 6

XXOthello 148 High St ☎3089
Closed Sun & Mon; 45seats French & Italian. Last dinner 10.30pm S% Lunch £2.80–£3.20&alc Dinner £3alc Wine £3 Credit cards 1 2 3

HENLEY-ON-THAMES Oxfordshire Map **4** SU78
★★★Red Lion (Inter-Hotel) ☎2161
28rm(18⇌ ⋒ 1▭) CTV in bedrooms 30P Last dinner 10pm S% sB&B fr£12 sB&B⇌⋒ fr£15 dB&B fr£18 dB&B⇌⋒ fr£25 Lunch £2.95–£3.95 Tea 25–50p Dinner fr£6&alc *xmas* Credit cards 2 5

XXRembrandt 60 Bell St ☎4892
50seats English & French. Last dinner 10pm S% Lunch £1.50–£5.25&alc Dinner £5.25&alc Wine £3.40 Credit cards 1 2 3 5

HEREFORD Hereford & Worcester Map **3** SO54
★★★Green Dragon Broad St (Trusthouse Forte) ☎2506 Telex no 35491
93rm(66⇌⋒) Lift CTV TV in bedrooms 90 Conference facilities available Last dinner 9.15pm S% sB&B £14 sB&B⇌⋒ £16 dB&B £19 dB&B⇌⋒ £23 *xmas* Credit cards 1 2 3 4 5 6

★★Litchfield Lodge Bodenham Rd ☎3258
10rm(5⇌⋒) 1▭ CTV 12P Last dinner 8pm sB&B £5.50–£6.50 sB&B⇌⋒ £7–£8 dB&B £11–£12 dB&B⇌⋒ £13–£14 Lunch £2.50–£3.50&alc Tea £1–£2.50&alc High Tea £1.50–£2.25&alc Dinner £3.50–£5&alc Wine £2.15

★★Merton Commercial Rd ☎65925
10rm(3⇌⋒) CTV CTV in bedrooms 6P Last dinner 9.30pm sB&B £12.96 sB&B⇌⋒ £15.65 dB&B £19.44 dB&B⇌⋒ £27 Lunch £1–£3 Dinner £6.05–£8.25 Wine £3.25 Credit card 1

★★Oaklands Bodenham Rd ☎2775
20rm(7⇌⋒) CTV TV in bedrooms 18P Last dinner 9pm S% sB&B £9.18–£10.26 sB&B⇌⋒ £10.26–£10.80 dB&B £16.74–£17.82 dB&B⇌⋒ £17.82–£18.36 Lunch £2.50&alc Dinner £3.50–£4&alc Wine £2.80 Credit card 3

XXGreyfriars Garden Greyfriars Ave ☎67274
Closed Sun; Dinner not served Mon; 150seats 100P English, French & Italian. Last dinner 9.30pm Lunch £3.10–£3.50&alc Dinner £5alc Wine £2.50 Credit cards 1 2 3 5

HERNE BAY Kent Map **5** TR16
★★Hotel St George Western Esp ☎3776
17rm(6⇌⋒) CTV TV available in bedrooms 30P Live music & dancing 3 nights wkly Cabaret wkly Last dinner 10pm *sB&B £9 dB&B £16 dB&B⇌⋒ £18.50 Lunch £3.10–£5&alc Dinner £3–£5&alc Wine *xmas* Credit cards 1 3 6

HERSTMONCEUX East Sussex Map **5** TQ61
XXSundial ☎2217
Closed Mon, Jan & 2wks Aug; Dinner not served Sun; 45seats 25P French. Last dinner 9.30pm *Lunch £4.50–£6&alc Dinner £10alc Wine £3.75 Credit cards 3 5

HERTFORD Hertfordshire Map **4** TL31
★★★White Horse Inn Hertingfordbury (1m W on A414) (Trusthouse Forte) ☎56791
Probably a farmhouse until it was converted in the 18th century. It has been modernised with a new wing of studio-style rooms.
30⇌⋒ TV in bedrooms 65P Last dinner 10.30pm S% sB&B⇌⋒ £17 dB&B⇌⋒ £23 *xmas* Credit cards 1 2 3 4 5 6

★★Salisbury Arms Fore St ☎53091
Old inn with beamed cocktail bar and wood-panelled dining room. It is said there has been an inn here since 1481, with medieval masonry in the cellar.
32rm(12⇌⋒) CTV 30P English & Chinese. Last dinner 9pm S% sB&B £10 sB&B⇌⋒ £12 dB&B £16 dB&B⇌⋒ £20 Lunch £3alc Dinner £4alc Wine £2.80 Credit cards 2 3 5

HESLEDEN Co Durham Map **8** NZ43
XGolden Calf Front St ☎Castle Eden 493
Closed Mon; dinner not served Sun; 50seats P bedrooms available International. Last dinner 9pm Lunch £4.50alc Dinner £7.50alc Credit cards 1 3 5

HESWALL Merseyside Map **7** SJ28
★★Victoria Gayton Rd ☎051–342 6021
15rm(3⇌⋒) CTV CTV available in bedrooms 80P 6 Last dinner 11pm S% sB&B £8.50 dB&B £14 dB&B⇌⋒ £16.50 Lunch £2.50 Tea 40p dinner fr£3.50&alc Wine £3.50 Credit cards 1 2 3

HEVERSHAM Cumbria Map **7** SD48
★★★Blue Bell at Heversham The Prince's Way ☎Milnthorpe 3159
An attractive 17th-C country inn, once a vicarage, with a history dating back to 1692.
Closed Xmas; 28rm(12⇌⋒) CTV 100p Last dinner 9.15pm S% sB&B £10.50 sB&B⇌⋒ £12 dB&B £16.50 dB&B⇌⋒ £18.50 Lunch fr£4 Tea fr£1.25 dinner fr£6.50 wine £3

HEXHAM Northumberland Map **12** NY96
★★*Beaumont* Beaumont St ☎2331
20rm(1⇌⋒) CTV Last dinner 10pm Credit cards 1 5

★★Royal Priestpopple ☎2270
25rm(14⇌⋒) CTV TV in bedrooms 20P English & French. Last dinner 9pm sB&B £9.70 sB&B⇌⋒ £12.65–£13.20 dB&B £18 dB&B⇌⋒ £22.50 Lunch £2.75–£3.50 High Tea £2.20–£2.50 Dinner £4–£6.50&alc Wine £2.70 Credit cards 1 3 6

HIGHBRIDGE Somerset Map **3** ST34
★George Church St ☎Burnham-on-Sea 783248
9rm CTV TV in bedrooms 20P Last dinner 8pm S% *sB&B £8.50 dB&B £13.50 Lunch £2–£2.50&alc Dinner £2.50–£3.50&alc Wine £2.20 Credit card 3

★Sundowner West Huntspill (1m SE on A38) ☎Burnham-on-Sea 784766
Closed 2wks May & 2wks Nov; 6rm CTV CTV in bedrooms 20P Last dinner 10pm sB&B fr£6.50 dB&B fr£12 Lunch fr£3&alc Dinner fr£.350&alc Wine £2.75 Credit card 6

HIGH LANE Greater Manchester Map **7** SJ98
XXRed Lion Buxton Rd ☎Disley 2061
60seats 70P Last dinner 10pm Lunch fr£2.95&alc Dinner £5.50alc Wine £2.60

HIGH WYCOMBE Buckinghamshire Map **4** SU89
★★Falcon ☎22173 Telex no 934900
A 14th-C inn of architectural and historical interest, adjoining the 18th-C Guildhall in the town centre.
12rm CTV in bedrooms 10 Last dinner 9.45pm S% sB&B £13 dB&B £21 Lunch £3&alc Dinner £3.50&alc Wine £3.50 Credit cards 1 2 3 5

HILLINGDON Greater London Map **4** TQ08
☆☆☆Master Brewer Motel Western Av (A40) ☎Uxbridge 51199
RS Xmas Day (no evening meal); 64⇌⋒ CTV in bedrooms 64P Conference facilities available last dinner 11.30pm S% sB&B⇌⋒ £19.50 dB&B⇌⋒ £22 Lunch £4.35–£7.05 Tea 75p alc Dinner £4.35–£7.05 Wine £3.05 Credit cards 1 2 3 5

IMLEY Staffordshire Map**7** SO89
★Himley House ☎Wombourne892468
S Sun eve (no restaurant); 17⇌🚿
nnexe: 7rm(1⇌🚿) ☽ 🍽TV in bedrooms ⊘ 250P ⚓
ive music & dancing Sat & every night in Dec
ast dinner9.45pm ♔ ✱sB&B£9.50
B&B⇌🚿£12 dB&B£14.50 dB&B⇌🚿 fr£17
unch£3&alc Dinner£3.95&alc Wine£2.40
redit cards 1 2 3 5 6

INDHEAD Surrey Map**4** SU83
Woodcock Inn Beacon Hill ☎4079
mall country inn situated outside Hindhead.
losed Xmas Day; Lunch not served Mon; 56seats
8P last dinner9.30pm Credit cards 2 3 5

INDON Wiltshire Map**3** ST93
Lamb at Hindon ☎225
ttractive creeper-clad 16th-C inn with traditional pen fireplace in bar.
losed 25&26Dec; 16rm(4⇌🚿) 1⊟ CTV ⊘ 12P ⚓
ast dinner9pm ♔ S% sB&B£13 (incl dinner)
B&B⇌🚿 fr£30 (incl dinner) Lunch£3–£3.50
inner£5–£7 Wine£2.30 ⊓ Credit cards 2 3

INSTOCK Salop Map**7** SJ62
Falcon Inn ☎Sambrook241
inner not served Sun; 46seats 80P ♀English & rench. Last dinner9.30pm Credit card 2

HINTLESHAM Suffolk Map**5** TM04

❀❀XXXHintlesham Hall ☎268
Extensive grounds, including a vegetable plot and a herb garden as pretty as the gardens of Versailles, surround this lovely 16th-century mansion which is owned by Robert Carrier. It offers some of the finest cooking in the country.
A fixed-price, seasonally changing, four-course menu is offered with delightfully-presented items and, needless to say with such a garden, full use is made of fresh vegetables. Pâté aux herbes, bouillabaise, fish salad, and rillette de anguille were amongst the first courses praised, while amongst the main ones were calves liver with avocado, sauté de boeuf à la moëlle and gigot de volaille.
Puddings are a delight to sample and the old favourite from Islington, Elizabeth Moxon's lemon posset, delightfully presented sorbets and a tulip of ice cream and pineapple in crisp tuille pastry, have all been acclaimed.
A fine selection of wines – some of good value – complement the food.
120seats 60P Live music Fri ♀International.
Last dinner10.30pm ✱Lunch£9.75alc
Dinner£11.20alc Wine£4.25 Credit card 2

HITCHIN Hertfordshire Map**4** TL12
★★★Blakemore Little Wymondley (2m SE A602)
☎Stevenage55821 Telex no825479
Georgian style house set in five acres of landscaped gardens and lawns.
41⇌🚿 Lift ☽ ⊞ 🍽CTV in bedrooms 200P 2🏠 ⚓
⊇(heated) sauna bath Live music & dancing Sat
Cabaret Sat Conference facilities available ♿
♀English & French. Last dinner10.30pm ♔ ♀
✱sB&B⇌🚿£19 dB&B⇌🚿£28 Lunch£4.50&alc
Tea30p–£1.50&alc High Tea£1.50–£2&alc
Dinner£4.50&alc Wine£4.25 ⊓ *xmas*
Credit cards 1 2 3 4 5 6

★★*Sun* Sun St ☎2092
16th-C coaching house said to have been visited by Oliver Cromwell.
28rm(2⇌🚿) 1⊟ ☽ 🍽CTV 50P Last dinner9pm ⊓
Credit cards 1 2 3 4 5 6

H

HOCKLEY HEATH West Midlands Map**7** SP17
☆☆☆**Barn Motel** Stratford Rd (Trophy Taverns) ☎Lapworth2144
Annexe:51⇌⋒ ☽ ⋔ CTV in bedrooms P ⚓ Disco Mon, Wed, Fri & Sat Live music & dancing Fri & Sat Last dinner10pm Credit cards 1 2 3 5

HODNET Salop Map**7** SJ62
★**Bear Inn** ☎214
Closed Xmas Day & 31Dec–3Jan; 5rm TV in bedrooms 100P ⚓ Disco twice wkly Cabaret wkly ♉English & Continental. Last dinner10.30pm ✿ S% sB&B£7 dB&B£11 Continental breakfast Lunch£2.95–£3.25 Dinner£2.75–£3.95&alc Wine£2.95 ⊓ Credit cards 1 2 3

HOGSTHORPE Lincolnshire Map**9** TF57
✕***Belmont*** ☎Skegness72288
Creeper-clad Victorian house with pleasant grounds.
60seats 36P bedrooms available ♉English & French. Last dinner9.30pm Credit cards 1 2 3

HOLFORD Somerset Map**3** ST14
★★**Alfoxton Park** ☎211
White 18th-C house, home of poet William Wordsworth in 1797, in 50 acres of parkland with views over Quantock Hills to Bristol Channel.
19rm(13⇌⋒) 5▭ CTV CTV available in bedrooms ✗ P ⚓ ⌂(heated) ⌂(hard) ∩ Last dinner10.30pm ✿ ♀ ✱sB&B£11–£13 sB&B⇌⋒£11–£13 dB&B£16–£18 dB&B⇌⋒£18.70–£22 Lunch£1.75–£3.50 Tea35p–£1 Dinner£5&alc Wine£2.90 ⊓ *xmas* Credit cards 1 2 3

★★**Combe House** ☎382
Pink-washed 17th-C house built as a tannery and retaining old water wheel.
15rm(8⇌⋒) ⋔ CTV 20P 2⌂ ⚓ ⌂(hard) Last dinner8.15pm ✿ ♀ sB&B£8.50–£10 sB&B⇌⋒£10–£12 dB&B£16–£18 dB&B⇌⋒£17..50–£20 Bar lunch£1.25–£1.50 Tea80–90p Dinner£3.85–£4.25 Wine£2.40 ⊓ Credit cards 1 2 3

HOLKHAM Norfolk Map**9** TF84
See also **Wells-next-the-Sea**
★***Victoria*** ☎Fakenham710469
Compact building, constructed of local traditional flints situated at entrance to Holkham Hall. Walled and lawned gardens.
8rm CTV 40P ⚓ ♉English & French. Last dinner8.30pm ✿ ⊓

HOLLINGBOURNE Kent Map**5** TQ85
★★★**Great Danes** Ashford Rd (Rank) ☎381 Telex no96198
78⇌⋒ ☽ ⋔ TV in bedrooms 250P ⚓ ⌂(heated) Live music & dancing Sat Conference facilities available ♉International. Last dinner11pm ✿ ♀ S% sB⇌⋒£16.50 (room only) dB⇌⋒£23.40 (room only) Lunch fr£4&alc Tea fr65p High Tea fr£1.10 Dinner fr£4&alc Wine£3.60 ⊓ *xmas* Credit cards 1 2 3 5

HOLMES CHAPEL Cheshire Map**7** SJ76
✕✕**Yellow Broom** Twemlow Green (1¾m NE A535) ☎33289
Closed Sun, Mon, 1wk late Jul & 1wk early Aug; ; Lunch not served; 45seats 30P ♉English & French. Last dinner9.30pm Dinner£9.50 Wine£5.87

HOLMROOK Cumbria Map**6** SD09
★**Lutwidge Arms** ☎230
Victorian fishing inn with grounds bordering River Irt. Two miles of water reserved for residents' use.
Closed Nov–Mar; RS Etr–mid Jan; 10rm ⋔ TV ✗ 20P 13⌂ ⚓ ↩ Children under 5yrs not accommodated Last dinner7pm ✱sB&B fr£6.75 dB&B fr£12.50 Bar lunch fr65p Dinner fr£4.05 Wine£2

HOLSWORTHY Devon Map**2** SS30
★**White Hart** Fore St ☎253475
7rm ⋔ CTV 20P Last dinner7.45pm ✿ S% sB&B£6.50 dB&B£13 Lunch£1.75alc Dinner£2–£3.50&alc Wine£2 Credit card 6

HOLT Norfolk Map**9** TG03
★★***Feathers*** 6 Market Pl ☎2318
Ancient coaching inn situated in town centre.
Closed Xmas Day; 23rm(6⇌⋒) CTV 60P 3⌂ ⚓ ⌂(grass) Last dinner8.45pm ♀ ✿ ⊓ Credit cards 1 2 3 5

HOLYWELL GREEN West Yorkshire Map**7** SE01
✕✕***Broad Carr House*** ☎Elland74512
Closed Tue; Dinner not served Sun; 50seats 30P ♉English & French. Last dinner9.30pm

HONILEY Warwickshire Map**4** SP27
✕✕***Honiley Boot Inn*** Honiley Rd ☎Haseley Knob234
190seats 300P Live music Sat ♉English & French. Last dinner10.30pm Credit cards 2 3 5

HONITON Devon Map**3** ST10
★★★***Deer Park*** Weston (2½m W off A30) ☎2064
Old stone manor-house, built in 1777 in its own grounds of 26 acres, including three miles of trout fishing.
17⇌⋒ ⋔ CTV TV available in bedrooms 60P 4⌂ ⚓ ⌂(heated) ⌂(hard) ↩ squash billiards sauna bath ♉English & French. Last dinner10.30pm ✿ ♀ Credit cards 1 2 3 4 5 6

★★***Kingslea*** Kings Rd ☎2921
9rm ☽ ⋔ CTV ✗ 30P Last dinner9.30pm ✿ ♀ Credit cards 1 3 5

★★**Monkton Court** Monkton ☎2309
Imposing old gabled rectory with mullioned

indows; standing in four acres of grounds.
m(3⇌⫙) ₩ TV available in bedrooms 40P ⚓
st dinner9.15pm ✿ ☡ sB&B£10
B&B⇌⫙£12 dB&B£14 dB&B⇌⫙£16
nch£3–£4 Tea50–80p Dinner£3–£4
ine£2.50 ⛿ Credit cards 1 2 3 4 5 6

★***New Dolphin*** High St ☎2377
rm(4⇌⫙) CTV ⊘ P Last dinner9.30pm ✿ ☡
redit cards 1 2 3

Angel High St ☎2829
omfortably appointed, small 17th-century coaching n.
S Sun; 7rm(1⇌⫙) ₩ CTV 20P ⊕ Children under
yrs not accommodated ♉ English & French.
st dinner9.30pm ✿

OOK Hampshire Map**4** SU75
✕**Raven Hotel** Station Rd ☎2541
seats 100P Live music & dancing 6 nights wkly
English & Italian. Last dinner10pm
nch fr£3.95&alc Dinner£8.50alc Wine£2.80
redit cards 1 2 3 4 5 6

OPE Derbyshire Map**7** SK18
✕**House of Anton** Castleton Rd ☎Hope
alley20390
seats 60P bedrooms available ♉ English &
ontinental. Last dinner9.30pm S%
unch£5.20–£8 Dinner£8.20–£10 Wine£4.50
redit cards 1 2 3 5

OPE COVE Devon Map**3** SX64
★**Cottage** ☎Galmpton555
losed 2–31 Jan; 37rm(10⇌⫙) ₩ CTV 50P ⊕ ⚓
ve music & dancing Sat in season ⛫
ast dinner8.45pm ✿ ☡ S% sB&B£5.35–£12
B&B⇌⫙£5.95–£16.95 dB&B£10.70–£24
B&B⇌⫙£11.90–£33.90 Lunch£4.70&alc
Tea45p–£1.20 Dinner£6&alc Wine£2.70 ⛿
xmas

★★**Sun Bay** ☎Galmpton371
Closed Oct–Mar; 12rm(5⇌⫙) ₩ CTV 12P ⊕ ⚓
Last dinner8.15pm ✿ ☡ S% sB&B£6–£7.50
sB&B⇌⫙£7–£8 dB&B£12–£14
dB&B⇌⫙£14–£16 Tea30–50p
Dinner£4–£4.50&alc

★**Greystone** ☎Galmpton233
Closed Oct–Mar; 13rm ₩ CTV 12P 4⌂ ⊕ ⚓ ⛫
Last dinner7.30pm ✿ ☡ S% ✱sB&B£6–£8
dB&B£12–£16 Lunch£2.50 Tea40p Dinner£4
Wine£2.36

HOPTON WAFERS Salop Map**7** SO67
✕**Crown Inn** ☎Cleobury Mortimer372
40seats 60P ♉ English & French.
Last dinner10.30pm ✱Lunch£3.50–£6
Dinner£5&alc Wine£3 Credit card 3

HORLEY Surrey Map**4** TQ24
Hotels are listed under Gatwick Airport

HORNCASTLE Lincolnshire Map**8** TF26
★★**Rodney** North St ☎3583
15rm CTV TV available in bedrooms 100P
Last dinner8.45pm ✿ S% sB&B£8 dB&B£15
Wine£2.30

★**Bull** Bull Ring ☎3331
16th-C inn, with arch into cobbled yard, modern extension and restored armoury. The banqueting hall, with its murals of the battle of Winceby (1643) is the scene of regular Tudor-style banquets.
8rm(1⇌⫙) CTV 30P ♉ French. Last dinner8.15pm
✿ S% sB&B£7.48 sB&B⇌⫙£8.67
dB&B£14.96 dB&B⇌⫙£17.34
Bar lunch85p–£1.20 Dinner£2–£3.95&alc
Wine£1.60 Credit cards 1 5

H

HORNCHURCH Greater London Map**5** TQ58
☆☆☆**Ladbroke Mercury Motor Inn** Southend Arterial Rd (Ladbroke) ☎Ingrebourne46789 Telex no897315
145 CTV available in bedrooms 150P Conference facilities available Last dinner10.30pm sB&B£22.50 dB&B£30.50 Lunch fr£5&alc Dinner fr£5.50&alc Wine£3.20 Credit cards 1 2 3 4 5 6

HORNING Norfolk Map**9** TG31
★★**Petersfield House** (Mount Charlotte) ☎630741
16rm(13) CTV in bedrooms 50P Live music & dancing wkly English, French & Italian. Last dinner9.30pm Lunch fr£3.25&alc Tea35–45p High Tea£1.50–£2.50 Dinner£4.50–£5.25&alc Wine£3.75 *xmas* Credit cards 1 2 3 5 6

HORNS CROSS Devon Map**2** SS32
★★**Foxdown Manor** ☎325
Closed 2 Jan–Mar; 6rm(5) 1 CTV TV available in bedrooms 20P (heated) (hard) sauna bath Disco wkly Live music & dancing wkly Children under 12yrs not accommodated French. Last dinner8.15pm sB&B£7–£9 sB&B£9–£11 dB&B£14–£18 dB&B£18–£22 Lunch fr£4&alc Tea fr£1.50&alc Dinner fr£6&alc Wine£2.30 *xmas* Credit card 1

★★***Hoops Inn*** ☎222
A charming 13th-century thatched inn with an ancient well and oak timbers.
Closed Oct–Mar; 6rm 1 TV 30P Children under 5yrs not accommodated Last dinner9.15pm Credit cards 1 2 3 5

HORSHAM West Sussex Map**4** TQ13
★★**Ye Olde King's Head** ☎3126
Part timbered, two storey inn situated on Carfax; established 1401. Cellars date from 12th-C
23rm(20) 1 CTV in bedrooms 40P English & French. Last dinner10pm sB&B fr£12.50 sB&B fr£13.50 dB&B fr£21.50 dB&B fr£22.50 Lunch£5.50alc Dinner£5.50alc Wine£2.75 Credit cards 1 3

HORSINGTON Somerset Map**3** ST72
★★**Horsington House** ☎Templecombe721
23rm(21) CTV TV available in bedrooms 50P (hard) Last dinner9pm S% *sB&B£11.50 sB&B£20 Lunch£2.50&alc Dinner£6alc Credit cards 1 2 3 5

HORTON Northamptonshire Map**4** SP85
✕✕**French Partridge** ☎Northampton870033
Closed Sun, Mon, 3wks Summer, & 2wks Xmas; Lunch not served; 50seats 50P French. Last dinner9.30pm S% Dinner£7 Wine£2.20

HORTON-CUM-STUDLEY Oxfordshire Map**4** SP51
★★★**Studley Priory** ☎Stanton St John203
Country-house, (partly 13th-C) with Elizabethan panelling and stone-moulding doorways. In 11 acres of grounds with extensive country views.
19 2 CTV in bedrooms 100P 3 (grass) English & French. Last dinner9.30pm S% sB&B£18.50–£26.50 dB&B£26–£40 Lunch£8alc Tea£1–£1.50 Dinner£8alc Wine£3.75 *xmas* Credit cards 1 2 3 5 6

HOTON Leicestershire Map**8** SK52
✕✕**Packe Arms** ☎Wymeswold880662
Closed Mon; Dinner not served Sun; 55seats 200P Last dinner10pm S% *Lunch£4.25–£5.75 Dinner£4.25–£5.75 Wine£3.50 Credit cards 1 2 3 5

HOUGHTON CONQUEST Bedfordshire Map**4** TL0
✕**Knife & Cleaver** ☎Bedford740387
Closed Sun; Lunch not served Sat; Dinner not serve Mon; 50seats 25P English & French. Last dinner10pm *Lunch£3.50alc Dinner£7alc Wine£2.85

HOUNSLOW Greater London Map**4** TQ17
☆☆☆**Master Robert Motel** Great West Road ☎01-5706261 Heathrow Plan**8**
RS Xmas Day; 64 CTV in bedrooms 64P International. Last dinner11.30pm S% sB&B£19.50 dB&B£22 Lunch£4.25&alc Tea75palc Dinner£4.25&alc Wine£3.05 Credit cards 1 2 3 5

✕**Hounslow Chinese** 261 Bath Rd ☎01-570 2161
Authentic Pekinese cuisine.
Closed Xmas; 80seats Pekinese. Last dinner11.30pm *Lunch£3alc Dinner£4alc Wine£2.70 Credit cards 1 2 3 5

HOVE East Sussex Map**4** TQ20
See also **Brighton**
★★★★**Dudley** Lansdowne Pl (Trusthouse Forte) ☎Brighton736266 Telex no87537
78 Lift CTV CTV in bedrooms 30P 30 Conference facilities available Last dinner10.30pm S% sB&B£21.50 dB&B£31.50 *xmas* Credit cards 1 2 3 4 5 6

★★★**Courtlands** The Drive ☎Brighton731055 Telex no87323
60rm(48) Annexe:2rm Lift CTV CTV in bedrooms 30P 4 English & French. Last dinner9.45pm S% sB&B£13–£15 sB&B£17.50–£21 dB&B£22–£30 dB&B£30–£36 Lunch£4–£4.50&alc Tea75p Dinner£4.75–£5.50&alc Wine£3 *xmas* Credit cards 1 2 3 5 6

★★★**Sackville** 189 Kingsway (Best Western) ☎Brighton736292
48 Lift CTV in bedrooms 12 French. Last dinner9pm S% sB&B£18–£19.50 dB&B£25–£33 Lunch fr£4.50&alc Tea fr£1 Dinner fr£5.90&alc Wine£3.50 *xmas* Credit cards 1 2 3 5

★★**Langfords** Third Avenue ☎Brighton738222
70rm(25) Lift CTV TV available in bedrooms Live music & dancing Sat English & French. Last dinner10.30pm S% sB&B£11.50 sB&B£13.50 dB&B£21 dB&B£25 Lunch£2.95&alc Tea75p Dinner£3.75&alc Wine£2.95 *xmas* Credit cards 1 2 3 5 6

★★**St Catherine's Lodge** Kingsway (Inter-Hotel) ☎Brighton778181
56rm(34) Lift CTV TV available in bedrooms 6P 4 Last dinner8.30pm S% sB&B£12 sB&B£14 dB&B£24 dB&B£28 Lunch£3.25–£3.50&alc Tea40–45p Dinner£4.85&alc Wine£3.85 Credit cards 1 2 3

✕✕✕**Eaton** Eaton Gdns ☎Brighton738921
Dinner not served Sun; 100seats 30P International. Last dinner10pm Lunch£5.50–£6&alc Dinner£6.50–£7.50&alc Credit cards 1 2 3 5 6

✕**Lawrence** 40 Waterloo St ☎Brighton772922
Closed Sun, Mon & 23–25Dec; Lunch not served; 19seats European. Last dinner10pm *Dinner£4.70–£5&alc Wine£2.60 Credit cards 2 3

✕**Vogue** 57 Holland Rd ☎Brighton775066
Closed Sun, Mon, 1st 2wks Mar & 3wks Sep; 34seats French. Last dinner9.30pm

HOVINGHAM North Yorkshire Map**8** SE67
★★**Worsley Arms** ☎234
Closed Xmas day; 14⇌⋒ 1⊟ ⋔ CTV 50P 5⌂ ⚓ ♀European. Last dinner9pm ✿ ♀ S% sB&B⇌⋒£11–£12 dB&B⇌⋒£19–£22 Lunch£3.25 Tea£1 Dinner£6 Wine£2.75 ⊓ Credit cards 1 3 6

HOW CAPLE Hereford & Worcester Map**3** SO63
★★***How Caple Grange*** ☎208
26rm(17⇌⋒) ⋔ TV 40P 2⌂ ⚓ ♀English & French. Last dinner8.30pm ✿ ♀ ⊓ Credit cards 1 2 3

HOWDEN Humberside Map**8** SE72
★★**Bowmans** Bridgegate ☎30805
13⇌⋒ ⋔ CTV in bedrooms 80P ♀English, French & Italian. Last dinner10.30pm ✿ ✱sB&B⇌⋒fr£14 dB&B⇌⋒fr£20 Lunch£3.75&alc Dinner£4.90&alc Wine£3
★**Wellington** 31 Bridgegate ☎30258
9⇌⋒ ⋔ CTV CTV in bedrooms 60P sauna bath Children under 5yrs not accommodated Last dinner8.30pm ✿ S% ✱sB&B⇌⋒£11.50 dB&B⇌⋒£20 Lunch£2.20–£3&alc Dinner£3.50–£5&alc ⊓

HOYLAKE Merseyside Map**7** SJ28
★★**Stanley** Kings Gap (Whitbread) ☎051–632 3311
Large public house with modern bedrooms.
16rm(2⇌⋒) ☽ ⋔ CTV 180P ⚓ Live music Sat & Sun; ♀English & French. Last dinner9.30pm ✿ ✱sB&B£10.15 sB&B⇌⋒£10.55 dB&B£18.40 dB&B⇌⋒£21 Lunch£3&alc Tea£2.50alc Dinner£4&alc Wine£2.40
✕**Libertys** 36 Market St ☎051–632 5101
Lunch not served; 60seats P ♀English & French. Last dinner10.45pm Dinner£3.75–£4.75&alc Wine£2.70 Credit cards 1 2 3 5

HUDDERSFIELD West Yorkshire Map**7** SE11
★★★**George** St George's Sq (Trusthouse Forte) ☎25444
62rm(36⇌⋒) Lift ☽ ⋔ TV in bedrooms 12P Last dinner9.45pm ✿ ♀ S% sB&B£4 sB&B⇌⋒£17 dB&B£19 dB&B⇌⋒£23 ⊓ Credit cards 1 2 3 4 5 6
★★★**Pennine President** Ainley Top (Ladbroke) ☎Elland75431 Telex no517346
118⇌⋒ Lift ☽ ⋔ CTV in bedrooms 300P ⊞ Conference facilities available ♀English & French. Last dinner10pm ✿ ♀ S% sB&B⇌⋒£19.50 dB&B⇌⋒£26 Lunch£3–£3.50&alc Tea50p Dinner£3.25–£3.75&alc Wine£3 ⊓ Credit cards 1 2 3 5
✕✕**Quo Vadis** 4 St Peter's Street ☎35440
Closed Sun & Public Hols; 50seats ♪ ♀French & Italian. Last dinner10.30pm ✱Lunch£3.30 Dinner£6.80 Wine£3 Credit card 1

HUGH TOWN St Mary's, Isle of Scilly (no map)
★★★**Bell Park** Church St ☎Scillonia22575
Closed Nov–2Mar; 17rm(15⇌⋒) CTV ⊘ ⌒(heated) Children under 2yrs not accommodated Last dinner8.30pm ✿ ♀ sB&B£11.75–£13 sB&B⇌⋒£11.75–£13 dB&B£23.50–£26 dB&B⇌⋒£23.50–£26 Lunch£1.75–£2.85 Dinner£4.50–£5.75 Wine£2.50 ⊓
★★★**Godolphin** Church St (Inter-Hotel) ☎Scillonia22316 Telex no45388
Once a large private residence, the Godolphin has now been tastefully converted to a holiday hotel.
Closed mid Oct–mid Mar; 29rm(22⇌) CTV CTV available in bedrooms ⊘ Children under 5yrs not accommodated Last dinner8.15pm ✿ ♀ S% sB&B£8.20 dB&B£16.40 dB&B⇌£18.80 Lunch£2.75 Tea45p Dinner£5.25 Wine£2.80

H

★★Tregarthens ☎Scillonia22540
Well-appointed, comfortable holiday hotel with country-house atmosphere.
Closed Nov–Mar; 33rm(20⇌⋒) CTV ⊗ ⚓ Children under 6yrs not accommodated Last dinner8pm ♁ ☐ sB&B£13–£18 dB&B£25–£35 dB&B⇌⋒£30–£40 Lunch£3.50–£4.50 Tea fr30p Dinner£5.50–£6.50 Wine£3.20 Credit cards 1 3

HULL Humberside Map**8** TA02
★★★★Royal Station Paragon Sq (British Transport) ☎29888 Telex no52450
108rm(90⇌⋒) Lift ☽ ⛫ CTV TV in bedrooms Conference facilities available ♿ ♡English & French. Last dinner10.30pm ♁ ☐ S% *sB&B⇌⋒ fr£23.45 dB&B⇌⋒ fr£35.15 Wine£3.15 ⊟ Credit cards 1 2 3 4 5 6

★★★Hull Centre Paragon St (Centre) ☎26462 Telex no52431
125⇌⋒ Lift ☽ ⛫ TV available in bedrooms ⊗ ₱ Conference facilities available Last dinner9.45pm ♁ ☐ S% *sB&B⇌⋒£14.75 dB&B⇌⋒£20.25 Continental breakfast Lunch£3.65 Dinner£3.65 Wine£3.40 ⊟ Credit cards 1 2 3 4 5 6

At **North Ferriby** (6m W on A63)
☆☆☆Hull Crest Motel (Crest) ☎645212
102⇌⋒ 200P

At **Willerby** (3¾m NW on A164)
★★★Willerby Manor Well Ln ☎Hull652616
37rm(22⇌⋒) 150P

HUNGERFORD Berkshire Map**4** SU36
★★Bear ☎2512
Said to date back to 1297. In 1643 the Bear was the headquarters of Charles I during the fighting around Newbury. The bodies of Lords Falkland, Sunderland and Carnarvon were brought here to await burial.
26rm(18⇌⋒) 2⊟ CTV CTV available in bedrooms 75P ⚓ ♿ ♡English & Continental. Last dinner10pm ♁ S% sB&B£14.50 sB&B⇌⋒£19.50 dB&B£19.50 dB&B⇌⋒£25.50 Lunch£4.15–£5&alc Dinner£6.15&alc Wine£3.25 ⊟ Credit cards 1 2 3 5

HUNSTANTON Norfolk Map**9** TF64
★★Le Strange Arms Sea front, Old Hunstanton ☎2810
28rm(7⇌⋒) CTV CTV available in bedrooms 350P 11⌂ ⚘ ⚓ billiards Last dinner9pm ♁ ☐ S% sB&B£9.50 sB&B⇌⋒£11.75 dB&B£19 dB&B⇌⋒£20.50 Lunch£3.75–£5.50&alc Tea30p–£1&alc High Tea£1.20–£2.50&alc Dinner£3.75–£6&alc Wine£3 *xmas* Credit card 5

★Lodge Cromer Rd ☎2896
16rm(4⇌⋒) CTV TV available in bedrooms 70P ⚓ ⛾ Live music & dancing Sat Cabaret Sat ♡French. Last dinner9pm ♁ sB&B£8.50 sB&B⇌⋒£9.50 dB&B£17 dB&B⇌⋒£19 Lunch£2.50–£3.50&alc Dinner£4.50&alc Wine£2.50 ⊟ *xmas* Credit cards 1 6

HUNTINGDON Cambridgeshire Map**4** TL27
★★★Old Bridge ☎52681
25rm(13⇌⋒) ☽ ⛫ CTV in bedrooms 100P ⚘ ⚓ ♡French & Italian. Last dinner10pm ♁ ☐ S% *sB&B fr£10 sB&B⇌⋒ fr£15 dB&B fr£18.50 dB&B⇌⋒ fr£22 Bar lunch£1alc Dinner£7alc Wine£3.80 ⊟ Credit cards 1 2 3 5

★★George George St (Trusthouse Forte) ☎53096
24rm(9⇌⋒) ⛫ TV in bedrooms 71P Last dinner10pm ♁ S% sB&B£12 sB&B⇌⋒£14.50 dB&B£18.50 dB&B⇌⋒£20.50 ⊟ *xmas* Credit cards 1 2 3 4 5 6

At **Brampton** (3m W junc A1/A604)
☆☆☆**Brampton** (Kingsmead) ☎810434
17⇌ 250P

HURLEY Berkshire Map**4** SU88
★★**Ye Olde Bell** ☎Littlewick Green4244
Remarkable two-storey black and white inn (1135), once a guesthouse of Benedictine monastery; still connected to the ruins by underground passage.
11⇌ CTV in bedrooms 100P 11
International. Specialities: poulet souvarov, caneton au cidre, châteaubriand. Last dinner10pm
*sB&B⇌£22 dB&B⇌£30
Continental breakfast Lunch£7.50alc
Tea£1.50alc Dinner£9.50alc Wine£6
Credit cards 2 3 5

HURSTBOURNE TARRANT Hampshire Map**4** SU35
✕***George & Dragon*** ☎277
Site used as an inn since 11th-C. Part of present building dates back to 16th-C or earlier. Original large fireplace in old part of building.
Closed Sun; Lunch not served Sat; Dinner not served Mon; 27seats 40P Last dinner9pm Credit card 3

HURST GREEN Lancashire Map**7** SD63
★★**Shireburn Arms** ☎Stonyhurst208
10rm(6⇌) Lift CTV TV available in bedrooms 18P Children under 13yrs not accommodated French & Italian.
Last dinner9.30pm sB&B fr£8.10
sB&B⇌ fr£12.10 dB&B fr£13.50
dB&B⇌ fr£19.45 Lunch£5.50alc
Dinner£5.50alc Wine£2.90 *xmas*
Credit card 3

HURSTPIERPOINT West Sussex Map**4** TQ21
✕***Barrons*** 120 High St ☎832183
Closed Sun; Lunch not served Sat; 20seats
English & French. Last dinner10.30pm
Credit card 1

HYTHE Hampshire Map**4** SU40
★**West Cliff Hall** ☎Southampton842277
A converted Victorian private country house overlooking Southampton Water to the docks.
47rm(11⇌) CTV 50P 6 squash
Last dinner9.30pm S% sB&B£8–£8.50
sB&B⇌£9.50 dB&B£13 dB&B⇌£15.50
Lunch£3–£3.50&alc Tea75p Dinner£3.50&alc
Wine£2.30 Credit cards 1 3

HYTHE Kent Map**5** TR13
★★★★**Hotel Imperial** Princes Parade (Prestige)
☎67441
Imposing sea-front building standing in 50 acres of own grounds, including 9-hole golf course.
87rm(70⇌) 1 Lift CTV CTV available in bedrooms 200P 10 (heated) squash billiards sauna bath Live music & dancing Sat (in season) Conference facilities available
International. Last dinner9.30pm
*sB&B£14.50–£16.50 sB&B⇌£14.50–£16.50
dB&B£29–£33 dB&B⇌£29–£33
Lunch£4.50–£5&alc Tea75–90p
Dinner£5–£5.50&alc Wine£2.50 *xmas*
Credit cards 1 2 3 5

★★★**Stade Court** West Pde (Inter-Hotel) ☎68263
32rm(25⇌) Lift CTV CTV available in bedrooms 20P 5 Disco Fri (high season) Live music & dancing Xmas & Etr Cabaret Xmas European.
Last dinner9pm sB&B£10.50–£11.75
sB&B⇌£11.25–£14 dB&B£18–£21
dB&B⇌£20–£25 Lunch£3–£3.50 Tea40p–£1
Dinner£4–£5.75&alc Wine£3.25 *xmas*
Credit cards 1 2 3 5

★★***Seabrook*** Seabrook (2m E A259) ☎67279
14rm(2⇌⋒) ⋈ CTV ⊘ 20P ⋈ Last dinner10pm
Credit cards ① ② ③ ⑤

★**Swan** High St ☎66236
9rm ⋈ TV 10P ⋈ Last dinner8.45pm ✱sB&B£6.50
dB&B£13 Lunch£1.70 Dinner£5alc *xmas*
Credit cards ① ② ③ ⑤

IBSLEY Hampshire Map**4** SU10
✕✕**Old Beams** ☎Ringwood3387
Closed 25&26Dec; Dinner not served Sun; 44seats
150P Last dinner9.45pm S% Lunch£3.60–£3.80
Dinner£6alc Wine£2.90

ILCHESTER Somerset Map**3** ST52
✕***Ivelchester Hotel Restaurant*** The Square ☎220
Closed Xmas; Dinner not served Sun; 48seats 40P
bedrooms available Last dinner9.30pm

ILFRACOMBE Devon Map**2** SS54
★★**Carlton** Runna Cleave Rd ☎62446
Closed Nov–Feb; RS Xmas & New Year;
46rm(7⇌⋒) Lift ☽ ⊞ ⋈ CTV ⊘ 25P Live music &
dancing nightly Cabaret twice wkly
Last dinner6.30pm ✿ S% sB&B£8–£9
sB&B⇌⋒£8.75–£10 dB&B£15.40–£19
dB&B⇌⋒£17.40–£20 Lunch£3 Dinner£3.50
Wine£3 *xmas* Credit cards ① ③

I

★★**Cliffe Hydro** Hillsborough Rd ☎63606
Closed Dec–Mar; RS Apr–May & Oct–Nov
(accommodation); 32rm(1⇌⋒) Lift CTV TV available
in bedrooms 10P ⚓ Disco 6 nights Live music &
dancing 6 nights Last dinner7pm ✿ ☡
sB&B£8.50–£9.50 dB&B£17–£19
dB&B⇌⋒£20.50–£21.50 Lunch£2–£2.50
Tea56p Dinner£3–£3.50&alc Wine£3.10

★★**Dilkhusa Grand** Wilder Rd (Travco) ☎63505
Closed Nov–Mar; 113rm(29⇌⋒) Lift ☽ CTV 30P
Disco twice wkly Live music & dancing twice wkly
Last dinner7.45pm ✿ ☡ sB&B£7.50–£8
sB&B⇌⋒£9–£9.50 dB&B£15–£16
dB&B⇌⋒£16.50–£17.50 Lunch fr£3
Dinner fr£3.50 Wine£2.25 ⋈ *xmas*
Credit cards ① ② ③ ⑤ ⑥

★★**Harleigh House** Wilder Rd ☎63850
Closed Mid Oct–Mar; 30rm(9⇌⋒) CTV ⋈ Disco
Mon & Thu Live music & dancing Thu ♡English &
Continental. Last dinner8pm ✿ ☡
sB&B£7.50–£8.50 sB&B⇌⋒£8.50–£9.50
dB&B£15–£17 dB&B⇌⋒£17–£19
Bar lunch80p–£1.20 Tea30–85p
Dinner£3.50–£4 Wine£2.90 ⋈ *xmas*

★★***Imperial*** ☎62536
Closed mid Oct–mid Apr; 98rm(39⇌⋒) Lift ☽ ⋈
CTV 12P Live music & dancing 5nights wkly
Last dinner8pm ☡

★★**Mount** Highfield Rd ☎62308
Closed Jan; RS Pub Hols, Nov, Dec, Feb & Mar;
72rm(6⇌⋒) Lift ☽ ⋈ CTV 30P 8⌂ ⚓ ⋈ ⋈(hard)
squash sauna bath Disco twice wkly Live music &
dancing 4nights cabaret wkly ⋈ Last dinner7.30pm
✿ ☡ sB&B£7.56–£8.64 dB&B£15.12–£17.28
dB&B⇌⋒£16.74–£18.90 Lunch fr£2.75 Tea fr£1
Dinner fr£3.50 Wine£2.80 ⋈ *xmas*

★★**St Helier** Hillsborough Rd ☎63862
Closed Oct–mid May; 29rm(6⇌⋒) CTV TV available
in bedrooms 20P 12⌂ ⚓ Disco twice wkly ⋈
♡English & Continental. Last dinner7.30pm ✿ ☡
S% sB&B£5.50–£6 sB&BB⇌⋒£6.50–£7.50
dB&B£11–£12 dB&B⇌⋒£13–£15
Lunch£2–£2.50 Tea70–80p
High Tea£1.30–£1.60 Dinner£2.50–£3.80
Wine£3 ⋈

Seven Hills Torrs Park ☎62207
Closed Oct–Mar; Unlicensed; 14rm(5) CTV 12P 1 Children under 3yrs not accommodated Lastdinner7.30pm S% sB&B£5.50–£6.50 sB&B£6.50–£7.50 dB&B£11–£13 dB&B£13–£15 Lunch£2–£2.25 Tea75p Dinner£2.75–£3.25 Creditcards 1 2 3 5

ILKLEY West Yorkshire Map**7** SE14
★★★**Craiglands** Cowpasture Rd (Trusthouse Forte) ☎607676
Mid 19th-C mansion with striking modern wing, on slopes of Ilkley Moor with nine acres of lawn and flower beds.
76rm(44) Lift TV in bedrooms 200P 8 billiards Lastdinner9.15pm S% sB&B£14.50 sB&B£16.50 dB&B£22 dB&B£24.50 *xmas*
Creditcards 1 2 3 4 5 6

★★**Lister's Arms** Skipton Rd ☎608698
18rm CTV 120P English & French. Lastdinner8.45pm sB&B£12 dB&B£20 Lunch£3.25 Lunch£3.25 HighTea£3.80 Dinner£5 Wine£2.85 *xmas*

★★***Troutbeck*** Crossbeck Rd ☎607425
14rm(6) CTV 60P Lastdinner8.30pm
Creditcards 2 3 5

XXX**Box Tree** Church St ☎608484
(See Chief Hotel Inspector's Article 'Four more of the Best' on page 9)
Closed Sun, Mon, 1st wk Feb & 1st 2wks Aug; Lunch not served; 50seats French. Lastdinner10pm ✱Dinner fr£12.50 Creditcards 1 2 3 5

ILMINSTER Somerset Map**3** ST31
☆☆☆***Horton Cross Motel*** ☎2144
23 CTV TV available in bedrooms 60P Disco Fri (Sep–Apr) Live music & dancing Sat (Sep–Apr) Lastdinner9.45pm
Creditcards 1 2 3 5

ILSINGTON Devon Map**3** SX77
★★**Haytor** ☎Haytor286
Gabled, stone-built house in own grounds of five acres.
15rm(3) CTV CTV available in bedrooms 20P S% ✱sB&B fr£8.75 sB&B fr£10.40 dB&B fr£17.17 dB&B fr£19.07 Lunch£2.85–£3.85&alc Tea50p–£1 Dinner£3.85£4.50&alc Wine£2.10 *xmas*

INGATESTONE Essex Map**5** TQ69
XXX**Heybridge Moat House** Roman Rd ☎3000
Dinner not served Sun; 120seats 200P Live music & dancing Thu–Sat Cabaret mthly International. Lastdinner11.30pm S% ✱Lunch£4&alc Dinner£8alc Wine£3.50 Creditcards 1 2 3 5

INSTOW Devon Map**2** SS43
★★★**Commodore** Marine Parade ☎860347
Modern, white stucco building in own grounds with views of estuary and sea.
20rm(18) TV in bedrooms 100P 2 Live music & dancing 3nights Lastdinner9.15pm ✱sB&B£10.50–£17 sB&B£17–£23 Lunch£4.15 Dinner£5.50&alc Creditcard 2

IPSWICH Suffolk Map**5** TM14
★★★**Belstead Brook** Belstead Rd (Inter-Hotel) ☎216456 Telex no987674
Closed 25Dec–1Jan; 25 CTV in bedrooms P English & French. Lastdinner9.30pm sB&B£21.60 dB&B£32.40 Lunch£6.50alc Dinner£6.50alc Wine£3.15
Creditcards 1 2 3 5 6

I

☆☆☆**Copdock International** (3½m SW A12) (Best Western) ☎Copdock444 Telex no987207
Closed 24–26Dec; 48rm(41⇌⋒) ☽ ▦ 🕅 CTV in bedrooms 400P ⚓ sauna bath Live music & dancing Sat Last dinner9.15pm ✿ ⚑ S%
✱sB&B£15.50 sB&B⇌⋒£17.50 dB&B£19.50 dB&B⇌⋒£24.50 Lunch fr£3.50 Tea fr50p Dinner fr£4.50&alc Wine£2.95 ⛿
Credit cards 1 3 5

★★★**Marlborough** 73 Henley Rd ☎57677
Former gentlemen's residence, with new wing. Situated in quiet residential area.
26rm(19⇌⋒) ☽ 🕅 CTV available in bedrooms 60P 1🏠 ⚓ ☋ English & Continental. Last dinner9pm ✿ ⚑ sB&B£14.75 sB&B⇌⋒£17.60 dB&B£23 dB&B⇌⋒£28 Lunch£4.80&alc Tea50p–£1 Dinner£4.80&alc Wine£3.25 ⛿
Credit cards 1 2 3 5 6

☆☆☆**Post House** London Rd (Trusthouse Forte) ☎212313
Modern holiday complex on southern outskirts of the town.
118⇌⋒ ☽ 🕅 CTV in bedrooms 175P ⚓ ⛱(heated) Last dinner9.45pm ✿ ⚑ S% sB&B⇌⋒£19.75 dB&B⇌⋒£28.50 ⛿ *xmas*
Credit cards 1 2 3 4 5 6

★★**Crown & Anchor** Westgate St (Henekey) ☎58506
50rm(6⇌⋒) ☽ CTV 30P ⛟ ☋ Mainly grills. Last dinner11.30pm ✿ S% sB&B£10.50 sb&B⇌⋒£13 dB&B£17 dB&B⇌⋒£20 ⛿ *xmas* Credit cards 1 2 3 4 5 6

★★**Great White Horse** Tavern St (Trusthouse Forte) ☎56558
Building with Georgian-style façade referred to by Dickens in Pickwick Papers. Records of distinguished visitors include George II in 1737.
55rm(10⇌⋒) 1▭ ☽ 🕅 CTV TV in bedrooms ⚑ Last dinner9.15pm ✿ ⚑ S% sB&B£12 dB&B£16.50 dB&B⇌⋒£20.50 ⛿ *xmas*
Credit cards 1 2 3 4 5 6

ISLE OF MAN
Details follow England

ISLES OF SCILLY
See under Scilly, Isles of

ISLE OF WIGHT
See Bembridge, Cowes, Freshwater, Newport, Ryde, St Helens, St Lawrence, Sandown, Shanklin, Totland Bay, Ventnor, Whippingham and Yarmouth.

IVER Buckinghamshire Map**4** TQ08
✕***Les Escargots*** High St ☎653778
Closed Sun & Bank Hols; Lunch not served Sat; 30seats ☋ French. Last dinner10.30pm
Credit cards 1 2 3 5

IVINGHOE Buckinghamshire Map**4** SP91
✕✕**Kings Head** ☎Cheddington668388
17th-C posting house for coaches using the old Roman road.
65seats 20P ☋ English & French.
Last dinner9.30pm ✱Lunch£7&alc Dinner£7&alc Wine£3.95 Credit cards 1 2 3 4 5 6

JERSEY
Details for Channel Islands follow England.

JEVINGTON East Sussex Map**5** TQ50
✕✕***Hungry Monk*** ☎Polegate2178
Closed last 2wks Sep; Lunch not served Mon–Sat; 30seats 14P ☋ French. Last dinner10.15pm Lunch£5.60 Dinner£6.40–£6.90 Wine£2.90

KEGWORTH Leicestershire Map**8** SK42
★★★**Yew Lodge** 33 Packington Hill ☎2518
38rm(26⇌⋒) Lift ☽ 🕅 CTV in bedrooms 72P Last dinner11pm ✿ ⚑ S% sB&B£14–£16 sB&B⇌⋒£16–£18 dB&B£24–£26 db&B⇌⋒£26–£28 Lunch£3–£3.20 High Tea£2.50–£2.80 Dinner£4.20–£4.60 Wine£3

KEIGHLEY West Yorkshire Map**7** SE04
★★**Beeches** Bradford Rd ☎607227
11rm(2⇌⋒) Annexe: 11rm(6⇌⋒) ☽ 🕅 CTV TV available in bedrooms 90P 3🏠 ⚓ Live music & dancing Sat ♿ Last dinner9pm ✿ ✱sB&B£11.24 sB&B⇌⋒£15.54 dB&B£22.48 dB&B⇌⋒£23.52 Lunch£3.50–£6.68&alc High Tea£1.30–£1.62 Dinner£3.50–£6.68&alc Wine£3.06 ⛿

KENDAL Cumbria Map**7** SD59
★★★**County** Station Rd (Open House) ☎22461
An early 19th-C building with extensively modernised interior. The Restaurant has an adjoining cocktail bar and the 'Parr' Bar has old-English style décor.
31rm(26⇌⋒) Lift ☽ 🕅 CTV TV in bedrooms 30P Last dinner9.30pm ✿ S% ✱sB&B£11 sB&B⇌⋒£13.50 dB&B£18 dB&B⇌⋒£22 Lunch fr£2.75&alc Dinner fr£4.50&alc Wine£2.80 ⛿ Credit cards 1 2 3 4 5 6

★★★**Woolpack Inn** Stricklandgate (Swallow) ☎23852 Telex no53168
The Crown Bar was once Kendal's wool auction room.
52⇌⋒ ☽ 🕅 CTV CTV in bedrooms 150P Conference facilities available Last dinner9pm ✿ ⚑ S% sB&B£9.35–£12.35 sB&B⇌⋒£13–£16.30 dB&B£15.75–£20.80 dB&B⇌⋒£19.70–£26.35 ⛿ Credit cards 1 2 3 5

★★**Kendal** Highgate ☎24103
46rm 6P Last dinner8pm ✿ S% sB&B£7.45–£11 dB&B£13.25–£18.50 Lunch fr£2.50 Dinner fr£3.50 Wine£2.75

★★Shenstone Country ☎21023
Situated 2 miles south of Kendal on the A6. An ivy-clad two-storey building in the style of a country-house, set in three acres of grounds, with lawns and beautiful trees.
13rm CTV 20P Last dinner8pm S%
sB&B£7.95 dB&B£14.90–£15.90 Lunch£2
Dinner£3.50 Wine£1.80

KENILWORTH Warwickshire Map**4** SP27
★★★★De Montfort Abbey End (De Vere) ☎55944
Telex no22121
Six-storey, red brick building (opened 1967) in centre of town. Colourful modern décor includes Simon de Montfort motifs and wall paintings.
97⇌ Lift TV in bedrooms 110P Conference facilities available English & Continental.
Last dinner10pm S% sB&B⇌£22
dB&B⇌£36.50 Lunch fr£5&alc Tea fr£1.30
Dinner fr£5&alc Wine£3.75
Credit cards 1 2 3 5 6

★★★Avonside Chesford Bridge ☎58331
48⇌ CTV in bedrooms 150P Live music & dancing Sat Conference facilities available
English & French. Last dinner10pm S%
sB&B⇌£14.58 dB&B⇌£21.06
Lunch£3&alc Dinner£4.25&alc Wine£2.60
xmas Credit cards 1 2 3 5

★★Clarendon House High St ☎54694
Low-ceilinged cottage with parts dating back to 16th-C.
Closed 26Dec & 1Jan; 13rm(6⇌) 2 CTV 14P
International. Last dinner9.30pm S%
sB&B£8.50 sB&B⇌£10 dB&B£14
dB&B⇌£18 Lunch£3.50 Dinner£4.50
Wine£2.20 Credit cards 1 2 3 5 6

★★Queen & Castle Castle Green ☎54153
18th-C inn situated on outskirts of town opposite castle.
Closed Xmas day Eve; 8rm TV 250P 5
sB&B£10.70 dB&B£21.40 Lunch fr£2.60
Wine£2.60

✕Restaurant Bosquet 97A Warwick Rd ☎52463
Closed Sun, Mon, 1wk Xmas & Etr, last wk Jul & 1st 3wks Aug; Lunch not served; 24seats French.
Specialities: Crêpe Bretonne; Vol au vent aux crevettes Jolivet; Crêpe aux fraises.
Last dinner10pm Dinner£7.95alc Wine£3.75

✕Ristorante Portofino Talisman Sq ☎57186
Closed Sun, Mon, Xmas & Etr; Lunch not served;
50seats French & Italian. Last dinner10pm S%
*Dinner£7alc Wine£3.40 Credit card 2

✕Romano's 60 Waverley Rd ☎57473
Closed Sun; Lunch not served Sat; 34seats 10P
English & Italian. Specialities: Tournedos Buonfustaio; Veal Romano's; Polto al geperone.
Last dinner10.30pm Lunch fr£2.50&alc
Dinner£5alc Wine£3 Credit card 2

KENNFORD Devon Map**3** SX98
☆☆☆Exeter Ladbroke Mercury Motor Inn (on A38) (Ladbroke) ☎832121
61⇌ CTV available in bedrooms 200P
Conference facilities available Last dinner10.30pm
sB&B⇌fr£17.50 dB&B⇌fr£26.50
Lunch fr£4.50&alc Dinner fr£5&alc Wine£3.20
Credit cards 1 2 3 4 5 6

★★Fairwinds ☎832911
Closed 15Dec–14Jan; RS 26Oct–14Dec & 15Jan–Mar; 7rm(2⇌) TV in bedrooms 9P
Last dinner8pm sB&B£9.45–£10.50
dB&B£14.30–£15.30 dB&B⇌£16–£17
Continental breakfast Lunch£1.50–£2.50
Tea£1–£1.50 Dinner£3.75–£5.10 Wine£2.40

✕*Haldon Thatch* Telegraph Hill (junc A38/A380)
☎832273
Closed Sun & 3wks Feb; 43seats 12P
bedrooms available English & French.
Last dinner10pm Credit cards 1 2 6

KERNE BRIDGE Hereford & Worcester Map**3** SO51
★Castle View ☎Symonds Yat 890329
8rm CTV 70P English & French.
Last dinner9.30pm S% sB&B fr£7.50
dB&B fr£13.50 Bar lunch60p–£1.50 Tea fr75p
High Tea fr£1.50 Dinner fr£3 Wine£2.50
xmas Credit cards 1 3 5

K

KESWICK Cumbria Map**11** NY22
See location atlas for details of other hotels in the vicinity
★★★Derwentwater Portinscale (Inter-Hotel)
☎72538
An 18th-C inn with recent additions, close to the shore of Derwentwater. The private gardens extend down to the lake itself.
43rm(21⇌) Lift CTV 60P Live music & dancing twice wkly Last dinner8.30pm
sB&B£10.75–£26 sB&B⇌£12.25–£17.50
dB&B£21.50–£32 dB&B⇌£24.50–£35
Bar lunch40p–£3&alc Tea60p–£1.50
Dinner£5–£5.50 Wine£2.70 *xmas*
Credit cards 1 2 3 5

★★★Royal Oak Station St (Trusthouse Forte)
☎72965
Originating in Elizabethan times, the Royal Oak was once the centre of a thriving pack-horse trade, later a posting house, it is now a centre for business and social functions of all kinds.
66rm(30⇌) Lift TV in bedrooms 42P
Last dinner9.15pm S% sB&B£11
sB&B⇌£15 dB&B£18.50 dB&B⇌£22.50
xmas Credit cards 1 2 3 4 5 6

★★**Chaucer House** Ambleside Rd ☎72318
A family-run hotel whose reputation has been built up over the last 35 years. Gives views of Skiddaw, Cat Bells, Grisedale and Lake Derwentwater.
Closed Nov–mid Mar; 35rm CTV 25P
Last dinner7.30pm sB&B£6.50–£7.50
dB&B£13–£15 dB&B⇌⋔£15–£16.50
Continental breakfast Dinner£5&alc Wine£3
Credit card 1

★★**George** St John's St (Mount Charlotte) ☎72076
A coaching inn of 17th-C origin, once frequented by the poets Wordsworth, Southey, and Coleridge.
17rm CTV 5P International. Last dinner8.15pm
sB&B fr£8.64 dB&B fr£17.28
Lunch£1.50–£2.70 Tea£2–£2.20
High Tea£2.25–£2.50 Dinner£4.37–£5.40
Wine£2.85 Credit cards 1 2 3

★★**Lake** Lake Rd ☎72069
Early 19th-C inn with covered patio, situated between the town centre and Derwentwater lake.
Closed Nov–Mar; 20rm(4⇌⋔) CTV 10P 12
Last dinner8pm S% sB&B fr£8.80
dB&B fr£17.60 db&B⇌⋔fr£19.60 Lunch fr£3.50
Dinner fr£3.50 Wine£3

★★**Millfield** Penrith Rd ☎72099
Closed Feb; 25rm(6⇌⋔) Lift CTV 20P 12
English & French. Last dinner8.30pm
sB&B£10.50 dB&B£20.50 dB&B⇌⋔£22.50
Bar lunch40p–£4.50 Dinner£4.60&alc
Wine£3.25

K

★★**Queen's** Main St ☎73333
Built of local stone and standing in the centre of the town, this is one of the oldest hotels in Keswick. In the early 1800s as the Queen's Head it enjoyed a high reputation as a posting house. Its name was changed to the Queen's Hotel in the 1860s.
Closed Nov; 35rm(12⇌⋔) Lift CTV CTV available in bedrooms 20 Last dinner8.30pm
sb&B£8.70–£10.80 sb&B£10.70–£12.80
dB&B£17.40–£21.60 dB&B⇌⋔£21.40–£25.60
Lunch£2.65–£4.10 Dinner£5.20–£6 Wine£4.50
Credit cards 1 2 3 5

★★**Red House** Skiddaw (on A591) ☎72211
Gabled, red painted, early-Victorian country house set in ten acres of gardens. Lovely mountain views.
Closed Dec–Feb; 24rm(9⇌⋔) CTV 25P 4
billiards last dinner7pm S%
sB&B£9.20–£10.15 dB&B£17.50–£19.40
db&B⇌⋔£19.20–£21.20 Lunch fr£2.50 Tea fr£1
Dinner fr£3.50 Wine£2.30

★★***Skiddaw*** Main St ☎72071
49rm(18⇌⋔) Lift TV available in bedrooms 20P
12 sauna bath Last dinner8.30pm
Credit cards 1 2 3 5

★★**Walpole** Station St ☎72072
About 100 years old and one of the finest examples of local slate work.
17rm(8⇌⋔) CTV 9P Last dinner8pm
sB&B fr£6.10 sB&B⇌⋔fr£7.18 dB&B fr£12.10
db&B⇌⋔fr£13.70 Lunch£2.50alc
Dinner fr£3.30&alc Wine£1.28 *xmas*

★**Crow Park** The Heads ☎72208
Closed Nov–Feb; 28rm CTV 13P Last dinner5pm
*sB&B£5.94 dB&B£11.88 Wine£2.40

★***Grange*** Manor Brow ☎72500
Occupies a commanding position, half a mile east of Keswick, overlooking the Derwentwater and Bassenthwaite valleys.
7rm CTV TV available in bedrooms 50P 2
English, French & Italian. Last dinner9.30pm
Credit cards 2 6

★**Lairbeck** Vicarage Hill ☎73373
Built of Lakeland stone, with good views of Skiddaw and surrounding countryside.
15rm(5⇌⋔) CTV 25P
Last dinner7.30pm sB&B£7.27–£9
sB&B⇌⋔£8.37–£10.10 dB&V£14.54–£18
dB&B⇌⋔£16.74–£20.20 Bar lunch£3.75
Tea£2.53 Dinner£5.80 Wine£3.42 *xmas*

KETTERING Northamptonshire Map**4** SP87
★★**George** Sheep St ☎2705
50rm(21⇌⋔) CTV 26P Last dinner9.30pm
S% *sB&B£9.99 sB&B⇌⋔£13.99
dB&B£14.85 dB&B⇌⋔£19.98 Lunch fr£3.51
Dinner fr£3.89 Wine£2.95 Credit cards 1 2 3 5

KETTLEWELL North Yorkshire Map**7** SD97
★★**Racehorses** ☎233
18th-C former coaching inn, with small garden.
16rm(3⇌⋔) CTV 20P Last dinner8.45pm
*sB&B£10.75 dB&B£20.50
dB&B⇌⋔£22.50 Lunch fr£3.60 Tea60p
Dinner fr£5.50 Wine£2.90 Credit card 1

★**Bluebell** Middle Ln ☎230
17th-C inn beside River Wharfe.
8rm(2⇌⋔) CTV 8P Last dinner8.30pm
S% *sB&B£8.30 dB&B£16.60
db&B⇌⋔£18.10 Bar lunch£1.75–£4
Dinner fr£4.50 Wine£2.30 Credit card 3

KEYNSHAM Avon Map**3** ST66
★**Grange** Bath Rd ☎2130
16rm(1⇌⋔) Annexe:20rm(10⇌⋔) CTV 36P
English & French. Last dinner9pm S%
sB&B fr£11.95 sB&B⇌⋔fr£13.15 db&B fr£19.50
dB&B⇌⋔fr£21.85 Lunch fr£4 Tea fr50p
High Tea fr£2.50 Dinner fr£4.50 Wine fr£3

KEYSTON Cambridgeshire Map**4** TL07
XXPheasant Inn ☎Bythorn241
Closed Xmas Day; 30seats 45P ♡English & French. Last dinner9.45pm S% Lunch£6alc Dinner£6alc Wine£3.65 Credit cards 1 2 3 5

KIDDERMINSTER Hereford & Worcester Map**7** SO87
★★★**Gainsborough House** Bewdley Hill (Inter-Hotel) ☎64041 Telex no336472
42⇌⋒ ☽ ⛫ CTV in bedrooms 127P Live music & dancing wkly ♡European. Last dinner9.30pm ✿ S% sB&B⇌⋒£16 dB&B⇌⋒£24 Lunch fr£3.50 Dinner fr£5 Wine£2.80 ⊟ Credit cards 1 2 3 5

XXXStone Manor Stone (2m SE on A448) ☎Chaddesley Corbett555
Converted Georgian house in spacious grounds.
100seats 400P bedrooms available Disco Tue & Fri Live music & dancing Sat ♡French.
Last dinner10pm Lunch£3.60&alc Dinner£8alc Wine£2.80 Credit cards 1 2 3 5

XX*Westley Court* Austcliffe Ln, Cookley (3m N off A449) ☎850629
Dinner not served Sun; 75seats P Live music & dancing Sat Cabaret Sat ♡English, French & Italian. Last dinner10pm

KIDSGROVE Staffordshire Map**7** SJ85
XOld Vicarage Newchapel (1m E on unclass road) ☎5270
Closed Mon; Lunch not served Tue–Sat; Dinner not served Sun; 45seats 20P ♡English & French. Last dinner10pm Lunch£3.50 Dinner£5alc Wine£2.35 Credit cards 1 3

KILDWICK West Yorkshire Map**7** SE04
XXXKildwick Hall Hotel ☎Crosshills32244
Closed 1st 3wks Jan; 60seats 40P bedrooms available ♡English & French.
Last dinner9.30pm S% Lunch£5.50 Tea85p Dinner£6.50&alc Wine£3.90 Credit cards 1 2 3 5

KINGHAM Oxfordshire Map**4** SP22
★★**Mill** ☎255
Converted mill and bakehouse, modern extensions behind, on outskirts of village.
Closed Jan; 11rm(3⇌⋒) ⛫ CTV 100P ⚓ ↬
Last dinner9.30pm ✿ ☕ sB&B£8.25–£9.25 sB&B⇌⋒£9.25–£10.25 dB&B£14–£15 dB&B⇌⋒£15.50–£17 Lunch£3.30–£3.60 Tea£1–£1.25 High Tea£2.50–£3 Dinner£3.95–£4.75&alc Wine£3.45 ⊟ *xmas*
Credit cards 2 3 5

★***Langston Arms*** ☎319
This hotel was built as a hunting lodge in the 19th-C and is located in the heart of the Cotswolds.
11rm(4⇌⋒) ⛫ CTV in bedrooms 30P 3⌂ ⚓ ∩
Disco wkly Live music & dancing wkly
Last dinner9.30pm ✿ ☕ ⊟
Credit cards 1 2 3 5

KINGSBRIDGE Devon Map**3** SX74
★★ **Buckland-Tout-Saints** (2½m NE on unclass road) (Best Western) ☎2586 Telex no45562
See page 43 for details

★★**Kings Arms** Fore St ☎2071
15th-C building first used as a coaching inn in 1775.
16rm(7⇌⋒) 11▭ CTV TV available in bedrooms 35P 2⌂ ⛟ Last dinner9.30pm ✿ ☕ S%
✻sB&B£8–£8.50 sB&B⇌⋒£9–£9.50 dB&B£16–£17 dB&B⇌⋒£17–£18 Lunch75p–£2.75 Tea35–65p High Tea fr£1.20 Dinner£1.75–£3.75 Wine£2.75 ⊟ *xmas*
Credit cards 1 2 3 5

K

☆☆**Kingsbridge Motel** The Quay ☎2540
20⇌ ⋒ ⋒ CTV CTV in bedrooms 8P 12 ⋒ ⋒ ⋒ ⋒ ♿
♡International. Last dinner9pm S%
sB&B⇌⋒£11.50 dB&B⇌⋒£17.75
Barlunch£2alc Dinner£4.50alc Wine£2 ⋒
Credit cards 1 2 5

★★**Pindar Lodge** The Promenade ☎2860
Closed Nov–Mar; 10rm(4⇌⋒) ⋒ CTV available in bedrooms 7P ⋒ Last dinner8.30pm ⋒ ⋒
sB&B£8.20 dB&B£16.14 dB&B⇌⋒£18.20
Barlunch40p Tea50p High Tea£1.20 Dinner£4
Wine£1.70 ⋒ Credit card 3

★★**Rockwood** Embankment Rd ☎2480
6⇌⋒ ⋒ TV in bedrooms ⋒ 5P 4⋒ ⋒ Children under 12yrs not accommodated ♡English & French.
Last dinner9pm S% sB&B⇌⋒£7.72
dB&B⇌⋒£14.26 Dinner£5.94 Wine£3.50
Credit cards 1 2 3 5

★★**Vineyard** Embankment Rd ☎2520
Closed mid Oct–Mar; 9rm(4⇌⋒) CTV 14P ⋒
♡International. Last dinner8.30pm ⋒
✱sB&B£7.50–£17 sB&B⇌⋒£8.50–£9.50
dB&B£15–£17 dB&B⇌⋒£17–£19
Barlunch75p–£2.50&alc Dinner£4.15&alc
Wine£2.75

✕✕***Old Brew House*** Union Rd ☎3232
Closed Sun; Lunch not served; 60seats 40P
Disco nightly ♡English & French. Last dinner10pm
Credit cards 1 2 3 5

K

KINGSKERSWELL Devon Map**3** SX86
✕✕**Pitt House** ☎3374
Closed Sun; Lunch not served Sat; 45seats 23P
Last dinner9.30pm ✱Lunch£3.80–£4.90&alc
Dinner£4–£5.20 Wine£4 Credit cards 1 3

KINGSLAND Hereford & Worcester Map**3** SO46
✕**Angel Inn** ☎355
Closed Xmas Day; 30seats 30P ♡English & French.
Last dinner9pm S% Lunch£3.50alc
Dinner£4.75alc Wine£2.30

KING'S LYNN Norfolk Map**9** TF62
★★★**Duke's Head** Tuesday Market Pl (Trusthouse Forte) ☎4996 Telex no817349
72⇌⋒ Lift ☽ ⋒ CTV in bedrooms 50P Conference facilities available Last dinner9.30pm ⋒ ⋒ S%
sB&B⇌⋒£19.50 dB&B⇌⋒£29.50 ⋒ *xmas*
Credit cards 1 2 3 4 5 6

★★**Mildenhall** ☎5146
Closed Xmas Day; 43rm(18⇌⋒) ☽ ⋒ CTV CTV available in bedrooms 50P Live music & dancing Sat
Cabaret Sat Last dinner10pm ⋒ ⋒ S%
✱sB&B fr£11.07 sB&B⇌⋒fr£12.15
dB&B fr£18.90 dB&B⇌⋒fr£20.79
Lunch fr£3.50&alc Tea fr50p Dinner fr£3.50&alc
Wine£4.21 Credit cards 1 2 3 6

★**Stuart House** Goodwins Rd ☎2169
Converted private residence with large garden, centrally located in residential area.
Closed 23Dec–1Jan; 14rm(7⇌⋒)
Annexe: 2rm(1⇌⋒) ⋒ CTV TV available in bedrooms
12P ⋒ ⋒ ⋒ Last dinner8.30pm ✱sB&B£8.50
sB&B⇌⋒£11 dB&B£14.75 dB&B⇌⋒£16.50
Barlunch50p–£2 Dinner£3.50–£5 Wine£2.50
Credit card 1

KINGSWEAR Devon Map**3** SX85
★★⋒***Redoubt*** ☎295
Closed Oct–7Apr; 21rm(2⇌⋒) ⋒ CTV 30P ⋒ ⋒
Children under 7yrs not accommodated
Last dinner9pm winter 11pm ⋒

KINGSWINFORD West Midlands Map**7** SO88
★★**Summerhill House** Swindon Rd (Ansells)
☎5254
10rm(3⇌⋒) ꟿ CTV ⊘ 200P ⇎ Last dinner9.15pm
S% sB&B£12.15 sB&B⇌⋒£13.50
dB&B£16.28 Lunch£3.85&alc Dinner£4.70&alc
Wine£3.20 ⊓ Credit cards [1] [2]

KINGTON Hereford & Worcester Map**3** SO25
★★**Burton** Mill St ☎230323
Early Victorian building, with attractive garden bordering River Arrow.
10rm(3⇌⋒) ꟿ CTV 30P 2⌂ billiards
Last dinner8.30pm ✧ S% ✱sB&B£6.75–£7.75
sB&B⇌⋒£7.75 dB&B⇌⋒£15.50
Lunch£2.50alc Dinner£3.50alc Wine£2.50
Credit card [3]

★★**Oxford Arms** Duke St ☎230322
10rm(3⇌⋒) ꟿ CTV 25P Children under 10yrs not accommodated Last dinner10pm ✧ ♀ S%
sB&B£6.43 sB&B⇌⋒£7.56–£8.64
dB&B£10.80–£15.12 dB&B⇌⋒£15.12
Lunch£2.50alc Tea50p Dinner£2.50–£5&alc
Wine£2.35 Credit cards [2] [4] [6]

★**Swan** Church St ☎230510
6rm TV 25P 2⌂ ⇎ Last dinner8pm ✧
✱sB&B£6.48 dB&B£12.96 Lunch fr£1.90
Dinner fr£3 Wine£2.90 Credit cards [1] [2] [3]

KINGTON (near Pershore) **Hereford & Worcester**
Map**3** SO95
✕***Red Hart Inn*** ☎Inkberrow792221
Dinner not served Sun; 60seats 80P
Last dinner9.30pm

KINTBURY Berkshire Map**4** SU36
✕✕***Dundas Arms*** ☎263
Closed Royal Ascot wk; Lunch not served; Dinner not served Sun & Mon; 40seats 50P bedrooms available ♡ English & French.
Last dinner9.15pm

KIRKBY Merseyside Map**7** SJ49
★★★**Golden Eagle** Cherryfield Dr (Embassy)
☎051–546 4355
79rm(75⇌⋒) Lift ☽ ꟿ CTV TV in bedrooms 75P
Conference facilities available Last dinner9.15pm
✧ S% sB&B£14 sB&B⇌⋒£16 dB&B⇌⋒£21
Lunch£4.50&alc Dinner£5.25&alc Wine£4.50
Credit cards [1] [2] [3] [4] [5] [6]

KIRKBY LONSDALE Cumbria Map**7** SD67
★★**Royal** Main St ☎71217
Originally built as a private residence, but converted into a coaching inn, 'The Rose and Crown' in the early 1900s. It was renamed the Royal following a visit by the Dowager Queen Adelaide in 1840.
20rm(10⇌⋒) ꟿ CTV CTV available in bedrooms 20P
6⌂ ⌒ Last dinner10pm ✧ ♀ ✱sB&B£7.50
sB&B⇌⋒£10.50–£12.50 dB&B£14–£15
dB&B⇌⋒£17.50–£20 Lunch£3–£4.50
Tea50p–£1.75 High Tea£2–£3.50
Dinner£6.50alc Wine£3 ⊓ *xmas* Credit card [1]

★**Red Dragon Inn** Main St ☎71205
17th-C inn with simple façade incorporating irregularly placed windows.
Closed Dec–Feb; 8rm CTV 6P 2⌂ Last dinner7pm
✧ S% sB&B£7 dB&B£12 Bar lunch£1.50–£2
High Tea£3 Dinner£4 Wine£2.50
Credit cards [1] [3] [5] [6]

KIRKBYMOORSIDE North Yorkshire Map**8** SE68
★★**George & Dragon** Market Pl ☎31637
Closed Xmas; 13rm(7⇌⋒) ꟿ CTV TV in bedrooms ⊘
22P Children under 5yrs not accommodated
Last dinner9.30pm ✧ sB&B£4.75–£9.50
sB&B⇌⋒£5–£10 dB&B£8–£16
dB&B⇌⋒£9.50–£19 Lunch£3–£3.50
Dinner£5&alc Wine£2.50 ⊓

KIRKBY STEPHEN Cumbria Map**12** NY70
★★**King's Arms** Market St ☎71378
A mid 18th-C inn Georgian façade. Of interest are an unusual powder closet on the landing, and framed tapestries worked by the proprietress.
12rm(1⇌⋒) ꟿ CTV 6P 9⌂ ♣ Last dinner9pm ✧
♀ sB&B£5.50–£13 dB&B£11–£26
dB&B⇌⋒£13–£30 Lunch£3 Tea£1.20
Dinner£6–£7 Wine£2.50 ⊓
Credit cards [1] [2] [3] [5] [6]

KIRK LANGLEY Derbyshire Map**8** SK23
★★**Meynell Arms** Ashbourne Rd ☎515
Closed Xmas day; RS 24 & 26–27Dec; 9rm(4⇌⋒)
1▭ ꟿ TV available in bedrooms 80P ⇎ ♣ Live music
Sat & Sun ♡ English & French. Last dinner10pm ✧
✱sB&B£6.50 sB&B⇌⋒£7 dB&B£10
dB&B⇌⋒£11 Bar lunch£1–£1.40&alc
Dinner£3.50–£3.75&alc Credit cards [1] [2] [3] [6]

KISLINGBURY Northamptonshire Map**4** SP65
✕✕✕**Cromwell Cottage** ☎Northampton830288
Closed Sun; 90seats 60P Last dinner9.45pm
✱Lunch£5alc Dinner£5alc Credit cards [1] [2] [3] [5] [6]

KNIGHTWICK Hereford & Worcester Map**3** SO75
★**Talbot** ☎235
Closed Xmas wk; 8rm(5⇌⋒) ꟿ 50P ⇎ ♣ ⌒ squash
Last dinner9.15pm ✧ sB&B£7.02
sB&B⇌⋒£10.26 dB&B£14.04 dB&B⇌⋒£16.20
Lunch fr50p Dinner£4.50alc Wine£2.50

KNOWLE West Midlands Map**7** SP17
★★★ **Chadwick Manor** Warwick Rd ☎2821
13⇌ ⋒ 1 CTV in bedrooms 200P 6 French. Last dinner10pm S%
✱sB&B⇌⋒£21 dB&B⇌⋒£26–£35
Lunch£4.60&alc Tea£1.20 Dinner£10alc
Wine£3.60 Credit cards 1 2 3 5 6

★★**Greswolde Arms** High St (Ansells) ☎2711
19rm(5⇌⋒) CTV 100P Mainly grills.
Last dinner10.30pm S% sB&B£12.30
dB&B£16.45 dB&B⇌⋒£18.85 Lunch£3.48
Dinner£3.75 Wine£3.20 Credit cards 1 2

KNOWL HILL Berkshire Map**4** SU87
✕✕**Bird in Hand** ☎Littlewick Green2781
60seats 100P English & French.
Last dinner10.15pm S% Lunch£4.50&alc
Dinner£7.50alc Wine£3.50 Credit cards 2 3 5

KNOWSLEY Merseyside Map**7** SJ49
☆☆☆**Liverpool Crest Motel** East Lancs Rd (Crest)
☎051–546 7531 Liverpool plan**10**
50⇌⋒ CTV in bedrooms 100P Conference facilities available Last dinner9.30pm S%
✱sB&B⇌⋒£15.17 dB&B⇌⋒£21.70
Continental breakfast Credit cards 1 2 3 4 5 6

KNUTSFORD Cheshire Map**7** SJ77
★**Rose & Crown** King St (Greenhall Whitley)
☎52366
Former coaching inn (built 1647, restored 1923) retaining Tudor style.
11rm CTV 40P Last dinner9.00pm
sB&B£10.50–£11.50 dB&B£14 Lunch£2.75
Tea40p High Tea£1.75 Dinner£3.50 Wine£2.80
Credit cards 1 2 3 5

K

✕✕**La Belle Époque** 60 King St ☎3060
Closed Sun & Public Hols; 80seats
bedrooms available Cabaret mthly French.
Last dinner10pm Dinner£7alc Wine£2.95
Credit cards 1 2 3 4 5 6

✕✕**David's Place** 10 Princess St ☎3356
Closed Sun & 2wks late Aug; Lunch not served Mon;
50seats English, French & Italian.
Last dinner10pm ✱Lunch£5.50alc Dinner£8alc
Wine£2.97 Credit cards 1 2 5

LACEBY Humberside Map**8** TA20
★★**Oaklands Hotel & Country Club**
☎Grimsby72248
48rm(43⇌⋒) 1 CTV TV available in bedrooms
250P squash sauna bath Live music & dancing wkly Cabaret wkly Last dinner9.30pm
S% sB&B£12 sB&B⇌⋒£14 dB&B£20
dB&B⇌⋒£24 Lunch£5alc Tea£1alc
High Tea£2alc Dinner£7alc Wine£3
Credit cards 2 5

LAMBOURN Berkshire Map**4** SU37
★★**Red Lion** ☎71406
Overlooks main square of Berkshire village famed for racehorse training.
12rm(7⇌⋒) CTV 45P Live music & dancing mthly French. Last dinner9pm sB&B£10
sB&B⇌⋒£11 dB&B£18 dB&B⇌⋒£19
Lunch£2.50&alc Tea50–85p Dinner£5&alc
Wine£3.25 Credit cards 1 2 3 5

LAMERTON Devon Map**2** SX47
★***Camplehaye*** ☎Tavistock2014
Detached house of part Georgian and part Victorian design.
9rm(1⇌⋒) CTV 20P English & Continental.
Last dinner8.30pm

LAMORNA COVE Cornwall Map**2** SW42
★★★ **Lamorna Cove** (Inter-Hotel)
☎Mousehole411
18⇌ 1 Lift CTV in bedrooms 25P
(heated) sauna bath Lastdinner9.30pm
S% sB&B⇌£15–£18
dB&B⇌£29.50–£32.50 Lunch£5–£7.50&alc
Tea£1–£1.75 Dinner£6.25–£9.50&alc
Wine£3.25 *xmas* Credit cards 1 2 3 5 6

★ **Menwinnion** Lamorna Valley ☎St Bunyan233
Closed Nov–Jan; 8rm(2⇌) CTV 12P 2
Children under 5yrs not accommodated
Lastdinner8pm S% ✱sB&B£8.64–£9.72
sb&B⇌£9.72–£10.80 dB&B£17.28–£19.44
dB&B⇌£19.44–£21.60 Lunch£2.70 Tea54p
Dinner£4.86 Wine£3.78

LANCASTER Lancashire Map**7** SD46
★★**Royal Kings Arms** Market St ☎2451
59rm Lift CTV 12P Lastdinner8pm S%
sB&B£7.45–£11 dB&B£13.25–£18.50
Lunch fr£2.50 Dinner fr£3.50 Wine£2.75

XX**Portofino** 23 Castle Hill ☎2388
Closed Sun; Lunch not served Sat; 60seats
Italian. Last dinner10.45pm
✱Lunch£2.20–£2.50&alc Dinner£6alc
Wine£3.50 Credit cards 1 2 3 5 6

LANCHESTER Co Durham Map**12** NZ14
XX***Kings Head Hotel*** ☎520054
Closed Mon; Dinner not served Sun; 44seats 200P
bedrooms available English & French.
Lastdinner9.15pm Credit cards 1 2 3 5

LAND'S END Cornwall Map**2** SW32
★★**Land's End** ☎Sennen271
Closed Oct–Mar; 43rm(9⇌) CTV 50P 4
Lastdinner8pm S% sB&B£6.50–£7.50
sB&B⇌£7.25–£8.25 dB&B£13–£15
dB&B⇌£14.50–£16.50 Lunch£2.75 Tea75p
Dinner£3.75 Wine£2.90

LANGDALE, GREAT Cumbria Map**11** NY30
★★★**Langdales** ☎253
Set in Langdale Valley, this is a two-storey stone and stucco building with attractive gardens bounded by the Langdale Beck.
22rm(11⇌) CTV 50P
Lastdinner8.15pm ✱sB&B fr£10
sB&B⇌fr£12 dB&B fr£20 dB&B⇌fr£40
Lunch fr£3 Tea fr20p Dinner fr£8 Wine£2.30
xmas

★**Pillar** Langdale Estate ☎656
The Pillar Hotel, which was originally a gunpowder mill, stands in 25 acres of private grounds in the Langdale Valley.
Closed Jan; RS Dec, Feb & Mar (open wknds only);
10rm(2⇌) TV 30P (grass) squash
Lastdinner7.30pm ✱sB&B£8–£9.50
dB&B£16–£19 dB&B⇌£20–£23 Tea40–60p
Dinner£4.75–£5.50

LANREATH Cornwall Map**2** SX15
★★***Punch Bowl Inn*** ☎218
Early 17th-C stone-built inn, embracing adjoining cottages. Previously courthouse, coaching inn, and smugglers' haunt. Sign by Augustus John.
Closed Nov–Mar; 16rm(9⇌) Annexe: 2⇌ 5
CTV 50P 4 Lastdinner9.30pm

LASTINGHAM North Yorkshire Map**8** SE79
★★ **Lastingham Grange** ☎345
17th-C country house of local stone, with extensive gardens; wing added during the last century. At edge of Spaunton Moor.

L

Closed mid Nov–Mar; 13rm(9⇌ ⋒) 🎮 ✗ 30P 2🏠 ♣ ⚓ ⛪ Last dinner8.30pm ✿ ☑ ✱sB&B£31 sB&B⇌⋒£14 dB&B£22 dB&B⇌⋒£25 Lunch£4–£4.50 Tea80p Dinner£5.50 Wine£2.50 ▮

LAUNCESTON Cornwall Map**2** SX38
★★***Eagle House*** Castle St ☎2036
Former Georgian mansion (built 1732) affording country views. Close to castle green and town centre.
19rm(1⇌⋒) 1▭ ☽ 🎮 CTV 60P Live music & dancing Sat Last dinner9pm ✿ ☑ ▮ Credit cards③⑤

LAVENHAM Suffolk Map**5** TL94
★★★**Swan** High St (Trusthouse Forte) ☎247477
Incorporates four picturesque Tudor houses with local history associations. Fascinating interior includes authentic beamed ceilings.
42⇌⋒ 🎮 CTV CTV in bedrooms 60P ⚓ Last dinner9.30pm ✿ ☑ S% sB&B⇌⋒£18.75 dB&B⇌⋒£30.50 ▮ *xmas*
Credit cards①②③④⑤⑥

LEAMINGTON SPA (ROYAL) Warwickshire Map**4** SP36
★★★★**Manor House** Avenue Rd (De Vere) ☎23251 Telex no22121
Four-storey gabled brick manor house with lawns and gardens backing onto the River Leam. Modern wing added 1963.
57rm(45⇌⋒) Lift ☽ 🎮 TV in bedrooms 120P ⚓ Conference facilities available ♀English & French. Last dinner10.30pm ✿ ☑ S% sB&B⇌⋒£16.50 dB&B⇌⋒£26 Lunch fr£4&alc Dinner fr£5.25&alc Wine£3.75 ▮
Credit cards①②③ ⑤⑥

★★★**Regent** 77 The Parade (Best Western) ☎27231
Regency building in centre of town. Past visitors include Queen Victoria, Duke of Wellington and Charles Dickens.
80⇌⋒ Lift ☽ 🎮 CTV CTV available in bedrooms 40P 25🏠 Disco 4nights wkly ♀International. Last dinner10.45pm ✿ ☑ S% sB&B⇌⋒£17.25 dB&B⇌⋒£25.50 Lunch£4.10 Dinner£5.75 Wine£3.50 ▮ *xmas*
Credit cards①②③ ⑤

❀★★**Mallory Court** Harbury Ln, Bishops Tachbrook (2m S off A452) ☎30214
See page 43 for details

★★**Abbacourt** 40 Kenilworth Rd ☎311188
18rm(5⇌⋒) 🎮 CTV TV in bedrooms ✗ 25P ♣ ♀International. Last dinner9pm ✿ S% sB&B£10.26 sB&B⇌⋒£11.34 dB&B£15.66 dB&B⇌⋒£16.74 Lunch£3.25 Dinner£4.75alc Wine£2.95

★★**Angel** Regent St ☎23683
Closed last wk Jul & 1st wk Aug; 14rm(8⇌⋒) 🎮 CTV CTV in bedrooms ✗ 18P ♀English, French & Italian. Last dinner10pm ✿ sB&B£8.50 sB&B⇌⋒£10.70 dB&B£17 dB&B⇌⋒£18.75 Continental breakfast Lunch£3&alc Dinner£3.50&alc Wine£2.60 Credit cards①②③⑤

★★**Berni Inn** Kenilworth Rd (Berni) ☎25151
23rm(3⇌⋒) Annexe: 8rm Lift ☽ 🎮 CTV 25P ♀Mainly grills. Last dinner11pm ✿ ▮
Credit cards①②③ ⑤⑥

★★**Clarendon** The Parade (Trusthouse Forte) ☎22201
Sturdy Regency terrace building with wrought-iron balcony and Doric columned entrance; opposite Beacham Gardens.
54rm(21⇌⋒) Lift ☽ 🎮 TV in bedrooms 50P ♿ Last dinner9pm ✿ S% sB&B£13 sB&B⇌⋒£14.50 dB&B£18.50 dB&B⇌⋒£22 ▮ *xmas* Credit cards①②③④⑤⑥

★★**Falstaff** 20 Warwick New Rd ☎21219
Neat Victorian house with attractive wood-faced modern extension and small garden. Sculptured mural on stairs, on Falstaff theme.
Closed Xmas wk; 34⇌ 1 Lift CTV TV in bedrooms 30P sauna bath Last dinner9pm S% ✱sB&B⇌£10.80–£14.04 dB&B⇌£18.36–£21.60 Lunch£3–£4 Tea fr25p Dinner fr£4&alc Wine£2.40 Credit cards 1 2 3

★***Amersham*** 34 Kenilworth Rd ☎21637
14rm CTV 14P Last dinner8.30pm

★**Chesford House** 12 Clarendon St ☎20924
10rm(4⇌) CTV 10P Last dinner8pm S% sB&B£8 dB&B£16 dB&B⇌£18 Continental breakfast Lunch£3.75–£6 Tea£1–£1.50 Dinner£3.75–£6 Wine£1.95 Credit card 2

★**Lansdowne** Clarendon St ☎21313
RS Xmas (B&B only); 9rm CTV 6P Last dinner7.30pm sB&B£7.13 dB&B£13.07 Continental breakfast Lunch£3.27 Tea£1–£1.50 High Tea£1.75–£2.50 Dinner£3.96

★**Park** 17 Avenue Rd ☎28376
16rm(5⇌) CTV 14P Last dinner8pm sB&B£6.75 sB&B⇌£7.75 dB&B£13.50 dB&B⇌£15.50 Lunch£3 Tea50p Dinner£3.75 Wine£2.70

XX**Blackdown** Sandy Ln ☎24761
Closed Sun & Public Hols; 300seats 150P Disco Sat French. Last dinner10.30pm Lunch fr£4.50&alc Dinner£10alc Wine£3.95 Credit cards 1 2 3 5

X***Quo Vadis*** 50 Clarendon St ☎24471
Italian 'trattoria' with colonnaded façade.
Closed Sun & Public Hols; 32seats English & Italian. Last dinner10.30pm Credit cards 1 2 3

LEATHERHEAD Surrey Map**4** TQ15
★★**New Bull** North St ☎72153
7rm(2⇌) CTV TV in bedrooms 80P Live music & dancing Sun Last dinner10pm S% ✱sB&B£12 sB&B⇌£13 dB&B£16 dB&B⇌£18 Lunch£2.85–£5.65&alc Tea60p High Tea£1.75 Dinner£2.85–£5.65&alc Wine£2.95 Credit cards 1 2 3 5

LECHLADE Gloucestershire Map**4** SU29
X**Trout** ☎52313
Small restaurant, beside River Thames, in an old Cotswold inn.
Closed Mon (except Public Hols); 40seats 40P Lunch£5.25alc Dinner£5.25alc Wine£2.30 Credit cards 1 3

LEDBURY Hereford & Worcester Map**3** SO73
★★**Feathers** High St ☎2600
Remarkable half-timbered black and white inn having oak beams, horse brasses and copper utensils.
13rm(1⇌) CTV 12P 10 squash English & French. Last dinner9.30pm S% sB&B£30.69–£12.47 dB&B£19–£23 dB&B⇌£21.38–£24.50 Lunch fr£4.16&alc Tea45p–£1 Dinner£5.76&alc Wine£3.45 *xmas* Credit cards 1 5

XX***Verzons*** Trumpet (3m W A438) ☎Trumpet381
Closed Sun & Mon; 50seats 50P English & French. Last dinner9.30pm

LEEDS West Yorkshire Map**8** SE33 **See plan**
☆☆☆☆**Ladbroke Dragonara** Neville St (Ladbroke) ☎442000 Telex no557143 Plan**3**
239⇌ Lift CTV in bedrooms 80 Live music & dancing Fri & Sat Conference facilities available International. Last dinner11pm

L

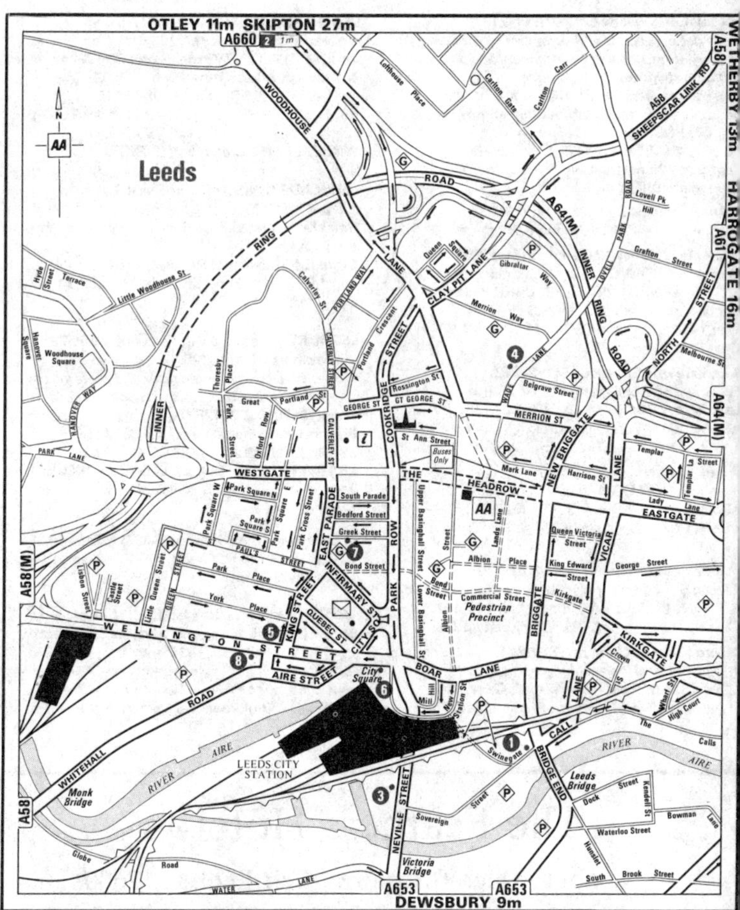

1 Golden Lion ★★
2 Hartrigg ★
3 Ladbroke Dragonara ✓ ☆☆☆☆
4 Merrion ★★★
5 Metropole ★★★
6 Queen's ★★★★
7 Terrazza ✕✕✕
8 Wellesley ★★

S% sB&B fr£26.75 dB&B fr£41.50 Lunch fr£3.50&alc Tea fr70p High Tea fr£2 Dinner fr£6.50&alc Wine£3.35 Credit cards 1 2 3 5

★★★★**Queen's** City Sq (British Transport) ☎31323 Telex no55161 Plan**6**
Impressive eight-storey building with Portland stone façade; adjoining city station.
193rm(174) Lift CTV in bedrooms sauna bath Conference facilities available English & French. Last dinner10.15pm S% *sB&B fr£26.50 dB&B fr£32 Wine£3.50 Credit cards 1 2 3 4 5 6

★★★**Merrion** Merrion Centre (Kingsmead) ☎39191 Telex no55459 Plan**4**
120 Lift CTV in bedrooms Conference facilities available. French. Last dinner10.30pm *sB&B £19 dB&B £24–£26 Continental breakfast Lunch fr£3.25 Dinner fr£3.75 Wine£4.25 Credit cards 1 3 4 5 6

★★★**Metropole** King St (Trusthouse Forte) ☎450841 Plan**5**
106rm(73) Lift TV in bedrooms 28P Conference facilities available Last dinner10pm S% sB&B£14 sB&B £16.50 dB&B£20.50 dB&B £22.50 Credit cards 1 2 3 4 5 6

☆☆☆**Windmill** Mill Green View, Seacroft (Reo Stakis) ☎732323 Not on plan
40 Lift CTV CTV in bedrooms 300P Disco 3nights wkly Live music & dancing wkly Conference facilities available English & French. Last dinner9.45pm S% *sB&B £16.50 dB&B £26 Lunch£7alc Tea fr30p Dinner£7alc Wine£3.10 Credit cards 1 2 3 5 6

★★**Golden Lion** Lower Briggate (Trusthouse Forte) ☎36454 Plan**1**
82rm(6) Lift TV in bedrooms Mainly grills. Last dinner9.30pm S% sB&B£12 sB&B £14 dB&B£16.50 dB&B £20 *xmas* Credit cards 1 2 3 4 5 6

★★**Wellesley** Wellington St (Henekey) ☎30431 Plan**8**
53rm(22⇌⋒) Lift ☽ 🍽 CTV 28P ♉ Mainly grills. Last dinner10.30pm ✿ S% sB&B£10.50 sB&B⇌⋒£13 dB&B£17 dB&B⇌⋒£20 ⊟ *xmas* Credit cards 1 2 3 4 5 6

★**Hartrigg** Shire Oak Rd, Headingley (2½m NW A660) ☎751568 Plan**2**
RS Public Hols (B&B only); 28rm CTV 18P 3⌂ ⇏ Last dinner7pm S% sB&B£8.37 dB&B£13.80 Lunch fr£2.50 High Tea fr£2.50 Dinner fr£3 Wine£2.20 Credit cards 1 3

XXX***Terrazza*** Minerva House, 16 Greek St ☎32880 Plan**7**
Closed Sun & Public Hols; Lunch not served Sat; 90seats P Disco Wed, Fri & Sat ♉ Italian. Last dinner11.45pm Credit cards 1 2 3 5 6

X**Rules** 188 Selby Rd ☎604564 Not on plan
Closed Sun & first 2wks Aug; Lunch not served; 36seats ₱ ♉ French. Last dinner11pm Dinner£5.50alc Wine£2.80 Credit cards 1 2 3 5

At **Garforth** (6m E junc A63/A642)
☆☆☆**Leeds Ladbroke Mercury Motor Inn** Garforth Roundabout (Ladbroke) ☎Leeds866556 Not on plan
156⇌⋒ 180P

At **Oulton** (6m SE on A639)
☆☆☆**Leeds Crest Motel** (Crest) ☎Leeds826201 Not on plan
40⇌⋒ 140P

LEEMING BAR North Yorkshire Map**8** SE28
☆☆☆**Motel Leeming** ☎Bedale2122
40⇌⋒ ☽ 🍽 TV in bedrooms 100P 14⌂ ⚓ Conference facilities available ♉ International. Last dinner9.45pm ✿ ♫ sB&B⇌⋒£15–£20 dB&B⇌⋒£24–£30 Lunch£3–£5.50 Tea75p–£1.50&alc High Tea65p–£2&alc Dinner£3.50–£5.50&alc Wine£2.10 ⊟ *xmas* Credit cards 1 2 3 5 6

LEE-ON-THE-SOLENT Hampshire Map**4** SU50
★★**Belle Vue** Marine Parade East ☎550258
Converted private houses with patio; views of Solent.
34rm(11⇌⋒) 🍽 CTV 80P ⇏ Live music & dancing Sat Cabaret Sat ♉ English & French. Last dinner8.45pm ✿ S% ✱sB&B£9 sB&B⇌⋒£10.50 dB&B fr£14.50 dB&B⇌⋒£16–£17 Lunch£3.79&alc Dinner£3.79&alc Wine£2.95 Credit card 5

LEICESTER Leicestershire Map**4** SK50
★★★★**Grand** Granby St (Embassy) ☎56222
93⇌⋒ Lift ☽ 🍽 CTV CTV available in bedrooms 50⌂ Last dinner9.30pm ✿ ♫ S% sB&B⇌⋒£18 dB&B⇌⋒£24 Continental breakfast Lunch£5&alc Dinner£6&alc Wine£5 ⊟ Credit cards 1 2 3 5 6

☆☆☆☆**Holiday Inn** St Nicholas Circle (Commonwealth) ☎51161 Telex no341281
190⇌⋒ Lift ☽ ⊞ 🍽 CTV CTV in bedrooms 300⌂ ▭(heated) sauna bath Live music & dancing Fri & Sat Conference facilities available ♉ International. Last dinner10.15pm ✿ ♫ ⊟ Credit cards 1 2 3 4 5 6

☆☆☆**Europa Lodge** Hinckley Rd (Grand Met) ☎394661
31⇌⋒ ☽ 🍽 TV available in bedrooms 120P ⚓ Live music & dancing Wed–Sun ♉ English & French. Last dinner9.45pm ✿ ♫ sB&B⇌⋒£14–£14.50 dB&B⇌⋒£18.50 ⊟ Credit cards 1 2 3 4 5 6

★★★**Hermitage** Wigston Rd, Oadby (3m SE A6) ☎719441
RS 24Dec–1Jan; 29⇌⋒ Lift ☽ 🍽 TV in bedrooms 80P ♉ English & French. Last dinner9.30pm ✿ sB&B⇌⋒£12–£17 dB&B⇌⋒£18–£25 Lunch£4.50–£5&alc Dinner£5–£5.50&alc Wine£2.60 ⊟ Credit cards 1 2 3 5

★★★**Leicester Centre** Humberstone Gate (Centre) ☎20471 Telex no341460
220⇌⋒ Lift ☽ 🍽 TV available in bedrooms ⇏ 20P Conference facilities available last dinner10.15pm ✿ ♫ S% ✱sB&B⇌⋒£15.25 dB&B⇌⋒£20.25 Continental breakfast Lunch£3.60 Dinner£3.60 Wine£3.40 ⊟ Credit cards 1 2 3 4 5 6

☆☆☆**Post House** Braunstone Lane East (Trusthouse Forte) ☎896688 Telex no341009
171⇌⋒ Lift ☽ 🍽 CTV in bedrooms 102P Last dinner9.45pm ✿ ♫ S% sB&B⇌⋒£19.75 dB&B⇌⋒£28.50 ⊟ Credit cards 1 2 3 4 5 6

★★***Belmont*** De Montfort St (Best Western) ☎24177
Late Victorian building beside tree-lined New Walk promenade.
35rm(19⇌⋒) Annexe: 20rm(10⇌⋒) Lift ☽ 🍽 CTV TV available in bedrooms Disco wkly Last dinner9.45pm ✿ ♫ ⊟ Credit cards 1 3

Ⓖ**Croft** 3 Stanley Rd ☎703220
28rm(2⇌⋒) 🍽 CTV CTV available in bedrooms 20P ⇏ Last dinner7pm ✿ ♫ S% sB&B£6.48 sB&B⇌⋒£7.02 dB&B£12.96 dB&B⇌⋒£13.50 Lunch£1.40 Tea£1 High Tea£1.40 Dinner£1.40

❀XXX**Manor** Glen Parva Manor, The Ford, Little Glen Rd, Glen Parva (3m SW A426) ☎774604
Closed Sun; Lunch not served Sat; 70seats 65P ♉ English, French & Italian. Specialities: Manor Smokies, Sole Walewska, Veal Marsala. Last dinner9.45pm Lunch£8alc Dinner£8alc Wine£3

XXX**White House** Scraptoft Ln ☎415951
Closed Mon; Dinner not served Sun; 140seats 85P Live music & dancing Sat (Fri also in winter) ♉ English, French & Italian. Last dinner9.30pm Lunch fr£3.80&alc Dinner£7.50alc Wine£3.85 Credit cards 1 2 3 5

L

✕✕**Girardot** Goscote Hotel, Birstall (2m N off A6) ☎674191
Closed Sun; Lunch not served Sat; Dinner not served Mon–Fri; 100seats 150P English & French. Lastdinner10pm S% Lunch£3–£3.50 Dinner£5.50–£6 Wine£3.50 Creditcards 1 2

LEIGH Greater Manchester Map**7** SJ69
☆☆☆**Greyhound Motor** East Lancs Rd (A580) (Embassy) ☎671256
64 Lift CTV TV in bedrooms 100P 8 Lastdinner9.30pm S% sB£16 (room only) dB£20 (room only) Lunch£4.50&alc Dinner£5&alc Wine£4.50 Credit cards 1 2 3 4 5 6

LEINTWARDINE Hereford & Worcester Map**7** SO47
✕***Lion*** ☎203
Closed Mar; 70seats 30P Lastdinner9.30pm

LENWADE (Great Witchingham) Norfolk Map**9** TG01
★★**Lenwade House** ☎Great Witchingham288
14 CTV CTV in bedrooms 40P (heated) (grass) squash Children under 5yrs not accommodated Lastdinner9.30pm sB&B fr£12 37 dB&B fr£20.30 Lunch fr£3.95 Dinner fr£3.95&alc Wine£2.95 *xmas* Creditcards 1 2 3 6

LEOMINSTER Hereford & Worcester Map**3** SO45
★★**Royal Oak** South St ☎2610
17th-C to 18th-C country inn situated in town centre. Minstrel's gallery in Assembly Room.
15rm(6) CTV TV available in bedrooms 40P Disco twice wkly Lastdinner9pm S% *sB&B£7.70–£8.80 sB&B£8.80–£9.50 dB&B£15.40–£18.70 dB&B£17.60–£18.70 Lunch£4.50alc Tea75palc High Tea75palc Dinner£4.50alc Wine£3 Creditcards 1 2 3

★★**Talbot** ☎2121
Closed Xmas day; 31rm(19) CTV CTV available in bedrooms 60P Lastdinner9.30pm S% sB&B£8.50 sB&B£11 dB&N£17.50 dB&B£19 Lunch£4.50alc Dinner£4.50alc Wine£2.25 Creditcards 1 2 3

LETCHWORTH Hertfordshire Map**4** TL23
★★★**Broadway** The Broadway (Crest) ☎5651
Built in Georgian style in the mid 1960s and situated in the centre of Letchworth.
32rm(12) Lift CTV in bedrooms 100P English & French. Lastdinner9.30pm S% *sB&B£12.96 sB&B£17.28 dB&B£20.52 dB&B£24.84 Creditcards 1 2 3 4 5 6

LEVENS (nr Kendal) Cumbria Map**7** SD48
★★**Heaves** (off A6 ½m from junc with A591) ☎Sedgwick60396
Georgian residence with older parts; situated in its own park and sheltered on the west by wooded hill. It stands 100ft above sea level giving fine views of Morecambe Bay, the Pennines and lakeland hills.
Unlicensed; 15rm(4) CTV TV available in bedrooms 30P 3 Lastdinner8.30pm S% sB&B£8–£9 sB&B£9–£10 dB&B£16–£18 dB&B£18–£20 Lunch£3alc Tea80palc Dinner£4alc Creditcards 1 2 3 6

LEWDOWN Devon Map**2** SX48
☆☆***Coach House*** (Inter-Hotel) ☎322
Closed Xmas; Annexe: 50 TV 200P Lastdinner9.30pm Creditcards 1 2 3

LEWES East Sussex Map**5** TQ41
★★★**Shelleys** High St (Mount Charlotte) ☎2361
20 1 CTV in bedrooms 24P 4 English & Continental. Lastdinner9.30pm S% *sB&B£17.30 dB&B£24.50

Lunch fr£3.75&alc Tea50p–£1.25
Dinner fr£5&alc Wine£3.75 xmas
Credit cards 1 2 3 4 5 6

★★White Hart High St (Best Western) ☎4676
18rm(6⇌) Annexe: 14⇌ CTV CTV available in bedrooms 50P French. Last dinner10.15pm
sB&B£11.88–£14.04 dB&B£17.28–£19.44
dB&B⇌ £22.68–£27 Lunch fr£3&alc Tea fr75p
Dinner£7alc Wine£4 xmas
Credit cards 1 2 3 5

✕La Cucina 13 Station Rd ☎6707
Closed Sun, Public Hols & 24Dec–1Jan; 50seats
Italian & Continental. Last dinner11pm
✻Lunch£4.20alc Dinner£5.10alc Wine£2.40
Credit cards 1 3

✕Trumps 19/20 Station St ☎3906
Closed Sun, Mon 1st 2wks Oct & Xmas wk; 30seats
Lunch not served English & French. Specialities: half fresh duck with black cherry sauce, fillet of beef Mexicana, veal steak pizzaiola au gratin.
Last dinner10pm ✻Dinner£10alc Wine£2.85

LICHFIELD Staffordshire Map7 SK10
★★★Little Barrow Beacon St ☎53311
26rm(24⇌) TV TV in bedrooms 40P
International. Last dinner10pm
sB&B⇌ £14.60 dB&B⇌ £21.40
Lunch£4&alc Dinner£6&alc Wine£2
Credit cards 1 2 3 5 6

★★Angel Croft Beacon St ☎23147
Rich, brown brick Georgian house, with one acre of ground, and situated close to Cathedral.
RS Sun; 13rm(5⇌) CTV 60P
Last dinner9pm S% sB&B fr£10
sB&B⇌ fr£12.25 dB&B fr£18
dB&B⇌ fr£21.50 Lunch fr£3.50 Tea fr65p
Dinner fr£4.40 Wine£3 Credit cards 1 3 5

★★George Bird St ☎55290
40⇌ CTV in bedrooms 50P 20 English & French. Last dinner10pm S%
✻sB&B⇌ £15.10 dB&B⇌ £21.95
Lunch£3.65–£4.95&alc Dinner£6alc Wine£3.20
Credit cards 1 2 3 5

★★Swan Bird St ☎55851
24⇌ CTV CTV in bedrooms 100P
Last dinner10pm S% ✻sB&B⇌ £14.10
dB&B⇌ £20.95 Bar lunch50p–£1.20 Tea35p
Dinner£5alc Wine£3.70 Credit cards 1 2 3 5

LIFTON Devon Map2 SX38
★★*Arundell Arms* (Best Western) ☎244
Early 19th-C building with old cockpit preserved in garden.
Closed Xmas; 23rm(15⇌) Annexe: 4rm CTV 80P English & French. Last dinner9pm
Credit cards 1 2 3 6

★Lifton Cottage ☎439
12 CTV 15P Last dinner6.30pm
S% sB&B£7.50–£8 dB&B£15–£16
Wine£2.50

LIMPLEY STOKE (nr Bath) Wiltshire Map3 ST76
★★★Cliffe (Best Western) ☎3226
Converted two-storey country residence, in three acres of wooded grounds with views of Avon valley.
Closed 22–28Dec; 10rm(8⇌) CTV in bedrooms 30P (heated) English & French.
last dinner8.30pm S%
sB&B£11.50–£12.50 sB&B⇌ £12.50–£30
dB&B£25–£28.50 dB&B⇌ £31.50–£38
Continental breakfast Lunch£4.95–£5.95&alc
Tea£2.50 Dinner£6.50–£7.50&alc Wine£3.50
Credit cards 1 2 3 5 6

✕✕Danielle ☎3150
A detached riverside building nestling low in the Avon Valley near to the famous Box Railway Tunnel.
Closed Mon (except Public Hols); Lunch not served Tue–Sat; Dinner not served Sun; 34seats 12P
French. Last dinner10.30pm
Lunch£6.50–£7&alc Dinner£8.50–£9.50&alc
Wine£2.15 Credit cards 1 2 3 5

LINCOLN Lincolnshire Map8 SK97
★★★★White Hart Bailgate (Prestige) ☎26222
Telex no56304
Early Georgian (1720) house with late-Victorian façade. Stands in shadow of Lincoln Cathedral.
62rm(53⇌) Lift CTV CTV in bedrooms 18P 40
Last dinner9.45pm S% sB&B£16.75
sB&B⇌ £19.25 dB&B£23.75 dB&B⇌ £35.25
Lunch£3.95&alc Tea£1 Dinner£4.50&alc
Wine£3.25 Credit cards 1 2 3 4 5 6

★★★Eastgate Eastgate (Trusthouse Forte) ☎20341
Telex no56316
Three-storey modern building and wing of Victorian mansion in own grounds, overlooking Lincoln Cathedral. Remains of North Tower of Roman eastgate in forecourt.
71⇌ Lift CTV in bedrooms 110P
Last dinner9.45pm S% sB&B⇌ £21.50
dB&B⇌ £30.50 xmas
Credit cards 1 2 3 4 5 6

★★Grand St Mary's Street ☎24211
51rm(31⇌) CTV 40P Last dinner10pm
S% sB&B£11 sB&B⇌ £13.50 dB&B£20
dB&B⇌ £23 Lunch£3&alc Tea£1&alc
High Tea£2&alc Dinner£3.50&alc Wine£2.50
Credit cards 1 3 5

At **Dunholme** (6m NE A46)
☆☆Four Seasons Scothern Ln ☎Welton60108
12⇌ 150P

LINFORD, GREAT Buckinghamshire Map**4** SP83
XXLinford Lodge Wood Ln
☎Newport Pagnell610971
Closed Sun; Lunch not served Sat; 65seats 30P
English & Continental. Lastdinner9.30pm S%
✻Lunch£6.50alc Dinner£6.50alc Wine£3.20
Creditcards 1 2 3 5

LINGFIELD Surrey Map**5** TQ34
XXRed Barn Inn Tandridge Ln (off B2029 1½m NW)
☎834272
52seats 290P Disco Sun Live music & dancing Sat
English, French & Italian. Lastdinner9.45pm
Lunch fr£3.75&alc Dinner£9alc Wine£3.50
Creditcards 2 3 5

LISKEARD Cornwall Map**2** SX26
★★Lord Eliot Castle St ☎42717
16rm(1⇌fl) CTV CTV available in bedroom 45P Live music & dancing Sat Lastdinner8.45pm
✻sB&B£9 dB&B£15 dB&B⇌fl£17.50
Lunch£1–£3 Tea40p–£1 High Tea75p–£3
Dinner£3.75 Wine£2.35

★★Webbs The Parade ☎43675
Pleasant Georgian-style hotel within this charter town.
16rm(10☎fl) 1 CTV 16P Lastdinner8.45pm

LITTLEBOROUGH Greater Manchester Map**7** SD91
★★*Dearnley Cottage* New Road, Dearnley ☎79670
9⇌fl CTV TV available in bedrooms 30P Live music & dancing 3nights wkly Cabaret 3nights wkly
English, French & Italian. Lastdinner10pm
Creditcards 1 2 3

★Sun Featherstall Rd ☎78957
8rm CTV 6P Lastdinner9.30pm S%
✻sB&B£7 dB&B£11–£12 Barlunch35p–£1.50
Dinner£3–£5 Wine£1.85

LITTLEHAMPTON West Sussex Map**4** TQ00
★★★Beach ☎7277
Three-storey rambling building with gables and rustic balconies; in walled garden of 1½ acres, 150yds from the beach.
35rm(20☎fl) CTV TV available in bedrooms 70P International. Lastdinner9.30pm
sB&B£7.50–£12.50 sB&B⇌fl£9.70–£13.90
dB&B£16.50–£22.70 dB&B⇌fl£18.50–£27.50
Lunch fr£2.50 Tea fr£1.50 High Tea fr£2.50
Dinner fr£4.90&alc Wine£2.50 *xmas*
Creditcard 5

★★Stetson St Catherines Rd ☎6081
Victorian building overlooking pleasant green between beach and town.
16rm(3⇌fl) CTV TV available in bedrooms 9P French. Lastdinner9pm
sB&B£9.50–£12.50 sB&B⇌fl£10.50–£15.50
dB&B£15–£20 dB&B⇌fl£16–£22.50
Lunch£2.50–£4.50 Tea45p Dinner£3.50–£6.50
Wine£3 Creditcards 1 3 5

LITTLE WEIGHTON Humberside Map**8** SE93
★★★Rowley Manor Rowley ☎Hull848248
15rm(13⇌fl) 2 CTV in bedrooms 100P English & French. lastdinner9.30pm
sB&B£12.50 sB&B⇌fl£13.50–£17.50
dB&B£19 dB&B⇌fl£23–£26
Lunch£4.25–£5.25 Dinner£5.50–£7.95
Wine£3.25 Creditcards 1 2 3 5

L

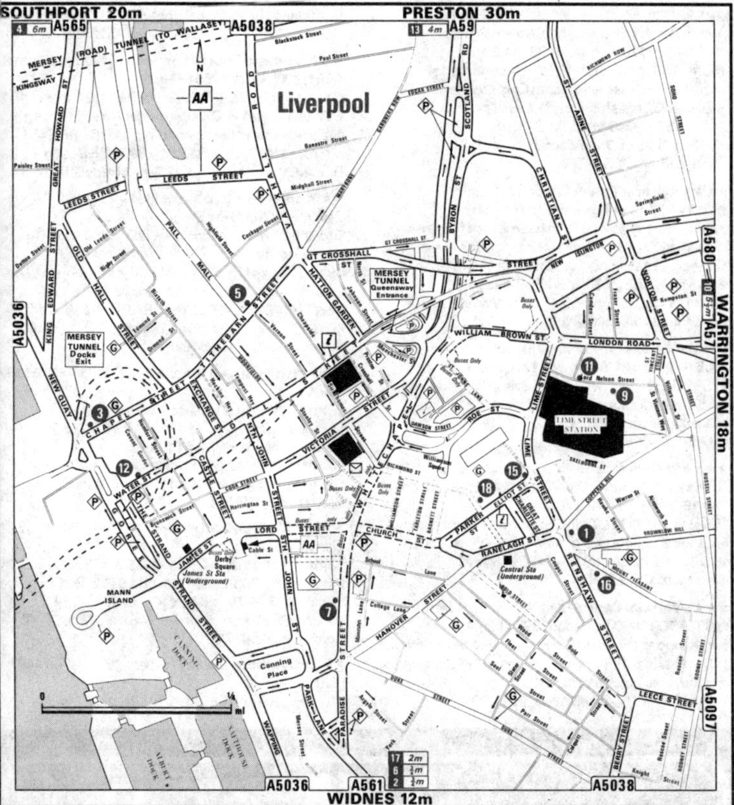

1 Adelphi ★★★★
2 Alexandria Court ★★
3 Atlantic Tower ★★★★
4 Blundellsands ★★★ *(see under Blundellsands)*
5 Bradford ★★
6 Green Park ★★
7 Holiday Inn ☆☆☆☆
9 Liverpool Centre ★★★
10 Liverpool Crest Motel ☆☆☆ *(see under Knowsley)*
11 Lord Nelson ★★
12 Oriel ❀XXX
13 Park ★★★ *(see under Netherton)*
15 St George's ★★★★
16 Shaftesbury ★★
17 Solna ★
18 Tower XXX

LIVERPOOL Merseyside Map**7** SJ39 **See plan**

★★★★**Adelphi** Ranelagh Pl (British Transport) ☎051-7097200 Telex no629644 Plan**1**
168rm(148⇌⋒) Lift ☽ TV in bedrooms 15P (heated) squash sauna bath Conference facilities available English & French. Last dinner10.30pm S% *sB&B⇌⋒ fr£23.70 dB&B⇌⋒ fr£31.05 Wine£3.50 Credit cards 1 2 3 4 5 6

★★★★**Atlantic Tower** Chapel St (Thistle) ☎051-2274444 Telex no627070 Plan**3**
226⇌⋒ Lift ☽ ▦ CTV in bedrooms Live music & dancing Thu-Sat Conference facilities available French. Last dinner10.30pm S% *sB&B⇌⋒ fr£25.30 dB&B⇌⋒ fr£37.60 Lunch fr£3.80 Dinner£5.40&alc Wine£3.15 Credit cards 1 2 3 4 5 6

☆☆☆☆***Holiday Inn*** Paradise St (Commonwealth) ☎051-7090181 Telex no627270 Plan**7**
273⇌⋒ Lift ☽ ▦ CTV available in bedrooms 20P (heated) sauna bath Conference facilities available last dinner10pm Credit cards 1 2 3 4 5 6

★★★★**St George's** St John's Precinct, Lime St (Trusthouse Forte) ☎051-7097090 Telex no627630 Plan**15**
155⇌⋒ Lift ☽ CTV in bedrooms Conference facilities available Last dinner10pm S% sB&B⇌⋒£22.50 dB&B⇌⋒£31.50 Credit cards 1 2 3 4 5 6

★★★**Liverpool Centre** Lord Nelson St (Centre) ☎051-7097050 Telex no627954 Plan**9**
Large modern hotel overlooking Lime Street Station.
170⇌⋒ Lift ☽ TV in bedrooms ⊘ 35P Conference facilities available Last dinner9.45pm S% *sB&B⇌⋒£13.75 dB&B⇌⋒£17.25 Continental breakfast Lunch£3.95 Dinner£3.95 Wine£3.40 Credit cards 1 2 3 4 5 6

★★**Alexandra Court** Alexandra Dr, Aigburth (2½m S [illegible] A561) ☎051-7272551 Plan**2**
Closed Public Hols; RS wknds (B&B); 24rm(8⇌⋒) CTV ⊘ 17P 3⌂ Children under 6yrs not accommodated Last dinner8pm *sB&B£9.45 sB&B⇌⋒£13.01 dB&B£15.33 dB&B⇌⋒£18.89 Dinner£4.16 Wine£3.50 Credit cards 1 2 3

★★**Bradford** Tithebarn St ☎051-2368782 Telex no627657 Plan**5**
Stone built hotel, dating back about 200 years, in centre of city.
49rm(23⇌⋒) Lift ☽ CTV CTV in bedrooms 12⌂ Last dinner8.30pm S% sB&B£9.50 sB&B⇌⋒£13 dB&B£15 dB&B⇌⋒£19 Lunch£3 Tea£1.25 High Tea fr£1.25 Dinner£4 Wine£2.60 Credit cards 2 3

★★**Green Park** 4-6 Greenbank Dr ☎051-7333382 Plan**6**
23rm ☽ CTV CTV in bedrooms 20P Last dinner9pm S% sB&B fr£7.50 sB&B⇌⋒ fr£8 dB&B fr£11.50 dbB&B⇌⋒ fr£12.50 Lunch£2alc Tea£1.25alc High Tea£1.50alc Dinner£2.75alc Wine£2 Credit cards 1 4 5 6

★★**Lord Nelson** Lord Nelson St ☎051-7094362 Plan**11**
63rm(12⇌⋒) Lift ☽ CTV ⊘ 16⌂ Last dinner9.30pm sB&B£12.75 sB&B⇌⋒£14.75 dB&B£18 dB&B⇌⋒£21 Lunch fr£3.50&alc Dinner fr£4&alc Wine£4 Credit cards 1 2 3 5

★★**Shaftesbury** Mount Pleasant ☎051-7094421 Plan**16**
RS Public Hols; 73rm(13⇌⋒) Lift ☽ CTV ⊘

English & French. Lastdinner9.15pm
% ✻sB&B£11.20 sB&B⇌⫪£12.70
B&B£16.50 dB&B⇌⫪£18 Lunch£3.25&alc
ea75p&alc HighTea£2&alc Dinner£4.10&alc
ine£4.30 Creditcards 1 2 3 5 6

Solna Ullet Rd, Sefton Park ☎051-733 1943
an**17**
osed Xmas; 22rm(1⇌⫪) TV in bedrooms 50P
Discowkly Lastdinner9.30pm
B&B£10-£12 sB&B⇌⫪fr£11 dB&B£18-£20
B&B⇌⫪£20-£22 Lunch£2.50-£3.50
nner£4-£4.50&alc Wine£3.60
redit cards 1 3 5 6

XXXOriel Water St ☎051-236 4664 Plan**12**
osed Sun & last 3wks Aug; Lunch not served Sat;
0seats 5P French. Lastdinner10.15pm
redit cards 1 2 3 5 6

XXTower St John's Precinct, Lime St
051-709 8895 Plan**17**
0seats French. Lastdinner10.30pm S%
unch£5.55&alc Dinner£6.55alc Wine£4.85

Knowsley (5m E off A580)
☆☆***Liverpool Crest Motel*** East Lancs Rd (Crest)
051-546 7531 Plan**10**
0⇌⫪ 100P

ZARD Cornwall Map**2** SW71
★Housel Bay Sea Front ☎417
7rm(10⇌⫪) CTV TV available in bedrooms
0P 5 Children under 11yrs not
ccommodated Lastdinner8.30pm S%
B&B£9.07-£10.43 dB&B£18.14-£20.86
B&B⇌⫪£23.59-£34.21 Lunch£3.50-£4
Tea50p-£1 Dinner£5.95-£6.50 Wine£3.24
Creditcard 1

★★Lizard ☎456
17th-C country inn with 19th-C additions in centre of village.
Closed Nov-Mar; 10rm CTV 20P 4 Live music & dancing wkly Lastdinner8pm S%
sB&B£6.50-£8 dB&B£13-£16 Lunch£2.50-£3
Dinner£3.25-£4 Wine£2

★★Polbrean ☎418
Closed Nov-Mar; 12rm(4⇌⫪) CTV TV available in bedrooms 20P 3 English & Italian.
Lastdinner8.30pm S% sB&B£7.42
dB&B£14.84 dB&B⇌⫪£16.63 Dinner£3.56
Wine£2.70

LOCKING Avon Map**3** ST35
XX*Coach House Inn* ☎Banwell822506
Closed Mon; Dinner not served Sun; 50seats 200P
English & French. Lastdinner10pm Creditcard 5

LOFTUS Cleveland Map**8** NZ71
★★★Grinkle Park ☎40515
20⇌⫪ CTV CTV in bedrooms 100P
Lastdinner8.30pm S%
✻sB&B⇌⫪£15-£18.95 dB&B⇌⫪£20.90-£24
Lunch fr£3.05 Tea36-91p Dinner fr£4.20
Wine£2.39 Creditcards 1 3

LOGGERHEADS Staffordshire Map**7** SJ73
XEl Catalán Newcastle Rd ☎Ashley2319
Closed Sun (except Jun, Jul & Aug) & Mon; 60seats
20P Spanish. Lastdinner11pm S%
Lunch£2.25&alc Dinner£5alc Wine£2.50
Creditcards 1 3 5 6

L

LONDON

Alphabetical list of London hotels and restaurants

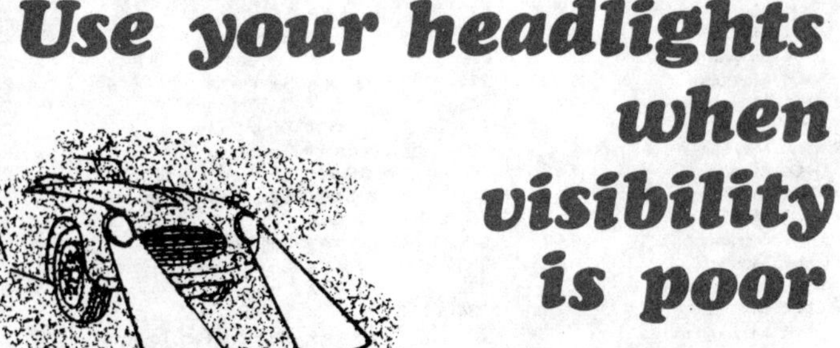
Use your headlights
when
visibility
is poor

ONDON Greater London Atlas Map**4**&**5**. For detailed maps of the central London area see pages 256–265.
Places within the London postal area are listed below. Other places within the county of London are listed under their respective place names.
A map of the London postal area appears on pages 266 & 267.
Hotels and restaurants in Central London are listed in postal district order commencing East then North, South and West, with a brief indication of the area covered. Establishments are indicated by number on the plans on pages 256–265.
A grid reference, eg (F1), is given after the number to help you find the location.
If more detailed information is required the *AA Motorists Map of London*, on sale at AA offices, is in two parts: the 'West End and the City' shows one-way systems, banned turns, car parks, stations, hotels, places of interest, etc; 'Outer London' gives primary routes, car parks at suburban stations, etc. A theatre map of the West End is included.
For London Airports see entry following:–

E1 Stepney *and east of the Tower of London*
★★★★Tower St Katharine's Way (EMI)
☎01–481 2575 Telex no 885934 Not on plan
826⇌⫼ Lift ☽ ▦ ᛗ CTV in bedrooms ⊘ 15P 90⌂
Conference facilities available ♀International.
Last dinner 11pm ✿ ☐ S% ✱sB&B⇌⫼£35
dB&B⇌⫼£45 Continental breakfast
Lunch £5.90&alc Tea £1alc Dinner £5.90&alc
Wine £3.50 ⊟ *xmas* Credit cards ① ② ③ ④ ⑤ ⑥

✕*Blooms* 90 Whitechapel High St ☎01–247 6001
Not on plan
Closed Sat; Dinner not served Fri; Unlicensed;
150seats 80P ♀Kosher.

E14 Poplar
✕*Good Friends* 139 Salmon Ln ☎01–987 5541 Not on plan
70seats ♀Cantonese. Last dinner mdnt

EC1 Clerkenwell, Farringdon
☆☆☆***Central City*** Central St ☎01–251 1565
Telex no 25181 Not on plan
RS Nov–Mar; 456rm(416⇌⫼) Lift ☽ ᛗ TV 15P 50⌂
Live music Thu–Sat Conference facilities available
Last dinner 10.30pm ✿ ☐
Credit cards ① ② ③ ⑤ ⑥

❀✕Bubb's 329 Central Markets ☎01–236 2435
Plan6: **2** A3
Closed Sat, Sun & Aug; 38seats **P** ♀French.
Last dinner 9.30pm ✱Lunch £9alc Dinner £9alc
Wine £2.80 Credit cards ① ③ ⑤

EC2 City of London; *Bank of England, Liverpool Street Station*
★★★Great Eastern Liverpool St (British Transport)
☎01–283 4363 Telex no 886812 Plan6: **8** A6
Victorian building designed by Barry; in heart of city.
156rm(125⇌⫼) Lift ☽ ᛗ TV in bedrooms 35P
Conference facilities available ♀English & French.
Last dinner 9pm ✿ ☐ S% ✱sB&B⇌⫼fr £31
dB&B⇌⫼fr £40 Wine £3.50 ⊟
Credit cards ① ② ③ ④ ⑤ ⑥

✕✕✕Baron of Beef Gutter Ln, Gresham St
☎01–606 6961 Plan6: **1** B4
Elegant city restaurant with traditional masculine mahogany and plush décor.
Closed Sat, Sun & Public Hols; 70seats **P**
Last dinner 10pm ✱Lunch £10alc Dinner £10alc
Wine £3.65 Credit cards ① ② ③ ④ ⑤ ⑥

❀❀✕✕✕Le Poulbot 45 Cheapside
☎01–236 4379 Plan6: **9** B4
An oasis of gastronomy in the City, this fine restaurant is owned by the Roux brothers and ably managed by their charmingly-attentive M Jean Cottard.
High-back booths provide a fair degree of privacy for confidential business talks – although it would be a pity to divert attention from the food. As befits a largely-masculine clientèle, the food is more robust than that at the Waterside at Bray or Le Gavroche in Chelsea under the same ownership; nevertheless the cooking shows real skill.
Specialities include pâté de Coquille St Jacques (this dish is particularly applauded); casserolettes d'escargots; and petits pâtés Poulbot – delicious when still warm from the oven. Among the main courses high praise has been given to the maigre de canard salardaise, poussin françoise, turbot St Germain, and filets de sole Léonora. An interesting dish for those who want to have the real taste of chicken is poulet de Bresse, specially imported from France.
The selection of puddings is not large but the fruit tarts and sorbets are always good; and, as there should be in an authentically French restaurant, a selection of French cheeses in immaculate condition is always available.
This is a busy restaurant with efficient but unobtrusive service. Jean Cottard – who seems to be everywhere – somehow always manages to find time to speak to all his customers.
Closed wknds & Public Hols; Dinner not served
55seats **P** ♀French. Last lunch 3pm
Lunch £20alc Credit cards ② ⑤

✕*Le Marmiton* 4 Blomfield St ☎01–588 4643 Not on plan
Closed Xmas, New Year & Public Hols; Dinner not served; 85seats ♀French.

EC3 City of London; *Monument, Tower of London*
✕✕✕*Viceroy* Colonial House, Mark Ln
☎01–626 2271 Plan6: **11** C6
Closed Sat, Sun & Public Hols; Dinner not served;
65seats ♀French. Credit cards ① ② ③ ⑤

✕✕✕*Wheelton Room* 62 Crutched Friars
☎01–709 9622 Not on plan
Closed Sat & Sun; Dinner not served; 120seats
♀English & Continental. Credit cards ① ② ③ ⑤ ⑥

EC4 City of London; *Blackfriars, Cannon Street and Fleet Street*
✕✕✕*Cotillion* Bucklersbury House, Cannon St,
Walbrook ☎01–248 4735 Plan6: **5** C3
Closed Sat, Sun & Public Hols; Dinner not served;
100seats ♀English & French. Last lunch 3pm
Credit cards ① ② ③

✕Le Gamin 32 Old Bailey ☎01–236 7931 Not on plan
Closed wknds & Public Hols; Dinner not served;
130seats **P** ♀French. Last lunch 3.30pm
Lunch £6alc Credit cards ① ② ③ ⑤

✕Ginnan 5 Cathedral Pl ☎01–236 4120 Plan6: **7** B4
Closed Sat, Sun, Public Hols, 2&3 Jan; 70seats **P**
♀Japanese. Last dinner 10pm
✱Lunch £2.60–£6.90&alc
Dinner £6.90–£8.25&alc Credit cards ① ② ③ ⑤

N1 Islington
❀✕✕✕Carriers 2 Camden Passage ☎01–226 5353
Not on plan
Double-fronted shop in quaint passage with modern-style restaurant on three floors. Owned by journalist Robert Carrier.
Closed Sun, Public Hols incl Etr Sat; 82seats **P**
♀International. Specialities: Saffron soup with fresh herbs, sauté d'agneau aux flageolets, amaretti soufflé glace. Last dinner 11.30pm
✱Lunch £10.27–£11.88 Dinner £11.88–£13.50
Wine £4.40 Credit card ②

✕✕Frederick's Camden Passage ☎01–359 2888 Not on plan
Closed Sun, Xmas & New Year's Day; 150seats ₱ ♡International. Last dinner 11.30pm S% Lunch£7.90alc Dinner£7.90alc Wine£2.48 Credit cards 1 2 3 4 5 6

✕M'Sieur Frog 31A Essex Rd ☎01–226 3495 Not on plan
Closed Sun, Public Hols & Aug; 50seats ₱ ♡French. Last dinner 11.15pm Dinner£9alc Wine£2.85

✕Portofino 39 Camden Passage ☎01–226 0884 Not on plan
Simple bottle-hung Italian restaurant.
Closed Sun & Public Hols; 56seats ₱ ♡English, French & Italian. Last dinner 11.30pm ✱Lunch£9alc Dinner£9alc Wine£2.55 Credit cards 1 2 3 5

N6 Highgate
✕✕*San Carlo* 2 High St ☎01–340 5823 Not on plan
Closed Mon; 120seats ♡Italian. Last dinner 11.30pm Credit cards 1 2 3 5 6

NW1 Regents Park; *Baker Street, Euston and Kings Cross Stations*
★★★Great Northern (British Transport) ☎01–837 5454 Telex no 299041 Not on plan
66rm(40⇌⋒) Lift ☽ ₩ CTV TV in bedrooms 10P ♡English & French. Last dinner 8.45pm ♁ ♖ S% ✱sB&B⇌⋒ fr£22.65 dB&B⇌⋒ fr£35.15 Wine£3.15 ₱ Credit cards 1 2 3 4 5 6

★★★Kennedy Cardington St (Grand Met) ☎01–387 4400 Telex no 28250 Not on plan
280⇌⋒ Lift ☽ ₩ CTV in bedrooms ⊘ ₱ Last dinner 11pm ♁ ♖ S% ✱sB⇌⋒£15.75–£19.25 (room only) dB⇌⋒£23.25–£28.25 (room only) ₱ Credit cards 1 2 3 4 5 6

❀★★★White House Albany St (Rank) ☎01–387 1200 Telex no 24111 Plan 1: **80** A2
587⇌⋒ Lift ☽ ₩ CTV in bedrooms ₱ Conference facilities available ♡French. Last dinner 11.30pm ♁ ♖ S% ✱sB&B⇌⋒£20.60–£23.60 dB&B⇌⋒£31.60–£36.60 Continental breakfast Lunch£8.50alc Dinner£8.50alc Wine£4 ₱ Credit cards 1 2 3 4 5 6

❀✕✕✕White House Hotel Restaurant Albany St ☎01–387 1200 Plan 1: **80** A2
Popular businessman's restaurant with striking canopied entrance.
Closed Sun; Lunch not served Sat; 110seats ₱ bedrooms available ♡French. Last dinner 11.30pm S% ✱Lunch£8.50alc Dinner£8.50alc Wine£4.25 Credit cards 1 2 3 4 5 6

✕Barque & Bite opp 15 Prince Albert Rd ☎01–485 8137 Not on plan
Closed Sun, Public Hols; Lunch not served Sat; 80seats ₱ ♡International. Last dinner 11.30pm S% ✱Lunch fr£5.40 Dinner fr£6.48 Wine£3.25 Credit cards 1 2 3 4 5 6

✕*Froops* 17 Princess Rd ☎01–722 9663 Not on plan
Closed Sun; Lunch not served; 44seats 10P ♡International. Last dinner 11.30pm Credit cards 2 3 5

NW3 Hampstead *and Swiss Cottage*
☆☆☆☆Holiday Inn 128 King Henry's Rd (Commonwealth) ☎01–722 7711 Telex no 267396 Not on plan
297⇌⋒ Lift ☽ ▦ ₩ CTV in bedrooms 100P 60⌂ ⊕ ⚓ ▭(heated) sauna bath Conference facilities available Open 24hours ♁ ♖ S% ✱sB&B⇌⋒ fr£33.50 dB&B⇌⋒ fr£43.50 Lunch fr£4.50 Dinner fr£6.50 Wine£3.75 ₱ *xmas* Credit cards 1 2 3 4 5

★★★Charles Bernard 5 Frognal ☎01–794 0101 Telex no 23560 Not on plan
57⇌⋒ Lift ☽ ₩ CTV CTV in bedrooms ⊘ 20P ⊕ ♡English & French. Last dinner 9pm S% sB&B⇌⋒£19.44–£21.60 dB&B£27–£29.70 Lunch£3.50–£5.50 Dinner£3.50–£5.50 Wine£2.70 ₱ Credit cards 1 2 3 4 5 6

☆☆☆Post House 217–221 Haverstock Hill (Trusthouse Forte) ☎01–794 8121 Telex no 262494 Not on plan
140⇌⋒ Lift ☽ ₩ CTV in bedrooms 70P Last dinner 10pm ♁ ♖ S% sB&B⇌⋒£21.25 dB&B⇌⋒£31 ₱ *xmas* Credit cards 1 2 3 4 5 6

★★★Swiss Cottage Adamson Rd ☎01–722 2281 Telex no 27950 Not on plan
64⇌⋒ Lift ☽ ₩ TV in bedrooms ⊘ 4P ⊕ sauna bath ♡English & Continental. Last dinner 8.45pm ♁ ♖ S% sB&B⇌⋒£16–£25 dB&B⇌⋒£24–£32 Lunch fr£2.50&alc Dinner fr£3.80 Credit cards 1 2 3 5 6

❀✕✕Keats 3 Downshire Hill ☎01–435 3544 Not on plan
Simple, intimate French restaurant with elegant décor.
Closed Sun, Public Hols & 3wks Aug; Lunch not served; 50seats ₱ ♡French. Specialities: Châteaubriand garni Keat, carre d'agneau, crépes de saumon fumé ciboulette. Last dinner 11.30pm ✱Dinner£12alc Wine£4.90 Credit cards 1 2 3 5

✕*Gullistan Tandoori* 73 Heath St ☎01–435 3413 Not on plan
36seats ✗ ♡Indian. Last dinner 11pm Credit cards 1 2 5

NW4 Hendon
★★★Hendon Hall Ashley Ln (Kingsmead) ☎01–203 3341 Not on plan
52rm(50⇌⋒) Lift ☽ ₩ CTV in bedrooms 80P ⚓ ♡English & French. Last dinner 10.30pm ♁ ♖ S% sB&B£17.50 sB&B⇌⋒£21 dB&B⇌⋒£27.50 Lunch fr£4.20&alc Dinner fr£4.20&alc Wine£3.25 ₱ Credit cards 1 2 3 4 5 6

NW6 Kilburn
✕Peter's Bistro 65 Fairfax Rd ☎01–624 5804 Not on plan
Closed 25&26Dec; Lunch not served Sat 44seats ₱ ♡French. Last dinner 11.30pm Lunch fr£2.25&alc Dinner£8alc Credit cards 3 5

✕Vijay 49 Willesden Ln ☎01–328 1087 Not on plan
Closed Xmas; 45seats ₱ ♡South Indian. Last dinner 10.30pm ✱Lunch£3alc Dinner£4alc Wine£2.90

NW7 Mill Hill
☆☆☆TraveLodge M1 Scratchwood Service Area (Access from motorway only) (Trusthouse Forte) ☎01–906 0611 Not on plan
Restaurant facilities in adjacent service area (mainly grills).
100⇌⋒ ₩ CTV in bedrooms 120P ♿ S% sB&B⇌⋒£14 dB&B⇌⋒£20 Continental breakfast ₱ Credit cards 1 2 3 4 5 6

✕*Kwan Yin* 143 Broadway ☎01–959 7011 Not on plan
Closed Good Friday & Xmas; 120seats 10P ♡Chinese. Last dinner 11.30pm Credit cards 1 2 3 4 5 6

NW8 St John's Wood
☆☆☆*Ladbroke Westmoreland* 18 Lodge Rd (Ladbroke) ☎01–722 7722 Telex no 23101 Not on plan
An ultra-modern hotel, with views of Regents Park

nd of Lord's Cricket ground.
46⇌ 🛁 Lift ☽ TV in bedrooms ⊘ 65P
Last dinner 10pm ♆ ♇

XXLords Rendezvous 24 Finchley Rd
☎01–722 4750 Not on plan
24seats 10P ♉Chinese. Credit cards 1 2 5 6

XXOslo Court Prince Albert Rd ☎01–722 8795 Not on plan
Closed Sun, Mon, 25–30Dec, 2wks Etr, last 2wks Aug & 1st wk Sep; Lunch not served Sat; 70seats ♭ ♉International. Last dinner 10.30pm
Lunch£9.50alc Dinner£9.50alc Wine£4

XXRosetti 23 Queens Gv ☎01–722 7141 Not on plan
50seats 30P ♉Italian. Last dinner 11.30pm
Lunch£8alc Dinner£10alc Wine£3
Credit cards 1 2 3 5 6

NW10 Harlesden, Willesden
X*Kuo Yuan* 217 High Rd, Willesden ☎01–459 2297
Not on plan
Closed Xmas; Lunch not served Mon–Fri; 80seats ♉Chinese. Last dinner 11pm

NW11 Golders Green
XXLuigi's 1–4 Belmont Pde, Finchley Rd
☎01–455 0210 Not on plan
Closed Mon; 90seats ♭ ♉Italian. Last dinner 11pm
S% ✱Lunch£2.70&alc Dinner£7.50alc
Credit cards 1 2 3 5

✿XL'Aubergade 816 Finchley Rd ☎01–455 8853
Not on plan
Closed Sun; 38seats ♭ ♉French.
Last dinner 11.30pm S% Lunch fr£4.50&alc
Dinner fr£4.50&alc Wine£2.80 Credit cards 1 3 6

X*Tung Hsing* 22 North End Rd ☎01–455 5990 Not on plan
100seats ♉Pekinese. Last dinner 11.30pm
Credit card 5

SE1 Southwark
X*South of the Border* Joan St ☎01–928 6374 Not on plan
Closed Sun; 60seats ♉French.

SE6 Catford
XCasa Comineti 129 Rushey Green ☎01–697 2314
Not on plan
Bright, street-level restaurant with comic French drawings on walls. Patronised by the famous since 1916.
Dinner not served Sun; 50seats ♭ ♉Continental.
Last dinner 9pm Lunch£8alc Dinner£8alc
Wine£3.70 Credit cards 1 2 3 4 5 6

SE11 Kennington
★★London Park Brook Dr, Elephant & Castle
☎01–735 9191 Telex no 919161 Not on plan
388rm(251⇌ 🛁) Lift ☽ 🍴 CTV TV available in bedrooms 16P Last dinner 8.45pm ♆ ♇ S%
✱sB&B£8 sB&B⇌ 🛁£9 dB&B£13.50
dB&B⇌ 🛁£15.20 Lunch£3.75&alc
Dinner£4.25&alc Wine£2.40 Credit cards 1 2 3 5

XX*Crispins* 7 Windmill Row ☎01–735 5455 Not on plan
A Victorian-style restaurant in basement, with ground-floor bar.
Closed Public Hols; 70seats ♉English & French.
Last dinner 11.30pm

SE13 Lewisham
XXCurry Centre 37 Lee High Rd ☎01–852 6544
Not on plan
60seats ♭ ♉Indian. Last dinner mdnt
✱Lunch£2.50–£5 Dinner£4–£8 Wine£2.90
Credit cards 1 3

SE22 East Dulwich
✿XChez Nico 148 Lordship Ln ☎01–693 8266 Not on plan
Closed Sun & Mon; Lunch not served; 40seats ♭ ♉French. Specialities: coq au vin jaune, poussin a l'eau de vie, mousse glacée. Last dinner 10pm
Dinner£6.70–£9 Wine£3.50

SW1 Westminster; *St James's Park, Victoria Station*
✿★★★★★ Berkeley Wilton Pl, Knightsbridge
☎01–235 6000 Telex no 919252 Plan5: **2** B2
See page 44 for details

✿★★★★★Carlton Tower Cadogan Pl
☎01–235 5411 Plan4: **15** C6
Tower building rising to eighteen storeys, with balconies above gardens of Cadogan Place.
244⇌ 🛁 Lift ☽ ▦ 🍴 CTV in bedrooms ⊘ 40🏠 ⛟ ⚓ Conference facilities available ♉English & French.
Open 24hours ♆ ♇ S%
✱sB&B⇌ 🛁£63.13–£69.65
dB&B⇌ 🛁£73.93–£80.45 Continental breakfast
Lunch£5alc Tea£4alc Dinner£5alc Wine£5.75
🅁 *xmas* Credit cards 1 2 3 4 5 6

★★★★★Hyde Park Knightsbridge (Trusthouse Forte) ☎01–235 2000 Telex no 262057 Plan4: **37** B5
Imposing brick and stone building with turrets, balconies, wrought iron-work and massive pillared porticos.
201⇌ 🛁 Lift ☽ 🍴 CTV in bedrooms ♭ ⛟ Conference facilities available ♿ Last dinner 10.30pm ♆ ♇
S% sB&B⇌ 🛁£51 dB&B⇌ 🛁£73
Credit cards 1 2 3 4 5 6

★★★★★**Sheraton Park Tower** 101 Knightsbridge ☎01–235 8050 Telex no 917222 Plan4: **71** B6
295⇌⋒ Lift ☽ ⊞ ⋈ CTV in bedrooms ⊘ ℙ Live music & dancing Tue–Sun Conference facilities available ♉French. Last dinner mdnt ♁ ♖ S% sB&B⇌⋒£74 dB&B⇌⋒£83 Lunch£5.50&alc Tea fr£2 Dinner£15alc Wine£5.50 ⊓ *xmas*
Credit cards 1 2 3 4 5 6

★★★★**Goring** Beeston Pl, Grosvenor Gdns ☎01–834 8211 Telex no 919166 Plan5: **9** C3
See page 47 for details

★★★★**Cavendish** Jermyn St (Trusthouse Forte) ☎01–930 2111 Telex no 263187 Plan1: **10** E3
255⇌⋒ Lift ☽ ⋈ CTV in bedrooms 10P 80⌂ Conference facilities available ♿ Open 24hours ♁ ♖ S% sB&B⇌⋒£41 dB&B⇌⋒£53 Continental breakfast ⊓ *xmas*
Credit cards 1 2 3 4 5 6

★★★★**Duke's** St James' Pl (Prestige) ☎01–491 3090 Telex no 28283 Plan5: **4** A4
Gracious building with brick-and-stone façade situated in quiet courtyard off St James's Park. Regency-style interior features prints of London Cries.
52⇌⋒ Lift ☽ ⋈ TV in bedrooms Guide dogs only ℙ ⊕ ♉French. Last dinner 10pm ♁ ♖ S% sB&B⇌⋒£38.50 dB&B⇌⋒£62 Lunch£8.50&alc Dinner£10.50alc Wine£6.50
Credit cards 1 2 3 4 5 6

☆☆☆☆**Holiday Inn Chelsea** Sloane St (Commonwealth) ☎01–235 4377 Telex no 919111 Not on plan
217⇌⋒ Lift ☽ ⊞ ⋈ CTV in bedrooms ⊡(heated) Live music & dancing Mon–Sat Conference facilities available ♉French. Last dinner 11pm ♁ ♖ S% ✱sB&B⇌⋒ fr£46.25 dB&B⇌⋒ fr£56.50 Continental breakfast Lunch fr£4.50 Tea fr£2.50 Dinner£6.50alc Wine£3.75 ⊓ *xmas*
Credit cards 1 2 3 4 5 6

★★★★**Ladbroke Belgravia** 20 Chesham Pl (Ladbroke) ☎01–235 6040 Plan5: **14** C2
110⇌⋒ Lift ☽ ⊞ CTV in bedrooms ℙ ⊕ ♉International. Last dinner 11pm ♁ ♖ S% sB&B⇌⋒£45.14–£48.59 dB&B⇌⋒£59.23–£62.68 Continental breakfast Lunch£6.61–£8.63 Tea£2.36 Dinner£8alc Wine£4.60 ⊓ Credit cards 1 2 3 5 6

★★★★**Quaglino's** Bury St, St James's (Trusthouse Forte) ☎01–930 6767 Plan1: **56** E3
41⇌⋒ Lift ☽ ⋈ CTV in bedrooms 37P ⊕ Live music & dancing 6 nights wkly Cabaret 6 nights wkly Conference facilities available ♿ Last dinner 11pm ♁ ♖ S% sB&B⇌⋒£41 dB&B⇌⋒£55 ⊓ *xmas* Credit cards 1 2 3 4 5 6

☆☆☆☆**Royal Westminster** 49 Buckingham Palace Rd (EMI) ☎01–834 1821 Telex no 916821 Plan5: **21** C3
136⇌⋒ Lift ☽ ⋈ CTV in bedrooms ⊘ ℙ Conference facilities available ♉International. Last dinner 10pm ♁ ♖ S% ✱sB&B⇌⋒£37 dB&B⇌⋒£49 Continental breakfast Lunch£5–£10alc Tea50p Dinner£5–£10alc Wine£3.60 ⊓
Credit cards 1 2 3 4 5 6

★★★★**St Ermins** Caxton St (Grand Met) ☎01–222 7888 Telex no 917731 Not on plan
235⇌⋒ Lift ☽ ⋈ CTV in bedrooms ⊘ 20P Conference facilities available Last dinner 10.30pm ♁ ♖ S% ✱sB⇌⋒£20–£25 (room only) dB⇌⋒£29–£36 (room only) ⊓
Credit cards 1 2 3 4 5 6

★★★**Lowndes** 19 Lowndes St (Thistle) ☎01–235 6020 Telex no 919065 Plan5: **15** C1
See page 48 for details

★★★**Eccleston** Eccleston Sq (Norfolk Capital) ☎01–834 8042 Telex no 23241 Plan5: **6** D4
120rm(63⇌⋒) Lift ☽ ⋈ CTV TV in bedrooms ℙ Conference facilities available ♉English & French. Last dinner 9.45pm ♁ ♖ S% sB&B£15.45 sB&B⇌⋒£21.25 dB&B£24 dB&B⇌⋒£32.80 Continental breakfast Lunch fr£2.25&alc Tea fr£1.50 High Tea fr£2 Dinner fr£3.80&alc Wine£4 ⊓ *xmas* Credit cards 1 2 3 5 6

★★★**Royal Court** Sloane Sq (Norfolk Capital) ☎01–730 9191 Telex no 23241 Plan5: **19** D2
101⇌⋒ Lift ☽ ⋈ CTV in bedrooms ℙ Last dinner 10pm ♁ ♖ S% sB&B⇌⋒£29.25 dB&B⇌⋒£44.50 Continental breakfast Lunch fr£3.25&alc Tea fr£1.25&alc Dinner fr£4.25&alc Wine£4 ⊓
Credit cards 1 2 3 5 6

★★★**Royal Horseguards** Whitehall Court (EMI) ☎01–839 3400 Telex no 917096 Not on plan
A five storey modern hotel with décor in the military style.
285⇌⋒ Lift ☽ ⋈ CTV in bedrooms ⊘ ℙ Conference facilities available ♉International. Last dinner 11pm ♁ ♖ S% ✱sB&B⇌⋒£31 dB&B⇌⋒£38.50 Continental breakfast Lunch£6.10&alc Tea£2 Dinner£7.60&alc Wine£3.50 ⊓
Credit cards 1 2 3 4 5 6

★★★**Rubens** Buckingham Palace Rd (Grand Met) ☎01–834 6600 Telex no 916577 Plan5: **22** C3
146⇌⋒ Lift ☽ ⋈ CTV in bedrooms ⊘ ℙ Conference facilities available ♉Mainly grills. ♿ Last dinner 9.30pm ♁ ♖ S% ✱sB&B⇌⋒£14.50–£17 (room only) dB&B⇌⋒£21.50–£24.50 (room only) ⊓
Credit cards 1 2 3 4 5 6

★★**St James** Buckingham Gate (Centre)
?01-834 2360 Telex no 919557 Not on plan
20⇌⋒ Lift ☽ ₩ TV in bedrooms ⊘ 20P Conference
acilities available Last dinner 10pm ♔ ♖ S%
sB&B⇌⋒£18.50 dB&B⇌⋒£24
ontinental breakfast Lunch£4.75 Dinner£4.75
Vine£3.40 ⊟ Credit cards 1 2 3 4 5 6

★★***Wilbraham*** Wilbraham Pl ☎01-730 8296
an5: **28** D1
5rm(37⇌⋒) Lift ☽ ₩ CTV TV available in bedrooms
⊘ ⊕ English & French. Last dinner 10pm ♔ ♖
redit cards 2 3 5

bury Court 26 Ebury St ☎01-730 8147 Plan5: **5** C3
ee page 50 for details

✕✕✕✕✕**Berkeley Hotel Restaurant** Wilton Pl,
nightsbridge ☎01-235 6000 Plan5: **3** B2
edrooms available ⊕ French. Prices on application
redit cards 1 6

✕✕✕✕✕**Carlton Tower Hotel (Chelsea Room)**
adogan Pl ☎01-235 5411 Plan4: **15** C6
'legant, spacious, modern restaurant with wide vindows overlooking gardens of Cadogan Place.
0seats ₱ bedrooms available ⊕ French.
pecialities: Salade nouvelle, Fricassée de turbot et omard aux concombres, Filets mignons de boeuf ux échalottes. Last dinner 11.15pm S%
✱Lunch£15alc Tea£4&alc Dinner£15alc
redit cards 1 2 3 4 5 6

✕✕✕✕**Stone's Chop House** Panton St
☎01-930 0037 Plan2: **39** D2
'he ground floor has traditional English atmosphere with sporting motifs, and the first floor decor is cool nd elegant with giant fountains on patio.
Closed Sun, Xmas Day & Good Fri; 250seats ₱
ast dinner 11.15pm Lunch fr£4.25&alc
)inner fr£4.25&alc Wine£3.90
redit cards 1 2 3 6

✕✕✕✕**Hunting Lodge** 16 Lower Regent St
☎01-930 4222 Plan2: **20** D2
Closed Sun; Lunch not served Sat; 100seats ₱
ast dinner 11.30pm S% Lunch£7.35&alc
)inner£7.35&alc Wine£4
redit cards 1 2 3 4 5 6

✕✕✕✕**Overton's** 5 St James's Street
☎01-839 3774 Plan5: **16** A4
Restaurant specialising in fish dishes.
Closed Sun; 90seats ₱ ⊕ French.
ast dinner 10.45pm Lunch£9.50alc
)inner£9.50alc Wine£3.75
Credit cards 1 2 3 4 5 6

✕✕✕✕***Quaglino's Hotel Restaurant*** Bury St
☎01-930 6767 Plan1: **56** E3
Closed Sun & Public Hols; Lunch not served Sat;
20seats 37P bedrooms available Live music & lancing Mon-Sat Cabaret Mon-Sat ⊕ French.
ast dinner 11pm Credit cards 1 2 3 4 5 6

✕✕✕✕**Sheraton Park Tower Hotel (Le Trianon)**
101 Knightsbridge ☎01-235 8050 Plan4: **71** B6
70seats ₱ bedrooms available Live music & dancing Tue-Sun; ⊕ French. Last dinner mdnt S%
Lunch£8.50&alc Dinner£15&alc Wine£4.50
Credit cards 1 2 3 4 5 6

✕✕✕***Duke's Hotel Restaurant*** St James's Pl
☎01-491 4840 Plan5: **4** A4
40seats bedrooms available ⊕ English & French.
Last dinner 10.30pm Credit cards 1 2 3 4 5 6

✕✕✕**Lafayette** 32 Kings St, St James's
☎01-930 1131 Plan1: **40** E3
Closed Sat & Sun; 90seats ✗ ⊕ Creole & French.
Last dinner 11.30pm Credit cards 1 2 3 5

❀❀❀✕✕✕**Le Gavroche** 61 Lower Sloane St
☎01-730 2820 Plan5: **7** E2
(See Chief Hotel Inspector's Article 'Four more of the Best' on page 13).
Closed Sun, Public Hols & 24Dec-1Jan; 50seats ₱
bedrooms available ⊕ French. Last dinner mdnt
Dinner£20alc Credit cards 2 5

✕✕✕**Kundan** 3 Horseferry Rd ☎01-834 3434 Not on plan
Closed Sun; 135seats P ⊕ Indian & Pakistani.
Last dinner 11.30pm ✱Lunch£6-£7
Dinner£7-£8 Wine£4.60
Credit cards 1 2 3 4 5 6

✕✕✕**Lockets** Marsham St ☎01-834 9552 Not on plan
Quiet restaurant within block of flats decorated in traditional and elegant style. Near Houses of Parliament. Division Bell can be seen.
Closed Sat & Sun; 130seats ₱ Last dinner 11pm
Lunch£10alc Dinner£6-£6.50&alc Wine£3.50
Credit cards 1 2 3 5

✕✕***L'Amico*** 44 Horseferry Rd ☎01-222 4680 Not on plan
Closed Sun; 70seats ⊕ Italian.

✕✕**Carafe** 15 Lowndes St ☎01-235 2525 Not on plan
Closed Mon; 75seats ⊕ French Fish dishes.
Last dinner 10.45pm S% ✱Lunch£10alc
Dinner&10alc Wine£3.20
Credit cards 1 2 3 4 5 6

✕✕**Lebanese Food Centre – Beirut** 11 Sloane St
☎01-235 2827 Plan4: **40** C6
⊕ Lebanese. Last dinner 11pm Dinner£5-£7
Wine£4.50 Credit cards 1 2 3 4 5 6

✕✕**Marcel** 14 Sloane St ☎01-235 4912 Plan4: **47** B6
Closed Sun & Public Hols; 60seats ₱ ⊕ French.
Last dinner 11.15pm ✱Lunch£8.75alc
Tea£1.30&alc Dinner£10alc Wine£3.35
Credit cards 2 5

XXMr Chow 151 Knightsbridge ☎01-589 7347 Plan4:**54** B6
Modern Chinese restaurant on two floors.
Closed Xmas 140seats P ♀Pekinese. Last dinner 11.45pm ✱Lunch£7alc Dinner£8alc Wine£3.20 Credit cards 1 2 3 4 5 6

❀XXPomegranates 94 Grosvenor Rd ☎01-828 6560 Not on plan
Closed Sun & Public Hols Lunch not served Sat 50seats P ♀International. Specialities: Gravad lax, Ronde de gigot, Honey and cognac ice cream Last dinner 11.15pm ✱Lunch£4.25-£4.75&alc Dinner£16alc Credit cards 1 2 3 5

XX*Tate Gallery* Millbank Embankment ☎01-834 6754 Not on plan
Closed Sun, Xmas, New Year, 15Apr & 1May; Dinner not served; 130seats. Last lunch 3pm

XArirang House 3-4 Park Cl ☎01-581 1820 Plan4:**4** B6
Closed Sun, Xmas & Etr 44seats P ♀Korean. Last dinner 11pm Lunch fr£1.50&alc Dinner£6alc Wine£1.55 Credit cards 1 2 3 4 5

XEatons 49 Elizabeth St ☎01-730 0074 Plan5:**4A** D2
Closed Sat & Sun 40seats P ♀French. Last dinner 11.15pm S% ✱Lunch£9.50 Dinner£9.50alc Wine£4.30 Credit cards 1 2 5

X*Overton's* 4-6 Victoria Bdgs ☎01-834 3774 Plan5:**17** C3
Closed Sun; 60seats ♀English & French. Last dinner 10.30pm Credit cards 1 2 3 5

X*Sale e Pepe* 13-15 Pavilion Rd, ☎01-235 0095 Plan4:**64A** B6
Closed Sun; 48seats ♀Italian. Last dinner mdnt

XTent 15 Eccleston St ☎01-730 6922 Plan5:**27** D3
Closed Sat 45seats P ♀Continental. Last dinner 11.15pm ✱Lunch£3.60-£4.80 Dinner£4.80

SW3 Chelsea

❀❀★★★★Capital Basil St, Knightsbridge ☎01-589 5171 Plan4:**14** B6
See page 46 for details

★★★Basil Street Basil St, Knightsbridge ☎01-581 3311 Plan4:**10** B6
See page 48 for details

❀XXXXWaltons 121 Walton St ☎01-584 0204 Plan4:**79** D5
Closed Public Hols; Dinner not served Sun; 60seats P ♀International. Specialities: Green vegetable pâté, Rack of Welsh lamb, Collops in the pan. Last dinner 11.30pm Lunch£5.50-£14 Dinner£10-£17 Wine£4.50 Credit cards 1 2 3 5

XXXBrompton Grill 243 Brompton Rd ☎01-589 8005 Plan4:**13** C5
Closed Public Hols; Lunch not served Sun; 76seats P ♀French. Last dinner 10.55pm ✱Lunch£4.50&alc Dinner£11alc Wine£5 Credit cards 2 3 5

❀XXXCapital Hotel Restaurant 22-24 Basil St, Knightsbridge ☎01-589 5171 Plan4:**14** B6
30seats P bedrooms available ♀French. Specialities: Mousseline de Coquilles St Jacques, Carré d'agneau persille aux herbes de provence, Sorbet à la fine champagne. Last dinner 10.30pm ✱Lunch£9.50alc Dinner£9.50alc Wine£4.25 Credit cards 1 2 3 4 5 6

XXX*Claudius* Chelsea Cloisters, Sloane Av ☎01-584 8608 Plan4:**16** D5
Lunch not served Sat; 80seats 6P ♀International. Last dinner 11.30pm Credit cards 1 2 3 5

XXXDrakes 2A Pond Pl, Fulham Rd ☎01-584 4555 Not on plan
Closed Xmas & Public Hols; 75seats P Last dinner 11pm (Sun 10.15pm) S% Lunch£8.50alc Dinner£8.50alc Wine£3.25 Credit cards 1 2 3 5 6

XXXParkes 4 Beauchamp Pl ☎01-589 1390 Plan4:**59** C5
Intimate basement with modern décor, including hessian walls and prints. Owner Tom Benson works in full view of one part of the restaurant.
Closed Sun, Xmas Day & Etr; Lunch not served Sat; 55seats P Last dinner 11pm Lunch£9alc Dinner£16alc Wine£4 Credit cards 1 2 6

XXChelsea Rendezvous 4 Sydney St ☎01-352 9519 Plan4:**19** D5
Closed Xmas & Public Hols; 92seats P ♀Pekinese. Last dinner 11.30pm Wine£3.10 Credit cards 2 3 4 5

❀XXDaphne's 112 Draycott Av ☎01-589 4257 Plan4:**23** D5
Small French twin-level restaurant with modern paintings and prints on light hessian-covered walls.
Closed Sun; 60seats P ♀French. Last dinner mdnt ✱Dinner£9alc Wine£3 Credit cards 1 2 3 5 6

XXEnglish House 3 Milner St ☎01-584 3002 Plan4:**29** D6
Closed Sun; 30seats P Last dinner 11.30pm S% Lunch£10alc Dinner£15alc Wine£4 Credit cards 1 2 3 5 6

XXLe Français 259 Fulham Rd ☎01-352 4748 Plan4:**30** E4
Small intimate French restaurant with simple décor; noted for its rare regional specialities.
Closed Sun; 65seats P ♀French. Last dinner 11pm S% Lunch fr£5&alc Dinner£12alc Wine£3.90 Credit cards 2 5

XX*Il Lando* 19 Elystan St ☎01-584 5248 Plan4:**17** E5
Closed Sun & Public Hols; Lunch not served; 50seats ♀Italian. Last dinner 11.30pm Credit cards 1 2 5 6

XXSan Frediano 62 Fulham Rd ☎01-584 8375 Plan4:**65** D4
White vaulted interior by Apicella.
Closed Sun; 85seats P ♀Italian. Last dinner 11.30pm ✱Lunch£7.40alc Dinner£7.40alc Wine£2.65 Credit cards 1 2 3 5 6

XXTandoori 153 Fulham Rd ☎01-589 7749 Plan4:**74** D5
Elegant and sophisticated Indian basement restaurant with paintings of Indian warriors.
Lunch not served Mon-Sat; 65seats P ♀North Indian. Last dinner 12.30am Lunch£7alc Dinner£7alc Wine£3 Credit cards 1 2 3 4 5 6

❀❀XXTante Claire 68 Royal Hospital Rd ☎01-352 6045 Plan4:**66** F6
(See Chief Hotels Inspector's Article 'Four more of the Best' on page 16).
Closed Sat, Sun, Public Hols, Xmas, New Year's Day & 2wks Summer; 38seats P ♀French. Last dinner 11pm S% ✱Lunch£7-£8&alc Dinner£12.20-£13.50alc Wine£4.50 Credit card 2

XAl Ben Accolto 48 Fulham Rd ☎01-589 0876 Plan4:**2** D4
Closed Sun & Public Hols; 50seats P ♀Italian. Last dinner 11.30pm Lunch£3-£7 Dinner£5-£7 Wine£2.70 Credit cards 1 2 5

XAu Fin Bec 100 Drayton Av ☎01-584 3600 Plan4:**8** D5
Closed Sun & Public Hols; 62seats P ♀French. Last dinner 10.45pm Lunch£10alc Dinner£10alc Wine£3 Credit cards 1 2 3 4 5 6

Bewick's 87–89 Walton St ☎01–584 6711
Plan4: **11** D5
Closed Sun, Xmas & Public Hols; Lunch not served Sat; 50seats P French. Last dinner 11.30pm
Lunch£6.50alc Dinner£8alc Wine£3.20
Credit cards 1 2 3 5 6

Da Angela 119 Sydney St ☎01–352 2718
Plan4: **22** E5
Closed Sun & Public Hols; Lunch not served; 35seats Live music & dancing Mon–Sat French.
Last dinner 2am Credit cards 1 2 3 4 5 6

Don Luigi's 33C King's Rd ☎01–730 3023
Plan4: **25** E6
50seats P Italian. Last dinner 11.30pm
*Lunch£8.50alc Dinner£8.50alc
Credit cards 1 2 3 4 5 6

Luba's Bistro 6 Yeoman's Row ☎01–589 2950
Plan4: **45** C5
Candle-lit, converted garage with extremely simple décor.
Closed Sun; Unlicensed; No corkage charge; 50seats P Russian & Continental.
Last dinner 11.30pm Lunch£2–£3&alc
Dinner£3.50–£5

✕Ma Cuisine 113 Walton St
☎01–584 7585 Plan4: **46** D5
The best value for money in London for French haute cuisine. This simply-decorated, but attractive, restaurant is run by Guy Mouilleron who looks after the kitchen, and his vivacious wife, Lucette, who looks after the front of the house.
On entering the restaurant one immediately senses the ambience that comes from a busy and successful restaurant. This success is thoroughly deserved, for the Mouillerons are serious in their approach to cooking and running a restaurant.
Highly acclaimed dishes have included the regular soupe de poisson et sa rouille, pâté d'anguille à la mousse de cresson and a delicious leek quiche. Amongst the main courses, ballotine de volaille Lucien Tendret, poularde Duc de Bourgogne, mousseline de St Jacques à l'orange and other daily dishes have been found to be absolutely delicious, although there have been variable reports about the noisettes d'agneau pastourelle. Fruit tarts with excellent buttery pastry are always enjoyed and so are the fresh fruit sorbets. There is an excellent selection of French cheeses and the coffee is very good too. The wine list is sensibly chosen and not unreasonably priced, but a few older wines would be welcome. Guy Mouilleron comes from south-west France and not surprisingly offers a selection of fine Armagnacs which make a fitting end to a superb meal.
Closed Sat, Sun, 23Dec–4Jan, 2wks Etr & 15Jul–15Aug; 30seats P French.
Last dinner 11pm *Lunch£9alc Dinner£9alc
Wine£4.95 Credit cards 2 5

✕*Marco Polo* 95 Kings Rd ☎01–352 0306 Plan4: **48** E5
Modern, attractive Chinese restaurant with an intimate atmosphere.
60seats Cantonese. Last dinner 11.45pm
Credit cards 1 2 3 4 5 6

✕*Poissonnerie de l'Avenue* 82 Sloane Av
☎01–589 2457 Plan4: **60** D5
Small, French fish restaurant with panelling and beams.
Closed Sun & Public Hols; 80seats French.
Last dinner 11.30pm Credit cards 1 2 3 5

✕*San Quintino* 45–47 Radnor Walk ☎01–352 2698
Not on plan
Closed Sun & Public Hols; 40seats Italian.
Last dinner 11.30pm Credit cards 1 2 3 5

✕*Shangri-La* 233 Brompton Rd ☎01–584 3658
Plan4: **67** C5
Closed Public Hols; Lunch not served Sun; 70seats Cantonese. Last dinner 11.25pm
Credit cards 1 2 3 5

✕Le Suquet 104 Draycott Ave ☎01–581 1785
Plan4: **73** D5
Closed Mon; Lunch not served Tue; 35seats P French. Last dinner 11.30pm *Lunch£10alc
Dinner£10alc Wine£4 Credit card 2

SW5 Earls Court

☆☆☆☆**London International** 147 Cromwell Rd, Kensington (Grand Met) ☎01–370 4200
Telex no 27260 Plan4: **42A** D2
418 Lift CTV in bedrooms P Conference facilities available Last dinner 10.30pm S%
*sB £18.75–£22.75 (room only)
dB £25.50–£30.50 (room only)
Credit cards 1 2 3 4 5 6

★★★**Barkston** 33–34 Barkston Gdns (Trusthouse Forte) ☎01–373 7851 Plan4: **9** D2
71 Lift TV in bedrooms P Conference facilities available Mainly grills.
Last dinner 9.30pm S% sB&B £24
dB&B £30.50 *xmas*
Credit cards 1 2 3 4 5 6

★★★**Elizabetta** Cromwell Rd ☎01–370 4282
Telex no 918978 Plan4: **28** D2
83 Lift TV available in bedrooms 10
International. Last dinner 10pm S%
sB&B £20.40–£25.26
dB&B £28.92–£33.42 Continental breakfast
Lunch£3.50alc Tea£1.60alc Dinner£4.25&alc
Wine£4 Credit cards 1 2 3 4 5 6

★★★**Hotel George** 11 Templeton Pl ☎01–370 1092
Telex no 8814825 Plan4: **36** D1
130 Lift CTV TV available in bedrooms
30P Last dinner 11pm S% sB&B £14–£22
dB&B £16–£28 Continental breakfast
Lunch£3.50–£7&alc Dinner£3.50–£7&alc
Wine£3 *xmas* Credit cards 1 2 3 5

✕*L'Artiste Affamé* 243 Old Brompton Rd
☎01–373 1659 Plan4: **7** E2
French bistro-style restaurant.
Closed Sun, Public Hols & Xmas; Lunch not served Sat; 50seats Live music twice wkly French.
Last dinner 11.15pm Credit cards 1 2 3 5

✕Kuo Yuan 139 Earls Court Rd ☎01–373 2233 Not on plan
80seats Mandarin Credit cards 2 3 5

✕*Naraine* 10 Kenway Rd ☎01–370 3853
Plan4: **55** D1/2
Closed Mon; 45seats Indian.
Credit cards 1 2 3 5

✕Le Truc 233 Earls Court Rd ☎01–373 7365
Plan4: **76A** E2
Closed Sun; French. Last dinner 1am
*Dinner£7alc Wine£4

SW6 Fulham

★★★**West Centre** Lillie Rd (Centre) ☎01–385 1255
Telex no 917728 Not on plan
510 Lift TV in bedrooms Conference facilities available Last dinner 10pm S%
*sB&B £17.75 dB&B £22.25
Continental breakfast Lunch£4.75 Dinner£4.75
Wine£3.40 Credit cards 1 2 3 4 5 6

✕Newton's 576 King's Rd ☎01–736 1804 Not on plan
Closed Sun; Lunch not served Sat; 55seats P English & French. Last dinner mdnt.
Lunch£3.80alc Dinner£4.75–£8 Wine£2.85
Credit cards 1 2 3

SW7 South Kensington

★★★★**Gloucester** 4–18 Harrington Gdns (Rank) ☎01–373 6030 Telex no 917505 Plan4: **34** D3 550⇌⋒ Lift ☽ ⊞ ♨ CTV in bedrooms 130 Conference facilities available English & Continental. Last dinner 10.45pm S% sB&B⇌⋒£39.15 dB&B⇌⋒£47.30 Continental breakfast Lunch £3.50&alc Tea £1.75 Dinner fr £3.50&alc Wine £3.80 *xmas* Credit cards 1 2 3 4 5 6

☆☆☆☆**London Penta** Cromwell Rd (Grand Met) ☎01–370 5757 Telex no 919663 Plan4: **43** D3 876⇌⋒ Lift ☽ ♨ CTV in bedrooms 90 Conference facilities available Last dinner 1am S% ✱sB⇌⋒£21 (room only) dB⇌⋒£26–£31 (room only) Credit cards 1 2 3 4 5 6

★★★**Eden Plaza** 68–69 Queens Gate ☎01–370 6111 Telex no 916228 Plan4: **27** D3 62⇌⋒ Lift ☽ ♨ CTV in bedrooms sauna bath English & Continental. Last dinner 9.45pm S% ✱sB&B⇌⋒£19.95 dB&B⇌⋒£28.95 Lunch fr £3.50 Tea fr 50p High Tea £3 Dinner £5alc Wine £2.85 Credit cards 1 2 3 5

★★★**Onslow Court** 109–113 Queens Gate (North) ☎01–589 6300 Telex no 262180 Plan4: **58** D4 *Large Victorian hotel situated in Queen's Gate.* Unlicensed; 150rm(89⇌⋒) Lift ☽ ♨ CTV Last dinner 8.30pm S% sB&B £9.45–£10.65 sB&B⇌⋒£12.45–£14 dB&B £14.90–£16.75 dB&B⇌⋒£19.90–£22.40 Lunch fr £3.40 Tea fr 85p Dinner fr £3.90 Credit cards 1 2 3 6

★★★**Rembrandt** Thurloe Pl (Grand Met) ☎01–589 8100 Telex no 917575 Plan4: **62** C5 184rm(73⇌⋒) Lift ☽ ♨ CTV in bedrooms Conference facilities available Last dinner 9.30pm S% ✱sB⇌⋒£14.50–£17 (room only) dB⇌⋒£21.50–£24.50 (room only) Credit cards 1 2 3 4 5 6

★★★**Stanhope Court** 46–52 Stanhope Gdns (North) ☎01–370 2161 Telex no 262180 Plan4: **72** D3 *Pleasant hotel only two minutes walk from Gloucester Road underground station.* Unlicensed; 125rm(54⇌⋒) Lift ☽ ♨ CTV Last dinner 8.30pm S% sB&B £9.45–£10.65 sB&B⇌⋒£12.45–£14 dB&B £14.90–£16.75 sB&B⇌⋒£19.90–£22.40 Lunch fr £3.40 Tea fr 85p Dinner fr £3.90 Credit cards 1 2 3 5

★★***Hotel Eden*** 27–33 Harrington Gdns (Inter-Hotel) ☎01–370 6161 Telex no 265731 Plan4: **26** D3 *Georgian-style hotel.* 125rm(67⇌⋒) Lift ☽ CTV TV available in bedrooms ⚓ Conference facilities available English, French & Italian. Last dinner 9.30pm Credit cards 1 2 3 4 5 6

★★**Leicester Court** 41 Queen's Gate Gdns, SW7 (North) ☎01–584 0512 Plan4: **41** C3 *The hotel is sited on the former London residence o the Earls of Strathmore.* Unlicensed; 67rm(8⇌⋒) Lift ☽ ♨ CTV Last dinner 8pm S% sB&B £9.45–£10.65 sB&B⇌⋒£12.45–£14 dB&B £14.90–£16.75 dB&B⇌⋒£19.90–£22.40 Lunch fr £3.40 Tea fr 85p Dinner fr £3.90 Credit cards 1 2 3 5

★★**Norfolk** Harrington Rd (Norfolk Capital) ☎01–589 8191 Telex no 23241 Plan4: **56** D4 *Imposing Victorian building in South Kensington, close to the Royal Albert Hall and Harrods.* 109⇌⋒ Lift ☽ ♨ CTV in bedrooms Last dinner 10pm S% sB&B⇌⋒£22.55 dB&B⇌⋒£32.20 Continental breakfast Lunch fr £3.25&alc Dinner fr £4.25&alc Wine £4 Credit cards 1 2 3 5 6

✕✕**Albasha** 171 Knightsbridge ☎01–581 3066 Plan4: **1** B5 Closed Xmas, New Year, & 3wks Aug; 120seats Lebanese. Last dinner 11.30pm Wine £5 Credit cards 1 2 5

✕✕***Il Giorno e La Notte*** 60 Old Brompton Rd ☎01–584 4028 Plan4: **33** D4 Closed Xmas Day, Etr & Public Hols; 80seats Italian. Last dinner 11.30pm Credit cards 1 2 3 5

✕✕**Shezan** 16–22 Cheval Pl ☎01–589 7918 Plan4: **68** C5 Closed Sun & Public Hols; 130seats Indian & Pakistani. Specialities: Murgh Tikka, Karahi Kebab, Gosht Khata Masala. Last dinner 11.30pm ✱Lunch £8–£10 Dinner £10–£12 Wine £4.25 Credit cards 1 2 3 4 5 6

✕***Bangkok*** 9 Bute St ☎01–584 8529 Plan4: **8A** D4 *Small, modern simply furnished Siamese restaurant.* Closed Mon, Xmas & Etr; 36seats Thai. Last dinner 11pm

✕**Chanterelle** 119 Old Brompton Rd ☎01–373 5522 Plan4: **18** E3 *Small restaurant with pleasant décor; divided into bays by natural wood partitions.* Closed 25 & 26Dec; 48seats English & French. Last dinner mdnt ✱Lunch £3–£8 Dinner £6–£10&alc Wine £3 Credit cards 1 2 5 6

✕**Gondolière** 3 Gloucester Rd ☎01–584 8062 Plan4: **35** C3 *A highly-coloured Trattoria with bright murals and paintings.* Closed Sun; Lunch not served Sat; 35seats Italian. Last dinner 11.30pm ✱Lunch £2.45&alc Dinner £5&alc Wine £3 Credit cards 1 3 4

SW8 South Lambeth
⊛××Alonso's 32 Queenstown Rd ☎01–720 5986 Not on plan
Closed Sun & Public Hols; P ♀French & Spanish. Specialities: Champagne and Camembert Soup, Rack of lamb with cherries and tangerines, Cold caramel and apple soufflé. Last dinner 11.30pm ✱Lunch £4.50 Dinner £7.25–£7.95 & alc
Credit cards 2 5

SW10 West Brompton
××*Nikita's* 65 Ifield Rd ☎01–352 6326 Not on plan
closed Xmas; 44seats ♀Russian.
Last dinner 11.30pm Credit cards 1 2 5

××Santa Croce 112 Cheyne Walk ☎01–352 7534 Not on plan
Italian restaurant on corner site.
Closed Sun; 120seats P ♀Italian.
Last dinner 11.15pm ✱Lunch £6alc Dinner £6alc
Wine £2.60 Credit cards 1 2 3 5 6

×La Croisette 168 Ifield Rd ☎01–373 3694 Not on plan
Closed Mon; Lunch not served Tue; 40seats P ♀French. Last dinner 11.30pm ✱Lunch £10
Dinner £10 Wine £4 Credit card 2

×La Fringale 4 Hollywood Rd ☎01–351 1011
Closed Sun; Lunch not served; 55seats P ♀French.
Last dinner 11.45pm Dinner £5alc Wine £2.30
Credit cards 3 5

×Provans 306B Fulham Rd ☎01–352 7343 Not on plan
Closed 25 & 26Dec; Lunch not served; 35seats P ♀English & French. Last dinner mdnt
Dinner £10alc Wine £3.20 Credit cards 1 2 5

×*William F's* 140 Fulham Rd ☎01–373 5534 Not on plan
Closed Sun; 36seats ♀English & French.
Last dinner 11.30pm

SW11 Battersea
×La Grenouille 515 Battersea Park Rd ☎01–228 5385 Not on plan
Closed Sun; Lunch not served; 45seats P ♀French.
Last dinner mdnt ✱Dinner £5.20alc Wine £2.50
Credit cards 1 2 3 5

×Hathaways 13 Battersea Rise ☎01–228 3384 Not on plan
Closed Sun & Public Hols; Lunch not served; 34seats P ♀English & North American.
Last dinner 10.30pm ✱Dinner £7.50alc Wine £3
Credit cards 1 2 3 5

×Lavender Hill 245 Lavender Hill ☎01–223 4129 Not on plan
Closed Sun & Mon; Lunch not served; 50seats P ♀French. Last dinner 10pm Dinner fr £8.75
Credit cards 1 2 3 6

×*Toto's Wine & Dine* 50 Battersea Rise ☎01–228 1206 Not on plan
Closed Sun; Lunch not served Sat; 54seats ♀French. Last dinner 11pm Credit cards 2 3 5

SW15 Putney
×*Cassis* 30 Putney High St ☎01–788 8668 Not on plan
Closed Sun; 40seats ♀French. Last dinner 11.15pm

×Wild Thyme 96 Felsham Rd ☎01–789 3323 Not on plan
Closed Sun, Mon & Aug; Lunch not served Sat; 44seats P ♀International. Last dinner 11pm S%
Lunch £5.50alc Dinner £6alc Wine £3
Credit cards 1 3 6

SW19 Wimbledon
⊛×Les Amoureaux 156 Merton Hall Rd ☎01–543 0567 Not on plan
Closed Sun & 3wks Aug; Lunch not served; 44seats ♀French. Last dinner 10pm ✱Dinner £5.40alc
Wine £2.50 Credit cards 1 2 3

×Le Café Royal 72 High St, Wimbledon Village ☎01–946 0238 Not on plan
Closed Sun; 50seats P ♀French.
Last dinner 10.30pm Lunch £10alc Dinner £10alc
Wine £3.20 Credit cards 1 2 3 5

W1 West End *Piccadilly Circus, St Marylebone and Mayfair*
★★★★★**Claridge's** Brook St ☎01–629 8860
Telex no 21872 Plan 1: **39** D2
See page 45 for details

⊛⊛⊛★★★★★**Connaught** Carlos Pl ☎01–499 7070
Plan 1: **15** D1
See page 44 for details

★★★★★**Dorchester** Park Ln ☎01–629 8888
Telex no 887704 Plan 1: **19** E1
See page 45 for details

★★★★★***Bristol*** 3 Berkeley St ☎01–493 8282
Telex no 24561 Not on plan
189⇌ Lift ☽ ⊞ CTV available in bedrooms 30 Live music Mon–Sat ♀French.
Last dinner 10.30pm
Credit cards 1 2 3 4 5 6

★★★★★**Churchill** Portman Sq ☎01–486 5800
Telex no 264831 Plan 3: **4** B5
Nine-storey building (opened 1970) occupying one side of Portman Square. Luxurious décor with a Regency flavour.
489⇌ Lift ☽ ⊞ CTV in bedrooms 80 Live music Mon–Sat; Conference facilities available ♿ ♀International. Last dinner 11pm S%
✱sB&B⇌ £56.76 dB&B⇌ £71.30
Lunch £12alc Tea £3.15&alc High Tea £5alc
Dinner £15alc Wine £4.60
Credit cards 1 2 3 4 5 6

★★★★★**Grosvenor House** Park Ln (Trusthouse Forte) ☎01–499 6363 Telex no 24871 Plan 1: **31** D1
Outstanding eight-storey building situated opposite Hyde Park.
478⇌ Lift ☽ CTV in bedrooms 20P 100 (heated) sauna bath Conference facilities available
Last dinner 11.30pm S%
sB&B⇌ £48.50 dB&B⇌ £70
Credit cards 1 2 3 4 5 6

★★★★★**Hilton** Park Ln ☎01–493 8000
Telex no 24873 Plan 5: **11** A2
Thirty-storey landmark (328ft) with Y-shaped ground plan and facing Hyde Park.
509⇌ Lift ☽ ⊞ CTV in bedrooms 350 Disco Mon–Sat Live music & dancing Mon–Sat Conference facilities available ♀English, French, Chinese & Polynesian.
✱sB&B⇌ £55–£59 dB&B⇌ £63–£67
Lunch £8alc Tea £2.50alc High Tea £6alc
Dinner £12alc Wine £5.80
Credit cards 1 2 3 4 5 6

★★★★★**Inn on the Park** 1 Hamilton Pl, Park Ln (Prestige) ☎01–499 0888 Telex no 22771 Plan 5: **12** A2/3
Spacious interior in traditional style. Four seasons luxury restaurant overlooks the Park Lane gardens.
228⇌ Lift ☽ ⊞ CTV in bedrooms 80 Live music & dancing nightly Conference facilities available ♿ ♀International. S%
✱sB&B⇌ £66.77 dB&B⇌ £82.62
Lunch £11alc Tea fr £3.30 Dinner £12.50alc
Wine £6.25 Credit cards 1 2 3 4 5 6

★★★★★**Inter-Continental** 1 Hamilton Pl, Hyde Park Corner ☎01-409 3131 Telex no 25853 Plan 5: **13** B2
497⇌⋒ Lift ☽ ⊞ ♛ CTV in bedrooms ⊘ 102⌂ sauna bath Disco Mon-Sat Cabaret nightly Conference facilities available ♉ International. Last dinner 11.30pm ♈ ♊
sB&B⇌⋒£66.46-£74.02
dB&B⇌⋒£78.92-£88.64 Continental breakfast Lunch £6.90-£11.50 Dinner £20alc Wine £6.50 Credit cards 1 2 3 4 5 6

★★★★★**May Fair** Berkeley St (Grand Met) ☎01-629 7777 Telex no 262526 Plan 1: **46** E2
Situated on site of Devonshire House in heart of Mayfair.
380⇌⋒ Lift ☽ ♛ CTV in bedrooms ⊘ ♬ Live music & dancing nightly Conference facilities available ♿ ♉ English, French & Polynesian.
Last dinner 10.30pm ♈ ♊ S%
✱sB⇌⋒£28-£34.50 (room only) dB⇌⋒£42-£48 (room only) ⊟ Credit cards 1 2 3 4 5 6

★★★★★***Ritz*** Piccadilly ☎01-493 8181 Telex no 267200 Plan 1: **59** E3
Elegant six-storey building (1906), in 17th-C French style. Overlooks Piccadilly & Green Park.
143⇌⋒ Lift ☽ ♛ CTV TV available in bedrooms ⊘ ⩩ Live music & dancing 6 nights wkly ♿ ♉ English & French. Last dinner 10.30pm ♈ ♊
Credit cards 1 2 3 5 6

★★★★ **Selfridge** Orchard St (EMI) ☎01-408 2080 Telex no 22361 Plan 1: **65** C1
See page 47 for details

★★★★**Athenaeum** Piccadilly (Rank) ☎01-499 3464 Telex no 261589 Plan 5: **1** A3
112⇌⋒ Lift ☽ ⊞ ♛ CTV CTV in bedrooms ♬ ⩩ Conference facilities available ♉ English & French. Last dinner 10.30pm ♈ ♊ S% ✱sB⇌⋒£44.70 (room only) dB⇌⋒£62.40 (room only)
Lunch £6.60-£7.15&alc Tea £2.75&alc
Dinner £11alc Wine £5.50 ⊟ *xmas*
Credit cards 1 2 3 4 5 6

★★★★**Britannia** Grosvenor Sq (Grand Met) ☎01-629 9400 Telex no 23941 Plan 1: **7** D1
434⇌⋒ Lift ☽ ♛ CTV in bedrooms ⊘ 10P Conference facilities available ♉ English & French. Last dinner 10pm ♈ ♊ S%
✱sB⇌⋒£30-£36.50 (room only) dB⇌⋒£42-£48 (room only) ⊟ Credit cards 1 2 3 4 5 6

★★★★**Brown's** Dover St, Albemarle St (Trusthouse Forte) ☎01-493 6020 Plan 1: **8** D3
Gracious building of white stucco and weathered brick founded in early 19th-C by a butler to Lord Byron's family.
127⇌⋒ Lift ☽ ♛ CTV in bedrooms ♬ ⩩ Conference facilities available Last dinner 10pm ♈ ♊ S%
sB&B⇌⋒£44.50 dB&B⇌⋒£63 *xmas*
Credit cards 1 2 3 4 5 6

★★★★**Cumberland** Marble Arch (Trusthouse Forte) ☎01-262 1234 Telex no 22215 Plan 3: **6** B5
Large stone-fronted building dating from 1932, facing Marble Arch and Park Lane.
894⇌⋒ Lift ☽ ♛ CTV in bedrooms ⊘ ♬ ⩩ sauna bath Conference facilities available
Last dinner 10.30pm ♈ ♊ S% sB&B⇌⋒£34
dB&B⇌⋒£46.50 Continental breakfast ⊟
xmas Credit cards 1 2 3 4 5 6

★★★★**Europa** Grosvenor Sq (Grand Met) ☎01-493 1232 Telex no 268101 Plan 1: **22** D1
275⇌⋒ Lift ☽ ♛ CTV in bedrooms ⊘ ♬ Live music Mon-Sat Conference facilities available ♉ English & French. Last dinner 11pm ♈ ♊ ⊟
Credit cards 1 2 3 4 5 6

☆☆☆☆***Holiday Inn*** George St (Commonwealth)
☎01–723 1277 Plan3: **11** B4
243⇌ ⋒ Lift ☽ ⊞ ⋈ CTV 82⌂ ▭(heated) sauna bath
Conference facilities available ♀International.
Last dinner 10.30pm ♆ ♗ ⊟
Credit cards [1] [2] [3] [5] [6]

★★★★**Park Lane** Piccadilly ☎01–499 6321
Telex no 21533 Plan5: **18** A3
Elegant building with pillared entrance portico; overlooking Green Park.
325⇌ ⋒ Lift ☽ ⋈ CTV in bedrooms ⊗ 180⌂
Conference facilities available ♀English & French.
Last dinner 10.45pm ♆ ♗ S%
sB&B⇌ ⋒£42.75 dB&B⇌ ⋒£58.75
Continental breakfast Lunch£6.95&alc Tea£1.85
Dinner£10alc ⊟ Credit cards [1] [2] [3] [5]

★★★★**Piccadilly** Piccadilly (Grand Met)
☎01–734 8000 Telex no 25795 Plan1: **54** D3
290⇌ ⋒ Lift ☽ ⋈ CTV in bedrooms ₱ Conference facilities available ♿ Last dinner 9.30pm ♆ ♗
S% ✱sB⇌ ⋒£26–£32 (room only)
dB⇌ ⋒£37.50–£43.50 (room only) ⊟
Credit cards [1] [2] [3] [4] [5] [6]

★★★★**Portman Inter-Continental** 22 Portman Sq
☎01–486 5844 Telex no 261526 Plan3: **22** B5
275⇌ ⋒ 8▭ Lift ☽ ⊞ ♪ ⋈ CTV in bedrooms ⊗ Live music Fri Conference facilities available ♀French.
Last dinner 11pm ♆ ♗ sB&B⇌ ⋒£58.50
dB&B⇌ ⋒£68.40 Lunch£9alc Dinner£12alc
Wine£4 ⊟ Credit cards [1] [2] [3] [4] [5] [6]

☆☆☆☆**Regent Centre** Carburton St (Centre)
☎01–388 2300 Telex no 22453 Plan1: **57** A2
350⇌ ⋒ Lift ☽ ⋈ CTV in bedrooms ⊗ 80⌂
Conference facilities available ♀Greek.
Last dinner 10pm ♆ ♗ S% ✱sB&B⇌ ⋒£20.50
dB&B⇌ ⋒£26.50 Continental breakfast
Lunch£4.20 Dinner£4.20 Wine£3.40 ⊟
Credit cards [1] [2] [3] [4] [5] [6]

★★★★**St George's** Langham Pl (Trusthouse Forte)
☎01–580 0111 Telex no 27274 Plan1: **62** B2
Skyscraper block opened in 1963.
85⇌ ⋒ Lift ☽ ⊞ ⋈ CTV in bedrooms 2P Conference facilities available Last dinner 10pm ♆ ♗ S%
sB&B⇌ ⋒£40 dB&B⇌ ⋒£53.50 ⊟
Credit cards [1] [2] [3] [4] [5] [6]

★★★★**Westbury** New Bond St (Trusthouse Forte)
☎01–629 7755 Telex no 24378 Plan1: **76** D2
Colourful décor, comfortable well-appointed rooms and convenient for West End shops.
270⇌ ⋒ Lift ☽ ⋈ CTV in bedrooms 18P Conference facilities available ♿ Last dinner 11pm S%
sB&B⇌ ⋒£44.50 dB&B⇌ ⋒£66.50
Credit cards [1] [2] [3] [4] [5] [6]

★★★**Chesterfield** 35 Charles S (Grand Met)
☎01–491 2622 Telex no 269394 Plan1: **11** E2
84⇌ ⋒ Lift ☽ ⋈ CTV in bedrooms ⊗ ₱
Last dinner 10.30pm ♆ ♗ S%
✱sB⇌ ⋒£22–£27 (room only) dB⇌ ⋒£31–£38 (room only) ⊟ Credit cards [1] [2] [3] [4] [5] [6]

★★★**Clifton-Ford** Welbeck St (Grand Met)
☎01–486 6600 Telex no 22569 Plan1: **14** B1
229⇌ ⋒ Lift ☽ ⋈ TV in bedrooms ⊗ Conference facilities available Last dinner 10.15pm ♆ ♗ S%
✱sB⇌ ⋒£18.75–£22.75 (room only)
dB⇌ ⋒£25.50–£30.50 (room only) ⊟
Credit cards [1] [2] [3] [4] [5] [6]

★★★**Londoner** Welbeck St (Grand Met)
☎01–935 4442 Telex no 22569 Plan1: **42** C1
143⇌ ⋒ Lift ☽ ⋈ CTV in bedrooms ⊗ ₱ ♀Mainly grills. Last dinner 9.30pm ♆ ♗ S%
✱sB⇌ ⋒£18.75–£22.75 (room only)
dB⇌ ⋒£25.50–£30.50 (room only) ⊟
Credit cards [1] [2] [3] [4] [5] [6]

★★★**Mount Royal** Bryanston St, Marble Arch (Grand Met) ☎01–629 8040 Telex no 23355 Plan3: **20** B5
702rm(696⇌ ⋒) Lift ☽ ⋈ CTV available in bedrooms ⊗ ₱ Conference facilities available ♆ ♗ S%
✱sB&B⇌ ⋒£20–£24 dB&B⇌ ⋒£28–£33 ⊟
Credit cards [1] [2] [3] [4] [5] [6]

★★★**Stratford Court** 350 Oxford St (Grand Met)
☎01–629 7474 Telex no 22270 Plan1: **66** C2
137⇌ ⋒ Lift ☽ ⋈ CTV in bedrooms ⊗ ₱ ♀Mainly grills. Last dinner 10.30pm ♆ ♗ S%
✱sB⇌ ⋒£15.75–£19.25 (room only)
dB⇌ ⋒£23.25–£28.25 (room only) ⊟
Credit cards [1] [2] [3] [4] [5] [6]

★★★**Washington** Curzon St ☎01–499 7030
Telex no 24540 Plan1: **75** E2
159⇌ ⋒ Lift ☽ ⋈ CTV in bedrooms ⊗ ₱ Conference facilities available Last dinner 9.30pm ♆ ♗ S%
✱sB⇌ ⋒£18.75–£22.75 (room only)
dB⇌ ⋒£25.50–£30.50 (room only) ⊟
Credit cards [1] [2] [3] [4] [5] [6]

★★**Green Park** Half Moon St (Grand Met)
☎01–629 7522 Telex no 28856 Plan5: **10** A3
174rm(90⇌ ⋒) Lift ☽ ⋈ TV in bedrooms ⊗ ₱ sauna bath Last dinner 10pm ♆ ♗ S%
✱sB⇌ ⋒£14.50–£17 (room only)
dB⇌ ⋒£21.50–£24.50 (room only) ⊟
Credit cards [1] [2] [3] [4] [5] [6]

★★**Mandeville** Mandeville Pl (Grand Met)
☎01–935 5599 Telex no 269487 Plan1: **43** C1
165⇌ ⋒ Lift ☽ ⋈ CTV in bedrooms ⊗ ₱ Conference facilities available Last dinner 9.30pm ♆ ♗ S%
✱sB⇌ ⋒£14.50–£17 (room only)
dB⇌ ⋒£21.50–£24.50 (room only) ⊟
Credit cards [1] [2] [3] [4] [5] [6]

★★**Mostyn** Portman St (Grand Met) ☎01–935 2361
Telex no 27656 Plan3: **19** B5/6
107rm(58⇌ ⋒) Lift ☽ ⋈ TV in bedrooms ⊗ ₱
Conference facilities available ♀Mainly grills.
Last dinner 9.30pm ♆ ♗ S%
✱sB⇌ ⋒£14.50–£17 (room only)
dB⇌ ⋒£21.50–£24.50 (room only) ⊟
Credit cards [1] [2] [3] [4] [5] [6]

★★**Regent Palace** Glasshouse St, Piccadilly (Trusthouse Forte) ☎01–734 7000 Telex no 23740
Plan1: **58** D3
1068rm Lift ☽ ⋈ CTV available in bedrooms ⊗ ₱
Last dinner 9pm ♆ ♗ S% sB&B⇌ ⋒£15.50
dB&B⇌ ⋒£24.50 Continental breakfast ⊟
xmas Credit cards [1] [2] [3] [4] [5] [6]

★★**Royal Angus** 39 Coventry St (EMI)
☎01–930 4033 Telex no 24616 Plan2: **33** C2
92⇌ ⋒ Lift ☽ ⋈ CTV in bedrooms ⊗ ₱
Last dinner 11pm ♆ ♗ S% ✱sB&B⇌ ⋒£24
dB&B⇌ ⋒£34 Continental breakfast
Lunch£3.75alc Tea80palc Dinner£3.75alc
Wine£2.20 ⊟ Credit cards [1] [2] [3] [4] [5] [6]

XXXXX***Café Royal (Grill Room)*** 68 Regent St
☎01–437 9090 Plan1: **9** D3
Celebrated grill room designed in 1865. Red plush interior with gilt ceiling and mirrors recall Edwardian splendours.
60 seats ♀English & French. Last dinner 11.30pm
✱Lunch£7.50–£20&alc Dinner£7.50–£20&alc
Wine£6.10 Credit cards [1] [2] [3] [5] [6]

XXXXX**Churchill Hotel Restaurant** Portman Sq
☎01–486 5800 Plan3: **4** B5
96 seats ₱ bedrooms available Live music Mon–Sat ♀International. Last dinner 11pm S%
✱Lunch£12alc Tea£3.15 Dinner£15alc
Wine£4.60 Credit cards [1] [2] [3] [4] [5] [6]

XXXXX***Claridge's*** Brook St ☎01–629 8860
Plan1: **13** D2
120 seats bedrooms available ♀French.
Last dinner 11pm Credit cards [1] [3] [6]

Enjoy Grand Metropolitan

Welcome all – children too! We invite everyone to use our many Hotel Restaurants – be you Hotel resident, just visiting, or up to London for the day.

As times of opening will vary slightly, here is a general guide:–
Breakfast 07.30 – 10.00hrs, Lunch 12.00 – 14.30hrs, Dinner 18.30 – 22.30hrs.

(N.B. Children's portions may always be obtained.)

Hotel	Restaurants
Britannia Hotel Grosvenor Sq., W1 Tel: 01-629 9400	CARLTON RESTAURANT Named after our Carlton Hotel at Cannes, this gracious restaurant shows style in every aspect of presenting superb French cuisine. A pleasurable experience! POWDER KEG An 'olde worlde' Cellar restaurant, featuring medium priced menu, specialising in grills, salads & English dishes. PARK COFFEE HOUSE A beautiful, spacious Coffee Shop. A good rendezvous.
May Fair Hotel Stratton St., W1 Tel: 01-629 7777 Reservations for Beachcomber: Tel: 01-493 1924	CHATEAUBRIAND RESTAURANT A fine French Provencal style restaurant combining the very best of regional & classic French cuisine. (Opening Summer '79) COFFEE SHOP A fashionable Mayfair meeting place. BEACHCOMBER London's original & famous Polynesian restaurant. Here you'll find unusual dishes of Chinese & Hawaiian origin – amazing South Sea Island decor – dancing to two live bands! A must to visit!
Europa Hotel Grosvenor Sq., W1 Tel: 01-493 1232	DIPLOMAT RESTAURANT An extremely elegant wood panelled restaurant with superb decor & French inspired menu. The food & service will prove a delight! COFFEE EXCHANGE A splendid little Coffee Shop.
Piccadilly Hotel Piccadilly, W1 Tel: 01-734 8000	Carvers' Table — Carve yourself a feast of meat at any Carvers' Table. Three courses all for a fixed price.
Chesterfield Hotel Charles St., W1 Tel: 01-491 2622	CHESTERFIELD RESTAURANT A truly superb restaurant, serving the very best of French cuisine in most attractive & civilised surroundings. THE BUTTERY An informal restaurant, open at lunch times only, with very good inclusive priced meals. Help yourself to interesting hot and cold dishes.
Drury Lane Hotel Drury Lane, WC2 Tel: 01-836 6666	MAUDIE'S RESTAURANT Attractive modern restaurant providing extremely good value. A speciality feature of Maudie's is an enormous help yourself – Hors d'oeuvre table – very delicious!
Mandeville Hotel Mandeville Pl., W1 Tel: 01-935 5599	LA COCOTTE RESTAURANT Here's food from the Mediterranean in plenty! Good selections of French, Italian & Spanish dishes—much atmosphere. ORANGERY COFFEE HOUSE As beautiful as its name. (Opening Spring 1980).
St. Ermin's Hotel Caxton St., SW1 Tel: 01-222 7888	CAXTON GRILL RESTAURANT This small intimate club like' restaurant offers traditional English grills and speciality dishes. A popular business lunch venue. Carvers' Table — Carve yourself a feast of meat at any Carvers' Table. Three courses, all for a fixed price.

Arrive hungry, carve as much meat as you like from prime joints of roast beef, lamb and pork – hot or cold – with unlimited vegetables or salads. First & third courses and coffee are served at your table.

All for a fixed price. - VAT included.

The above information is accurate at time of printing but may be subject to change during 1980

❀❀❀XXXXX**Connaught Hotel Restaurant** Carlos Pl ☎01-499 7070 Plan1:**15** D1
See Chief Hotels Inspector's 'Four more of the Best' on page 18.
75seats P bedrooms available ♀English & French. Last dinner10.30pm Credit cards 1 6

XXXXX**Dorchester Hotel Restaurant** Park Ln ☎01-629 8888 Plan1:**19** E1
Closed Sun; 185seats P bedrooms available Live music & dancing Mon-Sat ♀International. Last dinner11.30pm Credit cards 1 2 3 4 5 6

❀XXXXX**Grosvenor House Hotel (La Fontaine)** Park Ln ☎01-499 6411 Plan1:**31** D1
Closed Sun & Public Hols; Lunch not served Sat; 108seats bedrooms available ♀French. Last dinner11.30pm Credit cards 1 2 3 4 5 6

XXXXX**Hilton Hotel (Roof)** Park Ln ☎01-493 8000 Plan5:**11** A2
Luxurious split-level restaurant with bandstand and dance floor.
Closed Sun; Lunch not served 130seats P bedrooms available Disco Mon-Sat Live music & dancing Mon-Sat ♀French. Last dinner mdnt ✻Dinner£15alc Credit cards 1 2 3 4 5 6

XXXXX**Inn on the Park Hotel (Four Seasons)** Hamilton Pl, Park Ln ☎01-499 0888 Plan5:**12** A2/3
75seats P bedrooms available ♀French. Last dinner11pm S% ✻Lunch£11alc Dinner£12.50alc Wine£6.25 Credit cards 1 2 3 4 5 6

XXXXX**Inter-Continental Hotel (Le Soufflé)** 1 Hamilton Pl, Hyde Park Corner ☎01-409 3131 Plan5:**13** B2
85seats bedrooms available ✗ ♀French. Last dinner11.30pm Lunch£11.50&alc Dinner£20&alc Wine£7.50 Credit cards 1 2 3 4 5 6

❀❀XXXXX**Mirabelle** 56 Curzon St ☎01-499 4636 Plan1:**48** E2
With its ageing but still elegant décor, the Mirabelle is high on the list of London's smartest restaurants and one of the last of its type. It provides classic cooking, traditional service and an extensive à la carte menu which includes a good selection of 'Plats des Gourmets'. There is also a large number of wines – over 200 – with classic ones dating back to 1905. Praised dishes are too numerous to mention, but soups are good, as are the fish dishes – often served with delicious sauces. Among the main courses, médaillonsde boeuf Mirabelle, including Perigourdine sauce, and noisettes d'agneau Edward VII have pleased, in addition to the obsolescent pojarski à la crême which always delights those who choose it; we think that this is the only restaurant that regularly features a pojarski. Vegetables were very good as indeed were the puddings, which continue to please.
Closed Sun & Public Hols; 180seats P ♀International. Last dinner11pm Lunch£20alc Dinner£20alc Wine£7 Credit cards 1 2 3 5 6

XXXX**Athenaeum Hotel Restaurant** Piccadilly ☎01-499 3464 Plan5:**1** A3
50seats P bedrooms available ♀English & French. Last dinner10.30pm S% ✻Lunch£6.60&alc Tea£2.75&alc Dinner£11alc Wine£5.50 Credit cards 1 2 3 4 5 6

XXXX***Gennaros*** 44 Dean St ☎01-437 3950 Plan2:**16** B2
80seats Live music Mon-Sat; ♀Italian. Last dinner11.30pm Credit cards 1 2 3 4 5 6

XXXX**Hilton Hotel (Trader Vic's)** Park Ln ☎01-493 7586 Plan5:**11** A2
Exotic Polynesian setting, with bamboo huts, totems, Tahitian music and subdued lighting. Waiters and waitresses in traditional costume.
Closed Xmas Day; Lunch not served Sat; 170seats P ♀International. Last dinner11.30pm ✻Lunch£9alc Dinner£10alc Credit cards 1 2 3 4 5 6

XXXX***La Napoule*** 8-10 North Audley St ☎01-629 4178 Plan1:**50** D1
Closed Sun; Lunch not served Sat; 80seats ♀French. Last dinner10.50pm Credit cards 1 2 3 5 6

XXXX**Scott's** Mount St ☎01-629 5248 Plan1:**64** D1
Elegant restaurant with damask walls, old prints, gilt wall-brackets and Corinthian pillars.
Closed Public Hols; Lunch not served Sun; 100seats P ♀English & French. Last dinner11pm ✻Lunch£15alc Dinner£15alc Credit cards 1 2 3 5 6

XXXX**Selfridge Hotel (Fletcher's)** Orchard St ☎01-408 2080 Plan1:**65** C1
58seats P bedrooms available ♀International. Last dinner10.30pm ✻Lunch£6.20&alc Dinner£11.50alc Wine£5.40 Credit cards 1 2 3 4 5 6

XXXX**Tiberio** 22 Queen St ☎01-629 3561 Plan1:**69** E2
Elegant, modern Italian restaurant in white vaulted cellar. Impressive entrance with tropical plants and fountain.
Closed Sun; Lunch not served Sat; 90seats P Live music & dancing Mon-Sat; ♀Italian. last dinner1am ✻Lunch£12alc Dinner£15alc Credit cards 1 2 3 4 5 6

XXXX**Top of the Tower** Post Office Tower, Maple St ☎01-636 3000 Plan1:**71** B3
Comfortable, revolving restaurant at the PO Tower (600ft): turns a complete circle every twenty minutes, giving panoramic views of London.
Closed Xmas; 128seats P ♀Continental. Last dinner11.15pm ✻Lunch£6&alc Dinner£10alc Wine£3.50 Credit cards 1 2 3 4 5 6

XXXX***Westbury Hotel Restaurant*** New Bond St ☎01-629 7755 Plan1:**76** D2
70seats 25P bedrooms available ♀French. Last dinner11.30pm Credit cards 1 2 3 6

XXX**Braganza** 56 Frith St ☎01-437 5412 Plan2:**5** B2
Spacious restaurant on three floors with traditional masculine mahogany panelling and subdued wall lighting.
Closed Sun; 156seats P ♀French. Last dinner11.15pm S% ✻Lunch£10alc Dinner£10alc Wine£3.20 Credit cards 1 2 3 4 5 6

XXX**Chesa** (Swiss Centre) 2 New Coventry St ☎01-734 1291 Plan2:**9** C2
Closed Xmas Day; 70seats P ♀International. Last dinner mdnt S% ✻Lunch£7alc Dinner£10alc Wine£5 Credit cards 1 2 3 5

XXX***China Gardens*** 66-68 Brewer St ☎01-437 6500 Plan1:**12** D3
Elegant décor in black and beige with subdued spot-lighting, gold frieze, and wall mirrors.
Closed Sun, Public Hols & Xmas; 150seats Disco Mon-Sat ♀Cantonese. Last dinner12.45am Credit cards 1 2 3 4 5 6

XXX**Genevieve** 13–14 Thayer St ☎01–486 2244 Plan1: **28** C1
Elegant décor with red plush period chairs, carriage lamps and black and white drawings of the car Genevieve.
Closed Sun; 100seats P English & French. Last dinner 11pm Lunch £6–£6.50&alc Dinner £6–£6.50&alc Wine £9.50
Credit cards 1 2 3 5

XXX**Greenhouse** 27A Hay's Mews ☎01–499 3331 Plan1: **30A** E2
Closed Sun & Public Hols; 75seats P International. Last dinner 11pm Lunch £6.50alc Dinner £6.50alc Wine £3.75 Credit cards 1 2 3 5

❀XXX**Lacy's** 26 Whitfield St ☎01–636 2323 Plan1: **39** E3
Closed Sun; Lunch not served; 65seats
Last dinner 11.30pm Credit cards 1 2 3 5 6

XXX***Martinez*** 25 Swallow St ☎01–734 5066 Plan1: **45** D3
Spanish restaurant with colourful hand-painted tiled walls wrought-iron work, paintings and bulls head.
Closed Public Hols; 180seats Live music Mon–Sat; Continental. Last dinner 11.20pm
Credit cards 1 2 3 5

XXX***Masako*** 6–8 St Christopher Pl ☎01–935 1579 Plan1: **47** C1
Authentic Japanese décor with armour, bamboo walls, and hangings from ceilings. Waitresses in national costume.
Closed Sun; 120seats Japanese.
Credit cards 2 4 5

XXX***Portman Inter-Continental Hotel (Rôtisserie Normande)*** Portman Sq ☎01–486 5844 Plan3: **22** B5
Lunch not served Sat; 70seats bedrooms available Live music Sun French. Last dinner 11.30pm
Credit cards 1 2 3 4 5 6

XXX**Snooty Fox** 52 Hertford St ☎01–499 1150 Plan5: **25** A3
Elegant Mayfair restaurant with modern paintings on green baize walls.
Closed Sun; Lunch not served Sat; 50seats P French. Last dinner mdnt ✱Lunch £7.50alc Dinner £8alc Wine £4 Credit cards 2 3 5

XXX***Tandoori of Mayfair*** 37A Curzon St ☎01–629 0600 Plan1: **67** E2
closed Sun & Xmas; 100seats North Indian. Last dinner 12.30am Credit cards 1 2 3 4 5 6

XXX**Terrazza** 19 Romilly St ☎01–734 2504 Plan1: **41** B2
Soho restaurant on two floors, with cool, modern décor, tiled floor and murals.
180seats P Italian. Last dinner 11pm ✱Lunch £9.50alc Dinner £9.50alc
Credit cards 1 2 3 4 5 6

XXX**Veeraswarmy's** 99/101 Regent St ☎01–734 1401 Plan1: **72** D3
Closed Xmas Day & Good Fri; 150seats P Indian. Last dinner 11.30pm Lunch £9alc Dinner £9alc
Credit cards 1 2 3 4 5 6

XXX***Verreys*** 233 Regent St ☎01–734 4495 Plan1: **74** C3
Situated in basement, this 150-year-old restaurant has oak-panelled walls.
Closed Sun & Public Hols; 180seats English & French. Last dinner 11.15pm
Credit cards 1 2 3 5 6

❀XXX**White Tower** 1 Percy St ☎01–636 8141 Plan1: **81** B4
Closed Sat, Sun, Public Hols & 3 wks Aug; 80seats P Greek. Last dinner 10pm Lunch £8–£10 Dinner £8–£10 Wine £3.50 Credit cards 1 2 5

XX**Au Jardin des Gourmets** 5 Greek St ☎01–437 1816 Plan2: **2** A2
Closed Sun; Lunch not served Sat; 100seats P French. Last dinner 11.30pm
Lunch £6–£6.50&alc Dinner £6–£6.50&alc Wine £3.50 Credit cards 1 2 3 4 5

XX**Coq au Vin** 8 Harriet St, Lowndes Sq ☎01–235 3969 Plan4: **20** B6
Bright, street-level French restaurant in quiet street off Lowndes Square.
Lunch not served Sat; 50seats P French. ✱Lunch £12alc Dinner £12alc Wine £2.75
Credit cards 1 2 3 5 6

XX**La Cucaracha** 12 Greek St ☎01–734 2253 Plan2: **12** B2
Maze of small white-arched rooms with tiled floors; once the cellars of 18th-C monastery.
Closed Sun & Public Hols; Lunch not served Sat; 100seats P Live music 6 nights wkly Mexican. Last dinner 11.15pm ✱Lunch £6alc Dinner £6alc Wine £2.75 Credit cards 1 2 3 4 5 6

XX**Fisherman's Wharf** 73 Baker St ☎01–935 0471 Plan3: **7** A5
Closed Xmas; 66seats P French. Last dinner 10.30pm S% ✱Lunch £9.50alc Dinner £9.50alc Wine £3.15
Credit cards 1 2 3 4 5 6

XX**Gallery Rendezvous** 53 Beak St ☎01–734 0445 Plan1: **24** D3
Chinese paintings permanently exhibited in the restaurant.
Closed 25 & 26 Dec; 150seats P Pekinese. Last dinner 11pm ✱Lunch fr £4.50&alc Dinner fr £4.50&alc Wine £3.20 Credit cards 2 5

❀XX**Gay Hussar** 2 Greek St ☎01–437 0973 Plan2: **15** A2
Small, attractive restaurant decorated in Hungarian style.
Closed Sun & Public Hols; 35seats P Hungarian. Specialities: Paprika chicken, roast duck & red cabbage, veal goulash & galuska.
Last dinner 11.30pm Lunch £5.50&alc Dinner £8.50alc Wine £3

XX**Gaylord** 16 Albemarle St ☎01–629 9802 Plan1: **25** D3
100seats P Indian. Last dinner 11.30pm (Sun 11pm) ✱Lunch £5.50–£6&alc Dinner £5.50–£6&alc Wine £4.50
Credit cards 1 2 3 5 6

XX**Gaylord** Mortimer St ☎01–636 0808 Plan1: **26** C3
86seats 20P Indian. Last dinner 11.25pm Lunch £3.10–£4.15&alc Dinner £3.10–£4.15&alc
Credit cards 1 2 3 5 6

XX**Geetanjli of Mayfair** 23 Brook St ☎01–493 1779 Plan1: **27** D2
Closed 25, 26 Dec & 1 Jan; 54seats P Indian. Last dinner 11pm ✱Lunch £10alc Dinner £10alc Wine £3.50 Credit cards 1 2 3 5 6

XX**Golden Carp** 8A Mount St ☎01–499 3385 Plan1: **29** D2
Closed Sun & Public Hols; Lunch not served Sat 65seats P French & Italian. Last dinner 11pm S% ✱Lunch £6.75alc Dinner £6.75alc Wine £3.95 Credit cards 1 2 3 5 6

XX**Hostaria Romana** 70 Dean St ☎01–734 2869 Plan2: **19** B2
Closed Xmas Day; Lunch not served Easter Sun; 160seats P Italian. ✱Lunch £5.50alc Dinner £5.50alc Wine £3 Credit cards 1 2 3 4 5 6

XXIçi Paris 2A Duke St ☎01–935 1864 Plan1: **33** C1
An elegant basement restaurant with Louis XV furnishings.
Closed Sun, last wk Jul & 1st 2 wks Aug; Lunch not served Sat; 32seats P Live music & dancing nightly ♀French. Last dinner10.30pm S% Lunch£13.50alc Dinner£13.50alc Wine£4 Credit cards 2 3 4

XXLangan's Brasserie Stratton St ☎01–493 6437 Not on plan
Closed Sun; Lunch not served Sat; 180seats ♀French. Last dinner11.15pm S% Lunch£15alc Dinner£15alc Wine£3 Credit cards 2 5

XX*La Loggia* 39 Upper Berkeley St ☎01–723 0554 Plan3: **13** B5
An elegant restaurant with northern Italian décor.
Closed Sun; 60seats ♀Italian. Last dinner11.30pm

XXMarquis 121A Mount St, Grosvenor Sq ☎01–499 1256 Plan1: **44** D2
Closed Sun; 70seats P ♀French & Italian. Last dinner10.45pm Lunch£9alc Dinner£9alc Wine£4.45 Credit cards 1 2 3 5

XXMikado 110 George St ☎01–935 9320 Plan3: **18** B5
Closed Sun & Public Hols; Lunch not served Sat; 80seats P ♀Japanese. Last dinner10.30pm ✻Lunch£9.50–£15&alc Dinner£9.50–£15&alc Wine£6 Credit cards 2 3 5

❀XXOdin's 27 Devonshire St ☎01–935 7296 Plan1: **52** B1
Closed Public Hols; Lunch not served Sat & Sun; 40seats Last dinner11pm

XXTokyo 7 Swallow St ☎01–734 2269 Plan1: **70** D3
A modern, Japanese restaurant offering authentic cuisine.
85seats P ♀Japanese. Last dinner10.30pm S% ✻Lunch£2.60–£4.80&alc Dinner£4.50–£12&alc Wine£2.20 Credit cards 1 2 3 4 5 6

XXVendôme 20 Dover St ☎01–629 5417 Plan1: **73** D/E3
Closed Sat; 73seats P ♀French. Last dinner10.45pm S% ✻Lunch£10alc Dinner£10alc Wine£3.20 Credit cards 1 2 3 4 5 6

XXWheeler's 19 Old Compton St ☎01–437 2706 Plan2: **44** B2
Well-established fish restaurant on two floors, with quaint Victorian décor.
Closed Sun; 149seats P ♀French. Last dinner10.45pm S% ✻Lunch£10alc Dinner£10alc Wine£3.20 Credit cards 1 2 3 4 5 6

XArirang 31–32 Poland St ☎01–437 6633 Plan1: **1** C3
Closed Sun, Xmas & Etr; 75seats P ♀Korean. Last dinner11pm Lunch fr£1.50&alc Dinner£6.50alc Wine£1.50 Credit cards 1 2 3 4 5

XChuen Cheng Ku 17–23 Wardour St ☎01–734 3281 Plan2: **11** C2
400seats P ♀Chinese. Last dinner11.30pm (Sun 10.30pm) Lunch£2.50alc Dinner£3.50alc

X*Ganges* 40 Gerrard St ☎01–437 0284 Plan2: **14** C3
Closed Sun & Xmas day; 80seats ♀Indian. Credit cards 1 2 3 5

XKerzenstuberl 9 St Christopher's Pl ☎01–486 3196 Plan1: **37** C1
Closed Sun, Public Hols & mid Aug–mid Sep; Lunch not served Sat; 48seats P Live music Mon–Sat ♀Austrian. Last dinner11pm Lunch£10alc Dinner£10alc Wine£3.50 Credit cards 1 2 3 5 6

XLee Ho Fook 15/16 Gerrard St ☎01–734 9578 Plan2: **24** C2
125seats P ♀Cantonese. Last dinner11.30pm ✻Lunch£.350alc Dinner£5alc Wine£2.95 Credit cards 1 2 3 4 6

X*Little Acropolis* 10 Charlotte St ☎01–636 8198 Plan1: **41** B4
Small, intimate, candlelit Greek restaurant.
Closed Sun; Lunch not served Sat; 32seats ♀Greek. Last dinner10.30pm Credit cards 1 2 3 4 5 6

X*Okame* 30 Brook St ☎01–629 2730 Plan1: **52A** C2
Closed Sun; Lunch not served Sat; 40seats ♀Japanese. Last dinner10.30pm Credit cards 1 2 3 5

XOrient 43 Grafton Way ☎01–387 6363 Plan1: **52B** A3
Closed Xmas Day; 80seats P Cabaret Tue–Sun ♀Indian. Last dinner11.50pm Lunch£2.50–£5&alc Dinner£4–£8&alc wine£2.95 Credit cards 1 2 3 4 5 6

X*Panda House* 41–43 Wardour St ☎01–437 6279 Plan2: **25** C2
100seats ♀Cantonese. Last dinner mdnt

X*Pavilion* 165 Oxford St, W1 ☎01–437 8774 Plan1: **53** C3
Closed Sun; Lunch not served Sat; 45seats Live music nightly ♀Italian. Last dinner10.45pm Credit cards 1 2 3 5

XSaga 43 South Molton St ☎01–408 2236 Plan1: **63** C2
Closed Sun; 70seats P ♀Japanese. Last dinner10.30pm S% Lunch£3–£5&alc Dinner£8–£20&alc Credit cards 1 2 3 4 5 6

❀XSoho Rendezvous 21 Romilly St ☎01–437 1486 Plan2: **38** B2
Closed Public Hols, 25 & 26Dec; 80seats P ♀Pekinese. Specialities: Prawns with sesame seeds, crispy duck, sole in wine sauce.

Last dinner 11.45pm ✱Lunch £5.50alc Dinner £5.50alc Wine £3 Credit cards 1 2 3 4 5 6

×***Sol é Mar*** 77 Dean St ☎01-437 4206 Plan2:**38A** B2
Closed Sun; 75seats Portuguese.
Last dinner 11pm Credit cards 1 2 3 4 5 6

×***Tin Luk*** 11 Gerrard St ☎01-437 1163 Plan2:**42** C2
50seats Cantonese.

W2 Bayswater, Paddington

★★★★**Great Western Royal** Paddington Station (British Transport) ☎01-723 1551 Telex no 263972 Plan3:**9** B3
Imposing building with cream façade, classical frieze and twin towers, built by Younger Hardwick 1850-2.
163rm(140⇌ ⋒) Lift ☽ TV in bedrooms 8P Conference facilities available ♿ English & French.
Last dinner 9.15pm S%
✱sB&B⇌⋒ fr£29 dB&B⇌⋒ fr£38 ✱Wine £3.50
Credit cards 1 2 3 4 5 6

☆☆☆☆**London Embassy** 150 Bayswater Rd (Embassy) ☎01-229 1212 Telex no 27727 Plan3:**14** C1
193⇌⋒ Lift ☽ CTV in bedrooms 30P 25
Last dinner 9.45pm S% sB&B⇌⋒£27 dB&B⇌⋒£37 Continental breakfast
Lunch £5&alc Tea £1.50 Dinner £5.50&alc
Wine £4 Credit cards 1 2 3 4 5 6

★★★★**Royal Lancaster** Lancaster Ter (Rank) ☎01-262 6737 Telex no 24822 Plan3:**25** C3
436⇌⋒ Lift ☽ CTV in bedrooms 100P Live music & dancing Mon-Sat Conference facilities available ♿ English, French & Italian.
Last dinner 11.30pm S%
sB&B⇌⋒£35-£50 dB&B⇌⋒£55-£65
Continental breakfast Lunch £5.50alc Tea £2alc
Dinner £5.50alc Wine £4
Credit cards 1 2 3 4 5 6

☆☆☆***Central Park*** Queensborough Ter ☎01-229 2424 Telex no 27342 Plan3:**3** C2
299⇌⋒ Annexe:60⋒ Lift TV sauna bath Disco Sun Conference facilities available Mainly grills. Last dinner 11pm
Credit cards 1 2 3 5 6

★★★**Coburg** 129 Bayswater Rd (Best Western) ☎01-229 3654 Telex no 268235 Plan3:**5** C1
A traditional hotel overlooking Hyde Park.
RS Xmas; 125rm(70⇌⋒) Lift ☽ TV in bedrooms Conference facilities available ♿ International.
Last dinner 9.30pm S% sB&B fr£14 sB&B⇌⋒ fr£30 dB&B fr£21 dB&B⇌⋒ fr£32
Lunch £4&alc Tea £1 High Tea £2.50
Dinner £5&alc Wine £3
Credit cards 1 2 3 4 5 6

★★★**Park Court** Lancaster Gate (Trusthouse Forte) ☎01-402 4272 Telex no 23922 Plan 3:**21** C2
442⇌⋒ Lift ☽ CTV in bedrooms Conference facilities available. Last dinner 10.15pm
S% sB&B⇌⋒£20 dB&B⇌⋒£30
Continental breakfast *xmas*
Credit cards 1 2 3 4 5 6

☆☆☆**Post House** 104-105 Bayswater Rd (Trusthouse Forte) ☎01-262 4461 Telex no 22667 Plan3:**23** C2
175⇌⋒ Lift ☽ CTV in bedrooms 58
Last dinner 8.30pm S% sB&B⇌⋒£23.75 dB&B⇌⋒£33 *xmas* Credit cards 1 2 3 4 5 6

★★★**White's** Lancaster Gate (Trusthouse Forte) ☎01-262 2711 Plan3:**28** C2
Elegant, white, four-storey building, overlooking Hyde Park.
59⇌⋒ Lift TV in bedrooms 25P
Last dinner 10.15pm S% sB&B⇌⋒£25 dB&B⇌⋒£36.50 Continental breakfast
xmas Credit cards 1 2 3 4 5 6

☆☆**Grosvenor Court** Praed St (Grand Met) ☎01-262 3464 Plan3:**10** B3
93⇌⋒ Lift ☽ Mainly grills.
Last dinner 10pm S%
✱sB⇌⋒£12.25(room only) dB⇌⋒£18.25(room only) Credit cards 1 2 3 4 5 6

★★**Windsor** Lancaster Gate (Trusthouse Forte) ☎01-262 4501 Plan3:**29** C2
93rm(53⇌⋒) Lift ☽ CTV TV in bedrooms
Last dinner 8.30pm S% sB&B £14 sB&B £17 sB £B21 dB&B⇌⋒£24.50
Continental breakfast *xmas*
Credit cards 1 2 3 4 5 6

××××**Royal Lancaster Hotel (La Rosette)** Lancaster Ter ☎01-262 6737 Plan3:**25** C3
Lunch not served Sat & Sun; 80seats 100P bedrooms available Live music & dancing Mon-Sat English & Continental. Last dinner 11.30pm S%
Lunch £9alc Dinner £9.25&alc Wine £4.50
Credit cards 1 2 3 4 5 6

××**Bali** 101 Edgware Rd ☎01-262 9100 Plan3:**1** B4
Indonesian restaurant; exotic décor with ruined temple motif, Eastern goddess frieze, coconut palms and bamboo.
Closed Xmas; 100seats Indonesian.
Last dinner 11.30pm Lunch £4.70&alc
Dinner £5.20&alc Wine £2.90
Credit cards 1 2 3 4 5 6

××***Trat-West*** 143 Edgware Rd ☎01-723 8203 Plan3:**27** B4
70seats Italian. Last dinner 11.30pm
Credit cards 1 2 3 4 5 6

×**Chez Franco** 3 Hereford Rd ☎01-229 5079 Not on plan
Sma' pleasant ground-floor restaurant. Walls covered with photographs of well-known actors and actresses.

Closed Sun & last 3wks Aug; Lunch not served Sat; 38 seats P French & Italian. Last dinner 11.30pm S% Lunch£4.50&alc Dinner£4.50&alc Wine£2.95

X***Ganges*** 101 Praed St 01-723 4096 Plan3: **8** B3 Closed Mon; Lunch not served Tue-Fri 28seats Indian. Credit cards 1 2 3 5

X**Hungry Viking** 44 Ossington St 01-727 3311 Not on plan
Closed Mon; Lunch not served; 50seats Live music & dancing Tue, Thu, Sat & Sun Scandinavian. Last dinner 11.30pm Dinner£4.95 Wine£2.60 Credit cards 1 2 3 5

X***Kalamaras*** 76-78 Inverness Mews 01-727 9122 Plan3: **12** C1
Closed Sun; 150seats Live music Wed, Fri & Sat Greek. Last dinner mdnt Credit cards 2 5

X***Mandarin Kitchen*** 14-16 Queensway 01-727 9012 Plan3: **15** C1
90seats Chinese. Last dinner 11.15pm Credit card 2

W5 Ealing

☆☆☆**Carnarvon** Ealing Common 01-992 5399 Telex no935114 Not on plan
145 Lift TV in bedrooms 150P Conference facilities available International. Last dinner 9.30pm S% sB&B£14 sB&B £23 dB&B£21 dB&B £31 Lunch£5.50-£6.50&alc Tea50p-£2 Dinner£5.50-£6.50&alc Wine£3.50 Credit cards 1 2 3 5

W6 Hammersmith

☆☆☆☆***Cunard International*** 1 Shortlands 01-741 1555 Telex no934539 Not on plan
Closed Xmas wk; 640 Lift CTV in bedrooms 300 International. Last dinner 10.30pm Credit cards 1 2 3 4 5 6

W8 Kensington

★★★★★**Royal Garden** Kensington High St (Rank) 01-937 8000 Telex no2631651 Plan4: **63** B2
434 Lift CTV in bedrooms 140 Live music & dancing Mon-Sat Cabaret Mon-Sat Conference facilities available International. Last dinner 10.30pm S% *sB&B £35.60-£40.60 dB&B £45.20-£55.20 Continental breakfast Lunch£6.50 Tea£2.50 Dinner£6.50alc Wine£4.75 Credit cards 1 2 3 4 5 6

★★★★**Kensington Close** Wrights Ln, W8 (Trusthouse Forte) 01-937 8170 Telex no23914 Plan4: **38** C2
530 Lift CTV in bedrooms 120 (heated) sauna bath Conference facilities available Last dinner 10pm S% dB&B £25 dB&B £36 xmas Credit cards 1 2 3 4 5 6

★★★★***Kensington Palace*** De Vere Gdns 01-937 8121 Plan4: **39** B3
318 Lift CTV in bedrooms Conference facilities available English & French. Last dinner 8.30pm Credit cards 1 2 3 4 5 6

★★★**De Vere** 60 Hyde Park Gate (De Vere) 01-584 0051 Telex no8953644 Plan4: **24** B3
73 Annexe: 10 Lift TV in bedrooms Conference facilities available Mainly grills. Last dinner 9.30pm S% sB&B £26 dB&B £40 Continental breakfast Lunch£10alc Tea fr£1.25 Dinner£10alc Wine£3.75 Credit cards 1 2 3 5 6

☆☆☆**London Tara** Wrights Ln 01-937 7211 Telex no918835 Plan4: **44** C2
844 Lift CTV in bedrooms 70 Disco nightly Conference facilities available English & French. Last dinner 1.30am S% *sB&B £26.35 dB&B £31.64 Continental breakfast Credit cards 1 2 3 5 6

★★**Hotel Lexham** 32-38 Lexham Gdns 01-373 6471 Plan4: **42** C/D2
Four adjacent, three-storey private houses converted into a hotel.
Closed Xmas wk; Unlicensed; 64rm (15) Lift CTV English & Continental. Last dinner 8pm sB&B£11.30-£12.50 sB&B £12.50-£13.50 dB&B£17.25-£19 dB&B £22-£24 Lunch£2.30-£2.50 Tea50-60p Dinner£3.50-£3.80

XXX**Le Bressan** 14 Wrights Ln 01-937 8525 Plan4: **12** C2
Closed Sat, Sun, last 2wks Aug & 1st wk Sep; 50seats French. Last dinner 11.30pm Credit cards 1 2 3 4 5 6

XXX***Fu Tong*** 29 Kensington High St 01-937 1293 Plan4: **31** B2
Elegant, Chinese restaurant divided into several open-sided alcoves; with Chinese paintings and blossom trees.
115seats Chinese. Last dinner 11.20pm Credit cards 1 2 3 5 6

XXX***Trattoo*** 2 Abingdon Rd 01-937 4448 Plan4: **76** C1
Pleasant restaurant on two levels with stone-flagged floor and sloping glass roof.
85seats Live music 6 nights wkly Italian. Last dinner 12.30am Credit cards 1 2 3 4 5 6

XX**Alcove** 17 Kensington High St 01-937 1443 Plan4: **3** B2
Closed Sun; 95seats French. Last dinner 10.45pm

S% ✱Lunch£10alc Dinner£10alc
Credit cards 1 2 3 4 5 6

✕✕Sailing Junk 59 Marloes Rd ☎01–937 2589
Plan4: **64** C2
Designed as interior of richly decorated 'junk'; Chinese paintings, bamboo decorations and subdued lighting – partly from red, illuminated dragons.
45seats ₱ ✱Chinese. Last dinner 11.30pm
Dinner fr£6.18 Wine£2.90
Credit cards 1 2 3 4 5 6

✕✕La Toque Blanche 21 Abingdon Rd
☎01–937 5832 Plan4: **75** C1
Split-level French restaurant with cooking utensils and impressionists' prints on walls.
Closed Sat, Sun, Public Hols, Xmas, Etr & Aug; 42seats ₱ French. Last dinner 10.45pm
Lunch£10alc Wine£3.50 Credit cards 2 5

✕Ark 35 Kensington High St, ☎01–937 4294
Plan4: **5** B2
Closed Xmas & Etr; Lunch not served Sun; 75seats ₱ French. Last dinner 11.30pm Lunch£6.50alc
Dinner£7.50alc Wine£2.65 Credit cards 1 2 3 5

✕Armenian 20 Kensington Church St
☎01–937 5828 Plan4: **6** B2
Lunch not served Sat & Sun; 65seats ₱ Armenian.
Last dinner 11pm ✱Lunch£3.50alc
Dinner£3.50alc Wine£2 Credit cards 1 2 3 4 5 6

✕Il Barbino 32 Kensington Church St
☎01–937 8752 Plan4: **9A** B2
Closed Sun; Lunch not served Public Hols; 45seats ₱ Italian. Last dinner mdnt. S% Lunch£8alc
Dinner£8alc Wine£2.70 Credit cards 1 2 3 4 5 6

✕Holland Street 33C Holland St ☎01–937 3224
Plan4: **35A** B1
Closed Sat, Sun, Public Hols, Xmas & Etr; 20seats ₱
Last dinner 10pm Lunch£2.75–£3.50&alc
Dinner£5alc Wine£3 Credit cards 1 2 3 5 6

✕Siam 12 St Alban's Gv ☎01–937 8763 Plan4: **69** C2
Small restaurant decorated in traditional style.
Lunch not served Mon & Sat; 85seats ₱ Thai.
Last dinner 11.15pm Lunch£3–£4.80&alc
Dinner£3.50–£5.80&alc Wine£3.20
Credit cards 2 3 4 5

✕*Twin Brothers* 51 Church St ☎01–937 4152
Plan4: **77** B2
Closed Sun; Lunch not served; 32seats German.
Last dinner 11pm

W9 Maida Vale

★★★Clarendon Court Edgware Rd ☎01–286 8080
Telex no 07374 Not on plan
157rm(140⇌ ⋒) 2⊟ Lift ☽ ⋈ CTV in bedrooms ₱
sauna bath Conference facilities available
International. Last dinner mdnt S%
sB&B£11.88–£12.96 sB&B⇌⋒£21.14–£23.76
dB&B£24.84–£27 dB&B⇌⋒£32.18–£35.64
Continental breakfast Lunch£6–£6.50&alc
Dinner£6–£6.50&alc Wine£3.25 *xmas*
Credit cards 1 2 3 5

W11 Holland Park, Notting Hill

☆☆☆☆Hilton International Kensington Holland Park Av ☎01–602 3355 Telex no 919763 Not on plan
611⇌⋒ Lift ☽ ⊞ ⋈ CTV in bedrooms 100
International. Last dinner 10.30pm
✱sB&B⇌⋒£25.60–£29.90
dB&B⇌⋒£35.60–£38.60 Continental breakfast
Lunch£5.50–£6.50 Tea fr£2.20
Dinner£6.50–£7.50 Credit cards 1 2 3 4 5 6

❀✕✕✕Leith's 92 Kensington Park Rd
☎01–220 4481 Not on plan
Closed Xmas; Lunch not served; 95seats ₱
International Specialities: Leith's duckling, smoked trout mousse, chocolate roulade.
Last dinner mdnt ✱Dinner£9.90 Wine£3.50
Credit cards 1 2 3 5 6

❀✕✕Chez Moi 3 Addison Av ☎01–603 8267 Not on plan
Warm intimate French restaurant with subdued lighting.
Closed Sun, Public, Hols, last wk Dec–2nd wk Jan & last 3wks Aug; Lunch not served; 54seats ₱
French. Last dinner 11.30pm ✱Dinner£4,15alc
Wine£3.85

✕✕La Pomme d'Amour 128 Holland Park Av
☎01–229 8532 Not on plan
Closed Sat & Sun; ₱ French. Last dinner 10.45pm
✱Lunch fr£3.95&alc Dinner£10.50alc Wine£2.80
Credit cards 2 3 5

✕La Jardinière 148 Holland Park Av ☎01–221 6090
Not on plan
Closed Mon; Lunch served Sun only; 90seats ₱
French. Last dinner mdnt ✱Lunch fr£3.25&alc
Dinner£6.50alc Wine£2.70 Credit card 2

✕Singapore Mandarin 120–122 Holland Park Av
☎01–727 6341 Not on plan
Closed Xmas; 100seats ₱ Live music & dancing Fri & Sat Chinese & Malaysian. Last dinner 11.45pm
Lunch£1.75–£5 Dinner fr£5.25&alc Wine£2.60
Credit cards 2 5

W12 Shepherd's Bush

✕Shireen 270 Uxbridge Rd ☎01–749 5927 Not on plan
Closed Xmas; 35seats Indian.
Last dinner 11.30pm S% ✱Lunch£6alc
Dinner£8alc Wine£2.65 Credit cards 1 2 3 5 6

W14 West Kensington
★★★**Royal Kensington** 380 Kensington High St ☎01–603 3333 Telex no 22229 Not on plan
409⇌⋔ Lift ☽ ⊞ ♅ CTV in bedrooms ₱ Conference facilities available ♡ Continental.
Last dinner 12.30am ♉ ♊ S%
✱sB&B⇌⋔£25.38 dB&B⇌⋔£31.32
Continental breakfast Lunch £5alc Tea £1alc
High Tea £2alc Dinner £7alc Wine £4.50
Credit cards ①②③④⑤⑥

WC1 Bloomsbury, Holborn
☆☆☆☆***Imperial*** Russell Sq (Imperial)
☎01–837 3655 Telex no 263951 Plan 1: **34** B5
The bar on the ninth floor gives impressive views over London. There is a car park under the hotel but this is not operated by the Imperial.
450⇌⋔ Lift ☽ ⊞ ♅ CTV Conference facilities available ♡ English, French & Italian.
Last dinner 10.30pm ♉ ♊ Wine £2.75 ⊟
Credit cards ①②③④⑤⑥

☆☆☆☆***Royal National*** Bedford Way (Imperial)
☎01–637 2488 Telex no 263951 Plan 1: **60** A4
Modern building, situated adjacent to Russell and Tavistock Squares.
591⇌⋔ Lift ☽ ⊞ ♅ CTV TV available in bedrooms ⊘ Conference facilities available ♡ English, French & Italian. Last dinner 10.30pm ♉ ♊ Wine £2.75 ⊟
Credit cards ①②③④⑤⑥

★★★★**Russell** Russell Sq (Trusthouse Forte)
☎01–837 6470 Telex no 24615 Plan 1: **61** A5
Victorian building with towers and Dutch gables. Entrance hall and staircase are built of Griotti marble and the Carving Table Restaurant has fine marble pillars.
320⇌⋔ Lift ☽ ♅ CTV in bedrooms ₱ Conference facilities available Last dinner 10pm ♉ ♊ S%
sB&B⇌⋔£30 dB&B⇌⋔£42.50 ⊟ *xmas*
Credit cards ①②③④⑤⑥

★★★***Bedford*** Southampton Row (Imperial)
☎01–636 7822 Telex no 263951 Plan 1: **3** B5
250⇌⋔ Lift ☽ ♅ CTV ⊘ 75⌂ ♡ English, French & Italian. Last dinner 10.30pm ♉ ♊ Wine £2.75 ⊟
Credit cards ①②③④⑤⑥

★★★**Bloomsbury Centre** Coram St (Centre)
☎01–837 1200 Telex no 22113 Plan 1: **6** A5
250⇌⋔ Lift ☽ ♅ CTV TV in bedrooms ⊘ 80⌂
Conference facilities available Last dinner 10pm ♉
S% ✱sB&B⇌⋔£18.75 dB&B⇌⋔£25.75
Continental breakfast Lunch £4.75 Dinner £4.75
Wine £3.40 ⊟ Credit cards ①②③④⑤⑥

★★★**Kingsley** Bloomsbury Way (Trusthouse Forte)
☎01–242 5881 Telex no 21157 Plan 1: **38** B5
173rm(99⇌⋔) Lift ☽ CTV CTV in bedrooms ₱
Conference facilities available Last dinner 9pm ♉
♊ S% sB&B£14 sB&B⇌⋔£17 dB&B£21
dB&B⇌⋔£24.50 Continental breakfast ⊟
Credit cards ①②③④⑤⑥

★★★**London Ryan,** Gwynne Pl, King's Cross Rd
☎01–278 2480 Telex no 27728 Not on plan
Situated at Gwynne Place, which is named after Charles II's reputed mistress.
213⇌⋔ Lift ☽ ♅ CTV available in bedrooms 45P
Last dinner 10pm ♉ ♊ S%
sB&B⇌⋔£20–£24 dB&B⇌⋔£28–£33
Continental breakfast Bar lunch £2.25–£2.75
Dinner £4.25–£5 Wine £2.75
Credit cards ①②③④⑤⑥

☆☆☆***President*** Russel Sq (Imperial) ☎01–837 8844
Telex no 263951 Plan 1: **55** B5
Modernised, six-storied building adjoining the Imperial Hotel. The car park under the hotel is not operated by the hotel.
447⇌⋔ Lift ☽ ⊞ ♅ CTV ⊘ ♡ English, French & Italian. Last dinner 10.30pm ♉ ♊ Wine £2.75
⊟ Credit cards ①②③④⑤⑥

★★★**Royal Scot** 100 King's Cross Rd (Thistle)
☎01–278 2434 Telex no 27657 Not on plan
349⇌⋔ 8▭ Lift ☽ ⊞ ♅ CTV in bedrooms ⊘ 39P
Conference facilities available Last dinner 10.30pm
♉ S% sB&B⇌⋔ fr£24 dB&B⇌⋔ fr£33
Continental breakfast Lunch £5.95alc
Dinner £5.95alc Wine £2.75 ⊟
Credit cards ①②③④⑤⑥

★★★***Tavistock*** Tavistock Sq (Imperial)
☎01–636 8383 Telex no 263951 Plan 1: **68** A4
301⇌⋔ Lift ☽ ♅ CTV ⊘ 45⌂ Conference facilities available ♡ English, French & Italian.
Last dinner 10.30pm ♉ ♊ Wine £2.75 ⊟
Credit cards ①②③④⑤⑥

★★**Bedford Corner** Bayley St (Centre)
☎01–580 7766 Telex no 263561 Plan 1: **4** B4
85rm(45⇌⋔) Lift ☽ ♅ CTV ⊘ ₱
Last dinner 9.30pm S% ✱sB&B£10
sB&B⇌⋔£15.25 dB&B£15.25 dB&B⇌⋔£19.25
Continental breakfast Lunch £3.65 Dinner £3.65
Wine £3.40 ⊟ Credit cards ①②③④⑤⑥

★★***Cora*** Upper Woburn Pl ☎01–387 5111
Telex no 261591 Plan 1: **17** A4
150rm(52⇌⋔) Lift ☽ CTV TV available in bedrooms ⊘ ⛟ Conference facilities available ♡ English & Continental. Last dinner 9pm ♉ Credit cards ②③⑤

★★**Grand** 126 Southampton Row ☎01–405 2006
Telex no 25757 Plan 1: **30** B5
93rm(48⇌⋔) Lift ☽ ♅ CTV ₱ ♿ ♡ English & French. Last dinner 8.45pm ♉ ♊ ✱sB&B£9.10
dB&B£14 dB&B⇌⋔£17 Lunch £3.30&alc
Dinner £3.50&alc Credit cards ①②③④⑤⑥

★★**Ivanhoe** Bloomsbury St (Centre) ☎01–636 5601
Telex no 298274 Plan 1: **35** B4

50rm(28⇌⋒) Lift ☽ ⋒ CTV ⊘ P Last dinner9.30pm ♆ ♁ S% ✱sB&B£10 sB&B⇌⋒£15.25 dB&B£15.25 dB&B⇌⋒£19.25 Continental breakfast Lunch£3.60 Dinner£3.60 Wine£3.40 ⋒ Credit cards 1 2 3 4 5 6

★★**Kenilworth** 97 Great Russell St (Centre) ☎01-636 3283 Telex no 298274 Plan1: **36** B4 210rm(50⇌⋒) Lift ☽ ⋒ CTV ⊘ P Conference facilities available Last dinner9.30pm S% ✱sB&B£10 sB&B⇌⋒£15.25 dB&B£15.25 dB&B⇌⋒£19.25 Continental breakfast Lunch£3.30 Dinner£3.50 Wine£3.40 ⋒ Credit cards 1 2 3 4 5 6

★★**Montague** Montague St (Norfolk Capital) ☎01-637 1001 Telex no 23241 Plan1: **49** B5 121rm(27⇌⋒) Lift ☽ ⋒ CTV P Last dinner9pm ♆ S% sB&B£12.60 sB&B⇌⋒£17.30 dB&B£20 dB&B⇌⋒£25.20 Continental breakfast Lunch fr£3.25&alc Dinner fr£4.25&alc Wine£4 ⋒ *xmas* Credit cards 1 2 3 5 6

★★**White Hall, Bloomsbury Sq** ☎01-242 5401 Plan1: **78** B5
Georgian-style terraced hotel, close to the British Museum and London University.
60rm Lift ☽ ⋒ CTV ⊘ P Last dinner8pm ♆ ♁ sB&B fr£14.85 dB&B fr£25 Lunch fr£4.40 Dinner fr£4.40 Wine£2.40 Credit cards 1 2 3 4 5 6

★★**White Hall, 2-5 Montague St** ☎01-580 5871 Plan1: **79** B5
Pleasant, terraced house with own rear terrace and garden.
50rm Lift ☽ ⋒ CTV ⊘ P Last dinner8pm ♆ ♁ sB&B fr£33.55 dB&B fr£23.45 Lunch fr£4.40 Dinner fr£4.40 Wine£2.40 Credit cards 1 2 3 4 5 6

WC2 Covent Garden, *Leicester Square, Strand and Kingsway*

★★★★★**Savoy** Strand ☎01-836 4343 Plan2: **35** C5
See page 46 for details

★★★★**Charing Cross** Strand (British Transport) ☎01-839 7282 Telex no 261101 Plan2: **8** D4
Victorian building of brick and cream Stucco by Barry
206⇌⋒ Lift ☽ ⋒ CTV in bedrooms sauna bath Conference facilities available ♿ Last dinner10.30pm ♆ ♁ S% ✱sB&B⇌⋒ fr£34.50 dB&B⇌⋒ fr£48.25 Wine£3.50 ⋒ Credit cards 1 2 3 4 5 6

★★★★**Waldorf** Aldwych (Trusthouse Forte) ☎01-836 2400 Telex no 24574 Plan2: **43** B5/6
Impressive French-style, neo-Renaissance building.
310⇌⋒ Lift ☽ ⋒ CTV in bedrooms P Conference facilities available Last dinner11pm ♆ ♁ S% sB&B⇌⋒£41 dB&B⇌⋒£55.50 ⋒ Credit cards 1 2 3 4 5 6

★★★**Drury Lane** 10 Drury Ln (Grand Met) ☎01-836 6666 Telex no 8811395 Plan2: **12A** A4 129⇌⋒ Lift ☽ ⋒ TV available in bedrooms ⊘ P Last dinner11pm ♆ ♁ S% ✱sB⇌⋒£20-£25 (room only) dB⇌⋒£29-£36 (room only) ⋒ Credit cards 1 2 3 4 5 6

★★★**Pastoria** St Martin's Street, Leicester Sq (Grand Met) ☎01-930 8641 Plan2: **31** D3 53rm(40⇌⋒) Lift ⋒ CTV in bedrooms ⊘ P Last dinner10pm ♆ ♁ S% ✱sB⇌⋒£14.50-£17 (room only) dB⇌⋒£21.50-£24 (room only) ⋒ Credit cards 1 2 3 4 5 6

★★★**Strand Palace** Strand (Trusthouse Forte) ☎01-836 8080 Telex no 24208 Plan2: **40** C5 786⇌⋒ Lift ☽ ⋒ CTV CTV in bedrooms ⊘ P Conference facilities available Last dinner10.45pm ♆ ♁ S% sB&B⇌⋒£24.50 dB&B⇌⋒£36.50 Continental breakfast ⋒ *xmas* Credit cards 1 2 3 4 5 6

❀XXXXX**Savoy Hotel Grill** Embankment Gdns ☎01-836 4343 Plan2: **35** C5
Closed Sat; 120seats bedrooms available ♀International. Prices on application

XXXXX***Savoy Hotel Restaurant*** Strand ☎01-836 4343 Plan2: **35** C5
Closed Sun; 400seats bedrooms available ♀French. Last dinner2am Credit cards 1 2 3 6

❀XXXX**Inigo Jones** 14 Garrick St ☎01-836 6456 Plan2: **21** C4
On the first floor of old building in Covent Garden: the unusual ecclesiastical décor includes elegant Gothic arches, illuminated stained glass windows and wood carvings of prelates.
Closed Sun & Public Hols; Lunch not served Sat; 85seats P ♀French. Specialities: Blinis au saumon fumé d'Ecosse, carré d'agneau en croûte, steak tartare. Last dinner11.45pm ✱Lunch£7.80&alc Dinner£12.75alc Wine£4.85 Credit cards 1 2 3 5 6

XXXX***Simpsons*** 100 The Strand ☎01-836 9112 Plan2: **37** C5
Closed Sun & Xmas Day; 500seats last dinner10pm Credit cards 1 3

XXX***Boulestin*** 25 Southampton St ☎01-836 7061 Plan2: **4** C5
Elegant Edwardian-style French restaurant.
Closed Sat, Sun & 1st 3wks Aug; 60seats ♀French. Last dinner11pm Credit cards 1 2 5

XXX***La Bussola*** 42 St Martins Ln ☎01-240 1148 Plan2: **6** C3
Closed Sun; 150seats Live music & dancing Mon-Sat ♀Italian. Last dinner12.30am Credit cards 1 2 3 4 5 6

XXX**Grange** 39 King St ☎01-240 2939 Plan2: **17** C4
Closed Sun; Lunch not served Sat 65seats P ♀English & French. Last dinner11.30pm Lunch£6.70-£10.35 Dinner£6.70-£10.35 Wine£3.85 Credit card 2

XXX**PS Hispaniola** Victoria Embankment, River Thames ☎01-839 3011 Plan2: **18** E5
Restaurant on board a paddle steamer.
Lunch not served Sat; 400seats P ♀International. Last dinner11.30pm Lunch fr£6.50&alc Dinner£7 Credit cards 3 4 5

XXX**Ivy** 1-5 West St ☎01-836 4751 Plan2: **22** B3
A quiet restaurant in the heart of theatreland, popular with theatre clientèle.
Closed Sun & Public Hols; Lunch not served Sat; 120seats P ♀English & French. Last dinner11.15pm ✱Lunch£4-£6&alc Dinner£4-£6&alc Wine£3 Credit cards 1 2 3 4 5 6

XXX***Neal Street*** 26 Neal St ☎01-836 8368 Plan2: **29** B4
Closed Sat, Sun & Public Hols; 60seats ♀English & French. Last dinner11.30pm Credit cards 1 2 3 4 5 6

XXX***L'Opera*** 32 Great Queen St ☎01-405 9020 Plan2: **30** A5
Splendid plush Edwardian restaurant in gilt and crimson; on two floors in centre of theatreland.
Closed Sun; Lunch not served Sat; 100seats ✗ ♀International. Last dinner mdnt Credit cards 1 2 3 5

XXX**Rules** Maiden Ln, Strand ☎01-836 5314 Plan2: **34** C4
Elegant and plush Edwardian-style restaurant with velvet drapes, old prints and playbills.
Closed Sat, Sun & May; 120seats P Lunch£10alc Dinner£10alc Wine£4.20 Credit cards 1 3 5

XXX***Strand Palace Hotel (Carriage Room)*** Strand ☎01–836 7380 Plan2: **40** C5
Comfortable, modern surroundings with subdued, concealed lighting.
140seats bedrooms available Live music Mon–Sat; ♉English & French. Last dinner10.45pm
Credit cards 1 2 3 4 5 6

XX**Beotys** 79 St Martins Ln ☎01–836 8768 Plan2: **3** C3
Comfortable, spacious Greek restaurant.
Closed Sun; 100seats 🅿 ♉Greek.
Last dinner11.30pm Lunch fr£4.50&alc
Dinner£4.50alc Wine£2.40
Credit cards 1 2 3 4 6

XX***Chez Solange*** 35 Cranbourn St ☎01–836 0542 Plan2: **10** C3
Closed Sun; 150seats Live music 6 nights wkly ♉French. Last dinner2am
Credit cards 1 2 3 4 5 6

❀XX**Poon's** 41 King St ☎01–240 1743 Plan2: **31A** C4
Closed Sun; 120seats 🅿 ♉Chinese. Specialities: Wind dried meat, Crispy chicken.
Last dinner11.30pm Wine£3.30

XX***Terazza-Est*** 125 Chancery Ln ☎01–242 2601 Plan6: **10** B2
Closed Sat, Sun & Public Hols; 130seats ♉International. Last dinner11.30pm ✱
Credit cards 1 2 3 4 5 6

❀XX**Thomas de Quincey's** 36 Tavistock St ☎01–240 3972 Plan2: **41A** C5
Closed Sun & last 3wks Aug; Lunch not served Sat; 60seats 🅿 ♉French. Specialities: Casserolette de Quincey, Gratin de lotte et d'écrevisse au pistou de safran, Maigret de canard au poivre vert.
Last dinner11.15pm S% Lunch£13.50alc
Dinner£13.50alc Wine£3.50
Credit cards 1 2 3 5 6

X***Cellier de Medici*** 8 Mays Court ☎01–836 9180 Plan2: **7** D4
Closed Sun; Lunch not served Sat; 32seats ♉French & Italian. Credit cards 2 3 5

X**Manzi's** 1 Leicester St ☎01–437 4864 Plan 2: **27** C2
Edwardian-style sea food restaurant with an intimate atmosphere.
Closed Xmas; Lunch not served Sun; 120seats 🅿 bedrooms available Last dinner11.40pm
✱Lunch£7alc Dinner£7alc Wine£2.85
Credit cards 1 2 3 5 6

X**Mon Plaisir** 21 Monmouth St ☎01–836 7243 Plan2: **28** B3
Closed Sat, Sun, Public Hols & first 2wks Aug; 50seats 🅿 ♉French. Last dinner11pm
✱Lunch fr£4.50&alc Dinner£7.50alc Wine£2.90

X**New Rasa Sayang** 3 Leicester Pl ☎01–437 4556 Not on plan
♉Indonesian. Last dinner11.30pm ✱Lunch£10alc Dinner£10alc Wine£2.80

❀X**Poon's** 27 Lisle St ☎01–437 1528 Plan2: **32** C3
Unlicensed; 45seats ♉Chinese. Last dinner11.30pm

X***Sheekey's*** 29–31 St Martin's Court ☎01–836 4118 Plan2: **36** C3
Closed Sun, Xmas, Etr, Public Hols & last wk Jul–first wk Aug; Dinner not served Sat; 95seats
Last dinner8.30pm Credit cards 1 2 3 5 6

LONDON AIRPORTS See under Gatwick, Heathrow

Gazetteer continues on page 268

WARNING

Overseas visitors should not bring pets of any kind with them to Britain unless they are prepared for the animals to go into lengthy quarantine. Because of the continuing threat of rabies, penalties for ignoring the regulations are extremely severe.

London restaurants with specialised food

Chinese

C-Cantonese
P-Pekinese

Rating	Restaurant
XXX	China Garden (C)
XXX	Fu Tong (C)
XX	Chelsea Rendezvous (P)
XX	Gallery Rendezvous (P)
XX	Lords Rendezvous (P)
XX	Mr Chow (P)
❀XX	Poon's (King St) (C)
XX	Sailing Junk (C)
X	Chuen Cheng Ku (C)
X	Kuo Yuan (SW5) (P)
X	Kuo Yuan (NW10) (P)
X	Lee Ho Fook (C)
X	Mandarin Kitchen (C)
X	Marco Polo (C)
X	Panda House (C)
❀X	Poon's (Lisle St) (C)
X	Shangri La (C)
X	Singapore Mandarin (P)
❀X	Soho Rendezvous (P)
X	Tin Luk (C)
X	Tung Hsing (P)

English

Rating	Restaurant
XXXXX	Stone's Chop House
XXXX	Hunting Lodge
XXXX	Scott's
XXXX	Simpson's
XXX	Baron of Beef
XXX	Lockets
XXX	Neal Street
XXX	Rules
XX	Alcove
XX	English House
XX	Tate Gallery
X	Newton's
X	Holland Street
X	Toto's Wine & Dine

Fish dishes

Rating	Restaurant
XXXX	Overton's (St James's Street)
XXX	Braganza
XX	Alcove
XX	Fisherman's Wharf
XX	Golden Carp
XX	Wheeler's
X	La Croisette
X	Manzi's
X	Poissonnerie de l'Avenue
X	Sheekeys

French

Rating	Restaurant
XXXXX	Café Royal (*Grill Room*)
❀XXXXX	Carlton Tower Hotel (*Chelsea Room*)
XXXXX	Churchill Hotel Restaurant
❀❀❀XXXXX	Connaught Hotel Restaurant
XXXXX	Dorchester Hotel Restaurant
❀XXXXX	Grosvenor House Hotel (*La Fontaine*)
XXXXX	Hilton Hotel (*Roof*)
XXXXX	Inn on the Park Hotel (*Four Seasons*)
❀❀XXXXX	Mirabelle
XXXXX	Savoy Hotel Restaurant
XXXXX	Stone's Chop House
❀XXXX	Inigo Jones
XXXX	La Napoule
XXXX	Overton's
XXXX	Quaglino's Hotel Restaurant
XXXX	Royal Lancaster Hotel (*La Rosette*)
XXXX	Top of the Tower
XXXX	Westbury Hotel Restaurant
XXX	Boulestin
XXX	Braganza
❀XXX	Le Bressan
XXX	Brompton Grill
XXX	La Bussola
❀XXX	Capital Hotel Restaurant
❀XXX	Carriers
❀❀❀XXX	Le Gavroche
XXX	Genevieve
❀XXX	Lacy's
XXX	Lafayette
XXX	Neal Street
XXX	L'Opera
❀❀XXX	Le Poulbot
XXX	Snooty Fox
XXX	Strand Palace Hotel (*Carriage Room*)
❀XXX	White House Hotel Restaurant
XX	Au Jardin des Gourmets
❀XX	Chez Moi
XX	Chez Solange
XX	Le Coq au Vin
❀XX	Daphne's
XX	Le Français
XX	Frederick's
XX	Içi Paris
❀XX	Keats
XX	Marcel
XX	Marquis
XX	La Pomme D'Amour
❀❀XX	Tante Claire
❀XX	Thomas de Quincey's
XX	La Toque Blanche
❀X	Les Amoureaux
X	The Ark
X	Au Fin Bec
❀X	L'Aubergade
X	Barque & Bite
❀X	Bubb's
X	Cassis
X	Cellier de Medici
X	Chez Franco
❀X	Chez Nico
X	La Croisette
X	La Fringale
X	Le Gamin
X	Le Grenouille
X	La Jardinière
❀❀X	Ma Cuisine
X	Le Marmiton
X	M'sieur Frog
X	Overton's
X	Peters Bistro
X	Poissonnerie de l'Avenue
X	South of the Border
X	Le Suquet
X	Le Truc
X	Wild Thyme
X	William F's

Greek	❀XXX	White Tower	X	Kalamaras
	XX	Beoty's	X	Little Akropolis
Hungarian	❀XX	Gay Hussar		
Indian & Pakistani	XXX	Kundan	X	Ganges (Gerrard St W1)
	XXX	Veeraswamy's	X	Ganges (Praed St W2)
	XX	Curry Centre	X	Gullistan Tandoori
	XX	Gaylord (Albemarle St)	X	Naraine
	XX	Gaylord (Mortimer St)	X	Orient
	XX	Geetanjli	X	Shireen
	❀XX	Shezan	X	Vijay
	XX	Tandoori		
Indonesian	XX	Bali		
	X	New Rasa Sayang		
Italian	XXXX	Gennaros	XX	San Frediano
	XXXX	Tiberio	XX	Santa Croce
	XXX	Claudius	XX	Terrazza-Est
	XXX	Terrazza	X	Al Ben Accolto
	XXX	Trattoo	X	Il Barbino
	XX	L'Amico	X	Casa Comineti
	XX	Il Giorno e la Notte	X	Da Angela
	XX	Hostaria Romana	X	Don Luigi's
	XX	Il Lando	X	Portofino
	XX	La Loggia	X	Sale e Pepe
	XX	San Carlo	X	San Quintino
Japanese	XXX	Masako	X	Ginnan
	XX	Mikado	X	Okame
	XX	Tokyo	X	Saga
Jewish	X	Blooms		
Korean	X	Arirang House (SW1)		
Lebanese	XX	Albasha		
Mexican	XX	La Cucaracha		
Norwegian	X	Hungry Viking		
Original dishes	❀XXXX	Walton's	❀XXX	White Tower
	❀XXX	Carriers	❀XX	Daphne's
	❀XXX	Lacy's	❀XX	Odin's
	❀XXX	Leith's	X	Froops
	XXX	Parkes		
Polish & Russian	XX	Nikita's		
	X	Luba's Bistro		
Polynesian	XXXX	Hilton Hotel (*Trader Vic's*)		

Portuguese
- ✕ Sol É Mar

Siamese (Thai)
- ✕ Bangkok
- ✕ Siam

Spanish
- ✕✕✕ PS Hispaniola
- ✕✕✕ Martinez

Swiss
- ✕✕✕ Chesa (*Swiss Centre*)

London restaurants open Sundays in 1980

- ❀✕✕✕✕✕ Berkeley Hotel Restaurant
- ✕✕✕✕✕ Café Royal (*Grill Room*)
- ❀✕✕✕✕✕ Carlton Tower Hotel (*Chelsea Room*)
- ✕✕✕✕✕ Churchill Hotel Restaurant
- ✕✕✕✕✕ Claridge's
- ❀❀❀✕✕✕✕✕ Connaught Hotel Restaurant
- ✕✕✕✕✕ Inn on the Park Hotel (*Four Seasons*)
- ✕✕✕✕✕ Inter-Continental Hotel (*Le Soufflé*)
- ❀✕✕✕✕✕ Savoy Hotel Grill

- ✕✕✕✕ Athenaeum Hotel Restaurant
- ✕✕✕✕ Hilton Hotel (*Trader Vic's*)
- ✕✕✕✕ Royal Lancaster Hotel (*La Rosette*) (dinner only)
- ✕✕✕✕ Scotts (dinner only)
- ✕✕✕✕ Selfridges Hotel (*Fletcher's*)
- ✕✕✕✕ Sheraton Park Tower Hotel (*Le Trianon*)
- ✕✕✕✕ Top of the Tower
- ❀✕✕✕✕ Waltons (lunch only)

- ✕✕✕ Brompton Grill (dinner only)
- ❀✕✕✕ Capital Hotel Restaurant
- ✕✕✕ Chesa (*Swiss Centre*)
- ✕✕✕ Drakes
- ✕✕✕ PS Hispaniola
- ❀✕✕✕ Leith's
- ✕✕✕ Terrazza
- ✕✕✕ Veeraswamy's

- ✕✕ Albasha
- ✕✕ Bali
- ✕✕ Carafe
- ✕✕ Chelsea Rendezvous
- ✕✕ Le Coq au Vin
- ✕✕ Curry Centre
- ✕✕ Fisherman's Wharf
- ✕✕ Gallery Rendezvous
- ✕✕ Gaylord (Albemarle St)
- ✕✕ Gaylord (Mortimer St)
- ✕✕ Geetanjli
- ✕✕ Hostaria Romana
- ✕✕ Lebanese Food Centre – Beirut
- ✕✕ Luigi's
- ✕✕ Mr Chow
- ❀✕✕ Odin's (dinner only)
- ✕✕ Oslo Court
- ✕✕ Rosetti
- ✕✕ Sailing Junk
- ✕✕ Tandoori
- ✕✕ Tokyo
- ✕✕ Vendôme

- ✕ Ark (dinner only)
- ✕ Armenian (dinner only)
- ✕ Casa Comineti (lunch only)
- ✕ Chanterelle
- ✕ Chuen Cheng Ku
- ✕ La Croisette
- ✕ Don Luigi's
- ✕ Hungry Viking
- ✕ La Jardinière
- ✕ Kuo Yuan (SW5)
- ✕ Lee Ho Fook
- ✕ Manzi's (dinner only)
- ✕ New Rasa Sayang
- ✕ Orient
- ✕ Peter's Bistro
- ❀✕ Poons (Lisle St)
- ✕ Provans (dinner only)
- ✕ Shireen
- ✕ Siam
- ✕ Singapore Mandarin
- ❀✕ Soho Rendezvous
- ✕ Le Suquet
- ✕ Tent
- ✕ Vijay

London hotels & restaurants open for meals after 11pm

		Latest time for ordering
★★★★★	Dorchester	Midnight
✿★★★★★	Savoy	Midnight
✿★★★★★	Carlton Tower	24hr service
✿★★★★★	Grosvenor House	23.30
★★★★★	Inter-Continental	23.30
★★★★★	Sheraton Park Tower	Midnight

★★★★	Cavendish	24hr service
☆☆☆☆	Holiday Inn (NW3)	24hr service
☆☆☆☆	London Penta	01.00
★★★★	Royal Lancaster	23.30

★★★	Clarendon Court	Midnight
☆☆☆	London Tara	01.30
★★★	Royal Kensington	00.30
✿★★★	White House	23.30

✕✕✕✕✕	Café Royal (*Grill Room*)	23.30
✿✕✕✕✕✕	Carlton Tower Hotel (*Chelsea Room*	23.15
✕✕✕✕✕	Dorchester Hotel	23.30
✿✕✕✕✕✕	Grosvenor House Hotel (*La Fontaine*)	23.30
✕✕✕✕✕	Hilton Hotel (*Roof*)	Midnight
✕✕✕✕✕	Inter-Continental Hotel (*Le Soufflé*)	23.30
✕✕✕✕✕	Stone's Chop House	23.15

✕✕✕✕	Hilton Hotel (*Trader Vic's*)	23.30
✕✕✕✕	Hunting Lodge	23.30
✿✕✕✕✕	Inigo Jones	23.45
✕✕✕✕	Royal Lancaster Hotel (*La Rosette*)	23.30
✕✕✕✕	Sheraton Park Tower Hotel (*Le Trianon*)	Midnight
✕✕✕✕	Tiberio	01.00
✕✕✕✕	Top of the Tower	23.15
✿✕✕✕✕	Waltons	23.30

✕✕✕	Braganza	23.15
✿✕✕✕	Le Bressan	23.30
✿✕✕✕	Carriers	23.30
✕✕✕	Chesa (*Swiss Centre*)	Midnight
✿✿✿✕✕✕	Le Gavroche	Midnight
✕✕✕	Grange	23.30
✕✕✕	PS Hispaniola	23.30
✕✕✕	Ivy	23.15
✕✕✕	Kundan	23.30
✿✕✕✕	Lacy's	23.30
✿✕✕✕	Leith's	Midnight
✕✕✕	Snooty Fox	Midnight
✕✕✕	Veeraswamy's	23.30
✿✕✕✕	White House Hotel Restaurant	23.30

		Latest time for orderin
✕✕	Albasha	23.3
✿✕✕	Alonso's	23.3
✕✕	Au Jardin des Gourmets	23.3
✕✕	Bali	23.3
✕✕	Beoty's	23.3
✕✕	Chelsea Rendezvous	23.3
✿✕✕	Chez Moi	23.3
✕✕	La Cucaracha	23.1
✕✕	Curry Centre	Midnigh
✿✕✕	Daphne's	Midnigh
✕✕	English House	23.3
✕✕	Frederick's	23.3
✿✕✕	Gay Hussar	23.3
✕✕	Gaylord (Albemarle St)	23.3
✕✕	Gaylord (Mortimer St)	23.2
✿✕✕	Keats	23.3
✕✕	Langan's Brasserie	23.1
✕✕	Mr Chow	23.4
✿✕✕	Pomegranates	23.1
✿✕✕	Poons (King St)	23.3
✕✕	Rossetti	23.3
✕✕	Sailing Junk	23.3
✕✕	San Frediano	23.3
✕✕	Santa Croce	23.1
✿✕✕	Shezan	23.3
✕✕	Tandoori	00.3
✿✕✕	Thomas de Quincey's	23.1

✕	Al Ben Accolto	23.30
✕	Ark	23.30
✿✕	L'Aubergade	23.30
✕	Il Barbino	Midnight
✕	Barque & Bite	23.30
✕	Bewick's	23.30
✕	Chanterelle	Midnight
✕	Chez Franco	23.30
✕	Chuen Cheng Ku	23.30
✕	La Croisette	23.30
✕	Don Luigi's	23.30
✕	Eatons	23.15
✕	La Fringale	23.45
✕	Gondolière	23.30
✕	La Grenouille	Midnight
✕	Hungry Viking	23.30
✕	La Jardinière	Midnight
✕	Kalamaras	Midnight
✕	Lee Ho Fook	23.30
✕	Luba's Bistro	23.30
✕	Manzi's	23.40
✕	M'sieur Frog	23.15
✕	New Rasa Sayang	23.30
✕	Newton's	Midnight
✕	Orient	23.50
✕	Peter's Bistro	23.30
✕	Portofino	23.30
✕	Provans	Midnight
✕	Shireen	23.30
✕	Siam	23.15
✕	Singapore Mandarin	23.45
✿✕	Soho Rendezvous	23.45
✕	Le Suque	23.30
✕	Tent	23.15
✕	Tung Hsing	23.30
✕	William F's	23.30

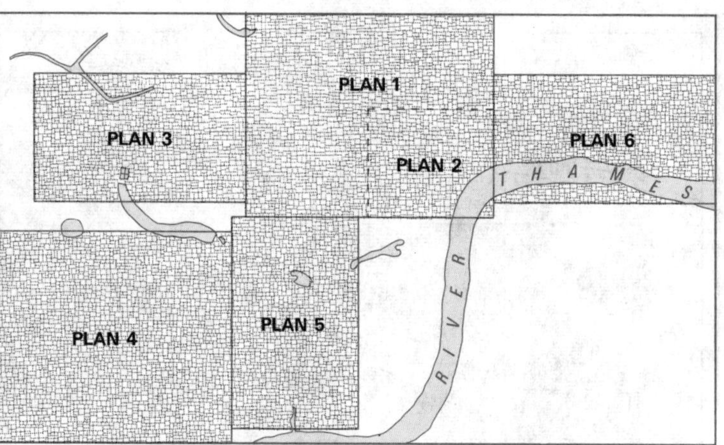

Seat belts save lives!

Remember a correctly adjusted seat belt can save your life. So whether you are travelling on a short or long journey, make sure you and your passenger are wearing seat belts. It's only common sense.

Use your headlights when visibility is poor

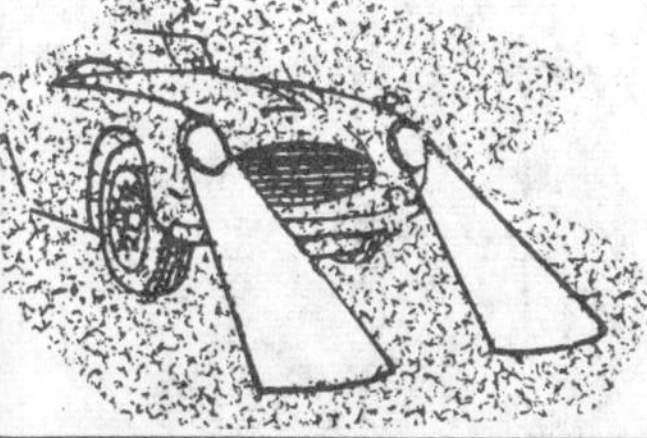

PLEASE MENTION THIS GUIDE WHEN YOU BOOK

London Plan 1

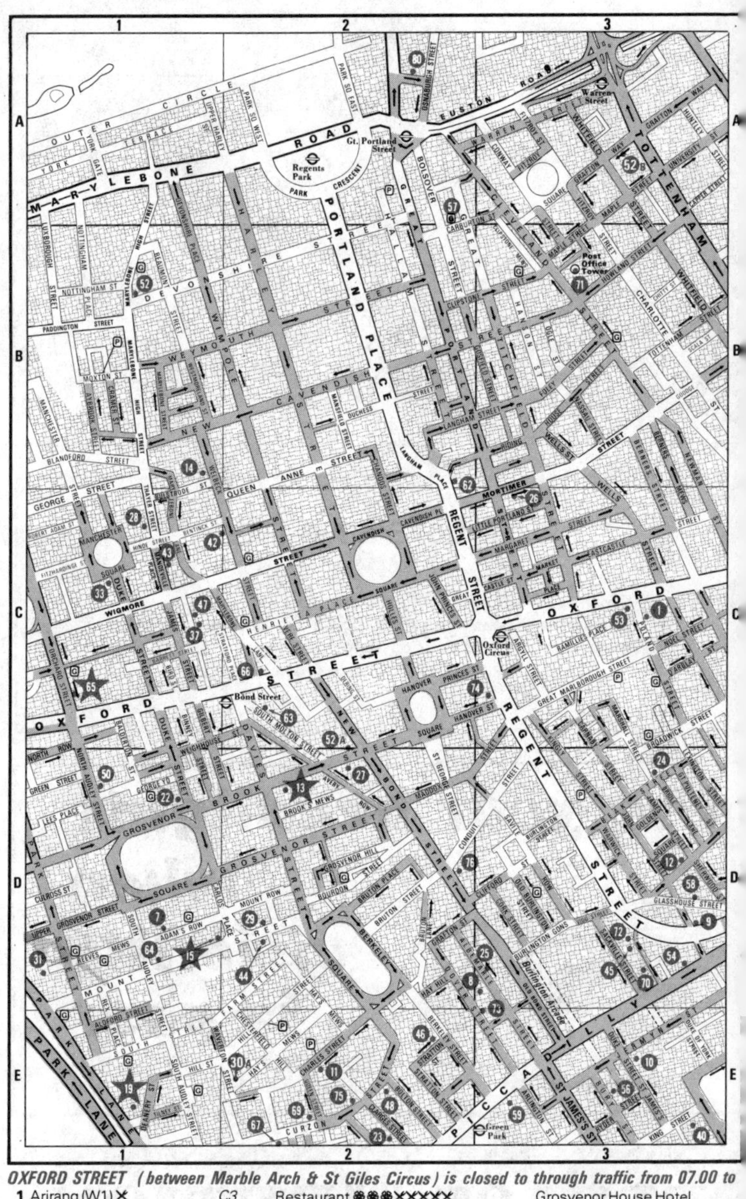

OXFORD STREET *(between Marble Arch & St Giles Circus) is closed to through traffic from 07.00 to*

1 Arirang (W1) ✕ *C3*
3 Bedford ★★★ *B5*
4 Bedford Corner ★★ *B4*
6 Bloomsbury Centre ★★★ *A5*
7 Britannia ★★★★ *D1*
8 Brown's ★★★★ *D3*
9 Café Royal *(Grill Room)* ✕✕✕✕✕ *D3*
10 Cavendish ★★★★ *E3*
11 Chesterfield ★★★ *E2*
12 China Garden ✕✕✕ *D3*
13 Claridge's ★★★★★ *D2*
Claridge's ✕✕✕✕✕
14 Clifton-Ford ★★★ *B1*
15 Connaught ❀❀❀★★★★★ *D1*
Connaught Hotel Restaurant ❀❀❀✕✕✕✕✕
17 Cora ★★ *A4*
19 Dorchester ★★★★★ *E1*
Dorchester Hotel ✕✕✕✕✕
22 Europa ★★★★ *D1*
24 Gallery Rendezvous ✕✕ *D3*
25 Gaylord (Albemarle Street) ✕✕ *D3*
26 Gaylord (Mortimer Street) ✕✕ *C3*
27 Geetanjli of Mayfair ✕✕ *D2*
28 Genevieve ✕✕✕ *C1*
29 Golden Carp ✕✕ *D2*
30 Grand ★★ *B5*
30A Greenhouse ✕✕✕ *E2*
31 Grosvenor House ❀★★★★★ *D1*
Grosvenor House Hotel *(La Fontaine)* ❀✕✕✕✕
33 Içi Paris ✕✕ *C1*
34 Imperial ☆☆☆ *B5*
35 Ivanhoe ★★ *B4*
36 Kenilworth ★★ *B4*
37 Kerzenstuberl ✕ *C1*
38 Kingsley ★★★ *B5*
39 Lacy's ❀✕✕✕ *B4*
40 Lafayette ✕✕✕ *E3*
41 Little Akropolis ✕ *B4*
42 Londoner ★★★ *C1*
43 Mandeville ★★ *C1*
44 Marquis ✕✕ *D2*
45 Martinez ✕✕✕ *D3*
46 May Fair ★★★★★ *E2*
47 Masako ✕✕✕ *C1*

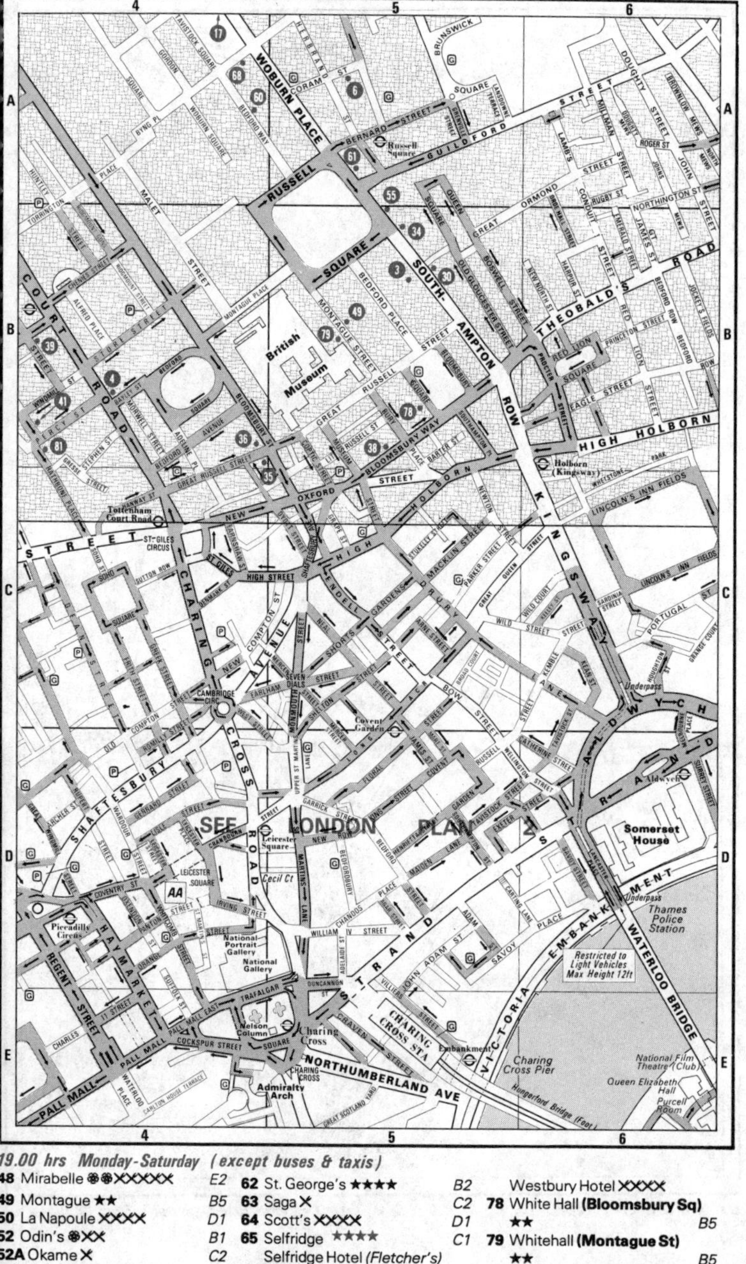

19.00 hrs Monday-Saturday (except buses & taxis)

- **48** Mirabelle ⊛⊛✕✕✕✕✕ — E2
- **49** Montague ★★ — B5
- **50** La Napoule ✕✕✕✕ — D1
- **52** Odin's ⊛✕✕ — B1
- **52A** Okame ✕ — C2
- **52B** Orient ✕ — A3
- **53** Pavilion — C3
- **54** Piccadilly ★★★★ — D3
- **55** President ☆☆☆ — B5
- **56** Quaglino's ★★★★ — E3
  Quaglino's Hotel Restaurant ✕✕✕✕
- **57** Regent Centre ☆☆☆ — A2
- **58** Regent Palace ★★ — D3
- **59** Ritz ★★★★★ — E3
- **60** Royal National ☆☆☆☆ — A4
- **61** Russell ★★★★ — A5
- **62** St. George's ★★★★ — B2
- **63** Saga ✕ — C2
- **64** Scott's ✕✕✕✕ — D1
- **65** Selfridge ★★★★ — C1
  Selfridge Hotel *(Fletcher's)* ✕✕✕✕
- **66** Stratford Court ★★★ — C2
- **67** Tandoori of Mayfair ✕✕✕ — E2
- **68** Tavistock ★★★ — A4
- **69** Tiberio ✕✕✕✕ — E2
- **70** Tokyo ✕✕ — D3
- **71** Top of the Tower ✕✕✕✕ — B3
- **72** Veeraswamy's ✕✕✕ — D3
- **73** Vendôme ✕✕ — D/E3
- **74** Verreys ✕✕✕ — C3
- **75** Washington ★★★ — E2
- **76** Westbury ★★★★ — D2
  Westbury Hotel ✕✕✕✕
- **78** White Hall **(Bloomsbury Sq)** ★★ — B5
- **79** Whitehall **(Montague St)** ★★ — B5
- **80** White House ⊛★★★
  White House Hotel Restaurant ⊛✕✕✕ — A2
- **81** White Tower ⊛✕✕✕ — B4

London Plan 2

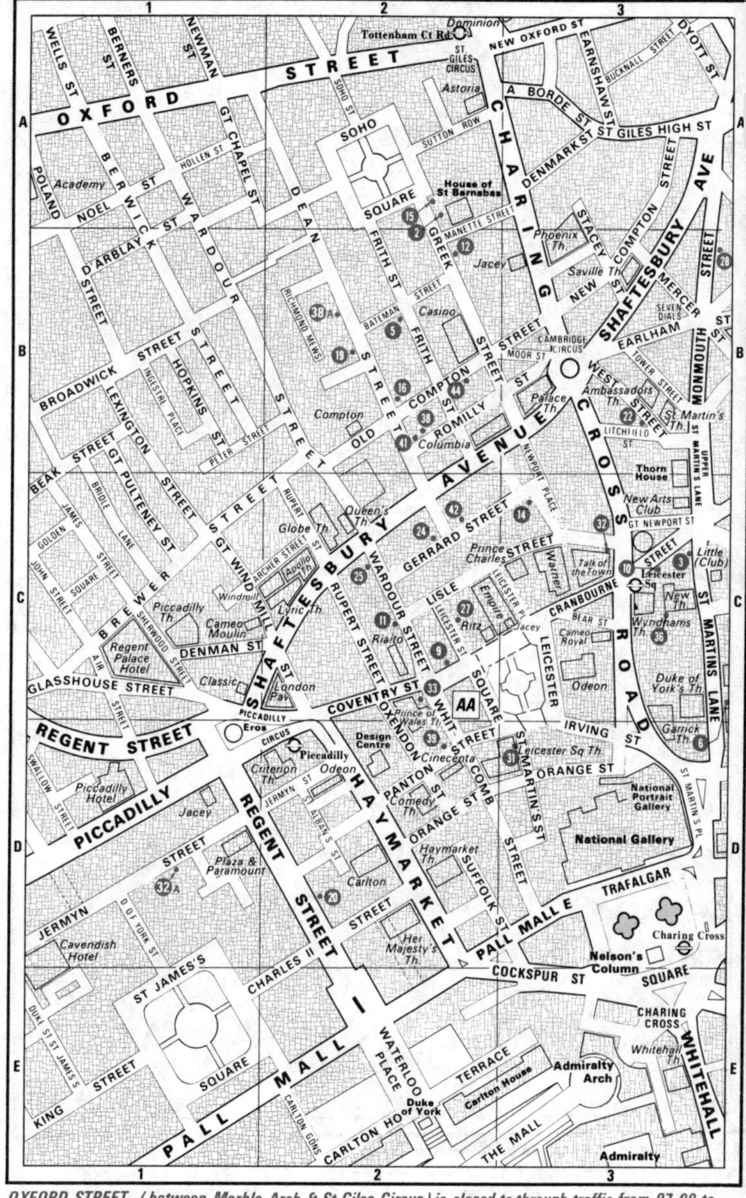

OXFORD STREET (between Marble Arch & St Giles Circus) is closed to through traffic from 07.00 to

2 Au Jardin des Gourmets ✕✕	A2	
3 Beotys ✕✕	C3	
4 Boulestin ✕✕✕	C5	
5 Braganza ✕✕✕	B2	
6 La Bussola ✕✕✕	C3	
7 Cellier de Medici ✕	D4	
8 Charing Cross ★★★★	D4	
9 Chesa ✕✕✕	C2	
10 Chez Solange ✕✕	C3	
11 Chuen Cheng Ku ✕	C2	
12 La Cucuracha ✕✕	B2	
12A Drury Lane ★★★	A4	
14 Ganges *(W1)* ✕	C3	
15 Gay Hussar ❁✕✕	A2	
16 Gennaros ✕✕✕✕	B2	
17 Grange ✕✕✕	C4	
18 Hispaniola ✕✕✕	E5	
19 Hostaria Romana ✕✕	B2	
20 Hunting Lodge ✕✕✕✕	D2	
21 Inigo Jones ❁✕✕✕✕	C4	
22 Ivy ✕✕✕	B3	
24 Lee Ho Fook ✕	C2	
27 Manzi's ✕	C2	
28 Mon Plaisir ✕	B3	
29 Neal Street ✕✕✕	B4	
30 L'Opera ✕✕✕	A5	
25 Panda House ✕	C2	
31 Pastoria ★★★	D3	
31A Poon's (King St.) ❁✕✕	C4	
32 Poon's (Lisle St.) ❁✕	C3	
33 Royal Angus ★★	C2	
34 Rules ✕✕✕	C4	

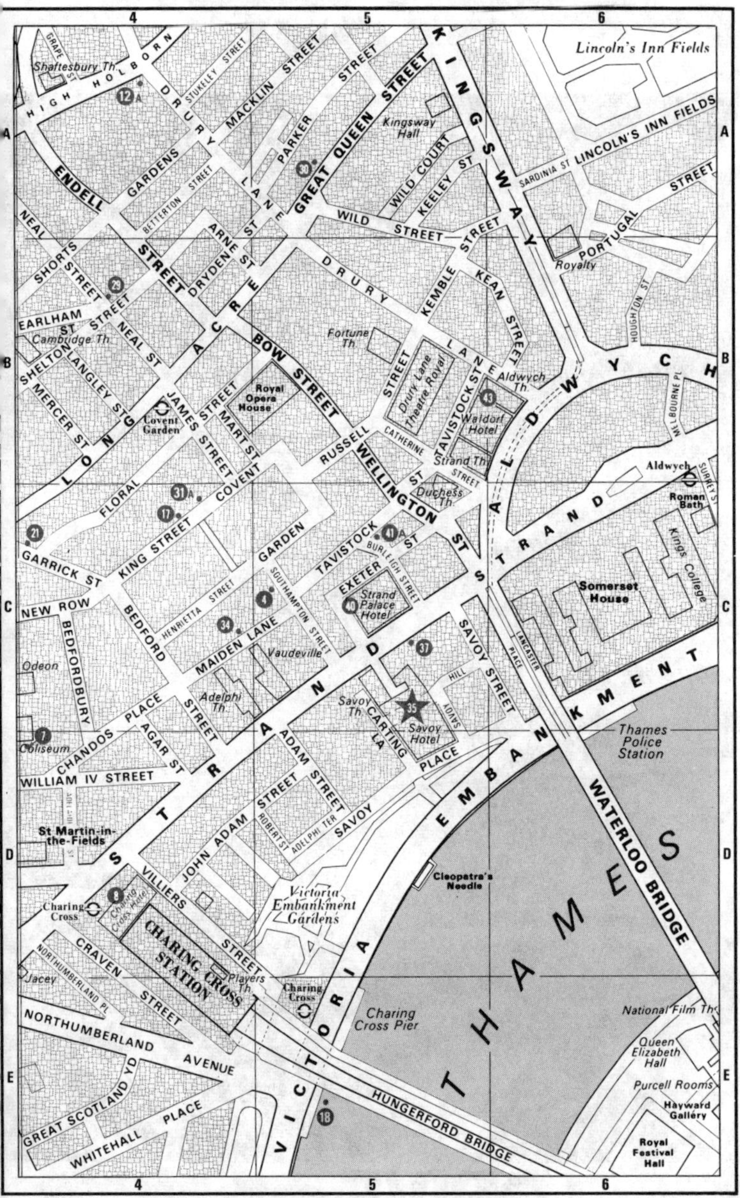

19.00 hrs Monday-Saturday (except buses & taxis)

35 Savoy ❁★★★★★ C5
Savoy Hotel Grill ❁✕✕✕✕✕
Savoy Hotel Restaurant ✕✕✕✕✕
36 Sheekey's ✕ C3
37 Simpsons ✕✕✕✕ C5
38 Soho Rendezvous ❁✕ B2
38A Sol é Mar ✕ B2
39 Stone's Chop House ✕✕✕✕✕ D2

40 Strand Palace ★★★ C5
Strand Palace Hotel *(Carriage Room)* ✕✕✕
41 Terrazza ✕✕✕ B2
41A Thomas de Quincey's ❁✕✕ C5
42 Tin Luk ✕ C2
43 Waldorf ★★★★ B5/6
44 Wheeler's ✕✕ B2

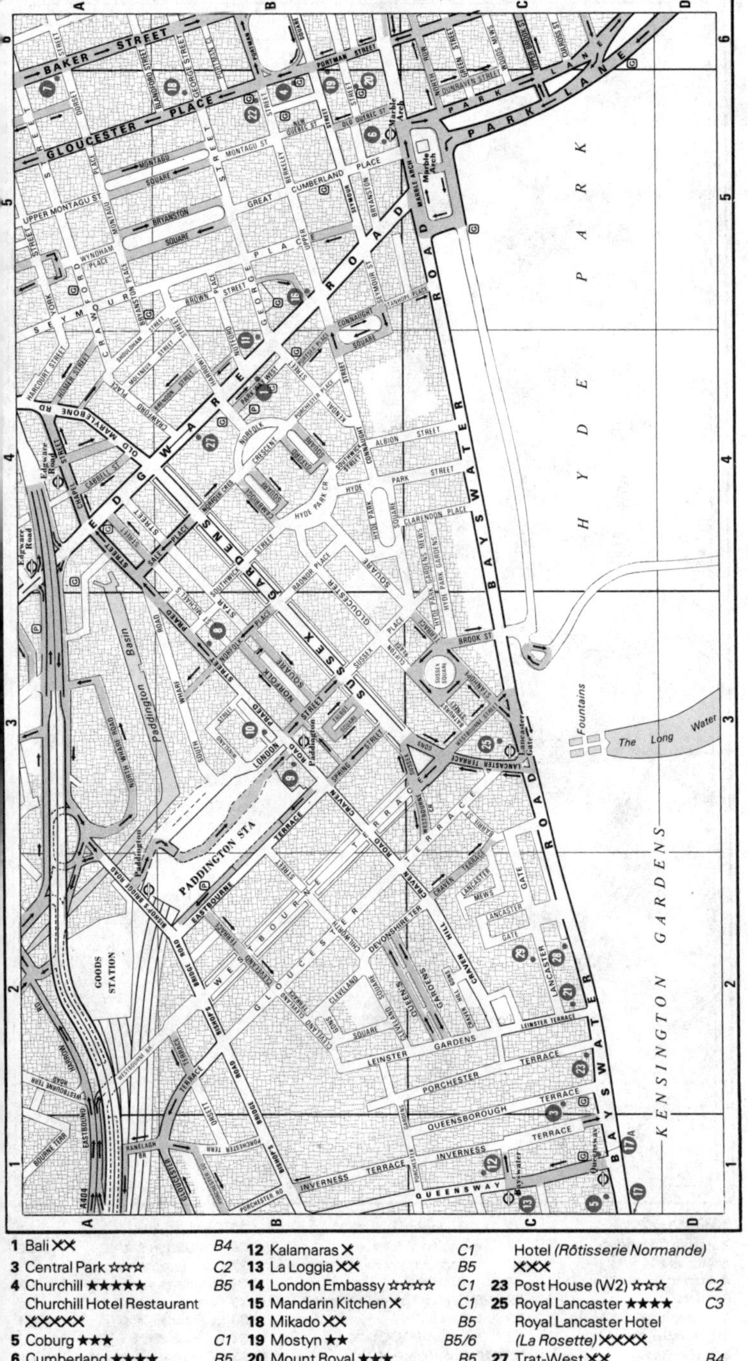

1 Bali ✕✕ B4
3 Central Park ☆☆☆ C2
4 Churchill ★★★★★ B5
Churchill Hotel Restaurant ✕✕✕✕✕
5 Coburg ★★★ C1
6 Cumberland ★★★★ B5
7 Fisherman's Wharf ✕✕ A5
8 Ganges (W2) ✕ B3
9 Great Western Royal ★★★★ B3
10 Grosvenor Court ☆☆ B3
11 Holiday Inn (W1) ☆☆☆☆ B4
12 Kalamaras ✕ C1
13 La Loggia ✕✕ B5
14 London Embassy ☆☆☆☆ C1
15 Mandarin Kitchen ✕ C1
18 Mikado ✕✕ B5
19 Mostyn ★★ B5/6
20 Mount Royal ★★★ B5
21 Park Court ★★★ C2
22 Portman Inter-Continental ★★★★ B5
Portman Inter-Continental Hotel *(Rôtisserie Normande)* ✕✕✕
23 Post House (W2) ☆☆☆ C2
25 Royal Lancaster ★★★★ C3
Royal Lancaster Hotel *(La Rosette)* ✕✕✕✕
27 Trat-West ✕✕ B4
28 White's ★★★ C2
29 Windsor ★★ C2

London Plan 4

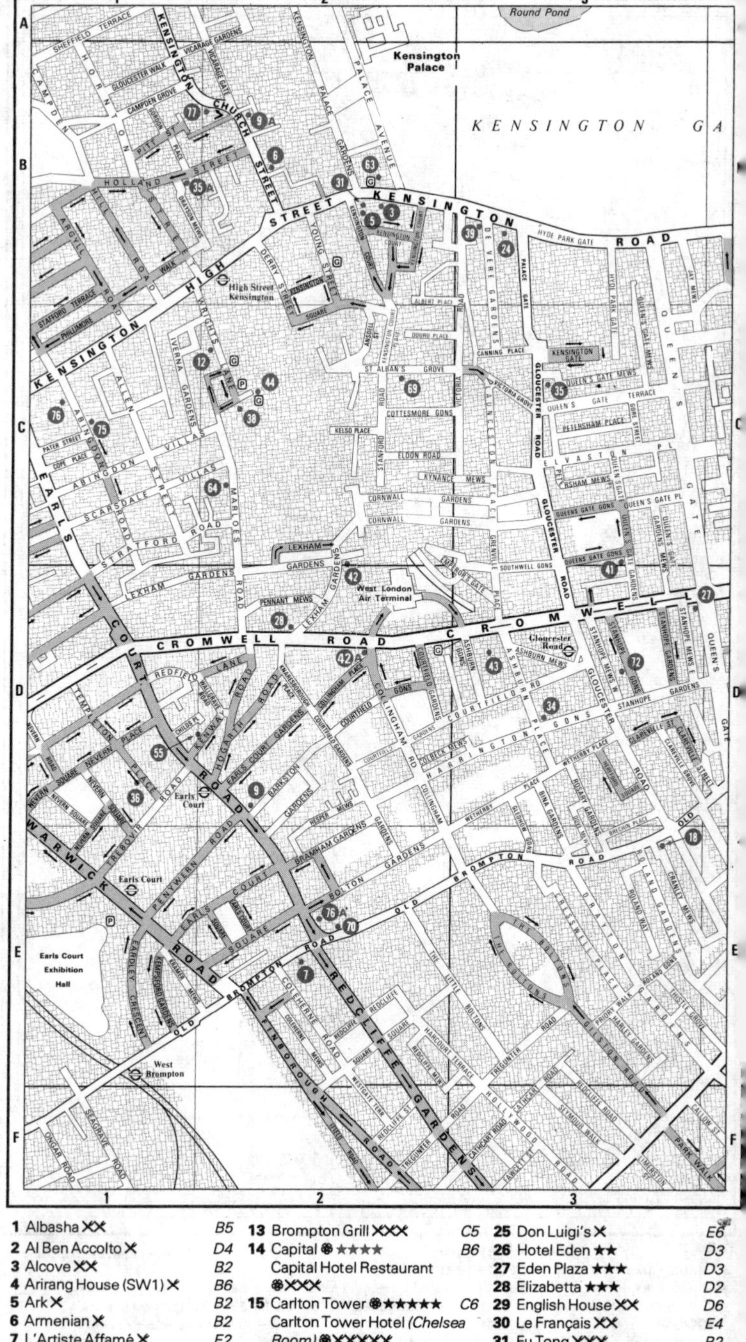

1 Albasha ✕✕ *B5*
2 Al Ben Accolto ✕ *D4*
3 Alcove ✕✕ *B2*
4 Arirang House (SW1) ✕ *B6*
5 Ark ✕ *B2*
6 Armenian ✕ *B2*
7 L'Artiste Affamé ✕ *E2*
8 Au Fin Bec ✕ *D5*
8A Bangkok ✕ *D4*
9 Barkston ★★★ *D2*
9A Il Barbino ✕ *B2*
10 Basil Street ★★★ *B6*
11 Bewick's ✕ *D5*
12 Le Bressan ⊛✕✕✕ *C2*
13 Brompton Grill ✕✕✕ *C5*
14 Capital ⊛★★★★ *B6*
Capital Hotel Restaurant ⊛✕✕✕
15 Carlton Tower ⊛★★★★★ *C6*
Carlton Tower Hotel *(Chelsea Room)* ⊛✕✕✕✕✕
18 Chanterelle ✕ *E3*
19 Chelsea Rendezvous ✕✕ *D5*
16 Claudius ✕✕✕ *D5*
20 Le Coq au Vin ✕✕ *B6*
22 Da Angela ✕ *E5*
23 Daphne's ⊛✕✕ *D5*
24 De Vere ★★★ *B3*
25 Don Luigi's ✕ *E6*
26 Hotel Eden ★★ *D3*
27 Eden Plaza ★★★ *D3*
28 Elizabetta ★★★ *D2*
29 English House ✕✕ *D6*
30 Le Français ✕✕ *E4*
31 Fu Tong ✕✕✕ *B2*
33 Il Giorno è la Notte ✕✕ *D4*
34 Gloucester ★★★★ *D3*
35 Gondolière ✕ *C3*
35A Holland Street ✕ *B1*
36 Hotel George ★★★ *D1*
37 Hyde Park ★★★★★ *B6*
38 Kensington Close ★★★★ *C2*

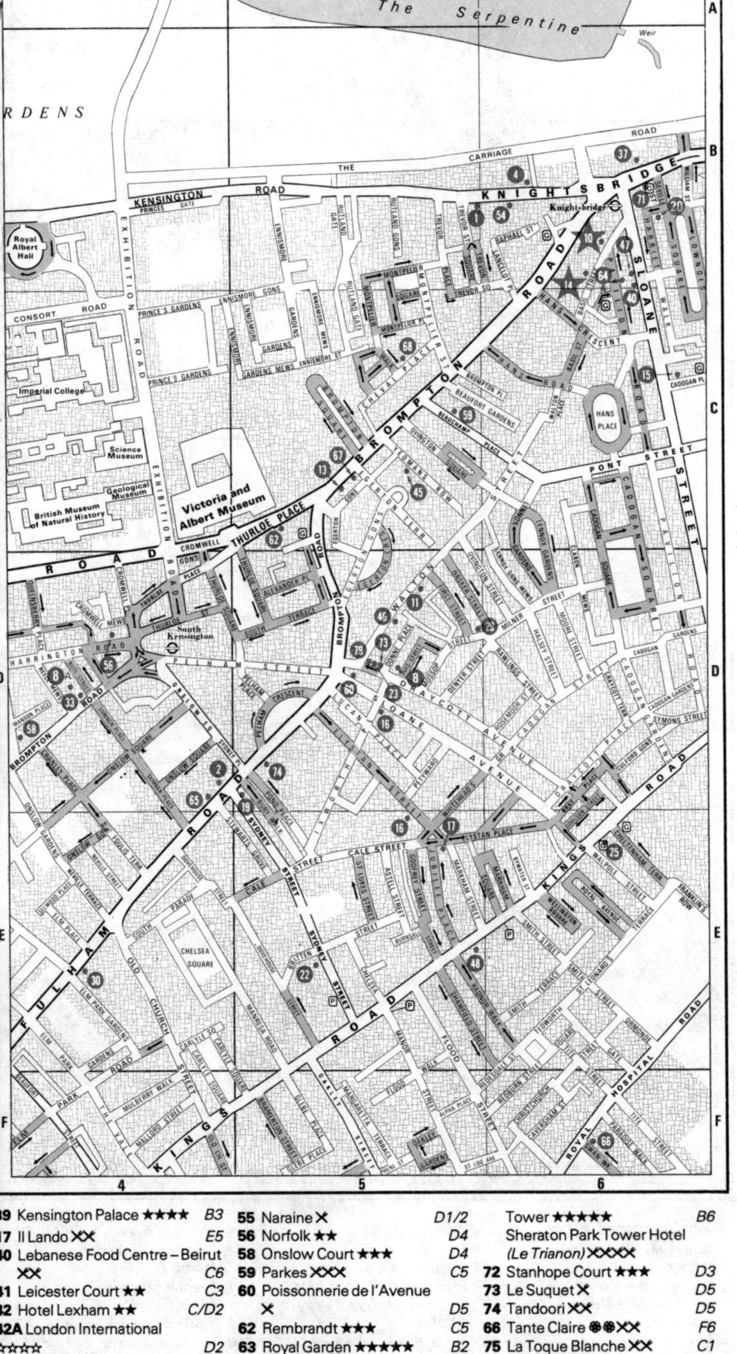

- **39** Kensington Palace ★★★★ B3
- **17** Il Lando ✕✕ E5
- **40** Lebanese Food Centre – Beirut ✕✕ C6
- **41** Leicester Court ★★ C3
- **42** Hotel Lexham ★★ C/D2
- **42A** London International ☆☆☆☆ D2
- **43** London Penta ☆☆☆☆ D3
- **44** London Tara ☆☆☆ C2
- **45** Luba's Bistro ✕ C5
- **46** Ma Cuisine ❀❀✕ D5
- **47** Marcel ✕✕ B6
- **48** Marco Polo ✕ E5
- **54** Mr. Chow ✕✕ B6
- **55** Naraine ✕ D1/2
- **56** Norfolk ★★ D4
- **58** Onslow Court ★★★ D4
- **59** Parkes ✕✕✕ C5
- **60** Poissonnerie de l'Avenue ✕ D5
- **62** Rembrandt ★★★ C5
- **63** Royal Garden ★★★★★ B2
- **64** Sailing Junk ✕✕ C2
- **64A** Sale è Pepe ✕ B6
- **65** San Frediano ✕✕ D4
- **67** Shangri-La ✕ C5
- **68** Shezan ❀✕✕ C5
- **69** Siam ✕ C2
- **71** Sheraton Park Tower ★★★★★ B6
- Sheraton Park Tower Hotel *(Le Trianon)* ✕✕✕✕
- **72** Stanhope Court ★★★ D3
- **73** Le Suquet ✕ D5
- **74** Tandoori ✕✕ D5
- **66** Tante Claire ❀❀✕✕ F6
- **75** La Toque Blanche ✕✕ C1
- **76** Trattoo ✕✕✕ C1
- **76A** Le Truc ✕ E2
- **77** Twin Brothers ✕ B2
- **79** Waltons ❀✕✕✕✕ D5

London Plan 5

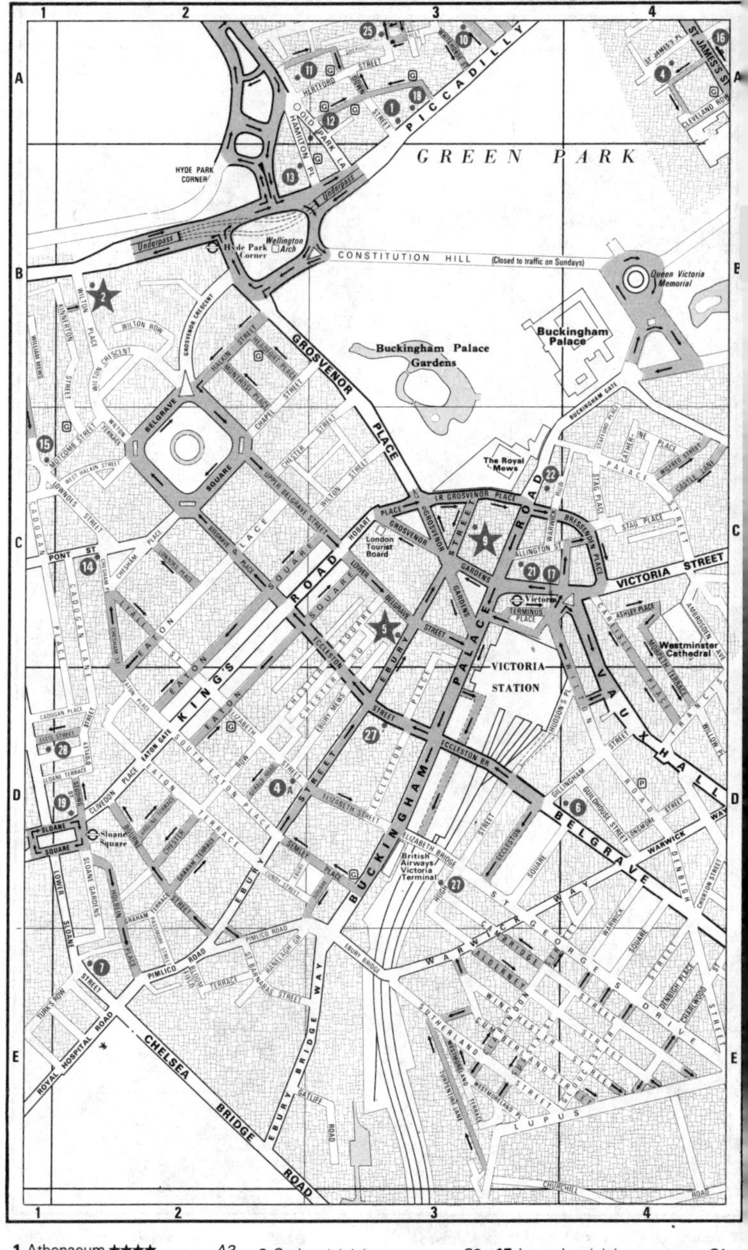

1 Athenaeum ★★★★ *A3*
Athenaeum Hotel Restaurant ✕✕✕✕

2 Berkeley ❀ ★★★★★ *B2*
Berkeley Hotel Restaurant ❀✕✕✕✕✕

4 Duke's ★★★★ *A4*
Duke's Hotel Restaurant ✕✕✕

4A Eatons ✕ *D2*

5 Ebury Court ★ *C3*

6 Eccleston ★★★ *D4*

7 Le Gavroche ❀❀❀✕✕✕ *E2*

9 Goring ★★★★ *C3*

10 Green Park ★★ *A3*

11 Hilton ★★★★★ *A2*
Hilton Hotel *(Roof)* ✕✕✕✕✕
Hilton Hotel *(Trader Vic's)* ✕✕✕✕

12 Inn on the Park ★★★★★ *A2/3*
Inn on the Park Hotel *(Four Seasons)* ✕✕✕✕✕

13 Inter-Continental ★★★★★ *B2*
Inter-Continental ✕✕✕✕✕

14 Ladbroke Belgravia ★★★★ *C2*

15 Lowndes ★★★ *C1*

16 Overton's (St. James) ✕✕✕✕ *A4*

17 Overton's (Victoria Buildings) ✕ *C3*

18 Park Lane ★★★★ *A3*

19 Royal Court ★★★ *D2*

21 Royal Westminster ☆☆☆☆ *C3*

22 Rubens ★★★ *C3*

25 Snooty Fox ✕✕✕ *A3*

27 Tent ✕ *D3*

28 Wilbraham ★★★ *D1*

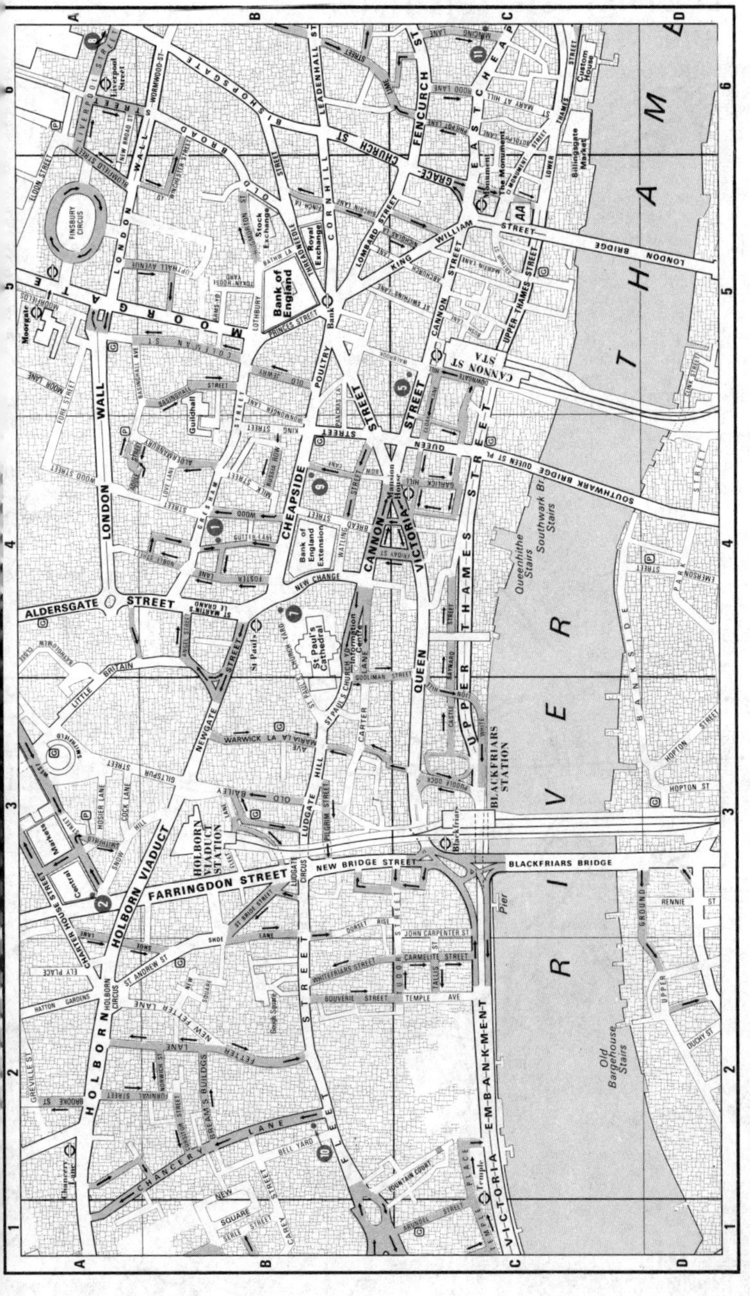

1 Baron of Beef ✕✕✕ B4	**7** Ginnan ✕ B4	**10** Terraza-Est ✕✕ B2
2 Bubb's ❁✕ A3	**8** Great Eastern ★★★ A6	**11** Viceroy ✕✕✕ C6
5 Cotillion ✕✕✕ C5	**9** Le Poulbot ❁❁✕✕✕ B4	

London Postal Districts and ways in & out of London

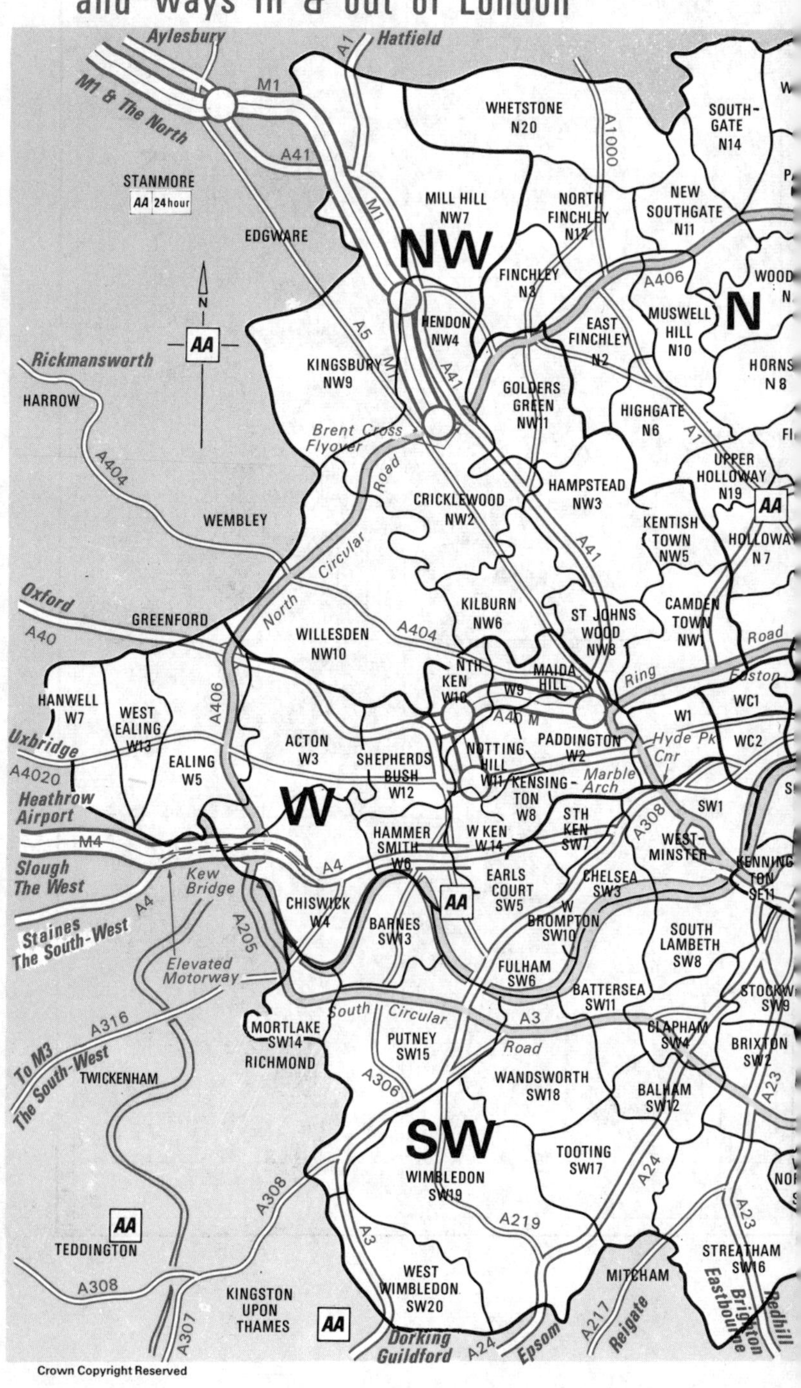

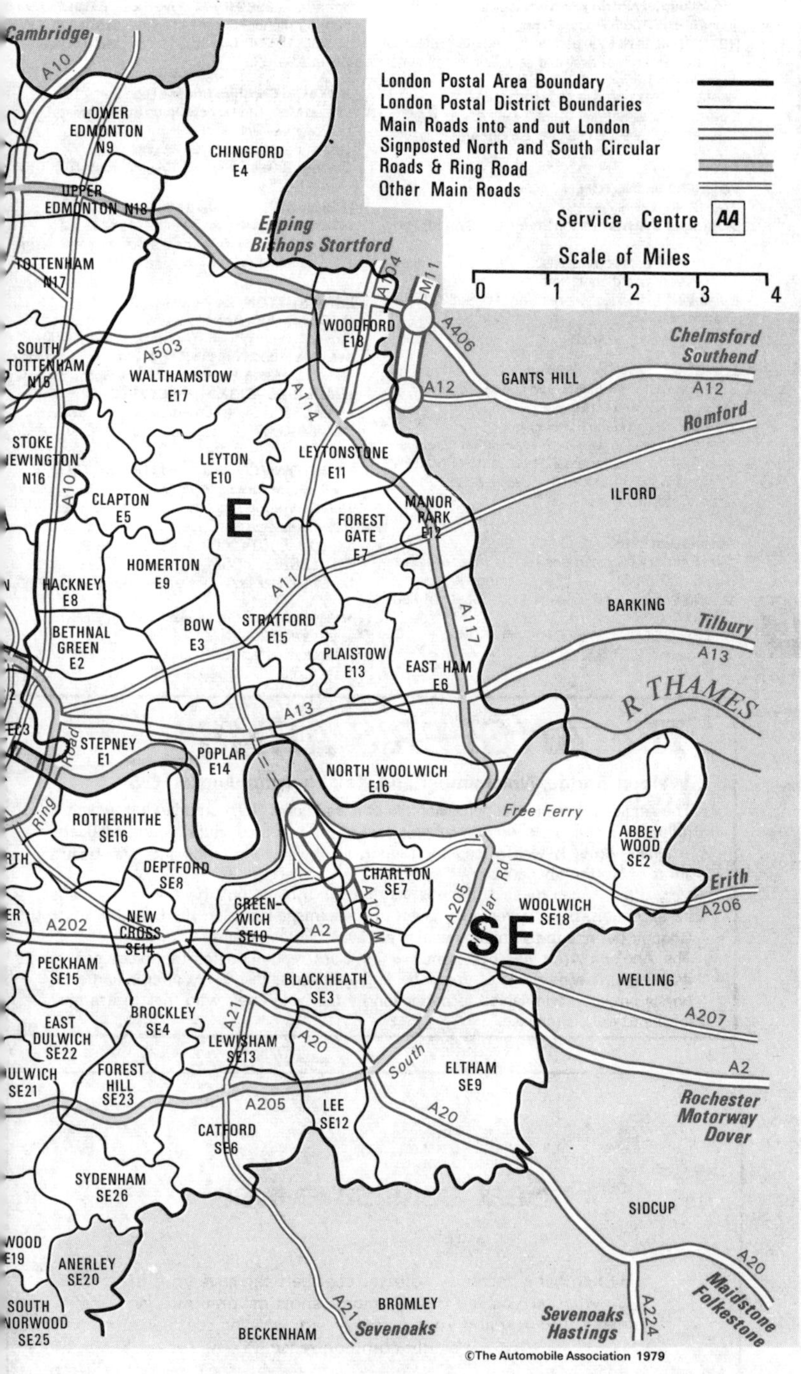
London Postal Area Boundary
London Postal District Boundaries
Main Roads into and out London
Signposted North and South Circular Roads & Ring Road
Other Main Roads
Service Centre AA
Scale of Miles
0 1 2 3 4
Cambridge
LOWER EDMONTON N9
CHINGFORD E4
UPPER EDMONTON N18
Epping Bishops Stortford
TOTTENHAM N17
WOODFORD E18
Chelmsford Southend
SOUTH TOTTENHAM N15
WALTHAMSTOW E17
GANTS HILL
Romford
STOKE NEWINGTON N16
LEYTON E10
LEYTONSTONE E11
ILFORD
CLAPTON E5
E
MANOR PARK E12
FOREST GATE E7
HOMERTON E9
HACKNEY E8
BARKING
BETHNAL GREEN E2
BOW E3
STRATFORD E15
Tilbury
PLAISTOW E13
EAST HAM E6
R THAMES
STEPNEY E1
POPLAR E14
NORTH WOOLWICH E16
Ring Road
Free Ferry
ROTHERHITHE SE16
ABBEY WOOD SE2
DEPTFORD SE8
CHARLTON SE7
Erith
GREENWICH SE10
WOOLWICH SE18
NEW CROSS SE14
SE
PECKHAM SE15
BLACKHEATH SE3
WELLING
BROCKLEY SE4
EAST DULWICH SE22
LEWISHAM SE13
South
ELTHAM SE9
DULWICH SE21
FOREST HILL SE23
Rochester Motorway Dover
LEE SE12
CATFORD SE6
SYDENHAM SE26
SIDCUP
NORWOOD SE19
ANERLEY SE20
Maidstone Folkestone
SOUTH NORWOOD SE25
BROMLEY
Sevenoaks
Sevenoaks Hastings
BECKENHAM
A10
A503
A104
M11
A406
A12
A114
A11
A117
A13
A102 M
A2
A205
A206
A202
A21
A20
A207
A224

LONG EATON Derbyshire Map**8** SK43
See also Sandiacre
☆☆☆**Novotel Nottingham** Bostock Ln (south of M1 junc 25) ☎60106 Telex no377585
122⇌ ⋔ Lift ⊞ ⋈ TV in bedrooms 180P ♣ ⇁(heated) Conference facilities available ♁ ♿ ☋International. Last dinner11.30pm ♆ ⚲ S%
✱sB&B⇌⋔£17.45 dB&B⇌⋔£22.40
Lunch£3.95 Tea45palc High Tea£1.20alc
Dinner£3.95 Wine£3.95 ⍐ Credit cards 1 2 3 5

LONGFRAMLINGTON Northumberland
Map**12** NU10
✕✕Angler's Arms Weldon Bridge (2m S off B6344) ☎655
40seats 70P bedrooms available ☋English, French & Portuguese. Last dinner10pm S%
Lunch£2.75–£5&alc Dinner£4alc Wine£2.75
Credit cards 2 3

LONG MELFORD Suffolk Map**5** TL84
During the currency of this guide Long Melford telephone numbers are liable to change.
★★★**Bull** (Trusthouse Forte) ☎494
15th-C with walled gardens in main street of village.
25⇌⋔ ⋈ TV in bedrooms 27P 3⌂ Last dinner10pm
♆ ⚲ S% sB&B⇌⋔£16 dB&B⇌⋔£25 ⍐
xmas Credit cards 1 2 3 4 5 6

★**Crown inn** ☎366
15th-century walled gardens in main street of village.
10rm(2⇌⋔) ⋈ CTV ⊘ 10P ⇎ Last dinner9.30pm
♆ sB&B fr£8.50 sB&B⇌⋔ fr£10 dB&B fr£14.50
dB&B⇌⋔ fr£16 Lunch fr£2.50
Dinner fr£2.95&alc Wine£3.25 ⍐
Credit cards 1 2 3 5 6

LONGNOR Staffordshire Map**7** SK06
★**Crewe & Harpur** ☎205
6rm ⋈ CTV 35P 2⌂ ⟲ ∩ Live music & dancing Sat & Sun Last dinner9.50pm ♆ S% sB&B£5.50–£7
dB&B£11–£14 Lunch£2.50 Dinner£3.50&alc
Wine£2.95 ⍐

✕✕Ye Old Cheshire Cheese High St ☎218
Closed Mon; Dinner not served Sun; 70seats 80P bedrooms available ☋English & French.
Last dinner9.45pm S% ✱Lunch£4alc
Dinner£7.50alc Wine£3 Credit cards 1 2 3 5 6

LONGRIDGE Lancashire Map**7** SD63
✕Corporation Arms Lower Rd ⇌2644
Closed Xmas Day; 60seats 60P Last dinner9.30pm
S% ✱Lunch£4alc Dinner£4alc Wine£3

LONG SUTTON Somerset Map**3** ST42
★★**Devonshire Arms** (Best Western) ☎271
Closed Xmas night; 4rm Annexe: 3rm ⋈ CTV TV available in bedrooms ⊘ 20P ♣ Live music & dancing wkly ☋English & French. Last dinner9pm ♆ S%
sB&B£10.95–£13.50 dB&B£21.90–£27
Lunch£3.85–£4.50 Dinner£4.50–£5.75&alc
Wine£2.95 ⍐ Credit cards 1 3

LONGTOWN Cumbria Map**11** NY36
★★**Graham Arms** English St ☎791213
Hotel with strong sporting associations, offering game fishing on the Border Esk River and tributaries.
14rm(2⇌⋔) CTV 20P 4⌂⟲ Last dinner9pm ♆
S% sB&B£8 dB&B£15 dB&B⇌⋔£18
Bar lunch£1–£1.50 Dinner£3–£5.50 Wine£2.50

★♔**March Bank** Scotsdyke (3m N A7 Galashiels road) ☎791325
RS 2wks mid Nov (B&B only); 6rm ⋈ CTV 25P ♣

L

Lastdinner8pm sB&B£9–£10 dB&B£18–£20 Lunch£4 Tea£1.20 High Tea£3.25 Dinner£5.50 *xmas*

LOOE Cornwall Map**2** SX25
★★★**Hannafore Point** Marine Dr, Hannafore ☎3273 Closed 2–23Jan; 40 CTV CTV available in bedrooms 60P Live music & dancing 4 nights (in summer) Conference facilities available English & Continental. Lastdinner9pm ✱sB&B£11–£16 dB&B£20–£28 Barlunch75p–£1.50 Tea60p Dinner£5–£6.30 Wine£2.95 *xmas* Credit cards 2 3 5

★★**Klymiarven** Barbican Hill ☎2333
Georgian manor house set in wooded gardens with unique views of harbour.
Closed Jan & Feb; 15rm(8) CTV 15P (heated) English & French. Lastdinner9.30pm S% sB&B£8.50–£11.70 sB&B£11.10–£14.75 dB&B£14.30–£19.70 dB&B£19.20–£26.50 Barlunch50p–£2.50 Tea30–80p Dinner£5–£6.50 Wine£2.25 *xmas*

L

★★***Rock Towers*** Hannafore Rd, Hannafore ☎2140
Detached, comfortable family hotel in elevated position overlooking Hannafore Point and Looe Harbour.
23rm(8⇌ ⋒) ⋈ CTV TV available in bedrooms ⊘ 12P 8⌂ ♀English, French & Italian. Last dinner9pm ♁

★**Portbyhan** West Looe Quay ☎2071
43rm Lift CTV ₱ ⊛ Last dinner7.30pm ♁ ⊛sB&B£5.75–£10.35 dB&B£11.50–£20.70 Lunch£2.75 Tea75p Dinner£3 Wine£2.50 *xmas*

LOSTWITHIEL Cornwall Map**2** SX15
★★**Carotel Motel** Hillside Gdns ☎872223
38rm ⋈ CTV CTV available in bedrooms 4P 2⌂ ⚓ Last dinner10pm ♁ sB&B⇌ ⋒£12.40 dB&B⇌ ⋒£19 Continental breakfast Lunch£3alc Dinner£4.50alc Wine£2.50 ⊓ Creditcards ① ② ③ ⑤

★★**Royal Oak Inn** ☎872552
An inn dating from the 13th-C, reputed to be an ale house used by smugglers in the past.
6rm CTV TV available in bedrooms 25P ⊛ Live music & dancing 3 nights wkly ♀English & French. Last dinner9.45pm ♁ S% sB&B£7.50–£8.50 dB&B£13–£16 Lunch£2.95–£3.50&alc Dinner£3.50–£4.50&alc Wine£2.25 ⊓ *xmas* Creditcards ① ③

★★**Royal Talbot** ☎872498
9rm ⋈ TV in bedrooms 30P Last dinner10pm ♁ ⊈ S% sB&B£8.50 dB&B£17 Lunch fr£2.50 Tea fr40p Dinner fr£3.50 Wine£2.90

LOUGHBOROUGH Leicestershire Map**8** SK51
★★★**King's Head** High St (Embassy) ☎214893
80rm(69⇌ ⋒) Lift Ↄ ⋈ CTV TV in bedrooms 100P Conference facilities available Last dinner9.30pm

✿ S% sB&B£11 sB&B⇌⋒£16 dB&B£18 dB&B⇌⋒£22 Lunch£5&alc Dinner£5.50&alc Wine£5 ⛿ Credit cards 1 2 3 4 5 6

★★Cedars Cedar Rd ☎214459
Closed 26–28Dec; 35rm(24⇌⋒) ⌘ TV in bedrooms 50P ⚓ ⌒(heated) Last dinner9pm ✿ ♪ ✱sB&B£7.50 sB&B⇌⋒£8.50 dB&B£13.50 dB&B⇌⋒£16 Tea60p–£1.70 Dinner£5.50alc Wine£2.70 ⛿

✕✕Harlequin 11 Swan St ☎215235
Closed Sun; 70seats ⚑ Live music & dancing Tue, Thu & Sat ♡Italian. Last dinner11pm ✱Dinner£6alc Wine£3.20 Credit cards 2 3 5

LOWESTOFT Suffolk Map**5** TM59
★★★*Victoria* Kirkley Cliff ☎4433
Spacious Victorian hotel with modern extensions on cliff top at southern end of town.
51rm(31⇌⋒) Lift ☽ ⌘ CTV TV available in bedrooms 50P 2🏠 ⛟ ⚓ ⌒(heated) Live music & dancing Sat Last dinner9pm ✿ ♪ ⛿ Credit cards 1 2 3 5 6

☆☆Golden Galleon Bridge Rd, Oulton Broad (2m W A1117) ☎2157
28⇌⋒ ☽ TV available in bedrooms 40P Last dinner10.30pm ✿ S% ✱sB&B⇌⋒£11.20–£11.70 dB&B⇌⋒£18.50–£19 Lunch fr£3.50&alc Dinner fr£3.50&alc Wine£2.30 ⛿ Credit cards 1 2 3 5

LOWESWATER Cumbria Map**11** NY12
★Grange ☎Lamplugh211
Formerly a 17th-C manor house but now converted to a comfortable country hotel situated in its own grounds at the head of Loweswater lake.
Closed Xmas; RS Dec & Jan; 8rm(1⇌⋒) Annexe:9rm(2⇌⋒) ⌘ CTV 20P 2🏠 ⛟ ⚓ Last dinner8pm ✿ ♪ sB&B£8.50–£9 sB&B⇌⋒£9–£9.50 dB&B£17–£18 dB&B⇌⋒£18–£19 Lunch£2.75–£3.50 Tea£1–£1.50 High Tea£2–£2.50 Dinner£4.50–£5.50 Wine£2.70 ⛿

LUDLOW Salop Map**7** SO57
★★★Feathers Bull Ring (Inter-Hotel) ☎2919
Telex no28905
36rm(33⇌⋒) 6▭ ☽ ⌘ CTV in bedrooms ⊘ 40P Last dinner9pm ✿ S% sB&B£15–£16 sB&B⇌⋒£18–£19 dB&B£28–£30 dB&B⇌⋒£34–£42 Lunch£5–£6&alc Tea fr£1 Dinner£6–£7&alc Wine£3 ⛿ *xmas* Credit cards 1 2 3 4 5 6

★★Angel Broad St (Trophy Taverns) ☎2531
Lord Nelson frequented the hotel and was made a freeman of the ancient borough.
18rm(4⇌⋒) ⌘ CTV 25P 8🏠 ⛟ ♡English & French. Last dinner8.30pm ✿ S% ✱sB&B£6.50–£8.50 sB&B⇌⋒£10.50–£12.50 dB&B£13–£17 dB&B⇌⋒£17–£21 Lunch fr£2.75 Dinner fr£4.75 ⛿ *xmas* Credit cards 1 3 5 6

★★Overton Grange (1½m S of Ludlow on A49) ☎3500
Closed 7 Jan–Feb; 17rm(5⇌⋒) ⌘ CTV 50P ⚓ Live music & dancing mthly. Last dinner8.30pm ✿ S% ✱sB&B£7.50–£9 dB&B£14–16.50 dB&B⇌⋒£19 Bar lunch£1.20alc Dinner£4.25&alc Wine£2.80 ⛿ *xmas*

★Cliff Dinham ☎2063
15rm ⌘ CTV ⊘ 20P ⚓ ♡Mainly grills. Last dinner8.30pm ✿ ♪ S% sB&B£7.50–£8.50 dB&B£15–£17 Lunch£3.25–£4.75 Tea£1.20–£1.50 Dinner£3–£6 Wine£4 ⛿ *xmas*

L

✕**Penny Anthony** 5 Church St ☎3282
Closed Sun & Thur; Dinner served Thur in summer; 50seats ☧ ♡Continental. Last dinner 10pm
✳Wine£2.10

LUDWELL Wiltshire Map**3** ST92
★**Grove House** ☎Donhead365
Closed 1–14 Nov; 12rm(2⇌⋒) ⚔ ₩ CTV 12P ⇎ ⚓
Children under 5yrs not accommodated
Last dinner 7pm ♆ ♈ S% sB&B£7.50–£8.50
dB&B£15–£17 dB&B⇌⋒£18–£20
Lunch£3–£4 Tea fr£1 Dinner£3.30–£4
Wine£2.30 ⊟ *xmas* Credit cards 1 3

LULWORTH Dorset Map**3** SY88
★★**Lulworth Cove** ☎West Lulworth333
14rm(2⇌⋒) ₩ TV in bedrooms 4P 2⌂ Live music & dancing Fri & Sun Last dinner 9.30pm ♆ S%
✳sB&B£6.25–£7.50 dB&B£12.50–£15
dB&B⇌⋒£13.50–£18 Lunch fr£2.50
Dinner fr£4.50 Wine£3.50 ⊟
Credit cards 1 2 3 4 5 6

LUMBY North Yorkshire Map**8** SE43
☆☆☆☆**Selby Fork Motor** (southern junc A1/A63) (Anchor) ☎South Milford682711 Telex no 858875
117⇌⋒ ☽ ₩ CTV in bedrooms 220P ⚓ ⊐(heated) ♂9 ✎(hard) sauna bath Live music & dancing Fri & Sat
Conference facilities available ⌂ ♆ ♈ S%
✳sB&B⇌⋒ fr£16 dB&B⇌⋒ fr£21.50
Lunch fr£3.50&alc Dinner fr£4&alc Wine£2.65
⊟ *xmas* Credit cards 1 2 3 4 5 6

LUSTLEIGH Devon Map**3** SX78
✕**Moorwood Cottage** ☎341
Thatched cottage set in four acres of grounds.
Closed Sun & Xmas Day; Lunch not served; 24seats
10P ♡European. Last dinner 9.30pm S%
✳Dinner£6alc Wine£3

LUTON Bedfordshire Map**4** TL02
☆☆☆☆**Luton EuroCrest** Dunstable Rd, Waller Av (Ansells) ☎55911 Telex no 825048
99⇌⋒ Lift ☽ ⊞ CTV in bedrooms 180P Conference facilities available Last dinner 9.50pm ♆ ♈ S%
✳sB&B⇌⋒£18.41 dB&B⇌⋒£27.21
Continental breakfast ⊟ Credit cards 1 2 3 4 5 6

☆☆☆☆**Strathmore** Arndale Centre (Thistle) ☎34199
Telex no 825763
151⇌⋒ Lift ☽ ₩ CTV in bedrooms ✈ ☧ Conference facilities available ♈International.
Last dinner 10.30pm ♆ ♈ S%
✳sB&B⇌⋒£18.90–£22.40
dB&B⇌⋒£25.30–£32.30 Lunch£5.55
Dinner£6.55&alc ⊟ Credit cards 1 2 3 4 5 6

☆☆☆**Luton Crest Motel** Dunstable Rd (Crest)
☎55955
139⇌⋒ Lift ☽ CTV in bedrooms 120P
Last dinner 10pm ♆ S% ✳sB&B⇌⋒£16.79
dB&B⇌⋒£23.32 Continental breakfast ⊟
Credit cards 1 2 3 4 5 6

★★**Red Lion** Castle St (Henekey) ☎413881
38rm(3⇌⋒) ☽ ₩ TV in bedrooms 20P ♡Mainly grills
Last dinner 10.30pm ♆ S% sB&B£10.50
sB&B⇌⋒£13 dB&B£17 dB&B⇌⋒£20 ⊟
xmas Credit cards 1 2 3 4 5 6

LYDBROOK Gloucestershire Map**3** SO61
✕✕***Courtfield Arms*** ☎207
Stone-built inn with oak beams, in woodland setting.
Closed Sun; 65seats 70P bedrooms available
♡English & Continental. Last dinner 10pm
Credit card 1

LYDFORD Devon Map**2** SX58
★♣**Lydford House** ☎347
Stone house built in 1880 standing in 1½ acres of grounds with views of Dartmoor.

Closed Xmas; 12rm(2⇌ ⋒) CTV 30P ⛟ ⚓ ∩ Children under 5yrs not accommodated ♡English & French. Lastdinner8.30pm ✪ S% ✻sB&B£6.50 dB&B 13 dB&B⇌⋒£15 Barlunch£2alc Dinner£2.85&alc Wine£2.55 ⊟ Credit cards 1 2 5 6

LYME REGIS Dorset Map**3** SY39 **See also Uplyme**

★★★Alexandra Pound St ☎2010
Once the residence of Dowager Countess Poulett and later owned by the Duc du Staspode. Dates back to 1735.
Closed Oct, Dec & Jan; RS Feb, Mar & Nov (no lunches); 23rm(11⇌⋒) ⋈ CTV ⊗ 15P 4⌂ ⛟ ⚓ ♡English & French. Lastdinner8.30pm ✪ ⊒ S% sB&B£11.50–£14.80 sB&B⇌⋒£12.50–£17 dB&B£24–£28 dB&B⇌⋒£25–£32 Lunch£3.50 Tea50p HighTea£1.50 Dinner£4.75 Wine£2.85 Credit cards 1 2 3 5 6

★★★High Cliff Sidmouth Rd ☎2300
Closed Jan & Feb; 12rm(5⇌⋒) ⋈ CTV TV available in bedrooms 25P 4⌂ ⛟ ⚓ Lastdinner8.30pm ✪ ⊒ ✻sB&B£11.90–£15 dB&B£16–£24 dB&B⇌⋒£24–£30 Lunch£3alc Tea fr40p&alc High Tea fr£1 Dinner fr£4.25&alc Wine£2 ⊟

★★★Mariners Silver St ☎2753
Mainly 17th-C building with sea views. 300 year old tulip tree in grounds. Buildings made famous by Beatrix Potter in The Tale of Little Pig Robinson.
Closed 27Dec–6Mar; 16rm(12⇌⋒) 22P ⛟ ♡English & Continental. Lastdinner8.30pm ✪ ⊒ S% sB&B£11.05–£12.70 dB&B£18.85–£24.70 dB&B⇌⋒£22.60–£25.40 Lunch fr£3.60 Tea fr30p Dinner fr£6.30&alc Wine£2.60 ⊟ *xmas* Credit cards 1 2 3 5 6

★★Bay Marine Pde ☎2059
Closed Nov–Feb; 31rm(2⇌⋒) ⋈ CTV 10P 20⌂ ⛟ Lastdinner8.30pm ✪ S% ✻sB&B£8.50–£9.50 dB&B£17–£19 dB&B⇌⋒£18.50–£21.50 Barlunch£1 Dinner£4.50 Wine£2.10 ⊟

★★Buena Vista Pound St (Inter-Hotel) ☎2494
Two-storey Regency house with white façade and first floor verandah. In own grounds overlooking the bay.
Closed Dec–Feb; RS Nov (no lunches); 20rm(8⇌⋒) CTV TV available in bedrooms 17P 2⌂ ⛟ ⚓ Lastdinner8pm ✪ ⊒ sB&B fr£12 dB&B fr£22 dB&B⇌⋒ fr£27 Lunch fr£3 Dinner fr£5 ⊟ Credit cards 1 2 3 4 5 6

★★Royal Lion Broad St ☎2768
Old coaching inn dating from 1603. Edward VII is reputed to have slept here.
23rm(6⇌⋒) 1⊟ ✗ CTV 30P 2⌂ Lastdinner8.30pm ✪ ✻sB&B£8.90–£10.70 dB&B£17.80–£21.40 dB&B⇌⋒£19.30–£22.90 Barlunch£1.75 Dinner£5 Wine£3 ⊟ *xmas* Credit card 3

★★St Michaels Pound St ☎2503
Closed Nov–Etr; 14rm(5⇌⋒) CTV 10P ⛟ Lastdinner7.15pm

★★Three Cups Broad St ☎2732
Closed Dec–Feb; 15rm(5⇌⋒) ⋈ CTV 25P ⛟ Lastdinner8pm ✪ sB&B£8.50–£9.50 dB&B£17–£19 dB&B⇌⋒£18.50–£21 Barlunch£1–£1.50 Dinner£4.50–£5 Wine£2 *xmas*

★Dorset Silver St ☎2482
Closed Nov–Mar; 13rm(4⇌⋒) CTV 13P ⛟ Lastdinner7.15pm ✪ ⊒ S% sB&B£5.83–£6.48 dB&B£11.66–£12.96 dB&B⇌⋒£13.16–£14.46 Lunch£2.6&alc

L

Tea90p&alc HighTea£1.62 Dinner£3.24&alc Wine£2.19 *xmas* Credit cards 1 2 3 4 5 6

★Stile House Pound St ☎2052
Closed Nov–Mar; 17rm CTV 18P Last dinner7pm S% sB&B£8–£9.80 dB&B£8–£10.50 Lunch£3.50 Tea80p Dinner£4–£4.90 Wine£1.60 Credit card 1

★Tudor House Church St ☎2472
Closed mid Oct–mid Mar; 17rm(4) CTV 12P Last dinner7.30pm S% sB&B fr£6.50 sB&B fr£7 dB&B fr£13 dB&B fr£14 Lunch£2 Dinner£3 wine£2.20

XX*Toni Ristorante Italiano* 14–15 Monmouth St ☎2079
Closed Sun & Oct–Etr; Lunch not served; 35seats Italian. Last dinner10.30pm ✱ Credit cards 1 3 5

LYMINGTON Hampshire Map**4** SZ39
★★★Passford House Mount Pleasant (2m NW on Sway Rd) ☎682398
Partly 17th-C white fronted country house, originally hunting lodge, set in 10 acres of woods and gardens.
51 CTV CTV in bedrooms 80P 4 (heated) (hard) sauna bath Last dinner8.30pm sB&B£13.50–£15.50 dB&B£27–£33 Lunch fr£3.20&alc Tea50p–£1.50 Dinner£5.20–£5.50&alc Wine£3.50 *xmas* Credit card 2

★★*Angel* 108 High St (Eldridge Pope) ☎72050
13th-C coaching inn reputedly haunted by coachman. Dining room hung with murals, depicting history of inn, painted by local artists.
16rm CTV 50P 8 English & French. Last dinner9.30pm Credit cards 1 2 5 6

★★Stanwell House ☎77123
Closed Xmas; 18rm(13) CTV in bedrooms English & French. Last dinner9.30pm S% sB&B£10–£12 sB&B£10.50–£12.50 dB&B£18–£20 dB&B£20–£22 Lunch£3.75–£4.20&alc Dinner£5.25–£6&alc Wine£3 Credit cards 1 2 3 5

XX*Slipway* The Quay ☎74545
50seats French. Last dinner10pm Credit cards 1 2 3 5

XFagan's High St ☎73074
Closed Tue; Lunch not served; 48seats French. Last dinner10.30pm ✱Dinner£5.50alc Wine£2.45

XLimpets 9 Gosport St ☎75595
Closed Mon & Nov; Lunch not served; 40seats Continental. Specialities: Filet de sole Noilly, tournedos Limpets, suprême de volaille Kiev. Last dinner10.30pm ✱Dinner£10alc Wine£3.30

LYMM Cheshire Map**7** SJ68
★★Lymm Whitbarrow Rd (Greenall Whitley) ☎2233
32rm(30) Annexe: 10rm(8) CTV in bedrooms 100P French. Last dinner9.30pm sB&B£12.50–£13 sB&B£14.85–£15.50 dB&B£17.50–£18 dB&B£20–£21 Lunch£3.50–£4&alc Tea50–60p Dinner£4–£4.50&alc Wine£3 1 2 3 5

L

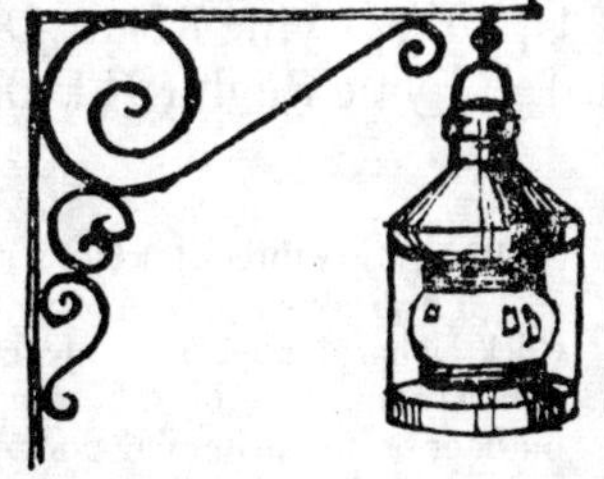

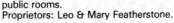

LYNDHURST Hampshire Map**4** SU30
★★★**Crown** High St ☎2722
Attractive Gothic-style gabled building with mullioned windows. Spacious interior includes warmly decorated restaurant overlooking small garden.
38⇌⋒ 1▭ Lift ☽ ₦ CTV CTV in bedrooms 41P 9🏠 ⇼ Live music & dancing Sat Conference facilities available Children under 5yrs not accommodated ♿ ♉English & French. Last dinner9.45pm ✿ ♊ S% ✳sB&B⇌⋒£15 dB&B⇌⋒£26.50 Lunch£4.75&alc Tea£1 Dinner£5.75–£6.95&alc Wine£2.90 ⊓ *xmas* Credit cards①②③⑤

★★★**Lyndhurst Park** High St (Best Western) ☎2824 Telex no47674
62rm(55⇌⋒) 4▭ Lift ☽ ₦ CTV in bedrooms 100P ⚓ ▭(heated) ⊸(hard) Live music & dancing Sat Conference facilities availalble Last dinner10pm ✿ sB&B£13.25–£17.25 sB&B⇌⋒£16.25–£18.75 dB&B£23.50–£28 dB&B⇌⋒£26.50–£31 Lunch fr£3 Dinner£4.25–£5.25&alc Wine£2.95 ⊓ *xmas* Credit cards①②③⑤.

★★★♛ **Parkhill** ☎2944
Closed Jan; 15⇌⋒ Annexe: 3⇌⋒ ₦ CTV in bedrooms ⊘ 40P ⇼ ⚓ ▭(heated) Children under 8yrs no accommodated ♉English & Continental. Last dinner9.30pm ✿ ✳sB&B⇌⋒£21 dB&B⇌⋒£28–£38 Lunch£4&alc Dinner£6&alc ⊓ *xmas* Credit cards①②③④⑤⑥

★★**Evergreens** Romsey Rd ☎2175
Closed 25 Dec–3 Jan; 18rm(8⇌⋒) ₦ CTV 35P ⚓ ▭ Children under 3yrs not accommodated Last dinner8pm ✿ ♊ S% sB&B£8–£9 sB&B⇌⋒£9.50–£10.50 dB&B£16–£18 dB&B⇌⋒£19–£21 Lunch£3–£4.50&alc Dinner£4–£4.50 Wine£2.15 ⊓

L

★★**Forest Lodge** Pikes Hill, Romsey Rd ☎2365
12rm(7⇌ ⋒) CTV CTV in bedrooms 40P 🐕 ⚓
(heated) ♀French. Last dinner 9pm ✿ ☕ S%
sB&Bfr£10.50 sB&B⇌⋒fr£11.75 dB&Bfr£21
dB&B⇌⋒£23.50 Lunch£3.95 Tea75p
Dinner£5.75&alc 🛏 *xmas* Credit cards 1 3 5

⊛**Forest Point** Romsey Rd (A337) ☎2420
Black and white timbered Tudor-style house with good views of the New Forest.
10rm(1⇌⋒) 🎬 CTV TV available in bedrooms 24P
4⌂ ⚓ 🍸 Last dinner 9.30pm ✿ ☕ sB&B£7–£8
dB&B£14–£15 dB&B⇌⋒£14–£15
Lunch£3–£4 Tea30–50p Dinner£4.25–£6
Wine£2.15 🛏 *xmas*

LYNMOUTH Devon Map**3** SS74
See also Lynton

★★★**Tors** ☎Lynton 3236
Stands in five acres of own grounds 200ft above sea-level, on heavily wooded slopes. Good views over bay.
Closed Oct–10 Apr; 42rm(27⇌⋒) Lift ☽ 🎬 CTV 38P
⚓ (heated) ♀French. Last dinner 9pm ✿ ☕
S% ✱sB&B£9.50–£10.65
sB&B⇌⋒£11.30–£12.10 dB&B£19–£21.30
dB&B⇌⋒£28.40–£31 Lunch fr£3.95 Tea fr70p
High Tea fr55p Dinner fr£4.95 Wine£3.20 🛏
Credit cards 1 2 3 5 6

★★**Bath** Sea Front ☎Lynton 2238
Closed Nov–Mar; 25rm(7⇌⋒) 🎬 CTV 13P 4⌂ 🍸
♀English & French. Last dinner 8.30pm ✿ ☕
S% sB&B£5.75–£8.80 dB&B£11.50–£17.60
dB&B⇌⋒£19–£20.90 Lunch£2.75 Tea40–80p
Dinner£4.50 Wine£2.80 🛏 Credit cards 1 2 5

L

★★ **Beacon** Countisbury Hill ☎Lynton3268
Closed Dec & Jan; 8rm(4⇌ ⋒) 10P
Children under 5yrs not accommodated
International. Last dinner8.30pm S%
✱sB&B⇌⋒£10.91 dB&B£15.66–£16.74
dB&B⇌⋒£18.36 Lunch£4.20alc Tea95palc
Dinner£4.05&alc Wine£3.10

★**Shelley's Cottage** ☎Lynton3219
Formerly known as Blackmoor's Lodging, Shelley wrote part of 'Queen Mab' here in 1812.
Closed Oct–Mar; 15rm CTV 2P Children under 8yrs not accommodated Last dinner7.55pm S% sB&B£6.45–£7.50 dB&B£12.90–£15 Lunch£2.50–£3.20 Tea80p Dinner£3–£3.70 Wine£2.80

LYNTON Devon Map**3** SS74
See also Lynmouth

★★**Crown** Sinai Hill (Inter-Hotel) ☎2253
Telex no45388
19rm(10⇌⋒) 4 CTV 20P English & French.
Last dinner8.15pm S% ✱sB&B£7.40–£8.60
sB&B⇌⋒£8.90–£10.10 dB&B£12.80–£15.20
dB&B⇌⋒£15.80–£18.20 Lunch£5alc
Dinner£3.95&alc Wine£2.60 *xmas*
Credit cards 1 3 5

★★**Lynton Cottage** ☎2342
Closed Nov–Feb 22rm(12⇌⋒) CTV 26P
Last dinner8.30pm S% ✱sB&B£8.80–£9.60
dB&B£14.70–£16.20 dB&B⇌⋒£17.10–£18.60
Bar lunch30p–£2 Dinner£4.25

★***Chough's Nest*** Northwalk ☎3315
Closed 21 Oct–Mar; 11rm (5⇌⋒) CTV 7P
Last dinner8.30pm

★🏰**Combe Park** Hillsford Bridge ☎2356
Stone built former hunting lodge set in six acres of woodlands.
Closed mid Oct–mid Mar; 10rm(7⇌🚿) CTV P Children under 14yrs not accommodated Last dinner8pm S% ✱sB&B£7–£7.50 sB&B⇌🚿£7.50–£8 dB&B£14–£15 dB&B⇌🚿£15–£16 Wine£3

★**Rockvale** ☎2279
Closed 25Oct–28Mar; 10rm(7⇌🚿) 1 CTV 10P Last dinner7pm S% sB&B£7.50 dB&B£15 dB&B⇌🚿£17.25 Bar lunch£1–£3 Dinner£3–£4.50 Wine£2.10

★**Sandrock** Longemead ☎3307
Closed Nov–Feb; 10rm(5⇌🚿) CTV CTV available in bedrooms 9P Last dinner7.30pm S% sB&B£6–£7 dB&B£12–£14 dB&B⇌🚿£15–£18 Bar lunch fr40p Tea fr30p Dinner fr£3.50 Wine £2

★**Seawood** North Walk ☎2272
Closed 5Oct–Mar; 12rm(6⇌🚿) 4 CTV 9P Last dinner7.30pm sB&B£7.50–£8.50 sB&B⇌🚿£8.60–£9.60 dB&B£15–£17 dB&B⇌🚿£17.20–£19.20 Lunch£2.50alc Dinner£4–£4.25 Wine £3

LYONSHALL Hereford & Worcester Map**3** SO35
✕**Penrhos Court** ☎Kington230720
Closed Mon & Jan–15Mar; 50seats 30P Last dinner9.30pm Dinner£2.50–£6.50&alc Wine£2.10 Credit card 1

LYTHAM ST ANNES Lancashire Map**7** SD32
Telephone exchanges Lytham or St Annes
★★★★**Clifton Arms** West Beach, Lytham (Whitbread & Best Western) ☎739898
43⇌🚿 Lift CTV CTV in bedrooms 50P Conference facilities available Continental. Last dinner10pm ✱sB&B⇌🚿£10.50–£15.84 dB&B⇌🚿£21–£30.80 Lunch£3.65&alc Tea£1.50 Dinner£4.50&alc Wine£2.51 *xmas* Credit cards 1 2 3

★★**Chadwick** South Prom, St Annes ☎720061
50⇌🚿 1 CTV CTV available in bedrooms 40P 1 Live music & dancing wkly (summer) mthly (winter) Conference facilities available Last dinner7.45pm S% sB&B⇌🚿£9–£10.50 dB&B⇌🚿£15–£17 Lunch£2.80–£3 Tea90p–£1 Dinner£3.80–£4.20 Wine£2.97 *xmas* Credit cards 1 2 5

★★**Fernlea** 15 South Prom, St Annes ☎726726
Telex no677150
92⇌🚿 Lift CTV CTV in bedrooms 60P (heated) squash sauna bath Live music & dancing twice wkly in season Conference facilities available Last dinner8pm SB&B⇌🚿£11–£11.50 dB&B⇌🚿£22–£23 Lunch£3–£3.50 Tea£1 High Tea£2.25 Dinner£4.50 Wine£2.50 *xmas* Credit cards 1 2 3 5

★★**Grand** South Prom, St Annes (Crest) ☎722155
37rm(9⇌🚿) Lift CTV CTV in bedrooms 150P Last dinner8.15pm S% ✱sB&B£10.58 dB&B£18.36 dB&B⇌🚿£23.76 Credit cards 1 2 3 4 5 6

★★**Hotel Glendower** North Prom, St Annes ☎723241
68rm(40⇌🚿) CTV P (heated) Last dinner6.30pm S% sB&B£12–£13 sB&B⇌🚿£13–£14 dB&B£24–£26 dB&B⇌🚿£26–£28 Lunch£3.50alc Tea75palc High Tea£2alc Dinner£4.50alc Wine£2.40 *xmas*

★★**Knight's** 365–367 Clifton Drive North, St Annes ☎720421
14rm(6⇌🚿) CTV available in bedrooms 16P

L

☺English & Continental. Lastdinner11pm ✿ ♖ ✱sB&B£9.18 sB&B⇌⋒£10.26 dB&B£18.36 dB&B⇌⋒£20.52 Lunch£3.25 Tea£1 Dinner£4.75&alc Wine£2.75 ⊓ *xmas*

★★Princes 40 North Prom, St Annes ☎725161 40rm(16⇌⋒) Lift CTV 30P billiards Live music wkly Lastdinner6.30pm ✿ ♖ ✱Lunch£3–£3.25 Tea20–25p Dinner£4–£4.25 ⊓ *xmas*

★★St Ives 7 South Prom, St Annes ☎720011 75rm(50⇌⋒) ☽ ⋈ CTV CTV available in bedrooms ⊘ 60P ▭(heated) Live music & dancing 4 nights in season Cabaret wkly ♧ Last dinner Nov–Apr9.30pm May–Oct 6.30pm ✿ ♖ sB&B fr£10 sB&B⇌⋒ fr£11 dB&B£16–£18 dB&B⇌⋒£18–£20 Lunch£2.80 Dinner£4.25&alc Wine£2.50 ⊓ *xmas* Credit card 1

★★*Savoy* 314 Clifton Drive North, St Annes ☎728441 18rm(13⇌⋒) Lift ☽ CTV 20P Children under 5yrs not accommodated ☺English & Continental. Lastdinner8pm Credit cards 2 6

★*Carlton* 61 South Prom, St Annes ☎721036 Closed Nov–Jan except Xmas; 22rm(4⇌⋒) ⋈ CTV ⊘ 12P Disco twice wkly Cabaret wkly Lastdinner6pm ⊓

★Lindum 65–67 South Prom, St Annes ☎721534 61rm(40⇌⋒) Lift ☽ CTV TV available in bedrooms 20P Live music & dancing Thu & Sun in season ♧ Lastdinner6.30pm ✿ ✱sB&B£7.13 sB&B⇌⋒£7.72 dB&B£14.26 dB&B⇌⋒£15.44 Lunch£2.97 Dinner£3.56 Wine£1.95 ⊓ *xmas*

★Oceandene South Prom, St Annes ☎726249 20rm(14⇌⋒) Annexe: 2⇌⋒ CTV ⊘ 14P 2⌂ Lastdinner6pm ✿ ♖ S% sB&B£6–£7 sB&B⇌⋒£6.50–£7.50 dB&B£12–£14 dB&B⇌⋒£13–£15 Lunch£2–£2.50 Tea£1.50–£2 Dinner£2.50–£6 ⊓ *xmas*

MADINGLEY Cambridgeshire Map**5** TL36
✕✕*Three Horseshoes* ☎221
Closed Xmas Day; 36seats 60P Credit cards 2 3 6

MAENPORTH Cornwall Map**2** SW73
★★★Trelawne ☎Mawnan Smith250226
Closed Nov–Feb; 18rm(11⇌⋒) ⚔ ⋈ CTV 20P ⚘ ⚓ ▭(heated) Lastdinner8.30pm ✿ ♖ S% sB&B£10–£12 sB&B⇌⋒£11.50–£14.50 dB&B£20–£24 dB&B⇌⋒£23–£29 Lunch£2.25alc Tea35p–£1.25 Dinner£5.50–£7.50 Wine£2.70 Credit cards 1 2 3 5

MAIDENCOMBE Devon **See under Torquay**

MAIDENHEAD Berkshire Map**4** SU88
☆☆☆☆Maidenhead EuroCrest Shoppenhangers Rd (Crest) ☎23444 Telex no 847502
193⇌⋒ Lift ☽ CTV CTV in bedrooms 300P ⚓ Conference facilities available ☺French. Lastdinner10pm ✿ S% ✱sB&B⇌⋒£19.76 dB&B⇌⋒£28.29 Continental breakfast ⊓ *xmas* Credit cards 1 2 3 4 5 6

★★Bear High St (Anchor) ☎25183 Telex no 858875
Three-storey coaching inn with gay awnings, patio and large black bear over porch.
12rm ⋈ CTV CTV in bedrooms ⚑ Lastdinner10pm ✿ ♖ S% ✱sB&B fr£13.25 dB&B fr£18 Lunch£2.95–£3.50 Dinner£2.95–£4.50 Wine£2.65 ⊓ Credit cards 1 2 3 4 5 6

★★Riviera Bridge Rd ☎25425
38⇌⋒ ☽ ⋈ CTV ⊘ 52P ⚓ ↳ Live music & dancing Wed & Sun ☺English & French. Lastdinner9.15pm ✿ S% ✱sB&B⇌⋒£11.25–£13 dB&B⇌⋒£15.50–£17.50 Lunch£4.50alc Dinner£4.50alc Wine£2.75 Credit cards 1 2 3 5 6

M

✕✕***La Riva*** Raymead Rd ☎33522
Closed Sun; 45seats 20P ♡Italian.
Last dinner10.30pm Credit cards 1 2 3 5 6

✕***Chef Peking*** 74 King St ☎32851
75seats ♡Chinese. Last dinner11pm

✕**Chez Michel et Valerie** Bridge Av ☎22450
Closed Mon, Good Fri, Public Hols & last 3wks Aug;
47seats P ♡French. Last dinner10.15pm
Lunch£10alc Dinner£10alc Wine£4
Credit cards 1 2 3 5 6

✕***Maidenhead Chinese*** 45–47 Queen St ☎24545
60seats ♡Chinese. Last dinner11.30pm

MAIDSTONE Kent Map**5** TQ75
★★**Boxley** Boxley (3m N between A229/A249)
☎52226 Telex no966192
Closed Public Hols; 10rm(6⇌ ⋒) Annexe: 4⇌ ⋒ 4▭
CTV 80P ⚘ (heated) billiards Disco Fri Live music & dancing Wed & Sat Last dinner8.45pm
S% ✱sB&B£15 sB&B⇌⋒£15 dB&B£20
dB&B⇌⋒£20 Dinner fr£3.75 Wine£2.90

★★**Royal Star** High St (Embassy) ☎55721
Old coaching inn in town centre, with modern interior.
37rm(14⇌⋒) D CTV TV in bedrooms 20P 100
Last dinner9.15pm S% sB&B£11.50
sB&B⇌⋒£16 dB&B£18 dB&B⇌⋒£22
Lunch£5&alc Dinner£5.50&alc Wine£5
Credit cards 1 2 3 4 5 6

✕✕**Running Horse** Sandling ☎52975
Tudor style roadhouse with small restaurant.
Closed Sun & Public Hols; 68seats 60P ♡English & Continental. Last dinner10pm Lunch£9.50alc
Dinner£9.50alc Wine£4 Credit cards 1 2 3 5

MALBOROUGH Devon Map**3** SX73
★★**Soar Mill Cove** Soar Mill Cove ☎Galmpton566
Closed Oct–Mar; 10rm(2⇌⋒) CTV 20P ⚘
♡English & Continental. Last dinner10pm
S% sB&B£12–£15 sB&B⇌⋒£12–£15
dB&B£24–£30 dB&B⇌⋒£24–£30
Lunch fr£3.50 Tea fr£1.25 High Tea fr£1.25
Dinner£6–£7&alc Wine£3.30 *xmas.*
Credit cards 1 3

MALDON Essex Map**5** TL80
★★**Blue Boar** Silver St (Trusthouse Forte) ☎52681
21⇌⋒ Annexe: 5⇌⋒ TV in bedrooms 43P
Last dinner10pm S% sB&B⇌⋒£15
dB&B⇌⋒£20.50 *xmas*
Credit cards 1 2 3 4 5 6

MALHAM North Yorkshire Map**7** SD96
★**Buck Inn** ☎Airton317
10rm(1⇌⋒) CTV TV available in bedroom 40P
Last dinner8.30pm S% ✱sB&B£6.40–£7
dB&B£12.80–£14 dB&B⇌⋒£13.80–£15
Lunch£1.50alc Tea60palc High Tea£2alc
Dinner£5alc Wine£2.60

MALMESBURY Wiltshire Map**3** ST98
★★★**Old Bell** Abbey Row ☎2344
Built of Cotswold stone, this hotel was once part of monastic property. The adjacent Abbey is of Norman design. Secluded rear gardens with views across river valleys.
19rm(9⇌⋒) TV in bedrooms 25P 2
Last dinner9.30pm sB&B£11.50–£12.50
sB&B⇌⋒£16–£17.50 dB&B£20–£22
sB&B⇌⋒£23–£25 Lunch£4.25–£4.75
Tea75palc Dinner£6.50alc Wine£3 *xmas*
Credit cards 1 2 3 5

★**Kings Arms** 29 High St ☎3383
Traditional coaching hostelry with archway and courtyard. Dates back several centuries.
Closed Xmas wk; 6rm CTV 15P ♡English &

Continental. Last dinner 9.30pm ♔ sB&B£7.70 dB&B£15.40 Lunch£5alc Dinner£5alc Wine£3

XXSuffolk Arms Tetbury Hill ☎2271
Cotswold stone inn, with low-beamed, panelled restaurant.
Closed Xmas & New Year's Day; Dinner not served Sun; 35 seats 80P Last dinner 10pm

MALTON North Yorkshire Map**8** SE77
★★Green Man Market Pl ☎2662
Closed Xmas; 25rm(15⇌ ⋒) ⋈ CTV 3P 2⌂
Last dinner 8.45pm ♔ ⊞ Credit card 2

★★Talbot Yorkersgate (Trusthouse Forte) ☎4031
24rm(7⇌ ⋒) CTV CTV in bedrooms 30P 6⌂
Last dinner 9.30pm ♔ ♕ S% sB&B£12 sB&B⇌ ⋒£14 dB&B£17.50 dB&B⇌ ⋒£21 ⊞
Credit cards 1 2 3 4 5 6

★Mount Yorkersgate ☎2608
11rm ⋈ TV ⊘ 20P ⌘ Last dinner 10pm ♔
sB&B£6–£7.50 dB&B£11–£14 Lunch£3&alc
Dinner£3&alc Wine £2.75 ⊞ Credit cards 1 3 5

★Wentworth Arms Town St, Old Malton ☎2618
Closed Xmas; 7rm ⋈ ⊘ 30P ⌘ Children under 6yrs not accommodated Last dinner 8.45pm ♔ ♕
sB&B£6–£8 dB&B£12–£16 Lunch£3alc
Tea£1.50alc High Tea£4.50alc Dinner£4.50alc
Wine£2

MALVERN, GREAT Hereford & Worcester Map**3** SO74
★★★Abbey Abbey Rd (De Vere) ☎3325
Telex no 22121
Imposing creeper-clad Gothic-style mansion with modern wing; close to priory church. Private gardens opposite.
106rm(84⇌ ⋒) Lift ☽ ⋈ CTV in bedrooms 120P ⚓
Conference facilities available ♿ Last dinner 8.30pm
♔ S% sB&B⇌ ⋒£16 dB&B⇌ ⋒£25.50
Lunch fr£3.75&alc Dinner fr£4.75&alc Wine£3.50
⊞ *xmas* Credit cards 1 2 3 5 6

★★Beauchamp Graham Rd ☎63411
16rm ⋈ CTV TV available in bedrooms 10P
Last dinner 8.30pm ♔ S% sB&B fr£10
dB&B fr£17.50 Lunch£3.95 Dinner£4.75&alc
Wine£2.40 ⊞ *xmas* Credit cards 1 3

★★Gold Hill Avenue Rd ☎4000
26rm(16⇌ ⋒) Lift ⋈ CTV TV available in bedrooms 25P ⊘ Last dinner 8.30pm ♔ ♕ ⊞
Credit card 3

★★Mount Pleasant Belle Vue Ter ☎61837
15rm(2⇌ ⋒) ⋈ CTV 20P ⚓ sauna bath
Last dinner 9pm ♔ ♕ S% sB&B£6–£8
sB&B⇌ ⋒£8.50 dB&B£14–£17 dB&B⇌ ⋒£18
Lunch fr£2.75&alc Tea fr40p High Tea fr£1.25
Dinner£5.75alc Wine£2.45 ⊞
Credit cards 1 2 5 6

★★Thornbury Avenue Rd ☎2278
Closed Xmas wk; 17rm Annexe: 4rm ✗ ⋈ CTV 12P
⌘ ⚓ Last dinner 8pm ♔ ♕ S% ✱sB&B£7.59
Lunch£3–£3.50 Tea50p–£1 High Tea£2.50
Dinner£3.30–£4 Wine£2.30

★Broomhill West Malvern Rd, Malvern West (2m W B4232) ☎64367
Closed Nov–Feb; 12rm(3⇌ ⋒) ⋈ TV 10P ⌘ Children under 5yrs not accommodated Last dinner 7.30pm
♔ ♕ ✱sB&B£7.25 dB&B£14.50
dB&B⇌ ⋒£16.50 Bar lunch£1.25 Tea£1
Dinner£4.75 Credit card 1

★Montrose Graham Rd ☎2335
Closed Nov; 14rm(6⇌ ⋒) ⋈ CTV 12P ⌘ ⚓
Last dinner 9.15pm ♔ ♕ S% sB&B£6.50–£8
sB&B⇌ ⋒£7.50–£9.50 dB&B£13–£16
dB&B⇌ ⋒£15–£19 Lunch£2.20 Tea£1
High Tea£1.50 Dinner£3.60 Wine£3.50 *xmas*

❀★Walmer Lodge 49 Abbey Rd ☎4139
(Rosette awarded for dinner only).
10rm(2⇌ ⋒) ⋈ CTV ⊘ 6P ⌘ ⚓ Children under 14yrs not accommodated ♡ English, French & Italian
Specialities: tournedos Maurice, escalope de veau Yorkaise. Last dinner 9pm sB&B£6.48
dB&B£15.12 dB&B⇌ ⋒£17.28 Dinner£6alc
Wine£3

MALVERN WELLS Hereford & Worcester Map**3** SO74
❀★★★Cottage-in-the-Wood Holywell Rd (Prestige) ☎3487
Closed 24–30 Dec; 12rm(9⇌ ⋒) Annexe: 8⇌ ⋒ 1▭
⋈ CTV in bedrooms ⊘ ⌘ Specialities: homemade soups & paté, fresh Wye salmon, various types of game in season. Last dinner 9pm ♔ ♕ S%
sB&B£14 sB&B⇌ ⋒£22.50 dB&B£27
dB&B⇌ ⋒£31–£41.50 Continental breakfast
Lunch£6&alc Tea£2 Dinner£8&alc ⊞
Credit cards 1 2 3 5 6

★★Essington Holywell Rd ☎61177
10rm(3⇌ ⋒) ⋈ CTV 30P ⌘ ⚓ Last dinner 8.15pm
♕ sB&B£8.70 dB&B£17.40 dB&B⇌ ⋒£21
Bar lunch£3 Dinner£5.50 Wine£2.75 ⊞ *xmas*
Credit cards 1 2 3

MALVERN (WYNDS POINT) Hereford & Worcester Map**3** SO74
★★Malvern Hills ☎Colwall40237
White-painted inn with panelled entrance; situated high in Malvern Hills with lovely views.
15rm CTV 25P 1 English & French. Lastdinner9.30pm S% sB&B£12 sB&B £14 dB&B£20 dB&B £23 Lunch£4 Tea£1 Dinner£5.50–£6.50&alc Wine£2.70 *xmas* Creditcards 1 5

MAN, ISLE OF Details follow England

MANCHESTER Greater Manchester Map**7** SJ89
See plan
★★★★★Hotel Piccadilly Piccadilly Plaza (Embassy) ☎061–236 8414 Telexno668765 Plan**8**
Fourteen-floor skyscraper block (1965) in city centre. Panoramic views from restaurant.
250 Lift CTV CTV in bedrooms 50P 50 Conference facilities available French. Lastdinner10.15pm S% sB £25(room only) dB £32(room only) Lunch£7.50alc Dinner£7.50alc Wine£5.50 Creditcards 1 2 3 4 5 6

★★★★Grand Aytoun St (Trusthouse Forte) ☎061–236 9559 Telexno667580 Plan**4**
A massive six-storey Victorian building, with towers and gables and an unusual Edwardian façade.
146rm131) Lift CTV in bedrooms Conference facilities available Lastdinner10.15pm S% sB&B £21.50 sB&B £32.50 dB&B £32.50 dB&B £33.50 Creditcards 1 2 3 4 5 6

★★★★Midland Peter St (British Transport) ☎061–236 3333 Telexno667797 Plan**7**
289rm(243) Lift TV in bedrooms Conference facilities available sauna bath Lastdinner10.15pm S% *sB&B fr£30 dB&B fr£41 Lunch fr£7 Dinner fr£7 Wine£3.50 Creditcards 1 2 3 4 5 6

★★★★Portland 3–5 Portland St, Piccadilly Gdns (Thistle) ☎061–228 3567 Telexno669157 Plan**9**
221 Lift CTV in bedrooms Conference facilities available French. Lastdinner10.15pm S% *sB&B £23.90 dB&B £29.90 Lunch£3.51&alc Dinner£5.40&alc Wine£3.15 *xmas* Creditcards 1 2 3 4 5 6

☆☆☆Post House Palatine Rd, Northenden (Trusthouse Forte) ☎061–998 7090 Telexno669248 Plan**10**
201 Lift CTV in bedrooms 243P Lastdinner10.30pm S% sB&B £21.25 dB&B £31 *xmas* Creditcards 1 2 3 4 5 6

★★★Willow Bank 340–2 Wilmslow Rd, Fallowfield ☎061–224 0461 Plan**9**
122rm(90) CTV CTV available in bedrooms 50P 50 Live music & dancing Sat European. Lastdinner10.15pm sB&B£14.50 sB&B £19 dB&B£20 dB&B £25 Lunch£3&alc Dinner£4.50&alc Wine£2 Creditcards 1 2 3 5 6

★★Simpsons 122 Withington Rd, Whalley Range ☎061–226 2235 Telexno667822 Plan**15**
38rm(8) CTV TV available in bedrooms 2 Lastdinner8.30pm sB&B£11 sB&B £13 dB&B£14 dB&B £16 Lunch£2.25–£2.75&alc Tea50p–£1 Dinner£4–£4.50 Wine£3 Creditcards 1 3 5 6

XXXL'Elysée 44 Princess St ☎061–236 1652 Plan**6**
Closed Sun; Lunch not served Sat; 100seats Disco Sat French. Lastdinner11pm S%

M

- Armenian✕
- Casa España✕✕
- Charlie Chans✕
- Grand ★★★★
- Isola Bella ✿✕✕
- L'Elysée✕✕✕
- Midland ✿★★★★
- Hotel Piccadilly★★★★★
- Portland ★★★★
- Post House ☆☆☆
- Rajdoot✕✕
- Royal Exchange✕
- Sam's Chop House✕
- Shish Kebab House✕✕
- Simpsons ★★
- Steak & Kebab✕
- Terrazza✕✕✕
- Truffles✕✕
- Willow Bank ★★★

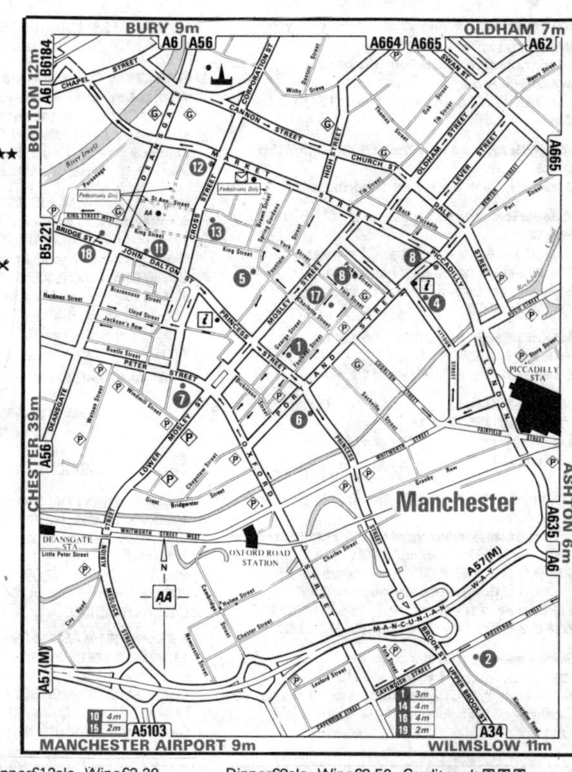

✱Lunch fr£2.80&alc Dinner£12alc Wine£3.20 Credit cards ② ③

✕✕✕Terrazza 14 Nicholas St ☎061–236 4033 Plan**17**
Closed Sun; Lunch not served Sat; 110seats 🅿 ♀Italian. ✱Lunch fr£3.50 Dinner£10alc Wine£3.05 Credit cards ① ② ③ ④ ⑤ ⑥

✕✕Casa España 100 Wilmslow Rd, Rusholme ☎061–224 6826 Plan**2**
Closed Sun & Public Hols; 53seats 🅿 ♀Spanish. Last dinner10.45pm ✱Lunch£1.95&alc Dinner£7alc Wine£2.75 Credit card ②

✿✕✕Isola Bella Booth St ☎061–236 6417 Plan**5**
Closed Sun; 65seats 🅿 ♀Italian Specialities: pollo Isola Bella, trota mandorla, vitello piemontese. Last dinner10.45pm S% Lunch£8alc Dinner£8alc Wine£3.50 Credit cards ② ③ ⑤

✕✕*Rajdoot* St James House, South Kings St ☎061–834 2176 Plan**11**
Closed Xmas; Lunch not served Sun & Public Hols; 76seats ♀North West Indian. Last dinner11.30pm Credit cards ① ② ③ ⑤

✕✕Shish Kebab House (Yerevan Suite) 125 Palatine Rd, Didsbury ☎061–434 1122 Plan**14**
Closed Sun; 70seats 100P ♀Armenian. Last dinner10.45pm Lunch£5.20alc Dinner£5.20alc Wine£3.95 Credit cards ① ② ⑥

✕✕Truffles 63 Bridge St ☎061–832 9393 Plan**18**
Closed Mon; Lunch served Wed, Thur & Sun; Dinner not served Sun; 50seats 🅿 Last dinner mdnt ✱Lunch£10.50alc Dinner£4–£4.50&alc Wine£3 Credit cards ① ② ③ ⑤

M

×Armenian (Granada Hotel) 404 Wilmslow Rd, Withington ☎061-434 3480 Plan**1**
Lunch not served Sat & Sun; 48seats 25P bedrooms available Armenian. Last dinner 11.15pm Lunch£5alc Dinner£5alc Wine£3.15 Credit cards 2 5

×*Charlie Chans* 41 George St ☎061-236 5750 Plan**3**
60seats Cantonese. Last dinner mdnt

×Royal Exchange St Annes Sq ☎061-833 9682 Plan**12**
Closed Sun & last 2wks Aug; Lunch not served Sat; 70seats English & French. Last dinner 11pm S% ✱Lunch£4alc Dinner fr£6.25alc Wine£3.50 Credit cards 1 3

×*Sam's Chop House* Back Pool Fold ☎061-834 1526 Plan**13**
Closed Sat, Sun & Public Hols; 130seats

×*Steak & Kebab* 846 Wilmslow Rd, Didsbury ☎061-445 2552 Plan**16**
Lunch not served Sat; 120seats International. Last dinner 11.30pm

MANCHESTER AIRPORT Greater Manchester Map**7** SJ78

☆☆☆☆**Excelsior** Wythenshawe (Trusthouse Forte) ☎061-437 5811 Telex no 668721
255 Lift CTV in bedrooms 250P (heated) Conference facilities available Last dinner 10.15pm S% sB&B £24.25 dB&B £33 Credit cards 1 2 3 4 5 6

★★★**Valley Lodge** Altrincham Rd ☎Wilmslow 529201 Telex no 666401
68 Lift CTV in bedrooms Disco Wed-Sat Conference facilities available International. Last dinner 10.30pm S% sB&B £16 dB&B £23 Lunch fr£3.50 Dinner£3.75 Wine£3.10 Credit cards 2 5

MARAZION Cornwall Map**2** SW53

★**Cutty Sark Inn** The Square ☎710334
11 CTV 30P Last dinner 9.30pm sB&B £7-£8 dB&B £14-£16 Lunch£3.50-£5 Dinner£3.75-£8&alc Wine£3.75 *xmas* Credit cards 2 3

MARGATE Kent Map**5** TR37

★★**Walpole Bay** Fifth Av, Cliftonville (1m E) (Best Western) ☎Thanet 21703
Closed Oct-Apr except Xmas; 45rm(18) Lift CTV Last dinner 8.30pm S% sB&B£11-£13 sB&B £12-£14 dB&B£20-£25 dB&B £22-£27 Lunch£4-£4.50 Tea50p Dinner£4.50-£5 Wine£2 *xmas*

★**Ye Olde Charles Inn** Northdown Rd, Cliftonville (1m E) ☎Thanet 21817
11rm CTV 60P 4 Mainly grills. Last dinner 9.45pm sB&B£10 dB&B£14.50 Lunch fr£3.50 Dinner fr£3.50 Wine£2.50 Credit cards 1 2 3 5 6

MARKET DRAYTON Salop Map**7** SJ63

★★***Corbet Arms*** High St ☎2037
Ancient inn with Georgian façade and pillared entrance.
RS 23-26 Dec; 8 CTV TV available in bedrooms 40P Last dinner 8.45pm Credit cards 1 3 6

★★**Tern Hill** (on A53) ☎Tern Hill 310
11rm(5) CTV 100P 4 Last dinner 9.15pm sB&B£8.91 dB&B £9.51 dB&B£17.82 dB&B £19.60 Lunch£2.50-£4 Dinner£3.50-£6&alc Credit cards 1 2 3 4 5 6

M

✕✕Four Alls Newport Rd ☎2995
Dinner not served Sun & Mon; 65seats 100P Last dinner9pm Lunch£2.85alc Dinner£5.50alc Wine£3

MARKET HARBOROUGH Leicestershire Map**4** SP78
★★Angel High St ☎63123
Closed Xmas; 17rm CTV TV available in bedrooms 50P 8⌂ Last dinner9.15pm ♁ S% ✱sB&B£8.95 dB&B£16 Lunch£3.20–£4.20 Tea fr40p Dinner£4.95–£5.25 Wine£3.25 ⊟

★★Grove Motel Northampton Rd ☎64082
16⇌⫙ ⫿ CTV in bedrooms ⊘ 40P ⊛ Disco Fri Last dinner9pm ♁ sB&B⇌⫙£11.88 dB&B⇌⫙£17.28 Lunch£1.75–£4&alc Wine£2.50 ⊟

★★Three Swans High St ☎66644
18⇌⫙ 2⊟ ⫿ CTV 50P 12⌂ ⊛ ☋English & French. Last dinner10pm ♁ sB&B⇌⫙£13.50–£14.50 dB&B⇌⫙£18–£21 Lunch£3.75–£4.50&alc Dinner£6.50alc Wine£2.95 ⊟ Credit cards 2 5

✕✕Peacock Inn The Square ☎62269
Closed Mon; Lunch not served Sat; Dinner not served Sun; 45seats 25P ☋English & French. Last dinner10pm Lunch£3.25–£4.25&alc Dinner£3.75–£4.50&alc Wine£3.10 Credit cards 1 3

MARKET RASEN Lincolnshire Map**8** TF18
During the currency of this guide, Market Rasen telephone numbers are liable to change.
★★Limes Gainsborough Rd ☎2357
10⇌⫙ ✕ ⫿ CTV ⊘ 40P ⚓ ⊸(grass) squash Last dinner8.45pm ♁ ⊒ S% ✱sB&B⇌⫙£9.50 dB&B⇌⫙£16.20 Lunch£4.30alc High Tea£2alc Dinner£5alc Wine£3.24 ⊟ Credit card 1

★Gordon Arms Queen St ☎2364
7rm CTV ⊘ 40P 2⌂ Last dinner8pm ♁ S% ✱sB&B fr£5.50 dB&B fr£10.50 Lunch fr£2.20 Dinner fr£2.75&alc Wine£1.45

MARKET WEIGHTON Humberside Map**8** SE84
★★*Londesborough Arms* ☎2219
10rm CTV ⊘ 50P Last dinner9.30pm ♁ ⊒ Credit cards 1 2 3 4 5 6

MARKSBURY Avon Map**3** ST66
❀★★★ **⚜Hunstrete House** (2m W off A368)
☎Compton Dando578
See page 50 for details

MARKS TEY Essex Map**5** TL92
☆☆☆Marks Tey London Rd ☎Colchester210001
Telex no987176
106⇌⫙ ☽ ⫿ CTV TV available in bedrooms 160P Conference facilities available ☋English & French. Last dinner10pm ♁ ⊒ S% ✱sB&B⇌⫙£13.99 dB&B⇌⫙£19.98 Lunch fr£3.51 Dinner fr£3.89 Wine£3.89 ⊟ *xmas* Credit cards 1 2 3 5

MARKYATE Hertfordshire Map**4** SP01
☆☆☆Hertfordshire Moat House London Rd (A5) (Queens) ☎Luton840840
97⇌⫙ ☽ ⫿ TV in bedrooms 200P Conference facilities available ☋French. Last dinner9.30pm ♁ S% sB&B⇌⫙£14–£19 dB&B⇌⫙£23–£26 Lunch£5.25&alc Dinner£5.25&alc Wine£3.75 ⊟ Credit cards 1 2 3 5

MARLBOROUGH Wiltshire Map**4** SU16
★★*Ailesbury Arms* High St (Inter-Hotel) ☎53451
30rm (8⇌⫙) ☽ ⫿ CTV TV available in bedrooms 24P 8⌂ ⚓ Last dinner10pm ♁ ⊒ ⊟ Credit cards 1 2 3 5

★★Castle & Ball High St (Trusthouse Forte) ☎52002
17th-C inn with tile-hung Georgian façade.
30rm (6⇌⫙) ⫿ CTV TV in bedrooms 50P Last dinner9.30pm ♁ ⊒ S% sB&B£11 dB&B£17.50 dB&B⇌⫙£20.50 ⊟ *xmas* Credit cards 1 2 3 4 5 6

MARLOW Buckinghamshire Map**4** SU88
★★★★Compleat Angler (Prestige) ☎4444
Telex no848644
42⇌⫙ ☽ ⫿ CTV CTV in bedrooms 100P 4⌂ ⚓ ⊸(hard) ↬ Conference facilities available ☋International. Last dinner9.30pm ♁ ⊒ S% sB&B⇌⫙£32.50 dB&B⇌⫙£44.50 Lunch£6&alc Tea£1.50 Dinner£15alc Wine£4.75 ⊟ Credit cards 1 2 3 5

★George & Dragon The Causeway ☎3887
RS Jan–Apr; 16rm (1⇌⫙) ⫿ CTV ⚑ ⊛ ☋English & French. Last dinner9.25pm S% sB&B£12 dB&B fr£22 dB&B⇌⫙ fr£26 Lunch£3.60–£4&alc Dinner£3.90–£4.30&alc Wine£3.50 Credit cards 1 2 3 5 6

✕✕Cavaliers (Restaurant Français) 24 West St ☎2544
Lunch not served Mon; 50seats ⚑ ☋French. Last dinner10pm Lunch£10alc Dinner£12alc Wine£3.75 Credit cards 1 2 3 5 6

✕*La Chandelle* 55 High St ☎2799
35seats ☋Continental. Last dinner10.30pm Credit cards 1 2 3 5

✕Dino's Trattoria (La Venezinia) ⇌4919
Closed Sun; 70seats ⚑ ☋English & Italian. Last dinner10.30pm S% ✱Lunch£8alc Dinner£8alc Credit cards 1 2 3 5 6

MARSDEN West Yorkshire Map**7** SE01
★★⚜Hey Green Waters Rd ☎Huddersfield844235
5⇌⫙ ⫿ CTV 50P ⚓ ☋English & French. Last dinner10pm ♁ sB&B⇌⫙£10 dB&B⇌⫙£18 Bar lunch£1.50 Dinner£7 Wine£3 ⊟ *xmas*

M

MARSTON TRUSSELL Northamptonshire Map**4** SP68
★★**Sun Inn** ☎Market Harborough65531
Closed 25 & 26 Dec; 10⇌⋒ ♛ CTV ⊗ 40P ♔ ♿
♕English, French & Italian. Last dinner9.30pm ✿
S% sB&B⇌⋒£16.50 dB&B⇌⋒£20.50
Lunch£4alc Dinner£5.50alc Wine£2.50 ⛿
Credit cards ② ⑤.

MARTOCK Somerset Map**3** ST41
★**White Hart** ☎2246
The building is of ham stone and stands in the Centre of town opposite the Corn Exchange.
8rm Lift CTV TV in bedrooms 20P 3⌂
Last dinner9.30pm ✿ S% sB&B fr£7
dB&B fr£14 Lunch£3.50alc Dinner£5.50alc
Wine£2.40 Credit card ①

MARYPORT Cumbria Map**11** NY03
★★**Waverley** Curzon St ☎2115
Recently modernised and pleasantly decorated, this hotel is near to the sea and within easy reach of the lakes and fells.
20rm(10⇌⋒) ♛ CTV ⚑ Last dinner8pm ✿ ☕
S% sB&B£9 sB&B⇌⋒£10–£11 dB&B£16
sB&B⇌⋒£18 Lunch£2.80 Tea£1
High Tea£2.20 Dinner£4.20 Wine£2.50
Credit cards ① ③ ⑥

MASHAM North Yorkshire Map**8** SE28
★★***King's Head*** Market Pl ☎295
Closed Xmas Day; 14rm ♛ CTV 40P 2⌂
Last dinner8pm ✿ ☕

MATLOCK Derbyshire Map**8** SK36
★★**New Bath** New Bath Rd (2m S A6) (Trusthouse Forte) ☎3275
58rm(56⇌⋒) ☽ ♛ CTV in bedrooms 250P ⚓
⊟(heated) ⤳(hard) sauna bath Last dinner10pm ✿
☕ S% sB&B⇌⋒£19 dB&B⇌⋒£24.50 ⛿
xmas Credit cards ① ② ③ ④ ⑤ ⑥

★★★**Riber Hall** Riber ☎2795
Annexe: 8⇌⋒ 8⊟ ⊞ ♛ CTV in bedrooms ⊗ 45P ⛟
⚓ Children under 10yrs not accommodated
♕English & French. Last dinner9.30pm ✿ ☕
✱sB&B⇌⋒£19.44 dB&B⇌⋒£23.76
Continental breakfast Lunch£4.32 Tea£1.50
Dinner£7.10 ⛿ Credit cards ① ② ③ ⑤

★**High Ror** Artists Corner, Dale Rd ☎2031
This hotel was built in approximately 1780, for Admiral Collingwood-Lord Nelson's successor.
18rm 4⊟ ♛ CTV TV available in bedrooms 20P 2⌂
sauna bath Last dinner8pm ✿ ☕ S%
✱sB&B£7–£8.50 dB&B£12–£17 Lunch fr£3
Tea fr£1 Dinner fr£3.25&alc Wine£2.95

MAWGAN PORTH Cornwall Map**2** SW86
★**Tredragon** ☎St Mawgan213
Closed mid Oct–Mar; 31rm(20⇌⋒) CTV 25P 2⌂ ⚓
Last dinner7.45pm ✿ ☕ sB&B£7–£9
dB&B£14–£18 dB&B⇌⋒£16.50–£20.50
Bar lunch75p–£2 Tea25–50p Dinner£3.50–£4
Wine£2.50

MAWNAN SMITH Cornwall Map**2** SW72
★★ ♜**Meudon** (1½m E unclass road) (Prestige)
☎250541
See page 51 for details

✕**Cockleshell** ☎250714
Closed Sun & Mon (Nov–Mar); 40seats 25P
♕English, French & Italian. Last dinner10pm
Lunch£1–£2.50&alc Dinner£6alc
Credit cards ① ② ③ ⑤ ⑥

MAYFIELD East Sussex Map**5** TQ52
★★**Middle House** ☎2146 Telex no95338
10rm(2⇌⋒) 1⊟ ♛ CTV ⊗ 20P ♔ ♕English & French. Last dinner9.30pm ✿ S%
sB&B£8.50–£9.50 sB&B⇌⋒£10–£12
dB&B£17–£19 dB&B⇌⋒£22–£24
Lunch£3.25–£4.50 Dinner£6alc Wine£3.25 ⛿
Credit cards ① ② ③ ④ ⑤ ⑥

MEALSGATE Cumbria Map**11** NY24
★★***Croft House*** ☎Low Ireby229
Closed Nov; RS Sun; 8rm ✗ ♛ CTV 15P ⚓
Last dinner8pm ✿

MEASHAM Leicestershire Map**8** SK31
☆☆**Measham Inn** Tamworth Rd ☎70095
RS Sun evenings (no meals); 32⇌⋒ ♛ CTV in bedrooms 200P Disco Wed Live music & dancing Sat
♕English & Continental. Last dinner9.30pm ✿
sB&B⇌⋒£8–£12.50 dB&B⇌⋒£16–£19
Lunch£2.65–£2.75&alc Dinner£3.89&alc
Wine£2.62 ⛿ Credit cards ① ② ③ ⑤ ⑥

MELBOURN Cambridgeshire Map**5** TL34
✕***Pink Geranium*** ☎Royston60215
Pink-washed thatched cottage.
Dinner not served Sun & Mon; 35seats 20P
♕English & French. Last dinner10pm

MELKSHAM Wiltshire Map**3** ST96
★***Kings Arms*** Market Pl ☎703217
Originally a coaching inn.
12rm CTV 50P Last dinner8.30pm ✿ ☕
Credit card ①

MELLING Lancashire Map**7** SD57
★★**Melling Hall** ☎Hornby21298
14rm(4⇌⋒) ♛ CTV CTV available in bedrooms 100P
⚓ ⤷ Disco wkly Live music & dancing wkly

ıstdinner10.30pm ✿ ⌂ *sB&B£7.50
3&B⇌⋒£10.50 dB&Bfr£15
3&B⇌⋒£20–£25 Lunch£3–£4.50
ea50p–£1.75 HighTea£2–£3.50
nner£6.50alc Wine£3 ⌂ *xmas*

ELTHAM West Yorkshire Map**7** SE01
★★Durker Roods ☎851413
2⇌⋒ ☽ CTV in bedrooms 100P
astdinner9.30pm ✿ sB&B⇌⋒£14.50
3&B⇌⋒£20 Lunch£3.56 Dinner£6alc Wine£3
reditcards 1 2 3 5

ELTON MOWBRAY Leicestershire Map**8** SK71
★George High St ☎2112
1rm(6⇌⋒) CTV CTV available in bedrooms 20P
astdinner10pm *sB&B£10.50 dB&B£18.75
3&B⇌⋒£22.75 Lunch£3.50alc Tea60palc
inner£3.50alc Creditcards 1 2 3 5

★Harboro' Burton St (Anchor) ☎68599
elex no858875
3rm(7⇌⋒) CTV CTV in bedrooms 30P Live music
dancing Sat Lastdinner10pm ✿ ⌂ S%
sB&B fr£10.85 sB&B⇌⋒ fr£14.50
3&B fr£18.50 dB&B⇌⋒ fr£22
unch fr£3.25&alc Tea fr30p Dinner fr£4&alc
/ine£2.65 ⌂ Creditcards 1 2 3 4 5 6

★Kings Head Nottingham St ☎2110
5rm(12⇌⋒) CTV 60P 12
astdinner8.30pm ✿ S% *sB&B£9.50
3&B⇌⋒£10.40 dB&B£19 dB&B⇌⋒£20.80
unch£3.56 Dinner£4.28 Wine£1.70

EMBURY Devon Map**3** ST20
Lee Hill Farm ☎Stockland388
Closed mid Jan–mid Feb; 6rm(2⇌⋒) CTV TV
vailable in bedrooms 20P 3
astdinner9.15pm ✿ ⌂ sB&B£7–£8
3&B⇌⋒£8–£9 dB&B£16–£18
B&B⇌⋒£18–£20 Lunch£2.50&alc
inner£2.75&alc Wine£2.25 ⌂ *xmas*
Creditcards 1 3

ERE Wiltshire Map**3** ST83
★★Old Ship Castle St (Inter-Hotel) ☎258
elex no45388
modernised double-fronted coaching hostelry, eaturing a high peaked exposed oak beam in the lining room.
2rm(4⇌⋒) Annexe: 11⇌⋒ 1 CTV TV in
edrooms 40P 3 Lastdinner9.30pm ✿ ⌂ S%
B&B£11.90 sB&B⇌⋒£13.40 dB&B£19.20
B&B⇌⋒£21.90–£23.90 Lunch fr£2.95&alc
ea fr95p Dinner fr£4.50&alc Wine£3.35 ⌂
mas Creditcards 1 2 3 5

Talbot ☎427
Originally the 'George Inn' where Charles II is said to ave dined. Now a black and white timbered hostelry.
7rm(2⇌⋒) CTV TV available in bedrooms 25P Live music & dancing Fri. Last dinner9pm ✿ S%
sB&B£7–£9 sB&B⇌⋒£7–£10 dB&B£14–£17
dB&B⇌⋒£14–£20 Lunch£2.85–£3.25
Dinner£3.50alc Creditcards 1 3

MERE BROW Lancashire Map**7** SD41
✕Crab & Lobster (Legh Arms) ☎Hesketh Bank2734
Old cottage converted in 1962 now extended.
Closed Sun, Mon, Xmas, New Year & 1st wk Jul; Lunch not served 50seats P Last dinner9.30pm
S% *Dinner£7alc Wine £2.80
Credit cards 1 2 3 4 5 6

MERIDEN West Midlands Map**4** SP28
★★★Manor (De Vere) ☎22735 Telex no22121
32⇌⋒ ☽ TV in bedrooms 260P (heated)
English & French. Last dinner10pm ✿ ⌂ S%
sB&B⇌⋒£22 dB&B⇌⋒£32 Lunch fr£4.50&alc
Dinner fr£5.25&alc Wine£3.50 ⌂
Creditcards 1 2 3 5 6

MESSING Essex Map**5** TL81
✕Old Crown Inn ☎Tiptree815575
Closed Sun & Public Hols; Lunch not served Sat; Dinner not served Mon; 50seats 30P English & Continental. Last dinner9.30pm Lunch£3–£4&alc
Dinner£8alc Wine£3.50

MEVAGISSEY Cornwall Map**2** SX04
★★Tremarne Polkirt Hill ☎2213
Closed Nov–Mar; 16rm(6⇌⋒) CTV TV available in bedrooms 14P (heated) Children under 5yrs not accommodated Last dinner 8pm ✿ ⌂
*sB&B£9.20–£10.25 dB&B£14.04–£17.28
dB&B⇌⋒£16.20–£19.44 Barlunch40p
Dinner£4.05 Wine£2.70 ⌂

★★*Trevalsa Court* Polstreath ☎2468
10rm(5⇌⋒) TV 15P Children under 12yrs not accommodated English & French.
Lastdinner9.30pm ⌂ ✿ ⌂
Creditcards 1 2 3 5

MICKLETON Gloucestershire Map**4** SP14
★★Threeways (Inter-Hotel) ☎231
49rm(29⇌⋒) CTV 60P English & French.
Lastdinner8.30pm ✿ sB&B£12
sB&B⇌⋒£15.65 dB&B£21 dB&B⇌⋒£27
Lunch£5–£5.50&alc Dinner£6&alc Wine£3 ⌂
Creditcards 1 2

MIDDLEHAM North Yorkshire Map**7** SE18
★Millers House Market Pl ☎Wensleydale22630
Closed 3 Jan–Feb 6rm(3⇌⋒) TV in bedrooms 10P English & Continental. Lastdinner9pm ✿
⌂ S% sB&B£8.25–£9.50
sB&B⇌⋒£9.75–£11.25 dB&B£16.50–£19
dB&B⇌⋒£19.50–£22.50 Lunch£4alc
Tea50–80p HighTea£2alc
Dinner£4.40–£5.50&alc Wine£3.50 ⌂
Creditcards 1 2 3 5

M

MIDDLESBROUGH Cleveland Map**8** NZ42
☆☆☆☆**Ladbroke Dragonara** Fry St (Ladbroke)
☎248133 Telex no58266
210⇌⋒ Lift ☽ ▦ CTV in bedrooms 300P 35⌂ Live music & dancing Mon–Sat Conference facilities available ♉English & French. Last dinner10.30pm ✿ ♨ S% ✱sB&B⇌⋒ fr£21.13 dB&B⇌⋒ fr£32.94 Lunch£3.78&alc Tea54p–£1.08 High Tea£1.08–£1.62 Dinner£7.02alc Wine£4.05 ⊟ Credit cards 1 2 3 5 6

☆☆☆**Blue Bell Motor Inn** Acklam (Swallow)
☎593939 Telex no53168
60⇌⋒ Lift ☽ ▦ CTV in bedrooms 300P ♉Mainly grills. Last dinner9.45pm ✿ S% sB&B⇌⋒£16 dB&B⇌⋒£21.50 ⊟ Credit cards 1 2 3 5

★★★**Marton** Stokesley Rd, Marton (3m S A172)
☎317141
54⇌⋒ ☽ ▦ CTV in bedrooms 400P billiards Live music & dancing wkly Last dinner9.45pm ✿ ♨ Lunch£2.50–£3&alc Tea35p–£1 High Tea£2.50–£3 Dinner£4&alc Wine£2.75 ⊟ Credit cards 3 6

☆☆☆**Middlesbrough Crest Motel** Marton Way (Crest) ☎87651
53⇌⋒ ☽ CTV in bedrooms 250P Conference facilities available Last dinner10pm ✿ S% ✱sB&B⇌⋒£15.17 dB&B⇌⋒£21.70 Continental breakfast ⊟ Credit cards 1 2 3 4 5 6

★★**Highfield** Marton Rd (Berni) ☎87638
26rm(7⇌) ☽ ▦ CTV ⊘ 100P ⚓ ♉Mainly grills. Last dinner11pm sB&B fr£9.45 sB&B⇌ fr£11.90 dB&B fr£16.20 dB&B⇌ fr£19 Lunch£2.75alc Dinner£5alc Wine£3 ⊟ Credit cards 1 2 3 5 6

MIDDLETON-IN-TEESDALE Co Durham Map**12** NY92
★★**Teesdale** Market Pl ☎537
Closed end Nov–Feb; 14rm(6⇌⋒) ▦ CTV 20P Last dinner8.30pm ✱sB&B£8 sB&B⇌⋒£9.50 dB&B£16 dB&B⇌⋒£19 Lunch fr£3.20&alc Dinner fr£3.20&alc Credit card 3

⊕ ♔**Heather Brae** (1½m N on unclass road) ☎203
Three-storey building of grey sandstone in three acres of secluded grounds 1,000ft above sea-level; panoramic views of countryside.
16rm ▦ CTV P ⚓ ♉English, French, German & Italian. Last dinner8.30pm ✿ ♨ sB&B fr£9.50 dB&B fr£19 Lunch£4.60 Dinner fr£5.40 Wine£3.50 ⊟ Credit card 3

MIDDLETON ONE ROW Co Durham Map**8** NZ31
★★**Devonport** ☎Dinsdale2255
19rm(9⇌⋒) ▦ CTV CTV in bedrooms 50P 5⌂ ⇏ Last dinner9pm ✿ sB&B£12 sB&B⇌⋒£14.50 dB&B£18 dB&B⇌⋒£22 Lunch fr£2.85&alc Dinner fr£5&alc Wine£2.75 Credit cards 1 2 3 5 6

MIDDLETON-ON-SEA (Nr Bognor Regis) West Sussex Map**4** SU90
★★**Villa Plage** Elmer Sands ☎2251
Overlooking sea, with private beach.
Closed Nov–Mar; 6rm(1⇌⋒) ▦ CTV ⊘ 12P ⇏ Children under 12yrs not accommodated

M

ast dinner8.15pm sB&B fr£10 dB&B fr£20
B&B⇌⋒ fr£24 Lunch£3.25&alc Tea70p
inner£3.75&alc Wine£3.25

Hotel International 28 Alleyne Way, Elmer Sands
2896
losed Oct–Nov; 12rm(3⇌⋒) CTV 12P 1
Children under 12yrs not accommodated
ast dinner7.30pm S% sB&B£8–£9
B&B£16–£18 dB&B⇌⋒£18–£20
ar lunch35p–£1.25 Dinner£3.50–£4
Vine£2.50 *xmas*

Manor Farm Elmer Sands 3154
losed Jan & Feb; 6rm(3⇌⋒) TV available in
edrooms 30P Children under 6yrs not
ccommodated Last dinner10pm Credit card 3

IIDDLETON STONEY Oxfordshire Map**4** SP52
★★***Jersey Arms*** 234
rm(1⇌⋒) Annexe: 4rm(4⇌⋒) CTV TV available
n bedrooms 100P 2 Last dinner9.30pm
Credit cards 1 2 3

IIDDLE WALLOP Hampshire Map**4** SU23
★★ **Fifehead Manor** Wallop566
See page 51 for details

IIDHURST West Sussex Map**4** SU82
★★**Spread Eagle** South St 2211 Telex no86853
Remarkable black-and-white, timbered inn dating from 1430. The interior has oak beams, open hearths, stained glass windows (early 17th-C) and wig closet adjoining four-poster bedroom.
23⇌⋒ 2 CTV in bedrooms P
Last dinner9.30pm *sB&B⇌⋒£20.30
dB&B⇌⋒£31.35–£54.64 Lunch£3.60&alc
Tea75p Dinner£5.20&alc Wine£3.50 *xmas*
Credit cards 1 2 3 5 6

★★**Angel** North St 2421
16th-C inn with delightful walled garden giving views of Cowdray Place. First-floor lounge used as courtroom up to 100 years ago.
18rm(8⇌⋒) 2 CTV TV in bedrooms 60P
Last dinner10pm S% dB&B fr£9.75
sB&B⇌⋒ fr£14 dB&B fr£17.80
dB&B⇌⋒ fr£18.70 Lunch fr£3.50&alc
Tea fr£1.25 Dinner fr£3.50&alc Wine£3.50
Credit cards 1 2 3 4 5 6

✕**Knockers** Knockhundred Row Midhurst3712
Small bistro-type restaurant.
Closed Sun; Lunch not served; 40seats French.
Last dinner10.30pm Dinner£11.50alc Wine£3.50
Credit cards 1 2 3 5 6

✕**Old Manor House** Church Hill 2990
Closed Mon; Dinner not served Sun; 70seats
English & French. Last dinner10pm
Lunch£2.75–£4 Dinner£6alc Credit cards 2 3

MILDENHALL Suffolk Map**5** TL77
★★**Bell** 712134
Once a coaching inn, part of which dates from 1600.
20rm(50⇌⋒) CTV CTV available in bedrooms 22P
English & Continental. Last dinner8.45pm
sB&B£10.50 sB&B⇌⋒£14.50 dB&B£16.50
dB&B⇌⋒£18.50 Lunch£3.50&alc Tea fr75p
Dinner fr£3.75&alc Wine£2.50
Credit cards 1 2 3 5 6

★★***Bull Inn*** Barton Mills (1m E A11) 713230
RS Xmas & Public Hols; 15rm(12⇌⋒) CTV 150P
Last dinner9pm Credit cards 1 6

★**Worlington Hall** Worlington (2m SW B1102)
712237
Closed Xmas Day; 8rm(2⇌⋒) CTV 100P
billiards Disco Fri Live music & dancing Sat Cabaret
Sat. Last dinner9.30pm S% sB&B£7.50
sB&B⇌⋒£9.50 dB&B£13 dB&B⇌⋒£15.50
Lunch£6&alc Tea50–70p&alc Dinner£6alc
Wine£2.75

MILFORD-ON-SEA Hampshire Map**4** SZ29
★**White Horse Inn** Keyhaven Rd 2360
6rm CTV TV available in bedrooms 60P
Last dinner9.30pm sB&B£7.12
dB&B£14.24–£15.44 Lunch£1.20–£1.70&alc
Dinner£3.50&alc Wine£2.10 Credit card 1

✕**Mill House** 1 High St 2611
Closed Mon, 27 Oct–9 Nov; Dinner not served Sun;
40seats English & French. Last dinner9.30pm
Lunch£2.20–£3&alc Dinner£6alc Wine£2.40
Credit cards 1 2 3 5 6

MILTON COMMON Oxfordshire Map**4** SP60
★★**Belfry** Brimpton Grange Great Milton381
Large, half-timbered, country house in acres of grounds. Banqueting hall adjoining.
46rm(40⇌⋒) 1 CTV TV in bedrooms 300P
Disco twice wkly Live music & dancing wkly
English & International. Last dinner10pm
sB&B£11.88 sB&B⇌⋒£14.26 dB&B£20.20
dB&B⇌⋒£22.58 Continental breakfast
Lunch£4&alc Dinner£4.50&alc Wine£2.50
Credit cards 1 2 3 5

M

MILTON DAMEREL Devon Map**2** SS31
★★★**Woodford Bridge** ☎252
A white-painted, thatched inn dating from 15th century. The River Torridge flows past the end of the garden offering facilities for fishing.
16rm(8⇌⋒) 🍽 CTV TV available in bedrooms 100P 2🏠 ⚓ ↳ Live music & dancing Wed & Sat ♡English & French. Last dinner 8.45pm ♁ ☕ *sB&B£8.80–£11 sB&B⇌⋒£9.50–£11.50 dB&B£16–£20 dB&B⇌⋒£20–£25 Lunch£4–£4.50 Tea75p–£1.50 Dinner£6–£6.50&alc Wine£3.25 ⊟ *xmas*

MILTON ERNEST Bedfordshire Map**4** TL05
✕✕**Milton Ernest Hall** ☎Oakley4111
Closed Mon, Public Hols, Xmas, Etr, 1st 2wks Jan & 1st wk Sep; Dinner not served Sun; 58seats 30P bedrooms available ♡English & French. Last dinner9.30pm *Lunch£7alc Dinner£7alc Credit card①

MILTON KEYNES Buckinghamshire Map**4** SP83
See under **Linford, Great and Stony Stratford**

MILTON ON STOUR Dorset Map**3** ST82
★★★**Milton Lodge** ☎Gillingham2262
Georgian house situated in 5½ acres of grounds.
10⇌⋒ 🍽 CTV TV available in bedrooms 60P ⚓ ⛱(heated) ↳ ∩ Last dinner9.15pm ♁ ☕ sB&B⇌⋒£11.50–£15.50 dB&B⇌⋒£23–£31 Lunch£2–£2.50&alc Tea30–75p Dinner fr£6&alc Wine£2.50 Credit card②

MINCHINHAMPTON Gloucestershire Map**3** SO80
See **Amberley**

MINEHEAD Somerset Map**3** SS94
★★★**Beach** The Avenue (Trusthouse Forte) ☎2193
41rm(19⇌⋒) 🍽 CTV TV in bedrooms 10P ⛱(heated) Last dinner9.45pm ♁ ☕ S% sB&B£14 sB&B⇌⋒£17 dB&B£23 dB&B⇌⋒£27 ⊟ Credit cards①②③④⑤⑥

★★**Benares** Northfield Rd ☎2340
Closed 21–31 Dec; 21rm(11⇌⋒) 🍽 CTV 20P 2🏠 ⚓ ↳ billiards ♡English & French. Last dinner7.30pm ♁ ☕ sB&B fr£11.50 dB&B fr£19.44 dB&B⇌⋒£23.22 Bar lunch75p–£2 Tea30–35p High Tea£2–£2.50 Dinner£4–£5 Wine£2.40 ⊟

★★**Wellington** Wellington Sq ☎4371
Red sandstone gabled building with slate roof, standing at corner of square in town centre.
30rm(9⇌⋒) ☽ CTV TV available in bedrooms 12P 6🏠 Live music & dancing twice wkly Cabaret wkly ♡English & French. Last dinner9.30pm ♁ ☕ sB&B£9.50–£10.50 sB&B⇌⋒£12.50–£14.45 dB&B£16.50 dB&B⇌⋒£21.50–£25 Lunch£2.50–£2.75 Tea80p–£1.45 High Tea£1.50–£2.50 Dinner£3.85–£4.50&alc Wine£2.10 ⊟ *xmas* Credit cards①②③⑤

★★**Winsor** The Avenue ☎2171
Closed Nov–Apr; 39rm(6⇌⋒) 🍽 CTV 26P Last dinner8pm ♁ S% sB&B£7.50 dB&B£15 dB&B⇌⋒£17.50 Lunch£2 Dinner£3.75 Wine£2.20 Credit cards①②③⑤⑥

★★**York** The Avenue ☎5151
20rm(10⇌⋒) 🍽 CTV 20P Children under 10yrs not accommodated Last dinner8.30pm ♁ ☕ S% sB&B£8–£9.50 dB&B£16–£19 dB&B⇌⋒£19–£21 Bar lunch£1–£2.50 Dinner£4.50&alc Wine£2.50 ⊟ *xmas* Credit cards①②③

★***Oak Lodge*** Martlet Rd ☎2100
15rm(2⇌⋒) 🍽 CTV 12P ⚓ Children not accommodated ♡English & French. Last dinner7pm

★**Kingsway** Ponsford Rd ☎2313
Closed mid Oct–Mar; 10rm 🍽 CTV 10P Children

M

ıder 5yrs not accommodated Last dinner7pm 3&B£9 dB&B£18 Lunch£3.80 Dinner£5 'ine£3.15

Merton Western Ln, The Parks ☎2375 osed Nov–Mar; 12rm(2⇌⋒) CTV 14P ⛟ ⚓ ıst dinner8pm ✿ ♀ S% sB&B fr£8 3&B fr£16 dB&B⇌⋒ fr£18 Lunch£3alc ea75palc Dinner£4.25alc Wine£2.75 *xmas*

INSTER LOVELL Oxfordshire Map**4** SP31
★Old Swan ☎Asthall Leigh614 rm ⋔ TV 50P ⛟ ⚓ ♀English & French. ıst dinner9.30pm ✿ ♀ *sB&B£6.50–£9 3&B£15–£17 Lunch£3–£4.20&alc Tea fr£1 Dinner£8.50alc Wine£3.30 ⊟ *xmas* Credit cards 1 2 3

MIRFIELD West Yorkshire Map**8** SE21
XXThree Nuns Inn Leeds Rd (2m W at junc A62/A644) ☎494233
86seats 150P Disco twice wkly Last dinner10pm Lunch£2.55–£3.15&alc Dinner£4.50alc Wine£2.70 Credit cards 1 6

MODBURY Devon Map**3** SX65
★*Modbury Inn* Brownston St ☎275
Old coaching inn with panelled lounge and restaurant.
Closed Xmas; 7rm ⋔ TV ⊗ 8P Children under 8yrs not accommodated ♀Mainly grills. Last dinner9pm ✿ ♀

M

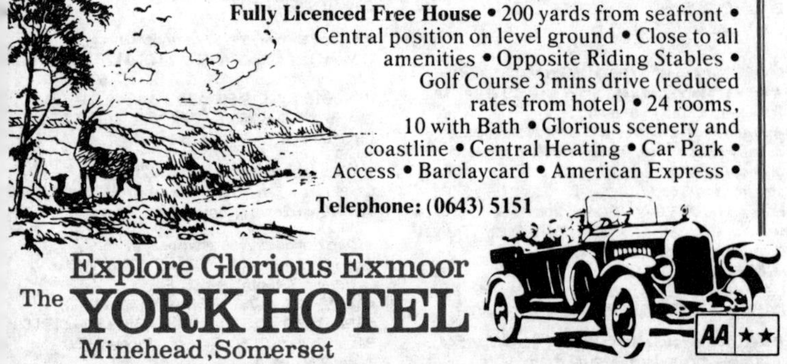

XX***Exeter Inn*** ☎239
50seats bedrooms available English & French. Lastdinner9.30pm Credit cards 2 5

MONK FRYSTON North Yorkshire Map**8** SE52
★★★**Monk Fryston Hall** ☎South Milford682369
24rm CTV in bedrooms 60P 3 Live music & dancing Sat Lastdinner9.30pm sB&B£17.60–£19 dB&B£25.30–£26.70 Lunch£4.07–£4.40&alc Tea55–66p Dinner£5.39–£5.72&alc Wine£3.50 *xmas*

MONTACUTE Somerset Map**3** ST41
XX**Milk House** The Borough ☎Martock3823
Old stonehouse with lattice windows, situated in attractive setting in the village square.
Closed Sun & Mon; Lunch not served; 50seats English & French. Lastdinner9.30pm S% ✱Dinner£6.50alc Wine£2.60 Credit card 3

MOOTA (BLINDCRAKE) Cumbria Map**11** NY13
☆☆**Moota Motel** ☎Aspatria20681
60rm(57) TV in bedrooms 250P 27 squash Disco Wed & Sat Live music & dancing Wed & Sat Lastdinner9.45pm S% sB&B£10–£11 sB&B£13–£14.50 dB&B£15.50–£16.50 dB&B£20–£21.50 Lunch£3–£3.50&alc High Tea£3–£4 Dinner£4.50–£5.50&alc
Credit cards 1 2 3 4 6

MORECAMBE Lancashire Map**7** SD46
★★★**Elms** Bare ☎411501
41rm(21) Lift CTV 80P 12 Live music & dancing 4 nights wkly (summer) 2 nights wkly (winter) Lastdinner8.15pm S% ✱sB&B£10 sB&B£11 dB&B£20 dB&B£22 Lunch£3–£4 Tea90p–£1 High Tea£2.75–£3 Dinner£4.50–£5.50 Wine£2.55 *xmas* Credit cards 1 3

M

★★★**Midland** Marine Rd (Inter-Hotel) ☎417180
44rm(22) Lift CTV in bedrooms 80P English & French. Lastdinner8.45pm S% sB&B£14–£15.50 sB&B£16–£17.50 dB&B£24–£26 dB&B£28–£30 Lunch£3.25–£3.60&alc Tea£1 Dinner£4.50–£5.50&alc Wine£2.70 *xmas*
Credit cards 1 2 3 5 6

★★**Clarendon** Promenade, West End ☎410180
31rm(2) Lift CTV CTV available in bedrooms sauna bath Lastdinner8.30pm S% ✱sB&B fr£7.30 sB&B fr£8.80 dB&B fr£14.60 dB&B fr£16.10 Lunch£2.40–£4&alc Dinner£3.25–£4&alc Wine£2.08 *xmas*

★★**Strathmore** Marine Road East ☎411314
66rm(16) Lift CTV 30P 12 English & French. Lastdinner10.45pm S% sB&B£10.50–£11.50 dB&B£21–£23 dB&B£24–£26 Lunch fr£3.50 Tea fr75p Dinner fr£3.75&alc Wine£3 *xmas*
Credit cards 1 2 3 5 6

MORETONHAMPSTEAD Devon Map**3** SX78
★★★★**Manor House** (2½ SW on B3212) (British Transport) ☎355 Telex no42794
An imposing building of mellow stone in Jacobean country-house style. The south-facing terrace overlooks 200 acres of parkland, with pools, trout streams and woods.
66rm Lift CTV CTV in bedrooms 60P 6 18 (hard) squash billiards English & French. Lastdinner8.45pm S% sB&B fr£29.30 dB&B fr£58.60 Lunch fr£6.45 Dinner fr£9 Wine£3.50 *xmas*
Credit cards 1 2 3 4 5 6

★★***Glebe House*** North Bovey (1½m SW) ☎544
In 20 acres of grounds, with own farm.
12rm(6) CTV 30P 3 International. Lastdinner10pm Credit card 2

★★**White Horse Inn** ☎242
9rm(3) CTV TV available in bedrooms Disco 3nights wkly Mainly grills. S% ✱sB&B£8.64 sB&B£10.80 dB&B£14.04 dB&B£17.28 Lunch£2.50–£4 Dinner£5alc Wine£2.75 *xmas* Credit cards 2 3 5

MORETON-IN-MARSH Gloucestershire Map**4** SP2
★★★**Manor House** High St (Best Western) ☎5050
Telex no837151
17th-C hotel of Cotswold stone situated in centre o small town. The hotel has been extensively modernised.
40rm(30) 1 Lift CTV CTV in bedrooms 35P 10 sauna bath English & French Lastdinner9.30pm S% ✱sB&B fr£13 sB&B fr£18 dB&B fr£23 dB&B fr£32 Lunch fr£4.50 Dinner fr£6.25 Wine£3.50 *xmas* Credit cards 1 2 3 4 5 6

★★**Redesdale Arms** (Crest) ☎50308
An old coaching inn by the side of the ancient Roma Fosse Way.
13rm(6) CTV TV in bedrooms 35P Lastdinner9.30pm S% ✱sB&B£10.80 sB&B£14.04 dB&B£19.33 dB&B£23.76 Credit cards 1 2 3 4 5 6

★★**White Hart Royal** High St (Trusthouse Forte) ☎50731
21rm(6) Annexe: 6rm CTV CTV in bedrooms 10 Lastdinner10pm S% sB&B£12 sB&B£14 dB&B£9 dB&B£21 *xmas* Credit cards 1 2 3 4 5 6

XX **Lambs** High St ☎50251
(Rosette awarded for dinner only.)
Closed Mon; Lunch not served Tue; Dinner not served Sun; 65seats English & French. Specialities: petit pots de champignons, best end of lamb 'en papillote'. Iced fruit soufflées. Lastdinner10.30pm Lunch£2.50alc Dinner£7.50alc Wine£3 Credit cards 1 2 3 5

MORPETH Northumberland Map**12** NZ18
★★***Queen's Head*** Bridge St (Scottish & Newcastle) ☎2083
23rm(10) CTV 7P 16 Live music & dancing mthly Lastdinner9pm
Credit cards 1 2 3 4 5 6

MORTEHOE Devon Map**2** SS44
★★★**Rockham Bay** ☎Woolacombe347
Closed mid Oct–Mar; 34rm(27) CTV CTV available in bedrooms 32P (heated) sauna bath Disco twice wkly Cabaret wkly English, Continental & Oriental. Lastdinner8.30pm sB&B£8–£19 sB&B£8–£19 dB&B£16–£38 dB&B£16–£38 Lunch£2–£3.50 Tea30p Dinner£3.50–£6

★★**Castle Rock** ☎Woolacombe465
Closed Oct–Apr; 30rm(5) CTV 12P 12 Lastdinner8.30pm sB&B£7.60–£9.40 dB&B£15.20–£18.80 dB&B£18.80–£21 Lunch fr£4 Tea fr40p Dinner fr£6 Wine£2.60 Credit cards 1 3

★★***Mortehoe*** ☎Woolacombe226
Closed Oct–Etr; RS Etr–May; 18rm(12) TV 18P 7 Lastdinner7.15pm

★**Glen Haven** ☎Woolacombe376
Closed Oct–2 Apr; 13rm(3) 3 CTV 7P Lastdinner7.45pm S% sB&B£5.25–£6.75 sB&B£6.25–£7.75 dB&B£10.50–£13.50 dB&B£12.50–£15.50 Bar lunch25p–£1.50 Tea50p Dinner£3.50 Wine£2.50

M

MOTTRAM ST ANDREW Cheshire Map**7** SJ87
★★★**Mottram Hall** (Greenall Whitley)
☎Prestbury (Cheshire) 828135 Telex no 668181
45⇌ ⋒ ☽ ⋈ CTV CTV in bedrooms 200P ⋈ ⚓ ⋄ billiards Conference facilities available ♀French. Last dinner 10pm ♁ ⚠ sB&B⇌⋒£24–£27 sB&B⇌⋒£28–£30 Lunch fr£3.50 Dinner£7.50–£8alc Wine£3.65 ⊟ Credit cards 1 2 3 4 5 6

MOULSFORD Oxfordshire Map**4** SU58
★**Beetle & Wedge** ☎Cholsey 651381
Old riverside inn standing in its own large gardens.
10⇌⋒ 1⊟ ⋈ CTV in bedrooms 40P ⚓ ♀English & French. Last dinner 10pm ♁ ⚠ sB&B⇌⋒£13.75 dB&B⇌⋒£27.50 Lunch£3.75&alc Tea40p–£1.25 Dinner£3.75&alc Wine£2.90 ⊟ *xmas* Credit cards 2 3 5

MOUSEHOLE Cornwall Map**2** SW42
★★**Lobster Pot** ☎251
Closed mid Nov–mid Feb; 14⇌⋒ ⋈ CTV Last dinner 9.45pm ♁ sB&B£5.75–£9 sB&B⇌⋒£6.50–£11 dB&B£11.50–£18 dB&B⇌⋒£13–£22 Lunch£3.50&alc Dinner£5.50&alc Wine£3.80

★**Cairn Dhu** Raginnis Hill ☎233 Telex no 45608
Closed 5Oct–23May; 7rm(2⇌⋒) CTV ⋈ 10P ⋈ Last dinner 9.45pm S% sB&B fr£9 sB&B⇌⋒ fr£10 dB&B fr£18 dB&B⇌⋒ fr£20 Dinner£5.50–£8.50 Wine£2.75 Credit cards 1 2 3 4 5 6

★**Old Coastguard** ☎222
14rm(4⇌⋒) 1⊟ CTV 5P ⋈ ⚓ Live music & dancing 4 nights wkly Last dinner 9.15pm ♁ ⚠ S% ✻sB&B£6.90–£10.40 dB&B£11.18–£19.20 dB&B⇌⋒£14.20–£20.80 Tea fr85p Dinner fr£4.40&alc Wine£2.75 ⊟ *xmas*

MUDEFORD Dorset see **CHRISTCHURCH**

N

MULLION Cornwall Map**2** SW61
★★★**Poldhu** Poldhu Cove (Inter-Hotel) ☎240339 Telex no 45137
Set in 20 acres of grounds on the headland overlooking Poldhu Cove and the Atlantic.
50rm(21⇌⋒) ☽ ⋈ CTV TV available in bedrooms 100P 12⌂ ⚓ ⌓(heated) ⛳ ⋈(hard) ⋄ billiards Live music & dancing twice wkly ♫ Last dinner 9pm ♁ ⚠ S% sB&B£17.40–£18.72 sB&B⇌⋒£18.72–£20 dB&B£34.80–£37.44 dB&B⇌⋒£37.44–£44 Lunch£4.50 Tea25p–£1 High Tea£2.75 Dinner£5&alc Wine£3 ⊟ *xmas* Credit cards 1 2 3 4 5 6

★★★**Polurrian** ☎240421
Closed 28Sep–2May 45rm(33⇌⋒) ☽ CTV TV available in bedrooms 40P ⋈ ⚓ ⌓(heated) ⋈(hard) squash Live music & dancing twice wkly ♫ ♀English, French & Italian. Last dinner 8.30pm ♁ ⚠ S% sB&B£11.50–£17.50 sB&B⇌⋒£13–£18 dB&B£22–£32.50 dB&B⇌⋒£23.50–£36 Lunch£5alc Tea£1–£1.10 High Tea50p–£1.55 Dinner£5.50–£6.50&alc Wine£3.10

★★**Mullion Cove** ☎240328
RS Oct–Mar; 45rm(8⇌⋒) ✗ CTV 100P 2⌂ ⚓ ⌓(heated) ⋈(hard) sauna bath Live music & dancing twice wkly ♫ Last dinner 8.15pm ♁ ⚠ sB&B£7.50–£11.50 sB&B⇌⋒£9–£15 dB&B£15–£22 dB&B⇌⋒£17–£28 Lunch£3.50alc Tea50–60p Dinner£4.50–£5&alc Wine£2.75 ⊟

MUNDESLEY-ON-SEA Norfolk Map**9** TG33
★★★**Continental** (Mount Charlotte) ☎720271
Closed Oct–9May; 44rm(27⇌⋒) Lift ☽ CTV TV available in bedrooms 60P 5⌂ ⚓ ⌓(heated) ⋈(hard) Disco wkly Live music & dancing twice wkly ♫ ♀English & French. Last dinner 9.30pm ♁ ⚠ sB&B£7.80–£11.80 sB&B⇌⋒£10.60–£17 dB£B£14–£24 dB&B⇌⋒£20–£34 Lunch£4 Dinner£5.50 ⊟ Credit cards 1 2 3

★★**Manor** ☎720309
25rm(11⇌⋒) ⋈ CTV 40P ⚓ ⌓(heated) sauna bath live music & dancing wkly Last dinner 9pm ♁ ⚠ S% sB&B£6.80–£7.90 dB&B£13.08–£15.30 dB&B⇌⋒£14.40–£16.60 Lunch£2.50–£2.75&alc Tea30p Dinner£3.50–£4.80&alc Wine£2.40 ⊟ *xmas*

NANTWICH Cheshire Map**7** SJ65
★★**Alvaston Hall** Middlewich Rd ☎64341
40rm(36⇌⋒) ☽ ⋈ CTV in bedrooms 200P ⚓ squash Live music & dancing Sat ♿ ♀English & French. Last dinner 10pm ♁ ⚠ sB&B£11 sB&B⇌⋒£13 dB&B£15 dB&B⇌⋒£18 Lunch£3&alc Tea£1 Dinner£4&alc Wine£2.36 ⊟ *xmas* Credit cards 1 2 3 5

★★**Lamb** Hospital St ☎65286
17rm(3⇌⋒) ⋈ CTV 12P 15⌂ Last dinner 9.30pm ♁ ⚠ S% sB&B£8.50 sB&B⇌⋒£11 dB&B£14 dB&B⇌⋒£16.50 Lunch£2.25&alc Tea80p Dinner£3.50&alc Wine£2.50 Credit cards 1 2 3 5 6

✕✕✕**Rookery Hall** Worleston (2m N B5074) ☎626866
Closed Mon, 21Jan–4Feb & 21Jul–4Aug; Lunch not served Tue–Sat; Dinner not served Sun; 70seats 35P bedrooms available ✗ ♀English & Continental. Last dinner 9pm S% Lunch£9.25 Dinner£12.50 Wine£5.35

✕✕***Churche's Mansion*** Hospital St ☎65933
Remarkable 16th-C half-timbered mansion, with beamed and panelled dining room.
Closed 25–28Dec; Dinner not served Sun; 60seats 30P Last dinner 8.30pm S%

ARBOROUGH Leicestershire Map4 SP59
Charnwood 48 Leicester Rd (Off A46 2m S of M1 nc 21) ☎Leicester862218
osed 1wk Xmas; 21rm(6⇌ ⋔) CTV 30P English & Continental. Last dinner8pm S% sB&B£8 sB&B⇌⋔£9.50 dB&B£13.50 dB&B⇌⋔£15.25 Lunch50p–£3.30 nner£3.20–£5.50 Wine£2.30

ATEBY Lancashire Map7 SD44
✕***Bowers*** ☎Garstang2120
n attractive, converted farmhouse with mullioned windows and beamed restaurant.
osed Sun; Lunch not served; 160seats 100P edrooms available Live music & dancing Thu & Sat st dinner10pm

EASHAM Co Durham Map8 NZ31
✕**Newbus Arms** Newbus Grange Darlington721071
seats 70P bedrooms available Disco Sat English French. Last dinner10pm Lunch fr£3.25&alc ea fr£1.25 Dinner fr£5.95&alc Wine£3.25 redit cards 1 2 3 5 6

EEDHAM MARKET Suffolk Map5 TM05
Limes ☎720305
riginally built in 1485 as a Boule house, a Georgian ontage was added in 1751.
losed Xmas; 6rm(1⇌⋔) CTV 50P English & rench. Last dinner9.30pm

ELSON Lancashire Map7 SD83
★**Great Marsden** Barkerhouse Rd ☎64749
4rm(4⇌⋔) Lift CTV 100P Children under yrs not accommodated Last dinner10pm B&B£7–£8.50 sB&B⇌⋔£8.50–£10 B&B£13–£14.50 dB&B⇌⋔£14.50–£16 unch£1.75–£2.75 Dinner£3.75–£4.50 Vine£1.95

ESSCLIFF Salop Map7 SJ31
Old Three Pigeons ☎279
losed Mon; 60seats 100P English & Continental. ast dinner9.30pm ✻Lunch fr£2.50&alc inner£4alc Wine£2.50

ETHERTON Merseyside Map7 SJ39
★★**Park** Dunnings Bridge Rd (off A5036) (Greenall Whitley) ☎051–525 7555 Liverpool plan**13**
2⇌⋔ Lift CTV in bedrooms 350P 3 Disco wice wkly Last dinner9.15pm S% B&B⇌⋔£17–£18 dB&B⇌⋔£22.50–£23.50 unch£3.50–£4&alc Tea50–75p inner£4–£5&alc Wine£3 redit cards 1 2 3 5 6

EWARK-ON-TRENT Nottinghamshire Map8 SK75
★**Midland** Muskham Rd ☎73788
0rm CTV 20P Last dinner8.45pm sB&B£8.64 dB&B£16.20 Lunch£2.50 inner£3.75&alc Wine£2.30

★**Ram** ☎702255
hree-storey brick inn listed as a building of historical terest.
2rm(1⇌⋔) CTV 6P 5 Last dinner8.30pm ✻sB&B£10.10 dB&B£20.20 B&B⇌⋔£22.50 Lunch£2.97 Dinner£4.28 Vine£1.70

★**Robin Hood** Lombard St (Anchor) ☎3858 elex no858875
Xmas; 21⇌⋔ CTV in bedrooms 40P ast dinner10pm S% ✻sB&B⇌⋔fr£16.50 B&B⇌⋔fr£24 Lunch fr£3.50 Dinner fr£4 Vine£2.65 Credit cards 1 2 3 4 5 6

✕✕**Queens Head** Market Pl ☎702327
6th-C inn overlooking the market square.
losed Mon; 70seats ✻Lunch£2.30–£2.60&alc inner£4alc Credit cards 1 2 3 5 6

NEWBOLD-ON-STOUR Warwickshire Map4 SP24
✕**White Hart** ☎Alderminster205
70seats 60P Last dinner10pm Lunch£4.50alc Dinner£5alc Wine£2.75 Credit cards 1 2 3 5

NEWBRIDGE **Cornwall** Map2 SW43
✕**Enzo** ☎Penzance3777
Lunch not served; 32seats 25P Italian. Last dinner10.30pm ✻Dinner£3.65–£6&alc Wine£2.60 Credit cards 1 2 5

NEWBRIDGE **Oxfordshire** Map4 SP40
✕✕***Rose Revived Inn*** ☎Standlake221
60seats 100P bedrooms available Live music & dancing twice wkly Last dinner9.30pm Credit cards 1 2 3 5

NEW BRIGHTON Merseyside Map7 SJ39
See Wallasey

NEWBURY Berkshire Map4 SU46
See also **Elcot**
★★★**Chequers** Oxford St (Trusthouse Forte) ☎43666
Once a well known posting house with stabling for 40 horses.
58rm(40⇌⋔) Annexe: 11⇌⋔ TV in bedrooms 60P Last dinner9pm S% sB&B£12 sB&B⇌⋔£16.50 dB&B£17.50 dB&B⇌⋔£22 *xmas* Credit cards 1 2 3 4 5 6

★**Bacon Arms** 10 Oxford St ☎40408
Old coaching inn with courtyard.
11rm(1⇌⋔) CTV 30P English & French. Last dinner9pm S% ✻sB&B£7.25 dB&B£12 dB&B⇌⋔£15 Lunch£3.25&alc Dinner£5alc Wine2.90 Credit cards 1 2 3 5

★**Queen's** Market Pl ☎47447
Closed Xmas Day; 11rm CTV 30P Mainly grills. Last dinner9pm S% sB&B£8.50–£9 dB&B£13.50–£14 Lunch fr£2.50&alc Dinner fr£2.50&alc Wine£3.55

✕**La Capannina** 81 Bartholomew St ☎47509
Closed Sun; 52seats Italian. Last dinner11pm ✻Lunch£3.50alc Dinner£5.50alc Wine£3.30 Credit cards 3 5

✕**La Riviera** 26 The Broadway ☎47499
Closed Wed, Xmas, Public Hols & 3wks Apr; 40seats Continental. Last dinner10.15pm Lunch£5alc Dinner£6.50alc Wine£3 Credit cards 3 5

NEWBY BRIDGE Cumbria Map7 SD38
★★★**Swan** (Inter-Hotel) ☎681 (May be prefixed by '31' during the currency of the guide)
36⇌⋔ TV 150P 9 Live music & dancing wkly International. Last dinner9pm S% ✻sB&B⇌⋔£12.50 dB&B⇌⋔£22 Bar lunch£1.50–£2.60 Tea60p–£1.20 Dinner£6&alc Wine£2.70 *xmas* Credit cards 3 5

NEWCASTLE-UNDER-LYME Staffordshire Map7 SJ84
★★★**Clayton Lodge** Newcastle Rd, Clayton (A519) (Embassy) ☎613093
54rm(40⇌⋔) CTV TV in bedrooms 100P Conference facilities available Last dinner9.15pm S% sB&B£11.50 sB&B⇌⋔£16 dB&B£18.50 dB&B⇌⋔£21 Lunch£5&alc Dinner£5.50&alc Wine£4.50 Credit cards 1 2 3 4 5 6

☆☆☆**Post House** Clayton Rd (Trusthouse Forte) ☎625151 Telex no36531
106⇌⋔ CTV in bedrooms 128P Last dinner10.30pm S% sB&B⇌⋔£19.75 dB&B⇌⋔£28.50 *xmas* Credit cards 1 2 3 4 5 6

N

★★**Borough Arms** King St (Crest) ☎616742
26rm(4⇌ ⋒) CTV CTV available in bedrooms 36P
French. Last dinner 8.30pm S%
*sB&B£10.80 sB&B⇌⋒£16.20 dB&B£16.47
dB&B⇌⋒£22.14 Credit cards 1 2 3 4 5 6

NEWCASTLE UPON TYNE Tyne & Wear Map **12**
NZ26 **See plan**

★★★★**Gosforth Park** High Gosforth Park, Gosforth (Thistle) ☎Wideopen 4111 Telex no 53655
Plan **4**
178⇌⋒ 1 Lift CTV in bedrooms 300P
(heated) squash Live music & dancing Tue–Sat
Cabaret Tue–Sat Conference facilities available
English & French. Last dinner 10.30pm
S% sB&B⇌⋒ fr£24.50 dB&B⇌⋒ fr£33
Continental breakfast Lunch fr£5.40 Tea fr85p
Dinner fr£6.75&alc Wine £3
Credit cards 1 2 3 4 5 6

★★★★**Royal Station** Neville St (British Transport)
☎20781 Telex no 53681 Plan **11**
113rm(92⇌⋒) Lift TV in bedrooms 10P
Conference facilities available English & French
Last dinner 10pm S%
*sB&B⇌⋒ fr£23.95 dB&B⇌⋒ fr£33
Wine £3.15 Credit cards 1 2 3 4 5 6

★★★**County** Neville St (Thistle) ☎22471
Telex no 537873 Plan **3**
120⇌⋒ Lift CTV CTV in bedrooms
Cabaret wkly Conference facilities available
English & Continental. Last dinner 9.30pm
Credit cards 1 2 3 4 5 6

★★★**Imperial** Jesmond Rd (Swallow) ☎815511
Telex no 537972 Plan **5**
130⇌⋒ Lift CTV in bedrooms 121P (heated)
sauna bath Conference facilities available
Last dinner 10.15pm S% sB&B⇌⋒ fr£18
dB&B⇌⋒ fr£24 *xmas* Credit cards 1 2 3 5

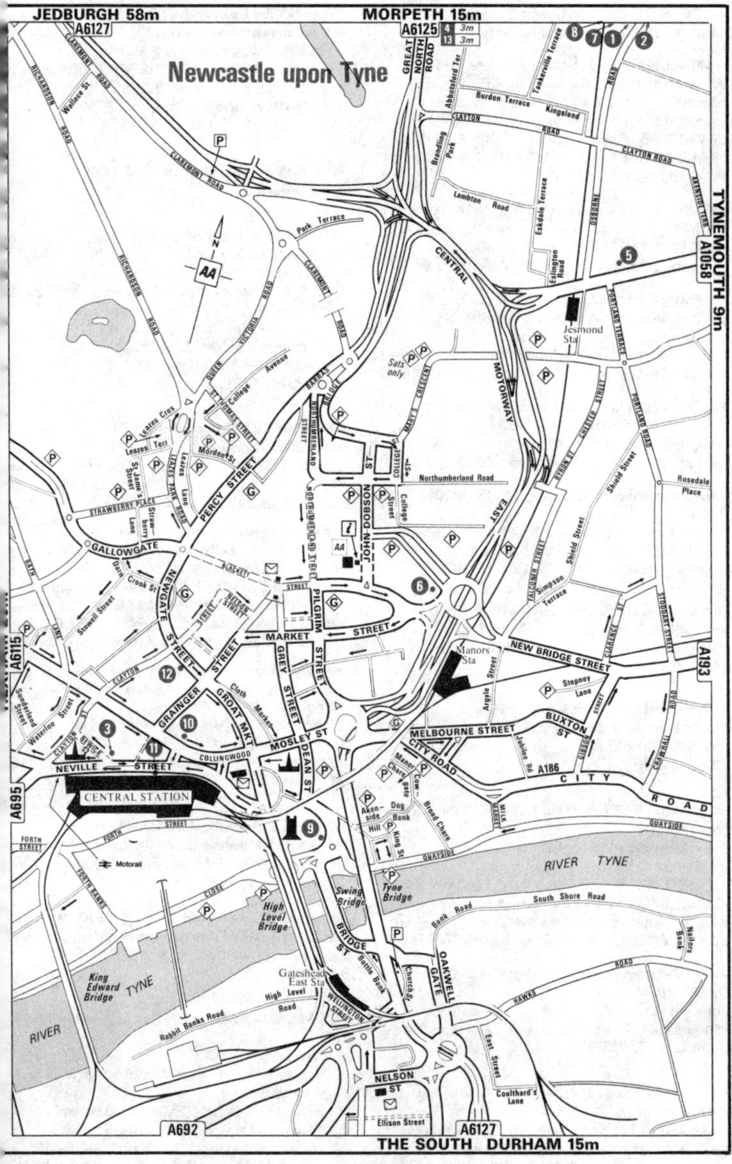

1 Avon ★★
2 Cairn ★★
3 County ★★★
4 Gosforth Park ❀★★★★
5 Imperial ★★★
6 Newcastle Centre ★★★
7 Northumbria ★★
8 Osborne ★
9 Partigi ✕✕
10 Ristorante Roma ✕
11 Royal Station ★★★★
12 Swallow ☆☆☆
13 Three Mile Inn ✕✕

★★**Newcastle Centre** New Bridge St (Centre) ☎26191 Telex no53467 Plan**6**
30⇌⋒ Lift ☽ ⋈ TV in bedrooms ⊘ sauna bath Last dinner9.45pm ✿ ♀ S% sB&B⇌⋒£16.75 dB&B⇌⋒£21.50 Continental breakfast Lunch£4 Dinner£4 Wine£3.40 ⊟ Credit cards 1 2 3 4 5 6

☆☆**Swallow** Newgate Arcade (Swallow) ☎25025 Telex no53168 Plan**12**
2⇌⋒ Lift ☽ ⋈ CTV in bedrooms 60P Live music & dancing Sat Conference facilities available Last dinner10.15pm ✿ S% sB&B⇌⋒fr£21.35 dB&B⇌⋒£27.70 ⊟ *xmas* Credit cards 1 2 3 5

★★**Avon** 64 Osborne Rd, Jesmond (Best Western) ☎814961 Telex no53636 Plan**1**
91rm(7⇌⋒) ☽ ⋈ CTV TV in bedrooms 50P 1⌂ Last dinner8.30pm S% sB&B£11.95–£13.15 sB&B⇌⋒£14.35–£16.65 dB&B£17.90–£19.70 dB&B⇌⋒£22.40–£24.70 ⊟
Credit cards 1 2 3 5 6

N

★★***Cairn*** 99 Osborne Rd, Jesmond ☎811358 Plan**2**
54rm CTV 35P Last dinner8.45pm

★★**Northumbria** 63 Osborne Rd, Jesmond (Best Western) ☎814961 Telex no53636 Plan**7**
69rm(45) Lift TV in bedrooms 30P sauna bath Last dinner10pm S%
sB&B£11.95–£13.15 sB&B£14.35–£16.65
dB&B£17.90–£19.70 dB&B£22.40–£24.70
Credit cards 1 2 3 5 6

★**Osborne** Osborne Rd, Jesmond ☎814778 Plan**8**
28rm CTV 6P 2 Last dinner8pm S%
sB&B£7–£8.50 dB&B£14 Tea fr50p
Dinner fr£3.25 Wine£1.25 Credit card 3

XX***Partigi*** Sandhill ☎20377 Plan**2**
Old building under Tyne bridge, with modern restaurant panelled in light wood.
Closed Sun; Lunch not served Sat; 50seats French & Italian. Last dinner11.30pm Credit cards 1 2 3 5

XX***Three Mile Inn*** Great North Road, Gosforth (3m N A1) ☎856817 Plan**13**
72seats 200P English & French.
Last dinner10.30pm Credit cards 1 3 5 6

X**Ristorante Roma** 22 Collingwood St ☎20612 Plan**10**
Closed Sun & Aug; 75seats French & Italian.
Last dinner11.30pm Lunch£1.95–£3.50&alc
Dinner£5.75alc Wine£2.75 Credit card 3

At **Seaton Burn** (6m N junc A1/A108)
☆☆☆☆**Holiday Inn** Great North Road (Commonwealth) ☎Wideopen5432 Not on plan
151 150P

At **Wallsend** (5m E junc A1058/A108)
☆☆☆☆**Europa Lodge** Coast Rd (Grand Met)
☎628989 Not on plan
182 200P

N

NEWCASTLE UPON TYNE AIRPORT Tyne & Wear Map**12** NZ17
☆☆☆☆***Airport*** Woolsington (Reo Stakis)
☎Ponteland24911
102 Lift CTV TV available in bedrooms 200P
Disco 5 nights wkly Live music & dancing twice wkly Conference facilities available
Last dinner10pm Credit cards 1 2 3 5 6

XX***Callerton*** Woolsington ☎Newcastle upon Tyne869254
Lunch not served Sat; Dinner not served Sun; 60seats 150P English & French. Last dinner9pm
Credit cards 1 2 3 5 6

NEWDIGATE Surrey Map**4** TQ14
XX**Forge** Parkgate Rd ☎582
Closed Sun, Mon, Boxing Day, 1st 2wks Jan & 1st 2wks Aug; Lunch not served Sat; 38seats 25P
French. Last dinner10pm Lunch£6alc
Dinner£10alc Wine£4.40 Credit cards 1 2 3 5 6

NEWENT Gloucestershire Map**3** SO72
X**Bistro One** Culver St ☎820896
Closed Sun & Mon; Lunch not served; 18seats
French. Last dinner9.30pm Dinner£10alc
Wine£2.95

NEW GRIMSBY Tresco Isles of Scilly (No map)
★**New Inn** ☎Scillonia22844
Stone and timber inn situated in rural area close to small harbour.
Closed Nov–Feb; 12rm(10) CTV (heated) English & French.
Last dinner8.15pm S% dB&B£21–£30
Lunch£2.75 Dinner£5.95 Wine£2.50

NEWHAVEN Derbyshire Map**7** SK16
★**Newhaven** ☎Hartington217
11rm CTV 200P Disco twice wkly
Last dinner1.30am sB&B£7 dB&B£13
Lunch fr£2.50&alc Tea fr75p&alc
High Tea fr£2.50&alc Dinner fr£2.50&alc
Wine£2.65 Credit cards 1 2 3 5 6

NEWHAVEN East Sussex Map**5** TQ40
See **Seaford**

NEWINGREEN Kent Map**5** TR13
☆☆**Royal Oak Motor** Ashford Rd (Whitbread)
☎Hythe (Kent)66580
27 TV in bedrooms 100P Live music & danci
Sat (Sep–May) Mainly grills. Last dinner9.15pm
S% sB&B£10 dB&B£21
Continental breakfast Lunch£3.80–£4.20
Dinner£2.80–£4.20 Wine£2.60
Credit cards 1 2 3 5

NEWMARKET Suffolk Map**5** TL66
★★***Bedford Lodge*** Bury Rd ☎3175
11rm(6) CTV TV available in bedrooms 100P
English & Continental. Last dinner9.30pm
Credit cards 1 2 3 4 5 6

★★**Rutland Arms** High St ☎4251
Main building is a Georgian coaching house, centre round a cobbled courtyard.
49rm(36) CTV 26P 8 Last dinner9pm
S% *sB&B£9.99 sB&B£13.99
dB&B£14.85 dB&B£19.98 Lunch fr£3.51
Dinner fr£3.89 Wine£2.95 Credit cards 1 2 3 5

★★**White Hart** High St (Trusthouse Forte) ☎3051
Three-storey gabled building (opened 1956) standing on site of 17th-C inn.
21rm(10) TV in bedrooms 50P 5
Last dinner10pm S% sB&B£11
sB&B£14.50 dB&B£17.50 dB&B£20.50
xmas Credit cards 1 2 3 4 5 6

NEW MILTON Hampshire Map**4** SZ29
★★★★★**Chewton Glen** Christchurch Rd (Prestige) ☎Highcliffe5341 Telex no41456
See page 52 for details

★**Carlton House** Barton Court Rd ☎612218
19rm(2) CTV TV available in bedroom 30P
Last dinner11am *sB&B£7.56
sB&B£8.37

NEWNHAM-ON-SEVERN Gloucestershire Map**3** SO61
★★**Victoria** ☎221
Early 17th-C house reputed to have been built by Sir John Vanburgh.
16rm(3) CTV CTV available in bedrooms 50P 3 Live music & dancing Sat & Sun
International. Last dinner9.30pm *sB&B£8
sB&B£9.50 dB&B£14 dB&B£16.50
Lunch£1.50–£3.50 Dinner£5–£8.50&alc
Wine£2.55

NEWPORT Gloucestershire Map**3** ST69
☆☆***Newport Towers Motel*** (on A38) ☎Berkeley57
60 TV in bedrooms 60P Conference facilities available Mainly grills.
Last dinner10pm Credit cards 1 2 3 5

NEWPORT Isle of Wight Map**4** SZ48
★**Wheatsheaf** St Thomas' Sq ☎523865
11rm(7) CTV English & French. Last dinner9pm sB&B£7.55
sB&B£8.55 dB&B£13.60 dB&B£14.60
Lunch£2.55–£3.40&alc Dinner£2.85–£3.90&alc
Wine£3.20

NEWPORT Salop Map**7** SJ71
★Royal Victoria St Mary's Street (Wolverhampton & Dudley) ☎810831
21rm(16⇨⋒) ☽ 🕅 CTV ⊘ 100P ♉English & French. Last dinner9.30pm ♉ ☕ S% ✻sB&B£10.35 sB&B⇨⋒£13.30 dB&B£17.50 dB&B⇨⋒£20.20 Lunch£3.45&alc Dinner£4.20&alc Wine£2.60 Credit cards 1 3

Barley Mow ☎810146
rm 🕅 CTV ⊘ 8P 1🏠 ♉ sB&B fr£6 dB&B fr£10 Lunch fr£2 Dinner fr£2.50 Wine£2 Credit card 3

NEWPORT PAGNELL Buckinghamshire Map**4** SP84
★★Swan Revived High St ☎610565
Pleasant hotel situated in town centre. Some famous names associated with the Swan are Samuel Pepys, the diarist, Sarah Siddons, the Georgian actress, also Disraeli used its portico for political addresses.
1⇨⋒ Lift ☽ 🕅 CTV CTV in bedrooms 20P ♉English & French. Last dinner10pm ♉ ☕ ✻sB&B⇨⋒ fr£16.60 dB&B⇨⋒ fr£22.22 Lunch£4.50&alc Tea fr70p Dinner£4.50&alc Wine£3.50 Credit cards 1 2 3 4 5 6

✕✕Glovers 18–20 St John Street ☎Goldcrest6398
Ground-floor restaurant with own courtyard and entrance.
Closed Sun, Mon, 25Dec–3Jan & first 3wks Aug; Lunch not served Sat; 38seats 8P ♉French & Continental. Last dinner10pm S% Lunch£10alc Dinner£12alc Wine£3.10 Credit cards 1 2 3 5

NEWPORT PAGNELL SERVICE AREA (M1 Motorway) Buckinghamshire Map**4** SP84
☆☆☆TraveLodge M1 Motorway Service Area (Trusthouse Forte) ☎610878
100⇨⋒ 🕅 CTV CTV in bedrooms 100P ⇎ ♿ ♉Mainly grills. sB&B⇨⋒£14 dB&B⇨⋒£17.50 Continental breakfast ⊟ Credit cards 1 2 3 4 5 6

NEWQUAY Cornwall Map**2** SW86 **See plan**
★★★Atlantic Dane Rd ☎2244 Plan**1**
Closed Oct–16May; 80rm(64⇨⋒) Lift ☽ 🕅 CTV TV available in bedrooms 100P 6🏠 ⇎ ⚓ ⊐(heated) billiards sauna bath Disco 3 nights wkly Live music & dancing twice wkly ♧ Last dinner9pm ♉ ☕ sB&B£12–£14 sB&B⇨⋒£13–£15 dB&B£24–£28 dB&B⇨⋒£26–£30 Lunch£5alc Tea fr75p Dinner fr£5.50&alc Wine£2.50 Credit cards 1 2 3 5 6

★★★Bay Esplanade Rd, Fistral Bay ☎2988 Plan**3**
Closed Nov–Feb except Xmas; 106rm(43⇨⋒) Lift ☽ 🕅 CTV 70P ⇎ Live music & dancing 6 nights wkly ♧ ♿ Last dinner8.30pm S% sB&B£6–£12 sB&B⇨⋒£7–£13 dB&B£12–£24 dB&B⇨⋒£16–£28 Lunch£2&alc Dinner£3.50&alc Wine£2.50 ⊟ *Xmas* Credit card 1

★★★Hotel Bristol Narrowcliff ☎5181 Plan**6**
Closed 3wks Oct; 104rm(62⇨⋒) Lift ☽ 🕅 CTV TV available in bedrooms 100P 5🏠 ⊡(heated) billiards Live music & dancing 4 nights wkly Conference facilities available ♿ Last dinner8.30pm ♉ ☕ S% sB&B£12.50–£13.50 sB&B⇨⋒£15.50–£16.50 dB&B£24–£26 Lunch£4.25&alc Tea90p Dinner£5&alc Wine£2.50 ⊟ *xmas* Credit card 2

★★★Edgcumbe Narrowcliff ☎2061 Plan**9** Closed Dec–Feb; 89⇨⋒ Lift ☽ 🕅 CTV CTV available in bedrooms 70P ⇎ ⊡ & ⊐(heated) billiards sauna bath Disco wkly Live music & dancing 3 nights wkly Cabaret twice wkly ♧ Last dinner8.30pm ♉ ☕ S% sB&B⇨⋒£9–£16 sB&B⇨⋒£18–£32 Lunch£3.90&alc Dinner£5.50&alc Wine£3 ⊟

N

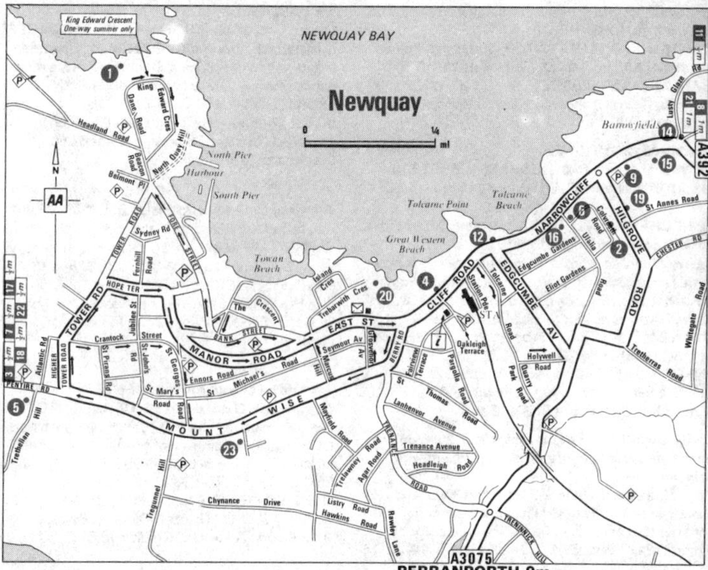

NEWQUAY BAY

Newquay

A3075 PERRANPORTH 9m

1 Atlantic ★★★
2 Barrowfield ★★
3 Bay ★★★
4 Beachcroft ★★
5 Bewdley ★★
6 Hotel Bristol ★★★
7 Corisande Manor ★★
8 Cross Mount ★★
9 Edgcumbe ★★★
11 Glendorgal ★★★
12 Great Western ★★
14 Hotel Riviera ★★★
15 Kilbirnie ★★★
16 Marina ★★
17 Minto House ★★
18 St Rumons ★★★
19 Sandy Lodge ★★
20 Trebarwith ★★★
21 Trevelgue ★★
22 Waters Edge ★★
23 Windsor ★★★

N

★★★***Glendorgal*** Lusty Glaze Rd ☎4937 Plan**11**
Secluded house on headland in twelve acres of ground.
Closed Oct–mid May; 30rm(16⇌ ⋒) CTV TV available in bedrooms 60P (hard) English, French & Swiss. Last dinner8.45pm Credit cards 2 3 5

★★★**Kilbirnie** Narrowcliff ☎5155 Plan**15**
Closed 3wks Nov & Xmas wk; 72rm(52⇌ ⋒) CTV CTV available in bedrooms 60P (heated) billiards sauna bath Disco wkly (Jun–Sep) Live music & dancing 4 nights wkly (Jun–Sep) Cabaret wkly (Jun–Sep) Last dinner8.15pm sB&B£9–£13 dB&B£18–£26 dB&B⇌ ⋒£22–£30 Lunch fr£3.50 Dinner fr£5.50 Wine£3

★★★**Hotel Riviera** Lusty Glaze Rd (Best Western) ☎4251 Plan**14**
Situated in cliff-top gardens overlooking sea.
Closed 25–27 Dec; 54rm(30⇌ ⋒) Lift CTV TV available in bedrooms 60P (heated) squash billiards sauna bath Live music & dancing 6 nights wkly (in summer) Cabaret 6 nights wkly (in summer) English & Continental. Last dinner9.30pm sB&B£11–£15.50 sB&B⇌ ⋒£13–£17.50 dB&B£22–£31 dB&B⇌ ⋒£26–£35 Lunch£1.65–£4 Tea£1&alc Dinner£6–£6.50&alc Wine£3 Credit cards 1 2 3 5

★★★**St Rumons** Esplanade Rd, Fistral Bay ☎2978 Plan**18**
Closed 28 Sep–2 May; 80rm(33⇌ ⋒) Lift CTV 55P 3 (heated) Live music & dancing 3night wkly

N

Last dinner8.30pm S% *sB&B£10–£13 sB&B £11–£14 dB&B£20–£26 dB&B £22–£28 Lunch£3.50–£4.50 Dinner£4.50–£5.50 Wine£3.30 Credit card 3

★★★**Trebarwith** Island Estate ☎2288 Plan**20**
Stands in own grounds among woodlands overlooking sea. Lawns, upper and lower sun deck, and private path to beach.
Closed 7 Oct–11 May 48rm(25) 5 CTV 30P (heated) billiards sauna bath Disco wkly Live music a& dancing 3 nights wkly Last dinner8.30pm S% sB&B£12.11–£17.64 dB&B£24.22–£25.28 dB&B £26.50–£37.50 Bar lunch75p–£1.50 Tea30p–£1 Dinner£5 Wine£2.75

★★★**Windsor** Mount Wise ☎5188 Plan**23**
Closed Dec–Mar; 51rm(25) CTV CTV available in bedrooms 40P (heated) squash sauna bath Disco twice wkly Live music & dancing 3 nights wkly Cabaret wkly Last dinner8.30pm S% sB&B£9–£12 sB&B £10.50–£13.50 dB&B£18–£24 dB&B £21–£27 Bar lunch£1–£1.80 Tea25p Dinner£4.50–£5.25 Wine£2.90

★★**Barrowfield** Hillgrove Rd ☎2560 Plan**2**
Closed Nov–Mar; 46rm(23) Lift CTV TV available in bedrooms 34P 20 (heated) sauna bath Disco nightly Live music & dancing twice wkly Cabaret twice wkly Last dinner8.30pm S% sB&B£9.50–£10.50

N

sB&B⇌ ⋒£10–£10.50 dB&B£18–£19 dB&B⇌ ⋒£19–£20 Lunch£2.30 Tea75p Dinner£3.75

★★**Beachcroft** Cliff Rd ☎2033 Plan**4**
Large hotel in own gardens.
Closed Oct–Mar; 70rm(42⇌ ⋒) Lift ☽ CTV 60P ⚓ ⇌(heated) (hard) sauna bath Disco wkly Live music & dancing 3 nights wkly Last dinner8pm sB&B£7.50–£10 sB&B⇌ ⋒£8–£8.50 dB&B£15–£22 dB&B⇌ ⋒£16–£24 Wine£2.50

★★***Bewdley*** Pentire Rd ☎2883 Plan**5**
Closed Dec–Jan; 36rm ☽ CTV 36P ⇌(heated) Disco wkly Live music & dancing twice wkly Last dinner6.30pm

★★**Corisande Manor** Riverside Av, Pentire ☎2042 Plan**7**
Closed Oct–mid May; 13rm Annexe: 10rm CTV 32P ⚓ Live music & dancing wkly Children under 3yrs not accommodated English, French & Italian. Last dinner7.30pm sB&B£6.50–£9 dB&B£13–£18 Barlunch£1–£3 Tea20–50p Dinner£5 Wine£2.50

★★**Cross Mount** Church St, St Columb Minor ☎2669 Plan**8**
Closed Nov–mid Dec & 24–27 Dec; 12rm(6⇌ ⋒) CTV 9P Last dinner9pm sB&B£8.75–£11 sB&B⇌ ⋒£11.25–£13.50 dB&B£17.50–£22 dB&B⇌ ⋒£20–£24.50

M

Lunch fr£2.75 Tea fr65p Dinner fr£3&alc Wine£3 Credit card 1

★★**Great Western** Cliff Rd ☎2010 Plan**12**
RS Nov–Mar; 45⇌ Lift CTV TV available in bedrooms 50P 20 Disco twice wkly Live music & dancing 3 nights wkly Cabaret wkly Last dinner10pm S% sB&B⇌£8.50–£10.50 dB&B⇌£17–£21 Lunch£2.90&alc Tea35p–£1 High Tea£1.50 Dinner£3.25&alc Wine£2.50 Credit cards 2 5

★★**Marina** Narrowcliff (Travco) ☎3012 Plan**16**
Closed Nov–Mar; 72rm(3⇌) CTV 16P 2 Last dinner8pm S% sB&B£7.50–£8 sB&B⇌£9–£9.50 dB&B£15–£16 dB&B⇌£16.50–£17.50 Lunch fr£3 Dinner fr£3.75 Wine£2.25 *xmas* Credit cards 1 2 3 5 6

★★**Minto House** 38 Pentire Cres, Pentire ☎3227 Plan**17**
Closed Oct–Mar; 25rm(17⇌) Annexe: 3rm(1⇌) CTV TV in bedrooms 20P sauna bath Disco wkly Live music & dancing 3 nights wkly Cabaret wkly Continental. Last dinner7.45pm sB&B£6–£15 sB&B⇌£6.50–£16 dB&B£12–£30 dB&B⇌£13–£32 Bar lunch£1–£3 Tea50p–£1.50 Dinner£5–£6.50 Credit cards 1 3

★★**Sandy Lodge** Hillgrove Rd ☎2851 Plan**19**
Closed 12Oct–26Apr; 46rm(10⇌) CTV 56P (heated) sauna bath Disco twice wkly Live music & dancing twice wkly Cabaret wkly Last dinner7.30pm S% sB&B£5.50–£7.50 dB&B£11–£15 dB&B⇌£13–£17 Lunch£2.50–£3.50&alc Tea60p–£1.25 Dinner£4–£5.75&alc Wine£2.30

★★**Trevelgue** Porth ☎2864 Plan**21**
28rm(1⇌) CTV 50P (heated) Disco wkly Live music & dancing twice wkly Last dinner8pm S% ✱sB&B£9–£10.20 dB&B£18–£20.40 Lunch£2.60–£3 Tea25–50p Dinner£4.50–£5 Wine£3.50

★★***Waters Edge*** Esplanade Rd, Fistral Bay ☎2048 Plan**22**
Closed Oct–Apr; 22rm(11⇌) CTV 22P Children under 5yrs not accommodated Last dinner8.15pm

NEW ROMNEY Kent Map**5** TR02

★★★**Dormy House** Marine Pde, Littlestone-on-Sea (1m E B2070) ☎3233
32rm(21⇌) CTV CTV in bedrooms 70P 4 (heated) (hard) Disco wkly Live music & dancing wkly English & French. Last dinner9.15pm S% sB&B£10.50–£11.50 sB&B⇌£11.70–£15 dB&B£21–£23 dB&B⇌ fr£23.40 Lunch£4–£4.80&alc Tea30p–£1.50 High Tea£1–£2 Dinner£4–£4.80&alc Wine£2.50 *xmas* Credit cards 2 5 6

Blue Dolphins Dymchurch Rd ☎3224
Closed 2wks Oct; 8rm(4⇌) CTV 10P 1 English & French. Last dinner9.15pm S% sB&B£8–£9 sB&B⇌£9–£9.50 dB&B£13–£14 dB&B⇌£15–£16 Lunch£3–£3.80 Dinner£3.50–£4.50&alc Wine£2.50 *xmas* Credit cards 1 2 6

Broadacre North St ☎2381
9rm CTV 12P Last dinner9pm S% ✱sB&B£8.30 dB&B£13.30 Lunch£3.50alc Dinner£3.20alc Wine£2.80 *xmas* Credit cards 1 3

N

NEWTON ABBOT Devon Map**3** SX87
★★**Globe** Courtenay St ☎4106
Old coaching inn in town centre with busy commercial trade.
24rm(3⇌⋒) ☽ ⋈ CTV ₽ Disco Fri & Sat
♀Mainly grills. Last dinner 9.45pm ♁ ☕
✻sB&B fr£7.25 sB&B⇌⋒£9.50–£12.25
dB&B fr£14 dB&B⇌⋒ fr£16.50
Lunch£1.50–£3&alc Tea85p–£1.35
Dinner£2.50–£4&alc 1 2 3 4 5 6

★★**Queens** Queen St (Inter-Hotel) ☎5216
Telex no 934900
38rm(12⇌⋒) ☽ ⋈ CTV in bedrooms 12P
Last dinner 9.30pm ♁ ☕ S% sB&B£12
sB&B⇌⋒£15 dB&B£21 dB&B⇌⋒£25.50
Lunch£3.50&alc Dinner£3.50&alc Wine£3.50
⊟ *xmas* 1 2 3 5

✕**Old Rydon Inn** Rydon Rd, Kingsteignton (1½ E A380) ☎4626
Closed Sun; Lunch not served Sat; Dinner not served Mon; 25seats 20P ♀International. Last dinner 10pm
✻Lunch£6alc Dinner£6alc Wine£2.75
Credit cards 1 2 3

✕***Vecchia Roma*** Worborough St ☎5884
Closed Sun; 50seats ♀Italian. Last dinner 11pm

NEWTON FERRERS Devon Map**2** SX54
★★**Court House** ☎Plymouth 872324
Creeper-clad manor in spacious terraced lawns and gardens. Rooms named after sailing ships of 16th- and 17th-centuries.
RS Dec & Jan; 9rm(5⇌⋒) CTV ⊘ 50P ⇌ ⚓
⊃(heated) ♤ ♀English & French. Last dinner 9pm
♁ ☕ S% ✻sB&B£10–£14

N

sB&B⇌⋒£12–£16 dB&B£20–£24 dB&B⇌⋒£22–£26 Lunch£3.75–£4.50 Tea75p–£1 Dinner£4.75–£6 Wine£3.20 ⊟

★★**River Yealm** Yealm Rd ☎Plymouth 872419
Gabled building with elaborate entrance porch; in own wooded grounds overlooking harbour. Own river frontage and jetty.
19rm(8⇌⋒) ♛ CTV 60P 1 ⌂ ⚓ Last dinner8.30pm ✿ ☕ S% sB&B fr£9.50 sB&B⇌⋒ fr£11.80 dB&B fr£19 dB&B⇌⋒ fr£23 Bar lunch fr£1&alc Tea fr50p&alc Dinner fr&5.50&alc Wine£2.25

NEWTON GREEN Suffolk Map**5** TL94
✕✕**Saracens Head** ☎Sudbury79036
Closed Sun & Mon; 40seats 20P bedrooms available Last dinner9.15pm S% Lunch£3.30&alc High Tea£2.50 Dinner£5&alc Wine£3 Credit cards 1 3

NEWTON SOLNEY Derbyshire Map**8** SK22
★★★**Newton Park** (Embassy) ☎Burton-on-Trent703568
26⇌⋒ ☽ ♛ CTV TV in bedrooms 100P ⚓ Last dinner9.15pm ✿ S% sB&B⇌⋒£15 dB&B⇌⋒£22 Lunch£5&alc Dinner£5.50&alc Wine£4.50 ⊟ Credit cards 1 2 3 4 5 6

NINFIELD East Sussex Map**5** TQ71
★★★**Moor Hall** ☎892330
Georgian country house in secluded grounds.
22rm(13⇌⋒) ♛ CTV 95P 3 ⌂ ⚓ ⌓(heated) sauna bath Live music & dancing mthly ♡English, French & Italian. Last dinner9pm ✿ S% sB&B£10.50–£12.50 sB&B⇌⋒£13–£14 dB&B£21–£25 dB&B⇌⋒£26–£28 Lunch fr£4&alc Tea50p–£1 High Tea£2–£2.50 Dinner£5&alc Wine£2.95 ⊟ *xmas* Credit cards 1 3

NORMAN CROSS Cambridgeshire Map**4** TL19
☆☆**Peterborough Crest Motel** Great North Road (Crest) ☎Peterborough240209
40⇌⋒ ☽ ⊞ ♛ CTV in bedrooms 80P ⚓ Last dinner9.30pm ✿ ☕ S% ✱sB&B☎⋒£16.25 dB&B⇌⋒£22.78 Continental breakfast ⊟ Credit cards 1 2 3 4 5 6

NORTHALLERTON North Yorkshire Map**8** SE39
★★**Golden Lion** Market Pl (Trusthouse Forte) ☎2404
29rm(9⇌⋒) ♛ CTV TV in bedrooms 100P Last dinner9.15pm ✿ ☕ S% sB&B£12 sB&B⇌⋒£14.50 dB&B£17.50 dB&B⇌⋒£20.50 ⊟ *xmas* Credit cards 1 2 3 4 5 6

NORTHAMPTON Northamptonshire Map**4** SP76
★★★**Saxon Inn** Silver St, Town Centre ☎22441 Telex no311142
140⇌⋒ Lift ☽ ♛ CTV in bedrooms 250P Live music & dancing Sat Conference facilities available ♡English & French. Last dinner10.30pm ✿ ☕ S% sB&B⇌⋒£17.02 dB&B⇌⋒£21.34 Lunch£3.30&alc Tea80p Dinner£3.80&alc Wine£3.50 Credit cards 1 2 3 5

★★★**Westone** Weston Favell (3m E off A45) (Grand Met) ☎406262
62rm(54⇌⋒) Lift ☽ ♛ TV available in bedrooms ⊘ 80P ⚓ ♣ Conference facilities available ♡English & French. Last dinner9.45pm ✿ ☕ ✱sB&B⇌⋒£14.50 dB&B⇌⋒£17.50 ⊟ *xmas* Credit cards 1 2 3 4 5 6

★★**Angel** Bridge St (Grand Met) ☎21661
45rm(2⇌⋒) 1 ▭ ☽ TV 20P ♡English & French. Last dinner9pm ✿ ☕ S% ✱sB&B⇌⋒£12.50 dB&B⇌⋒£17 ⊟ Credit cards 1 2 3 4 5 6

★★**Grand** Gold St ☎34416
52rm(15⇌⋒) Lift ☽ ⊞ ♛ CTV CTV in bedrooms 20P Last dinner9.30pm ✿ ☕ S% ✱sB&B fr£12.50 sB&B⇌⋒ fr£14 dB&B fr£17.50 dB&B⇌⋒ fr£19 Lunch fr£3.50 Tea fr35p Dinner fr£4 Wine£2.50 ⊟ Credit cards 1 3 5

✕**Casanova Inn** 16B Bridge St ☎36517
Closed Sun; Lunch not served Sat; 100seats 30P ♡Italian. Last dinner11pm ✱Lunch£1.50 Dinner£5alc Wine£2.50 Credit cards 1 2 3

✕**Napoleon's Bistro** 11 Welford Rd ☎713899
Closed Sun & Mon; Lunch not served Sat; 44seats ⚑ ♡French. Last dinner10pm S% Lunch£2.95–£3.95 Dinner£6.10alc Wine£3.30 Credit cards 1 3 5

✕**Vineyard** 7 Derngate ☎33978
Closed Sun & Mon; Lunch not served Sat; 32seats ⚑ ♡English & Continental. Last dinner10.30pm ✱Lunch£3.50alc Dinner£5alc Wine£2.10 Credit cards 1 3 5

At **Sywell** (6m NE off A43)
☆**Sywell Airport Motel** ☎Northampton491594
49⇌⋒ 100P

NORTH FERRIBY Humberside Map**8** SE92
☆☆☆**Hull Crest Motel** (Crest) ☎Hull645212
102⇌⋒ ☽ ♛ CTV CTV in bedrooms 200P ⚓ Last dinner10pm ✿ ☕ S% ✱sB&B⇌⋒£16.79 dB&B⇌⋒£22.78 Continental breakfast ⊟ Credit cards 1 2 3 4 5 6

NORTHIAM East Sussex Map**5** TQ82
★★**Hayes** Village Green ☎3142
An Elizabethan and Georgian building set in own ground.
Closed Feb; 7⇌⋒ 1 ▭ Lift ☽ CTV TV available in bedrooms 50P Last dinner9.30pm S% sB&B⇌⋒£11–£14 dB&B⇌⋒£15–£19.50 Bar lunch75p–£1.50 Dinner£4.25&alc Wine£2.85 ⊟ Credit cards 1 3 5

NORTHLEACH Gloucestershire Map**4** SP11
★**Wheatsheaf** ☎244
Creeper-clad, Cotswold inn with small garden.
8rm ♛ CTV 20P 3 ⌂ ⚓ Last dinner8pm ✿ ☕ sB&B£8.75 dB&B£13.90 Bar lunch35–90p Tea60p Dinner£2.50–£5&alc Wine£1.85

✕**Country Friends** Market Pl ☎421
Closed Mon; Dinner not served Sun; 18seats ⚑ Last dinner9.30pm Lunch£4–£4.50&alc Tea£1alc Dinner£7alc Wine£3.50 Credit card 3

NORTHREPPS Norfolk Map**9** TG23
✕✕ ***Northrepps Cottage*** ☎Overstrand202
Closed Mon; Dinner not served Sun; 250seats 100P Music & dancing Sat ♡English & French. Last dinner9pm

NORTH RIGTON North Yorkshire Map**8** SE24
✕✕✕**Square & Compass Inn** ☎Harrogate74228
Closed Mon; Dinner not served Sun; 80seats 87p Disco Sat ♡English, French & Italian. Last dinner9pm Lunch£2.05–£2.25&alc Dinner£5.50&alc Wine£3.75 Credit cards 1 3

NORTH STIFFORD Essex Map**5** TQ68
☆☆☆**Europa Lodge** (Grand Met) ☎Grays Thurrock71451
64⇌⋒ ☽ ♛ TV available in bedrooms 80P ⚓ ⚘(hard) Live music & dancing Sat Conference facilities available ♡French. Last dinner9.45pm ✿ ☕ S% ✱sB&B⇌⋒£14.50 dB&B⇌⋒£20 ⊟ *xmas* Credit cards 1 2 3 4 5 6

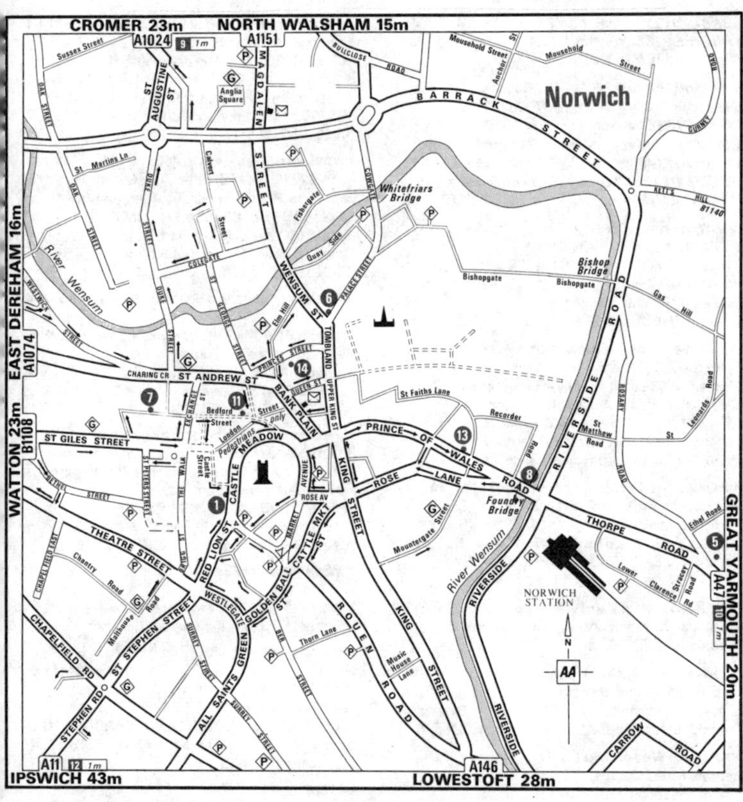

1 Castle ★★	**7** Marco's ✕✕	**10** Oaklands ★★	**13** Savoy ✕✕✕
5 Lansdowne ★★★	**8** Nelson ☆☆☆	**11** Parson Woodforde ✕✕	**14** Smedley's ✕✕
6 Maid's Head ★★★	**9** Hotel Norwich ☆☆☆	**12** Post House ☆☆☆	

NORTH TAWTON Devon Map**3** SS60
★**Kayden House** High St ☎242
8rm(3⇌⋒) ᛗ CTV TV available in bedrooms P
Last dinner9pm ♔ S% sB&B£7.70
sB&B⇌⋒£8.80 dB&B£14.40 dB&B⇌⋒£16.40
Bar lunch60p–£1.50&alc Dinner£3.50–£4.50&alc
Wine£2.35 ⊨ Credit cards 1 3

NORTH WARNBOROUGH Hampshire Map**4** SU75
✕✕**Mill House** ☎Odiham2953
Closed Sun, Mon, 1st 2wks in Jan; Dinner not served Xmas Day; 75seats 35P Last dinner9.50pm
Lunch£4.06&alc Dinner£7alc
Credit cards 1 3 5 6

NORTHWICH Cheshire Map**7** SJ67
★★★***Hartford Hall*** Hartford (2m SW off bypass A556) ☎75711
Gabled 16th-C country house in its own grounds.
21⇌⋒ ☽ ᛗ CTV 80P Last dinner10pm ♔ ⊨
Credit cards 1 4 5

★★**Woodpecker** London Rd ☎45524
RS Xmas; 31rm(22⇌⋒) ☽ ᛗ CTV in bedrooms
60P English & French. Last dinner10pm
sB&B£11–£12 sB&B⇌⋒£13.50–£14
dB&B£16.50–£17 dB&B⇌⋒£21–£22
Lunch£3.25–£4&alc Dinner£3.25–£4&alc
Wine£2.80 ⊨ Credit cards 1 2 3 5

NORWICH Norfolk Map**5** TG20 **See plan** See also **Caister St Edmund**
★★★**Lansdowne** 116 Thorpe Rd (Embassy)
☎20302 Plan**5**
45rm(21⇌⋒) Lift ☽ ᛗ CTV TV in bedrooms 60P
Last dinner9pm ♔ S% sB&B£11.50
sB&B⇌⋒£14.50 dB&B£18 dB&B⇌⋒£22
Lunch£5.50&alc Dinner£5.50&alc Wine£4.50
⊨ Credit cards 1 2 3 4 5 6

★★★**Maid's Head** Tombland (Queens) ☎28821
Telex no975080 Plan**6**
Part of hotel is more than 700 years old, showing original fireplace and King Pin Pillars.
82rm(79⇌⋒) 1 Lift ☽ ᛗ CTV in bedrooms 73P
27 Conference facilities available
Last dinner9.45pm ♔ sB&B£14
sB&B⇌⋒£19 dB&B⇌⋒£24.40
Lunch£3.75–£4.25&alc Tea95p–£1.20&alc
Dinner£4.25–£4.75&alc Wine£4 ⊨ *xmas*
Credit cards 1 2 3 5

☆☆☆**Nelson** Prince of Wales Rd. (Best Western)
☎28612 Telex no975203 Plan**8**
Stands on the banks of the River Wensum close to city centre. Relics, charts, manuscripts and prints of Nelson's history incorporated in the interior design.
94⇌⋒ Lift ☽ ᛗ CTV in bedrooms 100P 44
sauna bath Last dinner9.45pm ♔ S%

sB&B⇌⋒£21 dB&B⇌⋒£27 Lunch fr£4.25&alc Dinner fr£4.25&alc Wine£3.90 ⊓ *xmas* Credit cards ①②③⑤⑥

☆☆☆**Hotel Norwich** 121–131 Boundary Rd (Best Western) ☎410431 Telex no 975337 Plan **9**
85⇌⋒ ☽ ⊞ CTV in bedrooms ⊘ 150P sauna bath Conference facilities available ♉ English & French. Last dinner 9.45pm ♉ S% ✱sB&B⇌⋒£17.90 dB&B⇌⋒£22.65 Lunch fr£4&alc Dinner fr£4&alc Wine£2.95 ⊓ *xmas* Credit cards ①②③⑤

☆☆☆**Post House** Ipswich Rd (Trusthouse Forte) ☎56431 Telex no 975106 Plan **12**
120⇌⋒ ☽ ⊞ CTV in bedrooms 200P ⌂ (heated) Last dinner 9.45pm ♉ ♉ S% sB&B⇌⋒£19.75 dB&B⇌⋒£28.50 ⊓ *xmas* Credit cards ①②③④⑤⑥

★★**Castle** Castle Meadow (De Vere) ☎611511 Telex no 22121 Plan **1**
78rm(25⇌⋒) Lift ☽ CTV TV in bedrooms ₱ ♉ English & French. Last dinner 9.30pm ♉ ♉ S% sB&B⇌⋒£16.50 dB&B⇌⋒£21 Lunch£4.25&alc Tea fr£1.25 Dinner£4.25&alc Wine£3.75 ⊓ Credit cards ①②③⑤⑥

★★**Oaklands** 89 Yarmouth Rd ☎34471 Plan **10**
RS Xmas; 37rm(10⇌⋒) ⊞ CTV 70P ♣ ♉ English & French. Last dinner 10pm ♉ ♉ S% sB&B£8 sB&B⇌⋒£9.75 dB&B£13.80 dB&B⇌⋒£15.50 Lunch£2.75&alc Tea 20p Dinner£3.35&alc Wine£2.65 ⊓

XXX ***Savoy*** 50 Prince of Wales Rd ☎26662 Plan **13**
150 seats ♉ International. Last dinner midnight Credit cards ①②③⑤⑥

XX **Marco's** 17 Potter Gate ☎24044 Plan **7**
Closed Sun, Mon, Public Hols & Aug; 35 seats ₱ ♉ Italian. Last dinner 10pm S% Lunch fr£4&alc Dinner£15alc Wine£2.50 Credit cards ①②③⑤

XX **Parson Woodforde** 1 Old Post Office Yard, Bedford St ☎24280 Plan **11**
Dinner not served Sun; 46 seats 10P Last dinner 10.30pm ✱Lunch£3.50–£5&alc Dinner£8alc Wine£2.95 Credit cards ①③⑤⑥

XX **Smedley's** Princes St ☎23193 Plan **14**
Closed Sun & Public Hols; 95 seats ₱ ♉ English & French. Last dinner 10pm S% Lunch£4.20&alc Dinner£4.20&alc Wine£2.45 Credit cards ①②③⑤⑥

NOTTINGHAM Nottinghamshire Map **8** SK54 **See plan**

★★★★**Albany** St James's Street (Trusthouse Forte) ☎40131 Telex no 37211 Plan **1**
165⇌⋒ Lift ☽ ⊞ ⊞ CTV in bedrooms ₱ Conference facilities available Last dinner 11pm ♉ ♉ S% sB&B⇌⋒£28 dB&B⇌⋒£38.50 ⊓ *xmas* Credit cards ①②③④⑤⑥

★★★★**Victoria** Milton St (Reo Stakis) ☎49561 Telex no 37401 Plan **15**
167⇌⋒ Lift ☽ ⊞ CTV in bedrooms ₱ sauna bath disco twice wkly Conference facilities available ♉ French. Last dinner 11pm S% sB&B⇌⋒£18 dB&B⇌⋒£23 Lunch fr£3.25 Dinner fr£4.85 Wine£3.10 ⊓ Credit cards ①②③⑤⑥

★★★**George** George St ☎45641 Plan **6**
68rm(42⇌⋒) 1▭ Lift ☽ ⊞ CTV available in bedrooms ₱ ⊘ ♉ French. Last dinner 9pm ♉ ♉ S% sB&B fr£13.80 sB&B⇌⋒ fr£17.80 dB&B fr£17.80 dB&B⇌⋒ fr£24.15 Lunch fr£4&alc Dinner fr£4.50&alc Wine£3.75 Credit cards ①②③⑤⑥

★★★**Savoy** Mansfield Rd ☎602621 Telex no 377429 Plan **11**
125⇌⋒ Lift ☽ ⊞ CTV CTV in bedrooms ⊘ 150P 100⌂ Last dinner 11.30pm ♉ ♉ ✱sB&B⇌⋒£16.50 dB&B⇌⋒£22 Lunch£2.95–£5.25&alc Dinner£4.20–£7.10&alc Wine£2 Credit cards ①②⑤

★★★**Strathdon** Derby Rd (Thistle) ☎48501 Plan **12**
RS Xmas & New Years Day (restaurant closed); 67⇌⋒ Lift ☽ ⊞ CTV in bedrooms ₱ ♉ English & French. Last dinner 10pm ♉ ♉ S% sB&B fr£18.75 dB&B⇌⋒ fr£24.50 Lunch£3.75&alc Tea 85palc Dinner£5.50&alc Wine£2.75 ⊓ Credit cards ①②③④⑤⑥

★★***Edwalton Hall*** Edwalton (3½m S A606) ☎231116 Plan **3**
13rm(1⇌⋒) ⊞ CTV TV available in bedrooms 50P ♣ ♉ English & French. Last dinner 10pm ♉

★★**Flying Horse** Poultry (Berni) ☎52831 Plan **4**
58rm(31⇌⋒) ☽ ⊞ CTV TV in bedrooms 36⌂ Live music & dancing 5 nights wkly ♉ Mainly grills. Last dinner 11pm ♉ sB&B£9.20 sB&B⇌⋒£11.50 dB&B£15.80 dB&B⇌⋒£18.10 Lunch£1.62–£5.50 Dinner£1.62–£5.50&alc ⊓ Credit cards ①②③⑤

★★**Nottingham Knight** Loughborough Rd, Ruddington (junc A60/A614) (Henekey) ☎211171 Plan **8**
8rm(7⇌⋒) Lift ⊞ TV in bedrooms 400P ⊘ ♣ ♉ Mainly grills. Last dinner 10pm ♉ S% sB&B£10.50 sB&B⇌⋒£13 dB&B£17 dB&B⇌⋒£20 ⊓ *xmas* Credit cards ①②③④⑤⑥

★★**Portland** Carrington St ☎50208 Plan **9**
Closed Xmas; 45rm(8⇌⋒) Lift ☽ CTV TV in bedrooms ₱ ♉ English & French. Last dinner 9.30pm ♉ S% ✱sB&B£10 sB&B⇌⋒£13 dB&B£14.80 dB&B⇌⋒£20 Lunch£1.70&alc Dinner£3.55alc Wine£2.30 Credit cards ①③

XX **Casa Manuel** 4A Fletcher Gate ☎54879 Not on plan
Closed Sun; Lunch not served; 35 seats ₱

N

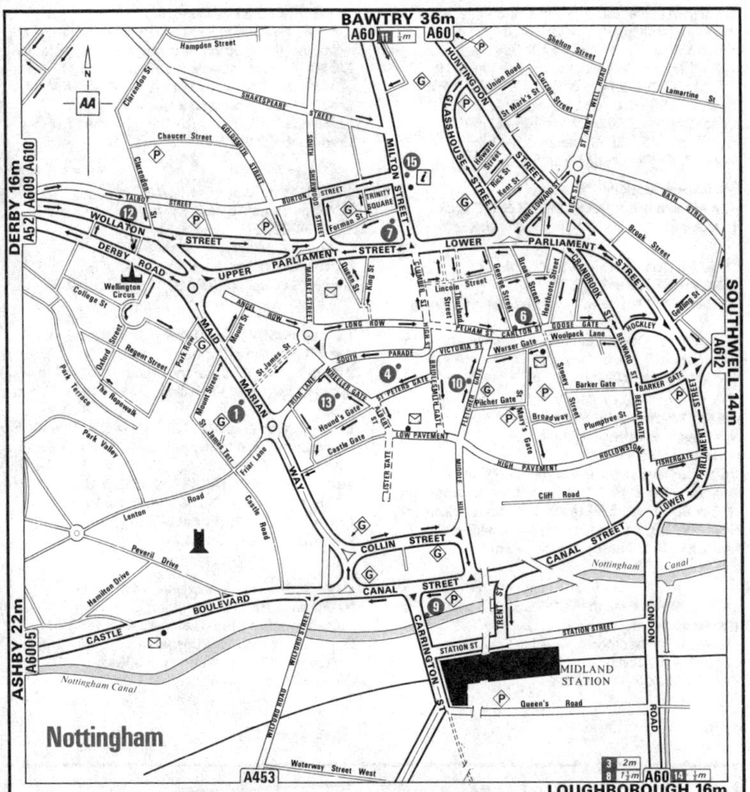

1 Albany ★★★★	**7** Moulin Rouge ✕	**10** Rhinegold ✕✕	**13** Trattoria Conti ✕✕
3 Edwalton Hall ★★	**8** Nottingham Knight ★★	**11** Savoy ★★★	**14** Trent Bridge Inn ✕✕
4 Flying Horse ★★	**9** Portland ★★	**12** Strathdon ★★★	**15** Victoria ★★★★
6 George ★★★			

Spanish. Last dinner 11.30pm S%
✱Dinner £14alc Wine £3.10

✕✕Rhinegold King John Chambers, Fletcher Gate ☎51294 Plan **10**
Closed Sun & 3–29Aug; Lunch not served; 75seats Continental. Last dinner 11pm S%
✱Dinner £3.60–£8.30&alc Wine £2.80
Credit card 2

✕✕Trattoria Conti 14–16 Wheeler Gate ☎44056 Plan **13**
Closed Sun & Public Hols; 80seats 30P (evening only) Italian. Last dinner 11.15pm ✱Lunch £2.50
Dinner fr £3.75 Credit cards 1 2 3 5

✕✕*Trent Bridge Inn* Radcliffe Rd, West Bridgford (1m S) ☎869831 Plan **14**
Dinner not served Sun; 80seats 200P Live music & dancing Sat Cabaret Sat English & French.
Last dinner 10pm Credit cards 1 2 6

✕Moulin Rouge Trinity Sq ☎42845 Plan **7**
Closed 26 & 27Dec & Public Hols; 44seats English & Continental. Last dinner 10pm S%
✱Lunch £5alc Dinner £6alc Wine £2.50
Credit cards 1 2 3 5

NUNEATON Warwickshire Map **4** SP39
★★Chase Higham Ln (Ansells) ☎383406
28 rm CTV TV in bedrooms 350P
Last dinner 10pm S% sB&B £16.25
dB&B £20.60 Lunch £3.75&alc
Dinner £4.30&alc Wine £3.20 Credit cards 1 2

★★Griff House Coventry Rd ☎382984
10rm(1) CTV CTV in bedrooms 100P
Last dinner 10pm S% sB&B £9–£11
sB&B £10–£12 dB&B £14–£16
dB&B £15–£17 Lunch £3–£4&alc
Tea fr £1.50 High Tea fr £2 Dinner £3–£4&alc
Wine £1.50

☆☆Nuneaton Crest Motel Watling St (Crest) ☎329711
47rm(23) CTV CTV in bedrooms 47P
S% ✱sB&B £15.17 dB&B £21.70
Continental breakfast Credit cards 1 2 3 4 5 6

OAKFORD BRIDGE Devon Map **3** SS92
✕*Bark House Hotel* ☎Oakford 236
Dinner not served Sun–Wed Oct–Mar; 20seats 12P bedrooms available Last dinner 10pm

OAKHAM Leicestershire Map**4** SK80
★★★**Crown** High St. (Best Western) ☎3631
RS 25 & 26Dec 25rm(18⇌⋔) ☽ CTV TV in bedrooms 30P ♉English & French. Last dinner10pm ♔ ☕ S% sB&B£12–£14 sB&B⇌⋔£13.50–£16 dB&B£16.50–£18 dB&B⇌⋔£18–£20 Lunch£2.85–£3.50&alc Tea80p–£1.50&alc High Tea£1.85–£3 Dinner£4.35–£5&alc Wine£2.85 ⛿ Credit cards 1 2 3 5

★★***George*** Market Pl ☎2284
4rm Annexe: 15rm(9⇌⋔) ⚑ 20P ♿ ♉French. Last dinner9.30pm ♔ ⛿ Credit cards 1 3

OAKLEY Bedfordshire Map**4** TL05
✕**Bedford Arms** ☎2280
Timber-built 17th-century inn with dining-room of stone.
Closed Xmas Day 40seats 100P Last dinner9.45pm S% Lunch£7.50alc Dinner£7.50alc Wine£2.95 Credit cards 1 2 3 5

OAKLEY Hampshire Map**4** SU55
★★**Beach Arms Motor Inn** (on B3400) ☎Basingstoke780210
RS Xmas Day Eve (no restaurant) 5rm(3⇌⋔) Annexe: 12⇌⋔ ⚑ CTV TV available in bedrooms ✈ 80P ♿ ⚓ ♉English & French. Last dinner10pm ♔ S% ✱sB&B£14 sB&B⇌⋔£14 dB&B⇌⋔£20 Lunch£4.75 Dinner£4.75&alc Wine£1.75 Credit cards 1 2 3 5 6

OCKHAM Surrey Map**4** TQ05
✕✕**Hautboy Inn** ☎Ripley (Surrey) 3353
150seats 80P bedrooms available ♉International Last dinner10.15pm Lunch£7alc Dinner£7alc Wine£3.50 Credit cards 3 5

ODSTOCK Wiltshire Map**4** SU12
❀✕**Yew Tree Inn** ☎Salisbury29786
Attractive thatched inn, with low-beamed restaurant.
Closed Sun & Mon 34seats 28P ♉French. Specialities: Poulet au vinaigre, rice & green salad, le veau 'St Trop', L'entrecôte aux échalotes. Last dinner9.45pm Lunch£7alc Dinner£7alc Credit cards 1 2 3 5 6

OLDBURY W Midlands Map**7** SO98
❀✕**Jonathans'** 16 Wolverhampton Rd, Quinton ☎021-429 3757
Closed Sun, Mon & Aug 35seats P Last dinner9.30pm Lunch£9.80alc Dinner£9.80alc Wine£2.80 Credit cards 3 5

OLD GRIMSBY Tresco Isles of Scilly (No map)
★★★**The Island** ☎Scillonia22883
Attractive hotel of stone and timber situated in own sub-tropical gardens and facing sea dotted with rocky islets.
Closed 13Oct–Feb 37rm(29⇌⋔) ⚑ CTV TV available in bedrooms ✈ ⚓ ⛆(heated) ⛳ ♔ ♉International. Last dinner8.30pm ♔ ☕ S% ✱sB&B£10–£16 sB&B⇌⋔£11.75–£17.75 dB&B£20–£32 dB&B⇌⋔£23.50–£38.50 Lunch fr£4.75 Dinner fr£7.72&alc Wine£3.30 Credit cards 1 2 3 4 5 6

OLDHAM Greater Manchester Map**7** SD90
✕✕**Inzievar Hotal** 5 Alexandra Rd ☎3830
Closed Sun, Bank Hols, Last wk Jun & 1st wk Jul Dinner not served Mon 65seats 10P ✂ Last dinner9.30pm ✱Lunch£3.50&alc Dinner£6.50alc Credit cards 1 2 3 5

O

OLD SODBURY Avon Map**3** ST78
★★Cross Hands ☎Chipping Sodbury313000
15rm(4⇌ ⋒) CTV in bedrooms 200P Mainly grills Last dinner10.30pm S% *sB&B fr£8.25 sB&B⇌⋒ fr£13 dB&B fr£15.30 dB&B⇌⋒ fr£18.50 Continental breakfast Lunch£2.09–£4.49 Dinner£2.09–£4.49 Wine£2.19 Credit cards 1 2 3 5

OLLERTON Nottinghamshire Map**8** SK66
★*Hop Pole* ☎Mansfield822573
Ivy-covered coaching inn.
10rm(⇌⋒) CTV 30P Last dinner9.30pm

OLNEY Buckinghamshire Map**4** SP85
XXFour Pillars 60 High St ☎Bedford711563
50seats 10P English, French & Italian. Last dinner10.30pm S% *Lunch£2.50–£3.50&alc Dinner fr£3.50 Wine£3 Credit cards 1 3 5

OMBERSLEY Hereford & Worcester Map**3** SO86
XXCrown & Sandys Arms ☎Worcester620252
Closed Sun, Mon, 26Dec–2Jan; 50seats 200P Last dinner10pm S% Lunch fr£2.50 Dinner fr£5.95 Wine£2.40 Credit cards 1 5

ORFORD (near Woodbridge) Suffolk Map**5** TM44
★★Crown & Castle (Trusthouse Forte) ☎205
18th-C posting house with a history of smuggling.
10rm Annexe: 10⇌⋒ TV in bedrooms 20P Last dinner9pm S% sB&B£12 sB&B⇌⋒£15 dB&B£17.50 dB&B⇌⋒£20.50 Credit cards 1 2 3 4 5 6

XXKings Head Inn ☎271
Remarkable, two-storey medieval inn, in shadow of St Bartholomew's church.
Closed Mon (except Public Hols); 32seats 100P bedrooms available English & Continental. Last dinner9pm Lunch£6alc Dinner£6alc Wine£3.90 Credit card 5

XButley-Oysterage Market Hill ☎277
Closed Xmas; Dinner not served Jan & Feb; 48seats Last dinner8.30pm S% Lunch£1.85–£6.50 High Tea£1.85–£6.50 Dinner£1.85–£6.50

OSWESTRY Salop Map**7** SJ22
★★★Wynnstay Church St (Trusthouse Forte) ☎5261
31rm(17⇌⋒) 70P Last dinner9.30pm S% sB&B£12 sB&B⇌⋒£14 dB&B£17 dB&B⇌⋒£20.50 *xmas* Credit cards 1 2 3 4 5 6

OTTERBURN Northumberland Map**12** NY89
★★★Percy Arms (Swallow) ☎20261 Telex no53168
32rm(15⇌⋒) CTV 50P Last dinner8.45pm S% sB&B£9.90–£12.55 sB&B⇌⋒£12.10–£15.45 dB&B£15.40–£22.20 dB&B⇌⋒£19.25–£25.80 *xmas* Credit cards 1 2 3 5

★★Otterburn Tower (Scottish & Newcastle) ☎20673
15rm(2⇌⋒) CTV 40P Last dinner8.30pm sB&B£7.65 dB&B£13.60–£15 dB&B⇌⋒£15 Continental breakfast Lunch£2.50&alc Tea35–70p High Tea£1.20 Dinner£3.10&alc Wine£1.95 Credit cards 1 2 3 5 6

OTTERY ST MARY Devon Map**3** SY19
★★★Salston (Best Western) ☎2310 Telex no42856
Country house of historical and architectural interest, standing in six acres of grounds.
23rm(12⇌⋒) 1 CTV in bedrooms 100P (heated) squash sauna bath Live music & dancing Sat French. Last dinner8.30pm sB&B£12.70–£14.70 sB&B⇌⋒£15.90–£17.90 dB&b£25.40–£29.40 dB&B⇌⋒£29.80–£33.80 Lunch£4&alc Tea30p Dinner£5.20–£5.45&alc Wine£3 *xmas* Credit cards 1 2 3 4 5 6

XXLodge Silver St ☎2356
Closed Mon, 1 wk Nov & 3 wks Jan/Feb; 20seats English & Continental. Last dinner9.30pm Lunch£7alc Dinner£7alc Wine£2.40

XXSalston Cellars (Salston Hotel) ☎2310
Closed Sun, Mon & 13–28Jan; 26seats 100P bedrooms available Live music & dancing Sat French. Last dinner10pm *Lunch£1–£4&alc Dinner£6.50alc Wine£3 Credit cards 1 2 3 4 5 6

OULTON West Yorkshire Map**8** SE32
☆☆☆Leeds Crest Motel The Grove ☎Leeds826201
40⇌⋒ CTV in bedrooms 136P 4 Last dinner10.30pm S% *sB&B⇌⋒£16.25 dB&B⇌⋒£22.78 Continental breakfast Credit cards 1 2 3 4 5 6

OUNDLE Northamptonshire Map**4** TL08
★★Talbot New St (Anchor) ☎3621
Period stone and slate building with original coaching entrance.
21rm(16⇌⋒) CTV in bedrooms 60P English & French. Last dinner9.30pm S% *sB&B fr£10.85 sB&B⇌⋒ fr£15 dB&B fr£18.50 dB&B⇌⋒ fr£22 Lunch£2.45–£3.50&alc Tea30p Dinner£3.75–£4.50&alc Wine£2.60 *xmas* Credit cards 1 2 3 4 5 6

OVERSTRAND Norfolk Map**9** TG24
★Overstrand Court High St ☎282
Country house designed by Lutyens; set in 2½ acres of woodland.
18rm(4⇌⋒) CTV TV available in bedrooms 50P International. Last dinner9.30pm

O

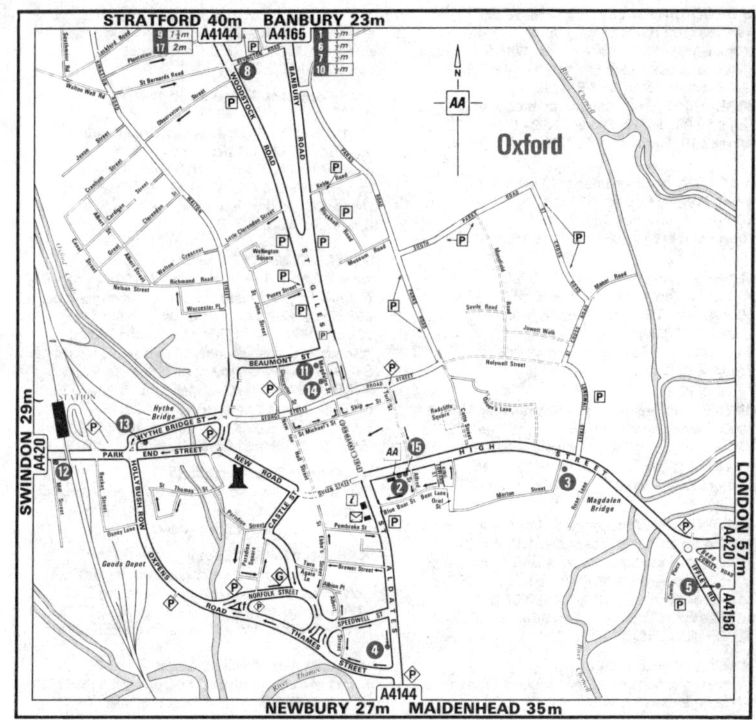

1 Cotswold Lodge ★★
2 Bleu Blanc Rouge ✕
3 Eastgate ★★
4 Elizabeth ❀❀✕✕
5 Isis ★★
6 Linton Lodge ★★★
7 Lotus House ✕
8 Luna Caprese ✕
9 Oxford Europa Lodge ☆☆☆
10 Les Quat'Saisons ❀❀✕
11 Randolph ★★★★
12 River ⊕
13 Royal Oxford ★★★
14 Saraceno ✕✕✕
15 La Sorbonne ❀❀✕✕
16 Soundings ✕✕
17 TraveLodge ☆☆☆

sB&B£9.34–£11.94 sB&B⇌⋒£10.74–£13.14 dB&B£18.68–£23.88 dB&B⇌⋒£21.48–£26.28 Lunch£2.40&alc Tea80p&alc High Tea£1.50&alc Dinner£3.24&alc Wine£2.40 ⊓ *xmas*

OVINGTON Northumberland Map**12** NZ06
★★Highlander Inn ☎Prudhoe32016
5rm(2⇌⋒) Annexe: 12⇌⋒ ⌘ CTV 25P ⚓ ♡French. Last dinner9pm ✪ sB&B£6.48 sB&B⇌⋒£7.56 dB&B£11.88 dB&B⇌⋒£12.96 Lunch£4.50alc Dinner£7.30–£9&alc Wine£2.95 ⊓ Credit card⑤

OWER Hampshire Map**4** SU31
☆☆☆New Forest Lodge (Grand Met) ☎333
43⇌⋒ ☽ TV available in bedrooms 100P ⚓ Conference facilities available ♡English & French. Last dinner9.30pm ♫ S%
✻sB&B⇌⋒£12–£13.50 dB&B⇌⋒£16–£18.50 ⊓ *xmas* Credit cards①②③④⑤⑥

OXFORD Oxfordshire Map**4** SP50 **See plan**
★★★★Randolph Beaumont Sq (Trusthouse Forte) ☎47481 Telex no83446 Plan**11**
Large, mid-Victorian building in Gothic style with pointed gables and lancet and dormer windows.
109⇌⋒ Lift ☽ ⌘ CTV in bedrooms 80⌂ Conference facilities available Last dinner10.15pm ✪ ♫ S% sB&B⇌⋒£23 dB&B⇌⋒£32.50 ⊓ *xmas* Credit cards①②③④⑤⑥

★★★Linton Lodge Linton Rd, Park Town (Myddleton & Best Western) ☎53461 Plan**6**
73rm(65⇌⋒) Lift ☽ ⌘ CTV in bedrooms 40P ⚓ ♡English & French. Last dinner9.45pm ✪ ♫ S% sB&B£14.50 sB&B⇌⋒£18.30 dB&B£21 dB&B⇌⋒£27 Continental breakfast Lunch£4.75–£6.25 Dinner£5.50–£6.50&alc Wine£3.25 ⊓ *xmas* Credit cards①②③⑤⑥

☆☆☆Oxford Europa Lodge Godstow Rd, Wolvercote Roundabout (Grand Met) ☎59933 Plan**9**
98⇌⋒ ☽ ⌘ TV available in bedrooms 180P ⚓ Live music Mon, Wed & Fri Conference facilities available ♡French. Last dinner9.45pm ✪ ♫ S%
✻sB&B⇌⋒£14 dB&B⇌⋒£21 ⊓ *xmas* Credit cards①②③④⑤⑥

★★★Royal Oxford Park End St (Embassy) ☎48432 Plan**13**
23rm(10⇌⋒) ☽ ⌘ CTV TV in bedrooms ⚑ Last dinner9pm ✪ S% sB&B£11.50 sB&B⇌⋒£15.50 dB&B£18.50 dB&B⇌⋒£22 Lunch£4.50&alc Dinner£5&alc Wine£4.50 ⊓ Credit cards①②③④⑤⑥

☆☆☆TraveLodge Pear Tree roundabout (junc A34/A43) (Trusthouse Forte) ☎54301 Telex no83202 Plan**17**
102⇌⋒ ⌘ CTV in bedrooms 80P ⚓ ⊡(heated) ♿ S% sB&B⇌⋒£14 dB&B⇌⋒£20 Continental breakfast ⊓ Credit cards①②③④⑤⑥

★★**Cotswold Lodge** 66A Banbury Rd ☎512121 Plan**1**
46rm(28⇌ ⋒) ☽ ⋈ CTV CTV in bedrooms ⊘ 60P Live music & dancing Sat ⊕ English, French & Greek. Last dinner 11pm S% ✱sB&B⇌ ⋒ £18 dB&B⇌ ⋒ £26 Lunch £3.78&alc Dinner £3.19&alc *xmas* Credit cards 1 2 3 5 6

★★**Eastgate** The High, Merton St (Anchor) ☎48244 Telex no 858875 Plan**3**
Late 19th-C building with overhanging leaded bay windows.
45rm(20⇌ ⋒) Lift ☽ ⋈ CTV CTV in bedrooms 30P ⊕ English & Continental. Last dinner 10pm S% ✱sB&B fr£11.50 sB&B⇌ ⋒ fr£16 dB&B fr£19.50 dB&B⇌ ⋒ fr£25 Lunch fr£2.75&alc Dinner fr£3.75&alc Wine £2.65 *xmas* Credit cards 1 2 3 4 5 6

★★**Isis** 47–53 Iffley Rd ☎48894 Plan**5**
35rm(6⇌ ⋒) ⋈ CTV 15P 8 Last dinner 8.30pm sB&B £10.50–£11.50 sB&B⇌ ⋒ £16–£17 dB&B £19–£20 dB&B⇌ ⋒ £22 Lunch £2.50–£3 Tea 75–95p High Tea £2.50–£2.95 Dinner £5–£5.50 Wine £3.15 Credit cards 1 3

River 17 Botley Rd ☎43475 Plan**12**
Closed Xmas & New Year; 18rm(4⇌ ⋒) ⋈ CTV 20P Last dinner 8pm sB&B fr£9 dB&B fr£17 dB&B⇌ ⋒ fr£20 dinner fr£3 Wine £3

✕✕✕**Saraceno** 15 Magdalen St ☎49171 Plan**14**
Italian restaurant, designed by Apicella, in cool, modern basement; tiled floor, white murals and original paintings.
Closed Sun; 100 seats ⊕ Italian. Last dinner 11.30pm Lunch £5.50alc Dinner £7.50alc Wine £3.10 Credit cards 1 3 5

✕✕**Elizabeth** 84 St Aldates ☎42230 Plan**4**
Antonio Lopez's efforts continue to succeed in providing excellent food in this attractive restaurant. Service is pleasant, particularly by the two Spanish waiters who have been here for so long. There can be delays but the fault lies with the kitchen's desire to cook to order and serve the food at its best
Dishes that never fail to please are the taramasalata, quenelles and Ittoro amongst the first courses, and l'entrecôte maison, entrecôte au poivre vert, poulet au Porto and casserole of quails amongst the main ones. Of the puddings, the sorbet au Champagne was lauded. The extensive wine has an excellent selection of château-bottled clarets as well as many other interesting items.
Closed Mon; Lunch not served; 35 seats ⊕ Spanish. Last dinner 11pm Credit card 6

✕✕**La Sorbonne** 130A High St ☎41320 Plan**15**
This simple but pleasing restaurant has a very French atmosphere and this French authenticity is carried through to the cooking. One must give the usual warning that it is the first-floor restaurant rather than the ground-floor bistro that we refer to – an occasional member still chooses the wrong room with consequent bewilderment.
M Chavagnon, the owner, supervises his kitchen skillfully and all his specialities are well worth sampling, particularly the game dishes in season – râble de lievre au poivrade was praised, as was the breast of wild duck with Armagnac. Quails, sea trout and entrecôte Bordelaise have also pleased, though quenelles de brochet have been found variable. Fruit tarts and soufflés are generally very good and an apple and calvados soufflé was perfect.
The wine list, mostly of French wines, is good – particularly strong on clarets and finer burgundies.
Closed Sun, last wk Aug & 1st wk Sep; 45 seats ⊕ French. Last dinner 10.30pm ✱Lunch £9alc Dinner £9alc Wine £4 Credit cards 2 5

O

✕✕***Soundings*** Elsfield Way ☎53191 Plan**16**
Closed Mon; Lunch not served Sun; 35seats
English & French. Last dinner11pm
✕**Bleu Blanc Rouge** 129A High St ☎42883 Plan**2**
Closed Tue, last wk Jul & 1st wk Aug; 60seats
French. Last dinner10.30pm ✻Lunch£3
Dinner£5.40 Wine£3.50 Credit cards 2 5
✕**Lotus House** 197 Banbury Rd, Park Town ☎54239 Plan**7**
Closed 25& 26Dec; 70seats Cantonese & Pekinese; Last dinner11.45pm
✻Lunch£1.20–£4.50&alc Dinner£2–£10&alc
Wine£3.30 Credit cards 2 3 5 6
✕***Luna Caprese*** 4 North Pde ☎54812 Plan**8**
Closed Xmas & Good Fri; 55seats Italian.
Last dinner11.30pm Credit cards 2 3
✕**Opium Den** 79 George St ☎48680 Not on plan
150seats Chinese. Last dinner11.45pm
Lunch£1.25alc Dinner£3alc Wine£2
Credit cards 1 2 3 5

✻✻✕**Les Quat' Saisons** 272 Banbury Rd, Summertown ☎53540 Plan**10**
Awarded a rosette in its first year of operation, this is indeed a rising star in the firmament of restaurants. Owned and run by a young Frenchman, Raymond Blanc, who cooks, and his English wife, Jenny, it is a simple restaurant in a parade of shops at Summertown and near the local radio station.
There is an à la carte menu containing a comprehensive selection of dishes, but complementing it is a page of daily dishes and it is here that you find the very fresh fish dishes and other seasonable items. M. Blanc's cooking is delicate and refined, sometimes to the point of blandness, but generally there is plenty of flavour to delight you. The fish dishes, whether to start or as a main dish, are consistently good, and entrecôte au poivre vert, poularde aux morilles and escalope de veau à la crême were popular. Vegetables and puddings are not neglected and a perfect soufflé has been reported as well as a very good feuilleté aux poires.
The wine list is not large – about 60 – but wines are well chosen and the lesser ones are very reasonably priced.
Closed Sun, Mon, Etr, 24Dec–6Jan & 15Jul–7Aug; 48seats French.
Last dinner10pm S% Lunch£2.50–£3&alc
Dinner£12.50alc Wine£3.20 Credit cards 3 4

OXTED Surrey Map**5** TQ35
★★**Hoskins** S ation Road West ☎2338
Gatwick plan**11**
10 CTV CTV in bedrooms 30P
Last dinner9.30pm S% sB&B£17
dB&B£24 Lunch£4–£5 Dinner£4–£5
Wine£2.50 Credit cards 1 2 3 5
✕***Golden Bengal*** 51 Station Rd East ☎7373
46seats Indian. Last dinner mdnt

PADSTOW Cornwall Map**2** SW97
★★★**Metropole** Station Road (Trusthouse Forte) ☎532486
42rm(33) CTV TV in bedrooms 40P
Last dinner8.30pm S% sB&B£13.50
sB&B£16.50 dB&B£20.50 dB&B£30
Credit cards 1 2 3 4 5 6
★★**Gulland Rock** North Quay ☎532369
Closed Oct–Mar; 30rm(9) CTV 50P
Last dinner8.30pm S%
sB&B£6.25–£9.25 sB&B£7.25–£10.25
dB&B£12.50–£18.50 dB&B£14.50–£20.50
Tea60p–£1.50 High Tea£1.25–£1.50
Dinner£3.75–£4 Wine£3.25
Credit cards 1 2 3 4 5 6

★★**Old Custom House Inn** South Quay ☎532359
13⇌ ⫙ ꟿ CTV ℙ Live music wkly Last dinner10pm
♔ ✻sB&B⇌⫙£9–£10 dB&B⇌⫙£14.50–£18
Lunch£3.25alc Dinner£5.50alc Wine£2.52
Credit cards ③ ⑥

★**Dinas** ☎532326
Overlooking Padstow and river estuary.
Closed Oct–Mar; 27rm(3⇌⫙) CTV 50P ⇻ ⚓ ⌂
Last dinner8.15pm ♔ ⚲ sB&B£6–£8
sB&B⇌⫙£6.80–£8.80 dB&B£12–£16
dB&B⇌⫙£13.60–£17.60 Lunch£2–£2.50
Tea30–60p Dinner£4–£4.50 Wine£1.60

✕**Blue Lobster** North Quay ☎532451
40seats ℙ Last dinner9.30pm Lunch£5.50alc
Dinner£8.50alc Wine£3.50

✕**Seafood** ☎532485
Closed Sun (except Jul & Aug) & mid-Oct–Good Fri;
Lunch not served; 60seats ℙ ☋English & French.
Last dinner9.45pm Dinner£7alc Wine£2.90
Credit cards ① ③

PAIGNTON Devon Map**3** SX86
★★★**Palace** Esplanade Rd (Trusthouse Forte)
☎555121
55rm(43⇌⫙) Lift ☽ ꟿ CTV TV in bedrooms 67P ⚓
⇌(heated) ⚫(hard) Conference facilities available
Last dinner8.45pm ♔ ⚲ S% sB&B£13.50
sB&B⇌⫙£17.50 dB&B£22.50 dB&B⇌⫙£28
⍐ *xmas* Credit cards ① ② ③ ④ ⑤ ⑥

★★★**Redcliffe** Marine Pde ☎556224
Unusual mid-Victorian building overlooking sea, with

P

central tower, pinnacles and battlements. Four acres of grounds; small private beach.
68rm(55⇌⋒) Lift ☽ ꟷ CTV 70P 7🏠 ✥ ⛳ ⊐(heated) ⚬(hard) Live music & dancing twice wkly ♧ Last dinner8.30pm ♧ ⚐ S% sB&B£10.50–£12.50 sB&B⇌⋒£11–£14 dB&B£21–£25 dB&B⇌⋒£22–£28 Lunch£3.50–£4&alc Dinner£4.50–£5&alc ⛿ *xmas* Credit card 2

★★Hunters Lodge Roundham Rd, Goodrington ☎557034
Closed Nov–Mar; 32rm CTV 40P 4🏠 Last dinner7.30pm ⚐ S% sB&B£8.50–£9.50 sB&B⇌⋒£9–£10 dB&B£16.50–£19 dB&B⇌⋒£18–£23 Bar lunch50p–£1 Tea50p–£1 Dinner£2.90–£3.90 Wine£2.90

★★St Annes Alta Vista Rd, Goodrington ☎557360
Closed Nov–Mar; 26rm(12⇌⋒) CTV 26P ⊐(heated) sauna bath Disco twice wkly ♀English & French. Last dinner6.15pm S% sB&B£7.20–£9 sB&B⇌⋒£8.45–£10.50 dB&B£14.40–£18 dB&B⇌⋒£17.30–£21 Dinner£4–£6 Wine£2.50 ⛿ Credit cards 1 3

★Alta Vista Alta Vista Rd, Roundham ☎551496
Closed 5Oct–Mar; 28rm(14⇌⋒) CTV ✥ 28P ⛳ Live music £ dancing twice wkly Last dinner7.30pm ♧ ⚐ sB&B£9–£12 sB&B⇌⋒£11–£14 dB&B£16–£20 dB&B⇌⋒£18–£24 Lunch£1–£2.50 Tea50p–£1.50 Dinner£4.50–£6.50 Wine£2.60 Credit cards 1 3

★Danethorpe 23 St Andrew's Rd ☎551251
Closed Nov & Mar; 12rm(1⇌⋒) ꟷ CTV 8P

P

Lastdinner6.30pm ♔ S% sB&B£6–£7 dB&B£12–£14 dB&B⇌⋒£14–£16 Dinner£3.80alc ⛿ *xmas*

★**Oldway Links** 21 Southfield Rd ☎559332 Closed Oct–Mar; 20rm 🍽 CTV 20P ⚓ Lastdinner7.30pm ♔ ♕ S% sB&B£7.25–£9 dB&B£14.50–£18 Lunch£1.75 Tea60p Dinner£3.50 Wine£2.25

★**Sunhill** Alta Vista Rd, Goodrington ☎557532 Closed Oct–Mar; 22rm CTV 14P ⚓ Lastdinner6.30pm S% sB&B£5.40–£6.48 dB&B£10.50–£12.96 Barlunch70p Tea70p Dinner£2.50 Wine£2.45 ⛿ *xmas*

☆**Torbay Holiday Motel** Totnes Rd ☎558226 66⇌⋒ 🍽 CTV CTV available in bedrooms 100P ⚓ ⇌(heated) Live music & dancing twice wkly ♡English & French. Lastdinner10pm S% dB&B⇌⋒fr£15.87 Credit card 1

PAINSWICK Gloucestershire Map**3** SO80
★★★**Cranham Wood** Kemps Ln ☎812160
Stone constructed country house with good restaurant.
18rm(9⇌⋒) 🍽 CTV CTV in bedrooms 30P ⚓ Lastdinner9.30pm ♔ ♕ sB&B£14 dB&B£22 dB&B⇌⋒£26 Continental breakfast Lunch£5.50&alc Tea£1.20 Dinner£5.50&alc Wine£3.50 ⛿ *xmas* Credit cards 1 2 3 5

✕**Country Elephant** ☎813564
Closed Mon, 1wk Etr, 1wk Xmas, & 3wks Oct–Nov; Lunch not served Tue–Sat; Dinner not served Sun; 36seats ⚑ Lastdinner10.30pm S% Lunch£4 Dinner£7alc Wine£2.95 Credit cards 2 3 5

PANGBOURNE Berkshire Map**4** SU67
★★★**Copper Inn** ☎2244
Formerly a posting house in the 19th century, situated near the Thames.
21⇌⋒ CTV in bedrooms ⊘ 29P ⚓ ♡English & French. Lastdinner10pm ♔ S% sB&B⇌⋒fr£19.50 dB&B⇌⋒£26.50 Lunch£2.50&alc Dinner£6alc Wine£2.50 ⛿ Credit cards 1 2 3 5

PARBOLD Lancashire Map**7** SD41
★★**Lindley** Lancaster Ln (Whitbread) ☎2804
10⇌⋒ 🍽 TV available in bedrooms 50P ⚓ ♡English & French. Lastdinner9.45pm ♔ S% sB&B⇌⋒fr£13.20 dB&B⇌⋒fr£17.80 Lunch£4alc Dinner£5.50alc Wine£2.65 Credit card 3

PARKGATE Cheshire Map**7** SJ27
★★**Parkgate** Boathouse Ln ☎051–3365101
RS Etr & Xmas; 24⇌⋒ 🍽 CTV CTV in bedrooms 100P ⚓ Live music Tue–Thur ♡English & French. Lastdinner9pm S% sB&B⇌⋒£6–£10 dB&B⇌⋒£12–£17 Lunch£1.80–£3 Dinner£3.50&alc ⛿ Credit cards 1 2 3 5

★★**Ship** The Parade (Anchor) ☎051–3363931 Telex no 858875
19⇌⋒ ☽ 🍽 CTV available in bedrooms ⊘ 100P Lastdinner9pm ♔ ♕ S% ✱sB&B⇌⋒fr&14.50 dB&B⇌⋒fr£22 Lunch fr£4&alc Dinner fr£4.20&alc Wine£2.65 ⛿ Credit cards 1 2 3 4 5 6

PARK GATE Hampshire Map**4** SU50
✕**Caborns** Park Lodge ☎Locksheath2614
54seats 30P bedrooms available ♡English & French. Lastdinner10.30pm ✱Lunch£5alc Dinner£7alc Wine£2.10 Credit cards 1 3 5

PATTERDALE Cumbria Map**11** NY31
★★**Patterdale** ☎Glenridding231
Lies at the foot of the Kirkstone Pass, facing Lake Ullswater and was once popular with the poet Wordsworth.
Closed Nov–Mar; 53rm(24⇌⋒) Annexe:6rm CTV ⊘ 50P 1🏠 ⚓ ↳ Lastdinner7.30pm ♔ ✱sB&B£7.35 sB&B⇌⋒£8.75 dB&B£14.70 dB&B⇌⋒£17.50 Lunch£2.85 Dinner£4 Wine£2.55 Credit card 2

PELYNT Cornwall Map**2** SX25
★★***Jubilee Inn*** ☎Lanreath312
A charming inn that has been completely modernised.
12rm(3⇌⋒) 🍽 CTV 50P 6🏠 Lastdinner9pm ♔

PENCRAIG Hereford & Worcester Map**3** SO52
★★**Pencraig Court** ☎Llangarron306
Closed Nov–Mar; 12rm(5⇌⋒) 1⊟ 🍽 CTV available in bedrooms ⊘ 25P 1🏠 ⚓ ♡English & French. Lastdinner8pm ♔ ♕ S% sB&B£10–£11.50 sB&B⇌⋒£11.50–£13 dB&B£16–£20 dB&B⇌⋒£19–£23 Barlunch fr£2 Tea fr£1 Dinner fr£6 Wine£2.50 Credit cards 1 3

PENDOGGETT Cornwall Map**2** SX07
★★**Cornish Arms** ☎Port Isaac263
7rm(1⇌⋒) 🍽 CTV ⊘ 50P ⚓ Live music & dancing Sun Children under 14 yrs not accommodated ♿ Last dinner 8.45pm in winter 9.30pm in summer ♔ ✱sB&B£15.18–£18.33 sB&B⇌⋒£16.13–£19.30 dB&B£20.88–£24.04 dB&B⇌⋒£22.78–£25.94 Lunch£3.45alc Dinner£6alc Wine£3.04 Credit cards 1 2 3 5

PENN STREET Buckinghamshire Map**4** SU99
✕✕***Hit or Miss*** ☎Holmer Green3109
Pleasant old coaching inn.
Closed Mon; Dinner not served Sun; 36seats 70P ♡International. Lastdinner9.30pm

P

PENPILLICK Cornwall Map**2** SX05
★★**Penpillick House** ☎Par2742
Small Georgian house standing 300ft above sea level with commanding views of St. Austell Bay and Luxulyan Valley.
11rm(5⇌⋒) ⊞ CTV 60P ⚓ ⊐(heated) ♂ ⚘(hard) ♡English & French. Last dinner10pm ✿ ⊥ S% ✱sB&B£7.30–£8.10 dB&B£14.60–£16.20 dB&B⇌⋒£16.50–£18.35 Lunch fr£3.75 Tea fr£2 Dinner fr£4.20&alc Wine£2.40 *xmas*

PENRITH Cumbria Map**12** NY53
See also **Edenhall**

★★***Clifton Hill*** Clifton (2¾m S A6) ☎62717
25⇌⋒ ⊞ TV 200P 25⌂ ⚓ Last dinner8.30pm ✿ ⊥ Credit card③

★★**George** Devonshire St ☎62696
31⇌⋒ ☽ CTV 30P Last dinner8.30pm ✿ ⊥ S% sB&B⇌⋒£8.50–£9.50 dB&B⇌⋒£18.50 Lunch£3 Tea£1.25 Dinner£4 Wine£2.80 ⚑

★★**Old Mansion House** Eamont Bridge (1m S A6) ☎65628
10rm ⊞ CTV TV available in bedrooms ⊘ 60P 4⌂ ⚡ Last dinner10pm ✿ ⊥ S% sB&B£10.62 dB&B£16.52 Lunch£4.20 Tea£1 Dinner£5alc Wine£2.50 ⚑ *xmas*

★★**Round Thorne Country** Beacon Edge ☎63952
Hillside Victorian house in own grounds with good mountain views.
6rm Annexe:7⇌⋒ ⊞ CTV 200P 2⌂ ⚓ ↬ Live music & dancing Fri–Sun ♣ ♿ Last dinner mdnt ✿ ⊥ sB&B£9.50 sB&B⇌⋒£9.50 dB&B£12–£15 dB&B⇌⋒£12–£15 Lunch£2.50&alc Tea£1–£2.50&alc High Tea£2–£3&alc Dinner£4–£5.50&alc Wine£2.50 ⚑ *xmas*
Credit cards①②③⑤

★★***Royal Hussar*** King St ☎64444
27rm(5⇌⋒) ⊞ CTV TV available in bedrooms 50P 10⌂ ♡English & French. Last dinner9pm ⊥ ✿ ⚑ Credit cards②③⑤

★★***Strickland*** Corney Sq ☎62262
Closed Xmas & New Year's Eve; 17rm(3⇌⋒) ⊞ CTV 13P Last dinner8pm ⊥ ✿ ⚑

★★**Waverley** Crown Sq ☎63962
7rm(1⇌⋒) ⊞ CTV 30P ⚡ Last dinner8pm ✿ S% sB&B fr£7.50 sB&B⇌⋒ fr£8.50 dB&B fr£14.50 dB&B⇌⋒ fr£15.75 Lunch fr£2.75 Dinner fr£3.75 ⚑ Credit cards①③

★***Abbotsford*** Wordsworth St ☎63940
Situated beneath the wooded Penrith Beacon.
10rm TV 10P ♡English & Italian. Last dinner9.30pm Credit card③

★***Carlton*** 38 Victoria Rd ☎62691
9rm ⊞ TV 12P 6⌂ ⚓ ♡English & Continental. Last dinner8.30pm ✿ Credit card①

★**Glen Cottage** Corney Sq ☎62221
White, stucco-faced cottage of charm and character, built in 1756 as three houses.
7rm(2⇌⋒) ⊞ CTV 3⌂ ⚡ Last dinner9pm ✿ sB&B fr£7 sB&B⇌⋒ fr8 dB&B fr£13 dB&B⇌⋒ fr£16 Lunch£2–£3 Dinner£2.75–£4 ⚑ Credit cards①②③⑤⑥

★**Old Victoria** 46 Castlegate ☎62467
9rm CTV 12P ♡English & Continental. Last dinner9pm ✿ S% sB&B£7–£8 dB&B£15–£16 Lunch£2.50–£4 Dinner£5.25–£8 Wine£3.50

★***Station*** Castlegate ☎62072
20rm CTV 10P 5⌂ Last dinner8pm ⊥ ✿

PENSHURST Kent Map**5** TQ54
★★**Leicester Arms** (Whitbread) ☎870551
A 17th-century inn located in picturesque village.
7⇌⋒ ⊞ TV in bedrooms ⊘ 30P ♡French. Last dinner9.30pm S% ✱sB&B⇌⋒£11.33 dB&B⇌⋒£19.08 Lunch£2.50–£4&alc Dinner£5alc Wine£2.60 ⚑
Credit cards①②③⑤⑥

PENZANCE Cornwall Map**2** SW43
★★★**Queens** The Promenade ☎2371
The hotel stands on the sea front offering exceptional views over Mounts Bay.
80rm(50⇌⋒) Lift ☽ ⊞ CTV TV available in bedrooms 150P Last dinner8.30pm ✿ ⊥ sB&B£9.50 sB&B⇌⋒£13.50 dB&B£19 dB&B⇌⋒£27 Credit cards①②③⑤

★★**Minalto** Alexandra Rd ☎2923
Closed Nov–Mar 10rm ⊞ CTV ⊘ 10P ⚡ ♡English & Continental. Last dinner8pm ✿ ⊥ S% sB&B£7.93 dB&B£15.86 Lunch£3.50&alc Tea£1.25&alc Dinner£4&alc Wine£2.90

★★**Mount Prospect** Britons Hill ☎3117
Conversion of two granite, three-storey houses overlooking sea.
29rm(8⇌⋒) ☽ CTV in bedrooms ⊘ 6P Live music & dancing Fri (summer) Last dinner8.30pm ✿ sB&B£9.18–£9.72 sB&B⇌⋒£10.53–£11.34 dB&B£18.36–£19.44 dB&B⇌⋒£21.06–£22.68 Lunch£3.53 Dinner£5.67 Wine£3.25 ⚑ *xmas*
Credit cards①②③⑥

★★***Union*** Chapel St ☎2319
30rm ⊞ CTV 10P 2/⌂ Last dinner8.15pm ⊥ ✿ Credit cards①②③

★**Chypons** Newlyn ☎2123
Fine views over Mounts Bay and Newlyn Harbour.
Closed Xmas Day; 14rm ⊞ CTV 20P ⚡ ⚓ Last dinner6.30pm ⊥ ✿

★**Pentrea** Alexandra Rd ☎2711
Closed Nov & Dec RS Jan–Mar 8rm ⊞ CTV 1⌂ ⚡ Children under 5yrs not accommodated Last dinner7pm ✿ S% sB&B£6.90–£7.45 dB&B£13–£14.50 Dinner£3.15–£3.80 Wine£2 Credit cards①③⑥

★**Yacht Inn** The Promenade ☎2787
Closed Dec & Jan 8rm CTV 8P ⚡ sauna bath Children under 5yrs not accommodated Last dinner8pm ✿ S% sB&B£6.61–£8.05 dB&B£13.22–£16.10 Lunch£2.50–£4 Dinner£3.50–£5 Wine£2.13

✕✕**Le Tarot** 19 Quay St ☎3118
Closed Sun & Jan Lunch not served 50seats ♡French. Last dinner10.25pm ✱Dinner£5.85alc Wine£1.80 Credit cards①③④⑥

PERRANARWORTHAL Cornwall Map**2** SW73
★★**Goonvrea** ☎Devoran863330
Georgian mansion, now hotel/country club. Standing in twelve acres of grounds.
14rm(1⇌⋒) 1⊟ ⊞ CTV ⊘ 60P ⚓ Live music & dancing Fri ♣ ♡English & French. Last dinner8pm ✿ ⊥ sB&B£11.50–£13 sB&B⇌⋒£12–£13.50 dB&B£24–£27 dB&B⇌⋒£25–£28 Lunch£5.25alc Tea25p–£1 High Tea£1.50–£3 Dinner£2–£8&alc Wine£1.50 ⚑ *xmas*
Credit cards①③

PERSHORE Hereford & Worcester Map**3** SO94
★★**Angel Inn** ☎2046
19rm(8⇌⋒) ⊞ CTV 60P ⚡ ⚓ ↬ Last dinner10pm ✿ sB&B fr£9.50 sB&B⇌⋒ fr£11 dB&B fr£16.75 dB&B⇌⋒ fr£17.75 Lunch fr£2 Dinner fr£4.75 Wine£3 ⚑ Credit cards①②③⑤

P

★★**Manor House** Bridge St ☎2713
3rm 🛏TV 40P 🐕 English & French.
Last dinner9.30pm S% sB&B£8.50
dB&B£17 Bar lunch75p–£4 wine£3
Credit cards 1 2 3 5

X***Zhivago's*** 22 Bridge S ☎3828
Closed Sun; 48seats English, French & Italian.
Last dinner10.30pm Credit cards 1 2 3 5

PETERBOROUGH Cambridgeshire Map**4** TL19
★★★**Great Northern** Station Rd (British Transport)
☎52331
50rm(26⇌🚿) 🛏TV in bedrooms 10P English & French. Last dinner8.30pm S%
*sB&B⇌🚿 fr£20.25 dB&B⇌🚿 fr£27.45
Wine£2.95 Credit cards 1 2 3 4 5 6

★★**Bull** Wes gate ☎61364
Former coaching inn with 17th-C façade. Extensive modernisation to ground floor and many rooms.
130rm(64⇌🚿) 🛏CTV 100P English & French.
Last dinner10.30pm S% *sB&B£9.99
sB&B⇌🚿£13.99 dB&B£14.85 dB&B⇌🚿£19.98
Lunch fr£3.51 Dinner fr£3.89 Wine£2.95
Credit cards 1 2 3 5

At **Norman Cross** (6m SW junc A1/A15)
☆☆**Peterborough Crest Motel** Great North Road (Crest) ☎Peterborough240209
40⇌🚿 80P

PETERLEE Co Durham Map**12** NZ44
★★★**Norseman** Bede Way (Open House) ☎862161
26⇌🚿 Lift 🛏TV in bedrooms 50P Disco twice wkly ♿ Last dinner9.45pm S%
*sB&B⇌🚿£14 dB&B⇌🚿£15.35–£21
Lunch£1–£2&alc Dinner£3.55–£3.95&alc
Wine£2.75 Credit cards 1 2 3 4 5

PETERSFIELD Hampshire Map**4** SU72
★★***Concorde*** Weston Rd ☎3442
RS Xmas Day; 12rm 🛏CTV 10P English, French & Italian. Last dinner9.30pm
Credit cards 1 3 5

★★**Red Lion** 3 College St ☎3025
12rm(2⇌🚿) 1 🛏CTV 30P Last dinner10pm
S% sB&B fr£9.75 sB&B⇌🚿 fr£14
dB&B fr£17.80 dB&B⇌🚿 fr£18.70
Lunch fr£3.50&alc Dinner fr£3.50&alc Wine£3.50
xmas Credit cards 1 2 3 4 5 6

X**Toby Jug** 22–26 Dragon St ☎3061
Closed Sun, Public Hols & 2wks May; Dinner not served; 50seats 15P Lunch£2.30–£6.50&alc
Tea25–75p&alc Wine£2.78

PETT BOTTOM Kent Map**5** TR15
X**Duck Inn** ☎Canterbury830354
Country inn nestling in hollow; has cosy dining room and wood fires.
Closed Mon, Tue, Xmas, 2wks Mar & 2wks Sep; 30seats 20P English & French.
Last dinner9.15pm S% Lunch£7–£8.50
Dinner£11alc Wine£3.50 Credit card 5

PETTY FRANCE Avon Map**3** ST78
★★**Petty France** ☎Didmarton361
Georgian, country house hotel set in 4½ acres of grounds.
Closed New Year's Day; 8⇌🚿 Annexe: 8⇌🚿 1 🛏
CTV in bedrooms 45P English & French.
Last dinner10pm S%
*sB&B⇌🚿£14–£14.80 dB&B⇌🚿£23–£27
Lunch£7alc Dinner£7alc Wine£3.95 *xmas*
Credit cards 1 2 3 5 6

PICKERING North Yorkshire Map**8** SE78
★★**Forest & Vale** ☎72722
17rm(5⇌🚿) Annexe: 6rm(2⇌🚿) 🛏 CTV 75P
Last dinner9pm sB&B£9 dB&B£18
dB&B⇌🚿£20 Lunch fr£3.50&alc
Dinner fr£4.50&alc Wine£4 *xmas*
Credit cards 1 3 6

PIDDLETRENTHIDE Dorset Map**3** SY79
★★**Old Bakehouse** ☎305
3⇌🚿 Annexe: 6⇌🚿 3 🛏TV in bedrooms 25P (heated) sauna bath Children under 12 yrs not accommodated English & French.
Last dinner9pm S% sB&B⇌🚿£11–£12
dB&B⇌🚿£16–£19 Dinner£6alc Wine£2.80
Credit card 3

PILLATON Cornwall Map**2** SX36
★★**Weary Friar** ☎St. Dominick50238
12th-C inn with oak beams and period furniture.
14⇌🚿 Lift 🛏CTV in bedrooms 60P Live music & dancing Fri Children under 5 yrs not accommodated International. Last dinner10pm
sB&B⇌🚿£13.25–£16.50 dB&B⇌🚿£26.50–£33
Lunch£4&alc Tea60p Dinner£5.75&alc
xmas Credit cards 1 2 3

PLAXTOL Kent Map**5** TQ65
XX**Forge** ☎446
16th-C forge converted into a German restaurant with a bar in the original hay-loft. On Thursday evenings (while customers are dining), blacksmiths make souvenir horseshoes.
Closed Mon; 54seats 25P International.
Last dinner10pm *Lunch£4.80&alc
Dinner£10.50alc Wine£4.25

PLUMLEY Cheshire Map**7** SJ77
XX***Golden Pheasant Inn*** Plumley Moor Rd ☎Lower Peover2261
Closed Mon; 97seats 90P Last dinner10pm
Credit cards 1 2 3

P

XXSmoker Inn Chester Rd ☎Lower Peover2338
Closed Mon; Dinner not served Sun; 80seats 100P
English & Continental. Lastdinner10pm
Lunch fr£3&alc Dinner fr£5&alc
Credit cards 1 2 3 5

PLYMOUTH Devon Map**2** SX45
☆☆☆☆**Holiday Inn** Armada Way (Commonwealth)
☎62866 Telex no45637
222⇌⋒ Lift ☽ ⊞ 🍽 CTV in bedrooms P (heated)
sauna bath Conference facilities available ♿
International. Lastdinner10.45pm
sB&B⇌⋒ fr£24.25 dB&B⇌⋒ fr£33 Lunch£3.95
Dinner fr£4.25&alc Wine£3.60 1 2 3 4 5

★★★**Duke of Cornwall** Millbay Rd (Best Western)
☎266256 Telex no45424
A splendid example of Victorian Gothic, built in heavy grey stone, with turrets, gables and wrought iron balconies.
RS 22–24 Dec; 70rm(46⇌⋒) Lift ☽ 🍽 CTV TV available in bedrooms 40P Disco Sat in winter Live music & dancing Sat Conference facilities available
English & French. Lastdinner9.45pm
S% sB&B fr£14 sB&B⇌⋒£15.50
dB&B fr£20.25 dB&B⇌⋒ fr£22.50
Lunch fr£4.50&alc Tea fr£1 Dinner fr£5&alc
Credit cards 1 2 3 5 6

☆☆☆**Mayflower Post House** Cliff Rd, The Hoe (Trusthouse Forte) ☎62828
104⇌⋒ Lift ☽ 🍽 CTV in bedrooms 149P (heated)
Lastdinner10.30pm S%
sB&B⇌⋒£20.75 dB&B⇌⋒£30 *xmas*
Credit cards 1 2 3 4 5 6

★★**Berni Grand** The Hoe (Berni) ☎61195
Large white-painted, five-storey building perched high on the Hoe overlooking sea.
76rm(26⇌⋒) Lift ☽ 🍽 CTV 20P Mainly grills.
Lastdinner11pm ✱sB&B£8.40 sB&B⇌⋒£11.90
dB&B£15.30 dB&B⇌⋒£19.75
Lunch£1.61–£4.23 Dinner£1.61–£4.23
Wine£1.33 Credit cards 1 2 3 5 6

★★**Elfordleigh** Plympton (3m E off A38) ☎33642
Closed 24 Dec–14 Jan; 18rm(8⇌⋒) 🍽 CTV 50P
(heated) (hard) Lastdinner8pm
sB&B£12.25 sB&B⇌⋒£13.50 dB&B£19.60
dB&B⇌⋒£22.10 Barlunch£1.50 Tea45p
Dinner£4.50 Wine £2.90

★★**Merchantman** Addison Rd ☎69870
14rm(3⇌) 🍽 CTV 6P English & Continental.
Lastdinner10pm S% sB&B£8
sB&B⇌£10 dB&B£14.50 dB&B⇌£16.50
Lunch£2alc Dinner£4.50alc Wine£3

★★**Highlands** Dean Cross Rd, Plymstock (3m SE off A379) ☎43643
Closed 24–30Dec; 8rm(5⇌⋒) Annexe:6⇌⋒ 🍽
CTV TV available in bedrooms 24P Disco Sat
Live music & dancing Sat English & French.
Lastdinner9pm S% sB&B£8–£9
sB&B⇌⋒£11–£14.50 dB&B£14–£15
dB&B⇌⋒£16–£17 Barlunch£1.25–£2.25
Dinner£3.50–£4&alc Wine£3.25
Credit cards 1 2 3

★**Merlin** 2 Windsor Villas, Lockyer St, The Hoe
☎28133
Closed 24Dec–1Jan; 18rm 🍽 CTV CTV available in bedrooms 15P International.
Lastdinner9.30pm sB&B£7.42–£8.61
dB&B£14.84–£17.22 Lunch£1.80–£2.50&alc
Tea75p–£1.50 Dinner£3.25–£4&alc Wine£3.50
Credit cards 1 2 3 5 6

XX**Green Lanterns** 31 New St, The Barbican
☎60852

P

Closed Sun; 35seats Last dinner10.30pm Wine£2.80 Credit cards 1 2 3 5

XXKhyber 44 Mayflower St ☎266036
Closed Xmas; 64seats P North Indian. Last dinner11pm Lunch£2.15–£3.15&alc Dinner£4.75–£7&alc Wine£2.85 Credit cards 1 2 3 5 6

X*Cooperage* Vauxhall St ☎64288
Closed Sun; 100seats English, French & Italian. Last dinner mdnt (1am Sat) Credit cards 1 2 3 5

POCKLINGTON Humberside Map**8** SE84
★★Feathers Market Sq (Scottish & Newcastle) ☎3155
Traditional three-storied coaching inn in the village.
8rm(3⇌ ⋒) Annexe:6⇌ ⋒ CTV CTV available in bedrooms 60P 6 Last dinner9.30pm S% sB&B£8.50–£10 sB&B⇌⋒£12–£14 dB&B£16–£18 dB&B⇌⋒£18.50–£22 Lunch£2.80–£4.50&alc Dinner£4.25–£7.50&alc Credit cards 1 2 3

POLKERRIS Cornwall Map**2** SX05
XRashleigh Inn (Rashleigh Room) ☎Par3991
(Rosette awarded for dinner only)
Closed Sun & Nov–Feb (except Xmas); 25seats 40P French. Specialities: Crêpe fruits de mer, pot au feu, blanquette de veau. Last dinner9pm Lunch£1.50alc Dinner fr£6 Wine£3.50

POLPERRO Cornwall Map**2** SX25
Claremont ☎72241
In elevated position overlooking picturesque village of Polperro.

P

Closed Nov–Mar; Unlicensed; 11rm(4⇌ ⋒) CTV 16P ⌘ sB&B£7–£10 dB&B fr£14 dB&B⇌ ⋒ fr£17

❀✕✕**House on Props** Harbour Side ☎72310
Closed Jan–mid Feb except New Year; Lunch not served Mon 22seats ♀French. Last dinner10.30pm

✕***Polmary*** The Coombs ☎72304
Closed Sun–Wed (Nov–Feb); 20seats 5P ♀English & French. Last dinner11pm Credit card ③

POOLE Dorset Map**4** SZ09 For hotel locations and additional hotels see **Bournemouth**

★★★**Dolphin** High St ☎3612 Bournemouth district plan**66**
RS Xmas Day; 74rm(49⇌ ⋒) Lift ☽ ⋔ CTV in bedrooms 100P Disco nightly Last dinner10pm ♁ S% sB&B£12.50 sB&B⇌ ⋒ £16 dB&B£19 dB&B⇌ ⋒ £24 Wine£2.30 ⊓
Credit cards ① ② ③ ⑤

★★★**Harbour Heights** 78 Haven Rd, Sandbanks ☎707272 Bournemouth district plan**69**
35rm(28⇌ ⋒) Lift ☽ ⋔ CTV available in bedrooms 100P ♀English & French. Last dinner9.30pm ♁ ⚐ S% sB&B fr£10.30 dB&B⇌ ⋒ fr£13.60 Lunch fr£3.50&alc Dinner fr£4.50&alc Wine£3.50 ⊓ *xmas* Credit cards ① ② ③ ④ ⑤

★★★**Sandbanks** Banks Rd, Sandbanks ☎707377 Bournemouth district plan**74**
142rm(81⇌ ⋒) Lift ☽ ⋔ CTV CTV available in bedrooms ⊗ 200P ▭(heated) sauna bath Disco 3 nights wkly ♔ Conference facilities available ♀International. Last dinner8.30pm ♁ ⚐ ✻sB&B£10.42–£15.17 sB&B⇌ ⋒ £11.50–£16.25 dB&B£19.22–£28.72 dB&B⇌ ⋒ £21.38–£30.89 Lunch fr£4 Dinner fr£5 Wine£3 ⊓ *xmas*

★★**Sea Witch** 47 Haven Rd, Canford Cliffs ☎707697 Bournemouth district plan**76**

P

9rm(7⇌fl) 🅃 CTV in bedrooms ⊗ 29P 🚗 ♀English & French. Last dinner9.30pm ♔ sB&B£11.50–£15.50 sB&B⇌fl£14–£18 dB&B£19–£22 dB&B⇌fl£22–£25 Lunch£3alc Dinner£7.50alc Wine£2.60 ♛ *xmas* Credit cards 1 2 3 4 5 6

Norfolk Lodge 1 Flaghead Rd, Canford Cliffs ☎708614 Bournemouth district plan**71**
Villa-type hotel in quiet residential area with well-kept secluded gardens and aviary.
12rm 🅃 CTV 2🏠 🚗 ⚓ ♀French. Last dinner7.30pm ♔ ☐ ✻sB&B£5–£8 dB&B£10–£16 Lunch fr£2.50 Tea fr£1 Dinner fr£3.50 Wine£3 *xmas*

XXGrovefield Hotel Pinewood Rd, Branksome Park ☎766798 Bournemouth district plan**68**
Closed Mon; Dinner not served Sun; 30seats 14P ♀English & French. Last dinner9pm Lunch£3.50–£4 Dinner£4.50–£5.50 Wine£3.30 Credit cards 2 3 5

XXWarehouse The Quay ☎77238 Bournemouth district plan**82**
Converted quayside warehouse with views across docks to Brownsea Island and Sandbanks.
Closed Sun, 23Dec–2Jan; Lunch not served Sat; 80seats P ♀French. Last dinner10pm Lunch£7.50alc Dinner£7.50alc Wine£2.80 Credit cards 1 2 3 5

XIsabel's 32 Station Rd, Parkstone ☎747885 Bournemouth district plan**84**
Closed Sun, Xmas & Oct; Lunch not served; 40seats 20P ♀French. Last dinner11pm Dinner£5.50alc Wine£3.30 Credit card 3

POOLEY BRIDGE Cumbria Map**12** NY42
★★★ Sharrow Bay Sharrow Bay (1¾m S unclass road) ☎301
For details see page 53

★★Chalet ☎215
Lies in the centre of the village, approximately 200 yards from Lake Ullswater, at its northern end.
8rm(4⇌fl) CTV 60P 🚗 ⚓ Children under 5yrs not accommodated ♀English & Italian. Last dinner9pm ♔ ☐ Credit cards 1 3

POOL-IN-WHARFEDALE West Yorkshire Map**8** SE24
XXXPool Court Pool Bank ☎Arthington842288
Closed Sun, Mon, 24Dec–7Jan & 27Jul–11Aug; Lunch not served; 90seats 50P ♀English & French. Specialities: Carrot & chervil gâteau, Fennel soup & sesame seed finger, fillet medaillons Nicholas. Last dinner9.30pm Dinner£8.50–£11&alc Wine£3.25 Credit cards 3 5

PORLOCK Somerset Map**3** SS94
★★Castle ☎862504
Closed 24–26Dec; 14rm(6⇌fl) CTV ⊗ 10P 🚗 ⚓ Last dinner8.30pm ♔ ✻sB&B£8.25 dB&B£15.50 dB&B⇌fl£18.50 Bar lunch£1.50alc Dinner£4alc Wine£2.50

★Oaks ☎862265
Stone house in own grounds overlooking Porlock Bay.
Closed Xmas; 12rm(2⇌fl) 🅃 CTV TV available in bedrooms ⊗ 14P 1🏠 🚗 ⚓ Children under 8yrs not accommodated Last dinner8pm ♔ S% sB&B£7.55–£9.65 dB&B£13.60–£17.80 dB&B⇌fl£16–£20.20 Dinner£5.50 Wine£3.10 ♛ Credit cards 1 3

PORLOCK WEIR Somerset Map**3** SS84
★★Anchor ☎Porlock862636

P

18rm(7⇌⋒) CTV in bedrooms 40P English & French. Last dinner8.45pm sB&B£10 sB&B⇌⋒£11 dB&B£18 dB&B⇌⋒£20 Lunch£3.50–£4 Dinner£5–£7.50 Wine£3

★Ship Inn ☎Porlock862753
3rm(2⇌⋒) (Annexe:3⇌⋒) CTV in bedrooms 11P English & French. Last dinner8.45pm S% *sB&B£9.50 sB&B⇌⋒£10.69 dB&B£19 dB&B⇌⋒£21.38 Lunch£3.50 Dinner£5.50 Wine£3

PORT GAVERNE Cornwall Map**2** SX08
★★Headlands ☎Port Isaac260
Closed Dec–Feb; 14rm(6⇌⋒) CTV 40P French. Last dinner8.30pm *sB&B£4.85–£7.35 sB&B⇌⋒£5.65–£8.20 dB&B£9.70–£14.70 dB&B⇌⋒£11.30–£16.40 Bar lunch70p–£2 Tea50p–£1.60 Dinner£4.50–£5.30&alc Wine£3.30

PORT ISAAC Cornwall Map**2** SW98
See also Port Gaverne & Trelights
★★Castle Park ☎300
In elevated position with commanding sea views, close to beach and town centre.
Closed Nov–Mar; 21rm(4⇌⋒) CTV 24P Last dinner8.30pm S% sB&B£5.50–£6.50 sB&B⇌⋒£6.50–£7.50 dB&B£11–£13 dB&B⇌⋒£13–£15 Lunch£4 Tea40p Dinner£5 Wine£2.56 Credit cards 1 5 6

★★St Andrews ☎240
Closed Nov–Mar; 15rm(1⇌⋒) CTV TV available in bedrooms 10P Last dinner9pm sB&B£5.50–£7.50 dB&B£11–£15 dB&B⇌⋒£13–£17 Lunch£3alc Tea20palc High Tea£1 Dinner£3.75–£4.75&alc Wine£2.55

PORTLAND Dorset Map**3** SY67
★★Pennsylvania Castle Pennsylvania Rd ☎820561
Mock castle with towers and battlements (built 1800), standing on cliff top. Remains of 11th-C 'Bow and Arrow' castle in grounds.
12rm(10⇌⋒) CTV P 9 Disco twice wkly Mainly grills. Last dinner9.45pm Credit cards 1 2 3 5 6

★★Portland Heights Yeates Corner (Best Western) ☎821361 Telex no418493
32⇌⋒ CTV in bedrooms 100P (heated) sauna bath English, French & German. Last dinner10pm sB&B⇌⋒£13.30–£16 dB&B⇌⋒£22–£27 Lunch£2.90–£3.50&alc Tea£1.35–£2.20 High Tea£2.20–£3.50 Dinner£6alc Wine£2.85 Credit cards 1 3

PORTLOE Cornwall Map**2** SW93
★★Lugger (Inter-Hotel) ☎Veryan322
Reputed to be a smugglers' inn dating from 17th-C, it stands on the water's edge with terrace over the harbour.
Closed mid Nov–mid Feb; 6rm TV 20P sauna bath Children under 12yrs not accommodated English & Continental. Last dinner9pm sB&B£10–£12.50 sB&B⇌⋒£11.50–£15 dB&B£20–£25 dB&B⇌⋒£23–£30 Bar lunch£3.30alc Dinner£6.25 Wine£3.15 Credit cards 1 2 3 5 6

PORTSCATHO Cornwall Map**2** SW83
★★★Rosevine Porthcurnick Beach ☎206
18rm(9⇌⋒) CTV 30P Live music & dancing fortnightly English & Continental. Last dinner8.45pm sB&B£17.60–£19.25(incl dinner)

P

B&B⇌⋒£17.60–£19.25(incl dinner)
B&B£35.20–£38.50(incl dinner)
B&B⇌⋒£37.40–£40.70(incl dinner)
ar lunch£1.20 Tea40p Dinner£7 Wine£3
redit card③

★★**Gerrans Bay** Gerrans ☎338
losed 4 Oct–Mar; 15rm(12⇌⋒) CTV 16P ⛟ ⚓
hildren under 10yrs not accommodated
ast dinner8.15pm S% sB&B£10.50–£12
B&B⇌⋒£11.50–£13 dB&B£22–£23
B&B⇌⋒£24.50–£27 Lunch£4.20 Dinner£6
redit cards①②③⑥

★★♛**Roseland House** Rose Vine ☎320
losed Mid Oct–Mar; 14rm(3⇌⋒) CTV 25P 3⌂ ⛟
⚓ Children under 10yrs not accommodated
♉English & Greek. Last dinner7.30pm S%
B&B fr£11.38(incl dinner)

dB&B fr£22.77(incl dinner)
dB&B⇌⋒ fr£25.28(incl dinner) Bar lunch fr95p
Dinner£5.75 Wine£2.95

✕**Cherry Tree** Gerrans ☎384
Closed Sun, Mon & 6 wks fr mid Oct; 30seats ₱
♉English & French. Last dinner8.30pm
✻Dinner fr£5.65 Wine£2.35

PORTSMOUTH AND SOUTHSEA Hampshire
Map**4** SZ69
Telephone exchange 'Portsmouth'
★★★**Pendragon** Clarence Pole, Southsea
(Trusthouse Forte) ☎23201 Telex no86376
56rm(36⇌⋒) Lift ☽ ⛫ TV in bedrooms 8⌂
Last dinner9pm ✧ S% sB&B£13.50
sB&B⇌⋒£15.50 dB&B£20 dB&B⇌⋒£23 ⛿
xmas Credit cards①②③④⑤⑥

★★★**Portsmouth Centre** Pembroke Rd (Centre) ☎27651 Telex no86397
180⇌⋒ Lift ☽ ♛ CTV in bedrooms ⊘200P
Conference facilities available Last dinner9.45pm
♆ ♒ S% ✱sB&B⇌⋒£15.50 dB&B⇌⋒£20
Continental breakfast Lunch£3.60 Dinner£3.60
Wine£3.40 ⊟ Credit cards 1 2 3 4 5 6

★★★**Royal Beach** South Pde, Southsea (Mount Charlotte) ☎731281 Telex no86719
114rm(52⇌⋒) Lift ☽ ♛ CTV TV available in bedrooms 50P Conference facilities available
Last dinner9.45pm ♆ ♒ S% sB&B fr£14.50
sB&B fr£16.75 dB&B fr£22.75 dB&B⇌⋒ fr£24
Lunch fr£4.25&alc Tea fr95p Dinner fr£5alc ⊟
xmas Credit cards 1 2 3 5

★★**Berkeley** South Pde, Southsea ☎735059
Closed 5Oct–18Apr; 46rm(13⇌⋒) Lift CTV 3P 6⌂
Children under 3yrs not accommodated
Last dinner7.30pm ♆ ♒ S% sB&B£9–£12
sB&B⇌⋒£10.20–£13.40 dB&B£18–£24
dB&B⇌⋒£20.40–£26.80 Lunch£4–£5.20
Dinner£4.75–£6 Wine£2.30

★★**Keppels Head** The Hard (Anchor) ☎21954
20rm(14⇌⋒) Lift ☽ ♛ CTV in bedrooms ⊘25P ⛟
Last dinner10pm ♆ ♒ S% ✱sB&B fr£11.50
sB&B⇌⋒ fr£15.50 dB&B fr£19 dB&B⇌⋒ fr£23
Lunch fr£2.95&alc Dinner fr£2.95&alc Wine£2.65
⊟ Credit cards 1 2 3 4 5 6

★★**Mayville** Waverley Rd, Southsea ☎732461
Closed 28Dec–13Jan; 20rm CTV 20P
Last dinner7pm ♆ ♒ S% sB&B£8.50
dB&B£16 Lunch£3 Dinner£4 Wine£4
Credit cards 1 3

★★**Ocean** St Helen's Pde, Southsea ☎734233
Closed 23Dec–1Jan; 50rm(7⇌⋒) Lift ♛ CTV CTV in bedrooms 30P ⛟ Last dinner10pm S%
sB&B£10.75 sB&B⇌⋒£11.75 dB&B£17.95
dB&B⇌⋒£18.95 Lunch£2.95&alc
Dinner£2.95&alc Wine£2.25 Credit card 3

★★**Saville** Clarence Pde, Southsea ☎27032
38rm ♛ CTV Live music & dancing twice wkly in season Children under 2½yrs not accommodated
Last dinner6.30 pm ♆ ♒ S% sB&B£9–£10.50
dB&B£17–£19.50 Lunch fr£3 Dinner fr£3.50
Wine£2.50 ⊟ *xmas*

★**Garden** South Pde, Southsea ☎732376
19rm ♛ CTV TV available in bedrooms 10P
Last dinner7.30pm ♆ ♒ S% ✱sB&B£11.04
dB&B£22.08 Wine£3.78 ⊟ *xmas* Credit card 3

★***Vermont*** South Pde, Southsea ☎733348
33rm ☽ ♛ CTV Disco 2 nights wkly Live music & dancing Wed–Sat Cabaret Fri & Sat Last dinner7pm
♆ ♒ ⊟ Credit card 3

Ⓖ ***Wairoa*** 2 Florence Rd, Southsea ☎732282
Unlicensed; 11rm TV ⛟ Last dinner6.45pm
Credit cards 1 2 3 4 5 6

✕✕***Murrays*** 27A South Pde, Southsea ☎732322
50seats ♉ English & Continental. Last dinner11pm
Credit cards 1 2 3 5 6

✕**Bamboo House** 110–114 Palmerston Rd, Southsea ☎22100
Closed 25 & 26Dec; 160seats ⚑ Live music & dancing Fri ♉ English & Chinese. Last dinner mdnt
✱Lunch£1.20alc Dinner£4alc Wine£2.60
Credit cards 2 5

✕***Golden Tundorioum*** 67 Palmerston Rd, Southsea ☎21739
80seats ♉ English, Continental & Indian.
Last dinner3am & 1am Sun Credit cards 1 2 3 5 6

P

OUNDISFORD Somerset Map**3** ST22
✕Well House ☎Blagdon Hill566
losed Mon; Lunch not served Tue & winter; Dinner
ot served Sun; 40seats P ♡English & French.
astdinner9pm Lunch£3–£6&alc
inner£5–£8&alc Wine£3.50

RAA SANDS Cornwall Map**2** SW52
★★Lesceave Cliff ☎Germoe2325
losed Jan; 17rm(9⇌ ⫿) ☽ ♛ CTV 10P 12⌂ ⚘ ⚓ ⌂
♡English & French. Last dinner10.30pm ⚘ ☗
% sB&B£8–£13 sB&B⇌ ⫿£9–£15
B&B£16–£26 dB&B⇌ ⫿£18–£30
ar lunch£1.75alc Tea£1alc Dinner£4.75&alc
Vine£2.75 ⛿ *xmas* Credit cards 1 2 3 5

★Prah Sands ☎Germoe2438
losed Oct–Mar; RS 1–23May & 21–30Sep;
4rm(9⇌ ⫿) CTV 30P ⚘ ⚲(hard) ⌂ Last dinner8pm
⚘ ☗ sB&B£8.64–£11.88
B&B⇌ ⫿£9.72–£12.96 dB&B£17.28–£23.76
B&B⇌ ⫿£19.44–£25.92 Lunch£3.20–£3.50
ea70–80p Dinner£5–£5.50 Wine£3

RESTBURY Cheshire Map**7** SJ97
✕✕✕Bridge ☎829326
losed Sun, Public Hols Mon & Good Fri; 80seats
0P Live music Tue–Sat ♡English & French.
ast dinner10pm Lunch£2.97–£3.29&alc
inner£7.29–£7.83&alc Wine£4.59
Credit cards 1 2 3 5

✕✕✕Legh Arms ☎829130
Dinner not served Xmas Day; 80seats 40P ♡French.
ast dinner10pm ✻Lunch£3.50–£4.15&alc
inner£10alc Credit cards 2 3 5

✕✕*White House* ☎829376
Closed Mon; Dinner not served Sun; 75seats 25P
Disco Wed, Fri & Sat ♡English & French.
ast dinner10.15pm Credit cards 1 2 3 5

RESTON Lancashire Map**7** SD52
☆☆☆Preston EuroCrest The Ringway (Crest)
☎59411 Telex no677147
133⇌ ⫿ Lift ☽ ♛ CTV in bedrooms 16P Conference
acilities available ♡English & French.
ast dinner10pm ⚘ ☗ S% ✻sB&B⇌ ⫿£17.06
dB&B⇌ ⫿£25.05 Continental breakfast ⛿
Credit cards 1 2 3 4 5 6

☆☆☆Tickled Trout Preston New Rd, Samlesbury
junc M6/A59) ☎Samlesbury671
RS Xmas; 66⇌ ⫿ ☽ ♛ CTV in bedrooms ⚮ 170P
0⌂ ⚘ Live music & dancing twice wkly Conference
acilities available Last dinner10.30pm ⚘
sB&B⇌ ⫿£16 dB&B⇌ ⫿£22 Lunch fr£3
Dinner£5.50alc Wine£2 ⛿ Credit cards 1 2 3 5

PRIDDY (near Wells) Somerset Map**3** ST55
✕Miners Arms ☎217
Small, white cottage at a crossroads on B3135. Simple white-walled restaurant hung with miners' lamps.
(Reservations essential)
Closed Mon, last 2wks nov & Xmas; Dinner not served Sun; 45seats 20P Last dinner9.30pm Lunch£3.20–£4.20&alc Dinner£7alc Wine£2.85 Credit card 3

PRINCETHORPE Warwickshire Map**4** SP37
★★Woodhouse ☎Marton632303
Closed 24–27Dec; 8rm(2⇌ ⫿) Annexe: 14rm ♛ TV available in bedrooms 100P ⚘ ⚓ ⛆(heated) ⚲(hard) Disco Sat ♡French. Last dinner10.30pm ⚘ ☗ S% sB&B£11 sB&B⇌ ⫿£16–£17.50 dB&B£20 dB&B⇌ ⫿£22.50–£25 Lunch fr£3.95&alc Dinner fr£5.50&alc Wine£2.95 Credit cards 1 2 5

PRIORS HARDWICK Warwickshire Map**4** SP45
✕✕Butcher's Arms ☎Byfield60504
Closed Xmas Day; Lunch not served Sat; Dinner not served Sun; 80seats 100P ♡English & Portuguese. Last dinner10pm Lunch£2.95–£4.95&alc Dinner£2.95–£4.95&alc Wine£3.10

PUDDINGTON Cheshire Map**7** SJ37
✕✕✕Craxton Wood Lodge Parkgate Rd (on A540 junc A550) ☎051-339 4717
Closed Sun, 23–30Dec & 19Aug–2Sep; 85seats 50P bedrooms available ♡French. Last dinner10pm ✻Wine£3.25 Credit cards 1 2 5

PUDSEY West Yorkshire Map**8** SE23
✕Tiberio 68 Galloway Ln ☎Bradford665895
Closed Sun & 23Jul–23Aug; Lunch not served; 40seats 20P ♡Italian. Last dinner11.30pm S% Credit cards 1 3

PURFLEET Essex Map**5** TQ57
★★Royal London Rd (Henekey) ☎5432
29⇌ ⫿ ♛ TV in bedrooms 30P Last dinner10.30pm ⚘ S% sB&B⇌ ⫿£13 dB&B⇌ ⫿£20 ⛿ *xmas* Credit cards 1 2 3 4 5 6

PUTSBOROUGH Devon Map**2** SS44
★★★*Putsborough Sands* ☎Croyde890555
Closed Oct–Apr, except Etr; 67rm(24⇌ ⫿) ☽ CTV 40P ⚘ ⛆(heated) squash sauna bath Disco twice wkly Live music wkly Last dinner8.30pm ☗ ⛿ Credit cards 1 3

RADLETT Hertfordshire Map**4** TL10
★★Red Lion Watling St (Henekey) ☎5341
17rm(7⇌ ⫿) ♛ TV in bedrooms ♡Mainly grills. Last dinner11pm ⚘ S% sB&B£12

R

sB&B⇌⋒£14 dB&B£17.50 dB&B⇌⋒£20.50 ⊟ *xmas* Credit cards 1 2 3 4 5 6

RAINFORD Merseyside Map**7** SD40
XXRoyal Oak East Lancs Rd ☎2465
Closed Sun; Lunch not served Sat; Dinner not served Mon; 50seats 150P English, French & Italian. Last dinner 10pm Lunch fr95p Dinner£4.60alc Wine£2.40 Credit cards 1 2 3 5

RAINHILL Merseyside Map**7** SJ49
See also St Helens
★**Rockland** View Rd ☎051-426 4603
13rm Annexe: 12rm(7⇌⋒) CTV TV available in bedrooms 30P billiards Last dinner 8.30pm sB&B£8.64 sB&b⇌⋒£10.26 dB&B£14.04 dB&B⇌⋒£15.66 Lunch£3-£5&alc Tea fr80p High Tea fr£1.60 Dinner£3-£5&alc Wine£3

RAKE Hampshire Map**4** SU82
XXLes Gourmets ☎Liss2377
Closed Sun, Mon, 8 days end of Oct & 10 days Feb; 40seats 40P French. Specialities: Filet en croute sauce madère, bar grille au penovil, crêpe écossaise. Last dinner 9.45pm ✱Lunch£8alc Dinner£12alc Wine£2.70 Credit cards 2 3 5

RAMPSIDE (nr Barrow-in-Furness) Cumbria Map**7** SD26
★**Clarke's Arms** (Whitbread) ☎Barrow-in-Furness20303
Small country hotel set in own grounds four miles from Barrow-in-Furness, overlooking Morecambe Bay.
7rm CTV 100P Mainly grills. Last dinner 9.45pm sB&B£7 dB&B£14 Lunch£3-£5 Dinner£3-£5 Wine£2.65

RAMSBOTTOM Greater Manchester Map**7** SD71
★★**Old Mill** Springwood ☎2991
Closed Xmas night; 15⇌⋒ TV 40P Live music & dancing twice wkly Cabaret wkly French. Last dinner 9.30pm S% sB&B⇌⋒ fr£12 dB&B⇌⋒ fr£16 Dinner£6alc Wine£2.60 Credit cards 1 2 3 5 6

RAMSBURY Wiltshire Map**4** SU27
XXBell The Square ☎230
Closed Mon, 1st 2wks Feb & last 2wks Aug; Dinner not served Sun; 50seats P Last dinner 9.45pm ✱Lunch£4.75&alc Dinner£5.50&alc Wine£3.50 Credit cards 2 5

RAMSGATE Kent Map**5** TR36
★★**Court Stairs Hotel & Country Club** Pegwell Rd, Westcliff ☎Thanet51850
Victorian Gothic country house with galleried entrance hall standing in gardens, woodland and two acres of lawns on cliff top, overlooking the sea.
17rm(8⇌⋒) CTV TV available in bedrooms 20P (hard) S% sB&B£10-£12 sB&B⇌⋒£12-£16 dB&B£16-£20 dB&B⇌⋒£20-£27 Continental breakfast Lunch£1.25-£2.50 Tea30-50p High Tea50-80p Dinner£6 £8 Wine£3.50 *xmas* Credit cards 1 3 5

★★**San Clu** Victorian Pde ☎Thanet52345
Situated on East Cliff overlooking sea.
50rm(19⇌⋒) Lift CTV TV available in bedrooms 15P English & French. Last dinner 8.20pm S% sB&B£9-£11 sB&B⇌⋒£13-£14 dB&B£14-£18 dB&B⇌⋒£22-£24 Lunch£4&alc Tea50palc High Tea£1.50alc Dinner£4.50&alc Wine£3 ⊟ *xmas* Credit cards 1 3 6

★★**Savoy** Grange Rd ☎Thanet52637
Closed Feb; 14rm(3⇌⋒) Annexe: 11⇌⋒ CTV CTV available in bedrooms 20P English & French. Last dinner 10pm S% sB&B£8-£10 sB&B⇌⋒£11.50-£13.50 dB&B£13-£15 dB&B⇌⋒£17.50-£20 Lunch fr£3&alc Tea fr45p Dinner£6.50alc Wine£2.30 ⊟ Credit cards 1 2 3 5 6

RANGEWORTHY Avon Map**3** ST68
Rangeworthy Court ☎347
Listed building. Ancient Cotswold manor, circa AD1342. Hotel run as country house, beautifully furnished with antiques.
Closed Xmas; 13rm(2⇌⋒) 1 CTV 50P (heated) (hard) Last dinner 9.30pm

RANTON Staffordshire Map**7** SJ82
XXXYew Tree ☎Seighford278
Dinner not served Sun; 120seats P French. Last dinner 9pm ✱Lunch£4.10&alc Dinner£5.50alc Credit cards 1 2 3 5

RAVENGLASS Cumbria Map**6** SD09
★**Pennington Arms** ☎222
A country inn in quiet village on estuary of Rivers Esk, Mite & Irt, famous in olden times for smuggling activities.
17rm(4⇌⋒) Annexe: 22rm CTV 50P 3 Last dinner 10pm sB&B£6.50-£7.75 sB&B⇌⋒£7.50-£8.75 dB&B£13-£15.50 dB&B⇌⋒£15-£17.50 Lunch£2.50alc Tea£1.50alc High Tea£2.50alc Dinner£3.50alc Wine£3.75

RAVENSCAR (near Scarborough) North Yorkshire Map**8** NZ90
★★**Raven Hall** ☎Scarborough870353
Closed mid Nov-mid Apr; 60rm(21⇌⋒) CTV 200P (heated) (hard) billiards Live music & dancing 4 nights wkly in season Last dinner 8.30pm sB&B£8.50-£12 sB&B⇌⋒£15-£17.50 dB&B£17-£24 dB&B⇌⋒£30-£35 Lunch£3-£4 Tea80p-£1 High Tea£2.50 Dinner£5-£6.50&alc Wine£2.70 ⊟

RAVENSTONEDALE Cumbria Map**12** NY70
★★**Black Swan** ☎Newbiggin-on-Lune204
6rm CTV 30P Disco Fri & Sat Live music & dancing Fri & Sat English & Continental. Last dinner 9pm sB&B£9.50 dB&B£16.50 Lunch£5.20&alc Tea80p Dinner£5.20&alc Credit card 3

READ Lancashire Map**7** SD73
XXBelvedere Hotel ☎Padiham72250
Closed Mon, 1st 3wks Jul; Lunch not served Sat & Sun; 100seats 35P Italian. Last dinner 9.30pm ✱Lunch£6alc Dinner£6alc

READING Berkshire Map**4** SU77
☆☆☆**Post House** 500 Basingstoke Rd (Trusthouse Forte) ☎85485 Telex no 849160
121⇌⋒ CTV in bedrooms 174P (heated) Last dinner 10.30pm S% sB&B⇌⋒£21.25 dB&B⇌⋒£31 ⊟ *xmas* Credit cards 1 2 3 4 5 6

★★**Caversham Bridge** Caversham Rd, Caversham ☎53793
Old Tudor-style hotel with lawns and rose gardens leading down to the River Thames.
11rm TV in bedrooms 120P P Live music & dancing Sat English & Continental. Last dinner 9.45pm S% sB&B£11.95 dB&B fr£21.90 Lunch£3.55 Tea30p Dinner£4.05&alc Wine£2.87 *xmas* Credit cards 1 5

★★**Ship** Duke St (Anchor) ☎583455 Telex no 858875
32rm(22⇌⋒) CTV CTV in bedrooms 30P Last dinner 9.30pm S% ✱sB&B fr£11.50

B&B⇌⋒ fr£16 dB&B⇌⋒ fr£22 Lunch fr£3.50 Dinner fr£4 Wine£2.65 ⊟ Credit cards ① ② ③ ④ ⑤ ⑥

REDBOURN Hertfordshire Map**4** TL11
☆☆☆**Aubrey Park** Hemel Hempstead Ln (Best Western) ☎2105 Telex no 847777
7⇌⋒ ☽ ▦ ⋔ CTV in bedrooms 100P ⚓ ⌂(heated) •(hard) Conference facilities available ♡English & French. Last dinner 10pm ✿ ♈ S% B&B⇌⋒ £15.75–£20 dB&B⇌⋒ £24–£29.50 Continental breakfast Lunch£6alc Tea50p Dinner£7alc Wine£3 ⊟ Credit cards ① ② ③ ④ ⑤ ⑥

REDCAR Cleveland Map**8** NZ62
☆☆☆***Royal York*** Coatham Rd ☎Middlesbrough 486221
1⇌⋒ Lift ☽ ⋔ TV ⊘ 300P Disco Fri & Sat Live music & dancing Fri & Sat Cabaret Fri & Sat ♿ Conference facilities available ♡English & Continental. Last dinner 10pm ✿ ♈ ⊟

★★**Clarendon** High St (Scottish & Newcastle) ☎Middlesbrough 484301
1rm CTV 20P ♡English & French. Last dinner 8.30pm ✿ S% sB&B£7.50 dB&B£14 Lunch£1alc Dinner£2.50–£2.70&alc Wine£2.20 ⊟ Credit cards ① ③

★★**Swan** High St (Crest) ☎Middlesbrough 483678
7rm (18⇌⋒) Lift CTV CTV available in bedrooms ♡Mainly grills. Last dinner 10pm ✿ S% ✱sB&B£10.80 dB&B£16.47 dB&B⇌⋒ £21.60 ⊟ Credit cards ① ② ③ ④ ⑤ ⑥

REDDITCH Hereford & Worcester Map**7** SP06
★★★**Southcrest** Mount Pleasant ☎41511 Telex no 338455
A beautiful old mansion built by Sir Charles Terry for entertaining royalty.
31⇌⋒ ☽ ⋔ TV in bedrooms 100P ⚓ ♡French. Last dinner 9.15pm ✿ ♈ S% ✱sB&B⇌⋒ £13.90–£16.90 dB&B⇌⋒ £20.80 Lunch fr£4&alc Dinner fr£4.50&alc Wine£3.35 ⊟ Credit cards ① ② ③ ⑤

REDHILL Surrey Map**4** TQ25
★★**Lakers** Redstone Hill ☎61043 Gatwick plan **13**
10rm CTV 30P Live music & dancing wkly Last dinner 8.45pm ✿ ♈ ✱sB&B£9.20 dB&B£16.50 Lunch£2.50&alc Tea50p Dinner£2.50 &alc Wine£2.50 Credit cards ① ③

REDRUTH Cornwall Map**2** SW74
XX**Basset Count House** Carnkie (2m SW off B3297) ☎215181
Closed Sun; 40seats 30P ✱Lunch£10alc Dinner£10alc Wine£3.20 Credit card ⑤

REIGATE Surrey Map**4** TQ25
☆☆☆**Ladbroke Mercury Motor Inn** (formerly Bridge House) Reigate Hill (Ladbroke) ☎46801 Gatwick plan **1**
Modern motor hotel with panoramic views of downlands. Private path to Colley Hill.
30⇌⋒ ☽ ▦ ⋔ CTV in bedrooms 100P ⌂(heated) Live music & dancing nightly Cabaret nightly Last dinner 11.30pm ✿ ♈ ✱sB&B⇌⋒ £15.75–£17.75 sB&B⇌⋒ £25 Lunch fr£4.10&alc Dinner fr£4.10&alc Wine£2.85 Credit cards ① ② ③ ⑤

RIBCHESTER Lancashire Map**7** SD63
XX**De Tabley Arms** ☎308
180seats 100P bedrooms available Disco Sat Live music Sat ♡English & French. Last dinner 9.30pm ✱Lunch£3.20 Dinner£6alc Wine£3

R

RICHMOND North Yorkshire Map**7** NZ10
★★**Frenchgate** 59–61 Frenchgate ☎2087
Closed Xmas, last 2wks Mar & Oct; RS Sun; 12rm(6⇌⋒) TV in bedrooms 8P Children under 7yrs not accommodated English & French. Last dinner8.30pm sB&B fr£11 sB&B⇌⋒ fr£12.50 dB&B fr£19 dB&B⇌⋒ fr£21 Lunch fr£4.50&alc Dinner fr£4.50&alc Wine£2.50

★★**King's Head** Market Sq (Swallow) ☎2311 Telex no53168
23rm(12⇌⋒) CTV TV in bedrooms 12P Last dinner9.30pm S% sB&B£9–£12.60 sB&B⇌⋒£11.40–£15.85 dB&B£15.75–£22 dB&B⇌⋒£18.15–£25.80 *xmas*
Credit cards 1 2 3 5

RICHMOND UPON THAMES Greater London Map**4** TQ17
★★★**Richmond Hill** 146–150 Richmond Hill ☎01-940 2247 Telex no21844
103rm(91⇌⋒) Lift CTV in bedrooms 150P squash English & French. Last dinner8.30pm S% sB&B fr£15.50 sB&B⇌⋒ fr£18.50 dB&B fr£19 dB&B⇌⋒ fr£22.50 Lunch£4.25&alc Tea35palc Dinner£4.25&alc Wine£3.30 *xmas* Credit cards 1 2 3 4 5 6

✕**Kew Rendezvous** 110 Kew Rd ☎01-948 4343
Closed 25 & 26Dec; 120seats Pekinese. Last dinner11.15pm *Lunch fr£4.50&alc Dinner£10&alc Wine£2.40 Credit cards 1 2 3 5

✕**Red Lion Chinese** 18 Red Lion St ☎01-940 2371
Closed 24, 25 & 26Dec; 84seats Pekinese. Last dinner11.15pm *Lunch£3.50–£5&alc Dinner£3.50–£5&alc Wine£2.70
Credit cards 1 3 5

✕**Richmond Rendezvous** 1 Paradise Rd ☎01-940 5114
Closed Xmas; 90seats Chinese. Last dinner11.15pm Lunch£.50–£10.00&alc Dinner£5.50–£10.00&alc Credit cards 1 2 3 5

✕***Valcheras*** The Quadrant ☎01-940 0648
Closed Xmas, Public Hols, last wk Jul & 1st wk Aug; Dinner not served Sun; 75seats Continental. Last dinner10.30pm Credit cards 3 5

RINGWOOD Hampshire Map**4** SU10
★★***Crown*** Southampton Rd (Eldridge Pope) ☎3326
8rm CTV 60P 3 Children under 5 yrs not accommodated English & French. Last dinner10pm Credit card 1

★★**Little Moortown House** Christchurch Rd ☎3325
Closed Dec–14Jan; 6rm(3⇌⋒) CTV 12P Children under 12yrs not accommodated English & Continental. Last dinner7.45pm
*sB&B£8.08–£9.08 sB&B⇌⋒£9.45–£10.45 dB&B£13.50–£14.50 dB&B⇌⋒£15.66–£16.66 Tea42–60p&alc Dinner£4–£6&alc Wine£2.40 Credit cards 1 2 3 5 6

★★***Original White Hart*** Market Pl (Eldridge Pope) ☎2702
12rm CTV 20P 5 Last dinner9.45pm
Credit cards 1 2 6

✕***Country Kitchen*** 10 High St ☎5075
42seats Last dinner10pm Credit cards 1 3 6

✕***Old Cottage*** West St ☎4283
Closed Mon; Lunch served Sun only; Dinner not served Sun; 48seats 8P Last dinner10.30pm
Credit card 3

RIPLEY Surrey Map**4** TQ05
✕✕✕***Clock House*** ☎2777
Dinner not served Xmas Day; 150seats Continental. Last dinner10pm
Credit cards 2 3 4 5

✕✕**Talbot Hotel Restaurant** ☎3188
An old inn (established in 1453) with beamed restaurant; contains seats used by Lord Nelson and Lady Hamilton.
Closed Mon; Dinner not served Sun; 50seats 200P International. Last dinner10.30pm S% Lunch£1–£4&alc Dinner£2.50–£6&alc Wine£2.60 Credit cards 1 2 3 4 5 6

RIPON North Yorkshire Map**8** SE37
★★★**Ripon Spa** Park St (Best Western) ☎2172
Late 19th-C country mansion in own grounds, on outskirts of town.
43rm(29⇌⋒) Lift CTV CTV in bedrooms 100P Live music & dancing mthly sB&B fr£11 sB&B⇌⋒ fr£15 dB&B fr£21 dB&B⇌⋒ fr£32 Lunch fr£3 Tea fr£1.10 Dinner fr£4.75 wine£2.80 *xmas* Credit cards 1 2 3

★★***Unicorn*** Market Sq ☎2202
28rm(13⇌⋒) CTV 6P 4 English & French. Last dinner9pm Credit cards 1 3

RIPPONDEN West Yorkshire Map**7** SE01
✕✕**Over The Bridge** Millfold ☎3722
Closed Sun; Lunch not served; Dinner not served Public Hols; 45seats 50P English & French. Last dinner9.30pm S% *Dinner£8 wine£3
Credit card 2

RISHWORTH West Yorkshire Map**7** SE01
★★**Royal** Oldham Rd ☎Ripponden2382
Closed Xmas Day; 9rm(7⇌⋒) CTV CTV available in bedrooms 70P Live music & dancing Sat International. Last dinner9.30pm S% sB&B£11–£12 sB&B⇌⋒£11–£12 dB&B£18.50–£20

R

dB&B⇌🛁£18.50–£20 Lunch£1.25–£2.50 Dinner£2.75–£4.50&alc Wine£2.40 ⊟
Creditcards 1 3

ROBIN HOOD'S BAY North Yorkshire Map**8** NZ90
★★**Grosvenor** Station Rd ☎Whitby880320
15rm CTV 12P Lastdinner8.15pm
sB&B£8.50–£9.50 dB&B£25–£26
Lunch£3.50–£4 Tea£1.50–£2
Dinner£5–£5.50&alc Wine£3.70 ⊟ *xmas*

★★**Victoria** ☎Whitby880205
Two storey, late Victorian villa in own small grounds on cliff top overlooking village and bay.
Closed mid Oct–Mar; 15rm(1⇌🛁) CTV 30P
Lastdinner8pm sB&B£9–£10
dB&B£18–£20 dB&B⇌🛁£20–£22
Barlunch35p–£2 Dinner£5–£5.50 Wine£3

ROCHDALE Greater Manchester Map**7** SD91
★★***Crimble*** Bamford (2½m W B6222)
☎Heywood68591
4rm Annexe:6rm CTV 100P Live music & dancing Sat English & Continental.
Lastdinner10pm

★★***Midway*** Manchester Rd ☎32881
Closed Xmas, New Year's Day & Etr; 29rm (10⇌🛁) TV available in bedrooms 200P Live music & dancing Sat Lastdinner9.30pm
Creditcard 2

ROCHESTER Kent Map**5** TQ76
★★***Royal Victoria & Bull*** High St ☎Medway46266
31rm(6⇌🛁) CTV Mainlygrills. Lastdinner11.30pm

ROCHESTER Northumberland Map**12** NY89
★**Redesdale Arms** ☎Otterburn20668
11rm 3 CTV 28P Continental.
Lastdinner9.15pm sB&B£7.60–£8.10
dB&B£15.10–£15.70 Barlunch40p–£3
Dinner£2.80–£5.50&alc Wine£2.95 ⊟
Creditcards 1 2

ROCK (near St Minver) Cornwall Map**2** SW97
★★**Roskarnon House** ☎Trebetherick2329
Solid house in own grounds leading to River Camel estuary.
Closed mid Oct–Feb; 16rm(4⇌🛁) CTV TV available in bedrooms 10P 2 English & French.
Lastdinner9pm sB&B£5–£10
sB&B⇌🛁£7–£14 dB&B£10–£20
dB&B⇌🛁£10–£20 Lunch£3.50–£5.50
Tea20–70p Dinner£4–£10 Wine£2 ⊟

★★**St Enodoc** ☎Trebetherick2311
Closed Feb; 16rm(8⇌🛁) CTV 17P
Lastdinner9pm sB&B£5.85–£9.50
sB&B⇌🛁£6.25–£10.25 dB&B£11.70–£19
dB&B⇌🛁£12.50–£20.50 Lunch£3.25–£4
Tea50p–£2 Dinner£4–£4.75&alc Wine£3 ⊟
xmas

ROKE Oxfordshire Map**4** SU69
✕✕**Home Sweet Home** ☎Wallingford38249
Attractive 16th-C stone-built inn on outskirts of village.
Closed Mon & 2wks Aug; Dinner not served Sun; 45seats 30P English, French & Italian.
Lastdinner9.30pm Lunch£6–£9&alc
Dinner£6–£10&alc Wine£4 Credit cards 1 2 3

ROMALDKIRK Co Durham Map**12** NY92
★**Rose & Crown** ☎Teasdale50213
Closed Xmas Day; 11rm(1⇌🛁) CTV 60P 5
Lastdinner10pm S% sB&B fr£11
sB&B⇌🛁 fr£12 dB&B fr£22 dB&B⇌🛁 fr£24
Lunch fr£4.50 Tea fr£1.25 High Tea fr£3
Dinner fr£6.75 Wine£3 ⊟

ROMILEY Greater Manchester Map**7** SJ99
✕**Waterside** 166 Stockport Rd ☎061–430 4302
Stone and brick built two-storey cottage approx 200 years old, beside the Peak Forest canal.
Closed Mon; Dinner not served Sun; 36seats 20P English & French. Lastdinner9.30pm S%
Lunch£3.25alc Dinner£7alc Wine£3.50
Creditcard 1

ROMSEY Hampshire Map**4** SU32
★★★**White Horse** Market Pl (Trusthouse Forte)
☎512431
The hotel was built on the site of the 12th-C Abbey Guest House in the reign of Henry VII and has a 16th-C wall painting.
33⇌🛁 CTV TV in bedrooms 60P
Lastdinner10pm S% sB&B⇌🛁£15.50
dB&B⇌🛁£22.50 ⊟ *xmas*
Creditcards 1 2 3 4 5 6

★***Dolphin*** Cornmarket ☎512171
7rm(2⇌🛁) CTV 20P Lastdinner10pm
Creditcards 1 2 3 5

✕✕**Edward (Royal Room)** 11 Bell St ☎512050
(classification awarded for dinner only)
120seats 30P Continental. Lastdinner11pm
Lunch90p–£4 Dinner£6.60 Wine£3.50
Creditcards 1 3 5 6

At **Ampfield** (4m E A31)
☆☆☆**Potters Heron** (Whitbread)
☎Chandlers Ford66611
42⇌🛁 120P

At **Ower** (4m SW A31)
☆☆☆**New Forest Lodge** (Grand Met) ☎Ower333
43⇌🛁 100P

ROSSINGTON South Yorkshire Map**8** SK69
★★**Mount Pleasant** Great North Rd (on A638)
☎Doncaster868219
Converted 18th-C estate house with 80 acres of woodland and farmland.
Closed 24 & 25Dec; 16rm(1⇌🛁)

R

Annexe:10rm(4⇌⋒) 1▭ ⚹ ⚲ TV TV available in bedrooms ⊘ 50P 10⌂ ⇝ ⚓ Last dinner9.30pm ♔ ⚲ sB&B£8–£8.50 sB&B⇌⋒£10–£15 dB&B£15–£16 dB&B⇌⋒£16–£17 Lunch£1.75–£4 Tea85p–£1.25 High Tea£2–£4 Dinner£3–£5

ROSS-ON-WYE Hereford & Worcester Map**3** SO62

★★★**Chase** Gloucester Rd (Queens) ☎3161
Georgian style country house dating from 1840. Set in 11 acres of lawns and gardens with lake and padlock.
38rm(30⇌⋒) 3▭ ☽ ⚲ CTV in bedrooms ⊘ 200P ⚓ ♀English, French & Italian. Last dinner9.45pm ♔ ⚲ S% sB&B£14–£16 sB&B⇌⋒£17–£18 dB&B£20–£23 dB&B⇌⋒£25–£28 Lunch£4–£5&alc Tea50p–£1.50 Dinner£6–£6.50&alc Wine£3.75 ⊟ *xmas* Credit cards 1 2 3 5 6

★★★**Pengethley** (4m N on A49 Hereford road) ☎Harewood End211
Small Georgian mansion standing in its own grounds in a peaceful spot in the Wye Valley overlooking National Trust parkland.
12⇌⋒ Annexe:2⇌⋒ ⚲ CTV CTV in bedrooms 70P 7⌂ ⚓ ⊃(heated) ⛳ ♀International. Last dinner9.30pm ♔ ⚲ S% ✱sB&B£12–£15 sB&B⇌⋒£20–£23 dB&B£19–£24 dB&B⇌⋒£26–£31 Lunch fr£5.25 Tea40p–£1 High Tea fr£1.50 Dinner£5.60–£6.75 Wine£3.75 ⊟ *xmas* Credit card 5

★★★**Royal** Palace Pound (Trusthouse Forte) ☎2769
32rm(21⇌⋒) ⚲ TV in bedrooms 30P ⚓ Last dinner9.30pm ♔ ⚲ S% sB&B£11 sB&B⇌⋒£13.50 dB&B£19 dB&B⇌⋒£21.50 ⊟ *xmas* Credit cards 1 2 3 4 5 6

★★★**Wye** Weston-under-Penyard (2m E A40) ☎3541
Spacious blue-shuttered country house set in 9 acres of grounds in lee of Penyard Hill.
53rm(36⇌⋒) ☽ ⚲ CTV CTV available in bedrooms 150P 10⌂ ⚓ squash ⛳ ♀English & Continental. Last dinner9.30pm ♔ ⚲ S% sB&B fr£15 sB&B⇌⋒ fr£18 dB&B fr£20 dB&B⇌⋒ fr£25 Lunch fr£4.50 Tea fr£1.50 High Tea fr£2 Dinner fr£5 Wine£2.90 ⊟ *xmas* Credit cards 1 2 3 4 5 6

★★ ⚘**Chasedale** Walford Rd ☎2423
16rm(7⇌⋒) CTV CTV available in bedrooms 30P ⇝ ⚓ ♀English & French. Last dinner8.30pm ♔ ⚲ S% sB&B£9 sB&B⇌⋒£11 dB&B£16 dB&B⇌⋒£18 Lunch£4.25 Tea50p–£2 High Tea£3–£4 Dinner£4.25 Wine£3.50

★★**Sandiway** Weston-under-Penyard (2m E A40) ☎2748
Originally 15th-C Hunsdon Manor, but with much later additions. Stands in 2½ acres of lawns and gardens.
Closed Jan; RS Oct–Mar (closed during lunchtimes) 13rm(6⇌⋒) ⚲ CTV ⊘ 50P ⚓ Last dinner8pm ♔ ⚲ sB&B£7.56 sB&B⇌⋒£11.50 dB&B£14.58 dB&B⇌⋒£16.74 Bar lunch65p–£2.50&alc Tea75p Dinner£3.50&alc Wine£1.95 ⊟

★★**Swan** Edde Cross St ☎2169
19rm(12⇌⋒) ⚲ CTV CTV in bedrooms 50P Last dinner9.30pm ♔ ⚲ S% sB&B£10.80–£11.88 sB&B⇌⋒£12.96–£14.26 dB&B£17.28–£20.20 dB&B⇌⋒£21.60–£24.95 Lunch£2.70–£3 Tea60–80p High Tea£1–£2 Dinner£4–£4.50&alc Wine£2.50 ⊟ *xmas* Credit cards 1 2 3 5 6

R

★**Brookfield House** Over Ross ☎2188
8rm(2⇨⋒) CTV 10P 5🏠 ⚓ Last dinner6.30pm ♡ ☕ S% sB&B£6.67–£8.37 dB&B£12.10–£15.12 dB&B⇨⋒£14.10–£15.12 Lunch fr£2.50 Tea fr£1 Dinner fr£3.75 Wine£2.70 ⛿

★**Rosswyn** 17 High St ☎2733
10rm(3⇨⋒) 3⊟ CTV ⚐ ⚘ ⚓ ♡International. Last dinner10pm ♡ S% sB&B£8–£8.50 sB&B⇨⋒£8–£8.50 dB&B£16 dB&B⇨⋒£16–£18 Bar lunch£1.80–£3 Dinner£5.50alc Wine£3 ⛿ *xmas*

★**Wilton Court** Wilton ☎2569
Manor house to Lords of Wilton, and local courthouse. Site of Roman ford across River Wye.
8rm(1⇨⋒) ⚿ CTV TV available in bedrooms 8P ⚘ ⚓ ⚲ Last dinner9pm ♡ S% ✻sB&B£8–£9 dB&B£15–£17 dB&B⇨⋒£16.50–£18.50 Bar lunch60p–£2.95 Dinner£3.75&alc Wine£2.50 ⛿

ROSTHWAITE Cumbria Map**11** NY21
See also Borrowdale and Grange-in-Borrowdale
★★***Scafell*** ☎Borrowdale208
RS mid Nov–mid Mar (bar only); 22rm(6⇨⋒) ⚿ 60P ⚘ ⚓ ⚘ ♡English & French. Last dinner8.30pm ♡ ☕

ROSUDGEON Cornwall Map**2** SW52
★**Courtlands** ☎Marazion710476
Closed Dec & Jan except Xmas; 15rm(3⇨⋒) CTV 20P Children under 7yrs not accommodated Last dinner7.30pm ♡ ☕ S% sB&B£10.20–£10.40 dB&B£19.40–£19.80 dB&B⇨⋒£21.40–£21.80 Lunch fr£2.55 Tea fr60p Dinner fr£3.90&alc Wine£2 ⛿ *xmas* Credit cards 1 3 6

ROTHBURY Northumberland Map**12** NU00
★★**Coquet Vale** Station Rd ☎20305
9rm CTV 30P ⚘ ♡English & French. Last dinner9pm ♡ S% sB&B£6.60 dB&B£12.20 Lunch£3.25 Dinner£3.95 Wine£2.90 ⛿

★**Queens Head** Town Foot ☎20470
11rm ⚿ CTV 12P 2🏠 Disco twice wkly Live music & dancing wkly Last dinner8pm ♡ ☕ ✻sB&B£6 dB&B£12 Lunch£2.50–£3.20 Tea95p High Tea£1.40–£1.50 Dinner fr£3.50&alc Wine£2.75

ROTHERHAM South Yorkshire Map**8** SK49
★**Brentwood** Moorgate Rd ☎2772
16rm(1⇨⋒) ⚿ CTV CTV available in bedrooms 50P ⚓ billiards Last dinner9pm ♡ S% sB&B£8.09 sB&B⇨⋒£9.20 dB&B£14.04 dB&B⇨⋒£19.44 Lunch£1.75–£3&alc Dinner fr£4&alc Wine£2.65 Credit cards 1 2 5

✕✕***Sitwell Arms*** Whiston (2m SE off A618) ☎77003
closed Xmas Day; Dinner not served Sun; 70seats 100P Last dinner9.45pm Credit cards 1 2 3 5

✕**Millgate** Corporation St ☎63311
Closed Sun & Public Hols; 80seats ⚐ ♡English & French. Last dinner11.30pm ✻Lunch£1.10–£1.95&alc Tea75p Dinner£6.50alc Wine£1.80 Credit cards 1 3

R

ROTHLEY Leicestershire Map**8** SK61
XX***Red Lion*** ☎Leicester302655
Lunch not served Sat; Dinner not served Sun; 56seats 100P English & French. Last dinner10pm
Credit cards 1 2 3 4 5 6

ROTTINGDEAN East Sussex Map**5** TQ30
★★***White Horse*** High St ☎Brighton31955
16rm(2⇌ ⋒) 1 Lift ☽ CTV TV available in bedrooms 60P Live music wknds English & French. Last dinner9.30pm
Credit cards 1 2 3 5 6

ROUSDON Devon Map**3** SY29
★★**Orchard Country House** ☎Lyme Regis2972
Closed Nov; 15rm(9⇌ ⋒) CTV 15P Children under 5yrs not accommodated Last dinner8pm sB&B£7.50–£7.75 sB&B⇌ ⋒£8.50–£8.75 dB&B£15–£15.50 dB&B⇌ ⋒£17–£19.50 Lunch£2.60 Tea75p Dinner£3.95&alc Wine£2.70 *xmas* Credit cards 2 5

ROWSLEY Derbyshire Map**8** SK26
★★★**Peacock** (Embassy) ☎Darley Dale3518
14⇌ ⋒ Annexe:6rm(1⇌ ⋒) ☽ CTV TV in bedrooms 50P Last dinner9.15pm S% sB&B£12 sB&B⇌ ⋒£16 dB&B£19 dB&B⇌ ⋒£24 Lunch£6&alc Dinner£7&alc Wine£5 Credit cards 1 2 3 4 5 6

ROYSTON Hertfordshire Map**5** TL34
★★**Banyers** Melbourn St ☎42110
Ivy-covered, Georgian-style building with 2½ acres of gardens.
11rm(1⇌ ⋒) CTV TV in bedrooms 20P Last dinner9.30pm sB&B£11.55 dB&B£17.05 dB&B⇌ ⋒£19.25 Lunch£2.75&alc Tea35p Dinner£10alc Wine£3.10 *xmas*
Credit cards 1 2 3 5

RUAN HIGH LANES Cornwall Map**2** SW93
★★**Pendower** Gerrans Bay ☎Veryan257
Closed Oct–Apr; 20rm(4⇌ ⋒) CTV 20P 10 Last dinner7.30pm sB&B£7.50–£8 dB&B£15–£16 dB&B⇌ ⋒£18–£20 Lunch fr£3.50 Dinner fr£4.50 Wine£2.50

★★**Polsue Manor** ☎Veryan270
Closed Oct–Mar; 13rm(11⇌ ⋒) ☽ CTV 20P English & French. Last dinner8.30pm S% sB&B£7.50–£8 sB&B⇌ ⋒£9–£9.50 dB&B£14–£16 dB&B⇌ ⋒£16.50–£18.50 Dinner£4.75–£6.50&alc Wine£2.35

★**Hundred House** ☎Veryan336
Closed Nov–Mar; 10rm(8⇌ ⋒) CTV 20P Children under 5yrs not accommodated Last dinner7.30pm sB&B£8.50–£9 sB&B⇌ ⋒£9.25–£9.75 dB&B£17–£18 dB&B⇌ ⋒£18.50–£19.50 Bar lunch£1.75 Dinner£4 Wine£2 Credit cards 1 5

RUGBY Warwickshire Map**4** SP57
★★★**Clifton Court** Lilbourne Rd, Clifton-upon-Dunsmore ☎65033
Closed 20Jul–6Aug; 14⇌ ⋒ CTV in bedrooms 150P Children under 14yrs not accommodated English & Continental. Last dinner9.30pm S% sB&B⇌ ⋒£16–£18 dB&B⇌ ⋒£23.50–£26 Lunch£3.85&alc Dinner fr£4.95&alc Wine£3.50 Credit card 1

★★★**Three Horse Shoes** Sheet St ☎4585
Old coaching inn with oak beams, panelling and stone fireplaces.
33⇌ ⋒ ☽ CTV CTV in bedrooms Live music & dancing Sat English & French. Last dinner10pm sB&B⇌ ⋒£15 dB&B⇌ ⋒£22 Lunch£3.75–£5 Dinner£5–£7&alc
Credit cards 1 2 3 4 5 6

X**Andalucia** 10 Henry St ☎76404
120seats Spanish. Last dinner10.30pm ✱Lunch£3&alc Dinner£7.50alc Wine£3.75
Credit cards 1 2 3 4 5 6

At **Crick** (6m E A428)
☆☆☆☆**Rugby Post House** (Trusthouse Forte) ☎Crick822101
96⇌ ⋒ 150P

RUGELEY Staffordshire Map**7** SK01
★★**Cedar Tree** Main Rd, Brereton ☎4241
12rm(3⇌ ⋒) CTV CTV available in bedrooms squash Disco Tue Live music & dancing Sat Cabaret Sat English & Continental. Last dinner9.30pm Credit card 2

★★**Eaton Lodge** Wolseley Rd (Wolverhampton & Dudley) ☎3454
12rm CTV 250P Last dinner8.45pm S% ✱sB&B fr£10.10 dB&B fr£17 Lunch£2.50&alc Dinner£3.15&alc Wine£2.60 Credit cards 1 3

RUNCORN Cheshire Map**7** SJ58
☆☆☆**Runcorn EuroCrest** Wood Ln, Beechwood (Crest) ☎714000 Telex no627426
142⇌ ⋒ Lift ☽ CTV in bedrooms 250P Conference facilities available English & French. Last dinner10pm S% ✱sB&B⇌ ⋒£16.52 dB&B⇌ ⋒£25.05 Continental breakfast
Credit cards 1 2 3 4 5 6

RUSHDEN Northamptonshire Map**4** SP96
★**Westward** Shirley Rd ☎2376
Closed 25 & 26Dec; 10rm Annexe:15rm CTV TV in bedrooms 12P (heated) Last dinner10pm ✱sB&B£8.30 dB&B£14.25 Bar lunch fr£1.50 Tea fr£1 High Tea fr£2.75 Dinner fr£3.50 Wine£2.25

RUSHYFORD Co Durham Map**8** NZ22
★★★**Eden Arms** (Swallow) ☎720541 Telex no53168

R

41rm(31⇌ ⋒) ☽ ⋒ CTV CTV available in bedrooms 150P Last dinner9.15pm ♧ ⚲ S% sB&B£14 sB&B⇌ ⋒£18.30 dB&B£21.50 dB&B⇌ ⋒£25.80 ⊟ *xmas* Credit cards 1 2 3 5

RUSTINGTON West Sussex Map**4** TQ00
★★**Broadmark** (Nicholsons) ☎4281
17rm(9⇌ ⋒) ⋒ CTV CTV in bedrooms 60P ⚓ Last dinner9.30pm ♧ ⚲ S% sB&B£9–£10 sB&B⇌ ⋒£10–£11 dB&B£13–£14 dB&B⇌ ⋒£14–£15 Lunch£2.50–£3.50&alc Dinner£3–£4&alc Wine£3.50 ⊟ *xmas* Credit cards 1 2 3 5

RYDE Isle of Wight Map**4** SZ59
★★**Yelf's** Union St (Trusthouses Forte) ☎64062
32rm(11⇌ ⋒) ⋒ TV in bedrooms ⚑ Last dinner8.45pm ♧ S% sB&B£11 sB&B⇌ ⋒£14 dB&B£16.50 dB&B⇌ ⋒£20.50 ⊟ Credit cards 1 2 3 4 5 6

RYE East Sussex Map**5** TQ92
★★**George** High St (Trusthouses Forte) ☎2114
Three storey inn, dating from Tudor times with Georgian façade. Interior has heavy oak beams and fireplaces. Dining room with minstrel's gallery, dates from 1818.
22⇌ ⋒ ⋒ CTV TV in bedrooms 17P Last dinner9pm ♧ S% sB&B⇌ ⋒£14.50 dB&B⇌ ⋒£21 ⊟ *xmas* Credit cards 1 2 3 4 5 6

★★**Hope Anchor** Watchbull St ☎2216
14rm(7⇌ ⋒) ☽ ⋒ CTV ⚑ ⛟ ♡English & French. Last dinner9pm ♧ ✱sB&B fr£7.50 dB&B fr£14 dB&B⇌ ⋒ fr£17 Lunch fr£3.25 Dinner£4–£6 Wine£2.85 *xmas* Credit cards 1 2 3 5

★★**Saltings** Hilders Cliff, High St ☎3838
19rm(7⇌ ⋒) ☽ ⋒ CTV ⊘ 35P ⛟ ♡English & Continental. Last dinner9.30pm ✱sB&B£7 dB&B£14.90 dB&B⇌ ⋒£15.90–£19.90 Lunch£2.95–£3.95&alc Dinner£4.95–£5.95&alc Wine£2.95 ⊟ *xmas* Credit cards 1 2 3 4 5 6

✕**Flushing Inn** Market St ☎3292
Closed Tue, 26Dec–3rd wk Jan, 1wk after Etr & 22Sep–22Oct; Dinner not served Mon; 36seats ⚑ Last dinner9.15pm Lunch£4.50–£8&alc Dinner£6.50–£8.50&alc Wine£4.30 Credit cards 1 3 4 5 6

✕**Monastery** 61 High St ☎3272
Closed Tue; Lunch not served winter (except Sun); 46seats ⚑ bedrooms available ♡English & French. Last dinner9.30pm ✱Lunch£3.90alc Dinner£5.50alc

RYE FOREIGN East Sussex Map**5** TQ82
☆☆***Rumpels Motel*** ☎Peasmarsh494
Annexe: 12⇌ ⋒ ⋒ TV available in bedrooms 35–40P 14⌂ ⚓ ♡English & French. Last dinner9.30pm ♧ ⚲ ⊟ Credit cards 1 2 3 5

ST AGNES Cornwall Map**2** SW75
★★**Lamorna House** Chapel Porth Rd, Goonvrea ☎2670
Closed Jan & Feb; 11rm CTV 12P ⛟ ⚓ Last dinner7.30pm ♧ ⚲ S% ✱sB&B£8.80–£9.40 dB&B£17.70–£18.85

★★ ⛨**Ross-in-Vale** Mithian ☎2202
Small Georgian country house standing in spacious grounds, surrounded by countryside and just outside the little village of Mithian.
Closed Oct–Mar; 15rm(8⇌ ⋒) CTV 25P ⛟ ⚓ ⌒(heated) Children under 5yrs not accommodated S% ✱sB&B£8.60–£9.20 sB&B⇌ ⋒£9.70–£10.30 dB&B£17.20–£18.40 dB&B⇌ ⋒£19.40–£20.60 Bar lunch fr30p Tea fr40p Dinner fr£4.25 Wine£2.90

★★**Rosemundy House** ☎2101
Closed 14Dec–5Jan; RS Nov–13Dec & 6Jan–Mar; 45rm(30⇌⋒) CTV TV available in bedrooms ⊘70P ⚓ ⛆(heated) Children under 5yrs not accommodated ♿ Last dinner 8pm ♉ sB&B£9.50 sB&B⇌⋒£11.50–£15.80 dB&B£19 dB&B⇌⋒£23–£31.60 Lunch£2.85 Dinner£4.25 Wine£3.25 ⊓ Credit card 3

ST ALBANS Hertfordshire Map**4** TL10
★★★**Noke** Watford Rd (2¼m S at junc A405/A412) (Thistle) ☎54252
57⇌⋒ ☽ ⋈ CTV in bedrooms 150P ⚓ ♉English & French. Last dinner 9.15pm ♉ ⚲ S% ✱sB&B⇌⋒£19.90 dB&B⇌⋒£28.80 Lunch£3.80 Tea50–60p Dinner£4.90 ⊓ Credit cards 1 2 3 5

★★★**Sopwell House** Cottonmill Ln (Best Western) ☎64477
18th-C mansion surrounded by three acres of gardens. Once owned by the Earl of Verulam and it is reputed that Princess Alice of Greece (Prince Philip's mother), was proposed to in the gardens.
18⇌⋒ ☽ ⋈ CTV in bedrooms ⊘80P ⛟ ⚓ ♉English & French. Last dinner 9.30pm ♉ sB&B⇌⋒£14.85–£18 dB&B⇌⋒£26.50–£36 Lunch£4.05–£4.50&alc Dinner£5.10–£5.50&alc Wine£3.75 ⊓ Credit cards 1 2 3 5

★★★**St Michael's Manor** Fishpool St ☎64444
Manor dating from 1512, carefully restored and improved by Newling Ward family since being taken over by them in 1965.
22rm(13⇌⋒) 1⊟ ☽ ⋈ CTV CTV in bedrooms 70P ⛟ ⚓ ♉English & French. Last dinner 7.30pm sB&B£12.40 sB&B⇌⋒£14 dB&B£17.30 dB&B⇌⋒£20 Lunch£3.50–£4 Dinner£4.90–£5.50&alc Wine£3.50 Credit cards 1 2 3

★★**White Hart** Holywell Hill ☎53624
10rm CTV 20P ⛟ Children under 5yrs not accommodated Last dinner 9.45pm ♉ S% sB&B£11 dB&B£15.50 Lunch£4.50alc Dinner£5alc Wine£2.95 ⊓ Credit cards 1 2 6

✕✕**Aspelia** 17 Heritage Cl ☎66067
Closed Sun; 100seats ▶ ♉Greek. Last dinner 11pm Lunch£3–£7 Dinner£3–£7 Wine£2.75 Credit cards 1 2 3 5 6

✕**Jade Garden** 16–20 Spencer St ☎56077
Closed 16Feb & 25–27Dec; 46seats ▶ ♉Cantonese. Last dinner 11.30pm S% Lunch£1.25–£4.03£alc Dinner£2.87–£4.03&alc Wine£3.80 Credit cards 1 2 3 5

ST ANNES Lancashire see **Lytham St Annes**

ST AUSTELL Cornwall Map**2** SX05
★★★**Porth Avallen** Sea Rd, Carlyon Bay ☎Par2802
Closed mid Dec–mid Jan; 26rm(19⇌⋒) ⋈ CTV CTV available in bedrooms ⊘50P ⛟ ⚓ ⛬ ♉English & French. Last dinner 8.30pm ♉ ⚲ S% ✱sB&B£10–£12.50 sB&B⇌⋒£12.50–£15 dB&B£20–£24.30 dB&B⇌⋒£21.50–£26.50 Lunch fr£3.50&alc Tea fr45p&alc High Tea fr£1.50&alc Dinner fr£3.50&alc Wine£2.40 ⊓ Credit cards 1 2

★★**Clifden** 36–39 Aylmer Sq ☎3691
Closed 23Dec–1Jan; 15rm ⋈ CTV CTV in bedrooms Last dinner 9pm ♉ ⚲ S% sB&B£9 dB&B£15 Lunch£1–£2&alc Tea fr25p Dinner£2.50–£5&alc Wine£2.25 Credit cards 1 3

★★**Cliff Head** Sea Rd, Carlyon Bay ☎Par2125
Closed Nov–Mar; 50rm(12⇌⋒) ⋈ CTV 60P ⚓ ⛆(heated) Last dinner 8pm ♉ S% sB&B£8–£9.50 sB&B⇌⋒£9.50–£11 dB&B£15–£18 dB&B⇌⋒£18–£21

S

Lunch£2–£3 Dinner£3.75–£4.50 Wine£3.50 ⛿ Credit cards ①③

★★**White Hart** Church St ☎2100
Closed 25 & 26Dec; 20rm(4⇌⋒) TV in bedrooms ℙ ⛟ Last dinner8.30pm ♁ sB&B£9.20 sB&B⇌⋒£10.10–£10.65 dB&B£16.10 dB&B⇌⋒£17.25–£18.40 Lunch£2.50&alc Dinner£4&alc Wine£2.45

★**Pier House** Harbour Front, Charlestown ☎5272
11rm(3⇌⋒) CTV 11⌂ ♡English & French. Last dinner10pm ♁ ♫ ✱sB&B£5.50–£6.50 dB&B£11–£13 dB&B⇌⋒£13–£15 Lunch fr£2.50&alc Tea fr75p Dinner£2.15–£2.45&alc

✕✕**Boscundle Manor** Tregrehan ☎Par3557
Closed Sun; Lunch not served Sat; 30seats 12P ♡International. Last dinner9.30pm ✱Lunch£6alc Dinner£6alc Wine£2.75 Credit cards ①②③⑥

ST BEES Cumbria Map**11** NX91
★***Manor House Inn*** Main St ☎425
The village and priory date back to 650AD and the hotel bears the date 1697. A gentle lady ghost has been seen, but her identity remains unknown.
7rm(2⇌⋒) ♛ TV 20P 1⌂ ♡English & Continental. Last dinner9pm ♁ ⛿ Credit cards ③⑥

ST HELENS Isle of Wight Map**4** SZ68
❀✕**Hay Loft** Upper Green ☎Bembridge2014
Closed Oct–May; Lunch not served; Dinner not served Sun (except Aug); 55seats ℙ Specialities: Hayloft terrine, local lobster thermidor, iced soufflés. Last dinner9.15pm Dinner£9alc Wine£2.16

ST HELENS Merseyside Map**7** SJ59 **See also Rainhill**
★★★**Fleece** Church St (Greenall Whitley) ☎26546
This modernised hotel dates back to 1729 when it was a coaching inn.
76rm(64⇌⋒) Lift ☽ ♛ TV in bedrooms Disco weekly ♿ Conference facilities available ♡English & French. Last dinner9.20pm ♁ S% sB&B£13–£14 SB&B⇌⋒£17–£18 dB&B£19–£20 dB&B⇌⋒£22–£23 Lunch£2.95–£4.20 Dinner£4–£5&alc Wine£2.95 ⛿ Credit cards ①②③⑤⑥

ST IVES Cambridgeshire Map**4** TL37
❀★★★**Slepe Hall** Ramsey Rd ☎63122
Closed Xmas; 15rm(9⇌⋒) 1⊟ ♛ TV in bedrooms 130P 2⌂ ♡International. Specialities: Fluffy mushroom flan, slepe smokies, Cromwellian pork loin. Last dinner10pm ♁ ♫ sB&B£15–£18.75 sB&B⇌⋒£18.75–£20 dB&B£22.85–£24 dB&B⇌⋒£24–£26 Lunch£5.25–£6&alc Tea£1.50–£3&alc Dinner£5.25–£6&alc Wine£3.95 ⛿ Credit cards ①②③⑤⑥

★★**Golden Lion** Market Hill ☎63159
20rm(16⇌⋒) ♛ CTV CTV available in bedrooms 70P ⛟ Last dinner9.30pm ♁ S% ✱sB&B£8.50 sB&B⇌⋒£10.50 dB&B£17.50 dB&B⇌⋒£19.50 Lunch£3–£3.75&alc Dinner fr£4.75&alc Wine£3.25 Credit cards ①③

☆☆**St Ives Motel** London Rd ☎63857
RS 25 & 26Dec; 16⇌⋒ ♛ TV in bedrooms 80P ⛟ ⚓ Last dinner7.30pm ♁ ♫ ✱sB&B⇌⋒ fr£14.55 dB&B⇌⋒ fr£20.50 Lunch fr£4.50 Dinner fr£6.50 Wine£2.65 Credit cards ①②③⑤

ST IVES Cornwall Map**2** SW54
★★★★**Tregenna Castle** (British Transport)
☎Penzance795254 Telex no45128
Imposing, stone-built, 18th-C castle standing in 100 acres of grounds.
84rm(69⇌⋒) Lift ☽ ♛ CTV TV in bedrooms 25P ⚓ ⇒(heated) ⛳ ⚲ squash ◯ billiards ⚘ conference facilities available ♡English & French. Last dinner9pm ♁ ♫ S% sB&B⇌⋒ fr£27.50 dB&B⇌⋒ fr£46 Lunch fr£5.85 Dinner fr£8.55 Wine£3.50 ⛿ *xmas* Credit cards ①②③④⑤⑥

★★★**Chy-an-Drea** The Terrace (Inter-Hotel)
☎Penzance795076
Closed Nov–Mar; 36rm(18⇌⋒) ♛ CTV TV available in bedrooms 5P 20⌂ ⛟ ⚓ Disco wkly Live music & dancing wkly Children under 4yrs not accommodated Last dinner8.30pm ♁ sB&B£9.25–£12.25 sB&B⇌⋒£10.25–£14 dB&B£18.50–£24.50 dB&B⇌⋒£20.50–£28 Lunch£3 Dinner£4.50 ⛿ Credit cards ①②③⑤

★★★**Garrack** Higher Ayr ☎Penzance796199
Secluded hotel with country house atmosphere; own extensive grounds; panoramic views of St Ives Bay.
Closed Oct–Mar; 19rm(9⇌⋒) Annexe: 2rm CTV 30P ⛟ ⚓ ⚘ ♡English & French. Last dinner8.30pm ♁ ♫ sB&B£8.80–£11 dB&B£17.60–£22 dB&B⇌⋒£24.50–£30 Lunch£4.75alc Dinner fr£5.50&alc Wine£2.60 ⛿ Credit cards ①②⑤⑥

★★★**Master Roberts** Street-an-Pol
☎Penzance796042
RS Nov–Mar (Restaurant closed); 18rm(10⇌⋒) 3⊟ CTV ⊘ 6P Disco 6 nights wkly Live music & dancing 4 nights wkly Last dinner10pm ♁ S% ✱sB&B£9.18–£11.88 sB&B⇌⋒£10.26–£12.96 dB&B£18.36–£23.76 dB&B⇌⋒£20.52–£25.92 Bar lunch65p–£1.75 Dinner£5–£7&alc Credit cards ③⑤

★★★**Porthminster** The Terrace ☎Penzance795221
50⇌⋒ Lift ☽ CTV CTV in bedrooms 27P 14⌂ ⛟ ⚓ ⇒(heated) sauna bath Live music & dancing twice

S

wkly ♣ Last dinner8.30pm ⚘ ☐ S%
sB&B⇌⋒£13.50–£16.50 dB&B⇌⋒£27–£33
Lunch£3.30&alc Tea75p Dinner£4&alc
Wine£2.50 *xmas* Credit cards 1 2 3 4 5

★★Boskerris Boskerris Rd, Carbis Bay ☎Penzance795295
Two-storey hotel in own gardens overlooking Carbis Bay.
Closed Oct–Mar; 22rm(8⇌⋒) CTV 20P ⚘ ♣ ☺English & French. Last dinner8pm ⚘ ☐ S%
sB&B£8.50–£9.50 dB&B£15–£19
dB&B⇌⋒£16.50–£21.50 Lunch£3alc
Tea60palc Dinner£4.50alc Wine£3 ⊓

★★Carbis Bay Carbis Bay ☎Penzance795311
Closed Nov–Mar; 28rm(18⇌⋒) CTV CTV available in bedrooms 100P ♣ ⊇(heated) Disco Mon Live music & dancing Fri ♣ ☺English & French.
Last dinner9pm ⚘ ☐ S%
✱sB&B£9.25–£15.50 sB&B⇌⋒£10–£17
dB&B£18.50–£31 dB&B⇌⋒£20–£34
Lunch£5alc Tea40p–£1 Dinner fr£5&alc
Wine£2.50 ⊓ Credit cards 1 2 3 4 5 6

★★Chy-an-Albany Albany Ter ☎Penzance796759
40rm(1⇌⋒) ☽ CTV CTV available in bedrooms ⊘ 30P Disco twice wkly Last dinner8pm ⚘ ☐
✱sB&B£9.50 sB&B⇌⋒£10.50 dB&B£19
dB&B⇌⋒£21 Tea fr£1 High Tea fr£1
Dinner fr£3.50 Wine£2.50 ⊓ *xmas*
Credit cards 1 2 3 5 6

★★Chy-an-Dour Treloyan Av ☎Penzance796436
RS 15Nov–15Mar; 29rm(21⇌⋒) Lift ☽ ♯ CTV 22P ♣ Last dinner8.15pm ⚘ sB&B£6.20–£9.50
sB&B⇌⋒£6.20–£10.90 dB&B£12.40–£19
dB&B⇌⋒£12.40–£21.80 Bar lunch80p–£2.50
Dinner£4 Wine£2.25 ⊓ Credit cards 2 3

★★Chy-Morvah The Belyars ☎Penzance796314
Closed Oct–Mar; 32rm(8⇌⋒) ♯ CTV ⊘ 25P ⚘ ♣ ⊇(heated) Live music & dancing nightly
Last dinner7.15pm ⚘ ☐ sB&B£7.90–£10.40
sB&B⇌⋒£9.20–£11.60 dB&B£15.80–£20.80
dB&B⇌⋒£18.40–£23.20 Lunch£2.25 Tea70P
Dinner£3 Wine£2.40

★★Hendra's Carbis Bay ☎Penzance795030
Three-storey building of Cornish granite.
37rm(13⇌⋒) ☽ CTV 16P 14⌂ ⚘ ♣ Live music & dancing wkly ♣ ♿ Last dinner8pm ⚘
✱sB&B£8–£10 sB&B⇌⋒£9–£11
dB&B£16–£20 dB&B⇌⋒£18–£22 Lunch£2.50
Dinner£3.50

★★Karenza Headland Rd, Carbis Bay ☎Penzance795294
Large, family hotel commanding views of Carbis Bay.
Closed 21Oct–19Mar; 13rm(8⇌⋒)
Annexe: 16rm(6⇌⋒) ♯ CTV 30P ⚘ ♣ ⊇(heated) Disco wkly Live music & dancing wkly ♣ ☺English & Continental. Last dinner8pm ⚘ ☐ S%
sB&B fr£10.20 sB&B⇌⋒ fr£11.05
dB&B fr£20.40 dB&B⇌⋒ fr£22.10 Lunch fr£2.75
Tea fr75p Dinner fr£4.30 Wine£3.50 ⊓

★★Pedn-Olva The Warren ☎Penzance796222
RS Nov–Mar; 26rm Annexe: 4rm ☽ CTV ⊘ 21P ♣ Live music & dancing wkly ♿ Last dinner7.15pm ⚘ ☐ sB&B£7.50–£8.50 dB&B£10,75–£12
Lunch£1–£2.75 Tea40p Dinner£4

★★St Ives Bay The Terrace ☎Penzance795106
Closed 15Oct–Apr; 53rm(12⇌⋒) Lift ☽ CTV ⊘ 20⌂ sauna bath Live music & dancing wkly Cabaret wkly Last dinner8.30pm ⚘ ☐ S%
sB&B£8.16–£9.72 sB&B⇌⋒£9.46–£11
dB&B£16.32–£19.44 dB&B⇌⋒£18.92–£22
Lunch£3.24–£3.82 Dinner£3.56–£4.53
Wine£2.75

★★St Uny Carbis Bay ☎Penzance795011
Castle-style residence, in own grounds and gardens, close to beach.
Closed 27Sep–16May; 34rm(17⇌⋒) Annexe: 2rm CTV 35P 5⌂ ⚘ ♣ Children under 5yrs not accommodated Last dinner8pm ⚘ ☐
sB&B£9.50–£10.50 dB&B£19–£22
dB&B⇌⋒£23–£26 Bar lunch fr£1 Tea fr75p
Dinner fr£7.50 Wine£4

★★*Western* Royal Sq ☎Penzance795277
Modernised old coaching inn.
Closed 30Sep–Mar; 23rm(7⇌⋒) CTV ⊘ 8⌂
Last dinner8pm ⚘

★Chy-an-Fore 28 Fore St ☎Penzance794155
12rm ♯ CTV ⊘ ℙ Last dinner4pm ☐ S%
sB&B£6.48–£8.69 dB&B£12.96–£17.38
Lunch£2–£2.50 Tea30p Dinner£2.50–£3
Wine£2.49 ⊓

★Ocean Breezes Clodgy View, Barnoon ☎Penzance795587
Closed Nov–Mar; 20rm(3⇌⋒) ♯ CTV CTV available in bedrooms 7P ⚘ Last dinner7.30pm ⚘ ☐ S%
✱sB&B£6.21–£8.64 sB&B⇌⋒£7.56–£10.26
dB&B£12.42–£17.28 dB&B⇌⋒£15.12–£20.25
Lunch£3.80&alc Tea£1.50alc Dinner£3.80&alc
Wine£2.60

★Trecarrell Carthew Ter ☎Penzance795707
Closed Nov–Mar; 15rm(2⇌⋒) ♯ CTV ⊘ 10P ⚘ Children under 3yrs not accommodated ☺English & French. Last dinner7.45pm ⚘ ☐ S%
sB&B£6.75–£11.45 sB&B⇌⋒£7.30–£12.70
dB&B£12.85–£22.25 dB&B⇌⋒£13.95–£22.25
dB&B⇌⋒£13.95–£24.30 Lunch fr£2.43
Tea fr75p Dinner fr£4.05 Wine£2.95 ⊓
Credit cards 1 2 3

Ⓗ *St Margarets* Carbis Bay ☎Penzance796453
Closed mid Oct–mid Apr; RS Mar–mid May; 18rm ♯ CTV 20P 1⌂ ⚘ Last dinner7.30pm ⚘ ☐ ⊓

✕*Le Matou* St Andrews Street ☎Penzance796661
Closed Mon; Lunch not served; 30seats ☺French.

✕Outrigger Street-an-Pol ☎Penzance795936
Closed Mon; Lunch not served; 30seats ℙ ☺English & French. Last dinner10.30pm ✱Dinner£6alc
Wine£2.95

ST LAWRENCE Isle of Wight Map4 SZ57

Ⓗ Rocklands ☎Ventnor852964
Closed Oct–14Nov; RS 15Nov–23May; 17rm(11⇌⋒) Annexe: 5rm 1▭ ♯ CTV CTV in bedrooms ⊘ 16P ⚘ ♣ ⊇(heated) ∩ billiards sauna bath ♣ Last dinner8.30pm ⚘ ☐ S%
sB&B£9–£10 sB&B⇌⋒£9–£10 dB&B£18–£20
dB&B⇌⋒£18–£20 Lunch fr£3 Tea fr55p
Dinner fr£7 Wine£2.50

ST LEONARDS Dorset Map4 SU00

★Avon Forest Ringwood Rd ☎Ferndown877764
Closed Jan 10rm ♯ CTV ⊘ 15P ⚘ ♣ Children under 10yrs not accommodated Last dinner9.30pm S%
sB&B£6 dB&B£12 Lunch£3alc Dinner£3.75alc
Wine£2.70 *xmas*

ST MARYCHURCH Devon Map3 SX96

See **Torquay**

S

ST MAWES Cornwall Map**2** SW83
★★★**Tresanton** ☎544
See page 52 for details

❀★★**Rising Sun** ☎233
See page 54 for details

★★**Green Lantern** Marine Pde ☎502
Closed mid Feb–mid Dec; 11rm(5⇌⫿) CTV CTV available in bedrooms ⊘ P ⊕ Children under 10yrs not accommodated ♀English & Continental. Last dinner9.30pm sB&B£8.50 sB&B⇌⫿£8.50 dB&B£17 dB&B⇌⫿£17 Lunch£3 Dinner£6 Wine£2.20 Credit cards ② ③ ⑤

★★**Idle Rocks** (Inter-Hotel) ☎771
Closed 6Nov–Feb; 15⇌⫿ ♛ CTV P ⊕ Children under 6yrs not accommodated ♀English & Continental. Last dinner8.30pm ♁ sB&B⇌⫿£11.50–£15 dB&B⇌⫿£23–£30 Lunch£3.30alc Dinner£6.25 Wine£3.15 ⊟ Credit cards ① ② ③ ⑤ ⑥

★★**Manor House** 11 The Square ☎392
RS Nov–Mar; 16rm(6⇌⫿) ♛ CTV 10P ♀English & Italian. Last dinner9pm ♁ sB&B£8–£9 sB&B⇌⫿£9–£10 dB&B£16–£18 dB&B⇌⫿£18 Dinner£5.25–£6.50&alc *xmas* Credit cards ① ③

★★**Ship & Castle** Harbourside ☎401
RS Dec–Feb; 36rm(33⇌⫿) Lift ♛ CTV 2P Live music & dancing twice wkly Cabaret wkly Last dinner8.30pm ♁ ☐ S% sB&B£6–£10 sB&B⇌⫿£8–£12 dB&B£12–£20 dB&B⇌⫿£16–£24 Lunch fr£2.65 Tea fr65p Dinner fr£3.95 Wine£2.95 ⊟ *xmas*

★***St Mawes*** ☎266
8rm(2⇌⫿) TV ⊕ Children under 3yrs not accommodated Last dinner8.15pm

S

ST MAWGAN Cornwall Map**2** SW86
★***Airways*** ☎329
8rm CTV 35P Last dinner9pm
Credit card 3

★***Pen-y-Morfa Country*** ☎363
11rm CTV P

ST NEOTS Cambridgeshire Map**4** TL16
XX**Chequers Inn** Eynesbury ☎Huntingdon72116
Closed Xmas Day; 40seats 35P English & French.
Last dinner10.30pm S% Lunch£7.75alc
Dinner£7.75alc Wine£3.70
Credit cards 1 2 3 4 5 6

ST WENN Cornwall Map**2** SW96
★ **Wenn Manor** ☎Roche240
8rm(5) CTV 20P 1 (heated)
Last dinner8.30pm sB&B£6.50–£8.50
dB&B£13–£17 dB&B £17–£19
Lunch£1.50alc Tea50p–£1&alc Dinner£4&alc
wine£2.30 *xmas* Credit cards 1 3

SALCOMBE Devon Map**3** SX73
★★★★**Marine** Cliff Rd (Prestige) ☎2251
Telex no45185
See page 54 for details

★★★**St Elmo** Sandhills Rd, North Sands ☎2233
Gabled, white-painted building perched high on cliffside, commanding views of Bolt Head and estuary.
Closed mid Oct–Apr; RS Etr; 27rm(11) CTV
30P Children under 6yrs not accommodated
English & French. Last dinner8.30pm
S% *sB&B£11–£13.50 sB&B £12.50–£15
dB&B£22–£27 dB&B £25–£30
Bar lunch60p–£3.50 Tea36p–£1.25
Dinner£5.75–£6.75 Wine£3

★★★**Salcombe** Fore St ☎2991
51rm(29) CTV 45P 4 (heated)
Last dinner8.30pm S%
sB&B£12.40–£21.40 (incl dinner)
dB&B£22.80–£45.50 (incl dinner)
dB&B £30.30–£48.30 (incl dinner)
Lunch£3.50 Tea£1 Dinner£7&alc *xmas*
Credit cards 2 5

★★★**Tides Reach** South Sands ☎2888
(Rosette awarded for dinner only)
Personally run, well-appointed holiday hotel. Impressive situation on South Sands Cove.
Closed Dec–Feb; 40rm(27) Lift CTV
available in bedrooms 100P Children under 8yrs
not accommodated English & Continental.
Specialities: fruits de mer, Bass, chicken Josephine.
Last dinner10pm *sB&B£10–£13
sB&B £14 dB&B£25–£30
dB&B £26–£40 Lunch£2.75–£4.50
Tea40–95p Dinner£6–£6.50&alc Wine£3
Credit cards 1 3 5

★★**Bolt Head** ☎2780
Built in the style of a Swiss chalet, standing 140ft above sea-level, overlooking sea and estuary.
Closed mid Oct–Mar; 22rm(19) CTV CTV
available in bedrooms 40P Children under
7yrs not accommodated English & French.
Last dinner10pm S% sB&B fr£10.50
sB&B fr£10.50 dB&B fr£12.50
dB&B fr£12.50 Bar lunch£1.10
Dinner£4.70&alc Wine£2.84
Credit cards 1 2 3 5

★★**Castle Point** Sandhills Rd ☎2167
Private grounds give access to estuary and ruins of Salcombe Castle.
Closed 15Oct–Mar; 20rm(7) CTV 40P 2

S

⚘ ⚓ Children under 6yrs not accommodated ♡French. Last dinner8pm ☆ ☐ sB&B£8–£15 dB&B£12–£30 dB&B⇌⋒£18–£35 Barlunch55p–£3 Tea55p–£1 Dinner£5–£6 Wine£3.25

★★Grafton Towers Moult Rd, South Sands ☎2882
In a peaceful situation, enjoying views of South Sands.
Closed 3Oct–Mar; 14rm(9⇌⋒) TV available in bedrooms 14P ⚘ ⚓ ⌂ ♡English & French. Last dinner8pm ☆ ☐ sB&B£11.66 sB&B⇌⋒£13.98 dB&B£23.32 dB&B⇌⋒£27.96 Lunch£2 Tea75p Dinner£4.25–£4.75 Wine£3 ⊟

★★South Sands ☎2791
Closed Oct–Mar; 17rm(14⇌⋒) ⅏ CTV 6P 13⌂ ⚘ ⌂ ♡English & French. Last dinner9pm ☆ ☐ ✱sB&B£9.42–£10.28 dB&B£10.28–£11 dB&B⇌⋒£12.57–£13.14 Barlunch40p–£2 Tea26–80p Dinner£3.50&alc Wine£2.94 ⊟ Credit cards 1 3 6

★Knowle Onslow Rd ☎2846
Closed Nov–Feb; 10rm(7⇌⋒) ⅏ CTV TV available in bedrooms 40P ⚘ ⚓ ⌂ ♡English & French. ☆ ☐ sB&B£7–£9 sB&B⇌⋒£8–£10 dB&B fr£14 dB&B⇌⋒ fr£16 Lunch£2.50–£3.50 Tea35p Dinner£3.75–£4 Wine£2.64 ⊟ Credit card 1

★Melbury Devon Rd ☎2883
Closed 27Sep–May; 14rm(4⇌⋒) CTV ⊘ 18P ⚘ ⚓ Children under 5yrs not accommodated Last dinner7pm ☆ S% sB&B£7.50–£9 sB&B⇌⋒£9–£10.50 dB&B£15–£18 dB&B⇌⋒£18–£21 Barlunch50p–£2 Dinner£4.50 Wine£2.50

S

★**Penn Torr** Herbert Rd ☎2234
Closed Oct–Mar; 11rm(4⇌⋔) 11P Children under 4yrs not accommodated S% dB&B£12–£13 dB&B⇌⋔£14–£15 Wine£2.50

★**Sunny Cliff** Cliff Rd ☎2207
Closed Nov–Mar; 15rm(2⇌⋔) Annexe: 2rm 14P 1 (heated) English & French. Last dinner 8pm S% sB&B£8–£10 dB&B£16–£20 dB&B⇌⋔£18–£22 Bar lunch 50p–£1.50 Tea 30–40p Dinner£4.25 Wine£3.10

★**Wells** Herbert Rd ☎2226 Closed Oct–Mar; 16rm(9⇌⋔) CTV 20P Children under 4yrs not accommodated Last dinner 7pm sB&B£9–£10 dB&B£18–£20 dB&B⇌⋔£20–£22 Lunch£3.50–£4 Dinner£5–£6

XX***Galley*** Main St ☎2828
Lunch not served; 50 seats Last dinner 10.30pm

SALFORD Greater Manchester Map**7** SJ89
See also Manchester
★★**Racecourse** Littleton Rd (Greenall Whitley) ☎061–792 1420
12rm(5⇌⋔) CTV 100P Last dinner 7.30pm *sB&B£10 sB&B⇌⋔£11 dB&B£15 dB&B⇌⋔£16 Lunch£2.50 Dinner£3.60 Wine£3.30 Credit cards 1 2 3 5

★**Beaucliffe** 254 Eccles Old Rd, Pendleton ☎061–789 5092
21rm(17⇌⋔) CTV 40P 3 Children under 6yrs not accommodated Last dinner 7.30pm S% *sB&B£7.56 sB&B⇌⋔£8.37 dB&B£14.04 dB&B⇌⋔£15.66 Lunch£2.40–£3.60&alc Dinner£3.25–£3.75&alc Wine£2.10 Credit cards 1 3

SALFORDS Surrey Map**4** TQ24 **See under Gatwick Airport**

SALISBURY Wiltshire Map**4** SU12
★★★**Rose & Crown** Harnham Rd (Grand Met) ☎27908
13th-C building with river-side lawns, with views of distant Salisbury Cathedral.
29rm(17⇌⋔) TV TV available in bedrooms 70P Live music & dancing Fri (Nov–Jan) Last dinner 9.30pm S% *sB&B⇌⋔£15.50–£17 dB&B⇌⋔£18–£20.50 *xmas* Credit cards 1 2 3 4 5 6

★★★**White Hart** St John Street (Trusthouse Forte) ☎27476
73rm(57⇌⋔) TV in bedrooms 85P Last dinner 10pm S% sB&B£14.50 sB&B⇌⋔£17.50 dB&B£21.50 dB&B⇌⋔£27 *xmas* Credit cards 1 2 3 4 5 6

★★**Cathedral** Milford St ☎20144
32rm(8⇌⋔) Lift CTV English & French. Last dinner 9.30pm S% sB&B fr£14.70 sB&B⇌⋔ fr£17.10 dB&B fr£20.80 dB&B⇌⋔ fr£26.90 Lunch fr£2.50 Tea fr50p High Tea fr£2.50 Dinner fr£4.50 Wine£3 Credit card 3

★★**Kings Arms** St John Street (Wessex Taverns) ☎27629
16th-C half-timbered and gabled inn near Cathedral.
13rm(6⇌⋔) CTV TV available in bedrooms Last dinner 10pm S% sB&B£9.50 dB&B£15 dB&B⇌⋔£18.75 Lunch£3.75alc Tea 75palc Dinner£3.75alc Wine£2.95 *xmas* Credit cards 1 2 3 4 5 6

★★Red Lion Milford St (Best Western) ☎22788
A coaching inn, built round a courtyard, dating from 1320.
58rm(30⇌ ⫚) 2▭ ☽ CTV 10P 12🏠 ♡English & French. Last dinner9.30pm ♁ ⚲
sB&B£12.50–£13.50 sB&B⇌⫚£15.50–£17.50
dB&B£19–£22 dB&B⇌⫚£22–£25
Lunch£3.75–£5&alc Tea50p–£1.25
Dinner£4.50–£5.50&alc Wine£3 ♜ *xmas*
Credit cards 1 2 5

★County Bridge St (Berni) ☎20229
Tudor-style hotel, in the centre of town with direct access to river.
Closed Xmas day; 36rm(2⇌⫚) ☽ CTV 25P ♡Mainly grills. Last dinner10.30pm ♁ ⚲
✱sB&B£7.25–£8 sB&B⇌⫚£9.95–£10.60
dB&B£13.20–£14.45 dB&B⇌⫚£15.90–£17.15
Lunch£1.80–£4.25 Tea90p Dinner£1.80–£4.25
Wine£2.44 ♜ Credit cards 1 2 3 5 6

XXHaunch of Venison Minster St ☎22024
Closed Sun, Mon, 2wks Feb & 2wks Jul; 37seats ⚑
Last dinner10pm Lunch£3.50&alc
Dinner£8.00alc Wine£2.50 Credit cards 1 2 5

XCranes 90 Crane St ☎3471
Closed Sun, Mon, 3wks Xmas & 3wks Jun; 32seats ♡Continental. Last dinner10.30pm

XProvençal Market Pl ☎28923
Closed Sun(Nov–Mar) & Xmas 34seats ⚑ ♡French.
Last dinner10.30pm S% ✱Dinner£10alc
Wine£3 Credit cards 2 3 5

SALTASH Cornwall Map**2** SX45
★Holland Inn ☎3635
30⇌⫚ ᛗ CTV in bedrooms 30P 🚗 ⚓
Last dinner9.30pm ♁ S% sB&B⇌⫚£10.50
dB&B⇌⫚£21 Lunch£3alc Dinner£3.50alc
Wine£2

SALTBURN-BY-THE-SEA Cleveland Map**8** NZ62
★★*Queen* Windsor Rd ☎3371
18rm(16⇌⫚) ᛗ TV 10P 1🏠 ♡English & French.
Last dinner9.45pm

SAMBOURNE Warwickshire Map**4** SP06
X*Green Dragon Inn* ☎Astwood Bank2465
Closed Sun last wk Jul & 1st wk Aug; Lunch not served Sat; Dinner not served Mon; 44seats 80P
Last dinner9.30pm

SAMPFORD PEVERELL Devon Map**3** ST01
★*Green Headland* ☎820255
6rm ᛗ CTV 100P ⚓ Last dinner8pm ♁ ⚲
Credit card 3

SANDBACH Cheshire Map**7** SJ76
★★★Chimney House Congleton Rd (Whitbread)
☎4141
22⇌⫚ ☽ ᛗ CTV TV available in bedrooms 80P ⚓
♡English & French. Last dinner9.45pm ♁ ⚲
sB&B⇌⫚ fr£13 dB&B⇌⫚ fr£17.25
Continental breakfast Lunch£3&alc
Dinner£3.50&alc Wine£2.65 ♜ *xmas*
Credit card 3

☆☆☆Saxon Cross Motel Holmes Chapel Rd (M6 junc 17) ☎2636
52⇌⫚ ☽ ᛗ CTV in bedrooms 200P ⚓ Conference facilities available Last dinner9.30pm ♁ ⚲ S%
sB&B⇌⫚ fr£13 dB&B⇌⫚ fr£18 Lunch fr£3
Tea fr75p Dinner£4alc ♜
Credit cards 1 2 3 4 5 6

★★Old Hall Newcastle Rd ☎3757
12⇌⫚ ᛗ CTV in bedrooms 100P 🚗 ⚓
Last dinner10pm S% sB&B⇌⫚£14
dB&B⇌⫚£19 Lunch£3.10 Tea40p
Dinner£4.50–£6.50 Wine£2.90 ♜
Credit cards 1 3

S

SANDBANKS Dorset See **Poole**

SANDERSTEAD Greater London Map**4** TQ36
★★★★**Selsdon Park** ☎01–657 8811
160⇌⋒ Lift ☽ 𝍖 CTV in bedrooms 200P 10🏠 ⚓ (heated) ⛳18 ⦿ ∩ billiards sauna bath Live music & dancing Sat Conference facilities available ♡International. Last dinner10.15pm S%
✱sB&B⇌⋒£22–£32 dB&B⇌⋒£34–£42
Lunch£6.25&alc Dinner£6.75&alc Wine£3.75
xmas Credit cards 1 2 3 5

SANDIACRE Derbyshire Map**8** SK43
See also Long Eaton
☆☆☆**Post House** Bostock Ln (N of M1 junc 25) (Trusthouse Forte) ☎Nottingham397800
Telex no377378
106⇌⋒ ☽ 𝍖 CTV in bedrooms 180P
Last dinner10pm S% sB&B⇌⋒£19.75
dB&B⇌⋒£28.50 Credit cards 1 2 3 4 5 6

SANDOWN Isle of Wight Map**4** SZ58
★★★**Broadway Park** Melville St ☎402007
Closed mid Sep–mid May; 54rm(37⇌⋒) Lift ☽ 𝍖 CTV 100P ⚓ (heated) (grass) Disco wkly Live music & dancing 6 nights wkly Children under 3yrs not accommodated ♡English & French.
Last dinner8.30pm sB&B£9.72–£10.80
sB&B⇌⋒£11.88–£12.96 dB&B£19.44–£21.60
dB&B⇌⋒£23.76–£25.92 Lunch fr£3.85
Dinner fr£6 Wine£3

★★★**Melville Hall** Melville St ☎403794
Closed Oct–Apr; 37rm(16⇌⋒) ☽ CTV 25P ⚓ (heated) Live music & dancing twice wkly in season Children under 5yrs not accommodated
Last dinner8.30pm sB&B£10.50–£14
dB&B£19–£25 dB&B⇌⋒£22–£32
Lunch£3.50–£4.25 Tea75p–£1.30
Dinner£4.25–£5.50 Wine£3.50 *xmas*

★★***Royal Cliff*** Beachfield Rd ☎402138
Closed Oct–mid Apr; 28rm(4⇌⋒) 𝍖 CTV 20P 4🏠 ⚓ Children under 4yrs not accommodated ♡English & French. Last dinner8pm

★**Rose Bank** 6 High St ☎403854
Closed Xmas; 10rm 𝍖 CTV **P** Children under 6yrs not accommodated Last dinner7pm
✱sB&B£7.02–£8.10 dB&B£14.04–£16.20
dB&B⇌⋒£17.28–£19.44 Lunch fr£2.43
Dinner fr£3.78&alc Wine£2.50

SANDWICH Kent Map**5** TR35
During the currency of this guide Sandwich telephone numbers are liable to change.
★★★**Bell** Upper Strand St ☎2836
Early 19th-C inn on quayside of River Stour.
28rm ☽ 𝍖 CTV in bedrooms 10P Last dinner10pm
S% ✱sB&B fr£12.75 sB&B⇌⋒ fr£15.16
dB&B fr£20.25 dB&B⇌⋒ fr£22.50
Lunch fr£3.40&alc Dinner fr£4.40 Wine£1.75
Credit cards 1 2 3 5

✕**Cave** Harnet St ☎2274
Closed Mon (except Public Hols); Lunch not served Sun; 40seats **P** ♡English & Continental.
Last dinner9.30pm Lunch£6alc Dinner£6alc
Wine£3.25 Credit cards 1 2 5

✕**Pilgrim's** Strand St ☎3358
Closed Sun; Lunch not served Sat; 40seats 14P bedrooms available ♡English & Continental.
Last dinner10pm ✱Lunch£2.50–£3.50&alc
Dinner£2.50–£3.50&alc Wine£3
Credit cards 1 2 3 5 6

SAUNTON Devon Map**2** SS43
★★★**Saunton Sands** (Percy R. Brend)
☎Croyde890212
96rm(69⇌⋒) Lift ☽ 𝍖 CTV CTV available in bedrooms 140P ⚓ (heated) (hard) squash

S

billiards sauna bath Disco twice wkly Live music & dancing 3 nights wkly English & French. Last dinner9.30pm S% sB&B£7.56–£14.85 sB&B£12.69–£16.20 dB&B£12.96–£26.46 dB&B£23.22–£34.02 Continental breakfast Lunch£3.78 Tea£1.50 Dinner£5.67 Wine£3.08 xmas Credit cards 1 2 3 5 6

SAVERNAKE Wiltshire Map**4** SU26
★★**Savernake Forest** (Best Western) Burbage810206
Victorian building in rural setting. Quiet location on fringes of Savernake Forest.
14rm(5) 60P Last dinner9pm S% sB&B£10 sB&B£13.50 dB&B£20 dB&B£22 Bar lunch£2.75alc Dinner£6.50alc Wine£2.25 Credit cards 1 2 3 5 6

SAWBRIDGEWORTH Hertfordshire Map**5** TL41
X ***Straw Hat*** London Rd Bishop's Stortford722434
Closed Mon; Dinner not served Sun; 45seats 35P English & Continental. Last dinner11.30pm

SAWLEY North Yorkshire Map**7** SD74
XXX ***Spread Eagle*** Clitheroe41202
Old stone coaching inn near River Ribble, with traditional restaurant giving country views.
180seats 60P English & French. Last dinner9pm

SCARBOROUGH North Yorkshire Map**8** TA08
★★★★**Crown** Esplanade 73491 Telex no52280
81 Lift CTV in bedrooms P 11 Last dinner8.45pm sB&B£15.33–£17.18 Continental breakfast Lunch£3.25alc Dinner£5.50alc Wine3.50 xmas Credit cards 1 2 3 5

S

★★★★***Holbeck Hall*** Seacliffe Rd ☎74374
29rm(25⇌ ⋔) ☽ ⋔ TV available in bedrooms ⊘ 52P 3⌂ ⇎ ⚓ Live music & dancing Sat Children under 12yrs not accommodated ♡ English & Continental. Last dinner 9pm ♡ ☐

★★***Carlton*** Belmont Rd ☎60938
45rm Lift ☽ ⋔ CTV ⇎ ⚓ Live music & dancing 3nights wkly Last dinner 11pm ♡ ☐

★★**Esplanade** Belmont Rd (Travco) ☎60382
Closed Nov–Mar except Xmas; 77rm(21⇌ ⋔) Lift ☽ CTV 30P ⚓ Live music & dancing twice wkly Cabaret wkly ⚘ Last dinner 7.30pm ♡ sB&B£9.50–£10 sB&B⇌ ⋔£11–£11.50 dB&B£19–£20 dB&B⇌ ⋔£20.50–£21.50 Lunch fr£3 Dinner fr£4 Wine£2.25 ⊟ *xmas* Credit cards ①②③⑤⑥

★★**Mayfair** 41–42 Esplanade ☎60053
18rm(14⇌ ⋔) Lift ☽ ✗ ⋔ CTV in bedrooms ⚓ Last dinner 7.30pm ♡ S% sB&B£7.50–£9.50 dB&B⇌ ⋔£15.50–£19.50 Lunch£2–£3 Dinner£3–£4 Wine£3 *xmas*

★★**Southlands** West St ☎61461
61rm(24⇌ ⋔) Lift ☽ ⋔ CTV TV available in bedrooms ⊘ 35P ⚓ Disco twice wkly Live music & dancing wkly ⚘ Last dinner 8.30pm ♡ ☐ S% sB&B£8.60–£10 dB&B£16–£19 dB&B⇌ ⋔£19–£22 Lunch£3 Dinner£4–£4.50 Wine£2.75 ⊟ *xmas* Credit cards ①②③⑤

★**Dorchester** Filey Rd ☎61668
Closed mid Sep–Apr; Unlicensed; 40rm(12⇌ ⋔) Annexe: 10rm Lift CTV TV available in bedrooms 30P ⇎ ♿ Last dinner 7pm ♡ ☐ S% sB&B£7.50–£8.50 dB&B£16–£18 dB&B⇌ ⋔£16–£19.50 Lunch£2.85 Tea£1 Dinner£4.50

✗✗**Lanterna** 33 Queen St ☎63616
Closed Sun & Mon; 36seats ⚑ ♡ Continental. Last dinner 9.30pm ✱Lunch£5.80alc Dinner£5alc Wine£3.50 Credit card ③

SCILLY, ISLES OF See **Hugh Town, New Grimsby and Old Grimsby**

SCOTCH CORNER (near Richmond) North Yorkshire Map**8** NZ20
★★★**Scotch Corner** Great North Road (Scottish Highlands) ☎Richmond (N. Yorks) 2943
Telex no 778215
Three-storey, red brick building with gardens and grounds on site of ancient Three Tuns Inn.
43rm(35⇌ ⋔) Lift ☽ ⋔ CTV 250P ⚓ Live music & dancing wkly (Oct–Apr) ♿ Last dinner 11pm ♡ ☐ S% sB&B£15.10 sB&B⇌ ⋔£17.95 dB&B£24.60 dB&B⇌ ⋔£30.30 Lunch£4.10 Tea£1.30 Dinner£6.25 Wine£3.25 ⊟ *xmas* Credit cards ①②③④⑤⑥

SCRATCHWOOD (M1 Motorway Service Area) **Access only from Motorway** Greater London Map**4** TQ19
☆☆☆**TraveLodge** see **London** under **NW7**

SCUNTHORPE Humberside Map**8** SE81
★★**Royal** Doncaster Rd (Anchor) ☎68181
Telex no 858875
28rm(24⇌ ⋔) ☽ ⋔ TV available in bedrooms 30P Last dinner 9.30pm ♡ ☐ S% ✱sB&B fr£11.25 sB&B⇌ ⋔ fr£15 dB&B fr£18.50 dB&B⇌ ⋔ fr£22 Lunch fr£3.50 Dinner fr£3.50 Wine£2.65 ⊟ Credit cards ①②③④⑤⑥

SEAFORD East Sussex Map**5** TV49
☆☆**Newhaven Ladbroke Mercury Motor Inn** (on A259) (Ladbroke) ☎891055
Annexe: 65⇌ ⋔ ☽ ⋔ CTV available in bedrooms 80P Conference facilities available Last dinner 10.30pm ♡ ☐ sB&B fr£17.50 dB&B⇌ ⋔ fr£26.50 Lunch fr£4.50&alc Dinner fr£5&alc Wine£3.20 ⊟ Credit cards ①②③④⑤⑥

✗**Masthead** 5 High St ☎896135
Closed Mon except Public Hols; Dinner not served Sun; 30seats ⚑ ♡ Continental. Last dinner 10pm Lunch£2.75–£5.95&alc Dinner£6alc Wine£3.20 Credit cards ①③⑤

SEAHOUSES Northumberland Map**12** NU23
★★***Dunes*** Sea Front ☎720378
Natural stone building on seafront overlooking beach and Farne Islands.
Closed Nov–Apr; 30rm(5⇌ ⋔) ⋔ CTV 30P 4⌂ ⇎ ⚓ Last dinner 7.45pm ♡ sB&B£7.50 sB&B⇌ ⋔£9.50 dB&B£17 dB&B⇌ ⋔£19.50 Lunch£3.50 Dinner£6.50 Wine£3

★**Beach House** Sea Front ☎720337
Closed Xmas; 16rm(3⇌ ⋔) 1⊟ ⋔ CTV TV in bedrooms 16P ⚓ Last dinner 7.30pm ♡ sB&B£6.50–£7.50 dB&B£13–£15 dB&B⇌ ⋔£16–£18 Dinner£3.35–£3.50 Wine£2.75 ⊟

★**Olde Ship** ☎720200
Closed mid Oct–last wk Mar; 7rm ⋔ CTV 10P 2⌂ ⇎ ⚘ Last dinner 8pm ♡ sB&B£7–£7.50 dB&B£14–£15 Lunch£2.50 Dinner£3.75 Wine£1.75 Credit cards ①③

⊕**Bamburgh Castle** ☎720283
Detached hotel with views across the harbour.
Closed 20Dec–Jan; 18rm CTV P 50⌂ ⚓ Last dinner 7.30pm ♡ sB&B£7.50–£8.50 dB&B£15–£17 Lunch£2.50–£3.50 Dinner£3.50–£4.50 Wine£2.50

SEALE Surrey Map**4** SU84
★★**Hog's Back** Hog's Back (on A31) (Embassy) ☎Runfold 2345

S

Converted private residence, with gardens and grounds. Tower room has views of six counties.
14rm(4⇌⋒) ☽ ⋔ CTV TV in bedrooms 100P ⚓
Last dinner9pm ♡ S% sB&B£11.50
sB&B⇌⋒£13 dB&B£18 dB&B⇌⋒£21
Lunch£5&alc Dinner£5.50&alc Wine£4.50 ⊨
Credit cards 1 2 3 4 5 6

SEASCALE Cumbria Map**6** NY00
★**Seafield** Drigg Rd ☎298
Closed 24–31 Dec; 10rm(3⇌⋒) ⋔ CTV 10P ⚓
Last dinner7.30pm ♡ sB&B£8.75–£9.50
dB&B£17.50–£19 dB&B⇌⋒£19.50–£21
Bar lunch£1.50alc Dinner£4alc Wine£2.75
★**Wansfell** ☎301
Offers distant views of the Isle of Man.
15rm(3⇌⋒) CTV 150P ♡English & French.
Last dinner8.30pm ♡ ♡ ✱sB&B£6.50
sB&B⇌⋒£7 dB&B£13 dB&B⇌⋒£14
Lunch£2–£2.85 Tea45p–£1
High Tea£1.50–£2.75 Dinner£4.85–£7&alc
Wine£2.90 ⊨

SEATON Devon Map**3** SY29
★★***Bay*** East Walk ☎20073
Closed mid Oct–mid Apr; 34rm(1⇌⋒) ⋔ CTV 60P
10⌂ Live music & dancing 3 nights wkly Children under 6yrs not accommodated Last dinner7pm ♡ ♡

✕✕**Copperfields** Fore St ☎22294
Dinner not served Sun; 38seats 8P ♡English & Continental. Last dinner10.30pm
✱Lunch£2.75–£7.50 Tea80palc
High Tea£1.20alc Dinner£5alc Wine£2.70
Credit cards 2 3

SEATON BURN Tyne & Wear Map**12** NZ27
☆☆☆☆**Holiday Inn** Great North Road
(Commonwealth) ☎Wideopen5432 Telex no53271
151⇌⋒ ☽ ⊞ ⋔ CTV CTV in bedrooms 300P ⚓
(heated) sauna bath Disco 6 nights wkly
Conference facilities available ♡English & French.
♡ ♡ S% ✱sB&B⇌⋒ fr£22.15
dB&B⇌⋒ fr£30.30 Lunch fr£4.25&alc
Tea£1.50alc Dinner£6.50alc Wine£3.75 ⊨
Credit cards 1 2 3 4 5

SEAVINGTON ST MARY Somerset Map**3** ST41
✕✕**Pheasant** ☎South Petherton40502
Closed Xmas, last 2wks Feb & last 2wks Sep; Lunch not served; Dinner not served Sun; 52seats P bedrooms available Last dinner9.30pm
✱Dinner£7alc Wine£2.50

SEDGEFIELD Co Durham Map**8** NZ32
★★★**Hardwick Hall** ☎20253
17⇌⋒ ⋔ CTV CTV in bedrooms ✈ 200P ⚓ Live music & dancing Sat Last dinner9.45pm ♡ S%
sB&B⇌⋒£18.50 dB&B⇌⋒£24.50 Lunch£5alc
Dinner£7.50alc Wine£3 ⊨
Credit cards 1 2 3 5 6

SEDLESCOMBE East Sussex Map**5** TQ71
★★**Brickwall** ☎253
Closed Jan; 16rm(10⇌⋒) ⋔ CTV 16P ⚓
(heated) Last dinner8.30pm ♡ ♡
✱sB&B£8.50–£9.50 sB&B⇌⋒£9.50
dB&B£17–£19 dB&B⇌⋒£19 Lunch fr£2.50&alc
Dinner£3.95–£4.50 Wine£3.10 ⊨ *xmas*
Credit cards 1 2 5

✕**Holmes House** ☎450
Small renovated cottage dating from 17th-C.
Closed Mon; Dinner not served Sun; 45seats 10P
♡International. Last dinner9pm Lunch£3.50&alc
Dinner£8alc Credit cards 1 2 3 5

SEIGHFORD Staffordshire Map**7** SJ82
✕Hollybush Inn ☎280
Dinner not served Sun; 40seats 150P
International. Last dinner9.30pm
✱Lunch£2.20–£3.80&alc Credit cards 1 3

SELBORNE Hampshire Map**4** SU73
★Queens ☎272
4rm(2 fl) Annexe: 5rm(4 fl) 1 CTV TV available in bedrooms 40P 2 Last dinner8.45pm S% sB&B£7 sB&B fl£9 dB&B£12 dB&B fl£14 Lunch£2.80–£3.80&alc Tea80p High Tea£1.30–£2 Dinner£3.80–£5&alc Wine£2.50 Credit cards 1 2 3 4

SELBY North Yorkshire Map**8** SE63
★Londesborough Arms Market Pl ☎707355
34rm(15 fl) Annexe: 3rm CTV CTV in bedrooms 20P 6 Last dinner9.30pm S% sB&B£10–£11.50 sB&B fl£12.50–£14.38 dB&B£15–£17.25 dB&B fl£19–£21.85 Lunch£2.50–£3&alc Dinner £3.50–£4&alc Wine£3 Credit cards 1 3

SELMESTON East Sussex Map**5** TQ50
✕Corin's Church Farm ☎Ripe343
Closed Mon; Lunch not served Tue–Sat; Dinner not served Sun; 24seats 24P English, French & Italian. Last dinner11pm Lunch£4 Dinner£6.50 Wine£3.50 Credit cards 1 3

SELSEY West Sussex Map**4** SZ89
★Conifers Seal Sq ☎2436
Closed 15Jan–Feb; 9rm(2 fl) CTV 10p S% sB&B£8 sB&B fl£9.50 dB&B£16 db&B fl£19 Continental breakfast Lunch£3.25–£4.25 Tea60p–£2 High Tea75p–£3 Dinner£4.25–£5.25 Wine£3 *xmas* Credit card 2

✕Thatched House 23 Warner Rd ☎2207
Lunch not served Mon & Tue; 35seats 20P bedrooms available English & French. Last dinner9.30pm ✱Lunch£3.60–£3.85 Dinner£4.50–£5.25 Wine£2.85 Credit cards 1 3 5

SENNEN Cornwall Map**2** SW32
★★Tregiffian ☎408
Comfortably modernised 17th-C farmhouse.
Closed Nov–Feb; 9rm(3 fl) CTV 20P Children under 5yrs not accommodated English & French. Last dinner8.30pm S% ✱sB&B£7.50–£8.50 dB&B£15–£17 Lunch£3.60&alc Tea£1 Dinner£3.60&alc Wine£2.40 Credit cards 1 3

SEVENOAKS Kent Map**5** TQ55
At Dunton Green
☆☆**Emma** London Rd ☎Dunton Green681
50 fl 140P

SHAFTESBURY Dorset Map**3** ST82
★★★Grosvenor The Commons (Trusthouse Forte) ☎2282
Old coaching inn (rebuilt 19th-C) with central archway leading to courtyard.
48rm(37 fl) TV in bedrooms Last dinner9pm S% sB&B£13 sB&B fl£15.50 dB&B£20 dB&B fl£24 Credit cards 1 2 3 4 5 6

★★★Royal Chase Royal Chase Roundabout (Best Western) ☎3355 Telex no417294
Originally a monastic residence converted into a hotel.
19rm(12 fl) 1 CTV CTV available in bedrooms 120P Disco Sat Live music & dancing Fri Last dinner10pm S% sB&B£10–£12.75 sB&B fl£14–£17 dB&B£18.50–£23.50 dB&B fl£22.50–£27.50 Lunch£3.25 4&alc Tea60palc High Tea£1.40alc Dinner£4.50alc Wine£3.10 *xmas* Credit cards 1 2 3 5

SHANKLIN Isle of Wight Map**4** SZ58
★★★Cliff Tops Park Rd ☎3262 Telex no86725
98rm(87 fl) Lift CTV CTV available in bedrooms 35P (heated) sauna bath Live music & dancing nightly in season English & French. Last dinner8.30pm S% sB&B£12–£15.25 sB&B fl£14–£19 dB&B£22.50–£30.50 dB&B fl£25–£38 Lunch fr£3.60 Tea fr50p Dinner fr£5.30&alc Wine£2.75 *xmas* Credit cards 1 2 3 6

★★★Shanklin Eastmount Rd ☎2286
RS Oct–Mar (no lunch); 69rm(47 fl) Lift CTV CTV available in bedrooms 40P Disco 6nights wkly Live music & dancing 5nights wkly in season English & French. Last dinner8.30pm sB&B£11.77–£14.25 sB&B fl£13.06–£15.44 dB&B£23.54–£27.32 dB&B fl£26.13–£29.10 Lunch fr£3.95 Tea fr£1 Dinner fr£5.88 Wine£3.75 *xmas* Credit card 2

★★Luccombe Hall Luccombe Rd ☎2719
Closed 16Dec–11Jan; RS Nov–15Dec & 12Jan–Mar (no lunch); 33rm(22 fl) CTV TV available in bedrooms 30P (heated) (grass) Last dinner8pm sB&B£7–£13.85 sB&B fl£7.50 dB&B£13.50–£24.60 dB&B fl£12.80–£28 Lunch£3.50–£4 Dinner£4.50–£5 Wine£2.45

★★Melbourne Ardenlea Queen's Rd ☎2283
Closed Nov–Mar; 52rm(6 fl) CTV 10P Live music & dancing twice wkly English & French. Last dinner7pm S% sB&B£6.48 sB&B fl£8.10 dB&B£12.96–£16.20 dB&B fl£17.28–£22.68 Lunch£4–£5 Dinner£6–£7 Wine£3

S

S

HAP Cumbria Map**12** NY51
★**Shap Wells** (situated 3m SW of Shap Village off 6) ☎628
osed 24Dec–22Feb; 63rm(14⇌⋒) 🍽 CTV 100P
⌂ ⚓ (hard) Last dinner 8.30pm
B&B fr£8.32 sB&B⇌⋒ fr£8.91 dB&B fr£16.64
B&B⇌⋒ fr£17.82 Lunch fr£2.40
nner fr£4.48&alc Wine£3
redit cards 2 3 4 5 6

HAPWICK Somerset Map**3** ST43
✕**Shapwick House** ☎Ashcott 201321
5seats 100P bedrooms available English &
rench. Last dinner 9.30pm S%
unch fr£3.50&alc Dinner fr£4.50&alc Wine£3
redit cards 1 2 4 5 6

HARDLOW Derbyshire Map**8** SK43
✕**Lady in Grey** Wilne Ln ☎Derby 792331
losed Mon & Public Hols; Dinner not served Sun;
2seats 50P bedrooms available English & French.
ast dinner 9.30pm Lunch£3.50–£3.75&alc
nner£5.50–£6.25&alc Wine£3
redit cards 1 2 3 5

HAWBURY Salop Map**7** SJ52
Bragg's Country Suppers Longley Farm, Stanton
eath (3m NE off A53) ☎250289
4seats 10P bedrooms available Last dinner 8pm

HEFFIELD South Yorkshire Map**8** SK38
★★★**Grosvenor House** Charter Sq (Trusthouse
orte) ☎20041 Telex no 54312
33rm(144⇌⋒) Lift 🍽 CTV in bedrooms 82⌂
isco 6nights wkly Conference facilities available
ast dinner 9.45pm S% sB&B£18.50
B&B⇌⋒£24.50 dB&B£26 dB&B⇌⋒£34.50
Credit cards 1 2 3 4 5 6

★★★**Hallam Tower** Manchester Rd, Broomhill
rusthouse Forte) ☎686031 Telex no 547293
47rm(135⇌⋒) Lift 🍽 CTV in bedrooms 120P
onference facilities available Last dinner 10pm
S% sB&B£17 sB&B⇌⋒£24.50
B&B⇌⋒£34.50 Credit cards 1 2 3 4 5 6

★★**Hotel St George** Kenwood Rd ☎583811
elex no 547030
6⇌⋒ Lift 🍽 CTV in bedrooms 120P ⚓
English & French. Last dinner 9.15pm
% ✱sB&B⇌⋒£15.18–£21.50
B&B⇌⋒£25.30–£31.62 Lunch fr£3.94
inner fr£4.31 Wine£3.22
redit cards 1 2 3 5 6

★★★**Mosborough Hall** High St ☎484353
2⇌⋒ 4 🍽 CTV in bedrooms 80P ⚓ Live
music & dancing Tue Last dinner 9.30pm
✱sB&B⇌⋒£14–£20 dB&B⇌⋒£22–£24
unch£3.60&alc Tea£2 Dinner£5.80&alc
Vine£3.39 Credit cards 1 2 3

★★★**Royal Victoria** Victoria Station Rd (British Transport) ☎24712
56rm(30⇌⋒) Lift 🍽 TV in bedrooms 200P
English & French. Last dinner 9.30pm
S% ✱sB&B⇌⋒ fr£24.60 dB&B⇌⋒ fr£32.90
Wine£3.15 Credit cards 1 2 3 4 5 6

★★**Roslyn Court** 178–180 Psalter Ln ☎661191
36⇌⋒ 🍽 CTV 50P Last dinner 9.30pm
S% ✱sB&B£12.96 sB&B⇌⋒£15.12
dB&B£19.44 dB&B⇌⋒£22.68
Bar lunch 65p–£1.50 Tea 60p–80p
Dinner£3–£3.80&alc Wine£2.50
Credit cards 1 2 3 5 6

★★**Rutland** 452 Glossop Rd, Broomhill ☎665215
82rm(45⇌⋒) Annexe: 17⇌⋒ Lift 🍽 CTV CTV available in bedrooms 80P ⚓ English &
French. Last dinner 9pm S%
sB&B£12.30–£14.50 sB&B⇌⋒£16.40–£19.65
dB&B£16.40–£20.50 dB&B⇌⋒£24–£26.85
Lunch£3.70–£6&alc Tea£1.50–£2
Dinner£4.75–£8&alc *xmas* Credit cards 1 3

★★**St Andrews** 46–48 Kenwood Rd ☎53082
Closed Xmas 31rm(12⇌⋒) 🍽 CTV 60P ⚓
Last dinner 8.30pm S% sB&B£12.96
sB&B⇌⋒£15.12 dB&B£19.44 dB&B⇌⋒£22.68
Bar lunch£2.50–£3.50&alc Tea 60p–80p
Dinner£3–£3.80&alc Wine£2.50
Credit cards 1 2 3 5 6

✕✕**Dore** Church Ln ☎365948
Dinner not served Sun; 90seats 15P French.
Last dinner 10pm ✱Lunch£3.50–£5&alc
Dinner£7.50alc Wine£2.80 Credit cards 1 2 5 6

SHENSTONE Hereford & Worcester Map**7** SO87
✕✕**Granary** Heath Ln ☎Chaddesley Corbett 535
Closed Mon; Lunch not served Sat; Dinner not served Sun; 50seats 35P Last dinner 9.15pm
Lunch£4.25 Dinner£6.50 Wine£3
Credit cards 1 2 3

SHEPTON MALLET Somerset Map**3** ST64
★★***Red Lion Inn*** Market Pl ☎2262
8rm(3⇌⋒) 🍽 TV available in bedrooms 50P
Disco Sat Live music Mon Last dinner 8.30pm
Credit cards 1 2 3 5

★★**Shrubbery** Commercial Rd ☎2555
7rm(4⇌⋒) 🍽 CTV 20P ⚓ Last dinner 9pm
✱sB&B fr£8.25 sB&B⇌⋒ fr£10.65
dB&B fr£14.90 dB&B⇌⋒ fr£17.60 Lunch£4alc
Dinner£5alc Wine£3 Credit cards 1 2 5

✕✕**Bowlish House** Bowlish (On the Wells road, A371) ☎2022
Building is a perfect example of a Palladian Georgian country house. Situated in a picturesque Mendip village.
Lunch not served Sat & Sun; 24seats 20P
bedrooms available International.
Last dinner 10.30pm Lunch£7.50alc
Dinner£7.50alc Wine£3

S

SHERBORNE Dorset Map**3** ST61
☆☆☆**Post House** Horsecastles Ln (Trusthouse Forte) ☎3191
60⇌⋒ ☽ ♛ CTV in bedrooms 100P ⚓
Last dinner9.45pm ♉ ☑ S% sB&B⇌⋒£19.75
dB&B⇌⋒£28.50 ⊟ *xmas*
Credit cards 1 2 3 4 5 6

★★**Eastbury** Long St ☎3387
16rm(5⇌⋒) TV 4⌂ ⚓ ✿ ☋English & Continental.
Last dinner8.15pm ♉ ☑ S% sB&B£8–£8.80
sB&B⇌⋒£12–£13 dB&B£14.60–£16
dB&B⇌⋒£16.60–£18 Lunch£2.30–£2.60
Tea45p–60p Dinner£3.50–£3.90 Wine£2.30 ⊟

★★**Half Moon** Half Moon St ☎2017
17rm ♛ CTV 65P ☋English & French.
Last dinner9.30pm ♉ S% sB&B£9.35
dB&B£15.25 Lunch£3.95alc Dinner£5.25alc
Wine£2.70

★**Saffron House** The Avenue ☎2734
Detached, mellow stone town house of 19th-C with character. Well-kept lawns and gardens at rear.
Closed Xmas; 6rm ♛ CTV 20P ⛟ ⚓ ☋English & French. Last dinner8pm S% sB&B£8.53
dB&B£17.06 Lunch£3.40–£3.75 Tea£1–£1.75
Dinner£3.70–£4.20 Wine£2.20

SHERBURN IN ELMET North Yorkshire Map**8** SE43
✕***Bon Viveur*** 19 Low St ☎South Milford682146
Closed Sun, Mon, 2wks Jan & 3wks Aug–Sep;
40seats 10p ☋French. Last dinner9.30pm

SHERINGHAM Norfolk Map**9** TG14
★★***Beaumaris*** South St ☎822370
Closed Nov–mid Apr; 28rm(8⇌⋒) ♛ CTV 30P ✿
Last dinner8pm ♉ ⊟

★★**Southlands** South St ☎822679
Closed Nov–Mar; 20rm(9⇌⋒) CTV 20P ⛟
Last dinner7.45pm ♉ ☑ S% sB&B fr£9
sB&B⇌⋒ fr£10.50 dB&B fr£18 dB&B⇌⋒ fr£21
Lunch£3.50 Tea80p Dinner£4.25 Wine£2.20

★**Two Lifeboats** Promenade ☎822401
Established in 1720, once used by smugglers.
RS 25Sep–21May; 21rm CTV **ℙ** ⛟
Last dinner8.15pm ♉ ☑ S% ✻sB&B£8–£9
dB&B£16–£18 Lunch£2.20alc Tea75palc
High Tea£2.70alc Dinner£4.50alc Wine£2.95

SHIFNAL Salop Map**7** SJ70
★★★**Park House** Park St ☎Telford460128
21⇌⋒ ☽ ♛ CTV in bedrooms 100P ⚓ ⏖(heated)
sauna bath Live music & dancing wkly ✿ ☋English & French. Last dinner9.30pm ♉ ☑ S%
sB&B⇌⋒£18–£22 dB&B⇌⋒£26–£30
Lunch£4&alc Tea£1.50 Dinner£6&alc
Wine£3.25 ⊟ *xmas* Credit cards 1 2 3 5

★★**Old Bell of Shifnal** Church St ☎Telford460475
Closed Sun; 6⇌⋒ TV in bedrooms ⊘ ⛟ ☋English & French. Last dinner9.30pm ♉ ☑ ✻sB&B£8.50
sB&B⇌⋒£10.50 dB&B£18.50 dB&B⇌⋒£22.50
Lunch£2.50–£2.85&alc Tea£1.20 Dinner£6alc
Wine£2.90 Credit cards 1 2 3 5 6

SHIPLEY Salop Map**7** SO89
✕✕**Thornescroft** Bridgnorth Rd
☎Pattingham700253
Georgian farmhouse with matching extension.
Closed Sun & Mon; 55seats P ☋Continental.
Last dinner9pm S% Lunch£2.95–£3.35&alc
Dinner£7alc Wine£3.25 Credit cards 1 2 5

SHIPSTON-ON-STOUR Warwickshire Map**4** SP24
★★***George*** Market Sq ☎61453
15rm(3⇌⋒) TV 20P Last dinner9.30pm ♉ ☑ ⊟
Credit cards 2 5

SHIPTON Gloucestershire Map**4** SP01
✕✕**Frogmill Inn** ☎Andoversford547
Built of local Cotswold stone.
Dinner not served Sun; 45seats 300P
bedrooms available Disco Thu ☋English & French.
Last dinner10pm S% ✻Lunch£1.30–£6
Dinner£1.30–£6 Wine£3.10 Credit card 2

SHIPTON-UNDER-WYCHWOOD Oxfordshire
Map**4** SP21
✕***Lamb Inn*** High St ☎830465
Closed Sun & Mon; Lunch not served; 16seats
☋French. Last dinner10pm

SHORNE Kent Map**5** TQ67
☆☆☆**Inn on the Lake** Watling St ☎3333
78rm(76⇌⋒) ☽ ♛ CTV CTV in bedrooms ⊘ 200P
Live music & dancing Sat Conference facilities available ☋English & French. Last dinner10pm ♉
sB&B⇌⋒£17.04–£19.17 dB&B⇌⋒£26.62
Lunch£5alc Dinner£8alc Wine£4.30 ⊟
Credit cards 1 2 3 5 6

SHREWSBURY Salop Map**7** SJ41
★★★**Ainsworth's Radbrook Hall** Radbrook Rd
☎4861
Original house of the Head of the Clan McPherson. Panelling built in the reign of Henry VIII.
31rm(26⇌⋒) Annexe: 5⇌⋒ ☽ ♛ CTV TV in bedrooms 200P ⚓ squash sauna bath Live music & dancing Sat Cabaret mthly Last dinner10.30pm ♉
☑ S% sB&B fr£8 sB&B⇌⋒ fr£14 dB&B fr£18
dB&B⇌⋒ fr£20 Lunch fr£2.99 Tea fr40p
High Tea fr£1.50 Dinner fr£3.06 Wine£3.50 ⊟
Credit cards 1 2 5 6

★★★**Lion** Wyle Cop (Trusthouse Forte) ☎53107
45rm(19⇌⋒) Lift ☽ ♛ TV in bedrooms 72P
Last dinner9.45pm ♉ S% sB&B£13.50
sB&B⇌⋒£15 dB&B£21.50 dB&B⇌⋒£24.50
⊟ *xmas* Credit cards 1 2 3 4 5 6

S

S

★★★***Prince Rupert*** Butcher Row ☎52461
Building dates back to the 15th-C and is named after the grandson of James I of England who made Shrewsbury his headquarters during the Civil War.
66rm(55⇌fl) Lift ☽ 🅼 CTV 1🏠 ♀English & French. Last dinner10pm

★★**Beauchamp** The Mount (Scottish & Newcastle) ☎3230
24rm(14⇌fl) 🅼 CTV CTV in bedrooms 70P ⚓ Live music Fri ♀English & French. Last dinner9pm
S% *sB&B£10.50–£11.50 sB&B⇌fl£11.50–£12 dB&B£17.05–£18.10 dB&B⇌fl£19.10–£20.20
Lunch£2.75–£4.50&alc Tea50p–£1.50 Dinner£2.75–£5&alc Wine£2.40 *xmas*
Credit cards 1 2 3 5

★★***Britannia*** Welsh Bridge (Greenall Whitley) ☎61246
25rm(6⇌fl) ☽ 🅼 CTV 40P 10🏠 Live music Sun ♀English, French & Italian. Last dinner9pm
Credit cards 1 2 3 5 6

★★**Lord Hill** Abbey Foregate (Greenhall Whitley) ☎52601
RS Xmas; 26rm(21⇌fl) ☽ 🅼 CTV in bedrooms 250P ⚓ ♀English & French. Last dinner9.30pm
sB&B£11–£12 sB&B⇌fl£13.50–£14 dB&B£16–£17 dB&B⇌fl£19–£20
Lunch£3.50–£4&alc Dinner£4–£4.50&alc
Wine£2.80 Credit cards 1 2 3 4 5 6

✕**Penny Farthing** Abbey Foregate ☎56119
Closed Sun, Mon & Public Hols; 35seats P ♀French. Last dinner9.30pm

SIDCOT Avon Map**3** ST45
★**Sidcot** ☎Winscombe2271
Late 1800's detached, stone-built property in some four acres of own grounds.
6rm CTV 30P English & French.
Lastdinner8.30pm S%
sB&B£7.50–£8.50 sB&B⇌⋒£8–£9
dB&B£14–£16 dB&B⇌⋒£15–£17
Lunch£2.75–£3.50 Tea50p–£1
HighTea80p–£1.30 Dinner£4.50alc Wine£2.60
Creditcards 1 3

SIDFORD Devon Map**3** SY19
★**Applegarth** Church St ☎Sidmouth3174
Closed end Oct–Nov; 6rm CTV 15P 1
English & French. Lastdinner9pm S%
sB&B£8–£10 dB&B£16–£20 Lunch£3–£3.50
Dinner£4.50&alc Wine£2.75 Creditcard 2

SIDMOUTH Devon Map**3** SY18
★★★★**Victoria** Esplanade ☎2651
Large, imposing building standing in its own grounds close to sea front with uninterrupted views of sheltered bay.
Closed 2Jan–10Mar; 65⇌⋒ Lift CTV CTV available in bedrooms 100P 4 (heated) (hard) Conference facilities available
Lastdinner9pm ✱sB&B⇌⋒£14–£18
dB&B⇌⋒£28–£36 Lunch£4&alc Tea40p
Dinner£5&alc wine£3.25 *xmas* Creditcard 2

★★★**Bedford** Esplanade ☎3047
Closed Nov–Mar; 43rm(22⇌⋒) Lift CTV TV available in bedrooms Lastdinner8.15pm
S% sB&B£9–£14.75 sB&B⇌⋒£12.50–£18.50
dB&B£18–£29.50 dB&B⇌⋒£20–£38
Lunch£3.50 Dinner£5.50 Wine£2.50
Creditcard 3

S

★★★**Belmont** Sea Front ☎2555
50⇌⋒ Lift ☽ ⅲ CTV 26P ⚓ Children under 2yrs not accommodated Last dinner8.30pm ☆ ☑ S%
sB&B⇌⋒£18–£19 dB&B⇌⋒£36–£38
Lunch£5 Tea£1 Dinner£6 Wine£4.50 ⊟

★★★**Fortfield** Station Rd (Best Western) ☎2403
55rm(24⇌⋒) Lift ☽ ⅲ CTV 60P ⇹ ⚓ ♿
Last dinner8.30pm ☆ ☑ S% sB&B£13–£15
sB&B⇌⋒£16–£18 dB&B£22–£26
dB&B⇌⋒£28–£36 Lunch£3.50 Dinner£4 ⊟
xmas Credit cards 1 2 3 5 6

★★★**Riviera** Esplanade ☎5201
37rm(21⇌⋒) Lift ☽ ⅲ CTV 9⌂ ⇹ ☋ English & French. Last dinner9pm ☆ ☑
*sB&B£8.50–£12.50 sB&B⇌⋒£9–£13.50
dB&B£17–£25 dB&B⇌⋒£18–£27
Lunch fr£3.50&alc Tea fr75p Dinner fr£4.25&alc
Wine£2.44 ⊟ *xmas* Credit cards 2 5 6

★★★***Royal York*** Esplanade ☎3043
38rm(15⇌⋒) Lift ⅲ CTV 5P ⇹ Last dinner8pm ☆
☑ ⊟

★★★**Salcombe Hill House** Beatland Rd ☎4697
33rm(16⇌⋒) Lift ⅲ CTV TV available in bedrooms
35P 5⌂ ⇹ ⚓ ⌓(heated) ⚘(grass) Children under3yrs not accommodated Last dinner8pm ☆
☑ *sB&B£8.50–£12 sB&B⇌⋒£9.50–£12.50
dB&B£17–£24 dB&B⇌⋒£19–£25
Lunch£3–£3.50 Tea60p Dinner£3.50–£4.50
Wine£2.50 ⊟

★★★**Westcliff** Manor Rd ☎3252
Building with balconies and terrace overlooking sea. Set in two acres of secluded lawns and gardens.
Closed 24Dec–14Feb; RS15–29Feb; 38rm(27⇌⋒)
Lift ☽ ⅲ CTV CTV available in bedrooms 50P ⇹
⌓(heated) Disco wkly

S

(high season) Live music & dancing wkly (high season) English & French. Last dinner8.30pm S% sB&B fr£9.55 sB&B⇌⋒ fr£11.28 dB&B fr£19.10 dB&B⇌⋒ fr£22.56 Lunch£3.75–£4 Tea60–80p Dinner£5.25–£6.25 Wine£2.60

★★**Abbeydale** Manor Rd ☎2060
Closed Nov–Mar; 16rm CTV 24P Children under 4yrs not accommodated Last dinner8pm sB&B£9.18–£11.34 dB&B£18.36–£22.68 Lunch£2.50–£4 Dinner£4–£6 Wine£2.20

★★ ***Brownlands*** Sid Rd ☎3053
Closed mid Oct–mid Apr; 17rm(6⇌⋒) CTV 25P 3 Last dinner7.30pm

★★**Byes Links** Sid Rd ☎3129
Closed Nov–Mar; 20rm(8⇌⋒) CTV 30P Live music & dancing twice wkly Last dinner8pm sB&B£11 sB&B⇌⋒£12 dB&B£20 dB&B⇌⋒£25 Lunch£2.50 Tea£1.25 High Tea£1 Dinner£3.75 Wine£2.10 Credit cards 1 3 5

★★***Faulkner*** Esplanade ☎3184
33rm(2⇌⋒) Lift CTV 5P Last dinner8pm

★★**Littlecourt** Seafield Rd ☎5279
Closed Dec–Feb; 20rm(9⇌⋒) CTV 20P 2 Last dinner8pm S% sB&B£7–£10 sB&B⇌⋒£8.50–£11.50 dB&B£14–£20 dB&B⇌⋒£17–£23 Lunch£2–£3.75 Tea50p–£1.50 Dinner£3.50–£4.50 Wine£2

★★**Royal Glen** Glen Rd ☎3221
35rm(20⇌⋒) TV TV available in bedrooms 30P 8 Children under8yrs not accommodated Last dinner8pm sB&B£8.24–£10 sB&B⇌⋒£10–£11.96 dB&B£16.24–£20 dB&B⇌⋒£20–£23.92 Lunch£2.50 Tea50P Dinner£2.70 Wine£2.80

★★**Woodlands** Station Rd ☎3120
30rm(15⇌⋒) CTV 25P Children under 3yrs not accommodated Last dinner7.30pm sB&B£7–£11 sB&B⇌⋒£8–£12 dB&B£14.25–£21.50 dB&B⇌⋒£16.75–£24 Lunch£2 Dinner£2.50 Wine£3.25 *xmas*

Wyndham House Esplanade ☎4167
Closed Nov–27Mar; 24rm(5⇌⋒) CTV English & International. Last dinner8pm

SILLOTH Cumbria Map **11** NY15

★★★**Skinburness** ☎31468
One of Cumbria's oldest and best loved hotels, affording a fine view of the Solway Firth and the Scottish mountains.
23rm(9⇌⋒) CTV 150P 5 Last dinner9.30pm sB&B£8.50 sB&B⇌⋒£9.70 dB&B£15.20 dB&B⇌⋒£17.40 Lunch£3–£5 Tea£1 High Tea£2.50–£3.50 Dinner£4–£6.20 *xmas*

★★**Golf** Criffel St ☎31438
23rm(14⇌⋒) CTV TV in bedrooms 6 sB&B£7.25–£8.75 sB&B⇌⋒£9–£12 dB&B£14–£18 dB&B⇌⋒£16–£20 Lunch£2.50–£3.50&alc Dinner£4.20–£5.70&alc Wine£3.30 Credit cards 1 2 6

★★**Queen's** Park Ter, Criffel St ☎31373
Situated on the seafront, offering excellent views of the Solway Firth and Scottish mountains.
16rm(1⇌⋒) CTV 10 Live music & dancing Sat Last dinner9pm S% *sB&B£5.75 dB&B£11 dB&B⇌⋒£13 Lunch fr£2.70 Tea fr£1.10 High Tea fr£1.25 Dinner fr£3.60 Wine£1.60 Credit cards 1 6

S

INDLESHAM Berkshire Map**4** SU76
✕✕**Sindlesham Mill** Mill Ln ☎Reading666370
losed Mon; Dinner not served Sun; 65seats 50P
isco Thu – Sat Cabaret ♕English & French.
astdinner9.45pm Lunch£4.80&alc
inner£7&alc Wine£3.50
redit cards ①②③④⑤⑥

ITTINGBOURNE Kent Map**5** TQ96
★★**Coniston** London Rd ☎23927
0rm(36⇌⋔) ☽ ⋈ CTV CTV in bedrooms 200P ⚓ ⚘
illiards ♕English & French. Lastdinner10.30pm
✿ sB&B£12.96 sB&B⇌⋔£15.12 dB&B£20.52
B&B⇌⋔£22.68 Lunch£10alc Dinner£4
Vine£3 Credit cards ①②⑤

IX MILE BOTTOM Cambridgeshire Map**5** TL55
★★★ **Swynford Paddocks** ☎234
2⇌⋔ 1⊟ ⋈ CTV CTV in bedrooms 30P ⚓
⚘(hard) ♕English & French. Lastdinner9pm ✿
B&B⇌⋔£20 – £26.50 dB&B⇌⋔£33.50 – £41
unch£5alc Dinner£6alc Wine£3 *xmas*
redit cards ①②③⑤

KEGNESS Lincolnshire Map**9** TF56
★★**County** North Pde ☎2461
47rm(9⇌⋔) Lift ⋈ CTV TV available in bedrooms 40P
3⌂ sauna bath ⚘ ♿ Lastdinner9.30pm ✿ ⌧
S% sB&B£10.10 sB&B⇌⋔£13.65
dB&B£16.05 dB&B⇌⋔£19.60 Lunch£3.60&alc
Dinner£3.60&alc Wine£2.75 ⛿ *xmas*
Credit cards ②⑤

★★***Crown*** Drummond Rd ☎3084
Overlooking the Seacroft Golf Links.
27rm(6⇌⋔) ⋈ CTV TV available in bedrooms 30P
3⌂ sauna bath Lastdinner10.30pm ✿ ⌧ ⛿
Credit cards ①③

★★**Links** Drummond Rd ☎3605
21rm(2⇌⋔) ⋈ CTV 35P ⚓ Live music & dancing
3nights wkly Lastdinner9pm ✿ ⌧ S%
sB&B£8.25 – £9.10 sB&B⇌⋔£9.60 – £10.70
dB&B£16.05 – £18.20 dB&B⇌⋔£18.75 – £21.40
Lunch£2.95 Tea32p High Tea£2.95 Dinner£3.70
Wine£2.65 ⛿ *xmas* Credit cards ①③

SKIPTON North Yorkshire Map**7** SD95
★**Midland** Broughton Rd ☎2781
11rm ⋈ CTV 20P ✿ S% ✻sB&B£7.50
dB&B£13 Continental breakfast Lunch fr£3
Tea fr£1 High Tea fr£2.50 Dinner fr£4.50
Wine£2.70 Credit card ②

✕***Le Caveau de la Bastille*** 86 High St ☎4274
Closed Thu & 2wks Oct; Lunch not served Sat & Sun;
24seats ♕French. Lastdinner10pm

SLEAFORD Lincolnshire Map**8** TF04
★**Carre Arms** ☎303156
14rm ⋈ CTV 20P 10⌂ Lastdinner9pm ✿
sB&B£10.62 dB&B£18.88 Lunch fr£2.50
Dinner fr£3 Wine£2.50

★**Lion** Northgate ☎302127
Small coaching inn with original entrance and courtyard.
10rm ⋈ CTV 8P 4⌂ Lastdinner8.15pm ✿
sB&B£9.50 dB&B£13.50 Bar lunch fr£1.20
Dinner fr£3.75 Wine£2.40 Credit cards ①③⑤

SLOUGH Berkshire Map**4** SU97
☆☆☆☆**Holiday Inn** Ditton Rd, Langley
(Commonwealth) ☎44244 Telex no848646
234⇌⋔ Lift ☽ ⊞ ⋈ CTV in bedrooms ⚓ ⊡(heated)
⚘(hard) sauna bath Conference facilities available ♿
♕Canadian. Lastdinner11pm ✿ ⌧ S%
✻sB&B⇌⋔ fr£24 dB&B⇌⋔ fr£33.50
Lunch fr£4.50 dinner fr£6.50 Wine£3.75 ⛿
xmas Credit cards ①②③④⑤

★★**Royal** Brunel Way (Trusthouse Forte) ☎23024
36rm(4⇌⋔) TV in bedrooms 25P
Lastdinner9.30pm ✿ S% sB&B£12
sB&B⇌⋔£14 dB&B£16.50 dB&B⇌⋔£20.50
⛿ *xmas* Credit cards ①②③④⑤⑥

SMALLWAYS North Yorkshire Map**12** NZ11
★***A66 Motel*** ☎Whorlton334
6rm(1⇌⋔) ⋈ CTV 45P ⚓ Lastdinner11pm

SNAINTON North Yorkshire Map**8** SE98
★★***Coachman Inn*** ☎Scarborough85231
10rm(8⇌⋔) ⋈ CTV TV available in bedrooms 60P ⚓
♕English & Continental. Lastdinner9pm ✿ ⛿
Credit cards ①③

SOLIHULL West Midlands Map**7** SP17
★★★**George** High St (Embassy) ☎021 – 704 1241
Hotel overlooks medieval bowling green.
46rm(42⇌⋔) ☽ ⋈ CTV TV in bedrooms 100P ⚓
Conference facilities available Lastdinner9.30pm
✿ S% sB&B£12 sB&B⇌⋔£18 dB&B£19
dB&B⇌⋔£22 Lunch£5&alc Dinner£5.50&alc
Wine£5 ⛿ Credit cards ①②③④⑤⑥

★★★**St John's** 651 Warwick Rd (Inter-Hotel)
☎021 – 705 6777 Telex no339352
218rm(190⇌⋔) Lift ☽ ⋈ CTV in bedrooms 370P
Conference facilities available ♿ ♕English & French.
Lastdinner10pm ✿ ⌧ S% sB&B fr£15.50
sB&B⇌⋔ fr£20 dB&B fr£20 dB&B⇌⋔ fr£25
Lunch£3.20 – £3.50&alc Dinner£4.50 – £5&alc
Wine£3.75 ⛿ Credit cards ①②③④⑤

★★**Fleming's** 141 Warwick Rd, Olton
☎021 – 706 0371
Closed 22 – 30Dec; 73⇌⋔ ☽ ⋈ CTV 92P ⚓ billiards
♕International. Lastdinner9.30pm ✿ ⌧ S%
sB&B£8.60 sB&B⇌⋔£12.25 dB&B⇌⋔£19.50
Lunch£2.75 Tea fr75p Dinner fr£4.50&alc
Wine£2.50 ⛿

S

XXXHillfield Hall Hillfield Rd ☎021-7049296
Closed Mon; Lunch not served Sat; Dinner not served Sun; 120seats 153P Live music & dancing Fri Last dinner10pm Lunch fr£4.40&alc Dinner£8alc Wine£3 Credit cards 1 2 3 5

SOMERTON Somerset Map**3** ST42
★★★Red Lion ☎72339 Telex no46240
16⇌⋒ 1⊟ ⧗ CTV TV in bedrooms 75P ♉English & French. Last dinner10pm ✿ sB&B⇌⋒£13–£15 dB&B⇌⋒£21–£23 Lunch£2.50–£3.50&alc Dinner£4alc Wine£2.40 ⊓ Credit cards 1 2 3 5

SOMPTING West Sussex Map**4** TQ10
XSmugglers West St ☎Worthing36072
Converted 16th-C cottages (believed to have been frequented by smugglers), once a hostelry known as the Brewers Arms.
Closed Sun & Mon; 50seats 16P ♉English & French. Last dinner9.30pm ✻Lunch£4.70–£4.90&alc Dinner£5.80–£6&alc Wine£3.40

SONNING Berkshire Map**4** SU77
★★★White Hart ☎Reading692277
Dates back to pre-Elizabethan times. The annexe, which is one of the 13th-C cottages, has an Elizabethan dining room. Set in lovely gardens leading down to the Thames, by the 900-year-old bridge.
11⇌⋒ Annexe:6⇌⋒ ☽ ⧗ CTV CTV in bedrooms 70P ⛟ ⚓ Live music & dancing wkly ♉English & French. Last dinner10pm ✿ ⌂ S% ✻sB&B⇌⋒£24.80 dB&B⇌⋒£33.90 Lunch£5.60&alc Dinner£5.60&alc Wine£3.50 ⊓ *xmas* Credit cards 1 2 3 5

SOUTHAM Warwickshire Map**4** SP46
★★*Craven Arms* ☎2452
Coaching inn with courtyard; has posting box with letters and token used for recording arrival and departure of coaches during coaching era.
7rm ⧗ CTV 110P ♉English & French. ⌂ Credit cards 1 3 6

★★Stoneythorpe 10 Warwick Rd ☎2365
Listed building which was the first free hospital in Warwick for the poor of the parish.
16rm(9⇌⋒) ⧗ CTV 30P ⚓ ⛳ Last dinner10pm ✿ ⌂ S% sB&B£8.50–£10.50 sB&B⇌⋒£10.50–£12.50 dB&B£17–£21 dB&B⇌⋒£21–£25 Lunch£2.50–£3.50&alc Tea70p–£1 High Tea£1.25–£2 Dinner£3.50–£5&alc Wine£1.40 ⊓ Credit cards 2 4 6

SOUTHAMPTON Hampshire Map**4** SU41
See plan
★★★★Polygon Cumberland Pl (Trusthouse Forte) ☎26401 Telex no47175 Plan**11**
120⇌⋒ Lift ☽ ⧗ CTV in bedrooms 166P 5⌂ ♿ Conference facilities available Last dinner9.15pm ✿ ⌂ S% sB&B⇌⋒£21.50 dB&B⇌⋒£32.50 ⊓ *xmas* Credit cards 1 2 3 4 5 6

★★★Berkeley 8–10 Cranbury Ter (Best Western) ☎23511 Plan**3** 40rm(28⇌⋒) ☽ CTV TV in bedrooms 12P ⚓ ♉International. Last dinner10.30pm ✿ ⌂ S% sB&B fr£13 sB&B⇌⋒ fr£14 dB&B fr£23 dB&B⇌⋒ fr£24.50 Lunch fr£4&alc Tea fr£1 Dinner fr£5&alc Wine£3.25 ⊓ *xmas* Credit cards 1 2 3 4 5 6

★★★Cotswold 119 Highfield Ln (Best Western) ☎559555 Telex no477476 Plan**5**
Closed 25 & 26Dec; 80rm(60⇌⋒) Lift ☽ ⊞ ⧗ TV in bedrooms 120P Live music & dancing Sat ♉Mainly grills. Last dinner11pm ✿ ⌂ S% sB&B£14.85 sB&B⇌⋒£17.05 dB&B£23.10 dB&B⇌⋒£27 Lunch£3.50–£5.30&alc Tea£1–£1.40 High Tea£1.50–£2.20 Dinner£3.85–£4.50&alc Wine£3.25 ⊓ Credit cards 1 2 3 4 5 6

★★★Dolphin High St (Trusthouse Forte) ☎26178 Plan**6**
Gracious four-storey, Georgian inn bearing arms of William IV.
72⇌⋒ Lift ☽ ⧗ TV in bedrooms 70P ♿ Conference facilities available Last dinner9.45pm ✿ ⌂ S% sB&B⇌⋒£18.75 dB&B⇌⋒£26.50 ⊓ *xmas* Credit cards 1 2 3 4 5 6

☆☆☆Post House Herbert Walker Ave (Trusthouse Forte) ☎28081 Telex no477368 Plan**12**
132⇌⋒ Lift ☽ ⧗ CTV in bedrooms 50P ⚓ ⛆(heated) Conference facilities available Last dinner10pm ✿ ⌂ S% sB&B⇌⋒£19.75 dB&B⇌⋒£28.50 ⊓ *xmas* Credit cards 1 2 3 4 5 6

★★★Royal Cumberland Pl ☎23467 Telex no47388 Plan**13**
100rm(48⇌⋒) Lift ☽ CTV TV available in bedrooms 12P Conference facilities available ♉English & French. Last dinner9.30pm ✿ ⌂ S% sB&B£12–£13 sB&B⇌⋒£13–£14 dB&B£23–£25 dB&B⇌⋒£25–£27 Lunch fr£3&alc Tea fr60p High Tea fr£1.75 Dinner fr£4&alc Wine£2.40 ⊓ Credit cards 1 2 3

★★Albany Winn Rd, The Avenue ☎554553 Plan**1**
RS 24–26Dec; 45rm(9⇌⋒) Annexe:2⇌⋒ Lift ☽ ⧗ CTV TV available in bedrooms 50P ⚓ Live music & dancing Sat (winter only) Last dinner9.15pm ✿ ⌂ S% sB&B£10–£11 sB&B⇌⋒£15–£16 dB&B£18–£19 dB&B⇌⋒£20–£21 Lunch£3–£3.50&alc Tea30p Dinner£3.75–£4.25&alc Wine£2.75 ⊓ Credit cards 1 3

★★Atlantic 28–30 Hill Ln ☎24612 Plan**2** 24rm ⧗ CTV 24P Last dinner7.15pm ✻sB&B fr£9.77 dB&B fr£16.10 Lunch fr£3.50 Tea35p Dinner fr£3.50&alc

S

S

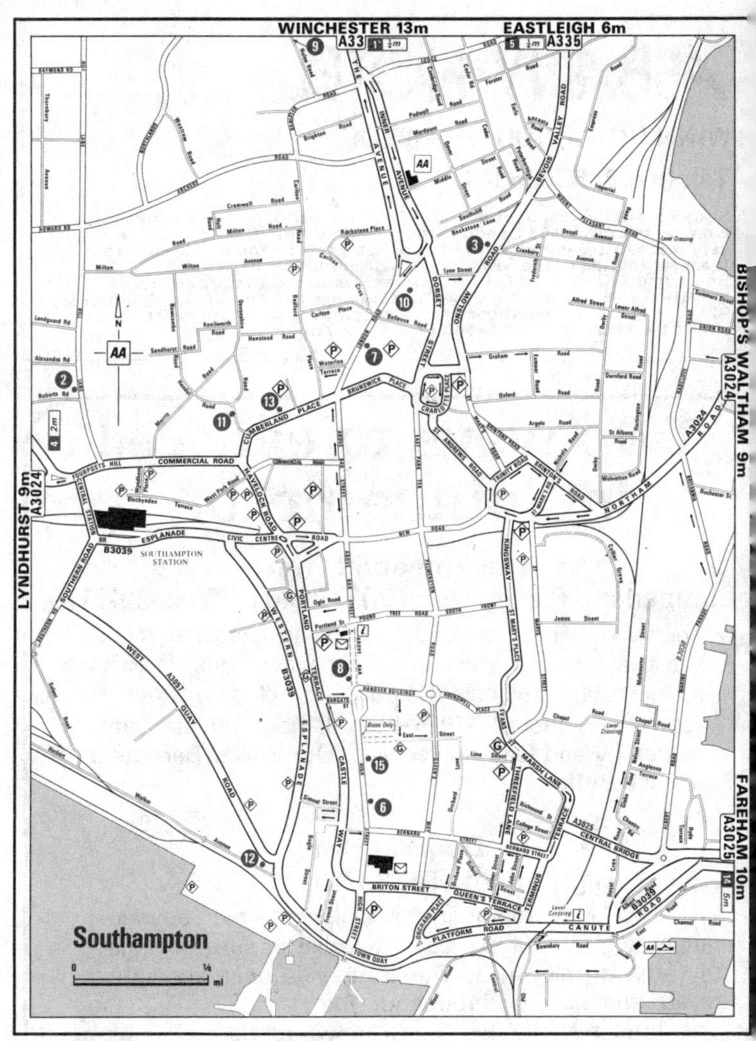

1 Albany ★★
2 Atlantic ★★
3 Berkeley ★★★
4 La Bodega ✕
5 Cotswold ★★★
6 Dolphin ★★★
8 Golden Palace ❀✕
9 Northlands ★★
10 Olivers ✕✕
11 Polygon ★★★★
12 Post House ☆☆☆
13 Royal ★★★
14 Solent ☆☆☆ (*see under Bursledon*)
15 Star ★★

★★**Northlands** Hulse Rd ☎28871 Plan**9**
21rm CTV 20P Last dinner8pm S%
sB&B£8.64 dB&B£17.28 Lunch£2alc Tea25palc dinner£3alc Wine£3.25

★★**Star** High St (Inter-Hotel) ☎26199
Telex no477777 Plan**15**
30rm(10⇌ ⫴) 1 Lift CTV TV available in bedrooms 26P 6 Last dinner8.45pm
S% ✻sB&B fr£12.50 dB&B fr£19.50
dB&B⇌ ⫴£21.50–£27.50 Lunch fr£2.50
Tea fr£1.25 Dinner fr£4&alc Wine£3.50
Credit cards 1 2 3

✕✕***Olivers*** Ordnance Rd ☎24789 Plan**10**
Closed Sun; Lunch not served Sat; 70seats 10P English & French. Last dinner11pm
Credit cards 1 2 3 5

✕**La Bodega** 294 Shirley Rd ☎772943 Plan**4**
Closed Sun; 36seats 50P English, French & Spanish. Last dinner mdnt Dinner£10alc
Wine£3.85 Credit cards 1 3

❀✕**Golden Palace** Above Bar St ☎26636 Plan**8**
Modern chinese style with large mirrors, paintings, and calligraphy.

25seats ☋English, Chinese & French. Last dinner mdnt Credit card 2

at **Bursledon** (6m SE A27)
☆☆**Solent** Hamble Ln ☎Bursledon2151 Plan: **14**
2⇌ 250P

SOUTHBOROUGH Kent Map**5** TQ54
✕***Marsal's*** 15A Church Rd ☎Tunbridge Wells39860
Closed Sun; Lunch not served Wed; 40seats
☋Spanish. Last dinner10pm Credit cards 1 3 5

SOUTH BRENT Devon Map**3** SX66
☆**Glazebrook House** ☎3322
Detached, two-storey house some 100 years old, set in 20 acres of grounds.
12rm(8⇌ ⋒) CTV TV available in bedrooms 80P billiards ☋English & French.
Last dinner10.30pm sB&B£9.50–£10.50
sB&B⇌⋒£10.50–£11.50 dB&B£19–£21
dB&B⇌⋒£21–£23 Dinner£3–£3.80&alc
Wine£2.90 Credit cards 1 2 3 5

SOUTHEND-ON-SEA Essex Map**5** TQ88
☆☆☆***Airport Moat House*** Aviation Way (Queens)
☎546344
Hotel is part of a leisure complex which includes the Historic Aircraft Museum.
Annexe: 65⇌⋒ CTV in bedrooms 350P
Disco 6nights wkly Live music & dancing wkly
Conference facilities available last Dinner9.50pm
Wine£3 Credit cards 1 2 3 5 6

☆**Roslin** Thorpe Esplanade, Thorpe Bay (2m E B1016) ☎586375 Telex no99450
20rm(24⇌⋒) Annexe: 8rm(6⇌⋒) CTV CTV available in bedrooms 24P Last dinner9.30pm
sB&B£10.26–£13.50
sB&B⇌⋒£13.50–£15.60 dB&B£17.90–£18.50
dB&B⇌⋒£20.50–£21.50 Lunch£3–£4&alc
Tea60p–£1.50 Dinner£4–£5&alc Wine£2.60
xmas Credit cards 1 2 3 5

✕✕**Schulers** 161 Eastern Esp ☎610172
Closed Mon; 75seats 15P ☋French.
Last dinner10pm Lunch fr£4.50&alc
Dinner fr£4.50&alc Wine£2.90
Credit cards 1 2 3 5

SOUTH GODSTONE Surrey Map**4** TQ34
★**Wonham House** Eastbourne Rd ☎3188 Gatwick plan **16**
18rm(8⇌⋒) TV available in bedrooms 50P
sauna bath Last dinner10pm S% sB&B£11
sB&B⇌⋒£13 dB&B£20 dB&B⇌⋒£24
Lunch£3–£4 Dinner£3.50&alc Wine£3
Credit cards 1 3

SOUTH MIMMS Hertfordshire Map**4** TL20
☆☆☆**South Mimms Crest Motel** Bignells Corner (junc A1/A6) (Crest) ☎Potters Bar43311
Telex no299162
112⇌⋒ CTV in bedrooms 150P Conference facilities available Last dinner10pm S%
*sB&B⇌⋒£17.33 dB&B⇌⋒£23.86
Continental breakfast Credit cards 1 2 3 4 5 6

SOUTH PETHERTON Somerset Map**3** ST41
✕✕**Oaklands** Palmer St ☎40272
Closed Mon; Lunch not served Tue–Sat; Dinner not served Sun; 40seats 14P bedrooms available
☋English & Continental. Specialities: Medaillons de boeuf chasseur, poached Devon salmon (in season).
Last dinner9pm Lunch£4.80 Dinner£7
Wine£2.60 Credit cards 2 5

SOUTHPORT Merseyside Map**7** SD31

★★★★Prince of Wales Lord St ☎36688
Telexno67415
Large, four-storey, brick building with gables, bay windows, architraves and glass entrance porch.
95rm(85⇌⋒) Lift ☽ ⚘ CTV in bedrooms 90P Conference facilities available Lastdinner10pm ♆ ♯ sB&B£16.50–£18 sB&B⇌⋒£20–£32 dB&B£30–£33 dB&B⇌⋒£33–£36 Lunch£3.50alc Tea£1.25–£1.75 Dinner£5.25–£6&alc Wine£2.50 ⊟ *xmas*
Creditcards ①②③④⑤⑥

★★★Royal Clifton Promenade ☎33771
Telexno.677415
117rm(66⇌⋒) 1⊟ Lift ☽ ⚘ CTV CTV in bedrooms 80P 4⌂ billiards Conference facilities available Lastdinner8.45pm ♆ sB&B£15.50–£17 sB&B⇌⋒£17.50–£19 dB&B£26–£29 dB&B⇌⋒£30.50–£33 Lunch£3.80–£4.50 Dinner£4.85–£5.75 Wine£2.50 ⊟
Creditcards ①②③④⑤⑥

★★Bold Lord St ☎32578
Former coaching house with small forecourt, situated on corner of northern end of the fashionable Lord Street.
29rm(12⇌⋒) ☽ ⊞ ⚘ CTV in bedrooms ⚯ Lastdinner9.45pm S% sB&B fr£10 sB&B⇌⋒ fr£13 dB&B fr£18 dB&B⇌⋒ fr£22 Lunch fr£2.25 Dinner£5alc Wine£3.75 *xmas*
Creditcards ①②③⑥

★★Red Rum 86–88 Lord St ☎35111
25rm(13⇌⋒) Lift ☽ ⚘ CTV in bedrooms 20P Lastdinner10pm ♆ sB&B£10 sB&B⇌⋒£13 dB&B£18 dB&B⇌⋒£22 Lunch fr£2.50 Dinner£3.50&alc Wine£2.55 ⊟ Creditcards ①②

★★Scarisbrick Lord St ☎38321
55rm(7⇌⋒) Lift ☽ CTV 40P 15⌂ Disco 6nights wkly ♿ ♡International. Lastdinner8.30pm ♆ S% sB&B£10.50–£13.50 sB&B⇌⋒£12.50–£15 dB&B£17–£22 dB&B⇌⋒£20–£25 Lunch£1.95–£2.75 Tea£1–£1.50 HighTea£2–£3 Dinner£4–£5 Wine£3.50 ⊟ *xmas* Creditcard ①②③④⑤⑥

★Metropole Portland St ☎36836
29rm(5⇌⋒) CTV TV available in bedrooms 12P ⚯ Lastdinner8.30pm ♆ S% ✱sB&B£8.60 sB&B⇌⋒£9.50 dB&B£16.60 dB&B⇌⋒£17.80 Lunch£1.75 Dinner£3–£3.50&alc Wine£2.50 *xmas* Creditcards ①②③⑥

XXSquires 78–80 King St ☎30046
Closed Sun & 2wks Jan; Lunch not served; 42seats ⚑ ♡French. Lastdinner10.30pm ✱Dinner£12alc Wine£3.25 Creditcards ①②③⑤

❀XLe Coq Hardi 1 Royal Ter, West St ☎38855
Closed Sun; Lunch not served; 26seats ⚑ ♡French. Specialities: Avocado façon du chef' Carre d'agneau provençale' caneton miel et amandes. Lastdinner9.30pm ✱Dinner£5.50alc Wine£2.70

SOUTHSEA Hampshire Map**4** SZ69
See **Portsmouth and Southsea**

SOUTH SHIELDS Tyne & Wear Map**12** NZ36

★★New Crown Mowbray Rd (Scottish & Newcastle) ☎553472
10rm(3⇌⋒) ⚘ TV in bedrooms 30P 4⌂ ♡English & French. Lastdinner9.15pm ♆ ♯ sB&B£10.20 sB&B⇌⋒£11.50 dB&B£15.60 dB&B⇌⋒£17.20 Lunch£4.25alc Tea£1.50 Dinner£4.50alc Wine£2.60 Creditcards ①②③④⑤⑥

★★**Sea** Sea Front (Swallow) ☎566227
Telex no53168
27⇌ⓜ Lift ☽ 🍽 CTV CTV in bedrooms 60P
Last dinner9.30pm ✿ ☑ S%
sB&B⇌ⓜ fr£16.75 dB&B⇌ⓜ fr£24 ☐
Credit cards 1 2 3 6

SOUTH STAINLEY North Yorkshire Map**8** SE36
✕✕✕***Red Lion*** ☎Harrogate770132
Georgian-style restaurant in a country inn.
Closed Xmas Day; 160seats 50P Last dinner5.15pm
Credit cards 1 2 3 5

SOUTH TAWTON Devon Map**3** SX69
★★**Wood Country** ☎Sticklepath230
15rm(3⇌ⓜ) CTV P (grass) billiards
Last dinner10pm ✿ ☑ sB&B£7.50–£10.50
sB&B⇌ⓜ£10.50–£11.50 dB&B£15–£21
dB&B⇌ⓜ£21–£23 Lunch£2.50–£3&alc
Tea75p–£1.25&alc High Tea75p–£1.25
Dinner£2.50–£3.50&alc Wine£2.65 ☐ *xmas*
Credit cards 1 2 3 5

SOUTHWELL Nottinghamshire Map**8** SK75
★★★**Saracens Head** Market Pl (Anchor) ☎812701
Telex no858875
Charles I surrendered to the Scots here in 1647.
23⇌ⓜ ☽ 🍽 CTV CTV in bedrooms 100P 3
International. Last dinner10pm ✿ S%
*sB&B⇌ⓜ£15.50 dB&B⇌ⓜ£23
Lunch fr£2.95&alc Dinner£3.50&alc Wine£2.80
☐ Credit cards 1 2 3 4 5 6

SOUTHWOLD Suffolk Map**5** TM57
★★★**Swan** Market Pl ☎722186
18th-C former coaching inn with original Georgian fireplace and door frames; many fine paintings, engravings and maps.
34rm(10⇌ⓜ) Annexe: 18⇌ⓜ Lift ☽ 🍽 CTV CTV available in bedrooms 60P 9 ♿
Last dinner8.30pm ✿ ☑ Wine£3
Credit cards 1 2 5

★★**Crown** High St ☎722275
Dates from the early Georgian period when it was a coaching house.
24rm(3⇌ⓜ) CTV 15P 9 French.
Last dinner8.30pm ✿ ☑ S%
*sB&B£9.35–£10.12 sB&B⇌ⓜ£11.22–£11.99
dB&B£18.70–£20.24 dB&B⇌ⓜ£20.57–£22.11
Lunch fr£3.50&alc Tea60p Dinner fr£4.15&alc
Wine£2.60 ☐

★★***Pier Avenue*** Pier Av ☎722632
12rm(3⇌ⓜ) CTV 20P 4 English & French.
Last dinner9pm ✿ ☑ ☐

★★**Randolph** Wangford Rd, Reydon ☎723603
In village only one mile from Southwold beach.
Closed mid Oct–Mar; 12rm(2⇌ⓜ) 🍽 TV in bedrooms 15P 2 Last dinner7.45pm S%
sB&B£5.75–£8.90 sB&B£11.50–£17.80
dB&B⇌ⓜ£13.50–£19.80 Bar lunch£1–£1.75
Dinner£3.50–£4 Wine£2.70

✕✕**Dutch Barn** Ferry Rd ☎723172
Closed Mon; Dinner not served Sun; 35seats 15P
French. Specialities: Beef medallions Nicholas, pork loin in cider and cream, Pigeon stroganoff.
Last dinner9.30pm Lunch£5alc Dinner£6alc
Wine£3.25 Credit cards 1 2

SOUTH ZEAL Devon Map**3** SX69
★★**Oxenham Arms** ☎Sticklepath244
12th-C inn of great character built of stone with slate roof.
Closed 20Nov–20Dec & 10Jan–15Feb; 9rm(5⇌ⓜ) CTV CTV available in bedrooms 10P English & French. Last dinner9pm ✿ sB&B£11–£11.50
sB&B⇌ⓜ£12.50–£13 dB&B£15–£16
dB&B⇌ⓜ£18–£19 Lunch£3.25alc
Dinner£5–£5.75 Wine£3 ☐ Credit cards 1 2 5

SPALDING Lincolnshire Map**8** TF22
★★**Red Lion** Market Pl ☎2869
Former coaching inn.
27rm(5⇌ⓜ) 🍽 CTV 25P 2 English, French & Italian. Last dinner9pm ✿ *sB&B£9.50
sB&B⇌ⓜ£13.07 dB&B£15.44 dB&B⇌ⓜ£17.82
Lunch£2.38–£3.09&alc Dinner£2.38–£3.09&alc
Credit cards 1 3 6

★★**White Hart** Market Pl (Trusthouse Forte) ☎5668
28rm(4⇌ⓜ) 🍽 TV in bedrooms 35P
Last dinner10pm ✿ ☑ S% sB&B£12
sB&B⇌ⓜ£14.50 dB&B£16.50 dB&B⇌ⓜ£20.50
☐ *xmas* Credit cards 1 2 3 4 5 6

✕✕***Springfields*** ☎4405
Bright, modern restaurant overlooking Springfield Gardens.
65seats 150P Last dinner9.30pm
Credit cards 1 2 3 5

SPEEN Buckinghamshire Map**4** SU89
✕***Old Plow Inn*** Flowers Bottom ☎Hampden Row300
Pleasant old country inn.
42seats 40P bedrooms available English & French.
Last dinner10pm

SPROTBROUGH South Yorkshire Map**8** SE50
✕**Edelweiss** 4 Main St ☎Doncaster853923
Closed Mon; Lunch not served Tue–Sun; 36seats
English & Continental. Last dinner10pm
Dinner£7.24&alc Wine£2.70 Credit cards 1 2 3 5

STABLEFORD Staffordshire Map**7** SJ83
✕✕✕***Cock Inn*** ☎Stoke-on-Trent680210
18th-C inn with original stone fireplace reputed to be haunted.
120seats 120P Live music & dancing Thu–Sat
International. Last dinner10.15pm Credit cards 1 2 3 4 5 6

STADDLE BRIDGE North Yorkshire Map**8** SE49
✕✕**McCoys (Tontine Inn)** ☎East Harsley207
Closed Sun; 80seats 80P bedrooms available
International. *Dinner£12alc Credit card 3

STAFFORD Staffordshire Map**7** SJ92
★★★**Tillington Hall** Eccleshall Rd (Greenall Whitley) ☎53531 Telex no36566
76⇌ⓜ Lift ☽ 🍽 CTV available in bedrooms 200P
Disco Thu Conference facilities available French.
Last dinner10pm ✿ ☑ S%
sB&B⇌ⓜ£20–£21 dB&B⇌ⓜ£25–£26.50
Lunch fr£3.75&alc Tea fr40p High Tea fr£2
Dinner fr£4.25&alc Wine£2.85 ☐
Credit cards 1 2 3 5

★★**Swan** Greengate St (Berni) ☎58142
30rm(1⇌ⓜ) ☽ 🍽 CTV 45P Mainly grills.
Last dinner11.30pm ✿ *sB&B£8.50
dB&B£15.10 dB&B⇌ⓜ£17.40 Lunch£3alc
Dinner£3.50alc Wine£2.52 ☐
Credit cards 1 2 3 5 6

★**Garth** Wolverhampton Rd, Moss Pit (Wolverhampton & Dudley) ☎51402
7rm(1⇌ⓜ) 🍽 CTV 50P Last dinner8.45pm ✿
☑ S% *sB&B£9.30 sB&B⇌ⓜ£12.75
dB&B£17.75 dB&B⇌ⓜ£20.20 Lunch£2.65&alc
Dinner£3.35&alc Wine£2.60 Credit cards 1 3

★**Romaline** 73 Wolverhampton Rd ☎54100
7rm 🍽 CTV 14P English & French.
Last dinner9.30pm ✿ S% *sB&B£7.25
dB&B£14.50 Lunch£1.35–£1.55 Dinner£3.50alc
Wine£2.50 Credit cards 1 5 6

★**Vine** Salter St (Wolverhampton & Dudley) ☎51071
23rm 🍽 CTV 10P Last dinner8.45pm ✿ ☑
S% *sB&B£10.10 dB&B£17.50 Lunch£3.15alc
Dinner£3.75alc Wine£2.60 1 3

S

XX***Minshull's*** Church Ln ☎3389
Closed Sun; 38seats English & French.
Last dinner 10pm Credit cards 1 2 3 5

STAINES Surrey Map**4** TQ07
★★**Pack Horse** Thames St (Anchor) ☎54221
Telex no 858875
Large, Victorian building with riverside patio, boat moorings and wide windowed dining room overlooking the Thames.
14rm CTV TV in bedrooms 60P
Last dinner 10.15pm S% *sB&B fr£12.75
dB&B fr£22 Lunch fr£3.50 Tea fr50p Dinner fr£4
Wine £2.65 *xmas* Credit cards 1 2 3 5 6

Swan The Hythe ☎52494
17th-C inn with historical associations. Samuel Pepys mentions it in his diary.
RS Xmas Day 8rm Lift 12P International.
Last dinner 9.45pm S% sB&B£11.50
dB&B£15 Lunch£5.75alc Dinner£5.75alc
Wine£3.05 Credit cards 1 2 3 5

STALISFIELD GREEN Kent Map**5** TQ95
X**Plough Inn** ☎Eastling256
Closed Mon; Lunch not served Tue–Sat; Dinner not served Sun; 28seats 60P Last dinner 9pm
*Lunch fr£3.50 Dinner£4.50alc Wine£2

STAMFORD Lincolnshire Map**4** TF00
★★★**George** St Martin's ☎2101 Telex no 32578
Old historic coaching inn, Royalty having stayed here many times, including Princess Anne for the Burghley Horse Trials European Three Day Event.
47rm(27) 1 CTV in bedrooms 100P
English, French & Italian. Last dinner 10.30pm
S% sB&B fr£13 sB&B fr£16
dB&B fr£20 dB&B fr£23 Bar lunch£1.50alc
Dinner£7.50alc Wine£3.90
Credit cards 1 2 3 5

★★**Crowne** ☎3136
18rm(7) CTV TV in bedrooms 30P English, French & Portuguese. Last dinner 10.30pm S%
sB&B fr£10.50 sB&B fr£15 dB&B fr£16
dB&B fr£17.50 Lunch fr£2.75
High Tea fr£2.75 Dinner fr£4.50 Wine£3
Credit cards 1 2 3 6

STANDISH Gt Manchester Map**7** SD51
☆☆☆**Cassinelli's Almond Brook Motor Inn** Almond Brook Rd ☎421504
44rm(42) CTV in bedrooms 200P Disco 4nights wkly Live music & dancing wkly Cabaret wkly
Italian. Last dinner 10pm S%
sB&B£15.50 sB&B£15.50 dB&B£22
dB&B£22 Lunch£2.50–£3.50&alc Tea50p
High Tea50p Dinner£4.50&alc Wine£2.40
xmas Credit cards 1 2 3 5 6

STANHOPE BRETBY Derbyshire Map**8** SK22
XX***Stanhope Arms*** Ashby Road East (on A50)
☎Burton-on-Trent 217954
Dinner not served Xmas Day; 110seats 250P bedrooms available English & French.
Last dinner 9.45pm

STAVERTON Devon Map**3** SX76
★★**Sea Trout Inn** ☎274
6rm CTV 70P 6 billiards Mainly grills.
Last dinner 9pm S% sB&B£10.50–£12.50
dB&B£21–£25 Lunch£3–£4.50
Dinner£4.50–£6.50&alc Wine£2.75 *xmas*
Credit cards 1 3

STEETON West Yorkshire Map**7** SE04
XXX**Currergate** Skipton Rd ☎53204
Closed Mon; Lunch not served Sat; 60seats 100P bedrooms available Disco Sat English & Italian.
Last dinner 10pm *Lunch fr£3&alc
Dinner fr£5.50&alc Wine£3 Credit cards 1 3 5

S

STEPPINGLEY Bedfordshire Map**4** TL03
✕French Horn ☎Flitwick2051
Closed Mon; Dinner not served Sun; 66 seats 60P ♀English & Continental. Last dinner10pm
✱Lunch£3&alc Dinner£7.50alc Wine£2.80
Credit cards 1 2 3 5

STEVENAGE Hertfordshire Map**4** TL22
★★★Cromwell High St, Old Town ☎59111
Originally 16th-C farmhouse, once owned by Oliver Cromwell's secretary. Cromwell himself stayed here occasionally, 1640–1650.
56⇌ ⋔ ☽ ⋔ CTV in bedrooms 100P ⋔ ♀English & French. Last dinner10pm ✿ ♀ S%
✱sB&B fr£15.75 sB&B⇌ ⋔ fr£18
dB&B⇌ ⋔ fr£25.60 Lunch£5.50alc Tea fr35p
Dinner£5.50alc Wine£3.50
Credit cards 1 2 3 4 5 6

☆☆☆Grampian The Forum ☎50661 Telex no825697
100⇌ ⋔ Lift ☽ ⋔ CTV in bedrooms ⚑ Conference facilities available ♀English & French.
Last dinner9.30pm ✿ ♀ S%
sB&B⇌ ⋔ £16.50–£19.50 dB&B⇌ ⋔ £23–£26
Lunch£3.50–£3.75&alc Tea£1
Dinner£4–£4.25&alc Wine£3 ▜ *xmas*
Credit cards 1 2 3 5

☆☆☆Roebuck Inn London Rd, Broadwater (Trusthouse Forte) ☎4171
Picturesque wayside inn dating back to 15th-C.
54⇌ ⋔ ☽ ⋔ TV in bedrooms 100P
Last dinner10.15pm ✿ S% sB&B⇌ ⋔ £16.50
dB&B⇌ ⋔ £23 ▜ *xmas* Credit cards 1 2 3 4 5 6

STEYNING West Sussex Map**4** TQ11
✕✕✕Springwells High St ☎812446
45seats 6P bedrooms available ♀French.
Last dinner9pm S% Lunch£4&alc Dinner£10alc
Wine£3.50 Credit cards 2 3 5

STINCHCOMBE Gloucestershire Map**3** ST79
★★ Stinchcombe Manor ☎Dursley2538
Telex no437193
6⇌ ⋔ ⊞ ⋔ CTV CTV in bedrooms 40P 2▲ ⇔ ⚓ ♤
♀International. Last dinner9.30pm ✿ ♀ S%
✱sB&B⇌ ⋔ £14–£25 dB&B£22–£26
dB&B⇌ ⋔ £25–£40 Lunch£4.50alc Tea£1.50alc
Dinner£4.50alc Wine£2.50 ▜ *xmas*
Credit cards 1 2 3 5 6

STOCKBRIDGE Hampshire Map**4** SU33
★★Grosvenor High St (Whitbread) ☎606
14rm(1⇌ ⋔) ⋔ CTV 50P 3▲ ⇔ ♀English & French.
Last dinner9pm ✿ ♀ ✱sB&B£9.07
dB&B£16.50 dB&B⇌ ⋔ £18 Lunch£3&alc
Tea30–65p Dinner£3.85&alc Wine£2.75 ▜
Credit cards 1 3 5 6

STOCKPORT Gt Manchester Map**7** SJ88
★★★Alma Lodge 149 Buxton Rd (Embassy)
☎061–483 4431
74rm(55⇌ ⋔) ☽ ⋔ CTV TV in bedrooms 100P
Conference facilities available Last dinner9.15pm
✿ S% sB&B£13 sB&B⇌ ⋔ £16 dB&B£17
dB&B⇌ ⋔ £22 Lunch£5&alc Dinner£5.50&alc
Wine£4.50 ▜ Credit cards 1 2 3 4 5 6

★★★Belgrade Dialston Ln ☎061–483 3851
Telex no667217
160⇌ ⋔ Lift ☽ ⋔ CTV CTV in bedrooms 300P
Conference facilities available ✿ ♀

★Acton Court Buxton Rd ☎061–483 6172
23rm(3⇌ ⋔) ✕ ⋔ CTV 200P 2▲ ⚓ Disco twice wkly
♤ Last dinner9.30pm ✿ ♀ Credit cards 2 3 5

STOCKTON-ON-TEES Cleveland Map**8** NZ41
☆☆☆☆Swallow 10 John Walker Sq (Swallow)
☎69721 Telex no53168
121⇌ ⋔ Lift ☽ ⋔ CTV available in bedrooms 200P
Conference facilities available Last dinner10.15pm
✿ ♀ sB&B⇌ ⋔ fr£20.50 dB&B fr£27.35 ▜
xmas Credit cards 1 2 3 5

★★★Billingham Arms Town Sq, Billingham (3m NE A19) (Thistle) ☎553661
64rm(55⇌ ⋔) Lift ☽ ⋔ CTV TV in bedrooms 200P
♀Continental. Last dinner10pm ✿ ♀ S%
SB&B£15.90 sB&B⇌ ⋔ £17.90 dB&B£24.30
dB&B⇌ ⋔ £26.30 Lunch£3.80&alc Tea£1.50
Dinner£4.90&alc Wine£2.95 ▜
Credit cards 1 2 3 4 5 6

☆☆☆Golden Eagle Trenchard Av, Thornaby-on-Tees (1m E A174) (Open House) ☎62511
57⇌ ⋔ Lift ☽ ⋔ CTV TV in bedrooms 80P Disco twice wkly Live music & dancing twice wkly
♀Continental. Last dinner9.45pm ✿ ♀ S%
✱SB&B⇌ ⋔ fr£14 dB&B⇌ ⋔ fr£21.50 Lunch£3
Tea£1 Dinner£4.30 Wine£2.35 ▜
Credit cards 1 2 3 5 6

☆☆☆Post House Low Ln, Thornaby-on-Tees (Trusthouse Forte) ☎591213 Telex58426
On A1044 close to interchange with A174 towards Yarm; 1m from new A19 diversion.
140⇌ ⋔ ☽ ⋔ TV in bedrooms 250P
Last dinner10.15pm ✿ ♀ S%
sB&B⇌ ⋔ fr£19.25 dB&B⇌ ⋔ fr£27 ▜
Credit cards 1 2 3 4 5 6

★★Parkmore 636 Yarm Rd, Eaglescliffe (3m S A19)
☎780324
39rm(35⇌ ⋔) ⋔ CTV CTV in bedrooms 70P ⚓
Last dinner9.45pm ✿ ♀ S%
sB&B£10.25–£11.25 sB&B⇌ ⋔ £11.25
dB&B£15.25 dB&B⇌ ⋔ &17.25 Lunch£3.60–£4

S

Tea£1.20–£1.50 HighTea£2–£3 Dinner£4.20–£6&alc Wine£3.65

★**Stonyroyd** 187 Oxbridge Ln ☎63133 13rm CTV 7P Last dinner7pm S% sB&B£7.50 dB&B£14 Tea fr£1 High Tea fr£2.20 Dinner fr£3.50 Wine£2.50

STOKE GABRIEL Devon Map**3** SX85
★★**Gabriel Court** ☎206
Features a long established, walled garden (c 1480) with yew arches, box hedges and magnolia trees.
25rm(17) CTV 13P 8 (heated) (grass) Last dinner8.30pm sB&B£11.85–£13 sB&B£12.95–£14.25 dB&B£23.70–£26 dB&B£25.90–£28.50 Lunch£4.50 Tea60p Dinner£5.65 Wine£3.50 *xmas*

STOKE HOLY CROSS Norfolk Map**5** TG20
✕✕**Old Mill** ☎Framlingham Earl3337
This restaurant was once a weatherboarded mill.
Closed Sun & Public Hols; Lunch not served Sat; 90seats 60P English & French. Last dinner10.30pm ✻Lunch£3.40–£7.35&alc Dinner£3.40–£7.35&alc Wine£2.80 Credit cards 1 2 3 5

STOKEINTEIGNHEAD Devon Map**3** SX97
✕✕***Harvest Barn*** ☎Shaldon3670
Closed Tue; 40seats 20P bedrooms available International. Last dinner10.15pm Credit cards 1 3

STOKE-ON-TRENT Staffordshire Map**7** SJ84
See also **Newcastle-under-Lyme**
★★★★**North Stafford** Station Rd (Trusthouses Forte) ☎48501 Telex no36287
70 Lift TV in bedrooms 120P Conference facilities available Last dinner9.45pm S% sB&B£20 dB&B£27.50 *xmas* Credit cards 1 2 3 4 5 6

★★**George** Swan Sq, Burslem (Embassy) ☎84021 36rm(5) CTV TV in bedrooms 8 Last dinner8.30pm S% sB&B£10 sB&B£12.50 dB&B£16 dB&B£18 Lunch£4.50&alc Dinner£5&alc Wine£4 Credit cards 1 2 3 4 5 6

★★**Grand** 66 Trinity St, Hanley (Trusthouse Forte) ☎22361
96rm(39) Lift TV in bedrooms 42P Last dinner9.15pm S% sB&B£13.50 sB&B£15.50 dB&B£19 dB&B£22 Credit cards 1 2 3 4 5 6

✕✕**Poachers Cottage** Stone Rd, Trentham (3m S A34) ☎657115
Closed Sun & Mon; 100seats 80P Last dinner9pm Lunch£2.60–£3 Dinner£6alc Wine£2.80

✕***La Taverne Provençale*** 13 Glebe St ☎411889
Closed Sun, Mon & Public Hols; 42seats 100P French, Italian & Spanish. Last dinner10.30pm

STOKESLEY North Yorkshire Map**8** NZ50
✕**Golden Lion Hotel** High St ☎710265
Dinner not served Sun; 60seats 10P bedrooms available French. Last dinner9.15pm Lunch£6.55alc Dinner£6.55alc Wine£3

STONE Staffordshire Map**7** SJ93
★★★***Crown*** High St ☎3535
13 TV available in bedrooms 200P English & French. Last dinner9pm

✕***La Casserole*** 6 Oulton Rd ☎4232
Closed Sun & Mon; Lunch not served; 50seats French.

STONE CROSS East Sussex Map**5** TQ60
★★★**Glyndley Manor** Hailsham Rd ☎Eastbourne843737
25 CTV CTV in bedrooms 50P (heated) Disco Sat Live music & dancing Sat English & French. Last dinner9.15pm ✻sB&B£9.40–£12.40 sB&B£18.80–£24.80 Lunch£3.75–£4.50&alc Tea£1.25–£1.75 Dinner£4–£4.75&alc Wine£4 *xmas* Credit cards 1 2 3 5 6

STONEY CROSS Hampshire Map**4** SU21
★★**Compton Arms** (Nicholsons) ☎Cadnam2134
Georgian-style inn standing in large lawns and gardens with good views over New Forest.
12 CTV in bedrooms 50P 5 Last dinner9.45pm S% sB&B£12.85–£14 dB&B£23.70–£28 Lunch£3.50–£4&alc Dinner£4–£5&alc Wine£3.50 *xmas* Credit cards 1 2 3 5

STONY STRATFORD Buckinghamshire Map**4** SP74
★★**Cock** Watling St ☎Milton Keynes562109
This famous old coaching inn was rebuilt after a fire in 1742 on the site of a much older building. A coachman's timetable is on display in the lounge bar.
Closed 24–26Dec; RS Sun; 13rm CTV P English & Continental. Last dinner9pm S% sB&B£13 dB&B£19–£22 Lunch£5.50–£7.35 Dinner£5.50–£7.35 Wine£2.90 Credit cards 1 2 3 5 6

STORRINGTON West Sussex Map**4** TQ01
✕✕**Manleys** Manleys Hill ☎2331
Closed Mon & 3wks Xmas; Dinner not served Sun; 40seats 15P Austrian & French. Specialities: crêpe pêcheur, steak de chevreuil à la maison. Last dinner10pm ✻Lunch£7alc Dinner£8alc Wine£3.50 Credit cards 1 2 6

S

STOURBRIDGE West Midlands Map**7** SO88
★★**Bell** Market St (Wolverhampton & Dudley) ☎5641
21rm CTV ⊘ 100P Last dinner8.45pm S% ✱sB&B£11.30 sB&B⇌⋒£12.75 dB&B£18 dB&B⇌⋒£20.20 Lunch£2.50 Dinner£3.45 Wine£2.60 Credit cards 1 3

★★**Talbot** High St (Wolverhampton & Dudley) ☎4350
20rm(6⇌⋒) 2 CTV ⊘ 30P Last dinner9.15pm S% ✱sB&B£11.25 sB&B⇌⋒£13.80 dB&B£18.35 dB&B⇌⋒£20.20 Lunch£2.35&alc Dinner£3.45&alc Wine£2.60 Credit cards 1 3

✱✕**Gallery** 121 Bridgnorth Rd, Wollaston ☎2788 *(Rosette awarded for dinner only)*.
Closed Sun, Mon & 25Dec–2Jan; Dinner served 31Dec; 40seats English & Continental. Last dinner9.30pm Lunch fr£2.50&alc Dinner£8alc Wine£3.20 Credit card 1

STOURPORT-ON-SEVERN Hereford & Worcester Map**7** SO87
★★★**Mount Olympus** 35 Hartlebury Rd ☎77333
43⇌⋒ CTV CTV in bedrooms ⊘ 150P (heated) (hard) squash Disco twice wkly Live music & dancing wkly Cabaret wkly English, French & Italian. Last dinner10.30pm S% sB&B⇌⋒£16.50–£17.50 dB&B⇌⋒£26–£28 Lunch£2.25–£3.50&alc Tea£1.25–£1.50 Dinner£3.75–£5.25&alc Wine£3.45 Credit cards 1 2 3 5

★★**Swan** High St (Ansells) ☎2050
33rm(26⇌⋒) CTV ⊘ 80P Last dinner9.45pm S% sB&B£11.60 sB&B⇌⋒£13.53 dB&B£15.80 dB&B⇌⋒£17.75 Lunch£2.40&alc Dinner£2.95&alc Wine£3.20 Credit cards 1 2

STOW-ON-THE-WOLD Gloucestershire Map**4** SP12
★★**Fosse Manor** ☎30354
Modernised Cotswold manor house situated one mile south of the historic market town.
19rm(12⇌⋒) Annexe:7rm(1⇌⋒) CTV 40P Last dinner9.30pm ✱sB&B£10 sB&B⇌⋒£12 dB&B£16.80 dB&B⇌⋒£22 Lunch£7alc Dinner£4.30&alc Wine£3.20 Credit cards 2 3 5

★★**Royalist** Digbeth St ☎30670
10rm(3⇌⋒) Annexe:4⇌⋒ 1 CTV 10P Last dinner9.30pm sB&B£10.69 sB&B⇌⋒£11.88 dB&B£15.44 dB&B⇌⋒£20.79 Bar lunch50p–£2 Dinner fr£3.95&alc Wine£3.50 *xmas* Credit cards 1 3

★★**Stow Lodge** The Square ☎30485
Closed Xmas–Feb; 20⇌⋒ TV in bedrooms ⊘ 30P Children under 5yrs not accommodated Last dinner9pm Credit cards 2 5

★★**Talbot** Market Sq (Crest) ☎30631
18th-C Cotswold inn of character. Used as a corn exchange as late as 1904. Still has letter box marked 'For Corn returns'.
36rm(11⇌⋒) CTV CTV available in bedrooms Last dinner9.45pm S% ✱sB&B£10.80 sB&B⇌⋒£14.04 dB&B£19.33 dB&B⇌⋒£23.76 Credit cards 1 2 3 4 5 6

★★**Unicorn** Sheep St (Crest) ☎30257
16th-C coaching inn.
19rm(8⇌⋒) CTV CTV in bedrooms 30P French. Last dinner9.30pm S% ✱sB&B£10.80 sB&B⇌⋒£14.04 dB&B£19.33 dB&B⇌⋒£23.76 Credit cards 1 2 3 4 5 6

★**King's Arms** Market Sq ☎30602
Stone-built 16th-C inn.
9rm CTV TV in bedrooms 9P Last dinner9.15pm

dB&B£28 Barlunch35p–£3 Dinner£5.50–£6.50 Wine£3.10 Credit cards 1 2 3 5

✕Rafter's Park St 30200
Closed Mon; Dinner not served sun; 40seats French. Last dinner10pm S% *Lunch£4alc Dinner£6.50alc Wine£2.75 Credit cards 1 2 3 5

STRATFIELD TURGIS Hampshire Map**4** SU66
★★Wellington Arms Turgis Green214
19rm(13) CTV 100P 4 Disco 3nights wkly English & French. Last dinner9pm S% sB&B£15 sB&B£15–£20 dB&B£18–£23 dB&B£20–£25 Lunch£8alc Dinner£8alc Wine£4

STRATFORD-UPON-AVON Warwickshire Map**4** SP25 **See plan**
★★★★Hilton Bridgefoot 67511 Telex no311127 Plan**9**
253 Lift CTV in bedrooms 350P Live music & dancing 6 nights wkly Conference facilities available International. Last dinner11.30pm
sB&B£22.85–£28.50
dB&B£30.60–£37.10
Lunch£3.80–£4.20&alc Tea£1.50–£2&alc High Tea£3–£3.50&alc Dinner£3.80–£4.20&alc Wine£4.20 *xmas* Credit cards 1 2 3 4 5 6

★★★★Shakespeare Chapel St (Trusthouse Forte) 294771 Telex no31181 Plan**15**
Historic black and white timbered building with many gables; dates from early 16th-C. Oak beams, hearths and bedrooms named after Shakespearian characters.
66 Lift CTV in bedrooms 35P Last dinner9.45pm S% sB&B£20 dB&B£32.50 *xmas*
Credit cards 1 2 3 4 5 6

★★★★Welcombe Warwick Rd (British Transport) 295252 Telex no31347 Plan**17**
Early 19th-C manor house with Jacobean style gables and chimneys in beautiful parkland setting of 40 acres with terrace and formal gardens.
84 CTV in bedrooms 150P 10 Conference facilities available Last dinner9.15pm S% sB&B fr£32 dB&B fr£48 Lunch fr£5.85 Dinner fr£7.60 Wine£3.50 *xmas* Credit cards 1 2 3 4 5 6

★★★Alveston Manor Clopton Bridge (Trusthouse Forte) 4581 Telex no31324 Plan**1**
Brick and timber, Tudor-style manor house with modern entrance and extensions behind. Beamed restaurant has tapestry hangings. First performance of 'A Midsummer Night's Dream' is said to have taken place on lawn.
112 TV in bedrooms 200P Conference facilities available Last dinner9.15pm S% sB&B£20 dB&B£30.50 *xmas*
Credit cards 1 2 3 4 5 6

★★★Arden Waterside (Inter-Hotel) 294949 Plan**2**
64rm(43) CTV TV available in bedrooms 40P Last dinner9pm S% *sB&B£10.65 sB&B£14.90 dB&B£20.20 dB&B£25 Lunch£3alc Dinner£4.80–£8.50 Wine£2.70 *xmas* Credit cards 1 2 3 5 6

★★★Falcon Chapel St (Grand Met) 5777 Plan**5**
The interior walls of this 15th-C timbered building are lined with oak panelling from New Place, Shakespeare's last home.
67rm(62) Lift TV available in bedrooms 120P Conference facilities available European. last dinner9pm *sB&B£17–£19 dB&B£24.50–£28.50 *xmas*
Credit cards 1 2 3 4 5 6

S

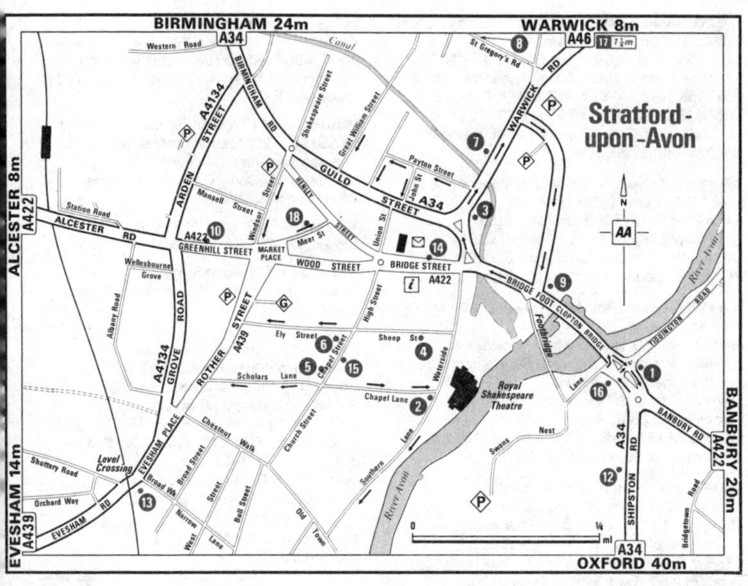

1 Alveston Manor ★★★
2 Arden ★★★
3 Buccaneer ✕
4 Christophi's ✕✕
5 Falcon ★★★
6 Giovanni ✕
7 Grosvenor House ★★★
8 Haytor ★★
9 Hilton ★★★★
10 Marianne ✕
11 Marlowe's ✕✕
12 Le Provençal ✕✕
13 Ravenhurst ★
14 Red House ★★
15 Shakespeare ★★★★
16 Swan's Nest ★★★
17 Welcombe ★★★★
18 White Swan ★★★

S

★★★**Grosvenor House** Warwick Rd (Best Western) ☎69213 Telex no311699 Plan**7**
closed 24–28Dec; 59rm(53⇌⋒) 2⊟ ☽ 🍴 CTV CTV in bedrooms 50P Last dinner9pm S% sB&B£10.80–£12 sB&B⇌⋒£12.50–£14 dB&B£18.50–£20.20 dB&B⇌⋒£21.70–£26 Lunch£3.50–£4&alc Dinner£4.40–£5&alc Credit cards 1 2 3 4 5 6

★★★**Swan's Nest** Bridgefoot (Trusthouse Forte) ☎66761 Telex no31419 Plan**16**
71rm(63⇌⋒) ☽ TV in bedrooms 100P Last dinner9.15pm S% sB&B£15 sB&B⇌⋒£17 dB&B£25.50 dB&B⇌⋒£27.50 *xmas* Credit cards 1 2 3 4 5 6

★★★**White Swan** Rother St (Trusthouse Forte) ☎297022 Plan**18**
Half-timbered 15th-C inn with original beams, oak panelling and James I fireplace. Rare murals of Tobias and the Angel (1550) in lounge.
55rm(23⇌⋒) ☽ TV in bedrooms Last dinner8.30pm S% sB&B£13 sB&B⇌⋒£15.50 dB&B£20 dB&B⇌⋒£22.50 *xmas* Credit cards 1 2 3 4 5 6

★★**Haytor** Avenue Rd ☎297799 Plan**8**
Closed 21Dec–6Jan; RS 7Jan–21Mar; 18rm(12⇌⋒) 1⊟ CTV 18P 3 Last dinner8pm S% sB&B fr£7.70 sB&B⇌⋒ fr£10.50 dB&B fr£17 dB&B⇌⋒ fr£21 Lunch fr£2.50 Tea fr35p Dinner fr£3.30 Wine£2.50 Credit card 2

★★**Red Horse** Bridge St (Norfolk Capital) ☎293211 Telex no23241 Plan**14**
American novelist Washington Irving lived and did much of his writing here.
70rm(30⇌⋒) ☽ CTV 40P Mainly grills. Last dinner9.30pm S% sB&B£11.70 sB&B⇌⋒£15.25 dB&B£22.85 dB&B⇌⋒£26.95 Lunch fr£3.25&alc Tea fr£1.50 High Tea fr£2 Dinner fr£3.80&alc wine£4 *xmas* Credit cards 1 2 3 5 6

★**Ravenhurst** Broad Walk ☎292515 Plan**13**
7rm CTV English & South American. Last dinner10pm S% sB&B£6–£6.90 dB&B£10.60–£12.20 Dinner£2.20–£3&alc Wine£3 *xmas*

✕✕**Christophi's** 21–23 Sheep St ☎293546 Plan**4**
closed Sun, 25 & 26Dec; Lunch not served; 120seats Greek. Last dinner11.30pm S% ✱Dinner£5.50alc Wine£2.75 Credit cards 1 2 3 5

✕✕**Marlowe's** 18 High St ☎4999 Plan**11**
150seats English & French. Last dinner11.30pm Lunch fr£3.50&alc Dinner£5.50–£8.50&alc Wine£4.20 Credit cards 1 2 3

✕✕**Le Provençal** Shipston Rd ☎297567 Plan**12**
Closed Sun, Mon & Dec–Feb; Lunch not served; 40seats 20P bedrooms available French. Last dinner11.30pm ✱Dinner£6alc Wine£2.80 Credit card 2

✕**Buccaneer** 11 Warwick Rd ☎292550 Plan**3**
Closed Mon & Feb; Lunch not served; 32seats bedrooms available Continental. Last dinner11.30pm Dinner£7alc Wine£3.10 Credit cards 1 2 3 5

✕**Giovanni** Ely St ☎297999 Plan**6**
Closed Sun; Italian. Last dinner11.30pm

✕***Marianne*** 3 Greenhill St ☎293563 Plan**10**
Closed Sun; 50seats French. Last dinner11.30pm Credit card 5

STRATTON Cornwall Map**2** SS20
★**Stamford Hill House** ☎Bude2709
closed Oct–Mar; RS Xmas; 14rm CTV 20P Children under 1yr not accommodated Last dinner9pm S% sB&B£5–£6.50 sB&B⇌⋒£5.25–£6.75 dB&B£10–£13 dB&B⇌⋒£10.50–£13.50 Lunch£2.50–£3.50&alc Tea£1–£1.50 Dinner£2.80–£3.85&alc Wine£2 *xmas*

STREET Somerset Map**3** ST43
☆☆☆**Wessex** ☎43383
50⇌⋒ Lift ☽ CTV in bedrooms 40P 20 Live music & dancing Sat Conference facilities available Last dinner9.45pm S% sB&B⇌⋒fr£17.07 dB&B⇌⋒ fr£25.12 Lunch£1.50alc High Tea£1.50alc Dinner£5alc Wine£2.95 *xmas* Credit cards 1 2 3 5 6

★★**Bear** High St ☎42021
Stone building dating from late 19th-C; on site of old cider house.
Closed 21–30Dec; 11rm(6⇌⋒) CTV 16P Last dinner8pm S% sB&B£11 sB&B⇌⋒£12.50 dB&B£20 dB&B⇌⋒£21.50 Lunch£3 Dinner£4alc Wine£2.40

✕✕**Mullions** 41 High St ☎45110
Closed 25 & 26Dec; 60seats 20P bedrooms available English, French & Italian. Last dinner10.30pm ✱Lunch fr£4.95 Dinner£10alc Wine£3.50

STREETLY West Midlands Map**7** SP09
☆☆**Parson & Clerk Motel** Chester Rd (junc A452/B4138) (Ansells) ☎021–353 1747
31rm(30⇌⋒) CTV 200P Last dinner10pm S% sB&B⇌⋒£14.60 dB&B⇌⋒£18.50 Lunch£3.50&alc Dinner£3.75&alc Wine£3.20 Credit cards 1 2

STRETE Devon Map**3** SX84
✕**Laughing Monk** ☎Stoke Fleming639

S

Lunch served Sun only; 45seats 20P Lastdinner10pm Lunch£4alc Dinner£6alc Wine£2.90 Creditcards 1 2 3

STROUD Gloucestershire Map**3** SO80
See also Amberley

★★★Bear of Rodborough Rodborough Common (½m SW) (Anchor) ☎Amberley3522
Character hotel set in cotswold countryside, with extensive grounds adjoining National Trust land.
32rm(30⇌⋒) ☽ CTV in bedrooms 60P 10 Lastdinner9.15pm S% ✱sB&B fr£12 sB&B⇌⋒ fr£15.50 dB&B fr£20 dB&B⇌⋒ fr£24 Lunch£5.50alc Tea90palc Dinner£6.50alc Wine£2.65 *xmas* Creditcards 1 2 3 4 5 6

★★*Burleigh Court* Brimscombe (2½m SE off A419) ☎Brimscombe3804
11rm(4⇌⋒) CTV TV available in bedrooms 40P Lastdinner8.45pm S%

★Alpine Lodge Stratford Rd ☎4949
10rm(4⇌⋒) CTV 20P Mainlygrills. Lastdinner9.30pm S% sB&B£7 dB&B£13 dB&B⇌⋒£16 Barlunch30p–£1.50&alc Dinner£4alc Wine£2.60

★Imperial (Berni) ☎4077
Closed Xmas; 18rm CTV 15P Mainlygrills. Lastdinner10.30pm ✱sB&B fr£7.20 dB&B fr£13.20 Lunch£1.61–£4.74 Dinner£1.61–£4.74 Wine£2.44 Creditcards 1 2 3 5

XX*Mr Baillie's* 203 Slad Rd ☎5331
Country mansion set in landscaped grounds

overlooking Slad Valley.
Closed Mon, Tue after Public Hols & 2–23Jan; Dinner not served Sun; 34seats 15P ♕International. Lastdinner9pm Creditcard⑤

STUDLAND Dorset Map**4** SZ08
★★★***Knoll House*** Ferry Rd ☎251
Delightfully situated amid pine trees, a rambling building set back from road in lawns and gardens; extending to the beach.
Closed 22Oct–1Apr; 112rm(82⇌⋒) ☽ ⅏CTV 100P ⚓ ⌓(heated) ⛳ ⚽(hard) ∩ Disco wkly in season ♕English & French. Lastdinner8.30pm ♔ ⚿

★★⚜**Manor House** ☎288
Charming gabled and turreted Gothic-style manor house, standing in 12 acres of secluded gardens and grounds which overlook the sea and cliffs.
Closed Mar–mid Oct; 19rm(15⇌⋒) 1⊟ ⅏ CTV 25P ⊛ ⚓ Children under 5yrs not accommodated Lastdinner7.45pm ♔ ⚿ S% ✱sB&B£8–£9 sB&B⇌⋒£9–£10 dB&B£15–£18 dB&B⇌⋒£17–£24 Barlunch60p–£1.75 Tea35p–65p HighTea£1.50–£2 Dinner£4.75–£5.50 Wine£3

STURMINSTER NEWTON Dorset Map**3** ST71
❀✕✕**Plumber Manor** (2m SW on Hazelbury Bryan road) ☎72507
17th-C, grey stone manor house in 15 acres parkland.
Closed Mon, Feb & 1st 2wks Nov; Lunch not served; Dinner not served Sun (Nov–Mar); 56seats 25P bedrooms available ♕International. Specialities: game in season, lamb Shrewsbury, beef Wellington. Lastdinner9.30pm ✱Dinner£7.50–£8 Wine£3.40

✕✕**Townhouse Gigi** Church Rd ☎72874
Renovated double-fronted small house with colour washed frontage.
Closed Sun; 36seats ℙ ♕English, French & Italian. Lastdinner10pm ✱Lunch£2.10alc Dinner£5.50–£7.50&alc Wine£2.50

SUDBURY Suffolk Map**5** TL84
★★★**Mill** Walnut Tree Ln ☎75544 Telexno919161 46⇌⋒ Annexe:4⇌⋒ ☽ ⅏CTV CTV in bedrooms 80P 6⌂ ♕English & French. Lastdinner9.30pm ♔ ⚿ S% ✱sB&B⇌£13.50 dB&B⇌⋒£20.50 Lunchfr£3.50&alc Dinnerfr£4.50&alc Wine£2.40 ⊨ *xmas* Creditcards①②③⑤

★★**Four Swans** North St ☎72793
5rm Annexe: 12⇌⋒ ⅏CTV 20P Lastdinner9.30pm & 10.30 Sat ♔ S% sB&B£10.30 sB&B⇌£13.50 dB&B£18 dB&B⇌⋒£21.50 Lunch£3.25–£4&alc Dinner£3.25–£4&alc ⊨ Creditcards②⑤

SULGRAVE Northamptonshire Map**4** SP54
✕**Thatched House Hotel** ☎232
Built in 17th-C of Cotswold stone, this restaurant stands in remote country village.
50seats 10P bedrooms available ♕English & French. Lastdinner9.15pm ✱Lunch£3.60–£5.75 Tea85p–£1.50 Dinner£5–£7.75 Wine£2.75 Creditcards①②③⑥

SUNBURY-ON-THAMES Surrey Map**4** TQ16
✕**Castle** 21 Thames St ☎83647
Converted 17th-C small inn, close to River Thames.
100seats 50P ✗ Live music & dancing Fri ♕European. Lastdinner10pm ✱Lunch£4.25–£10 Dinner£6–£15 Wine£4.50 Creditcards①③

SUNDERLAND Tyne & Wear Map**12** NZ35
★★★**Mowbray Park** Borough Rd (Thistle) ☎78221 60rm(34⇌⋒) Lift ☽ ⅏ CTV CTV in bedrooms ℙ

S

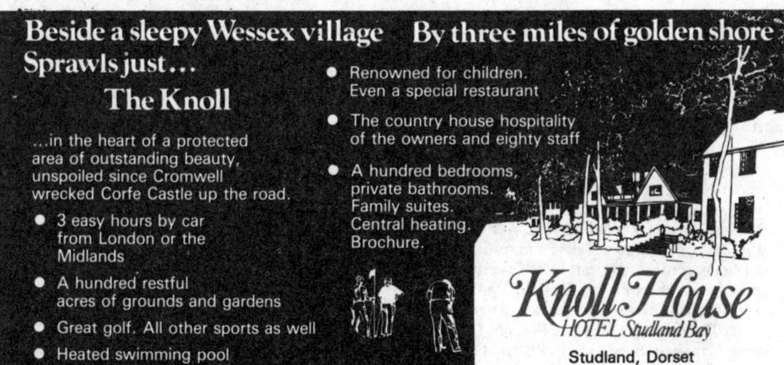

French. Last dinner 9.45pm ♁ ⊡ S%
✱sB&B£13.50–£13.90 sB&B⇌⋒£17
dB&B£19.50 dB&B⇌⋒£24
Lunch£3.25–£3.60&alc Tea40p
Dinner£4.35–£4.70&alc Wine£2.75 ⊟
Credit cards 1 2 3 4 5 6

★★★**Seaburn** Queen's Pde, Seaburn (Swallow)
☎292041 Telex no 53168
58rm(47⇌⋒) Lift ☽ ⋈ CTV in bedrooms 300P
Last dinner 9.30pm ♁ ⊡ S% sB&B⇌⋒fr£18
dB&B fr£19.80 dB&B⇌⋒fr£25.63 ⊟ *xmas*
Credit cards 1 2 3 5

★★**Roker** Roker Ter (Berni) ☎71786
48rm ☽ ⋈ CTV TV in bedrooms ⊘ 150P 20⌂
Mainly grills. Last dinner 11pm ♁ S%
✱sB&B£9.20 sB&B⇌⋒£11.50 dB&B£15.80
dB&B⇌⋒£18.10 Lunch£1.62–£4.34
Dinner£1.62–£4.34 Wine£2.52 ⊟
Credit cards 1 2 3 5

★**Gelt House** St Bede's Ter ☎72990
Closed Xmas; 15rm ⋈ CTV TV available in bedrooms
14P sauna bath ♁ S% sB&B£8.64
dB&B£15.12 Lunch£4 Dinner£4.50&alc ⊟

SUNNINGDALE Berkshire Map**4** SU96
✕***La Paloma*** 61 Chobham Rd ☎Ascot 20414
Lunch not served Mon; Dinner not served Sun;
34seats Spanish. Last dinner 10.15pm
Credit cards 1 2 3

SUTTON COLDFIELD West Midlands Map**7** SP19
★★★★**Penns Hall** Penns Ln (Embassy)
☎021–351 3111
Handsome mansion of mellow brick, dating from 1720; situated in own secluded grounds with lake.
70rm(56⇌⋒) Lift ☽ ⋈ CTV TV in bedrooms 200P ⚓
Conference facilities available Last dinner 9.15pm
♁ S% sB&B£14 sB&B⇌⋒£18 dB&B£18
dB&B⇌⋒£24 Continental breakfast
Lunch£5&alc Dinner£5.50&alc Wine£5 ⊟
Credit cards 1 2 3 4 5 6

★★★**Moor Hall** Moor Hall Dr, Four Oaks (Best Western) ☎021–308 3751
55rm(50⇌⋒) ☽ ⋈ CTV in bedrooms 200P ⚓ ⛳18
Disco Wed, Fri & Sun Live music & dancing Sat
Conference facilities available English & French.
Last dinner 10.30pm ♁ ⊡ S% sB&B fr£19
sB&B⇌⋒fr£20.50 dB&B⇌⋒fr£23.50
Lunch fr£3.75 Dinner fr£5 Wine£3.95 ⊟ *xmas*
Credit cards 1 2 3 4 5 6

✕✕**Le Bon Viveur** 65 Birmingham Rd
☎021–355 5836
Closed Sun & Mon; 48seats 20P French.
Last dinner 10.30pm S%
✱Lunch£2.35–£2.95&alc Dinner£8alc
Wine£2.80 Credit cards 1 2 3 5

✕✕**La Gondola** Lichfield Rd, Mere Green
☎021–308 6782
Closed Sun; 100seats 100P Italian.
Last dinner 10.30pm ✱Lunch£2.25–£2.95&alc
Dinner£10alc Credit cards 1 2 3 5

SUTTON-ON-SEA Lincolnshire Map**9** TF58
★★**Bacchus** High St ☎41204
22rm(6⇌⋒) ⋈ CTV 50P 8⌂ ⚓ Last dinner 8.30pm
♁ ⊡ S% ✱sB&B£9.50–£10.10
sB&B⇌⋒£10.40–£11.30 dB&B£19–£20.20
dB&B⇌⋒£20.80–£22.60 Lunch£2.97 Tea90p
Dinner£4.28 Wine£1.70 ⊟

SWAFFHAM Norfolk Map**5** TF80
★★**George** Station St (Grand Met) ☎21238
Georgian coaching house with stucco front.
27⇌⋒ ⋈ TV 20P English & French.
Last dinner 9pm ♁ ⊡ S% ✱sB&B⇌⋒£12.50
dB&B⇌⋒£16.50 ⊟ *xmas*
Credit cards 1 2 3 4 5 6

SWANAGE Dorset Map**4** SZ07
★★★**Corrie** De Moulham Rd ☎3104
Long, low, pebble-dash building with enclosed verandah and sun balcony overlooking sea.
49⇌⋒ Lift ☽ ⋈ CTV TV available in bedrooms 36P
8⌂ (heated) sauna bath Disco 3 nights wkly Live music & dancing 4 nights wkly Last dinner 7.45pm
♁ ⊡ ✱sB&B⇌⋒£11.50–£15.53
dB&B⇌⋒£19.55–£29.90 Lunch fr£4.03&alc
Tea fr35p&alc High Tea fr£2.30&alc
Dinner fr£5.18&alc Wine£2.95 *xmas*

★★★**Grosvenor** ☎2292
In private grounds with own beach affording panoramic views across Swanage Bay.
Closed Nov–Mar; 107rm(63⇌⋒) Annexe: 13rm Lift
☽ CTV CTV available in bedrooms ⊘ 100P ⚓
(heated) (heated) (hard) sauna bath Disco twice wkly Live music & dancing wkly ♿
International. Last dinner 8.30pm ♁ ⊡ S%
✱sB&B£9.45–£14.52 sB&B⇌⋒£10.53–£15.60
dB&B£17.28–£27.43 dB&B⇌⋒£19.44–£29.59
Lunch£4 Tea fr30p Dinner£5 Wine£3

★★★**Pines** 1 Burlington Rd ☎2166
Adjoining houses of Purbeck stone; situated on cliff top, with good sea views.
50rm(48⇌⋒) Lift ⋈ CTV CTV available in bedrooms
50P ⚓ Live music & dancing twice wkly (in season) English & Continental. Last dinner 8pm
♁ ⊡ sB&B£10–£11.50 sB&B⇌⋒£10–£12.50
dB&B£20–£23 dB&B⇌⋒£20–£25
Lunch£3.50–£4 Tea30p–35p High Tea£1–£2
Dinner£4.50–£5 Wine£2.75 ⊟ *xmas*

★★***Cliff Top*** 8 Burlington Rd ☎2091
Purbeck stone building on cliff top location with fine views across Bay.

S

Closed Nov–Etr; 15rm(7⇌🛁) 🛏 CTV 10P 3🏠 🚫 ♀English & Austrian. Last dinner7.30pm ♀

★★**Grand** Burlington Rd ☎3353
In elevated position on cliff top with fine views across Swanage Bay.
Closed Nov–Mar; 61rm(9⇌🛁) Lift ☽ 🛏 CTV ✂ 8P 6🏠 ⚓ Discowkly Live music & dancing 3nights wkly Lastdinner7.15pm ♀ ♀ S% sB&B£9–£11 sB&B⇌🛁£10.30–£12.30 dB&B£17–£21 dB&B⇌🛁£19.60–£23.60 Lunch£2–£2.50 Tea60p Dinner£4.50 Wine£2.50 🅱 *xmas*
Creditcards 1 3

★★***Ship*** The Square (Whitbread) ☎2078
15rm CTV 6P Lastdinner9pm ♀ ♀ 🅱
Creditcards 1 3

★**Suncliffe** Burlington Rd ☎3299
Closed Oct–Mar; 15rm(4⇌🛁) CTV TV available in bedrooms ✂ 15P 2🏠 🚫 ⚓ Lastdinner7.30pm ♀ ♀ S% sB&B£8.20–£9.75 dB&B£16.40–£19.50 dB&B⇌🛁£17.90–£21 Barlunch75palc Tea50p–£1 HighTea£1.55–£2 Dinner£2.50–£3.50 Wine£2.20 🅱

Ⓐ**Malverns** Park Rd ☎2575
19rm(1⇌🛁) 🛏 CTV 8P Lastdinner6.30pm S% sB&B fr£5.27 sB&B⇌🛁 fr£5.41 dB&B fr£6.70 dB&B⇌🛁 fr£11.68 Lunch£1.30–£1.40 Dinner£1.65–£1.75 Wine£1.70 *xmas*

Ⓐ**York** Cauldron Av ☎2704
Closed 8Oct–Mar; Unlicensed; 24rm(4⇌🛁) 🛏 CTV ✂ 20P 4🏠 🚫 ⚫(hard) ♨ Lastdinner8pm ♀ ♀ S% sB&B£7.50–£8.50 sB&B⇌🛁£8.50–£9.50

sB&B£15–£17 dB&B⇌⋒£16–£18 Tea60–75p Dinner£3–£3.75

✕La Trattoria High St ☎3784
Closed Nov–Mar (except Fri & Sat); Lunch not served; 30seats P Italian. Last dinner10.30pm
✱Dinner£6.50alc Wine£3.15 Credit cards 2 5

SWAY Hampshire Map**4** SZ29
★★★ ***White Rose*** Station Rd ☎2754
10rm(7⇌⋒) Lift TV 50P (heated) English & French. Last dinner10.15pm
Credit cards 1 3 5

SWINDON Wiltshire Map**4** SU18
★★★**Blunsdon House** Blunsdon (3m N off A419) ☎721701 Telex no44833
Modernised Victorian country house with new wing, set in 33 acres of gardens and grounds.
87rm(27⇌⋒) Lift CTV available in bedrooms 200P English & Continental.
Last dinner10pm S% ✱sB&B fr£11 sB&B⇌⋒ fr£14.50 dB&B⇌⋒ fr£20
Lunch fr£3.75&alc Dinner fr£4.25&alc Wine£3 *xmas* Credit cards 1 2 3 4 5 6

★★★**Goddard Arms** High St, Old Town (Anchor) ☎692313 Telex no858875
Grey-tiled, creeper-clad inn in old part of town; modern motel block in grounds.
65⇌⋒ CTV in bedrooms 100P
Last dinner9.15pm S% ✱sB&B fr£11 sB&B⇌⋒ fr£16 dB&B fr£19 dB&B fr£23
Lunch fr£3.40&alc Dinner fr£3.75&alc Wine£2.65 *xmas* Credit cards 1 2 3 4 5 6

☆☆☆**Post House** Marlborough Rd (Trusthouse Forte) ☎24601
103⇌⋒ CTV in bedrooms 177P (heated)
Last dinner10pm S% sB&B⇌⋒£19.75 dB&B⇌⋒£28.50 *xmas*
Credit cards 1 2 3 4 5 6

☆☆☆**Swindon Crest Motel** Stratton St Margaret (3m NE A420) (Crest) ☎822921
50⇌⋒ CTV in bedrooms 150P
Last dinner10pm S% ✱sB&B⇌⋒£15.71 dB&B⇌⋒£22.24 Continental breakfast
Credit cards 1 2 3 4 5 6

☆☆☆**Wiltshire** Fleming Way (Kingsmead) ☎28282 Telex no444250
85⇌⋒ Lift CTV in bedrooms P Live music & dancing Sat Cabaret Sat Conference facilities available English & French. Last dinner10.30pm
✱sB&B⇌⋒ fr£18.50 dB&B⇌⋒ fr£26
Continental breakfast Lunch£3.50&alc Tea50p Dinner£3.75&alc *xmas* Credit cards 1 3 4 5

SYMONDS YAT (EAST Hereford & Worcester Map**3** SO51
★★***Royal*** ☎890238
23rm(11⇌⋒) 40P sauna bath English & French. Last dinner9pm

SYMONDS YAT (WEST (nr Ross-on-Wye) Hereford & Worcester Map**3** SO51
★★**Old Court** ☎890367
Stone manor house, mainly 15th to 16th-century but with some parts dating from 12th century. The beamed Tudor banqueting hall is the centre of regular Elizabethan style feasts.
17rm(10⇌⋒) CTV 80P Live music & dancing Sat French. Last dinner9.30pm
sB&B fr£9 sB&B⇌⋒ fr£11.50 dB&B fr£15 dB&B⇌⋒ fr£17 Lunch£3alc Tea75palc
High Tea£1.50alc Dinner£4.50alc Wine£2.60
xmas Credit cards 1 3

★★**Paddocks** ☎890246
White, three-storey building with attractive modern extensions giving pleasant views of the gardens bordering river and surrounding hills.
Closed Nov–Feb; 30rm(6⇌⋒) CTV 200P (hard) Live music & dancing Wed Last dinner8pm
sB&B£9.07 sB&B⇌⋒£10.17 dB&B£18.14 dB&B⇌⋒£20.34
Lunch£3.02–£3.85&alc Tea£1.10–£1.21
High Tea£1.21–£3.30 Dinner£5.50–£6.22
Wine£3.50

★★**Wye Rapids** ☎890366
Secluded, rambling building with sun lounge, terrace and gardens overlooking gorge of River Wye; Yat rock, Longstone Rock and Bowless Hole Rock in view.
17rm(6⇌⋒) CTV 25P Last dinner8.30pm
S% ✱sB&B£11–£12.50 dB&B£18–£20 dB&B⇌⋒£24–£26 Tea30p Dinner fr£4&alc
xmas Credit cards 1 2 3 5

SYWELL (nr Northampton) Northamptonshire Map**4** SP86
☆**Sywell Airport Motel** ☎Northampton491594
49⇌⋒ CTV 100P Disco Fri, Sat & Sun; Conference facilities available Last dinner10pm
S% ✱sB&B⇌⋒£8.20–£10.20 dB&B⇌⋒£13.65–£15.15 Lunch£3.70–£4.60alc
Dinner£3.70–£4.60alc Wine£2.20
Credit cards 2 5

TADDINGTON Derbyshire Map**7** SK17
✕✕***Waterloo*** ☎230
Dinner not served Sun & Public Hols; 250seats 150P
Last dinner8.30pm

TALLAND BAY Cornwall Map**2** SX25
★★★**Talland Bay** (Inter-Hotel) ☎Polperro72667
Telex no45388
Closed 20Dec–14Feb; 16rm(9⇌⋒) CTV available

T

in bedrooms 20P 🚗 ⚓ ⇌(heated) Children under 5yrs not accommodated ♡French. Last dinner8.30pm ✿ ⚐ S% sB&B£10.50–£14.50 sB&B⇌⋒£12–£19.25 dB&B£19.25–£27.50 dB&B⇌⋒£26.50–£38.50 Lunch£3.50 Tea£1 Dinner£6&alc Wine£2.50 ⊟ Credit cards①②⑤

TANGMERE West Sussex Map**4** SZ90
✕**Old Timbers** Arundel Rd ☎Halnater294
Closed Sun, Tue, 10 days after Etr & 2wks Oct; 65seats 30P ♡English & French. Last dinner10.30pm ✱Lunch£2.65–£3&alc Dinner£6.50alc Wine£2.85

TARPORLEY Cheshire Map**7** SJ56
★★**Swan** 50 High St ☎2411
9rm 🛏CTV TV in bedrooms 50P Last dinner9.15pm ✿ sB&B£9 dB&B£15 Lunch fr£3.25&alc Dinner fr£4.15&alc Wine£3 Credit cards①②③⑤

TAUNTON Somerset Map**3** ST22
★★★**Castle** Castle Green (Prestige) ☎2671 Telex no46488
Impressive, stone-turreted castle, parts of which are medieval.
47rm(40⇌⋒) 5⊟ Lift ☽ 🛏CTV in bedrooms 30P 10🏠 ⚓ Last dinner9.30pm ✿ ⚐ S% ✱sB&B⇌⋒£27 dB&B£39.50 dB&B⇌⋒£48 Lunch fr£5.25&alc Tea fr£2 Dinner fr£6.25&alc Wine£3 ⊟ *xmas* Credit cards①②③④⑤⑥

★★★**County** East St (Trusthouse Forte) ☎87651
76rm(38⇌⋒) Lift ☽ 🛏CTV TV in bedrooms 111P 2🏠 Last dinner9.30pm ✿ ⚐ S% sB&B£14 sB&B⇌⋒£16.50 dB&B£21.50 dB&B⇌⋒£25 ⊟ *xmas* Credit cards①②③④⑤⑥

★★**Corner House** Park St ☎84683
Closed Xmas; 23rm(2⇌⋒) 🛏 CTV 30P 🚗 Last dinner7.45pm ✿ S% sB&B£9.50–£10.50 sB&B⇌⋒£12–£13 dB&B£16.50–£18 dB&B⇌⋒£17–£20.50 Lunch fr£3.20 Dinner fr£4.15

★★**Falcon** Henlade (2m E on A358 Yeovil road) ☎442502
11rm(3⇌⋒) 🛏CTV 20P 2🏠 ⚓ Last dinner8.45pm ✿ ⚐ S% sB&B£7.50–£8 sB&B⇌⋒£10–£11 dB&B£14–£15 dB&B⇌⋒£15–£16 Lunch£2.75–£3.50&alc Dinner£3–£3.75&alc Wine£2.85 ⊟

★★**St Quintin** Bridgwater Rd, Bathpool ☎73016
6rm Annexe: 4rm CTV 🐕 30P 🚗 ⚓ Last dinner8pm ✿ ⚐ sB&B£8.95–£11.25 dB&B£17.90–£22.50 Bar lunch£1.80–£3.60&alc Tea£1–£1.30&alc High Tea£3–£4.75&alc Dinner£4–£6.60&alc Wine£4 ⊟ Credit cards①②③⑤

TAVISTOCK Devon Map**2** SX47
★★★**Bedford** Plymouth Rd (Trusthouse Forte) ☎3221
35rm(21⇌⋒) 🛏TV in bedrooms 12🏠 ⚓ Last dinner9pm ✿ ⚐ S% sB&B£13 sB&B⇌⋒£15.50 dB&B£20.50 dB&B⇌⋒£23 ⊟ *xmas* Credit cards①②③④⑤⑥

TEBAY (WEST SERVICE AREA (M6 Motorway) Cumbria Map**12** NY60
Access to northbound traffic only
☆☆**Tebay Mountain Lodge** ☎Orton351
Affords good views of Cumbrian mountains, located between the Lake District and Yorkshire Dales.
32⇌⋒ ☽ 🛏CTV CTV in bedrooms 40P ♡English & French. Last dinner9pm ✿ ✱sB&B⇌⋒ fr£13.28 dB&B⇌⋒ fr£18.46 Continental breakfast Wine£3.15 ⊟ Credit cards①②③⑤⑥

TEDBURN ST MARY Devon Map**3** SX89
★★**King's Arms** ☎224
16th-C inn situated in centre of village.
6rm 🛏 CTV 40P 2🏠 Last dinner9.30pm ✿ sB&B fr£7.50 dB&B fr£14 Lunch£2.75 Dinner£3.75alc Wine£2.45

TEES-SIDE AIRPORT Co Durham Map**8** NZ31
★★★**St George** Middleton St George ☎Dinsdale2631
56⇌⋒ ☽ 🛏CTV CTV in bedrooms 200P 14🏠 🚗 ⚲(hard) squash sauna bath Cabaret Sun Conference facilities available ♡French. Last dinner9.45pm ✿ ⚐ S% sB&B⇌⋒£18.25 dB&B⇌⋒£28 Lunch£6.20–£9&alc Tea90p Dinner£6.20–9&alc Wine£3 ⊟ Credit cards①②③⑤

TEIGNMOUTH Devon Map**3** SX97
★★**Glendaragh** Barn Park Rd ☎2881
10rm(6⇌⋒) 🛏CTV CTV in bedrooms 11P 1🏠 🚗 ⚓ Last dinner8pm S% ✱sB&B£7.50–£9 dB&B£15–£18 dB&B⇌⋒£17–£20 Bar lunch fr£1.35 Dinner£3.75 Wine£2.50 ⊟

★★***Ivy House*** Sea Front ☎2735
RS Oct–May; 15rm(3⇌⋒) 🛏 CTV 10P Last dinner6.30pm ✿ ⊟

★★**London** Bank St ☎2776
26rm(22⇌⋒) Lift ☽ 🛏 CTV CTV available in bedrooms 12P ⇌(heated) sauna bath Disco 3nights wkly Live music & dancing twice wkly Cabaret wkly ♧ ♡English & French. Last dinner9pm ✿ ⚐ sB&B£10–£11.50 sB&B⇌⋒£11.50–£13 dB&B£18–£20 dB&B⇌⋒£19.50–£21.50 Tea60p High Tea£1.50 Dinner£5 Wine£3 ⊟ *xmas*

T

❀★★♛**Venn Farm** Higher Exeter Rd (Best Western) ☎2196
Rosette awarded for dinner only).
RS Nov–Mar; 10rm(8⇌⋒) ₩ CTV in bedrooms ⊘ 50P ⇔ ⚓ Specialities: West Country peppered steak, half duckling in orange and honey sauce. Last dinner8.30pm ♁ ♀ ✱sB&B fr£10.35 sB&B⇌⋒ fr£11.50 dB&B fr£19.40 dB&B⇌⋒ fr£20.70 Bar lunch fr£2.50 Tea fr£1 Dinner fr£5&alc Wine£3.50 ⊟ *xmas* Credit cards①③

★**Belvedere** Barn Park Rd ☎4561
Closed Nov–Mar; 15rm(2⇌⋒) ₩ CTV 10P Last dinner10pm ♁ ♀ S% sB&B£6.50–£7.50 sB&B⇌⋒£7.50–£8.50 dB&B£13–£15 dB&B⇌⋒£15–£17 Lunch£3–£3.80&alc Tea£1 High Tea£1.50 Dinner£3–£3.80&alc Wine£2.60 ⊟ *xmas* Credit cards①③

★**Carlton** Sea Front ☎6929
Closed Nov, Jan & Feb; 33rm(3⇌⋒) ₩ CTV 14P Live music & dancing Wed Cabaret Wed Children under 9yrs not accommodated Last dinner6pm S% ✱sB&B£8–£10 dB&B£16–£20 dB&B⇌⋒£20–£24 Wine£2.25 ⊟ *xmas* Credit cards②⑤

★**Portland** Sea Front ☎2761
RS Nov–Mar; 28rm Lift ₩ CTV 6P Last dinner6pm ♀ ✱sB&B£6.50–£7.50 dB&B£13–£15 ⊟ *xmas*

✕✕**Churchills** Den Rd ☎4311
Closed Mon; Lunch not served Sat; Dinner not served Sun in winter; 36seats ₱ ♀French. Last dinner10.30pm ✱Lunch fr£3.18&alc Dinner£8.64alc Wine£2.80 Credit cards①③

✕✕**Minadab** 60 Teignmouth Rd ☎2044
Small, well-restored Regency-style restaurant.
Closed Tue & 19Oct–9Nov; Lunch not served Sat; Dinner not served Sun; 30seats 7P bedroom available ♀French & Italian. Last dinner10pm S% ✱Lunch£2.95–£5&alc Tea70p–£1.05&alc Dinner£3.50–£7&alc Wine£2.80 Credit cards③⑥

TELFORD Salop Map**7** SJ60
★★★♛**Buckatree Hall** Ercall Ln, Wellington ☎51821
26⇌⋒ ☽ ₩ CTV in bedrooms 140P ⚓ ♿ ♀French. Last dinner10pm ♁ ♀ sB&B fr£17.82 dB&B fr£23.76 Lunch fr£4.05&alc Tea fr54p Dinner fr£4.59&alc Wine£2.90 ⊟ *xmas* Credit card③

★★**Charlton Arms** Wellington (Greenall Whitley) ☎51351
31rm(7⇌⋒) ☽ ₩ CTV TV available in bedrooms 100P ♀English & French. Last dinner9.30pm ♁ ♀ sB&B£11.50 sB&B⇌⋒£13.30 dB&B£17 dB&B⇌⋒£19 Lunch£3.50–£4&alc Tea fr40p Dinner£4–£4.50&alc Wine£3 ⊟ Credit cards①②③⑤⑥

★★**Falcon** Holyhead Rd, Wellington ☎55011
14rm(1⇌⋒) ₩ CTV ⊘ 36P ⇔ Children under 3yrs not accommodated Last dinner9pm ♁ sB&B£11 sB&B⇌⋒£12 dB&B£15.50 dB&B⇌⋒£17 Bar lunch fr£1&alc Dinner fr£4&alc Wine£2.90

★***White House*** Wellington Rd, Donnington (off A518) ☎Lilleshall4276
Unlicensed; 7rm TV 100P 2🏠 ⇔ ⚓ Last dinner9.30pm

TENBURY WELLS Hereford & Worcester Map**7** SO56
★**Royal Oak** ☎810417
Timber-framed building dating from 16th century.
Closed Xmas; 6rm ₩ CTV 50P Last dinner9pm ♁ sB&B£8–£9 dB&B£13–£16 Lunch£3–£4 Dinner£5alc Wine£2.50 Credit card⑤

TETBURY Gloucestershire Map**3** ST89 See also **Westonbirt**
★★★**White Hart** (Snooty Fox) Market Pl ☎52436
10⇌⋒ ₩ CTV in bedrooms ₱ ♀English & French. Last dinner9.45pm ♁ ♀ sB&B⇌⋒£16 dB&B⇌⋒£26–£30 Lunch£2.95alc Tea45palc Dinner£5.50alc wine£3.20 ⊟ *xmas* Credit cards①②③⑤⑥

❀★★**Close** 8 Long St (Prestige) ☎52272
See page 55 for details

TETFORD Lincolnshire Map**8** TF37
★**White Hart** ☎255
6rm ₩ CTV ⊘ 50P 2🏠 ⇔ ⚓ ⌂ Last dinner9.45pm ♁ S% sB&B fr£6.50 dB&B fr£10.50 Lunch£3alc Dinner£3.50alc Wine£2.75 ⊟ Credit cards①③

TEWIN Hertfordshire Map**4** TL21
✕**Plume of Feathers** ☎7265
Attractive 16th century inn panelled restaurant.
80seats 60P ♀Mainly grills. Last dinner9.30pm S% ✱Lunch£8alc Dinner£8alc Wine£2.75 Credit cards①②③⑤⑥

TEWKESBURY Gloucestershire Map**3** SO83
☆☆☆**Tewkesbury Park Golf & Country Club** Lincoln Green Ln ☎295405 Telex no449205
30⇌⋒ ☽ ₩ CTV 250P ⇔ ⚓ ⊏(heated) ⛳18 squash billiards sauna bath Disco Thu & Sat ♀English & French. Last dinner10pm ♁ ♀ S% sB&B⇌⋒£21 dB&B⇌⋒£26 Lunch fr£3.70&alc Tea fr£1 High Tea fr£1 Dinner fr£4.90&alc Wine£2.80 ⊟ *xmas* Credit cards①②③

★★**Bell** Church St ☎293293
30rm(13⇌⋒) 2⊟ ₩ TV TV in bedrooms 35P 7🏠 ⌂ ♀English & French. Last dinner10pm ♁ ♀ sB&B£12.80 sB&B⇌⋒£17.50 dB&B£20.50 dB&B⇌⋒£28 Lunch£3.80–£4.25 Tea50p–£1

High Tea£3 Dinner£5–£6&alc Wine£4 xmas Credit cards 1 2 3 4 5 6

★★**Royal Hop Pole** Church St (Crest) ☎293236
25rm(10) CTV CTV in bedrooms 15P English & French. Last dinner9.30pm S% *sB&B£10.26 sB&B£15.12 dB&B£19.33 dB&B£23.76 Credit cards 1 2 3 4 5 6

★***Tudor House*** High St ☎293129
Timbered building dating from 1540. Present dining room was Court of Justice in reign of James I.
11rm(1) CTV 6 Last dinner9pm

THAKEHAM West Sussex Map**4** TQ11
★★**Abingworth Hall** ☎West Chiltington2257
A delightful country hotel set in the heart of the Sussex Downs. Standing in own grounds by the side of a natural lake.
14rm(10) CTV 60P 6 (heated) (hard) billiards English & French. Last dinner9.30pm S% *sB&B£10.80 sB&B£11.88 dB&B£21.60 dB&B£23.76 Lunch£2.75–£3.50&alc Tea30–95p Dinner£3.75&alc Wine£2.80 *xmas* Credit card 1

THAME Oxfordshire Map**4** SP70
★★★***Spread Eagle*** Cornmarket (Best Western) ☎3661
29rm(16) CTV 80P Disco twice wkly Live music & dancing mthly French. Last dinner9.30pm Credit cards 1 3

★***Black Horse*** The Cornmarket ☎2886
7rm CTV 12P Last dinner9.15pm

THATCHAM Berkshire Map**4** SU56
X***Slades*** 7 High St ☎63344
Closed Sun & Mon; Lunch not served Sat; 40seats English & French. Last dinner9.45pm Credit cards 1 3 5

THETFORD Norfolk Map**5** TL88
★★★**Bell** King St (Trusthouse Forte) ☎4455
42rm TV in bedrooms 65P Last dinner9.15pm S% sB&B£17 dB&B£24 *xmas* Credit cards 1 2 3 4 5 6

★**Anchor** Bridge St ☎3329
20rm(12) CTV TV available in bedrooms 60P English & Continental. Last dinner9pm S% sB&B£9.50–£10.50 sB&B£13–£14.50 dB&B£15.50–£16.50 dB&B£18–£18.50 Lunch£3.50–£4&alc Dinner£3.95–£4.50&alc Wine£3.50 Credit cards 1 2 3

THIRLSPOT Cumbria Map**11** NY31
★★***Kings Head*** ☎Keswick72393
15rm(6) CTV 80P Last dinner8.30pm

THIRSK North Yorkshire Map**8** SE48
★★**Golden Fleece** Market Pl (Trusthouse Forte) ☎23108
20rm(6) TV in bedrooms 50P 2 Last dinner9pm S% sB&B£12 sB&B£14.50 dB&B£17.50 DB&B£20.50 Credit cards 1 2 3 4 5 6

★★**Three Tuns** Market Pl ☎23124
12rm(7) CTV 20P 3 English & Continental. Last dinner9.30pm S% sB&B£11.50 sB&B£12.50 dB&B£18 dB&B£19.50 Lunch fr£3.50 Dinner£4.75alc Wine£3.70 Credit cards 1 3 6

THORNBURY Avon Map**3** ST69
XXXX**Thornbury Castle** ☎412647
Two years ago we featured Kenneth Bell and his renowned restaurant in 'Four of the Best'. Since then, standards have remained high.
The menu is not too large for the kitchen to cope with, so that one can be sure that each dish is near-perfectly prepared. Amongst the dishes particularly praised were the dariole de gibier which is a mould lined with veal forcemeat and filled with diced game – mostly pheasant and hare on this occasion, and root vegetables, and cooked and served with a delightful sauce; others were the mousseline de sole served with a lobster sauce, and mousse of salmon, both universal favourites. Amongst the main courses are the breast of chicken, stuffed with chopped walnuts, veal and ham, flambéed in Pernod and finished with a lovely cream sauce; or paupiette of veal with Madeira sauce – a scallop of veal in which was rolled a tasty stuffing of chopped apricots, mushrooms, almonds and sage and then cooked and served with an excellent sauce that is light, limpid and frothy. Another is the cotelettes d'agneau farcies en croute – lamb cutlets wrapped in the lightest of pastry, baked and served with a delicate red wine sauce.
Vegetables have been praised, as have been such puddings as marquise de chocolat, which is a loaf tin mould lined with sponge, filled with a rich chocolate mixture, then turned out and sliced. Or the hazlenut meringue with raspberry purée, biscuity-beige in colour and a little gooey inside; the meringue flavoured with hazlenuts filled with fresh cream, and served with a fresh-tasting (even in February) purée of raspberries. One inspector reported that the chocolate mousse, deliciously rich-tasting and flavoured with Grand Marnier, was the best he had ever sampled.
Kenneth Bell's judgement and appreciation of wine is outstanding and his cellars abound with some of the finest. Particularly pleasing is the large number of half bottles available.
Closed Mon & Xmas; Lunch not served Tue–Sat; Dinner not served Sun; 60seats 25P Continental. Last dinner9.30pm Lunch£11.50alc Dinner£11.50alc Wine£4.50 Credit cards 1 2 3

THORNE South Yorkshire Map**8** SE61
★★**Belmont** Horsefair Green ☎812320
Closed Xmas; 26rm(8) CTV 30P Last dinner8pm *sB&B£6.50–£7 sB&B£7.50–£8 dB&B£11–£12 dB&B£12.50–£13.50 Lunch£1.45–£3.45 Dinner£1.75–£3.75 Wine£2

THORNTHWAITE Cumbria Map**11** NY22
★★**Swan** ☎Braithwaite256
17th-C coaching inn amidst some of the finest mountain scenery overlooking the Lakes Bassenthwaite and Skiddaw.
Closed mid Nov–Mar; 15rm(2) CTV 60P 3 Last dinner8.15pm S% dB&B fr£7 dB&B fr£14 dB&B fr£18 Lunch fr£2 Tea fr60p Dinner fr£5 Wine£2.50

★★**Thwaite Howe** ☎Braithwaite281
Victorian villas built for the owners of local lead mines on the edge of a forest.
Closed Dec–Feb; 8 CTV 20P Last dinner5pm dB&B fr£17 Dinner£4–£5 Wine£2.90

THORNTON West Yorkshire Map**7** SE03
XX**Cottage** 869 Thornton Rd ☎Bradford832752
Closed Tue; Lunch not served Sat; 85seats 100P French. Last dinner10pm Lunch£5.50alc Dinner£7.50–£12.50 Wine£4.70 Credit cards 1 2 3

THORNTON CLEVELEYS Lancashire Map**7** SD34
X**River House** Skippool Creek, Thornton-le-Fylde (2m E A585) ☎Poulton-le-Fylde883497
Detached mid-Victorian house on the bank of the River Wyre.
Closed Mon, 25 & 26Dec, 1Jan, 1st wk Feb & last 2wks Sep; 45seats 20P bedrooms available Last dinner9.30pm *Lunch£3.75 Tea fr£1.20

High Tea£1.54–£3.45 Dinner£5.50&alc
Credit card 2

THORNTON DALE North Yorkshire Map **8** SE88
★**New Inn** ☎226
3rm CTV 6P Last dinner 8.45pm
sB&B fr£7.50 dB&B fr£12 Lunch fr£2.20
Dinner£3.20–£5.50 Wine£1.75 Credit card 1

THORNTON WATLASS North Yorkshire Map **8** SE28
★**Buck Inn** ☎Bedale 2461
6rm CTV P Live music Sat *sB&B£4.50
dB&B£7

THORPE (DOVEDALE) Derbyshire Map **7** SK15
★★★**Izaac Walton** (1m W on Ilam road)
☎Thorpe Cloud 261
Converted 18th-C farmhouse with modern wing.
26rm(21) CTV 100P Disco wkly
French & Italian. Last dinner 9.30pm
sB&B fr£10 sB&B fr£15 dB&B fr£16.50
dB&B fr£22 Lunch£3.50&alc Tea45p
Dinner£5&alc Wine£3.30 *xmas*

★★★**Peveril of the Peak** (Trusthouse Forte)
☎Thorpe Cloud 333
32rm(26) TV in bedrooms 120P (hard)
Last dinner 9.30pm S% sB&B£13
sB&B£16 dB&B£19 dB&B£21
xmas Credit cards 1 2 3 4 5 6

THORPE BAY Essex
See **Southend-on-Sea**

THURLESTONE Devon Map **3** SX64
★★★**Thurlestone** (Best Western) ☎382
Telex no 45151
Spacious hotel, built, owned and managed by the Grose family for 90 years. Fine country and sea views.
Closed 2–11 Jan; 74rm(62) Lift CTV CTV available in bedrooms 35P 20 (heated) squash billiards sauna bath Disco twice wkly (summer) wkly (winter) Conference facilities available Last dinner 8.30pm
sB&B£14–£22.25 sB&B£16–£27.50
dB&B£28–£48 dB&B£32–£57.50
Lunch£3.30–£4.50&alc Tea40p–£1.50
Dinner£5.50–£6&alc Wine£2.75 *xmas*
Credit cards 1 2 3 4 5 6

★**Furzey Close** ☎333
Closed Dec & Jan; RS Nov & Feb–Apr; 10rm(3)
CTV 12P Last dinner 7.30pm
sB&B£8.70–£10.20 dB&B£17.40–£20.40
dB&B£20.36–£23.60 Bar lunch 50p–£1
Tea30–60p Dinner£4.50 Wine£2.40

TINTAGEL Cornwall Map **2** SX08
★★**Bossiney House** ☎240
Closed 5 Oct–Mar; 20rm(14) CTV 30P
Last dinner 7.45pm S% sB&B£7.80–£10
sB&B£8.80–£11 dB&B£15.60–£20
dB&B£17.60–£22 Bar lunch 80p Tea50p
Dinner£3.25 Wine£3

★**Atlantic View** Treknow ☎221
Closed 2 Jan–Feb; 12rm(6) 1 CTV CTV available in bedrooms 20P (heated) English & French. Last dinner 7.30pm S%
*sB&B£9–£11 dB&B£12–£20
dB&B£13–£21 Lunch£3–£3.50
Tea£1–£1.50 High Tea£2 2.50
Dinner£4.50–£5.50 Wine£2.50 *xmas*

★**El Condado** Trewarmett ☎460
Closed Nov–Feb; 6rm(1) TV 8P 2
S% Lunch£1alc Dinner£5alc Wine£2.16
Credit cards 1 2 3

TITCHFIELD Hampshire Map **4** SU50
★***Queens Head*** ☎42154
6rm TV & TV available in bedrooms 26P
Last dinner 9.30pm Credit cards 1 3

TITCHWELL Norfolk Map **9** TF74
★★***Manor*** ☎Brancaster 221
Closed Feb 14–28 & Xmas; 6rm Annexe: 3 TV
30P Last dinner 9.30pm Credit cards 1 6

TIVERTON Devon Map **3** SS91
☆☆☆**Tiverton Motel** Blundells Rd ☎3427
30rm(29) CTV in bedrooms 100P
Last dinner 9.30pm S% sB&B£14
dB&B£19 Continental breakfast
Tea£1–£2&alc High Tea£1.50–£3&alc
Dinner£3–£6&alc Wine£2.75
Credit cards 1 2 3 5

★★**Boars Head** Bampton St ☎2313
10rm CTV 10 Disco wkly Live music & dancing mthly Last dinner 7pm S%
sB&B£9–£10 dB&B£14.50–£15.50
Lunch£1.50–£2.50 Dinner£3–£5&alc
Wine£2.25 Credit cards 1 3 5

★★**Hartnoll** Bolham Rd ☎2777
12rm(5) CTV 3 Last dinner 9.30pm
S% *sB&B fr£9.50 sB&B fr£10.70
dB&B fr£16.65 dB&B fr£17.85
Credit cards 3 5

✕✕**Lowman** 45 Gold St ☎57311
Closed Thu; Dinner not served Wed; 29 seats
International. Specialities: medaillons of pork fillet, steak 'Glengarry', quail dauphinoise.
Last dinner 10pm *Lunch£3alc Dinner£4.50alc
Wine£2

T

TONBRIDGE Kent Map**5** TQ54
★★**Rose & Crown** High St (Trusthouse Forte) ☎357966
Early 18th-C building of blue and red chequered brick. Interior has panelling and oak beams.
46⇌ ⋒ ☽ 🍽 TV in bedrooms 50P Last dinner10pm ♆ ⊈ S% sB&B⇌⋒£18.50 dB&B⇌⋒£23 ⊟ *xmas* Credit cards 1 2 3 4 5 6

TORBAY Devon **See under Brixham, Churston Ferrers, Paignton & Torquay**

TORCROSS Devon Map**3** SX84
★★**Torcross** ☎206
RS Nov–Feb (accommodation); 20rm(12⇌⋒) CTV 12P 20⌂ Live music & dancing Thu ⌂ Last dinner8pm ♆ ⊈ ✳sB&B£7.50–£10 sB&B⇌⋒£7.50–£10 dB&B£15–£20 dB&B⇌⋒£15–£20 Bar lunch50p–£2.10 Tea20–80p Dinner£3.50 Wine£2.30 ⊟

Grey Homes ☎220
Closed Nov–Mar; 7rm CTV 15P 3⌂ ⚓ (grass) Last dinner6pm ♆ ⊈ ✳sB&B£6.70–£7.78 dB&B£13.40–£15.56 Bar lunch45p–£1.20 Tea fr54p Dinner£3.46–£3.78 Wine£3.02 ⊟

TORQUAY Devon Map**3** SX96
See Central and District plans
★★★★★**Imperial** Park Hill Rd (Trusthouse Forte) ☎24301 Telex no42849 Central plan**19**
168⇌⋒ Lift ☽ CTV CTV in bedrooms 200P 60⌂ ⚓ ⊏&⊐(heated) (hard) squash sauna bath Conference facilities available ♿ Last dinner9pm ♆ ⊈ S% sB&B⇌⋒£28.25 dB&B⇌⋒£34 *xmas* Credit cards 1 2 3 4 5 6

★★★★**New Grand** Sea Front ☎25234
Telex no42891 Central plan**27**
110⇌⋒ Lift ☽ 🍽 CTV in bedrooms P 50⌂ ⚓ ⊐(heated) (hard) sauna bath Live music & dancing Sat Conference facilities available ⌂ English & Continental. Last dinner9.15pm ♆ ⊈ ✳sB&B⇌⋒£14–£21 dB&B⇌⋒£28–£42 Lunch£4–£6&alc Tea85p High Tea£1.75 Dinner£6&alc Wine£2.50 ⊟ *xmas* Credit cards 1 2 3 4 5 6

★★★★**Osborne** Meadfoot Beach ☎22232
Telex no42573 District plan**58**
Gracious Regency Crescent, with balconies, canopies and fluted Corinthian columns. 5 acres of peaceful gardens sloping down to the beach. Swimming pool and tennis court overlooking sea.
85⇌⋒ Lift ☽ 🍽 CTV in bedrooms 70P ⚓ ⊐(heated) (hard) billiards Conference facilities available ⌂ ♿ International. Last dinner10pm ♆ ⊈ S% sB&B⇌⋒fr£11 dB&B⇌⋒fr£22 Lunch£4.25&alc Tea fr40p High Tea fr£1 Dinner£5.50&alc Wine£4.50 ⊟ *xmas* Credit cards 1 2 3 5 6

★★★★**Palace** Babbacombe Rd ☎22271
Telex no42606 District plan**61**
138rm(112⇌⋒) Lift ☽ 🍽 CTV CTV available in bedrooms 100P 40⌂ ⚓ ⊏&⊐(heated) (hard) squash billiards sauna bath Live music & dancing 6nights wkly Conference facilities available ⌂ ♿ English & French. Last dinner9.15pm ♆ ⊈ sB&B£16.74 sB&B⇌⋒£18.90 dB&B£29.16 dB&B⇌⋒£33.48 Lunch fr£4.32&alc Tea fr£1.08 Dinner fr£6.48&alc Wine£3.24 ⊟ *xmas* Credit cards 1 2 3 4 5 6

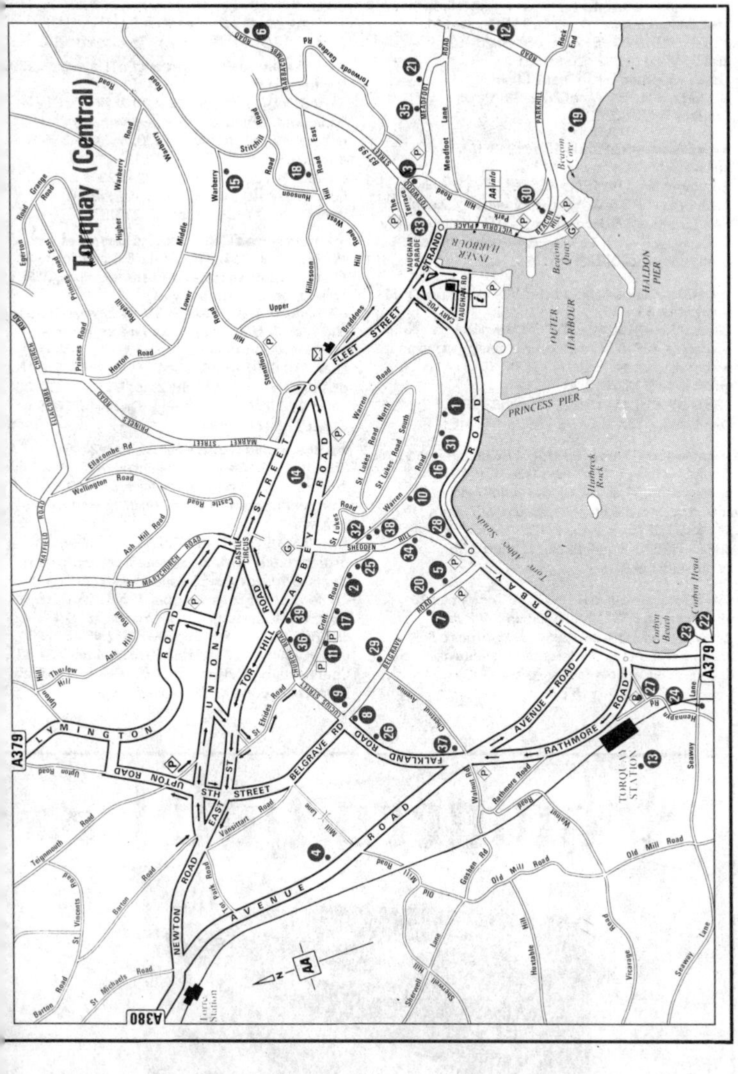

1 Alpine ★★
2 Alvanley ★
3 Ardmoor ★★
4 Bancourt ★★
5 Belgrave ★★★
6 Burlington ★★
7 Bute Court ★★
8 Carlton ★
9 Cavendish ★★
10 Conway Court ★★
11 Crofton House ★★
12 Devonshire ★★★
13 Elmington ★★
14 Fanny's Dining Room ✕✕✕
15 Fonthill ★★
16 Homers ★★★
17 Howden Court ★★
18 Hunsdon Lea ★★
19 Imperial ★★★★★
20 Kistor ★★★
21 Lincombe Hall ★★★
22 Livermead Cliff ★★★
23 Livermead House ★★★
24 Manor House ★★★
25 Nepaul ★★★
26 Nethway ★★
27 New Grand ★★★★
28 Palm Court ★★★
29 Rainbow House ★★★
30 Regina ★★
31 Rock Wall ★
32 Hotel Roseland
33 Royal ★
34 Sheddon Hall ★★
35 Sydore ★★
36 Templestowe ★★
37 Toorak ★★★
38 Vernon Court ★★
39 Windsor ★★

★★★**Belgrave** Sea Front ☎28566 Central plan**5**
57rm(47⇌⋒) Lift ☽ ✕ CTV CTV available in bedrooms 80P 6⌂ ⚓ ⩘(heated) Last dinner8.30pm ✿ ⚐ sB&B£8.75–£13.80 sB&B⇌⋒£10.50–£16.50 dB&B£17.50–£27.60 dB&B⇌⋒£21–£33 Lunch fr£3.25&alc Tea fr25p Dinner fr£4.50&alc Wine£3 ⚑ *xmas*
Credit cards 1 2 3 5

★★★**Corbyn Head** Sea Front, Livermead ☎27867 District plan**49**
Large, rambling building with white, wood façade; has small garden overlooking sea. Unusual round entrance hall with Round Room restaurant above roof garden.
56rm(38⇌⋒) ☽ ✕ CTV TV available in bedrooms 60P 6⌂ ⚓ ⩘(heated) Live music & dancing 3nights

T

(summer) wkly (winter) ♿ English & French. Lastdinner8.30pm sB&B£9.50–£11 sB&B⇌fl£10.80–£12.50 dB&B£20–£22 dB&B⇌fl£22–£32 Lunch£3.80 Tea30–50p&alc HighTea£2.50alc Dinner£5.50&alc Wine£2.70 xmas Creditcards 1 2 3 5 6

★★★***Devonshire*** Park Hill Rd ☎24850 Telexno42712 Central plan**12**
RS Nov–Mar; 57rm(33⇌fl) CTV TV available in bedrooms 70P 3 (heated) (hard) Live music wkly Live music & dancing 5nights wkly Cabaretwkly English & French. Lastdinner8.30pm Credit cards 1 2 3 5 6

★★★**Gleneagles** Asheldon Rd, Wellswood ☎23637 District plan**51**
Closed Nov–Mar; 42⇌fl CTV TV available in bedrooms 40P (heated) Live music & dancing twice wkly Lastdinner8pm sB&B⇌fl£9.72–£12.96 dB&B⇌fl£19.44–£25.92 Lunch£3.75–£4.25 Tea55–95p Dinner£4.75–£5.75 Wine£3

★★★**Homers** Warren Rd ☎25139 Central plan**16**
Closed 16Nov–14Mar; 18rm(13⇌fl) CTV in bedrooms 5P Children under 7yrs not accommodated French. Lastdinner8.30pm *sB&B£15 sB&B⇌fl£16 dB&B£26 dB&B⇌fl£28 Lunch£2.95 Dinner£6.95 Wine£4.25

★★★**Kistor** Belgrave Rd ☎23219 Central plan**20**
46⇌fl Lift CTV CTV in bedrooms 40P (heated) sauna bath Disco wkly Live music & dancing twice wkly Conference facilities available English & Continental. Lastdinner8.30pm S% sB&B⇌fl£9–£15.55 dB&B⇌fl£18–£31.10 Lunch£3–£3.50 Tea30p–£1.20 High Tea60p–£2.50 Dinner£4–£4.50 xmas Credit cards 1 2

★★★**Lincombe Hall** Meadfoot Rd (Travco) ☎2230[illegible] Central plan**21**
Closed Oct–Mar; 28rm(13⇌fl) CTV CTV in bedrooms 30P 5 (heated) (hard) Cabaret wkly Lastdinner8.30pm S% sB&B£9.50–£10 sB&B⇌fl£11–£11.50 dB&B£19–£20 dB&B⇌fl£22–£23 Lunch fr£3&alc Tea fr£1 Dinner fr£4&alc Wine£2.25 Credit cards 1 2 3 5 6

★★★**Livermead Cliff** Torbay Rd (Best Western) ☎22881 Telexno42918 Central & District plans**22**
Castellated, three storey, red-stone building with grounds enclosed by sea wall.
62rm(48⇌fl) Lift CTV TV available in bedroom[s] 60P 12 (heated) Conference facilities available Lastdinner8.30pm S% sB&B£10.65–£13.75 sB&B⇌fl£12.80–£16.15 dB&B£21.30–£27.55 dB&B⇌fl£25.60–£32.30 Lunch fr£3.95&alc Tea fr55p Dinner fr£5.60&alc Wine£2.85 xmas

★★★**Livermead House** Torbay Rd ☎24361 Telexno42918 Central & District plans**23**
Three-storey building on sea front, in red Devon stone with mansard roof. Set in three acres of grounds.
76rm(56⇌fl) Lift CTV CTV available in bedrooms 90P 15 (heated) (hard) billiards sauna bath Live music & dancing wkly (summer) Conference facilities available ♿ English & Continental. Lastdinner8.30pm S% sB&B£9.75–£13.60 sB&B⇌fl£12.45–£15.95 dB&B£19.45–£27.20 dB&B⇌fl£24.84–£31.85 Continental breakfast Lunch fr£3.95&alc Tea fr55p Dinner fr&5.60&alc Wine£2.85 xmas

T

The Osborne Hotel

TORQUAY

S. DEVON

Telephone: (0803) 213311 Telex: 42573

The Osborne is a renowned holiday and business centre set in 5½ acres of woods and gardens sweeping down to the beach. Luxurious suites, bedrooms, Time Ownership Apartments and a Conference Centre are concealed within a gracious Regency Crescent overlooking superb views of Torbay. Open all the year round.

85 Bedrooms, all with private bathroom, colour TV, radio, baby listening system, telephone etc. Many bedrooms with balconies offering glorious sea and coastal views.

Haute Cuisine Restaurant. Private dining rooms, modern Conference rooms, two bars, hard tennis court, heated swimming pool, billiards, games room, central heating, lifts, night porter, ample parking, most credit cards accepted.

Golf, fishing, riding, sailing nearby.

T

42 Anchorage ★★
43 Ansteys Lea ★★
44 Ashley Rise ★
45 Hotel Balmoral
46 Brigantine Motor
47 Coniston ★★
48 Coppice ★★
49 Corbyn Head ★★★
50 Dartmoor Maiden ★★
51 Gleneagles ★★★
52 Lansdowne ★★
22 Livermead Cliff ★★★
23 Livermead House ★★★
53 Maidencombe House ★★
54 Meadfoot Bay ★★
55 Norcliffe ★
56 Orestone House ★
58 Osborne ★★★★
59 Oswald's ★★★
60 Overmead ★★
61 Palace ★★★★
62 Penrhyn ㊌
63 Sunray ★★
64 Viscount ★★
65 Woodland Park ★

Torquay (District)

TEIGNMOUTH 8m A379 · Maidencombe · Watcombe Head · Watcombe · Barton · EXETER 22m A380 · Hele · A3022 · A397 · Petit Tor Point · St Marychurch · B3199 · B3200 · Babbacombe · Long Quarry Point · Anstey's Cove · Torre · Wellswood · B3199 · Kilmorie · Meadfoot Beach · Livermead Sands · London Bridge · A379 DARTMOUTH 11m

T

T

★★★***Manor House*** Seaway Ln ☎65164 Telexno42759 Centralplan**24**
27rm(21⇌⋒) ⅏ CTV ⊘ 40P ⚓ Children under 5yrs not accommodated Lastdinner8.15pm ✿ ♀

★★★**Nepaul** Croft Rd ☎22745 Centralplan**25**
36rm(35⇌⋒) Lift ☽ ⅏ CTV CTV in bedrooms 15P 4⌂ ▭(heated) billiards Discowkly Live music & dancing wkly Lastdinner8.30pm ✿ ♀ sB&B£7.50–£14.50 sB&B⇌⋒£7.50–£14.50 dB&B£15–£28 dB&B⇌⋒£15–£28 Lunchfr£2.50&alc Dinnerfr£3.75&alc Wine£1.50 ⊟ *xmas*

★★★**Oswald's** Palermo Rd, Babbacombe ☎39292 Districtplan**59**
55rm(23⇌⋒) Lift ☽ ⅏ CTV 30P ⚓ ♂9 Cabaretwkly Lastdinner8pm ✿ Lunch£3.50 Dinner£4.50 Wine£3 *xmas* Creditcards 1 3

★★★**Palm Court** Torbay Rd ☎24881 Telexno42987 Centralplan**28**
72rm(40⇌⋒) Lift ☽ ⅏ CTV CTV in bedrooms 15P ⛟ billiards Conference facilities available ♀French. Lastdinner9pm ✿ ♀ S% sB&B£9.72–£13.50 sB&B⇌⋒£11.64–£15.39 dB&B£19.44–£27 dB&B⇌⋒£22.68–£32.94 Lunch£3.50 Tea25–65p Dinner£5.50&alc Wine£3 ⊟ *xmas* Creditcards 1 2 3 4 5 6

★★★**Rainbow House** Belgrave Rd ☎211161 Telexno42731 Centralplan**29**
Turreted, white building with mansard-roof and attractive modern lounges overlooking patio.
80rm(⇌⋒) Annexe: 20⇌⋒ Lift ☽ ⊞ ⅏ CTV TV available in bedrooms 100P ⚓ ▭&▭(heated) squash Disco wkly (Etr–Oct) Live music & dancing 5nights wkly Cabaret nightly (Etr–Oct) Conference facilities available ⚘ ♀Continental. Lastdinner9.15pm ✿

T

♀ *sB&B fr£9.25 sB&B⇌⋒ fr£11.25 dB&B fr£16.50 dB&B⇌⋒ fr£20.50 Lunch£2.95 Dinner£4.75 Wine£2.95 ⊟ *xmas* Credit cards 1 2 3 4 5 6

★★★**Toorak** Chestnut Av ☎27135 Central plan**37**
A comfortable hotel, personally run.
Closed 1–10Jan; 69rm(43⇌⋒) Annexe: 11rm(5⇌⋒) ☽ ⋒ CTV 60P 15⋒ ⋒ ♣ ⋒(heated) ⋒(hard) billiards Live music & dancing twice wkly Conference facilities available ⋒ ♀ English & Continental. Last dinner 8.15pm ⋒ ♀ S% sB&B£13–£18.50 sB&B⇌⋒ £14.50–£20 dB&B£2–£37 dB&B⇌⋒ £29–£40 Lunch£4.25&alc Tea£1 Dinner£6.25&alc Wine£3 ⊟ *xmas*

★★**Alpine** Warren Rd ☎27612 Central plan**1**
18rm(9⇌⋒) Lift ⋒ CTV TV available in bedrooms 4⋒ ♀ English, French & Italian. Last dinner 8.30pm ♀ ⋒

★★**Anchorage** Cary Av, Babbacombe ☎36175 District plan**42**
Closed 2Nov–17Mar; 50rm(23⇌⋒) ☽ CTV ⋒ 50P ♣ Live music & dancing 3 nights wkly Children under 5yrs not accommodated Last dinner 8.30pm ⋒ ♀ sB&B£8.10–£10.26 sB&B⇌⋒ £9.18–£11.34 dB&B£15.12–£19.48 dB&B⇌⋒ £17.28–£21.64 Lunch£2.50–£3 Tea£1 Dinner£3.50–£4.50 Wine£2.05 ⊟

★★**Ansteys Lea** Wellswood ☎24843 District plan**43**
Closed mid Oct–Feb (except Xmas) 28rm(8⇌⋒) ⋒

CTV 20P (heated) Last dinner7.30pm S% ✻sB&B£7.05–£9.05 sB&B £8.05–£10.05 dB&B£13–£17 dB&B £15–£19 Bar lunch£1.25alc Tea75palc Dinner£3.50 Wine£2.50 *xmas*

★★**Ardmore** Asheldon Rd, Wellswood ☎24792 Central plan**3**
32rm(9) CTV 40P (heated) Last dinner7pm S% sB&B£6–£8 dB&B£12–£16 dB&B £14–£18 Bar lunch50p–£1 Tea25p–£1 Dinner£2.50–£3.50 Wine£3 *xmas*

★★***Hotel Balmoral*** Meadfoot Sea Rd ☎23381 District plan**45**
Closed Nov–Dec; 18rm CTV 18P British & French. Last dinner8.30pm Credit cards 1 3

★★**Bancourt** Avenue Rd ☎25077 Central plan**3**
Closed Nov–Mar; 42rm(20) CTV 35P (heated) Live music & dancing 3nights wkly Cabaret wkly Last dinner7.30pm S% sB&B£6.60–£9 sB&B £7.80–£10.20 dB&B£13.20–£18 dB&B £15.60–£20.40 Bar lunch£2.75 Dinner£4.80 Wine£2.90 Credit cards 2 4 6

★★**Brigantine Motor** 56 Marlchon Rd, Shiphay ☎63162 District plan**46**
10rm(3) CTV TV in bedrooms 40P 1 (heated) Children under 8yrs not accommodated Mainly grills. Last dinner10pm S% sB&B fr£7.56 sB&B fr£8.31 dB&B fr£11.88 dB&B fr£14.04 Lunch£2.75–£3.25&alc Tea75p–£1&alc High Tea75p–£2&alc Dinner£3&alc Wine£2 *xmas* Credit cards 1 3 6

★★**Burlington** 462–466 Babbacombe Rd ☎24374 Central plan**6**
Closed Nov–Mar(except Xmas); 44rm(10) CTV 30P Live music & dancing 3nights wkly Last dinner8pm S% sB&B£6.60–£10.25 sB&B £7.60–£11.90 dB&B£12–£18.50 dB&B £14–£22 Lunch£2.50–£3 Tea50p–£1 Dinner£3–£4 Wine£3 *xmas* Credit cards 3 6

★★**Bute Court** Belgrave Rd ☎23771 Central plan**7**
White painted, Victorian building with spacious interior, modern lounge and dining-rooms giving views over garden to sea.
50rm(23) Lift CTV 35P 5 (heated) billiards Disco wkly Live music & dancing wkly Last dinner8pm S% sB&B£7.25–£11 sB&B £7.95–£12.25 dB&B£14.50–£22 dB&B £15.90–£24.50 Lunch£2–£3 Tea25p&alc High Tea£1–£2 Dinner£3–£4 Wine£2.35 *xmas* Credit cards 1 2 3 6

★★**Cavendish** Belgrave Rd ☎23682 Central plan**9**
Closed 11Oct–3Apr; 60rm(13) CTV 24P (heated) Live music & dancing 3nights wkly in summer Cabaret wkly in summer Children under 5yrs not accommodated English & Continental. Last dinner7.45pm sB&B£11–£15 sB&B £13.20–£18.50 dB&B£22–£30.15 dB&B £25.10–£35.90 Lunch£4.25–£7 Tea£1.10 Dinner£5.30–£10.10 Wine£2.95

★★***Coniston*** Stanley Rd, Babbacombe ☎37280 District plan**47**
RS Nov–Mar; 24rm CTV 20P (heated) Last dinner7.30pm Credit cards 1 3

★★**Conway Court** Warren Rd ☎25363 Central plan**10**
Closed Nov–Mar; 38rm(15) 6 CTV TV available in bedrooms Live music & dancing twice

T

wkly Cabaret 3nights wkly Last dinner7.15pm ✿ ☐ S% sB&B£6.85–£11.25 sB&B⇌⋒£7.93–£12.33 dB&B£13.90–£22.50 dB&B⇌⋒£15.86–£24.66 Barlunch60p–£3 Tea25p–£1 Dinner£4.32 Wine£2.90 ⊟

★★Coppice Barrington Rd ☎27786 Central plan**48**
Closed mid Sep–Feb; 27rm(18⇌⋒) ⊞ ⋈ CTV 25P ⚓ ⌂(heated) ⌂ Last dinner7.30pm ✿ ☐ S% *sB&B£4.70–£8.20 dB&B£9.40–£16.40 dB&B⇌⋒£11.40–£18.40 Barlunch50p–£2 Tea50p–£1.50 High Tea£1–£2 Dinner£2.50–£6 Wine£2.60

★★Crofton House 17 Croft Rd ☎23761
Central plan**11**
RS Nov–Feb (except Xmas); 39rm(21⇌⋒) Annexe: 2⇌⋒ ⋈ CTV 12P ⚓ ⌂(heated) Disco wkly Cabaret wkly Last dinner7pm ✿ ☐ S% sB&B£6.50–£8.50 sB&B⇌⋒£7.50–£9.50 dB&B£12–£16 dB&B⇌⋒£13–£18 Lunch£1.50 Tea£1 Dinner£2.50 ⊟ *xmas*

★★Dartmoor Maiden Maidencombe ☎38760
District plan**50**
6rm(2⇌⋒) CTV TV available in bedrooms ⊘ 16P ⌂ ⚓ Children under7yrs not accommodated ♡French. Last dinner9.30pm ✿ sB&B£6 dB&B£12–£13 dB&B⇌⋒£14–£16 Lunch35p–£4&alc Dinner£5&alc Wine£2.80 ⊟ *xmas*
Credit cards 1 2 3 5

★★Elmington St Agnes Ln ☎65192(605192 fr Feb80) Central plan**13**
Stands in about 1 acre of gardens; overlooking Tor Bay.
Closed Nov–Mar (except Xmas); 22rm(6⇌⋒) Annexe: 8rm ☽ CTV 20P ⚓ ⌂(heated) Cabaret twice weekly Last dinner7.30pm ✿ ☐ sB&B£5.85–£10.50 dB&B£11.50–£21 dB&B⇌⋒£14–£25 Lunch£1.75–£2.50 Tea45–65p Dinner£2.50–£3.75 Wine£3.50 ⊟ *xmas*

★★Fonthill Lower Warberry Rd ☎23894
Central plan**15**
Closed mid Oct–early May; 32rm(22⇌⋒) CTV 26P ⚓ ⌂(heated) Disco Tue ♡English & Continental. Last dinner7.45pm ✿ ☐ S% sB&B£6.20–£8.65 sB&B⇌⋒£7–£9.65 dB&B£12.40–£17.30 dB&B⇌⋒£14–£19.30 Barlunch£1.25–£2 Tea60p Dinner£3.25 Wine£2.30 ⊟

★★Howden Court Croft Rd ☎24844 Central plan**17**
Closed Nov–Mar; 32⇌⋒ CTV 20P ⚓ Last dinner7.30pm ✿ ☐ S% sB&B⇌⋒£9.20–£12.55 dB&B⇌⋒£18.40–£25.10 Lunch fr£2.75 Tea fr£1.50 Dinner fr£3.75 Credit card 3

★★Hunsdon Lea Hunsdon Rd ☎26538
Central plan**18**
Closed mid Oct–Mar (except Xmas); 18rm(9⇌⋒) CTV CTV available in bedrooms ⊘ 12P ⌂(heated) Live music & dancing twice wkly Last dinner7pm ✿ ☐ S% sB&B£10–£16 sB&B⇌⋒£11.50–£17.50 dB&B£18–£24 dB&B⇌⋒£21–£27 Lunch£3–£4.75&alc Tea75p–£1 Dinner£3.50–£5.50&alc Wine£1.70 ⊟ *xmas*

★★*Lansdowne* Babbacombe Rd ☎22822
District plan**52**
Closed Nov–Mar; 33rm(22⇌⋒) ⋈ CTV 30P ⚓ ⌂(heated) Disco Thu ♡English & French. Last dinner8pm ✿ ☐ ⊟

★★*Maidencombe House* Teignmouth Rd, Maidencombe ☎36611 District plan**53**
Buildings of natural stone and stucco standing in 1½ acres of terraced lawns.

T

rm(19⇌⋒) ℳ CTV ⊘ 50P ⚓ ⇀(heated) Live music dancing Sat Cabaret Sat Last dinner8.30pm ✿ Credit cards 1 5

★**Meadfoot Bay** Meadfoot Sea Rd ☎24722 strict plan**54**
osed Nov–Mar; 26rm(9⇌⋒) ℳ CTV TV available in drooms 20P Children under 3yrs not commodated Last dinner7pm
&B£5.80–£10.30 dB&B£11–£20
&B⇌⋒£13.30–£25 Lunch£3.25
nner£4.25&alc Wine£3.50 ⊟

★**Morningside** Sea Front, Babbacombe Downs 37025 Not on plan
osed Oct–Mar; 18rm(1⇌⋒) ℳ CTV ⊘ 14P ⇌ ildren under5yrs not accommodated
st dinner7pm ✿ ☐ sB&B£6.50–£8.50
B&B£13–£17 dB&B⇌⋒£15–£19
nch£2–£3 Tea£1–£2 Dinner£3–£5 Wine£3

★★**Nethway** Falkland Rd ☎27630 Central plan**26**
RS Jan–Mar; 24rm(16⇌⋒) ☽ ✗ ℳ TV TV available in bedrooms 15P 1⌂ ⚓ ⇀ ♂ billiards Disco twice wkly Live music & dancing twice wkly Cabaret wkly ♧ ☺ English & French. Last dinner7.30pm ✿ ☐
✱sB&B£6.95–£9 sB&B⇌⋒£7.95–£10
dB&B£12.96–£16.40 dB&B⇌⋒£15.86–£20
Bar lunch fr£1 Tea50p–£1
Dinner£3.24–£5.10&alc Wine£2 ⊟ *xmas*

★★**Overmead** Daddyhole Rd ☎27633
District plan**60**
Closed Oct–Apr; 60rm(12⇌⋒) Lift ☽ ℳ CTV ⊘ 7P 13⌂ ⚓ ⇀ billiards Live music & dancing 3nights wkly Cabaret wkly Last dinner8pm ✿ ☐ S%
sB&B£9–£11 sB&B⇌⋒£10.30–£12.30
dB&B£17–£21 dB&B⇌⋒£19.60–£23.60
Bar lunch40p–£1 Tea60p Dinner£4.50
Wine£2.50 ⊟ *xmas* Credit cards 1 3

T

★★**Regina** Victoria Pde ☎22904 Central plan**30**
Opposite harbour, overlooking sea. Elizabeth Barrett Browning lived here 1833–1841 when it was known as Bath House.
Closed Oct–Mar; 63rm(17⇌⋒) Lift ☽ ⋈ CTV 6⌂ Last dinner8pm ✿ ☕ ✳sB&B£5.40–£8.20 sB&B⇌⋒£6–£9.50 dB&B£10.80–£16.40 dB&B⇌⋒£12–£19 Lunch£2.50 Tea25p Dinner£3.25 ▤

★★**Hotel Roseland** Warren Rd ☎24614 Central plan**32**
Closed 17Oct–4May; 30rm(14⇌⋒) ⋈ TV in bedrooms ⊘ 6⌂ Last dinner7.30pm ✿ S% sB&B£7.08–£9.18 sB&B⇌⋒£8.16–£10.24 dB&B£14.16–£18.36 dB&B⇌⋒£16.32–£20.54 Bar lunch£1.65–£2.20 Dinner£4–£4.75 Wine£2.80 ▤ *xmas*

★★***Shedden Hall*** ☎22964 Central plan**34**
Closed 30Sep–Apr; 25rm(12⇌⋒) CTV TV available in bedrooms 20P ⌒(heated) Children under 2yrs not accommodated Last dinner7pm ✿ ☕ ▤

★★**Sunray** Aveland Rd, Babbacombe ☎38285 District plan**63**
Closed Dec–Feb; RS Nov & Mar; 24rm(8⇌⋒) ⋈ CTV CTV available in bedrooms 15P Disco twice wkly ♡English & French. Last dinner8pm ✿ ☕ S% sB&B£5.50–£6.50 dB&B£11–£13 dB&B⇌⋒£13–£15 Lunch£2.50 Dinner£3.50 Wine£2.40 ▤

★★***Sydore*** Meadfoot Rd ☎24758 Central plan**35**
15rm(3⇌⋒) ⋈ CTV TV available in bedrooms ⊛ ⚓ Last dinner8.30pm ▤

★★***Templestowe*** Tor Church Rd ☎25145 Central plan**36**
Closed Nov–mid Apr; 100rm(27⇌⋒) Lift ☽ CTV 60P ⚓ ⌒(heated) ⊸(hard) Live music & dancing twice wkly Last dinner7.15pm

★★**Vernon Court** Warren Rd ☎22676 Central plan**38**
Closed Nov–Apr; 19rm(9⇌⋒) TV in bedrooms ⊘ 9P ⊛ ⚓ Last dinner7.15pm S% sB&B£7.50–£11 dB&B£14–£22 dB&B⇌⋒£15–£24 Bar lunch£3 Tea50p Dinner£5 Wine£2.80

★★**Viscount** St Albans Rd, Babbacombe ☎37444 District plan**64**
Closed Nov–Apr; 20rm(5⇌⋒) CTV TV in bedrooms 20P ⊛ Children under3yrs not accommodated Last dinner7.30pm ✿ ☕ S% sB&B£6–£11.30 dB&B£12–£22.60 dB&B⇌⋒£14.16–£24.76 Lunch£2.50 Tea£1 Dinner£5 Wine£2.90

★★**Windsor** Abbey Rd ☎23757 Telex no42906 Central plan**39**
Rs Nov–Mar; 45rm(7⇌⋒) ☽ ⋈ CTV 30P ⌒(heated) disco Mon Live music & dancing Thu Last dinner8pm ✿ ☕ *xmas* Credit cards ①③

★**Alvanley** Croft Rd ☎22466 Central plan**2**
Closed Nov–Mar (except Xmas) 20rm(6⇌⋒) ⋈ CTV 14P Last dinner7pm ✿ sB&B£5.75–£7.50 sB&B⇌⋒£6.50–£8.25 dB&B£11.50–£15 dB&B⇌⋒£13–£16.50 Bar lunch75p–£2 Dinner£2.50–£3.50&alc Wine£2 ▤ *xmas*

★**Ashley Rise** 18 Babbacombe Rd, Babbacombe ☎37282 District plan**44**
RS Oct–Feb; 28rm(2⇌⋒) ⋈ CTV 14P 3⌂ Live music & dancing twice wkly Last dinner7pm ✿ ☕ S% sB&B£7–£11 dB&B£13–£21 dB&B⇌⋒£15–£23 Dinner fr£3 *xmas*

★**Carlton** Falkland Rd ☎22008 Central plan**8**
Closed 25Oct–Mar; 32rm(5⇌⋒) ☽ CTV 20P ⚓ ⌒(heated) Disco wkly (twice wkly in season) Last dinner7.15pm ✿ ☕ sB&B£4.15–£7.85 dB&B£15.70 dB&B⇌⋒£18 Lunch£1.85 Tea55p Dinner£2.30 Wine£2.70 *xmas*

T

T

★Norcliffe Sea Front, Babbacombe ☎38456 District plan**55**
Closed Nov–Mar; 22rm(8⇌ ⋔) 🍽 CTV 17P ⇎
🍷English & French. Last dinner7.30pm ♁ ☕
S% sB&B£8–£10.80 dB&B£16–£21.60
dB&B⇌ ⋔£18–£25.60 Bar lunch80p–£2
Tea£1–£1.20 Dinner£3.50–£4.50
Wine £2.50

★Orestone House Rockhouse Ln, Maidencombe ☎38099 District plan**56**
Closed Oct & Feb; RS Nov–Jan & Mar; 14rm(6⇌ ⋔)
CTV ✈ 18P 🍽 ⚓ ⌂(heated) 🍷English & French.
Last dinner8.30pm ♁ ☕ sB&B£8.50–£9.50
dB&B£17–£19 dB&B⇌ ⋔£19–£21
Bar lunch£1.50alc Tea60palc Dinner£4.75&alc
Wine£3 ⊟

★Rock Walk Warren Rd ☎28775 Central plan**31**
Closed Nov–Mar; 31rm(19⇌ ⋔) 🍽 CTV TV available in bedrooms 10P Live music & dancing twice weekly
Cabaret twice weekly ♫ Last dinner7.15pm ♁ ☕
sB&B£8.70–£12.20 sB&B⇌ ⋔£9.78–£13.28
dB&B£16.50–£23.50 dB&B⇌ ⋔£17.58–£24.58
Lunch£2.50 Dinner£3.50 ⊟

★Royal The Stand ☎23124 Central plan**33**
Situated opposite harbour, with view of harbour and Tor Bay.
16rm(4⇌ ⋔) 🍽 CTV P ⇎ Children under 5yrs not accommodated Last dinner8.30pm ♁ ☕ S%
sB&B£7–£10 dB&B£14–£20
dB&B⇌ ⋔£15–£21 Lunch£2.75&alc
Tea£1–£1.50&alc Dinner£3&alc Wine£2.40 ⊟
xmas

★**Woodland Park** Babbacombe Rd, Babbacombe ☎38043 District plan **65**
Closed Oct–Mar; 18rm(5⇌ ⋒) CTV 20P ⛟
Last dinner 7pm ♁ ☕ sB&B£6.50–£7.50
sB&B⇌ ⋒£7.50–£8.50 dB&B£13–£15
dB&B⇌ ⋒£15–£17 Bar lunch 45p–£1.50
Tea 40–75p Dinner £2–£2.50 Credit cards 3 6

⊕ ***Penrhyn*** Carry Park, Babbacombe ☎37385
District plan **62**
Closed 16 Oct–Etr; Unlicensed; 20rm CTV 15P 6🏠
⚓ billiards Live music & dancing Wed
Last dinner 7pm

✕✕✕**Fanny's Dining Room** 55 Abbey Rd ☎28605
Central plan **14**
Closed Sun; 40 seats ₱ ♡ English & French.
Last dinner 9.30pm S% Dinner £15alc
Wine £3.75 Credit cards 1 2 3 4 5 6

✕**Les Escaliers** 1A Fleet St ☎26937 Not on plan
Closed Sun, Mon, 1wk Oct & 2wks Feb; Lunch not served Tue & Sat; 30 seats ₱ ♡ English & French.
Last dinner 10.30pm ✱Lunch £2alc
Dinner £5.50alc Wine £2.52

TORRINGTON, GREAT Devon Map **2** SS41
★★***Castle Hill*** South St ☎2339
14rm(4⇌ ⋒) CTV 30P ⚓ Last dinner 9pm ♁

TOTLAND BAY Isle of Wight Map **4** SZ38
★★**Sentry Mead** ☎Freshwater 3212
Closed Nov–Mar except Xmas; 13rm(4⇌ ⋒) CTV
12P ⛟ ⚓ ♡ English & French. Last dinner 8.15pm
♁ ☕ S% ✱sB&B£8.37–£9.18
dB&B£16.74–£18.36 dB&B⇌ ⋒£18.90–£20.52
Lunch £2.90–£3.25 Tea 40–60p Dinner £4–£4.25
Wine £2.16 *xmas*

TOTNES Devon Map**3** SX86
★★★**Seymour** Bridgetown ☎864686
Spacious hotel situated beside River Dart.
30rm(17⇌⋒) ☽ ꟿCTV P ⥲ billiards
Lastdinner8.30pm ✿ ⊈ ✱sB&B£12.50
sB&B⇌⋒£13.75 dB&B£18 dB&B⇌⋒£20.50
Lunch£3&alc Tea25p Dinner£4.50 Wine£3.15
⊟ *xmas* Creditcards 1 2 3 4 5

★★**Royal Seven Stars** ☎862125
An attractive old coaching inn, dating from the 17th-C.
18rm(8⇌⋒) CTV 25P Live music & dancing twice wkly Cabaret twice wkly Lastdinner9.15pm ✿
sB&B£11–£13 sB&B⇌⋒£13.50–£15
dB&B£18 20 dB&B⇌⋒£21–£23
Lunch£3.75–£4.25&alc Dinner£5.50–£6.50&alc
Wine£3.25 ⊟ *xmas* Creditcard 5

XX***Elbow Room*** ☎863480
Dinner not served Sun & Mon (except Public Hols)
30seats ♡International. Lastdinner9.30pm
Creditcards 2 3 6

XX**Ffoulkes** 30 High St ☎863853
Closed Sun, 2wks Nov & 2wks Mar; Lunch not served 36seats ₱ ♡French. Lastdinner10.15pm
S% Dinner£11alc Wine£3.25
Creditcards 1 2 3 5 6

TOTON Nottinghamshire Map**8** SK53
XX***Grange Farm*** ☎Long Eaton69426
Old stone farmhouse with traditional décor including display cabinet with porcelain figures.
Closed Sun, Xmas, New Year & Public Hols;
150seats 130P Music & dancing Sat Cabaret Sat
Lastdinner9pm

TREBETHERICK Cornwall Map**2** SW97
★★**St Moritz** (Inter-Hotel) ☎2242
60rm(36⇌⋒) ꟿ CTV CTV in bedrooms 300P ⚓ Live music & dancing wkly ⌂ ♡English & French.
Lastdinner9pm ✿ ⊈ S% sB&B£10–£12
sB&B⇌⋒£12–£15 dB&B£16–£18
dB&B⇌⋒£20–£22 Lunch£4–£4.50&alc
Tea50p–£1 Dinner£5&alc Wine£3.50 ⊟ *xmas*
Creditcards 1 2 3 5

★**Fore Dore** ☎3471
Ideally situated between Polzeath Beach and Daymer Bay. Own grounds incorporate 9-hole putting green.
Closed Nov–Mar; 11rm CTV 10P ⇛ ⚓
Lastdinner8.30pm ✿ ⊈ S% sB&B£6.17
dB&B£12.34 Lunch£2.16 Dinner£3.24 Wine£2

TREGONY Cornwall Map**2** SW94
XX**Kea House** Main St ☎642
Closed Sun; Lunch not served; 32seats ₱
♡European. Lastdinner10.30pm
✱Dinner£5.25alc Wine£2.95 Creditcard 1

TRELIGHTS Cornwall Map**2** SW97
★**Long Cross** ☎Port Isaac243
Closed Nov–Mar; 15rm(5⇌⋒) ⚔ CTV 50P ⇛ ⚓
Disco Sat Live music & dancing Fri Lastdinner8pm
✿ S% ✱sB&B fr£5 dB&B fr£10
dB&B⇌⋒ fr£12 Barlunch50p–£1
Dinner£2–£2.50 Wine£1.75 Creditcards 1 3

TREVONE Cornwall Map**2** SW87
★**Trevone Bay** (off B3276) ☎St Merryn 520243
Closed Nov–Mar; 15rm CTV 12P ⇛ ⌂
Lastdinner7.15pm ⊈ sB&B£5.25–£7
dB&B£10.50–£14 Barlunch£1.10–£2.50
Tea50p–£1.10 Dinner£3–£3.50 Wine£1.70

TREYARNON BAY Cornwall Map**2** SW87
★★**Waterbeach** St Merryn ☎520292
Closed Oct–Apr; 16rm(7⇌ ⫚) CTV 40P 3 (hard) Last dinner8.15pm S%
✱sB&B£10–£15 dB&B£20–£30
dB&B⇌ ⫚£23–£33 Lunch£2.50alc
Dinner£5.60–£6.50 Wine£2.40

TRING Hertfordshire Map**4** SP91
★★**Rose & Crown** High St (Trusthouse Forte) ☎4071
Built by Rothschild in early 20th-C in style of Tudor coaching house.
16rm(8⇌ ⫚) TV in bedrooms 40P
Last dinner9.30pm S% sB&B£12
dB&B£17.50 dB&B⇌ ⫚£20.50 *xmas*
Credit cards 1 2 3 4 5 6

✕**Waterfall** 75 High St ☎5283
Closed Xmas 65seats Pekinese.
Last dinner11pm Dinner£5–£10&alc Wine2.60
Credit cards 1 2 3 5

TROTTON West Sussex Map**4** SU82
★★★**Southdowns** ☎Rogate521
12rm(8⇌ ⫚) CTV CTV available in bedrooms 80P
Live music & dancing twice mthly
Last dinner9.30pm S%
sB&B£15.50–£18.50 sB&B⇌ ⫚£18.50–£21.50
dB&B£18.50–£21.50 dB&B⇌ ⫚£21.50–£24.50
Lunch£3.75–£4&alc Tea£1–£1.50
Dinner£5.50–£6&alc Wine£4.20 *xmas*
Credit cards 1 2 3 5 6

TROWBRIDGE Wiltshire Map**3** ST85
★**Polebarn House** Polebarn Rd ☎65624
9rm(2⇌ ⫚) CTV TV available in bedrooms 12P
5 English & French. Last dinner9pm
S% sB&B£9.18 dB&B£14.58 dB&B⇌ ⫚£15.66
Bar lunch£1alc Tea75palc Dinner£5.50alc
Wine£2.90 Credit card 1

TRURO Cornwall Map**2** SW84
★★**Brookdale** Tregolls Rd ☎3513
33rm(10⇌ ⫚) Annexe: 23rm(7⇌ ⫚) CTV TV in bedrooms 60P 10 English, French & Italian.
Last dinner8.45pm S%
sB&B£9.45–£10.05 sB&B⇌ ⫚£11.34–£12
dB&B£18.90–£20.10 dB&B⇌ ⫚£22.68–£24
Lunch£2.20–£2.50&alc Tea30p–£1
Dinner£3.70–£4 Wine£3 *xmas*
Credit cards 1 2 3 5

★★**Carlton** Falmouth Rd ☎2450
Closed 1–21 Oct & 25 Dec–1 Jan; 25rm(10⇌ ⫚) CTV 30P Last dinner8pm S%
✱sB&B⇌ ⫚£8.32 dB&B£13.78
dB&B⇌ ⫚£17.46 Dinner£3.45&alc Wine£2.32
Credit card 1

TUNBRIDGE WELLS (Royal) Kent Map**5** TQ53
★★★**Calverley** Crescent Rd ☎26455
Queen Victoria stayed here as a child.
39rm(22⇌ ⫚) Lift CTV TV available in bedrooms 40P Last dinner8.30pm sB&B£11.80
sB&B⇌ ⫚£14 dB&B£21 dB&B⇌ ⫚£23
Lunch£3&alc Tea60p Dinner£3.50&alc
Wine£2.10 Credit cards 1 2 3 5 6

★★★**Spa** Mount Ephraim (Best Western) ☎20331
Telex no957188
80rm(58⇌ ⫚) Lift CTV CTV available in bedrooms 150P 4 Conference facilities available English & French. Last dinner9.30pm
S% sB&B£13.75–£14.50
sB&B⇌ ⫚£21–£22 dB&B⇌ ⫚£35

T

Continental breakfast Lunch£4.50–£5&alc Tea£1–£1.25 High Tea£4 Dinner£5–£5.50&alc xmas Credit cards 1 2 3 4 5 6

★★**Beacon** Tea Garden Ln ☎24252
9rm(7⇌) CTV 40P Disco Sat Last dinner7.45pm S% sB&B fr£9 sB&B⇌ fr£11 dB&B⇌ fr£18 Bar lunch£1alc Tea fr60p Dinner fr£4 Credit cards 1 3 6

★★**Royal Wells Inn** Mount Ephraim ☎23414
14⇌ 2 CTV 29P English & French. Last dinner9.30pm S% sB&B⇌ £9.50 dB&B⇌ £18.50 Lunch£3.50–£7.50&alc Dinner£3.50–£7.50&alc Wine£3 Credit cards 1 3 5

★★**Wellington** Mount Ephraim ☎20286
67rm(31⇌) 1 Lift CTV 25P Last dinner8.15pm S% sB&B£9–£10 sB&B⇌ £12.50–£14 dB&B£19–£20 dB&B⇌ £22–£24 Lunch£3–£3.50&alc Tea75p–£1 Dinner£3.50–£4&alc Wine£2.60 xmas Credit cards 1 2 3 5

✕**Alpine Rose** 9–11 Langton Rd ☎21575
Swiss restaurant with authentic Swiss décor imported from Switzerland to create an 'Apres-Ski' atmosphere.
Closed Mon; 60seats French & Swiss. Last dinner10pm Lunch£3.20&alc Dinner£7.50alc Credit cards 1 3 5

TURVEY Bedfordshire Map**4** SP95
★**Laws** ☎213
Closed Sun (Nov–Apr), Xmas wk, Public Hols; RS Sun (May–Oct); 11rm(1⇌) CTV 100P English & French. Specialities: Suprême chicken

T

tarragon, scampi galvani, éscalop brillat-savarin. Lastdinner9pm sB&B£12 sB&B⇌⋒£14 dB&B£18 Lunch£6alc Dinner£6alc Wine£2.80 Credit cards ① ⑤

TUTBURY Staffordshire Map**8** SK22
★★Ye Olde Dog & Partridge High St ☎Burton-on-Trent813030
Remarkable 14th-C timbered inn with elegant period décor.
Closed 25 & 26 Dec & New Year's Day; RS Sun & Mon; 3⇌⋒ Annexe: 14⇌⋒ 2 ☽ CTV CTV in bedrooms 100P 1 Live music nightly Children under 10yrs not accommodated English & French. Lastdinner9.45pm sB&B⇌⋒£16 dB&B⇌⋒£20–£35 Lunch£7alc Dinner£4&alc Wine£2.50 Credit cards ① ② ③ ⑤

TUXFORD Nottinghamshire Map**8** SK77
★★Newcastle Arms ☎870208
16rm(8⇌⋒) TV in bedrooms 80P 2 Lastdinner9.45pm sB&B£11.50 sB&B⇌⋒£12.50 dB&B£15 dB&B⇌⋒£17 Lunch£4 Tea£1 Dinner£5 Wine£4.50 Credit cards ① ② ③ ⑤ ⑥

TYNEMOUTH Tyne and Wear Map**12** NZ36
★★★Grand Grand Pde ☎North Shields72106
38rm(31⇌⋒) Lift ☽ CTV CTV in bedrooms 28P 4 Disco 3nights wkly English & French. Lastdinner10pm sB&B£12–£15 sB&B⇌⋒£16–£18 dB&B£18–£21 dB&B⇌⋒£21–£24 Lunch£3–£3.50&alc Tea75p–£1.50 High Tea£1.50–£2 Dinner£3.75–£4.50&alc Wine£2.90 *xmas* Credit cards ① ② ③ ④ ⑤ ⑥

T

★★**Park** Grand Pde (Open House)
☎North Shields71406
28rm(9☎) ☽ TV available in bedrooms 240P
English & French. Last dinner10pm S%
sB&B£13.50 sB&B⇌£16.75 dB&B£20.75
dB&B⇌£24 Lunch£3.75&alc Dinner£5&alc
Wine£2.85 Credit cards 1 2 3 4 5

TYTHERLEIGH Devon Map**3** ST30
✕**Tytherleigh Arms** ☎South Chard20214
Closed Sun & Xmas Day; 35seats 70P
International. Last dinner9.30pm
✱Lunch£1.50alc Dinner£4.75&alc
Credit cards 1 2 3

UCKFIELD East Sussex Map**5** TQ42
✕**Sussex Barn** Ringles Cross ☎3827
Attractive, tile-hung white-painted cottage, with pleasant beamed dining-room.
Closed Mon; Dinner not served Sun; 26seats 20P
English & Continental. Last dinner9.15pm
✱Lunch£3.85&alc Dinner£8.20alc Wine£3.50
Credit cards 2 3

ULLSWATER Cumbria
See **Glenridding, Howtown, Pooley Bridge** and **Watermillock**

ULVERSTON Cumbria Map**7** SD27
★★**Lonsdale House** Daltongate ☎52598
Originally built as an 18th-C town house, but now converted into a family run hotel.
19rm(11⇌) CTV CTV available in bedrooms P
French. Last dinner8.30pm sB&B£10
sB&B⇌£12 dB&B£16 dB&B⇌£18
Lunch£3.25alc Dinner£5alc Wine£2.60
Credit card 2

★**Railway** Princes St ☎52208
A small hotel near to the sea and Birkrigg Common, an open expanse of two thousand bracken acres.
8rm CTV 40P 2 Last dinner8.15pm S%
sB&B£8–£9 dB&B£13–£15 Lunch£2.20–£3.50
Dinner£4–£5 Wine£2.10

UMBERLEIGH Devon Map**2** SS62
★★**Rising Sun** (Wessex Taverns)
☎High Bickington447
Closed Nov–Jan; 6rm(4⇌) Annexe: 2rm CTV 20P
4 Children under 8yrs not accommodated
Last dinner8.30pm S% sB&B fr£9
sB&B⇌ fr£10 dB&B fr£16 dB&B⇌ fr£18
Bar lunch50p–£1 Dinner£5–£6 Wine£3.20
Credit cards 1 3

UNDERBARROW Cumbria Map**7** SD49
✕✕**Greenriggs Country House Hotel**
☎Crosthwaite387
Closed Jan; Lunch not served; Dinner not served Sun; 45seats 30P bedrooms available
Last dinner8pm Dinner£7–£7.50 Wine£2.80

UPLYME Devon Map**3** SY39
★★★**Devon** ☎Lyme Regis3231
16th-C hotel standing in eight acres of ground, originally a monastery.
Closed Nov–Feb except Xmas; RS Mar; 21⇌ CTV 30P (heated) English & French.
Last dinner8.30pm S%
✱sB&B⇌£10.50–£16 dB&B⇌£21–£32
Lunch£3.50 Tea45p Dinner£4.50 Wine£3.05
xmas Credit cards 2 3

★***Black Dog*** ☎Lyme Regis2634
RS 2wks Nov & 2wks Mar; 6rm CTV 16P 3
Children under 5yrs not accommodated
Last dinner7.15pm

UPPER BENEFIELD Northamptonshire Map**4** SP98
✕✕***Benefield Wheatsheaf*** ☎254
Closed Sun; Dinner not served Mon; 36seats 50P
Last dinner9pm Credit cards 1 2 3

UPPER SLAUGHTER Gloucestershire Map**4** SP12
★★★**Lords of the Manor** ☎Bourton-on-the-Water20243 Telex no83147
Dating from the 17th-C in 7½ acres of beautiful grounds.
15rm(11⇌) 1 CTV 15P
Last dinner9.45pm S% sB&B£18.50
sB&B⇌£19.90 dB&B£37 dB&B⇌£41
Lunch£4.90 Dinner£8alc Wine£4.90 *xmas*
Credit cards 1 2 3 5 6

UPPINGHAM Leicestershire Map**4** SP89
★★★**Falcon** High St ☎3535
Closed Xmas night 21rm(10⇌) 1 ☽ CTV 20P
squash English & Continental.
Last dinner9.30pm ✱Lunch£3.78&alc
Tea35p&alc Dinner£6alc Wine£3.56
Credit cards 2 3 5 6

Central High St ☎2352
Closed 24Dec–6Jan 14rm(2⇌) CTV P
Last dinner8.30pm sB&B£7.50
sB&B⇌£9 dB&B£14 dB&B⇌£17
Lunch£2.50–£3 Tea50p–£1.50
Dinner£3.20–£3.50&alc Wine£2.60
Credit cards 1 2 3

UPTON NOBLE Somerset Map**3** ST73
✕**Lamb Inn** ☎308
Closed Sun & Mon; Lunch not served; 18seats 8P
Last dinner10.30pm ✱Dinner£6.75alc Wine£2.30

UPTON-ON-SEVERN Hereford & Worcester Map**3** SO84
★★**White Lion** High St ☎2551
14rm(6⇌) CTV CTV in bedrooms 25P
English & French. Last dinner9pm
sB&B fr£11 sB&B⇌ fr£12 dB&B fr£18
dB&B⇌ fr£20 Lunch£3–£4 Dinner£6alc
Wine£3 Credit card 1

T

UTTOXETER Staffordshire Map**7** SK03
★★★**White Hart** Carter St (Ansells) ☎2437
16th-C coaching inn. Dutch linenfold panelling is of particular interest.
13rm(8⇌⋒) 𝍤 CTV ⊘30P ⊞ Last dinner10pm ♁ ⊈ S% sB&B£13.10 sB&B⇌⋒£14.95 dB&B£17.40 dB&B⇌⋒£19.50 Lunch£3.50–£5 Dinner£4–£6 Wine£3.20 ⊟ Credit cards 1 2

UXBRIDGE Gt London Map**4** TQ08
✕✕✕**Giovanni's** Denham Lodge, Oxford Rd ☎31568
Closed Sun & Public Hols; Lunch not served Sat; 100seats 30P ♀Italian. Last dinner10.30pm ✱Lunch£8alc Dinner£8alc Wine£3.50 Credit cards 1 2 3 4 5 6

At **Hillingdon** (2m NE A40)
☆☆☆**Master Brewer** Western Av ☎Uxbridge51199
64⋒ 64P

VENTNOR Isle of Wight Map**4** SZ57
★★★**Royal** Belgrave Rd (Trusthouse Forte) ☎852186
59rm(35⇌⋒) Lift CTV TV available in bedrooms 56P ⚓ ⌒(heated) Disco 6nights wkly (twice wkly in winter) ♿ Last dinner9pm ♁ ⊈ S% sB&B£13 sB&B⇌⋒£15 dB&B£20.50 dB&B⇌⋒£23 ⊟ Credit cards 1 2 3 4 5 6

★★★**Ventnor Towers** Madeira Rd ☎852277
Victorian building with a modern extension; stands in five acres of lawns and wooded grounds reaching to the cliff top.
32rm(16⇌⋒) 𝍤 CTV 40P ⊞ ⚓ ⌒(heated) ⦿(hard) Last dinner8.30pm ♁ sB&B£9.80–£12.30 sB&B⇌⋒£10.85–£13.35 dB&B£19.60–£24.60 dB&B⇌⋒£21.70–£26.70 Lunch£3.25 Tea50p Dinner£5.15 Wine£2.75 ⊟

★★ ⚘**Winterbourne** Bonchurch (1m E) ☎852535
See page 55 for details.

★★**Bonchurch Manor** Bonchurch (1m E) ☎852868
Closed Nov–Jan except Xmas; 11rm(6⇌⋒) 𝍤 CTV ⊘15P ⊞ ⚓ ⌒ ♀English & French. Last dinner9pm ♁ ⊈ S% sB&B£10.50–£12 dB&B£21–£24 dB&B⇌⋒£24–£27.60 Lunch£2–£4.50 Tea50p Dinner£4.50–£5.50&alc Wine£2.75 *xmas* Credit cards 1 2 3 5

★★**Metropole** Esplanade ☎852181
Closed Nov–Feb except Xmas; 36rm(7⇌⋒) Lift CTV 10P 6⌂ sauna bath Live music & dancing twice wkly Cabaret twice wkly ♫ Last dinner8.30pm ♁ ⊈ sB&B£7.50–£9.50 sB&B⇌⋒£9–£11 dB&B£15–£19 dB&B⇌⋒£18–£22 Lunch£3 Tea75p Dinner£4.30 Wine£3.25 ⊟ *xmas* Credit cards 1 3

✽★★⚘**Peacock Vane** Bonchurch (1m E) ☎852019
Closed mid Jan–mid Feb; 6rm(3⇌⋒) Annexe: 5⇌⋒ 2▭ TV 20P ⊞ ⚓ ⌒(heated) ♀English & French. Last dinner9.30pm Credit cards 1 2 3 5

★⚘**Madeira Hall** Trinity Rd ☎852624
Closed mid Oct–mid Mar; Unlicensed; 12rm CTV 12P ⊞ ⚓ ⌒(heated) Last dinner7pm ♁ S% sB&B£6.38–£7.69 dB&B£12.76–£15.38 Lunch£1.45–£1.51 Dinner£2.17–£3.32

⊕**Lake** Bonchurch (1m E) ☎852613
Closed Oct–mid Mar; 20rm CTV 20P ⊞ ⚓ Last dinner7pm ♁ ⊈ S% sB&B£6–£6.75 dB&B£12–£13.50 Lunch£2.25–£3 Tea70p–£1.50 Dinner£3.50–£5 Wine£3 ⊟

VERYAN Cornwall Map**2** SW93
★★★**Nare** ☎279
Closed Nov–Mar; 37rm(24⇌⋒) 𝍤 CTV TV available in bedrooms ⊘40P ⊞ ⚓ ⌒(heated) ⦿(hard) billiards sauna bath Last dinner8.30pm ♁ ⊈ sB&B£9–£11 sB&B⇌⋒£11–£13 dB&B£18–£22 dB&B⇌⋒£22–£26 Lunch£2.50 Dinner£6.50 Wine£3 Credit cards 1 2 5

★★**Elerkey House** ☎261
Small country-house hotel situated in ancient picturesque Cornish village.
Closed 5Oct–Mar; 9rm(3⇌⋒) 𝍤 CTV CTV available in bedrooms ⊘12P ⊞ ⚓ Children under 6yrs not accommodated Last dinner8pm ♁ S% ✱sB&B£7.50 dB&B£14 dB&B⇌⋒£16 Lunch£1–£1.50 Dinner£4.50 Wine£2.35

WADDESDON Buckinghamshire Map**4** SP71
★**Five Arrows** ☎302
6rm 𝍤 CTV 50P 3⌂ ⚓ Last dinner9pm S% ✱sB&B£7.55 dB&B£15.10 Lunch fr£3.50&alc Dinner fr£3.50&alc

★**White Lion** High St ☎227
RS Xmas; 7rm 𝍤 TV 40P ⊞ ⚓ Last dinner8.30pm ♁ S% sB&B fr£7.50 dB&B fr£14 Lunch£3–£5&alc Dinner£3.20–£5&alc Wine£2.90 Credit cards 2 4 6

WADEBRIDGE Cornwall Map**2** SW97
★★**Molesworth Arms** Molesworth St ☎2055
Original 16th-C coaching inn, comfortably furnished, offering a relaxed atmosphere. Ideally located for touring.
16rm(11⇌⋒) 𝍤 CTV 50P 4⌂ Disco twice wkly Live music & dancing 3nights wkly Children under 8yrs not accommodated Last dinner9.30pm ♁ ⊈ S% ✱sB&B£6–£8 sB&B⇌⋒£7–£9 dB&B£12–£16 dB&B⇌⋒£14–£18 Lunch£1.50–£2.50&alc Tea50p–£1 Dinner£3.50–£4&alc Wine£1.80 ⊟ Credit cards 1 3

W

WAKEFIELD West Yorkshire Map**8** SE32
☆☆☆☆**Post House** Queen's Dr, Ossett (Trusthouse Forte) ☎276388 Telex no55407
96⇌⋒ Lift ☽ ⋒ CTV CTV in bedrooms 140P Conference facilities available Last dinner10.30 ♉ ☑ S% sB&B⇌⋒£21.25 dB&B⇌⋒£31.50 ⊟ *xmas* Credit cards 1 2 3 4 5 6

★★★**Swallow** Queens St (Swallow) ☎72111 Telex no53168
66rm(51⇌⋒) Lift ☽ ⋒ TV in bedrooms 20P Last dinner9.15pm ♉ S% sB&B fr£13.30 sB&B⇌⋒£17.50 dB&B fr£20.75 dB&B⇌⋒ fr£24 ⊟ *xmas* Credit cards 1 2 3 5

★★**Stoneleigh** 211–217 Doncaster Rd ☎61598
24rm(19⇌⋒) ☽ ⋒ CTV CTV available in bedrooms 50P ⊕ ♘ English, French & Italian. Last dinner10pm ♉ ☑ sB&B£12 sB&B⇌⋒£14.50 dB&B£18 dB&B⇌⋒£20 Lunch£3.75&alc Tea85p Dinner£6.50alc Wine£3.15 Credit cards 1 3

WALBERSWICK Suffolk Map**5** TM47
★★**Anchor** ☎Southwold722112
Gabled mock-Tudor exterior with Scandinavian-style lounge and dining room; chalets are in garden setting.
6rm(2⇌⋒) Annexe: 10⇌⋒ ⋒ CTV 60P ⊕ ⚓ ♘ ♿ Last dinner8.30pm ♉ ☑ ✱sB&B£9.15–£10 dB&B£18.30–£20 dB&B⇌⋒£20.10–£22 Lunch£3.35–£4.15 Tea25–65p Dinner£4.20–£5&alc Wine£2.60 ⊟ *xmas* Credit cards 1 2 3 5 6

WALBERTON West Sussex Map**4** SU90
★★★**Avisford Park** Yapton Ln ☎Yapton551215
60rm(53⇌⋒) ☽ ⋒ CTV in bedrooms ⊘ 200P ⚓ ⇒(heated) ➶(grass) squash billiards Live music & dancing wkly Conference facilities available ♘ English & French. Last dinner9.30pm S% sB&B£13 sB&B⇌⋒£16–£17.25 dB&B£19 dB&B⇌⋒£24–£25 Continental breakfast Lunch£4.25&alc Tea75p Dinner£5.25–£6.50&alc Wine£3.25 ⊟ *xmas* Credit cards 1 2 3 6

WALFORD (nr Ross-on-Wye) Hereford & Worcester Map**3** SO52
★⚚**Walford House** ☎Ross-on-Wye3829
6rm Annexe: 10rm ⋒ CTV 75P ⚓ Last dinner10pm ♉ ☑ S% sB&B fr£8 dB&B fr£12.75 Lunch fr£4 Tea75p–£1.40 High Tea£1.25–£1.50 Dinner£5–£6&alc Wine£2.95 ⊟ *xmas* Credit cards 1 3 5

WALL Northumberland Map**12** NY96
★★**Hadrian** ☎Humshaugh232
A creeper-clad building built in 1740 from the stones of Hadrian's Wall.
8rm CTV 40P 4⌂ ⊕ ⚓ ♘ English & Continental. Last dinner9.45pm ♉ sB&B£11.50–£11.90 dB&B£19.50–£23 Lunch£3.50–£3.75 Dinner£7alc Wine£3

WALLASEY Merseyside Map**7** SJ29
★★***St Hilary*** Grove Rd ☎051–639 3947
16rm ⋒ CTV 25P ⚓ ♘ English & French. Last dinner10pm

★**Belvidere** Seabank Rd, New Brighton ☎051–6398145
30rm(5⇌⋒) ☽ ⋒ CTV 30P 3⌂ Last dinner8pm ♉ ☑ S% sB&B£7.51 sB&B⇌⋒£11.10 dB&B£13.75 dB&B⇌⋒£18.50 Lunch£1.75–£3 Tea75p–£1.25 Dinner£3–£4.75 Wine£2.25

WALLINGFORD Oxfordshire Map**4** SU68
★★★**George** High St (Kingsmead) ☎36665
Timbered and gabled Tudor inn with courtyard and rear garden. Dick Turpin is said to have had a room above the archway. Access to car park from Oxford Rd at rear of hotel.
18rm(9⇌⋒) CTV in bedrooms 120P Disco Fri & Sat ♘ English & French. Last dinner10pm ♉ ☑ sB&B£14 sB&B⇌⋒£18 dB&B£23 dB&B⇌⋒£27 Lunch£3.50–£4.25&alc Tea50p Dinner£3.50–£4.25&alc Wine£2.95 ⊟ *xmas* Credit cards 1 2 3 5 6

★★**Shillingford Bridge** Shillingford (2m N A329) ☎Warborough8567
Closed Xmas Day; 24rm(14⇌⋒) 1⊟ ⋒ TV in bedrooms 80P ⚓ ⇒(heated) ↬ squash Live music & dancing twice wkly Cabaret mthly Last dinner10pm ♉ ☑ sB&B fr£11 sB&B⇌⋒ fr£13 dB&B fr£18 dB&B⇌⋒ fr£20 Lunch fr£4.50 Tea fr£1 Dinner fr£4.50 Wine£2.75 Credit cards 1 2 3 5 6

WALLSEND Tyne & Wear Map**12** NZ26
☆☆☆☆**Europa Lodge** Coast Rd (Grand Met) ☎628989 Telex no53583
182⇌⋒ Lift ☽ ⋒ CTV in bedrooms 200P ⚓ Live music & dancing 4nights wkly ♘ International. Last dinner9.45pm ♉ ☑ S% ✱sB&B⇌⋒£14.50 dB&B⇌⋒£19 ⊟ Credit cards 1 2 3 4 5 6

WALSALL West Midlands Map**7** SP09
★★★**Barons Court** Walsall Rd, Walsall Wood (3m NE A461) ☎Brownhills6543 Telex no338212
78rm(75⇌⋒) 11⊟ Lift ☽ ⋒ CTV in bedrooms 160P Live music & dancing Fri & Sat ♘ English & French. Last dinner9.45pm ♉ sB&B fr£14.50 sB&B⇌⋒ fr£18 dB&B fr£21 dB&B⇌⋒ fr£26 Lunch fr£4.50&alc Dinner fr£5.25&alc Wine£3.75 ⊟ Credit cards 1 2 3 5 6

☆☆☆**Walsall Crest Motel** Birmingham Rd (Crest) ☎33555
106⇌⋒ Lift ☽ CTV in bedrooms 300P ♡English & French. Last dinner 10pm ✿ ☐ S% ✻sB&B⇌⋒£16.25 dB&B⇌⋒£22.78 Continental breakfast ⊟ Credit cards 1 2 3 4 5 6

★★**County** Birmingham Rd (Queens) ☎32323
Large house with Tudor façade and half-timbered gabled modern extension, situated on main road close to town centre.
47rm(3⇌⋒) ☽ ⋈ CTV CTV in bedrooms 35P ♡French. Last dinner 9.45pm ✿ S% sB&B£12 sB&B⇌⋒£13 dB&B£16.50 dB&B⇌⋒£17.50 Lunch£4.25&alc Dinner£4.75&alc Wine£3.25 ⊟ Credit cards 1 2 3 5 6

★★***Royal*** Ablewell St ☎24555
36⇌⋒ Lift ☽ ⋈ TV in bedrooms ⊘ 40P Disco Fri Last dinner 9.30pm ✿ ☐ Credit cards 1 2 3 5

XX***Kubilays*** 110 Lichfield St ☎35699
Closed Sun, Mon & Public Hols; 52seats ♡English, French & Turkish. Last dinner 10pm

WALSHFORD North Yorkshire Map**8** SE45
❀XXX**Bridge Inn** (Byron Room) Great North Road ☎Wetherby62345
Closed Mon, 1st wk Jan, last wk Jul & 1st wk Aug; Dinner not served Sun; 60seats 100P ♡International. Specialities: Hot creamed shrimps, guinea fowl with juniper berries, fresh lemon posset. Last dinner 10pm S% ✻Lunch£4.25–£8.95 Dinner£7.25–£10.95 Credit cards 1 2 3 4 5

WALTHAM, GREAT Essex Map**5** TL61
XX***Windmill*** Chelmsford ☎360292
Small country pub with Victorian atmosphere.
Closed Sun (Public Hol wknds only); Lunch not served Sat; 50seats 50P Last dinner 9.30pm

WANSFORD Cambridgeshire Map**4** TL09
★★**Haycock Inn** ☎Stamford782223
Datestone over the lounge fireplace shows 1632, the date when this ancient posting house was rebuilt. It contains a Brew House, cock fighting loft, Elizabethan granary and a large courtyard.
20rm(6⇌⋒) Annexe: 5rm(1⇌⋒) 3⊟ ☽ ⋈ CTV in bedrooms ⊘ 100P 2⌂ ⚓ Last dinner 10pm ✿ ☐ S% sB&B fr£11 dB&B fr£18.50 dB&B⇌⋒ fr£22 Bar lunch£1.50alc Dinner£7.50alc Wine£3.90 ⊟ Credit cards 1 2 3 5

WANTAGE Oxfordshire Map**4** SU48
★★**Bear** Market Pl ☎66366
18rm(2⇌⋒) ⋈ TV in bedrooms 6P 2⌂ Live music & dancing Sat Last dinner 10pm ✿ ☐ Wine£3.25 ⊟ *xmas* Credit cards 1 3

WARE Hertfordshire Map**5** TL31
☆☆☆**Cannons Moat House** Baldock St (Queens) ☎5011
Modern two-storied brick building, with good car parking.
Closed Xmas; 50⇌⋒ Lift ☽ ⋈ CTV CTV available in bedrooms ⊘ 100P Live music & dancing Fri & Sat Conference facilities available ♡English & French. Last dinner 9.30pm ✿ ☐ S% sB&B⇌⋒ fr£18.50 dB&B⇌⋒ fr£25 Lunch fr£4.50 Dinner fr£4.50 Wine£4 ⊟ Credit cards 1 2 3 5 6

WAREHAM Dorset Map**3** SY98
★★★**Priory** Church Green ☎2772
Credit cards 1 2 3
(No further information available at time of going to press)

★***Black Bear*** South St (Eldridge Pope) ☎3280
Double-fronted, bow-windowed inn with stone porch, situated near river.
12rm(1⇌⋒) ⋈ CTV 4P Last dinner 9pm ✿ ☐ Credit cards 1 6

★**Red Lion** The Square ☎2843
14rm CTV ⊘ 8P Last dinner 9.30pm ✿ ⊟

WARK Northumberland Map**12** NY87
★**Battlesteads** ☎30209
Converted 16th-C farmhouse, stone-built, standing on outskirts of small village.
Closed Xmas Day; 6rm ⋈ TV 50P ⚓ Last dinner 9pm ✿ ✻sB&B fr£7.50 dB&B fr£12.50 Lunch£3.50 Dinner£5alc Wine£2.50 ⊟

WARMINSTER Wiltshire Map**3** ST84
★★★♔**Bishopstrow House** Boreham Rd (2m SE A36) ☎212312
(See page 56 for details)

★★**Old Bell** Market Pl ☎212097
18rm(5⇌⋒) ⋈ CTV in bedrooms ⊠ ♡Mainly grills. Last dinner 10.30pm ✿ ✻sB&B£11 sB&B⇌⋒£13 dB&B£17.50 dB&B⇌⋒£19 Lunch£4alc Dinner£4alc Wine£2.50 ⊟ Credit cards 1 3 5 6

WARRINGTON Cheshire Map**7** SJ68
★★★**Paddington House** Old Manchester Rd ☎Padgate816767
36⇌⋒ Lift ☽ ⋈ TV in bedrooms 100P 2⌂ ⚓ Disco wkly Live music & dancing wkly ♿ ♡English & French. Last dinner 9.30pm ✿ ☐ sB&B⇌⋒£12.95 dB&B⇌⋒£19.50 Lunch£3.75&alc Tea£1.50–£2.60 Dinner£4.75&alc Wine£2

W

★★**Patten Arms** Parker St (Greenall Whitley) ☎36602
Tall brick-built hotel with modern extension. Close to the railway station and town centre.
Closed Xmas Day; 46rm(27⇌⋒) ☽ CTV TV in bedrooms 25P ♀English & French. Last dinner9pm S% sB&B£12.50–£15 sB&B⇌⋒£15.50–£18 dB&B£17.50–£20 dB&B⇌⋒£21–£25 Lunch£3–£4&alc Dinner£4.75–£6&alc Wine£3.20
Credit cards ① ② ③ ⑤

★**Rockfield** 3 Alexandra Rd, Grappenhall (1¾m SE off A50) ☎62898
9rm Annexe: 8rm(2⇌⋒) CTV 25P
Last dinner9pm sB&B£9.50 sB&B⇌⋒£13 dB&B£16 dB&B⇌⋒£20 Lunch£3–£3.50&alc Dinner£3.78–£4.10&alc Wine£3
Credit cards ① ③ ⑥

WARWICK Warwickshire Map**4** SP26

★★**Crown** Coventry Rd ☎42087
18th-C coaching inn of two-storeys, with pillared entrance porch. Dovecote in courtyard.
12rm CTV 12P Last dinner9pm S% sB&B£7 dB&B£14 Lunch£3.25&alc Tea35p Dinner£3.80&alc Wine£2.10

★★**Lord Leycester** Jury St (Norfolk Capital) ☎41481 Telex no23241
44rm(14⇌⋒) ☽ CTV 35P Last dinner9.45pm S% sB&B£11.70 sB&B⇌⋒£15.25 dB&B£19.90 dB&B⇌⋒£23.40
Lunch fr£3.25&alc Tea fr£1.25 Dinner fr£4.25&alc Wine£4 *xmas* Credit cards ① ② ③ ⑤ ⑥

★★***Warwick Arms*** High St ☎42759
18th-C stone coaching inn close to 16th-C Leycester Hospital.
30rm(6⇌⋒) CTV 30P ♀English & French. Last dinner9pm Credit cards ① ② ③ ⑤

★★**Woolpack** Market Pl (Crest) ☎41684
Early 18th-C three storey building with small courtyard; some original beams and panelling.
26rm(6⇌⋒) CTV CTV in bedrooms 50P 250 Last dinner9.30pm S% ✱sB&B£10.80 sB&B⇌⋒£15.66 dB&B£17.82 dB&B⇌⋒£23.22 Credit cards ① ② ③ ④ ⑤ ⑥

✕✕✕**Saxon Mill** Guys Cliffe ☎42255
Ancient stone mill, partly Norman, with working water-wheel; in pleasant setting on banks of Avon.
Closed Mon; Dinner not served Sun; 120seats 100P Disco Tue & Sat ♀English & French. Last dinner9.30pm ✱Lunch£3.50alc Dinner£7.15alc Wine£2.50
Credit cards ① ② ③ ⑤ ⑥

✕✕✕**Westgate Arms** Bowling Green St ☎42362
Large white building housing a traditional restaurant of red plush and panelling, with large windows giving views of lawns and surrounding countryside.
Closed Sun; 75seats 50P ♀English & French. Specialities: Filet de boeuf choron, filet de sole royale mousseline, canard au champagne. Last dinner10.30pm ✱Lunch£3.50&alc Dinner£6alc Wine£2.55 Credit cards ① ② ③ ⑤ ⑥

✕✕***Aylesford*** High St ☎42799
Closed Sun, Public Hols & last 3wks Jul; 85seats ♀Continental. Last dinner10pm
Credit cards ① ② ③ ⑤

WASHINGTON Tyne & Wear Map**12** NZ35

☆☆☆**Post House** (Trusthouse Forte) ☎462264 Telex no537574
145⇌⋒ Lift ☽ CTV in bedrooms 198P 3 Conference facilities available Last dinner10.30pm S% sB&B⇌⋒ fr£19.75 dB&B⇌⋒ fr£28.50 *xmas* Credit cards ① ② ③ ④ ⑤ ⑥

WATCHET Somerset Map**3** ST04
★**Downfield** St Decuman's Rd ☎31267
Closed Xmas 8rm CTV 12P Last dinner8pm
sB&B£8.50–£10 dB&B£17–£20
Dinner£5.50–£7.50 Wine£2.90

WATERBEACH West Sussex Map**4** SU80
★★★**Richmond Arms** (Kingsmead) ☎Halnaker361
Ivy-clad country inn in quiet situation close to Goodwood Park and Duke of Richmond's estates.
20rm(12⇌ ⋒) CTV 100P English & French.
Last dinner10pm *sB&B£13
sB&B⇌ ⋒£16.50 dB&B⇌ ⋒£24
Lunch£3.65–£3.85 Tea40p
Dinner£3.65–£4.20&alc Wine£3.25 *xmas*
Credit cards 1 2 3 5 6

WATERGATE BAY Cornwall Map**2** SW86
★★**Tregurrian** ☎St Mawgan280
Closed Oct–Apr 28rm(10⇌ ⋒) CTV 22P
(heated) Children under 2yrs not accommodated
Last dinner7pm S% sB&B£7–£10
dB&B£14–£20 dB&B⇌ ⋒£18–£24
Bar lunch30palc Tea20palc Dinner fr£3.50
Wine£2.55

★**Cleavelands** ☎St Mawgan273
Closed Nov–Apr 28rm(9⇌ ⋒) CTV 40P
Cabaret wkly Last dinner7.30pm S%
Lunch£1–£5 Tea50p–£1 Dinner£4–£6
Wine£2.70

WATERMILLOCK Cumbria Map**12** NY42
★★★**Leeming House** Ullswater
☎Pooley Bridge444
A small Georgian residence, elegantly furnished and run more as a country residence than a hotel.
Closed Dec–14Feb; 17rm(13⇌ ⋒) 1 CTV
CTV available in bedrooms 50P Children
under 8yrs not accommodated English & French.
Last dinner9pm S% *sB&B£16.50
sB&B⇌ ⋒£18.50 dB&B£28 dB&B⇌ ⋒£35
Lunch£3.95–£5.50&alc Tea85palc
High Tea85palc Dinner£6.15–£6.80&alc
Wine£3.50 Credit cards 1 2 3 4 5 6

WATFORD Hertfordshire Map**4** TQ19
☆☆☆**Caledonian** St Albans Rd ☎29212
85⇌ ⋒ Lift CTV in bedrooms Disco wkly
Conference facilities available English & French.
Last dinner9.15pm S% *
SB&B⇌ ⋒£15.50 dB&B⇌ ⋒£21 Lunch£3.25
Dinner£3.75&alc Wine£3.20 *xmas*
Credit cards 1 2 3 5

At **Bushey** (2m SE A41)
☆☆☆**Watford Ladbroke Mercury Motor Inn** Elton Way, Watford bypass (A41) ☎Watford35881
188⇌ ⋒ 200P

WATTON AT STONE Hertfordshire Map**4** TL31
XX***George & Dragon*** ☎285
Closed Sat & Sun; Lunch not served Mon; 32seats
40P Last dinner9.30pm

WEEDON Northamptonshire Map**4** SP65
★★**Crossroads** ☎40354
Closed 25 & 26Dec; 11rm(6⇌ ⋒) CTV in
bedrooms 50P Last dinner10pm
*sB&B fr£12.25 sB&B⇌ ⋒ fr£13.50
dB&B fr£17.25 dB&B⇌ ⋒ fr£19.30
Continental breakfast Lunch£5.50alc
Dinner£6.50alc Wine£3 Credit cards 1 2 3 4 5 6

WELLESBOURNE Warwickshire Map**4** SP25
★★**Kings Head** ☎Stratford-on-Avon840206
Rs 25 & 26Dec 11rm(4⇌ ⋒) CTV CTV available in
bedrooms 40P Live music wkly English &
French. Last dinner9pm S%
sB&B£9–£10 sB&B⇌ ⋒£11–£12
dB&B£16.50–£18.50 dB&B⇌ ⋒£18.50–£20.50
Bar Lunch£2.50–£3.50 Dinner£7.50–£8.50
Wine£3 Credit cards 1 2 3

WELLINGBOROUGH Northamptonshire Map**4** SP86
★**Columbia** 19 Northampton Rd ☎222094
Closed 22Dec–8Jan; 34rm(11⇌ ⋒) CTV 12P
sauna bath Mainly grills. Last dinner7.45pm
S% sB&B£10.80 sB&B⇌ ⋒£12.42
dB&B£15.12 dB&B⇌ ⋒£17.28 Lunch£2.16
Tea80p Dinner£3.50&alc Wine£2

WELLINGTON Salop Map**7** SJ61
See Telford

WELLINGTON Somerset Map**3** ST21
See also Burlescombe
★★**Beam Bridge** Sampford Arundel (2½m SW A38)
☎Greenham672223
7rm CTV 100P English & Continental.
Last dinner9.30pm S% sB&B£7.50–£8
dB&B£14–£16 Lunch fr£2.75&alc
Dinner fr£3.50&alc Wine£2.50
Credit cards 1 2 3 5

WELLS Somerset Map**3** ST54
★★★**Crown** Market Pl ☎73457
14rm(9⇌ ⋒) 4 CTV 14P squash
Last dinner9.30pm sB&B fr£11.50
sB&B⇌ ⋒ fr£13.50 dB&B fr£20.50
dB&B⇌ ⋒ fr£22.50 Lunch£2.80–£4 Tea£1
Dinner£6 Wine£2.85 *xmas*
Credit cards 1 2 3 5 6

★★★**Swan** Sadler St (Best Western) ☎78877
Telex no449658
Three storey building (partly 16th-C and partly Victorian); overlooks west front of Cathedral.
27rm(26⇌ ⋒) 4 CTV TV available in bedrooms

20P Last dinner9.30pm ⚘ ⊡ S% sB&B⇌⋒ fr£15.90 dB&B⇌⋒ fr£28 Lunch£5&alc Tea£1 Dinner£6&alc Wine£3.50 ▤ *xmas* Credit cards 1 2 3

★★White Hart Sadler St ☎72056
10rm(3⇌⋒) Annexe: 5⇌⋒ CTV 10P 5🏠 ⛟ Last dinner8.30pm ⚘ S% sB&B£10–£11 dB&B⇌⋒£14–£15 dB&B£15–£16 dB&B⇌⋒£20–£21 Lunch£2.60–£2.75 Dinner£4alc Wine£2.60 ▤ Credit cards 1 3

★Ancient Gate House Sadler St ☎72029
Gate House in the precincts of Wells Cathedral dating from 1473; faces west front of Cathedral.
Closed 25 & 26Dec; 9rm 📺 CTV ⚐ ♈English & Italian. Last dinner10.30pm ⚘ S% ✱sB&B£8 dB&B£16 Lunch£3.20–£3.50 Dinner£4–£5 Wine£2.95 ▤ Credit cards 1 3 5

WELLS-NEXT-THE-SEA Norfolk Map**9** TF94
★Crown The Buttlands ☎Fakenham710209
13rm 📺 TV 8P 4🏠 ⚓ Last dinner8.30pm ⚘ ⊡ sB&B£10.50 dB&B£21 Bar Lunch£2alc ⛟ Tea33p–36p Dinner£4.50 Wine£3.09 ▤ *xmas*

WELWYN Hertfordshire Map**4** TL21
☆☆Clock Motel ☎6911
Annexe: 21⇌⋒ 📺 CTV in bedrooms ⊘ 350P Live music & dancing Fri & Sat Cabaret Fri & Sat ♿ ♈English & French. Last dinner10pm ⚘ ⊡ sB&B⇌⋒£15 dB&B⇌⋒£20 Lunch fr£3.35&alc Tea fr£1 Dinner fr£4.35&alc Wine£3.95 ▤ *xmas* Credit cards 1 2 3 5 6

☆☆Heath Lodge Motel Danesbury Park Rd (off B197) ☎5101
Converted country house, set in 14 acres of well maintained grounds.
Closed 24Dec–2Jan; Rs Sun; 21rm(17⇌⋒) 📺 CTV in bedrooms 50P 6🏠 ⛟ ⚓ Live music & dancing Sat Last dinner8.50pm S% sB&B£9.18 sB&B⇌⋒£12.96 dB&B⇌⋒£21.60 Lunch fr£3.75 Dinner fr£3.75 Wine£3.50 ▤ Credit cards 2 5

WELWYN GARDEN CITY Hertfordshire Map**4** TL21
★★★Homestead Court Homestead Ln ☎24336 Telex no25102
Modern brick building with garden, situated off Great North Road, close to open country.
Closed Xmas & Public Hols; 58⇌⋒ Lift ☽ 📺 CTV in bedrooms 200P 4🏠 Last dinner9.30pm ⚘ ⊡ S% sB&B⇌⋒£15 dB&B⇌⋒£21 Lunch£4 Tea£2.25 Dinner£5.50 Wine£3.90 Credit cards 1 2 3 6

★★Garden Guessens Court ☎24383
34rm(30⇌⋒) 📺 CTV in bedrooms ⊘ 50P ⛟ ♈French. Last dinner10pm S% sB&B£14 sB&B⇌⋒£14–£16 dB&B£20 dB&B⇌⋒£20 Lunch£8alc Dinner£8alc Wine£2.90 Credit cards 1 2 3 5 6

WEMBLEY Gt London Map**4** TQ18
☆☆☆☆London EuroCrest Empire Way (Crest) ☎01-902 8839 Telex no24837
335⇌⋒ Lift ☽ CTV in bedrooms 30P 200🏠 ♈English & French. ⚘ ⊡ S% ✱sB&B⇌⋒£21.92 dB&B⇌⋒£34.77 ▤ Credit cards 1 2 3 4 5 6

WEMBURY Devon Map**2** SX54
★★🏛*Langdon Court* Down Thomas ☎Plymouth862358
Modernised Elizabethan mansion.
Closed Xmas; 21⇌⋒ CTV 100P ⛟ ⚓ Children under 5yrs not accommodated Last dinner8.30pm ⚘ Credit cards 1 2 3 4 5 6

W

/ENTBRIDGE (nr Pontefract) West Yorkshire Map**8**
:E41
★★★♛**Wentbridge House** ☎Pontefract620444
converted country mansion with pleasant well-kept
rounds situated in quiet village.
:S Xmas; 17rm(13⇌⋒) Annexe: 3rm 1▭ CTV TV in
edrooms 75P 6🏠 ⚓ ♿ 🍷English & French.
ast dinner9.30pm ☕ S% ✱sB&B fr£14.58
;B&B⇌⋒ fr£17.82 dB&B£19.44–£22.14
B&B⇌⋒£25.92–£38.88 Lunch fr£5.13&alc
)inner fr£6.21&alc Wine£4
:redit cards 1 2 3 4 5 6

✕✕✕**Swiss Cottage** (off A1 on B6474)
☎Pontefract620300
50seats 50P Live music wkly 🍷English & French.
.ast dinner9.45pm Lunch£3–£4&alc
)inner£6&alc Wine£2.95 Credit cards 1 2 3 5

WEOBLEY Hereford & Worcester Map**3** SO45
★★**Red Lion** ☎220
14th-C timbered inn situated in village centre.
7⇌⋒ 🛏 CTV in bedrooms 100P 🍷English &
Continental. Last dinner10pm ☕ S%
sB&B⇌⋒£15 dB&B⇌⋒£20 Lunch£3.50
Dinner£6alc Wine£2.75 Credit cards 2 5

★★**Unicorn** ☎230
Closed Nov & mid Jan–Feb; RS Dec–mid Jan; 13rm
CTV ⊘ 100P 🍷English, Chinese & Indian.
Last dinner9pm ✱sB&B fr£7.13 dB&B fr£13.07
Lunch£2–£3 Dinner£2.50–£4 Wine£2.20
Credit cards 1 3

WEST BAY Dorset See **Bridport**

WEST BROMWICH West Midlands Map**7** SP09
☆☆☆**Europa Lodge** Birmingham Rd (Grand Met)
☎01-553 6111 Telex no336232
133⇌⋒ Lift ☽ 🛏 TV available in bedrooms 200P Live
music & dancing Tue & Sun 🍷English & French.
Last dinner10pm ☕ 🍸 S% ✱sB&B⇌⋒£14.50
dB&B⇌⋒£19 🅱 Credit cards 1 2 3 4 5 6

WESTBURY Wiltshire Map**3** ST85
★★**Lopes Arms** Market Pl ☎822403
8rm(2⇌⋒) 🛏 CTV TV available in bedrooms ⊘ 12P
🐕 🍷Mainly grills. Last dinner9.45pm ☕ S%
✱sB&B£11 sB&B⇌⋒£12 dB&B£16
dB&B⇌⋒£17 Lunch£1–£3&alc
Dinner£2.50–£4.50&alc Wine£1.70

WEST CHILTINGTON West Sussex Map**4** TQ01
★★**Roundabout** (1½m S) Monkmead Ln (Best
Western) ☎3123
Tudor style hotel with period furniture, set in
attractive gardens.
Closed 1–23Jan; 18⇌⋒ 2▭ 🛏 CTV 35P 🐕 ⚓
Children under 3yrs not accommodated 🍷 English &
French. Last dinner9pm ☕ S%
sB&B⇌⋒£13.50–£16 dB&B⇌⋒£19.90–£25.15
Lunch£4.50–£4.80 Tea£1.20–£1.50
Dinner£5.60–£6 Wine£3.60 🅱 *xmas*
Credit cards 1 3 4 5 6

WEST COKER Somerset Map**3** ST51
☆☆**Coker Motel** ☎2555
16rm(6⇌⋒) 🛏 CTV TV in bedrooms 90P 8🏠 ⚓ ♿
Live music & dancing Fri & Sat 🍷English & French.
Last dinner9.30pm ☕ sB&B£8.70
sB&B⇌⋒£11.70 dB&B£14.90 dB&B⇌⋒£17.90
Continental breakfast Lunch£2.50alc
High Tea£1.25 Dinner£3.50&alc Wine£2.70
Credit cards 1 2 3 4 5 6

WESTERHAM Kent Map**5** TQ45
★★**Kings Arms** Market Sq ☎63246
Late 18th-C former coaching house standing in
Market Square.
RS Xmas 16rm(2⇌⋒) 🛏 TV TV in bedrooms 30P 6🏠
⚓ Last dinner10pm ☕ 🍸 S% ✱sB&B£10
sB&B⇌⋒£12 dB&B£14 dB&B⇌⋒£16
Lunch£2.85–£5.65&alc Tea60p High Tea£1.75
Dinner£2.85–£5.65&alc Wine£2.95 🅱
Credit cards 1 2 3 5

WESTGATE-ON-SEA Kent Map**5** TR37
★★**Ivyside** 25 Sea Rd ☎Thanet31082
50rm(42⇌⋒) Lift ☽ 🛏 CTV TV in bedrooms ⊘ 35P
⚓ ▭& ⊇(heated) squash sauna bath Disco twice
wkly Live music & dancing twice wkly 🎪
Last dinner9pm ☕ 🍸 sB&B£10–£11
sB&B⇌⋒£10–£11 dB&B⇌⋒£20–£22
Lunch£3.50 Tea80p Dinner£5.25&alc
Wine£2.50 🅱 *xmas*

WEST HARTLEPOOL Cleveland Map**8** NZ53
See **Hartlepool**

WEST KIRBY Merseyside Map**7** SJ28
★★***Dee*** 44 Grange Rd ☎051-625 5532
10rm 🛏 TV 20P Credit card 3

WEST LULWORTH Dorset Map**3** SY88
See Lulworth

WESTON Salop Map**7** SJ52
★★★**Hawkstone Park** (Best Western)
☎Lee Brockhurst611
37rm(9⇌⋒) Annexe: 16⇌⋒ ☽ 🛏 CTV 300P ⚓
⊇(heated) ⛳18 🎾(grass) billiards 🎪 ♿
Last dinner9.30pm ☕ 🍸 sB&B£13
sB&B⇌⋒£15.50 dB&B£26 dB&B⇌⋒£31
Lunch£3.90 Tea£1 High Tea£3.50 Dinner£5
Wine£2.92 🅱 *xmas* Credit cards 1 2 3 5

WESTONBIRT Gloucestershire Map**3** ST89
See also **Tetbury**
★★★**Hare & Hounds** (Best Western) ☎233
Built of Cotswold stone; stands in 9 acres of grounds,
adjacent to 500 acre arboretum.
24rm(19⇌⋒) 🛏 CTV 50P 10🏠 ⚓ 🎾(hard) squash 🎪
Last dinner9pm ☕ 🍸 S% sB&B£12
sB&B⇌⋒£15–£17 dB&B£22
dB&B⇌⋒£26–£28 Lunch£3.50–£4.50&alc
Tea£1 Dinner£5.25–£6&alc Wine£2.50 🅱
xmas Credit cards 1 3 6

WESTON-ON-THE-GREEN Oxfordshire Map**4** SP51
★★★***Weston Manor*** (Best Western)
☎Bletchington621
Impressive 14th-C stone manor house with many
historical associations; standing in own grounds; oak
panelled restaurant.
16rm(8⇌⋒) Annexe: 5rm(3⇌⋒) 2▭ 🛏 CTV 100P 🐕
⚓ ⊇(heated) squash Live music Sat 🍷English &
French. Last dinner9pm ☕ 🍸 🅱
Credit cards 1 2 3 5

WESTON-SUPER-MARE Avon Map**3** ST36
★★★**Grand Atlantic** Beach Rd (Trusthouse Forte)
☎26543
79⇌⋒ Lift ☽ 🛏 CTV TV in bedrooms 250P ⚓
⊇(heated) 🎾(hard) Conference facilities available
Last dinner9pm ☕ 🍸 S% sB&B⇌⋒£17.50
dB&B⇌⋒£31 🅱 *xmas* Credit cards 1 2 3 4 5 6

★★★**Royal** South Pde (Norfolk Capital) ☎23601
Telex no23241
35rm(25⇌⋒) Lift ☽ 🛏 CTV 40P ⚓
Last dinner8.30pm ☕ 🍸 S% sB&B£13.50
sB&B⇌⋒£16.40 dB&B£21.65 dB&B⇌⋒£28.70
Lunch fr£3.25&alc Tea fr£1.25 Dinner fr£4.25&alc
Wine£4 🅱 *xmas* Credit cards 1 2 3 5 6

★★★**Royal Pier** Birnbeck Rd ☎26644
Closed Nov–Mar; 48rm(23⇌⋒) Lift ☽ 🛏 CTV TV
available in bedrooms ⊘ 30P 🐕 billiards
Last dinner8.15pm ☕ 🍸 S%

sB&B£13.50–£14.75 sB&B⇌⋒£14.50–£16.50 dB&B£27–£29.50 dB&B⇌⋒£29–£33 Lunch fr£3.75 Tea fr40p Dinner fr£4.25 Wine£3 Credit cards ① ③

★★Albert Beach Rd ☎21363
Closed 2wks Xmas; 71rm(21⇌⋒) Lift ☽ CTV 24P Last dinner7.30pm ✿ ♕ sB&B£8.40–£10.20 sB&B⇌⋒£11.30–£12.70 dB&B£16.80–£20.40 dB&B⇌⋒£22.60 –£25.40 Lunch fr£3 Dinner fr£3.75 Wine£3 ⊟

★★*Commodore* Sand Bay, Kewstoke ☎28161
20rm(2⇌⋒) ⋈ CTV 50P Live music & dancing wkly Last dinner9pm ✿ ♕ ⊟ Credit cards ① ② ③

★★Dauncey's Claremont Cres ☎21144
Closed 1Jan–7Jan; 48rm(9⇌⋒) Lift CTV ₱ Last dinner6.45pm ✿ ♕ ✱sB&B£7.50 sB&B⇌⋒£8.70 dB&B£15 dB&B⇌⋒£16.20 Lunch£2.40 Tea45p Dinner£3 Wine£2.15 ⊟ *xmas*

★★Grand Panorama 57 South Rd ☎24980
23rm(⇌⋒) CTV CTV available in bedrooms 20P Children under 5yrs not accommodated ♀English & French. Last dinner7.30pm ✿ ♕ sB&B£8.12 dB&B£16.24 dB&B⇌⋒£18.56 Lunch£1.50–£3.50&alc Tea fr45p Dinner£3.49&alc Wine£3.20

★Monte Bello 48 Knightstone Rd ☎22303
Closed 4Oct–Mar; 32rm(9⇌⋒) Lift CTV ⊘ ₱ Last dinner9pm ✿ ♕ sB&B£6.50–£7 sB&B⇌⋒£7–£7.50 dB&B£13–£14 dB&B⇌⋒£14–£15 Lunch£2–£2.50&alc Tea60p–90p High Tea£2–£2.50&alc Dinner£2–£2.50&alc Wine£2.50 Credit cards ① ② ③ ⑥

WEST RUNTON Norfolk Map**9** TG14
★★★*Links Country Park* (Best Western) ☎691
Four-storey, Tudor-style building with own sheltered gardens.
22⇌⋒ Lift ☽ ⋈ 100P ⚘ ♂9 ⌂ ♀English & French. Last dinner10pm ✿ ♕ Wine£3 ⊟ Credit cards ① ② ③ ⑤

❀XXMirabelle Station Rd ☎396
Closed Mon; Dinner not served Sun (Nov–May); 50seats 25P ♀French. Specialities: lobster thermidor, entrecôte tyrolienne, sauté of beef Mirabelle. Last dinner9pm Lunch fr£3.25&alc Dinner fr£5.50&alc Wine£2.75 Credit card ②

WESTWARD HO! Devon Map**2** SS42
★★Buckleigh Grange Buckleigh Rd ☎Bideford4468
Closed Nov & Dec; RS Jan & Feb; 14rm(8⇌⋒) ⋈ CTV TV available in bedrooms 22P ⇎ ⚘ ➹(grass) Last dinner7.30pm S% sB&B£8.80 sB&B⇌⋒£9.90 dB&B£17.60 dB&B⇌⋒£18.70 Lunch£2.20 Tea45p Dinner£3.25 Wine£2.30 ⊟

WEST WITTERING West Sussex Map**4** SZ79
★★Roman Way Hotel & Country Club ☎2229
2⇌⋒ Annexe:8⇌⋒ ⋈ CTV 60P ⋈ ⚘ ⊡(heated) ♂9 ➹(hard) squash sauna bath Disco Fri Last dinner10pm sB&B⇌⋒£19.50 dB&B⇌⋒£25 Continental breakfast Lunch£3.75 Dinner£5.50 Wine£3.75 ⊟ Credit cards ① ② ③ ⑤

WEST WITTON North Yorkshire Map**7** SE08
★Wensleydale Heifer ☎Wensleydale22322
7rm(3⇌⋒) ⋈ CTV 30P ⇎ Last dinner9.30pm ✿ sB&B£10–£12 sB&B⇌⋒£11–£13 dB&B£17–£19 dB&B⇌⋒£19–£21 Lunch£2.50–£3.50 Dinner£3.50&alc Wine£2.50 ⊟ *xmas* Credit card ⑤

W

WEST WOODBURN Northumberland Map**12** NY88
★**Bay Horse Inn** ☎60218
6rm CTV 30P 3 Last dinner9pm
sB&B£6.50–£7.50 dB&B£13–£15 Lunch£2–£4
Dinner£3–£5 Wine£2.50

★**Fox & Hounds** ☎60210
10rm CTV 40P Last dinner7.45pm
sB&B fr£5.40 dB&B fr£10 Lunch fr£1.20
Dinner£2.80–£4 Wine£2.50

WETHERAL Cumbria Map**12** NY45
★★**Crown** ☎60208
Situated in its own grounds, close to the River Eden, famous for its salmon and trout fishing. Within easy distance of some of the finest scenery.
20rm TV 10P 6 Last dinner8.30pm
S% sB&B£9 dB&B£18 Lunch£1.90–£3
Tea40p Dinner£4.80 Wine£2.40

✕**Fantails** ☎60239
Closed Feb; Lunch not served Nov–Mar; 70seats
20P English & French. Last dinner9.30pm
✱Lunch £5.50alc Dinner£5.50alc Wine£2.60
Credit cards 1 2 3 5 6

WETHERBY West Yorkshire Map**8** SE44
☆☆☆**Wetherby Turnpike Motor Inn** (junc A1/A58)
☎63881
72 ☽ CTV in bedrooms 120P Disco wkly (winter) Conference facilities available
International. Last dinner10pm S%
sB&B £18.90–£22.40
dB&B £26.30–£31.80 Lunch£4–£4.75
Dinner£6alc Wine£3.95
Credit cards 1 2 3 5 6

✕✕✕**Cardinal** 16 Bank St ☎62751
Closed Mon, last wk Jul & 1st wk Aug; 75seats 8P
French. Last dinner11pm ✱Dinner£6.95–£8.60
Wine£3.25 Credit cards 1 2 3 5

WETHERINGSETT Suffolk Map**5** TM16
★★**Wetheringsett Manor** ☎Mendlesham545
Country house built in 1843, standing in 20 acres of grounds; ½m from A140.
9rm(5) CTV CTV available in bedrooms 40P
4 English & French. Last dinner9pm
✱sB&B£12 sB&B £13.50 dB&B£16.50
dB&B £17.50 Lunch£3&alc Tea25p
High Tea£1.25–£2.50 Dinner fr£3.50&alc
Wine£2.10 Credit card 1

WEYBOURNE Norfolk Map**9** TG14
★★**Maltings** ☎275
Formerly a manor, malting house and dairy. Original Norfolk flintstone house dates from the 16th century.
12rm(7) CTV in bedrooms 100P sauna bath
French. Last dinner9.30pm
Continental breakfast Credit card 2

✕✕**Gasche's Swiss** ☎220
Closed Mon; Dinner not served Sun; 65seats 40P
English & Continental. Last dinner9pm
✱Lunch£3.45–£3.95&alc
Dinner£5.50–£6.50&alc Wine£2.95 Credit card 2

WEYBRIDGE Surrey Map**4** TQ06
★★★**Oatlands Park** 146 Oatlands Dr (North)
☎47242 Telex no262180
Part Georgian, part Victorian unlicensed hotel with over 60 permanent residents. Set in 35 acres of splendid grounds.
Unlicensed; 145rm(92) 1 Lift ☽ CTV 40P
12 (hard) squash Live music & dancing mthly in winter Conference facilities available
Last dinner8.30pm S% sB&B fr£13
sB&B fr£15 dB&B fr£22.50
dB&B fr£25.50 Lunch fr£4.10 Tea fr£1
Dinner fr£4.65 *xmas* Credit cards 1 2 3 6

★★★**Ship** Monument Green (Thistle) ☎48364
RS Xmas; 39⇌⋒ ☽ ⊞ CTV available in bedrooms 65P Disco wkly Live music & dancing wkly
Last dinner 10pm ♁ ⚐ Credit cards 1 2 3 5 6

✕✕**Casa Romana** 2 Temple Hall, Monument Hill ☎43470
Closed Mon; Lunch not served Sat; 75seats 20P ♕Italian. Last dinner 10.45pm ✱Lunch fr£3.25&alc Dinner£8alc Wine£2.95

✕***Chez Antoine*** Oaklands Village ☎43131
Closed Mon; Lunch not served Sun; 36seats 50P ♕French. Last dinner 11pm Credit cards 2 3 5

WEYMOUTH Dorset Map **3** SY67

★★★**Ingleton** Greenhill ☎785804 Telex no 418225
Closed 22Dec–5Jan; n13rm(5⇌⋒) ⊞ CTV TV available in bedrooms ⊘ 20P ♣ Children under 6 mths not accommodated ♔ ♕French.
Last dinner 9pm ♁ ⚐ sB&B fr£9
sB&B⇌⋒ fr£12 dB&B fr£18 dB&B⇌⋒ fr£24
Lunch£3.50–£4.50 Tea45–65p
High Tea75p–£1.75 Dinner£4.50–£6 Wine£2.25

★★**Crown** 51–52 St Thomas Street ☎785695
51rm(2⇌⋒) Lift ☽ ⊞ CTV 2P 8⌂ Last dinner 7pm ♁ ✱sB&B£6.75–£7.56 sB&B⇌⋒£7.83–£8.64 dB&B£11.88–£13.50 dB&B⇌⋒£12.96–£14.58 Lunch£1.40–£5&alc Dinner fr£2.75&alc Wine£2.15 ⊟ Credit cards 1 3

★★***Golden Lion*** St Edmonds Street ☎786778
Closed Oct–May; 19rm(1⇌⋒) ⊞ CTV ⊕
Last dinner 9.45pm ♁

★★***Kingswood*** Rodwell Rd ☎784926
16rm(3⇌⋒) ⊞ CTV ♣ Live music & dancing twice wkly Cabaret wkly Last dinner 7.30pm ♁ ⚐ ⊟
Credit card 5

★★**Prince Regent** 139 Esplanade ☎71313
Georgian terraced façade on seafront opposite pier.
50rm(14⇌⋒) Lift CTV TV available in bedrooms ⊘ 2⌂ Disco wkly in summer Live music & dancing 3 nights wkly in summer ♕English & French.
Last dinner 8pm ♁ ⚐ S% ✱sB&B£9–£10
sB&B⇌⋒£12–£13 dB&B£18–£20
dB&B⇌⋒£21–£23 Lunch£2.95–£3.50&alc
Tea35p–£1.50 Dinner£3.45–£4&alc Wine£3 ⊟
Credit cards 1 2 3 5

★★**Rembrandt** 12 Dorchester Rd ☎786253
16rm(10⇌⋒) ⊞ CTV TV in bedrooms 30P ⛱ ♕English & French. Last dinner 10pm ♁ ⚐ ✱sB&B£6.50–£7.50 sB&B⇌⋒£8.50–£9.50 dB&B£13–£15 dB&B⇌⋒£17–£19
Lunch£2–£3&alc Tea75p–£1.25
Dinner£2.75–£3&alc Wine£2.90 ⊟ *xmas*
Credit cards 1 3 5

★★**Hotel Rex** 29 The Esplanade ☎73485
Closed 25–26Dec; 20⇌⋒ Lift ☽ ⊞ CTV 8⌂ ⊕ ♕English & French. Last dinner 10.30pm ♁ ⚐ sB&B⇌⋒£7.80–£10 dB&B⇌⋒£14–£18.40 Tea45p Dinner fr£2.25&alc Wine£2.15 ⊟

★★**Streamside** 29 Preston Rd ☎833121
Closed Nov–Mar; RS Apr; 18rm(13⇌⋒)
Annexe: 4rm ⊞ CTV 22P ♣ Live music & dancing twice wkly ♔ Last dinner 7.45pm ♁ ⚐ ✱sB&B£10.50–£12.50 sB&B⇌⋒ fr£12.50 dB&B fr£15 dB&B⇌⋒ fr£18 Tea25p
Dinner fr£3.95&alc Wine£2.50 Credit cards 1 3

★***Weatherbury*** 7 Carlton Road North ☎783484
15rm ⊞ CTV 30P Live music 4 nights wkly
Last dinner 7.30pm ♁ ⚐ Credit card 1

Ⓖ**Bay View** 35 The Esplanade ☎782083
10rm(5⇌⋒) ⊞ CTV in bedrooms P ⊕

Last dinner9.30pm S% sB&B£6.50–£7.50 dB&B£13–£15 dB&B⇌⋒£14.50–£17 Bar lunch60p–£6 High Tea£2.50–£4 Dinner£3alc Wine£1.92 Credit card 1

×Pullinger's Pier Bandstand ☎782021
Modern restaurant on pier head offering panoramic views.
150seats Last dinner10pm ✱Lunch fr£2&alc Tea fr£1&alc Dinner£2–£6&alc Credit cards 1 3

×Sea Cow Bistro Custom House Quay ☎783524
Closed Sun, 9Oct–1Nov & 15Aug; 60seats International. Last dinner10.15pm ✱Lunch£4.50 Dinner£7.50alc Wine£2.70 Credit cards 1 3 5

×Spinnaker Custom House Quay ☎782767
Closed Sun (Oct–May); Lunch not served Sun (Jun–Sep); 80seats 5P English, French, Italian & Spanish. Last dinner10.30pm Lunch£4.50alc Dinner£4.50alc Credit cards 1 3 4 6

WHIPPINGHAM Isle of Wight Map**4** SZ59
★★Padmore House Beatrice Av ☎Cowes293210
11rm(7⇌⋒) CTV in bedrooms 50P (heated) Children under 8yrs not accommodated English & French. Last dinner9pm sB&B£10.25 sB&B⇌⋒£13.25 dB&B£20.50 dB&B⇌⋒£30 Lunch£3.95–£4.95 Tea55p–£1 Dinner£5.50–£7.50 Wine£3.25 Credit cards 1 2 3 5

WHIPSNADE Bedfordshire Map**4** TL01
××Old Hunters Lodge ☎872228
Pleasant thatched cottage in own grounds, near The Downs and Whipsnade Zoo.
Closed Mon; 50seats 30P English & French. Last dinner9.30pm Lunch£4–£4.50&alc Dinner£8.50alc Wine£2.60 Credit card 5

WHITBY North Yorkshire Map**8** NZ81
★★*Royal* West Cliff ☎2234
135rm(66⇌⋒) Lift CTV Disco nightly Live music & dancing nightly in season Last dinner8pm

★Marvic White Point Rd ☎2400
Closed Nov–Mar; 28rm CTV 50P
Last dinner7.30pm sB&B£8.50 dB&B£17 Lunch£3 Tea45p Dinner£4 Wine£2.25

★Saxonville Ladysmith Av (off Argyle Rd) ☎2631
Closed Nov–Mar; RS May & Oct; 22rm(4⇌⋒) CTV CTV available in bedrooms 20P Children under 4yrs not accommodated Last dinner7.15pm S% sB&B fr£8 dB&B fr£16 dB&B⇌⋒ fr£18 Lunch fr£2.50 Dinner fr£4.25 Wine£2.50

★White House Upgang Ln, West Cliff ☎2098
RS Oct–May; 12rm(2⇌⋒) CTV 30P Last dinner7pm S% sB&B£7.50–£9.50 dB&B£15–£19 dB&B⇌⋒£18–£23 Bar lunch70p–£1.75 Tea fr£1 Dinner£4–£5.50 Wine£2.50

WHITCHURCH Hampshire Map**4** SU44
★★White Hart Newbury St ☎2900
7rm Annexe:8rm CTV 25P 8 English & French. Last dinner9.30pm sB&B£12 dB&B£18 Lunch£7alc Tea fr£1.25 Dinner£8alc Wine£3.50 Credit cards 1 2 3 5 6

WHITCHURCH Hereford & Worcester Map**3** SO51
★*Doward* Crockers Ash ☎Symonds Yat890267
8rm CTV 50P English & French.
Last dinner9.30pm Credit cards 2 4 5

W

WHITCHURCH Salop Map**7** SJ54
See also **Redbrook, Clwyd, Wales**
★★**Dodington Lodge** Dodington ☎2539
9rm(3⇌ ⋒) ⌘ CTV 4P 2⌂ ⚓ ♡English & French.
Last dinner9pm ♁ ⌼ sB&B£9.50–£14
sB&B⇌⋒£12.50–£17 dB&B£15–£19
dB&B⇌⋒£18–£22 Lunch£2–£3&alc
Tea40p–£1.50&alc High Tea75p–£3
Dinner£3–£4.50&alc Wine£3.20 ⊟ Credit card 3

★★**Victoria** High St ☎2031
8rm TV 20P 3⌂ Last dinner9pm ♁ ⌼
sB&B£7.50 dB&B£15 Lunch£2.50–£3
Tea50p–£1 High Tea£2.50alc Dinner£6alc
Wine£3.75

★**Hollies Motel** 23 Chester Rd ☎2184
Closed Xmas; 6rm Annexe: 10⇌ ⋒ ⌘ CTV CTV available in bedrooms 70P ⌗ ♡Mainly grills.
Last dinner10pm sB&B£12 sB&B⇌⋒£15
dB&B£17 dB&B⇌⋒£20 Lunch£4alc
Dinner£5alc Wine£2.65 Credit cards 1 2 3 4 5 6

★***Witch Ball*** Prees Heath (2½m S A41) ☎3234
7rm ⌘ CTV 100P ⚓ ⌓ Last dinner9.30pm ♁ ⌼

WHITEHAVEN Cumbria Map**11** NX91
★★**Chase** Corkickle ☎3656
18rm(4⇌ ⋒) ⌘ CTV CTV available in bedrooms 60P
⚓ ⌘ ♡English & French. Last dinner9pm ♁ ⌼
sB&B£7.50 sB&B⇌⋒£8.50 dB&B£15
dB&B⇌⋒£16.50 Lunch£2.80 Tea60p
Dinner£3.50&alc Wine£3.25 Credit cards 1 3 5

★★**⚘Roseneath** Low Moresby (3m NE off A595)
☎61572
Closed Xmas Day; 6rm(4⇌ ⋒) ⌘ TV available in bedrooms ⊘ 25P ⌗ ⚓ Children under 12yrs not accommodated Last dinner7.45pm S%
sB&B fr£8.50 sB&B⇌⋒ fr£11 dB&B fr£19
dB&B⇌⋒ fr£21 Lunch fr£3.95 Tea fr£1.20
Dinner fr£6.95 Wine£2.60 Credit cards 1 2 3

★★**Waverley** Tangier St ☎4337
24rm(1⇌ ⋒) ⌘ CTV TV available in bedrooms ⊘ 14P
♡Mainly grills. Last dinner8pm ♁ S%
✱sB&B£8.10–£10.26 sB&B⇌⋒£10.26
dB&B£15.12–£16.20 dB&B⇌⋒£18.36
Lunch£3.50alc Dinner£4alc Wine£2.23
Credit cards 1 3

WHITLEY BAY Tyne & Wear Map**12** NZ37
★★**Holmedale** Park Av ☎523121
Closed 25Dec–1Jan; 25rm CTV TV available in bedrooms 10P ⌗ ♡English & French.
Last dinner9.50pm ♁ S% ✱sB&B£7.13
dB&B£11.88 Dinner£4alc Wine£2.45
Credit cards 1 3

★**Newquay** South Pde ☎532211
17rm(3⇌ ⋒) ⌘ CTV TV in bedrooms ⊘ 18P
Last dinner7.50pm ♁ ⌼ S% sB&B£8.50
sB&B⇌⋒£10 dB&B£16 dB&B⇌⋒£18
Lunch£2&alc Tea£1.50 Dinner£3.75&alc
Wine£2.50 ⊟ *xmas*

WHITSTABLE Kent Map**5** TR16
★★**Marine** Marine Pde, Tankerton (1m E) ☎272672
32rm(4⇌ ⋒) ⌘ CTV 20P 3⌂ ⌗ billiards
Last dinner8.15pm ♁ ⌼ S% sB&B£11–£12
sB&B⇌⋒£13–£15 dB&B£21–£23
dB&B⇌⋒£24–£26 Lunch£3.50&alc
Dinner£4.75&alc Wine£2.90 ⊟ Credit cards 1 3

XX***Giovanni's*** 49–51 Canterbury Rd ☎273034
Closed Mon; 55seats 14P ♡English, French & Italian. Last dinner10.45pm Credit cards 1 3 5 6

XX**Windmill** Borstal Hill ☎272866
Closed Sun; Lunch not served Sat; 45seats 30P
bedrooms available ♡English & French.
Last dinner7pm Lunch fr£3.50&alc Dinner£10alc
Wine£3 Credit cards 1 3 5 6

❀X**Le Pousse Bedaine** 101 Tankerton Rd, Tankerton (1m E) ☎272056
(Rosette awarded for dinner only)
Closed Sun & Mon; Lunch not served Tue–Fri;
36seats P ♡French. Last dinner11pm
Credit cards 1 3 5 6

WHITTINGTON Salop Map**7** SJ33
★**Ye Olde Boot Inn** (Frederic Robinson)
☎Oswestry62250
7rm ⌘ CTV 100P Last dinner9.30pm ♁ S%
sB&B£5.50 dB&B£11 Lunch fr£2.70&alc
Dinner fr£2.85&alc Wine£2.50

WHITTINGTON Staffordshire Map**7** SO88
XX**Whittington Inn** (on A449) ☎Kinver2110
Closed Sun & Mon; 40seats 230P ♡French.
Wine£4 Credit cards 2 5

WHITTLESEY Cambridgeshire Map**4** TL29
XX**Falcon** London St ☎Peterborough203247
Closed Xmas Day; 36 seats 40P
Last dinner10.30pm S% Lunch£7.75alc
Dinner£7.75alc Wine£3.70
Credit cards 1 2 3 4 5 6

WHITWELL-ON-THE-HILL North Yorkshire Map**8** SE76
★★**⚘Whitwell Hall** ☎551
12⇌ ⋒ Annexe: 8⇌ ⋒ 1⊟ ⌘ CTV available in bedrooms 40P 4⌂ ⚓ ⚘(hard) Children under12yrs not accommodated Last dinner8.30pm ♁ ⌼
✱sB&B⇌⋒£8–£14 dB&B⇌⋒£26–£28
Lunch£3.70 Tea60p High Tea fr£3 Dinner£6.50
Wine£2.75 ⊟ *xmas* Credit cards 1 2 3 5

WICKEN (Milton Keynes, Bucks) Northamptonshire Map**4** SP73
★★**⚘Wicken** Cross Tree Rd ☎239
Closed 25 & 26Dec; 13rm(5⇌ ⋒) ⌘ CTV CTV in bedrooms 10P ⌗ ⚓ ⌓(heated) Last dinner9.15pm
♁ ⌼ ✱sB&B£12.50 sB&B⇌⋒£13.50

W

3&B£19 dB&B⇌⋒£21 Lunch£3.80alc
a fr50p&alc High Tea fr70p&alc Dinner£4.75alc
ine£3.15 Credit cards 1 2 3 5

ICKHAM Hampshire Map 4 SU51
★★**Old House** ☎833049
osed Xmas wk, 2wks Etr, 2wks Jul/Aug; 10⇌⋒ ⋈
TV ⊘ 12P ⇌ ♔ French. Specialities: mousseline
sole au beurre blanc, bouillabaisse de poulet au
ernod, agneau farci en croûte. Last dinner 9.30pm
% sB&B⇌⋒£17 dB&B⇌⋒£26 Dinner£8alc
ine£3.95 Credit cards 1 3

ICKHAM MARKET Suffolk Map 5 TM35
★**White Hart** (Best Western) ☎746203
5th-C coaching inn on A12.
0rm CTV 25P ⚓ English & Continental.
ast dinner 8.30pm ✿ sB&B£13.60
3&B£22.55 Lunch£1.65–£4.25
nner fr£4.50&alc Wine£2.50 ⊟
redit cards 1 2 3 5

IDECOMBE-IN-THE-MOOR Devon Map 3 SX77
★**Wooder Manor** (Best Western) ☎240
elex no 8814912
arly Georgian manor house in 2½ acres of wooded rounds, situated ½ mile north of village on Moretonhampstead road. Fine antique furniture. uperb views of Dartmoor landscape.
osed Dec–Feb; 10rm(5⇌⋒) ⋈ TV ⊘ 20P 3⌂ ⇌
Last dinner 8.30pm ✿ S%
3&B£8.50–£12.15 sB&B⇌⋒£9.50–£13.50
3&B£17–£21.60 dB&B⇌⋒£19–£24.30
ar lunch£1.35 Dinner£5.40 Wine£3 ⊟
redit cards 1 2 3 4 5 6

IDEMOUTH BAY Cornwall Map 2 SS20
★**Trelawny** Marine Dr ☎328
losed Oct–Mar; RS Apr (no lunch); 10rm ✕ CTV
5P ⚓ Children under 4yrs not accommodated
ast dinner 7pm ✿ S% ✱sB&B£8.50–£10.50
3&B£17–£21 Bar lunch 70p–£1.50
inner£3.50–£6 Wine£1.70 ⊟ Credit cards 1 3

Brocksmoor ☎207
ungalow, country-house style hotel, within own rounds with spacious lawns, putting green and utdoor swimming pool.
losed Oct; 10rm(1⇌⋒) ⋈ CTV ⊘ 20P ⇌ ⚓ ⇨
hildren under 3yrs not accommodated English &
ontinental. Last dinner 10pm ✿ ☕ S%
3&B£8.50–£9.50 dB&B£17–£20
ar lunch 50p–£1.25 Tea 50p–£1
inner£3–£4.50&alc Wine£3 ⊟ *xmas*

IDMERPOOL Nottinghamshire Map 8 SK62
Pullman Inn ☎Kinoulton 300
converted railway station with a restaurant on the latform. Trains still run through station during the ay as it is a BR test track.
losed Sun; Lunch not served Sat; 50seats 200P
English & French. Last dinner 10pm S%
unch£4.75alc Dinner£6.50alc Wine£4.25
redit cards 1 2 3 5 6

IGAN Gt Manchester Map 7 SD50
★★★**Brocket Arms** Mesnes Rd (Embassy) ☎46283
4rm(22⇌⋒) ☽ ⋈ CTV TV in bedrooms 60P
ast dinner 9pm ✿ S% sB&B⇌⋒£15
B&B⇌⋒£18.50 Lunch£5.50&alc
inner£5.50&alc Wine£4.50
redit cards 1 2 3 4 5 6

★★***Bellingham*** 149 Wigan Ln ☎43893
8rm(13⇌⋒) ⋈ CTV TV available in bedrooms 25P
⚓ English & Scottish. Last dinner 8.30pm ✿ ☕
redit card 3

★***Bel Air*** 236 Wigan Ln ☎41410
2rm(7⇌⋒) ⋈ CTV TV available in bedrooms 6P
English & French. Last dinner 10pm
redit cards 1 6

At **Standish** (4m NW A49)
☆☆☆**Cassinelli's Almond Brook Motor Inn** Almond Brook Rd ☎Standish 421504
42rm(44⇌⋒) 200P

WIGTON Cumbria Map 11 NY24
★★**Greenhill Mansion** Red Dial (2m S off A595)
☎3304
8rm(1⇌⋒) 2⊟ ⋈ CTV TV available in bedrooms
100P ⚓ English & French. Last dinner 9.30pm ✿
☕ ✱sB&B£7.50–£10.50 dB&B£15–£18.50
dB&B⇌⋒£17–£22 Lunch£3.50–£4.50
Tea 50p–£1.50 High Tea£2.50–£4
Dinner£4.50–£6.50&alc Wine£2.60 Credit card 1

★★**Kildare** High St ☎2182
8rm(1⇌⋒) CTV TV available in bedrooms ⊘ 20P ⇌
English & French. Last dinner 10.30pm ✿ ☕
S% sB&B fr£8.50 dB&B fr£14,50 Lunch fr£3.50
Tea fr£1.35 Dinner fr£4.50 Wine£2
Credit cards 1 3 6

WILLERBY Humberside Map 8 TA03
★★★**Willerby Manor** Well Ln ☎Hull 6532616
RS Xmas; 37rm(22⇌⋒) ☽ ⋈ CTV TV in bedrooms ⊘
150P ⚓ French. Last dinner 9.45pm ✿ S%
✱sB&B£11.85 sB&B⇌⋒£13.75
dB&B⇌⋒£21.60 Lunch fr£3.50
Dinner£3.75–£4.75 Wine£2.85 ⊟
Credit cards 1 2 3 5 6

WILLITON Somerset Map 3 ST04
★★***White House*** Long St ☎32306
Closed Nov–Apr; 8rm(1⇌⋒) Annexe: 5rm(4⇌⋒) ⋈
CTV 21P ⇌ French. Last dinner 8.15pm

WILMCOTE Warwickshire Map 4 SP15
★★**Swan House** ☎Stratford-upon-Avon 67030
Small inn (partly 18th-C) with courtyard and well.
Closed Xmas Day; 7rm(1⇌⋒) ⋈ CTV ⊘ 35P
English & French. Last dinner 9.30pm ✿ ☕
S% ✱sB&B£9.44 dB&B£18.82
dB&B⇌⋒£21.20 Bar lunch£1.35alc Tea 80palc
Dinner£5.75alc Wine£3.20 Credit cards 1 3

WILMINGTON Devon Map 3 SY29
★★**Home Farm** ☎278
Converted, colour-washed, thatched cottages in pleasant rural setting off A35.
Closed Jan & Feb; 7rm(3⇌⋒) ⋈ CTV 25P 2⌂ ⇌ ⚓
French. Last dinner 9.30pm S% sB&B£15–£17
sB&B⇌⋒£17.50 dB&B£22–£26
dB&B⇌⋒£28–£30 Lunch£4.50–£6&alc
Dinner£7.50–£8.50&alc Wine£3.50 ⊟ *xmas*

WILMSLOW Cheshire Map 7 SJ88
★★**Stanneylands** Stanneylands Rd ☎525225
25rm(13⇌⋒) ☽ ⋈ CTV in bedrooms ⊘ 120P ⇌ ⚓
International. Last dinner 10pm ✿ ☕ S%
✱sB&B£15.25 sB&B⇌⋒£20.50 dB&B£22.50
dB&B⇌⋒£28.50 Lunch fr£4.75&alc Dinner£8alc
⊟ Credit cards 1 2 3 4 5 6

✕✕**Mandarin** Parsonage Green ☎24096
Closed Xmas; 80seats 27P Chinese.
Last dinner 11.30pm ✱Lunch£1.30–£1.80&alc
Dinner£5alc Wine£3.30 Credit card 3

WILTON Wiltshire Map 4 SU03
★★**Pembroke Arms** ☎3127
Mellow, brick, creeper-clad building close to historic Wilton House.
RS Xmas Day; 8rm CTV 50P ⚓ ⟿ Disco Sat English
& French. Last dinner 10pm ✿ S%
sB&B£7.85–£8.85 dB&B£12.65–£14.50
Lunch fr£2.50&alc Dinner£4.35alc Wine£2.35
Credit card 1

1 Chantry Mead ★★
2 Elizabethan ✕✕
3 Momtaj Mahal ✕
4 Oriel ★★
5 Royal ★★★
6 Splinters ✕✕
8 Stanmore ★★
9 Wessex ★★★
10 Westacre ★★
11 Winchester ★★
12 Winton Court ★★

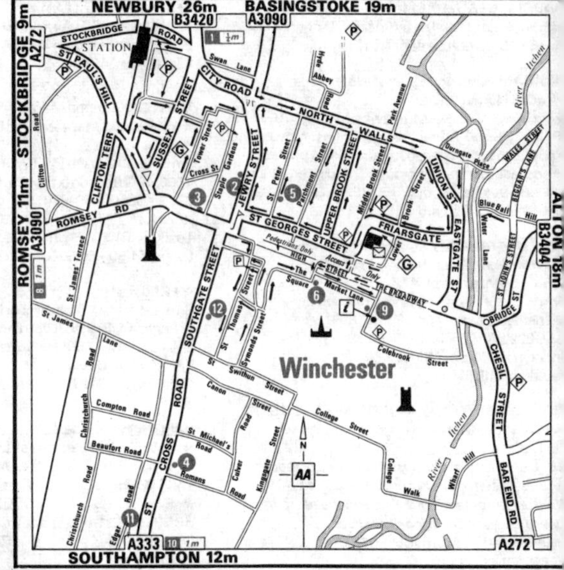

WIMBORNE MINSTER Dorset Map**4** SZ09
★★★**King's Head** The Square (Trusthouse Forte) ☎880101
28rm(10⇌⋒) Lift ⚗ CTV TV in bedrooms 25P Last dinner9.15pm ✿ ⊈ S% sB&B£12 sB&B⇌⋒£15 dB&B£19 dB&B⇌⋒£22 ⊟ *xmas* Credit cards 1 2 3 4 5 6

At **Ferndown** (4m E junc A31/A348)
☆☆**Coach House Motel** Tricketts Cross ☎Ferndown89122
32⋒ 285P

WINCANTON Somerset Map**3** ST72
★★**Dolphin** High St ☎32215
Stone-built, single-storey terraced building with lattice windows and courtyard.
10rm(4⇌⋒) CTV 10P 2⌂ Last dinner8.30pm ✿ sB&B£10 sB&B⇌⋒£11 dB&B£20 dB&B⇌⋒£22 Lunch£2.50alc Tea75p Dinner£3.50alc Wine£2.25 Credit card 1

★★**Holbrook House** Castle Cary Rd (Best Western) ☎32377
Large country house (dating from 1685) in wooded grounds.
20rm(10⇌⋒) ⚗ CTV 40P 6⌂ ⚘ ⚓ ⌒(heated) ⚲(hard/grass) squash Last dinner8.30pm ✿ ⊈ S% sB&B£12–£12.50 sB&B⇌⋒£14–£14.50 dB&B£24–£25 dB&B⇌⋒£28–£29 Lunch£3.50–£4.50&alc Tea40–75p High Tea£1–£3 Dinner£4.50–£5&alc Wine£3.20 ⊟ *xmas* Credit cards 1 2 3 4 6

WINCHCOMBE Gloucestershire Map**4** SP02
★★**George Inn** High St ☎602331
This fine old inn dates back some 700 years. It has a courtyard with lion-headed door and in the lounge is a Tudor fireplace.
12rm(3⇌⋒) Annexe:4rm CTV ⊘ 12P ⚘ ⚓ Last dinner8.45pm ✿ ⊈ sB&B fr£10.75 sB&B⇌⋒ fr£12 dB&B fr£21.50 sB&B⇌⋒ fr£24 Lunch fr£4.50&alc Dinner fr£6.25&alc Credit cards 2 3 6

WINCHESTER Hampshire Map**4** SU42 **See plan**
★★★★**Wessex** Paternoster Row (Trusthouse Forte) ☎61611 Telex no47419 Plan**9**
Modern, two-storey brick building in pillars in Cathedral precincts.
94⇌⋒ Lift ☽ ⚗ CTV in bedrooms 40P Conference facilities available Last dinner10pm ✿ ⊈ S% sB&B⇌⋒£25 dB&B⇌⋒£33.50 ⊟ Credit cards 1 2 3 4 5 6

★★★**Royal** St Peter Street ☎3468 Plan**5**
Originally a private house, but became a convent in 18th century. A raised altar is still visible in one of the bedrooms.
30rm(10⇌⋒) 1⊟ ☽ ⚗ CTV CTV available in bedrooms 25P 10⌂ ⚓ Last dinner8.45pm ✿ ⊈ S% sB&B£11–£11.50 sB&B⇌⋒£12.50–£13.50 dB&B£18–£20 dB&B⇌⋒£19.50–£21.50 Lunch£2.75–£3.85 Tea30–50p High Tea75p–£1.25 Dinner£4.50–£5.50 Wine£2.50 *xmas* Credit cards 1 2 3 6

★★**Chantry Mead** Bereweeke Rd ☎2767 Plan**1**
Closed 24Dec & 1Jan; 21rm(8⇌⋒) ⚗ CTV 22P ⚘ ⚓ Last dinner8.30pm ✿ sB&B£7.90 sB&B⇌⋒£13.55 dB&B£15.70 dB&B⇌⋒£22.80 Lunch£3 Dinner fr£3.50 Wine£2.50 Credit cards 1 6

★★**Oriel** 17 St Cross Rd ☎4819 Plan**4**
14rm(2⇌⋒) ⊞ ⚗ CTV ⊘ 50P ⚘ ⚓ ⊕English & Hungarian. Last dinner9.30pm S% sB&B£10 dB&B£16 dB&B⇌⋒£17 Lunch£3–£5 Dinner£4–£6 Wine£3

★★***Stanmore*** (Eldridge Pope) ☎2720 Plan**8**
12rm(3⇌⋒) ⚗ CTV 100P ⚓ Last dinner10.30pm ✿ ⊈ Credit cards 1 2 6

★★**Westacre** Sleepers Hill ☎68403 Plan**10**
17rm(4⇌⋒) ⚗ CTV CTV available in bedrooms 60P ⚓ Live music & dancing 6 nights wkly Children under 12yrs not accommodated ⊕English & Hungarian. Last dinner9.30pm ✿ ⊈ S% *sB&B£9 dB&B£15 dB&B⇌⋒£18 Lunch£2.75–£4.50 Tea£1 Dinner£4.50&alc Wine£2.90

★★**Winchester** St Cross Rd ☎3507 Plan**11**
40rm(6⇌⋒) CTV CTV available in bedrooms 40P billiards Last dinner7pm ✿ ⊈ S% sB&B£7.56–£8.10 sB&B⇌⋒£10.80 dB&B£14.58–£16.20 dB&B⇌⋒£17.28–£19.44 Bar lunch£1.25–£2 Tea75p–£1

gh Tea£1.25–£2 Dinner£3 Wine£3 ⊟
edit cards 1 2

★**Winton Court** Southgate St ☎3664 Plan**12**
rm(10⇌ ⋒) Lift ⊒ ⋔ CTV TV available in bedrooms
4 ⌂ sauna bath Disco wkly ♿ ☺English &
ontinental. Last dinner 8.30pm ✿ sB&B£11.56
&B⇌⋒£12.64 dB&B£17.28 dB&B⇌⋒£18.90
nch fr£3.24 Dinner fr£1.89 Wine£2.81 ⊟

×**Elizabethan** 18–19 Jewry St ☎3566 Plan**2**
uilding approximately 400 years old, originally arders' cottages attached to the old prison in Jewry
.
osed Mon, Good Fri & Xmas Day; Dinner not
rved Sun; 60seats 16P ☺English & French.
st dinner 10pm Lunch£2.60–£3.20&alc
nner£7alc Wine£2.50 Credit cards 1 2 3 5

××**Splinters** 9 Great Minster St ☎64004 Plan**6**
Closed Sun, 25 & 26Dec & Feb; 42seats **P** ☺French.
Last dinner 10.30pm ✱Lunch£5alc
Dinner£7.80alc Wine£2.75 Credit card 2

×**Momtaj Mahal** 84 High St ☎4841 Plan**3**
Closed Xmas Day; 54seats **P** ☺English, Indian &
Spanish. Last dinner 11pm Lunch£1.15–£3.00
Dinner£1.60–£4.50 Wine£2.40
Credit cards 1 2 3 5 6

WINCHMORE HILL Buckinghamshire Map**4** SU99
××**Plough Inn** ☎Amersham 21333
Lunch not served Sat; Dinner not served Sun;
60seats 40P Live music & dancing Wed & Fri
☺English, French & Italian. Last dinner 9.45pm
✱Lunch£3.75–£3.95&alc Dinner£7alc
Credit cards 1 2 3 5

1 Applegarth ⓟ
2 Aquarius ✕✕✕
3 Beech Hill ★★★
4 Belsfield ★★★
5 Bordriggs ★★
6 Burn How Motel ★★★
7 Burnside ★★
8 Cranleigh ★
9 Elleray ★★
10 Grey Walls ★★
11 Hideaway ★★
12 Hydro ★★★
13 Knoll ★
14 Langdale Chase ★★★
15 Linthwaite ★★
16 Low Wood ★★★
17 Miller Howe ❁❁ ★★
18 Mortal Man ★★
19 Old England ★★★★
20 Porthole Eating House ❁✕
21 Priory ★★★
22 Ravensworth ★
23 Royal ★★
24 St Martin's ★★
25 Stag's Head ★★
26 Sun ★★
27 Wild Boar ★★★
28 Willowsmere ⓟ
29 Winander ★★

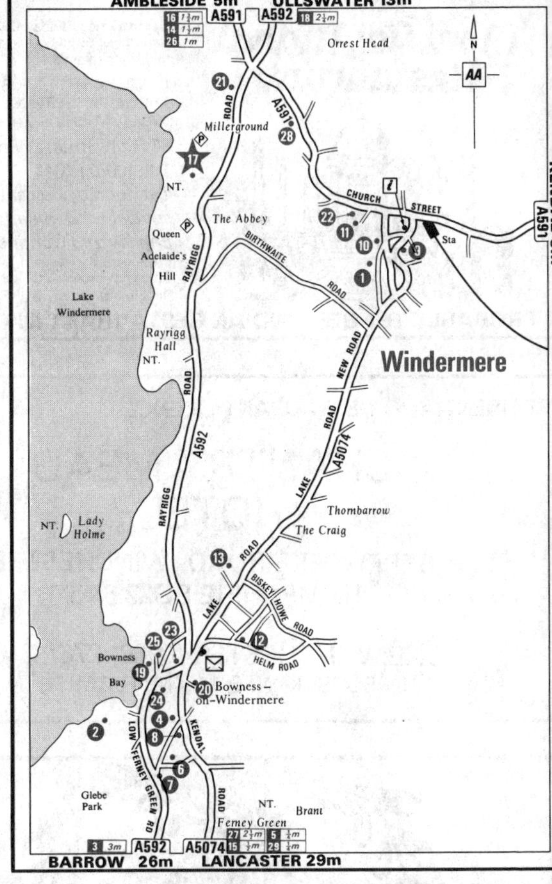

WINDERMERE Cumbria Map**7** SD49
See plan

★★★**Old England** Bowness on Windermere (Trusthouse Forte) ☎2444 Telex no65194 Plan**19**
Large rambling four-storey hotel by waterside with fine views of lake and fells beyond. New wing added 1970.
90⇌⋒ Lift ☽ ⋈ CTV in bedrooms 60P ⚓ ⌂(heated) Conference facilities available ♿ Last dinner9.15pm ✿ ⌧ S% sB&B⇌⋒£24 dB&B⇌⋒£35.50 ⊟ *xmas* Credit cards 1 2 3 4 5 6

★★★**Beech Hill** Cartmel Fell ☎2137 Telex no67415 Plan**3**
A luxury hotel overlooking Lake Windermere. Leisure facilities include an indoor heated pool, games room, sauna and solarium and private floating dock for sailing enthusiasts. Conference accommodation is available.
50⇌⋒ ☽ ⋈ CTV CTV in bedrooms 50P ⌂(heated) sauna bath Disco twice wkly Conference facilities available ♣ ♡International. Last dinner8.45pm ✿ ⌧ sB&B⇌⋒£19–£21 dB&B⇌⋒£32–£35 Lunch£3.50–£4 Tea£1.10–£2 Dinner£5–£6 Wine£2.50 ⊟ *xmas* Credit cards 1 2 3 4 5 6

★★★**Belsfield** Bowness on Windermere (Trusthouse Forte) ☎2448 Telex no65238 Plan**4**
A 19th-C building with white façade standing in six acres of grounds which slope down to the ferry landing stage at Bowness. It has its own indoor heated swimming pool.
73rm(67⇌⋒) Lift ☽ ⋈ TV in bedrooms 80P ⚓ ⌂(heated) Conference facilities available ♿ Last dinner9.30pm ✿ ⌧ S% sB&B£17 sB&B⇌⋒£20 dB&B£28 dB&B⇌⋒£30.50 ⊟ *xmas* Credit cards 1 2 3 4 5 6

★★★**Burn How Motel** Back Belsfield Rd, Bowness on Windermere ☎4486 Plan**6**
Situated in the centre of Bowness amid secluded gardens, and close to the lake and shops.
Closed Jan–Feb; 18⇌⋒ ⋈ CTV in bedrooms 18P ⚓ ♣ ♡English & French. Last dinner9pm ✿ ⌧ S% sB&B⇌⋒£15–£26 dB&B⇌⋒£22–£26 Continental breakfast Lunch£3 Tea£1 Dinner£6 Wine£3.20 ⊟ *xmas* Credit cards 2 5

★★★**Hydro** Bowness on Windermere ☎4455 Telex no65196 Plan**12**
A Victorian hotel, modernised to today's standards. It is set above the village of Bowness, overlooking the northern reaches of Lake Windermere, with the craggy Langdale Pikes and the Cumbrian mountains in the distance.
97⇌⋒ Lift ☽ ⋈ CTV CTV in bedrooms 100P Conference facilities available Last dinner8.30pm ✿ ⌧ S% ✻sB&B⇌⋒£12–£16 dB&B⇌⋒£24–£32 Lunch fr£3.75 Dinner£5.25–£8 *xmas* Credit cards 1 2 3 5 6

★★★**Langdale Chase** ☎Ambleside2201 Plan**14**
A large, late-Victorian country house hotel with oak panelling and antique style furnishings. Set in extensive grounds with terrace and lawns

W

escending to the lake shore, where the hotel has its wn pier.
9rm(19⇌ ⋒) ☽ CTV TV in bedrooms 40P 3 ⚓ (grass) International. Last dinner 8.45pm S% *sB&B£12.50–£16 sB&B⇌⋒£16–£19 B&B£22–£28 dB&B⇌⋒£28–£36 Lunch£3.95 ea£1.50 Dinner£6.75 Wine£3 xmas redit cards 1 2

★★★Low Wood Ambleside ☎Ambleside 3338 elex no 65273 Plan **16**
One of the original coaching inns, visited by John Ruskin as a boy of twelve over 100 years ago. It tands on the northern banks of Lake Windermere, with spacious lawns and gardens extending to the ake side.
Closed mid Nov–mid Mar; 143rm(58⇌⋒) ☽ CTV 00P ⚓ Live music & dancing Sat in winter English & French. Last dinner 10.30pm S% sB&B£8.70–£12.15 B&B⇌⋒£9.95–£13.40 dB&B£17.40–£24.30 dB&B⇌⋒£19.90–£26.80 Lunch£3.75 ea60p–£1 Dinner£6&alc Wine£2.50 redit cards 1 2 3 5

★★★Priory Rayrigg Rd, Bowness on Windermere ☎4377 Telex no 67415 Plan **21**
n six acres of private grounds one mile from the entre of Windermere. Having a lakeside frontage with jetty, the hotel's own power boat is available for water ski-ing or cruises on the famous Lake Windermere.
15⇌⋒ CTV CTV in bedrooms 25P ⚓ billiards ast dinner 8.45pm sB&B⇌⋒£19–£21 dB&B⇌⋒£32–£35 Lunch£3.50–£4.50 Dinner£5–£6 Wine£2.50 xmas Credit cards 1 2 3 4 5 6

★★★Wild Boar Crook (2½m S of Windermere on B5284 Crook road) ☎5225 Plan **27**
A converted 17th-C house, situated 2 miles from Bowness in a setting of woodlands and fell slopes. The dining room features a natural rock formation. The name arises from a legend that the last wild boar of the old county of Westmorland met its death here.
38⇌⋒ 1 CTV CTV available in bedrooms 60P 4 ⚓ Live music & dancing Sat (Oct–Mar) English & French. Last dinner 8.45pm S% sB&B⇌⋒£10.60–£15.40 dB&B⇌⋒£21.20–£30.80 Lunch£4.75&alc Tea75p–£1 Dinner£7.75&alc Wine£2.50 xmas Credit cards 1 2 3 5

❀❀★★ Miller Howe Rayrigg Rd ☎2536 Plan **17**
See page 57 for details

★★Bordriggs Longtail Hill, Bowness on Windermere ☎3567 Plan **5**
10⇌⋒ CTV 14P ⚓ Last dinner 7.30pm dB&B⇌⋒£20 Lunch fr£4.50 Tea fr£1.50 Dinner fr£5 Wine£3.10 Credit card 3

★★Burnside Bowness on Windermere (Trusthouse Forte) ☎2211 Plan **7**
Occupies a prominent position, offering sweeping views of Lake Windermere and the surrounding hills, and is set in 5 acres of its own garden and woodland.
31rm(26⇌⋒) CTV TV in bedrooms 70P ⚓ Last dinner 9pm S% sB&B£15 sB&B⇌⋒£17 dB&B£24 dB&B⇌⋒£27.50 xmas Credit cards 1 2 3 4 5 6

★★Elleray Cross St ☎3120 Plan **9**
A small hotel in the centre of town, close to both rail and bus stations.
13rm CTV CTV available in bedrooms 6P

Lastdinner8pm S% sB&B£6–£7.50 dB&B£12–£15 Barlunch£1.75 Dinner£4.50 Wine£2.40

★★Grey Walls Elleray Rd ☎3741 Plan**10**
A large country house in two acres of grounds in a setting of natural rocks, with lawns and gardens formed by tall evergreens.
Closed Dec–Feb; 18rm(15⇌⋒) ⋈ CTV 18P 4⌂ ⇏ ⚓ ♡ ⊈ sB&B⇌⋒ fr£9.40 dB&B fr£17.80 dB&B⇌⋒ fr£18.80 Barlunch fr£1 Tea fr50p Dinner fr£5 Credit cards[1] [2] [5]

★★Hideaway Phoenix Way ☎3070 Plan**11**
A charming country house hotel occupying a secluded position. Once the home of an international painter, this hotel dates back to 1828. The hotel was originally part of the Old College of which one of its more notable pupils was actor James Mason.
Closed Xmas–Mar; 12⇌⋒ ⋈ CTV ⊘ 15P ⇏ ⚓ Lastdinner8pm ♡ ⊈ S% sB&B⇌⋒£8 dB&B⇌⋒£16 Lunch£3 Tea£1 HighTea£1 Dinner£4.50 Wine£3 ⊟

★★ *Linthwaite* Bowness on Windermere ☎3688 Plan**15**
A stone country house hotel, 1 mile from Bowness, standing in 7½ acres of grounds with beautiful gardens and woodland.
Closed Nov–mid Apr; 13rm(11⇌⋒) ⋈ TV available in bedrooms ⊘ 25P ⇏ ⚓ Children under 8yrs not accommodated ♀English & French. Lastdinner7.30pm ♡ ⊈

★★Mortal Man Troutbeck (2½m N off A592) ☎Ambleside3193 Plan**18**
A delightful old lakeland inn, built in 1689, and originally known as the White House. In 1889 this building was incorporated in a new one.
Closed mid Nov–mid Feb; 11rm CTV 30P ⇏ ⚓ Children under 5yrs not accommodated Lastdinner8pm ♡ S% sB&B£15 dB&B£30 Lunch£4.25 Dinner£6 Wine£2.20

★★Royal Bowness on Windermere (Best Western) ☎3045 Plan**23**
A 16th-C hotel, once known as the White Lion, but renamed the Royal after a visit by Queen Adelaide in 1840. The Hotel, although modernised, retains its old world charm. There is a secluded garden.
30rm(15⇌⋒) 1⊟ ⋈ CTV 6P 5⌂ ⚓ Live music & dancing Thu & Fri ♀English & French. Lastdinner10.30pm ♡ ⊈ S% sB&B£8.70–£12.75 sB&B⇌⋒£9.95–£14 dB&B£17.40–£25.50 dB&B⇌⋒£19.90–£28 Lunch£4&alc Tea75p–£1 Dinner£6.25&alc Wine£2.50 ⊟ Credit cards[1] [2] [3] [5]

★★St Martins ☎3731 Plan**24**
A pleasant, comfortably furnished family hotel, situated in the centre of the village, close to Bowness Bay.
Closed Nov–mid Mar; 16rm(3⇌⋒) CTV 12P ⇏ Lastdinner8pm ♡ S% sB&B fr£8 dB&B fr£16 dB&B⇌⋒ fr£18 Lunch fr£3 Dinner fr£4.75 Wine£2.50

★★ *Stags Head* Church Rd, Bowness on Windermere (Best Western) ☎3132 Plan**25**
An old-world hotel designated as a building of special architectural or historic interest by the Department of the Environment.
17rm(7⇌⋒) ⋈ CTV TV available in bedrooms Lastdinner8.45pm ⊟ Credit cards[1] [2] [3] [4] [5] [6]

★★Sun Troutbeck Bridge (2m N) ☎3274 Plan**26**
Old posting house on main Windermere/Keswick road, in sheltered hillside position.
8rm ⋈ CTV 10P 1⌂ Lastdinner9.30pm ♡ S% *sB&B£7.50 dB&B£13 Barlunch40p–£3.20 Dinner£4&alc ⊟ Credit cards[1] [3] [5]

★★Winander Ferry View, Bowness on Windermere ☎3835 Plan**29**
A small comfortable hotel, easily reached from the motorway, one mile from ferry and village.
13rm(4⇌⋒) ⋈ CTV 20P ⇏ ♀Mainly grills. ♡ *sB&B£9.78 dB&B£17.25 dB&B⇌⋒£19.55 Barlunch£1.28alc Dinner£4.25&alc Wine£2.55 ⊟ Credit card[5]

★Cranleigh Kendal Rd ☎3293 Plan**8**
Situated in peaceful surroundings, close to the shops and lakes.
Closed Jan & Feb; RS Dec; 11rm(3⇌⋒) CTV ⊘ 8P ⇏ Children under 5yrs not accommodated Lastdinner7pm ⊈ S% sB&B£8–£9 sB&B⇌⋒£8.50–£9.50 dB&B£22–£24 dB&B⇌⋒£24–£26 Tea£1–£1.50 Dinner£4.50–£6.50 Wine£3.30 ⊟ *xmas*

★Knoll Bowness on Windermere ☎3756 Plan**13**
Surrounded by pleasant wooded grounds, and offering fine views of the northern end of the Lake Windermere and the fells.
Closed Nov–Feb; 12rm(3⇌⋒) ⋈ CTV ⊘ 20P ⇏ ⚓ Children under 3yrs not accommodated Lastdinner7pm S% *sB&B fr£7 dB&B fr£14 dB&B⇌⋒ fr£15 Lunch fr£2.50 Tea fr£1.25 Dinner fr£3.50 Wine£2.40

★Ravensworth Ambleside Rd ☎3747 Plan**22**
In a sheltered position on the main Ambleside road close to railway station, buses and village centre. Because of the sheltered position, semi-tropical plants such as bamboos thrive in the open. Noted for its imaginative cuisine.
Closed mid Nov–mid Dec & mid Jan–Feb; 12rm(11⇌⋒) ⋈ TV in bedrooms 12P ⇏ ♀English & Ausrian. Lastdinner7pm ♡ S% sB&B£7–£9 sB&B⇌⋒£8.40–£11 dB&B⇌⋒£16.80–£22 Dinner£3.50–£4.50&alc Wine£2 ⊟ *xmas* Credit cards[1] [6]

Applegarth College Rd ☎3206 Plan**1**
An elegant mansion house built in 1890 of individual character and elegance of yester-year. Quietly situated, but within easy reach of all amenties.
Closed Oct–Mar; 12rm CTV 6P
Last dinner7pm

Willowsmere Ambleside Rd ☎3575 Plan**28**
Situated on the main Windermere to Ambleside road (A591), close to shops and railway station. Has its own sheltered garden.
Closed Nov–Feb; 14rm(5) CTV TV available in bedrooms 20P Children under 5yrs not accommodated English & Austrian.
Last dinner7pm sB&B£6.50–£7.50 dB&B£12.50–£14 dB&B£14–£16 Tea£1 Dinner£3.75 Wine£2 Credit cards 1 2 3 5

XXX**Aquarius** Glebe Rd, Bowness on Windermere ☎4040 Plan**2**
Closed Mon (winter only); 120seats 30P Live music & dancing Sat French. Last dinner10pm S% *Lunch fr£3.95&alc Dinner fr£5.95&alc Wine£2.70 Credit cards 1 2 3 4 5 6

X**Porthole Eating House** 3 Ash St, Bowness on Windermere ☎2793 Plan**20**
Closed Tue, Dec–mid Feb; Lunch not served; 42seats English, French & Italian. Specialities: suprême chicken saltinbocca escalope of veal with mushrooms, boeuf McCarthy. Last dinner10.30pm *Dinner£8alc Wine£4 Credit card 2

WINDSOR Berkshire Map**4** SU97
See also **Datchet**
★★★**Castle** High St (Trusthouse Forte) ☎51011 Telex no849220
83 Lift TV in bedrooms 130P Conference facilities available Last dinner10pm S% sB&B£21.50 dB&B£31 *xmas*
Credit cards 1 2 3 4 5 6

★**Royal Adelaide** Kings Rd (Crest) ☎63916
18th-C building with plaque commemorating stay of Edward VII.
34rm(9) CTV CTV available in bedrooms 16P Last dinner8.30pm S% *sB&B£11.12 sB&B£15.66 dB&B£18.90 dB&B£22.68 Credit cards 1 2 3 4 5 6

XX***Don Peppino*** 30 Thames St ☎60081
Closed Sun; 80seats English, French & Italian. Last dinner11pm Credit cards 1 2 3 5

XX***Windsor Peking*** 14 High St ☎64942
110seats Disco twice wkly Live music four night wkly Pekinese. Last dinner11.30pm
Credit cards 1 2 3 5 6

WINKTON Dorset Map**4** SZ19
★★***Fishermans Haunt*** Salisbury Rd ☎Christchurch484071
RS Xmas; 4rm(2) Annexe:5rm(2) CTV 100P Last dinner10pm
Credit cards 1 3

WINSFORD Somerset Map**3** SS93
★★**Royal Oak Inn** ☎232
Thatched inn with 12th-C origins, standing in village centre.
Closed mid Dec–mid Feb; RS Nov–mid Dec & mid Feb–Mar; 9rm(5) Annexe;6 TV 15P 5 Last dinner9pm S% sB&B£14.50 sB&B£16 dB&B£23.50 dB&B£26.50 Bar lunch60p–£2 Dinner£4.50–£8 Wine£3 *xmas* Credit cards 1 2 3 5 6

WINTERSLOW Wiltshire Map**4** SU23
★★**Pheasant** (Nicholsons) ☎862374
11rm(2) CTV 60P 4 Last dinner10.30pm S% sB&B£8.35–£9.65

W

sB&B⇌⋒£8.85–£10.35 dB&B£15.70–£17.30 dB&B⇌⋒£16.70–£19 Lunch£2.75&alc Dinner£3&alc Wine£3.50 ⊟ *xmas*
Credit cards ① ② ③ ⑤

WISBECH Cambridgeshire Map**5** TF40
★★**Rose & Crown** Market Pl (Best Western) ☎3187
16rm(8⇌⋒) ⧖ CTV in bedrooms 10P ♉English & French. Last dinner9.15pm ✿ ⊡
sB&B£9.75–£11.25 sB&B⇌⋒£11.50–£13.95 dB&B£16.90–£18.95 dB&B⇌⋒£20.50–£22.95 Lunch£2.95–£3.75&alc Tea80p–£1.25 Dinner£6.75alc Wine£2.75 ⊟ *xmas*
Credit cards ① ② ③ ⑤

★★**White Lion** South Brink ☎4813
Once a coaching inn, this modernised hotel is centrally situated and overlooks River Nene.
20rm(9⇌⋒) ☽ ⧖ CTV 20P ♉French.
Last dinner8.45pm ✿ S% sB&B£11.25 sB&B⇌⋒£13.60 dB&B£18.50 dB&B⇌⋒£20.95 Lunch£3.50–£5&alc Dinner£3.50–£5&alc Wine£3.50 Credit cards ① ⑥

WISHAW Warwickshire Map**7** SP19
★★★★**Belfry** Lichfield Rd (A446) ☎Curdworth 70301
Telex no338848
59⇌⋒ 3⊟ ☽ ⧖ CTV in bedrooms P ♪18 Disco 3 nights wkly Conference facilities available ♉English & French. Last dinner10.30pm ✿ ⊡ S%
*sB&B⇌⋒£18.50 dB&B⇌⋒£24 Lunch£2.50–£4.65&alc Tea£1–£1.75 High Tea£3–£4.75 Dinner£6.95&alc Wine£2.80
⊟ Credit cards ① ② ③ ⑤

✕✕✕**Moxhull Hall** Holly Ln ☎021–329 2056
Closed Sun, Mon, 22–31 Dec & 2wks Aug; 70seats 50P ✗ ♉English & French. Last dinner9.45pm S%
*Lunch£6.50alc Dinner£6.50alc Wine£2.75
Credit cards ① ② ③ ④ ⑤

WITHAM Essex Map**5** TL81
☆☆**Rivenhall Motor Inn** Rivenhall End ☎516969
Telex no99414
RS Sat & Sun; 8rm(5⇌⋒) Annexe: 18⇌⋒ ☽ ⧖ CTV in bedrooms 100P ♉English & Continental.
Last dinner9.30pm ✿ ⊡ *sB&B£12 sB&B⇌⋒£12 dB&B£16 dB&B⇌⋒£17.50 Continental breakfast Lunch£3.75 dinner£3.75 Wine£3.13 Credit cards ① ② ⑤

★★ ***White Hart*** Newland St ☎512245
14rm(13⇌⋒) ⧖ CTV 45P Live music Wed ♉English & French. Last dinner10pm ✿ ⊡
Credit cards ① ② ③ ⑤

★**Spreadeagle** Newland St ☎512131
RS Sun; 8rm Annexe: 6rm CTV 50P ♉English & French. Last dinner9pm S% sB&B fr£9 dB&B fr£14 dB&B⇌⋒ fr£14.50 Lunch fr£3&alc Dinner£6alc Wine£2.60 ⊟ Credit cards ① ③ ⑤

WITHERIDGE Devon Map**3** SS81
★★ ***Mitre*** 2 The Square ☎395
9rm(1⇌⋒) ⧖ CTV TV available in bedrooms 10P 3⌂ ♉Mainly grills. ✿ ⊡

WITHERNSEA Humberside Map**8** TA32
★★**Queen's** ☎2212
17rm ⧖ CTV ⊘ 50P ⇼ Last dinner9.45pm ✿ S%
*sB&B£7.50 dB&B£11 Lunch£2 Dinner£1.50–£5&alc Wine£2

WITHINGTON Gloucestershire Map**4** SP01
✕✕**Mill House** ☎204
Small restaurant in converted water mill.
Dinner not served Sun; 62seats 80P bedrooms available ♉English & French.
Last dinner9.45pm S% Lunch£2.50–£3.50&alc Dinner£6.95&alc Wine£3.30 Credit cards ① ② ③ ⑤

WITHYPOOL Somerset Map**3** SS83
★♛**Wester Close Country House** ☎Exford 302
Family hotel in pleasant grounds with fine views of Exmoor.
10rm(6⇌⋒) 1⊟ ⧖ CTV 20P ⇼ ⚓ ⌂
Last dinner9pm ✿ ⊡ sB&B£8.50 sB&B⇌⋒£9.50 dB&B£16 dB&B⇌⋒£18 Lunch£4 Tea£1 Dinner£5.25&alc Wine£3 *xmas*

WITLEY, GREAT Hereford & Worcester Map**7** SO76
❀✕✕**Hundred House** ☎215
(Rosette awarded for dinner only)
Dinner not served Sun & Mon; Lunch not served Xmas Day; 80seats 80P ♉English & French.
Specialities: fresh fish. Last dinner9.15pm
*Dinner£7.75alc Wine£2.50 Credit cards ① ② ③

WIVELISCOMBE Somerset Map**3** ST02
★***Courtyard*** High St ☎23737
7rm(4⇌⋒) ⧖ TV Last dinner10pm ✿ ⊡
Credit cards ① ③ ⑤

WIVENHOE Essex Map**5** TM02
✕**Smugglers** 47 High St ☎3582
Closed Sun, Mon & 1wk Feb; 30seats P ♉Austrian, French & Swiss. Last dinner10.30pm
Dinner£5.50alc Wine£2.70

WOBURN Bedfordshire Map**4** SP93
★★★**Bedford Arms** George St (Kingsmead) ☎441
Tastefully-modernised Georgian coaching inn, with stables and modern new wing. Situated not far from the Abbey and wild animal park.
41rm(25⇌⋒) ☽ CTV in bedrooms 60P 8⌂ ⚓ ♉English & French. Last dinner10.30pm ✿ ⊡
S% sB&B£17–£18.50 sB&B⇌⋒£18.75–£20 dB&B£23–£25 dB&B⇌⋒£26–£28 Lunch£3.50–£4.25&alc Tea50p Dinner£3.75–£4.25&alc ⊟ *xmas*
Credit cards ① ② ③ ⑤ ⑥

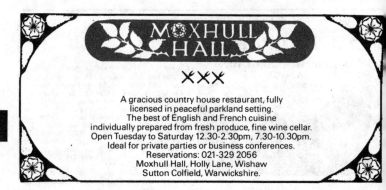

W

WOLVERHAMPTON West Midlands Map**7** SO99
★★Connaught Tettenhall Rd ☎24433
Telex no338490
20rm(52⇌⋒) Lift ☽ ⋒ TV & TV available in bedrooms 100P sauna bath Disco 3 nights wkly Live music & dancing wkly English & French. Last dinner9.30pm Credit cards 1 2 5 6

★★Goldthorn Penn Rd ☎29216
71rm(29⇌⋒) ☽ TV in bedrooms 84P 4 French. Last dinner9.30pm S% sB&B£10 sB&B⇌⋒£13.50 dB&B£14.95 dB&B⇌⋒£18.45 Lunch£3.50&alc Dinner£3.50&alc Wine£2.50 Credit card 1

★★★Mount Mount Rd, Tettenhall Wood (2½mW off A454) (Embassy) ☎752055
62rm(47⇌⋒) ☽ CTV TV in bedrooms 150P Conference facilties available Last dinner9.15pm S% sB&B£11.50 sB&B⇌⋒£16 dB&B£17 dB&B⇌⋒£22 Lunch£4.75&alc Dinner£5.50&alc Wine£4.50 Credit cards 1 2 3 4 5 6

★★★Park Hall Park Dr, Goldthorn Park (2m S off A459) (Embassy) ☎31121
57rm(49⇌⋒) ☽ CTV TV in bedrooms 150P Conference facilities available Last dinner9pm S% sB&B£11.50 sB&B⇌⋒£16 dB&B£17 dB&B⇌⋒£22 Lunch£4.50&alc Dinner£5&alc Wine£4.50 Credit cards 1 2 3 4 5 6

★★★Castle Croft Castlecroft Rd (Ansells) ☎761264
26rm(20⇌⋒) CTV TV in bedrooms 70P Last dinner9.30pm S% sB&B£9.25 sB&B⇌⋒£12.26 dB&B£12.25 dB&B⇌⋒£15.85 Lunch£3.37&alc Dinner£4&alc Wine£3.20 Credit cards 1 2

★★Fox School St (Wolverhampton & Dudley) ☎21680
29⇌⋒ ☽ TV in bedrooms 20P Last dinner9.30pm S% *sB&B⇌⋒£13.60 dB&B⇌⋒£20.75 Lunch£2.50&alc Dinner£3.25&alc Wine£2.60 Credit cards 1 3

★★Ravensholt Summerfield Rd (Wolverhampton & Dudley) ☎24140
17rm Annexe: 12rm CTV 40P Last dinner9pm S% *sB&B fr£11.40 dB&B fr£18 Lunch£3.65&alc Dinner£4&alc Wine£2.60 Credit cards 1 3

✕Tandoor 46 Queen St ☎20747
Closed Xmas; Lunch not served Sun & Public Hols; 90seats Indian. Last dinner 12.15am S% Lunch£1.80–£2.50&alc Dinner£6alc Wine£3.90 Credit cards 1 2 3 5

WOODBRIDGE Suffolk Map**5** TM24
★★★Melton Grange ☎4147
Country mansion with parts 800 years old, set in own parkland and woods on outskirts of Woodbridge.
32rm(29⇌⋒) CTV 100P English & French. Last dinner9pm S% sB&B£15 sB&B⇌⋒£15 dB&B£23 dB&B⇌⋒£23 Lunch£3.25&alc Dinner£3.75&alc Wine£2.65 *xmas* Credit cards 1 2 3 5

★★★Seckford Hall ☎5678
Large, well-preserved, brick-built, Elizabethan house, converted by Sir Ralph Harwood.
Closed Xmas Day; 24rm(20⇌⋒) 3 CTV CTV available in bedrooms 100P 3 Children under 2yrs not accommodated English & French. Last dinner9pm S% sB&B£12–£13

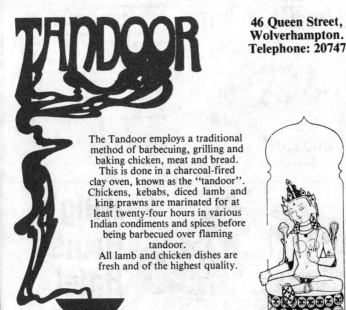

W

sB&B⇨⋒£14.50–£15.50 dB&B£21 dB&B⇨⋒£24 Lunch£3.95–£4.50&alc Dinner£5alc Wine£3 ⊟ Credit cards 1 2 3 5 6

★★Crown Thorofare (Trusthouse Forte) ☎4242
Centrally situated, fully-modernised old coaching inn, parts of which date back to 1532.
15rm Annexe: 10⇨⋒ ₥ TV in bedrooms 36P Last dinner10pm ♉ ⊻ S% sB&B£12 sB&B⇨⋒£15 dB&B£17.50 dB&B⇨⋒£20.50 ⊟ *xmas* Credit cards 1 2 3 4 5 6

XXLe Provençal 42 Market Hill ☎5726
Closed Sun, Mon, 2wks Xmas–New Year & 3wks Sep; 30seats P ♡French. Last dinner10.30pm S% Dinner£10alc

WOODFORD GREEN Greater London Map**5** TQ49
☆☆☆Waltham Forest Oak Hill (Queens) ☎01-505 4511
50⇨⋒ Lift ☽ ₥ CTV in bedrooms 100P 10⌂ Live music & dancing Sat Cabaret Sat Last dinner9.45pm ♉ S% sB&B⇨⋒£14.90–£18.85 dB&B⇨⋒£19.80–£24.75 Lunch fr£3.50&alc Dinner fr£3.50&alc Wine£3.50 ⊟ *xmas* Credit cards 1 2 3 5 6

WOODHALL SPA Lincolnshire Map**8** TF16
★★Golf The Broadway (Crest) ☎52434
57rm(9⇨⋒) ☽ CTV in bedrooms 70P 4⌂ ⚓ ⛳18 Last dinner9.30pm ♉ S% ✱sB&B£10.80 sB&B⇨⋒£16.20 dB&B£17.82 dB&B⇨⋒£23.76 ⊟ Credit cards 1 2 3 4 5 6

WOODHOUSE EAVES Leicestershire Map**8** SK51
XXTudor Home Maplewell Rd ☎890318
Lunch not served Sat; Dinner not served Sun & Mon; 85seats 25P ♡English & French. Last dinner9.30pm S% ✱Lunch£3&alc Dinner£5&alc Wine£2.80 Credit cards 1 3 5

XX*Ye Olde Bull's Head* ☎890255
Closed Mon; Dinner not served Sun; 70seats 150P ♡English & Continental. Last dinner9.45pm Credit card 1

WOODLANDS Hampshire Map**4** SU31
★★Busketts Lawn 174 Woodlands Rd ☎Ashurst2272
17rm(13⇨⋒) ☽ ₥ CTV CTV available in bedrooms 50P ⚓ ⥾(heated) ♧ ♡English & Continental. Last dinner8pm ♉ ⊻ S% sB&B£10.75 sB&B⇨⋒£10.75 dB&B£19.50 dB&B⇨⋒£21.50 Lunch£4.50 Tea£1.25 High Tea£1.85 Dinner£5&alc Wine£4 ⊟ *xmas* Credit cards 3 5

★★*Woodlands Lodge* Bartley Rd ☎Ashurst2257
11rm ₥ TV available in bedrooms 50P ⚓ Last dinner9pm ♉ ⊻ ⊟ Credit cards 1 2 3 5

WOODSTOCK Oxfordshire Map**4** SP41
★★★Bear Park St ☎811511
See page 56 for details

★★King's Arms ☎811412
8rm ₥ CTV 4P Last dinner9.30pm ♉ ⊻ sB&B£12–£15 dB&B£20–£30 Lunch£3–£3.75 Tea80p–£1 High Tea£2–£3 Dinner£4alc Wine£3.10 ⊟ Credit cards 1 2 3 5

★★*Marlborough Arms* Oxford St ☎811227
Coaching inn (partly 16th-C) mentioned as George Inn in Sir Walter Scott's 'Woodstock'. Cobbled courtyard.
14rm ₥ CTV TV available in bedrooms 12P Last dinner9pm ♉ ⊻ ⊟ Credit cards 2 3 5

W

WOODY BAY Devon Map**3** SS64
★Woody Bay ☎Parracombe264
4rm(4⇌🛁) 2▭ 🍽 CTV 20P 🐕 Live music & dancing wkly 🍷English & French. Last dinner9.30pm ☕ % sB&B£10–£11 sB&B⇌🛁£11–£12 dB&B£20–£22 dB&B⇌🛁£22–£24 Barlunch£2.20–£7.25 Tea40p Dinner£6&alc Wine£3.25 ⊟ *xmas* Credit cards 1 2 3 5 6

WOOLACOMBE Devon Map**2** SS44
★★★Narracott Grand ☎418
Closed Nov–Feb; 107rm(92⇌🛁) Lift ☽ 🍽 CTV CTV in bedrooms P 🐕 ⊃(heated) squash sauna bath Disco 6 nights wkly Live music & dancing 5 nights wkly ♧ Conference facilities available Last dinner8pm ✿ ☕ ✱sB&B£9.50–£18 sB&B⇌🛁£12.50–£19.50 dB&B£19–£36 dB&B⇌🛁£25–£39 Lunch£3alc Tea30p High Tea£2alc Dinner£4alc Wine£2.50

★★★Watersmeet ☎333
Closed mid Oct–Apr; 40rm(17⇌🛁) CTV ⊘ 30P 20🏠 🐕 ⚓ ⊃(heated) ⚫(grass) Disco wkly Live music & dancing wkly 🍷English & Continental. Last dinner8.30pm ✿ ☕ ✱sB&B£8–£9 sB&B⇌🛁£9.50–£10.50 dB&B£16–£18 dB&B⇌🛁£18–£20 Lunch£4.50–£5.50 Tea45p Dinner£6.50–£7.50 Wine£2.90 Credit card 5

★★★Woolacombe Bay ☎388
Closed Nov–Mar; 52rm(37⇌🛁) Lift ☽ CTV CTV in bedrooms 70P 🐕 ⚓ ⊃(heated) ♂9 billiards disco wkly Live music & dancing 3 nights wkly ♧ Last dinner8.30pm ✿ ☕ ✱sB&B£10.80–£16.97 (incl dinner) sB&B⇌🛁£12.34–£18.51 (incl dinner) dB&B£21.60–£33.94 (incl dinner) dB&B⇌🛁£24.78–£37 (incl dinner) Lunch£3 Tea30p Dinner£4 Wine£2.70 ⊟

W

★★**Atlantic** Sunnyside Rd ☎469
Closed Oct–Mar; 15rm CTV 12P ⚓ Disco Wed Last dinner 7pm ♁ ♁ S% sB&B£6–£8.50 dB&B⇌⋔£6.50–£9 dB&B£12–£17 dB&B⇌⋔£12.50–£17.50 Lunch fr£3 Tea fr£1.50 Dinner fr£4 Wine£2.50 ⊟

★★***Beach*** Sea Front ☎449
Closed mid Oct–mid Apr; 36rm(20⇌⋔) ⚔ CTV 28P 4⌂ ⊡(heated) Disco Sat Live music & dancing Sun & Wed Cabaret Sat Last dinner 8pm ♁ ♁

★★**Rathleigh** Beach Rd ☎404
Closed Oct–Apr; RS May & Sep; 19rm TV available in bedrooms 20P ⌂ Last dinner 7.30pm ♁ ♁ sB&B£6–£8.50 sB&B⇌⋔£6.50–£8.75 dB&B£12–£16 dB&B⇌⋔£13–£17 Bar lunch 50p £1 Dinner£4–£5 Wine£3

★★***Sands*** Bay View Rd ☎550
White stucco building with Spanish-style exterior. situated in quiet road overlooking sea and beach.
Closed Oct–Mar (except Xmas); 23rm(4⇌⋔) CTV 18P ⌂ Last dinner 8pm ♁ ♁

★★**Whin Bay** Bay View Rd ☎475
Closed Nov–Mar; 17rm(5⇌⋔) ♁ CTV 18P ⌂ Last dinner 9pm S% sB&B£7.85–£10.71 dB&B£15.71–£21.43 dB&B⇌⋔£17.14–£22.85 Bar lunch 50p–£1 Dinner£1.50–£3 Wine£2.10

★**Crossways** The Esplanade ☎395
Closed Sep–Feb; 9rm ♁ CTV 10P ⌂ Last dinner 6pm ♁ sB&B£6.50–£8 dB&B£13–£16 Wine£1.50

★**Headlands** Beach Rd ☎320
closed Oct–Mar; 11rm(1⇌⋔) Annexe: 5rm CTV 15P ⌂ ⌂ Last dinner 7.30pm ♁ ♁ S% *sB&B£6.50–£9.50 sB&B⇌⋔£7.30–£10.50 dB&B£13–£19 dB&B⇌⋔£15–£21 Dinner fr£4.60 Wine£2.70 ⊟

★**Little Beach** The Esplanade ☎398
Closed Nov–Feb; 10rm(8⇌⋔) ♁ CTV 12P 1⌂ ⌂ sauna bath ♁ English & Continental. Last dinner 8pm ♁ ♁ S% sB&B£9.75–£12.35 sB&B⇌⋔£13.25–£15 dB&B£19.50–£21.85 dB&B⇌⋔£21.20–£30 Bar lunch 75p–£1.75 Tea 75p–£1.10 Dinner£5.50 Wine£3 ⊟ Credit card 1

★**Sunnyside** Sunnyside Rd ☎267
Closed mid Sep–mid May; 18rm CTV 12P ⌂ ⚓ Disco wkly Last dinner 7.15pm sB&B£5–£6 dB&B£10–£12 Dinner£3.50–£4.50 Wine£2.50 ⊟

WOOLER Northumberland Map **12** NT92

★★**Tankerville Arms** Cottage Rd ☎581
16rm(4⇌⋔) ♁ CTV CTV available in bedrooms 100P 3⌂ ⚓ ⌂ Last dinner 9pm ♁ S% *sB&B£9–£9.75 dB&B£15.50–£17.50 dB&B⇌⋔£17.50–£19.50 Lunch£2.50–£3 Dinner£4–£5.50 Wine£2.25 ⊟ *xmas*

WOOLFARDISWORTHY Devon Map **2** SS32

★★★**Moorhead** ☎Clovelly 461 Telex no 46474
Two-storey hotel in own grounds of some ten acres.
closed Nov–Mar; 13⇌⋔ ♁ CTV TV available in bedrooms ⌀ 50P ⌂ ⚓ ⊡(heated) Last dinner 9pm ♁ ♁ *sB&B⇌⋔£8.50–£12 dB&B⇌⋔£13–£20 Bar lunch fr£2.50 Tea fr50p High Tea fr£1.75 Dinner fr£4&alc Wine£3.20 Credit cards 1 2 3

WOOTTON BASSETT Wiltshire Map **4** SU08

XX**Magnolia Room** High St ☎3121
Closed Mon; 100 seats 20P Live music & dancing Sat ♁ English & French. Last dinner 10pm Lunch£1.50–£3.00&alc Dinner£5.50&alc Wine£2.75 Credit cards 1 3 5

'OOTTON WAWEN Warwickshire Map**4** SP16
Ye Olde Bull's Head ☎Henley-in-Arden2511
osed Mon; Dinner not served Sun; 70seats 100P
Continental. Last dinner10pm
Lunch£3.70–£4.10&alc Dinner£7alc
ine£2.18 Credit cards 1 3

'ORCESTER Hereford & Worcester Map**3** SO85
★★Giffard High St (Trusthouse Forte) ☎27155
elex no338869
right, modern interior and fine views of Cathedral nd surrounding countryside.
)4 Lift CTV in bedrooms Conference
icilities available Last dinner9.15pm S%
3&B £18 dB&B £26.50 xmas
redit cards 1 2 3 4 5 6

★Diglis Riverside ☎353518
lose Xmas; Rs Sun; 15rm(5) CTV 80P
ast dinner8.30pm sB&B fr£8.50 dB&B fr£17
3&B fr£18.50 Lunch£2–£6
inner£3.50–£6 Wine£4.50

★Star Foregate St (Wolverhampton & Dudley)
;24308
3rm Lift CTV 70P Last dinner9.45pm
S% *sB&B fr£11.43 dB&B fr£18
unch£3.45&alc Dinner£3.95&alc Wine£2.60
Credit cards 1 3

★Ye Olde Talbot Friar St (Trophy Taverns) ☎23573
Aodern brick façade with beamed older building.
3rm(1) CTV Mainly grills.
ast dinner9.15pm S% *sB&B£9.40
B&B £10.10 dB&B£16.70 dB&B £18.20
unch£2.75&alc Dinner£6alc Wine£2.65
redit cards 1 3

Park House 12 Droitwich Rd ☎21816
rm CTV 10P Last dinner8pm S%
sB&B£7–£8.50 dB&B£14–£17 Lunch£2.30–£3
Tea£1.50–£2 Dinner£3–£4 Wine£2

★Talbot 8–10 Barbourne Rd ☎21206
14rm CTV 40P Last dinner10pm S%
sB&B£7.25–£9.40 dB&B£13.50 Lunch£5–£8
Dinner£5–£8 Wine£2.50

XXKing Charles II New St ☎22449
Closed Sun, Public Hols, 25 & 26 Dec & New Year;
35seats English, French & Italian.
Last dinner9.30pm Lunch£3.75&alc
Dinner£12alc Wine£4 Credit cards 1 2 3 4 6

WORKINGTON Cumbria Map**11** NX92
★★★Westland Braithwaite Rd ☎4544
A modern hotel, situated 2 miles outside Workington, just off the A595.
30rm(17) CTV 200P Live music & dancing wkly French. Last dinner10pm

★★Green Dragon Portland Sq ☎3803
A family and commercial hotel, situated in the industrial and market town of Workington.
11rm(1) CTV 15 Last dinner8.15pm
S% sB&B£10.78 dB&B£18.80
dB&B £20.80 Lunch fr£3 Dinner fr£4.80&alc
Wine£2.80

WORPLESDON Surrey Map**4** SU95
★★Worplesdon Place Perry Hill ☎2407
15rm(9) CTV 100P Live music & dancing
Sat in winter English & French. Last dinner10pm
Credit cards 3 5

WORSLEY Greater Manchester Map**7** SD70
XXCasserole 21 Worsley Rd ☎061–794 2660
Closed Sun & Mon; Lunch not served Sat; 55seats
12P English & French. Last dinner10pm S%
*Lunch£4.05&alc Dinner£5.13&alc Wine£2.50
Credit card 5

WORTHING West Sussex Map **4** TQ10
★★★**Beach** Marine Pde ☎34001
Three-storey white 1930s-style building with uninterrupted view of sea. Terrace and balcony run the length of building.
97rm(82⇌⋒) Lift ☽ ⋔ CTV in bedrooms ⊗ 55P Conference facilities available Children under 8 yrs not accommodated Last dinner 8.45pm ♁ ⊈ S% sB&B fr£10.25 sB&B⇌⋒ fr£12.25 dB&B fr£21.20 dB&B⇌⋒ fr£22.05 Lunch £3.90&alc Tea £1 Dinner £5.25&alc Wine £3 ⊟ *xmas* Credit cards 1 2 3

★★★**Berkeley** Marine Pde (North) ☎31122 Telex no 262180
Converted Victorian terraced houses, considerably extended, with glass-shielded sun terrace overlooking the sea. Dining room with modern panelling and alcoves.
Unlicensed; 96rm(45⇌⋒) Lift ☽ ⚔ ⋔ CTV 20P Last dinner 8pm ♁ ⊈ S% sB&B fr£9 sB&B⇌⋒ fr£12 dB&B fr£16.50 dB&B⇌⋒ fr£20.50 Lunch fr£3.75 Tea fr75p Dinner fr£4 ⊟ Credit cards 1 2 3 6

★★★**Chatsworth** The Steyne (Inter-Hotel) ☎36103
The hotel has an attractive Georgian frontage, situated in a terrace overlooking Steyne gardens and the sea.
90rm(76⇌⋒) Lift ☽ ⋔ CTV in bedrooms ⚑ billiards Conference facilities available ♡ English & French. Last dinner 9.15pm ♁ ⊈ ✱sB&B £8.50–£10.50 sB&B⇌⋒ £11.50–£13.50 dB&B £17–£19 dB&B⇌⋒ £20–£22 Lunch £4 Tea £1.25 Dinner £5 Wine £2.65 ⊟ *xmas* Credit cards 1 2 3 6

★★★**Eardley** Marine Pde ☎34444
Modernised and extended Victorian terraced houses

W

the end of the parade and overlooking the sea.
6rm(49⇌ ⌂) Lift ☽ CTV in bedrooms 20P 2
Conference facilties available Last dinner9.45pm
sB&B£9.50–£12.50
B&B⇌ ⌂£12.50–£15 dB&B£18–£22
B&B⇌ ⌂£20–£24 Lunch fr£3.50 Tea fr60p
Dinner fr£4.50&alc Wine£2.70 xmas
Credit cards 1 2 3

★★Warnes Marine Pde ☎35222
Georgian-style hotel overlooking sea.
0rm(50⇌ ⌂) Lift ☽ CTV CTV in bedrooms 20P 2
Billiards Conference facilities available English,
French & Italian. Last dinner8.30pm
B&B£10–£11 sB&B⇌ ⌂£13.50–£15.50
dB&B£20–£22 dB&B⇌ ⌂£24.50–£27.50
Continental breakfast Lunch£4.25&alc Tea£1.25
High Tea£2 Dinner£5&alc Wine£3.50 xmas
Credit cards 1 2 3 5

★Ardington Steyne Gdns ☎30451
Pleasantly situated facing Steyne gardens, adjacent to promenade and shopping centre.
Closed Xmas; 44rm (17⇌ ⌂) ☽ CTV TV available in bedrooms Last dinner8pm ✱sB&B£9
sB&B⇌ ⌂£10 dB&B£18 dB&B⇌ ⌂£20
Lunch£3–£3.50 Tea45p Dinner£3.50

★Beechwood Hall Park Cres, Wykeham Rd
☎32872
Regency period house set in wooded and lawned gardens, close to town centre and sea front.
5rm(3⇌ ⌂) CTV P Children under 5yrs not accommodated Last dinner7.30pm S%
sB&B fr£8.50 dB&B fr£17 dB&B⇌ ⌂ fr£20
Lunch fr£3 Tea75p–£1 Dinner fr£4 Wine£2.74

★Kingsway Marine Pde ☎37542
3rm(13⇌ ⌂) Lift TV in bedrooms 6P Children under 3yrs not accommodated Last dinner8.30pm
sB&B£9–£10 sB&B⇌ ⌂£9.75–£12.80
dB&B£18–£22.60 dB&B⇌ ⌂£22–£26.60
Lunch fr£2.75&alc Tea45p Dinner£4–£4.50&alc
Wine£2.72 xmas Credit cards 2 3 5

XXParade Wine Lodge Marine Pde ☎33825
Bright and airy modern restaurant with small bar on enclosed balcony overlooking sea.
Closed Mon; Dinner not served Sun; 100seats
Last dinner9.30pm ✱Lunch£3.20–£3.50&alc
Dinner£3.95–£4.95&alc Wine£2.95
Credit cards 1 3 5

XXParagon Continental 9/10 Brunswick Rd
☎33367
Closed Sun & Tue; 36seats Continental.
Last dinner10pm ✱Lunch£3.80&alc
Dinner£12alc Wine£2.80 Credit cards 2 3

WOTTON-UNDER-EDGE Gloucestershire Map**3** ST79
★★Swan Market St ☎2329
White-painted inn with enclosed courtyard.
26rm(19⇌ ⌂) CTV in bedrooms Live music & dancing wkly Continental. Last dinner9.45pm
S% sB&B£18 sB&B⇌ ⌂ fr£20.50 dB&B£26
dB&B⇌ ⌂ fr£28 Lunch£6 Dinner£7 xmas
Credit cards 1 2 3 5 6

WRAFTON Devon Map**2** SS43
XXPoyers Farm ☎Braunton812149
Late 16th-C converted farm cottage with white walls, ships' timbers and thatched roof.
Closed Mon & 3wks Oct; Dinner not served Sun; 42 seats 24P English, French & Italian.
Last dinner9.30pm

WROXHAM Norfolk Map**9** TG31
★★ *Wroxham* Broads Centre, Hoveton ☎2061
Morris dancing is held on hotel terrace every year in July.
18rm(14⇌ ⌂) CTV TV available in bedrooms 100P
Live music & dancing Sat (in winter) English & French. Last dinner9.30pm
Credit cards 1 2 3 4 5 6

WROXTON Oxfordshire Map**4** SP44
★★Wroxton House ☎Wroxton St Mary482
14rm(8⇌ ⌂) CTV CTV in bedrooms 50P
International. Last dinner10pm
sB&B£11.50–£12.50 sB&B⇌ ⌂£15.50–£16.50
dB&B£22–£25 dB&B⇌ ⌂£25–£28
Lunch£3.75&alc Dinner£4.25–£4.95&alc
Wine£3.30 Credit cards 1 2 3 5 6

WYE Kent Map**5** TR04
★*Kings Head* Church St ☎812418
9rm CTV 2P 5 English & French.
Last dinner10pm

XXWife of Bath ☎812540
Small cottage restaurant with low-ceilinged rooms hung with modern paintings.
Closed Sun, Mon & Xmas; 50seats 14P French.
Last dinner10pm

WYKEHAM (nr Scarborough) N Yorks Map**8** SE98
★★Downe Arms ☎Scarborough 862471
Telex no527192
6rm Lift CTV 200P 4 Disco 4nights wkly in summer Live music & dancing wkly English & French. Last dinner9pm S% sB&B£6–£7.50
Bar lunch75p–£2 Dinner£5–£7 Wine£2.60
Credit cards 1 2 3 4 5 6

WYMONDHAM Norfolk Map**5** TG10
★★Abbey Church St ☎602148
Small modernised hotel, part of which dates from late 16th century; quiet location adjacent to Wymondham Abbey.
Unlicensed; 33rm(14⇌ ⌂) Lift ☽ CTV 22P 3
Last dinner8.30pm S% sB&B fr£6.83
sB&B⇌ ⌂ fr£8.13 dB&B fr£13.07
dB&B⇌ ⌂ fr£14.37 Lunch£1.50–£1.75 Tea fr75p
High Tea fr£1.80 Dinner fr£3
Credit cards 1 2 3 5

XBullen's 16 Damgate St ☎603533
Closed Sun & Mon; Lunch not served; 24seats
English & French. ✱Dinner£5.75 Wine£2.25
Credit cards 1 3

WYRE PIDDLE Hereford & Worcester Map**3** SO94
★Avonside Main Rd ☎Pershore2654
7rm(3⇌ ⌂) CTV TV in bedrooms 10P
(heated) Children under 5yrs not accommodated Last dinner9pm S%
sB&B£10.35–£11.50 sB&B⇌ ⌂£12.65–£13.80
dB&B£15.52–£18.40 dB&B⇌ ⌂£18.97–£21.85
Dinner£5.17–£6.03 Wine£3.40

YARCOMBE Devon Map**3** ST20
★★Yarcombe Inn ☎Upottery218
A white-painted, thatched building dating from the 14th century.
RS Xmas Day; 7rm CTV 50P
Last dinner9.30pm S% ✱sB&B fr£7
dB&B fr£14 Lunch£3.45 Dinner£4.25&alc
Wine£1.95 Credit cards 1 3

★Belfry ☎Upottery234
Rosette awarded for dinner only
Closed 3wks Xmas, 1wk Spring & 1wk summer; RS Sun; 6⇌ CTV 10P Children under 14yrs not accommodated Last dinner7.15pm ✱
sB&B⇌£10.40–£14.10 dB&B⇌£18.10–£24.50
Dinner£5.50 Wine£3

YARMOUTH Isle of Wight Map**4** SZ38
★★George Quay St ☎760331
24rm(8⇌ ⌂) CTV 6P 6 Live music & dancing Sat in winter Last dinner9.15pm
S% sB&B fr£7.50 sB&B⇌ ⌂ fr£9.50

dB&B fr£15 dB&B⇌⋒ fr£19 Lunch£3.25–£3.50 Tea75p–£1.50 Dinner£4.95–£5.50 Wine£2.50 ⊟ *xmas* Credit cards 1 2 3 5 6

YARMOUTH, GREAT Norfolk Map**5** TG50

★★★**Carlton** Marine Parade South (Inter-Hotel) ☎55234 Telex no 97249
96rm(72⇌⋒) Lift ☽ ⫶ CTV CTV available in bedrooms 25⌂ Conference facilities available Last dinner9.15pm ✿ ♫ ✻sB&B fr£13.50 sB&B⇌⋒ fr£16.50 dB&B fr£19 dB&B⇌⋒ fr£24.50 Lunch fr£4 Tea fr90p Dinner fr£5.25 Wine£3 ⊟ *xmas* Credit cards 1 2 3 4 5 6

★★★**Star** Hall Quay (Grand Met) ☎2294
Centrally-situated, three-storey, half-timbered inn dating back to 1666, overlooking quayside and River Yare.
42rm(21⇌⋒) Lift ☽ ⫶ TV TV available in bedrooms 18P ♉English & French. Last dinner9.45pm ✿ ♫ S% ✻sB&B⇌⋒£12.50 dB&B⇌⋒£19 ⊟ *xmas* Credit cards 1 2 3 4 5 6

★★**Burlington** North Dr ☎4568
Closed Nov–Mar; 32rm(22⇌⋒) Lift ⫶ CTV CTV available in bedrooms ⊘ 40P Last dinner8pm ✿ ♫ S% sB&B£8.50–£14 sB&B⇌⋒£10–£16 dB&B£16–£28 dB&B⇌⋒£18–£30 Lunch£3–£4.50 Tea40p Dinner£4.50–£6 ⊟ *xmas* Credit card 1

★★**Cliff** Gorleston-on-Sea (2m S A12) ☎62179
30rm(11⇌⋒) ☽ ⫶ CTV CTV available in bedrooms 50P ⚓ ⌂ Last dinner9pm ✿ ♫ S% ✻sB&B£10.26 sB&B⇌⋒£12.42 dB&B£18.36 dB&B⇌⋒£22.68 Lunch£2.95&alc Dinner£3.78&alc Wine£2.70 ⊟ *xmas* Credit cards 1 2 3 6

★★**Imperial** North Dr ☎2000
53rm(23⇌⋒) Lift ☽ ⫶ CTV 40P ⌂ ♉English & French. Last dinner10.30pm ✿ S% sB&B£10.50–£12.50 sB&B⇌⋒£12.50–£15 dB&B£17–£21 dB&B⇌⋒£21–£25 Lunch fr£3&alc Dinner fr£5&alc Wine£3 ⊟ *xmas* Credit cards 1 2 3 5 6

★***Marine View*** North Dr ☎2879
52rm Lift CTV 25P 5⌂ Live music Fri Cabaret Fri Last dinner6.30pm Credit card 3

YATTENDON Berkshire Map**4** SU57

★**Royal Oak** ☎Hermitage201325
Pleasant 16th-C inn with oak beams and open log fires, situated in the tiny village of Yattendon.
6rm(3⇌⋒) ⫶ CTV in bedrooms 30P ⊛ ⚓ ♉English & French. Last dinner9.30pm ✿ S% sB&B£20 sB&B⇌⋒£20 dB&B£30 dB&B⇌⋒£30 Lunch£7alc Dinner£7alc Wine£2.35 ⊟ Credit cards 1 2 3 5 6

YELDHAM, GREAT Essex Map**5** TL73

XX**White Hart** ☎237250
An old coaching inn built in 1510. Samuel Pepys endorsed the first application for license to sell beer here.
60seats 60P Last dinner9.30pm Lunch£10alc Dinner£10alc Wine£2.95 Credit cards 1 2 3

YELVERTON Devon Map**2** SX56

★★★**Moorland Links** ☎2245
27rm(16⇌⋒) ☽ ⫶ CTV in bedrooms 140P ⚓ ⊐ ⊸(hard) ∩ ♉French. Last dinner9pm ✿ ♫ S% ✻sB&B⇌⋒ fr£21 dB&B⇌⋒ fr£29.16 Lunch£4.86&alc Tea80p Dinner£5.90&alc Wine£3.12 ⊟ *xmas* Credit cards 1 2 3 5 6

★***Retreat*** Tavistock Rd ☎2099
8rm CTV 40P 4⌂ ⊛ ⚓ Last dinner9pm ✿ ♫ ⊟ 1 2 3 4 5 6

Y

YEOVIL Somerset Map**3** ST51
★★★**Manor** Hendford (Crest) ☎23116
A manor house dating from 1800 with a mellow stone front.
24rm(14⇌⋒) ☽ ⋒ CTV in bedrooms 100P
Mainly grills. Last dinner 10pm S%
✱sB&B⇌⋒£16.20 dB&B⇌⋒£23.76
Credit cards 1 2 3 4 5 6

★★***Mermaid*** High St ☎23151
A modernised inn, situated in the town centre, it has a beamed ceiling in the restaurant and bars.
Closed Xmas; 15rm(3⇌⋒) CTV 8P
Mainly grills. Last dinner 10pm ☎
Credit cards 2 3 5

★★***Three Choughs*** Hendford (Eldridge Pope) ☎4886
39rm(7⇌⋒) CTV Live music & dancing Sat English & French. Last dinner 9.45pm ☎
Credit cards 1 2 5 6

★**Preston** Preston Rd ☎4400
6rm(1⇌⋒) CTV CTV in bedrooms 36P 7
Last dinner 9.15pm sB&B£8.85
sB&B⇌⋒£10.60 dB&B£17.50 dB&B⇌⋒£20
Lunch fr£3.60&alc Tea fr70p&alc
High Tea fr£1.20&alc Dinner fr£3.80&alc
Wine£2.90 Credit card 3

XX**Little Barwick House** (2m S off A37) ☎23902
Closed Sun; 27seats 15P bedrooms available
English & French. Last dinner 9.30pm
Lunch£4.85 Dinner£6.50alc Wine£2.95
Credit cards 1 2 3 5

At **West Coker** (3m W A30)
☆☆**Coker Motel** ☎West Coker 2555
16⇌⋒ 98P

YORK North Yorkshire Map**8** SE65
★★★★**Royal Station** Station Rd (British Transport) ☎53681 Telex no 57912
Massive railway palace rising to six storeys and standing in own ample gardens within sight of the Minster.
130rm(111⇌⋒) Lift ☽ CTV TV in bedrooms 100P
Conference facilities available
Last dinner 9.30pm S%
sB&B⇌⋒ fr£25.40 dB&B⇌⋒ fr£40.50
Dinner fr£6.45 Wine£3.15 *xmas*
Credit cards 1 2 3 4 5 6

★★★★**Viking** North St (Grand Met) ☎59822
Telex no 57937
110⇌⋒ Lift ☽ TV available in bedrooms 85P
Conference facilities available English & French.
Last dinner 9.30pm S% ✱sB&B⇌⋒£22
dB&B⇌⋒£32 *xmas* Credit cards 1 2 3 4 5 6

★★★**Abbey Park** The Mount (Myddleton) ☎25481
Telex no 57993
84rm(75⇌⋒) Lift ☽ CTV in bedrooms 50P Live music & dancing Sat in winter Last dinner 8.45pm
S% ✱sB&B£12.50 sB&B⇌⋒£16.60
dB&B£21 dB&B⇌⋒£26.20 Lunch fr£3.75
Dinner fr£4.95 Wine£3 *xmas*
Credit cards 1 2 3 5 6

★★★**Chase** Tadcaster Rd ☎707171
Closed Xmas; 80rm(56⇌⋒) Lift ☽ CTV CTV in bedrooms 100P 12 Live music & dancing Sat in winter Conference facilties available
Last dinner 8.45pm sB&B fr£14.96
sB&B⇌⋒ fr£17.82 dB&B fr£22.57
dB&B⇌⋒ fr£27.32 Continental breakfast
Lunch fr£3.40 Dinner fr£5.40 Wine£3
Credit cards 1 2 3 5 6

★★★**Dean Court** Duncombe Pl ☎25082
35⇌⋒ Lift ☽ CTV in bedrooms 5
Last dinner 9pm ☎ S% sB&B⇌⋒£17
dB&B⇌⋒£34 Lunch£4 Tea25p–£1.50
Dinner£6 Wine£3.22 *xmas*
Credit cards 1 2 3 5

☆☆☆**Post House** Tadcaster Rd (Trusthouse Forte) ☎707921 Telex no 57798
104⇌⋒ Lift ☽ TV in bedrooms 180P Conference facilities available Last dinner 10pm S%
sB&B⇌⋒£21.25 dB&B⇌⋒£30 *xmas*
Credit cards 1 2 3 4 5 6

★★**Ashcroft** 294 Bishopthorpe Rd ☎59286
Closed 24–31 Dec; 12rm CTV 40P
Last dinner 8.15pm sB&B£8.80–£10.50
sB&B⇌⋒£9.90–£12 dB&B£16.40–£19
dB&B⇌⋒£17.50–£22 Lunch£3–£3.50
Tea£1.08–£1.27 High Tea£2.70–£3
Dinner£3.78–£4.30

★★**Beechwood Close** Shipton Rd ☎58378
12rm CTV CTV available in bedrooms 36P
Last dinner 9pm sB&B£9 dB&B fr£18
Lunch£2.75 Tea35p–£1 High Tea70p–£1.50
Dinner£4.25alc Wine£2.80

★★**White Swan** Piccadilly (Centre) ☎28851
30rm Lift ☽ P Last dinner 9pm S%
✱sB&B£10 dB&B£16 Lunch£3.25 Dinner£3.25
Wine£3.40 Credit cards 1 2 3 4 5 6

★**Town House** 100–104 Holgate Rd ☎36171
16rm(8⇌⋒) CTV TV available in berooms 15P
English & French. Last dinner 9.30pm
S% sB&B fr£8.50 sB&B⇌⋒ fr£10 dB&B fr£15
dB&B⇌⋒ fr£18.50 Lunch fr£2.75 Tea fr£1.50
Dinner fr£5&alc Wine£3.25 *xmas*
Credit cards 1 2 3 5

XXX**Tanglewood** Malton Rd (6m NE on A64)
☎Flaxton Moor 318
Closed Mon; Dinner not served Sun; 100seats 60P
English & French. Last dinner 9.45pm
Lunch£6.50alc Dinner£8.75alc Wine£4
Credit cards 1 2 3 5

Y

ALDERNEY (No map)

★★Grand Island The Butes, St Ann ☎2848
Closed Oct–Apr; 34rm(16) CTV 25P (heated) (hard) Live music & dancing nightly International. Last dinner 9.30pm sB&B£10.60–£13 dB&B£18.80–£23.60 dB&B£21.20–£26 Lunch£3.35–£3.65&alc Dinner£5.15–£6.05&alc Credit cards 1 3 5

★★Hotel Chez Andre 45 Victoria St ☎2777
Closed Oct–Feb; 14rm(7) CTV CTV available in bedrooms Live music & dancing 5 nights wkly French. Last dinner 8pm sB&B£10.50–£12 sB&B£11.75–£13.25 dB&B£21–£28 dB&B£23.50–£30 Tea90p–£1.10 Dinner£4.50–£5&alc Wine£2.20 Credit cards 1 3 5 6

GUERNSEY (No map)

CÂTEL

★★Hotel de Beauvoir Rue Cohu ☎Guernsey 54750
29rm(20) CTV 40P English & French. Last dinner 7.30pm S% sB&B£8–£10 sB&B£8.50–£10.50 dB&B£16–£20 dB&B£17–£21 Lunch£2.50 Tea30P Dinner£3.75–£4.75&alc Wine£2 Credit cards 1 2 3

FERMAIN BAY

★★★Le Chalet ☎Guernsey 35716
Closed 21Oct–14Apr; 40 CTV in bedrooms 40P English, French & Austrian. Last dinner 8.30pm S% sB&B£11.50–£13.20 dB&B£21–£24.12 Lunch£2.75–£3 Dinner£4.25–£5&alc Wine£2.50 *xmas* Credit cards 1 2 3 4 5 6

★★La Favorita ☎Guernsey 35666
Peacefully situated building with terraced gardens, overlooking bay.
Closed Nov–Mar; 30rm(17) CTV 30P Last dinner 7.30pm S% sB&B£9.75–£12.90 sB&B£10.40–£13.65 dB&B£15–£20 dB&B£16–£21 Lunch£3–£3.75 Tea60p–£1 Dinner£3.90–£4.90 Wine£3 Credit card 3

PETIT BÔT

★Manor ☎Guernsey 37788
62rm(20) Lift CTV 28P Children under 10yrs not accommodated English & French. Last dinner 7.30pm S% sB&B£6.60–£7 sB&B£7.60–£8 dB&B£13.20–£14 dB&B fr£15.20 Lunch fr£2.20 Tea fr50p High Tea fr80p Dinner fr£3 Wine£2.10 Credit card 3

ST MARTIN

★★★Green Acres Les Hubits ☎Guernsey 35711
48 CTV in bedrooms 50P (heated) Live music & dancing Mon Last dinner 8.30pm S% sB&B fr£8.50 dB&B fr£17 Lunch fr£1.75 Tea fr25p Dinner fr£3&alc Wine£2.75 *xmas*

★★★Ronnie Ronalde's St Martin's Hotel, Les Merriennes ☎Guernsey 35644
58rm Lift CTV in bedrooms 150P (heated) (hard) Live music & dancing 5 nights wkly Conference facilities available English & French. Last dinner 9.30pm S% sB&B fr£11 dB&B fr£22 Lunch£3&alc Tea50p High Tea£1 Dinner£3.50&alc Wine£2 Credit cards 1 2 3 5

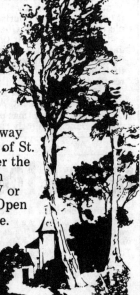

★★★***St Margarets Lodge*** Forest Rd ☎Guernsey35757 Telexno418144 42⇌ Lift ☽ CTV TV available in bedrooms 150P ⚓ (heated) Live music & dancing 3nights wkly (in summer) Conference facilities available English, French & Italian. Last dinner10pm Credit cards 1 2 3 5 6

★★***Bella Luce*** La Fosse ☎Guernsey38764 25⇌ CTV 30P ⚓ (heated) sauna bath English & French. Last dinner8.30pm Credit card 1

★★***La Villette*** La Rue des Marettes ☎Guernsey38454 43rm(32⇌) CTV TV available in bedrooms 100P ⚓ (heated) Live music 5 nights wkly Live music & dancing 3nights wkly ♿ English & Continental. Last dinner8pm

★***Saints Bay*** Icart ☎Guernsey38888 Closed Nov–Mar; 27rm(15⇌) CTV 50P ⚓ (heated) Last dinner8pm

ST PETER PORT

★★★★**Duke of Richmond** Cambridge Park ☎Guernsey26221 Telexno4191462 75⇌ Lift ☽ CTV in bedrooms (heated) Live music & dancing 6 nights wkly Conference facilities available ♿ Continental. Last dinner9.30pm S% sB&B⇌£14.50–£19.50 dB&B⇌£25–£34 Lunch£3.25–£3.50&alc Lunch£3.25–£3.50&alc Tea30p–£1 High Tea£1.50–£3 Dinner£5–5.25&alc Wine£2.85 *xmas* Credit cards 1 2 3 5 6

★★★★**Old Government House** Ann's Place (Prestige) ☎Guernsey24921 Telexno4191144 74⇌ 1 Lift ☽ CTV CTV available in bedrooms

40P ⛱(heated) Conference facilities available ♡French. Lastdinner9.15pm S% sB&B£11.50–£16.40 dB&B£23–£32.80 Lunch fr£3.25 Tea fr30p Dinner fr£4 Wine£2.05 xmas Credit cards 1 2 3 5 6

★★★La Frégate Les Côtils ☎Guernsey24624 13 15P Children under 14yrs not accommodated Lastdinner9.30pm *sB&B£13–£15.50 dB&B£24–£29 Lunch£3.50–£3.75&alc Dinner£4.50&alc Wine£2 Credit cards 1 2 3 5

★★★Royal Glategny Esp ☎Guernsey23921 Telex no4191221 *Four storey hotel facing harbour with views of Herm, Jethou and Sark.* 79rm(70) Lift CTV CTV in bedrooms 120P (heated) Live music & dancing 5 nights wkly Conference facilities available ♡International. Lastdinner9.30pm S% sB&B£12–£17 sB&B£13–£18 dB&B£24–£34 dB&B£26–£36 Lunch£3.50&alc Dinner£4&alc Wine£1.89 xmas Credit cards 1 2 3 4 5 6

★★Dunchoille Guelles Rd ☎Guernsey22912 Closed Jan–Mar; 24rm(10) CTV 16P Children under 4yrs not accommodated Lastdinner7.15pm sB&B£6.50–£7.50 sB&B£7.50–£8.50 dB&B£13–£15 dB&B£16–£16.50 Bar lunch40p–£1.25 Dinner£2.50–£3.50 Wine£1.80

★★Grange Lodge Grange Rd ☎Guernsey25161 Closed mid Oct–mid Mar; 38rm(14) CTV 50P (heated) sB&B£7.50–£9 sB&B£8–£9.50 dB&B£15–£18 dB&B£16–£19 Bar lunch50p–£1.40 Tea25p–40p Dinner£3 Wine£1.15 Credit cards 1 3

★★Hotel de Havelet Havelet ☎Guernsey22199 *Georgian house with modern extension and sun terrace; set in extensive gardens overlooking harbour and sea.* 35rm(28) CTV CTV in bedrooms 40P Children under 7yrs not accommodated Lastdinner9.30pm S% *sB&B£8.90–£9.75 sB&B£9.75–£11 dB&B£17.80–£19.50 dB&B£19.50–£22 Lunch£2.25–£2.75&alc Tea fr30p Dinner£3.25–£3.75&alc Wine£1.95 xmas Credit cards 1 2 3 5 6

★★Moore's Pollet ☎Guernsey24452 40rm(11) Lift CTV CTV available in bedrooms ♡English & French. Lastdinner8.15pm S% sB&B£9.95–£12 dB&B£17.90–£21.50 dB&B£11–£26.40 Lunch£2.95–£4.25 Dinner£3.95–£4.50 Credit cards 1 2 3 4 6

XXX Le Français Market St ☎Guernsey20963 Closed Sun 15Jan–16Feb; Lunch not served Sat; 40seats ♡French. Lastdinner9.45pm S% *Lunch£3.65&alc Dinner£8alc Wine£2.60 Credit cards 1 2 3 5 6

XXX Le Nautique Pier Steps ☎Guernsey21714 Closed Sun (Nov–Feb); 66seats ♡French. Lastdinner10.30pm Lunch£7.60alc Dinner£7.60alc Wine£2.15 Credit cards 1 2 3 5

X Nino's Ristorante Italiano Lefevre St ☎Guernsey23052 *Simple restaurant with open-plan grill kitchen.* 75seats 4P ♡English & Italian. Lastdinner11pm Lunch fr£2.50&alc Dinner fr£4.50&alc Wine£2.10 Credit cards 1 2 3 4 5 6

JERSEY (No map)

ARCHIRONDEL

★★Les Arches Archirondel Bay ☎Jersey53839 Telex no4192085 53rm(30) 120P (heated) Disco 6nights wkly Live music & dancing 6nights wkly Cabaret wkly Conference facilities available ♡Continental. Lastdinner8.30pm S% sB&B£11.70–£16 sB&B£13.20–£18 db&B£23.40–£32 dB&B£26.40–£36 Lunch£4.50–£5.50&alc Tea40p–£1 Dinner£5.50–£7.50&alc Wine£2.20 Credit cards 1 2 3

BEAUMONT

★★Hotel l'Hermitage ☎Jersey33314 Telex no41570 Closed Dec–Feb; 111 CTV TV in bedrooms 85P (heated) sauna bath Disco wkly Live music & dancing wkly Cabaret wkly Children under 14yrs not accommodated ♡International. Lastdinner7.30pm S% sB&B£6.25–£12 dB&B£12.50–£24 Lunch£2.40 Dinner£3 Wine£1.65

BOULEY BAY

★★★★Water's Edge ☎Jersey62777 Telex no4191462 Closed Jan–Apr; 56 Lift CTV CTV in bedrooms 24P (heated) sauna bath Live music & dancing 5nights wkly ♡English & Continental. Lastdinner9.45pm S% Credit cards 1 2 3 5

CORBIÈRE

XXX *Sea Crest Hotel Restaurant* Petit Port ☎Jersey42687 55seats 40P bedrooms available ♡English, French & Italian. Lastdinner10pm Credit cards 1 3

GOREY

★★★ ***Old Court House*** ☎Jersey54444
Modern building with well-kept gardens including aviary; situated near bay.
Closed 6Nov–6Dec; RS 28Oct–5Nov & 7Dec–Apr except Xmas, New Year & Etr; 27rm(27⇌ ⋒) ☽ ⅏ CTV TV available in bedrooms ⊘ 60P ⚓ ⛱(heated) sauna bath ♡International. Last dinner 9.30pm ☐ ⊟ Credit cards 1 2 3 5

★★ ***Dolphin*** Gorey Pier ☎Jersey53370 Telex no41385
17rm(15⇌ ⋒) ☽ ⅏ CTV TV available in bedrooms ⊘ Live music 6nights wkly ♡English, French & Italian. Last dinner 10.15pm ♁ Wine£2.20 ⊟ Credit cards 3 6

× ***Galley*** ☎Jersey53456
Small restaurant overlooking harbour. Nautical décor includes fishing nets and buoys.
Dinner not served Mon; 40seats bedrooms available ♡English & French. Last dinner 10.15pm

GROUVILLE BAY

★★ **Beausite** ☎Jersey54164 Telex no4192128
Closed Dec–Mar; 56rm(54⇌ ⋒) TV TV available in bedrooms 36P ⛱ Disco wkly Live music & dancing wkly ♧ Last dinner 8.30pm ♁ ☐ S%
sB&B£6–£8 sB&B⇌ ⋒£6.50–£8.50
dB&B£12–£16 dB&B⇌ ⋒£13–£17
Bar lunch 50p–£2.50 Tea 30p–£1
High Tea £1.50–£1.75 Dinner£3–£4 Wine£1.75
⊟

★★ ***Woodlands*** ☎Jersey54510
24rm(10⇌ ⋒) ☽ ⅏ CTV 50P ⚓ ⛱(heated) Disco 5nights wkly Live music & dancing 5nights wkly Cabaret 3–5nights wkly ♡English, French & Italian. Last dinner 10.30pm ♁ ☐ ⊟ Credit cards 1 2 5

L'ETACQ

××× **Lobster Pot** ☎Jersey82888
Attractive stone-built cottage restaurant.
Dinner not served Sun 100seats 50P ♡English, French & Italian. Last dinner 10pm Lunch£8alc Dinner£10alc Wine£2.80 Credit cards 1 2 3 5 6

ST AUBIN

×× **Old Court House Inn** St Aubin's Harbour ☎Jersey41156
60seats **P** bedrooms available Live music nightly ♡English & French. Last dinner 11pm S% ✱Lunch£7alc Dinner£10alc Wine£2.70

ST BRELADE

★★★★ **Atlantic** La Moye ☎Jersey44101
Modern purpose-built hotel, standing in own grounds with elevated position offering views across lawns and trees to the sea.
Closed 16Jan–Feb; 46⇌ ⋒ Lift ☽ ⅏ CTV in bedrooms 50P ⚓ ⛱(heated) ♪(hard) Disco twice wkly Conference facilities available ♡French. Last dinner 9.15pm ♁ ☐ S%
sB&B⇌ ⋒£15.70–£26.70 Lunch£3.75&alc
Tea£1.50 Dinner£6.75&alc *xmas*
Credit cards 1 2 3 4 5 6

★★★★ **Hotel l'Horizon** St Brelade's Bay ☎Jersey43101 Telex no4192281
90⇌ ⋒ Lift ☽ ⅏ CTV in bedrooms ⊘ 66P ⛟ ⛱(heated) sauna bath Live music & dancing nightly Conference facilities available ♡English, French & Italian. Last dinner 10.45pm ♁ ☐
✱sB&B⇌ ⋒£12.50–£17 dB&B⇌ ⋒£25–£40
Lunch£5 Tea£1alc Dinner£6 Wine£2 *xmas*
Credit cards 1 2 3 4 5 6

★★★★ **La Place** Route du Coin la Haule ☎Jersey44261
Closed Nov–10Apr 42⇌ ⋒ ☽ ⅏ CTV CTV in

bedrooms ⇌(heated) sauna bath ♡French. Last dinner9pm ✿ ☐ S% ✱sB&B⇌⋔£14.50–£16.50 dB&B⇌⋔£29–£33 Lunch£4&alc Tea£1.50 High Tea£2 Dinner£4.50&alc Credit cards ① ② ③ ⑤

★★★**Château Valeuse** Rue de Valeuse, St Brelades Bay ☎Jersey43476
Detached modernised villa standing in an elevated position in quiet location with views across the bay.
Closed Jan; 26rm(23⇌⋔) ☽ ♛ CTV ⊘ 80P ⚓ ⇌(heated) Children under 5yrs not accommodated ♡French. Last dinner10pm ✿ ☐ S% ✱sB&B£8–£8.50 sB&B⇌⋔£9–£9.50 dB&B£17–£18 dB&B⇌⋔£18–£19 Lunch£2.50–£3.50&alc Tea30p–£1&alc Dinner£3–£4&alc Wine£2.30 *xmas* Credit card ③

✕**Herbie's Inn** St Brelades Bay ☎Jersey41081
Closed Mon; 75seats 35P ♡English & Continental. Last dinner10.30pm ✱Lunch£2.50&alc Dinner£5.80&alc Wine£2.35 Credit card ③

ST CLEMENT'S BAY

★★★**Ambassadeur** La Greve d'Azette ☎Jersey24455
Closed Oct–Apr; 41rm(26⇌⋔) ☽ CTV 30P Live music nightly Cabaret wkly ♡International Last dinner9.15pm ☐ ✿ S% sB&B£7.50–£12 sB&B⇌⋔£9.50–£14.50 dB&B£15–£24 dB&B⇌⋔£19–£29 Lunch£3&alc Dinner£4&alc Wine£2.75 ⊟ Credit cards ① ② ③ ④ ⑤ ⑥

✕✕✕**Shakespeare Hotel Restaurant** Coast Rd, Samares ☎Jersey51915
Closed 16Dec–13Feb; 95seats 60P bedrooms available ♡English & French. Last dinner9.45pm ✱Lunch£3.30–£4&alc Dinner£8alc Wine£1.80 Credit cards ① ② ③

ST HELIER
★★★★**Hotel La Plage** Havre des Pas ☎Jersey23474
Telexno4192356
97⇌⋒ Lift ☽ CTV in bedrooms ⊗80P 10⌂ Live music & dancing nightly Cabaret Sat ♡English & French. Lastdinner9pm ✿ ♨
sB&B⇌⋒£16.50–£18.75
dB&B⇌⋒£31.65–£42.50 Lunch£3.50–£4&alc
Tea50p–£1.50 Dinner£4.85–£5.50&alc
Wine£2.20 ⊨ *xmas* Creditcards 1 2 3 4 5 6

★★★**Apollo** St Saviour's Rd ☎Jersey25441
Telexno4192086
53⇌⋒ Lift ☽ ⅢCTV CTV in bedrooms 40P Live music & dancing twice wkly ♡French.
Lastdinner8.30pm ✿ ♨ S%
✻sB&B⇌⋒£14–£18.50 dB&B⇌⋒£11–£16.50
Lunch fr£3.50 Tea fr30p Dinner fr£4&alc
Wine£2.20 ⊨ *xmas* Creditcards 1 2 3

★★★**Beaufort** Green St ☎Jersey32471
Telexno4192160
50⇌⋒ Lift ☽ Ⅲ CTV in bedrooms ⊗20P Live music 6nights wkly ♡English, French & Italian.
Lastdinner9pm ✿ ♨ S%
Lunch£2.50–£4.50&alc Tea35–70p
Dinner£4.50–£6&alc Wine£2.50 *xmas*
Creditcards 1 2 3 5 6

★★★**Ommaroo** Havre des Pas ☎Jersey23493
Telexno419225
85rm(74⇌⋒) Lift ☽ Ⅲ CTV TV available in bedrooms 80P ⚓ Discowkly Live music & dancing twice wkly Cabaretwkly Conference facilities available ⌂
Lastdinner8.30pm ✿ ♨ S% ✻sB&B£11–£15
sB&B⇌⋒£13–£17 dB&B⇌⋒£26–£34
Lunch fr£4&alc Tea fr75p Dinner fr£5&alc *xmas*
Creditcards 2 3

★★**Hotel Savoy** Rouge Bouillon ☎Jersey30012
RS Nov–Feb; 68rm(29⇌ ⋒) ☽ ♛ CTV 65P ⊃(heated) Live music & dancing wkly Cabaret wkly Last dinner8pm ✿ ☕ S% sB&B£8.75–£10.25 sB&B⇌⋒£10.25–£11.75 dB&B£17.50–£20.50 dB&B⇌⋒£20.50–£23.50 Lunch£3&alc Tea25p Dinner£4.50&alc Wine£2.60 *xmas*
Credit cards ① ③

★★**Mountview** St John's Rd ☎Jersey30080
Telex no4192341
Closed Nov–Mar; 35rm(19⇌ ⋒) Lift ☽ CTV 8P Live music & dancing wkly ♡International.
Last dinner8.30pm ✿ S% sB&B£8.25–£16 sB&B⇌⋒£9.25–£17 dB&B£16.50–£26.40 dB&B⇌⋒£18.50–£28.40 Lunch fr£3 Dinner fr£4 Wine£2

★★**Pomme d'Or** The Weighbridge ☎Jersey20501
Telex no4192356
On corner site in old part of town, overlooking harbour.
Closed 27Sep–Mar 62⇌⋒ Lift ☽ ♛ CTV in bedrooms ⊗ Live music & dancing 3 nights wkly Conference facilities available ♡English & French.
Last dinner8.30pm ✿ ☕ S%
dB&B⇌⋒£22.50–£24.70 Lunch£3.50–£4 Tea fr50p High Tea fr£2.50 Dinner£4–£4.50&alc Wine£2.50 Credit cards ① ② ③ ④ ⑤ ⑥

★★***Royal Yacht*** The Weighbridge ☎Jersey20511
47⇌⋒ Lift ☽ ♛ CTV TV available in bedrooms ♿ ✿ ☕

❀✕✕**La Capannina** 67 Halkett Pl ☎Jersey34602
Closed Sun & 24Dec–5Jan; 96seats ₱ ♡French & Italian. Specialities: saddle of lamb, Italian pastas, selection of fresh local fish. Last dinner10pm ✳Dinner£5alc Wine£2.40 Credit cards ① ② ③ ⑤

✕✕**Le Coq au Vin** 6 Cheapside ☎Jersey33705
Closed Sun & Jan; 55seats bedrooms available ♡French & Italian. Last dinner10.30pm Lunch£3.50&alc Dinner£5.50alc
Credit cards ② ③ ⑤

❀✕✕**Mauro's** 37 La Motte St ☎Jersey20147
Closed Sun, Public Hols, last wk Dec & Jan. 50seats ₱ ♡French & Italian. Specialities: melon parma ham, bisque d'homard flambé, caneton a l'orange.
Last dinner10pm ✳Lunch£9alc Dinner£9alc Wine£2.05

ST LAWRENCE

✕✕✕**Little Grove Hotel Restaurant** Rue d'Haut ☎Jersey25321
Dinner not served Mon; 60seats 40P bedrooms available ✗ Live music & dancing 4nights wkly ♡French. Last dinner10pm S% ✳Lunch fr£3&alc Tea20p–£1 Dinner£4–£5&alc
Credit cards ① ② ③ ⑤

ST PETER

★★★★**Mermaid** Airport Rd ☎Jersey41255
Telex no4192249
69⇌⋒ ☽ ♛ CTV CTV in bedrooms 200P ⚓ ⊃(heated) ⊃ Disco 3nights wkly Live music & dancing 3nights wkly Cabaret 3nights wkly Conference facilities available ♡French. ✿ ☕ S% Lunch fr£3.50 Tea fr£1.20 High Tea fr£2.20&alc Dinner fr£4 Wine£2.90 *xmas* Credit cards ① ② ③

✕✕✕**Mermaid Grill** (Mermaid Hotel) Airport Rd ☎Jersey41255
140seats 200P bedrooms available Disco 3nights wkly Live music & dancing 3nights wkly Cabaret

3nights wkly French. Last dinner9pm S%
*Lunch fr£3.50&alc Tea fr£1.20 High Tea fr£2.20
Dinner fr£4 Wine£2.90 Credit cards 1 3 4

ST SAVIOUR
★★★★ **Longueville Manor** (off St Helier/Grouville road, A3) Jersey25501
See page 58 for details

SARK (No map)

XX**Aval du Creux Hotel Restaurant** Harbour Hill 2036
Closed 5Oct–Apr 60seats P bedrooms available
Last dinner8.30pm S% Lunch£3–£3.50&alc
Dinner£4–£4.50&alc Wine£2.90

Isle of Man

ANDREAS Map**6** SC49
XX**Grosvenor** Kirk Andreas 576
Closed Tue & Oct; Dinner not served Sun; 40seats
60P International. Last dinner9pm
*Lunch£1.75–£3.75 Dinner£6alc

BALLASALLA Map**6** SC26
XXX**Coach House** Silverburn Bridge
Castletown2343
Closed Sun & 29Oct–10Nov; 105seats 35P
English & French. Last dinner10.30pm
*Lunch£4.50&alc Dinner£6.50alc Wine£2.70
Credit cards 2 3

CASTLETOWN Map**6** SC26
★★★**Golf Links** Fort Island 2201 Telex no627636
On peninsula at most southerly tip of island, with golf course on three sides of building.
Closed Oct–Mar; 75 CTV CTV available in bedrooms 100P (hard) billiards French.
Last dinner9.30pm sB&B £14.50–£16
dB&B £25–£28 Lunch£4.50 Tea£1
Dinner£5.50&alc

DOUGLAS Map**6** SC37
★**Hydro** Queens Promenade 6870
Closed Oct–Apr; 71rm Lift CTV
Last dinner6.30pm S% sB&B£8.25–£9.90
dB&B£11.40–£12 Lunch£1.50 Tea40p
High Tea£2 Dinner£2.50&alc Wine£2.15
Credit card 3

★**Woodbourne** Alexander Dr 21766
Closed Nov–May; 12rm CTV Children under 15yrs not accommodated Last dinner9.30pm S%
sB&B£10.88 dB&B£16.65 Lunch£2.50–£5.85
Dinner£2.50–£5.85&alc Wine£4.95

XXX***Julian's*** King Edward Rd, Onchan 5626
Closed Sun Oct–Mar, Mon in season & 2wks Oct/Nov; 65seats P English & French.
Last dinner10pm

X**Inner Man** 25 Nelson St 3646
Closed 1Nov–2Mar; Lunch not served Sat & Sun;
42seats P Live music & dancing 3nights wkly
English & French. Last dinner10pm Lunch£5alc
Dinner£7.50alc Wine£2.60

PEEL Map**6** SC28
X**Lively Lobster** The Harbour 2789
Closed mid Oct–mid May; 60seats P
Last dinner9pm *Lunch£5alc Dinner£7.50
Wine£2.50

PORT ERIN Map**6** SC16
X**The Restaurant** Station Rd 3566
Closed Mon & 31Oct–1Apr; Dinner not served Sun;
110seats 40P English & French.
Last dinner9.30pm Lunch£2.50–£3.75&alc
Tea fr85p High Tea£1–£3.50 Dinner£4–£5&alc
Wine£2.65

WALES

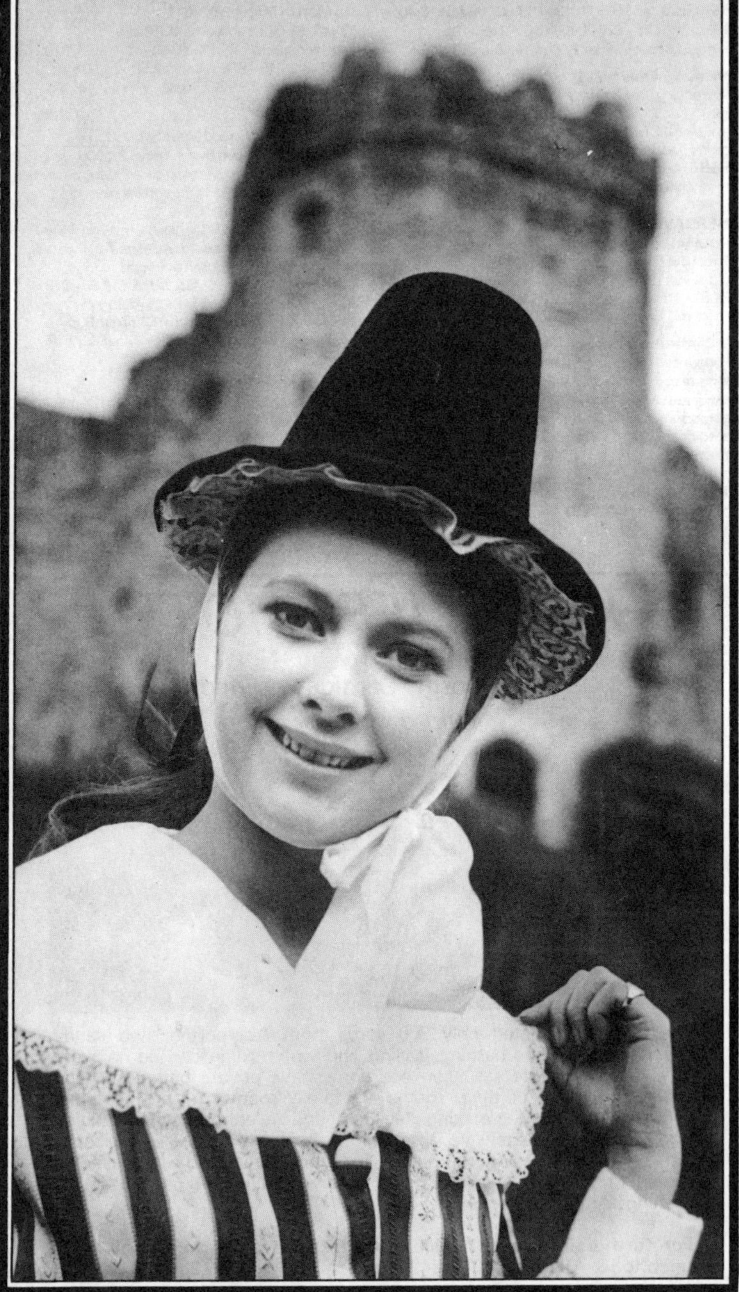

A

ABERDARON Gwynedd Map**6** SH12
★★**Ship** ☎204
Closed Nov–Feb; 8rm(3⇌⋒) TV ♀French. Lastdinner8.30pm ✿ S% sB&B fr£9 dB&B fr£18 Dinner£5alc Wine£3

ABERDOVEY Gwynedd Map**6** SN69
★★★**Treffeddian** ☎213
Closed 14Oct–Mar; 48rm(33⇌⋒) Lift CTV 28P 17🏠 ⚓ ⇌(heated) ♿ Lastdinner8.30pm ✿ ☕ S% sB&B£8.20 sB&B⇌⋒£13–£13.50 dB&B£16.40 dB&B⇌⋒£26–£27 Lunch fr£4 Tea fr70p Dinner fr£6&alc Wine£2.90 Credit card 1

★**Penhelig Arms** ☎215
Overlooking the sea, early 19th-C former coaching inn.
6rm(3⇌⋒) CTV 12P Children under 8yrs not accommodated Lastdinner8.30pm S% dB&B£14–£16 dB&B⇌⋒£13–£15 Bar lunch40p–£1.75 Dinner£5alc Wine£2.85

ABERGAVENNY Gwent Map**3** SO21
★★**Angel** Cross St (Trusthouse Forte) ☎2613
31rm(10⇌⋒) TV in bedrooms 27P Lastdinner10pm ✿ ☕ S% sB&B£13 sB&B⇌⋒£15 dB&B£15.50 dB&B⇌⋒£21.50 *xmas* Credit cards 1 2 3 4 5 6

✕✕**Clytha Arms** (6m E on A40) ☎Gobion206
Modernised roadside inn with a garden and open views of the surrounding area.
Dinner not served Tue (winter only); 40seats 40P bedrooms available ♀Continental. Lastdinner9.30pm ✻Lunch£5alc Dinner£6alc Wine£3.75 Credit cards 1 3

ABERMULE Powys Map**7** SO19
★★***Dolforwyn Hall*** ☎221
Country house dating back to 1640.
Closed Xmas wk; 8rm(3⇌⋒) CTV 40P ⚓ ♀English & French. Lastdinner9.30pm ☕

ABERPORTH Dyfed Map**2** SN25
★★**Highcliffe** ☎810534
6rm(4⇌⋒) Annexe: 6⇌⋒ CTV TV in bedrooms 20P Lastdinner8.30pm ✿ ✻sB&B⇌⋒ fr£8.50 dB&B⇌⋒ fr£17 Bar lunch65p–£1.85 Dinner£4.25&alc Wine£2.30

☆☆**Morlan Motel** ☎810611
17⇌⋒ TV in bedrooms 44P 8🏠 ♿ Lastdinner9pm ✿ ☕ sB&B⇌⋒£9.50–£10 dB&B⇌⋒£15–£16 Lunch£2.50–£3.50&alc Tea£1 Dinner£3.50–£4&alc Wine£2.14 Credit cards 1 2 3

ABERSOCH Gwynedd Map**6** SH32
★★★**Porth Tocyn** Bwlch Tocyn ☎2966
Low, white building set amid gardens and pastures, with views of the Welsh mountains beyond St Tudwal's Bay.
Closed Nov–Xmas; RS Xmas & Etr; 17rm (15⇌⋒) CTV CTV available in bedrooms P ⚓ ⇌(heated) (hard) ♀Welsh, English & French. Lastdinner9.30pm ✿ ☕ sB&B£12.50–£15 sB&B⇌⋒£14–£17 dB&B£25–£28 dB&B⇌⋒£27–£30 Lunch fr£3 Tea fr80p High Tea fr£2 Dinner fr£8&alc Wine£3.50 *xmas* Credit cards 1 2

★★**Harbour** ☎2406
Closed Oct Mar; 10rm(5⇌⋒) Annexe: 11rm(5⇌⋒) CTV 60P ⚓ Disco 6nights wkly Live music & dancing wkly ♀English & French. Lastdinner9pm ✿ ☕ sB&B£7.50–£10.25 sB&B⇌⋒£7.50–£11.50 dB&B£15–£20.50 dB&B⇌⋒£15–£23 Lunch£2 Tea£1–£1.50 Dinner£6.75alc Wine£2.80 Credit cards 2 5 6

★★*Neigwi* Sarn Rd ☎2363
A popular yachting centre is located in nearby bay.
Closed Nov–Feb; 11rm(3⇌ ⫙) CTV ⊗ 30P ⇛ ♀English & French. Lastdinner9pm ⊟
Creditcards 1 6

★**Manor** ☎2272
Closed Dec–Jan; 9rm(2⇌ ⫙) ⨯ CTV P ⇛ ⚓ Live music Sat ♀English & Welsh. Lastdinner7pm ✿
S% sB&B£8–£9 sB&B⇌ ⫙£10.75–£11.75 dB&B£16–£18 dB&B⇌ ⫙£21.50–£23.50 Barlunch£1.20–£2 Dinner£3.25&alc Wine£2.60 ⊟ *xmas*

✕**Sandpiper** High St ☎2151
Closed Jan & Feb; Dinner not served Sun 85seats 10P Lastdinner10pm Lunch£2.30alc Dinner£5alc Wine£2.35 Creditcards 1 3

ABERYSTWYTH Dyfed Map**6** SN58
★★★**Conrah** Chancery ☎617941
Country mansion (rebuilt 1912) set in 18 acres of grazing land and shrubbery, with private trout pool. Mountain views. Closed Nov; RS Dec–Feb; 13rm(11⇌ ⫙) Annexe:13rm(7⇌ ⫙) Lift ⨯ ⫙ CTV ⊗ 60P 3⌂ ⚓ Children not accommodated Lastdinner9pm ✿ S% sB&B£8.50–£9.50 sB&B⇌ ⫙£10.50–£12 dB&B£21–£25 dB&B⇌ ⫙£24–£28 Lunch£3.75 Dinner£5.75 Wine£2.80 Creditcards 1 3 5

★★*Belle Vue Royal* Marine Ter ☎617558
Occupies a fine position on the promenade overlooking the sea.
Closed Xmas; 50rm(11⇌ ⫙) ☽ ⫙ CTV 9P 14⌂ ♀English & Continental. Lastdinner9pm ✿ ⊟
Creditcards 1 2 3 4 5 6

★★**Cambrian** Alexandra Rd ☎612446
RS Xmas (accommodation); 14rm ⊞ ⫙ CTV P Lastdinner8pm ✿ ✱sB&B£7.25–£7.75 dB&B£14.50–£15 Lunch£3–£3.50 Dinner£3–£4.50 Wine£2.40 ⊟
Creditcards 2 4 6

★★**Seabank** Victoria Ter ☎617617
Closed 3 wks Xmas; 22rm(12⇌ ⫙) Lift ⫙ CTV CTV available in bedrooms P ⇛ Lastdinner8pm ✱sB&B fr£9.72 sB&B⇌ ⫙ fr£11.88 dB&B fr£13.50 dB&B⇌ ⫙ fr£18.36 Lunch£3.03–£4.64 Dinner£3.24–£4.86 Wine£2.60

Ⓖ**Groves** 44–46 North Pde ☎617623
Closed 23Dec–3Jan; RS last 2wks Oct; 15rm(1⇌ ⫙) ⫙ CTV 8P Children under 3yrs not accommodated Last dinner summer9pm winter7.30pm ✿ ✱sB&B£6.25–£7 dB&B£12.50–£14 dB&B⇌ ⫙£14.50–£16 Barlunch40p–£2 Dinner£3.25–£5.25 Wine£2.50

Ⓖ**Marine** Marine Pde ☎612444
Closed Xmas; 34rm(15⇌ ⫙) ⫙ CTV 8P 12⌂ Lastdinner10pm ✿ ⊥ sB&B£9–£10 sB&B⇌ ⫙£10–£12 dB&B£17–£18.50 dB&B⇌ ⫙£19–£21 Lunch£3–£3.50 Tea fr85p Dinner fr£4 Wine£2.30 Creditcard 3

AMLWCH Gwynedd Map**6** SH49
★★**Dinorben Arms** Dinorben Sq (Inter-Hotel) ☎830358
Former coaching house, with garden, in centre of town.
20rm(15⇌ ⫙) ⫙ CTV CTV available in bedrooms 60P Lastdinner8.30 ✿ S% sB&B£12 sB&B⇌ ⫙£14.25 dB&B£19 dB&B⇌ ⫙£20.95 Lunch£4.50 Tea75p High Tea£2.50 Dinner£5&alc Wine£3.20 ⊟ Creditcards 2 3

★★**Trecastell** Bull Bay (Frederick Robinson) ☎830651
Two-storey hotel situated on high ground with magnificent views over Bull Bay.
16rm CTV 90P ⚓ Lastdinner9pm ✿ ⊥ sB&B£6.50 dB&B£13 Lunch£2.50–£4&alc Tea£1–£2&alc High Tea£1–£2&alc Dinner£3.50–£4.50 Wine£2.50 ⊟

BABELL Clwyd Map**7** SJ17
✕**Black Lion Inn** ☎Caerwys239
16th-C country inn with small, beamed dining room.
Closed Sun, Mon, mid 2wks Aug & 1st wk Nov; Lunch not served Sat; 54seats 80P ♀English & Continental. Lastdinner10pm Lunch£2.35alc Dinner£7.95alc Wine£3.35 Creditcard 2

BALA Gwynedd Map**6** SH93
★★**Bala Lakeside Motel** (1m S on B4403 Llangower road) ☎520344
Modern hotel situated outside town with views of the lake.
Closed Feb; 14rm(12⇌ ⫙) ⫙ CTV 40P 10⌂ ⇛ ⚓ ⛵ &9 Lastdinner8.30pm ✿ ⊥ S% ✱Lunch£3–£5.50 Tea£1 Dinner£4.50–£6 Wine£3

★★*Plas Coch* High St ☎520309
Three-storey building in main street of town.
10rm(1⇌ ⫙) ⫙ TV ⊗ 10P ⇛ Lastdinner8pm ✿
Creditcards 1 2 3

★★**White Lion Royal** High St (Greenall Whitley) ☎520314
Closed Xmas–New Year; 22⇌ ⫙ CTV 40P Lastdinner8.30pm ✿ ⊥ sB&B⇌ ⫙£13.75–£15 dB&B⇌ ⫙£18–£20 Lunch£3.50–£4&alc Tea50–75p Dinner£4–£4.75&alc Wine£2.80 ⊟
Creditcards 1 2 3 5

B

BANGOR Gwynedd Map**6** SH57
★★**British** High St ☎4911
Three-storey city type hotel situated on busy road ½m from city centre.
59rm(31⇌ ⥰) Lift ⊞ ⥰ CTV ⊘ 50P 3⌂ ♿
Last dinner8.30pm ✿ S% sB&B£10–£12
sB&B⇌⥰£11–£13 dB&B£20–£24
dB&B⇌⥰£22–£26 Lunch£2.50–£4&alc
Dinner£3.50–£4.50&alc Wine£1.40 *xmas*
Credit card[6]

★★**Ty Uchaf** Tal-y-Bont (2m E off A55) ☎52219
Closed Xmas–Mar; 10rm(4⇌⥰) ⥰ CTV ⊘ 30P ⊕ ⚓
Last dinner9pm ✿ sB&B£6.25 sB&B⇌⥰£7.25
dB&B£12.50 dB&B⇌⥰£14.50 Bar lunch£2alc
Dinner£4alc Wine£2.50

★**Waverley** Holyhead Rd ☎2017
Closed Xmas; 16rm(2⇌⥰) CTV 25P
Last dinner8.30pm ✿ ⊈ Credit card[3]

BARMOUTH Gwynedd Map**6** SH61
★★**Cors y Gedol** ☎280402
30rm(5⇌⥰) Lift ⊞ ⥰ CTV in bedrooms 140P
sauna bath Disco twice wkly Live music & dancing
3nights wkly ♿ ♡English & French.
Last dinner8.15pm ✿ ⊈ *sB&B£9
sB&B⇌⥰£11 dB&B£18 dB&B⇌⥰£20
Lunch£3.75 Tea£1–£1.75 High Tea£1.50
Dinner£4.65&alc Wine£2.10 ⊟ *xmas*
Credit cards[1][6]

★★**Lion** High St ☎280324
Closed Nov–Feb; 15rm CTV TV available in
bedrooms ₱ Children under 3yrs not accommodated
Last dinner8.30pm ✿ sB&B£8.50–£9.50
dB&B£16–£19 Lunch£3.50 Dinner£4.50&alc
Wine£2.45 ⊟

★★⚑**Plas Mynach** Llanaber Rd ☎280252
Closed Nov–Mar; 10rm(2⇌⥰) CTV CTV available in
bedrooms 20P ⊕ ⚓ ♡Continental.
Last dinner7.45pm ✿ ⊈ S% *sB&B£7
dB&B£17 Lunch£3–£4.50 Tea40p–80p
Dinner£3–£4.50 Wine£2.50

★**Ty'r Craig Castle** Llanaber Rd ☎280470
Closed mid Oct–Mar except Xmas; RS Xmas; 12rm
⥰ TV available in bedrooms 20P ⊕ ⚓ ♡English &
French. Last dinner8.15pm ✿ ⊈ S%
sB&B£6.50–£7.50 dB&B£12–£14
Lunch£3–£3.50&alc Tea£1.20
Dinner£3.50–£4&alc Wine£2.75

ⓐ**Min-y-Mor** Promenade ☎280555
Closed Oct–May; 50rm(11⇌⥰) CTV ⊘ P ⚓
Children under 2yrs not accommodated ♿
Last dinner7.30pm ✿ ⊈ sB&B£8–£10
dB&B£16–£20 dB&B⇌⥰£23–£25.20
Bar lunch£1alc Dinner£3.75 Wine£2.65

BARRY South Glamorgan Map**3** ST16
★★★**International** Port Rd, Rhoose (2½m W A426)
☎710787
32⇌⥰ ☽ ⥰ CTV in bedrooms 250P ⚓ Disco wkly
Live music & dancing 4nights wkly ♡French.
Last dinner10.30pm ✿ ⊈ S%
sB&B⇌⥰£12.50 dB&B⇌⥰£17.50
Lunch£3&alc Tea85p&alc High Tea£1.85&alc
Dinner£4.50alc Wine£2.65 ⊟
Credit cards[1][2][3][6]

★★★**Water's Edge** The Knap ☎733392
38⇌⥰ Lift ☽ ⥰ CTV in bedrooms 600P Live music &
dancing wkly ♡French. Last dinner10pm ✿ ⊈
sB&B⇌⥰£16.50 dB&B⇌⥰£21 Lunch fr£3.50
Tea fr£1 High Tea fr£2&alc Dinner fr£3.75
Wine£2.75 ⊟ Credit cards[1][2][3]

★★**Mount Sorrel** (Inter-Hotel) ☎740069
35rm(29⇌ ⋒) Annexe: 4⇌ ⋒ ☽ ⋒ CTV CTV in bedrooms 17P Live music & dancing Sat Last dinner 9pm ✿ S% sB&B£12.50 sB&B⇌ ⋒£14.50 dB&B£16.50 dB&B⇌ ⋒£18.50 Lunch£2.50–£3.50&alc Dinner£4.50–£5&alc Wine£2.75 ⊨ Credit cards 1 2 3 4 5 6

✕✕***Casa Paco*** 1/2 Broad Street Pde ☎732009
Closed Sun & Mon; Lunch not served Sat; 40seats P ♀English & French. Last dinner 11.15pm

BEAUMARIS Gwynedd Map**6** SH67
★★★**Bulkeley Arms** Castle St ☎810415
Stone, two-storey building scheduled as of special architectural and historical interest, facing Menai Strait with views of Snowdonia.
42rm(18⇌ ⋒) Lift ⋒ CTV TV available in bedrooms ⊗ 30P ⇜ Last dinner 8.15pm ✿ ⊈ ⊨ *xmas*

★★**Henllys Hall** ☎810412
24rm(6⇌ ⋒) 8⊟ ✕ ⋒ CTV ⊗ 200P 3⌂ ⚓ ⇀(heated) ⇝(hard) ♀International. Last dinner 10.30pm ✿ ⊈ sB&B£9.50 sB&B⇌ ⋒£15.50 dB&B£9.50 dB&B⇌ ⋒£15.50 Bar lunch£1 Tea£1 High Tea£1.50–£3 Dinner£4.50&alc Wine£3.50 ⊨ *xmas* Credit cards 1 2

★**Liverpool Arms** Castle St ☎810362
12rm ⋒ CTV 12P Last dinner 8.30pm ⊈ sB&B£6.25–£6.87 dB&B£12.50–£13.75 Lunch£1.10–£2 Dinner fr£2.75&alc

★**White Lion** Castle Sq ☎810589
10rm ⋒ CTV ⊗ 12P ♀Mainly grills. Last dinner 9.30pm S% sB&B£6 dB&B£12 Lunch 60p–£2&alc Dinner£2–£6&alc Wine£1.45

✕***Hobson's Choice*** 13–13A Castle St ☎810323
Classification awarded for dinner only.
Closed Sun; Lunch not served Sep–May; 80seats

Live music Fri & Sat ♡International. Lastdinner10pm Creditcard 1

BEDDGELERT Gwynedd Map**6** SH54
★★★***Royal Goat*** ☎224
29rm(11⇌⋒) CTV ✈ 50P ↬ Live music Sat Lastdinner9.30pm (8.30pm winter) ✿ ♫ ☰ Creditcards 1 2 3 5 6

★★**Saracen's Head** ☎223
Situated at the foot of Snowdon overlooking the River Glaslyn, with the Aberglaslyn pass in the background.
21rm(7⇌⋒) Annexe:3⇌⋒ CTV 30P ♡English & French. Lastdinner9.30pm ✿ ♫ sB&B£9.50 dB&B£19 dB&B⇌⋒£22 Lunch£3 Tea30p–£1 Dinnerfr£4&alc Wine£3 Creditcards 1 2 3

★★**Bryn Eglwys** Railbridge ☎210
In the heart of Snowdonia National Park, this hotel is set in its own grounds overlooking the River Glaslyn.
Closed Jan; 12rm(2⇌⋒) ⚿ CTV CTV available in bedrooms ✈ 36P ♣ ♡English & French. ✿ ♫ sB&B£6.50–£7 dB&B£13–£14 dB&B⇌⋒£14–£15 Lunch£3–£3.50 Tea90p–£1 HighTea£2–£2.50&alc Dinner£4.25–£4.50&alc Wine£2.90 ☰ *xmas*

BENLLECH BAY Gwynedd Map**6** SH58
★★**Bay Court** Beach Rd ☎Tynygongl 2573
Modern purpose built hotel in good position overlooking the sands of Benllech Bay.
19rm(1⇌⋒) Annexe:4⇌⋒ ⊞ ⚿ CTV 65P Lastdinner8.30pm ✿ ♫ S% sB&B£8.50–£10 sB&B⇌⋒£9.50–£11 dB&B£17–£20 dB&B⇌⋒£19–£22 Lunch£2–£3.50&alc Tea£1 HighTea£1 Dinner£4–£4.50&alc Wine£2.35 ☰

★★**Glanrafon** ☎Tynygongl 2364
Blue-washed three storey Victorian building with front lawns and walled garden, overlooking the bay.
24rm(12⇌⋒) ⚿ CTV 70P ♣ Disco twice wkly Lastdinner8.30pm ✿ ♫ S% sB&Bfr£7.25 dB&Bfr£14.50 dB&B⇌⋒fr£16.50 Lunchfr£2.50 Dinnerfr£3 Wine£3 ☰

★★**Golden Sands** ☎Tynygongl 2384
RS Oct; 9rm(5⇌⋒) Annexe:3rm ⚿ CTV CTV 15P ♡English & French. Lastdinner10.30pm ✿ sB&B£7.50 sB&B⇌⋒£8.50 dB&B£14–£15 dB&B⇌⋒£15.60–£17.50 Lunch£2.20–£2.50 Dinner£3–£3.50&alc Wine£2.85 ☰ *xmas* Creditcards 1 2 3

BETHESDA Gwynedd Map**6** SH66
★★**Snowdonia Park Motel** Nant Ffrancon ☎600548
Modern chalets situated at side of A5 trunk road.
Annexe:30⇌⋒ ⚿ CTV available in bedrooms 30P ⇎ ♣ Lastdinner9.30pm S%
✱sB&B⇌⋒£11–£13.75 dB&B⇌⋒£15–£22 Continental breakfast Dinner£5alc Wine£3.50 Creditcards 1 2 3 5 6

BETWS-Y-COED Gwynedd Map**6** SH75
★★**Craig-y-Dderwen Country House** ☎293
Large Tudor style house set amongst wooded land 400yd from main road.
6rm(14⇌⋒) ⚿ CTV TV in bedrooms 30P 2⌂ ♣ δ9 ↬ ∩ Live music & dancing Tue & Fri ⌂ ♡Welsh & French. Lastdinner8.30pm ✿ ♫ sB&Bfr£6.50 sB&B⇌⋒fr£7.50 dB&Bfr£13.50 dB&B⇌⋒fr£15.50 Lunchfr£3.50&alc Teafr£1.50&alc HighTeafr£1.50&alc Dinnerfr£4.50&alc Wine£1.35 ☰ *xmas* Creditcards 1 2 3 4 5 6

★★**Park Hill** Llanrwst Rd ☎540
10rm(6⇌⋒) ⚿ TV 10P ⇎ ♣ Children under 6yrs not accommodated Lastdinner7.30pm ✿ ♫ sB&B£6–£7 dB&B£12–£14 dB&B⇌⋒£14–£16 Teafr65p Dinnerfr£4 Wine£3 ☰ *xmas* Creditcards 1 2

★★**Royal Oak** Holyhead Rd ☎219
Closed Jan & Feb; 36rm(17⇌⋒) 8▭ ⚿ CTV 200P 2⌂ ♣ Lastdinner8.30pm ✿ S% sB&B£12 sB&B⇌⋒£13 dB&B£20 dB&B⇌⋒£22 Barlunch£1.30–£1.50 Dinner£7–£8 Wine£4 *xmas* Creditcards 1 2 3 4 6

☆☆**Waterloo Motor** ☎411
5⇌⋒ Annexe:21⇌⋒ ⚿ 26P ♣ δ18 ↬ ⌂ ♡French. Lastdinner9.30pm ✿ sB&B⇌⋒£10.26–£13.50 dB&B⇌⋒£14.58–£21.06 Lunch£2.95–£3.50 Dinner£2.50–£10&alc Wine£3 ☰ *xmas* Creditcards 1 2 3 4 5 6

BLACKWOOD Gwent Map**3** ST19
★★★**Maes Manor** ☎224551
10rm(7⇌⋒) Annexe:17rm(13⇌⋒) ☽ ⚿ CTV CTV in bedrooms 100P ♣ Live music & dancing Sat Cabaret Sat ♡English & French. Lastdinner10pm ✿ ♫ S% sB&Bfr£14 sB&B⇌⋒fr£15 dB&B⇌⋒£23 Lunchfr£3.50&alc Teafr£1.25 Dinnerfr£5&alc Wine£2.85 ☰ *xmas* Creditcards 1 2 3 5

BLAENAU FFESTINIOG Gwynedd Map**6** SH74
★**Queens** ☎338
13rm ⚿ CTV ✈ P Lastdinner8.15pm ✿ sB&Bfr£8.10 dB&Bfr£16.20 Barlunch30p–£1.60 Dinner£2.75–£5 Wine£2

BODELWYDDAN Clwyd Map**6** SJ07
✕✕***Faenol Fawr Manor*** ☎Rhuddlan 590784
Closed 1wk Feb; Dinner not served Sun & Mon;

B

50seats 3P bedrooms available Disco Fri & Sat ☋International. Last dinner10pm Credit cards ① ②

BONTDDU Gwynedd Map**6** SH61
★★★Bontddu Hall ☎661
Built in country house style, with 2½ acres of grounds overlooking Mawddach estuary. Views of Cader Idris.
Closed Nov–Apr; 18⇌ ⋒ Annexe: 8⇌ ⋒ CTV CTV in bedrooms 50P ⛟ ⚓ Children under 3yrs not accommodated ☋International. Last dinner9.15pm ✿ ⊒ sB&B⇌ ⋒£5.95–£12.85 dB&B⇌ ⋒£11.90–£26.80 Lunch£5alc Tea50palc Dinner fr£5.45&alc Wine£3.70 Credit cards ② ⑤

BRECHFA Dyfed Map**2** SN53
✕✕Ty Mawr Hotel Restaurant ☎332
Closed Sun, Mon, 1st 2wks Feb & 1st 2wks Nov; Lunch not served; 52seats 120P bedrooms available ☋French. Last dinner9pm S% Dinner£5–£7.50&alc Wine£3

BRECON Powys Map**3** SO02
★George George St ☎3422
One of the Brecon's oldest hotels, adapted for comfort. Conveniently situated near Brecon Beacons National Park.
10rm ꟾꟾ CTV ⊘ 18P Last dinner6.15pm ✿ ⊒ S% sB&B£8.64 dB&B£15.12 Lunch£3.50–£4.50&alc Dinner£4–£4.75&alc Credit cards ② ③

★Lansdowne The Watton ☎3321
Closed mid Nov–Feb; 12rm(1⇌ ⋒) 2⊟ ꟾꟾ CTV P ☋Mainly grills. Last dinner8.30pm in Winter 9.30pm in summer ✿ ⊒ ✻sB&B fr£6.50 dB&B fr£11 dB&B⇌ ⋒ fr£18 Lunch fr£1.85&alc Dinner fr£2.90&alc Wine£2.50 ⊓ Credit cards ① ③

At **Libanus** (4m SW A470)
☆☆Mountains ☎4242
26⋒

BROADHAVEN Dyfed Map**2** SM81
★♔Rosehill Country Portfield Gate (3m NE off B4341) ☎304
Closed mid Oct–Etr; Annexe: 5rm CTV 25P ⛟ ⚓ Last dinner7pm ✿ ⊓

BURTON Dyfed Map**2** SM90
★★Beggars Reach ☎Neyland600700
10⇌ ⋒ ꟾꟾ CTV ⊘ P ⛟ ⚓ Live music & dancing wkly ☋English & French. Last dinner9.30pm ✿ ⊒ ✻sB&B⇌ ⋒ fr£11.95 dB&B⇌ ⋒ fr£18.95 Dinner£6.40alc Wine£2.80 ⊓ Credit cards ② ⑤

CAERLEON Gwent Map**3** ST39
★★Priory (Nicholsons) ☎421241
Priory dating from 12th-C, with 15th-C stained glass windows in Nun's Court. Gardens and grounds.
25⇌ ⋒ ꟾꟾ CTV CTV in bedrooms 100P ⚓ ♿ Last dinner10pm ✿ S% sB&B⇌ ⋒£13–£14.80 dB&B⇌ ⋒£18–£22 Lunch£3.50&alc Dinner£4&alc Wine£3.50 ⊓ *xmas* Credit cards ① ② ③ ⑤

CAERNARFON Gwynedd Map**6** SH46
★★★Royal ☎3184
58⇌ ⋒ Lift ☽ ꟾꟾ CTV TV available in bedrooms 250P ♿ Conference facilities available Last dinner8.45pm ✿ ⊒ S% ✻sB&B⇌ ⋒£10.50 dB&B⇌ ⋒£20 Lunch£2.75 Tea75p Dinner£3.75&alc Wine£1.90 Credit card ①

★★Prince of Wales Bangor St (Scottish & Newcastle) ☎3367
Hotel with modern exterior, situated on the main Caernarfon to Bangor road.

3rm CTV 9P Disco 3nights wkly Last dinner8.15pm S% *sB&B£7.10 dB&B£13.70 Lunch£2.25–£2.50 Dinner£3.50alc Wine£2.45 Credit cards 1 2 3 5

Menai Bank North Rd ☎3297
5rm(1⇌ ⋒) ⋔ CTV 12P Last dinner8pm S% *sB&B£6.50–£7 dB&B£12–£13 B&B⇌ ⋒£15–£16 Lunch fr£2 Dinner fr£3.50 Wine£1.60 *xmas* Credit card 1

Muriau Park South Rd ☎4647
Country style hotel situated one mile from town centre.
rm(1⇌ ⋒) ⋔ CTV 12P 2 English & French. Last dinner9.30pm Credit cards 1 2 3

CAERPHILLY Mid Glamorgan Map**3** ST18
☆☆**Griffin Inn Motor** Rudry (3m E unclass road) ☎883396
Closed Xmas; 20⇌ ⋒ ⋔ CTV in bedrooms 120P (heated) Live music & dancing Fri & Sat Mainly grills. Last dinner10pm S% sB&B⇌ ⋒ fr£14.50 dB&B⇌ ⋒ fr£20 Lunch£5alc Dinner£6.50alc Wine£3.10 Credit cards 1 2 3 5

C

CAERSWS Powys Map**6** SO09
★★**Maesmawr Hall** (Inter-Hotel) ☎255
Dates back to the 16th-C and is secluded as an ancient monument. Stands in 5½ acres of wooded grounds on the River Severn.
13rm(8⇌ ⋒) Annexe: 6⇌ ⋒ ⋔ CTV TV available in

bedrooms 100P 2🏠 ⚓ ⇝ Disco Wed & Sat Live music & dancing Wed & Sat ♿ Lastdinner9pm ✿ ☕ sB&B£10.26–£11.34 sB&B⇌⋒£11.88–£12.96 dB&B£17.28–£19.44 dB&B⇌⋒£20.52–£22.68 Lunch fr£3.51 Tea fr80p High Tea fr£1 Dinner fr£4.86 Wine£2.43 🅿 *xmas* Credit cards 1 2 3 5 6

C

CARDIFF South Glamorgan Map**3** ST17 **See plan**

★★★★Angel Castle St (Trophy Taverns & Best Western) ☎32633 Telex no49132 Plan**1** 98rm(82⇌⋒) Lift ☽ ⋈ CTV CTV in bedrooms 30P Conference facilities available ♡International. Lastdinner10pm ✿ ☕ sB&B£14.50 sB&B⇌⋒£22.50 dB&B£25.50 dB&B⇌⋒£30 Lunch£5&alc Tea£1 Dinner£6.50&alc Wine£3.50 🅿 Credit cards 1 2 3 4 5 6

★★★Cardiff Centre Westgate St (Centre) ☎38868 Telex no497258 Plan**2** 160⇌⋒ Lift ☽ ⋈ CTV in bedrooms ⊗ 🅿 Conference facilities available Lastdinner9.45pm ✿ ☕ S% ✻sB&B⇌⋒£15.50 dB&B⇌⋒£20 Continental breakfast Lunch£3.55 Dinner£3.55 Wine£3.40 🅿 Credit cards 1 2 3 4 5 6

★★★Park Park Pl (Mount Charlotte) ☎23471 Telex no497195 Plan**5** Closed 25–27Dec; 109rm(82⇌⋒) Lift ☽ ⋈ TV in bedrooms 32🏠 Live music & dancing Fri & Sat (Oct–Apr) ♡European. Lastdinner9.45pm ✿ ☕ S% sB&B£15 sB&B⇌⋒£19–£23.50 dB&B£20 dB&B⇌⋒£24–£32 Lunch£4.50&alc Dinner£5&alc Wine£3.65 🅿 Credit cards 1 2 3 5

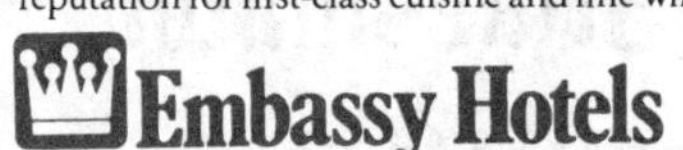

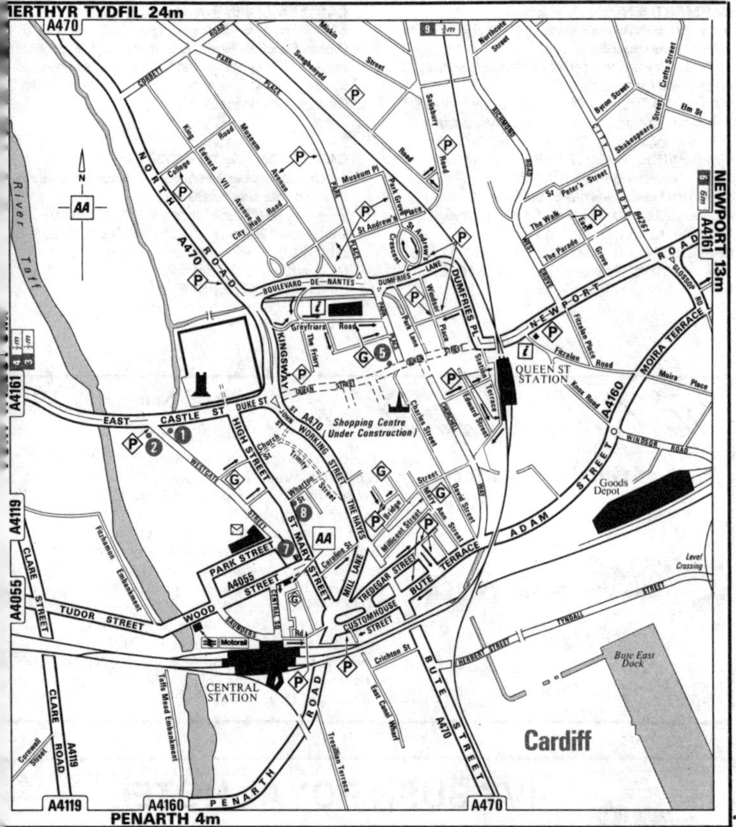

1 Angel ★★★★
2 Cardiff Centre ★★★
3 Gibsons ❀✕
4 Harvesters ✕
5 Park ★★
6 Post House ☆☆☆
7 Royal ★★
8 Sandringham ★★
9 Yr Ystafell Gymraeg ✕

☆☆☆**Post House** Church Rd, Pen wyn (Trusthouse Forte) ☎750121 Telex no 497633 Plan **6**
Purpose-built modern hotel with contemporary décor situated on the outskirts of the city
150⇌⋒ Lift ☽ ⅏ CTV in bedrooms 210P ♿
Last dinner 10.15pm ✿ ☑ S%
sB&B⇌⋒£19.75 dB&B⇌⋒£28.50 ▣
Credit cards 1 2 3 4 5 6

★★★**Royal** 87 St Mary Street (Embassy) ☎23321 Telex no 49576 Plan **7**
68rm(37⇌⋒) Lift ☽ ⅏ CTV TV in bedrooms **P** Last dinner 9.15pm ✿ S% sB&B£12 sB&B⇌⋒£16 dB&B£19 dB&B⇌⋒£24 Lunch £4.75&alc Dinner £5.50&alc Wine £4.50 ▣
Credit cards 1 2 3 4 5 6

★★**Sandringham** 21 St Mary Street ☎32161 Plan **8**
28rm(6⇌⋒) ☽ CTV **P** ☺ Mainly grills.
Last dinner 11pm ✿ sB&B£12.75
sB&B⇌⋒£14.25 dB&B£15.75 dB&B⇌⋒£20.25
Lunch £3.30alc Dinner £3.30alc Wine £3 ▣
Credit cards 1 2 3 5 6

❀✕**Gibsons** Romilly Cres ☎41264 Plan **3**
Closed Sun & Mon; 36seats 3P ☺ French.
Specialities: stuffed chicken breast with Pernod & cream, steak in overcoat, roast quails with sage & Madeira. Last dinner 10pm ✱Lunch £6alc Dinner fr £6.75&alc Wine £3.60 Credit cards 1 3 6

✕**Harvesters** 5 Pontcanna St ☎32616 Plan **4**
Closed Sun, Mon, Xmas & 3wks Aug; Lunch not served; 38seats **P** Last dinner 11pm Dinner £7alc Wine £3.15

✕***Ty Mawr Arms*** Craig Rd, Lisvane ☎754456 Not on plan
Dinner not served Sun; 70seats 100P bedrooms available Disco 3nights wkly ☺ French & Italian. Last dinner 11pm Credit cards 1 2 3 5 6

✕**Yr Ystafell Gymraeg** 74 Whitchurch Rd, Cathays ☎42317 Plan **9**
Closed Sun; Lunch not served Sat; 44seats **P** Last dinner 11.30pm S% ✱Lunch £3.45alc Dinner £6.20alc Wine £2.70 Credit cards 1 2 3

CARDIGAN Dyfed Map **2** SN14
See also **Gwbert-on-Sea**
★***Angel*** St Mary Street ☎2561
11rm CTV 8P 4⌂ ⇎ Last dinner 7.30pm

C

CARMARTHEN Dyfed Map**2** SN42
★★★**Ivy Bush Royal** Spilman St (Trusthouse Forte) ☎5111 Telexno48520
15th-C building considerably extended, with small garden and forecourt.
103rm(70⇌🚿) Lift ☽ 👥 CTV CTV in bedrooms 63P 3🏠 ⚓ sauna bath Conference facilities available Last dinner9pm ♔ ☕ S% sB&B£14 sB&B⇌🚿£15 dB&B£20 dB&B⇌🚿£22 ⛿ *xmas* Credit cards 1 2 3 4 5 6

★★**Boars Head** Lammas St ☎6043
Closed 25Dec; 10rm(1⇌🚿) TV 20P 13🏠 🐕 Last dinner8pm ♔ ☕ sB&B£8.50 sB&B⇌🚿£11.40 dB&B£15 dB&B⇌🚿£19.80 Lunch£2.20alc Tea60palc Dinner£2.20alc Wine£1.72

CASTLE MORRIS Dyfed Map**2** SM93
❀✕**Y Gwesty Bach** ☎Letterston337
Closed Sun, Feb & mid Oct – mid Nov; Lunch not served; Dinner not served Mon – Wed in winter; 33seats 12P ☕Cosmopolitan. Last dinner9.30pm Dinner£7.75 Wine£2.70

CASTLETON Gwent Map**3** ST28
☆☆**Cardiff Ladbroke Mercury Motor Inn** Wentloog Castle (Ladbroke) ☎680591
55⇌🚿 ☽ 👥 CTV in bedrooms 75P sauna bath Last dinner10.30pm ♔ ☕ sB&B⇌🚿 fr£18 dB&B⇌🚿 fr£24 Lunch fr£4.50&alc Dinner fr£5&alc Wine£3.20 ⛿ Credit cards 1 2 3 4 5 6

EPSTOW Gwent Map**3** ST59
★★***Two Rivers*** Newport Rd ☎5151
7⇔ Lift ☽ ▦ CTV 150P sauna bath Music
ights wkly Last dinner10.30pm
redit cards 1 2 3 5

★**Beaufort** Beaufort Sq ☎5074
2rm(2⇔) CTV 12P Last dinner9.30pm
% sB&B£11.50–£12.50 sB&B⇔£13–£14
B&B£17.80–£19.80 dB&B⇔£20.70–£22
unch£4.50–£5&alc Dinner£5–£6&alc
redit cards 1 2 3 5

★**Portwall** Welsh St ☎2050
uilt 1840, with Norman town wall as garden oundary.
5rm(2⇔) TV in bedrooms 25P
ast dinner9pm sB&B£11.50
B&B⇔£12.50 dB&B£17.50 dB&B⇔£19.50
Lunch fr£2.50 Tea fr£1.25 High Tea fr£1.25
Dinner fr£4 Wine£2.20 *xmas*
Credit cards 1 2 3 5

★★**George** Moor St (Trusthouse Forte) ☎2365
17th-C building near a small trout stream believed to have been used by the monks from the Abbey.
20rm(6⇔) TV in bedrooms 25P
Last dinner9.30pm S% sB&B£11
sB&B⇔£14.50 dB&B£17.50 dB&B⇔£20.50
xmas Credit cards 1 2 3 4 5 6

✕***Manor House*** Bank St ☎2926
Closed Sun; 40seats 300P Continental.
Last dinner10.30pm Credit cards 1 2 3 5 6

CHIRK Clwyd Map**7** SJ23
★★***Hand*** ☎2479
14rm(3⇔) CTV 45P 4 Last dinner9pm

C

CHURCH STOKE Powys Map**7** SO29
★★ ***Mellington Hall*** ☎456
Closed Nov & Feb; 8rm(3⇌⋒) TV 100P
Lastdinner8.30pm ♁ ⊡

COLWYN BAY Clwyd Map**6** SH87
★★★**Hopeside** Princes Dr ☎33244 Telex no61254
Closed Xmas & New Year; 20⇌⋒ ✗ ₩ CTV in bedrooms 35P ⛟ Children under 6yrs not accommodated Lastdinner8.30pm ♁ ⊡ S% sB&B⇌⋒£13.50–£14.50 dB&B⇌⋒£26–£28 Lunch£4–£4.50 Tea£1–£1.50 HighTea£2.50–£3 Dinner£5.75–£6.75&alc Wine£3 ⊟ Credit cards 1 3 6

★★★**Norfolk House** Princes Dr ☎31757 Telex no61254
White painted, two storey building situated ¼mile from the town centre and ¼mile from the beach.
Closed 24Dec–7Jan; 35rm(31⇌⋒) Lift ☽ CTV CTV available in bedrooms 40P ⛟ ⚓ Lastdinner8.30pm ♁ ✱sB&B£12.25 sB&B£13 dB&B£21.50 dB&B⇌⋒£23 Barlunch fr£1.50 Dinner fr£5.75 Wine£2.45 ⊟ Credit cards 1 2 3 6

★★★**Rhos Abbey** 111 Rhos Prom (Inter-Hotel) ☎46601
Large three-storey building situated on the seafront and within a short walking distance of village.
30rm(22⇌⋒) Lift ☽ TV in bedrooms 80P ⇌ sauna bath Disco Fri & Sat Live music & dancing Tue & Thur Cabaret Thu Lastdinner9pm ♁ ⊡ S% sB&B£12–£13 sB&B⇌⋒£14–£15 dB&B£22–£24 dB&B⇌⋒£26–£28 Lunch£3.25–£3.60 Dinner£4.50–£5.50&alc Wine£2.70 ⊟ *xmas* Credit cards 1 2 3 5 6

☆☆☆**Hotel 70°** Penmaenhead ☎56555
44⇌⋒ ☽ ₩ CTV in bedrooms 250P ⛟ Live music & dancing Wed–Sat (summer only) ♡English & French. Lastdinner9.15pm ♁ ⊡ S% sB&B⇌⋒£15 dB&B⇌⋒£28 Lunch£4.55–£5.25 Dinner£9alc Wine£3.75 *xmas* Credit cards 1 2 3 4 5 6

★**Commodore** Conway Rd ☎2720
Closed Oct–Apr; 23rm CTV 20P ⚓ Lastdinner6pm ♁ ⊡ S% sB&B£5.75–£6.50 dB&B£11.50–£13 Lunch£2–£2.75 Tea95p–£1.25 Dinner£2.70–£3.25 Wine£1.45

★**Marine** West Prom ☎30295
Closed Sep–Mar; 16rm(8⇌⋒) ✗ CTV CTV available in bedrooms 13P Lastdinner7.30pm ♁ ⊡ S% ✱sB&B£7–£9 sB&B⇌⋒£8–£10 dB&B£14–£18 dB&B⇌⋒£16–£20 Lunch£3–£4 Dinner£3–£4 Wine£2 ⊟ Credit card 3

★**Melfort** Llannerch Road East, Rhos-on-Sea ☎44390
Closed Xmas; 17rm(2⇌⋒) ✗ CTV 18P ♁ ⊡ S% sB&B£6 sB&B⇌⋒£7 dB&B£12 dB&B⇌⋒£14 Lunch£2 Tea80p HighTea£2 Dinner£3.50 Wine£1.80 Credit cards 1 3 5

★***St Enoch's*** Promenade ☎2031
23rm(1⇌⋒) ✗ CTV 8P ⛟ ⚓ ♡English. Lastdinner7.30pm ♁ ⊡ ⊟

⊛**Edelweiss** Lawson Rd ☎2314
25rm CTV ⊘ 30P ⚓ Lastdinner6.30pm S% sB&B£5.50–£6.50 dB&B£11–£13 Continental breakfast Lunch£1.80–£2.50 Dinner£2–£2.50 Wine£3

⊛**St Margaret's** Prince Dr ☎2718
14rm(2⇌⋒) ₩ CTV TV available in bedrooms 14P Lastdinner7pm ♁ ⊡ S% sB&B£6.48–£7 sB&B⇌⋒£7.30–£8.50 dB&B£12.96–£14 dB&B⇌⋒£14.60–£17 Lunch£2.25–£3 Tea70p–£1 High Tea70p–£1 Dinner£3.25–£4 Wine£3 *xmas* Credit cards 1 3 6

ONWY Gwynedd Map**6** SH77
★★Castle High St (Trusthouse Forte) ☎2324
An important coaching house at the beginning of the 19th-C with a red tile façade.
28rm(20⇌⋒) TV in bedrooms 42P
Last dinner9.15pm S% sB&B£11
sB&B⇌⋒£14 dB&B£17 dB&B⇌⋒£20.50
xmas Credit cards①②③④⑤⑥

XXAlfredo Lancaster Sq ☎2381
Early 17th-C inn of historical interest.
Dinner not served Sun; 220seats English, French & Italian. Last dinner10pm S%
Lunch£3–£4.50&alc High Tea£3.50–£4.50
Dinner£7alc Wine£3.60

CORWEN Clwyd Map**6** SL04
★★Glan Deva Carrog (2½m E B5437)
☎Glyndwr608
7rm TV in bedrooms 12P international.
Last dinner10pm S% sB&B£7
dB&B£14 Lunch£2.95 Tea60P
Dinner£3.75–£7.50 Wine£2.95 *xmas*
Credit card②

COWBRIDGE South Glamorgan Map**3** ST07
★★Bear High St ☎2169
15th-C coaching inn retaining much original character.
24rm(10⇌⋒) CTV CTV in bedrooms 40P
French. Last dinner10pm S%
*sB&B£10.50 sB&B⇌⋒£12.50 dB&B£15
dB&B⇌⋒£20 Lunch fr£3&alc Dinner£4.50&alc
Wine£2.75 *xmas* Credit cards①③

COYCHURCH Mid Glamorgan Map**3** SS97
XXXCoed y Mwstwr Hotel Restaurant
☎Pencoed860621

Closed 24–27Dec & Public Hols; Lunch not served Sat; Dinner not served Sun; 70seats 70P bedrooms available Live music & dancing Thu–Sat English & French. Last dinner10.30pm S% Lunch£10alc Dinner£10alc Wine£3.20 Credit cards 1 2 3 5 6

C

CRICCIETH Gwynedd Map**6** SH43
★★★**Bron Eifion** ☎2293
19rm(17⇌ ⋒) CTV TV available in bedrooms 100P 4 Children under 3yrs not accommodated English & Continental. Last dinner9pm S% *sB&B£18–£21.50 (incl dinner) sB&B⇌⋒£20.50–£21.50 (incl dinner) dB&B fr£36 (incl dinner) dB&B⇌⋒£41–£43 (incl dinner) Lunch£3.50 Tea35p Dinner£5.50 Wine£3.50 *xmas*

★★**George IV** ☎2168
40rm Lift CTV 50P Last dinner9pm *sB&B£7.50–£9 dB&B£15–£18 Lunch£2–£3 Tea70–80p Dinner£3.50–£4&alc Wine£2.60 *xmas*

★★***Lion*** Y Maes (Inter-Hotel) ☎2460
38rm(9⇌⋒) Lift CTV 20P 14 Last dinner8.15pm Dinner£3.75 Credit cards 1 2 3 5 6

★★**Parciau Mawr** High St ☎2368
Closed 19Oct–Feb; 7rm(2⇌⋒) Annexe: 6⇌⋒ CTV TV available in bedrooms 30P Children under 5yrs not accommodated English & French. Last dinner8.30pm S% sB&B£9.02–£9.92 sB&B⇌⋒£11.44–£12.41 dB&B£18.04–£19.84 dB&B⇌⋒£20.24–£22.26 Dinner fr£5&alc Wine£2.40

★★**Plas Gwyn** Pentrefelin (1m NE A497) ☎2559
Single storey hotel 1 mile from town and set close to the A497.
15rm CTV CTV available in bedrooms 40P 4 Last dinner9pm sB&B£7 dB&B£14–£14.50 Lunch£3 Dinner£4–£6&alc Wine£3

★**Abereistedd** West Pde ☎2710
Closed Nov–Feb; 15rm(3⇌⋒) CTV 7P 2 Last dinner9pm S% sB&B£5–£7 sB&B⇌⋒£6.50–£8.50 dB&B£10–£14 dB&B⇌⋒£13–£17 Lunch£1.50–£2&alc Tea70p–£1.50 Dinner£2–£2.50&alc Wine£2.40

★**Bodlondeb** Porthmadog Rd ☎2249
closed Nov–Feb; 12rm CTV TV available in bedrooms 15P 5 Last dinner9pm S% *sB&B£6.50–£7.50 dB&B£13–£14 Lunch fr£2.50 Tea fr£1 Dinner fr£2.50&alc Wine£3.10 Credit card 5

★**Caerwylan** ☎2547
Closed Nov–Mar; 34rm(3⇌⋒) Lift CTV 9P 14 Last dinner7.30pm sB&B£5.25–£5.50 dB&B£10.25–£11 dB&B⇌⋒£10.50–£12.50 Lunch fr£2.30 Tea fr45p Dinner fr£3.30

★**Henfaes** Porthmadog Rd ☎2396
closed Nov–Mar; 14rm(9⇌⋒) CTV TV available in bedrooms Last dinner7.30pm sB&B£7.02–£7.56 dB&B£14.04–£15.12 dB&B⇌⋒£14.04–£18.36

Bron Aber Pwllheli Rd ☎2539
Closed end Oct–Mar; 16rm CTV 15P

astdinner7.30pm ✻sB&B£6–£6.50 dB&B£12
innerfr£3 Winе£3

Glyn-y-Coed Porthmadog Rd ☎2870
nlicensed; Closed end Sep–Mar; 10rm CTV 10P
astdinner8pm sB&B£4.86 dB&B£9.72
unch£2.26 dinner£3.40

CRICKHOWELL Powys Map**3** SO21
★★Cliffaes ☎Bwlch730371
Closed Jan–14Mar; 21rm(10⇌⋒) CTV 30P
(hard) billiards Lastdinner8.45pm S%
B&B£9.20–£10.40 sB&B⇌⋒£10.40–£13.70
B&B£18–£20.80 dB&B⇌⋒£20.80–£27.40
unchfr£4.25 Teafr£1.40 Dinnerfr£6 Wine£2.75

★Bear ☎810408
RS Sun; 12rm(8⇌⋒) CTV 12P English &
rench. Lastdinner8.45pm
✻sB&B£6.50–£7.50 sB&B⇌⋒£8.50–£10.75
dB&B£12–£14 dB&B⇌⋒£14–£17
Barlunch£1.50–£3.50 Dinner£4.50–£7&alc
Wine£2

CROSSGATES Powys Map**3** SN06
☆☆Park Motel ☎Penybont201
Closed Nov–Feb; RS Mar; Annexe:7⇌⋒ CTV TV
available in bedrooms 60P Lastdinner9pm
sB&B⇌⋒£8.80–£11
dB&B⇌⋒£10.56–£13.20
Lunch£1.90–£2.20&alc Tea80palc
Dinner£2.75–£4&alc Wine£2.80

CRUGYBAR Dyfed Map**2** SN63
★★Glanrannel Park ☎Talley230
A country home overlooking a small lake in 23 acres of grounds.
Closed Nov–Mar; 8rm CTV 40P 3
Lastdinner7.30pm S% sB&B fr£9.50
dB&B fr£18 Barlunchfr£1 Teafr50p
High Teafr£1.50 Dinnerfr£4.50 Wine£3

CWMBRAN Gwent Map**3** ST29
★★★*Hotel Commodore* Mill Ln, Llanyravon ☎4091
24⇌⋒ Lift CTV TV available in bedrooms 250P
10 Live music & dancing Sat Cabaret Sat
English & French. Lastdinner10pm
Creditcards 1 3 4 5 6

DEGANWY Gwynedd Map**6** SH77
★★Bryn Cregin Ty Mawr Rd ☎83402
Hotel set in its own grounds in a quiet position just off the main road.
24rm(17⇌⋒ 1) CTV TV available in bedrooms
French. Lastdinner10pm
✻sB&B£7.50–£15.50 sB&B⇌⋒£8.50–£16.50
dB&B£15–£31 dB&B⇌⋒£17–£33
Lunch£4.50–£6.50 Tea£1–£2
High Tea£2.50–£4.50 Dinner£5.50–£7.50&alc
Wine£3.95 *xmas*

★★Deganwy Castle ☎83358
Views across the Conwy estate to Conwy castle and the mountains of Snowdonia.
33rm(6⇌⋒) CTV TV available in bedrooms 100P
Lastdinner9pm S% sB&B£14
sB&B£16 dB&B£24 dB&B⇌⋒£30
Barlunch£1–£2 Dinner£4.75–£5.50&alc
Wine£2.50 *xmas* Creditcards 1 2 3

DENBIGH Clwyd Map**6** SJ06
★★Bull Hall Sq ☎2582
14rm(1⇌⋒) CTV 15P Lastdinner8.30pm
✻sB&B£8.01–£8.31 sB&B⇌⋒£10–£10.50
dB&B£16.02–£16.62 dB&B⇌⋒£17.82–£19
Lunch£2.75–£4.50&alc Tea£1–£1.50
Dinner£3–£4&alc Wine£2.50 Creditcards 1 3 6

DEVIL'S BRIDGE Dyfed Map**6** SN77
★★Devil's Bridge ☎Ponterwyd232
Early 19th-C country inn built in style of a Swiss

chalet. Flower gardens overlook famous beauty spot. 22rm(1⇌⋒) CTV ⊘ 200P 8⌂ ⚓ ↬ Disco fortnightly Lastdinner8.15pm sB&B£9.50–£10.30 dB&B£16.70–£17.50 Lunch£2.80–£4.50 Tea50p–80p Dinner£4.50–£6&alc Wine£3.40 ⊟ *xmas* Creditcards ① ② ③ ④ ⑤ ⑥

DINAS MAWDDWY Gwynedd Map**6** SH81
★***Dol-Brawd-Maeth*** Cheltenham Rd ☎333
Small country-type hotel set by side of main road. 8rm ⅏ CTV 200P ⚓ ↬ Live music & dancing Wed & Sat Lastdinner7.30pm ♉ ⚑ Creditcards ① ③ ⑤

D

DINAS POWIS South Glamorgan Map**3** ST17
✕✕***Earls*** The Square, Station Rd ☎514146
Closed Mon; Lunch not served; 44seats 10P ♉Continental. Lastdinner11.30pm

DOLGELLAU Gwynedd Map**6** SH71
★★★**Golden Lion Royal** Lion St ☎422579
Regency coaching inn, with orchard and rose garden. Closed 3Dec–1Jan; 23rm(8⇌⋒) Annexe:5⇌⋒ 2⊟ CTV TV available in bedrooms 10P Lastdinner9pm ♉ ⚑ Wine£3.30 Creditcards ② ③

★★**Royal Ship** (Frederic Robinson) ☎422209
21rm(5⇌⋒) Lift ⅏ CTV ⊘ 8P 3⌂ Lastdinner9pm ♉ ⚑ ✻sB&B£9 sB&B⇌⋒£11 dB&B£18 dB&B⇌⋒£22 Lunch fr£2.75 Tea fr£1 Dinner fr£4.50 ⊟

DOLWYDDELAN Gwynedd Map**6** SH75
★★**Elen's Castle** ☎207
18th-C coach house with spectacular scenery situated in the Lledr Valley.
Closed Nov–Mar except Xmas; 10rm(2⇌⋒) 1⊟ ✕

40P 2🏠 🚗 ⚓ 🐕 Last dinner7pm ✿ ☕ S% B&B£7–£8 dB&B£14–£16 dB&B⇌🛁£16–£18 Lunch£2–£3&alc Tea50p&alc High Tea£1.50&alc Dinner£3–£4&alc Wine£2 xmas

EGLWYSFACH Dyfed Map**6** SN69
★★🏠Ynyshir Hall ☎Glandyfi209
Famous for its situation in a garden of heathers, rhododendrons, magnolias and camellias. Grounds extend over several acres and share part of the Dovey Valley with the bird sanctuary owned by the Royal Society for the Protection of Birds.
10rm(6⇌🛁) ✗ 🍽 20P 1🏠 🚗 ⚓
Last dinner10.30pm sB&B£12.75–£15 sB&B⇌🛁£16–£17 dB&B£25–£32 dB&B⇌🛁£28–£36 Barlunch£1–£2.75 Dinner£7.50&alc Wine£3.20 🅱 *xmas*
Credit cards 1 2 3 5 6

ERBISTOCK Clwyd Map**7** SJ34
✗Boat Inn ☎Overton-on-Dee243
60seats 80P 🍷English & French.
Last dinner9.15pm S% Lunch£7.15alc Dinner£8.45alc Wine£4 Credit cards 1 2 3 5

FAIRBOURNE Gwynedd Map**6** SH61
★★Springfield Beach Rd ☎378
19rm(6⇌🛁) 🍽 TV 300P Last dinner9pm ✿ ☕ S% ✱sB&B£7.50 dB&B£15 dB&B⇌🛁£16

F

Lunch fr£2.70&alc Tea80p Dinner fr£3.75&alc Wine£2.29

FISHGUARD Dyfed Map**2** SM93
★★★ ***Fishguard Bay*** Goodwick ☎873571
Telex no48503
62rm(30⇌ ⋒) Lift ☽ ⋔ CTV TV available in bedrooms 70P billiards Live music & dancing Thu
Last dinner10pm ✿ ⊈ ⊟
Credit cards 1 2 3 4 5 6

★★**Cartref** High St ☎872430
16rm ☽ CTV ⊘ 2P ⇔ Children under 7yrs not accommodated Last dinner8pm ✿ S%
sB&B£7.50–£8.50 dB&B£14–£15.50
Lunch£2–£2.25 Tea75p–£1 Dinner£3.50–£4
Wine£2.75 Credit cards 1 3

★**Manor House** Main St ☎873260
Three storey Georgian terrace in town centre. Views of Fishguard harbour.
Closed 2wks Nov; 7rm CTV ⊘
Last dinner8.30pm ✿ ⊈ S%
sB&B£6.48–£7.02 dB&B£11.88–£12.96
Bar lunch£2.20–£3.20 Dinner£3.20–£3.80
Wine£3.50 ⊟ *xmas*

FOUR MILE BRIDGE Gwynedd Map**6** SH27
★★**Anchorage** ☎Valley740168
One storey building situated within easy reach of beach and golf courses.
RS Sun; 13rm(5⇌ ⋒) ⋔ CTV ⊘ 50P ⇔ Children under 3yrs not accommodated Last dinner9.15pm
✿ S% sB&B£7.50 sB&B⇌ ⋒£8.50 dB&B£14
dB&B⇌ ⋒£16 Lunch£5.50alc Dinner£7alc
Wine£3

GLASBURY Powys Map**3** SO13
★★ ***Maesllwch Moat House*** ☎226
On banks of River Wye.
10rm(3⇌ ⋒) ⋔ TV 60P Last dinner9pm ⊈
Credit cards 1 3 5

GWBERT-ON-SEA Dyfed Map**2** SN15
★★★**Cliff** (Best Western) ☎Cardigan3241
Telex no48440
Stands in 30 acres of grounds, overlooking Cardigan Bay and the Teifi estuary; direct access to sandy beaches.
54⇌ ⋒ Annexe: 16⇌ ⋒ 2 ☽ ⋔ CTV CTV available in bedrooms 100P ⚓ ⊐(heated) squash Live music & dancing Sat Conference facilities available
English & French. Last dinner9pm ✿ ⊈ S%
sB&B⇌ ⋒£12–£22 dB&B⇌ ⋒£24–£44
Lunch£4.50–£5&alc Dinner£5.75–£6.50&alc ⊟
xmas Credit cards 1 2 3 5

HARLECH Gwynedd Map**6** SH53
★★ ***St David's*** ☎366
80rm(14⇌ ⋒) Lift ☽ CTV 50P 50 ⚓ ⊐(heated) billiards ♿ Last dinner8.30pm ✿ ⊈ ⊟

HAVERFORDWEST Dyfed Map**2** SM91
★★**Hotel Mariners** Mariners Sq (Embassy) ☎3353
17th-C inn with stables and old coaching post, situated in centre of market town.
29rm(11⇌ ⋒) ☽ ⋔ CTV TV in bedrooms 50P
Last dinner8.45pm ✿ S% sB&B£10
sB&B⇌ ⋒£13 dB&B£17 dB&B⇌ ⋒£20
Dinner£5&alc Wine£4.50 ⊟
Credit cards 1 2 3 4 5 6

★**Pembroke House** Spring Gdns ☎3652
osed Xmas Day; 25rm(15⇌ fl) 5 CTV
V in bedrooms 30P English & French.
stdinner10.30pm S% sB&B£9
B&B⇌ fl£10 dB&B£16 dB&B⇌ fl£19
nch£3 Dinner£3&alc Wine£2.50
edit cards ①②③⑤⑥

AY-ON-WYE Powys Map**3** SO24
Crown Broad St ☎820435
ctorian building on banks of River Wye.
rm(2⇌ fl) CTV 35P 1 Lastdinner8pm
% sB&B£7.50–£8 dB&B£14–£15
B&B⇌ fl£15–£16 Lunch£3–£3.50&alc
inner£4.20–£5 Wine£3 Creditcard③

Old Black Lion Lion St ☎820841
seats 20P bedrooms available European.
Lastdinner9pm ✻Lunch£4.40alc Dinner£4.40alc
Wine£2.90 Creditcards③⑥

KNIGHTON Powys Map**7** SO27
★★★***Norton Arms*** Broad St ☎528321
Old established hotel situated in town centre.
11rm(7⇌ fl) Lift CTV TV available in bedrooms 40P
billiards Lastdinner9pm

LAMPETER Dyfed Map**2** SN54
★★**Black Lion Royal** (Inter-Hotel) ☎422172
18rm(8⇌ fl) 50P 1 Welsh & French.
Lastdinner9pm ✻sB&B£9–£10
sB&B⇌ fl£10–£11.50 dB&B£17–£29
dB&B⇌ fl£19–£22 Lunch fr£3.30
Dinner£4.30&alc Wine£2.89 Creditcards①③⑤⑥

LAMPHEY Dyfed Map**2** SN00
★★**Lamphey Hall** ☎672394
12rm(2⇌⋔) ☽ ⋔ CTV CTV in bedrooms ⊘ 22P ⚓
Disco Wed Live music & dancing Fri
Last dinner9.30pm ✿ ⊒ ✻sB&B£11.90
sB&B⇌⋔£12 dB&B£21 dB&B⇌⋔£23
Lunch£1.25–£3.75&alc Tea75p–£1.25
Dinner£1.75–£3.50&alc Wine£2.95 ⊟ *xmas*

LANGLAND BAY West Glamorgan Map**2** SS68
See also **Mumbles and Swansea**
★★★**Osborne** Rotherslade Rd (Embassy)
☎Swansea66274
43rm(21⇌⋔) Lift ☽ ⋔ CTV TV in bedrooms 25P
♀French. Last dinner9pm ✿ S% sB&B£11
sB&B⇌⋔£15.50 dB&B£17 dB&B⇌⋔£23
Lunch£4.50&alc Dinner£5.25&alc Wine£4 ⊟
Credit cards 1 2 3 4 5 6

★★**Langland Court** Langland Court Rd
☎Swansea68505
Closed Xmas Day; 14rm(2⇌⋔)
Annexe:17rm(13⇌⋔) ☽ ⋔ CTV CTV available in bedrooms ⊘ 40P 5 ⚓ billiards ♀English & Continental. Last dinner8pm ✿ ⊒
sB&B£13–£16 sB&B⇌⋔£15–£18
dB&B£24–£27 dB&B⇌⋔£31.50–£35
Lunch£3–£5 Tea£1 High Tea£3–£5
Dinner£4–£6 Wine£3 ⊟ Credit card 2

★**Ael-y-Don** ☎Swansea66466
Closed Nov–Feb; 16rm(6⇌⋔) ⋔ CTV ⊘ 12P 4
⚓ Children under 6yrs not accommodated
Last dinner7.30pm ✿ ✻sB&B fr£7
sB&B⇌⋔ fr£7.75 dB&B fr£14
dB&B⇌⋔ fr£15.50 Bar lunch95p Dinner£3.50
Wine£2.25

LANGSTONE Gwent Map**3** ST38
☆☆**New Inn Motel** (Ansells)
☎Newport (Gwent)412426
30⇌⋔ ⋔ CTV TV in bedrooms ⊘ 200P
Last dinner10.15pm S% sB&B⇌⋔£13.75
dB&B⇌⋔£17.85 Lunch£3.20&alc
Dinner£3.50&alc Wine£3.20 ⊟ Credit cards 1 2

LIBANUS Powys Map**3** SN92
☆☆**Mountain's** ☎Brecon4242
26⇌⋔ ☽ ⋔ CTV CTV in bedrooms Disco wkly
♿ Last dinner9.30pm ✿ ⊒ ✻sB&B⇌⋔£11.90
dB&B⇌⋔£17.80 Continental breakfast
Lunch£3.25–£3.50&alc Tea60p–£1
High Tea£1–£1.50 Dinner£3.50–£3.75&alc
Wine£2.50 ⊟ *xmas* Credit cards 1 2 3 5

LITTLE HAVEN Dyfed Map**2** SM81
★★**Haven Fort** ☎Broad Haven401
Closed Oct–Feb; 15rm(10⇌⋔) ⋔ CTV CTV available in bedrooms ⊘ 60P Children under 5yrs not accommodated ♀International. Last dinner7pm
✿ ⊒ ✻sB&B£10.75 sB&B⇌⋔£11.50
dB&B£20.40 dB&B⇌⋔£22.60
Bar lunch55p–£1.50 Tea fr65p
Dinner£3.80–£5&alc Wine£2.80

★★**Little Haven** Strawberry Hill ☎Broad Haven285
Modern, three-storey building situated in spacious gardens on headland overlooking St Brides Bay.
Closed mid Oct–end Mar; 9rm(6⇌⋔)
Annexe:5rm(2⇌⋔) ☽ ⋔ CTV 50P ⚓ ♀English & French. Last dinner9.30pm ✿ ⊒
sB&B£7.70–£8.50 sB&B⇌⋔£8.70–£9.50
dB&B£15.40–£17 dB&B⇌⋔£17.40–£19
Bar lunch fr£1.45 Dinner fr£4.25&alc ⊟

LLANARMON-DYFFRYN-CEIRIOG Clwyd Map**7** SJ13
★★★Hand ☎666
Closed Feb; 15rm(12⇌fl) Annexe: 1rm CTV 50P Last dinner8.30pm S% sB&B£10 sB&B⇌fl£12 dB&B£20 dB&B⇌fl£20 Lunch£3.50–£5.50&alc Tea40p–£1 Dinner£4.50–£6&alc Wine£3 Credit card②

★★West Arms ☎665
Country hotel over 400 years old, situated in a small picturesque village 950ft above sea level.
15rm(5⇌fl) CTV 15P 2 Last dinner8.45pm S% sB&B£9.50 sB&B⇌fl£10 dB&B£19 dB&B⇌fl£20–£22 Lunch£2.50–£3 Tea35–70p Dinner£4.25–£5.25 Wine£2.70 Credit card②

LLANBEDR Gwynedd Maps**6** SH52
★Cae Nest Hall ☎349
16th-C country house, standing in own grounds, about a mile from the sea.
Closed Jan–Mar; 9rm(1⇌fl) CTV 15P English & French. Last dinner9.15pm sB&B£8.75–£9.75 dB&B£16–£17.50 dB&B⇌fl£19–£21 Lunch£3.50 Tea£1 Dinner fr£4.80&alc Wine£2.70 *xmas* Credit card③

LLANBEDROG Gwynedd Map**6** SH33
★★Bryn Derwen ☎257
Closed Dec & Jan; 10rm(9⇌fl) CTV TV in bedrooms 25P Last dinner9pm sB&B£8.25–£10 sB&B⇌fl£8.25–£10

L

dB&B£16.50–£20 dB&B⇌⋒£16.50–£20 Lunch£3–£4 Tea£1–£2 High Tea£2.50–£3 Dinner£5–£7.50 Wine£2.50 Credit cards 1 3

LLANBERIS Gwynedd Map**6** SH56
★★Gallt-y-Glyn ☎370
10rm CTV 12P Last dinner8.30pm S% sB&B£8.87–£10.12 sB&B⇌⋒£9.87–£11.12 dB&B£7.60–£8 dB&B⇌⋒£8.10–£8.50 Lunch£3.50&alc Tea60–80p Dinner£4.25&alc Wine£2.80 *xmas* Credit cards 1 2 3 5

LLANDDEWI SKYRRID Gwent Map**3** SO31
✕Walnut Tree Inn (3m NE of Abergavenny) ☎Abergavenny2797
Closed Sun; 45seats International. Last dinner10.30pm

LLANDEILO Dyfed Map**2** SN62
★★Cawdor Arms ☎3500
16⇌⋒ 2 CTV in bedrooms 9P sauna bath Last dinner9.30pm S% sB&B⇌⋒£15.50–£16.50 dB&B⇌⋒£25–£27.50 Lunch fr£5 Tea£1–£2 Dinner£5.50–£8.50 Wine£3.75 Credit cards 1 2 3

LLANDISSLIO (WEST) Dyfed Map**2** SN12
★★Nantyffin Motel ☎Clynderwen329
15rm(7⇌⋒) Annexe:6rm Lift TV TV in bedrooms 150P 7 Conference facilities available English & French. Last dinner9pm S% sB&B fr£7.50 sB&B⇌⋒ fr£8.50 dB&B fr£15 dB&B⇌⋒ fr£17 Lunch£2.50–£4 Tea fr75p Dinner fr£3.75 Wine£2.20 Credit cards 1 2 3 5 6

L

LLANDOGO Gwent Map**3** SO50
☆☆*Old Farmhouse* ☎St Briavels303
Modernised 15th-C homestead with motel wing. Set in wooded slopes of Wye Valley.
8rm Annexe: 15⇌⋒ CTV TV available in bedrooms 65P Last dinner10pm Credit cards 1 2 3 5

LLANDOVERY Dyfed Map**3** SN73
★★Llanfair Grange ☎20495
Closed Xmas; 6rm(1⇌⋒) CTV CTV available in bedrooms 60P 2 Last dinner9.15pm sB&B£9 dB&B£16 dB&B⇌£18.20 Lunch£3.75–£5&alc Tea fr50p Dinner£3–£6.50&alc Wine£2.50

★Picton Court ☎20320
A country house built 1898 set in 15 acres.
11rm(4⇌⋒) 1 CTV 25P 5 Last dinner10pm S% sB&B£8 dB&B£16 dB&B⇌⋒£20 Lunch£1–£3&alc Tea50p–£1 Dinner£3.75&alc Wine£2 *xmas*

LLANDRINDOD WELLS Powys Map**3** SO06
★★Hotel Commodore Spa Rd ☎2288
62rm(48⇌⋒) Lift CTV CTV available in bedrooms 100P Last dinner8.30pm S% sB&B£9.50–£12 sB&B⇌⋒£10.50–£12.50 dB&B£16–£18 dB&B⇌⋒£12–£24 Bar lunch65p–£1.50 Tea75p–£1.50 High Tea£1–£2 Dinner£4–£5 Wine£2.50 *xmas* Credit cards 1 2 3 6

★★Glen Usk South Cross (Mount Charlotte) ☎2085
Closed Nov–3Apr; 85rm(33⇌⋒) Lift CTV 10P Disco 3nights wkly Last dinner8.30pm S% sB&B£11.15 sB&B⇌⋒£12.50 dB&B£19.90 dB&B⇌⋒£22.35 Lunch£3.40&alc Tea£1.25 Dinner£5&alc Wine£3.50 Credit cards 1 2 3 5 6

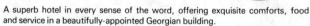

LLANDUDNO Gwynedd Map**6** SH78 **See plan**

★★★Empire Church Walks ☎77260 Telexno617161 Plan**9**
Closed 21Dec–6Jan; 51⇌⋒ 3⊟ Lift ▦ CTV in bedrooms 24P 12🏠 ⇌ ▭(heated) sauna bath Live music & dancing Sat Lastdinner8.30pm ♁ ⊥ S% sB&B⇌⋒£11–£18 dB&B⇌⋒£22–£30 Lunch£5 Dinner£6 Wine£4 ⊨ Credit cards 1 2 3

★★★Gogarth Abbey West Shore ☎76212 Not on plan
Holiday hotel set back onto Great Orme and facing the West Shore.
Closed Jan & Feb; 41rm(20⇌⋒) ☽ ▦ CTV 50P ▭(heated) sauna bath Live music & dancing twice wkly Lastdinner8.30pm ♁ ⊥ S% sB&B£9–£11 sB&B⇌⋒£10.30–£12.30 dB&B£17.21 dB&B⇌⋒£19.60–£23.60 Lunch£3–£3.50 Tea60p HighTea£2 Dinner£4.50 Wine£2.50 ⊨ *xmas* Credit cards 1 3

★★★Hydro Promenade (Travco) ☎77241 Plan**14**
94rm(37⇌⋒) Lift ☽ ▦ CTV in bedrooms 70P 14🏠 ⚓ billiards sauna bath Live music & dancing twice wkly Cabaret twice wkly ♡French & Italian. Lastdinner8.30pm ♁ ⊥ sB&B£9.50–£10 sB&B⇌⋒£11–£11.50 dB&B£19–£20 dB&B⇌⋒£20.50–£21.50 Lunchfr£3.30 Dinnerfr£4.45 Wine£2.25 ⊨ *xmas* Credit cards 1 2 3 5 6

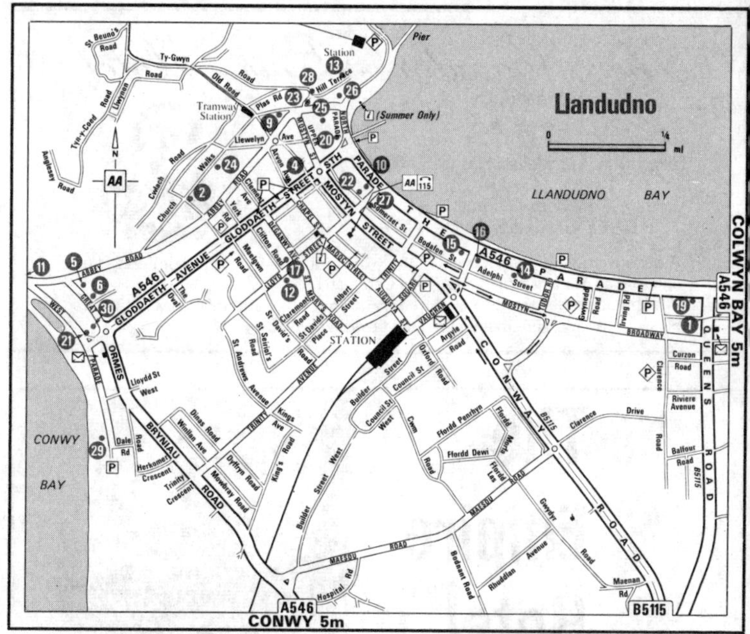

1 Bromwell Court ★
2 Bron Orme ★
4 Clarence ★★
5 Clontarf ★
6 Cranleigh ★
9 Empire ★★★
10 Esplanade ⊕
12 Gwesty Leamore ★
13 Headlands ★
14 Hydro ★★★
15 Imperial ★★★
16 Marine ★★★
17 Oak Alyn
18 Min-y-Don ★
19 Ormescliffe ★★
20 Osborne ★
21 Ravenhurst ★
22 Richmond ★
23 Rothesay ★
24 Royal ★★
25 St George's ★★★
26 St Tudno ★★
27 Somerset ★
28 Southcliffe ★
29 Sunnymede ★
30 Tan-Lan

★★★**Imperial** Promenade ☎77466 Plan**15**
150rm(79⇌⋒) Lift ☽ ₩ CTV CTV available in bedrooms 50P Live music & dancing nightly ⌂ Conference facilities available Last dinner 8.30pm ✿ ⊈ S% ✱sB&B£9.50–£12 sB&B⇌⋒£11.75–£14.25 dB&B£19–£24 dB&B⇌⋒£23.50–£48 Lunch fr£4 Tea fr£1.75 High Tea fr£2.85 Dinner fr£5 Wine£3.25 ⊟ *xmas* Credit cards ① ③

★★★**Marine** Promenade (Trusthouse Forte) ☎77521 Plan**16**
79rm(54⇌⋒) Lift ☽ ₩ TV in bedrooms 36P Conference facilities available Last dinner 9pm ✿ ⊈ S% sB&B£13 sB&B⇌⋒£14.50 dB&B£19.50 dB&B⇌⋒£24.50 ⊟ *xmas* Credit cards ① ② ③ ④ ⑤ ⑥

★★★**St George's** Promenade (Best Western) ☎77544 Telex no 61520 Plan**25**
75⇌⋒ Lift ☽ ₩ CTV CTV in bedrooms 40P Last dinner 8.15pm ✿ ⊈ S% sB&B⇌⋒ fr£10.50 dB&B⇌⋒ fr£18 Lunch fr£3.75 Tea fr£1.10 Dinner fr£6 Wine£3.50 ⊟ *xmas* Credit cards ① ② ③ ⑤

★★**Clarence** Gloddaeth St ☎76485 Plan**4**
Closed mid Oct–Mar; 74rm Lift ☽ CTV ₱ Last dinner 8.30pm ✿ ⊈ S% sB&B£8–£10 dB&B£16–£20 Lunch£2.50–£2.90 Dinner£3–£3.50 Wine£2.70 ⊟ Credit cards ① ② ③ ⑤ ⑥

★★**Ormescliffe** Promenade ☎77191 Plan**19**
558rm(28⇌⋒) Lift CTV 15P Live music & dancing nightly (summer only) ⌂ Last dinner 8pm ✿ ⊈ sB&B£10–£11 sB&B⇌⋒£12–£13 dB&B£20–£22 dB&B⇌⋒£24–£26 Lunch fr£3.50 Dinner fr£4.50 Wine£3.50 ⊟ *xmas* Credit cards ① ③ ⑤ ⑥

★★**Royal** Church Walks ☎76476 Plan**24**
Closed Nov–Jan; RS Feb–Apr & Oct; 38rm(6⇌⋒) Lift CTV 35P ⚓ Last dinner 7.30pm ✿ ⊈ ✱sB&B£6.25–£8.50 sB&B⇌⋒£7–£10 dB&B£12.50–£17 dB&B⇌⋒£14–£20 Lunch£2.25 Tea35p Dinner£3.15 Wine£2.50 ⊟

★★**St Tudno** North Pde ☎76309 Plan**26**
Closed Nov–Mar; 18rm(9⇌⋒) Lift ₩ CTV TV in bedrooms ₱ ⇋ ♉ English & French. Last dinner 7.30pm ✿ ⊈ sB&B£8.25–£10.35 dB&B£16.70–£20.70 dB&B⇌⋒£20.15–£24 Lunch£3.75 Tea fr35p Dinner£4.90 Wine£2.60

★***Branksome*** Lloyd St ☎75989 Not on plan
Closed Nov–Mar; 24rm(4⇌⋒) ₩ CTV 8P 1⌂ Last dinner 7pm ✿

IMPERIAL HOTEL

VAUGHAN STREET
Tel: Llandudno (0492) 77466

Situated in a central position on the Promenade. 150 bedrooms, 80 with private bath. The Hotel is approximately 5 minutes' from the main shopping centre and the railway station. The Penthouse floor has all rooms with private bath, colour TV, radio and telephone. Resident band and entertainment seven nights a week during season.

ST GEORGE'S HOTEL

A member of Best Western Hotels

LLANDUDNO Tel: (0492) 77544 Telex: 61520

This magnificent hotel is open all year. Situated in the centre of the Promenade with easy access to shops and leisure facilities.

Bedrooms:
All bedrooms have shower or bathroom, coloured television, radio, telephone, full central heating. There is a passenger lift to all floors and full fire precautions are installed and a fire certificate issued.

Restaurants:
The Wedgewood Restaurant offers excellent cuisine and promises to delight the most discriminating with table d'hôte and à la carte menus. On the lower ground level the Cock and Hen Tavern offer a quick service of popular dishes, excellent coffee and superb home-made gateaux and pastries.

Bars:
Terrace Bar, with its panoramic view of the sea, offers a wide choice of spirits, liqueurs and beers. The Dragon Bar adjoins the Restaurant, has easy access from St George's Place and is ideal for meeting friends in very comfortable surroundings.

Free car parking facilities at the rear of the hotel.

THE Ormescliffe LLANDUDNO

On sea front overlooking bay.
60 bedrooms many with private bath or shower & tea/coffee making facilities.
Ballroom with dancing or entertainment in season.
Fully licensed to Residents.
Games Room.
Free parking facilities at rear of Hotel.

Children's holidays a speciality. Cots, high-chairs provided.
Washing facilities. Special baby teas. Listening service every night.
Fire Certificate.

We are here to make your stay a happy one.

Ring or write for Brochure and Tariff — Telephone 77191

★Bromwell Court Promenade ☎78416 Plan**1**
Closed 21Nov–Jan; RS Feb; 12rm(3⇌⋒) ₩CTV CTV available in bedrooms 𝐏 ⊜ Children under 6yrs not accommodated Last dinner6.30pm ✿ S% sB&B£6.75–£7 sB&B⇌⋒£7.75–£8 dB&B£13–£14 dB&B⇌⋒£15–£16 Lunch£2–£2.25 Dinner£3–£3.50 Wine£3.25 ⊟ Credit cards ② ③ ⑥

★Bron Orme Church Walks ☎76735 Plan**2**
Hotel at foot of Great Orme, short distance from beach and town centre.
Closed Nov–Feb; Rs Oct–Apr; 11rm CTV ⊘ 𝐏 ⊜ Children under 2yrs not accommodated ♉French. Last dinner7pm ⊈ sB&B£5.40–£5.94 dB&B£9.72–£10.80 Lunch£3.50–£6 Tea fr30p Dinner£3–£5&alc Wine£2.50 Credit cards ① ③ ⑥

★Clontarf West Shore ☎77621 Plan**5**
Closed mid Oct–Mar; 10rm(3⇌⋒) ₩CTV ⊘ 12P 1⌂ ⊜ Children under 12yrs not accommodated Last dinner6pm ✿ ⊈ ✱sB&B£6.50 dB&B£12.50 dB&B⇌⋒£17 Lunch£4.25alc Tea£1.50alc Wine£3

★Cranleigh Great Ormes Rd ☎77688 Plan**6**
Closed mid Oct–Mar; 13rm(2⇌⋒) ₩CTV 13P ⊜ Children under 5yrs not accommodated Last dinner7pm ✿ ⊈ sB&B£6.10–£7.50 dB&B£11.04–£14.60 dB&B⇌⋒£13.20–£16.76 Lunch fr£2.50 Tea fr£1 Dinner fr£3.50 Wine£2.30

★Gwesty Leamore 40 Lloyd St ☎75552 Plan**12**
Closed Dec–Mar; 12rm CTV ⊘ 5P Last dinner6pm ✿ S% sB&B£6–£6.90 dB&B£12–£13.80 Bar lunch£1–£2.50 Tea45p–£1 Dinner£2.80–£3.45 ⊟ Credit cards ① ② ③

★Headlands Hill Ter ☎77485 Plan**13**
Situated at foot of Great Orme with views over Llandudno Bay.
Closed Oct–mid May; 19rm(3⇌⋒) CTV 6P Last dinner6.45pm ✿ ⊈ ✱sB&B£7.50 sB&B⇌⋒£8.75 dB&B£15 dB&B⇌⋒£17.50 Bar lunch fr50p Dinner fr£3.50 Wine£2.30

★Min-Y-Don North Pde ☎76511 Plan**18**
Closed Oct–Mar; 20rm(2⇌⋒) CTV ⊘ 5P ⊜ Children under 3yrs not accommodated Last dinner7pm sB&B fr£6 dB&B fr£12 dB&B⇌⋒ fr£13.50 Bar lunch fr50p Dinner fr£3 Wine£2

★Oak Alyn Deganwy Av ☎76497 Plan**17**
Closed Dec–Jan; 17rm ₩CTV 17P Last dinner7pm ✿ ⊈ sB&B£6–£8 dB&B£12–£16 Lunch80p–£2 Dinner£1.50–£3 Wine£2.25 ⊟ *xmas* Credit cards ① ③

★Osborne North Pde ☎77087 Plan**20**
Closed Oct–15Apr; 29rm(8⇌⋒) ☽ CTV 9⌂ Last dinner8pm ✿ ⊈ Lunch fr£2.75 Dinner fr£3.25 Wine£2.25 *xmas* Credit cards ① ② ③ ④ ⑤ ⑥

★Ravenhurst West Pde ☎75525 Plan**21**
Closed Dec–Feb; 23rm(5⇌⋒) Annexe: 2rm CTV 14P Last dinner7pm ✿ ⊈ S% ✱sB&B£6.60–£7.70 sB&B⇌⋒£7.75–£8.90 dB&B£13–£15.30 dB&B⇌⋒£15.30–£16.50 Lunch£1.60–£3.60&alc Tea60p–£2&alc Dinner£2.40–£3.50&alc Wine£2.50 ⊟

★*Richmond* St Georges Pl ☎76347 Plan**22**
Closed Oct–mid Apr; 26rm(4⇌⋒) Lift CTV ⊘ ⊜

★Rothesay 83 Church Walks ☎76844 Plan**23**
Closed Oct–Mar; 23rm(1⇌⋒) CTV 𝐏 Last dinner5pm ✿ ⊈ S% sB&B£6.50 dB&B£13.61 Dinner fr£2.70 ⊟ *xmas*

L

★Somerset Central Promenade ☎76540 Plan27
Closed Oct–Mar; 38rm(5⇌fl) Lift CTV TV available in bedrooms 24P Last dinner7pm sB&B£10–£12 dB&B£20–£24 dB&B⇌£20–£26 Lunch£2–£2.50 Dinner£3–£3.50 Wine£1.25

★Southcliffe Hill Ter ☎76277 Plan28
32rm(4⇌fl) Lift CTV 3P International. Last dinner7.30pm sB&B£6.25–£6.75 sB&B⇌fl£7.50–£8.50 dB&B£12.50–£13.50 dB&B⇌fl£13.75–£14.75 Lunch£3–£4.50&alc Tea50p–£2&alc High Tea£1–£3&alc Dinner£2.50–£6.50&alc Wine£1.75 Credit card 3

★Sunnymede West Pde ☎77130 Plan29
Closed Oct–Feb; 12rm CTV 12P Last dinner6pm S% sB&B£6.50–£7.70 dB&B£13–£15.50 Lunch£1.50–£3&alc Tea50p High Tea75p Dinner£3–£3.50&alc Wine£2.20

★Tan-Lan Great Ormes Rd ☎75981 Plan30
Closed Nov–Feb; 19rm CTV 8P Last dinner6.30pm sB&B fr£6 dB&B fr£12 Lunch fr£2.50 Tea fr£1 Dinner fr£3.50

★*Villa Marina* Craigside ☎49366 Not on plan
Closed Jan; 10rm Lift 15P Children under 3yrs not accommodated Last dinner7pm Credit cards 1 3

Esplanade Promenade ☎76687 Plan10
60rm(25⇌fl) Lift CTV 30P Last dinner7.30pm S% sB&B£8–£10 sB&B⇌fl£10–£12 dB&B£16–£18.50 dB&B⇌fl£20–£23 Lunch£3.50 Dinner£5 Wine£3.50 *xmas* Credit cards 1 2 3 6

L

Fairhaven Craigydon Pde ☎76123 Not on plan Closed Nov–Mar; 11rm(3⇌ ⋒) CTV CTV available in bedrooms 7P Children under 6yrs not accommodated Last dinner 6.30pm S% sB&B£6–£6.95 sB&B⇌⋒£7–£7.95 dB&B£12–£13 dB&B⇌⋒£14–£14.95 Lunch£2–£2.50 Dinner£3–£3.75 Wine£2 Credit card 6

LLANDUDNO JUNCTION Gwynedd Map**6** SH87
★★Station (Whitbread) ☎Deganwy 81259
Situated opposite station ½m from village.
18rm(8⇌⋒) TV in bedrooms P Last dinner 10pm *sB&B£6.90 sB&B⇌⋒£8 dB&B£15 dB&B⇌⋒£15 Lunch£1.60&alc Dinner£2.50alc Wine£2.35 Credit card 3

LLANELLI Dyfed Map**2** SN50
★★★Stradey Park Furnace (Trusthouse Forte) ☎58171 Telex no 48521
80⇌⋒ Lift CTV in bedrooms 120P Conference facilities available Last dinner 9.30pm S% sB&B⇌⋒£15 dB&B⇌⋒£22 *xmas*
Credit cards 1 2 3 4 5 6

★★Diplomat Ael-y-Bryn ☎56156
12rm Lift CTV CTV in bedrooms 150P Live music & dancing Sat English & French. Last dinner 9.45pm S% sB&B⇌⋒£12–£14.50 dB&B⇌⋒£15–£17 Lunch£3–£3.75&alc Tea£1–£1.50 Dinner£3.50–£3.75&alc Wine£2.50 *xmas* Credit cards 1 2 3 5

LLANFAIRFECHAN Gwynedd Map**6** SH67
Myrtlewood Penmaenmawr Rd ☎680735
RS Oct–Mar (B&B only); Unlicensed; 9rm CTV TV available in bedrooms 12P Last dinner 5pm S% sB&B£5.50 dB&B£11 Dinner£3

L

LLANFYLLIN Powys Map**6** SJ11
★★Bodfach Hall ☎272
17th-C country house with oak panelling. Adam fireplace and original William Morris wallpaper. Situated in 33-acre estate with 4 acres of garden.
Closed Jan & Feb; RS Nov & Dec; 9rm(3⇌⋒) CTV TV available in bedrooms 30P Last dinner 9pm S% sB&B fr£9.25 dB&B fr£18.50 dB&B⇌⋒ fr£20.90 Dinner fr£4.50 *xmas*

★★Cain Valley ☎366
15th-C country inn with Jacobean stairway.
12rm(10⇌⋒) CTV TV available in bedrooms 20P 4 English & German. Last dinner 9.30pm S% sB&B£8.65 sB&B⇌⋒£10.65 dB&B£14.35 dB&B⇌⋒£15.95 Lunch£2.75–£3.75 Dinner£3.65–£4.95&alc

LLANGADOG Dyfed Map**3** SN72
★★Plas Glansevin ☎238
Closed 24 & 25Dec; RS Nov–Mar; 7rm(2⇌⋒) 50P Last dinner 8pm S% sB&B£9.50 sB&B⇌⋒£11.50 dB&B£19 dB&B⇌⋒£23 Bar lunch 95p 45p–£1.70 Dinner£5.75–£6.50 Wine£4.50
Credit cards 1 2 3 5

LLANGAMMARCH WELLS Powys Map**3** SN94
★★★Lake ☎202
Victorian country house in 45 acres of wooded grounds, including a 2-acre lake.
Closed mid Oct–mid Mar; 27rm(12⇌⋒) CTV 35P 6 18 (hard) billiards Last dinner 8.45pm sB&B£7.75–£8.50 sB&B⇌⋒£8.75–£9.50 dB&B£15–£16 dB&B⇌⋒£16–£18 Lunch£3–£3.50&alc Tea 50p–£1 Dinner£5.25–£5.75&alc Wine£2

LLANGOLLEN Clwyd Map**7** SJ24
★★★Bryn Howel (2¾m E A539) ☎860331
Set amid hills overlooking the River Dee and Shropshire canal.
39rm(21⇌⋒) TV TV available in bedrooms 250P English & Continental. Last dinner 10pm S% sB&B£10 sB&B⇌⋒£14 dB&B£18 dB&B⇌⋒£23 Lunch£3.50&alc Tea£1 Dinner£5&alc Wine£2.85

★★★Hand (Mount Charlotte) ☎860303
Three-storey coaching inn overlooking river.
60rm(48⇌⋒) CTV in bedrooms 50P Live music & dancing wkly Cabaret wkly Welsh, English & French. Last dinner 10pm S% sB&B£9.85–£11.85 sB&B⇌⋒£12.85–£14.80 dB&B£16.50–£19.80 dB&B⇌⋒£19.75–£23.50 Lunch fr£3.55&alc Tea fr95p High Tea fr£1.95 Dinner fr£4.55&alc Wine£3.25 *xmas*
Credit cards 1 2 3 4 6

★★★Royal Bridge St (Trusthouse Forte) ☎860202
Two-storey stone-built hotel standing on the banks of the River Dee near the 14th-C bridge.
39rm(23⇌⋒) TV in bedrooms 23P 2 Last dinner 9pm S% sB&B£11 sB&B⇌⋒£13.50 dB&B£17.50 dB&B⇌⋒£20.50 *xmas* Credit cards 1 2 3 4 5 6

★★Chain Bridge ☎860215
35rm(22⇌⋒) Lift TV 100P Disco Tue Live music & dancing Sat Last dinner 9.30pm sB&B fr£10.10 sB&B⇌⋒ fr£13.65 dB&B fr£20.20 dB&B⇌⋒ fr£27.30 Lunch fr£3&alc Dinner fr£3.80 Wine£2.90 *xmas* Credit cards 1 2 3 5 6

★★Ty'n-y-Wern (1m E on A5) ☎860252
18th-C farmhouse in 7 acres of lawns and grazing

land overlooking River Dee and Vale of Llangollen.
10rm(2⇌ ⋒) ⋈ CTV 100P ⚓ ♡English & French. Last dinner 9.30pm ✿ S% ✻sB&B£8–£9 dB&B£16–£17.50 dB&B⇌⋒£18–£19 Bar lunch£1.75–£3.50 Dinner£4.25–£5&alc Wine£2.50 ⊟ Credit card 3

LLANGURIG Powys Map**6** SN98
★★**Black Lion** ☎223
4⇌⋒ Annexe:6⇌⋒ ⋈ TV 40P 2 ⌂ ⇌ ♣ ♿ Last dinner 8.30pm ✿ ⊥ ✻sB&B⇌⋒ fr£18 dB&B⇌⋒ fr£13 Lunch fr£1.80 Tea 35–60p High Tea 60p–£1 Dinner£3.80–£4.90 *xmas* Credit card 3

★***Glan Severn Arms*** Pant Mawr ☎240
Small country style inn situated at roadside with panoramic views from rear of building.
Closed Xmas wk; 6rm ⋈ 20P ⇌ ♣ ✿

LLANGYNIDR Powys Map**3** SO11
★***Red Lion*** ☎Bwlch730223
RS Xmas; 9rm TV ⊘ 40P ⇌ ⚓ Last dinner 10pm

LLANGYNOG Powys Map**6** SJ02
★**New Inn** ☎Pennant229
8rm ⋈ TV 50P 2 ⌂ ♣ Last dinner 7.30pm ✿ S% sB&B£5.50–£6 dB&B£11–£12 Lunch fr£2.50 High Tea fr£1.80 Dinner fr£3.50 Wine£2 ⊟ *xmas*

LLANDILOES Powys Map**6** SN98
★**Red Lion** Longbridge St ☎2270
7rm ⋈ CTV 12P Last dinner 7.30pm ✿ S% sB&B£6–£6.60 dB&B£12–£12.50 Lunch£2.35–£3.50 Tea£1–£1.50 High Tea£2–£3 Dinner£4–£5.25 Wine£2.95 Credit cards 1 3

LLANRHAEADR Clwyd Map**6** SJ06
★★★**Bryn Morfydd** ☎Llanynys280
Country mansion half a mile from main road set amongst green fields and trees.
17⇌⋒ Annexe:8⇌⋒ ☽ ✂ ⋈ CTV TV in bedrooms 100P ⚓ ⌒(heated) ●(hard) Live music & dancing Sat ♣ ♡Welsh, English & French. Last dinner 9pm ✿ ⊥ S% sB&B⇌⋒£16 dB&B⇌⋒£28 Lunch£6alc Tea 50–75p Dinner£6alc Wine£3.50 ⊟ *xmas*

LLANRWST Gwynedd Map**6** SH76
★★★ **Gwesty Plas Maenan** Maenan (3m N) ☎Dolgarrog232
14⇌⋒ ⋈ TV in bedrooms ⊘ 150P ⚓ ♣ Live music & dancing wknds Cabaret wknds Last dinner 10pm ✿ ⊥ S% sB&B⇌⋒£8–£10.75 dB&B⇌⋒£15.50–£19 Lunch£2.75–£5&alc Tea£1.20–£2.50 High Tea£2.75–£3.95 Dinner£3.75–£5.70 Wine£2.90 ⊟ *xmas*

★★**Eagles** ☎640454
18rm(7⇌⋒) CTV 60P 3 ⌂ ⚓ Last dinner 8.30pm ✿ ⊥ S% sB&B£9–£11 sB&B⇌⋒£10–£12 dB&B£17–£19 dB&B⇌⋒£19–£21 Lunch£2.50–£3.75 Tea 90p Dinner£4.25–£5.25 Wine£3.20 ⊟ *xmas* Credit cards 2 3

✕✕**Meadowsweet Hotel Restaurant** Station Rd ☎640732
Closed Oct–Etr; 36 seats 8P bedrooms available ♡French. Last dinner 9.30pm ✻Lunch£3.30 Dinner£5.50&alc Wine£2.70 Credit cards 1 2 3

L

LLANSANNAN Clwyd Map**6** SH96
★**Saracen's Head** (Frederic Robinson) ☎212
Small country inn set in centre of village in the heart of the countryside.
8rm Lift 🅼 CTV 6P Last dinner9.30pm ♁ S%
✱sB&B£6.50 dB&B£13 Lunch85p–£1
High Tea£2.50–£2.50 Dinner£4 Wine£3

LLANTWIT MAJOR South Glamorgan Map**3** SS96
✕✕✕**Colhugh Villa** Flanders Rd ☎2022
Situated in centre of village in an elevated position.
Closed Mon, Xmas & New Year's Day; Lunch not served Tue–Sat; Dinner not served Sun; 55seats 30P ♡English & French. Last dinner9.30pm
✱Lunch£3.40 (Sun only) Dinner£6.50&alc
Wine£3.50 Credit cards 1 2 3 5

LLANWRTYD WELLS Powys Map**3** SN84
★**Neuadd Arms** ☎236
18rm CTV ⊘ 14P 1⌂ ⌗ ∩ Children under 1yr not accommodated ♡International. Last dinner8.30pm
♁ ⊥ S% sB&B£7.50–£8 dB&B£15–£16
Lunch£3–£3.50 Tea75p–£1
Dinner£4–£4.50&alc ⊨ *xmas*

LLWYNMAWR Clwyd Map**7** SJ23
★★**Golden Pheasant** (Inter-Hotel) ☎Glyn Ceirig281
18th-C building with much character, situated in small country village.
14⇌fl TV 40P ⚓ ⌂ ∩ Last dinner8.30pm ♁ ⊥
S% sB&B⇌fl£11–£12 dB&B⇌fl£22–£24
Lunch£5alc Tea£1alc High Tea£3alc
Dinner£6alc Wine£3 ⊨ *xmas* Credit cards 1 2

MACHYNLLETH Powys Map**6** SH70
★★**White Lion** Pentrehedryn St ☎2048
Three-storey building situated in town centre by town clock.
20rm(3⇌fl) ☽ CTV 200P ⚓ ♡Continental & Oriental. Last dinner10pm ♁ S%
✱sB&B£6.60–£8.60 sB&B⇌fl£8.20–£10.20
dB&B£12.60–£15.20 dB&B⇌fl£13.20–£16.80
Lunch£3.10&alc Dinner£3.45&alc Wine£2.65
⊨ Credit cards 1 3

★★**Wynnstay** Maengwyn St (Trusthouse Forte) ☎2003
26rm(10⇌fl) TV in bedrooms 42P
Last dinner9.30pm ♁ ⊥ S% sB&B£11
sB&B⇌fl£14 dB&B£17.50 dB&B⇌fl£21 ⊨
xmas Credit cards 1 2 3 4 5 6

MAENTWROG Gwynedd Map**6** SH64
★★***Oakeley Arms*** Tan-y-Bwlch ☎277
9rm(8⇌fl) 🅼 CTV TV available in bedrooms ⊘ 30P ⌗ ⚓ ♡Italian. Last dinner8.30pm ♁

MALLWYD Gwynedd Map**6** SH81
★***Brigand's Inn*** ☎Dinas Mawddwy208
Small country inn by side of road to Dolgellau and Machynlleth.
Closed Nov–Mar except Xmas; 12rm(2⇌fl) TV P 3⌂ ⚓ ⌂ Last dinner8.30pm ♁

MANORBIER Dyfed Map**2** SS09
⊕***Castle Mead*** ☎358
Closed Nov–Etr; 8rm(5⇌fl) Annexe: 4rm(1⇌fl) 🅼 CTV 20P ⌗ ⚓ Last dinner7.30pm ♁ ⊥

MENAI BRIDGE Gwynedd Map**6** SH57
★★**Anglesey Arms** Mona Rd ☎712305
Late Victorian three-storey building with gardens. Extensive views of the Menai Strait.
17rm(7⇌fl) 🅼 CTV ⊘ 30P ⚓ Last dinner8.30pm
♁ ⊥ S% sB&B fr£9.25 dB&B fr£18.50
dB&B⇌fl fr£20.50 Lunch fr£3.25 Dinner fr£4.30
Wine£3 ⊨

★★**Gazelle** Glyngarth (2m NE A545) (Frederic Robinson) ☎Glyngarth713364
14rm(1⇌ ⋒) 🍴 20P Lastdinner9pm
✱sB&B£7.50 sB&B⇌⋒£8.50 dB&B£15 dB&B⇌⋒£17 Lunch£2.25 Tea80p Dinner£4.50

MERTHYR TYDFIL Mid Glamorgan Map**3** SO00
★★**Castle** Castle St ☎2327
Modern hotel close to town centre.
50⇌⋒ Lift 🍴CTV CTV in bedrooms Live music & dancing Sat English & French. Lastdinner10pm ✱sB&B⇌⋒£14.85 dB&B⇌⋒£20.79 Lunch£1.80–£3.60&alc Tea45p Dinner£3.60&alc Wine£2.50 *xmas* Creditcards 1 2 3

MILFORD HAVEN Dyfed Map**2** SM90
★★**Lord Nelson** Hamilton Ter (Wessex Taverns) ☎3265
An historic inn with memories of the great Admiral, overlooking Milford Haven.
27rm(7⇌⋒) 🍴CTV 20P Lastdinner10pm sB&B£11 sB&B⇌⋒£12 dB&B£20 dB&B⇌⋒£22 Lunch£2–£3 Tea fr50p Dinner£3–£5&alc Wine£1.50 Creditcards 1 2 3 5

☆☆**Sir Benfro** Herbrandston (3m W on unclass road) ☎4242
12⇌⋒ 🍴 TV TV in bedrooms 50P (heated) French. Lastdinner9.30pm

M

sB&B⇌ ⫙£9.50 dB&B⇌ ⫙£18
Lunch£3.50–£4&alc Tea£1–£1.50 HighTea£2
Dinner£3.95–£5&alc Wine£2.99

MILTON Dyfed Map**2** SN00
★Milton Manor ☎Carew398
21rm(15⇌ ⫙) CTV 30P International.
Lastdinner9.30pm S%
sB&B£8.50–£9.25 sB&B⇌ ⫙£9.25–£10
dB&B£17–£18.50 dB&B⇌ ⫙£18.50–£20
Lunch£3.25 Tea£1alc HighTea£2.50alc
Dinner£4&alc Wine£2.60 *xmas*

MOELFRE Gwynedd Map**6** SH58
✕Old Ship's Bell ☎693
Closed Oct–Mar; Lunch not served Sun; 50seats bedrooms available English, French & Italian.
Lastdinner9.30pm Lunch£3 Dinner£6alc
Wine£1.50

MOLD Clwyd Map**7** SJ26
★★Bryn Awel Denbigh Rd ☎3285
Closed 25 & 26Dec & New Year's Day; 7rm
Annexe: 12rm(2⇌ ⫙) CTV 70P 7 Live music & dancing Sun Lastdinner10.30pm
sB&B£7.50 sB&B⇌ ⫙£8.50 dB&B£12.50
dB&B⇌ ⫙£13.75 Lunch£5alc Tea£1.05alc
Dinner£7alc Wine£2.40 Creditcard 5

MONMOUTH Gwent Map**3** SO51
★★Beaufort Arms Agincourt Sq (Trusthouse Forte)
☎2411
Early 18th-C coaching inn with Georgian façade adjoining old Shire-Hall.
26rm(3⇌ ⫙) CTV TV in bedrooms 40P
Lastdinner9pm S% sB&B£10.50
dB&B£17.50 dB&B⇌ ⫙£20.50 *xmas*
Creditcards 1 2 3 4 5 6

★★King's Head Agincourt Sq (Best Western)
☎2177 Telexno497294
17th-C inn where Charles I is reputed to have stayed.
25rm(4⇌ ⫙) 1 CTV in bedrooms 20P
Lastdinner9pm sB&B£12 sB&B⇌ ⫙£17
dB&B£20 dB&B⇌ ⫙£25 Lunch£3.50–£4.15&alc
HighTea£2.50 Dinner£4.75–£5.25&alc Wine£3
xmas Creditcards 1 2 3 5

★*Talocher Farmhouse* Wonastow Rd
☎Dingestow236
9rm CTV 40P 2 saunabath Children under 5yrs not accommodated Lastdinner8pm

★White Swan Priory St ☎2045
Closed 25 & 26Dec; 19rm(4⇌ ⫙) CTV 7P 10
English & French. Lastdinner9.30pm
sB&B fr£9.50 sB&B⇌ ⫙ fr£11 dB&B fr£16
dB&B⇌ ⫙ fr£19 Lunch£2.25
Dinner£3.50–£7&alc Wine£2.80
Creditcards 2 3

MORFA NEFYN Gwynedd Map**6** SH24
★★*Woodlands Hall* Edern ☎Nefyn720425
13rm(5⇌ ⫙) CTV 100P Live music & dancing wkly
Lastdinner9.30pm

MUMBLES (nr Swansea) West Glamorgan Map**2** SS68
See also **Langland Bay** and **Swansea**
★*St Anne's* Western Ln ☎Swansea69147
Modern hotel in quiet position, near the town and overlooking Swansea Bay.
Closed 24–31Dec; 21rm(13⇌ ⫙) CTV TV available in bedrooms

✕✕*Norton House* Norton Rd ☎Swansea66174
Closed Sun & Etr; 80seats 150P bedrooms available French. Lastdinner10pm Creditcard 1

EATH West Glamorgan Map**3** SS79
★★Cimla Court Motel Cimla Rd ☎3771
RS Xmas Day; 3rm Annexe: 13rm(12⇌⋒) CTV 60P Live music & dancing Sat Cabaret Sat Last dinner9.30pm ✱sB&B£8.50 sB&B⇌⋒£10 dB&B£15 dB&B⇌⋒£18 Lunch£2.60alc Dinner£2.60alc Wine£2.80

EFYN Gwynedd Map**6** SH34
★★*Nanhoron Arms* St Davids Rd ☎720203
20rm(3⇌⋒) CTV TV available in bedrooms 120P 3 Disco Fri & Sat in season Live music & dancing Fri & Sat in season Last dinner9.30pm

Caeau Capel Rhodfar Mor ☎720240
Closed Oct–Mar; RS Mar–mid May 21rm(4⇌⋒) CTV 40P (grass) Last dinner7.30pm S% ✱sB&B£5.40–£7.56 sB&B⇌⋒£6.48–£8.64 dB&B£10.80–£15.12 dB&B⇌⋒£12.96–£17.28 Barlunch36p–£2.16 Tea21p–54p Dinner£3.24–£4.86

NEWBRIDGE-ON-WYE Powys Map**3** SO05
★*New Inn* ☎211
9rm(1⇌⋒) TV 60P English & French.

NEWCASTLE EMLYN Dyfed Map**2** SH34
★★Emlyn Arms (Inter-Hotel) ☎710317
20rm(10⇌⋒ Annexe: 20⇌⋒ CTV CTV available in bedrooms 150P English & French. Last dinner8.30pm S% sB&B£8.25 sB&B⇌⋒£9–£13.25 dB&B£15 dB&B⇌⋒£16.50–£21.50 Lunch£3&alc Tea35p–80p Dinner£4.20&alc Wine£1.40 *xmas* Credit cards 1 2 3 5

NEWPORT Gwent Map**3** ST38
☆☆☆**Gateway Motor** The Coldra ☎412777
120⇨⋒ ☽ ⋈ CTV available in bedrooms ⊘ 300P ⚓ ⌂ ♡French. Last dinner 10pm ✿ ♫ S%
sB&B⇨⋒£18.34 dB&B⇨⋒£26.39
Lunch£3.25–£4.25 Dinner£3.75–£4.75
Wine£2.95 ⊟ Credit cards 1 2 3 4 5 6

★★**Queens** Bridge St (Anchor) ☎62992
Telex no 858875
42rm(12⇨⋒) ☽ CTV CTV in bedrooms P
Last dinner 10pm ✿ ♫ S% ✱sB&B fr£11
sB&B⇨⋒ fr£14.50 dB&B fr£18 dB&B⇨⋒ fr£20
Lunch fr£2.95 Dinner fr£2.95 Wine£2.65 ⊟
Credit cards 1 2 3 4 5 6

★★**Westgate** Commercial St (Trusthouse Forte)
☎66244 Telex no 49173
68rm(17⇨⋒ Lift ☽ ⋈ TV in bedrooms P
Last dinner 10pm ✿ ♫ S% sB&B£13
sB&B⇨⋒£15.50 dB&B£17.50 dB&B⇨⋒£20.50
⊟ Credit cards 1 2 3 4 5 6

At **Castleton** (6m W A48)
☆☆**Cardiff Ladbroke Mercury Motor Inn**
(Ladbroke) ☎Castleton(Gwent)680591
55⇨⋒ 75P

At **Langstone** (4m E A48)
☆☆**New Inn Motel** (Ansells)
☎Newport(Gwent)412426
30⇨⋒ 200P

NEW QUAY Dyfed Map**2** SN35
★**New Quay** ☎560282
RS Oct–Mar; 14rm(1⇨⋒) ⋈ CTV TV available in bedrooms P ⇔ Last dinner 8.30pm ✿ S%
✱sB&B£5.50–£7 sB&B⇨⋒£6.50–£8.50
dB&B£11–£14 dB&B⇨⋒£13–£17
Bar lunch 65p–£1.60 Dinner£2–£3.50
Wine£2.10 ⊟

NEWTOWN Powys Map**6** SO19
★★★**Bear** Broad St ☎26964
Coaching inn dating from Tudor times, situated in town centre.
43rm(32⇨⋒) ☽ ⋈ CTV CTV available in bedrooms
60P Last dinner 9.30pm ✿ ♫ S%
✱sB&B⇨⋒£8.25 dB&B⇨⋒£10.50
Lunch fr£2.50 Dinner fr£4 Wine£3 ⊟ *xmas*
Credit cards 1 2 3 5

NORTHOP HALL Clwyd Map**7** SJ26
★★★**Chequers** (Inter-Hotel) ☎Deeside 816181
Telex no 8951994
Converted house over 100 years old, set in its own grounds.
18⇨⋒ ⋈ CTV CTV in bedrooms 200P 2⌂ ⇔ ⚓ Live music & dancing Sat ♡Welsh & French.
Last dinner 9.45pm. ✿ S% dB&B⇨⋒£13–£15
dB&B⇨⋒£21–£25 Lunch£3–£5.50&alc
Dinner£5–£6 Wine£2.45 ⊟ *xmas*
Credit cards 1 2 3 5 6

PEMBREY Dyfed Map**2** SN40
★★**Ashburnham** Ashburnham Rd ☎Burry Port 2328
A small informal hotel quietly situated opposite Ashburnham golf course.
10rm(4⇨⋒) ⋈ CTV 40P Disco wkly
Last dinner 9.30pm ✿ sB&B£6.75
sB&B⇨⋒£7.75 dB&B£13.50–£14.50
dB&B⇨⋒£14.50 Lunch fr£5alc Wine£2.15
Credit cards 1 2 3

PEMBROKE Dyfed Map**2** Sm90
★★**Lion** ☎4501
30rm(1⇨⋒) CTV 40P Last dinner 9.30pm ✿ S%
✱sB&B£9.75 sB&B⇨⋒£12 dB&B£14
dB&B⇨⋒£18 Bar lunch£1.25alc Dinner£5alc
Wine£2.60 Credit cards 1 2 3 5

N

★*Old King's Arms* Main St ☎3611
S Xmas–New Year's Day; 21⇌⋒ TV available in edrooms 21P ♡International. Lastdinner10pm
Credit cards ① ② ③

EMBROKE DOCK Dyfed Map**2** SM90
★**Commodore** The Old Dockyard
☎Pembroke3981 Telex no48497
4rm(13⇌⋒) ☽ CTV TV in bedrooms 50P
auna bath ♡French. Lastdinner10pm
% sB&B£10.45 sB&B⇌⋒£14.25
B&B⇌⋒£19.25 Lunchfr£3&alc Teafr£1.15
ligh Tea fr£1.75 Dinnerfr£4.95&alc Wine£2.70
Creditcards ① ③ ⑤

★★**Dolphin** Pembroke St ☎Pembroke5581
⇌⋒ CTV available in bedrooms 14P
astdinner10pm ✱sB&B⇌⋒£9–£11
dB&B⇌⋒£21 Lunch£6alc Tea£1.75
High Tea£2.50 Dinner£5.25&alc Wine£3.25

PENARTH South Glamorgan Map**3** ST17
★**Glendale** 8–10 Plymouth Rd ☎708302
17rm(8⇌⋒) CTV CTV available in bedrooms
♡Italian. Lastdinner9.30pm S%
sB&B£6.50–£7.50 sB&B⇌⋒£8.50–£9.50
dB&B£12–£13 dB&B⇌⋒£14–£16
Lunchfr£1.50&alc Dinnerfr£3&alc Wine£1.65
xmas

★**Walton House** 37 Victoria Rd ☎707782
RSXmas; 11rm(1⇌⋒) CTV 12P
Lastdinner7.30pm ✱sB&Bfr£6.50
dB&Bfr£11.50 dB&B⇌⋒fr£14
Lunch£2.50–£3.50&alc Teafr£1.50 High Teafr£2
Dinner£2.50–£4&alc Wine£3

P

✻XXX**Caprice** The Esplanade ☎702424
Closed Sun & Public Hols; 76seats English, French & Italian. Specialities: lobster thermidor, fresh roast duckling, veal cutlets in rosemary.
Lastdinner11pm ✻Lunch£4.75&alc
Dinner£10alc Wine£3.15 Creditcards 1 2 3 5

PENNAL Gwynedd Map**6** SH60
★★**Llugwy** (1m E on A483) ☎228
Gracious Elizabethan country house set in own grounds.
10rm(8) 25P Lastdinner10pm sB&B£10.50–£13.35
sB&B£11.50–£14.35 dB&B£21–£26.70
dB&B£23–£28.70 Barlunch£1.25 Tea50p
Dinner£6alc Wine£2.90 *xmas*
Creditcards 1 2 3 5 6

★**Riverside** ☎285
9rm CTV 40P 6 Lastdinner8.45pm
sB&B£8–£8.75 dB&B£16–£17.50
Barlunch£1–£2.50 Tea70p–£1.50
Dinner£3.95–£5.50 Wine£2.75 Creditcard 3

PENRHYNDEUDRAETH Gwynedd Map**6** SH63
★★★***Portmeirion*** (Prestige) ☎228 Telexno61467
This Italianate village, grouped around an old mansion, overlooks the sea.
Closed Jan–mid Apr; RS Nov & Dec; 18rm(11)
Annexe: 32rm(26) CTV TV available in bedrooms 400P (heated) Children under 9yrs not accommodated International.
Lastdinner9.15pm Creditcards 1 2 3 5 6

PONTARGOTHI Dyfed Map**2** SN52
★★**Cothi Bridge** ☎Nantgaredig251

6rm(7⇌⋒) ⋈ CTV 40P ⇌ ⚓ ⇜ Last dinner 9pm ⚲ ☋ S% ✱sB&B fr£7 sB&B⇌⋒ fr£8.50 dB&B fr£12 dB&B⇌⋒ fr£15 Bar lunch 70p–£2 Tea 30p–£1 Dinner £3.50–£4.50&alc Wine £2.40 ≡ *xmas* Credit cards 1 2 3 5

PONTERWYD Dyfed Map **6** SN78
★★Dyffryn Castell ☎237
Historical coaching house set at side of A44 in the heart of the countryside.
RS Nov & Feb; 6rm(1⇌⋒) ⋈ CTV 40P Children under 10yrs not accommodated Last dinner 8.30pm ⚲ S% sB&B £10.03 sB&B⇌⋒ £11.53 dB&B £15.44 dB&B⇌⋒ £17.44 Bar lunch 55p–£3.45 Dinner £5–£11&alc Wine £3.96 ⊟

PORT DINORWIC Gwynedd Map **6** SH56
★Sea Horse 20 Snowdon St ☎670546
Closed Sun & Oct; 30seats ⚑ ☋French.
Last dinner 9.30pm Dinner £4.65alc Wine £3.20
Credit cards 1 3

PORTHCAWL Mid Glamorgan Map **3** SS87
★★Fairways Sea Front ☎2085
A traditional hotel offering panoramic views of the Bristol Channel and close to beaches and the Royal Porthcawl Golf Club.
24rm(4⇌⋒) Lift ⋈ CTV 20P 3⌂ Last dinner 9pm ⚲ S% sB&B £7.70–£9.50 sB&B⇌⋒ £11–£12 dB&B £14.60–£17 dB&B⇌⋒ £19.20–£21.75 Bar lunch 35p–£1.50 Dinner £3.50&alc Wine £3 ⊟

★Rose & Crown Nottage (2m N B4283) ☎4850
A well-appointed and informal small hotel with all the character of a village inn.
8⇌⋒ ⋈ CTV ⊘ 25P Last dinner 10.30pm ⚲ sB&B⇌⋒ £12 dB&B⇌⋒ £22 Lunch £2.50–£3.50 Dinner £3.50–£4.50&alc Wine £1.50
Credit cards 1 3 5

PORTHMADOG Gwynedd Map **6** SH53
★★Royal Sportsman High St (Trusthouse Forte) ☎2015
Centrally situated two-storey stone-fronted hotel.
21rm(5⇌⋒) CTV TV in bedrooms 20P
Last dinner 9.15pm ⚲ ☋ S% sB&B £10.50 dB&B £18.50 dB&B⇌⋒ £21 ⊟ *xmas*
Credit cards 1 2 3 4 5 6

★★Tyddyn Llwyn Black Rock Rd ☎2205
Modern purpose-built hotel set amongst green pastureland, just off the main road.
RS Oct–May; 11rm ⋈ CTV ⊘ 20P ⚓ Children under 2yrs not accommodated ☋English, French & Italian.
S% ✱sB&B fr£7 dB&B fr£14 Lunch fr£3
Dinner fr£3.50&alc Wine £2.38

PORT TALBOT West Glamorgan Map **3** SS79
☆☆☆Executive Princess Margaret's Way, Aberavon (2m SW) ☎4949
69⇌⋒ Lift ☽ ⊞ ⋈ CTV in bedrooms ⊘ 150P Disco twice wkly Conference facilities available ♨ ♿ ☋French. Last dinner 9.45pm ⚲ ☋ S% sB&B⇌⋒ £17.28 dB&B⇌⋒ £24.84
Lunch fr£4.25&alc Tea fr£2&alc
Dinner fr£4.25&alc Wine £2.80 ⊟
Credit cards 1 2 3 4 5 6

★★★Twelve Knights Margam Rd, Margam (2m SE A48) (Inter-Hotel) ☎2381
11⇌⋒ ☽ ⋈ CTV in bedrooms ⊘ 200P ⇌
Last dinner 10pm ⚲ S% sB&B⇌⋒ £17.50 dB&B⇌⋒ £25 Lunch £3.75&alc Dinner £5&alc
Wine £3 ⊟ Credit cards 1 2 3 5

P

PRESTEIGNE Powys Map**3** SO36
★★Radnorshire Arms High St (Trusthouse Forte) ☎406
Originally a private residence, converted into a hotel in 1792.
8rm(5⇌⋒) Annexe: 9rm(8⇌⋒) TV in bedrooms 20P 8⌂ ⚓ Last dinner 9.15pm ✿ ⊻ S% sB&B£11 sB&B⇌⋒£14 dB&B£18.50 dB&B⇌⋒£21 ⊟ *xmas* Credit cards 1 2 3 4 5 6

★Bull St Davids Street ☎488
Small, old building standing in part of the old town cross site, at the western end of the town.
6rm(2⇌⋒) ⋈ CTV 1⌂ Children under 8yrs not accommodated Last dinner 9pm ✿ sB&B£7.50–£8.50 dB&B⇌⋒£12–£13.50 Lunch£3–£3.50&alc Dinner£3.50–£4.50&alc Wine£3 ⊟

PUMSAINT Dyfed Map**3** SN64
★*Dolauchothi Arms* ☎204
Old coaching inn with some original oak beams and good views of surrounding hills. Garden with lawns and 4½m of private fishing.
Closed Xmas; 6rm ⋈ CTV 50P ⚓ Last dinner 8.30pm ✿

REDBROOK Clwyd Map**7** SJ54
★★*Redbrook Hunting Lodge* Wrexham Rd ☎Redbrook Maelor 204
12rm(4⇌⋒) 1⊟ CTV P ⚓ Music & dancing Sat ♿ ♡English & French. Last dinner 10pm ✿ ⊻

RED WHARF BAY Gwynedd Map**6** SH58
★Min-y-Don ☎Tynygongl 2596
Holiday hotel set as edge of bay with views of Red Wharf Bay.
18rm(3⇌⋒) ⋈ CTV 120P Last dinner 9pm ✿ ⊻ S% sB&B£7.50–£10 sB&B⇌⋒£9.50–£12 dB&B£15–£20 dB&B⇌⋒£19–£24 Bar lunch£1–£3 Tea£1–£2 High Tea£1–£2 Dinner£3.50–£4.50&alc Wine£2 ⊟ *xmas*

RHAYADER Powys Map**6** SN96
★★Elan Valley Elan Valley (2½m SW B4518) ☎810448
Closed mid Oct–mid Mar; 12rm ⋈ CTV 50P 6⌂ ⚓ Last dinner 8pm ✿ ⊻ S% sB&B£8.50 dB&B£17 Lunch£3.60 Tea£1 Dinner£4.50 Wine£2.50 Credit card 2

★Elan West St ☎810373
Closed 1st 2wks Feb; 15rm(1⇌⋒) CTV 14P ♡English & French. Last dinner 8pm ✿ ⊻ sB&B£5.50–£7.50 dB&B£11–£15 dB&B⇌⋒£13–£17 Lunch£2.50–£3.50 Tea30p–£1 Dinner£3.75–£5 Wine£2.65

★*Lion Royal* ☎810202
Closed 2wks Xmas; RS Oct–Mar; 20rm TV 15P 15⌂ Last dinner 8pm ✿ ⊻ ⊟

RHOS Dyfed Map**2** SN33
★★Lamb ☎Velindre 370576
8⇌⋒ ⋈ CTV in bedrooms 100P Last dinner 10pm ✿ S% sB&B⇌⋒£12–£13 dB&B⇌⋒£20–£22 Lunch£1.80–£2.80 Dinner£5–£10 Wine£3 Credit cards 1 3 5

RHOSNEIGR Gwynedd Map**6** SH37
★★Bay ☎810332
RS Oct–Mar; 30rm(6⇌⋒) ✗ CTV 40P 8⌂ ⚓ (hard) Disco wkly Last dinner 8.30pm ✿ ⊻ ✳sB&B£7.20–£9.60 sB&B⇌⋒£8–£10.60 dB&B£14.40–£19.20 dB&B⇌⋒£16–£21.20 Lunch£1.50–£1.80 Tea40–60p Dinner£3.50–£4.50&alc Wine£3.50 ⊟ *xmas*

★*Maelog Lake* ☎810204
13rm ⋈ CTV P ⚓ Live music wkly ♡English. Last dinner 8pm ✿ ⊻ ⊟ Credit cards 1 3

RHOSSILI West Glamorgan Map**2** SN00
★★Worms Head ☎Gower 512
Closed 25 & 26Dec; 21rm(5⇌⋒) ⋈ CTV 20P Last dinner 8pm ✿ sB&B fr£6.75 dB&B fr£13.50 dB&B⇌⋒ fr£15.50 Lunch£3alc Dinner fr£4.25 ⊟

RHYDWYN Gwynedd Map**6** SH38
✗Lobster Pot Church Bay ☎Llanfaethlu 241
Closed Sun & Nov–Mar; 64seats P Last dinner 9.45pm Dinner£7alc Wine£2.46 Credit cards 1 2

RHYDYMAIN Gwynedd Map**6** SH82
❀✗✗Rossi Ristorante ☎667
(Rosette awarded for dinner only)
40seats 30P bedrooms available ✗ ♡Italian. Last dinner 9pm ✳Lunch£2–£4.50&alc Dinner£12alc Wine£2.75 Credit cards 1 2 3 5 6

RHYL Clwyd Map**6** SJ08
★★★Westminster East Pde (Greenall Whitley) ☎2241
Three-storey building situated near town centre and opposite promenade.
55rm(27⇌⋒) Lift ☽ ⋈ CTV in bedrooms 11P ♡English & French. Last dinner 8.45pm ✿ ⊻ S% sB&B£13–£14 sB&B⇌⋒£15–£16 dB&B£17.50–£18.50 dB&B⇌⋒£20.50–£21.50 Lunch£3.50–£3.75&alc Tea50p High Tea£2–£2.50 Dinner£4–£4.25&alc Wine£3.20 ⊟ *xmas* Credit cards 1 2 3 4 5 6

ROBESTON WATHEN Dyfed Map**2** SN01
✗✗Robeston House ☎Narberth 860392
Closed Sun & Xmas; 51seats 50P bedrooms available ♡English & Continental. Last dinner 9.30pm ✳Lunch£6.50 Tea75p Dinner£6.50 Wine£2.50 Credit cards 1 6

ROSSETT Clwyd Map**7** SJ35
✗✗Golden Grove ☎570445
Closed Sun & Mon; 40seats 250P ♡International. Last dinner 9.45pm S% ✳Lunch£5.50alc Dinner£6.75alc Wine£4 Credit cards 1 2 3 5 6

RUABON Clwyd Map**7** SJ34
★★Wynnstay Arms High St ☎822187
9rm ⋈ CTV in bedrooms 80P 2⌂ ♡English & French. Last dinner 9.45pm ✿ S% sB&B£11.75 dB&B£23.75 Lunch£2.95 Dinner£3.50&alc Wine£2.75 ⊟ Credit card 1

RUTHIN Clwyd Map**6** SJ15
★★★Castle (Inter-Hotel) ☎2479
Part 14th and 18th-C historical building situated in town square.
27rm(16⇌⋒) ⋈ TV available in bedrooms 40P ♡International. Last dinner 9.30pm ⊻ ✿ ⊟ Credit cards 1 2 3 5

★★★Ruthin Castle ☎2664 Telex no 61169
64⇌⋒ Lift ☽ ⋈ CTV 200P ⚓ Live music & dancing Sat out of season ♡International. Last dinner 9pm ✿ ⊻ sB&B⇌⋒£15–£17.25 dB&B⇌⋒£30–£34.50 Lunch fr£3.75 Tea fr95p Dinner fr£6&alc Wine£3 ⊟ *xmas* Credit cards 1 2 3 5

ST ASAPH Clwyd Map**6** SJ07
★★Oriel House Upper Denbigh Rd ☎582716
Modernised hotel set in own grounds with private stretch of river.
19rm(18⇌⋒) 1⊟ ⋈ TV in bedrooms 150P ⚓ ♿ ♡English & French. Last dinner 9.30pm ✿ ⊻ S% sB&B⇌⋒£15 dB&B£26 dB&B⇌⋒£27–£33 Lunch£6alc Dinner£6alc Wine£4 Credit cards 1 3

★★Talardy The Roe ☎583766
14rm(9⇌⋒) ☽ ✗ ⋈ CTV 500P ⚓ Disco nightly Live music & dancing twice wkly ♡English & French. ✿

sB&B£7 sB&B⇌⫼£9 dB&B£12
B&B⇌⫼£15 Lunch£1.40–£2.50
inner£1.50–£8&alc Wine£2.50
redit cards 1 2 3 5 6

T DAVID'S Dyfed Map**2** SM72
★★Warpool Court (Inter-Hotel) ☎300
arly 19th-C country house in 7 acres of secluded alian gardens, with views of St Brides Bay. ollection of hand painted tiles depict heraldic hields.
losed Jan; 25⇌⫼ CTV in bedrooms 60P
(heated) Live music & dancing Sat (winter) Cabaret ri (winter) English & French.
ast dinner9.30pm S%
sB&B⇌⫼£14.90 dB&B⇌⫼£25.20
unch£2–£3.95 Dinner fr£5.90&alc Wine£2.55
xmas Credit cards 1 2

★★★Whitesands Bay ☎403
Overlooking sea, St David's Head, and island of Ramsey.
Closed mid Oct–Apr; 18rm(10⇌⫼)
Annexe: 12rm(2⇌⫼) CTV CTV in bedrooms 100P 4 (heated) sauna bath English & French. Last dinner8.30pm
sB&B£12–£24 sB&B⇌⫼£13.50–£25.50
dB&B£24–£50 dB&B⇌⫼£25.50–£52.50
Lunch£4–£5 Tea£1.25–£1.75
Dinner£5.50–£6.50&alc Wine£3
Credit cards 1 2 3

★★Grove High St ☎341
Closed Xmas; 10rm(9⇌⫼) 2 CTV 65P
Children under 7yrs not accommodated
Last dinner8.30pm *sB&B£7.50–£11
sB&B⇌⫼£9–£12.50 dB&B£13–£16
dB&B⇌⫼£14.50–£17.50 Lunch fr£2.50
Tea fr75p Dinner fr£4.25 Wine£2.60

★★***Old Cross*** Cross Sq ☎387
18th-C house, recently extended, facing market cross in square.
Closed Nov–mid Mar; 17⇌⋔ ⋈ CTV ⊗ 22P ⋓ English & French. Last dinner 8.30pm ✿ Credit cards 1 3

★★**St Non's** ☎239
On the fringes of St David's in close proximity to the Cathedral and Bishop's Palace.
20⇌⋔ ⋈ CTV 50P ⚓ ⋓ International. Last dinner 9.30pm ✿ ⊈ sB&B⇌⋔£10–£15 dB&B⇌⋔£20–£26 Bar lunch £2.50 Tea fr 50p Dinner £7alc Wine £2.65 *xmas* Credit cards 1 3 5

★**Twr-y-Felin** ☎265
Just outside St David's with fine views of St Brides Bay with numerous islands including Grassholm the famous bird sanctuary.
Closed Nov–Feb; Unlicensed; 13rm CTV 30P ⚓ Last dinner 8pm ✿ ⊈ S% sB&B fr £9 dB&B fr £18 Lunch fr £3 Tea fr 35p Dinner fr £5

ST MELLONS South Glamorgan Map **3** ST28
★★**St Mellons Hotel & Country Club** (Best Western) ☎Castleton 680355
12⇌⋔ ☽ CTV TV in bedrooms ⊗ 200P ⚓ ⇌(heated) squash sauna bath ⋓ French. Last dinner 9.45pm ✿ ⊈ ✻sB&B⇌⋔£9–£18 dB&B⇌⋔£18–£23 Lunch £3.50&alc Dinner £5alc Wine £2.75 ⊨ Credit cards 1 2 3 5

SALEM Dyfed Map **2** SN62
✕**Angel Inn** ☎Llandeilo 3394
Closed Sun; Lunch not served; 32 seats 50P bedrooms available ⋓ English & French. Last dinner 10pm ✻Dinner £5&alc Wine £2.60 Credit cards 3 5

SAUNDERSFOOT Dyfed Map **2** SN10
★★★**St Brides** St Bride's Hill (Inter-Hotel) ☎812304 Telex no 48350
50rm(33⇌⋔) ☽ ⋈ CTV in bedrooms 75P ⚓ ⇌(heated) Live music & dancing twice wkly (summer) wkly (winter) Children under 2½yrs not accommodated ⋓ Welsh, English & French. Last dinner 9pm ✿ ⊈ S% sB&B £12.50–£13.50 sB&B⇌⋔£14–£16.50 dB&B £19–£21 dB&B⇌⋔£24–£28 Lunch £3.50alc Dinner £5.25&alc Wine £3.25 ⊨ *xmas* Credit cards 1 2 3 5 6

★★**Glen Beach** Swallow Tree Wood ☎813430
RS Jan & Feb; 14rm(5⇌⋔) CTV 50P ⚓ Live music & dancing Wed & Fri Cabaret Sat (Sep–May) ⋓ English & French. Last dinner 10pm ✿ ⊈ sB&B £8–£12 sB&B⇌⋔£9–£13 dB&B £16–£24 dB&B⇌⋔£18–£26 Bar lunch 60p–£3 Tea 80p High Tea £1.20 Dinner £4.75&alc Wine £2.50 ⊨ *xmas* Credit cards 1 6

SKENFRITH Gwent Map **3** SO42
☆☆**Priory Motel** ☎210
Small, modern hotel located in its own grounds in the Monmouth valley overlooking the old village and Castle of Skenfrith.
Annexe: 8⇌⋔ ⊞ ⋈ TV in bedrooms 100P Live music & dancing Sat & Sun ✿ ⊈ sB&B⇌⋔ fr £13.47 dB&B⇌⋔ fr £18.82 Lunch £1.20–£1.50 Dinner £7alc Wine £3.50 ⊨ *xmas* Credit cards 1 3

SOUTHGATE West Glamorgan Map **2** SS58
★★**Heatherslade Bay** Westcliff ☎Bishopston 3328
15⇌⋔ ⋈ CTV CTV available in bedrooms 10P ⚓ Last dinner 8pm ✿ ⊈ S% sB&B⇌⋔£10–£12 dB&B⇌⋔£20–£24 Lunch £1.80–£3.50&alc Tea 95p&alc High Tea £1.20&alc Dinner £3&alc ⊨

WARPOOL COURT HOTEL

An old stone house of historic interest, the hotel stands in a magnificent position overlooking the broad sweep of St Bride's Bay. Within 5 minutes walk of both the tiny city of St Davids and the famous Pembrokeshire coastal path, and with spacious grounds of its own, its situation is perfect. Peace and quiet is the keynote here and gracious surroundings, good food, a convivial cellar bar and a happy atmosphere make it the perfect centre to enjoy all that lovely St Davids peninsula has to offer. The resident proprietors, Grahame and David Lloyd, ensure this by aiming for a standard of service that is as generous and as warm as it is skilled and efficient. All rooms have a bath and colour television, and there is a private hotel boat and a heated swimming pool.

Highly recommended in all Food Guides.

ST.DAVIDS, DYFED

Tel: St Davids 300

St Non's Hotel

ST DAVIDS — PEMBROKESHIRE
Telephone: St Davids 239

Andrew Stirling and Sandy Falconer, trained at Catering College, have for many years been running this small hotel owned by the Stirling Family.

THE HOTEL which is double glazed throughout has full central heating, contains 20 bedrooms all with private bathroom, a public lounge bar, a resident's lounge bar and television room. It is situated on the fringe of the cathedral city of St Davids, in close proximity to the cathedral and bishop's palace. Within easy reach are the beautiful Pembrokeshire coastline and islands, sandy beaches and numerous cliff walks — the area has many sites of interest which due to the comparatively mild weather can be viewed all the year round.

THE KITCHEN is under the control of Simon Periam, who uses as many fresh commodities as possible, to the extent that the majority of the vegetables are produced in our own gardens.

THE SERVICE: we aim to be efficient, yet friendly, so as to make your stay a pleasant one which we hope will encourage you to return.

S

Twr-Y-Felin Hotel

St Davids, Dyfed. Tel: St Davids 265
Guests: St Davids 553

St David's Premier Hotel

Established over 50 years & renowned for good food, comfort & personal attention. 2 lounges & 1 TV lounge. The hotel where guests return for annual visits. Situated in a fine position in its own grounds about 6 minutes' walk from Caerfai Bay. The hotel is a member of BHRA & S Wales Tourist Council. Your comfort and well-being is the personal interest of the resident proprietors: Mr & Mrs RN Lewis. Brochure available on request.

SWANBRIDGE South Glamorgan Map**3** ST16
XXXX***Sully House*** ☎Sully530448
Closed Sun; 72seats 30P bedrooms available
French. Lastdinner10.30pm Creditcards 1 2 3

SWANSEA West Glamorgan Map**3** SS69
☆☆☆☆**Dragon** 39 The Kingsway (Trusthouse Forte)
☎51074 Telexno48309
118 Lift CTV CTV in bedrooms 40P
Conference facilities available Lastdinner9.30pm
S% sB&B £21.50 dB&B £32.50
xmas Creditcards 1 2 3 4 5 6

★★★**Dolphin** Whitewalls (Trophy Taverns & Best Western) ☎50011
Closed Xmas Day; 65 Lift CTV in bedrooms
Conference facilities available English & French.
Lastdinner9.45pm S%
sB&B £9.75–£16.75 dB&B £19.50–£24
Lunch fr£3.50&alc Dinner fr£4.30&alc Wine£3.50
Creditcards 1 2 3 5

XX***Apollo*** 8 Craddock St ☎43526
Closed Sun; 60seats English, French & Italian.
Lastdinner11pm Creditcards 1 3 6

XX**Drangway** Wind St ☎461397
Closed Sat, Sun & 1st 2wks Aug; 48seats
French. Lastdinner10pm S%
Lunch£3.45–£7.25&alc Dinner£6.45&alc
Wine£3.95 Creditcards 1 2 3 5

TALSARNAU Gwynedd Map**6** SH63
★★**Maes-y-Neuadd** ☎Harlech780200
The original wing of this country house was built in

S

T

the 14th century. Cromwell is said to have visited here.
Closed mid Oct–Mar; 13rm(11⇌ ⋒) ⋈ TV in bedrooms 50P ⋕ ♣ Children under 5yrs not accommodated Last dinner 8pm ✿ S% sB&B£11.80 sB&B⇌⋒£12.80 dB&B⇌⋒£23.60 Dinner£5alc Wine£3

TALYBONT Dyfed Map**6** SN68
★White Lion ☎245
Small country inn situated in village centre.
RS Sun (Oct–Mar); 6rm CTV 12P 1⌂ Last dinner 9pm ✿ sB&B£7.50 dB&B£14 Lunch£4&alc Dinner£4&alc Wine£3.50

TAL-Y-BONT Gwynedd Map**6** SH76
☆☆Lodge (Inter-Hotel) ☎Tyn-y-Groes476
Closed Jan & Feb; 10⇌⋒ ⋈ CTV TV in bedrooms ⊘ 30P ⋕ ♣ ♀English & French. Last dinner 9pm ✿ ♀ S% sB&B⇌⋒£12.50–£15 dB&B⇌⋒£20–£25 Continental breakfast Lunch£3.50–£5&alc Tea£1–£1.50&alc Dinner£6–£7.50&alc Wine£2.25 ⊨ Credit cards 1 2 3 5

TAL-Y-LLYN Gwynedd Map**6** SH70
★★Tynycornel ☎Abergynolwyn282
RS 4Nov–24Mar (wkns only); 6rm(1⇌⋒) Annexe: 11⇌⋒ ⋈ 4P ⋕ ♣ ⌂ ♀English & French. Last dinner 9pm ✿ ✱sB&B fr£9.95 sB&B⇌⋒ fr£10.95 dB&B fr£17.50 dB&B⇌⋒ fr£19.80 Bar lunch£1.50alc Dinner fr£5.90 Wine£3.40 ⊨ Credit cards 1 3

TENBY Dyfed Map**2** SN10
★★★Imperial The Paragon (Best Western) ☎3737
Telex no 48444
48rm(46⇌⋒) Lift ☽ CTV in bedrooms 16P 16⌂ Live music & dancing Wed & Sat ♀English & French

T

Lastdinner9.30pm ♨ ☕
✱sB&B⇌⫙£12.50–£15 dB&B£25–£36
Lunch£4.25&alc Tea35p–£1 Dinner£5.50&alc
Wine£2.95 ⊟ *xmas* Creditcards 1 2 3 5

★★Atlantic The Esplanade ☎2881
Closed 25Oct–Mar; 46rm(20⇌⫙) ⊞ ♛ CTV 30P ⛟
⚓ Discowkly Lastdinner8.30pm ♨ ☕ S%
✱sB&B£10–£12 sB&B⇌⫙£13 dB&B£20–£24
dB&B⇌⫙£22–£28 ⊟

★★Fourcroft The Croft ☎2516
Part of Georgian terrace, with attractive cliffside gardens, overlooking bay and harbour.
Closed mid Oct–Mar; 45rm(19⇌⫙) Lift ♛ CTV TV in bedrooms ℙ ⛱ 🍷International. Lastdinner8pm ♨
☕ S% sB&B£8.50–£10.50
sB&B⇌⫙£9.50–£11.50 dB&B£16–£20
dB&B⇌⫙£18–£22 Lunch£2.50–£3.50 Tea fr£1
High Tea fr£1.50 Dinner£4.50–£6 Wine£2.50
Creditcard 1

★★*Royal Lion* ☎2127
Closed Dec–Feb; 35rm(13⇌⫙) CTV 20P ⊟
Creditcards 1 3

★★*Tenby House* Tudor Sq ☎2000
Closed 12–26Oct; 17rm(3⇌⫙) CTV 10P ⛟
Lastdinner8.30pm ♨ ☕

★*Abbey* Penally (2m SW A4139) ☎2143
Closed Oct & Xmas; RS Nov–Apr; 8rm(4⇌⫙) ♛
CTV 20P ⚓ Lastdinner10pm ♨

★*Croft* ☎2576
Closed Nov–Apr; 20rm(4⇌⫙) CTV 5P
Lastdinner7pm ♨ ☕ Creditcards 1 3

THREE COCKS Powys Map**3** SO13
★★Three Cocks ☎Glasbury215
Small, very old roadside inn situated 5 miles from nearest village.
Closed 1–14Jan; 7rm ♛ CTV 40P ⛟ ⚓ 🍷English & French. Lastdinner10pm ♨ ✱sB&B£7.70
dB&B£14.30 Lunch£5.44&alc Dinner£6.40alc
Wine£2.97 Creditcards 1 3 4 5 6

TINTERN Gwent Map**3** SO50
★★Beaufort (Embassy) ☎202
27⇌⫙ ☽ ♛ CTV TV in bedrooms 40P ⚓
Lastdinner9pm ♨ ☕ S% sB&B⇌⫙£12
dB&B⇌⫙£20 Lunch£4.50&alc Dinner£4.50&alc
Wine£3.50 Creditcards 1 2 3 4 5 6

★★Royal George (Trusthouse Forte) ☎205
19rm(15⇌⫙ ♛ TV in bedrooms 30P ⚓
Lastdinner9.30pm ♨ ☕ S% sB&B£11
sB&B⇌⫙£14 dB&B£17.50 dB&B⇌⫙£20.50
⊟ *xmas* Creditcards 1 2 3 4 5 6

TREARDDUR BAY Gwynedd Map**6** SH27
★★★Beach ☎860332
26⇌⫙ Lift ☽ ♛ TV in bedrooms 200P squash
sauna bath Disco 6nights (summer) 4nights (winter)
🍷International. Lastdinner9.30pm ♨ ☕
sB&B⇌⫙£11 dB&B⇌⫙£17.82
Continental breakfast Lunch£4.75alc Tea75palc
High Tea£1.50alc Dinner£5alc Wine£3 ⊟
xmas Creditcards 1 2 3 5 6

★★★Trearddur Bay (Best Western) ☎860301
Telex no 61609
Hotel with good views situated in its own grounds next to beach.
28rm(19⇌⫙) ☽ ♛ CTV TV in bedrooms 200P ⚓
⊡(heated) 🍷French. ♨ ☕ S%
✱sB&B£9.18–£10.26 sB&B⇌⫙£12.42–£14.58
dB&B£18.36–£20.52 dB&B⇌⫙£24.84–£31.32
Lunch£3.24–£4.32&alc Tea£1.08
High Tea£2–£3 Dinner£4.54–£5.20&alc Wine£3
⊟ *xmas* Creditcards 1 2 3 5

T

***Seacroft** Ravenspoint Rd ☎860348
rm(4⇌🛁) 🛏CTV 30P English & French.
Last dinner9.15pm

TREGARON Dyfed Map**3** SN65
Talbot ☎208
Closed Oct–Mar; 14rm(4⇌🛁) 🛏TV
Last dinner9pm S% sB&B£10.95
sB&B⇌🛁£10.95 dB&B£21.90 dB&B⇌🛁£21.90
Lunch fr£4.30 Dinner fr£5.75&alc Wine£3.15

TREMADOG Gwynedd Map**6** SH54
★Madoc ☎Porthmadog2021
Early 19th-C inn, with oak beams and Welsh granite fireplace, at foot of Tremadog rocks. Fine views of Moel-y-Gest.
4rm(2⇌🛁) Annexe: 7rm CTV 14P 4
Last dinner8.30pm S%
sB&B£8.25–£8.75 sB&B⇌🛁£8.75–£9.25
dB&B£16.50–£17.50 dB&B⇌🛁£17–£18
Lunch£2.75–£3.75 Tea85p High Tea£1.50
Dinner fr£4&alc Wine£2.60 *xmas*
Credit cards 1 2

TYWYN Gwynedd Map**6** SH50
★Corbett Arms Corbett Sq (Inter-Hotel) ☎710264
Situated close to town centre.
Closed Nov–Mar; 35rm(5⇌🛁) 🛏CTV 50P 20
Last dinner8.45pm S%
sB&B£9.50–£12.50 sB&B⇌🛁£16–£18
dB&B£19–£22 dB&B⇌🛁£22–£26 Lunch£3.50
High Tea£3.50 Dinner£5.40–£7&alc Wine£2.35
xmas Credit cards 1 2 3 4 5 6

★Ddraig Goch Marine Pde ☎710141
Closed 24 & 25Dec; 12⇌🛁 Lift 🛏TV in bedrooms
12P English & Continental. Last dinner8pm
S% *sB&B⇌🛁£6.50–£8.50
dB&B⇌🛁£13–£17 Bar lunch40p–£1.50
Tea20–45p Dinner£5.20&alc Wine£2.45
Credit cards 1 3 5 6

★Gorlan Marine Pde ☎710404
9rm CTV 2P English. Last dinner9pm
Credit card 3

USK Gwent Map**3** SO30
★★Glen-yr-Afon Pontypool Rd ☎2302
Closed 25Dec–1Jan; 14rm(9⇌🛁) 🛏CTV 24P
Last dinner8.30pm S% sB&B£8.37
sB&B⇌🛁£9.72 dB&B£12.50 dB&B⇌🛁£13.50
Lunch£3.50&alc Tea75p Dinner£4&alc
Wine£2.70

★★Three Salmons Bridge St ☎2133
14rm(11⇌🛁) Annexe: 17rm(12⇌🛁) 2 🛏CTV CTV in bedrooms 50P International.
Last dinner9.45pm S% *sB&B£12–£12.50
sB&B⇌🛁£15.25–£16 dB&B£16.50–£17
dB&B⇌🛁£22 Lunch£3&alc Dinner£6.50alc
Wine£2.95 Credit cards 1 3

VALLEY Gwynedd Map**6** SH27
★★Valley ☎740203
21rm 🛏TV 80P 2 billiards English & French.

WHITEBROOK Gwent Map**3** SO50
★★Crown at Whitebrook ☎Trelleck254
Closed 20Jan–Feb; 8⇌🛁 🛏 40P French.
Last dinner10pm S% sB&B⇌🛁£12.50
dB&B⇌🛁£25 Lunch£10alc Tea£1alc
Dinner£10alc Wine£4 Credit cards 1 2 6

W

WOLF'S CASTLE Dyfed Map**2** SM92
★**Wolfcastle Country** ☎Treffgarne225
12rm(4⇌ 𝍢) 🍽 CTV in bedrooms 10P ⛟ ⚓ squash
🍷International. Last dinner9.30pm ☕ 🍵
❋sB&B£8–£12 sB&B⇌ 𝍢£8–£12
dB&B£14–£16.80 dB&B⇌ 𝍢£14–£16.80
Bar lunch£1.50alc Tea50palc High Tea£2alc
Dinner£6alc Wine£2.80 🏨 Credit cards 1 3

WREXHAM Clwyd Map**7** SJ34
☆☆☆**Wrexham Crest Motel** High St/Yorke St
(Crest) ☎53431
Modern hotel with original frontage situated in the town centre.
80⇌ 𝍢 Lift ☽ 🍽 CTV in bedrooms 40P 24🏠
Last dinner9.30pm ☕ 🍵 S%
❋dB&B⇌ 𝍢£15.71 dB&B⇌ 𝍢£22.24
Continental breakfast 🏨 Credit cards 1 2 3 4 5 [

SCOTLAND

A

ABERDEEN Grampian *Aberdeenshire* Map**15** NJ90 **See plan**

☆☆☆☆**Holiday Inn** Old Meldrum Rd, Bucksburn (3m N A947) (Commonwealth) ☎713911 Telexno71308 Plan**10**
99⇌⋒ Lift ☽ ⊞ ⋈ CTV in bedrooms 180P ▭(heated) Disco Sun Cabaret Sun Conference facilities available ♡International. Lastdinner10.30pm ✿ ⌧ sB&B⇌⋒£29.13–£31.43 dB&B⇌⋒£40.43–£42.72 Lunch£2–£3.50&alc Dinner£3.75–£5&alc Wine£4.50 ⊟ Creditcards 1 2 3 4 5 6

★★★★**Station** Guild St (British Transport) ☎27214 Telexno73161 Plan**19**
57rm(41⇌⋒) Lift ☽ ⋈ CTV in bedrooms 22P ♿ ♡English & French. Lastdinner9.30pm ✿ ⌧ S% ✱sB&B⇌⋒ fr£29.70 dB&B⇌⋒ fr£39.80 Dinner fr£7.90 Wine£3.15 ⊟ Creditcards 1 2 3 4 5 6

★★★**Caledonian** 10 Union Ter (Thistle) ☎29233 Telexno73758 Plan**1**
Five storey, traditional Victorian stone building, lying just off Union Street.
79rm(56⇌⋒) 1▭ Lift ☽ ⋈ CTV CTV in bedrooms 17P ♡French. Lastdinner9.45pm ✿ ⌧ S% sB&B£16.90–£18.30 sB&B⇌⋒£22.40–£26 dB&B£23.90–£26.70 dB&B⇌⋒£29.40–£35.50 Lunch£3.50&alc Tea45p–90p Dinner£5.40&alc Wine£2.75 ⊟ Creditcards 1 2 3 4 5

★★★**Imperial** Stirling St (Swallow) ☎29101 Telexno73365 Plan**11**
110rm(101⇌⋒) Lift ☽ ⋈ CTV in bedrooms ⚑ Live music & dancing nightly ♿ ✿ S% sB&B⇌⋒ fr£20.85 dB&B⇌⋒ fr£28.40 *xmas* Creditcards 1 2 3 5

★★★**Marcliffe** Queens Ter ☎51281 Telexno73225 Plan**13**
A granite faced, terraced building situated on the western approach road to Aberdeen with modern furnishings and décor.
41⇌⋒ Lift ☽ ⋈ CTV in bedrooms 40P ⛟ ♡French. Lastdinner9.45pm ✿ ⌧ S% sB&B⇌⋒£20 dB&B⇌⋒£27 Lunch fr£3.50&alc Tea fr£1.20 Dinner fr£5&alc Wine£4.20 ⊟ Creditcards 1 2 3 5

☆☆☆***Royal Darroch*** Cults (3m SW A93) (Reo Stakis) ☎48811 Telexno739138 Plan**17**
67⇌⋒ Lift ☽ ⋈ CTV TV available in bedrooms 200P Conference facilities available Lastdinner9.50pm ⊟ Creditcards 1 2 3 5

★★**George** 2–4 Bon Accord Ter (Open House) ☎27266 Plan**6**
52rm(8⇌⋒) ☽ ⋈ CTV CTV available in bedrooms ⚑ Disco nightly Lastdinner10pm ✿ ⌧ S% sB&B£11.50 sB&B⇌⋒£15.50 dB&B£19 dB&B⇌⋒£23 Lunch£1.25 Tea45p High Tea£1.95 Dinner£3.35&alc Wine£2.35 ⊟ *xmas* Creditcards 1 2 3 4 5 6

★★**Gloucester** 102 Union St (Allied Scotland) ☎29095 Telexno76357 Plan**8**
82rm(24⇌⋒) Lift ☽ ⋈ TV available in bedrooms ⚑ Disco nightly Live music & dancing 6nights Lastdinner9pm ✿ ⌧ S% sB&B fr£12.50 sB&B⇌⋒ fr£15 dB&B fr£25 dB&B⇌⋒ fr£30 Lunch fr£2.75 Tea fr£1.50 Dinner fr£4 Wine£3.50 ⊟ *xmas*· Creditcards 1 2 3 4 5 6

★★**Gordon** Wellington Rd (Clansmans) ☎873012 Plan**9**
21rm(12⇌⋒) ⋈ CTV CTV available in bedrooms 80 ⛟ Lastdinner10pm ✿ ⌧ sB&B£30.55–£11.45 sB&B⇌⋒£12.60–£13.50 dB&B£17.85–£18.70 dB&B⇌⋒£19.95–£20.50 Lunch£2.15–£4.30 Tea70p–£1 High Tea£1.85–£3.15 Wine£2.15–£4.30 Wine£2.80 ⊟ Creditcards 1 2 3 5

★★**Lang Stracht** Lang Stracht (Open House) ☎38712 Plan**12**
Modern concrete structure, just off ring road.
41rm(2⇌⋒) Lift ☽ CTV Disco wkly Live music & dancing wkly ♡Mainly grills. Lastdinner8.45pm ✿ ⌧ S% sB&B£30.50 dB&B£18.75 dB&B⇌⋒£20 Lunch£1.75–£2.75 Tea fr75p High Tea£1.70–£2.20 Dinner&4alc ⊟ Creditcards 1 2 3 4 5 6

★★**Northern** Kittybrewster (Swallow) ☎43342 Telexno53168 Plan**14**
34rm(4⇌⋒) Lift ☽ ⋈ CTV 50P ⛟ ✿ S% sB&B fr£13.15 sB&B⇌⋒ fr£15.40 dB&B fr£26.20 dB&B⇌⋒ fr£27.70 ⊟ Creditcards 1 2 3 5

✕✕✕**Le Dodo** 15 Crown St ☎26916 Plan**4**
Closed 25 & 26Dec; Lunch not served Sat & Sun; 65seats ⚑ ♡French. Lastdinner11pm S% Lunch£2.75–£3.25&alc Dinner£10.50alc Wine£2.95 Creditcards 1 2 3 5

✕✕✕**Fiddlers** 1 Portland St ☎52050 Plan**5**
Closed Sun; Lunch not served Sat; 45seats 15P ♡International. Lastdinner10.30pm Lunch£10alc Dinner£10alc Wine£4.50 Creditcards 2 3 4 5

✕✕**Chivas** 387 Union St ☎53135 Plan**2**
Closed Sun; 90seats ⚑ Lastdinner10pm S% ✱Lunch£1.80–£2.40&alc High Tea£2.25 Dinner£4.25&alc Wine£2.95 Creditcard 5

✕✕**Dickens** 347 Union St ☎20318 Plan**3**
89seats ⚑ ♡International. Lastdinner11pm Lunch£3–£4.50&alc Dinner£7.50alc Wine£3.50 Creditcards 1 2 3 5

1 Caledonian★★★
2 Chivas✕✕
3 Dickens✕✕
4 Le Dodo✕✕✕
5 Fiddlers✕✕✕
6 George★★
7 Gerard's✕✕
8 Gloucester★★
9 Gordon★★
10 Holiday Inn☆☆☆☆
11 Imperial★★★
12 Lang Stracht★★
13 Marcliffe★★★
14 Northern★★
15 Poldino's✕
16 Raja✕
17 Royal Darroch☆☆☆
18 Shapla✕✕
19 Station★★★★

✕✕**Gerard's** 50 Chapel St ☎571782 Plan**7**
Closed Sun; 120seats. 🍷 French.
Last dinner 11pm Lunch£2.25&alc Dinner£8alc
Wine£3.75 Credit cards 1 2 3 4 5

✕✕**Shapla** 13 King St ☎55999 Plan**18**
100seats 🍷 Indian. Last dinner 11.30pm S%
Lunch fr£1.75&alc Dinner fr£5.50&alc Wine£3.50
Credit cards 2 3 6

✕**Poldino's** 7 Little Belmont St ☎27777 Plan**15**
A modern Italian restaurant in a quiet back street near the city centre.
Closed Sun; 75seats 🍷 Italian.
Last dinner 10.45pm S% Lunch£2.50&alc
Dinner£5alc Credit card 1

✕**Raja** 62 Shiprow ☎26949 Plan**16**
150seats 20P Disco 4nights wkly Live music & dancing 4nights wkly Cabaret 4nights wkly
English, French & Indian. Last dinner 12.30pm
Lunch£2.25–£8&alc Dinner£2.75–£10.70&alc
Wine£1.90 Credit cards 1 2 3 5

ABERDEEN AIRPORT Grampian *Aberdeenshire* Map**15** NJ81
☆☆☆☆**Aberdeen Airport** Skean Dhu, Argyll Rd
☎Aberdeen 725252 Telex no 739239
148⇌ 🌙 CTV in bedrooms 250P (heated)
♿ Conference facilities available Last dinner 9.45pm
S% ✻sB&B⇌£22.55–£23.45
dB&B⇌£28.55–£29.45 Lunch£3.75&alc
Dinner£4.85–£8.10&alc Wine£3.50 *xmas*
Credit cards 1 2 3 5 6

ABERDOUR Fife *Fife* Map**11** NT18
★★**Woodside** High St ☎860328
Attractive palm tree fronted hotel. Interesting cocktail bar was once a lounge in the Orient Line vessel Orontes.
14rm CTV TV in bedrooms 35P
International. Last dinner 8.45pm
✻Lunch£7.50alc Dinner£7.50alc
Credit cards 1 2 3 6

ABERFELDY Tayside *Perthshire* Map**14** NN84
★★**Palace** ☎359
Four storey grey and red stone Victorian building just outside town centre, in market town by River Tay.
Closed 4Jan–Mar; 18rm(3⇌) CTV 30P
Live music & dancing twice wkly Scottish, English & French. Last dinner 8.30pm
sB&B£9–£10 dB&B£18–£20
dB&B⇌£20–£22 Lunch£2.20–£2.50
Tea 50–75p High Tea£2.20–£2.50
Dinner£3.50–£4.50&alc Wine£2.10

★★Weem Weem (1m NW on B846) (Inter-Hotel) ☎381
RS Jan–16Mar; 12rm(1⇌⋒) TV 30P ⛟ Last dinner8.30pm ✿ sB&B£8.50–£10 dB&B£17–£20 dB&B⇌⋒£18–£21 Bar lunch£1.50alc Dinner£4–£8 Wine£3 Credit card ②

★Cruachan ☎545
Closed Dec–Feb; RS Nov & Mar; 10rm(1⇌⋒) ♛ CTV 30P ⛟ ⚓ Last dinner8pm ✿ ☕ ✱sB&B£8–£9 dB&B£13–£16 dB&B⇌⋒£15–£18 Lunch fr£2.50 Tea fr80p Dinner fr£4 Wine£2.40 Credit cards ① ③

⊕Station Dunkeld St ☎372
7rm CTV ⊘ 24P 7⌂ Last dinner7.30pm ✿ ☕ S% sB&B£5–£5.50 dB&B£10–£11 Lunch£2–£2.50&alc Tea£1–£1.30 High Tea£1.50–£2.50 Dinner£2.75–£3&alc Wine£2.50 ⚐

✕*Ailean Chraggen* Weem (1m N B846) ☎346
Closed Nov–Etr; 50seats 35P bedrooms available ☋English & French. Last dinner8.30pm

ABERLADY Lothian *East Lothian* Map**12** NT47
★★Kilspindie House Main St ☎319
13rm(5⇌⋒) ♛ CTV TV available in bedrooms 40P 3⌂ ⛟ ⚘ Last dinner9pm ✿ ☕ S% sB&B£8.30–£9.30 sB&B⇌⋒£9.30–£10.30 dB&B£15–£17 dB&B⇌⋒£18–£20 Lunch£2.70 Tea45–75p High Tea£2.10–£3.50 Dinner fr£4.25&alc Wine£2.75 ⚐

ABERLOUR Grampian *Banffshire* Map**15** NJ24
★★★★Aberlour High St ☎287
Centrally situated three storey hotel.
18rm(10⇌⋒) ♛ CTV 15P 6⌂ Last dinner8.30pm ✿ ☕ sB&B£10.50–£11.50 sB&B⇌⋒£11.50–£12.50 dB&B£17–£18 dB&B⇌⋒£18–£19 Lunch£2.85 Tea80p High Tea£1.75alc Dinner£4.90 ⚐

★★Dowrans ☎488
13rm(10⇌⋒) ♛ CTV 30P 3⌂ ⚘ Last dinner8.15pm ✿ ☕ ✱sB&B£8–£9 sB&B⇌⋒£8–£9 dB&B£16–£18 dB&B⇌⋒£16–£18 Lunch£2.75 Tea60–80p Dinner£5 Wine£2.40

⊕Lour ☎224
Popular for fishing and surrounded by distilleries.
10rm ♛ CTV ⊘ ⛟ High Tea6pm sB&B£6.50 sB&B⇌⋒£7.50 dB&B£13 dB&B⇌⋒£15 Lunch fr£2.50 Tea fr75p High Tea£2 Dinner fr£4 Wine£2.40

ABOYNE Grampian *Aberdeenshire* Map**15** NO59
★★*Balnacoil House* ☎2252
Country house type hotel standing in own grounds on the banks of the River Dee.
15rm(5⇌⋒) ♛ CTV TV available in bedrooms 40P 3⌂ ⛟ ⚓ Last dinner8.30pm ✿ ☕ Credit card ⑤

★★Birse Lodge ☎2253
Victorian granite dower house of Huntly estate. Standing in 5½ acres of private grounds near village green and River Dee.
Closed mid Oct–Mar; 13rm(8⇌⋒) Annexe: 4⇌⋒ ♛ CTV 30P ⛟ ⚓ ♿ Last dinner8.30pm ✿ ☕ sB&B£10 sB&B⇌⋒£11.50 dB&B£20 dB&B⇌⋒£23 Bar lunch£1.20 Tea75p Dinner£6 Wine£2.60

★★Huntley Arms (Inter-Hotel) ☎2101
Hotel stands beside field in which the Aboyne Games are played.
Closed Xmas & New Year's day; 56rm(16⇌⋒) ☽ ♛ CTV TV available in bedrooms 127P 2⌂ ⚓ billiards sauna bath Disco Fri, Sat & Sun ⚘ Last dinner9pm ✿ S% sB&B£7–£9 sB&B⇌⋒£9–£12 dB&B£14–£20 dB&B⇌⋒£18–£25 Lunch£3.50–£4.50&alc Dinner£3.50–£5&alc Wine£2.90 ⚐ Credit cards ① ② ③ ⑤ ⑥

★*Charleston* ☎2475
Small converted private house, just off the main road, overlooking field where the Aboyne Games are played.
7rm TV 30P ⛟ Music Sat Music & dancing Sun Last dinner7pm ✿ ☕ Credit cards ② ③

ACHNASHEEN Highland *Ross & Cromarty* Map**14** NH15
★★Achnasheen ☎243
Original building (1870) has close associations with Inverness to Kyle of Lochalsh railway line. Of special interest to railway enthusiasts, as it is part of the station.
14rm(7⇌⋒) CTV 30P Last dinner8.15pm ✿ ☕ S% sB&B£8.25–£9 sB&B⇌⋒ fr£14.50 dB&B fr£17 dB&B⇌⋒ fr£21 Lunch fr£3.75 Tea fr45p High Tea fr£3 Dinner fr£5.50 Wine£3.50 ⚐ Credit cards ① ② ③ ④ ⑤

★★♚*Ledgowan* (Best Western) ☎252
Fine solidly built red sandstone building, formerly a shooting lodge, set amid tall pines overlooking Strath Bran.
Closed Dec–Feb; RS Nov, Mar & Apr; 17rm(7⇌⋒) ♛ TV 30p ⛟ ⚓ Last dinner8.30pm ✿ ☕ Credit cards ① ② ③ ⑤ ⑥.

AIRDRIE Strathclyde *Lanarkshire* Map**11** NS76
★★Tudor Alexander St (Clansmans) ☎64144
21rm(7⇌⋒) ☽ ♛ CTV CTV in bedrooms 150P ⛟ ☋European. Last dinner9.30pm ✿ ☕ ✱sB&B£10.50 sB&B⇌⋒£13.20 dB&B£17.20 dB&B⇌⋒£20.50 Lunch£4.20alc Tea80p–£1 Dinner£6.20alc Wine£2.80 ⚐ Credit cards ① ② ③ ⑤ ⑥

XX**Postillion** 8–10 Anderson St ☎67525
Closed New Year's Day; Lunch not served Sat & Sun; 46seats P bedrooms available Last dinner9.30pm Lunch£8alc dinner£8alc Credit cards 1 3

ALMONDBANK Tayside *Perthshire* Map**11** NO02
★★**Huntingtower** Crieff Rd (off A85) ☎241 Perth plan**4**
8rm(4⇌ ⫴) CTV 50P Scottish & French. Last dinner9.30pm sB&B£12–£14 sB&B⇌⫴£15–£16.50 dB&B£20–£24 dB&B⇌⫴£24–£28 Lunch£3.75–£5&alc Dinner£7–£8&alc Wine£3.50
Credit cards 1 2 3 5 6

ALNESS Highland *Ross & Cromarty* Map**14** NH66
X**Tall Pines** ☎882445
Closed Tue (Sep–Jun) 50seats 30P
Last dinner9.45pm ✻Lunch£3.15alc
High Tea£3.15alc Dinner£6.50alc Wine£2.64

ALYTH Tayside *Perthshire* Map**15** NO24
★★★**Lands of Loyal** Loyal Rd ☎2481
Originally built by William Deilvy in 1850, this three storey building stands on elevated ground above Alyth, with fine views over Strathmore towards Sidlaw Hills.
Closed Xmas & New Year; 14rm(7⇌⫴) 1 TV 15P 4 British & French. Last dinner8.30pm ✻sB&B fr£11 sB&B⇌⫴ fr£13 dB&B fr£19 dB&B⇌⫴ fr£21.50 Lunch£4.50 Tea£1.30 Dinner£7 Wine£2.40
Credit cards 2 5

ANNAN Dumfries & Galloway *Dumfriesshire* Map**11** NY16

★★**Queensbury Arms** (Osprey) ☎2024
A whitewashed, two storey building in the centre of Annan which is 10 miles from the English border.
27rm(4⇌⫴) Lift CTV TV available in bedrooms 30P 6 Live music & dancing twice wkly
Last dinner9pm S% ✻sB&B£11 sB&B⇌⫴£14 dB&B£17 dB&B⇌⫴£21 Lunch£2.60&alc Tea30p High Tea£2.60 Dinner£3.90&alc Wine£2.41 *xmas*
Credit cards 1 2 3 5

ANSTRUTHER Fife *Fife* Map**12** NO50
★★★***Craw's Nest*** Bankwell Rd ☎310691
A resort hotel in small east Fife fishing village.
31⇌⫴ CTV 80P 3 Music & dancing Sat
Last dinner8.45pm Credit cards 1 2 3 5 6

★★***Smugglers Inn*** High St ☎310506
Original inn dates back to 1300 and in the days of Queen Anne it was a noted tavern.
10rm(4⇌⫴) CTV 16P English & French.
Last dinner9.30pm Credit cards 1 2 3 5 6

★**Royal** Rodger St ☎310581
9rm(2⇌⫴) CTV 9P High Tea6.15pm S% sB&B£8.50 sB&B⇌⫴£9.50 dB&B£17 dB&B⇌⫴£19 Bar lunch£1.75 High Tea£2.75 Wine£1.65

ARBROATH Tayside *Angus* Map**12** NO64
★★**Hotel Seaforth** Dundee Rd ☎72232
19rm(6⇌⫴) CTV 150P Live music & dancing Sat
Last dinner9.30pm sB&B£9–£10.50 sB&B⇌⫴£11.50–£13 dB&B£15.50–£17 dB&B⇌⫴£20–£22.50 Lunch£2.50–£3 Tea90p–£1.20 High Tea£2–£3.20 Dinner£8alc Wine£3.50

A

★Towerbank James St ☎75987
6rm CTV 12P Last dinner10.45pm S%
✱sB&B£7 dB&B£14 Lunch£1–£3.50&alc
Dinner£3.50–£8&alc Wine£3 *xmas*

ARDENTINNY Strathclyde *Argyll* Map**10** NS18
★★Ardentinny (Inter-Hotel) ☎209
RS Nov–Mar (open wknds only) 8rm(3) CTV 20P
British & Continental. Last dinner10pm S%
sB&B£10.50–£14 dB&B£15–£24
Bar lunch£1–£3&alc High Tea£1.15–£2.50
Dinner£5–£6 Wine£3.50 *xmas*
Credit cards 2 6

ARDLUI Strathclyde *Dunbartonshire* Map**10** NN31
★★Ardlin ☎Inverglas243
Three-storey white painted house, with gardens running down to shores of Loch Lomond.
11rm(1) CTV 50P Live music & dancing 6nights
Last dinner8.30pm sB&B£11.30
dB&B£20.40 dB&B£22.20
Bar lunch£2.40alc Tea50p Dinner£5.50alc
Wine£2.29

ARDRISHAIG Strathclyde *Argyll* Map**10** NR88
★★Royal ☎239
On northern edge of town, looking out across Loch Fyne.
20rm(4) CTV 60P French. Last dinner 9pm
S% sB&B£8–£9 sB&B£8.75–£10
dB&B£16–£18 dB&B£17.50–£20
Lunch£2.50–£3.50 High Tea£3–£4
Dinner£5–£7 Wine£3.20

ARDROSSAN Strathclyde *Ayrshire* Map**10** NS24
★★Eglinton Arms Princes St ☎65112
One of the original buildings in the town. Situated in a development area and conveniently placed for the harbour.
10rm(1) CTV 20P Last dinner8.45pm
✱sB&B fr£7.60 sB&B fr£8.85 dB&B fr£15.20
dB&B fr£17.70 High Tea£2–£3.50
Dinner£4.50–£5.50 Wine£2.50

★High Tide Parkhouse Rd (Scottish & Newcastle)
☎61527
Small, modern hotel with brick exterior, set on main road on the edge of town.
10rm CTV 60P Last dinner9pm S%
✱sB&B£6.50 dB&B£13 Lunch£2
Dinner£3.10&alc Wine£2.10 Credit cards 1 2 5

ARDUAINE Strathclyde *Argyll* Map**10** NM80
★★★Loch Melfort ☎Kilmelford233
Closed Nov–Mar; 28rm(23) CTV 50P
Last dinner8.30 sB&B£15–£20
sB&B£15–£22 dB&B£22–£24
dB&B£26–£30 Continental breakfast
Lunch£5 Tea50p Dinner£7–£10 Wine£3
Credit cards 1 2

ARINAGOUR Isle of Coll, Strathclyde *Argyll*
Map**13** NM26
★Isle of Coll ☎Coll334
9rm TV 30P sauna bath Last dinner8pm
sB&B£10.80 dB&B£21.60 Lunch£5.25
Tea£1.25 Dinner£6&alc Wine£2.05
Credit cards 1 5 6

ARRAN, ISLE OF Strathclyde *Bute* Map**10**
See **Brodick, Corrie, Lamlash** and **Whiting Bay.**

ARROCHAR Strathclyde *Dunbartonshire* Map**10**
NN20
★★Arrochar (Inter-Hotel) ☎222 Telex no 777205
White-painted building on shores of Loch Long with good views of surrounding hills.
RS Nov–Mar except wnds, Xmas & New Year;
65rm(33) Lift TV 100P Live music &

A

dancing 6nightly (in season) ♿ Lastdinner8.30pm
☆ ☐ ⊟ Creditcards 1 2 3 4 5 6

AUCHENCAIRN Dumfries & Galloway *Kirkcudbrightshire* Map**11** NX75
★★★Balcary Bay ☎217
Closed Nov–Mar; 12rm(5⇌⋒) 2⊟ CTV CTV available in bedrooms P 2 billiards Scottish, French & Italian. Lastdinner9.30pm S%
sB&B£12.50 sB&B⇌⋒£14.50 dB&B£25
dB&B⇌⋒£29 Lunch£6alc Tea£1alc
Dinner£6–£6.50&alc Wine£2.50
Creditcards 1 2 3 5 6

AUCHTERARDER Tayside *Perthshire* Map**11** NN91
★★★★★ **Gleneagles** (British Transport) ☎2231
See page 58 for details

★★*Ruthven Tower* Abbey Rd ☎2578
Converted private house in quieter part of town, within own grounds.
Closed New Year's Day; 10rm(2⇌⋒) Annexe: 8⇌⋒ CTV TV available in bedrooms 40P ♿ English. Lastdinner9pm

★Crown 112–114 High St ☎2375
13⇌⋒ CTV 12P English & French.
Lastdinner8.45pm ✱sB&B⇌⋒£5–£9.18
dB&B⇌⋒£10–£16.20 Lunch£4alc Tea75p
High Tea£1.50–£3 Dinner£4.80&alc Wine£2.95
Creditcards 1 3 5

AULTBEA Highland *Ross & Cromarty* Map**14** NG88
★★Drumchork Lodge (Inter-Hotel) ☎242
18rm(3⇌⋒) Annexe: 4⇌⋒ CTV 50P 4 English & Continental. Lastdinner8pm
S% sB&B fr£8.80 sB&B fr£8.80
sB&B⇌⋒ fr£9.80 dB&B fr£16.50
dB&B⇌⋒ fr£17.50 Barlunch fr£1.60 Tea fr£1.20
Dinner fr£4.20 Wine£2.70
Creditcards 1 2 3 5

★Aultbea ☎201
RS Oct–Mar; 8rm(1⇌⋒) Annexe: 11rm TV 30P
Lastdinner8pm sB&B fr£7
sB&B⇌⋒ fr£8.50 dB&B fr£14
dB&B⇌⋒ fr£15.50 Lunch fr£2.50 Tea fr£1
High Tea fr£2.25 Dinner fr£4.50 Wine£2.25

AVIEMORE Highland *Inverness-shire* Map**14** NH81
★★★★Coylumbridge (Reo Stakis) ☎810661
Telex no 75272
133⇌⋒ TV CTV in bedrooms 180P Live music & dancing 6nights wkly Conference facilities available International. Lastdinner9.15pm
✱sB&B⇌⋒£18 dB&B⇌⋒£30 *xmas*
Creditcards 1 2 3 5

★★★★Strathspey (Thistle) ☎810681
Telex no 75213
Six storey ultra modern building of spacious design standing within Aviemore Sports Centre.
90⇌⋒ Lift CTV CTV in bedrooms 150P (heated) squash sauna bath Disco twice wkly Live music & dancing 6nights wkly Cabaret 6nights wkly Conference facilities available Scottish & French. Lastdinner9.15pm S%
sB&B⇌⋒£16–£19.50 dB&B⇌⋒£19–£27.50
Lunch£2.50–£3.50 Tea45–50p Dinner£5.40
Wine£3.24 *xmas* Creditcards 1 2 3 5 6

★★★Badenoch (Osprey) ☎810261
New building of ultra-modern design, situated within Aviemore Sports Centre.
77rm(61⇌⋒) Lift CTV TV available in bedrooms 40P billiards sauna bath Disco 4nights wkly
Lastdinner9.30pm S% ✱sB&B£9.95
sB&B⇌⋒£17.40 dB&B£16.40 dB&B⇌⋒£24
Lunch fr£3.10 Tea fr30p Dinner fr£4.50 Wine£3
xmas Creditcards 1 2 3 5

A

☆☆☆**Freedom Inn** Aviemore Centre ☎810781
93⇌⋒ Lift ☽ ⋈ TV in bedrooms ⊘ 100P Conference facilities available ♡International.
Last dinner9.30pm sB&B⇌⋒£15.10–£27.60
dB&B⇌⋒£27.60–£35.20 Bar lunch£1–£1.50
Dinner£5.25 Wine£3.50 *xmas*
Credit cards 1 2 3 5

☆☆☆**Post House** Aviemore Centre (Trusthouse Forte) ☎810771
103⇌⋒ Lift ☽ ⋈ CTV in bedrooms 140P Conference facilities available Last dinner9.30pm ♡ ⊈ S%
sB&B⇌⋒£19.75 dB&B⇌⋒£30 *xmas*
Credit cards 1 2 3 4 5 6

★★**Alt-Na-Craig** ☎810217
A red sandstone Victorian villa with modern extension standing in own grounds on main road in centre of highland village.
10rm(1⇌⋒) CTV 15p 1⌂ ♣ Last dinner8pm ♡
⊈ S% sB&B£12–£12.50 dB&B£24–£24.50
dB&B⇌⋒£25.50–£26 Lunch£3 Tea fr25p
Dinner£4 Wine£2.40

★★**Cairngorm** (Best Western) ☎810233
Telex no 75261
Victorian stone house with modern extension, situated on main road, and adjacent to Aviemore Centre.
24rm(12⇌⋒) CTV 30P 4⌂ ♣ Last dinner9pm ♡
⊈ S% sB&B£12 sB&B⇌⋒£13.50 dB&B£24
dB&B⇌⋒£27 Bar lunch£1–£3.50
Dinner£6.50–£7.50 Wine£2.75 ⊟
Credit cards 1 2 3 4 5 6

★★**Lynwilg** ☎810207
18th-C coaching inn with small modern extension. Beside the main road approximately 2 miles south of Aviemore village and overlooking Loch Alvie.
Closed 29Oct–18Feb; 12rm(2⇌⋒) ⋈ CTV 50P 6⌂
⊕ ♣ ⌒ Last dinner8.30pm ♡ ⊈ S%
sB&B£12.10–£13.10 sB&B⇌⋒£13.10–£14.10
dB&B£20.90–£23.50 dB&B⇌⋒£21.90–£24.50
Bar lunch£1–£2.70 Dinner£5.50–£7 Wine£2.50
Credit cards 2 5

XX**Winking Owl Roadhouse** ☎810646
Converted cottage in own grounds situated in Aviemore village.
Closed Sun, Nov & 1st 2wks Dec; 70seats 50P
Last dinner9.15pm Dinner fr£5 Wine£2.90
Credit cards 1 2 3 5

⊛X**Bumbles** Grampian Rd ☎810392
Rosette awarded for dinner only.
Closed Wed, 9Nov–14Dec & 3rd wk May; 45seats
P Specialities: Garlic mushroom tartlet with Bearnaise sauce, rabbit with mustard and white wine, Elizabethan pork râgout. Last dinner9.30pm
Lunch£3alc Dinner£7alc Wine£3

AYR Strathclyde *Ayrshire* Map**10**NS32 **See plan**

★★★**Belleisle** Belleisle Park ☎42331 Plan**2**
16rm(14⇌⋒) 1⊟ ☽ ⋈ CTV CTV in bedrooms 40P ♣

♫ Live music & dancing wkly ♡French.
Last dinner8.45pm ♡ ⊈ sB&B⇌⋒£12–£15
dB&B£20–£24 dB&B⇌⋒£22–£26
Lunch£2.50–£2.75&alc Tea£1–£1.25
High Tea£2–£2.25 Dinner£5.50&alc Wine£2.70
xmas Credit cards 1 2

☆☆☆**Caledonian** Dalblair Rd (Allied Scotland) ☎69331 Telex no 76357 Plan**6**
121⇌⋒ Lift ☽ ⋈ CTV TV available in bedrooms ⊘
100P sauna bath Disco 4nights wkly Conference facilities available Last dinner10pm ♡ ⊈ S%
sB&B⇌⋒ fr£16 dB&B⇌⋒ fr£30 Lunch fr£3
Tea fr£1.50 Dinner fr£5.50 Wine£4 ⊟ *xmas*
Credit cards 1 2 3 4 5 6

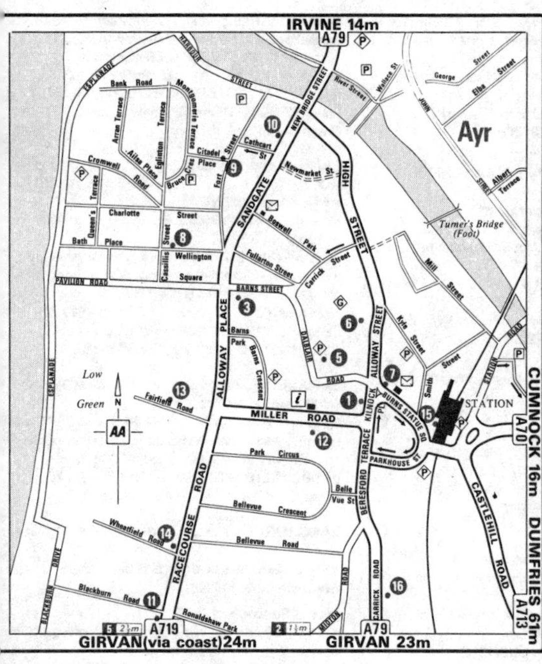

1 Ayrshire & Galloway★★
2 Belleisle★★★
3 Berkeley★★
4 Bumbles✕
5 Burns Monument★★
6 Caledonian☆☆☆
7 Carle's✕
8 County★★
9 Fort Lodge★
10 Fouter's Bistro✕
11 Gartferry★★
12 Kylestrome Hotel Restaurant✕✕
13 Marine Court★★
14 Savoy Park★★★
15 Station★★★
16 Struan★

★★Pickwick 19 Racecourse Rd ☎60111 Not on Plan
2(2⇌⋒) ☽ ▥ CTV CTV in bedrooms 60P ⚓ ☋English & French. Last dinner9.30pm ✿ ♖ S% ✱sB&B⇌⋒£13.50 dB&B⇌⋒£24 Bar lunch£1.50alc Tea35p Dinner£4.45–£5.45&alc Wine£2.25 *xmas* Credit cards 1 2 3 5

★★★Savoy Park Racecourse Rd ☎66112 Plan**14**
Red sandstone building standing in 3 acres of gardens.
0rm(13⇌⋒) ☽ ▥ TV available in bedrooms 100P ⚓ ♣ ☋French. Last dinner8.30pm sB&B£14.25 sB&B⇌⋒£15.25 dB&B£28.50 dB&B⇌⋒£30.50 Lunch£3–£4 Dinner£6.50&alc ⊟ Credit card 1

★★★Station Burns Statue Sq (Reo Stakis) ☎63268 Plan**15**
4⇌⋒ Lift ☽ ▥ CTV CTV in bedrooms 100P Disco nights wkly Live music & dancing Sun Conference facilities available Last dinner9.15pm ✿ ♖ S% ✱sB&B⇌⋒£15 dB&B⇌⋒£24 Lunch£3.25&alc Tea fr35p High Tea£2.25 Dinner£4.85&alc Wine£3.10 ⊟ *xmas* Credit cards 1 2 3 5

★★Ayrshire & Galloway 1 Killoch Pl (Open House) ☎62626 Plan**1**
24rm(8⇌⋒) ☽ CTV TV available in bedrooms 15P Last dinner9pm ✿ ♖ S% ✱sB&B£10.50 sB&B⇌⋒£13 dB&B£16 dB&B⇌⋒£19.50 Lunch£2.40 High Teas£1.50–£2.81 Dinner£4 ⊟ *xmas* Credit cards 1 2 3 5

★★Berkeley Barns St ☎63658 Plan**3**
10rm(2⇌⋒) ▥ CTV ⊘ 18P ⊕ ⚓ ☋French. Last dinner8.45pm ✿ ♖ sB&B fr£9.50 sB&B⇌⋒ fr£11 dB&B fr£16.50 dB&B⇌⋒ fr£18 Lunch fr£2.75&alc Tea fr85p High Tea fr£2.50 Dinner fr£4.75&alc Wine£2.95 *xmas* Credit cards 1 3

★★*Burns Monument* Alloway (2m S B6024) ☎42466 Plan**5**
3rm(1⇌⋒) ▥ CTV ⊘ 10P ⚓ ↬ Live music & dancing Sat (in winter) ♣ Last dinner9.30pm ✿

★★County Wellington Sq (Open House) ☎63368 Plan**8**
An attractive two-storey hotel, near sea.
31rm(2⇌⋒) ☽ ▥ CTV TV available in bedrooms 25P Last dinner8.45pm ✿ S% ✱sB&B£11 dB&B£17 dB&B⇌⋒£19.50 Lunch£2.70 High Tea£3.50 Dinner£3.70 Wine£1.95 ⊟ Credit cards 1 2 3 4 5 6

★★*Gartferry* Racecourse Rd ☎62768 Plan**11**
Built in late 18th-C using stone from the original Ayr prison. Hotel is situated on south side of the town.
13rm(7⇌⋒) ▥ CTV 200P ⚓ Live music & dancing Sun Cabaret Sun ☋British & Continental. Last dinner9.30pm ✿ ♖ Credit cards 1 2 3 5

★★*Marine Court* Fairfield Rd ☎65261 Plan**13**
15rm(11⇌⋒) Annexe:6⇌⋒ ☽ ▥ CTV 70P ⊕ ⚓ Music & dancing Sat ☋English & French. ✿ ♖

★*Fort Lodge* 2 Citadel Pl ☎65232 Plan**9**
6rm ▥ CTV ⊘ 7P ⊕ Last dinner7pm ✿ Credit cards 1 2 3 5 6

★Struan 37 Carrick Rd ☎65679 Plan**16**
Detached Victorian villa on main road, one mile south of town centre.
8rm(5⇌⋒) ▥ CTV 40P Last dinner8pm S% ✱sB&B£7–£8.50 sB&B⇌⋒£8.50–£10 dB&B£11–£12 dB&B⇌⋒£13–£15 Bar lunch£2alc High Tea£2alc Dinner£5alc Wine£3

✕✕Kylestrome Hotel Restaurant Miller Rd ☎62474 Plan**12**
100seats 40P bedrooms available Last dinner10pm ✱Lunch£3alc Dinner£6alc Wine£2.95

✕*Bumbles* Dalblair Arcade ☎60993 Plan**4**
Closed Sun, Xmas & New Year's Day; Lunch not served; 38seats 100P ☋French. Last dinner10.15pm Credit cards 1 2

✕*Carle's* 27 Burns Statue Sq ☎62740 Plan**7**
Closed Sun; Unlicensed; 70seats ☋International. Last dinner9.45pm (7.30pm mid Oct–May)

B

✕Fouter's Bistro 2A Academy St ☎61391 Plan**10**
Situated in narrow cobbled street; stone floor with authentic 'Bistro' atmosphere.
Closed Mon, last wk Sep & First wk Oct; Lunch not served Sun; 42seats French & Italian. Last dinner10pm Lunch£2.75alc Dinner£7alc Wine£2.75 Credit cards 1 2 4 6

BALLACHULISH Highland *Argyll* Map**14** NN05
See **North Ballachulish**
★★★Ballachulish (Best Western) ☎239
Large Victorian building on roadside; gardens overlook Loch Linnhe and Ardgour Mountains.
Closed 8Oct–Apr; 35rm(16⇌🛁) CTV 30P International. Last dinner8.30pm S% sB&B£13 sB&B⇌🛁£15 dB&B£26 dB&B⇌🛁£30 Tea45p Dinner£6&alc Wine£4 Credit cards 1 2 3 4 5 6

BALLATER Grampian *Aberdeenshire* Map**15** NO39
★★Craigard 3 Abergeldie Rd ☎445
Closed 25Oct–4Apr; 16rm(9⇌🛁) CTV 24P 2🏠 Last dinner8pm S% *sB&B£6.40–£9 sB&B⇌🛁£7.20–£10.25 dB&B£12.80–£18 dB&B⇌🛁£14.40–£20.50 Bar lunch£1.70alc Tea40p–£1 Dinner£5.40 Wine£2.60 Credit cards 1 5

★★Darroch Learg ☎443
Attractive red stone house standing on hillside in 4 acres of garden and woodland overlooking golf course and River Dee.
Closed Nov–Feb; 15rm(9⇌🛁) Annexe: 10rm(1⇌🛁) CTV 25P Last dinner8pm S% sB&B£9 sB&B⇌🛁£10.50 dB&B£18 dB&B⇌🛁£21 Lunch£2.75&alc Tea90p High Tea£2 Dinner£5 Wine£2.50

BALLOCH Strathclyde *Dunbartonshire* Map**10** NS3
★★Balloch (Clansmans) ☎Alexandria52579
13rm(6⇌🛁) CTV 30P European. Last dinner8.30pm *sB&B£8.95 sB&B⇌🛁£10.30 dB&B£15.25 dB&B⇌🛁£17.75 Lunch£3.45alc Dinner£3.45alc Wine£2.70 Credit card 1

BALMACARA Highland *Ross & Cromarty* Map**14** NG82
★★Balmacara ☎283
Roadside inn with fine views across Loch Alsh towards Skye.
RS Nov–Mar; 31rm(20⇌🛁) TV 50P Live music wkly Scottish & French. Last dinner8.30pm S% *sB&B£6.50–£8.95 sB&B⇌🛁£6.50–£10.45 dB&B£13–£17.90 dB&B⇌🛁£13–£20.90 Lunch£2.50 Tea45p Dinner£4.75 Wine£2.75 Credit card 2

BANAVIE Highland *Inverness-shire* Map**14** NN17
★★Moorings ☎Corpach550
RS Oct–May; 12rm(2⇌🛁) CTV 25P Children under 12yrs not accommodated Last dinner8pm sB&B£7.50–£9.50 dB&B£16–£22.50 dB&B⇌🛁£18–£24 Bar lunch£1.50–£3.75 Dinner£4.80–£8 Wine£2.85

BANCHORY Grampian *Kincardineshire* Map**15** NO69
★★★ Banchory Lodge ☎2625
See page 62 for details
★★★ Raemoir ☎2622
18th-C mansion set in own grounds in elevated position 3 miles north of town.
18rm(13⇌🛁) Annexe: 5⇌🛁 CTV TV available in bedrooms 200P 8🏠 International.

Last dinner9.30pm ♆ ♇ sB&B fr£14 sB&B⇌⋒ fr£15 dB&B fr£28 dB&B⇌⋒ fr£30 Lunch fr£3 Tea fr40p High Tea fr£2.50 Dinner fr£6.50 Wine£2.95 Credit card 5

★★★Tor-na-Coille ☎2242
20rm(15⇌⋒) Annexe: 2rm Lift CTV CTV in bedrooms 60P squash English & French. Last dinner9.30pm sB&B£9–£13 sB&B⇌⋒£14–£19 dB&B£18–£29 dB&B⇌⋒£23–£33 Bar lunch£2.75–£3.50&alc Tea50p–£1 Dinner£6–£6.50&alc Wine£3.50 *xmas* Credit cards 1 2 3 5 6

★★Burnett Arms ☎2545
Rough cast and granite fronted building in main street of pleasant Deeside town.
13rm(5⇌⋒) CTV 40P 6 Live music & dancing Sat Last dinner7.45pm Credit cards 3 5

BANFF Grampian *Banffshire* Map**15** NJ66
☆☆☆Banff Springs Golden Knowes Rd ☎2881
Well-appointed modern hotel, standing to the West of the town, on hillside with splendid views over Moray Firth.
30⇌⋒ CTV CTV in bedrooms P Last dinner8.30pm S% sB&B⇌⋒ fr£15 dB&B⇌⋒ fr£29 Credit cards 1 2 3 5 6

★★County High St ☎2846
Closed Jan & Feb 7rm(4⇌⋒) 2 TV in bedrooms 25P English & French. Last dinner9pm S% sB&B£13.50–£14.50 sB&B⇌⋒£15.50–£16.50 dB&B£22.50–£24.50 dB&B⇌⋒£25–£26 Dinner fr£6alc Wine£4 Credit cards 1 2 3 5

★Fife Lodge Sandyhill Rd ☎2436
6rm CTV TV available in bedrooms 100P Live music & dancing wkly Last dinner8.15pm

BANKFOOT Tayside *Perthshire* Map**11** NO03
XXHunters Lodge ☎325
50seats 50P bedrooms available Last dinner9pm S% Lunch£8alc High Tea£3.50alc Dinner£10alc Wine£3.20 Credit cards 1 2 3 5

BARRA, ISLE OF Western Isles *Inverness-shire* Map**13** **See Tangusdale**

BARRHEAD Strathclyde *Renfrewshire* Map**11** NS45
★★Dalmeny Park Lochlibo Rd ☎041–881 9211
18rm(10⇌⋒) CTV CTV in bedrooms 100P billiards Live music & dancing Fri French. Last dinner9.30pm S% *sB&B fr£15 sB&B⇌⋒ fr£15 dB&B fr£21 dB&B⇌⋒ fr£21 Lunch fr£3 Dinner£5alc Wine£3 *Xmas* Credit cards 1 2 3 5 6

★Barrhead 1 Robertson St (Scottish & Newcastle) ☎041–881 3288
A brick faced building situated on a corner site.
10rm CTV P Scottish & French. Last dinner9pm Credit card 1

BATHGATE Lothian *West Lothian* Map**11** NS96
☆☆☆Golden Circle Blackburn Rd (Swallow) ☎53771 Telex no72606
75⇌⋒ Lift CTV in bedrooms 150P Conference facilities available Last dinner9.30pm S% sB&B⇌⋒ fr£17.30 dB&B⇌⋒ fr£24.50 Credit cards 1 2 3 5

★★Dreadnought Whitburn Rd (Scottish & Newcastle) ☎630791
18rm(11⇌⋒) CTV 26P Last dinner9pm S% *sB&B fr£6.50 sB&B⇌⋒ fr£8 dB&B fr£12 dB&B⇌⋒ fr£16 Lunch£3alc Dinner£3alc Wine£1.80 Credit cards 1 2 3 4 5 6

✕✕✕Balbairdie Bloomfield Pl ☎55448
Closed Sun 40seats ♡Scottish & French
Last dinner10pm S% Lunch£5–£7&alc
Dinner£10alc Wine£5 Credit cards 1 2 3 5

✕✕✕Bridge Castle Hotel Restaurant
☎Armadale30228
A fine castle, dating from 12th-C, which has been converted into a hotel. There are bars in the outhouses.
60seats 180P bedrooms available ♡French
Last dinner10pm ✱Lunch£3.50&alc
Dinner£6&alc Wine£3.50 Credit cards 1 2 3 5

BEARSDEN Strathclyde *Dunbartonshire* Map**11** NS57
☆☆Burnbrae Milgavie Rd (Reo Stakis)
☎041-942 5951
15rm(13⇌⋒) ☽ ⋈ CTV in bedrooms 70P
Last dinner10pm ✿ ⌂ S% ✱sB&B£11.50
sB&B⇌⋒£15 dB&B⇌⋒£23 Bar lunch
65p–£1.05 Tea35p–£1 Dinner£4alc
Credit cards 1 2 3 5

❀✕✕La Bavarde 9 New Kirk Rd ☎041-942 2202
Closed Sun & Mon, 1st wk Jan & last 3wks Jul
50seats Last dinner9.30pm Credit cards 1 5

✕Ristorante da Riccardo 130 Drymen Rd
☎041-943 0960
Closed Sun & Mon 38seats P ♡Italian.
Last dinner10.30pm Lunch£1.75–£6
Dinner£4–£8&alc Credit card 1

BEATTOCK Dumfries & Galloway *Dumfriesshire* Map**11** NT00
★★Auchen Castle (Inter-Hotel) ☎407
Closed mid Dec–mid Feb; 20rm⇌⋒
Annexe: 10⇌⋒ ⋈ CTV CTV in bedrooms 40P 3⌂ ⚓
⇜ ⌂ ♡English & French. Last dinner9pm ✿ ⌂
S% ✱sB&B⇌⋒£11–£14 dB&B⇌⋒£18–£24
Lunch£3.25 Tea30p Dinner£5.90 Wine£3.10
⊟ Credit cards 1 2 3 5

★★Beattock House ☎403
8rm(3⇌⋒) ⋈ CTV 25P ⚓ ⇜ Last dinner9pm ✿
⌂ S% ✱sB&B£11.50 sB&B⇌⋒ fr£12.50
dB&B fr£23 dB&B⇌⋒ fr£25 Lunch fr£3.50
Tea fr£1.50 High Tea fr£3 Dinner fr£6.95
Wine£4.25 ⊟

★★Old Brig Inn ☎401
7rm(1⇌⋒) ⋈ CTV 20P 4⌂ Last dinner8.30pm ✿
⌂ S% sB&B£9.50 dB&B£17
dB&B⇌⋒£20.50 Lunch£4 Tea£1–£1.50
Dinner£6 Wine£3.50 ⊟ Credit cards 1 5

BEAULY Highland *Inverness-shire* Map**14** NH54
★★Lovat Arms ☎2313
An impressive red sandstone building with ornate stonework, standing on main road in the centre of town.
18rm(3⇌⋒) TV 20P Live music Sat & Sun
Last dinner9.30pm ✿ ⌂

★★Priory The Square ☎2309
12rm(6⇌⋒) ⋈ CTV **P** Cabaret twice wkly
Last dinner9pm ✿ ⌂ S% sB&B£8.50–£10.50
sB&B⇌⋒£9–£11 dB&B£15–£20
dB&B⇌⋒£16–£21 Lunch£2.40&alc Tea75p
High Tea£2.20 Dinner£4.50&alc Wine£2.30 ⊟
Credit cards 1 2 3 4 5 6

BELLSHILL Strathclyde *Lanarkshire* Map**11** NS76
★Hattonrigg Hattonrigg Rd (Scottish & Newcastle)
☎748488
8rm(4⇌⋒) ☽ ⚔ ⋈ CTV ⊘ 100P Disco twice wkly
Live music & dancing twice wkly Cabaret wkly
Last dinner10pm ✿ S% sB&B fr£8.60
sB&B⇌⋒ fr£9.70 dB&B fr£17.50
dB&B⇌⋒ fr£17.50 Lunch fr£2.30
Dinner£4.50alc Wine£2.90 Credit cards 1 2 3 5

BETTYHILL Highland *Sutherland* Map**14** NC76
★★Bettyhill ☎352
Victorian hotel, now extended, set on coastal road offering superb views over Torrisdale Bay and sands.
22rm(5⇌⋒) TV 40P 3⌂ ⊘ ⇜ Last dinner8pm ✿
⌂ ✱sB&B£7 dB&B£14 dB&B⇌⋒£17
Lunch£4 Tea50p Dinner£4.50 Wine£2.30

BIELDSIDE Grampian *Aberdeenshire* Map**15** NJ80
✕✕Murtle Mill North Deeside Rd ☎Aberdeen48877
Converted grain mill with white painted walls and mill wheel. An extension incorporates a craft centre.
80seats 50P ♡International. Last dinner10.30pm
S% Lunch£6.50alc Dinner£8alc Wine£3.95
Credit cards 1 2 3 5

BIGGAR Strathclyde *Lanarkshire* Map**11** NT03
★★Toftcombs ☎20142
8rm ⋈ CTV P ⚓ Live music & dancing Sat
Last dinner8.30pm ✿ ⌂ S% ✱sB&B£7
dB&B£14 Lunch fr£3 Tea fr80p High Tea fr£2.50
Dinner fr£4.50 Wine£2.30 Credit cards 1 2 3

BLACKFORD Tayside *Perthshire* Map**11** NN80
★★Blackford Moray St ☎246
RS Nov–Feb; 6rm(1⇌⋒) ⋈ CTV 20P ⊘ Disco wkly
Children under 5yrs not accommodated
Last dinner9pm ✿ ⌂ S% sB&B£7.50
dB&B£15 dB&B⇌⋒£17 Lunch fr£2.50
Tea fr£1.25 Dinner£5.50alc *xmas* Credit card 5

BLAIR ATHOLL Tayside *Perthshire* Map**14** NN86
★★Atholl Arms ☎205
Large greystone roadside hotel, built and furnished in traditional Scottish style.
28rm(3⇌⋒) ⊞ CTV 25P 8⌂ Cabaret twice wkly

Last dinner 8.30pm ✱sB&B£5.95–£6.45 dB&B£11.90–£12.90 dB&B⇌⋒£12.90–£13.90 Lunch£2.10–£2.50 Dinner£3.75–£5.50 Wine£2.80 Credit cards 1 3

★★***Tilt*** Bridge of Tilt ☎333
Two-storey stone building with attractive modern extension, good views of surrounding countryside.
29rm(3⇌⋒) CTV 6 Music & dancing wkly Last dinner 8.30pm Credit cards 2 4 5

BLAIRGOWRIE Tayside *Perthshire* Map **11** NO14
★★**Angus** ☎2838 Telex no 76526
70rm(62⇌⋒) Lift CTV in bedrooms 30P (heated) squash sauna bath Cabaret wkly Last dinner 8.30pm S% sB&B£8.50–£10 sB&B⇌⋒£8.50–£10 dB&B£17–£20 dB&B⇌⋒£17–£20 Lunch£2.75–£4.75 Tea£1.70 High Tea£1.10–£2.30 Dinner£3.75–£5.75 Wine£3 *xmas* Credit cards 1 2 3 6

★**Golf View** Rosemont ☎2895
5rm(1⇌⋒) CTV TV in bedrooms 60P Last dinner 9pm ✱sB&B£9.50 dB&B£17 dB&B⇌⋒£23 Bar lunch£1.75alc High Tea£2alc Dinner£5alc Wine£2 Credit cards 3 5

★**Stormont Lodge** Upper Allan St ☎2853
8rm(3⇌⋒) CTV TV available in bedrooms 40P Last dinner 8.30pm ✱sB&B£8.80 dB&B£15.60 dB&B⇌⋒£18.60 Lunch£3.50&alc Tea90p High Tea£2.50 Dinner£4.50&alc Wine£4

BLAIRLOGIE Central *Stirlingshire* Map **11** NS89
✕✕**Blairlogie House Hotel Restaurant** ☎Alva 61441
Closed 1–30 Jan; 40 seats 30P bedrooms available Last dinner 9pm ✱Lunch£4alc Dinner£5.95alc Wine£3 Credit cards 1 3 6

BOAT OF GARTEN Highland *Inverness-shire* Map **14** NH91
★★**Boat** ☎258
Grey stone building dating from 1898 and offering good scenic views, situated adjacent to railway station.
36rm(32⇌⋒) CTV CTV in bedrooms 35P 5 Last dinner 9pm S% sB&B£10.52–£11.75 sB&B⇌⋒£11.27–£12.50 dB&B£29.84–£32.04 dB&B⇌⋒£31.34–£33.54 Lunch£3.25 Dinner£5.50&alc Wine£3.05 *xmas* Credit cards 1 3 6

★★**Craigard** Kinchurdy Rd ☎206
Late Victorian shooting lodge converted to hotel in 1931. Situated in 2½ acres of grounds with direct access to golf course.
22rm(8⇌⋒) CTV 30P 4 Last dinner 8pm sB&B£9.75–£10.75 dB&B£19.50–£21.50 dB&B⇌⋒£22–£24 Lunch£3.25 Tea45p Dinner£5.25–£5.50

BONAR BRIDGE Highland *Sutherland* Map **14** NH69
★★**Bridge** ☎Ardgay 204
Two-storey stone house on main road, with views of Kyle of Sutherland.
16rm(5⇌⋒) CTV 20P Scottish & French. Last dinner 9pm ✱sB&B£8–£9 sB&B⇌⋒£9.50–£10.50 dB&B£14–£16 dB&B⇌⋒£17–£19 Bar lunch£1.20alc Tea40palc High Tea£2.25alc Dinner£4.75alc Wine£2.40 Credit cards 1 2 3 5

★★***Caledonian*** ☎Ardgay 214
Two-storey, stone building standing on main road, overlooking Kyle of Sutherland.
8rm(6⇌⋒) CTV 20P Last dinner 8pm

BORGUE Dumfries & Galloway *Kirkcudbrightshire* Map **11** NX64
★★**Senwick House** Brighouse Bay ☎236
6rm(2⇌⋒) CTV 50P Last dinner 9.30pm S% ✱sB&B£9.50–£11.50 sB&B⇌⋒£11–£13 dB&B£19–£23 dB&B⇌⋒£22–£26 Lunch fr£3.50 Tea fr£1.50 Dinner fr£5.40 Wine£2.60 *xmas*

BOTHWELL Strathclyde *Lanarkshire* Map **11** NS75
✕✕✕**Da Luciano** 2 Silverwells Cres ☎852722
Closed Mon; Lunch; 40P English, French & Italian. Last dinner 10.45pm ✱Lunch fr£2.50&alc Dinner£5.50alc Wine£3 Credit cards 1 2 3 5 6

BOWMORE Isle of Islay, Strathclyde *Argyll* Map **10** NR35
★***Bowmore*** ☎218
8rm TV 10P Last dinner 8.30pm

★**Lochside** Shore St ☎244
7rm(2⇌⋒) TV Last dinner 10pm S% sB&B fr£11.50 dB&B fr£23 dB&B⇌⋒ fr£26.50 Bar lunch fr50p Dinner£4alc Wine£2.90

BRAEMAR Grampian *Aberdeenshire* Map **15** NO19
★★★**Invercauld Arms** ☎605 Telex no 73448
Large stone-built, early Victorian building on outskirts of village. Built on the site where the Old Pretender's standard is said to have been raised.
Closed Nov–Feb; 57rm(40⇌⋒) Lift TV TV available in bedrooms 100P 1 Live music & dancing wkly Last dinner 9pm ✱sB&B£5.40–£12.96 sB&B⇌⋒£8.64–£21.60 dB&B£10.80–£23.76 dB&B⇌⋒£17.28–£32.40 Lunch fr£4.15&alc Tea fr85p Dinner fr£6.50&alc Wine£2.75 Credit cards 1 2 3 5

BRECHIN Tayside *Angus* Map **15** NO56
★★**Northern** Clerk St ☎2156
Closed 25 Dec & 1 Jan; 24rm(16⇌⋒) CTV 26P 3

B

Last dinner 8pm ✿ ✱sB&B£6 sB&B⇌⋒£7–£8 dB&B£12 dB&B⇌⋒£14 Lunch£2.16–£2.70 High Tea£1.40–£2.70 Dinner£3.70–£3.78 Wine£2

BRIDGE OF ALLAN Central *Stirlingshire* Map**11** NS79
★★★Royal Henderson St (Best Western) ☎832284 Telex no 778982
Large building dating from 1836 standing on main road in centre of town.
32rm(14⇌⋒) Lift ☽ ⋔ CTV TV available in bedrooms 100P ☙ International. Last dinner 8.45pm ✿ ☐ S% sB&B fr&15 sB&B⇌⋒ fr£17 dB&B fr£25.50 dB&B⇌⋒ fr£27.50 Lunch fr£3.50&alc Tea fr45p High Tea fr£3 Dinner fr£6&alc Wine£3.50 ⊟ *xmas* Credit cards 1 2 3 4 5 6

BRIDGE OF CALLY Tayside *Perthshire* Map**15** NO15
❀★ Bridge of Cally ☎231
See page 62 for details

BRIDGE OF EARN Tayside *Perthshire* Map**11** NO11
★★Moncrieffe Arms ☎2216
Closed 1 Jan; 13rm(4⇌⋒) ⋔ CTV 50P 2⌂ ⚓ ☙ Scottish & French. Last dinner 9pm ✿ ☐ ✱sB&B£11 sB&B⇌⋒£12 dB&B£18 dB&B⇌⋒£20 Lunch£3.50&alc Tea50p High Tea£2.75 Dinner£4.50&alc Wine£2.76 ⊟ Credit card 2

BROADFORD Isle of Skye, Highland *Inverness-shire* Map**13** NG62
★★Broadford ☎204
Original inn dating from 1611, considerably altered and extended.
19rm(9⇌⋒) Annexe: 9⇌⋒ CTV 60P ⚓ ↬ ♿ Last dinner 8.45pm ✿ ☐ S% sB&B£11–£12.30 sB&B⇌⋒£14.50–£15.80 dB&B£21.80–£28 dB&B⇌⋒£25.30–£31.50 Bar lunch fr£1.50 Tea fr40p Dinner fr£5.40 Wine£1.95

BRODICK Isle of Arran, Strathclyde *Bute* Map**10** NS03
★★★Douglas (Swallow) ☎2155
25rm(9⇌⋒) ☽ CTV TV in bedrooms 65P ⚓ billiards sauna bath Live music & dancing Fri, Sat & Sun ⌬ ☙ English & French Last dinner 8pm ✿ ☐ S% ✱sB&B£8–£8.70 sB&B⇌⋒£9–£10.05 dB&B£14–£17.35 dB&B⇌⋒£17.50–£20.10 Lunch fr£3 Tea fr30p High Tea fr£1.25 Dinner fr£4.25 Wine£2.95 ⊟ *Xmas* Credit cards 1 2 3 5

⊛Glenartney ☎2220
Two-storey rough-cast house on hill overlooking Brodick Bay.
Closed Oct–Feb; 19rm ⋔ CTV 10P Last dinner 7.30pm ✿ sB&B fr£6 dB&B fr£12 Lunch fr£2.50 Dinner fr£3.50 Wine£1.45 ⊟

BRORA Highland *Sutherland* Map**14** NC90
★★Royal Marine Golf Rd ☎252
Closed 1–4 Jan; 9rm(7⇌⋒) ⋔ CTV TV available in bedrooms 40P 3⌂ ⚓ ⌬ Last dinner 8pm ✿ ☐ S% ✱sB&B£10.75 sB&B⇌⋒£11.75 dB&B£21.50 dB&B⇌⋒£23.50 Lunch£2.90 Tea75p–95p High Tea£2.85–£3.55 Dinner£4–£5 Wine£2.45 ⊟ Credit cards 1 2 3 5 6

BROUGHTON Borders *Peeblesshire* Map**11** NT13
★★Greenmantle ☎301
Modern building with cottage-type exterior in centre of village. Set in two acres of grounds off the main road.
6rm(2⇌⋒) CTV 50P ⚓ ☙ Scottish & French. Last dinner 9pm ✿ ☐ sB&B fr£8.50 sB&B⇌⋒ fr£10 dB&B fr£16 dB&B⇌⋒ fr£25 Lunch fr£3.30 Tea fr80p High Tea fr£2.30 Dinner fr£5 Credit cards 3 5

BUCKIE Grampian *Banffshire* Map**15** NJ46
★★Cluny High St ☎32922
Closed 1 Jan; 7⇌⋒ CTV in bedrooms ⚑ Last dinner 10pm ✿ ☐ sB&B⇌⋒£10.50 dB&B⇌⋒£20.50 Lunch fr£2 High Tea fr£1.75 Dinner fr£4.70 Wine£2.80 ⊟ Credit cards 1 5 6

BUNESSAN Isle of Mull, Strathclyde *Argyll* Map**10** NM32
★★*Argyll Arms* ☎Fionnphort 240
9rm ⊘ 30P ⇼ ↬ Live music wkly Cabaret wkly Last dinner 8pm ✿ ☐

BUTE, ISLE OF Strathclyde *Bute* Map**10**
See Rothesay

CAIRNBAAN Strathclyde *Argyll* Map**10** RN89
★★Cairnbaan Motor Inn ☎Lochgilphead 2488
Old inn with extensions; situated near Crinan Canal.
Annexe: 24rm(14⇌⋒) ⋔ CTV 80P 6⌂ ☙ Scottish & French. Last dinner 9pm ✿ ☐ ✱sB&B£8.64–£9.18 sB&B⇌⋒£12.96–£14.04 dB&B£17.28–£18.36 dB&B⇌⋒£20.52–£22.68 Lunch£1.25–£3 Dinner£5.50 Wine£2.90 ⊟ *Xmas* Credit cards 1 2 3 4 5

CALLANDER Central *Perthshire* Map**11** NN60
★★★⚑Roman Camp ☎30003
Closed Nov–Mar; 10rm(5⇌⋒) 1⊟ CTV in bedrooms 30P 3⌂ ⚓ Last dinner 8.45pm ✿ ✱sB&B fr£14.25 sB&B⇌⋒ fr£16.60 dB&B fr£28.50 dB&B⇌⋒ fr£33.50 Lunch fr£5.40 Dinner fr£7 Wine£3.50 Credit card 2

★★Ancaster Arms Main St (Open House) ☎30167
A red sandstone Victorian building with tower standing in main street of Scottish country town.
26rm CTV 40P Live music & dancing wkly Last dinner9pm S% ✱sB&B£10 dB&B£16 Lunch£3.27–£5.37&alc Tea75p &alc High Tea£2.16&alc Dinner£3.27–£5.37&alc Wine£2.85 xmas Credit cards 1 2 3 5

★Pinewood Leny Rd, Strathyre Rd ☎3011
RS Nov–Mar; 16rm(2⇌ ⋒) CTV 30P Last dinner8.30pm sB&B£7.72–£8.31 sB&B⇌ ⋒£8.91–£9.50 dB&B£15.44–£16.62 dB&B⇌ ⋒£17.82–£19 Lunch£2.97–£3.26 Tea32p–38p Dinner£4.44–£4.75&alc Wine£1.75 Credit cards 1 3

★Waverley Main St ☎30245
A conversion of three adjoining sandstone terraced houses, in centre of country town.
Closed Oct–Mar; 13rm CTV Last dinner8pm S% sB&B£8–£8.50 dB&B£16–£17 Lunch£2.75–£3 Tea70p–80p High Tea£2.20–£4 Dinner£4.50–£5

✕*Brackinn Falls* Main St ☎30622
Closed Mon–Thu (Nov–Etr); 100 seats Music & dancing Sat (in winter) Mainly grills. Last dinner9pm

CAMPBELTOWN Strathclyde *Argyll* Map**10** NR72
★★Ardshiel Kilkerran Rd ☎2133
Three-storey Victorian house occupying gabled end of small row in quiet residential area not far from town centre and harbour.
Closed 2wks Oct & 1wk Feb; 12rm CTV 12P Last dinner8pm S% sB&B fr£9.50 dB&B fr£19 Lunch fr£2.75 High Tea fr£2.50 Dinner fr£4.50 Wine£3 Credit cards 1 3

CAMPSIE GLEN Strathclyde *Stirlingshire* Map**11** NS67
✕✕✕Campsie Glen ☎Lennoxtown310666
100seats 45P bedrooms available French & Italian. Last dinner10.30pm ✱Lunch£2.50–£2.75 Dinner£5–£8&alc Wine£3.60 Credit cards 1 2 3 5

CANNICH Highland *Inverness-shire* Map**14** NH33
★★Glen Affric ☎214
Closed Nov–Mar; 23rm(5⇌ ⋒) CTV 40P Last dinner7.45pm S% sB&B£7 sB&B⇌ ⋒£9 dB&B£14 dB&B⇌ ⋒£18 Lunch£2.50 Tea60p High Tea£2 Dinner£5.50 Wine£2.75

CANONBIE Dumfries & Galloway *Dumfriesshire* Map**11** NY37
★Cross Keys ☎205
8rm CTV 20P 1 Last dinner8.30pm S% sB&B£7.50 dB&B£14 Lunch£3.50alc Dinner£5.20alc Wine£3

CARFRAEMILL (by Lauder) Borders *Berwickshire* Map**12** NT55
★★Carfraemill (Osprey) ☎Oxton200
9rm(2⇌ ⋒) Lift CTV TV available in bedrooms 20P Last dinner9pm S% ✱sB&B£9.50 sB&B⇌ ⋒£13 dB&B£16 dB&B⇌ ⋒£21 Lunch fr£2.60 Tea fr30p High Tea fr£2.60 Dinner fr£3.90 Wine£2.36 xmas Credit cards 1 2 3 5

CARNOUSTIE Tayside *Angus* Map**12** NO53
★★★Bruce Links Pde ☎52364
36rm(24⇌ ⋒) CTV CTV available in bedrooms 40P 6 French. Last dinner9pm sB&B£14.75 sB&B⇌ ⋒£17 dB&B⇌ ⋒£32 Lunch fr£3.75 Tea fr95p Dinner fr£5.50&alc Wine£3.50 xmas Credit cards 2 5

★★*Earlston* 24 Church St ☎52352
21rm(7⇌ ⋒) CTV 75P Last dinner10pm Credit cards 1 3

★★Glencoe Links Pde ☎53273
Three-storey stone house with modern extensions overlooking sea and golf course.
11rm(7⇌ ⋒) CTV 10P Scottish & French. Last dinner9pm S% sB&B£7–£8 dB&B⇌ ⋒£16–£17 Lunch£2.50–£5 Tea35p–£1 High Tea£2–£3.50 Dinner£4.50–£7 Wine£3.50 Credit card 1

★Station ☎52447
12rm CTV 20P 6 Live music & dancing Sat Cabaret Sat Last dinner9pm S% sB&B£5.50–£6.50 dB&B£11–£12 Lunch£1.75–£2.50 Tea75p–£1 High Tea£1.50–£2.10 Dinner£3–£4 Wine£2.80 Credit cards 1 6

Carlogie House ☎53185
8rm(3⇌ ⋒) CTV 150P Last dinner8pm

CARRADALE Strathclyde *Argyll* Map**10** NR83
★★Carradale ☎223
RS Nov–Feb; 16rm(2⇌ ⋒) Annexe: 6rm(3⇌ ⋒) CTV 25P Last dinner8pm S% ✱sB&B£7–£7.50 sB&B⇌ ⋒£8.30–£10.50 dB&B£14–£15 dB&B⇌ ⋒£19.20–£21 Lunch£2.50 Tea55p High Tea£2.10–£2.80 Dinner£4–£5 Wine£2.15

CARRBRIDGE Highland *Inverness-shire* Map14 NH92
Rowan Lea ☎212
RS Nov–mid May (except Xmas & Etr); 10rm TV 20P Last dinner8pm Credit cards 1 2 3

✕*Landmark* ☎613
100seats 120P Last dinner9pm

CARSPHAIRN Dumfries & Galloway *Kirkcudbrightshire* Map**11** NX59
★★Salutation ☎250
RS Oct–Mar; 18rm(2⇌ ⋒) CTV 12P Last dinner8pm S% sB&B£6–£8.50 dB&B£12–£17 dB&B⇌ ⋒£13–£18 Lunch£1.75–£2.50 Tea50–75p High Tea£1.50–£2.75 Dinner£3.75–£5&alc Wine£2 xmas

CASTLE DOUGLAS Dumfries & Galloway *Kirkcudbrightshire* Map**11** NX76
★★★Douglas Arms King St (Best Western) ☎2231
White-painted former coaching inn standing in town centre.
27rm(11⇌ ⋒) CTV TV available in bedrooms P 12 Last dinner9pm S% ✱sB&B£12.30–£14.50 sB&B⇌ ⋒£14.30–£16.50 dB&B£24.60–£29 dB&B⇌ ⋒£28.60–£33 Lunch£3.50–£4.50 Tea£1.25–£1.50 High Tea£1.75–£7 Dinner£5.50–£8&alc Wine£3.50 Credit cards 1 2 3 5

★★Imperial King St ☎2086
14rm CTV 40P 9 Children under 2½yrs not accommodated Last dinner7pm S% sB&B£8–£9.50 dB&B£16–£19 Bar lunch£1–£2 High Tea£1.30–£3 Wine£3

★★King's Arms St Andrew's Street ☎2626
17rm(4⇌ ⋒) CTV 17P Children under 1yrs not accommodated French. Last dinner8pm S% sB&B£7.50–£9.50 dB&B£15–£19 dB&B⇌ ⋒£21–£26.50 Bar lunch£1.40 High Tea£2.60–£4.20 Dinner£5–£5.75 Credit cards 2 5 6

CHARLESTOWN Fife *Fife* Map**11** NT08
★*Elgin* (off A985) ☎Limekilns257

5rm Annexe: 2⇔ 🚿 TV 40P 2 English & French. Last dinner 9.30pm Credit cards 1 6

CHIRNSIDE Borders *Berwickshire* Map **12** NT85
★★ **Chirnside** ☎219
Early Victorian country mansion set in 56 acres of tree-studded grounds.
15rm 1 Lift CTV 30P Last dinner 8.30pm Lunch £2.40–£3.12 Tea 72p–£1.08 High Tea £1.80–£2.84 Dinner £3.60–£6 Wine £2.38 Credit cards 2 5

CLACHAN-SEIL Strathclyde *Argyll* Map **10** NM71
❀★ **Willowburn** (Inter-Hotel) ☎Balvicar 276
Rosette awarded for dinner only.
Closed Nov; 6rm (1⇔🚿) CTV TV available in bedrooms 20P English & French. Specialities: Boeuf bourguignonne, Atholl Brose, Malakoff pudding. Last dinner 8pm sB&B dB&B £18 dB&B⇔🚿 £21 Bar lunch fr45p Dinner £5.50 Wine £1.90 Credit cards 1 2 3 5

CLEISH Tayside *Kinross-shire* Map **11** NT09
❀✕✕ **Nivingston House** ☎Cleish Hills 216
Closed Mon & Oct; 54 seats 35P bedrooms available Continental. Last dinner 9pm Credit cards 2 3

CLOVA Tayside *Angus* Map **15** NO37
★★ ***Ogilvy Arms*** Glenclova (Clova Village) ☎222
7rm (4⇔🚿) TV 25P Last dinner 8.15pm

CLYDEBANK Strathclyde *Dunbartonshire* Map **11** NS56
☆☆☆ **Radnor** Kilbourie Rd (Osprey) ☎041–952 2875
Modern four-storey brick building occupying fine site overlooking Clydeside.
12⇔🚿 Lift CTV CTV in bedrooms 30P Live music & dancing wkly Cabaret wkly Last dinner 8.45pm S% *sB&B⇔🚿 £13 dB&B⇔🚿 £21 Lunch fr£2.60 Tea fr30p High Tea fr£2.60 Dinner fr£3.90 Wine £2.60 *xmas* Credit cards 1 2 3 5

★★ **Boulevard** 1710 Great Western Rd (Open House) ☎Duntocher 72381
Roadhouse style hotel situated on north side of A82 dual-carriageway.
13rm CTV 200P Disco nightly Mainly grills. Last dinner 9pm S% *sB&B £10 dB&B £15.50 Lunch £2.80 Dinner £3.80 Credit cards 1 2 3 4 5 6

CLYNDER Strathclyde *Dunbartonshire* Map **10** NS28
★★ **Clynder** (Osprey) ☎248
11rm CTV 20P Live music & dancing twice wkly Last dinner 8.45pm S% *sB&B £9 dB&B £15 Lunch fr£2.60 Tea fr30p High Tea fr£2.60 Dinner fr£3.90 Wine £2.60 *xmas* Credit cards 1 2 3 5

COATBRIDGE Strathclyde *Lanarkshire* Map **11** NS76
☆☆☆ **Coatbridge** Glasgow Rd (Open House) ☎24392
Modern custom-built hotel set on west side of town overlooking Drumpelier golf course.
22⇔🚿 CTV CTV in bedrooms 150P Disco Thu & Sun Live music & dancing Sat French. Last dinner 9.30pm S% Lunch £2.90&alc Dinner £4&alc Credit cards 1 2 3 5

★ **Georgian** Lefroy St (Scottish & Newcastle) ☎21888
8rm CTV 30P Disco wkly Last dinner 8.30pm S% sB&B £7 dB&B £14 Lunch £5alc Tea fr50p Dinner £5alc Wine £3 Credit cards 1 3

COCKBURNSPATH Borders *Berwickshire* Map **12** NT77
★ **Cockburnspath** ☎217
Small, white-painted coaching inn (18th century) with attractive interior décor, situated on main road of village.
4rm Annexe: 2rm TV 30P Last dinner 8.30pm sB&B fr£6.50 dB&B fr£13 Lunch fr£3.20 Tea fr85p High Tea fr£2 Dinner fr£3.20 Wine £2.30

COLDSTREAM Borders *Berwickshire* Map **12** NT83
★ **Majicado** 71 High St ☎2112
7rm CTV Mainly grills. Last dinner 9pm sB&B fr£5 dB&B fr£10 Lunch £2.50alc Tea 50p alc High Tea £1.50alc Dinner £3alc Credit card 6

COLL, ISLE OF Strathclyde *Argyll* Map **13**
See Arinagour

COLONSAY, ISLE OF Strathclyde *Argyllshire* Map **10**
See Scalasaig

COMRIE Tayside *Perthshire* Map **11** NN72
★★ **Comrie** Drummond St ☎239
Attractive ivy-clad roadside hotel in quiet central Highland village.
Closed Nov–Mar; 10rm (4⇔🚿) Annexe: 2⇔🚿 CTV 26P Children under 5yrs not accommodated Last dinner 8.30pm S% sB&B £7–£9 sB&B⇔🚿 £9.50–£11 dB&B £14–£18 dB&B⇔🚿 £19–£22 Lunch £2.75&alc Tea 50p Dinner £5.50&alc Wine £2

★★ **Royal** ☎200
Built in 1765. Prints of photographs in cocktail bar recall visits by Queen Victoria and her much-loved servant John Brown, and Lloyd George.
10rm (5⇔🚿) Annexe: 5⇔🚿 1 CTV TV available in bedrooms 30P 2 Scottish & French. Last dinner 9pm sB&B £8.50 sB&B⇔🚿 £9.50 dB&B £17 dB&B⇔🚿 £19 Bar lunch £2–£3 Dinner £5.50&alc Wine £3.25 Credit card 1

ONNEL Strathclyde *Argyll* Map **10** NM93
★Falls of Lora ☎483
osed Oct–Apr; 32rm(10⇌ ⋒) CTV 50P 6⌂ ⌗ ⚓ ∩
Last dinner 8.15pm ✿ ☐ ✻sB&B£7–£10
B&B⇌⋒£8.50–£10.50 dB&B£14–£20
B&B⇌⋒£19–£21 Bar lunch £1.50–£2.50
nner£4.75 Wine£2.40

★Lochnell Arms Connel North ☎408
rm(2⇌⋒) 50P ⌗ ⚓ Last dinner 10pm ✿ ☐
% sB&B£6–£9 sB&B⇌⋒£6.50–£9.50
B&B£12–£18 dB&B⇌⋒£13–£19
nch£2.25–£3 Tea75p Dinner£4.50–£5.50
ine£2.90 *xmas*

★Ossians Connel North ☎322
odern architect designed hotel situated some 50yds from northern end of Connel Bridge and oking across Loch Etive.
osed 20 Oct–9 Apr; 14rm(4⇌⋒) CTV 50P ⌗
English & French. Last dinner 7.30pm ✿ ☐
% sB&B£9.84 dB&B£19.68 dB&B⇌⋒£21.43
ar lunch £1.40alc Tea70p High Tea£2.34
inner£4.67 Wine£2.60

ONTIN Highland *Ross & Cromarty* Map **14** NH45
★Craigdarroch Lodge Craigdarrock Drive
Strathpeffer265
9rm(11⇌⋒) CTV 20P ⌗ ⚓ billiards Scottish
Continental. Last dinner 8.30pm ✿ ☐ S%
B&B£12.50 sB&B⇌⋒£12.50 dB&B£23
B&B⇌⋒£25 Lunch£3.50–£4.50 Tea70p
inner£7 *xmas* Credit cards 1 2 3 5 6

Achilty ☎Strathpeffer355
losed Oct–Mar; 10rm TV 10P 2⌂ ⌗ ⚓ billiards
Last dinner 8pm ✿ sB&B£6.60 dB&B£13.20
unch£3 Dinner£4.40 Wine£2.70

ORRIE Isle of Arran Strathclyde *Bute* Map **10** NS04
★★*Corrie* ☎273
oadside hotel some 20 yards from sea in quaint little oastal village, on eastern side of Isle of Arran.
SOct–Mar; 19rm CTV TV available in bedrooms
0P ⚓ Last dinner 8.30pm ✿ ☐
Credit cards 1 3

ORSOCK Dumfries & Galloway *Kirkcudbrightshire*
Map **11** NX77
★★*Glaisters Lodge* ☎245
Closed mid Nov–mid Jan; 6rm(1⇌⋒) 9P ⌗ ⚓
ast dinner 8pm

ORTACHY Tayside *Angus* Map **15** NO35
★★*Royal Jubilee Arms* Dyke Head ☎225
1⇌⋒ Annexe: 15⇌⋒ CTV 100P Cabaret wknds
ast dinner 11pm ✿ ☐ Credit card 3

OVE Strathclyde *Dunbartonshire* Map **10** NS28
★★*Knockderry* ☎Kilcreggan2283
3rm(5⇌⋒) CTV 50P ⌗ ⚓ Live music Sat
(Jun–Aug) Last dinner 8.30pm ✿ ☐
Credit cards 1 2 3 5

CRAIGELLACHIE Grampian *Banffshire* Map **15** NJ24
★★★Craigellachie ☎204
Well established fishing hotel in Highland distillery village. Fine views towards River Spey.
Closed Oct–Feb; 31rm(17⇌⋒) CTV 40P ⌗
Last dinner 8.30pm ✿ S% sB&B£8.50–£10.50
sB&B⇌⋒£10.50–£12.50 dB&B£17–£20
dB&B⇌⋒£20–£24 Lunch£2.80 Tea75p
Dinner£4–£4.50 Wine£2.40

CRAIGHOUSE Isle of Jura, Strathclyde *Argyll* Map **10** NR56
★★Jura ☎Jura243
Overlooks sheltered bay.
18rm(4⇌⋒) CTV 12P 4⌂ ⌗ ⚓
Last dinner 8pm ☐ ✻sB&B fr£13
sB&B⇌⋒fr£14.50 dB&B fr£26 dB&B⇌⋒fr£29
Lunch fr£2.75 Tea fr80p Dinner fr£5 Wine£2.50
Credit cards 1 2 3 5

CRAIGNURE Isle of Mull, Strathclyde *Argyll* Map **10** NM73
★★★Isle of Mull (Scottish Highlands & Best Western) ☎351 Telex no 778215
Modern hotel, ½mile from car ferry terminal, looking out across Craignure Bay to the distant mainland.
closed 14Oct–24Apr; 60⇌⋒ CTV 50P ⚓
Last dinner 8.15pm ✿ ☐ S% sB&B⇌⋒£17.95
dB&B⇌⋒£30.30 Lunch£4.10 Tea40p–£1.30
Dinner£6.25 Wine£3.25
Credit cards 1 2 3 4 5 6

CRAIL Fife *Fife* Map **12** NO60
★Croma Nethergate ☎239
10rm(2⇌⋒) CTV P ⌗ ⚓ Last dinner 10pm ✿
☐ S% sB&B£5.50–£6 sB&B⇌⋒£6–£6.50
dB&B£11–£12 dB&B⇌⋒£12–£13
Tea50–65p&alc High Tea£2&alc
Dinner£4.32–£4.86&alc

★Marine Nethergate ☎207
12rm CTV P ⚓ Children under 6yrs not accommodated Last dinner 8.30pm ✿ ☐ S%
sB&B£6.48 dB&B£12.96 Bar lunch 75p–£1.50
Tea fr50p Dinner£5.40alc Wine£2.40

CRAWFORD Strathclyde *Lanarkshire* Map **11** NS92
★Crawford Arms ☎267
Closed New Year's Day; 6rm CTV 80P
Last dinner 8pm ✿ sB&B£6.75 dB&B£13
Lunch£2.20 Dinner£2.60&alc Wine£3
Credit card 5

CREETOWN Dumfries & Galloway *Kirkcudbrightshire* Map **11** NX45
★★Ellangowan ☎201
8rm CTV 3P 5⌂ Last dinner 9.30pm ✿ ☐ S%
sB&B£6–£6.50 dB&B£12–£13 Wine£2.10

CRIANLARICH Central *Perthshire* Map**10** NN32
★★**Crainlarich** ☎272
Coaching house dating from 1780 in hills of West Perthshire.
Rs Nov–Feb; 31rm CTV 40P Live music & dancing wkly last dinner8pm sB&B fr£10 dB&B fr£20

C

CRIEFF Tayside *Perthshire* Map**11** NN82
★★**Arduthie** Perth Rd ☎3113
Closed mid Feb–Mar; RS Nov–mid Feb; 8rm Annexe: 4 CTV 30P Last dinner8pm sB&B£8.50–£9.50 dB&B£17–£19 dB&B £17–£19 Lunch£3 High Tea£2.50–£3 Dinner£5.30 Wine£3 Credit card 3

★★**Cultoquhey** ☎3253
Closed Nov–Mar; 12rm CTV 50P 2 Last dinner8pm sB&B fr£7 dB&B fr£14 Lunch£2.75 Tea85p High Tea£2.35 Dinner£4.85 Wine£3.75 Credit card 3

★★**Drummond Arms** James Sq ☎2151
32rm(9) Lift CTV 30P 3 Live music & dancing Tue & Fri Last dinner9pm S% sB&B£8–£9.50 sB&B £9.75–£10.75 dB&B£16–£19 dB&B £19.50–£21.50 Lunch fr75p High Tea£2.25–£3.50 Dinner£4–£5.75 Wine£2.65 *xmas* Credit cards 1 2 3

★★**George** King St ☎2089
28rm(4) CTV 4P Live music & dancing Tue & Fri Last dinner8.30pm S% sB&B£6.50–£8.50 sB&B £7.50–£9.75 dB&B£13–£17 dB&B £15–£19.50 Lunch fr£2.25 Tea fr75p High Tea£1.95–£2.75 dinner£3.75–£4.75 Wine£2.65 *xmas*

★★***Murray Park*** Connaught Ter ☎3731
15rm(9) CTV 60P Last dinner9.15pm

★**Gwydyr** Comrie Rd ☎3277
Closed 21Dec–3Jan; RS Nov–20Dec & 4Jan–Mar; 9rm CTV 16P 2 Last dinner8.30pm sB&B fr£6.48 dB&B fr£11.88 Bar lunch fr£2.16 High Tea fr£1.60 Dinner fr£3.75&alc Wine£2.95 Credit cards 3

★**Leven House** Comrie Rd ☎2529
Rs Nov–Mr; 13rm CTV 5P 2 European. Last dinner7pm S% ✻sB&B£5.50 dB&B£10 Lunch£2.20 High Tea£1.75 Dinner£3 Wine£3

★**Star** East High St ☎2632
10rm(1) CTV 20P 2 sauna bath British & French. Last dinner9pm ✻sB&B£6–£8 sB&B £7.50–£9.50 dB&B£12–£16 dB&B £13.50–£17.50 Lunch£1.30–£5.40&alc Tea85p High Tea£1.60&alc Dinner£4&alc Wine£2.60 Credit cards 1 2 5

CRINAN Strathclyde *Argyll* Map**10** NR79
★★★***Crinan*** ☎235 Telex no 778817
20 Lift CTV 30P sauna bath Last dinner9pm Credit cards 1 2 3 5

CROCKETFORD Dumfries & Galloway *Kirkcudbrightshire* Map**11** NX87
★★**Galloway Arms** Stranraer Rd ☎240
Closed mid Oct–mid Nov; 11rm(1) CTV 50P Scottish & French. Last dinner9.45pm sB&B£8–£8.80 dB&B£15–£17.50 dB&B £17–£18.50 Lunch£3–£4.50 Tea£1–£1.40 High Tea£2.50–£4 Dinner£5–£7.50 Wine£3.50

CROFTAMIE Strathclyde *Dunbartonshire* Map**11** NS48
✕**Red House Grill** ☎Drymen358
Closed Mon & Nov; 48seats 30P Last dinner9.30pm Dinner£7alc Wine£3

CROMARTY Highland *Ross & Cromarty* Map**14** NH76
★★***Royal*** Marine Ter ☎217
13rm TV 12P 14 Music wkly International. Last dinner9pm Credit card 3

CROSSMICHAEL Dumfries & Galloway *Kirkcudbrightshire* Map**11** NX76
★★**Culgruff House** ☎230
Baronial mansion set in secluded, wooded grounds the heart of farming land, high above the village of Crossmichael.
16rm(1) CTV 50P 8 Last dinner8pm sB&B£8.64 sB&B £9.18 dB&B£16.20 dB&B £17.28 Lunch£3.24 Tea£1.35 High Tea£2.70 Dinner£5.40 Wine£3.80 Credit cards 1 2 3

CULLEN Grampian *Banffshire* Map**15** NJ56
★★★***Seafield Arms*** Seafield St (Best Western) ☎40791
25rm(7) CTV 20P Last dinner9.30pm Credit cards 1 2 3 4 5 6

★★**Cullen Bay** ☎40432
18rm(1) CTV 80P Last dinner8.30pm sB&B£8.10–£9.18 dB&B£16.20–£18.36 dB&B £18.20–£20.36 Lunch£1.45–£1.70 Tea50–65p Dinner£3.78&alc Wine£2.59 *xmas* Credit cards 2 5

CUMNOCK Strathclyde *Ayrshire* Map**11** NS51
★★**Dumfries Arms** Glaisnock St ☎20282
7rm(2) CTV CTV available in bedrooms 75P Disco twice wkly Cabaret wkly Last dinner9.30pm sB&B fr£8 sB&B fr£10 dB&B fr£14 dB&B fr£16 Lunch£1.20alc Tea fr25p High Tea£1.20alc Dinner£1.20alc Wine£2.25

★★**Royal** 1 Glaisnock St ☎20822
11rm CTV 8P 2 Last dinner9pm sB&B£7.50 dB&B£15 Lunch£2.50–£3.50 Tea50p–£1 High Tea£2–£3 Dinner£3.50–£5.50 Wine£3.50 Credit card 1

DALBEATTIE Dumfries & Galloway *Kirkcudbrightshire* Map**11** NX86
★**Burnside** John St ☎610219
7rm CTV 20P Disco wkly Live music & dancing twice wkly Mainly grills. Last dinner7.30pm S% sB&B£5–£6.50 dB&B£11–£13 Lunch£2–£3.50 High Tea£2–£4 Dinner£3–£5 Wine£2.80 *xmas*

DALMALLY Strathclyde *Argyll* Map**10** NN12
★★**Carraig-Thura** Lochawe (3m W A85) ☎210
RS Dec–Mar; 22rm(6) TV 50P European. Last dinner8.30pm sB&B£8.50–£9.50 sB&B £9.75–£10.25 dB&B£17–£18 dB&B £19.50–£20.50 Bar lunch£1.30–£2 Tea50p Dinner£6.50–£7

★★**Dalmally** ☎249
RS Nov–Mar; 56rm CTV 200P 2 Live music & dancing twice wkly Last dinner8.45pm S% sB&B£8.50–£10 dB&B£16–£19 Lunch fr£2.50 Tea fr40p Dinner fr£3.50 Wine£2.90

DALRY Dumfries & Galloway *Kirkcudbrightshire* Map**11** NX68
★★**Lochinvar** ☎210
18rm(2) CTV 30P 1 Children under 3yrs not accommodated Last dinner7.30pm S% ✻sB&B fr£6.50 sB&B fr£7.50 dB&B fr£13 dB&B fr£15 Lunch fr£1.80 Dinner fr£4 Wine£1.20

★★**Milton Park** ☎286
18rm CTV 50P 4 (hard) Last dinner7.30pm sB&B fr£8 dB&B fr£16 Bar lunch fr43p

D

Tea fr£1.08 High Tea fr£4.32 Dinner fr£6.48 Wine£2.75 xmas Credit card 3

DAVIOT Highland *Inverness-shire* Map **14** NH73
★★**Meallmore Lodge** ☎206
Situated on the main north road, south of Daviot, this converted sandstone and granite shooting lodge was built in 1869 for the Mackintoshes of Moy.
12 Annexe: 8rm CTV 60P 4 Last dinner 9pm sB&B£7–£8.50 sB&B£8–£9 dB&B£14–£16 dB&B£15–£19 Lunch fr£3.50 Tea 25–70p Dinner£4–£5.40&alc Wine£2.60 Credit cards 2 5

DINGWALL Highland *Ross & Cromarty* Map **14** NH55
★★**National** High St ☎2166
A handsome red sandstone building dating from 1900 in main shopping street.
42rm(3) CTV CTV available in bedrooms 50P 5 Last dinner 8.45pm S% *sB&B fr£9.96 dB&B fr£19.91 dB&B fr£24.29 Lunch fr£3 Tea fr£1 Dinner fr£4.30 Wine£2.40 Credit cards 1 3

★**Royal** High St ☎2130
Three-storey stone building in main street.
19rm CTV Disco twice wkly Last dinner 9pm S% sB&B£8.35 dB&B£14.85 Lunch£2.25 Tea fr60p High Tea£1.50–£3.75 Dinner£4 Wine£2.50 xmas Credit card 5

DIRLETON Lothian *East Lothian* Map **12** NT58
★★★**Open Arms** ☎241
Small select hotel in picturesque setting by village green, close to 13th-C castle ruin.
7 CTV in bedrooms 60P Scottish & Continental. Last dinner 10pm sB&B£20 dB&B£32.50 Lunch fr£3.50 Tea fr£1.25 Dinner£8 Wine£2.50 Credit cards 2 3 5

DORNOCH Highland *Sutherland* Map **14** NH78
★★★**Royal Golf** Castle St ☎283
Three-storey stone building standing in own grounds on outskirts of town. Views across Dornoch Firth to hills of Easter Ross.
Closed Feb–mid Mar; 28rm(22) CTV 20P Scottish & French. Last dinner 9.30pm sB&B£14–£20.50 sB&B£15.50–£22.80 dB&B£24–£35 dB&B£27–£39.60 Credit cards 1 2 3

★★**Burghfield House** ☎212
Scottish baronial-style turreted mansion built for Lord Rothermere in 1910, standing in 5½ acres of tree-studded grounds.
Closed 16Oct–3Apr; 16rm(4) Annexe: 31rm(3) CTV 100P billiards Disco twice wkly Scottish & French. Last dinner 8.30pm *sB&B£9.20–£10.50 sB&B£10.35–£11.65 dB&B£18.40–£21 dB&B£20.70–£23.30 Lunch fr£3.40 Dinner fr£5.40 Wine£2.50 Credit cards 2 3 5

★★**Dornoch** ☎351 Telex no 75160
Closed Nov–Mar; 107rm(20) Lift CTV 50P 20 (hard) Live music & dancing twice wkly Last dinner 9pm S% sB&B£13.50–£19 sB&B£15.50–£21 dB&B£23–£33 dB&B£27–£37 Credit cards 1 2 3

★★**Dornoch Castle** Castle St ☎216
450-year-old castle, former seat of Bishops of Caithness; standing in centre of town overlooking Dornoch Firth.
Closed Oct–Mar; 21rm(11) Lift CTV 16P Last dinner 8pm sB&B£9.72 dB&B£19.44 dB&B£21.06 Lunch£3.50alc Tea 65palc Dinner£5.25 Wine£2

DOUGLAS Strathclyde *Lanarkshire* Map **11** NS83
★***Douglas Arms*** ☎322
5rm(4) CTV TV available in bedrooms 60P Last dinner 8pm

DRUMMORE Dumfries & Galloway *Wigtownshire* Map **10** NX13
★***Queens*** Mill St ☎300
A village hotel which looks out across Luce Bay.
7rm CTV Live music Fri & Sat Last dinner 8pm Credit card 1

DRUMNADROCHIT Highland *Inverness-shire* Map **14** NH53
★★ **Polmaily House** ☎343
See page 64 for details

★★***Drumnadrochit*** Loch Ness ☎218
26rm TV (hard) English & Continental. Last dinner 8pm

★**Benleva** ☎288
7rm CTV 30P Live music & dancing wkly Last dinner 9.30pm S% sB&B£6.50–£8.50 dB&B£12–£16 Bar lunch fr£1.50 Tea£1 Dinner fr£5 Wine£2.80 Credit cards 1 2 3

DRYBURGH Borders *Berwickshire* Map **12** NT53
★★★**Dryburgh Abbey** ☎St Boswells 2261 Telex no 537174
Turreted mansion dating from 1848 standing in 11 acres of parkland on the banks of the River Tweed.
29rm(16) 3 Lift CTV 100P 4 Last dinner 8.30pm S% sB&B£12.60–£15.80 sB&B£17–£19.60 dB&B£24.20–£29.50 dB&B£27.50–£31.50 Lunch£3.95 Tea£1 Dinner£6.60 Wine£2.14 Credit cards 1 2 3 5

DRYMEN Central *Stirlingshire* Map**11** NS48
★★**Buchanan Arms** (Scottish Highlands) ☎588
Telexno778215
Originally an 18th-C coaching inn, now modernised and extended, set by roadside in centre of small village.
24rm(15⇌⋒) ☽ CTV 50P ⇹ ⚓ Lastdinner9.15pm ✪ 🍷 S% sB&B£15.85 sB&B⇌⋒£18.70 dB&B£26.10 dB&B⇌⋒£31.80 Lunch£4.40&alc Tea£1.30 Dinner£7&alc Wine£3.25 ▤ *xmas* Creditcards 1 2 3 4 5 6

✕**Reivers** 5–7 Stirling Rd ☎205
45seats 3P bedrooms available ♡Scottish & French. Lastdinner9pm Lunch£2.25alc Tea£1.10alc Dinner£5alc Wine£2.35 Creditcards 1 3

DULNAIN BRIDGE Highland *Moray* Map**14** NH92
✪★★**Muckrach Lodge** ☎257
Rosette awarded for dinner only.
10rm ⋕ ⊘ 50P 3⌂ ⇹ ⚓ ♡French. Specialities: smoked or fresh salmon, venison, homemade pâtés. Lastdinner7.30pm ✪ 🍷 sB&B£8.50 dB&B£17 Barlunch£1.65alc Tea25p–35p Dinner£6.50–£7.50 Wine£4.20 *xmas*

DUMBARTON Strathclyde *Dunbartonshire* Map**10** NS37
★★**Dumbuck** Glasgow Rd (Open House) ☎63818
Closed 1Jan; 25rm(10⇌⋒) ☽ ⋕CTV in bedrooms 100P ⚓ Live music & dancing Sun
Lastdinner9.30pm ✪ sB&B£11.50 sB&B⇌⋒£14 dB&B£17 dB&B⇌⋒£21 Lunch£2.80–£3.50&alc Dinner£3.80–£4.20&alc Wine£2.75 ▤ Creditcards 1 2 3 4 5 6

✕***Upstairs Downstairs*** Riverside Ln ☎67828
Closed Sun & New Year's Day; 36seats ♡Mainlygrills. Lastdinner9.30pm

DUMFRIES Dumfries & Galloway *Dumfriesshire* Map**11** NX97
★★★**Cairndale** English St (Best Western) ☎4111
Closed 1Jan; 44rm(29⇌⋒) Lift ☽ ⋕CTV in bedrooms 60P 1⌂ ⇹ ♿ Lastdinner9pm ✪ 🍷 S% sB&B£17.40 sB&B⇌⋒£21.40 dB&B£32.60 dB&B⇌⋒£36.60 Lunch£4–£5&alc Tea£1.50 HighTea£2.50–£6.50 Dinner£6.25–£7.25&alc Wine£3.50 Creditcards 1 2 3 4 5 6

★★★**Station** 49 Lovers' Walk ☎4316
30rm(18⇌⋒) Lift ☽ ⋕CTV CTV in bedrooms 60P Live music & dancing Sat (winter) ♿ ♡Scottish, French & Italian. Lastdinner9pm ✪ 🍷 sB&B£13.50 sB&B⇌⋒£15 dB&B£18.50 dB&B⇌⋒£20 Lunch£3.20&alc Tea80p HighTea£3 Dinner£5.50&alc Wine£2.20 ▤ Creditcards 1 2 3 4 5 6

★★**County** High St (Inter-Hotel) ☎5401
Telexno777205
The lounge was Bonnie Prince Charlie's HQ in 1745.
50rm(23⇌⋒) Lift ☽ CTV available in bedrooms 20P Lastdinner10.30pm ✪ S% sB&B£11–£12 sB&B⇌⋒£13–£15 dB&B£18–£20 dB&B⇌⋒£22–£24 Lunch£2.60–£3.25 HighTea £2.20–£4 Dinner£4.50–£6.50 Wine£2.80 ▤ Creditcards 1 2 3 5 6

★***Embassy*** Newbridge (2½m NW on A76) (Scottish & Newcastle) ☎Newbridge233
Small Regency country house standing in 16 acres of gardens with own trout stream.
6rm(1⇌⋒) CTV 40P Musicwknds
Lastdinner8.30pm ✪ 🍷 Creditcards 2 3 4 5 6

★**Nithsdale** 9 St Mary Street ☎3452
13rm ⋕CTV ⇹ HighTea7pm ✪ S% sB&B£8.75 dB&B£15.70 Lunch£3.25 HighTea£2–£3.50 Creditcards 1 2 3 4 5 6

★**Skyline** 123 Irish St ☎62416
10rm(3⇌⋒) ⋕CTV TV available in bedrooms 20P Disco twice wkly Live music & dancing twice wkly Lastdinner9pm ✪ 🍷 S% sB&B£7–£7.50 sB&B⇌⋒£8–£8.50 dB&B£14–£15 dB&B⇌⋒£16–£17 Lunch£2.50–£4.50&alc Tea£1–£1.50&alc HighTea£2.50–£4.50&alc Dinner£4.20&alc Wine£2.80 ▤ Creditcards 2 3 4 5 6

★**Swan at Kingholm** Kingholm Quay ☎3756
RS 25Dec & 1Jan; 9rm CTV 40P ⚓
Lastdinner9.30pm ✪ 🍷 S% sB&B£6.25–£7.25 dB&B£12–£13 Lunch£2.75–£3.75&alc Tea65p–£1.25&alc HighTea£2.75–£3.75&alc Dinner£3.50–£5&alc Wine£2.50

★**Winston** Rae St ☎4433
Closed 30Dec–4Jan; 14rm ⋕CTV 6P
Lastdinner7pm ✪ sB&B£6.48–£6.80 dB&B£12.96–£13.60 Lunch fr£2.16 Dinner fr£3.24 Wine£2.30 ▤

✕✕***Bruno's*** Balmoral Rd ☎5757
Closed Tue; 70seats ♡English, French & Italian. Lastdinner9.15pm

DUNBAR Lothian *East Lothian* Map**12** NT67
★★★**Roxburghe** Queens Rd ☎62755
46rm(24⇌⋒) CTV TV available in bedrooms 50P 6⌂ ⋕Conference facilities available ♡English & French. Lastdinner9pm ✪ 🍷 sB&B£9.50–£14.50 sB&B⇌⋒£12.50–£15.50 dB&B£19–£29 dB&B⇌⋒£25–£31 Lunch fr£4.50&alc Tea fr£1.50 HighTea fr£3 Dinner fr£6&alc Wine£4.50 ▤ *xmas* Creditcard 2

D

★★Bayswell Bayswell Park ☎62225
Closed 16Oct–Mar; 14rm(5⇌⋒) CTV 20P ⚘
Last dinner8.30pm ♡ S% sB&B£9
sB&B⇌⋒£12.50 dB&B£18 dB&B⇌⋒£22
Lunch fr£2.65 High Tea fr£2 Dinner fr£5 Wine£2
Credit cards 1 3

DUNBLANE Central *Perthshire* Map**11** NN70
★★★Dunblane Hydro (Reo Stakis) ☎822551
126⇌⋒ Lift ☽ ▦ CTV in bedrooms 300P ⚘
(heated) (hard/grass) sauna bath Disco wkly Live music & dancing nightly in summer Cabaret twice wkly Last dinner10pm ♡ S%
sB&B⇌⋒£16–£17 dB&B⇌⋒£28–£30
Lunch£3.25–£3.75&alc Tea50p–70p
Dinner£4.50–£5.50&alc Wine£3.10 ⊟ *xmas*
Credit cards 1 2 3 5

DUNDEE Tayside *Angus* Map**11** NO33
★★★Angus 101 Marketgait (Thistle) ☎26874
Telex no 76456
Modern hotel forming part of shopping centre.
58rm(43⇌⋒) Lift ☽ ▦ CTV in bedrooms 7P
Last dinner10pm ♡ S% sB&B£19
sB&B⇌⋒£24 dB&B£29 dB&B⇌⋒£34
Lunch£4–£4.50&alc Tea£1
Dinner£6–£6.50&alc Wine£2.75 ⊟
Credit cards 1 2 3 4 5 6

☆☆☆Invercarse 371 Perth Rd, Ninewells (Thistle) ☎69231
Extended private house, standing in own grounds.
28⇌⋒ ☽ ▦ CTV CTV in bedrooms 200P ⚘
Disco Sun Live music & dancing Sat French.
Last dinner10pm ♡ S% *sB&B⇌⋒ fr£18
dB&B⇌⋒ fr£25.50 Continental breakfast
Lunch fr£3.35&alc Dinner fr£5.40&alc Wine£2.80
⊟ Credit cards 1 2 3 5

☆☆☆Swallow Kingsway West, Invergowrie (3½m W off A972 Dundee Ring Road) (Swallow) ☎641122
Telex no 53168
69⇌⋒ 2 ☽ ▦ CTV in bedrooms 80P ⚘ British & French. Last dinner9.30pm ♡
*sB&B⇌⋒£19.30–£28.60
dB&B⇌⋒£26.90–£34.30 Lunch£3.80&alc
Tea40p Dinner£4.25&alc Wine£2.50 ⊟
Credit cards 1 2 3 5 6

★★Kellyfield Drumgeith Rd (Reo Stakis) ☎454522
A converted private house standing in own grounds in the midst of a housing estate.
8rm(1⇌⋒) ☽ ▦ CTV 100P ⚘ Mainly grills.
Last dinner9pm ♡ S% *sB&B fr£9
sB&B⇌⋒ fr£10 dB&B fr£16 dB&B⇌⋒ fr£18
Lunch£2.50alc Dinner£2.50alc

★★Cambustay 8 Dalhousie Rd, Broughty Ferry (3m E A930) (Clansmans) ☎79290
A converted and extended private house, in own grounds on east side of town.
8rm ▦ CTV 70P ⚘ Last dinner9.30pm ♡
sB&B£8.45 dB&B£14.55 Lunch£2.45–£3.75
High Tea£1.85–£3.15 Dinner£2.45–£3.75
Wine£2.80 ⊟ Credit cards 1 2 3 5

★★Queen's 160 Nethergate (Trusthouse Forte) ☎22515
Five storey city centre hotel, on Tay Road Bridge approach road.
56rm(11⇌⋒) Lift ☽ ▦ CTV in bedrooms 40P
Last dinner9.15pm ♡ S% sB&B£12
sB&B⇌⋒£15.50 dB&B£19 dB&B⇌⋒£21.50
⊟ Credit cards 1 2 3 4 5 6

★★Tay Whitehall Cres ☎21641 Telex no 76296
Five-storey city centre hotel, on Tay Road Bridge approach road.
87rm(30⇌⋒) Lift ☽ ▦ CTV CTV in bedrooms

Disco 6nights wkly ♉French & Italian. Last dinner9.30pm ✿ ⚐ S% sB&B£31.75 sB&B⇌⫙£16.75 dB&B£18.95 dB&B⇌⫙£24.55 Lunch£2.75–£3.25&alc Tea50p–£1.50 High Tea£1.80–£2.25 Dinner£3.30–£3.60&alc Wine£2.50 ⊟ Credit cards 1 2 3 5

★★**Tay Park** Broughty Ferry (3m E A930) ☎78924
Fine country mansion, situated in its own terraced grounds commanding magnificent views of the River Tay estuary and opposite Fife shore.
12rm(4⇌⫙) ☽ ⌘ TV CTV in bedrooms 80P ⚓ Last dinner9.30pm ✿ S% sB&B fr£7.50 dB&B⇌⫙ fr£18 Continental breakfast Lunch£3.50&alc Dinner fr£4.50&alc Credit card 2

DUNDONNELL Highland *Ross & Cromarty* Map**14** NH08
★★**Dundonnell** (Inter-Hotel) ☎204
RS Nov–Feb; 26rm(20⇌⫙) ⌘ 60P ⛟ Last dinner8.30pm ✿ ⚐ ✱sB&B£8.50–£10 sB&B⇌⫙£10.50–£13 dB&B£17–£20 dB&B⇌⫙£21–£24 Bar lunch£1.25–£1.75 Tea90p–£1.10 Dinner£4.75–£5.75 Wine£2.40 Credit cards 2 5

DUNFERMLINE Fife *Fife* Map**11** NT08
☆☆☆**King Malcolm** Queensferry Rd, Wester Pitcorthie (Thistle) ☎22611
48⇌⫙ ☽ ⌘ CTV CTV in bedrooms 60P Disco Sun ♉English & French. Last dinner9.30pm ✿ ⚐ sB&B⇌⫙ fr£17.50 dB&B⇌⫙ fr£25 Lunch£3.25&alc Tea85p Dinner£4.90&alc Wine£2.75 ⊟ Credit cards 1 2 3 4 5 6

★★**Brucefield** Woodmill Rd ☎22199
9rm(7⇌⫙) ⌘ CTV TV available in bedrooms 100P Last dinner8pm ✿ ⚐ S% ✱sB&B fr£10.99 sB&B⇌⫙ fr£12.48 dB&B fr£13.09 dB&B⇌⫙£18.42 Lunch fr£2.50 Tea fr75p High Tea fr£2 Dinner fr£4.45 Wine£2.50

★★**City** 18 Bridge St ☎22538
17rm(10⇌⫙) ☽ ⌘ CTV ⊘ 20P Last dinner9pm ✿ ⚐ S% sB&B fr£8.50 sB&B⇌⫙ fr£10.50 dB&B fr£15 dB&B⇌⫙ fr£19.50 Lunch£2.50 Tea75p High Tea£3.50 Dinner£4.50 Wine£2.25 ⊟ *xmas*

At **Kingseat** (3m NE on B912)
☆☆**Halfway House** ☎Dunfermline31661
10⇌⫙ 200P

DUNKELD Tayside *Perthshire* Map**11** NO04
★★★ ♛**Dunkeld House** ☎243
See page 64 for details

★★**Atholl Arms** Bridgehead ☎219
Closed Xmas; 24rm CTV 20P ⚓ ♉British & Continental. Last dinner8.30pm ✿ ⚐ S% sB&B£7.56–£8.80 dB&B£15.12–£17 Bar lunch£1.40–£1.80 Tea75p–£1 Dinner£4.86–£5.30 Wine£2.90 ⊟ Credit cards 1 2 3 4 5 6

⊛**Taybank** Tay Ter ☎340
RS Nov–Feb; 7rm CTV 30P ⛟ ⚓ Last dinner8pm ✱sB&B£6 dB&B£12 Bar lunch60p–£1.50 Dinner£4–£4.50 Wine£2.90

DUNNET Highland *Caithness* Map**15** ND27
★★**Northern Sands** ☎Barrock270
13rm(2⇌⫙) CTV 40P ⛟ ⚓ ↩ Live music & dancing Sat ♣ ♉French. Last dinner10pm ✿ ⚐ ✱sB&B£6 sB&B⇌⫙£6.50 dB&B£12 dB&B⇌⫙£12.50 Lunch80p–£4.50 Tea70p–£1.50 High Tea£1–£4 Dinner£4–£5.50 Wine£3.20 Credit card 3

DUNOON Strathclyde *Argyll* Map**10** NS17
★★**Abbeyhill** Dhailling Rd ☎2204
12rm(9⇌⫙) ⌘ CTV 40P ⚓ Last dinner8pm ✿ ⚐ S% ✱sB&B£8.10 sB&B⇌⫙£10.26 dB&B£16.20 dB&B⇌⫙£18.36 Lunch£2.70–£3 Tea60p High Tea£1.80–£2 Dinner£3.50–£5.50 Wine£2.27 ⊟

★★**Argyll** ☎2059
In central situation close to pier.
28rm(6⇌⫙) CTV ℙ Last dinner8pm ✿ ⚐ S% sB&B£10.10 sB&B⇌⫙£11 dB&B£17.23 dB&B⇌⫙£19.01 Lunch£2.61 Tea£1.08 High Tea£2.20 Dinner£4.16 ⊟ *xmas* Credit cards 1 6

★★**McColl's** West Bay (Osprey) ☎2764
58rm(12⇌⫙) Lift ☽ ⌘ CTV TV available in bedrooms 30P ⚓ Disco 3nights Live music & dancing wkly ♿ Last dinner9pm ✿ ⚐ S% ✱sB&B£11 sB&B⇌⫙£13.70 dB&B£17 dB&B⇌⫙£21 Lunch fr£2.60&alc Tea fr30p High Tea£2.60 Dinner fr£3.90&alc Wine£2.46 ⊟ *xmas* Credit cards 1 2 3 5

★★**Queens** Marine Pde, Kirn ☎4224
Substantial stone building overlooking Firth of Clyde.
22rm ⌘ CTV 30P ⛟ ⚓ Last dinner8.15pm ✿ ⚐ ✱sB&B£8.50–£9 dB&B£17–£18 Bar lunch75p–£1.50 Dinner fr£3.75 Wine£1.98

★★**Royal Marine** Sea Front, Hunter's Quay (2m N A815) ☎3001
34rm(2⇌⫙) ☽ ⌘ CTV ⊘ 25P ⌘ Last dinner8pm ✿ ⚐ S% ✱sB&B£9.50–£10.50 sB&B⇌⫙£10.50–£11.50 dB&B£19–£21 dB&B⇌⫙£21–£23 Lunch£5alc Tea50p–£2 Dinner£5alc Wine£2.25 ⊟ *xmas*

★**Caledonian** Argyll St ☎2176
13rm ⌘ CTV in bedrooms ℙ ⛟ Children under 3yrs not accommodated Last dinner8pm ✿ ⚐ sB&B fr£6.75 dB&B fr£12 Bar lunch fr75p Dinner fr£3.50 Wine£2.40 Credit card 6

DUNTOCHER Strathclyde *Dunbartonshire* Map**11** NS47
★★**Maltings** Dunbarton Rd ☎75371
25⇌⫙ ☽ ⌘ CTV 100P Disco 2nights wkly ♉English & French. Last dinner9.30pm ✿ ⚐ ✱sB&B⇌⫙£10 dB&B⇌⫙£16.50 Lunch£4&alc Tea£1–£2 Dinner£4–£8&alc Wine£2.80 Credit cards 2 3 5

DUNVEGAN Isle of Skye, Highland *Inverness-shire* Map**13** NG24
★★***Dunvegan*** ☎202
6rm Annexe: 10rm(3⇌⫙) ⌘ 50P ⛟ ⚓ ↩ ∩ Live music 6nights wkly Live music & dancing 3nights wkly Cabaret 2nights wkly Children under 1yr not accommodated Last dinner8pm ✿ ⚐ Credit cards 1 3

DUROR Highland *Argyll* Map**14** NM95
★★**Stewart** (Inter-Hotel) ☎268 Telex no 727582
29⇌⫙ ⌘ CTV TV available in bedrooms 40P ⌘ Last dinner9pm ✿ ⚐ sB&B⇌⫙£11.75–£14.50 dB&B⇌⫙£19–£23.50 Bar lunch fr£1.75 Tea40p Dinner£6 Wine£2.50 ⊟ *xmas* Credit cards 1 2 3

DYCE Grampian *Aberdeenshire* Map**15** NJ81
☆☆☆**Skean Dhu** ☎Aberdeen723101 Telex no 73473
222⇌⫙ ☽ ⌘ CTV in bedrooms 300P Live music & dancing Sun Conference facilities available ♉International. Last dinner11pm ✿ ⚐ S% ✱sB&B⇌⫙£19.90–£23.95 dB&B⇌⫙£21.90–£25.50 Lunch fr£3.95&alc Tea£1.20alc High Tea£1.80alc Dinner fr£4.50&alc Wine£3.20 ⊟ Credit cards 1 2 3 5 6

EAGLESHAM Strathclyde *Renfrewshire* Map**11** NS55

★★**Eglinton Arms** Gilmour St (Open House) ☎2631
12 CTV in bedrooms 50P Disco Sun Live music & dancing Mon French. Last dinner9.30pm S% sB&B£15.50 dB&B£22 Lunch£3 High Tea£3 Dinner£5.50alc Wine£2.80
Credit cards 1 2 3 5 6

XX***Pepper Pot*** Cross Keys Inn ☎2002
Closed Sun; 70seats 40P Last dinner10pm
Credit card 1

EASDALE Strathclyde *Argyll* Map**10** NM71

★★**Dunmor House** ☎Balvicar203
Delightful, white-painted house with views of the Atlantic and Isle of Scarba.
Closed 18Oct–30Apr; 11rm(5) TV 25P 6
Last dinner6pm ✱sB&B£12 dB&B£19.60 dB&B£24–£25.80 Bar lunch£2alc Tea£1.20&alc Dinner fr£6 Wine£3.20

★***Inshaig Park*** ☎Balvicar256
7rm TV 8P Children under 8yrs not accommodated English. Last dinner7.30pm

EAST KILBRIDE Strathclyde *Lanarkshire* Map**11** NS65

☆☆☆☆**Bruce** Cornwall St (Swallow) ☎29771
Telex no 778428
Modern custom-built hotel forming part of new town complex.
65 Lift CTV in bedrooms 24P Conference facilities available Last dinner9.45pm S% sB&B£20.60 dB&B£27.10
Credit cards 1 2 3 5

☆☆☆***Stuart*** Cornwall Way (Thistle) ☎21161
29 Lift TV 200P Music & dancing Sat Last dinner9.30pm
Credit cards 1 2 3 4 5 6

★★***Crutherland Country House*** Strathaven Rd ☎24611
2rm Annexe: 9rm(2) CTV 200P
English. Last dinner10pm

★★**Torrance** Main St (Open House) ☎25241
Large 200 year old former coaching inn, in centre of original village of East Kilbride.
26rm(7) CTV TV available in bedrooms 100P Last dinner9pm S% ✱sB&B£12 sB&B£13.50 dB&B£18 dB&B£21 Lunch£2.15&alc Dinner fr£3.35&alc Wine£2.85
Credit cards 1 2 3 5 6

EAST LINTON Lothian *East Lothian* Map**12** NT57

★★★**Harvesters** (Best Western) ☎395
Telex no 8814912
An intimate Georgian house standing in 3½ acres of well-tended gardens beside the River Tyne. The interior is well decorated, and personal service from the proprietors can be enjoyed.
Closed 18Dec–20Jan; 6rm(4)
Annexe: 7rm(4) CTV 45P 1
Last dinner8.30pm S% sB&B£15–£18.75 sB&B£17–£21 dB&B£24.50–£32 dB&B£26–£36.50 Lunch£5.25&alc Dinner£7.50&alc Wine£3.35
Credit cards 1 2 3 5 6

EDDLESTON Borders *Peeblesshire* Map**11** NT24

XX***Horse Shoe Inn*** ☎225
50seats 40P Last dinner10pm Credit cards 1 2 3 5

EDINBURGH Lothian *Midlothian* Map**11** NT27
See plan

★★★★**Caledonian** Princes St (British Transport) ☎031–225 2433 Telex no 72179 Central plan**3**
210rm(202) Lift TV in bedrooms 150P Conference facilities available English & French. Last dinner10.30pm S% sB&B fr£32 dB&B fr£55.95 Dinner fr£7.35 Wine£3.50
Credit cards 1 2 3 4 5 6

★★★★**George** George St (Grand Met) ☎031–225 1251 Telex no 72570 Central plan**14**
156 Lift CTV available in bedrooms 24P Live music & dancing Tue, Fri, Sat & Sun Conference facilities available Scottish, English & French. Last dinner10pm S%
✱sB&B£16.75–£23 dB&B£27–£32
xmas Credit cards 1 2 3 4 5 6

★★★★**North British** Princes St (British Transport) ☎031–556 2414 Telex no 72332 Central plan**22**
A traditional style railway hotel, located in the city centre. There is a Scottish speciality restaurant in the basement.
193rm(171) Lift TV in bedrooms 16P Conference facilities available English & French. Last dinner10.30pm S% sB&B fr£32 dB&B fr£55.40 Wine£3.50
Credit cards 1 2 3 4 5 6

☆☆☆☆**Royal Scot** 111 Glasgow Rd (Swallow) ☎031–334 9191 Telex no 727197 District plan**53**
258 Lift CTV in bedrooms 300P sauna bath Conference facilities available Last dinner10.30pm S% sB&B fr£21.35 dB&B fr£32.40 Credit cards 1 2 3 5

★★★**Barnton** Queensferry Rd, Barnton (Thistle) ☎031–339 1144 District plan**34**
Hotel occupies good position on A90 4½miles NW of the city centre.
48rm(45) Lift CTV in bedrooms 120P International. Last dinner10pm S% sB&B£19.50 dB&B£32.80 Lunch£4.50&alc Tea60p High Tea£2.75 Dinner£5.80&alc Wine£3.50
Credit cards 1 2 3 4 5 6

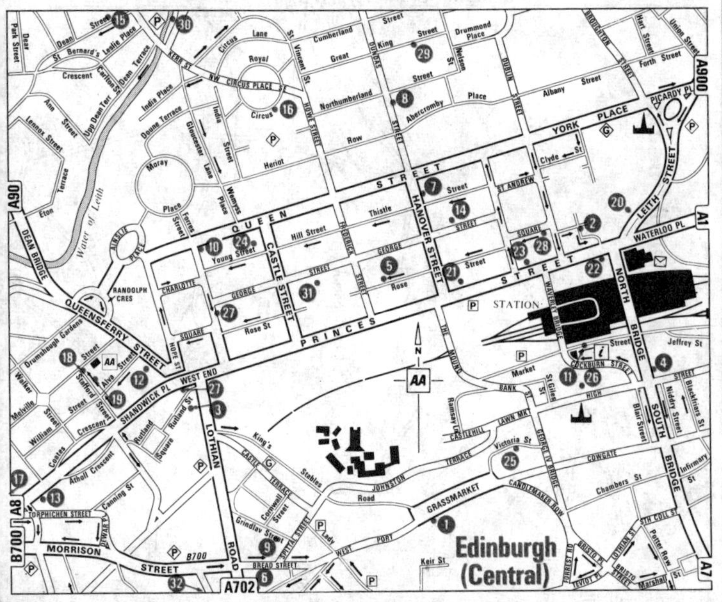

1 Beehive✕✕
2 CaféRoyal✕✕✕
3 Caledonian★★★★
4 Carlton★★★
5 Casa Española✕
6 Casa Siciliana✕
7 Cousteous Sea Food✕✕
8 Le Caveau✕
9 Creperie Restaurant Française✕
10 Denzler's✕✕
11 Doric Tavern✕
12 Edinburgh Rendezvous✕
13 Flapper's❀✕
14 George★★★★
15 Georgian★
16 Gordon★
17 Grosvenor Centre★★
18 Handsel✕✕
19 Howtodie❀✕✕
20 King James☆☆☆
21 Mount Royal★★
22 North British★★★★
23 Old Waverley★★
24 Ristorante Cosmo✕✕✕
25 Ristorante Milano✕✕
26 Rosie's✕
27 Roxburghe★★★
28 St Andrew★★
29 Scotia★★
30 Snobs✕
31 Town & Country✕✕
32 Vitos✕✕

★★★***Braid Hills*** Braid Rd, Braid Hills (2½m S A702) (Inter-Hotel) ☎031–447 8888 District plan**35**
Built in 1886 and standing in own grounds, off A702, hotel offers wide panorama of Edinburgh and Pentland Hills.
51rm ☽ CTV TV available in bedrooms 40P ⛟ ⚓ Last dinner8.45pm ♉ ♅ ▜

★★★**Bruntsfield** Bruntsfield Pl ☎031–229 1393 District plan**36**
Conversion of six adjoining houses, dating from 1862, overlooking Bruntsfield Links.
50rm(37⇌⋒) Lift ☽ ⚲ CTV TV available in bedrooms 25P Last dinner9.45pm ♉ ♅ S% sB&B£13–£15 sB&B⇌⋒£15–£17 dB&B£22–£25 dB&B⇌⋒£25–£28 Lunch£4.50–£5&alc Dinner£4.50–£5&alc Wine£3.25 ▜ *xmas* Credit card ①

★★★**Carlton** North Bridge (Scottish Highlands) ☎031–556 7277 Telex no 778215 Central plan**4**
92⇌⋒ Lift ☽ ⚲ CTV in bedrooms ⚑ Conference facilities available ♿ Last dinner9pm ♉ ♅ S% sB&B⇌⋒£18.70 dB&B⇌⋒£31.80 Lunch£6.15&alc Tea40p–£1.30 Dinner£6.15&alc Wine£3.25 ▜ *xmas* Credit cards ① ② ③ ④ ⑤ ⑥

☆☆☆**Edinburgh EuroCrest** Queensferry Rd (Crest) ☎031–332 2442 Telex no 72541 District plan**41**
Modern hotel situated 1m from city centre on main road from Edinburgh to Forth Road Bridge.
120⇌⋒ Lift ☽ ⚲ CTV in bedrooms 170P Conference facilities available ♀French Last dinner10pm ♉ ✻sB&B⇌⋒£18.14 dB&B⇌⋒£32.61 Continental breakfast ▜ Credit cards ① ② ③ ④ ⑤ ⑥

★★★**Ellersly House** Ellersly Rd (Allied Scotland) ☎031–337 6888 Telex no 76357 District plan**42**
Former private mansion, now extended, west of city centre close to A8.
57⇌⋒ Lift ☽ CTV P ⚓ Live music & dancing three nights wkly ♿ Last dinner9pm ♉ ♅ S% sB&B⇌⋒fr£15 dB&B⇌⋒fr£29 Lunch fr£3.50 Tea fr£1.50 Dinner fr£5.50 Wine£4 ▜ *xmas* Credit cards ① ② ③ ④ ⑤ ⑥

☆☆☆***King James*** 107 Saint James Centre (Thistle) ☎031–556 0111 Telex no 727200 Central plan**20**
Modern hotel centrally situated among shops.
160⇌⋒ Lift ☽ ⚲ CTV in bedrooms 6P Live music Mon–Sat Live music & dancing Sat (winter) Cabaret wkly (summer) Conference facilities available ♿ ♀Scottish & French. Last dinner10pm ♉ ♅ ▜ Credit cards ① ② ③ ④ ⑤ ⑥

★★★**Oratava** 41–43 Craigmillar Park ☎031–667 9484 Telex no 727401 District plan**49**
54⇌⋒ Lift ☽ ⚲ CTV in bedrooms 80P Live music & dancing Mon–Sat Cabaret Mon–Sat ♿ ♀International. Last dinner10pm ♉ ♅ sB&B⇌⋒£13–£20 dB&B⇌⋒£19–£31 Lunch£2.80–£3.10&alc Dinner£5.70–£6.80&alc Wine£3.50 ▜ *xmas* Credit cards ① ② ③ ④ ⑤ ⑥

E

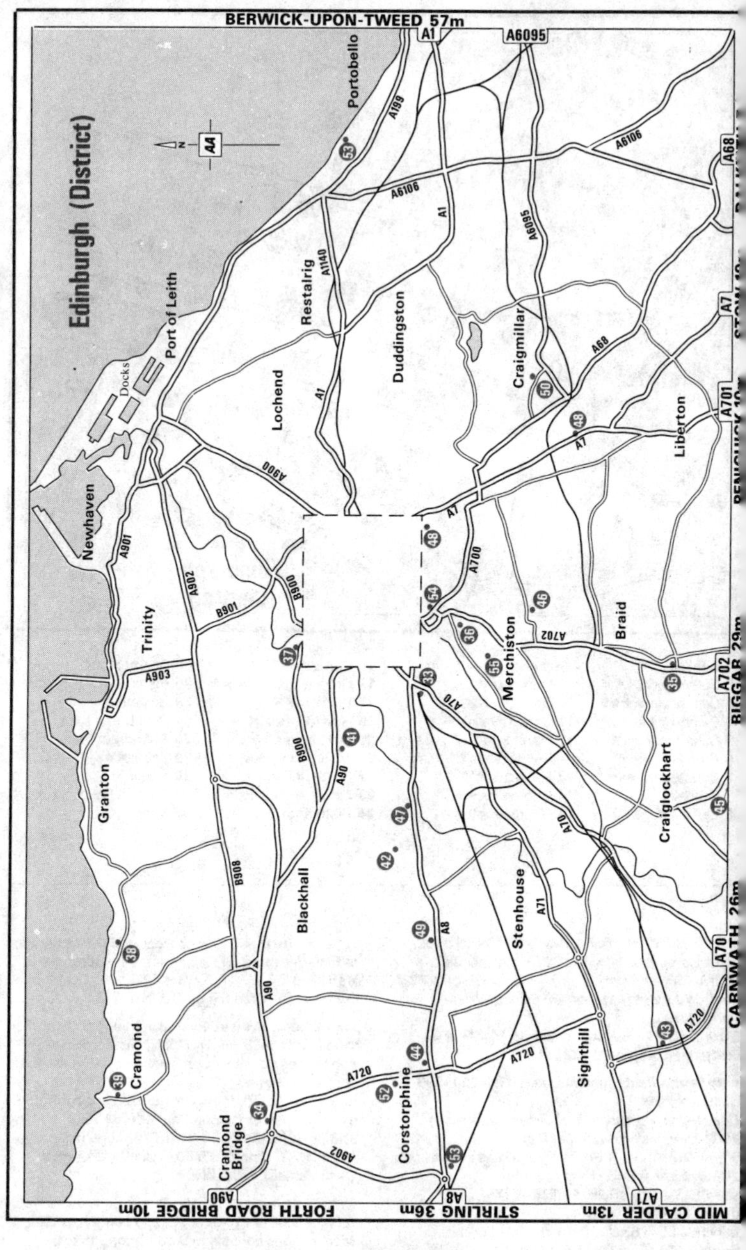

33 Anatolian✕
34 Barnton★★★
25 Braid Hills★★★
36 Bruntsfield★★★
37 Chez Julie✕
38 Commodore☆☆
39 Cramond Inn✕✕
41 Edinburgh EuroCrest☆☆☆
42 Ellersly House★★★
43 Hailes★★
44 Harp★★
45 Hunter's Tryst✕✕
46 Iona★★
47 Murrayfield★★
48 Old Bell Inn✕
49 Oratava★★★
50 Post House☆☆☆
51 Prestonfield House✕✕✕
52 Rainbow✕✕✕
53 Royal Scot☆☆☆☆
54 Shamiana✕✕

★★★**Post House** Corstorphine Rd (Trusthouse Forte) ☎031–334 8221 Telex no 727103 District plan **50**
208⇌⋒ Lift ☽ ꟿ CTV in bedrooms 158P Conference facilities available ♿ Last dinner 10.15pm ♈ ☕ sB&B⇌⋒ £21.25 dB&B⇌⋒ £31.50 ⛿ *xmas* Credit cards 1 2 3 4 5 6

★★★**Roxburghe** Charlotte Sq (Prestige) ☎031–225 3921 Central plan **27**
78rm(61⇌⋒) Lift ☽ ꟿ CTV in bedrooms ⚑ ♿ ♀ Scottish & French. Last dinner 10pm ♈ ☕ S% sB&B£11–£20 sB&B⇌⋒ £13.50–£25 dB&B£20–£40 dB&B⇌⋒ £22–£50 Continental breakfast Lunch fr£3.50&alc Tea£1.20alc High Tea£2.50alc Dinner fr£5&alc Wine£3.50 ⛿ Credit cards 1 2 3 4 5 6

★★★**Commodore** West Marine Dr, Cramond Foreshore (Reo Stakis) ☎031–336 1700 District plan **38**
Set in parkland on the Cramond foreshore; the hotel overlooks Firth of Forth.
49⇌⋒ Lift ☽ ꟿ CTV CTV in bedrooms 75P Conference facilities available Last dinner 9.45pm ♈ ☕ S% sB&B⇌⋒ fr£16 dB&B⇌⋒ fr£27 Lunch £3.25&alc Tea 40p Dinner £4.85&alc Wine£3.10 ⛿ Credit cards 1 2 3 5

★★**Grosvenor Centre** Grosvenor St (Centre) ☎031–226 6001 Telex no 72445 Central plan **17**
170rm(37⇌⋒) Lift ☽ ꟿ CTV ⚑ Last dinner 10pm ♈ ☕ S% ✱sB&B£10 sB&B⇌⋒ £16.25 dB&B£14 dB&B⇌⋒ £22.50 Continental breakfast Lunch £3.65 Dinner £3.65 Wine£3.40 ⛿ Credit cards 1 2 3 4 5 6

★★**Hailes** 2 Wester Hailes Centre (Scottish & Newcastle) ☎031–442 3382 District plan **43**
A modern hotel adjoining a new shopping centre set within a housing scheme.
20⇌⋒ ꟿ CTV 20P Disco wkly Live music & dancing wkly Cabaret wkly Last dinner 9pm ♈ S% sB&B⇌⋒ £10.50 dB&B⇌⋒ £19.80 Lunch £1.50–£3.50&alc Dinner £2.50–£5&alc Wine£3.45 Credit cards 1 3 5

★★**Harp** St John's Rd, Corstorphine (3½m W on A8) (Osprey) ☎031–334 6241 District plan **44**
20rm(8⇌⋒) ☽ CTV CTV available in bedrooms 40P Live music & dancing twice wkly ♀ French Last dinner 9.15pm ♈ ☕ S% ✱sB&B£11 sB&B⇌⋒ £14 dB&B£17 dB&B⇌⋒ £21 Lunch fr£2.60&alc Tea fr30p High Tea fr£2.60 Dinner fr£3.90&alc Wine£2.20 ⛿ *xmas* Credit cards 1 2 3 5

★★**Iona** Strathearn Pl ☎031–447 6264 District plan **46**
Situated in quiet district on south side of Edinburgh.
17rm ꟿ CTV 20P ♣ Last dinner 8.30pm sB&B£9 dB&B£16 Lunch £2.50 Tea £1 High Tea £2.50 Dinner £4.50alc Wine£3

★★**Mount Royal** 53 Princes St (Allied Scotland) ☎031–225 7161 Telex no 727641 Central plan **21**
156rm(146⇌⋒) Lift ☽ ꟿ CTV ⚑ Last dinner 8.30pm ♈ ☕ S% sB&B⇌⋒ fr£16.50 dB&B⇌⋒ fr£24.20 Continental breakfast Lunch fr£3.50 Tea fr£1.50 Dinner fr£5.50&alc Wine£4 ⛿ Credit cards 1 2 3 4 5 6

★★**Murryfield** 18 Corstorphine Rd (Clansmans) ☎031–337 2207 District plan **47**
An attractive ivy-clad building in residential area of

city close to Rugby International Ground.
22rm(7⇌⋒) ☽ CTV CTV in bedrooms 40P
Last dinner 10pm ✿ ⊻ sB&B£11.50
sB&B⇌⋒£13.50 dB&B£19.50 dB&B⇌⋒£22.50
Lunch£2.45–£3.75 High Tea£1.85–£3.15
Dinner£2.45–£3.75 Wine£2.80 ⊟
Credit cards ① ② ③ ⑤

★★Old Waverley Princes St (Scottish Highlands)
☎031–556 4648 Telex no 778215 Central plan **23**
72rm(52⇌⋒) Lift ☽ CTV ℙ Last dinner 8.45pm ✿
⊻ S% sB&B£13.30–£15.10
sB&B⇌⋒£16.05–£17.95 dB&B£21–£24.60
dB&B⇌⋒£26.50–£30.30 Bar lunch£1.50–£2.50
Tea40p–£1.30 Dinner£6.25 Wine£3.25 ⊟
xmas Credit cards ① ② ③ ④ ⑤ ⑥

★★St Andrews 8–10 South St Andrew Street
☎031–556 8774 Central plan **28**
A traditional hotel, set in the city centre, just off Princes Street.
40rm(9⇌⋒) Lift ☽ ⅏ CTV CTV available in bedrooms
ℙ ♉Scottish & French. Last dinner 9pm ✿
sB&B£13–£16 sB&B⇌⋒£15–£18
dB&B£22–£28 dB&B⇌⋒£26–£32
Lunch£3.50–£4 Dinner£4–£4.50 Wine£2.85 ⊟
Credit cards ① ② ③ ④

★★*Scotia* 5–11 Great King St (Inter-Hotel)
☎31–556 3266 Telex no 727572 Central plan **29**
48rm)15⇌⋒) Lift ☽ ⅏ CTV Last dinner 9pm ✿ ⊟
Credit cards ① ② ③ ④ ⑤ ⑥

★Georgian 5–6 Dean Ter ☎031–332 4520
Central plan **15**
12rm(5⇌⋒) TV available in bedrooms ℙ ⇌
Last dinner 7pm S% sB&B£10–£12.50
dB&B£17.50–£15 dB&B⇌⋒£20–£23
Bar lunch£3–£4.50 Dinner£4.50–£6 Wine£3.90
⊟

★Gordon 7–9 Royal Circus ☎031–225 3000
Central plan **16**
Closed Nov–Mar; CTV 7⌂ ⇌ Last dinner 7pm ✿
⊻ S% sB&B£11.50–£14 dB&B£17.25–£22
Tea46p Dinner£4–£4.50 Wine£3

XXXXPrestonfield House Priestfield Rd ☎031-667 8000 District plan **51**
200P bedrooms available ♉French & Italian.
Last dinner 10.30pm ✱Lunch£9.50alc
Dinner£9.50alc Wine£2.95
Credit cards ① ② ③ ④ ⑤

XXXCafé Royal West Register St ☎031–556 4124
Central plan **2**
Closed Sun; 150seats ℙ ♉French.
Last dinner 10pm Lunch£3.60 Dinner£10alc
Wine£2.99 Credit cards ① ② ③ ④ ⑤ ⑥

XXXRainbow Drum Brae South ☎031–339 8262
District plan **52**
Modern restaurant and bars set on hillside overlooking city, towards Pentland Hills.
Closed Sun; 80seats 80P live music & dancing mthly
Last dinner 9.45pm ✱Lunch £3 Dinner£6.50&alc
Wine£2.75 Credit cards ① ② ③ ⑤

XXXRistorante Cosmo 58A North Castle St
☎031–226 6743 Central plan **24**
Italian restaurant situated in new town of Edinburgh, five minutes' walk from Princes St.
Closed Sun, Mon, Xmas Day, New Year's Day, Public Hols & 1–15 Jul; Lunch not served Sat; 62seats ℙ
♉Italian. Last dinner 10pm ✱Lunch£6alc
Dinner£8alc Wine£3.70 Credit cards ① ③ ⑥

XX*Beehive* Grassmarket ☎031–225 7171
Central plan **1**
1st floor restaurant in old stone building, situated in the older part of the city in front of Edinburgh Castle.
Closed Sun; 60seats Disco Fri & Sat ♉Mainly grills.
Last dinner 10.30pm Credit cards ① ② ③ ⑤ ⑥

×**Cousteaus Sea Food** 109 Hanover St
031–226 3355 Central plan**7**
osed Sun, Mon & 1st wk Jan; 53seats P French
a Food. Last dinner 11pm S%
Lunch£3.57&alc Dinner£6–£8&alc Wine£2.95
edit cards 1 2 3 4 5 6

Cramond Inn Cramond Village ☎031–336 2035
strict plan**39**
tractive inn in setting close to harbour. Oak-eamed ceilings and rough east wall.
osed Sun; 60seats 65P Last dinner 10pm
nch£5 Dinner£7alc Wine£2.90
edit cards 1 2 3 4 5

×**Denzler's** 80 Queen St ☎031–226 5467
entral plan**10**
osed Sun, Xmas, 1–2Jan & Public Hols; 130seats
Swiss. Last dinner 9.45pm Lunch£6.60&alc
nner£7.50alc Wine£3.50

×**Handsel** 22 Stafford St ☎031–225 5522
entral plan**18**
osed Sun; 58seats British, French & Italian.
ast dinner 9.45pm S% Lunch£3.90alc
inner£3.90alc Wine£3.20

××**Howtowdie** 27A Stafford St ☎031–225 6291
entral plan**19**
osed Sun; 45seats P Scottish & French.
pecialities: Oyster soup, duck in heather honey & ast almonds, pot roast pheasant in apricot.
ast dinner 10.30pm Lunch£7alc Dinner£12alc
ine£3.50 Credit cards 1 2 3 4 5 6

×***Hunters Tryst*** Oxgangs Rd ☎031–445 3132
istrict plan**45**
Modernised former coaching inn.
losed Sun & Mon; 80seats 100P Scottish & nglish. Last dinner 10pm Credit cards 1 2 3 5 6

××**Old Bell Inn** 233 Causewayside ☎031–668 1573
District plan**48**
Closed Sun 40seats P British & French.
Last dinner 10pm ✱Lunch fr£2.75&alc
Dinner£6.50alc Wine£3.80

××**Ristorante Milano** 7 Victoria St ☎031–226 5260
Central plan**25**
Closed Sun; 65seats P Italian. Last dinner 11pm
Lunch£5alc Dinner£7alc Wine£3
Credit cards 2 3 4 5

××**Shamiana** 14 Brongham St ☎031–229 5578
District plan**54**
Closed Sun, Xmas day & New Year's day; 42seats P North Indian. Last dinner 11.30pm Dinner£7alc
Wine£2.50 Credit cards 1 2 3 4 5

××***Town & Country*** 72 Rose St, North Ln
☎031–225 3106 Central plan**31**
Closed Sun; 30seats International.
Last dinner 11pm Credit cards 1 2 3 5

××***Vitos*** 109 Fountain Bridge ☎031–229 2747
Central plan**32**
Lunch served Sun only; Dinner not served Sun; 45seats Italian. Last dinner 11pm
Credit cards 1 2 3

×**Anatolian** 13 Dalry Rd ☎031–346 0204 District plan**33**
Closed Sun; Lunch not served; 32seats Turkish.
Last dinner 11.30pm Dinner£6.50alc Wine£3.30
Credit cards 2 3 5

×**Casa Española** 61–65 Rose St ☎031–225 5979
Central plan**5**
Closed Sun & Public Hols; 65seats Spanish.
Last dinner 10.40pm ✱Lunch£2.50&alc
Dinner£5alc Wine£2.50 Credit cards 1 3 6

E

×***Casa Siciliana*** 11 Lochrin Ter ☎031–229 1690 Central plan**6**
Closed Sun; 50seats ♀International. Last dinner 11pm Credit card 2

×**Le Caveau** 13B Dundas St ☎031–556 5707 Central plan**8**
Closed Sun & 1st 2wks; 50seats P ♀French. Last dinner 10pm Lunch£4.50alc Dinner£5.50alc

×**Chez Julie** 110 Raeburn Pl ☎031–332 2827 District plan**37**
Closed Sun, Xmas, 1–2Jan; Dinner not served Mon; 38seats P ♀British & French. Last dinner 10pm ✱Lunch£2.15–£2.65&alc Dinner£5.50alc Wine£2

×***Creperie Restaurant Française*** 8A Grindley St ☎031–229 5405 Central plan**9**
Closed Sun & Mon; 45seats bedrooms available ♀French. Last dinner 10.50pm

×**Doric Tavern** 15/16 Market St ☎031–225 1084 Central plan**11**
Closed Sun; 44seats P ♀Scottish & French. Last dinner 9.30pm Lunch fr£1.20&alc Dinner fr£2&alc Wine£2.80

×**Edinburgh Rendezvous** 10A Queensferry St ☎031–225 2023 Central plan**12**
Closed 25 & 26Dec; 200seats P ♀Pekinese. Last dinner 11.30pm ✱Lunch fr£1.20&alc Dinner fr£3.50&alc Wine£2.30 Credit cards 2 5

❀×**Flappers** 8 West Maitland St ☎031–228 1001 Central plan**13**
Closed Sun; Lunch not served Sat; 32seats P ♀French & Italian. Specialities: Scaloppine Fantasia, Entrecôte de Boeuf Madagascar, Scampi Breva. Last dinner 10.45pm ✱Lunch£7.50alc Dinner£7.50alc Wine£3.20 Credit card 2

×**Rosie's** Jackson's Cl, 209 High St ☎031–225 8748 Central plan**26**
Closed Sun; 40seats P Last dinner 10.30pm ✱Lunch£6alc Dinner£6alc Wine£3.50

×**Snobs** 1 Dean Bank Ln ☎031–332 0003 Central plan**30**
Closed Sun, Xmas Day & New Year Day; 26seats ♀Italian. Last dinner 11pm Lunch£5.50alc Dinner£7alc Wine£3.05 Credit cards 1 2

EDZELL Tayside *Angus* Map**15** NO56

★★★***Glen Esk*** High St ☎319
24rm(10⇌ ⫪) 𝍖 CTV 100P 8⌂ ⛟ ⚓ ⛳18 ⥬ Music & dancing wkly Last dinner 9pm ⛫ ⊈

★★**Central** ☎218
A small three-storey hotel, standing in a quiet street in this village which lies to the south of the Grampian Mountains.
24rm(2⇌ ⫪) ⊞ 𝍖 CTV 80P 2⌂ ⚓ Last dinner 9pm ⛫ ⊈ sB&B£7 sB&B⇌ ⫪£8.25 dB&B£13.90 dB&B⇌ ⫪£14.45 Lunch£1.90–£2.10 Tea85p High Tea£1.75–£2.50 Dinner£2.50–£3&alc Wine£2.50

★★***Panmure Arms*** High St (Inter-Hotel) ☎420 Telex no 76534
Attractive mock Tudor-style hotel situated in quiet village on edge of the Highlands.
17rm(12⇌ ⫪) 1⊟ ☽ 𝍖 CTV TV available in bedrooms 40P ⥬ squash billiards sauna bath Live music & dancing wkly Last dinner 9pm ⛫ ⊟ Credit cards 3 5

ELGIN Grampian *Moray* Map**15** NJ26

☆☆☆**Eight Acres** Sheriffmill ☎3077
45⇌ ⫪ ☽ 𝍖 CTV TV in bedrooms 200P ⚓ Conference facilities available Last dinner 9pm ⛫ sB&B⇌ ⫪ fr£17 dB&B⇌ ⫪ fr£31 Lunch fr£3.50 High Tea fr£4 Dinner fr£6.50 Wine£2.50 ⊟ Credit cards 1 2 3 5 6

★★**Laichmoray** Station Rd ☎2558
Greystone hotel standing opposite goods station in south end of town.
Closed 1Jan; 23rm(3⇌ ⫪) 𝍖 CTV 60P ⚓ ⥬ Live music & dancing Fri & Sat ⌂ Last dinner 8.30pm ⛫ ⊈ S% ✱sB&B£10.26–£11.34 dB&B£19.44–£21.60 dB&B⇌ ⫪£19.44–£21.60 Lunch£2.70–£3.24 Tea43–65p High Tea£1.30–£3.78 Dinner£5.40–£6.48 Credit cards 1 3 5

★***Grove*** Pluscarden Rd ☎2958
7rm CTV 10P ⚓ Last dinner 8.30pm ⛫ ⊈ ⊟ Credit cards 1 2 3

★**St Leonards** Duff Av ☎7350
Converted private house standing in own grounds in residential area of town.
17rm(8⇌ ⫪) 𝍖 CTV 60P ⚓ ⌂ ♀Scottish, English & French. Last dinner 8.30pm ⛫ ⊈ S% sB&B£8 sB&B⇌ ⫪£10 dB&B£15 dB&B⇌ ⫪£19 Lunch£1.75–£2 Tea60p High Tea£1.50–£3.50 Dinner£4.50 Wine£3 *xmas*

××**Enrico's** 15 Grey Friars St ☎2849
Closed Sun; 66seats P ♀International. Last dinner 10pm ✱Lunch fr£1.62&alc Dinner£5–£10 Credit cards 3 5

ELIE Fife *Fife* Map**12** NO40

★★**Golf** Bank St ☎330209
19rm(7⇌ ⫪) 𝍖 CTV 50P ⛟ ⚓ Live music & dancing wkly Cabaret wkly Last dinner 9pm ⛫ ⊈ ✱sB&B£7.29–£9.72 dB&B£14.58–£29.16 dB&B⇌ ⫪£16.74–£31.32 Bar lunch£1.40 Tea£1 High Tea£2.50 Dinner£4.50&alc Wine£2.30 ⊟ *xmas* Credit cards 1 3 6

×**Upstairs Downstairs** 51 High St ☎330374
30seats 8P bedrooms available ♀Scottish & French. Last dinner 7.30pm Lunch£1.65–£1.85 Tea£1.25

igh Tea£2.10–£3.25 Dinner£4–£4.50&alc Wine£2.75

LLON Grampian *Aberdeenshire* Map**15** NJ93
☆☆**Ellon Ladbroke Mercury Motor Inn**
(Ladbroke) ☎20666 Telex no739200
40⇌⋒ ☽ 🕅CTV available in bedrooms 100P
Conference facilities available Last dinner10pm ♈
☋ sB&B⇌⋒£18–£20.50
dB&B⇌⋒£24.50–£29 Lunch fr£4.50&alc
Dinner fr£5&alc Wine£3.20 ☰
Credit cards 1 2 3 4 5 6

Buchan ☎20208
7rm(14⇌⋒) CTV TV available in bedrooms 60P
Last dinner6.30pm ♈ ☋ S% sB&B£6.62
sB&B⇌⋒£8.77 dB&B£17.54 dB&B⇌⋒£20.70
Lunch£1.90 Tea85p High Tea£1.80 Dinner£2.75
Wine£3.50

★**New Inn** Market St ☎20425
12rm(2⇌⋒) 🕅CTV 68P High Tea7pm ♈ ☋ S%
✻sB&B£7–£8 sB&B⇌⋒£8–£8.50
dB&B£14–£16 dB&B⇌⋒£16–£17
Lunch£1.35–£2 Tea45–55p High Tea£2
Wine£2.56 Credit cards 1 2 3 5

ERSKINE Strathclyde *Renfrewshire* Map**11** NS47
☆☆☆☆**Glasgow EuroCrest** North Bar, Inchinnan
(Crest) ☎041–812 0123 Telex no35353
200⇌⋒ Lift ☽ ▦ 🕅CTV in bedrooms 300P ♣ ♿
Conference facilities available ♡French.
Last dinner10pm ♈ ☋ S% ✻sB&B⇌⋒£17.06
dB&B⇌⋒£25.59 Continental breakfast ☰
Credit cards 1 2 3 4 5 6

E

E

ETTRICK BRIDGE Borders *Selkirkshire* Map**11** NT32
★★Ettrick Shaws Lodge ☎229
Closed Nov–Apr; 6⇌ 1 CTV 20P
Scottish & Continental. Last dinner 8pm
sB&B⇌£18 dB&B⇌£29 Lunch£7alc
Tea75p Dinner£5&alc Wine£3.50
Credit cards 1 2 5

EVANTON Highland *Ross & Cromarty* Map**14** NH66
★★*Novar Arms* ☎210
Two-storey building standing alongside main road in centre of village.
14rm CTV 20P Last dinner 7.45pm
Credit card 3

FAIRLIE Strathclyde *Ayrshire* Map**10** NS25
✕*Mudhook* Main St ☎432
36 seats Last dinner 10.30pm

FALKIRK Central *Stirlingshire* Map**11** NS87
☆☆☆*Park* Arnot Hill, Camelon Rd (Reo Stakis)
☎28331
55⇌ Lift CTV TV available in bedrooms
200P Live music & dancing Sat Cabaret Sat
Conference facilities available Last dinner 10pm
Credit cards 1 2 3 4 5 6

✕✕*Hatherley* Arnothill Ln ☎25328
Closed Sun; Lunch not served Wed; 32 seats 25P
Danish. Last dinner 9.30pm

FALKLAND Fife *Fife* Map**11** NO20
✕✕Covenanter ☎224
Closed Mon & last 2wks Jul; 40 seats
bedrooms available French. Last dinner 9pm S%
Lunch£2.80 Dinner£5.60alc Wine£2.85

FEARNAN Tayside *Perthshire* Map**11** NN74
★Tigh-an-Loan ☎Kenmore249
Closed Oct–Mar; 10rm TV 20P
Last dinner 7pm sB&B£7.50 dB&B£15
Bar lunch£2 Tea£1 Dinner£4.50 Wine£3
xmas

FENWICK Strathclyde *Ayrshire* Map**11** NS44
★★Fenwick ☎478
12rm(2⇌) CTV CTV in bedrooms 120P
Disco Sun Live music & dancing Sat Cabaret Thu
International. Last dinner 9.30pm S%
sB&B£10 sB&B⇌£11 dB&B£17.50
dB&B⇌£17.50 Lunch£2.75 Tea30–50p
Dinner£7alc Wine£4 Credit cards 1 5

FOCHABERS Grampian *Moray* Map**15** NJ35
★★Gordon Arms ☎820508
15rm(7⇌) Annexe: 2⇌ CTV CTV available in
bedrooms 50P Last dinner 9.30pm
sB&B£14–£18 sB&B⇌£16–£20
dB&B£24–£28 dB&B⇌£26–£30
Lunch fr£2.50 Tea fr£1.50 High Tea fr£2.50
Dinner fr£6 Wine£2.80

FORFAR Tayside *Angus* Map**15** NO45
★★*County* Castle St ☎2878
10rm CTV Last dinner 9pm

★★Royal Castle St ☎62691
Closed 1 & 2 Jan; 21rm(10⇌) CTV 20P Disco
Fri, Sat & Sun International. Last dinner 10pm
S% sB&B fr£10.95 sB&B⇌ fr£13.25
dB&B fr£19.55 dB&B⇌ fr£29.25
Lunch£2.75–£4.25 High Tea£2.35–£4.15
Dinner£5.45&alc Wine£2.55

FORRES Grampian *Moray* Map**14** NJ05
★★Ramnee ☎72410
Fine, two-storey stone villa standing back from main road in well kept grounds.
Closed Jan; 20rm(10⇌) CTV TV available in
bedrooms 50P 1 French & Italian.
Last dinner 9pm sB&B fr£9.72
sB&B⇌ fr£11.25 dB&B fr£18.36
dB&B⇌ fr£21.06 Bar lunch fr £1 Dinner fr£5.40
Wine£2.70

★★Royal ☎72617
Three-storey stone building with wrought iron entrance porch and balcony, standing in quiet area of the town opposite market and adjacent to station.
Closed Xmas and New year; 20rm CTV 40P
billiards Live music & dancing twice wkly
Last dinner 8.30pm ✻sB&B fr£9.18
dB&B fr£18.36 Lunch£2.87 Tea90p
High Tea£2.19–£4.26 Dinner£5.75 Wine£2.41
Credit cards 1 6

✕✕*Elizabethan Inn* Mundole ☎2526
Located west of Forres this converted and extended cottage stands on the banks of the River Findhorn.
Closed last 2wks May & last wk Sept–1st wk Oct;
Dinner not served Wed; 45 seats 30P bedrooms
available Last dinner 8.30pm

FORSINARD Highland *Sutherland* Map**14** NC84
★★Forsinard ☎Halladale221
13rm(11⇌) TV 30P Last dinner 8.30pm
sB&B£13 sB&B⇌£13 dB&B£26
dB&B⇌£26 Lunch£4 Tea95p High Tea£3.75
Dinner£6.60 Wine£2.60

FORT AUGUSTUS Highland *Inverness-shire* Map**14**
NH30
★★Inchnacardoch Lodge Loch Ness (Inter-Hotel)
☎6258
17rm 1 TV 50P 2 Live music & dancing
Sat Last dinner 8.30pm S%
sB&B£8.80–£9.90 dB&B£17.60–£19.60
Lunch£2–£2.50 Tea30–60p
Dinner£4–£4.50&alc Wine£2.10 *xmas*
Credit cards 1 2 3 4 5 6

★Lovat Arms ☎6206
eat, stone-built house with extensive views of Loch Ness and surrounding mountains.
losed Nov; 25rm(3⇌ ⋒) Annexe: 6rm CTV 50P ⚘ ast dinner 8pm ♁ ⊻ S% sB&B£10–£11 sB&B⇌ ⋒£11.50–£12.50 dB&B£20–£22 dB&B⇌ ⋒£23–£25 Lunch fr£3.50 Tea fr90p Dinner fr £5.50 Wine£1.95 ⊟

FORT WILLIAM Highland *Inverness-shire*
Map **14** NN17

❀❀❀★★★★ **Inverlochy Castle** (3m NE A82)
☎2177
See page 59 for details

★★★**Alexandra** ☎2241 Telex no 778869
Conversion and extension of purpose-built Victorian stone hotel standing on corner site. Situated just outside main shopping centre of town and adjacent to railway station.
89rm(68⇌ ⋒) Lift ☽ CTV 40P Last dinner 8.30pm ♁ ⊻ S% sB&B£10–£15 sB&B⇌ ⋒£11.50–£18 dB&B£20–£24 dB&B⇌ ⋒£23–£29 Lunch£3.50 Dinner£5.85 Wine£3.25 ⊟ Credit cards 1 2 3 5 6

☆☆☆**Ladbroke Mercury Motor Inn** (on A82) (Ladbroke) ☎3117
Modern low rise building standing by main road, on southern outskirts of town, with splendid hill views over Loch Linnhe.
60⇌ ⋒ ☽ TV available in bedrooms 60P sauna bath Last dinner 10pm ♁ ⊻ sB&B⇌ ⋒£15.50–£17.50 dB&B⇌ ⋒£27–£30 Lunch fr£4.50&alc Dinner fr£5&alc Wine£3.20 ⊟ Credit cards 1 2 3 4 5 6

★★**Grand** Gordon Sq ☎2928
This pre-war, three-storey hotel, stands on a corner site in the shopping centre.
31rm(18⇌ ⋒) ☽ CTV 25P Last dinner 8.30pm ♁ ⊻ sB&B£8–£12.50 sB&B⇌ ⋒£7.50–£15

dB&B£15–£23 dB&B⇌⋒£15–£25 Lunch£2.75–£3.50 Dinner£4.50–£6.50 Wine£2.20 ⊟ Credit cards 1 2 3 5 6

★★**Highland** Union Rd ☎2291
An imposing Victorian structure with ornate panelled main hall and stairway. Hill-side situation with panoramic views over town, Lock Linnhe and Ardgour Hills.
Closed Nov–Mar; 51rm(12⇌⋒) ☽ ⋈ CTV ⊘ 18P ⚓ Live music & dancing twice wkly Cabaret wkly Last dinner8.15pm ♡ ☐ S% sB&B£9–£11 sB&B⇌⋒£10.30–£12.30 dB&B£17–£21 dB&B⇌⋒£19.60–£23.60 Lunch£2–£2.50 Tea60p Dinner£4.50 Wine£2.50 ⊟ Credit cards 1 3

★★**Imperial** Fraser's Sq ☎2040
An extended three-storey Victorian building standing in a side street off the main shopping area, with views over Loch Linnhe.
37rm ⋈ CTV 24P Last dinner8.15pm ♡ ☐ S% *sB&B£6.50–£7.83 dB&B£13–£15.12 Lunch£2.50–£2.80 Tea40–70p High Tea£2.50–£3 Dinner£3.75–£4.30 Wine£2.19 ⊟

★★**Milton** ☎2331 Telex no778869
RS Oct–Apr; 61rm(10⇌⋒) ☽ CTV 100P ⚓ Disco Fri Last dinner8.30pm ♡ ☐ S% sB&B£9.50–£14 sB&B⇌⋒£11–£17 dB&B£19–£22 dB&B⇌⋒£22–£27 Lunch£3.25 Dinner£5.50 Wine£3.25 ♿ Credit cards 1 2 3 5 6

★★**Nevis Bank** Belford Rd ☎2595
23rm(6⇌⋒) ⋈ CTV 20P Last dinner8pm ♡ S% sB&B fr£11.40 dB&B fr£22.80 dB&B⇌⋒fr£27.50 Lunch fr£1.90 Dinner fr£5 Wine£3.40

FOYERS Highland *Inverness-shire* Map **14** NH42
★**Foyers** ☎Gorthleck216
10rm(2⇌⋒) ⋈ CTV 25P 2🏠 ⚘ ⚓ ⚐ Last dinner7.15pm ♡ ☐ S% sB&B£6.50 dB&B£12.50 dB&B⇌⋒£13.50 Lunch fr£2.50 Tea fr75p Dinner fr£3.75&alc Wine£2.80

FRASERBURGH Grampian *Aberdeenshire* Map **15** NJ96
★★**Royal** Broad St ☎2524
15rm(8⇌⋒) ⋈ CTV ⚑ Last dinner8.45pm ♡ sB&B£8–£10 sB&B⇌⋒£10–£12 dB&B£15–£18 dB&B⇌⋒£19–£23 Lunch£2–£2.50 High Tea£1.75–£3.25 Dinner£4.25–£4.75&alc Wine£3

FREUCHIE Fife *Fife* Map **11** NO20
★**Lomond** Parliament Sq ☎Falkland329
9rm ⋈ CTV CTV in bedrooms 60P ♡ Scottish & French. Last dinner9pm ♡ ☐ S% sB&B£8–£10 sB&B⇌⋒£9–£11 dB&B£16–£20 dB&B⇌⋒£18–£22 Lunch£2–£4 Tea40p–£1.25 High Tea£2.30alc Dinner£6.50alc Wine£3.25 ⊟ Credit card 3

GAIRLOCH Highland *Ross & Cromarty* Map **14** NG8
★★★**Gairloch** (Scottish Highlands) ☎2001 Telex no778215
Three storey red sandstone Victorian building standing on the edge of Loch Goil in West Highland village.
Closed 14Oct–24Apr; 50rm(33⇌⋒) Lift ☽ CTV 50P ⚓ ⚘ ⚐ Last dinner9pm ♡ ☐ S% sB&B£13.30–£15.10 sB&B⇌⋒£16.05–£17.95 dB&B£21–£24.60 dB&B⇌⋒£26.50–£30.30 Bar lunch£1.50–£2.50 Tea40p–£1.30&alc Dinner£6.25 Wine£3.25 ⊟ Credit cards 1 2 3 4 5 6

☆☆☆**Gairloch Sands** (Scottish Highlands) ☎2131 Telex no778215
Closed 14Oct–24Apr; 36⇌⋒ ☽ CTV 50P ⚓ Last dinner8.30pm ♡ ☐ S% sB&B⇌⋒£17.95 dB&B⇌⋒£30.30 Lunch£4.10 Tea40p–£1.30 Dinner£6.25&alc Wine£3.25 ⊟ Credit cards 1 2 3 4 5 6

★**Cragg Mor** Charlestown ☎2068
9rm(2⇌⋒) CTV ⊘ 20P ⚘ ⚓ ⚐ Last dinner8pm ♡ ☐ S% *sB&B£8.75–£9.62 dB&B£14.30–£15.73 dB&B⇌⋒£17.50–£19.25 Bar lunch fr60p Tea fr50p Dinner£5.20 Wine£2.50 *xmas* Credit card 6

GALASHIELS Borders *Selkirkshire* Map **12** NT43
★★***Douglas*** Channel St (Open House) ☎2189
Centrally situated in main shopping street, red sandstone faced building with wrought iron work on roof ridges.
40rm(11⇌⋒) Lift ☽ ⋈ CTV TV available in bedrooms 10P 15🏠 Disco wkly Live music 2nights wkly Last dinner10pm ♡ ☐ ⊟ Credit cards 1 2 3 4 6

★★**Kings Knowes** Selkirk Rd ☎3478
Red sandstone mansion dating from 1869 in nine acres of grounds overlooking River Tweed. Interior reflects Italian influence.
10rm(5⇌⋒) ⋈ CTV CTV in bedrooms 18P ⚘ ⚓ ⚘ Last dinner9.30pm ♡ S% sB&B£16.05 sB&B⇌⋒£17.82 dB&B£21.38 dB&B⇌⋒£23.76 Lunch£5.50alc Dinner£5.50alc Wine£3.50 Credit cards 1 2 5 6

★**Royal** Channel St (Scottish & Newcastle) ☎2918
Three-storey stone building with decorative wrought iron work balcony to second floor, situated in main shopping thoroughfare.
22rm(1⇌⋒) CTV ⚑ Last dinner8.45pm ♡ S% sB&B£8 dB&B£15.50 dB&B⇌⋒£20.50 Lunch£3.50alc Dinner£3.50alc Wine£2.75 ⊟ Credit cards 1 3 6

×**Redgauntlet** 36 Market St ☎2098
Closed Tue; 33seats English, French & Italian. Last dinner 10pm S% Dinner £5alc Wine £3

GARVE Highland *Ross & Cromarty* Map **14** NH36
See also **Aultguish**

★★★**Strathgrave Lodge** ☎204
Closed 2Oct–Apr; 16rm(12) 30P 4 English & Continental. Last dinner 8.30pm *sB&B£10 sB&B£12 dB&B£21 dB&B£22–£24 Bar lunch fr£1&alc Tea fr90p Dinner £6.50 Wine £2.80

★★**Garve** ☎205
Large, three-storey white-painted building standing on main road in shadow of Ben Wyvis.
33rm(16) TV 60P 3 Scottish & French. Last dinner 8.30pm S% *sB&B£8.50–£9.75 sB&B£10–£11.75 dB&B£17–£19.50 dB&B£20–£23.50 Lunch £3.50–£5 Tea 90p–£1.25 High Tea £2.50–£4.50 Dinner £5.50–£7 Wine £2.83 *xmas* Credit cards 1 3

★★**Inchbae Lodge** (5m N A835) ☎Aultguish269
Formerly a shooting lodge.
Closed mid Oct–Mar; 7rm(3) Annexe: 6 35P sB&B£7–£8 sB&B£8–£9 dB&B£14–£16 dB&B£16–£18 Lunch £4–£5 Tea 45p High Tea £2.50–£5 Dinner £6–£7.50 Wine £3.50 Credit card 5

GATEHOUSE OF FLEET Dumfries & Galloway *Kirkcudbrightshire* Map **11** NX55
★★★**Murray Arms** (Best Western) ☎Gatehouse207
Telex no 8814912
A modernised and extended 17th-C posting house. Burns wrote 'Scots wha Hae' whilst staying here.
12rm(10) Annexe: 14rm(6) CTV 20P (hard) Last dinner 9pm S% sB&B£13–£34.50 sB&B£14.50–£16 dB&B£26–£29 dB&B£29–£32 Lunch £2.75 Tea £1 High Tea fr£2.50 Dinner £6&alc Wine £3 *xmas* Credit cards 1 2 3 5

★★**Anwoth** Fleet St ☎Gatehouse217
8rm(3) CTV 15P Last dinner 8pm sB&B£7 sB&B£8.50 dB&B£14 dB&B£17 Bar lunch 60p–£1.60 Tea 50p Dinner £4 Wine £2.69 *xmas* Credit card 6

GIFFNOCK Strathclyde *Renfrewshire* Map **11** NS55
★★★**MacDonald** Eastwood Toll (Thistle)
☎041–638 2225
Modern sandstone building at Eastwood Toll roundabout (A77), on southern outskirts of Glasgow.
58 CTV CTV in bedrooms 200P billiards Live music & dancing Fri & Sat Austrian, French, German & Italian. Last dinner 9.45pm *sB&B£21.90 dB&B£30.80 Lunch £4&alc Dinner £5&alc Wine £3.15 Credit cards 1 2 3 4 5 6

★★**Redhurst** Eastwood Mains Rd (Reo Stakis)
☎041–638 6465
Modern custom-built L-shaped building in residential suburb about 5 miles from Glasgow city centre.
16rm(10) CTV CTV in bedrooms 60P Last dinner 10.30pm *sB&B fr£12 sB&B fr£15 dB&B fr£23 Lunch fr£3.50&alc Tea fr85p Dinner fr£5.10&alc Wine £2.75 Credit cards 1 2 3 5 6

GIFFORD Lothian *East Lothian* Map **12** NT56
★★***Tweeddale Arms*** ☎240
8rm(2) CTV 12P Music & dancing Sat English & French. Last dinner 10pm Credit cards 2 5

★**Goblin Ha'** ☎244
7rm TV Last dinner 9pm S% sB&B£7.50–£8.20 dB&B£15–£16.40 Lunch £3 Tea 80p High Tea £2.70–£3.10 Dinner £4.90–£6.60

GIRVAN Strathclyde *Ayrshire* Map **10** NX19
★★**Kings Arms** Dalrymple St (Clansmans) ☎3322
31rm(6) CTV CTV available in bedrooms 60P European. Last dinner 10pm *sB&B£8.50 sB&B£9.60 dB&B£17 dB&B£19.20 Lunch £2.75alc Tea 30palc Dinner £4.50alc Wine £2.70 Credit cards 1 2 3 5

★**Ailsa Arms** Old St (Clansmans) ☎3754
8rm CTV 30P Mainly grills. High Tea 6.45pm *sB&B£7.50 dB&B£15 Bar lunch 45p–£1.50 High Tea £1.80–£3.15 Wine £1.65 Credit cards 1 3

★**Carrick Arms** Dalrymple St ☎2261
7rm CTV 18P High Tea 7.30pm S% sB&B£5.25–£6.95 dB&B£10–£12.95 Lunch £1.95–£5 High Tea £2–£4 Credit cards 1 2 5

★**Hamilton Arms** (Osprey) ☎2182
11rm CTV 8P 1 S% sB&B fr£8 dB&B fr£16 Lunch £1.85–£2.50 High Tea £1.60–£1.90 Dinner £2.50–£4.20 Wine £2.89

GLAMIS Tayside *Angus* Map **15** NO34
××**Strathmore Arms** ☎248
Situated in Strathmore Valley, this old coaching inn lies near Glamis Castle.
Closed Sun; 80seats 50P Last dinner 9pm Lunch £3–£3.50&alc Dinner £5.50alc Wine £3.25

G

GLASGOW Strathclyde *Lanarkshire* Map**11** NS56
See plan

★★★★**Albany** Bothwell St (Trusthouse Forte) ☎041–248 2526 Telex no 77440 Plan**1**
248 Lift CTV CTV in bedrooms 25P Last dinner 10.45pm S% sB&B £29.50 dB&B £39.50 Credit cards 1 2 3 4 5 6

★★★★**Central** Gordon St (British Transport) ☎041–221 9680 Telex no 777771 Plan**7**
(Rosette awarded to the Malmaison Restaurant)
204rm(163) Lift TV in bedrooms English & French. Last dinner 10.45pm S% ✱sB&B fr£30 dB&B fr£41 Wine£3.50 Credit cards 1 2 3 4 5 6

★★★**Bellahouston** 517 Paisley Rd West (Swallow) ☎041–427 3146 Telex no 778795 Not on plan
72 Lift CTV in bedrooms 150P Conference facilities available Last dinner 9.20pm S% sB&B fr£19.15 dB&B fr£27 Credit cards 1 2 3 5

☆☆☆**Glasgow Centre,** Argyle St, Anderston (Centre) ☎041–248 2355 Telex no 779652 Plan**12**
125 Lift TV in bedrooms Conference facilities available Last dinner 9.15pm S% ✱sB&B £15.75 dB&B £20.25 Continental breakfast Lunch£2.80 Dinner£2.80 Wine£3.40 Credit cards 1 2 3 4 5 6

☆☆☆**Ingram** Ingram St (Reo Stakis) ☎041–248 4401 Plan**13**
90 Lift CTV in bedrooms 30P Disco nightly Conference facilities available French. Last dinner 9.45pm S% ✱sB&B £18 dB&B £28 Lunch£3.25&alc Dinner£4.85&alc Credit cards 1 2 3 5

★★★**North British** George Sq (British Transport) ☎041–332 6711 Telex no 778147 Plan**15**
Gracious, white five-storey building near City chambers; overlooks gardens of square.
130rm(100) Lift TV in bedrooms Conference facilities available English & French. Last dinner 9.30pm S% ✱sB&B fr£20 dB&B fr£34 *xmas* Credit cards 1 2 3 4 5 6

☆☆☆***Pond*** Great Western Rd (Reo Stakis) ☎041–334 8161 Not on plan
Modern hotel on north-west suburbs of city.
137 Lift CTV TV available in bedrooms 150P Live music & dancing Sat (winter) British & French. Last dinner 10.30pm Credit cards 1 2 3 5

★★★**Royal Stuart** 316 Clyde St ☎041–248 4261 Telex no 778833 Plan**21**
115rm(75) Lift CTV CTV in bedrooms 30P Live music & dancing wkly Cabaret wkly Conference facilities available International. Last dinner 9.30pm sB&B £12 sB&B £15.50 dB&B £22 Lunch£2.75&alc Dinner£3.75&alc Credit cards 1 2 3 4 5 6

★★★**Tinto Firs** 470 Kilmarnock Rd (Thistle) ☎041–637 2353 Not on plan
This modern hotel is situated on the A77, in a residential area south of the city.
30rm(24) CTV in bedrooms 40P Live music & dancing Fri French. Last dinner 9.30pm S% ✱sB&B fr£17.90 sB&B fr£20.90 dB&B fr£29.80 Lunch fr£3.80&alc Tea fr£1 Dinner fr£5.40&alc Wine£2.85 Credit cards 1 2 3 4 5 6

★★**Blythswood** 320 Argyle St (Mount Charlotte) ☎041–221 4133 Plan**5**
60rm(4) Lift CTV CTV available in bedrooms Last dinner 7.45pm S% sB&B fr£10 sB&B fr£11.50 dB&B fr£18 dB&B fr£22 Lunch fr£2.50&alc Tea fr£1.20 High Tea fr£1.75 Dinner fr£3 Wine£3.50 *xmas* Credit cards 1 2 3 5

★★***Ewington*** Queens Dr, Queens Park ☎041–423 1152 Not on plan
48rm(12) Lift CTV billiards Last dinner 8.30pm

★★**Lorne** 923 Sauchiehall St (Open House) ☎041–334 4891 Not on plan
86rm(48) Lift CTV in bedrooms 8P 22 Mainly grills. Last dinner 9.30pm S% ✱sB&B £13 sB&B £16 dB&B £20 dB&B £24 Lunch£4alc Dinner£4.50alc Wine£2.50 Credit cards 1 2 3 4 5 6

★★**Newlands** 260 Kilmarnock Rd (Scottish & Newcastle) ☎041–632 9171 Not on plan
Set in the southern suburbs of the city, this small hotel is conveniently situated on the A77 road and adjacent to a commuter station.
17rm(15) CTV Last dinner 9.30pm S% ✱sB&B £9.30 dB&B £17.20 Lunch£3.50alc Tea£1 Dinner£3.50alc Wine£2.75 Credit cards 1 2 3 5

★★**Royal** 106 Sauchiehall Rd (Osprey) ☎041–332 3416 Plan**20**
Centrally situated on pedestrianised section of Sauchiehall Street.
45rm(15) Lift CTV CTV available in bedrooms Last dinner 8.45pm S% ✱sB&B £11 sB&B £14 dB&B £17 dB&B £21 Lunch fr£2.60 Tea fr30p High Tea fr£2.60 Dinner fr£3.90 Wine£2.40 *xmas* Credit cards 1 2 3 5

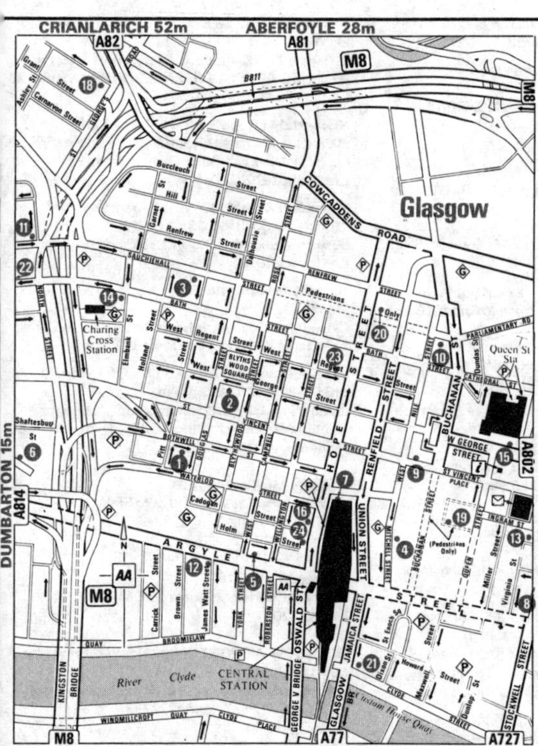

1 Albany★★★★
2 Ambassador✕✕✕
3 Andreas✕✕
4 L'Ariosto✕✕
5 Blythswood★★
6 Buttery✕
7 Central❁★★★★
8 Colonial❁✕✕
9 Danish Food Centre✕
10 Ferrari✕✕
11 Fountain✕✕✕✕
12 Glasgow Centre☆☆☆
13 Ingram☆☆☆
14 Loon Fung✕
15 North British★★★
16 Oriental✕
18 Pendulum✕✕
19 Le Provençal✕✕
20 Royal★★
21 Royal Stuart★★★
23 Tandoor Mahal✕
24 Trattoria Lanterna✕

☆☆**Shawlands** 30 Shawlands Sq, Shawlands Shopping Centre (Open House) ☎041–632 9226 Not on plan
Closed 25, 26 & 31 Dec, 1 Jan; RS Sun; 20⇌⋒ Lift ☽ ▦ ⛿ TV in bedrooms P ♀French.
Last dinner 8.45pm ♁ ♖ S% ✱sB&B⇌⋒£14 dB&B⇌⋒£22 Bar lunch £1–£1.75 Tea 40–70p Dinner £3.50–£5.50alc Wine £3
Credit cards 1 2 3 4 5 6

★★**Sherbrooke** 11 Sherbrooke Av, Pollokshields ☎041–427 4227 Not on plan
7rm(5⇌⋒) ⛿ CTV CTV in bedrooms ⊘ 50P ⌗ ⚓ ♀Mainly grills. Last dinner 10.30pm ♁ sB&B£13 sB&B⇌⋒£16 dB&B£19.50 dB&B⇌⋒£24
Lunch £3–£4&alc Dinner £4.75&alc Wine £3.50

★★***Stepps*** 3 Stepps Rd (Scottish & Newcastle) ☎041–774 3434 Not on plan
24rm(17⇌⋒) Lift ☽ ⛿ CTV 40P ⌗
Last dinner 9.45pm ♁ Credit cards 1 2 3 5

★***Levern Water*** 231 Cleaves Rd, Nitshill (6m SW A726) (Scottish & Newcastle) ☎041–881 5791 Not on plan
Small modern hotel forming part of Sitolliner precinct in southern suburb of Glasgow.
10⇌⋒ ☽ CTV ⊘ 6P ♀Scottish & English.
Last dinner 9pm Credit cards 2 3 5

✕✕✕✕***Fountain*** Charing Cross ☎041–332 6396 Plan **11**
Closed Sun, last 2wks Jul, Public Hols; Lunch not served Sat; 50seats 22P Live music Tue–Sat
Last dinner 10.15pm Credit cards 1 2 3 4 5

✕✕✕**Ambassador** 19–20 Blythswood Sq ☎041–221 2034 Plan **2**
Closed Sun; 100seats **P** ♀French & Italian.
Last dinner 11pm S% Lunch £4.10&alc Wine £3.65 Credit cards 1 2 3 5

✕✕**Andreas** 377 Sauchiehall St ☎041–331 1277 Plan **3**
Lunch not served Sat & Sun; 60seats **P** ♀French & Greek. Last dinner 1am S% Lunch fr £1.75&alc Dinner £6–£10 Wine £3.50
Credit cards 1 2 3 4 5 6

✕✕**L'Ariosto** Mitchell St ☎041–221 0971 Plan **4**
Closed Sun; 150seats Live music & dancing 6nights wkly ♀French & Italian. Last dinner 10.45pm S% Lunch £3&alc Dinner £8.50alc
Credit cards 1 2 3 4 5 6

❁✕✕**Colonial** 25 High St ☎041–552 1923 Plan **8**
Closed Sun & Public Hols; 68seats **P** ♀French.
Last dinner 11pm S% Lunch £3.20–£6&alc Dinner £7alc Wine £1 Credit cards 1 2 3 5 6

✕✕**Duke of Touraine** 1342 Duke St ☎041–554 4158 Not on plan
Closed Sun; 85seats 10P Disco Tue Live music & dancing Wed, Thu, Fri & Sat Cabaret mthly ♀English, French & Italian. Last dinner 10.45pm
Lunch £2.20&alc Dinner £2.75–£5.75&alc Wine £3.20 Credit cards 1 2 3 5

✕✕**Ferrari** Sauchiehall St ☎041–332 8414 Plan **10**
Italian restaurant set between shops in pedestrian precinct at east end of Sauchiehall Street.
Closed Sun 25 Dec & 1 Jan; 50seats **P** ♀French & Italian. Last dinner 11.30pm S% ✱Lunch £5alc Dinner £5alc Wine £3.60 Credit cards 1 2 3 5

✕✕***Pendulum*** 17 West Princes St ☎041–332 1709 Plan **18**
Closed 3rd & 4th wk Jul; Lunch not served Sat;

Dinner not served Mon; 50seats French & Italian. Last dinner 10.30pm Credit card 1

××**Le Provençal** 21 Royal Exchange Sq ☎041–221 0798 Plan**19**
Closed Sun & Public Hols; 48seats P French. Last dinner 11pm Lunch £1.20–£4.10 Dinner £3.25–£5.65 Wine £2.95 Credit cards 1 2 3 5

××**Shish Mahal** 45 Gibson St ☎041–334 7899 Not on plan
110seats P Indian & Pakistani. Last dinner 11.30pm Lunch £2alc Dinner £2.75alc Credit cards 1 2 3 5 6

×**Buttery** 654 Argyll St ☎041–221 8188 Plan**6**
Popular restaurant and tavern close to Charing Cross Road complex.
Closed Sun 55seats 100P Continental. Last dinner 9.30pm Lunch £2.50&alc Dinner £3.50&alc Credit card 5

G

×**Danish Food Centre** 50/60 St Vincent Street ☎041–221 0518 Plan**9**
Closed Sun & Public Hols; 100seats bedrooms available Danish. Last dinner 9pm S% *Lunch £4.35alc Dinner £5.80alc Credit cards 1 2 3 5

×**Jasmine House** 124 Busby Rd, Clarkston ☎041–644 3096 Not on plan
100seats 50P Chinese. Last dinner 1.30am (mdnt Sun) Credit cards 1 2 3 5 6

×**Koh-I-Noor** 4 Gibson St ☎041–339 4275 Not on plan
Closed Xmas Day; Unlicensed; corkage charge 102seats P Indian. Last dinner 11.59pm S% Lunch fr £1.40&alc Dinner fr £3.50&alc Credit cards 1 2 3 5 6

×**Loon Fung** 417 Sauchiehall St ☎041–332 1240 Plan**14**
110seats P Cantonese. Last dinner 11.45pm *Lunch £1.02–£1.19 Dinner £2.90alc Wine £3.70 Credit cards 2 5

×**Oriental** 41 Hope St ☎041–221 1950 Plan**16**
60seats P Chinese. Last dinner 11.30pm S% Lunch £1.10–£1.40&alc Dinner £4alc Credit cards 1 2 3 5

×***Tandoor Mahal*** 142 West Regent St ☎041–221 5043 Plan**23**
60seats English & Indian. Last dinner 11.30pm Credit cards 1 6

×**Trattoria Lanterna** 35 Hope St ☎041–221 9160 Plan**24**
Closed Sun; 70seats P bedrooms available Italian. Last dinner 10.30pm Credit cards 2

×**Ubiquitous Chip** Ashton Lane, Off Byres Rd ☎041–334 5007 Not on plan
Closed Sun, 1/2 Jan & last 2 wks Jul; 130seats International. Last dinner 10.45pm *Lunch £3alc Dinner £5alc Wine £1.95

At **Bearsden** (6m NW A81)
☆☆**Burnbrae** Milngavie Rd (Reo Stakis) ☎041–942 5951
15rm (13 ⇌ fl) 70P

At **Stepps** (5m E A80)
☆☆☆**Garfield** (Open House) ☎041–779 2111
21 ⇌ fl 120P

GLASGOW AIRPORT Strathclyde *Renfrewshire*
Map**11** NS46
★★★★**Excelsior** Abbotsinch (Trusthouse Forte) ☎041–887 1212 Telex no 777733

307⇌⋒ Lift ☽ ▦ ⋈ CTV in bedrooms 35P ♿ Conference facilities available Last dinner 10pm ✿ S% sB&B⇌⋒£24.25 dB&B⇌⋒£37.50 ▤ Credit cards 1 2 3 4 5 6

☆☆☆☆**Normandy** (2m NE A8) Inchinnan Rd, Renfrew (Reo Stakis) ☎041–886 4100 Telex no 778897
143⇌⋒ Lift ☽ ▦ ⋈ CTV CTV in bedrooms 800P ♣ Disco nightly Conference facilities available ♡European. Last dinner 11pm ✿ ☐ S% ✱sB&B⇌⋒£19 dB&B⇌⋒£28 Lunch fr£3.30 Tea fr65p High Tea fr£2 Dinner fr£4.85 Wine£3 ▤ *xmas* Credit cards 1 2 3 5

★★★**Dean Park** (3m NE A8) 91 Glasgow Rd, Renfrew ☎041–886 3771 Telex no 779032
130rm(122⇌⋒) ☽ ⋈ CTV CTV available in bedrooms 250P ♣ Live music & dancing Sat Cabaret Wed Conference facilities available ♡French. Last dinner 9.30pm ✿ S% ✱sB&B⇌⋒£16 dB&B⇌⋒£22.50 Lunch£2.95&alc Dinner£3.95&alc Wine£3.15 *xmas* Credit cards 1 2 3 5

★★★**Glynhill** (2m E A741) Paisley Rd, Renfrew ☎041–886 5555
55⇌⋒ ☽ ⋈ CTV CTV in bedrooms 130P Live music & dancing 4 nights wkly Conference facilities available ♡Continental. Last dinner 10pm ✿ ☐ S% sB&B£10.80 sB&B⇌⋒£14.60 dB&B£15.15 dB&B⇌⋒£19.45 Lunch fr£3&alc Tea fr40p High Tea fr£3 Dinner fr£5&alc Wine£3.50 ▤ Credit cards 1 3

★★**Rockfield** (2m SE A741) 125 Renfrew Rd, Paisley (Clansmans) ☎041–889 6182
19rm(17⇌⋒) ⋈ CTV CTV in bedrooms 75P ♡European. Last dinner 9pm ✿ ☐ ✱sB&B£10.50 sB&B⇌⋒£13.20 dB&B£17.20 dB&B⇌⋒£20.50 Lunch£4.20alc Dinner£4.20alc Wine£2.80 ▤ Credit cards 1 2 3 5

★★***Silver Thread*** (3m S) Paisley (Scottish & Newcastle) ☎041–887 2196
A modern brick and concrete-built hotel, situated about five minutes' walk from the town centre.
14⇌⋒ Lift ⋈ CTV 30P Disco 5nights wkly Live music 4nights wkly Last dinner 10pm ✿ ▤ Credit cards 1 2 3 5 6

☆☆**Watermill** (3m S) Lonend, Paisley (Reo Stakis) ☎041–889 3201 Telex no 778704
Pleasantly located in the centre of Paisley, this four-storey hotel is a conversion from the original mill and stable buildings. A waterfall at the rear adds to its character.
51⇌⋒ Lift ☽ ⋈ CTV CTV in bedrooms 100P ♡Mainly grills. Last dinner 10.15pm ✿ ☐ S% ✱sB&B⇌⋒£16 dB&B⇌⋒£24 Lunch£2.75alc Tea75palc High Tea£3alc Dinner£3alc Wine£2.70 ▤ *xmas* Credit cards 1 2 3 5

XXX**Ristorante Piccolo Mondo** (3m NE) 63 Hairst St, Renfrew ☎041–886 3055
Italian restaurant and function suite with modern red-brick façade; set on corner site in town centre.
Closed Sun; 300seats 60P Live music & dancing nightly Cabaret Wed–Fri ♡Italian. Last dinner 10.15pm ✱Lunch£2.75&alc Dinner£4.75–£5.75&alc Credit cards 1 2 3 5 6

XX**Shish Mahal** (3m S) 8 New St, Paisley ☎041–887 6877
78seats ℙ ♡European & Indian. Last dinner 11.20pm ✱Lunch£1.15&alc Dinner£2.80alc Wine£3 Credit cards 1 2 3

At **Erskine** (4m NW A8)
☆☆☆☆**Glasgow EuroCrest** North Bar, Inchannan ☎041–812 0123
200⇌⋒ 300P

GLENBORRODALE Highland *Argyll* Map **13** NM66
❀★★**Clan Morrison** ☎232
(Rosette awarded for dinner only)
Closed end Oct–mid Mar; 6⇌⋒ ⋈ 60P ⛟ ♣ ⌂ ♿ Specialities: Duckling with liqueur sauce, roast haunch of venison with port/brandy sauce, sole belle meunière. Last dinner 8pm ✿ ☐ S% sB&B⇌⋒£12.10 dB&B⇌⋒£22.20 Bar lunch£1–£3 Dinner£8.47 Wine£2.20

★★♜**Glenborrodale Castle** ☎266
Closed Nov–Mar; 21rm(2⇌⋒) Annexe: 3rm CTV in bedrooms 40P ⛟ ♣ Last dinner 9.30pm ✿ ☐ S% ✱sB&B£12–£13.50 dB&B£20–£21 dB&B⇌⋒£26–£27.50 Bar lunch£2.50 Tea45–90p High Tea fr£1.50 Dinner£5–£7 Wine£2.80 ▤ Credit cards 1 2 3 4 5 6

GLENCAPLE Dumfries & Galloway *Dumfriesshire* Map **11** NX96
★★**Nith** ☎213
10rm(3⇌⋒) TV available in bedrooms 60P Disco Sat Live music & dancing Sat Last dinner 8.30pm ✿ ☐ dB&B£7 sB&B⇌⋒£8 dB&B£14 dB&B⇌⋒£15 Bar lunch£1.60 Tea90p High Tea£2.20–£3.75 Dinner£3.95 Wine£2.70 ▤ Credit card 1

GLENCARSE Tayside *Perthshire* Map **11** NO12
❀★★★**Newton House** ☎250
Former dower house situated on the edge of the village, bordering the main Perth to Dundee road.
7rm ⋈ CTV ⊘ 30P ⛟ ♣ ♡Scottish & French. Last dinner 9pm ✿ sB&B£10.03–£10.62 dB&B£17.70–£18.29 Lunch£3.54–£4.72&alc Dinner£8alc Wine£2.50

GLENCOE Highland *Argyll* Map **14** NN15
★★***Glencoe*** ☎Ballachulish 245
A roadside, painted stone building, which has been modernised and extended. It stands at the head of

Glencoe overlooking Loch Leven and the mountains. 13rm(2⇌ ⋒) Annexe: 5rm ⋈ CTV 30P ⚓ Last dinner 7.45pm ✿ ☑

★★Kings House (12m SE A82) ☎Kingshouse259 *Stone inn dating from early 1700's; used as a barracks for George III after Battle of Culloden (1746).* Closed Nov–Feb; 22rm(10⇌ ⋒) 100P ⚓ ♿ ♡Scottish & Newcastle. Last dinner 8.15pm ✿ ☑ sB&B£10 dB&B£20 dB&B⇌ ⋒£22 Bar lunch fr30p Tea35p Dinner£5 Wine£3.05 Credit card 2

★Clachaig Inn ☎Ballachulish252 Closed Nov; 13rm(4⇌ ⋒) 50P ⛟ Last dinner 8.30pm ✿ ☑ S% sB&B£8.50–£9.50 dB&B£15–£17 dB&B⇌ ⋒£17–£19 Bar lunch£3 Dinner£3.50–£5 Wine£3

GLENDEVON Tayside *Perthshire* Map **11** NN90
★Tormaukin ☎252 7rm(2⇌ ⋒) CTV ⊘ 100P ⛟ ⚓ ♡International. Last dinner 9.15pm ✿ ⊟

G

GLENEAGLES Tayside *Perthshire* Map **11** NN91
See Auchterarder

GLENFARG Tayside *Perthshire* Map **11** NO11
★★Bein Inn ☎216 10rm(7⇌ ⋒) ⋈ TV available in bedrooms 70P 8⌂ ⛟ ⚓ Last dinner 9.45pm ✿ sB&B£8–£12 sB&B⇌ ⋒£13–£14 dB&B£12.50–£13.50 dB&B⇌ ⋒£17.50–£18.50 Bar lunch£2alc Dinner£5.50alc Wine£4 ⊟ *xmas* Credit card 1

★★Glenfarg ☎241 16rm CTV 20P 2⌂ ⚓ billiards Last dinner 8.30pm ✿ ☑ sB&B£6.90–£8 dB&B£13.80–£16 Lunch£2.30–£3&alc Tea75p–£1&alc High Tea£1.75–£2&alc Dinner£3.45–£7.45&alc Wine£3 ⊟ *xmas*

GLENLUCE Dumfries & Galloway *Wigtownshire* Map **10** NX15
★King's Arms Main St ☎219 *Small hotel set in centre of village on main road between Newton Stewart and Stranraer.* Closed Nov–Mar; 8rm(2⇌ ⋒) TV 16P ⛟ Last dinner 9pm ✿ sB&B£6 dB&B£12 dB&B⇌ ⋒£14 Lunch£2.50 High Tea£1–£13 Dinner£3 Wine£2.70

GLENROTHES Fife *Fife* Map **11** NO20
★★★ *Balgeddie House* Leslie Rd ☎742511 Closed New Year's Day; 19⇌ ⋒ ⋈ CTV TV available in bedrooms ⊘ 75P ⛟ ⚓ Live music & dancing wkly Last dinner 9pm ✿ Credit card 3

★★Golden Acorn Central Av (Osprey) ☎752292 *Modern hotel beside new town shopping centre.* 24rm(20⇌ ⋒) Lift ☽ ⋈ CTV CTV in bedrooms 40P Live music & dancing twice wkly Last dinner 9pm ✿ ☑ S% ✱sB&B£11 sB&B⇌ ⋒£13.70 dB&B£17 dB&B⇌ ⋒£21 Lunch fr£2.60&alc Tea fr30p High Tea fr£2.60 Dinner fr£3.90&alc Wine£2.30 ⊟ Credit cards 1 2 3 5

★★Greenside High St, Leslie (2m W A911) ☎743453 16rm(10⇌ ⋒) ⋈ CTV CTV available in bedrooms 60P ⛟ Last dinner 9pm ✿ sB&B£9–£10 sB&B⇌ ⋒£12.50–£13.50 dB&B£16–£18 dB&B⇌ ⋒£18.50–£20 Lunch£2.10–£2.50 Dinner£2.75–£5.50&alc Wine£3.20 Credit cards 2 4 6

★★Rothes Arms South Parks Rd (Open House) ☎753701 16rm(7⇌ ⋒) ☽ ⋈ CTV in bedrooms 50P ⛟ Disco twice wkly Live music & dancing 5 nights wkly Last dinner 9pm ✿ ☑ S% ✱sB&B£12 sB&B⇌ ⋒£13.50 dB&B£18 dB&B⇌ ⋒£21 Lunch£3&alc Tea fr30p Dinner£3&alc Wine£2.75 ⊟ Credit cards 1 2 3 4 5 6

GOLLANFIELD Highland *Inverness-shire* Map **14** NH75
✕Old Smiddy ☎Ardersier2749 Closed Jan; Dinner not served Sun; 45 seats 30P ♡Scottish & English. Last dinner 10pm Lunch£2–£3 Tea75p Dinner£6.50alc Wine£3.70

GOLSPIE Highland *Sutherland* Map **14** NH89
★★Golf Links ☎408 *A converted red stone manse dating from 1870. Sea front location, near to harbour and golf course.* 10rm(3⇌ ⋒) ⋈ CTV 18P ⛟ ⚓ Last dinner 8pm ✿ ☑ S% ✱sB&B£9 dB&B£17 dB&B⇌ ⋒£19.50 Dinner£5 Wine£2.75

★★Sutherland Arms Old Bank Rd ☎216 17rm(1⇌ ⋒) ⋈ CTV P ⛟ ⚓ ♿ ♡French & Italian. Last dinner 8pm ✿ ☑ sB&B fr£11 sB&B⇌ ⋒ fr£11 dB&B fr£20 dB&B⇌ ⋒ fr£20 Lunch fr£4.50 Tea fr£1.35 High Tea£4alc Dinner fr£6 Wine£2.80

★Ben Bhraggie ☎242 6rm ⋈ CTV ⊘ 15P 4⌂ ⛟ ⚓ ♡International. Last dinner 9.30pm ✿ S% ✱sB&B fr£6 dB&B fr£12 Lunch fr£2.50 Dinner£4alc

GOUROCK Strathclyde *Renfrewshire* Map **10** NS27
☆☆☆Gantock Cloch Rd (Reo Stakis) ☎34671 *Modern building situated one mile southwest of town, with views out across the Clyde.* 63⇌ ⋒ ☽ ⋈ CTV CTV in bedrooms 150P Live music & dancing Sat Conference facilities available Last dinner 10pm ✿ ☑ S% ✱sB&B⇌ ⋒£16 dB&B⇌ ⋒£16 dB&B⇌ ⋒£26 Lunch fr£3.25&alc Tea fr75p High Tea fr£2.70 Dinner fr£4.85&alc Wine£2.75 ⊟ *xmas* Credit cards 1 2 3 4 5 6

GRANDTULLY Tayside *Perthshire* Map**14** NN95
★Grandtully ☎Strathtay207
9rm(2⇌ ⋒) 40P Children under 10 yrs not accommodated Last dinner8.30pm sB&B fr£12.95 dB&B fr£25 dB&B⇌⋒ fr£25.50 Bar lunch£1alc Dinner£5.75&alc Wine£3.25

GRANGEMOUTH Central *Stirlingshire* Map**11** NS98
★★Leapark Boness Rd ☎6733
Detached stone mansion, standing in own grounds, close to town centre.
33rm(5⇌⋒) CTV TV in bedrooms 150P 1 Disco Sun Live music & dancing Sat Cabaret Tue Last dinner9.30pm S% sB&B£14.04 sB&B⇌⋒£16.20 dB&B£25.92 dB&B⇌⋒£28.08 Lunch£2.50 Tea£1 High Tea£1.75–£2.50 Dinner£3.50–£6 Wine£2.50 *xmas* Credit cards 1 2 3 5 6

GRANTOWN-ON-SPEY Highland *Moray* Map**14** NJ02
★★★*Grant Arms* The Square ☎2526
Large Victorian building in Scottish baronial style, with imposing frontage standing in square close to main shopping centre of small town.
Closed Nov–mid Apr; 60⇌⋒ 1 Lift CTV TV available in bedrooms 25P 12 Last dinner9pm Credit cards 1 2 3 5 6

★★Ben Mhor High St. ☎2056
An extended red sandstone building, dating from 1876, standing on main road in town centre.
24⇌⋒ TV TV in bedrooms P Last dinner8.30pm S% sB&B⇌⋒£10–£13 dB&B⇌⋒£20–£24 Lunch£2.50–£3.50 Tea50p–£1 High Tea£2–£3.50 Dinner£5–£7 Wine£2.50 *xmas* Credit cards 1 3 5 6

★★Coppice Grant Rd ☎2688
Detached two-storey stone building dating from 1890, standing in two acres of grounds.
24rm CTV 30P Last dinner8pm S% sB&B£7.50–£8.50 dB&B£15–£17 Bar lunch£1–£2.50 Dinner£3.50–£4.50 Wine£2.70 *xmas*

★★Craiglynne ☎2597
Three converted late Victorian houses linked by modern extension and standing in well maintained gardens at Southern end of Speyside town.
61rm(14⇌⋒) CTV 75P Live music & dancing twice wkly in season Last dinner8.30pm S% sB&B£10.50–£12.30 sB&B⇌⋒£12–£13.80 dB&B£21–£24.60 dB&B⇌⋒£24–£27.60 Bar lunch fr£1.20 Tea fr30p Dinner£4.50&alc Wine£3.50 *xmas* Credit cards 1 2 3 5 6

★★Garth Castle Rd ☎2836
Charming conversion of 18th-C house.
14rm Annexe:3⇌⋒ CTV 10P 1 Last dinner8pm ✻sB&B£6.65 sB&B⇌⋒£8.65 dB&B£13.30 dB&B⇌⋒£17.30 Bar lunch 50p–£2.50 Dinner£4.50–£4.95&alc Wine£2.30 Credit cards 2 3 4 5 6

★★Seafield Lodge Woodside Av ☎2152
Converted detached house dating from 1910 standing in quiet residential street.
RS Nov–Mar; 14rm(9⇌⋒) CTV 50P 1 Last dinner8.15pm sB&B£7.56–£9.72 dB&B£15.12–£20.24 dB&B⇌⋒£17.28–£22.40 Bar lunch fr£2.16 Dinner fr£5.40 Wine£3.60 Credit card 2

Dunvegan Heathfield Rd ☎2301
Closed 21 Dec–4 Jan; 9rm CTV 9P 1 Last dinner7.30pm S% sB&B£6.60–£7.25 dB&B£13.20–£14.50 Bar lunch 35p–£1 Tea50–75p Dinner£3.60 Wine£2.75

Holmhill Woodside Av ☎2645
10rm CTV 10P 2 Children under 3 mths not accommodated Last dinner8.15pm S% sB&B£6.50–£7.95 dB&B£33–£15.90 Dinner£3.25 Wine£2.85 *xmas*

Ravenscourt Seafield Av ☎2286
Unlicensed; 8rm CTV 15P Last dinner7.30pm sB&B£6.90–£7.48 dB&B£13.80–£14.95 *xmas* Credit card 3

GREENOCK Strathclyde *Renfrewshire* Map**10** NS27
★★★Tontine 6 Ardgowan Sq (Best Western) ☎23316 Telex no779801
19th-C building, with extension wing, situated on square in west end of town.
44rm(31⇌⋒) CTV in bedrooms 15P 15 Last dinner9pm S% sB&B fr£16.50 sB&B⇌⋒ fr£19 dB&B fr£25 dB&B⇌⋒ fr£29 Lunch fr£4.20&alc Tea fr£1.25 High Tea fr£3 Dinner fr£5.50&alc Credit cards 1 2 3 5 6

✕*La Taverna* 6 West Blackhall St ☎25391 Closed Sun; 48seats Last dinner9.45pm Credit cards 1 5

GRETNA Dumfries & Galloway *Dumfriesshire* Map**11** NY36
★★Gretna Chase (¼m S on B721 in England) ☎517
6rm(1⇌⋒) CTV 50P English & French. Last dinner9.30pm sB&B£10 dB&B£18 dB&B⇌⋒£20 Bar lunch£1.40–£2.40 Dinner£5alc Wine£3.15

★★Royal Stewart Motel ☎210
Bungalow-style motel on the outskirts of the town which is now bypassed.
Closed Sep; RS Oct, Feb & Mar; 13rm(8⇌⋒) CTV CTV available in bedrooms 17P Last dinner9pm S% sB&B£6–£8 sB&B⇌⋒£8–£10 dB&B£12–£14 dB&B⇌⋒£14–£18 Lunch£2 Dinner£3.50–£4.50 Wine£2.20

★★Solway Lodge Annan Rd ☎266
3rm Annexe: 10rm(7⇌⋒) TV 25P ⚓
Last dinner 8.30pm ✿ S% sB&B⇌⋒£9.50
dB&B⇌⋒£17 Lunch £2.20–£3.50
High Tea £2–£3.80 Dinner £2.80–£5 Wine £2.50

GRETNA GREEN Dumfries & Galloway
Dumfriesshire Map **11** NY36
★★Gretna Hall ☎257
The original marriage house of Gretna Green; catering mainly for tourists.
50rm(6⇌⋒) 1⊟ ☽ CTV 100P 2🏠 ⚓ Live music & dancing 4nights wkly (summer) Last dinner 9.30pm
✿ S% sB&B£8.50–£9.50
sB&B⇌⋒£10–£10.50 dB&B£17–£19
dB&B⇌⋒£20–£21 Lunch fr£3.50 Dinner fr£4.50
Wine £2.48 ⊓ *xmas* Credit cards 1 2 5 6

GULLANE Lothian *East Lothian* Map **12** NT48
★★★ Greywalls Duncur Rd ☎842144
See page 60 for details

★★Bissets ☎842230
Victorian building in two acres of grounds situated in the centre of small village.
28rm CTV TV available in bedrooms 30P 3🏠 ⚓
Live music & dancing wkly Last dinner 8.30pm
✿ ♀ sB&B£12–£20 dB&B£10–£35
Lunch £2.75–£3.50 Tea £1–£1.50
High Tea £2.75–£3.50 Dinner £5–£10.50
Wine £3.50 ⊓ *xmas* Credit cards 1 2 3 5

✕Golf Inn 72 Main St ☎843259
Formerly a stone farmhouse, this inn was converted in 1843. Situated on the roadside in centre of village.
45seats 9P bedrooms available ♀International.
Last dinner 9.30pm S% ✱Lunch fr£1.45
Dinner £4.50alc Wine £1.90

✿✕La Potiniere Main St ☎843214
Small restaurant with wishing well at the entrance.
Closed Wed & Oct; Lunch not served Sat; Dinner not served Sun–Fri 32seats 3P ♀French. S%
Lunch £4–£4.50 Dinner £6 Wine £3

HADDINGTON Lothian *East Lothian* Map **12** NT57
★★George ☎3372
Hotel built over 300 years ago, standing at east end of High Street.
13rm(3⇌⋒) CTV CTV available in bedrooms 10P
Last dinner 8.30pm ✿ S% sB&B fr£7.60
sB&B⇌⋒ fr£9.50 dB&B fr£15.20
dB&B⇌⋒ fr£18 Lunch fr£2.20 Dinner fr£3.60
Wine £2.35

HAMILTON Strathclyde *Lanarkshire* Map **11** NS75
★★Commercial 29 Townhead St (Osprey) ☎282757
18rm(10⇌⋒) ☽ CTV CTV available in bedrooms
20P Last dinner 8.30pm ✿ ♀ S%
✱sB&B fr£9.50 sB&B⇌⋒ fr£13 dB&B fr£16
dB&B⇌⋒£21 Lunch fr£2.60&alc Tea fr30p
High Tea fr£2.60 Dinner fr£3.90&alc Wine £2.31
⊓ *xmas* Credit cards 1 2 3 5

★Royal New Cross (Clansmans) ☎285926
Small hotel on corner site above shops in centre of town.
6rm(1⇌⋒) CTV ♀Mainly grills.
Last dinner 8.45pm ✿ ♀ ✱sB&B£8.75
dB&B£14.50 Lunch £3.50alc
High Tea £1.90–£3.40 Dinner £3.50alc
Wine £2.70 Credit card 5

✕Il Frate (Friar Tuck) 4 Barrack St ☎284379
Closed Sun; 52seats ♀Italian. Last dinner 11pm
Wine £4.20

HARDGATE Strathclyde *Dunbartonshire* Map **11** NS47
★★Cameron House Main St ☎Duntocher 73535
17⇌⋒ Lift ☽ TV in bedrooms 65P
Last dinner 9.30pm ✿ S% sB&B⇌⋒£11.50
dB&B⇌⋒£16 Lunch £1.80–£2&alc
Dinner £3.80–£4&alc

HARRAY Orkney Map **16** HY31
★★Merkister ☎366
RS Oct–Mar; 19rm(2⇌⋒) CTV 30P ⚓
Last dinner 9pm ✿ ♀ S% sB&B£9–£10.50
sB&B⇌⋒£10–£11.50 dB&B£18–£21
dB&B⇌⋒£20–£23 Lunch £2.50–£4.50
Tea £1.50–£3 High Tea fr£2.50
Dinner £5–£6.50&alc Wine £4.95 ⊓

HARRIS, ISLE OF Western Isles *Inverness-shire*
Map **13** **See Tarbert**

HAWICK Borders *Roxburghshire* Map **12** NT51
★★Crown High St (Osprey) ☎3344
Centrally situated in main shopping street adjoining 19th-C stone buildings.
32rm(6⇌⋒) ☽ CTV 10🏠 Live music & dancing wkly Last dinner 8.30pm ✿ ♀ S%
✱sB&B£9.50 sB&B⇌⋒£13 dB&B£16
dB&B⇌⋒£21 Lunch fr£2.60&alc Tea fr30p
High Tea fr£2.60 Dinner fr£3.90&alc Wine £2.36
⊓ *xmas* Credit cards 1 2 3 5

★★Kirklands West Stewart Pl ☎2263
Late Victorian sandstone house standing in quiet residential area of town.
Rs Sun; 6rm(3⇌⋒) CTV TV in bedrooms 20P ⚓
♀English & French. Last dinner 8.30pm ✿
sB&B£10.80–£11.88 sB&B⇌⋒£11.88
dB&B£18.36 dB&B⇌⋒£19.44
Lunch £3.50–£5&alc Dinner £5.94&alc
Wine £2.80 ⊓

HELENSBURGH Strathclyde *Dunbartonshire* Map **10** NS28
★★★Queen's East Clyde St ☎3404
Originally established by Henry Bell, the pioneer of steam navigation.

21rm(10⇌ 🚿) ☽ 📺 CTV CTV available in bedrooms 60P 🐕 ⚓ ♡French. Last dinner9pm ♡ ☕ Wine£4 Credit cards 1 2 3

★★***Cairndhu*** Rhu Road Lower ☎3388
13rm(5⇌ 🚿) ☽ 📺 CTV ⊗ 60P ⚓ Last dinner9pm ♡ Credit cards 2 3 5

✕**Ruby Chinese** West Clyde St ☎4080
82seats P ♡Chinese & European. Last dinner11.30pm Lunch£1.20–£1.50 Dinner£2.50–£3&alc Wine£2.90

HOLLYBUSH Strathclyde *Ayrshire* Map**10** NS31
★★★**Hollybush House** ☎Dalrymple214
Closed Xmas; 12rm(7⇌ 🚿) 📺 CTV 40P 8🏠 🐕 ⚓ ⇒ ♨ ♡English & French. Last dinner9.30pm ♡ ☕ S% ✻sB&B£14.25 sB&B⇌ 🚿£15.45 dB&B£23.75 dB&B⇌ 🚿£26.15 Lunch£3alc Tea£1.08alc Dinner£5alc Wine£3.25 Credit cards 1 2 3 6

HOWGATE Lothian *Midlothian* Map**11** NT25
✕✕**Old Howgate Inn** Wester Howgate ☎Penicuik74244
Old coaching house reputed to have been used by pilgrims on their way south from Edinburgh.
Closed Sun; 45seats 40P ♡Danish. Last dinner10pm ✻Lunch£5alc Dinner£7alc Wine£2.85

HUNTLY Grampian *Aberdeenshire* Map**15** NJ53
★★♣**Castle** ☎2696
Closed Jan & Feb; 24rm(9⇌ 🚿) 1▭ 📺 CTV 20P 3🏠 ⚓ ⇒ Last dinner9.30pm ♡ ☕ sB&B£10–£12 sB&B⇌ 🚿£11.50–£13.50 dB&B£20–£24 dB&B⇌ 🚿£23–£27 Lunch£2.80–£3.50 Tea£1 High Tea£3 Dinner£5–£5.50 Wine£3 Credit cards 3 5

★★**Gordon Arms** The Square (Open House) ☎2536
14rm ▦ 📺 CTV Last dinner8pm ♡ ☕ ✻sB&B fr£8.50 dB&B fr£15.50 Lunch£2.20alc Tea50palc High Tea£1.10alc Dinner£3.50alc Wine£2.85 ♬ Credit cards 1 2 3 5

★★***Huntly*** 18 The Square (Scottish & Newcastle) ☎2703
13rm 📺 CTV 4P Last dinner7pm ♡ ☕ Credit cards 1 3

INCHNADAMPH Highland *Sutherland* Map**14** NC22
★★***Inchnadamph*** ☎Assynt202
Closed Nov–Feb; 30rm(7⇌ 🚿) TV 30P 4🏠 🐕 ⇒ Last dinner8pm ♡ ☕

INVERARAY Strathclyde *Argyllshire* Map**10** NN00
★**Fernpoint** Ferryland ☎2170
Closed 21Oct–14Apr; 6rm(4⇌ 🚿) 📺 CTV ⊗ 15P 🐕 ⚓ Last dinner10pm ♡ sB&B£11.50–£13.75 sB&B⇌ 🚿£11.50–£13.75 dB&B£23–£27.50 dB&B⇌ 🚿£23–£27.50 Lunch£2–£3alc Dinner£5–£6alc Wine£3.25 Credit cards 1 3

INVERGARRY Highland *Inverness-shire* Map**14** NH30
★★♣**Glengarry Castle** ☎254
A Victorian mansion with ruins of Invergarry Castle in the grounds.
Closed 17Oct–2Apr; 30rm(9⇌ 🚿) 📺 CTV 30P 3🏠 🐕 ⚓ 🎾(hard) ⇒ Last dinner8.15pm ♡ ☕ S% sB&B£9.75–£11 dB&B£17.60–£20.50 dB&B⇌ 🚿£21–£24 Lunch£3–£3.50 Tea£1–£1.15 Dinner£4.75–£5.50 Wine£2.50 Credit cards 1 2 3

INVERKEITHING Fife *Fife* Map**11** NT18
★**Queens** Church St ☎413075
13rm 📺 CTV 40P 🐕 ♡English & French.

I

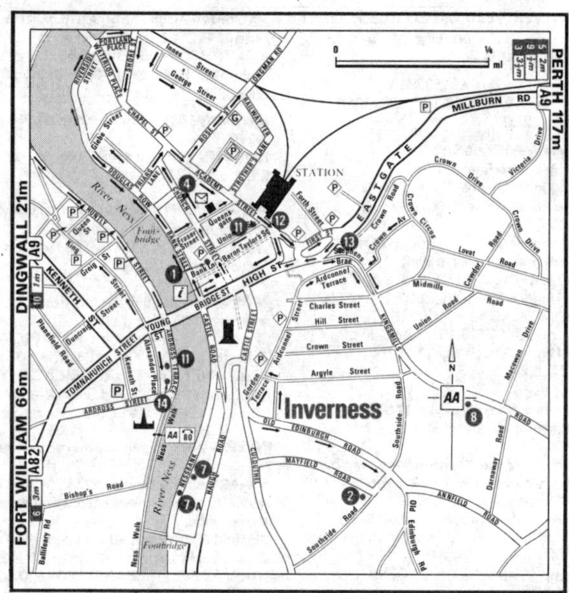

1 Caledonian☆☆☆☆
2 Craigmore★★
3 Culloden House★★★★
4 Cummings★★
5 Drumossie★★
6 Dunain Park★★
7 Glen Mhor★★
8 Kingsmills★★★
9 Ladbroke Mercury Motor Inn☆☆☆
10 Muirtown★★
11 Palace★★
12 Royal★★
13 Station★★★
14 La Toscana✕
15 Tower

Lastdinner9pm sB&B£8.48 dB&B£16 Lunch fr£2.70 Tea fr50p High Tea fr£1.50 Dinner fr£3.75&alc Wine£2.50

INVERKIP Strathclyde *Renfrewshire* Map**10** NS27
★★Langhouse Langhouse Rd ☎Wemyss Bay521211
Closed New Year's Day; 8rm(3⇌⋒) CTV 30P (hard) European. Last dinner8.30pm S% ✱sB&B£7.50 sB&B⇌⋒£9 dB&B£13 dB&B⇌⋒£15.50 Lunch£2.50 Dinner£3.50 Wine£2.30

INVERMORISTON Highland *Inverness-shire* Map**14** NH41
★*Glenmoriston Arms* Glenmoriston ☎Glenmoriston206
9rm(2⇌⋒) TV 30P Music Tue & Wed
Children under 5yrs not accommodated
Last dinner8.15pm Credit cards 1 3

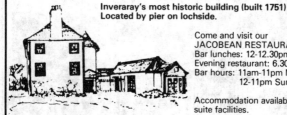

INVERNESS Highland *Inverness-shire* Map**14** NH64
See plan

★★★★ **Culloden House** Culloden Moor (2m E off A96) (Prestige) ☎Culloden Moor461 Telex no75402 Plan**3**
21⇌⋒ ☽ ♔ CTV in bedrooms 100P ⚘ ⚓ sauna bath Last dinner11pm ✿ ⚠ ✱sB&B⇌⋒ fr£35 dB&B⇌⋒ fr£5 Lunch£5.50&alc Tea£1.80 Dinner£7.50&alc Wine£3.50 *xmas* Credit cards 1 2 3 5 6

☆☆☆**Caledonian** Church St (Allied Scotland) ☎37181 Telex no76357 Plan**1**
120⇌⋒ Lift ☽ ♔ CTV TV available in bedrooms P Disco twice wkly Cabaret 6nights Conference facilities available Last dinner9pm ✿ ⚠ S% sB&B⇌⋒ fr£17.50 dB&B⇌⋒ fr£32 Lunch fr£3.50 Tea fr£1.50 Dinner fr£5.50 Wine£4 ⊟ *xmas* Credit cards 1 2 3 4 5 6

★★★**Kingsmills** Damfield Rd (Best Western) ☎37166 Plan**8**
Conversion of 18th-C Provost's House standing in 3 acres of gardens.
46rm(38⇌⋒) ☽ ♔ CTV CTV available in bedrooms 100P ⚘ ⚓ squash ♿ English & French. Last dinner10pm ✿ ⚠ S% sB&B£15–£18 sB&B⇌⋒£18.50–£25 dB&B£18.50–£26 dB&B⇌⋒£24–£42.50 Lunch£3.50–£6 Tea£1–£1.50 Dinner£6.50–£7.50&alc Wine£4.50 ⊟ Credit cards 1 2 3 5 6

☆☆☆**Ladbroke Mercury Motor** (junc of A9/A96) Nairn Rd (Ladbroke) ☎39666 Telex no75377 Plan**9**
84⇌⋒ Lift ☽ ♔ CTV in bedrooms 150P Conference facilities available Last dinner10.30pm ✿ sB&B⇌⋒£17–£20 dB&B⇌⋒£26–£32 Lunch fr£4.50&alc Dinner fr£5.50&alc Wine£3.20 ⊟ Credit cards 1 2 3 4 5 6

★★★**Station** Academy St (British Transport) ☎31926 Telex no75275 Plan**13**
63rm(52⇌⋒) Lift ☽ ♔ TV in bedrooms 5P English & French. Last dinner9pm ✿ ⚠ S% dB&B⇌⋒ fr£26.35 dB&B⇌⋒ fr£46.85 Dinner fr£8.60 Wine£3.15 ⊟ Credit cards 1 2 3 4 5 6

❀★★ **Dunain Park** ☎30512 Plan**6**
See page 60 for details

★★**Craigmonie** Annfield Rd (Open House) ☎31649 Plan**2**
Gabled and turreted red sandstone mansion dating from 1832 with modern extension.
10rm ♔ CTV 30P Live music & dancing Sun Last dinner8.30pm ✿ ⚠ S% sB&B£11.50 dB&B£17.50 Bar lunch£1.50 Tea50p High Tea£2 Dinner£5 Wine£2.85 Credit cards 1 2 3 4 5 6

★★**Cummings** Church St ☎32531 Plan**4**
38rm(5⇌⋒) Lift ☽ ♔ CTV 25P Cabaret 6nights wkly Last dinner8pm S% sB&B£10–£12 dB&B£19–£23 dB&B⇌⋒£23–£27 Lunch£2.50–£3.50 High Tea£2.50–£3.50&alc Dinner£4.50–£5.50 Wine£2.20 ⊟

★★**Drumossie** Perth Rd (Inter-Hotel) ☎36451 Plan**5**
82rm(49⇌⋒) Annexe: 20⇌⋒ ☽ CTV CTV available in bedrooms 80P ⚓ Live music & dancing 3nights wkly Conference facilities available European. Last dinner8.30pm ✿ sB&B£9.50–£14 sB&B⇌⋒£11–£16 dB&B£18–£26 dB&B⇌⋒£20–£30 Lunch£3.25 Dinner£5.25 Wine£3.25 ⊟ *xmas* Credit cards 1 2 3 5

★★**Glen Mhor** 10 Ness Bank ☎34308 Plan**7**
Conversion of Tarradale stone mansion dating from

I

1870. Set in quiet residential area of town.
Closed 1–3Jan; 22rm(5⇌ ⋒) ☽ 🅿CTV CTV available in bedrooms 16P Live music & dancing twice wkly ♡European. Last dinner8.30pm ✿ ♀ ✳sB&B£8–£9.95 sB&B⇌ ⋒£10–£13.50 dB&B£16–£19 dB&B⇌ ⋒£20–£30 Continental breakfast Lunch fr£3.50 Tea fr75p High Tea fr£2 Dinner fr£5.45 Wine£3.30 ▤ Credit cards 1 2 3 5

★★***Muirtown*** 11 Clachnaharry Rd (Open House) ☎34860 Plan**10**
Low rise complex with the accommodation in modern timber-clad chalets. On main road to north of town overlooking river.
Annexe: 36⇌ ⋒ 🅿 120P Last dinner8.30pm ✿ ♀ ▤ Credit cards 1 2 3 4 5 6

★★**Palace** Ness Walks ☎223243 Telex no778869 Plan**11**
40rm(9⇌ ⋒) Lift ☽ CTV 20P Last dinner8.30pm ✿ ♀ S% sB&B£30–£15 sB&B⇌ ⋒£11.50–£18 dB&B£20–£24 dB&B⇌ ⋒£23–£29 Lunch£3.50 Dinner£5.85 Wine£3.25 ▤ Credit cards 1 2 3 5 6

★★**Royal** Academy St (Trusthouse Forte) ☎30665 Plan**12**
48rm(19⇌ ⋒) Lift ☽ TV in bedrooms 🅿 Last dinner9.15pm ✿ ♀ S% sB&B£13.50 sB&B⇌ ⋒£16.50 dB&B£20.50 dB&B⇌ ⋒£25 ▤ Credit cards 1 2 3 4 5 6

⊕**Tower** Ardross Ter ☎32765 Plan**15**
On a corner site at the end of a terraced row, dated 1875, and near the town centre, overlooking the River Ness and the Castle.
9rm 🅿CTV 4P ⇌ High Tea7.30pm ✿ ♀ S% sB&B£6.50–£7 dB&B£13–£14 Lunch£2.50–£3 Tea80p–£1 High Tea£2.50–£3 Wine£2.50

✕**La Toscana** East Gate ☎37402 Plan**14**
Closed Sun (Mon Jun–Sep); Lunch not served Oct–May; 35seats 🅿 bedrooms available ♡Italian. Last dinner10pm ✳Lunch£1–£2.50 Dinner£8.50alc Wine£2.39

INVERSHIN Highland *Sutherland* Map**14** NH59
★★**Aultnagar Lodge** (2½ m N A836) ☎245
26rm(12⇌ ⋒) Lift TV 50P 4🏠 ⇌ ♣ Live music & dancing Wed Cabaret Wed Last dinner8.30pm ✿ ♀ sB&B£7.50 sB&B⇌ ⋒£8.50 dB&B£15 dB&B⇌ ⋒£17–£18 Lunch£2.50 Tea£1–£1.50 High Tea£3–£3.50 Dinner£4.75 Wine£1.90 *xmas* Credit card 2

★★**Invershin** ☎202
Closed New Year; 12rm(3⇌ ⋒) Annexe: 12rm(6⇌ ⋒) 🅿CTV available in bedrooms 35P 2🏠 ♣ ↺ ∩ Last dinner9.15pm ✿ ♀ S% sB&B£7–£9 sB&B⇌ ⋒£8–£10 dB&B£14–£18 dB&B⇌ ⋒£15–£19 Lunch£2.50–£3.50 Tea£1–£1.50 High Tea£3–£4.50 Dinner£4–£6 Wine£1.90 ▤ Credit cards 1 3 5 6

INVERURIE Grampian *Aberdeenshire* Map**15** NJ72
★**Gordon Arms** The Square ☎20314
11rm CTV ⇌ Last dinner7.45pm ✿ S% sB&B£7.90 dB&B£15.80 Lunch fr£2.40 High Tea£1.80–£2.80 Dinner fr£3.60 Wine£2.90 ▤ *xmas*

✕**J. G's** Market Pl ☎21378
Closed Sun; Dinner not served Mon & Tue 50seats 30P ♡French. Last dinner9.45pm Lunch£1–£3.50&alc Tea40p–£1.10 High Tea£2.15–£3 Dinner£4.35–£5.50&alc Wine£2.80

IRVINE Strathclyde *Ayrshire* Map**10** NS33
★★Redburn (Osprey) ☎79389
11rm(2⇌ ⋒)CTV 100P ⚓ Lastdinner8pm ✿ ⚲
S% ✱sB&B£6.90 dB&B fr£14.50
dB&B⇌⋒fr£17 Lunch£1.50–£5 Tea50p–£2
High Tea£1.60–£2.50 Dinner£5–£6&alc
Credit cards 1 2 3 5 6

ISLAY, ISLE OF Strathclyde *Argyll*
See Bowmore, Port Askaig and Port Ellen

ISLE OF WHITHORN Dumfries & Galloway
Wigtownshire Map**11** NX43
★Queens Arms ☎369
10rm(4⇌⋒) CTV ⊘ 10P ⊞ Lastdinner8.45pm ✿
sB&B£7–£8 dB&B£14–£16 dB&B⇌⋒£16–£18
Bar lunch30p–£3alc Dinner£4.50–£4.75&alc
Wine£2.35

ISLE ORNSAY Isle of Skye, Highland *Inverness-shire*
Map**13** NG61
★★Kinlock Lodge ☎214 Telex no75442
Closed Nov–Mar; 12rm(6⇌⋒) ⋔ TV 30P ⊞ ⚓ ⚲
Lastdinner8.15pm ✿ ⚲ S% sB&B£10.50
sB&B⇌⋒£12.50 dB&B£21 dB&B⇌⋒£25
Lunch£3 Tea£1 Dinner£6.50 Wine£2.90 ⊟

★Tigh-Osda Eilean Iarmain Camus Croise, Sleat
☎266 Telex no75252
8rm Annexe: 5rm 2⊟ 20P ⊞ Live music & dancing
monthly Cabaret monthly Lastdinner8.30pm ✿
⚲ sB&B£6.50–£9.50 dB&B£13–£19
Lunch£2.80–£3.50 Tea75p–£1
High Tea£2.80–£3.50 Dinner£5.50–£6.50
Wine£2.80 ⊟ *xmas*

JEDBURGH Borders *Roxburghshire* Map**12** NT62
★★Jedforest Country House ☎Camptown274
Mansion, dating from 1870, standing in 50 acres of tree-studded parkland bordering the River Jed.
7rm CTV CTV available in bedrooms 50P ⚓ ⚲ ∩
billiards Lastdinner8.30pm ✿ ⚲ S%
sB&B fr£8.90 sB&B⇌⋒£12.50 dB&B fr£15.45
dB&B⇌⋒fr£20.20 Lunch fr£3 Tea fr60p
Dinner fr£3.95&alc Wine£2.65 ⊟

✕Carter's Rest ☎3414
Closed Sun (Oct–Mar); 80seats P ☉Mainly grills.
Lastdinner9.30pm Lunch£4–£7&alc
Dinner£4–£7&alc

JOHN O'GROATS Highland *Caithness* Map**15** ND37
★★John O'Groats House ☎203
Closed 2Oct–Mar; 17rm ⋔ CTV 50P ⚓ ⚲ ☉Scottish
& French. Lastdinner8.45pm ✿ ⚲ S%
sB&B£6–£10 sB&B⇌⋒£7–£12 dB&B£14–£24
dB&B⇌⋒£30–£35 Lunch£1–£3&alc
Dinner£2.50–£5&alc Wine£3 Credit cards 1 3

★Sea View ☎220
This stone building stands on the roadside overlooking Pentland Firth and Isles of Stroma and Orkney.
9rm ⋔ CTV 20P 2⌂ ⚲ Lastdinner8pm ✿ ⚲
✱sB&B fr£5.80 sB&B⇌⋒fr£6.30 dB&B fr£11.60
dB&B⇌⋒fr£12.60 Lunch fr£2.75 Tea fr55p
High Tea fr£2.50 Dinner fr£4 Wine£3.25

JOHNSTONE BRIDGE Dumfries & Galloway
Dumfriess-shire Map**11** NY19
★★Dinwoodie Lodge Main Rd ☎289
A lodge house on the A74 positioned at the turn off for Newton Wamphray.
8rm ☽ ⋔ TV TV available in bedrooms 100P 4⌂ ⚓ ⚲
♿ Lastdinner9.30pm ✿ ⚲ ✱sB&B£8–£9
dB&B£16–£18 Lunch£2.50 Tea80p
High Tea£2–£3.75&alc Dinner£3.50–£3.75&alc
Wine£2.90 Credit cards 3 5

JURA, ISLE OF Strathclyde *Argyll* **See Craighouse**

KEITH Grampian *Banffshire* Map**15** NJ45
★★Royal Church Rd ☎2528
Commercial hotel in town centre.
14rm(3⇌⋒) ✕ ⋔ CTV 20P 4⌂ Disco Sat Live music
& dancing Sat Lastdinner9pm ✿ ⚲
sB&B£8–£9 sB&B⇌⋒£10–£12 dB&B£16–£18
dB&B⇌⋒£20–£24 Lunch£2.50–£3
Tea60p–80p High Tea£2.25–£2.50
Dinner£5.50–£6 Wine£3 ⊟ *xmas* Credit card 1

KELSO Borders *Roxburghshire* Map**12** NT73
★★★Cross Keys The Square (Inter-Hotel) ☎3303
20rm(13⇌⋒) Lift ☽ ⊞ ⋔ CTV CTV in bedrooms 12P
Live music & dancing twice wkly ♿ ☉French.
Lastdinner9.30pm ✿ ⚲ ✱sB&B£12–£13.50
sB&B⇌⋒£13–£14.50 dB&B£22–£25
dB&B⇌⋒£24–£27 Lunch£1.75–£3 Tea30p–£1
High Tea£3 Dinner£3–£5.50 Wine£3.80 ⊟
Credit cards 1 2 3 4 5 6

★★★Ednam House Bridge St ☎2168
Large Georgian house built in 1761, set in three acres of grounds, on the banks of the River Tweed.
Closed 1wk New Year; 32rm(18⇌⋒) ⋔ CTV 60P 2⌂
⊞ ⚓ Lastdinner9pm ✿ ⚲ sB&B fr£12.45
sB&B⇌⋒ fr£14.69 dB&B fr£3.10 Tea fr£1
High Tea fr£2 Dinner£5.50 Wine£2.30

★★★Woodside ☎2152
Small Georgian house standing in tree-studded grounds on the outskirts of border town.
5⇌⋒ Annexe: 6rm(5⇌⋒) ⋔ TV in bedrooms 30P
10⌂ ⊞ ⚓ ☉English, French & Italian.
Lastdinner9pm sB&B⇌⋒£18–£24
dB&B⇌⋒£18–£26 Dinner£6–£8&alc
Wine£2.50 ⊟ Credit cards 2 3 5 6

K

★★**House o'Hill** ☎2594
6rm(2⇌⋒) CTV CTV in bedrooms 100P
Children under 3yrs not accommodated English & French. Last dinner 9pm s% *sB&B£12.53 sB&B⇌⋒£13.29 dB&B£20.24 dB&B⇌⋒£22.77 Lunch fr£5&alc Dinner fr£6.33&alc Wine£3.65 Credit card 6

★★**Queens Head** Bridge St ☎2636
Coaching inn, dating from 1780, standing in centre of border town.
8rm(1⇌⋒) CTV Scottish & French. Last dinner 8pm S% sB&B£5.60–£7.20 sB&B⇌⋒£6.60–£8.20 dB&B£11.20–£14.50 dB&B⇌⋒£13.20–£16.40 Bar lunch £1.50–£2 High Tea £1.85–£1.95 Dinner £3.70–£3.95 Wine £2.25 Credit card 1

KENMORE Tayside *Perthshire* Map **14** NN74
★★★***Kenmore*** Village Sq ☎205
Reputed to be Scotland's oldest inn. Robert Burns is said to have stayed here.
30rm(18⇌⋒) Lift TV 70P
Last dinner 9pm

KILCHOAN Highland *Argyll* Map **13** NM46
★★**Kilchoan** ☎200
7rm(5⇌⋒) TV in bedrooms 30P
Last dinner 8pm S% sB&B£8–£10 sB&B⇌⋒£9–£11 dB&B£16–£20 dB&B⇌⋒£18–£22 Lunch £1.50 Tea 40–80p Dinner £5.50 Wine £2.17

KILCHRENAN Strathclyde *Argyll* Map **10** NN02
★★**Taychreggan** Lochaweside ☎211
Closed 13Oct–Mar; 22rm(11⇌⋒) TV 40P
International. Last dinner 8.45pm sB&B£11–£12.50 sB&B⇌⋒£12.50–£14 dB&B£22–£25 dB&B⇌⋒£25–£28 Lunch £3 Tea 75p Dinner £6 Wine £3 Credit cards 1 2 3 5 6

KILCREGGAN Strathclyde *Dunbartonshire* Map **10** NS28
★★**Kilcreggan** ☎2243
Closed 1 Jan; 8⇌⋒ CTV 40P
Last dinner 8pm S% *sB&B⇌⋒£12–£13 dB&B⇌⋒£21.50–£23 Lunch £1–£3&alc Dinner £5–£6&alc Wine £3 Credit cards 1 3

KILLEARN Central *Stirlingshire* Map **11** NS58
★★**Black Bull** (Clansmans) ☎50215
Inn dating from 1880 in small country town. Garden at rear.
12rm(4⇌⋒) CTV 40P European.
Last dinner 9pm *sB&B£8.95 sB&B⇌⋒£10.30 dB&B£15.25 dB&B⇌⋒£17.75 Lunch £4.20alc Tea 65palc High Tea £1.80–£3.15 Dinner £4.20alc Wine £2.80
Credit cards 1 2 3 5

KILLIECRANKIE Tayside *Perthshire* Map **14** NN96
★★**Killiecrankie** ☎220
Set amidst woodland and well-tended gardens, this attractive white-painted house is located near to National Trust beauty spot.
Closed mid Oct–Mar; 12rm(10⇌⋒) CTV 30P
Last dinner 8.30pm sB&B£9.35 sB&B⇌⋒£10.55 dB&B£18.70 dB&B⇌⋒£21.10 Bar lunch fr£1 Tea fr40p Dinner fr£5.75 Wine £2.70

KILLIN Central *Perthshire* Map **11** NN53
★★**Bridge of Lochay** ☎272
18th-C drovers' inn on outskirts of town close to River Lochay.
Closed Nov–Mar; 18rm(4⇌⋒) CTV 40P 3
Last dinner 8.15pm S% sB&B fr£8 dB&B fr£16 dB&B⇌⋒ fr£20 Lunch fr£2.70 Dinner fr£5 Wine £2.50

★★**Killin** ☎296
25rm(3⇌⋒) Annexe: 5⇌⋒ Lift CTV 50P 4
Live music & dancing wkly Last dinner 9.15pm sB&B£8.50–£9 dB&B£16.75–£17.60 dB&B⇌⋒£21.20–£22.80 Lunch £3–£3.50 Tea 60p–£1 Dinner £5.40–£5.75 Wine £2.10 *xmas*

★★**Morenish Lodge** ☎258
Originally a shooting lodge built in 1820, for the Earl of Breadalbane, set in 10 acres of grounds.
Closed Oct–Apr; 13rm(3⇌⋒) TV 25P 4
Children under 5yrs not accommodated
Last dinner 8pm S% sB&B£9–£10 dB&B£18 dB&B⇌⋒£20 Bar lunch £1.80–£2.20 Dinner £5.50–£6 Wine £3

★**Craigard** ☎285
Closed Nov–Mar; 10rm CTV 15P Last dinner 9pm sB&B£5.50–£6.25 dB&B£9.80–£10.85 Lunch £3.20alc Tea fr70p High Tea £2–£4 Dinner £4 Wine £2.50

★**Falls of Dochart** Main St ☎237
Closed Nov–Mar; 8rm(4⇌⋒) CTV 50P 2
Last dinner 8.30pm S% *sB&B&6 sB&B⇌⋒£7 dB&B£12 dB&B⇌⋒£14 Lunch £2.40 High Tea £2.40 Dinner £4.50 Wine £2.45

★**Tighnabruaich** Main St ☎216
8rm 3 CTV 15P Last dinner 8pm S% sB&B£6.50 dB&B£13 Lunch £2.25 Tea 60p High Tea £1.25–£2.50 Dinner £4.60–£6&alc Wine £2 *xmas* Credit cards 2 3

KILMARNOCK Strathclyde *Ayrshire* Map **10** NS43
☆☆☆**Howard Park** Glasgow Rd (Swallow) ☎31211
Telex no 53168
50⇌⋒ Lift CTV in bedrooms 400P Conference facilities available Last dinner 9.30pm S% sB&B⇌⋒£17.20 dB&B⇌⋒£23.25
Credit cards 1 2 3 5

Coffee Club 30 Bank St ☎22048
Closed Sun; Unlicensed; No corkage charge
00seats Last dinner 10pm *Lunch £1.75
Tea fr £1.70 High Tea fr £1.70 Dinner £6alc

KILMARTIN Strathclyde *Argyll* Map **10** NR89
✕Cairn ☎254
Rosette awarded for dinner only.
Closed 24 & 25Dec, 1Jan, Feb & 1st 2wks Nov; Dinner not served Sun; 60seats 20P International. Last dinner 9.30pm *Lunch £3alc Tea 60palc Dinner £4alc Wine £3.30 Credit cards 2 3 5

KILWINNING Strathclyde *Ayrshire* Map **10** NS34
✕✕High Smithstown (off A737 1m N of Kilwinning Station) ☎53689
Rosette awarded for dinner only.
Closed Sun, Mon & 14–31 Oct; Lunch not served; 50seats 16P French. Specialities: Pâté du chef, poulet rôte a l'Estragou, mousse au chocolat à l'orange. Last dinner 9.30pm Dinner £7&alc Wine £4 Credit card 2

KINCLAVEN Tayside *Perthshire* Map **11** NO13
★★★ *Ballathie House* ☎Meikleour 268
Telex no 727096 (Ballathie)
Closed Dec–14Jan; 23 CTV in bedrooms 50P (hard) Last dinner 9pm
Credit cards 1 2 6

KINCRAIG Highland *Inverness-shire* Map **14** NH80
★★Ossian ☎242
Closed Jan; 9rm TV 20P Last dinner 9pm S% sB&B £9 dB&B £18 Dinner £5&alc Wine £3 *xmas*

Suie ☎344
9rm 3 P Children under 10yrs not accommodated Last dinner 7pm sB&B £7.50 dB&B £15 Bar lunch 50–75p Dinner £4–£5 Wine £3 Credit cards 2 3

✕✕*Invereshie House* ☎332
Closed Nov–Etr; Lunch not served; 24seats 20P bedrooms available International. Last dinner 10pm

KINGSEAT Fife *Fife* Map **11** NT19
★★Halfway House ☎Dunfermline 31661
10 CTV CTV in bedrooms 200P Live music & dancing Fri–Sun Last dinner 9.30pm
sB&B £11.25–£15 dB&B £18.50–£22
Lunch £2.50–£3.50 High Tea £2.25–£3.25
Dinner £3.95–£6.50 Wine £2.40
Credit cards 1 2 3

KINGSKETTLE Fife *Fife* Map **11** NO30
★★★ *Annfield House* ☎Ladybank 245
Closed 1st 2wks Nov; RS 14Nov–31 Mar (closed Mondays); 9rm(7) CTV 50P
Last dinner 9pm Wine £2.35

KINGUSSIE Highland *Inverness-shire* Map **14** NH70
★★Duke of Gordon Newtonmore Rd (Best Western) ☎302
An Edwardian building with a tower, topped by wrought iron and a pair of stone lions at entrance.
47rm(9) Lift CTV CTV available in bedrooms 90P billiards Live music & dancing nightly in summer Cabaret twice wkly in summer Last dinner 8.30pm S% sB&B £9.10–£11.10 dB&B £17–£21 dB&B £21–£24 Lunch £2.30–£2.75 Tea 35p–£1 Dinner £5.35 Credit cards 1 2 3 5

KINLOCHBERVIE Highland *Sutherland* Map **14** NC25
★★Kinlochbervie ☎275
Modern, two-storey white-painted building on hillside overlooking sea.
Closed Xmas & New Year; 10 Annexe: 2 CTV in bedrooms 40P Last dinner 8pm S% *sB&B fr £12.10 dB&B fr £24.20 Tea fr 60p Dinner fr £6.50 Wine £3.80

KINLOCH RANNOCH Tayside *Perthshire* Map **14** NN65
★★Dunalastair ☎323
24rm(6) CTV 20P 6 Last dinner 8.30pm S%
sB&B £7.50–£9.85 sB&B £9.66–£12.05
dB&B £15–£19.70 dB&B £19.33–£24.10
Lunch £2.75–£3.05 Tea 75p–£1.20
Dinner £4.45–£5.45 Wine £2.95
Credit cards 1 2 3 5

★★Loch Rannoch ☎201
Impressive late 19th-C hillside hotel with views of Loch Rannoch.
21rm(9) CTV 40P International. Last dinner 8.30pm S% sB&B fr £12.50 sB&B fr £15 dB&B fr £21 dB&B fr £25 Lunch fr £4 Tea fr 50p High Tea fr £1 Dinner fr £5 Wine £2.50 *xmas* Credit cards 1 2 3 5

KINROSS Tayside *Kinross-shire* Map **11** NO10
★★★Green 2 The Muirs (Best Western) ☎63467
Fully modernised former coaching inn standing in 6 acres of gardens.
50rm(48) CTV CTV available in bedrooms 60P (heated) (hard) squash sauna bath Live music & dancing Fri & Sat Scottish & French. Last dinner 9pm S%
sB&B £14.85–£16.50 dB&B £29.50–£32
Dinner £6&alc Wine £3.50 *xmas*
Credit cards 1 2 3 6

★★*Bridgend* ☎63413
10rm(3) CTV 50P Music & dancing 3nights wkly Last dinner 8pm

★Kirklands High St ☎63313
9rm TV 30P High Tea 8pm S%
sB&B £8.50 dB&B £17 Lunch £2–£2.25 Tea £1
High Tea £2–£3.50 Wine £2.90

K

××**Windlestrae** ☎63217
Closed Tue, Jan & 1st wk Oct; 50seats 50P bedrooms available ♡French. Last dinner9pm S% Lunch£4.05–£4.20 Dinner£9alc Wine£3.30 Credit cards 1 2 3 5

KIPPEN Central *Stirlingshire* Map**11** NS69
×***Vinery*** (Cross Keys Hotel) Main St ☎293
20seats 8P Live music Sun Last dinner9.30pm Credit card 3

KIPPFORD Dumfries & Galloway *Kirkcudbrightshire* Map**11** NX85
★**Anchor** ☎205
RS Nov–Mar; 15rm Annexe: 4rm(1⇌ ⋒) ♛ CTV 25P Last dinner8.30pm ♁ sB&B fr£8 dB&B fr£16 dB&B⇌ ⋒ fr£18 Bar lunch20p–£2 Dinner fr£5&alc Wine£2

KIRKCALDY Fife *Fife* Map**11** NT29
★★**Station** 4 Bennochy Rd (Osprey) ☎62461
34rm(9⇌ ⋒) ☽ ♛ CTV 10▲ Last dinner9pm ♁ ♖ S% ✱sB&B£9.50 sB&B⇌ ⋒£13 dB&B£16 dB&B⇌ ⋒£21 Lunch fr£2.60&alc Tea fr30p High Tea fr£2.60 Dinner fr£3.90&alc Wine£2.45 ⊟ *xmas* Credit cards 1 2 3 5

★**Victoria** ☎60117
Closed 1 & 2Jan; 9rm(1⇌ ⋒) CTV TV available in bedrooms ⊘ 30P Live music & dancing Wed Children under 12yrs not accommodated Last dinner7pm ✱sB&B£8.64 dB&B£17.28 dB&B⇌ ⋒£21.60 Lunch£2.16 High Tea£2.16–£3.78 Dinner fr£4.32 Wine£3 Credit cards 1 6

KIRKCOLM Dumfries & Galloway *Wigtownshire* Map**10** NX06
★★♣**Knocknassie House** Ervie (3½m W off B738) ☎Ervie217
8rm(1⇌ ⋒) CTV TV available in bedrooms 20P ⛟ ♣ ♠ Last dinner9pm S% sB&B£7–£7.50 dB&B£14–£15 Bar lunch£2alc Dinner fr£3.50&alc Wine£3.40 ⊟ *xmas* Credit card 2

★***Corsewall Arms*** Main St ☎228
12rm(1⇌ ⋒) ♛ CTV 40P ⛟ Last dinner8pm ♖ Credit cards 1 2 3 4 5 6

KIRKCUDBRIGHT Dumfries & Galloway *Kirkcudbrightshire* Map**11** NX65
★★**Royal** St Cuthbert Street ☎30551
20rm(7⇌ ⋒) ♛ CTV 6P 5▲ ⛟ Last dinner9pm ♁ ♖ S% sB&B£6–£6.50 sB&B⇌ ⋒£6.75–£7.25 dB&B£12–£13 dB&B⇌ ⋒£13.50–£14.50 Lunch£2–£2.80&alc Tea35p–£1 High Tea£1.60–£3 Dinner£3.50–£4.05 Wine£2.95 *xmas*

★★**Selkirk Arms** High St ☎30402
Robert Burns wrote the 'Selkirk Grace' here.
17rm(2⇌ ⋒) Annexe; 10rm(2⇌ ⋒) CTV 18▲ ⛟ ♣ ↬ Live music & dancing Tue Last dinner7.30pm ♁ S% sB&B£8.35–£9.61 dB&B£16.70–£19.22 dB&B⇌ ⋒£19.22–£23.02 Bar lunch60p–£3 Dinner£5–£5.80 Wine£2.70 ⊟ Credit card 1

❀×**Ingle** St Mary Street ☎30606
Rosette awarded for dinner only.
Closed Mon & Feb; Lunch not served Sun–Thu; 55seats Live music & dancing Fri & Sat ♡Continental & Italian. Specialities: Lasagne, Entrecôte pizzaiola. Last dinner9.30pm ✱Lunch£1.50–£3.05alc Dinner£5–£10alc Wine£3.80 Credit card 2 5

KIRKMICHAEL Tayside *Perthshire* Map**15** NO06
★★**Log Cabin** ☎Strathardle288
13rm(8⇌ ⋒) ♛ CTV CTV available in bedrooms 60P ♣ ⌂(heated) ⌒(hard) ↬ ∩ Live music & dancing Wed, Fri & Sat ♠ ♡Scottish, Continental & English. Last dinner9pm ♁ ♖ S% sB&B fr£10.10 dB&B£20.20–£42 dB&B⇌ ⋒£23–£45 Bar lunch fr£2 Tea fr45p Dinner fr£5.50 Wine£3 ⊟ *xmas* Credit cards 1 2 3 5

★**Strathlene** ☎Strathardle347
RS Nov–Jan; 8rm(1⇌) ♛ CTV 3P ⛟ Last dinner9pm ♁ sB&B£7.15–£8.80 sB&B⇌£8.15–£9.80 dB&B£14.30–£16 dB&B⇌£15.30–£17 Lunch£3 Tea25–60p Dinner£4.50 Wine£2.35 ⊟

Ⓖ**Aldchlappie** ☎Strathardle224
RS Nov–Mar; 7rm CTV 25P 4▲ ⛟ ♣ ↬ Last dinner9pm ♁ ✱sB&B fr£7.30 dB&B fr£14.60 Bar lunch fr£1.50 Dinner fr£5 Wine£2.50

KIRKWALL Orkney Map**16** HY41
★★**Ayre** Ayre Rd ☎2197
27rm(4⇌ ⋒) ♛ CTV 24P ⛟ sauna bath Disco wkly Live music & dancing wkly Last dinner8.30pm ♁ ♖ S% ✱sB&B£10.30 sB&B⇌ ⋒£12.40 dB&B£18.60 dB&B⇌ ⋒£22.90 Lunch£1.28alc Dinner£4.82alc Wine£2.70 *xmas* Credit cards 1 2 3

★★**Kirkwall** Harbour St (Allied Scotland) ☎2232 Telex no76357
Stone building near pier head with views over bay.
39rm(12⇌ ⋒) Lift ☽ ♛ CTV TV available in bedrooms P Disco twice wkly ♿ Last dinner8pm ♁ ♖ S% sB&B fr£10 sB&B⇌ ⋒ fr£12 dB&B fr£20 dB&B⇌ ⋒ fr£24 Lunch fr£3 Tea fr£1.50 Dinner fr£4.50 Wine£3.50 Credit cards 1 2 3 4 5 6

KIRRIEMUIR Tayside *Angus* Map**15** NO35
★**Airlie Arms** St Malcolm's Wynd ☎2847
Homely hotel in town centre.
7rm ♛ CTV ♁ ♖ S% ✱sB&B fr£5.20 dB&B fr£10.40 Bar lunch fr£1.75 Tea fr£1.15 High Tea fr£1.85 Dinner fr£3.45 Wine£3

KNOCK Isle of Skye, Highland *Inverness-shire* Map**13** NG60
★★**Toravaig House** Knock Bay (Inter-Hotel) ☎Isle Ornsay231
Closed Dec–Feb; 11rm(2⇌ ⋒) 20P 2▲ ⛟ ♣ ♠ Last dinner8pm ♁ ♖ S% ✱sB&B£6–£8.50 dB&B£12–£17 dB&B⇌ ⋒£15–£21 Lunch£2.50 Tea50p Dinner£5 Wine£2.30 Credit card 2

KYLE OF LOCHALSH Highland *Ross & Cromarty* Map**13** NG72
★★★**Lochalsh** (British Transport) ☎Kyle4202
White-painted building in prominent position, with fine views across Kyle of Lochalsh to Skye.
45rm(29⇌ ⋒) Lift ☽ ♛ CTV 4P 12▲ ♿ ♡English & French. Last dinner8.30pm ♁ ♖ S% sB&B⇌ ⋒ fr£22.60 dB&B⇌ ⋒ fr£41.70 Dinner fr£7.90 Wine£3.15 ⊟ *xmas* Credit cards 1 2 3 4 5 6

KYLEAKIN Isle of Skye, Highland *Inverness-shire* Map**13** NG72
★★**Marine** ☎Kyle4585
RS15Oct–15Mar; 25rm CTV 12P Last dinner8.15pm ♁ ♖ sB&B£7–£8 dB&B£14–£16 Lunch£2.50–£3.25 Tea35–45p Dinner£4.50–£5.50 Wine£2.36

LAGGAN BRIDGE Highland *Inverness-shire* Map**14** NN69
★***Gaskmore House*** ☎250
8rm TV 25P ♡International.

AIRG Highland *Sutherland* Map**14** NC50
★★**Sutherland Arms** (Scottish Highlands) ☎2291
elex no778215
tone hotel with views over River Shin and Dam.
losed 14Oct–24Apr; 27rm(20⇌⋒) Annexe: 5⇌⋒
CTV available in bedrooms 30P
ast dinner8.30pm S%
3&B£13.30–£15.10 sB&B⇌⋒£16.05–£17.95
3&B£21–£24.60 dB&B⇌⋒£26.50–£30.30
ar lunch£1.50–£2.50 Tea40p–£1.30
inner£6.25 Wine£3.25
redit cards 1 2 3 4 5 6

AMLASH Isle of Arran, Strathclyde *Bute* Map**10**
IS03
Lamlash ☎208
mall hotel on village main street, looking out across ay to Holy Isle.
S Oct–Mar; 11rm TV available in bedrooms 50P
ast dinner8pm Credit card 1

3X**Carraig Mhor** ☎453
'osette awarded for dinner only
losed Sun, Mon, last 2wks Feb & 1st 3wks Nov;
7seats bedrooms available Specialities: Roast uckling and orange sauce, scallops St Jacques, fillet f pork in cream sauce. Last dinner9pm
unch£2alc Dinner£6alc Wine£2.35

ANARK Strathclyde *Lanarkshire* Map**11** NS84
★***Cartland Bridge*** ☎4426
5rm CTV 300P Live music & dancing Sat
ast dinner9.15pm Credit cards 1 2

★★**Clydesdale** Bloomgate (Clansmans) ☎3565
rm(1⇌⋒) TV in bedrooms 100P Live music & ancing wkly European. Last dinner9pm
3&B£7.50 sB&B⇌⋒£9 dB&B£15
B&B⇌⋒£18 Lunch£4.20alc Tea50palc
ligh Tea£1.80–£3.15 Dinner£4.20alc
Vine£2.80 Credit cards 1 2 3 5

★***Caledonian*** Bannatyne St ☎3084
rm CTV TV available in bedrooms
ast dinner8pm Credit card 5

ANGBANK Strathclyde *Renfrewshire* Map**10** NS37
★★★**Gleddoch House** (Best Western) ☎711
elex no779801
Closed 26Dec & 1–2Jan; 19rm(18⇌⋒) 1
CTV CTV in bedrooms 100P 3 (heated)
quash sauna bath Last dinner9pm S%
B&B£10 sB&B⇌⋒£20 dB&B⇌⋒£25
unch£4–£4.50 Dinner£7.25–£8 Wine£3.50
mas Credit cards 1 2 3 4 5 6

ANGHOLM Dumfries & Galloway *Dumfriesshire*
Map**11** NY38
★★**Eskdale** Market Pl ☎357
2rm(2⇌⋒) CTV 16P Last dinner8pm

sB&B fr£6.90 sB&B⇌⋒ fr£8 dB&B fr£13.80
dB&B⇌⋒ fr£36 Lunch fr£2.15 Tea fr80p
High Tea fr£2.15 Dinner fr£3.90 Wine£2.12
Credit card 1

★**Crown** High St ☎247
8rm CTV 6P Disco twice wkly
Last dinner7.30pm sB&B£6.50 dB&B£13
Lunch fr£3.50&alc Dinner fr£3.50&alc Wine£3.50
Credit card 3

★***Holmwood House*** Holmwood Dr ☎211
7rm(3⇌⋒) TV 20P Live music 6nights wkly Live music & dancing wkly Last dinner6.30pm

LARGS Strathclyde *Ayrshire* Map**10** NS25
★★★**Marine & Curlinghall** Broomfields (Inter-Hotel)
☎674551
Originally two hotels, now linked to form one building. Situated in own grounds on sea front, with views of islands in Firth of Clyde.
58rm(30⇌⋒) 1 CTV CTV available in bedrooms 150P billiards Live music & dancing Sat
Last dinner9.30pm S% sB&B£14
sB&B⇌⋒£16 dB&B£23 dB&B⇌⋒£29
Lunch£3.75 Tea£1.15 Dinner£5.95
Credit cards 1 2 5 6

★★**Castle** Broomfields (Osprey) ☎673302
Two storey building overlooking sea and the Greens.
40rm(14⇌⋒) CTV 40P Live music & dancing twice wkly Cabaret twice wkly Last dinner8.45pm
S% ✱sB&B£9 sB&B⇌⋒£13 dB&B£15
dB&B⇌⋒£21 Lunch fr£2.60 Tea fr30p
High Tea fr£2.60 Dinner fr£3.90 Wine£2.46
xmas Credit cards 1 2 3 5

★★***Elderslie*** Broomfields ☎672251
25rm CTV 60P Last dinner9pm

★★**Mackerston** ☎673264
Closed Nov–Feb; 56rm(2⇌⋒) Lift CTV P
Last dinner8pm sB&B fr£9.50
sB&B⇌⋒ fr£9.50 dB&B fr£19 dB&B⇌⋒ fr£19
Lunch fr£2.25 Dinner fr£3.50 *xmas*
Credit cards 1 2 3

★★***Queens*** North Esp ☎673253
14rm CTV TV 60P sauna bath
Last dinner8.30pm Credit cards 2 4 6

★★**St Helens** Greenock Rd ☎672328
Detached stone building with gardens; set back off the main road and looking out across Firth of Clyde.
28rm(4⇌⋒) CTV 32P Children under 5yrs not accommodated Scottish & Italian.
Last dinner8pm sB&B£10.15–£11.40
sB&B⇌⋒£11.40–£12.65 dB&B£19–£20.25
dB&B⇌⋒£20.25–£22.80 Lunch£3.45–£4.05
Tea70–95p High Tea£2.30–£3
Dinner£4.60–£4.95 Wine£3.50 *xmas*

★★**Springfield** Greenock Rd ☎673119
40rm(16⇌⋒) Lift CTV 80P Live music &

dancing wkly Cabaret twice wkly Last dinner8pm ☕ S% sB&B£7–£7.70 sB&B⇌⋒£8–£9 dB&B£13–£14.50 dB&B⇌⋒£15–£16.50 Lunch fr£2.50 Tea fr50p High Tea fr£1.75 Dinner fr£3.50&alc Wine£3 ⛟ *xmas* Credit cards 1 2 3 5 6

⊕**Haylie** 108 Irvine Rd ☎672572
Detached stone house with extensions on southern side of town with views out across Clyde.
12rm ⚲ CTV ⊘ 8P ⚓ Last dinner7pm ⚘ ☕ S% ✱sB&B£5.25–£6 dB&B£10.50–£12 Tea80p High Tea£2.50–£3 Dinner£3–£3.50 Wine£2.10 ⛟

LATHONES Fife Map**12** NO40
★**Lathones** ☎Peat Inn219
Annexe: 6rm(5⇌⋒) ⚲ TV 40P ⛟ Live music wkly Last dinner9.30pm ⚘ ☕ S% sB&B⇌⋒£9.60 dB&B⇌⋒£18 Bar lunch£1.20 Dinner£5.50–£6 Wine£2.50 *xmas* Credit cards 1 2 3 4 5 6

LAUDER Borders *Berwickshire* Map**12** NT54
★**Lauderdale** 1 Edinburgh Rd ☎231
11rm(3⇌⋒) ⚲ CTV 60P 2⌂ ⚓ ☋ Mainly grills. Last dinner8.30pm ⚘ S% sB&B£7–£8 dB&B£12–£14 dB&B⇌⋒£14–£16 Lunch£2&alc High Tea£1–£2.50 Dinner£2.50–£3.50&alc Wine£2.25 ⛟

★**Loanside** 2 Edinburgh Rd ☎305
10rm CTV 40P Live music & dancing Sat Last dinner8pm ⚘ ☕ S% sB&B£8.50 dB&B£15 Bar lunch£1.70–£2 Tea£1 High Tea£2–£3 Dinner£5–£6 Wine£3.20 ⛟ *xmas*

LECKMELM Highland *Ross & Cromarty* Map**14** NH19
★⚑**Tir-Aluinn** ☎Ullapool2074
Closed Oct–May; 16rm(3⇌⋒) CTV 50P ⛟ ⚓ ♿ ⚘ ☕ S% sB&B fr£8.64 dB&B fr£17.28 dB&B⇌⋒fr£19.44 Bar lunch fr80p Tea fr£1 Dinner fr£4 Wine£2.35

LEDAIG Strathclyde *Argyll* Map**10** NM93
★★★⚑**Isle of Eriska** ☎205
See page 61 for details

LERWICK Shetland Map**16** HU44
★★★**Kveldsro House** ☎2195
Closed Xmas & New Year;
14rm(8⇌⋒) ⚲ CTV in bedrooms ⊘ 28P ⌂ Children under 12 not accommodated Last dinner8.30pm ⚘ ☕ sB&B£16.50 sB&B⇌⋒£22.50 dB&B£24.50 dB&B⇌⋒£31 Lunch£3alc Dinner£5.50alc Wine£2.85

★★★**Lerwick** Scalloway Rd (Thistle) ☎2166
Telex no75128
24⇌⋒ ☽ ⚲ CTV CTV in bedrooms ⊘ 60P Last dinner9pm ⚘ S% sB&B⇌⋒£28.20 dB&B⇌⋒£38.90 Lunch£4 Dinner£6.25&alc Wine£3.25 Credit cards 1 2 3 4 5 6

★★***Grand*** Commercial St ☎2018
27rm CTV TV available in bedrooms Last dinner8pm ⚘ ☕

★★**Queens** ☎2826
23rm ⚲ CTV ₱ Last dinner8.30pm ⚘ ☕ sB&B£16–£18 dB&B£24–£27 Lunch£2.50&alc Tea£1.20 Dinner fr£5.50&alc Wine£2.70

THAM Fife *Fife* Map **11** NO31
★ **Fernie Castle** ☎209 Telex no 727369
h-C fortified house standing in secluded grounds h a small lake.
1 CTV in bedrooms 80p Live music & ncing Sat Scottish & French.
st dinner 9.15pm
B&B £15.75–£24.25
&B £31.50–£33 Lunch £3.75–£7
nner £7.50alc Wine £3.15 Credit cards 1 2

TTERFINLAY Highland *Inverness-shire* Map **14**
29
Letterfinlay Lodge (off A82) ☎Invergloy 222
sed Nov–Feb; 12rm CTV 100P
st dinner 8pm sB&B £6–£9
&B £14–£18 Bar lunch £2 Tea £1.50 Dinner £5
ne £3

VEN Fife *Fife* Map **11** NO30
Caledonian High St (Osprey) ☎24101
rm(16) CTV CTV available in bedrooms
P 12 Disco 4 nights wkly. Last dinner 9pm
S% *sB&B £9.50 sB&B £13 dB&B £16
&B £21 Lunch fr £2.60&alc Tea fr 30p
h Tea fr £2.60 Dinner fr £3.90&alc Wine £2.40
xmas Credit cards 1 2 3 5

WIS, ISLE OF Western Isles *Ross & Cromarty*
p **13 See Shieldinish and Stornoway**

LITHGOW Lothian *West Lothian* Map **11** NS97
XX **Champany** (2m NE of A904)
Philipstoun 532
sed Sun & 1–3 Jan; 65 seats 40P International.
ecialities: Creamed tripe and onions; pork nderloin; crofter's fish pie. Last dinner 9.45pm
% *Lunch £4.10–£4.60&alc Dinner £8alc
ne £4 Credit cards 2 5

NWOOD Strathclyde *Renfrewshire* Map **10** NS46
Golden Pheasant Moss Rd (Clansmans)
Johnstone 21266
urpose-built hotel standing at the edge of this all commercial industrial town.
CTV CTV in bedrooms 100P Mainly grills.
st dinner 8.30pm *sB&B £10.25
&B £17.70 Lunch £3.45alc Dinner £3.45alc
ne £2.70 Credit cards 1 2 5

CHBOISDALE Isle of South Uist, Western Isles
verness-shire Map **13** NF71
Lochboisdale ☎332
vo stone buildings dating from approx 1850, anding close to rocky foreshore and harbour.
rm(6) TV 30P International.
st dinner 8.30pm S% sB&B £9.50–£11
&B £10.50–£12 dB&B £19–£22
&B £21–£24 Lunch fr £3.75
gh Tea fr £3.50 Dinner fr £5.35 Wine £2.50
edit cards 1 2 3

LOCHCARRON Highland *Ross & Cromarty* Map **14** NG93
★ **Lochcarron** ☎226
7rm(3) TV 20P Last dinner 7.30pm
*sB&B £7–£8.75 sB&B £8–£10
dB&B £14–£17.50 dB&B £16–£20
Bar lunch £1–£1.20 Tea 75p Dinner £5–£5.50
Wine £1.90

LOCHEARNHEAD Central *Perthshire* Map **11** NN52
★★★ **Lochearnhead** ☎237
Three-storey building overlooking Loch Earn.
Closed Nov–Jan; 45 CTV 100P 6
(hard) squash International.
*sB&B £8–£10 sB&B £9–£11
dB&B £18–£20 dB&B £18–£22
Lunch fr £2.60 Tea fr 75p High Tea fr £2
Dinner fr £5.50 Wine £2 Credit cards 1 2 3 5 6

★★ **Clachan Cottage** Lochside ☎247
A modernised conversion and extension of two 250 year-old cottages, overlooking Loch Earn and surrounding Perthshire Hills.
Closed Nov–Feb; 33rm(10) CTV 60P
Disco Sat Last dinner 8.30pm
*sB&B £7–£8.50 sB&B £7.50–£9
dB&B £15–£18 dB&B £15.50–£18.50
Lunch £2.25–£2.50 Tea 50p–£1 High Tea £2.50
Dinner £4.50 Wine £2.10 *xmas*
Credit cards 1 2 3 6

Mansewood Country House ☎213
Closed Feb; RS Nov–Jan; 6rm(3) TV 10P
International. Last dinner 8pm S%
sB&B £7–£11.50 sB&B £8.50–£13.50
dB&B £12–£16.50 dB&B £18.50 Lunch £4alc
Tea 50p Dinner £6 Wine £2 *xmas*

LOCHGAIR Strathclyde *Argyll* Map **10** NR99
★★ **Lochgair** (Inter-Hotel) ☎233
19rm(9) CTV 60P Live music & dancing
Fri & Sat Scottish & French. Last dinner 8.30pm
S% sB&B fr £11.50 sB&B fr £13.50
dB&B fr £21 dB&B fr £23 Bar lunch £1.75alc
Tea fr 45p Dinner fr £6.50 Wine £2.95 *xmas*
Credit cards 1 2 3 5 6

LOCHGILPHEAD Strathclyde *Argyll* Map **10** NR88
★★ ***Stag*** Argyll St ☎2496
RS Nov–Feb; 25rm CTV 16P Last dinner 8pm
Credit cards 1 3

LOCHINVER Highland *Sutherland* Map **14** NC02
★★ **Culag** ☎209
Closed 16 Oct–14 May; 48rm(19) Lift CTV 40P
Last dinner 8.30pm S%
sB&B £10.75 dB&B £22 dB&B £24.50
Lunch fr £3.50 Tea fr £1.30 Dinner fr £6.75
Wine £2.70 Credit cards 1 2 3 5

L

LOCHMADDY Isle of North Uist, Western Isles *Inverness-shire* Map**13** NF96
★★***Lochmaddy*** ☎331
20rm(1⇌ ⫙) ⩩ TV 50P ↬ Live music twice wkly
Last dinner9pm ♆ ⌧

LOCHWINNOCH Strathclyde *Renfrewshire* Map**10** NS36
✕***Gable End*** 45 High St ☎842775
Closed Mon & Tue; 40seats 20P Last dinner9pm
Credit cards 1 2

LOCKERBIE Dumfries & Galloway *Dumfriesshire* Map**11** NY18
★★**Dryfesdale** ☎2427
11rm(5⇌ ⫙) Annexe: 4rm(1⇌ ⫙) Lift ☽ ⩩ CTV TV available in bedrooms 100P ⛟ ⚓
Last dinner8.30pm ♆ ⌧ S% sB&B£12.50 sB&B⇌⫙£13.75 dB&B£17 dB&B⇌⫙£20
Lunch£2.50–£5 Tea40–70p Dinner£4.50–£7
Wine£2.30 ⛿

★★***Lockerbie House*** ☎2610
30rm(16⇌⫙) CTV 150P ⚓ Live music & dancing Sat
Last dinner8.45pm ♆

★★**Somerton House** Carlisle Rd ☎2583
6rm(3⇌⫙) ⩩ CTV 100P 1⌂ ⛟ ⚓ ♉ Mainly grills.
Last dinner8pm ♆ ⌧ sB&B£10.25
sB&B⇌⫙£10.90 dB&B£14.50 dB&B⇌⫙£16
Lunch£2–£4 Tea45–75p High Tea£1.65–£1.95
Dinner£4–£4.60 Wine£3.20

★**Blue Bell** ☎2309
12rm ⩩ CTV 12P Last dinner8pm ♆ ⌧
✻sB&B£6.48 dB&B£12.96 Lunch£2.37
Tea fr43p High Tea£3.45 Dinner fr£3.45 Wine£3
Credit card 3

★**Kings Arms** ☎2410
16rm CTV 8⌂ ⚓ Last dinner8.45pm ♆
✻sB&B£6 dB&B£12 Continental breakfast
Lunch90palc Dinner£2.85alc Wine£3.12
Credit cards 1 3

★**Townhead** Townhead St ☎2298
RS Dec–Mar; 11rm ⩩ CTV 30P Last dinner7.30pm
♆ ⌧ S% sB&B£5.40–£7 dB&B£10–£12
Lunch£2.20&alc Tea75p High Tea£2alc
Dinner£2.50alc Wine£2

LOGIERAIT Tayside *Perthshire* Map**14** NN95
★**Logierait** ☎Ballinluig253
Small roadside hotel, beside River Tay.
7rm ⩩ CTV 100P 3⌂ ⛟ ⚓ ↬ Live music & dancing
Sat & Sun Last dinner8pm ♆ ⌧ sB&B£7–£7.5
dB&B£14–£15 Bar lunch fr75p Tea fr50p
Dinner fr£5 Wine£2.30 ⛿

LOSSIEMOUTH Grampian *Moray* Map**15** NJ27
★★**Stotfield** ☎2011
Closed mid Oct–mid Apr; 50rm(13⇌⫙) ☽ ⩩ CTV
CTV available in bedrooms 20P 6⌂ Live music & dancing Wed & Fri Last dinner8pm ♆
sB&B£5.95–£9.95 sB&B⇌⫙£6.95–£10.95
dB&B£10.95–£19 dB&B⇌⫙£12.95–£21
Lunch£2.95 Dinner£4.50&alc Wine£2.20 ⛿

LOWER LARGO Fife *Fife* Map**12** NO40
✕✕**Crusoe Hotel Restaurant** ☎Lundin Links3207
60seats 30P bedrooms available Last dinner9pm
Dinner£6–£8&alc Wine£2.65

LUNAN BAY Tayside *Angus* Map**15** NO65
★★**Lunan Bay** ☎Inverkeilor265
Closed 1–3Jan; 8⇌⫙ ⩩ CTV CTV in bedrooms ⊗

L

0P 5 French & Italian. Last dinner9pm
S% ✱sB&B£13.65 sB&B⇌⋒£14.85
B&B£21.38 dB&B⇌⋒£23.76
nch£3.50–£6&alc High Tea£2–£2.50
nner£9alc Wine£3 Credit cards 1 2 3 5 6

UNDIN LINKS Fife *Fife* Map**12** NO40
★***Lundin Links*** ☎320207
rm(9⇌⋒) CTV 100P Last dinner9pm
Credit cards 1 2 3 6

Beach 55 Levens Rd ☎320368
rm(7⇌⋒) CTV 50P Scottish &
ench. Last dinner8.30pm S%
B&B£10–£11 sB&B⇌⋒£11–£12.50
B&B£19–£20 dB&B⇌⋒£21–£22
nch£3.25–£4 Dinner£5.25–£6 Wine£3.15
nas

USS Strathclyde *Dunbartonshire* Map**10** NS39
★***Colquhoun Arms*** ☎225
rm(1⇌⋒) CTV 50P Last dinner9.15pm
Credit cards 2 5

MACDUFF Grampian *Banffshire* Map**15** NJ76
★**Fife Arms** Shore St ☎32408
ituated in town centre, overlooking harbour.
rm(6⇌⋒) CTV 12P Last dinner8pm
B&B fr£9 sB&B⇌⋒ fr£10 dB&B fr£17
B&B⇌⋒ fr£19 Bar lunch fr£1.75 Tea fr75p
igh Tea fr£1.80 Dinner fr£5 Wine£2.60

Deveron House 27 Union Rd (Inter-Hotel) ☎32309
rm(12⇌⋒) CTV in bedrooms 18P Disco twice
kly Live music & dancing twice wkly
ast dinner7.30pm sB&B£8.50–£9.50
B&B⇌⋒£9.50–£10.50 dB&B£14–£17
B&B⇌⋒£17–£18.50 Lunch fr£2.75 Tea fr£1
igh Tea fr£2.50 Dinner fr£4.90&alc Wine£2.75
xmas Credit cards 1 2 3 5

MAIDENS Strathclyde *Ayrshire* Map**10** NS20
Bruce ☎Turnberry401
mall, modern hotel in coastal village, with views ver harbour and bay.
rm(2⇌⋒) CTV 40P Live music wknds
ast dinner10pm Credit card 1

MALLAIG Highland *Inverness-shire* Map**13** NM69
★**Marine** ☎2217
djacent to harbour and railway station.
rm(6⇌⋒) CTV 8P Last dinner8pm
B&B fr£9 sB&B⇌⋒ fr£10 Bar lunch fr£1
inner fr£4 Credit card 2

★***West Highland*** ☎2210 Telex no778869
arge stone building, dating from 1900, standing on aised site overlooking fishing port and islands of hum, Eigg and Skye.
rm(7⇌⋒) CTV 30P Last dinner8.30pm
Credit cards 1 2 3 5 6

MEIGLE Tayside *Perthshire* Map**11** NO24
★★**Kings of Kinloch** ☎273
Imposing 18th-C mansion set in own grounds of A94 situated 1½ miles W of Meigle. Rear views across Strathmore.
Closed 11–31 Jan; 7rm(1⇌⋒) TV available in bedrooms 45P 2 Live music & dancing Sat
Cosmopolitan. Last dinner9pm
sB&B£10 sB&B⇌⋒£11 dB&B£20
dB&B⇌⋒£22 Lunch£3.50–£5 High Tea£3.50alc
Dinner£5alc Wine£3.50

★**Meigle** ☎270
7rm CTV 60P 1 Disco Fri Live music & dancing Sat & Sun Last dinner8pm S%
sB&B£5.40–£6.50 dB&B£10.80–£13 Lunch£3
High Tea£2–£3 Dinner£3–£5 Wine£3 *xmas*

MELROSE Borders *Roxburghshire* Map**12** NT53
★★★**George & Abbotsford** (Swallow) ☎2308
Telex no53168
Three-storey stone coaching inn standing on main road in centre of Border town.
22rm(13⇌⋒) CTV 40P Last dinner9pm
S% sB&B£11.55–£12.50
sB&B⇌⋒£12.65–£15.45 dB&B£18.70–£22.10
dB&B⇌⋒£19.25–£25.80 *xmas*
Credit cards 1 2 3 5

★★**Burt's** The Square ☎2285
Dating from 1722, this converted town house is of architectural interest.
21rm(5⇌⋒) CTV 24P Last dinner8.30pm
sB&B£7.75 sB&B⇌⋒£9.25 dB&B£15.50
dB&B⇌⋒£18.50 Lunch£3.50–£4.50
Dinner£5–£6 Wine£2.80 Credit cards 1 2 3

★***Bon-Accord*** The Square ☎2645
Conversion of two adjoining stone houses dating from 1805, with shuttered windows.
8rm CTV Live music Sun Live music & dancing Sat
Last dinner8pm

MILNATHORT Tayside *Kinross-shire* Map**11** NO10
★**Thistle** New Rd ☎Kinross63222
6rm CTV 40P Live music & dancing 3nights wkly
Last dinner8pm S% ✱sB&B£5.50 dB&B£11
Lunch£2.50alc High Tea£2.40–£2.60
Dinner£3.50&alc Wine£2.80

MILNGAVIE Strathclyde *Dunbartonshire* Map**11** NS57
★★★**Black Bull** Main St (Thistle) ☎041–956 2291
27rm(26⇌⋒) CTV in bedrooms 65P
Scottish & French. Last dinner9.30pm
✱sB&B£16.50 sB&B⇌⋒£18.50 dB&B£25
dB&B⇌⋒£27 Lunch£3–£4 Tea50p
Dinner£4.50–£5.50&alc
Credit cards 1 2 3 5 6

M

MOCHRUM Dumfries & Galloway *Wigtownshire* Map**10** NX34
★**Greenmantle** ☎Port William357
This 17th-C building was formerly a manse and was converted to an hotel some ten years ago, in its own gardens in centre of small country village.
7rm(6⇌ ⫙) TV 30P Last dinner8.30pm sB&B⇌⫙£9 dB&B⇌⫙£18 Lunch£2.75&alc Dinner£6.60&alc Wine£2.50

MOFFAT Dumfries & Galloway *Dumfriesshire* Map**11** NT00
☆☆☆**Ladbroke Mercury Motor Inn** Ladyknowe (Ladbroke) ☎20464
A modern two-storey building at the foot of the main square.
51⇌⫙ CTV CTV available in bedrooms 70P Last dinner10pm sB&B⇌⫙£14.50–£17 dB&B⇌⫙£22.50–£27 Lunch fr£4.50&alc Dinner fr£5.50&alc Wine£3.20 Credit cards 1 2 3 4 5 6

★★**Annandale** High St ☎20013
Three storey hotel situated in the main square
Closed Xmas Day & Jan–Mar; 30rm CTV TV available in bedrooms 50P Last dinner8.30pm sB&B£10 sB&B⇌⫙£16 dB&B£19 dB&B⇌⫙£23 Continental breakfast Lunch fr£3.50 Dinner fr£5.75 Wine£3.50 Credit cards 1 2 3 5 6

★★**Balmoral** High St ☎20288
Two storey hotel with characteristic shutters.
20rm(3⇌⫙) CTV 20P Last dinner9pm sB&B£8 sB&B⇌⫙£9 dB&B£16 dB&B⇌⫙£18 Lunch fr£2.40 Tea fr80p High Tea fr£2.40 Dinner£4.25 Wine£2.42 Credit cards 1 2 3 5 6

★★**Beechwood Country House** ☎20210
8rm(3⇌⫙) CTV 20P Last dinner9pm sB&B£8–£10 sB&B⇌⫙£9–£11 dB&B£16–£20 dB&B⇌⫙£18–£22 Lunch£2.50–£3.50 Tea£1–£1.50 Dinner£5–£6 Wine£2.50

★★**Moffat House** High St ☎20039
14rm(5⇌⫙) CTV 30P 10 Scottish, English, French & Italian. Last dinner8.45pm S% sB&B£8.50–£10 sB&B⇌⫙£9.50–£11 dB&B£17–£20 dB&B⇌⫙£19–£22 Lunch£3.25 High Tea£3 Dinner£5.50&alc Wine£3.75 Credit cards 2 3 5

MONIAVE Dumfries & Galloway *Dumfriesshire* Map**11** NX79
★★**Woodlea** ☎209
Closed Nov; 13rm(2⇌⫙) CTV 20P (heated) (grass) sauna bath Last dinner8.30pm S% sB&B£8.50–£9.78 dB&B£17–£19.55 dB&B⇌⫙£21–£24.15 Lunch£2.90–£3.19 Tea90–99p Dinner£4.80–£5.28&alc Wine£2.45

★**Craigdarroch Arms** ☎205
9rm CTV 8P Last dinner9pm *sB&B£5.90–£6.90 dB&B£11.80–£13.80 Lunch£2.50–£3 Tea50–65p High Tea£1.80–£3 Dinner£3–£4 Wine£2.20 Credit cards 1 3 5

MONKTON Strathclyde *Ayrshire* Map**10** NS32
★★★***Adamton House*** ☎Prestwick70678
30⇌⫙ CTV 80P Live music & dancing Sat English & French. Last dinner9.30pm Credit cards 1 2 3 5

MONTROSE Tayside *Angus* Map**15** NO75
★★★**Links** Mid Links ☎2288
22rm(18⇌⫙) CTV TV available in bedrooms 40P Disco 5 nights wkly Live music & dancing twice wkly Last dinner10.45 S% sB&B⇌⫙fr£14 dB&B⇌⫙fr£20 Lunch£2.50&alc Dinner£4.50alc Wine£3.50 Credit cards 1 3 5 6

★★★**Park** John St ☎3415 Telex no76367
59rm(41⇌⫙) CTV CTV in bedrooms 100P Last dinner9pm S% sB&B£14.50 sB&B⇌⫙£20 dB&B£24 dB&B⇌⫙£26 Lunch fr£3.30&alc Tea£1 High Tea fr£3 Dinner fr£4.40&alc Wine£3.50 Credit cards 2 3 5

★**Corner House** 134 High St ☎3126
12rm(2⇌⫙) CTV Last dinner9pm *sB&B£9–£11 sB&B⇌⫙£11 dB&B£16–£18 dB&B⇌⫙£20–£22 Lunch£2 Tea80p High Tea£2.50–£3 Dinner£5alc Wine£2.80

MONYMUSK Grampian *Aberdeenshire* Map**15** NJ61
★★**Grant Arms** ☎226
Closed Nov–Mar; 10rm(1⇌⫙) CTV 20P Live music & dancing Fri, Sat & Sun Last dinner9pm sB&B£9.50 sB&B⇌⫙£10.70 dB&B£17 dB&B⇌⫙£21.40 Lunch£2.75 Tea95p Dinner£6 Wine£3.17 Credit card 5

MORAR Highland *Inverness-shire* Map**13** NM69
★★**Morar** ☎Mallaig2346
Closed 20Oct–Apr; 27rm TV 50P Last dinner8.30pm S% sB&B£8.91–£11 dB&B£16.08–£20 Lunch£3 Tea40p Dinner£5 Wine£2.50

MOTHERWELL Strathclyde *Lanarkshire* Map**11** NS75 **See also Wishaw**
★★★**Garrion** Merry St (Open House) ☎64561
52rm(35⇌⫙) Lift CTV in bedrooms 200P Disco Fri & Sat Last dinner9.15pm S% *sB&B fr£13 sB&B⇌⫙fr£15.25 dB&B fr£19.50 dB&B⇌⫙fr£21 Lunch fr£3&alc Tea fr40p High Tea fr£2 Dinner fr£3.75&alc Wine£2.75 Credit cards 1 2 3 5

M

UIRHEAD Strathclyde *Lanarkshire* Map**11** NS66
★Crow Wood House (Scottish & Newcastle)
☎041-779 3861
B⇌⋒ ☽ ⋈ CTV 100P Last dinner 9pm ☆ S%
sB&B⇌⋒£9.20 dB&B⇌⋒£18.40
unch£2.50alc High Tea£1.45 Dinner£3.40alc
Vine£2.80 Credit cards 2 3

✕*La Campágnola* 112 Cumbernauld Rd
☎041-779 3405
losed Sun; 60 seats P ♡Continental.
ast dinner 10.45pm Credit cards 1 3 5

UIR OF ORD Highland *Ross & Cromarty* Map**14**
H55
★Ord Arms ☎286
losed 1 & 2 Jan; 15rm(7⇌⋒) ⋈ CTV CTV in
edrooms 80P ⊕ ⚓ Live music & dancing mthly ♧
♡International. Last dinner 9.30pm ☆ ⊥ S%
B&B£8.31–£9 sB&B⇌⋒£10.69–£11.50
B&B£16.63–£18 dB&B⇌⋒£19–£21
unch£2.75–£3 Tea75P–£1
igh Tea£1.75–£3.80 Dinner£5alc Wine£3.10

ULL, ISLE OF See **Bunessan, Craignure, Salen nd Tobermory**

AIRN Highland *Nairnshire* Map**14** NH85
★★★Golf View Seabank Rd ☎52301
57rm(50⇌⋒) Lift ☽ CTV CTV in bedrooms 35P 2⌂
⊕ ⚓ ⌓(heated) ⚲(hard) sauna bath Live music &
ancing 3 nights wkly Cabaret wkly ♧ ♡International.
ast dinner 9pm ☆ ⊥ sB&B£14–£17
B&B⇌⋒£16–£19 dB&B£28–£34
B&B⇌⋒£32–£38 Lunch£3.75 Tea fr£1
Dinner fr£5.75&alc Wine£3.50 ⊨ *xmas*
Credit cards 1 2 3 5

★★★★Newton ☎53144
Closed Nov–Mar; 31⇌⋒ Lift ☽ ⋈ CTV CTV available in bedrooms 60P ⊕ ⚓ ⚲(hard) sauna bath ♿ ♡International. Last dinner 9.30pm ☆ ⊥ S%
✱sB&B⇌⋒£14–£19 dB&B⇌⋒£28–£38
Lunch£3.95&alc Tea£1 High Tea£3.50–£4
Dinner£6.50&alc Wine£2.20 ⊨
Credit cards 1 2 5

★★★Royal Marine (Scottish Highlands) ☎53381
Telex no 778215
Closed 14 Oct–24 Apr; 43rm(32⇌⋒) Lift ☽ CTV 40P ⚓ ♿ Last dinner 8.30pm ☆ ⊥ S%
sB&B£13.30–£15.10 sB&B⇌⋒£16.05–£17.95
dB&B£21–£24.60 dB&B⇌⋒£26.50–£30.30
Bar lunch£1.50–£2.50 Tea40p–£1.30
Dinner£6.25 Wine£3.25 ⊨
Credit cards 1 2 3 4 5 6

★★*Alton Burn* Alton Burn Rd ☎52051
26rm CTV 40P ⚓ ⌓(heated) May–Sep ⚲(hard)
Last dinner 8pm ☆ ⊥ ⊨

★★Clifton ☎53119
A conversion of two adjoining three-storey buildings on corner site near to sea front.
Closed Nov–mid Mar; 19rm(5⇌⋒) 1⊟ CTV 20P ⊕ ⚓ ♡French. Last dinner 9.30pm ☆ ⊥
✱sB&B£9 sB&B⇌⋒£10.50–£12.50 dB&B£18
dB&B⇌⋒£21–£25 Bar lunch£3.90alc
Tea40p–£1.20 Dinner fr£7 Wine£2.95

★★Windsor Albert St ☎53108
48rm(4⇌⋒) ⋈ CTV TV available in bedrooms 20P 6⌂ Last dinner 9pm ☆ ⊥ sB&B£7–£8
dB&B£14–£16 dB&B⇌⋒£18–£20 Lunch fr£3
Tea fr£1 High Tea fr£2.50 Dinner fr£4&alc
Wine£3.50 ⊨ Credit card 3

N

Invermarine Thurlow Rd ☎53160
4rm CTV 40P Last dinner8.30pm
% *sB&B£6–£7.25 dB&B£11–£13.50
unch£2.50 Tea£1 Dinner£3–£3.50&alc
Vine£3.75

Ross House Seabank Rd ☎53731
RS Oct–Mar; 17rm CTV 17P Live music & dancing Fri
ast dinner8pm sB&B£5.50–£6
B&B⇌⋔£5.75–£6.20 dB&B£11–£12
B&B⇌⋔£11.50–£12.40 Lunch£1.75–£2
Tea30–45p Dinner£4–£4.25 Wine£2

Taste Bud 44 Harbour St ☎52743
Closed Oct; Lunch not served in winter; 48seats
International. Last dinner9pm

ETHY BRIDGE Highland *Inverness-shire* Map**14**
NJ02
★★★Nethy Bridge (Best Western) ☎203
Telex no75261
Closed mid Oct–Mar; 66rm(54⇌⋔) Lift CTV TV available in bedrooms 40P 10 billiards Live music & dancing twice wkly Scottish & French. Last dinner9pm S% sB&B£14
sB&B⇌⋔£16 dB&B£28 dB&B⇌⋔£30
Bar lunch£2–£4 Dinner£6–£7.50 Wine£2.75
Credit cards [1][2][3][5][6]

★Mount View ☎324
Situated in three acres of secluded tree-studded grounds on outskirts of village.
Closed Oct–26Dec; 11rm CTV 20P
Last dinner8pm S% sB&B£8.33
dB&B£16.66 Dinner£5.54 Wine£2.10

NEW ABBEY Dumfries & Galloway
Kirkcudbrightshire Map**11** NX96
★*Abbey Arms* 1 The Square ☎215
7rm CTV 6P Last dinner6.30pm

NEWARTHILL Strathclyde *Lanarkshire* Map**11** NS75
★*Silverburn* Loanhead Rd (Scottish & Newcastle)
☎Holytown732503
Closed New Year's Day; 6⇌⋔ CTV 60P
Disco Sun Continental. Last dinner8.30pm
Credit cards [1][3][5][6]

NEWBRIDGE Lothian *Midlothian* Map**11** NT17
★★Norton ☎031–3331275
9rm(3⇌⋔) CTV CTV available in bedroom 50P
Last dinner9pm

NEW GALLOWAY Dumfries & Galloway
Kirkcudbrightshire Map**11** NX67
★★Kenmure Arms ☎360
17rm CTV 15P Last dinner7.30pm S%
sB&B fr£7 dB&B fr£14 Lunch fr£3
Dinner fr£4.50 Wine£3

★Crosskeys ☎218
RS 2wks Nov; 9rm TV 8P 2 Last dinner8pm
sB&B£6.90–£7.45 dB&B£13.80–£14.90
Lunch£3.20–£3.50 Tea70p Dinner£4.75–£5.35
Credit cards [1][3]

NEWTON MEARNS Strathclyde *Renfrewshire*
Map**11** NS55
XXMearns House Mearnskirk ☎041–639 7576
Lunch not served Mon–Thu; 36seats 20P French.
Last dinner10.45pm S% Lunch£3.25–£3.50&alc
Dinner£8alc Wine£3.25 Credit cards [1][2][3]

NEWTONMORE Highland *Inverness-shire* Map**14**
NN79
★★Highlander Motel (Inter-Hotel) ☎341
33⇌⋔ CTV TV available in bedrooms 100P
Disco wkly Live music & dancing twice wkly
Food served 24hrs S%
sB&B⇌⋔£8–£10.85 dB&B⇌⋔ fr£14.85
Lunch fr£2.50 Tea fr50p High Tea fr£1.50
Dinner fr£4.50&alc Wine£2.50 *xmas*
Credit cards [1][2][3][4][5][6]

★★Macdonald Lodge Fort William Rd ☎256
12rm Annexe: 6rm(3⇌⋔) TV 20P
Last dinner8pm S% sB&B£10.30
sB&B⇌⋔£10.30 dB&B£20.60 dB&B⇌⋔£20.60
Bar lunch£1.25&alc Tea45palc
High Tea£1.90&alc Dinner£5alc Wine£3.50

★★Mains ☎206
34rm(5⇌⋔) CTV 50P 20 Disco wkly Live music & dancing wkly Last dinner9pm
sB&B£7.56–£8.74 sB&B⇌⋔£9.56–£10.74
dB&B£15.12–£17.48 dB&B⇌⋔£17.12–£19.48
Lunch£3.50–£4.35 Tea75p–85p
Dinner£4.60–£6.25 Wine£3.25 *xmas*
Credit cards [1][2][3][5]

★Glen Main St ☎203
Converted small stone house with modern extension to side and front.
9rm(2⇌⋔) CTV 25P Last dinner7.30pm
S% sB&B£6.50 dB&B£13 dB&B⇌⋔£17
Bar lunch£1.50alc Dinner£7alc Wine£3

Badenoch Station Rd ☎246
Closed early Oct–late Mar; Unlicensed; 7rm 12P

NEWTON STEWART Dumfries & Galloway
Wigtownshire Map**10** NX46
★★★Bruce Queen St ☎2294
22rm(16⇌⋔) CTV TV available in bedrooms 20P
6 French. Last dinner8.45pm S%
sB&B£9–£13 sB&B⇌⋔£10–£14
dB&B£18–£26 dB&B⇌⋔£20–£28
Lunch£2–£3.30 High Tea£3
Dinner£5–£5.50&alc Wine£2.35 *xmas*
Credit cards [1][2][3][5]

N

★★**Crown** 101 Queen St ☎2727
RS Nov–Mar; 13rm(1⇌⫶) ♨ CTV ⊘ 20P ⊞
Last dinner 8pm ✿ S% sB&B fr£7.50
dB&B fr£14 dB&B⇌⫶ fr£16 Lunch fr£2.40
Dinner fr£3.75 Wine£2.90

★★**Galloway Arms** Victoria St ☎2282
Old building set between shops in centre of market town.
21rm(14⇌⫶) ☽ ♨ CTV 10P 12⌂ ⚓ ♡ Mainly grills.
Last dinner 8pm ✿ ♖ S% Lunch£2alc
Tea60p alc High Tea£2.50alc Dinner£4.50alc
Wine£3.50

★★**Kirroughtree** Minnigaff ☎2141
This 18th-C mansion is set in an elevated position in parkland, 2m outside town.
24rm(12⇌⫶) CTV in bedrooms 60P ⚓ ♡ Scottish & French. Last dinner 9.30pm ✿ sB&B£8.30–£10
sB&B⇌⫶£9.30–£11 dB&B£12.50–£20
dB&B⇌⫶£14.50–£22 Lunch fr£4.50&alc
Dinner fr£5.50&alc Wine£3 ▤ *xmas*
Credit cards 1 5 6

★**Cairnsmore** Victoria St ☎2162
11rm CTV 12P 4⌂ ⚓ ♡ Mainly grills.
Last dinner 7pm ✿ S% sB&B£5.50
dB&B£10–£13 Lunch£2alc High Tea£2alc
Dinner£3alc Wine£2.10 Credit card 1

★**Glencairn** 14 Arthur St ☎2355
10rm(3⇌⫶) CTV 14P Cabaret wkly
Last dinner 10pm ✿ ♖ sB&B£5.50–£7
dB&B£11–£14 Lunch fr£2.50&alc
Tea75p–£1.50 High Tea£2–£2.90&alc
Dinner£3.75–£4.25&alc Wine£2

NORTH BALLACHULISH Highland *Inverness-shire*
Map **14** NN06
★***Loch Leven*** ☎Onich236
RS Nov–Feb; 7rm TV 50P ⊞ ⚓ Last dinner 10pm ✿

NORTH BERWICK Lothian *East Lothian* Map **12** NT58
★★★**Marine** Cromwell Rd (Trusthouse Forte)
☎2406 Telex no 727363
Hotel in grand resort style, with excellent views across Firth of Forth.
85⇌⫶ Lift ☽ ♨ CTV TV in bedrooms 150P ⚓
⌒(heated) ⚘(hard) squash sauna bath
Last dinner 9pm ✿ ♖ S%
sB&B⇌⫶£14–£15.50 dB&B⇌⫶£23 ▤ *xmas*
Credit cards 1 2 3 4 5 6

★★***Blenheim House*** Westgate ☎2385
6rm(3⇌⫶) CTV 30P ⊞ ⚓ ♿ Last dinner 9pm ✿

★★***Nether Abbey*** Dirleton Av ☎2802
Closed Nov–Feb; 18rm(2⇌⫶) CTV 70P ⊞ ⚓
Last dinner 8pm Credit card 3

★★**Point Garry** West Bay Rd ☎2380 Closed
Nov–Feb; 15rm(8⇌⫶) ♨ CTV 15P ⊞ billiards
Last dinner 8.30pm ✿ ♖ sB&B£8.50
sB&B⇌⫶£9.50 dB&B£16 dB&B⇌⫶£18
Lunch£3 Tea75p Dinner£4.05&alc Wine£2.50

✕**Al Vagabondo** 35 High St ☎3434
Closed Mon (Nov–Mar); Lunch not served Sun;
50seats ♡ Italian. Last dinner 10.45pm
✻Lunch£2.20–£2.60&alc Dinner£6alc
Wine£2.90 Credit cards 1 3 4 5

NORTH UIST, ISLE OF Western Isles *Inverness-shire* Map **13**
See **Lochmaddy**

OBAN Strathclyde *Argyll* Map **10** NM83
★★★**Alexandra** Corran Esp (Scottish Highlands)
☎2381 Telex no 778215
Stone building with gables, tower and Regency style porch leading to front. Views of Oban Bay.
Closed 14Oct–24Apr; 59rm(33⇌⫶) Lift ☽ CTV 30P
20⌂ ⊞ ♿ Last dinner 8.30pm ✿ ♖ S%
sB&B£13.30–£15.10 SB&B⇌⫶£16.05–£17.95
dB&B£21–£24.60 dB&B⇌⫶£26.50–£30.30
Bar lunch£1.50–£2.50 Tea40p–£1.30
Dinner£6.25 Wine£3.25 ▤
Credit cards 1 2 3 4 5 6

★★★**Caledonian** Station Sq ☎3133 Telex no 778869
Set in town centre close to railway and bus station, this five-storey Victorian building overlooks the bay and harbour.
Closed 16Oct–Apr; 72rm(31⇌⫶) Lift ☽ CTV ₱
Last dinner 9pm ✿ ♖ S% sB&B£10–£15
sB&B⇌⫶£11.50–£18 dB&B£20–£24
dB&B⇌⫶£23–£29 Lunch£3.50 Dinner£5.85
Wine£3.25 ▤ Credit cards 1 2 3 5 6

★★★**Great Western** The Esplanade (Scottish Highlands) ☎3101 Telex no 778215
Large traditional hotel with imposing frontage, situated on Esplanade looking out across Oban Bay.
Closed 14Oct–24Apr; 76rm(58⇌⫶) Lift ☽ CTV 20P
Disco 3 nights Conference facilities available
Last dinner 8.30pm ✿ ♖ S%
sB&B£13.30–£15.10 sB&B£16.05–£17.95
dB&B£21–£24.60 dB&B⇌⫶£26.50–£30.30
Lunch£4.10 Tea40p–£1.30 Dinner£6.25
Wine£3.25 ▤ Credit cards 1 2 3 4 5 6

★★★**Regent** The Esplanade ☎2341
Narrow sandstone building at end of Esplanade overlooking Oban Pier.
31rm(24⇌⫶) Lift ☽ ♨ CTV ₱ Last dinner 8.30pm
✿ ♖ sB&B£8.77–£12.61
sB&B⇌⫶£10.24–£16.24 dB&B£16.45–£24.13
dB&B⇌⫶£19.38–£31.39 Lunch fr£3.99
Dinner fr£5.53 Wine£2.75 ▤ Credit cards 1 2

★Columba North Pier ☎2183
›osed 19Oct–12Apr; 55rm Lift ☽ ⚿ CTV 9P Live
ısic & dancing Tue, Fri, Sat & Sun Last dinner8pm
 S% sB&B£8.10–£9.72
&B£16.14–£19.64 Lunch£2.30 Dinner£3.80
ne£3.25

★Lancaster Corran Esp ☎2587
›one building with fine views of Oban Bay and
›rrara Island.
›rm(5⇌⋒) CTV 20P ⛟ ⊡(heated) sauna bath
›st dinner7.30pm ✿ ♔ ✱sB&B£9 dB&B£18
&B⇌⋒£19 Lunch fr£2.50 Dinner fr£4
ne£2.30

★Marine The Esplanade ☎2211
›ilding in style of 1930s, situated on sea front
›erlooking bay and islands.
›osed Oct–Mar; 44rm(11⇌⋒) Lift ☽ CTV 12P ⛟ ♿
›st dinner8.15pm ✿ ♔ sB&B fr£10
&B fr£19 dB&B⇌⋒ fr£22.50 Lunch fr£2.75
›nner fr£5.25 Wine£2.95 Credit cards 1 2 3 5

★Park The Esplanade ☎3621
›rm(39⇌⋒) Lift ☽ CTV 16P Live music & dancing
›ice wkly ♁European. Last dinner8.30pm ✿
&B£9.50–£14 sB&B⇌⋒£11–£16
&B£18–£26 dB&B⇌⋒£20–£30
›nch fr£3.25 Dinner fr£5.25 ⊟ *xmas*
›edit cards 1 2 3 5

★*Rowan Tree* George St ☎2954
›rm(16⇌⋒) ☽ ⚿ CTV TV available in bedrooms
P ✿ ♔ ⊟

Palace George St ☎2294
›licensed; 18rm(6⇌⋒) ⚿ CTV Last dinner8pm

King's Knoll Dunollie Rd ☎2536
›nverted stone manse, with well maintained
›rdens, overlooking Oban Bay.
›osed Nov–Mar; 18rm ⚿ CTV 12P ⛟ ⚓
›st dinner7.45pm ✿ sB&B£6.50–£7.50
&B£13–£15 Bar lunch60p–£2
›nner£4–£4.50&alc ⊟ Credit cards 1 2 3

✕*Le Bistro* Breadalbane St ☎3823
›osed Oct–May; Lunch not served; 85seats Music
›ights wkly Cabaret wkly ♁English & French.
›st dinner11pm Credit card 1

LD KILPATRICK Strathclyde *Dunbartonshire*
›ap**11** NS47
Telstar ☎Duntocher72938
›osed Sun; Lunch not served Sat; 50seats 60P
Scottish, French, & Italian. Last dinner9.15pm
Lunch£1.75–£2.50&alc Dinner£5alc
›ine£3.50 Credit cards 2 5

LD RAYNE Grampian *Aberdeenshire* Map**15** NJ62
Lodge ☎205
›osed New Year's Day; 2rm Annexe:4⇌⋒ ⚿ CTV
60P Last dinner8pm ✿ ♔ ✱sB&B£6
sB&B⇌⋒£10 dB&B£12 dB&B⇌⋒£16 Bar
lunch£2 Tea50p High Tea£1.90 Dinner£5alc
Wine£2.40 ⊟

ONICH Highland *Inverness-shire* Map**14** NN06
★★Allt-Nan-Ros ☎210
In own grounds with splendid views over Loch Linnhe and surrounding hills.
Closed Nov–Mar; 20rm ⚿ CTV 30P ⚓
Last dinner8.30pm ✿ ♔ S% sB&B£6.50
dB&B£13 Dinner fr£4 Credit card 3

★★Creag Dhu ☎238
Closed 27Oct–Mar; 19rm(4⇌⋒) ⚿ CTV 25P ⛟ ⚓
Children under 1 year not accommodated
Last dinner8pm ✿ ♔ S% sB&B£10–£12
dB&B£18–£22 dB&B⇌⋒£21–£25 Bar
Lunch£2alc Tea35p–£1 Dinner£5.50–£7&alc
Wine£2.70

★★Onich ☎214
Conversion of two adjoining houses, dating from 1880, with modern extension, standing on lochside in own grounds. Views over Loch Linnhe and surrounding hills.
Closed 15 Oct–25Apr; 25rm CTV 50P ⚓
Last dinner8pm ✿ ♔ S% ✱sB&B£8–£9
dB&B£16–£19 Bar lunch£2 Tea£1.25 Dinner£6
Wine£2.90 Credit cards 1 2

ORKNEY Map**16**
see **Harray, Kirkwall, St Margaret's Hope and Stromness**

OVERSCAIG Highland *Sutherland* Map**14** NC42
★★Overscaig ☎Merkland203
RS Nov–Mar; 14rm(5⇌⋒ ⚿ TV 30P 3⌂ ⛟ ⚓ ↬
♁Scottish & French. Last dinner10pm ✿ S%
sB&B£10–£11 sB&B⇌⋒£22–£24
Bar lunch£2–£3.50 Dinner fr£6&alc Wine£3 ⊟
Credit card 2

PAISLEY Strathclyde *Renfrewshire* Map**11** NS46
Hotels and restaurants are listed under Glasgow Airport

PATHHEAD Lothian *Midlothian* Map**11** NT36
★★Stair Arms (Open House) ☎Ford (Midlothian) 320277
Old coaching inn with tastefully renovated interior, retaining its old-world atmosphere. An old coach stands by the car park. Location is on the A68 to Edinburgh.
7rm ⚿ CTV 100P 2⌂ ⚓ Live music & dancing Sat
Last dinner9.30pm ✿ Credit cards 1 2 3 4 5 6

PEAT INN Fife *Fife* Map**12** NO40
✕✕Peat Inn ☎206
Closed Mon; 46seats 40P ♁French.
Last dinner9.30pm Dinner£6alc Wine£2.40
Credit cards 2 6

P

PEEBLES Borders *Peeblesshire* Map**11** NT24
★★★**Park** Innerleithen Rd (Swallow) ☎20451
Telex no53168
Traditional Scottish building with modern extension overlooks the River Tweed and Border hills.
18⇌⋒ ☽ CTV CTV in bedrooms 50P ⚓
Last dinner9pm ✿ ☕ S%
sB&B⇌⋒£12.65–£17.25
dB&B⇌⋒£20.35–£26.45 ⛿ *xmas*
Credit cards 1 2 3 5

★★★**Peebles Hydro** ☎20602 Telex no72568
An impressive late Victorian building set in 30 acres of grounds with fine views over the River Tweed, surrounding hills and pine forests.
Closed 5days before Xmas & 5days after New Year; 145rm(127⇌⋒) Lift ☽ ⛭CTV TV available in bedrooms ⊗ 150P ⚓ ▭(heated) (hard) squash ⌒ billiards sauna bath Live music & dancing twice wkly Conference facilities available Last dinner8.30pm ✿ ☕ S% sB&B£14.65–£15.75
sB&B⇌⋒£16.85–£18 dB&B£24.75–£27
dB&B⇌⋒£29.25–£41.50 Lunch£3.50–£4.75
Tea fr35p Dinner£5.75–£7.50 Wine£4.25 ⛿
xmas

★★★**Tontine** High St (Trusthouse Forte) ☎20892
37⇌⋒ ☽ ⛭CTV TV in bedrooms 30P 6⌂
Last dinner9.30pm ✿ ☕ S% sB&B⇌⋒£15.50
dB&B⇌⋒£24.50 ⛿ *xmas*
Credit cards 1 2 3 4 5 6

★★ **Cringletie House** ☎Eddleston233
See page 61 for details

★★ **Venlaw Castle** Edinburgh Rd ☎20384
Built in 1872 this converted, Baronial-style, storehouse stands in 6½ acres of wooded hill country on the site of the keep of the old Smithfield castle.

P

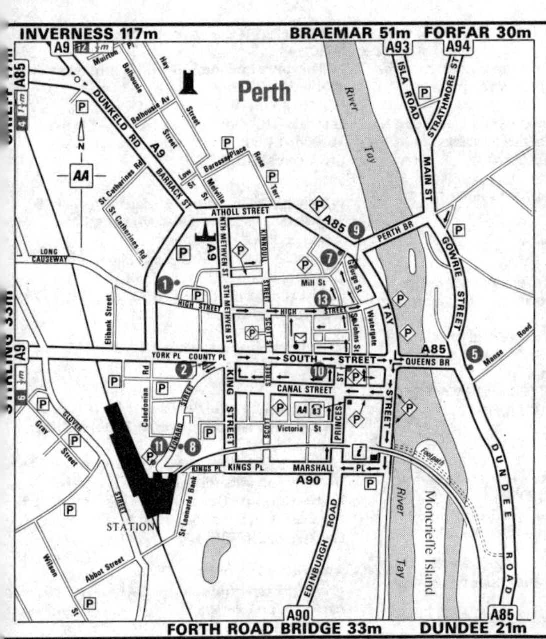

1 City Mills☆☆☆
2 County★
4 Huntingtower★★ (*see under Almondbank*)
5 Isle of Skye★★★
6 Lovat House★★
7 Penny Post✕
8 Queen's★★
9 Royal George★★★
10 Salutation★★
11 Station★★★★
12 Tay Motel★★
13 Timothy's✕✕

losed 20Oct–Mar; 12rm(5⇌ ⋒) CTV 20P 2
Last dinner8pm S%
B&B£8.50–£9.50 sB&B⇌⋒£9.75–£10.75
B&B£16–£17 dB&B⇌⋒£18.50–£19.50
ar lunch£1.50–£3 Tea40–60p Dinner£4–£5.50
Vine£3 Credit cards 1 2 4 5 6

County High St (Scottish & Newcastle) ☎20595
Centrally situated in Border town, stone-built inn dating from 14th-C, featuring vaulted 'Bastel House'.
rm TV 3P Children under 4yrs not accommodated
ast dinner8.45pm S% sB&B£5.80
B&B£10.50 Lunch£2–£4 High Tea£2–£3.50
inner£2–£5 Wine£3.50 Credit card 1

Kingsmuir Springhill Rd ☎20151
0rm CTV CTV available in bedrooms 30P
Last dinner8pm S% sB&B£8
B&B£14 Lunch£3–£4.50 Tea£1 Dinner£4–£5
Vine£2.50 Credit cards 1 3 6

★**Riverside** Neidpath Rd ☎20776
Converted three-storey manse dating from 1865 with terraced gardens leading to banks of River Tweed.
8rm TV 40P 1 Last dinner8pm
*sB&B£6.50–£7.50 dB&B£12–£14
Lunch£2–£2.50 Dinner£3.50–£4 Wine£2.80

PERTH Tayside *Perthshire* Map **11** NO12 **See plan**
★★★★**Station** Leonard St (British Transport) ☎24141 Telex no 76481 Plan **11**
Traditional Victorian building adjacent to station.
53rm(40⇌⋒) Lift CTV CTV in bedrooms P
English & French. Last dinner9pm
S% sB&B fr£23.45 sB&B⇌⋒ fr£23.45
dB&B fr£41 dB&B⇌⋒ fr£41 Lunch fr£5.85
Dinner fr£7 Wine£3.15 *xmas*
Credit cards 1 2 3 4 5 6

P

☆☆☆**City Mills** West Mill St (Reo Stakis) ☎28281 Plan**1**
Built around an old mill. The mill stream passes under the hotel and can be seen in parts through glass floors.
40⇌⫙ ☽ ♛CTV CTV in bedrooms 60P Live music & dancing wkly Conference facilities available ♡Mainly grills. Last dinner10.15pm ✿ ⊡ S% sB&B⇌⫙£16 dB&B⇌⫙£26 Lunch fr£3.25 High Tea fr£2.50 Dinner fr£4.70 Wine£3.10 ▤ Credit cards[1][2][3][5]

★★★**Isle of Skye** Queen's Bridge, Dundee Rd ☎24471 Plan**5**
The hotel is on north bank of river, opposite bridge.
45rm(35⇌⫙) ☽ ♛ CTV in bedrooms 70P Live music & dancing Sat ♡Scottish & French. Last dinner10pm ✿ ⊡ S% sB&B£10.50 sB&B⇌⫙£11.50 dB&B£19.80 dB&B⇌⫙£22 Lunch£3.50–£3.80&alc Tea75p High Tea£2–£2.75 Dinner£4.50&alc Wine£3.50 ▤ *xmas* Credit cards[1][2][3][4][5][6]

★★★**Royal George** Tay St (Trusthouse Forte) ☎24455 Plan**9**
Three storey stone building overlooking River Tay.
43⇌⫙ ☽ ♛ TV in bedrooms 20P 12⌂ Last dinner9pm ✿ ⊡ S% sB&B⇌⫙£16.50 dB&B⇌⫙£25 ▤ Credit cards[1][2][3][4][5][6]

★★**Lovat House** Glasgow Rd ☎36555 Plan**6**
Converted and extended private house on southern approach road (A9) to Perth.
23rm(7⇌⫙) ☽ ♛ CTV TV available in bedrooms ⊘ 40P Live music & dancing Sat ♡French. Last dinner9.30pm ✿ ⊡ S% ✱sB&B£10.53–£16.20 dB&B£16.20 dB&B⇌⫙£16.20–£20.52 Lunch£2.20–£2.50 Tea£1.50 High Tea£1.60–£3.75 Dinner£5alc ▤ Credit cards[1][3][5]

★★**Queens** Leonard St (Travco) ☎25471 Plan**8**
55rm(7⇌⫙) Lift ☽ ♛ CTV 20P Last dinner8.15pm ✿ sB&B£7.50–£8 sB&B⇌⫙£9–£9.50 dB&B£15–£16 dB&B⇌⫙£16.50–£17.50 Lunch fr£2.50 High Tea fr£1.95 Dinner fr£3.30 Wine£2.25 ▤ Credit cards[1][2][3][5][6]

★★**Salutation** South St (Allied Scotland) ☎22166 Telex no76357 Plan**10**
Established in 1699, this was the temporary HQ of Prince Charles Edward Stuart.
62rm(55⇌⫙) ☽ ♛CTV TV available in bedrooms ₱ Live music & dancing 5nights wkly Last dinner8.30pm ✿ ⊡ S% sB&B⇌⫙fr£12 dB&B fr£20 dB&B⇌⫙fr£24 Lunch fr£3 Tea fr£1 Dinner fr£4.50 Wine£3.50 ▤ *xmas* Credit cards[1][2][3][4][5][6]

★★***Tay Motel*** Dunkeld Rd (Open House) ☎22804 Plan**12**
Annexe: 20⇌⫙ ☽ ♛CTV TV available in bedrooms 150P ⚓ Live music monthly Music & dancing monthly. Last dinner8.30pm ✿ ⊡ ▤ Credit cards[1][2][3][4][5][6]

★***County*** New Row (Scottish & Newcastle) ☎23618 Plan**2**
Two-storey building in town centre, near Motorail terminal.
9rm CTV 6P ♡Mainly grills. Last dinner8.45pm ✿ ▤ Credit cards[1][2][3][5][6]

✕✕**Timothy's** 24 St John Street ☎26641 Plan**13**
Closed Sun & Mon; 56seats ₱ ♡Danish. Last dinner10pm ✱Lunch£1.50alc Dinner£3alc Wine£3.10

✕**Penny Post** 80 George St ☎20867 Plan**7**
So named as building housed one of Perth's first post offices in 1773.
Closed Sun; 32seats ₱ ♡Mainly grills. Last dinner10pm S% Lunch£2.40alc Dinner£4.80&alc Wine£2.60 Credit cards[2][5]

PETERCULTER Grampian *Aberdeenshire* Map**15** NJ80
✕**Ristorante Italiano** 309–311 North Deeside Rd ☎Aberdeen733289
Closed Mon; 115seats 25P ♡Italian. Last dinner10.30pm ✱Lunch£2.50–£4&alc Tea80p–£1.50 Dinner£10alc Wine£3.70 Credit cards[1][2][3][5][6]

PETERHEAD Grampian *Aberdeenshire* Map**15** NK1[illegible]
★★★**Palace** Prince St (Swallow) ☎4821 Telex no53168
59rm(49⇌⫙) Lift ☽ ♛CTV in bedrooms 60P Last dinner9pm ✿ S% sB&B£18.50 sB&B⇌⫙£20.45 dB&B£24.60 dB&B⇌⫙£28.40 Credit cards[1][2][3][5]

○**Waterside Inn** Fraserburgh Rd ☎71121
117⇌⫙

PITLOCHRY Tayside *Perthshire* Map**14** NN95
★★★**Atholl Palace** (Trusthouse Forte) ☎2400 Telex no76406
118rm(105⇌⫙) Lift ☽ ♛ CTV TV in bedrooms 180P ⚓ ⇌(heated) ◢(hard) sauna bath Conference facilities available Last dinner9.30pm ✿ ⊡ S% sB&B⇌⫙£16.50 dB&B⇌⫙£26 ▤ *xmas* Credit cards[1][2][3][4][5][6]

★★★**Fishers** Atholl Rd ☎2000
Well-established four storey building in town centre backed by fine gardens.
76rm(48⇌⫙) Lift ☽ ♛ CTV CTV available in bedrooms ⊘ 60P 5⌂ ⚓ Last dinner8.30pm ✿ ⊡ S% sB&B fr£11 sB&B⇌⫙fr£14 dB&B fr£21.60 dB&B⇌⫙fr£26.50 Lunch fr£3.50 Tea fr65p High Tea fr£2 Dinner fr£5 Wine£2 ▤ Credit cards[1][2][3][5]

★★★**Green Park** ☎2537
An extended country house hotel, standing on the banks of Loch Faskally, and backed by woodland.
Closed Nov–mid Mar; 41rm(24⇌⫙) CTV ⊘ 40P 4⌂ ⚓ ♡International. Last dinner8pm ✿ ⊡ S% dB&B fr£8.50 sB&B⇌⫙fr£10.50 dB&B fr£17 dB&B⇌⫙fr£21 Lunch fr£2.80 Dinner fr£5.50 Wine£3

★★★**Pine Trees** Strathview Ter ☎2121
Closed 14Oct–6Apr; 18⇌⫙ ☽ CTV CTV available in bedrooms 40P 10⌂ ⚓ Last dinner9pm ✿ ⊡ S% ✱sB&B£9.50–£10.50 sB&B⇌⫙£12–£13.50 Lunch fr£3.50&alc Tea40p–£1 High Tea fr£1.25 Dinner£5.50–£8.50&alc Wine£2.95 ▤ Credit cards[1][2][3][4][5][6]

★★★**Pitlochry Hydro** (Scottish Highlands) ☎2666 Telex no778215
Set in own grounds, the hotel offers commanding views over the southwest of town and valley.
Closed 14Oct–24Apr; 62rm(58⇌⫙) Lift ☽ CTV 60P 6⌂ ⚓ ♂18 ◢(hard) Last dinner8.30pm ✿ ⊡ S% sB&B£14–£15.85 sB&B⇌⫙£16.85–£18.70 dB&B£22.40–£26.10 dB&B⇌⫙£28.10–£31.80 Bar lunch£1.50–£2.50 Tea40p–£1.30 Dinner£6.25 Wine£3.25 ▤ *xmas* Credit cards[1][2][3][4][5][6]

★★★**Scotland's** 40 Bonnethill Rd (Best Western) ☎2292
51rm(33⇌⫙) Lift ☽ CTV CTV available in bedrooms 50P Last dinner9pm ✿ ⊡ S% sB&B£10.20–£18.20 sB&B⇌⫙£12.20–£20.20 dB&B£17.30–£31.10 dB&B⇌⫙£21.30–£35.10 Lunch fr£4.70 Dinner fr£6.50 Wine£3.50 ▤ Credit cards[1][2][3][5][6]

★★**Burnside** West Moulin Rd ☎2203
Centrally situated in a quiet part of the town within sight of Pitlochry Festival Theatre.

P

Closed early Nov–mid Nov; 16rm(12⇌⋒)
Annexe: 6rm ♛ CTV 30P ⚓ Last dinner8pm ✿ ☕
S% sB&B£10.05 sB&B⇌⋒£11.30
dB&B£17.60 dB&B⇌⋒£20.10 Barlunch fr£1.25
Tea fr55p Dinner fr£4.75 Wine£2.75 ▣
Credit cards 2 5

★★Craigvrack West Moulin Rd ☎2399
19rm(10⇌⋒) ♛ CTV 20P 2🏠 ⛟ ⚓ Children under 3yrs not accommodated Last dinner8.30pm ✿ ☕
S% sB&B£8.90–£10.80 sB&B⇌⋒£10–£12.30
dB&B£17.80–£21.60 dB&B⇌⋒£20–£24.60
Lunch£1.69 Tea35p Dinner£5.25&alc
Wine£2.20 ▣ *xmas* Credit card 1

★★Dundarach ☎2862
Formerly a private mansion house, set in ten acres of wooded grounds, with views over river and surrounding hills, yet within ¼ mile of town centre.
22rm(16⇌⋒) ✗ CTV TV available in bedrooms 20P 6🏠 ⚓ Last dinner8.30pm ✿ ☕ sB&B£8–£8.50
sB&B⇌⋒£8.50–£9 dB&B£16–£17
dB&B⇌⋒£17–£18 Lunch£2.75–£3
Tea£1–£1.25 Dinner£4.75–£5 Wine£2.90 ▣
xmas

★★*Moulin* ☎2196
Charming little hotel on hillside above town. History dates back to 1700.
Closed Nov–Mar; 18rm(9⇌⋒) CTV 40P ⛟ ⚓
Last dinner8pm ✿ ☕

★★Wellwood West Moulin Rd ☎2879
Closed Nov–Mar; 14rm CTV CTV available in bedrooms 20P 1🏠 ⛟ ⚓ Children under 10yrs not accommodated ♡International. Last dinner7.30pm
sB&B fr£8 dB&B fr£16 Barlunch£1.25–£2.50
Dinner£5.75 Wine£2.60 ▣

★Airdanair 160 Atholl Rd ☎2266
Closed 20Oct–Mar; 10rm(1⇌⋒) ♛ CTV ⊘ 14P ⚓
Last dinner7.30pm ✿ ☕ S%
*sB&B£8.10–£8.60 dB&B£12.20–£13.20
dB&B⇌⋒£14.20–£15.20 Barlunch£1.50
Tea fr40p Dinner£3.85 Wine£2.75

★Birchwood 2 East Moulin Rd ☎2477
12rm(7⇌⋒) ♛ CTV 20P ⚓ Last dinner6.30pm
sB&B£10.50–£12.50 sB&B⇌⋒£11.50–£13.50
dB&B£25–£29 dB&B⇌⋒£28–£32
Dinner fr£5.50 Wine£3.20

★Brae Knowe Knockard Rd ☎2147
Closed Nov–Mar; 15rm(13⇌⋒) ♛ ⊘ 20P ⛟ ⚓ Live music & dancing Sat Last dinner8pm ✿ ☕
sB&B£7.50 sB&B⇌⋒£7.75 dB&B£15
dB&B⇌⋒£16 Barlunch£1–£2 Tea75p
Dinner£5.50&alc Wine£2.95 ▣ Credit card 3

★Claymore 162 Atholl Rd ☎2888
Closed mid Oct–Mar; 8rm(2⇌⋒) CTV 30P ⛟ ⚓
Children under 5yrs not accommodated
Last dinner8.30pm S% sB&B£8.40–£9.40
dB&B£16–£18.20 dB&B⇌⋒£19.50–£21.70
Barlunch£2.30alc Dinner fr£4.50 Wine£2.40

★⛰Dunfallandy House Logierait Rd (2m S unclass road) ☎2648
8rm ♛ TV ⊘ 24P ⛟ ⚓ ♡European. Last dinner8pm
*sB&B£7.25 dB&B£14.50 Barlunch£2alc
Dinner£5alc Wine£2.60 ▣

POLMONT Central *Stirlingshire* Map **11** NS97
★★★Inchyra Grange Grange Rd (Inter-Hotel) ☎711911
A converted mansion of considerable age and character standing in nine acres of grounds with views over Grangemouth and Firth of Forth.
29rm(26⇌⋒) ☽ ♛ CTV in bedrooms 100P ⚓ Live music & dancing Sat & Sun Cabaret Sat & Sun
♡Scottish & French. Last dinner9.15pm ✿
*sB&B£10.50 sB&B⇌⋒£14.30 dB&B£15.75
dB&B⇌⋒£21.50 Lunch£3&alc Dinner£4&alc
Wine£3 ▣ Credit cards 1 2 3 5 6

PORT APPIN Strathclyde *Argyll* Map **14** NM94
★★*Airds* ☎Appin236
Formerly an old Ferry Inn, situated in a little coastal village, looking out to the Island of Lismore and the distant mountains.
Closed Nov–mid Mar; 14rm(5⇌⋒) ♛ ⊘ 26P
Last dinner8.30pm ✿ ☕ ▣

PORT ASKAIG Isle of Islay, Strathclyde *Argyll* Map **10** NR46
★Port Askaig ☎Kildalton245
Picturesque Highland inn.
10rm(4⇌⋒) ♛ CTV 10P ⚓ Children under 6yrs not accommodated Last dinner8.30pm ✿ S%
sB&B fr£10 dB&B fr£16 dB&B⇌⋒ fr£18
(Continental breakfast) Lunch fr£3 Dinner fr£5.30
Wine£1.80

PORT ELLEN Isle of Islay *Strathclyde Argyll* Map **10** NR34
★★Dower House Kildalton (3m E A846) ☎225
5⇌⋒ ♛ CTV 12P ⛟ ⚓ Last dinner8.30pm ✿ ☕
sB&B⇌⋒£9.60–£11.50
dB&B⇌⋒£18.15–£21.50 Lunch£4.30–£5.15
Tea45p–50p Dinner£6.35–£7.50

PORTMAHOMACK Highland *Ross & Cromarty* Map **14** NH98
★★Caledonian ☎345
18⇌⋒ ♛ CTV TV in bedrooms 20P Disco twice wkly Live music & dancing twice wkly Cabaret twice wkly
♡French. Last dinner9pm ✿
sB&B⇌⋒£11.88–£12.96 dB&B⇌⋒£17.28
Lunch£2.50–£3.50 High Tea£2–£2.50
Dinner£4.50–£5.50 Wine£1.95
Credit cards 1 2 3 6

P

PORTPATRICK Dumfries & Galloway *Wigtownshire* Map **10** NX05

★★★ **Knockinaam Lodge** (2m S on unclass road) ☎471
Closed Jan & Feb; 10rm(8⇌ ⋒) CTV CTV available in bedrooms 100P French. Last dinner 8.30pm ✻sB&B fr£18.11 sB&B⇌⋒ fr£36.22 Bar Lunch £2–£2.50 Tea 80p–£1 High Tea £1.50–£3 Dinner £6–£7 Wine £3 *xmas*

★★ **Fernhill** ☎220
Closed Dec–Feb; 11rm(7⇌⋒) CTV 40P Last dinner 8.30pm sB&B £9–10.50 dB&B £16–£19 dB&B⇌⋒ £18–£21 Bar lunch £2.50 Tea 50p Dinner £5.50–£6.75 Wine £3

★★ **Portpatrick** (Mount Charlotte) ☎333
Large building on cliffside with fine views down onto town and harbour.
Closed 21 Oct–Mar; 63rm(31⇌⋒) Lift CTV ⇌(heated) billiards Disco Tue Live music & dancing Thu Last dinner 9pm S% ✻sB&B £8.05–£12.65 sB&B⇌⋒ £9.20–£13.80 dB&B £16.10–£25.30 dB&B⇌⋒ £18.40–£27.60 Lunch £3.75 Tea 90p Dinner £4.50 Wine £3.40 Credit cards 1 2 3

★ **Mount Stewart** South Cres ☎291
9rm TV available in bedrooms 9P Last dinner 9.30pm ✻sB&B £9.50–£10.50 dB&B £19–£21 Lunch fr£2.50 Tea fr17p High Tea fr£2.50 Dinner fr£3.50 Wine £2.40

PORTREE Isle of Skye, Highland *Inverness-shire* Map **13** NG44

★★★ **Coolin Hills** ☎2003
Converted shooting lodge, with fine views over Portree Bay.
19rm(18⇌⋒) Annexe: 10rm(4⇌⋒) CTV 50P Last dinner 8pm sB&B £9–£10 sB&B⇌⋒ £10–£11 dB&B 18–£22 dB&B⇌⋒ £20–£22 Lunch £3.70 Tea 60p Dinner £4.15 Wine £2.20

★★ **Caledonian** ☎2641
14rm(4⇌⋒) CTV 14P Last dinner 7.30pm S% dB&B fr£13 dB&B⇌⋒ fr£15 Dinner £3.50–£4

★★ **Rosedale** ☎2531
Closed 13 Oct–11 May; 17rm(4⇌⋒) TV 12P Children under 8 yrs not accommodated Last dinner 8pm sB&B £8–£9.50 dB&B £16–£19 dB&B⇌⋒ £19–£22 Dinner £4.50–£5

★★ ***Royal*** ☎2525
26rm(17⇌⋒) TV 20P 6 Last dinner 8pm

PORT WILLIAM Dumfries & Galloway *Wigtownshire* Map **10** NX34

★★ **Monreith Arms** ☎232
13rm(1⇌⋒) CTV 8P 3 Last dinner 9.30pm sB&B fr£6.50 dB&B fr£13 dB&B⇌⋒ fr£14 Lunch fr£2.25 Tea fr90p Dinner fr£3.45 Wine £2.50

POWFOOT Dumfries & Galloway *Dumfriesshire* Map **11** NY16

★★ **Powfoot Golf** Links Av ☎Cummertrees 254
A golfing hotel with views of the Solway.
20rm(7⇌⋒) CTV 40P Last dinner 8.15pm S% sB&B £8–£11 sB&B⇌⋒ £9.50–£12 dB&B £15–£18 dB&B⇌⋒ £19–£20 Lunch £1.20alc Tea 50p–80p Dinner £4.50–£6 Wine £2.10 *xmas*

PRESTWICK Strathclyde *Ayrshire* Map **10** NS32

☆☆ **Carlton Motor** (Osprey) ☎76811
37⇌⋒ CTV CTV in bedrooms 40P Live music & dancing twice wkly Last dinner 9.30pm S% ✻sB&B⇌⋒ £14 dB&B⇌⋒ £21 Lunch fr£2.60&alc Tea fr30p High Tea fr£2.60 Dinner fr£3.90&alc Wine £2.36 *xmas* Credit cards 1 2 3 5

★★ **Links** Links Rd ☎77792
Traditional seaside hotel overlooking Prestwick Championship Golf Course.
9rm(5⇌⋒) CTV CTV available in bedrooms 100P 2 Last dinner 8.30pm sB&B fr£7.56 sB&B⇌⋒ fr£9.72 dB&B fr£15.12 dB&B⇌⋒ fr£19.44 Lunch £3–£4.50 Tea £1 High Tea £3–£5 Dinner £5–£6.50 Wine £3

★★ **Parkstone** Esplanade ☎77286
Detached building situated on Esplanade looking out to Isle of Arran.
12rm CTV 60P Last dinner 8.30pm S% sB&B £8.95–£9.75 dB&B £17.50–£19.50 Lunch £2.95 Tea 75p High Tea £2.50 Dinner £4.55 Wine £3.15 Credit card 2

★★ ***Queen's*** Esplanade ☎70501
28rm(12⇌⋒) CTV 4 Live music & dancing Sat Last dinner 9pm Credit cards 1 3 5

★★ **St Nicholas** 41 Ayr Rd ☎79568
13rm(4⇌⋒) CTV TV available in bedrooms 40P billiards Last dinner 9.30pm S% sB&B £6.90–£7.90 sB&B⇌⋒ £7.90–£8.90 dB&B £13.80–£15.80 dB&B⇌⋒ £17.80 Lunch £1.60–£2.50 Tea 75p–£1.20 High Tea £1.80–£3.40 Dinner £3.50&alc Wine £2.25 *xmas* Credit card 2

P

★***Auchen Coyle*** Links Rd ☎78316
8rm(3⇌⋒) 🍽CTV ⊘20P Live music twice wkly
Last dinner9pm Credit cards② ③

★***Golden Eagle*** Main St ☎77566
rm 🍽 CTV 20P ♡Mainly grills. Last dinner8pm ♁ ⊥ ⊟

★**North Beach** Links Rd ☎79069
Overlooks the golf links, near to the shore.
9rm 🍽 CTV TV available in bedrooms 20P Disco 3nights wkly Live music & dancing twice wkly Last dinner8pm ⊥ S% sB&B£6.48–£7.29 dB&B£12.96–£14.58 Lunch£1.50–£3.50 Tea75p High Tea£1.50–£3.50 Dinner£2.50–£4 Wine£2.50

QUEENSFERRY (SOUTH) Lothian *West Lothian* Map**11** NT17
☆☆☆**Forth Bridges Lodge** Forth Road Bridge (Grand Met) ☎031–331 1199 Telex no727430
Low rise modern complex situated close to southern approach to Forth road, affording splendid views over the Firth of Forth.
98⇌⋒ ☽ 🍽 TV available in bedrooms 200P 20🏠 ⚓ Disco Fri, Sat & Sun Conference facilities available Last dinner10pm ♁ ⊥ S% ✱sB&B⇌⋒£14.50–£16.50 dB&B⇌⋒£22–£25.50 ⊟ Credit cards① ② ③ ④ ⑤ ⑥

❀★★**Hawes Inn** (Swallow) ☎031–331 1990 Telex no53168
Historic inn overlooking the Firth of Forth. Robert Louis Stevenson is said to have started 'Kidnapped' whilst staying here.
9rm(2⇌⋒) CTV 150P last dinner9pm ♁ Credit cards① ② ③ ⑤

RATHO Lothian *Midlothian* Map**11** NT17
✕**Bridge Inn** ☎031–333 1320
Closed Sun; 50seats 40P ♡English & French. Last dinner10pm S% ✱Lunch£1.50–£2.88&alc Dinner£4.50alc Wine£2.56 Credit cards② ⑤

RENFREW Strathclyde *Renfrewshire* Map**11** NS56
For hotels and restaurants see Glasgow Airport

RHU Strathclyde *Dunbartonshire* Map**10** NS28
★★★**Rosslea Hall** ☎684
15rm(13⇌⋒) ⊞ 🍽 CTV available in bedrooms ⊘ 40P ⚓ ♡French. Last dinner8.30pm ♁ ⊥ S% sB&B£8.64 sB&B⇌⋒£15.12 dB&B£27–£30.24 dB&B⇌⋒£27–£30.24 (Continental breakfast) Lunch£3.25 Tea fr50p Dinner£5&alc Wine£2.90 ⊟ Credit cards① ② ③ ⑤

★**Ardencaple** (Clansmans) ☎200
8rm(3⇌⋒) CTV 40P ♡European. Last dinner10pm ♁ ⊥ ✱sB&B£8.25 sB&B⇌⋒£9.70 dB&B£13 dB&B⇌⋒£16.50 Lunch£4.20alc Tea45p–65p High Tea£1.80–£3.15 Dinner£4.20alc Wine£2.80 ⊟ Credit cards① ③ ⑤

ROCKCLIFFE Dumfries & Galloway *Kirkcudbrightshire* Map**11** NX85
★★★**Barons Craig** ☎225
Closed mid Oct–Mar; 27rm(18⇌⋒) 🍽 CTV 50P 4🏠 ⚓ ♡International. Last dinner9pm ♁ ⊥ sB&B£13.80 sB&B⇌⋒£19.32 dB&B£26.90 dB&B⇌⋒£32.40 Lunch fr£4.80 Tea fr£1.25 Dinner fr£6.50 Wine£2.50

ROSEBANK Strathclyde *Lanarkshire* Map**11** NS84
★★★**Popinjay** ☎Crossford441
34rm(31⇌⋒) 1⊟ ☽ 🍽 CTV in bedrooms 100P ⚓ Live music & dancing 5 nights wkly Last dinner9.30pm ♁ S% sB&B fr£12.50 sB&B⇌⋒fr£15 dB&B fr£20.50 dB&B⇌⋒fr£25 Lunch fr£3 Dinner fr£5 Wine£3 ⊟ Credit cards① ② ③ ⑤

ROSEMARKIE Highland *Ross & Cromarty* Map**14** NH75
★★**Marine** ☎Fortrose20253
Closed Oct–Mar; RS Etr–30Apr; 50rm(14⇌⋒) CTV 50P 10🏠 ⚓ Last dinner8.30pm ♁ sB&B£9 sB&B⇌⋒£10.60 dB&B£18 dB&B⇌⋒£21.20 Lunch£3.50 Dinner£4.70 Wine£2.50 ⊟

ROSLIN Lothian *Midlothian* Map**11** NT26
✕**Ye Olde Original Rosslyne Inn** Main St ☎031–440 2384
60seats 24P bedrooms available ♡Mainly grills. Last dinner9pm Lunch£1–£3&alc Dinner£3–£8&alc Wine£2.40

ROTHES Grampian *Moray* Map**15** NJ24
★★★**Rothes Glen** ☎254
Closed mid Nov–Mar; 20rm(8⇌⋒) 1⊟ 🍽 CTV CTV available in bedrooms 25P ⚓ Last dinner8.30pm ♁ ✱sB&B£14.65 sB&B⇌⋒£15.75 dB&B£29.30 dB&B⇌⋒£31.50 Lunch£3.30 Dinner£6.60&alc Wine£2.25

★***Station*** 51 New St ☎240
12rm CTV 8P 4🏠 Last dinner8.30pm

ROTHESAY Strathclyde *Bute* Map**10** NS06
★★★**Glenburn** Glenburn Rd ☎2500 Telex no778982
Imposing stone building with terraced lawns and fine view out across Rothesay Bay.

R

101rm(45⇌ ⋒) Lift ☽ CTV 60P billiards Disco 3nights wkly Live music & dancing wkly Cabaret 3nights wkly Lastdinner8.30pm S% *sB&B fr£12 sB&B⇌⋒fr£14 dB&B fr£33 dB&B⇌⋒fr£35 Lunch£2.50–£3.25 Tea50p–75p Dinner£5.25–£5.75 Wine£2.95 *xmas* Creditcards 1 2 3 4 5

★★Royal Albert Pl (Osprey) ☎3044
21rm ☽ CTV P Disco 3nights wkly Live music & dancing nightly Lastdinner9pm S% *sB&B£8 dB&B£14 Lunch fr£2.60 Tea fr30p High Tea fr£2.60 Dinner fr£3.90 Wine£2.40 *xmas* Creditcards 1 2 3 5

★★Victoria Victoria St (Osprey) ☎3553
23rm(1⇌⋒) ☽ CTV P Lastdinner9.30pm S% *sB&B£8 dB&B£14 Lunch fr£2.60 Tea fr30p High Tea fr£2.60 Dinner fr£3.90 Wine£2.39 *xmas* Creditcards 1 2 3 5

★Ardmory House Ardmory Rd, Ardbeg ☎2346
11rm CTV TV available in bedrooms 20P Lastdinner7pm

ROWARDENNAN Central *Stirlingshire* Map**10** NS39
★★Rowardennan ☎Balmaha273
9rm(1⇌⋒) CTV 50P Lastdinner8.45pm S% sB&B£9.50 sB&B⇌⋒£10.50 dB&B£17 dB&B⇌⋒£18 Barlunch50p–£2.50 Tea fr£1 Dinner£4.50–£6 Wine£4 *xmas*

ROY BRIDGE Highland *Inverness-shire* Map**14** NN28
★★Glen Spean Lodge ☎Spean Bridge224
15rm(1⇌⋒) TV 30P 3 Lastdinner8pm

RUMBLING BRIDGE Tayside *Kinross-shire* Map**11** NT09
★★Rumbling Bridge ☎Fossoway325
A country hotel with a long established coaching inn history.
Closed Nov; 26rm⇌⋒ CTV 60P Lastdinner9.30pm S% sB&B⇌⋒£7 Lunch fr£2&alc Tea65p–£1 High Tea£2–£3.50 Dinner£4–£4.50&alc Wine£3.10 *xmas*

RUTHERGLEN Strathclyde *Lanarkshire* Map**11** NS66
★★Burnside East Kilbride Rd, Burnside, Cambuslang (Reo Stakis) ☎041–634 1276
16rm(8⇌⋒) ☽ CTV CTV in bedrooms 100P Disco twice wkly Lastdinner9pm *sB&B£12 sB&B⇌⋒£14 dB&B£19.50 dB&B⇌⋒£22 Lunch£2.50–£4.25&alc Tea75p–£1.25 Dinner£2.50–£4.25&alc Wine£3.10 Creditcards 1 2 3 5

★★Mill Mill St (Open House) ☎041–647 5491
30rm(10⇌⋒) ☽ CTV 100P Live music wkly Scottish, English & French. Lastdinner8.30pm Creditcards 1 2 3 5

★Cathkin East Kilbride Rd, Burnside (1¼m S on A749) (Scottish & Newcastle) ☎041–634 1077
Flat-roofed building adjacent to housing estate. 4 miles south east of Glasgow city centre.
6⇌⋒ CTV 100P Live music Fri–Sun Lastdinner7.30pm Creditcards 1 3

ST ANDREWS Fife *Fife* Map**12** NO51
★★★★Old Course (British Transport) ☎74371
Telex no76280
Interesting modern building alongside 17th hole of Old Course. Fine views over golf course to St Andrews Bay.
68⇌⋒ Lift ☽ CTV CTV in bedrooms 100P Conference facilities available English & French. Lastdinner9.45pm S%

R

sB&B⇌ fr£29.55 dB&B⇌ fr£50.35 Dinner£8.20 Wine£3.15 Credit cards 1 2 3 4 5 6

★★★★**Rusacks Marine** ☎74321
Closed Nov–Mar; 50⇌ Lift CTV in bedrooms 30P Scottish & French. Last dinner 9pm sB&B⇌ £20–£25 dB&B⇌ £35–£40 Lunch £4.50 Tea £1.50 Dinner £7–£8.50 Wine £4 Credit card 2

★★★**Rufflets** ☎72594
Closed mid Jan–mid Feb; 19rm(14⇌) 100P 6 Scottish & French. Last dinner 9pm sB&B£12 sB&B⇌ £14 dB&B£24 dB&B⇌ £27 Lunch fr£2.75&alc Tea fr50p Dinner fr£6&alc Wine£3.50 *xmas* Credit cards 2 3 5 6

★★★**St Andrews** 40 The Scores (Inter-Hotel) ☎72611
Situated on the sea front with views over sandy beach and rock pools.
RS Nov–Mar (no lunches); 26rm(18⇌) Lift CTV in bedrooms sauna bath Live music & dancing Sat Last dinner 9pm S% sB&B£8–£13.50 sB&B⇌ £8–£15 dB&B£16–£24 dB&B⇌ £16–£27 Lunch£3.50&alc Tea£1.25 High Tea£3.50 Dinner£5.95&alc Wine£4.35 *xmas* Credit cards 1 2 3 4 5 6

★★★**Scores** ☎72451
41rm(22⇌) Lift CTV Last dinner 9pm S% sB&B£9.50–£11 sB&B⇌ £10.50–£14 dB&B£19–£22 dB&B⇌ £21–£28 Lunch£3–£3&alc Tea35p–60p&alc Dinner£6–£8.50&alc Wine£3.50 *xmas* Credit cards 2 3 5

★★**Cross Keys** 83 Market St ☎72185
18rm(3⇌) CTV 10P Last dinner 8.15pm sB&B£9.35 dB&B£18.70 dB&B⇌ £20.70 Lunch fr£1.50&alc Tea fr50p High Tea fr£1.60 Dinner fr£5&alc Credit cards 1 3

★★**Star** ☎75701
Modernised coaching inn dating from early 1800's.
26rm(22⇌) CTV in bedrooms Last dinner 9pm S% sB&B£7.50–£12 sB&B⇌ £7.50–£13.50 dB&B⇌ £15–£24 Tea£1.25 Dinner£5.95&alc *xmas* Credit cards 1 2 5

★**Russell** The Scores ☎73447
Closed Nov–Mar; 12rm TV available in bedrooms Children under 4yrs not accommodated Last dinner 8pm S% sB&B£6.50–£8 dB&B£13–£16 Bar lunch£1 Dinner£3.50–£4.50 Wine£2.25 Credit cards 1

✕✕**Grange Inn** Grange ☎72670
64seats 60P Scottish & French. Specialities: Mussel and onion stew, Stilton and mushroom crêpes. Last dinner 9.45pm ✱Lunch£7alc Dinner£12alc Wine£3.20 Credit cards 1 2 3 5 6

✕***Pepita's*** 11 Crails Ln ☎74084
Closed Sun; Dinner not served Mon; 60seats French. Last dinner 10pm

ST BOSWELLS Borders *Roxburghshire* Map **12** NT53

★★**Buccleuch Arms** ☎2243
15rm 1 CTV CTV available in bedrooms 60P Last dinner 9.30pm sB&B£6–£9.90 dB&B£12–£19.80 Lunch£2.50–£3.50 Tea£1 High Tea£2.25–£2.75 Dinner£5.50–£6.50 Wine£3.50 Credit cards 1 2 3 4 5 6

ST COMBS Grampian *Aberdeenshire* Map **15** NK06

★★**Tufted Duck** ☎Inverallochy 2481
18⇌ TV in bedrooms 100P Scottish &

French. Last dinner9.30pm
sB&B⇌⋔ fr£14.50 dB&B⇌⋔ fr£25 Lunch fr£3
Tea fr50p Dinner fr£4.25 Wine£3.50
Credit cards 2 3 5 6

ST FILLANS Tayside *Perthshire* Map**11** NN62
★★★**Four Seasons** ☎281
Closed Nov–Mar; 12⇌⋔ TV in bedrooms 50P
Live music & dancing nightly International.
Last dinner9.45pm S%
sB&B⇌⋔£15–£19.50 dB&B⇌⋔£30–£39
Lunch£3.95–£4.95&alc Tea£1.30
Dinner£4.95–£5.95&alc Wine£3.10
Credit cards 1 2 3

★★***Drummond Arms*** (Inter-Hotel) ☎212
Four-storey turreted grey stone roadside hotel in attractive position overlooking wooded shore of Loch Earn, with steeply rising hills to rear.
Closed mid Oct–Mar; 40rm(8⇌⋔) CTV 50P
Last dinner8.15pm Credit cards 1 2 5

ST MARGARET'S HOPE Orkney Map**16** ND49
✕**Creel** Front St ☎311
Closed Sun & Wed; Lunch not served; 30seats
bedrooms available English & French.
Last dinner10.30pm ✱Dinner£6alc Wine£2.50

ST MARY'S LOCH Borders *Selkirkshire* Map**11** NT22
★★**Rodono** ☎Cappercleuch232
Shooting lodge dating from 1866, standing on hillside overlooking St. Mary's Loch and border hills.
Closed Nov–Feb; 11rm CTV 30P Scottish, English & French. Last dinner9.30pm
✱sB&B£8.90 dB&B£17.80
Lunch£2.30–£5.50&alc Tea£1.01–£1.25
High Tea£2–£2.85 Dinner£5.30–£6.50&alc
Wine£2.95

SALEN Isle of Mull, Strathclyde *Argyll* Map**10** NM54
✕**Puffer Aground** Main Rd ☎Aros389
Closed Sun & Mon (in winter) mid Jan–mid Mar; Dinner by reservation only Wed–Sat mid Oct–mid Jan; 45seats 12P Last dinner9pm
✱Lunch£1.25&alc Dinner£3.70&alc Wine£2.75

SANQUHAR Dumfries & Galloway *Dumfriesshire* Map**11** NS70
★★**Mennockfoot Lodge** ☎382
4rm Annexe:8rm(2⇌⋔) CTV 30P
Last dinner8.45pm S% sB&B£9–£11
sB&B⇌⋔£9.50–£12 dB&B£18–£22
dB&B⇌⋔£19–£23 Lunch£3.50–£5
High Tea£2.50–£4 Dinner£5–£6.50 Wine£2.50

SCALASAIG Isle of Colonsay, Strathclyde *Argyllshire* Map**10** NR39
★**Colonsay** ☎Colonsay316
RS Nov–Feb; 11rm(1⇌⋔) 30P 1 18
European. Last dinner8pm S%
sB&B£8.50–£10.20 sB&B⇌⋔£8.50–£10.20
dB&B£14–£16.80 dB&B⇌⋔£14–£16.80
Bar lunch£1–£2 Tea60p–£1 High Tea£3
Dinner fr£6 Wine£2.80

SCONE Tayside *Perthshire* Map**11** NO12
★★★**Murrayshall House** Montague ☎51171
7⇌⋔ CTV CTV in bedrooms 50P
Last dinner10.30pm sB&B⇌⋔£15.50
dB&B⇌⋔£23 Lunch£3.50 Tea75p
Dinner£5.50&alc Wine£3 Credit cards 2 3 5

SCOURIE Highland *Sutherland* Map**14** NC14
★★**Scourie** ☎2396
A shingle-clad building occupying the site and part of 17th-C Tower House, standing on rugged coastal line overlooking Scourie Bay.
Closed 21 Oct–Feb; 22rm(10⇌⋔ 30P
Last dinner8.30pm sB&B£8.50–£10
sB&B⇌⋔£10.80–£12.50 dB&B£17–£20
dB&B⇌⋔£19.30–£22.50 Lunch£2.40–£2.70
Tea35–40p Dinner£4.50–£5 Wine£1.98
Credit card 3

SEAMILL Strathclyde *Ayrshire* Map**10** NS24
★★**Inverclyde** 31 Ardrossan Rd
☎West Kilbride823124
Small detached building set close to roadside in Clyde coast village.
10rm CTV TV available in bedrooms 30P
International. Last dinner9pm S% sB&B£8
sB&B⇌⋔£9 dB&B£16 dB&B⇌⋔£18
Lunch£2.95 High Tea£2.20–£3
Dinner fr£3.50&alc Wine£2.60

. Borders *Selkirkshire* Map**12** NT42
Heatherlie Hill ☎21200
Closed Oct–Apr; 9rm CTV 15P
Last dinner8pm Credit cards 1 3

SHETLAND Map**16**
See **Lerwick & Virkie**

SHIELDINISH Isle of Lewis, Western Isles *Ross & Cromarty* Map**13** NB21
★**Claitair** ☎Balallan345
8rm CTV 20P Mainly grills.
Last dinner9pm S% sB&B£9.50
dB&B£16 Lunch fr£2.50 Tea fr50p High Tea fr£2
Dinner fr£3.75&alc Wine£2.90

S

SKEABOST BRIDGE Isle of Skye, Highland *Inverness-shire* Map**13** NG44
★★★⚑Skeabost House ☎202
Closed Nov–mid Apr; 22rm(10⇌) ☽ 🀫 CTV 40P 2⌂ ⚘ ⚓ ↬ billiards Lastdinner8pm ✿ ♫ sB&B£8.90 sB&B⇌⋒£13.80 dB&B£17.80 dB&B⇌⋒£27.60 Lunch£3.05 Tea55p–£1.20 Dinner£5.95

SKELMORLIE Strathclyde *Ayrshire* Map**10** NS16
★★★⚑Manor Park ☎Wemyss Bay520832
Imposing mansion set in its own grounds and formal gardens two miles south of Skelmorlie. The well and cupola above reception hall is a feature.
RS Jan; 8rm(6⇌⋒) 🀫 CTV in bedrooms ⊘ 150P ⚘ ⚓ Lastdinner9pm ✿ ♫ sB&B£15 sB&B⇌⋒£15 dB&B£30 dB&B⇌⋒£30 Lunch£4.50 Tea£1.50 Dinner£6.50 ⊓ *xmas*

XXRedcliffe Hotel Restaurant 25 Shore Rd ☎Wemyss Bay521036
40seats 25P ♭ bedrooms available ♀French & Swiss. Lastdinner10pm Lunch£2.50–£5&alc Dinner£5.50&alc Wine£2.90 Credit cards 1 2

SKINFLATS Central *Stirlingshire* Map**11** NS98
XDutch Inn Main Rd ☎Grangemouth3015
Closed Sun; 80seats 150P ♀Mainly grills. Lastdinner8pm S% Lunch£3alc Dinner£3alc

SKYE, ISLE OF Highland *Inverness-shire* Map**13**
See **Broadford, Dunvegan, Isle Ornsay, Knock, Kyleakin, Portree, Skeabost Bridge, Sligachan (below) and Uig.**

SLIGACHAN Isle of Skye, Highland, *Inverness-shire* Map**13** NG42
★★★Sligachan ☎204
Closed 13Oct–Mar; 23rm(9⇌⋒) 🀫 20P 6⌂ ⚘ ⚓ ↬ Children under 8yrs not accommodated Lastdinner8pm ✿ ♫ S% sB&B£13.75 sB&B⇌⋒£15 dB&B£26.50 dB&B⇌⋒£30 Lunch£2.80alc Tea£1.70 Dinner£7.80 Wine£2.90

SOUTH UIST, ISLE OF Western Isles *Inverness-shire* Map**13**
See Lochboisdale

SPEAN BRIDGE Highland *Inverness-shire* Map**14** NN28
See also **Letterfinlay** *and* **Roy Bridge**
★★Spean Bridge ☎250
9rm(2⇌⋒) CTV 40P ⚘ ↬ Lastdinner9pm ✿ ♫ sB&B fr£8.80 dB&B fr£17.60 dB&B⇌⋒ fr£22.80 Lunch fr£2.90 Tea fr70p Dinner fr£5.60 Wine£3 Credit card 5

STEPPS Strathclyde *Lanarkshire* Map**11** NS66
☆☆☆Garfield Cumbernauld Rd (Open House) ☎041–779 2111
21⇌⋒ ☽ 🀫 CTV in bedrooms 120P ⚘ Live music & dancing Sat ♀French. Lastdinner9pm ✿ ♫ ✱sB&B⇌⋒£15.50 dB&B⇌⋒£23 Lunch£2.40 Tea50p Dinner£5&alc Wine£2.85 ⊓ Credit cards 1 2 3 4 5 6

STEWARTON Strathclyde *Ayrshire* Map**10** NS44
★★★⚑Chapeltoun House ☎2696
Closed 25 & 26Dec & 1–5Jan; 6rm(4⇌⋒) 🀫 CTV in bedrooms 50P ⚘ ⚓ ↬ Children under 12yrs not accommodated ♀International. Lastdinner9.30pm ✿ sB&B£15 sB&B⇌⋒£18 dB&B£26 dB&B⇌⋒£30 Lunch£4.25&alc Dinner£7.50 Wine£3.25

STIRLING Central *Stirlingshire* Map**11** NS79
★★★Golden Lion King St ☎5351
59rm(43⇌⋒) Lift ☽ 🀫 CTV in bedrooms 35P Live music & dancing Mon & Wed in season Cabaret Mon & Wed in season Lastdinner9pm ✿ ✱sB&B£9.72 sB&B⇌⋒£14.04 dB&B£17.28 dB&B⇌⋒£22.68 Lunch fr£2.3 Dinner fr£4.50 Wine£2.50 ⊓ *xmas* Credit cards 1 2 6

☆☆King Robert Glasgow Rd (Open House) ☎811666
Modern low rise building, lying on outskirts of town, adjacent to Bannockburn Monument and battlefield.
21⇌⋒ ☽ 🀫 CTV in bedrooms 120P ⚓ Disco nightly Lastdinner8.45pm ✿ S% ✱sB&B⇌⋒£14 dB&B⇌⋒£21 Lunch£3.75alc Dinner£4.50alc Credit cards 1 2 3 4 5 6

★★Station 56 Murray Pl (Reo Stakis) ☎2017
Conversion of adjoining buildings, the earliest being a former coaching inn. Standing on corner site in town centre adjacent to railway station.
25⇌⋒ ☽ 🀫 CTV CTV in bedrooms 15P Lastdinner10.30pm ✿ S% ✱sB&B⇌⋒£14 dB&B⇌⋒£24 Lunch£3alc High Tea£2.20 Dinner£3alc Wine£3.10 ⊓ Credit cards 1 2 3 5 6

★★Terraces 4 Melville Ter ☎2268
12rm(10⇌⋒) ☽ 🀫 CTV 20P Lastdinner9pm ✿ ♫ S% sB&B⇌⋒£10.25–£11.25 dB&B£17.25–£18.25 dB&B⇌⋒£18.25–£19.25 Lunch fr£2.65&alc High Tea fr£1.50 Dinner£4.15–£5&alc Wine£2.60 ⊓

★King's Gate 5 King St ☎3944
15rm(5⇌⋒) 🀫 CTV 4P ⚘ Lastdinner8.30pm ✿ ♫ S% ✱sB&B£8–£9 sB&B⇌⋒£9–£11

S

dB&B£12–£16 dB&B⇌⋔£14–£18
Lunch fr£2.50 Tea fr75p High Tea fr£2
Dinner fr£4 Wine£3.20

★Royal Queen St ☎5137
RS Sun (no dinner); 12rm(4⇌⋔) CTV P
Mainly grills. Last dinner8.45pm S%
sB&B£9 sB&B⇌⋔£10 dB&B£15
dB&B⇌⋔£16 Bar lunch90palc Tea35palc
Dinner£4.50alc Wine£1.60 Credit cards 1 2 3

XXHeritage 16 Allan Park ☎3660
An 18th-C painted stone building of architectural interest situated in town at the foot of Castle Rock.
Closed 25, 26Dec, 1 & 2Jan; 70seats 12P
bedrooms available French. Last dinner9.30pm
Lunch fr£3.50&alc Dinner fr£7&alc Wine£2.80

XXHollybank Glasgow Rd ☎812311
Closed Sun, Mon & 3wks Oct; Lunch not served;
45seats 40P bedrooms available International.
Last dinner9pm ✳Dinner£7–£10 Wine£3.40
Credit card 5

XRiverways Kildean Market ☎5734
300seats P Live music & dancing Sat International.
Last dinner7pm Tea£1–£1.50&alc Dinner£4.50
Wine£2.65

XTrattoria La Romantica 4 Viewfield Pl ☎64521
Closed Sun & Mon; 35seats Italian.
Last dinner11pm Credit cards 1 2 3 5

STONEHAVEN Grampian *Kincardineshire* Map**15** NO88

☆☆☆Commodore Cowie Park ☎62936
Telex no73911
40⇌⋔ TV CTV in bedrooms 80P Disco 4nights
wkly Live music & dancing wkly International.
Last dinner10pm sB&B⇌⋔£19.95
dB&B⇌⋔£21.95 Lunch£3.25&alc Tea50–75p
Dinner£4.95–£5.95&alc Wine£3.25 *xmas*
Credit cards 1 2 3 5 6

★★St Leonards Bath St ☎62044
14rm(4⇌⋔) CTV TV in bedrooms 40P
French. Last dinner9pm S%
✳sB&B£12–£15 sB&B⇌⋔£13–£16
dB&B£24–£30 dB&B⇌⋔£26–£32
Lunch£3.50&alc Dinner£5&alc Wine£3.40
Credit card 3

★Crown 26–30 Allardice St ☎62296
18rm CTV CTV in bedrooms 18P
Last dinner8.30pm S% sB&B£9–£12
sB&B⇌⋔£10–£13 dB&B£15 dB&B⇌⋔£16
Lunch fr£1.30 Tea fr50p High Tea fr£1.95
Dinner fr£2.50&alc Wine£2.60

STORNOWAY Isle of Lewis, Western Isles *Ross & Cromarty* Map**13** NB43

★★★Caberfeidh ☎2604
37⇌⋔ Lift CTV 50P billiards Live music & dancing 4nights wkly European.
Last dinner9.30pm S%
✳sB&B⇌⋔£11.50–£12.50 dB&B⇌⋔£20
Lunch£3.50&alc Dinner£6&alc Wine£2.60
Credit cards 1 2 3 5

★★★Seaforth James St ☎2740
30rm(25⇌⋔) Lift CTV 30P British & French.
Last dinner10pm S% ✳sB&B£10.50
sB&B⇌⋔£12.50 dB&B fr£22 dB&B⇌⋔£24
Lunch fr£3 Tea fr75p Dinner fr£3.50 Wine£3.10
Credit cards 1 2 3 5

★★*Royal* Cromwell St (Scottish & Newcastle)
☎2109
A pleasant two-storey painted stone building overlooking inner harbour and Lewis Castle.
17rm CTV P Last dinner8.30pm
Credit cards 1 3

STRACHUR Strathclyde *Argyll* Map**10** NN00

★★Creggans Inn ☎279
A 15th-C inn offering views over Loch Fyne.
26rm(13⇌⋔) CTV TV available in bedrooms 150P
Scottish & French. Last dinner8.15pm
✳sB&B fr£14.30 sB&B⇌⋔fr£17.60
dB&B fr£25.30 dB&B⇌⋔fr£28.60 Lunch fr£4.95
Tea fr£1.10 High Tea fr£3.20 Dinner fr£7
Wine£3.45 *xmas* Credit cards 2

XXInver Cottage Strathlachlan
☎396
A roadside cottage situated on Loch Fyne six miles SW of Strachur.
Closed Mar–Oct; 60seats Scottish & French.
Last dinner9.30pm ✳Lunch65p–£2.50&alc
Dinner£2.50&alc Wine£2.50

STRANRAER Dumfries & Galloway *Wigtownshire* Map**10** NX06

★★★*George* George St (Best Western) ☎2487
Former coaching inn showing fine examples of Victorian/Edwardian architecture.
28rm(12⇌⋔) Lift CTV 30P Last dinner9.15pm
Credit cards 1 2 3 4 5 6

★★★North West Castle ☎2644 Telex no777088
79rm(71⇌⋔) Lift CTV 100P (heated)
billiards sauna bath Live music & dancing Sat
Conference facilities available Last dinner10pm
S% sB&B fr£10 sB&B⇌⋔fr£10 dB&B fr£16
dB&B⇌⋔fr£16 Lunch fr£2.25 Dinner fr£4
Wine£2.60 *xmas*

★Bucks Head Hanover St ☎2064
Homely hotel situated in town centre.
14rm CTV 14P 6 Live music & dancing Sat & Sun
Last High Tea7.30pm

XXL'Aperitif London Rd ☎2991
Closed Sun & mid Sep–mid Oct; 50seats 40P
International. Last dinner9pm Lunch£3–£3.25
High Tea£3–£3.25 Dinner fr£4.50 Wine£2.80

×Bay House Cairnryan Rd ☎3786
osed Mon 1st 2wks Oct–May, 1–14 Feb & 14–28
ct; 55seats 20P International.
ast dinner9.30pm S% *Lunch£2.50alc
inner£5alc Wine£2.75 Credit cards 1 2 3

TRATHAVEN Strathclyde *Lanarkshire* Map**11**
S74
★***Strathaven*** Hamilton Rd ☎21778
rm TV 300P French. Last dinner9pm
redit cards 3 5

TRATHBLANE Central *Stirlingshire* Map**11** NS57
★**Kirkhouse Inn** ☎Blanefield70621
Modernised coaching inn.
9rm(12⇌ ⋒) 1 CTV CTV available in
edrooms 300P French. Last dinner10pm
sB&B£10 sB&B⇌⋒£11.75 dB&B£16
B&B⇌⋒£18.50 Lunch£3–£3.50&alc
ea45–70p High Tea£1.80–£2.20
inner£4–£4.50&alc Wine£3
redit cards 2 3 5

××**Country Club** ☎Branefield70491
0seats 40P bedrooms available Last dinner9pm
unch fr£2.65&alc Dinner£7alc Wine£2.84
redit cards 1 2 3 5

TRATHDON Grampian *Aberdeenshire* Map**15**
J31
Colquhonnie ☎210
0rm TV 40P 6 Last dinner8.30pm

TRATHPEFFER Highland *Ross & Cromarty* Map**14**
H45
★★**Highland** ☎457 Telex no 75160
losed mid Nov–mid Mar except Xmas & New Year;
27rm(86⇌⋒) Lift CTV 50P Live music &
ancing twice wkly Last dinner9.30pm
% sB&B⇌⋒£18–£24.50 dB&B£30–£43
B&B⇌⋒£30–£43 *xmas* Credit cards 1 2 3

★★**Strathpeffer** ☎200
losed 21 Oct–Mar; 34rm(5⇌⋒) CTV 30P
illiards sauna bath Last dinner8pm S%
B&B£7.25 dB&B£15.50 dB&B⇌⋒£18.50
unch£2.50 Tea£1 Dinner£5 Wine£3

★**Holly Lodge** ☎254
losed Oct–Apr; 7rm(5⇌⋒) CTV 15P billiards
Children under 12 yrs not accommodated
ast dinner8pm S% sB&B£9–£10
B&B⇌⋒£9–£10 dB&B£20–£24
B&B⇌⋒£24–£30 Bar lunch£1.25 Tea60p
Dinner£4–£5 Wine£2.50 Credit cards 1 2 3

★***Richmond*** ☎300
7rm (4⇌⋒) 14P CTV Last dinner9.30pm

STRATHTUMMEL Tayside *Perthshire* Map**14** NN86
★★**Loch Tummel** ☎Tummel Bridge272
RS Nov–Mar; 8rm(3⇌⋒) TV 35P 2
British & French. Last dinner9pm S%
sB&B£10.80 sB&B⇌⋒£11.88 dB&B£21.60
dB&B⇌⋒£23.76 Lunch£3alc Tea45palc
High Tea£3alc Dinner£10alc Wine£2.45

★★**Port-An-Eilean** ☎Tummel Bridge233
Closed mid Oct–mid Apr; 12rm(5⇌⋒) 20P 2
Last dinner9pm sB&B£7–£8
sB&B⇌⋒£8–£9 dB&B£14–£16
dB&B⇌⋒£16–£18 Bar lunch£2.75alc
Tea50p–£1 Dinner£4.50–£5.50 Wine£2.80

STRATHYRE Central *Perthshire* Map**11** NN51
★**Ben Sheann** Main Rd ☎272
Purpose-built Victorian hotel set on roadside in centre of small Highland village overlooking pine-clad hills.
13rm(2⇌⋒) CTV 26P 1 Last dinner9.30pm
S% *sB&B£8 sB&B⇌⋒£9.75
dB&B£16 dB&B⇌⋒£19.50 Lunch£3alc
Tea£1.20alc Dinner£4alc Wine£2.20 *xmas*

★**Munro** ☎229
RS Nov–Mar; 12rm 30P 5 Last dinner8pm
sB&B£8–£9 dB&B£15–£17
dB&B⇌⋒£17.50–£19.50 Bar lunch75p&alc
Dinner£3alc Wine£3

STRICHEN Grampian *Aberdeenshire* Map**15** NJ95
Freemasons High St ☎218
6rm CTV 20P Last dinner7pm S%
sB&B fr£7 dB&B fr£11 Lunch fr£1.65 Tea fr50p
High Tea fr£1.65 Dinner fr£2.50 Wine£2.50

STROMNESS Orkney Map**16** HY20
★★**Stromness** ☎850298
Victorian four-storey sandstone building in narrow main street, overlooking harbour.
Closed Jan–Mar; RS Nov & Dec; 40rm(35⇌⋒) Lift
CTV 6P billiards Last dinner8pm
sB&B⇌⋒ fr£9.94 dB&B fr£15.64
dB&B⇌⋒ fr£16.64 Lunch fr£2.16 Tea fr£1
High Tea fr£1.62 Dinner fr£4.65 Wine£2.80

STRONTIAN Highland *Argyll* Map**14** NM86
★★**Kilcamb Lodge** ☎2257
Situated on outskirts of village with grounds stretching down to Loch Sunart.
Closed Nov; 11rm(3⇌⋒) CTV 30P
Last dinner7pm sB&B£8–£9.25
dB&B£13.90–£16 dB&B⇌⋒£16–£18.50
Lunch£3.50 Tea70p Dinner£4.50

★★**Loch Sunart** ☎2471
Situated in small Highland village on Loch Sunart, the hotel looks out over the bay and down the loch.
Closed end Nov–Mar except Xmas & New Year;
11rm(5⇌⋒) CTV 20P Last dinner7pm
S% sB&B£9–£10 sB&B⇌⋒£10–£11
dB&B£17–£19 dB&B⇌⋒£18–£20
Bar lunch£1.50–£2 Dinner£5–£6

STRUY Highland *Inverness-shire* Map**14** NH43
★★**Cnoc** Erchless Castle Estate ☎264
Closed 16 Oct–19 Nov; 10rm 60P
Last dinner10pm
sB&B£12.50–£14(incl dinner)
dB&B£25–£28(incl dinner) Bar lunch fr£2.50
Tea fr50p Dinner fr£6 Wine£2.95

××***Mauldbridge House*** ☎222
35seats 20P bedrooms available Last dinner9pm

SYMINGTON Strathclyde *Lanarkshire* Map**11** NS93
★★**Tinto** (Open House) ☎Tinto454
Closed 1 Jan; 34rm(3⇌⋒) CTV 100P billiards
Live music & dancing Sat Last dinner8.30pm
S% *sB&B£12.25 sB&B⇌⋒£14.25
dB&B£19.25 dB&B⇌⋒£22.25 Lunch£2.70&alc
Tea95p High Tea£2 Dinner£3.78&alc
Wine£3.85 *xmas* Credit cards 1 2 3 4 5

★★**Wyndales House** (2m SW A73) ☎Tinto207
11rm 1 40P Last dinner9pm S%
sB&B£15.44 dB&B£19.60 Lunch£1–£2
Dinner£3.50–£6.75 Credit cards 1 3 5

TAIN Highland *Ross & Cromarty* Map**14** NH78
★★**Royal** Main St ☎2013
22rm(8⇌⋒) CTV CTV available in bedrooms 40P
Scottish & French. Last dinner9pm S%
sB&B£9 sB&B⇌⋒£11 dB&B£18
dB&B⇌⋒£22 Lunch fr£2.75 Tea fr80p
High Tea fr£2.75 Dinner fr£4.75&alc Wine£2
Credit cards 1 3 5

TALLADALE Highland *Ross & Cromarty* Map**14**
NG97
★★**Loch Maree** ☎Loch Maree200

T

Closed Nov–Feb; 15rm 10P 5 Last dinner8pm *sB&B£10.75–£11.75 dB&B£18–£19 Lunch£3.10 Tea60p Dinner£4.50–£5 Wine£2.44

TANGUSDALE Barra, Isle of, Western Isles *Inverness-shire* Map**13** NF60
★★★Isle of Barra (Scottish Highlands & Best Western) Castlebay383 Telexno778215
RS 14Oct–24Apr; 41 CTV 30P Last dinner8.15pm S% sB&B £17.95 dB&B £30.30 Barlunch£1.50–£2.50 Tea40p Dinner£6.25 Wine£3.25 Credit cards 1 2 3 4 5 6

TARBERT Harris, Isle of, Western Isles *Inverness-shire* May**13** NB10
★★Harris Harris2154
Closed Dec–Feb; 24rm(12) TV 20P Lastdinner8pm S% *sB&B£7.50–£8.50 dB&B£13–£15 dB&B £18–£19.50 Lunch£3 Tea80p–£1 Dinner£4–£4.50 Wine£2.50

TARBERT Loch Fyne Strathclyde *Argyll* Map**10** NR86
★★★Stonefield Castle 207
Stone castle in a 100 acres of wooded grounds surrounded by hills, overlooking Loch Fyne.
Closed end Oct–Mar; 34rm(32) Lift CTV 50P (heated) (hard) sauna bath Last dinner9pm *sB&B£11.34–£12.96 sB&B £16.20–£17.82 dB&B £22.68–£36.72 Bar lunch50p–£2 Tea40–60p High Tea£1–£2.50 Dinner£6.50–£9.50 Wine£3 Credit cards 1 2 3 4 5 6

TAYNUILT Strathclyde *Argyll* Map**10** NN03
★Polfearn 251
12rm TV 20P Children under 3yrs not accommodated Last dinner8pm S% sB&B£8–£9 dB&B£14–£16 Bar lunch30p–£2.50 Tea fr50p Dinner fr£5

THORNHILL Dumfries & Galloway *Dumfriesshire* Map**11** NX89
★★Buccleuch & Queensberry 30215
10rm(4) CTV 35P 4 Last dinner8pm S% sB&B£9.75–£10.75 sB&B £12.25–£13.25 dB&B£17.75–£19.75 dB&B £20.25–£22.25 Bar lunch£1.50alc Tea75–85p High Tea£2.50alc Dinner£4.50alc Wine£3

★George 30326
7rm CTV 20P Last dinner7.30pm sB&B fr£7 dB&B fr£14 Lunch£2.75 Tea75p High Tea£2–£3 Dinner£3–£4 Wine£2

THURSO Highland *Caithness* Map**15** ND16
★★Pentland Princes St 3202
40rm(4) CTV Last dinner8.15pm S% sB&B fr£8.35 sB&B fr£9.50 dB&B fr£16.65 Lunch£2.50alc Tea50palc High Tea£2.25alc Dinner£4alc Wine£2.40

★★Royal Trall St 3191 Telexno75160
88rm(18) Lift CTV 10P Last dinner9pm S% sB&B£10–£15 sB&B £13.50–£18.50 dB&B£18–£27 dB&B £22–£38 Credit cards 1 2 3

★St Clair Sinclair St 3730
27rm(6) CTV TV available in bedrooms 6 Last dinner8pm S% sB&B£7.72 sB&B £8.91 dB&B£15.44 dB&B £17.82 Lunch£2.16 Tea40p High Tea£2.16 Dinner£3.78 Wine£2.95 Credit card 6

TOBERMORY Isle of Mull, Strathclyde *Argyll* Map**13** NM55
★★★Western Isles 2012
29rm(11) CTV 20P 6 Last dinner8.45pm S% *sB&B£10.80–£12.96 dB&B£19.44–£23.76 dB&B £24.84–£27 Bar lunch£1–£3&alc Tea40–50p Dinner£5.25–£6.75 Wine£3.45 Credit cards 1 2 3 6

TOMINTOUL Grampian *Banffshire* Map**15** NJ11
★★Gordon Arms The Square 206
Situated in village square with views of surrounding hills.
35rm(6) CTV Last dinner8pm *sB&B£8.50–£10 sB&B £10.50–£12 dB&B£16–£19 dB&B £18–£21 Lunch fr£2.50 Tea fr50p Dinner fr£4 Wine£2.50

★★Richmond Arms 209
27rm(7) TV 25P 3 Last dinner8.30pm Credit card 3

TONGUE Highland *Sutherland* Map**14** NC55
★★Ben Loyal 216
13rm(2) Annexe:6rm TV 18P Last dinner8pm sB&B£5.75–£8 dB&B£11–£16 dB&B £15.50–£19 Bar lunch£1.25 Tea90p High Tea£1.70 Dinner£4.50 Wine£2.10

★★Tongue (Scottish Highlands) 206 Telexno778215
Built in 1876, with Victorian décor and furnishings.
Closed 14Oct–24Apr; 21rm(10) CTV 30P Last dinner8.30pm S% sB&B£13.30–£15.10 sB&B £16.05–£17.95 dB&B£21–£24.60 dB&B £26.50–£30.50 Lunch£1.50–£2.50 Tea40p–£1.30 Dinner£6.25 Wine£3.25 Credit cards 1 2 3 4 5 6

TROON Strathclyde *Ayshire* Map**10** NS33
★★★★Marine (Scottish Highlands) 314444 Telexno778215

a fine position on the coast, overlooking golf course.
3⇌⋒ Lift ☽ ⋈ CTV CTV available in bedrooms 50P ⚘ ⛳ ♠ Live music & dancing wkly ♿ ♡Scottish & French. Last dinner10.15pm ♁ ♫ S% B&B⇌⋒£22 dB&B⇌⋒£38.40 Lunch£5.30&lac Tea£1.30 Dinner£7–£8.20&alc Wine£3.25 ⊟ *xmas* Credit cards ① ② ③ ④ ⑤ ⑥

★★Sun Court Crosbie Rd ☎312727
Spacious former home of wealthy industrialist, overlooking sea. Real tennis court.
0rm(17⇌⋒) ⋈ CTV 70P ⚘ ⛳ ♠(hard) squash ♟ ♡Scottish & French. Last dinner9.30pm ♁ S% B&B£13 sB&B⇌⋒£15 dB&B£20 dB&B⇌⋒£22 Lunch£3.50&alc Dinner£5&alc Wine£2.50 ⊟ Credit card ②

★★Ardneil St Meddans Street ☎311611
rm(3⇌⋒) CTV CTV available in bedrooms ⊘ 20P Last dinner8pm ♁ ♫ ✻sB&B fr£8 B&B⇌⋒ fr£9 dB&B fr£16 dB&B⇌⋒ fr£18 Lunch£3 Tea60p High Tea£2.75 Dinner£4.50 Wine£3 Credit card ①

★★Craiglea South Beach ☎311366
12rm(12⇌⋒) ⋈ CTV CTV available in bedrooms 12P ⌂ ⚘ Live music & dancing Sat Last dinner8.45pm ♁ ♫ sB&B£9.50–£11 sB&B⇌⋒£10–£11.50 dB&B£18–£21 dB&B⇌⋒£19–£23 Lunch£3–£4.50&alc Tea35p Dinner£4.75–£5.25&alc Wine£3.25 ⊟ *xmas* Credit cards ① ②

★★Piersland Lodge Craigend Rd ☎314747
11rm(6⇌⋒) CTV CTV available in bedrooms ⊘ 50P ⛳ ♠(grass) ♡International. Last dinner9.30pm ✻sB&B£11.25 sB&B⇌⋒£13.25 dB&B£18 dB&B⇌⋒£20.75 Lunch£3.05alc Tea75p alc High Tea£3alc Dinner£10.65alc ⊟

★★South Beach South Beach Rd ☎312033
25rm(6⇌⋒) ⋈ CTV CTV available in bedrooms 40P ⛳ Live music & dancing Sat Last dinner8.30pm ♁ ♫ sB&B£9–£10 sB&B⇌⋒£10–£11 dB&B£18–£20 dB&B⇌⋒£19–£21 Lunch£3–£3.50 Tea50p High Tea£3–£4 Dinner£5–£6 Wine£2.20 Credit cards ① ② ③ ⑤ ⑥

⊛XXL'Auberge de Provençe (Marine Hotel) Crosbie Rd ☎314444
Closed Sun & Mon; Lunch not served 45seats 100P ♡French. Specialities: Tranche de poulet fumé, medaillons de veau forestière, pêche recamier. Last dinner10pm Dinner£9alc Credit cards ① ② ③ ⑤ ⑥

TURNBERRY Strathclyde *Ayrshire* Map**10** NS20
★★★★Turnberry (British Transport) ☎202
Telex no777779
Gracious white building set in extensive grounds with tennis courts and two 18-hole golf courses. Fine views over Firth of Clyde.
122⇌⋒ Lift ☽ ⋈ CTV CTV available in bedrooms 100P 4⌂ ⛳ ⛆(heated) ⛳9 ♠ billiards Live music & dancing twice wkly ♿ Conference facilities available ♡English & French. Last dinner9.15pm ♁ ♫ S% sB&B⇌⋒ fr£28.25 dB&B⇌⋒ fr£44.55 Lunch fr£7 Dinner fr£9 Wine£3.50 ⊟ *xmas* Credit cards ① ② ③ ④ ⑤ ⑥

TWEEDSMUIR Borders *Peeblesshire* Map**11** NT12
★★*Crook Inn* ☎272
Pre-war building in country setting occupying site of the old Crook Inn dating from 1604.
8rm(4⇌⋒) ⋈ TV 60P ⚘ ⛳ Last dinner9pm ♁ ♫

TWYNHOLM Dumfries & Galloway *Kirkcudbrightshire* Map**11** NX65
★Burnbank ☎244
Small village hotel situated in hollow beside the local burn.
5rm ⋈ CTV 12P ♡French. Last dinner9.30pm S% sB&B fr£6 dB&B fr£12 Bar lunch40p–£2.65 Dinner£3.75–£5.75&alc Wine£2.50 ⊟ Credit card ③

TYNET Grampian *Banffshire* Map**15** NJ36
★★Mill Hotel ☎Clochan233
Converted mill on main road between Fochabers and the fishing town of Buckie.
Annexe: 11⇌⋒ ⋈ CTV in bedrooms 200P Live music & dancing Wed & Sat Last dinner8.30pm ♁ ♫ sB&B⇌⋒£10.80 dB&B⇌⋒£19.44 Lunch fr£2.50 Tea fr80p High Tea£1–£3 Dinner fr£4.50 Wine£2.50 ⊟ Credit cards ② ⑤

UIG Isle of Skye, Highland *Inverness-shire* Map**13** NG36
★★Uig ☎205
Closed Oct–Mar; 12⇌⋒ Annexe: 13⇌⋒ ⋈ P ⛳ Children under 12 yrs not accommodated ♿ Last dinner8pm ♁ ♫ ✻sB&B⇌⋒ fr£12.50 dB&B⇌⋒ fr£25 Bar lunch fr£1.50 Tea fr75p Dinner fr£5 Wine£3 Credit cards ① ② ③ ⑤ ⑥

★Ferry Inn ☎242
6rm(1⇌⋒) ⋈ 18P ⚘ Last dinner8pm ♁ ♫ S% ✻dB&B£14.25 dB&B⇌⋒£15.44 Bar lunch fr40p Tea75p Dinner fr£3.50 Wine£1.80

UIST (NORTH), ISLE OF Western Isles *Inverness-shire*
See **Lochmaddy**

UIST SOUTH, ISLE OF Western Isles *Inverness-shire*
See **Lochboisdale**

ULLAPOOL Highland *Ross & Cromarty* Map**14** NH19
☆☆☆Ladbroke Mercury Motor Inn North Rd (On A835) (Ladbroke) ☎2314

Modern low rise complex standing on main north road on outskirts of fishing port.
Closed Nov–Mar; 60⇌ ⋒ ☽ ♨ CTV TV available in bedrooms 80P ♣ Conference facilities available Last dinner 10pm ♡ ⊻ sB&B⇌ ⋒ £14.50–£17 dB&B⇌ ⋒ £23–£28 Lunch fr£4.50&alc Dinner fr£5.50&alc Wine£3.20 ⊟ Credit cards 1 2 3 4 5 6

★★★Royal (Best Western) ☎2181
Closed Nov–Mar; 60rm(45⇌ ⋒) ☽ ♨ TV 135P ♣ ♧ ♿ ♡ Scottish & French. Last dinner 9.30pm ♡ ⊻ sB&B£11.55–£12.50 sB&B⇌ ⋒ £14.50–£15 dB&B£22–£24 dB&B⇌ ⋒ £27.50–£34 Lunch£7alc Tea fr50p Dinner fr£6&alc Wine£3 ⊟ Credit cards 1 2

★★Caledonian (Scottish Highlands) ☎2306
Telex no 778215
Large stone building dating from 1905 with modern extensions. Situated on corner site in West Highland fishing village overlooking harbour.
Closed 14Oct–24 Apr: 39rm(18⇌ ⋒) ☽ CTV 30P ♣ Last dinner 8.30pm ♡ ⊻ S% sB&B£13.30–£15.10 sB&B⇌ ⋒ £16.05–£17.95 dB&B£21–£24.60 dB&B⇌ ⋒ £26.50–£30.30 Lunch£4.10 Tea 40p–£1.30 Dinner£6.25 Wine£3.25 ⊟ Credit cards 1 2 3 4 5 6

★★Ceilidh Place West Argyle St ☎2103
RS Nov–Apr; 15rm(6⇌ ⋒) ☽ ♨ CTV TV available in bedrooms 30P ♣ (hard) Disco wkly Live music & dancing twice mthly Cabaret twice wkly Last dinner 9.30pm ♡ ⊻ sB&B£6–£10 sB&B⇌ ⋒ £7–£12 dB&B£12–£20 dB&B⇌ ⋒ £14–£24 Lunch£3–£5&alc Tea£2alc Dinner£5.50–£6&alc Wine£3.25 ⊟ *xmas* Credit card 5

★Ferry Boat Inn Shore St ☎2366
Closed mid Nov–Feb; 12rm CTV
Last dinner 9pm ✱sB&B£5.50–£7 dB&B£11–£14 Bar lunch 80p–£1.25 Dinner£3.50–£4.50 Wine£2.63 Credit cards 1 6

UPHALL Lothian *West Lothian* Map **11** NT07
★★★Houstoun House ☎Broxburn 853831
Telex no 727148
RS Xmas Day & New Year's Day; 27⇌ ⋒ 7 ♨ CTV in bedrooms 100P ♣ ♡ International. Last dinner 9pm ♡ ⊻ S% sB&B⇌ ⋒ £20–£23 dB&B⇌ ⋒ £30–£35 Lunch£5 Dinner£8 Wine£3

VIRKIE Shetland Map **16** HU31
★*Meadowvale* ☎Sumburgh 240
11rm(3⇌ ⋒) ♨ CTV 25P Last dinner 7.30pm ♡ ⊻

WAMPHRAY Dumfries & Galloway *Dumfriesshire* Map **11** NY19
★Red House ☎Johnstone Bridge 214
Closed Nov–Mar; 6rm TV 20P Last dinner 8.30pm ♡ sB&B fr£8.30 dB&B fr£16.60 Lunch fr£3.05 Dinner fr£4.55 Wine£2.50 Credit card 5

WESTHILL Grampian *Aberdeenshire* Map **15** NJ80
☆☆☆Westhill Inn ☎Aberdeen 740388
Telex no 73784
39⇌ ⋒ Lift ♨ CTV CTV in bedrooms 250P sauna bath Conference facilities available Last dinner 10pm ♡ ⊻ S% ✱sB&B⇌ ⋒ £14.50 dB&B⇌ ⋒ £21 Lunch fr£2.25&alc Tea fr£1 High Tea fr£2 Dinner fr£4.20 Wine£3.15 ⊟ Credit cards 1 2 3 5

WHITEBRIDGE Highland *Inverness-shire* Map **14** NH41
★★Whitebridge ☎Gorthleck 226
Closed 20Oct–Jan; RS Feb–Apr; 12rm(3⇌ ⋒) ♨ 40P 2 Last dinner 8pm ♡ ⊻ S% sB&B£7.48–£8.19 sB&B⇌ ⋒ £8.67–£9.38

U

dB&B£14.96–£16.39 dB&B⇌⋒£17.34–£18.77 Lunch£3.60–£4 Dinner£5.52–£6&alc Wine£2.60 ⊟

WHITHORN Dumfries & Galloway *Wigtownshire* Map**10** NX44
★***Castlewigg*** ☎213
7rm ⊞ CTV ⊘ 30P ⚓ Live music Sat Last dinner9pm ✿ ⊡

WHITING BAY Isle of Arran, Strathclyde *Bute* Map**10** NS02
★★**Whiting Bay** ☎247
A two storey building on the sea front.
Closed Nov; 22rm(5⇌⋒) ⊞ CTV TV available in bedrooms 60P ⚓ Disco 3nights wkly Live music & dancing Fri Cabaret Fri Last dinner11pm ✿ ⊡ sB&B£6.50–£9.50 sB&B⇌⋒£8–£11 dB&B£13–£19 dB&B⇌⋒£16–£22 Lunch£2.50–£3.50 Tea50–75p High Tea£2.50–£4 Dinner£3.75–£4.50 Wine£3 ⊟ *xmas* Credit cards 1 2 3 5

WICK Highland *Caithness* Map**15** ND35
★★**Ladbroke Mercury Motor Inn** Riverside (on A9) (Ladbroke) ☎3344
30⇌⋒ ☽ ⊞ CTV TV available in bedrooms 30P Conference facilities available Last dinner10pm ✿ ⊡ sB&B⇌⋒£14.50–£18 dB&B⇌⋒£22.50–£27.50 Lunch fr£4.50&alc Dinner fr£5.50&alc Wine£3.20 ⊟ Credit cards 1 2 3 4 5 6

★★**Station** Bridge St ☎4545
56rm(10⇌⋒) Lift ☽ CTV CTV available in bedrooms 50P Disco 4nights wkly Live music & dancing 3nights wkly Cabaret twice wkly ♡ English & French. Last dinner8.30pm ✿ ⊡ S% sB&B£11.50–£13.50 sB&B⇌⋒£14.50–£16.50 dB&B£18.50–£22.50 dB&B⇌⋒£24.50–£28.50 Lunch£3.50–£4&alc Tea£1–£1.50 High Tea£3–£4 Dinner£5.50–£6.50 Wine£3 Credit cards 1 2 3 4 5 6

Ⓡ**Rosebank** Thurso St ☎3244
21rm(6⇌⋒) ☽ CTV 14P 2⌂ ⇎ Disco 3nights wkly Live music & dancing wkly Cabaret wkly Last dinner8pm ✿ ⊡ S% sB&B£8 sB&B⇌⋒£12 dB&B£16 dB&B⇌⋒£24 Lunch£3.50&alc High Tea£1.80–£4.50&alc Dinner£4–£6&alc Wine£3 ⊟ Credit card 4

WIGTOWN Dumfries & Galloway *Wigtownshire* Map**10** NX45
★**Galloway** Main St ☎2218
8rm(2⇌⋒) CTV 10P Last dinner8pm ✿ ⊡ S% sB&B£5.60 sB&B⇌⋒£6.90–£7.90 dB&B£11.20 dB&B⇌⋒£13.80–£15.80 Lunch£2.50alc Tea£1 High Tea£2–£3.50 Dinner£4.25alc Wine£2.75

WISHAW Strathclyde *Lanarkshire* Map**11** NS75
See also Motherwell
★★**Horse & Anchor** 206–212 Cambusnethan St ☎75603
7rm(6⇌⋒) ⊞ CTV ⊘ P 3⌂ ⇎ S% ✱sB&B£8.95 sB&B⇌⋒£8.95 dB&B⇌⋒£13.95 Lunch fr£3 Dinner fr£3.50 Credit cards 1 2 3

★**Coltness** Coltness Rd (Clansmans) ☎79491
Closed 1Jan; 11rm ⊞ CTV 150P ⚓ Live music Fri & Sat Last dinner8.30pm ✿ ✱sB&B£9.30 dB&B£15.45 Lunch£2.35 Dinner£3.50alc Wine£2.80 *xmas* Credit cards 1 2 3 5

WORMIT Fife *Fife* Map**11** NO32
★★***Sandford Hill*** ☎Newport-on-Tay541802
5rm(3⇌⋒) ⊞ CTV TV available in bedrooms 50P ⇎ ⚓ ⊸(hard) Last dinner9pm ✿ ⊡ Credit card 1

W

The National Grid

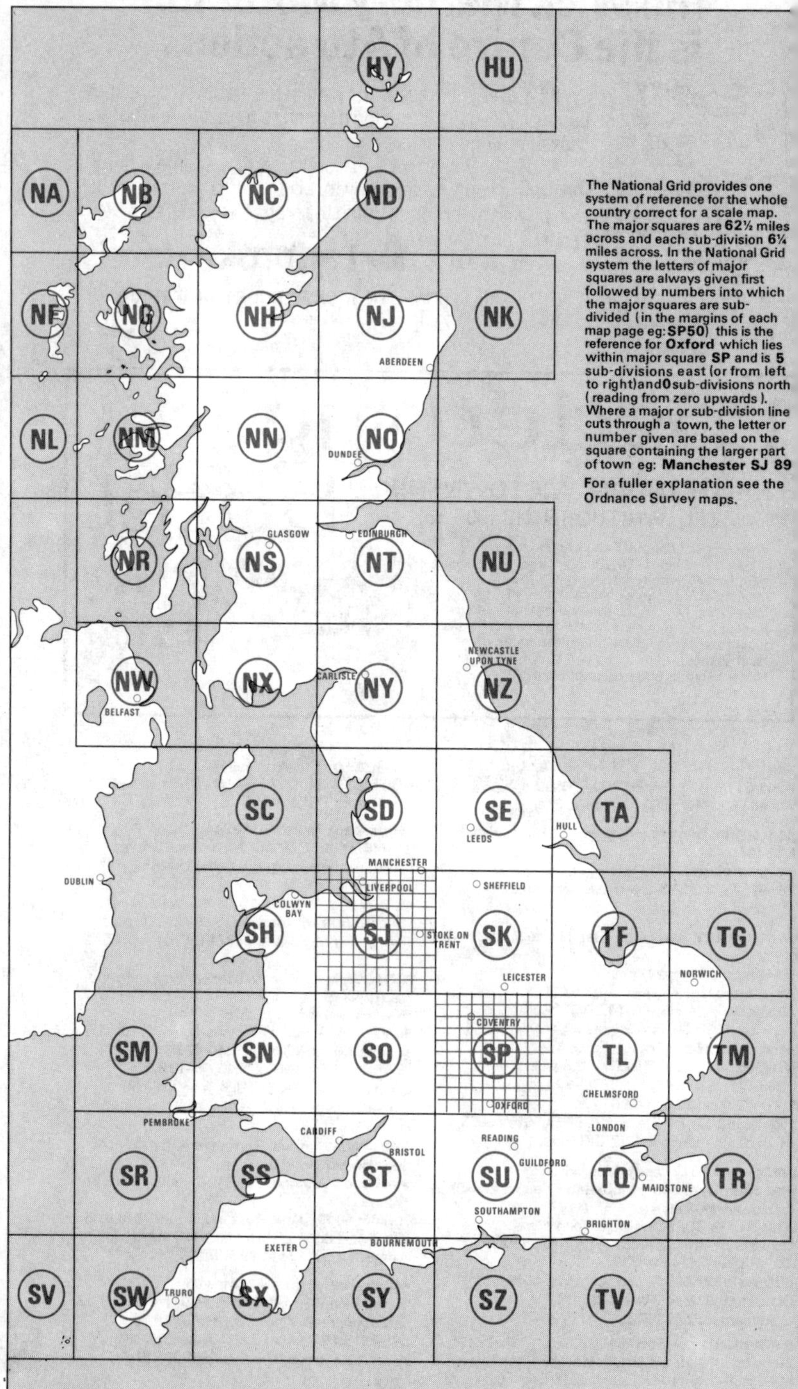

The National Grid provides one system of reference for the whole country correct for a scale map. The major squares are **62½** miles across and each sub-division **6¼** miles across. In the National Grid system the letters of major squares are always given first followed by numbers into which the major squares are sub-divided (in the margins of each map page eg: **SP50**) this is the reference for **Oxford** which lies within major square **SP** and is **5** sub-divisions east (or from left to right) and **0** sub-divisions north (reading from zero upwards). Where a major or sub-division line cuts through a town, the letter or number given are based on the square containing the larger part of town eg: **Manchester SJ 89**

For a fuller explanation see the Ordnance Survey maps.

Key to Atlas

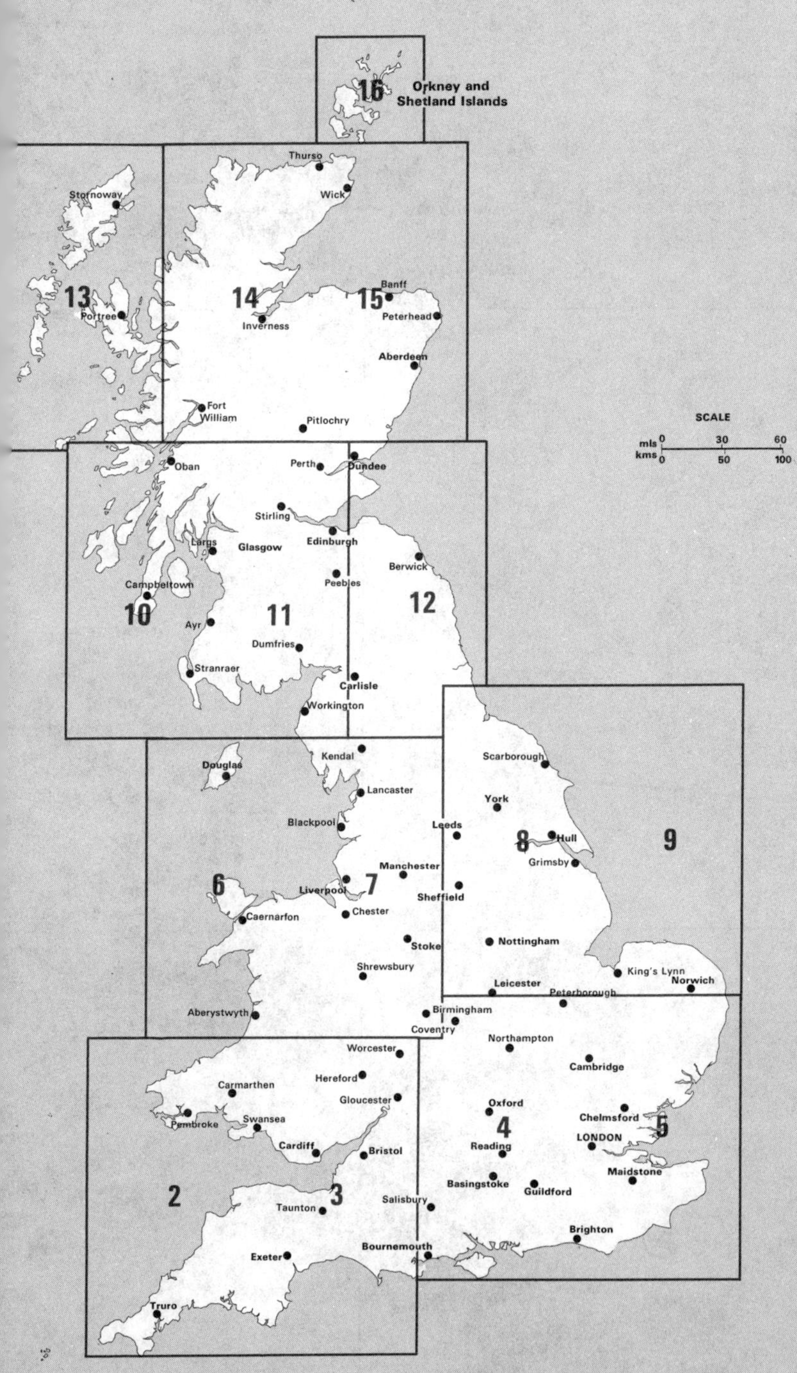

This atlas is for location purposes Only: see Member's Handbook for current road and AA road services information

Maps produced by the AA Cartographic Department (Publications Division), Fanum House, Basingstoke, Hampshire RG21 2EA

SM
SN
SR
SS
SW
SX
ABERAERON
NEW QUAY
Gwbert-on-Sea
Aberporth
CARDIGAN
LAMPETER
NEWCASTLE EMLYN
Rhos
Brechfa
FISHGUARD
Castle Morris
St David's
Wolf's Castle
CARMARTHEN
Llandissilio
HAVERFORDWEST
Broadhaven
Little Haven
Robeston Wathen
NARBERTH
AMMANFO
MILFORD HAVEN
NEYLAND
Burton
Milton
Saundersfoot
KIDWELLY
Pembroke Dock
PEMBROKE
Lamphey
Pembrey
TENBY
BURRY PORT
GORSEINON
Manorbier
Southgate
Rhossili
A487
A40
A478
A477
A485
A484
A48
ILFRACOMBE
Mortehoe
Woolacombe
Putsborough
Saunton
Wrafton
BARNSTAPLE
Appledore
Westward Ho!
Instow
NORTHAM
Fairy Cross
Clovelly
BIDEFORD
Hartland
Horns Cross
Woolfardisworthy
GREAT TORRINGTON
Bradworthy
Kilkhampton
Milton Damerel
BUDE
STRATTON
Hatherleigh
Widemouth Bay
HOLSWORTHY
Clawton
OKEHAMPTON
Crackington Haven
Boscastle
Tintagel
Bridestowe
Lewdown
LAUNCESTON
Lydford
Port Isaac
Port Gaverne
Camelford
Lifton
Pendoggett
Trebetherick
Trelights
Treyone
Harlyn Bay
Rock
Lamerton
Constantine Bay
PADSTOW
Treyarnon Bay
Wadebridge
Gulworthy
TAVISTOCK
Hellandbridge
Gunnislake
Mawgan Porth
St Wenn
BODMIN
Yelverton
Watergate Bay
St Mawgan
LISKEARD
NEWQUAY
Pillaton
Crantock
LOSTWITHIEL
SALTASH
Penpillick
Lanreath
TORPOINT
PLYMOUTH
Pelynt
ST AUSTELL
Golant
Downderry
St Agnes
LOOE
Cawsand
Bodinnick
FOWEY
Polkerris
Polperro
Talland Bay
Wembury
Newton Ferrers
TRURO
Tregony
Mevagissey
Bigbury-on-Sea
CAMBORNE
REDRUTH
Perranarworthal
Portloe
ST IVES
Carbis Bay
Veryan
Halsetown
Hayle
Portscatho
Ruan High Lanes
Botallack
Newbridge
PENRYN
ST JUST
FALMOUTH
St Mawes
Marazion
Rosudgeon
PENZANCE
Maenporth
Sennen
Praa Sands
HELSTON
Mawnan Smith
Mousehole
Gillan
Land's End
Lamorna Cove
Helford
Mullion
Coverack
Lizard
A30
A39
A38
A386
A388
A3072
A390
A361
A3071
A394

Hotel
Restaurant
Hotel & Restaurant
Other Towns for Location only

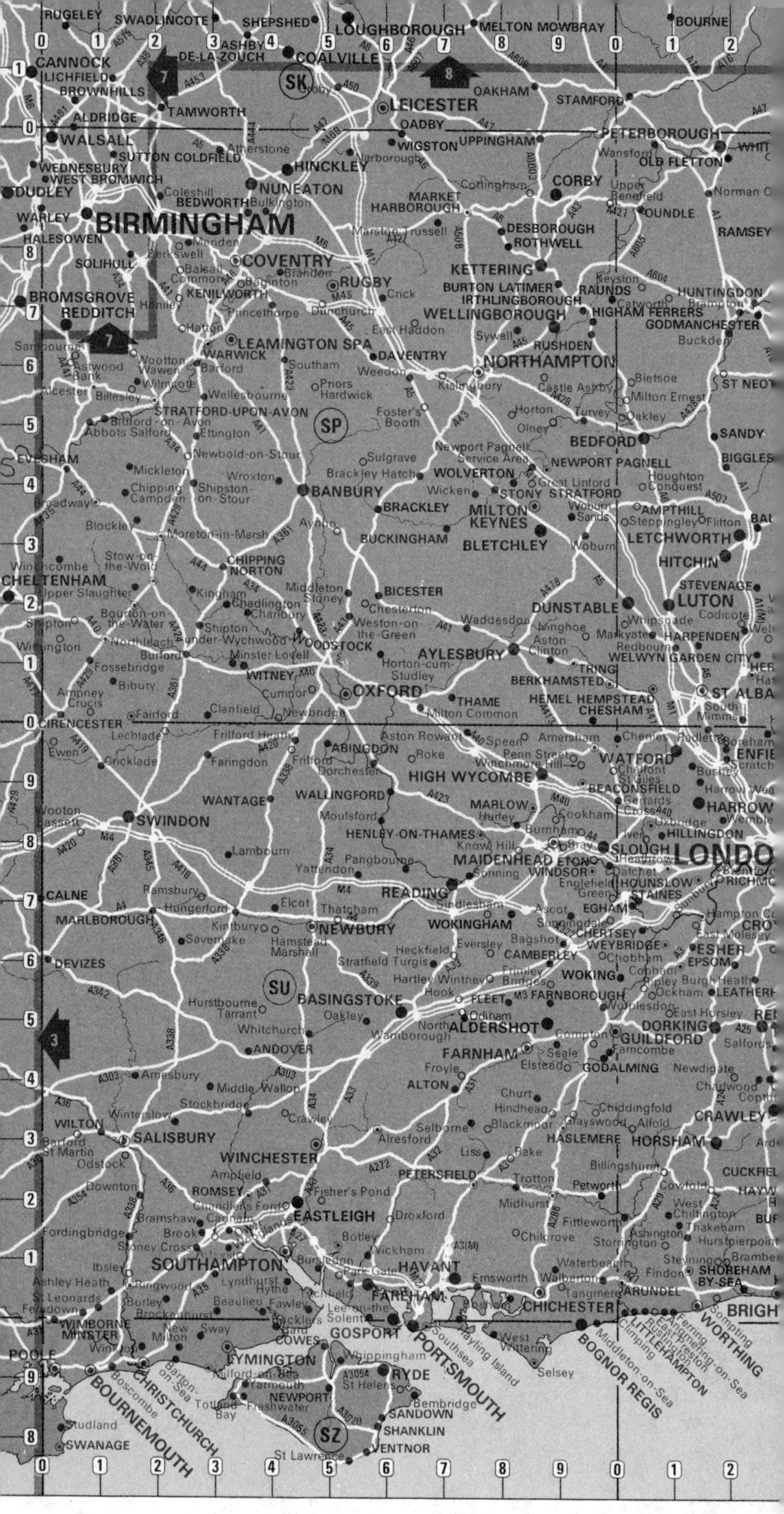

RUGELEY
SWADLINCOTE
SHEPSHED
LOUGHBOROUGH
MELTON MOWBRAY
BOURNE
ASHBY-DE-LA-ZOUCH
COALVILLE
CANNOCK
LICHFIELD
BROWNHILLS
TAMWORTH
ALDRIDGE
SK
LEICESTER
OAKHAM
STAMFORD
OADBY
WIGSTON
UPPINGHAM
PETERBOROUGH
WALSALL
SUTTON COLDFIELD
Atherstone
HINCKLEY
Narborough
Wansford
OLD FLETTON
WEDNESBURY
WEST BROMWICH
DUDLEY
Coleshill
NUNEATON
Cottingham
CORBY
Upper Benefield
Norman Cross
BEDWORTH
Bulkington
MARKET HARBOROUGH
OUNDLE
WARLEY
BIRMINGHAM
HALESOWEN
Meriden
Marston Trussell
DESBOROUGH
ROTHWELL
RAMSEY
Berkswell
COVENTRY
SOLIHULL
Balsall Common
Brandon
Baginton
KETTERING
KENILWORTH
RUGBY
BURTON LATIMER
RAUNDS
Keyston
HUNTINGDON
BROMSGROVE
REDDITCH
Honiley
Crick
IRTHLINGBOROUGH
Catworth
Brampton
Princethorpe
Dunchurch
WELLINGBOROUGH
HIGHAM FERRERS
GODMANCHESTER
Hatton
East Haddon
Sywell
Buckden
Sambourne
LEAMINGTON SPA
WARWICK
RUSHDEN
Astwood Bank
Wootton Wawen
Barford
Southam
DAVENTRY
NORTHAMPTON
Weedon
Kislingbury
Bletsoe
Alcester
Bilesley
Wilmcote
Wellesbourne
Priors Hardwick
Castle Ashby
Milton Ernest
ST NEOTS
STRATFORD-UPON-AVON
Foster's Booth
Horton
Turvey
Oakley
Bidford-on-Avon
Abbots Salford
Ettington
SP
Olney
BEDFORD
SANDY
Newbold-on-Stour
Newport Pagnell Service Area
NEWPORT PAGNELL
BIGGLESWADE
EVESHAM
Mickleton
Sulgrave
Brackley Hatch
WOLVERTON
Great Linford
Houghton Conquest
Wroxton
Chipping Campden
Shipston-on-Stour
BANBURY
Wicken
STONY STRATFORD
Broadway
BRACKLEY
MILTON KEYNES
Woburn Sands
AMPTHILL
Steppingley
Flitton
Blockley
Aynho
BUCKINGHAM
BLETCHLEY
LETCHWORTH
Moreton-in-Marsh
Woburn
HITCHIN
Winchcombe
Stow-on-the-Wold
CHIPPING NORTON
CHELTENHAM
Upper Slaughter
Kingham
Middleton Stoney
BICESTER
STEVENAGE
Bourton-on-the-Water
Chadlington
Charlbury
Chesterton
DUNSTABLE
LUTON
Shipton
Shipton-under-Wychwood
Weston-on-the-Green
Waddesdon
Whipsnade
Codicote
Withington
Northleach
WOODSTOCK
Ivinghoe
Markyate
HARPENDEN
Burford
Minster Lovell
Aston Clinton
Redbourn
WELWYN GARDEN CITY
Fossebridge
AYLESBURY
Horton-cum-Studley
TRING
WITNEY
BERKHAMSTED
Bibury
Cumnor
OXFORD
HEMEL HEMPSTEAD
ST ALBANS
Ampney Crucis
THAME
Fairford
Clanfield
Newbridge
Milton Common
CHESHAM
South Mimms
CIRENCESTER
Lechlade
Frilford Heath
Aston Rowant
Speen
Amersham
Chenies
Radlett
Ewen
Cricklade
Faringdon
ABINGDON
Roke
Penn Street
WATFORD
ENFIELD
Frilford
Dorchester
Winchmore Hill
Chalfont St Giles
Bushey
HIGH WYCOMBE
BEACONSFIELD
Harrow Weald
WANTAGE
WALLINGFORD
Gerrards Cross
Wootton Bassett
MARLOW
Hurley
HARROW
SWINDON
Moulsford
Cookham
Wembley
Uxbridge
HENLEY-ON-THAMES
Burnham
HILLINGDON
Lambourn
Knowl Hill
Bray
Iver
SLOUGH
LONDON
Pangbourne
MAIDENHEAD
ETON
Heathrow
Datchet
Yattendon
Sonning
WINDSOR
Englefield Green
HOUNSLOW
RICHMOND
Ramsbury
READING
CALNE
Hungerford
Elcot
Thatcham
Sindlesham
Ascot
EGHAM
STAINES
MARLBOROUGH
NEWBURY
WOKINGHAM
Sunningdale
CHERTSEY
Hampton Court
Kintbury
Savernake
Hamstead Marshall
Heckfield
Eversley
Bagshot
WEYBRIDGE
East Molesey
DEVIZES
Stratfield Turgis
CAMBERLEY
Chobham
ESHER
EPSOM
Hartley Wintney
Frimley Bridges
WOKING
Cobham
SU
Hook
FLEET
FARNBOROUGH
Ripley
Burgh Heath
Ockham
LEATHERHEAD
Hurstbourne Tarrant
BASINGSTOKE
Worplesdon
East Horsley
Oakley
ALDERSHOT
DORKING
Whitchurch
North Warnborough
Compton
GUILDFORD
ANDOVER
FARNHAM
Seale
Farncombe
Salfords
Elstead
GODALMING
Newdigate
Froyle
Amesbury
Middle Wallop
ALTON
Charlwood
Churt
Stockbridge
Hindhead
Chiddingfold
Wintersiow
Crawley
Blackmoor
Grayswood
Alfold
CRAWLEY
WILTON
Selborne
SALISBURY
Barford St Martin
Alresford
HASLEMERE
HORSHAM
Liss
Rake
Odstock
WINCHESTER
Billingshurst
Ampfield
PETERSFIELD
Trotton
Petworth
Cowfold
CUCKFIELD
Downton
ROMSEY
Fisher's Pond
Midhurst
West Chiltington
Chandler's Ford
EASTLEIGH
Droxford
Fittleworth
Thakeham
Bramshaw
Cadnam
Fordingbridge
Brook
Chilgrove
Storrington
Ashington
Hurstpierpoint
Stoney Cross
Botley
Wickham
Steyning
Bramber
Ibsley
SOUTHAMPTON
Bursledon
Park Gate
HAVANT
Waterbeach
Findon
SHOREHAM-BY-SEA
Ashley Heath
Ringwood
Lyndhurst
Hythe
Titchfield
Emsworth
Walberton
St Leonards
Burley
Beaulieu
Fawley
FAREHAM
Tangmere
ARUNDEL
Ferndown
Brockenhurst
Lee-on-the-Solent
Bosham
CHICHESTER
BRIGHTON
WIMBORNE MINSTER
New Milton
Sway
Bucklers Hard
COWES
GOSPORT
PORTSMOUTH
Southsea
Hayling Island
West Wittering
BOGNOR REGIS
Middleton-on-Sea
Climping
LITTLEHAMPTON
Rustington
East Preston
Angmering-on-Sea
Ferring
Sompting
WORTHING
POOLE
LYMINGTON
Whippingham
Selsey
BOURNEMOUTH
CHRISTCHURCH
Barton-on-Sea
Milford-on-Sea
Yarmouth
RYDE
Boscombe
NEWPORT
St Helens
Totland Bay
Freshwater
Bembridge
SANDOWN
Studland
SHANKLIN
SWANAGE
SZ
VENTNOR
St Lawrence

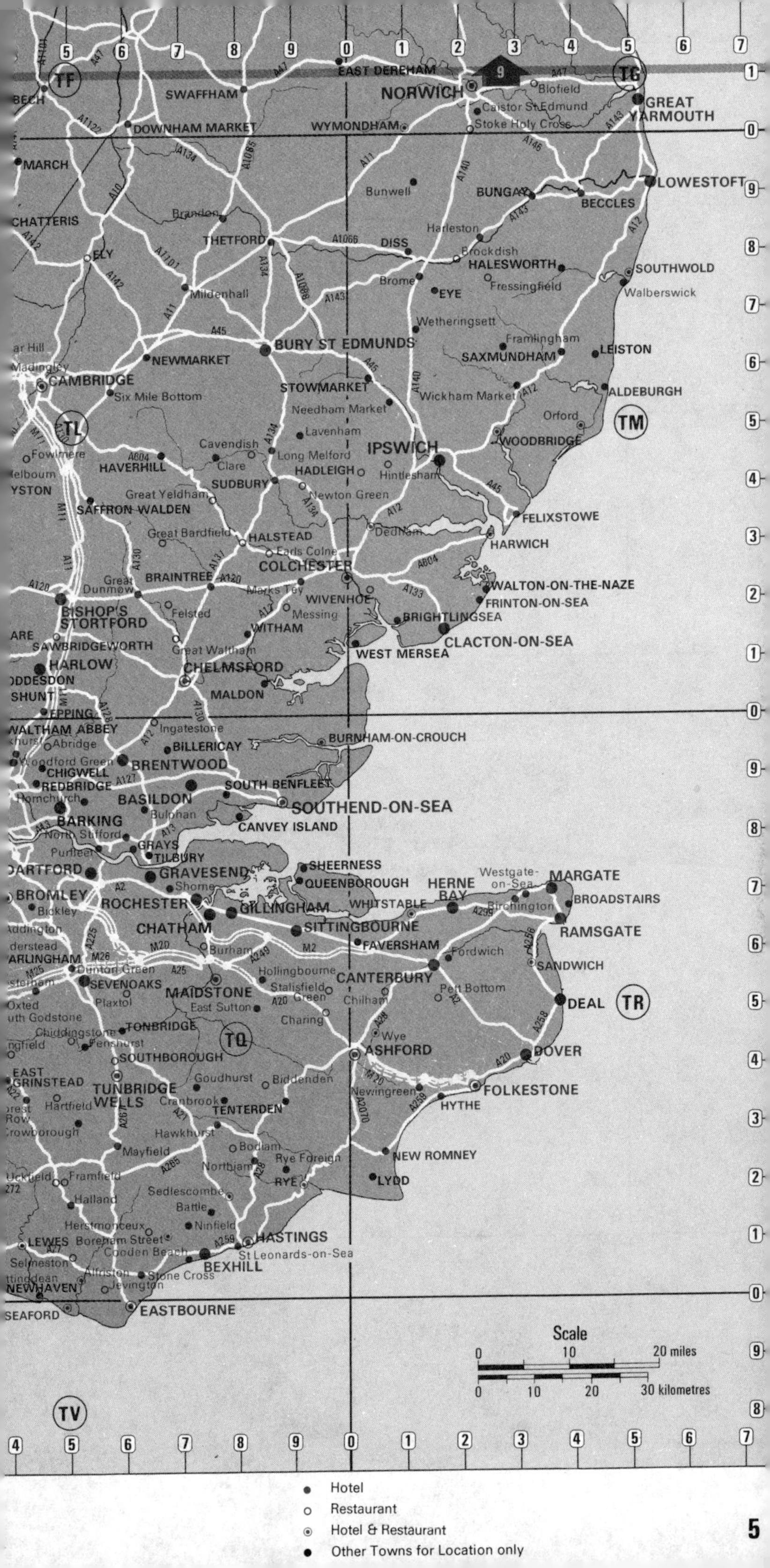

TF
TG
TL
TM
TQ
TR
TV
9
EAST DEREHAM
NORWICH
Blofield
GREAT YARMOUTH
Caistor St Edmund
Stoke Holy Cross
SWAFFHAM
DOWNHAM MARKET
WYMONDHAM
MARCH
CHATTERIS
Brandon
THETFORD
Bunwell
BUNGAY
BECCLES
LOWESTOFT
Harleston
DISS
Brockdish
HALESWORTH
SOUTHWOLD
Fressingfield
Walberswick
ELY
Brome
EYE
Mildenhall
Wetheringsett
BURY ST EDMUNDS
Framlingham
SAXMUNDHAM
LEISTON
NEWMARKET
CAMBRIDGE
STOWMARKET
Wickham Market
ALDEBURGH
Six Mile Bottom
Needham Market
Orford
WOODBRIDGE
Lavenham
Cavendish
IPSWICH
Clare
Long Melford
HAVERHILL
HADLEIGH
Hintlesham
SUDBURY
Great Yeldham
Newton Green
SAFFRON WALDEN
FELIXSTOWE
Dedham
Great Bardfield
HALSTEAD
HARWICH
Earls Colne
COLCHESTER
BRAINTREE
Great Dunmow
Marks Tey
WALTON-ON-THE-NAZE
WIVENHOE
FRINTON-ON-SEA
Felsted
Messing
BISHOP'S STORTFORD
BRIGHTLINGSEA
WITHAM
SAWBRIDGEWORTH
CLACTON-ON-SEA
Great Waltham
WEST MERSEA
HARLOW
CHELMSFORD
MALDON
EPPING
WALTHAM ABBEY
Ingatestone
Abridge
BURNHAM-ON-CROUCH
BILLERICAY
Woodford Green
BRENTWOOD
CHIGWELL
REDBRIDGE
SOUTH BENFLEET
Hornchurch
BASILDON
SOUTHEND-ON-SEA
BARKING
Bulphan
CANVEY ISLAND
North Stifford
Purfleet
GRAYS
TILBURY
SHEERNESS
DARTFORD
GRAVESEND
Westgate-on-Sea
MARGATE
Shorne
QUEENBOROUGH
HERNE BAY
BROMLEY
ROCHESTER
WHITSTABLE
Birchington
BROADSTAIRS
Bickley
GILLINGHAM
CHATHAM
SITTINGBOURNE
RAMSGATE
Burham
FAVERSHAM
Fordwich
Dunton Green
Hollingbourne
SANDWICH
SEVENOAKS
CANTERBURY
Stalisfield Green
Pett Bottom
MAIDSTONE
Plaxtol
Chilham
DEAL
East Sutton
Charing
TONBRIDGE
Chiddingstone
Penshurst
Wye
SOUTHBOROUGH
ASHFORD
DOVER
EAST GRINSTEAD
Goudhurst
Biddenden
Newingreen
FOLKESTONE
TUNBRIDGE WELLS
Hartfield
Cranbrook
TENTERDEN
HYTHE
Crowborough
Hawkhurst
Mayfield
Bodiam
NEW ROMNEY
Rye Foreign
Northiam
Framfield
RYE
LYDD
Halland
Sedlescombe
Battle
Herstmonceux
Ninfield
HASTINGS
LEWES
Boreham Street
Cooden Beach
St Leonards-on-Sea
Selmeston
BEXHILL
Alfriston
Stone Cross
Jevington
NEWHAVEN
EASTBOURNE
SEAFORD
Scale
0 10 20 miles
0 10 20 30 kilometres
Hotel
Restaurant
Hotel & Restaurant
Other Towns for Location only

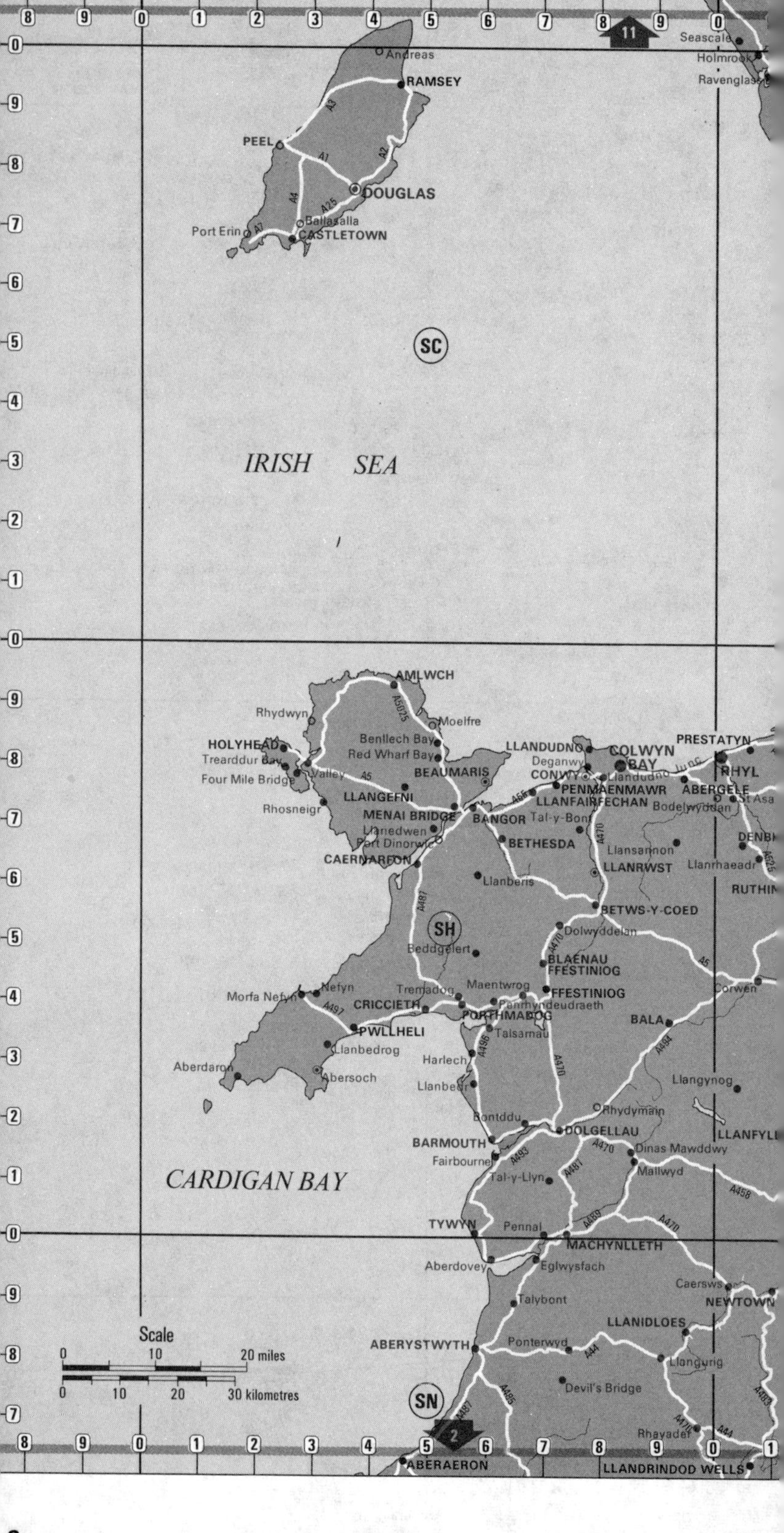

Andreas
RAMSEY
PEEL
DOUGLAS
Ballasalla
Port Erin
CASTLETOWN
Seascale
Holmrook
Ravenglass
SC
IRISH SEA
AMLWCH
Rhydwyn
Moelfre
Benllech Bay
Red Wharf Bay
HOLYHEAD
Trearddur Bay
Four Mile Bridge
Valley
BEAUMARIS
LLANGEFNI
Rhosneigr
MENAI BRIDGE
Llanedwen
Port Dinorwic
CAERNARFON
LLANDUDNO
COLWYN BAY
PRESTATYN
RHYL
Deganwy
CONWY
Llandudno Junc
PENMAENMAWR
ABERGELE
LLANFAIRFECHAN
Bodelwyddan
St Asaph
BANGOR
Tal-y-Bont
BETHESDA
Llansannon
DENBIGH
LLANRWST
Llanrhaeadr
Llanberis
RUTHIN
BETWS-Y-COED
SH
Dolwyddelan
Beddgelert
BLAENAU FFESTINIOG
Morfa Nefyn
Nefyn
Tremadog
Maentwrog
FFESTINIOG
Corwen
CRICCIETH
Penrhyndeudraeth
PORTHMADOG
BALA
PWLLHELI
Talsarnau
Llanbedrog
Harlech
Aberdaron
Abersoch
Llanbedr
Llangynog
Rhydymain
Bontddu
DOLGELLAU
LLANFYLLIN
BARMOUTH
Dinas Mawddwy
Fairbourne
Mallwyd
Tal-y-Llyn
CARDIGAN BAY
TYWYN
Pennal
MACHYNLLETH
Aberdovey
Eglwysfach
Caersws
Talybont
NEWTOWN
LLANIDLOES
ABERYSTWYTH
Ponterwyd
Llangurig
Devil's Bridge
Rhayader
SN
ABERAERON
LLANDRINDOD WELLS
Scale
0 10 20 miles
0 10 20 30 kilometres

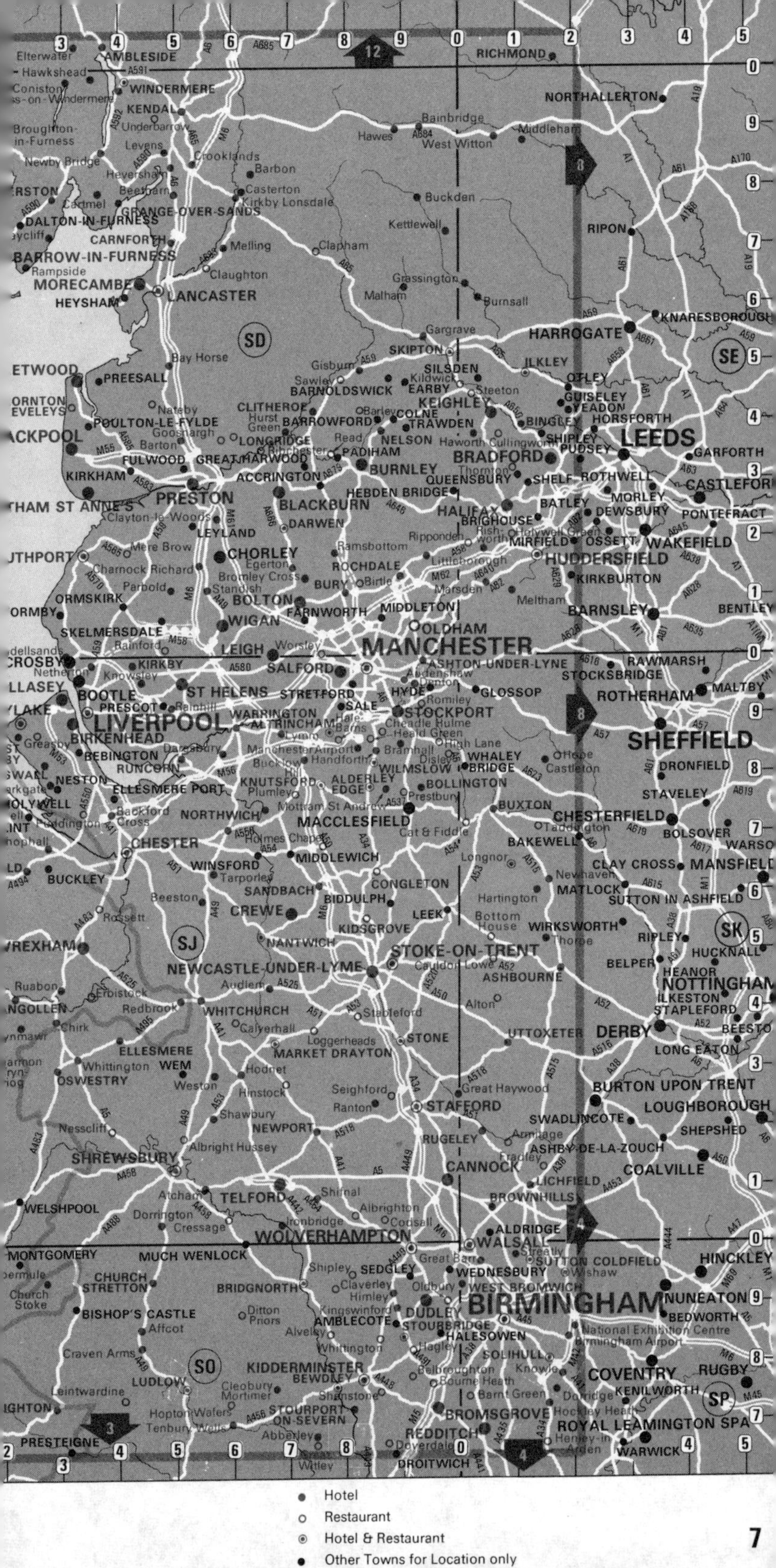

AMBLESIDE
WINDERMERE
KENDAL
RICHMOND
NORTHALLERTON
Hawes
Bainbridge
West Witton
Middleham
Crooklands
Barbon
Casterton
Kirkby Lonsdale
GRANGE-OVER-SANDS
DALTON-IN-FURNESS
BARROW-IN-FURNESS
CARNFORTH
Buckden
Kettlewell
RIPON
Melling
Clapham
MORECAMBE
HEYSHAM
LANCASTER
Claughton
Grassington
Malham
Burnsall
KNARESBOROUGH
Gargrave
HARROGATE
SKIPTON
ILKLEY
SILSDEN
Bay Horse
PREESALL
Gisburn
BARNOLDSWICK
EARBY
Steeton
OTLEY
GUISELEY
YEADON
KEIGHLEY
CLITHEROE
BARROWFORD
COLNE
TRAWDEN
HORSFORTH
BINGLEY
LEEDS
POULTON-LE-FYLDE
LONGRIDGE
NELSON
SHIPLEY
PUDSEY
GARFORTH
FULWOOD
GREAT HARWOOD
PADIHAM
BRADFORD
BURNLEY
KIRKHAM
ACCRINGTON
QUEENSBURY
SHELF
ROTHWELL
CASTLEFORD
PRESTON
HEBDEN BRIDGE
MORLEY
BLACKBURN
HALIFAX
BATLEY
DEWSBURY
PONTEFRACT
LEYLAND
DARWEN
BRIGHOUSE
MIRFIELD
OSSETT
WAKEFIELD
CHORLEY
Ramsbottom
HUDDERSFIELD
ROCHDALE
ORMSKIRK
BURY
KIRKBURTON
BOLTON
Marsden
Meltham
BARNSLEY
FARNWORTH
MIDDLETON
BENTLEY
SKELMERSDALE
WIGAN
OLDHAM
MANCHESTER
LEIGH
Worsley
CROSBY
KIRKBY
SALFORD
ASHTON-UNDER-LYNE
RAWMARSH
STOCKSBRIDGE
MALTBY
BOOTLE
ST HELENS
STRETFORD
HYDE
GLOSSOP
ROTHERHAM
PRESCOT
SALE
STOCKPORT
LIVERPOOL
WARRINGTON
ALTRINCHAM
BIRKENHEAD
SHEFFIELD
BEBINGTON
RUNCORN
Manchester Airport
WILMSLOW
WHALEY BRIDGE
Castleton
DRONFIELD
NESTON
ELLESMERE PORT
KNUTSFORD
ALDERLEY EDGE
BOLLINGTON
STAVELEY
NORTHWICH
MACCLESFIELD
BUXTON
CHESTERFIELD
BOLSOVER
CHESTER
Cat & Fiddle
BAKEWELL
MIDDLEWICH
WINSFORD
CLAY CROSS
MANSFIELD
BUCKLEY
SANDBACH
CONGLETON
MATLOCK
SUTTON IN ASHFIELD
CREWE
BIDDULPH
LEEK
WIRKSWORTH
RIPLEY
KIDSGROVE
HUCKNALL
NANTWICH
STOKE-ON-TRENT
BELPER
NEWCASTLE-UNDER-LYME
ASHBOURNE
HEANOR
NOTTINGHAM
ILKESTON
STAPLEFORD
WHITCHURCH
STONE
UTTOXETER
DERBY
LONG EATON
ELLESMERE
WEM
MARKET DRAYTON
OSWESTRY
BURTON UPON TRENT
LOUGHBOROUGH
STAFFORD
SWADLINCOTE
SHEPSHED
NEWPORT
RUGELEY
ASHBY-DE-LA-ZOUCH
SHREWSBURY
CANNOCK
COALVILLE
LICHFIELD
WELSHPOOL
TELFORD
BROWNHILLS
ALDRIDGE
WOLVERHAMPTON
WALSALL
MONTGOMERY
MUCH WENLOCK
SEDGLEY
SUTTON COLDFIELD
HINCKLEY
CHURCH STRETTON
BRIDGNORTH
WEDNESBURY
WEST BROMWICH
NUNEATON
BIRMINGHAM
BEDWORTH
BISHOP'S CASTLE
AMBLECOTE
DUDLEY
STOURBRIDGE
HALESOWEN
National Exhibition Centre
Birmingham Airport
SOLIHULL
RUGBY
KIDDERMINSTER
BEWDLEY
COVENTRY
LUDLOW
KENILWORTH
STOURPORT-ON-SEVERN
BROMSGROVE
REDDITCH
ROYAL LEAMINGTON SPA
PRESTEIGNE
DROITWICH
WARWICK
SD
SE
SJ
SK
SO
SP
Hotel
Restaurant
Hotel & Restaurant
Other Towns for Location only

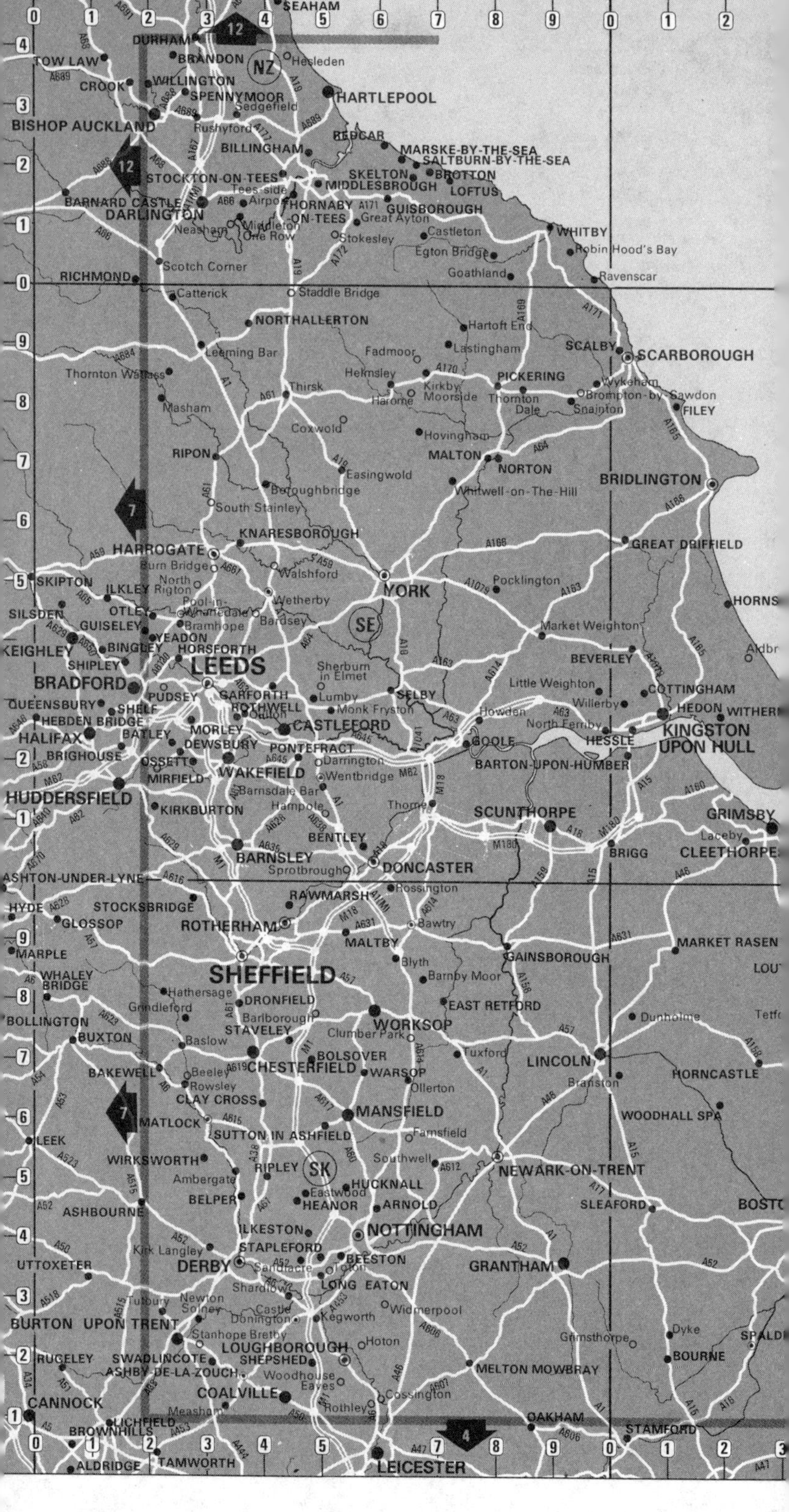

SEAHAM
DURHAM
TOW LAW
BRANDON
Hesleden
WILLINGTON
CROOK
SPENNYMOOR
HARTLEPOOL
Sedgefield
BISHOP AUCKLAND
Rushyford
REDCAR
BILLINGHAM
MARSKE-BY-THE-SEA
SALTBURN-BY-THE-SEA
STOCKTON-ON-TEES
SKELTON
BROTTON
MIDDLESBROUGH
LOFTUS
BARNARD CASTLE
DARLINGTON
THORNABY-ON-TEES
GUISBOROUGH
Great Ayton
Stokesley
Castleton
WHITBY
Robin Hood's Bay
Egton Bridge
Goathland
Ravenscar
Scotch Corner
RICHMOND
Catterick
Staddle Bridge
NORTHALLERTON
Hartoft End
Leeming Bar
Fadmoor
Lastingham
SCALBY
SCARBOROUGH
Thornton Watlass
Helmsley
Kirkby Moorside
PICKERING
Wykeham
Brompton-by-Sawdon
Thirsk
Harome
Thornton Dale
Snainton
FILEY
Masham
Coxwold
Hovingham
RIPON
MALTON
NORTON
Easingwold
BRIDLINGTON
Boroughbridge
Whitwell-on-The-Hill
South Stainley
KNARESBOROUGH
HARROGATE
GREAT DRIFFIELD
Burn Bridge
Walshford
North Rigton
YORK
Pocklington
SKIPTON
ILKLEY
Wetherby
HORNSEA
SILSDEN
OTLEY
Pool-in-Wharfedale
Bardsey
GUISELEY
Bramhope
Market Weighton
KEIGHLEY
YEADON
BINGLEY
HORSFORTH
BEVERLEY
SHIPLEY
LEEDS
Sherburn in Elmet
BRADFORD
Little Weighton
COTTINGHAM
PUDSEY
GARFORTH
SELBY
QUEENSBURY
SHELF
ROTHWELL
Lumby
Monk Fryston
Howden
Willerby
HEDON
HEBDEN BRIDGE
Oulton
North Ferriby
KINGSTON UPON HULL
HALIFAX
BATLEY
MORLEY
CASTLEFORD
HESSLE
DEWSBURY
PONTEFRACT
GOOLE
BRIGHOUSE
OSSETT
Darrington
BARTON-UPON-HUMBER
MIRFIELD
WAKEFIELD
Wentbridge
HUDDERSFIELD
Barnsdale Bar
Hampole
Thorne
SCUNTHORPE
GRIMSBY
KIRKBURTON
Laceby
BENTLEY
BRIGG
CLEETHORPES
BARNSLEY
DONCASTER
Sprotbrough
ASHTON-UNDER-LYNE
Rossington
RAWMARSH
HYDE
STOCKSBRIDGE
GLOSSOP
ROTHERHAM
Bawtry
MALTBY
MARKET RASEN
MARPLE
GAINSBOROUGH
Blyth
WHALEY BRIDGE
SHEFFIELD
Barnby Moor
Hathersage
DRONFIELD
EAST RETFORD
Grindleford
Barlborough
WORKSOP
Dunholme
BOLLINGTON
STAVELEY
Clumber Park
BUXTON
Baslow
Tuxford
LINCOLN
BOLSOVER
CHESTERFIELD
WARSOP
HORNCASTLE
BAKEWELL
Beeley
Rowsley
Branston
Ollerton
CLAY CROSS
MANSFIELD
WOODHALL SPA
MATLOCK
Famsfield
SUTTON IN ASHFIELD
LEEK
Southwell
WIRKSWORTH
NEWARK-ON-TRENT
RIPLEY
Ambergate
HUCKNALL
BELPER
Eastwood
HEANOR
ARNOLD
SLEAFORD
ASHBOURNE
ILKESTON
NOTTINGHAM
Kirk Langley
STAPLEFORD
BEESTON
UTTOXETER
DERBY
Sandiacre
Toton
GRANTHAM
Shardlow
LONG EATON
Tutbury
Newton Solney
Castle Donington
Widmerpool
Kegworth
BURTON UPON TRENT
Stanhope Bretby
Hoton
Grimsthorpe
Dyke
LOUGHBOROUGH
RUGELEY
SWADLINCOTE
SHEPSHED
BOURNE
ASHBY-DE-LA-ZOUCH
MELTON MOWBRAY
Woodhouse Eaves
COALVILLE
Cossington
CANNOCK
Measham
Rothley
OAKHAM
LICHFIELD
BROWNHILLS
STAMFORD
ALDRIDGE
TAMWORTH
LEICESTER
NZ
SE
SK
12
7
4

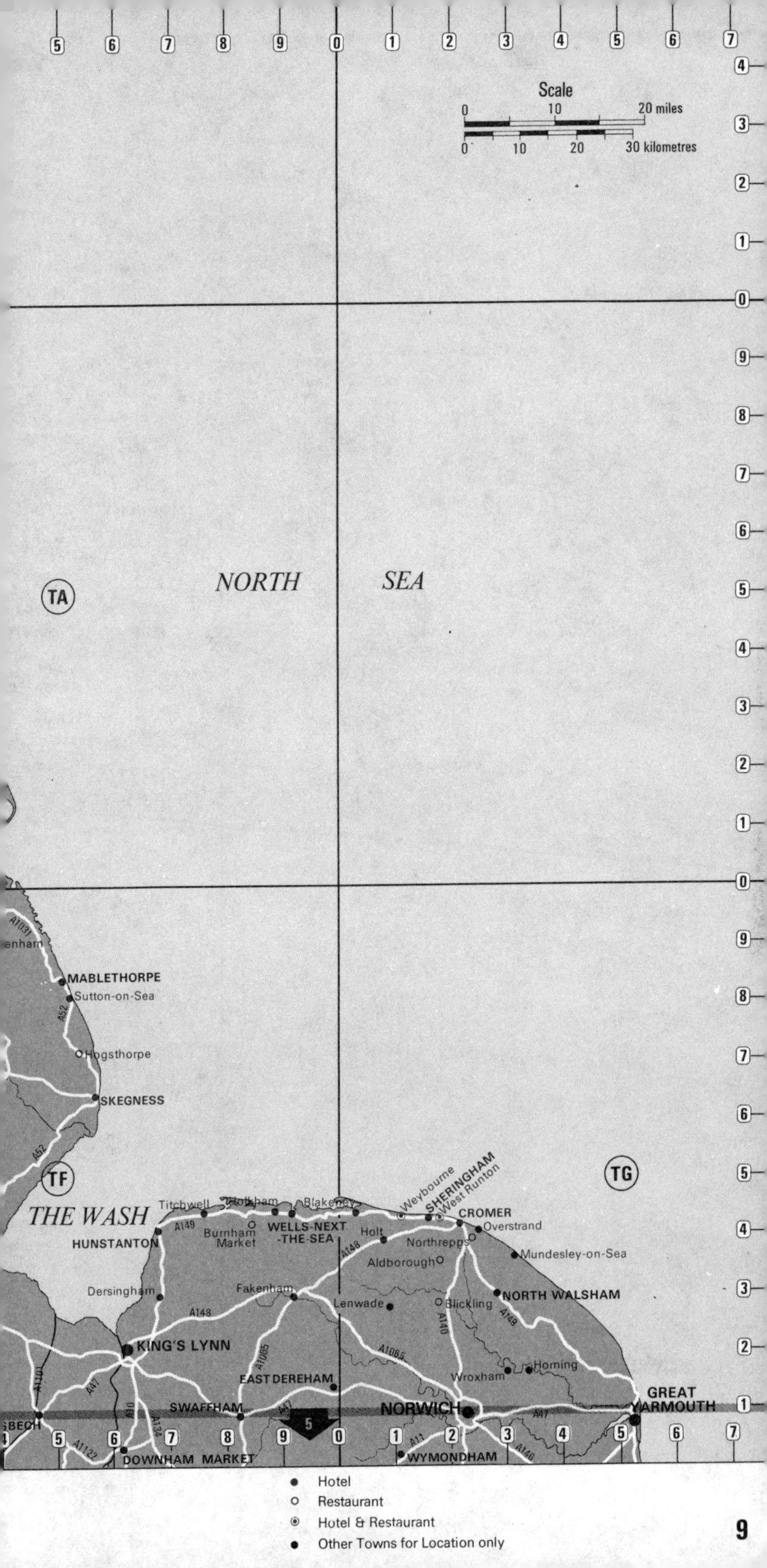
Scale
0 10 20 miles
0 10 20 30 kilometres
NORTH SEA
TA
TF
TG
THE WASH
MABLETHORPE
Sutton-on-Sea
Hogsthorpe
SKEGNESS
Titchwell
Holkham
Blakeney
Weybourne
SHERINGHAM
West Runton
CROMER
Overstrand
HUNSTANTON
Burnham Market
WELLS-NEXT -THE-SEA
Holt
Northrepps
Mundesley-on-Sea
Aldborough
Dersingham
Fakenham
Lenwade
Blickling
NORTH WALSHAM
KING'S LYNN
Horning
Wroxham
EAST DEREHAM
SWAFFHAM
NORWICH
GREAT YARMOUTH
DOWNHAM MARKET
WYMONDHAM
Hotel
Restaurant
Hotel & Restaurant
Other Towns for Location only

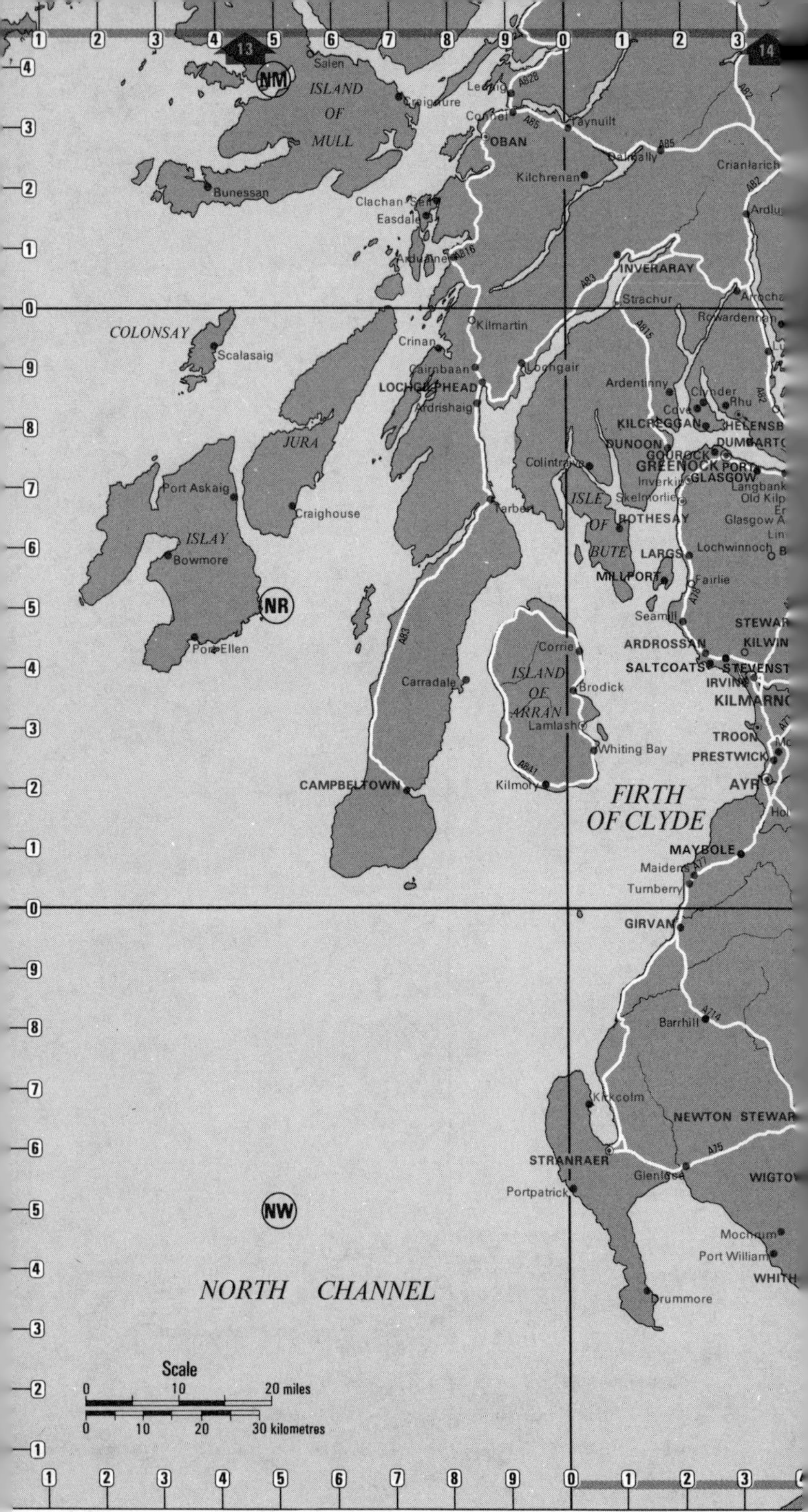

ISLAND OF MULL
Salen
Craignure
Bunessan
OBAN
Taynuilt
Dalmally
Kilchrenan
Crianlarich
Easdale
INVERARAY
Strachur
COLONSAY
Scalasaig
Kilmartin
Crinan
Cairnbaan
LOCHGILPHEAD
Ardrishaig
JURA
Craighouse
ISLAY
Port Askaig
Bowmore
Port Ellen
Ardentinny
KILCREGGAN
DUNOON
GOUROCK
GREENOCK
PORT GLASGOW
Colintraive
ISLE OF BUTE
ROTHESAY
LARGS
MILLPORT
Fairlie
Seamill
ARDROSSAN
SALTCOATS
IRVINE
TROON
PRESTWICK
AYR
Carradale
ISLAND OF ARRAN
Corrie
Brodick
Lamlash
Whiting Bay
Kilmory
CAMPBELTOWN
FIRTH OF CLYDE
MAYBOLE
Maidens
Turnberry
GIRVAN
Barrhill
Kirkcolm
NEWTON STEWART
STRANRAER
Glenluce
Portpatrick
Port William
Drummore
NORTH CHANNEL
NM
NR
NW
Scale
0 10 20 miles
0 10 20 30 kilometres

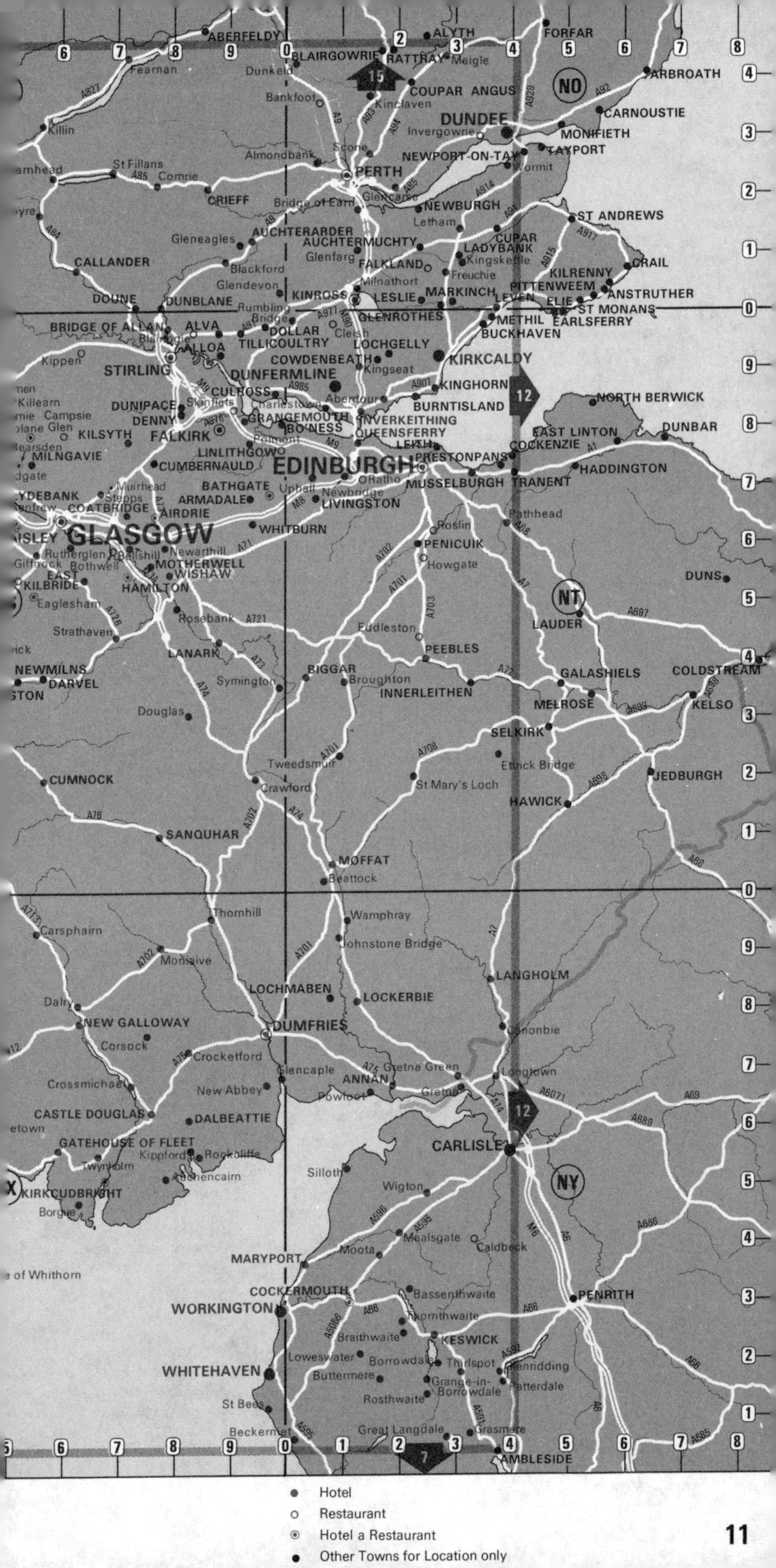

ABERFELDY
ALYTH
FORFAR
BLAIRGOWRIE
RATTRAY
Meigle
Fearnan
Dunkeld
15
ARBROATH
NO
COUPAR ANGUS
Bankfoot
Kinclaven
DUNDEE
CARNOUSTIE
Killin
Invergowrie
MONIFIETH
Scone
NEWPORT-ON-TAY
TAYPORT
Almondbank
Wormit
St Fillans
PERTH
Comrie
Glencarse
CRIEFF
Bridge of Earn
NEWBURGH
Letham
ST ANDREWS
Gleneagles
AUCHTERARDER
CUPAR
AUCHTERMUCHTY
LADYBANK
Glenfarg
Kingskettle
CALLANDER
FALKLAND
CRAIL
Blackford
Freuchie
KILRENNY
Glendevon
Milnathort
PITTENWEEM
ANSTRUTHER
KINROSS
LESLIE
MARKINCH
LEVEN
ELIE
ST MONANS
DOUNE
DUNBLANE
Rumbling Bridge
GLENROTHES
METHIL
EARLSFERRY
BRIDGE OF ALLAN
ALVA
DOLLAR
Cleish
BUCKHAVEN
Blairlogie
ALLOA
TILLICOULTRY
LOCHGELLY
Kippen
COWDENBEATH
KIRKCALDY
STIRLING
DUNFERMLINE
Kingseat
CULROSS
KINGHORN
12
NORTH BERWICK
Killearn
DUNIPACE
Charlestown
Aberdour
BURNTISLAND
Campsie
Glen
DENNY
GRANGEMOUTH
INVERKEITHING
DUNBAR
KILSYTH
FALKIRK
BO'NESS
QUEENSFERRY
EAST LINTON
Bearsden
Polmont
LEITH
COCKENZIE
MILNGAVIE
LINLITHGOW
PRESTONPANS
CUMBERNAULD
EDINBURGH
Ratho
HADDINGTON
Muirhead
BATHGATE
Uphall
Newbridge
MUSSELBURGH
TRANENT
YDEBANK
Stepps
ARMADALE
LIVINGSTON
COATBRIDGE
AIRDRIE
Pathhead
Roslin
GLASGOW
WHITBURN
PENICUIK
Rutherglen
Bellshill
Newarthill
Giffnock
Bothwell
MOTHERWELL
Howgate
EAST KILBRIDE
WISHAW
DUNS
HAMILTON
NT
Eaglesham
Rosebank
LAUDER
Strathaven
Eddleston
LANARK
PEEBLES
NEWMILNS
DARVEL
BIGGAR
GALASHIELS
COLDSTREAM
Symington
Broughton
INNERLEITHEN
MELROSE
KELSO
Douglas
SELKIRK
Tweedsmuir
Ettrick Bridge
CUMNOCK
Crawford
St Mary's Loch
JEDBURGH
HAWICK
SANQUHAR
MOFFAT
Beattock
Thornhill
Wamphray
Carsphairn
Johnstone Bridge
Moniaive
LANGHOLM
Dalry
LOCHMABEN
LOCKERBIE
NEW GALLOWAY
DUMFRIES
Canonbie
Corsock
Crocketford
Glencaple
ANNAN
Gretna Green
Longtown
Crossmichael
New Abbey
Powfoot
Gretna
CASTLE DOUGLAS
DALBEATTIE
GATEHOUSE OF FLEET
Kippford
Rockcliffe
CARLISLE
Twynholm
Auchencairn
Silloth
NY
KIRKCUDBRIGHT
Wigton
Borgue
Mealsgate
Caldbeck
Moota
MARYPORT
COCKERMOUTH
Bassenthwaite
PENRITH
WORKINGTON
Thornthwaite
Braithwaite
KESWICK
Loweswater
Borrowdale
Thirlspot
Glenridding
WHITEHAVEN
Buttermere
Grange-in-Borrowdale
Patterdale
Rosthwaite
St Bees
Great Langdale
Grasmere
Beckermet
7
AMBLESIDE
A827
A9
A93
A94
A929
A92
A85
A914
A91
A84
A915
A917
A977
A91
M90
A9
A985
A907
A921
M9
A876
A1
M8
A71
A702
A701
A703
A68
A7
A697
A721
A73
A72
A74
A708
A699
A698
A6089
A76
A702
A74
A68
A7
A713
A702
A701
A75
A712
A6071
A69
A689
A596
A595
M6
A6
A686
A66
A5086
A592
A591
A595
A66
A6
A685
Hotel
Restaurant
Hotel a Restaurant
Other Towns for Location only

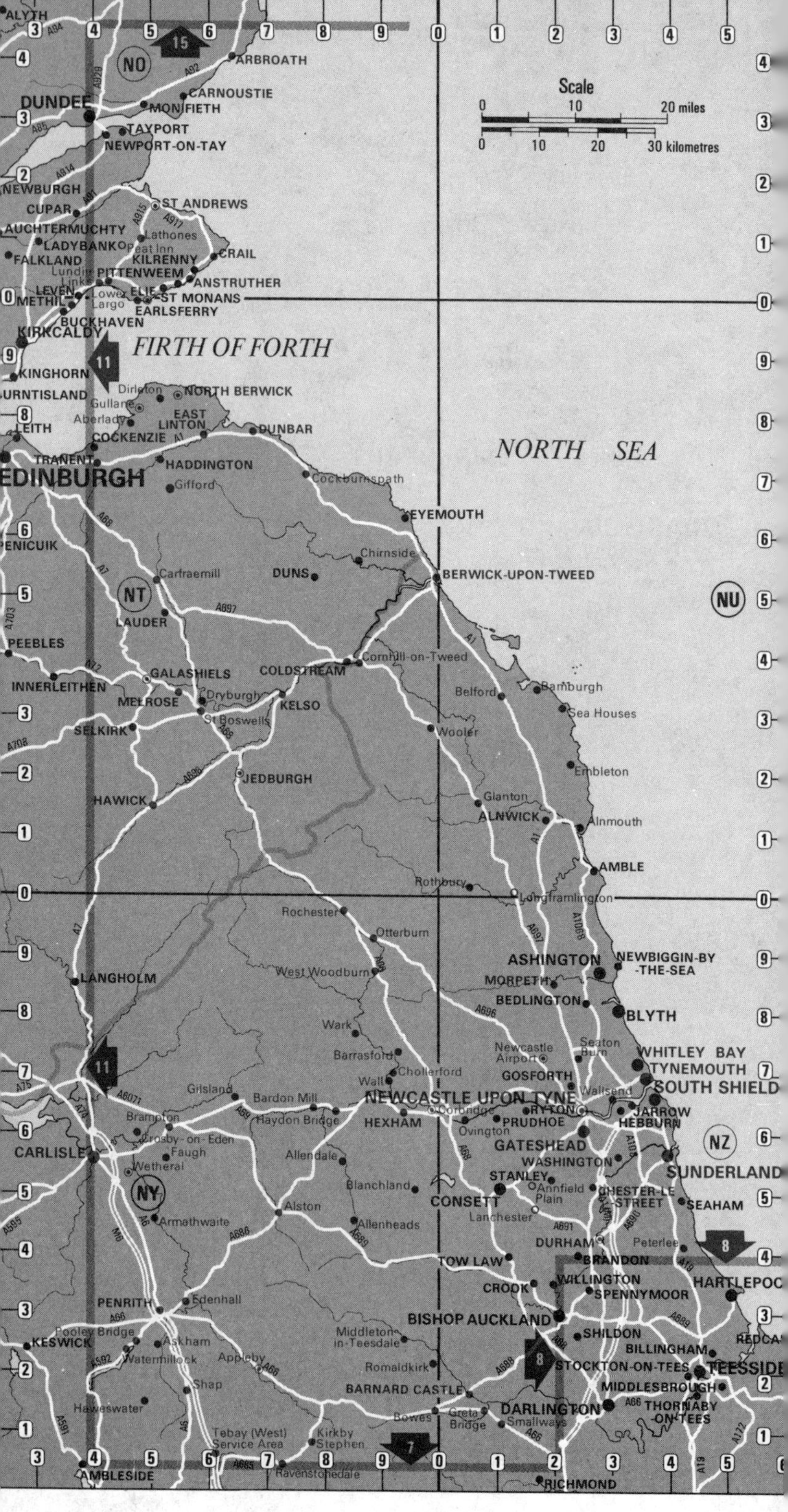
Scale
0 10 20 miles
0 10 20 30 kilometres
NORTH SEA
FIRTH OF FORTH
NO
NT
NU
NY
NZ
ALYTH
ARBROATH
CARNOUSTIE
DUNDEE
MONIFIETH
TAYPORT
NEWPORT-ON-TAY
NEWBURGH
CUPAR
ST ANDREWS
AUCHTERMUCHTY
LADYBANK
Peat Inn
Lathones
FALKLAND
KILRENNY
CRAIL
PITTENWEEM
ANSTRUTHER
LEVEN
METHIL
Lower Largo
ELIE
ST MONANS
EARLSFERRY
BUCKHAVEN
KIRKCALDY
KINGHORN
BURNTISLAND
Dirleton
NORTH BERWICK
Gullane
Aberlady
EAST LINTON
DUNBAR
LEITH
COCKENZIE
TRANENT
HADDINGTON
EDINBURGH
Gifford
Cockburnspath
EYEMOUTH
PENICUIK
Chirnside
Carfraemill
DUNS
BERWICK-UPON-TWEED
LAUDER
PEEBLES
Cornhill-on-Tweed
COLDSTREAM
GALASHIELS
INNERLEITHEN
MELROSE
Dryburgh
KELSO
Belford
Bamburgh
Sea Houses
St Boswells
SELKIRK
Wooler
Embleton
JEDBURGH
HAWICK
Glanton
ALNWICK
Alnmouth
AMBLE
Rothbury
Longframlington
Rochester
Otterburn
ASHINGTON
NEWBIGGIN-BY-THE-SEA
LANGHOLM
West Woodburn
MORPETH
BEDLINGTON
BLYTH
Wark
Newcastle Airport
Seaton Burn
WHITLEY BAY
TYNEMOUTH
Barrasford
Chollerford
GOSFORTH
Wall
Wallsend
SOUTH SHIELDS
Gilsland
Bardon Mill
NEWCASTLE UPON TYNE
Brampton
Haydon Bridge
Corbridge
RYTON
JARROW
HEXHAM
PRUDHOE
HEBBURN
Ovington
Crosby-on-Eden
CARLISLE
Faugh
GATESHEAD
Allendale
WASHINGTON
SUNDERLAND
Wetheral
STANLEY
Annfield Plain
Blanchland
CHESTER-LE-STREET
SEAHAM
CONSETT
Alston
Lanchester
Armathwaite
Allenheads
DURHAM
Peterlee
TOW LAW
BRANDON
WILLINGTON
HARTLEPOOL
CROOK
SPENNYMOOR
PENRITH
Edenhall
BISHOP AUCKLAND
Pooley Bridge
Middleton-in-Teesdale
SHILDON
KESWICK
Askham
BILLINGHAM
REDCAR
Watermillock
Appleby
Romaldkirk
STOCKTON-ON-TEES
TEESSIDE
Shap
BARNARD CASTLE
MIDDLESBROUGH
Haweswater
DARLINGTON
THORNABY-ON-TEES
Bowes
Greta Bridge
Smallways
Tebay (West) Service Area
Kirkby Stephen
AMBLESIDE
Ravenstonedale
RICHMOND
A94
A92
A929
A85
A914
A91
A915
A917
A1
A68
A7
A697
A703
A72
A708
A698
A1068
A696
A75
A74
A6071
A69
A6
M6
A595
A686
A689
A591
A592
A66
A688
A19
A172
A167
A690
A691
A1(M)
A685
15
11
8
7

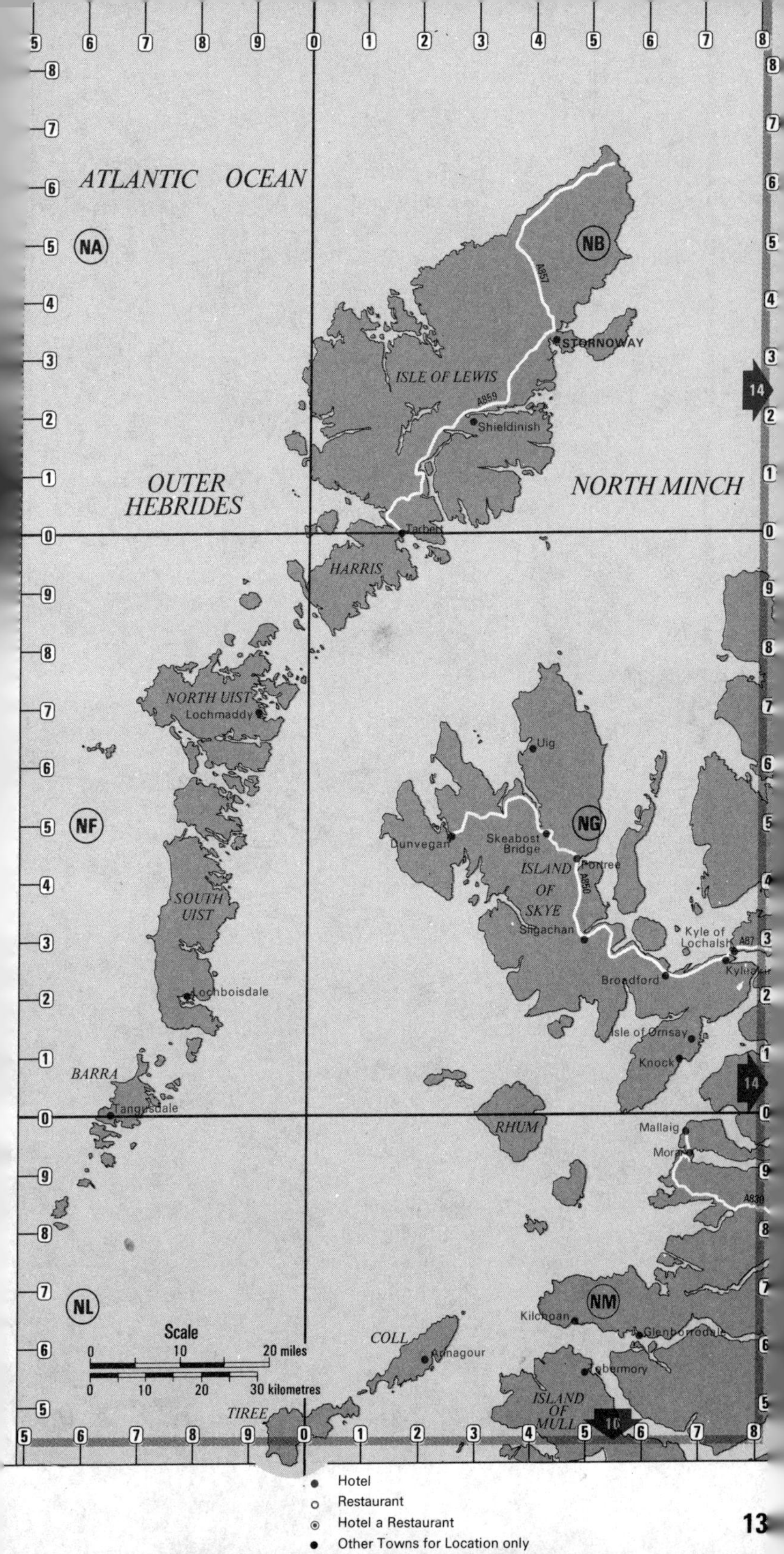

● Hotel
○ Restaurant
◉ Hotel a Restaurant
● Other Towns for Location only

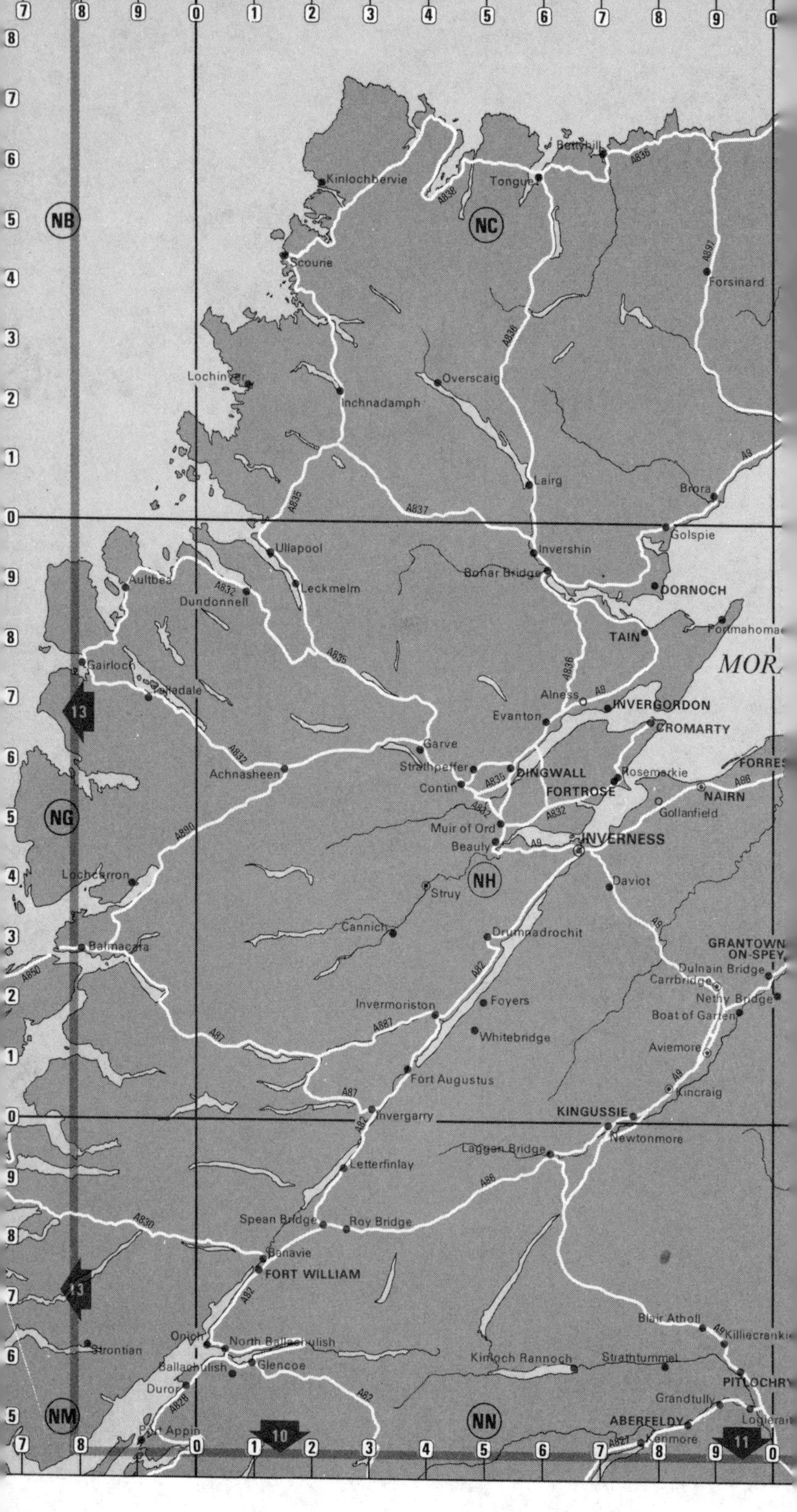
NB
NC
NG
NH
NM
NN
Kinlochbervie
Tongue
Bettyhill
Scoune
Forsinard
Lochinver
Overscaig
Inchnadamph
Lairg
Brora
Golspie
Ullapool
Invershin
Bonar Bridge
Aultbea
Leckmelm
Dundonnell
DORNOCH
TAIN
Portmahomac
MORA
Gairloch
Talladale
Alness
INVERGORDON
Evanton
CROMARTY
Garve
Strathpeffer
DINGWALL
Rosemarkie
Achnasheen
Contin
FORTROSE
NAIRN
FORRES
Gollanfield
Muir of Ord
Beauly
INVERNESS
Lochcarron
Struy
Daviot
Cannich
Drumnadrochit
Balmacara
GRANTOWN-ON-SPEY
Dulnain Bridge
Carrbridge
Nethy Bridge
Invermoriston
Foyers
Boat of Garten
Whitebridge
Aviemore
Fort Augustus
Kincraig
Invergarry
KINGUSSIE
Newtonmore
Laggan Bridge
Letterfinlay
Spean Bridge
Roy Bridge
Banavie
FORT WILLIAM
Blair Atholl
Killiecrankie
Onich
North Ballachulish
Strontian
Kinloch Rannoch
Strathtummel
Ballachulish
Glencoe
Duror
PITLOCHRY
Grandtully
Logierait
ABERFELDY
Kenmore
Port Appin
A838
A836
A897
A835
A837
A9
A832
A890
A850
A87
A887
A82
A86
A830
A828
A827

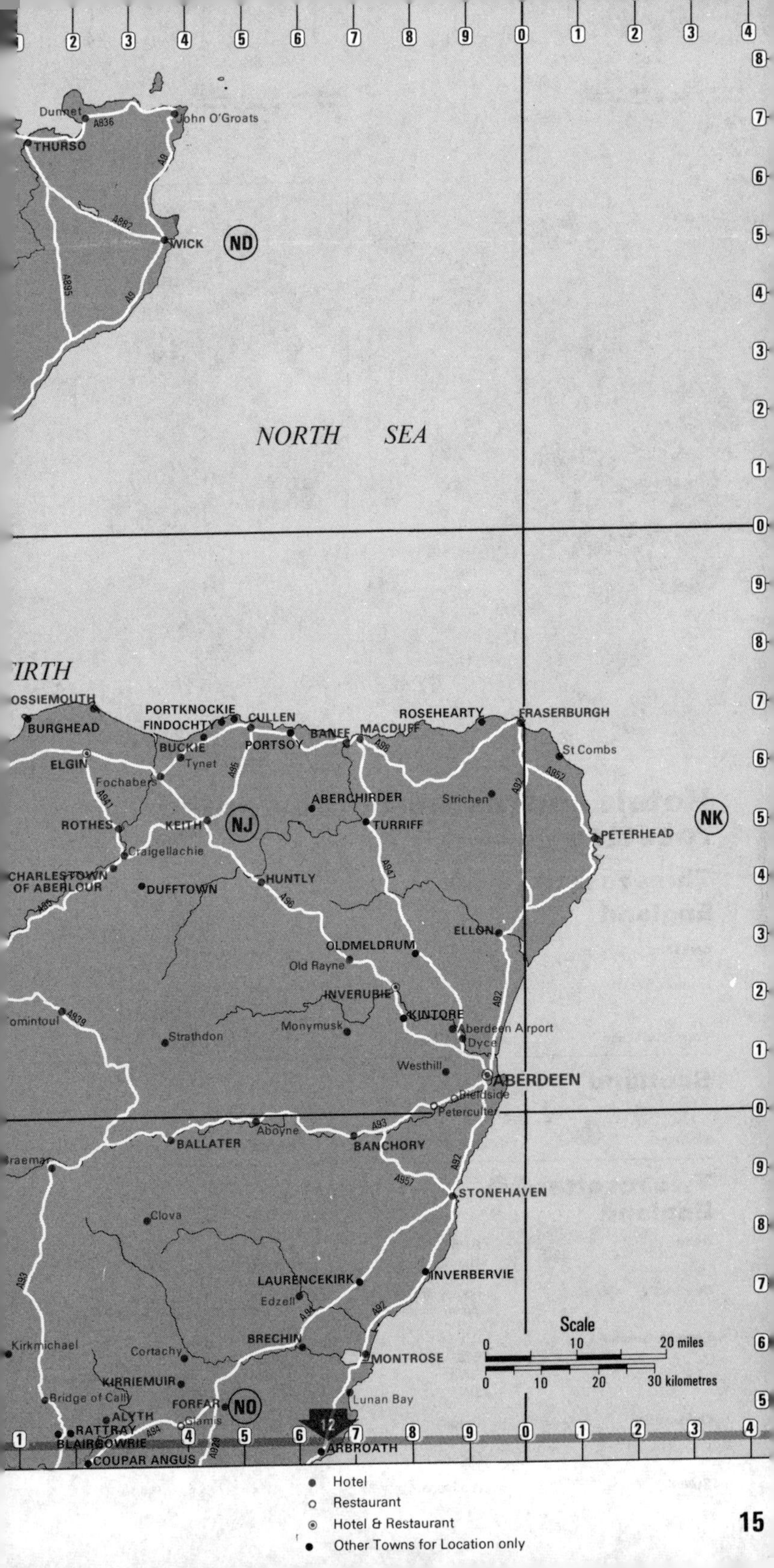

● Hotel
○ Restaurant
◎ Hotel & Restaurant
● Other Towns for Location only

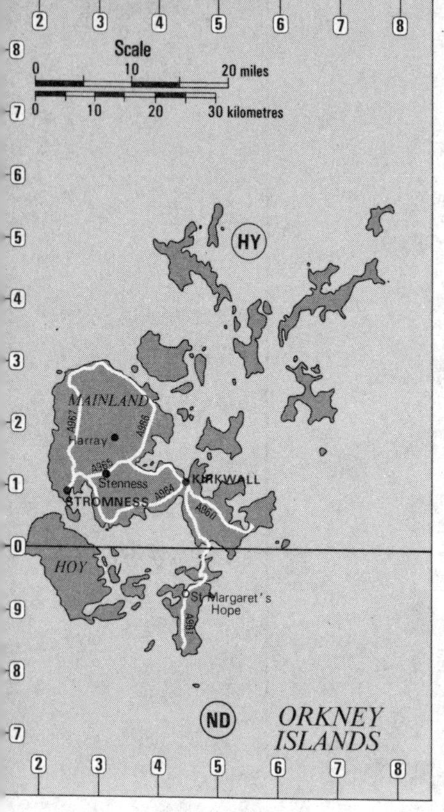

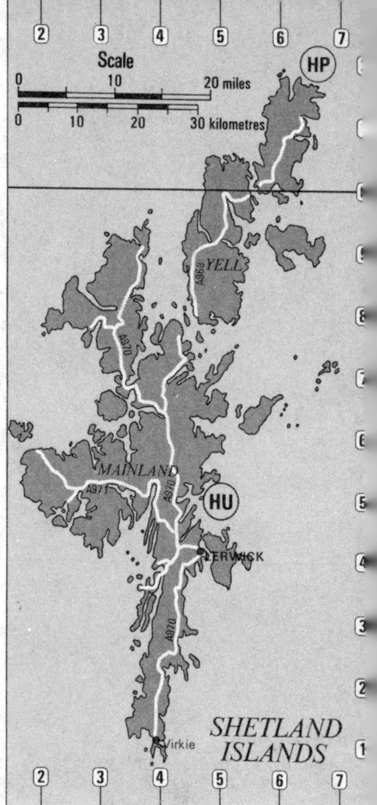

Hotels and restaurants awarded rosettes

Three rosettes ❀❀❀

England

Berkshire	Bray	XXXX	Waterside
London, Greater	W1	XXXXX	Connaught Hotel
	SW1	XXX	Le Gavroche
Yorkshire, West	Ilkley	XXX	Box Tree

Scotland

Highland	Fort William	★★★★	Inverlochy Castle (Dinner only)

Two rosettes ❀❀

England

Avon	Bath	XXX	Popjoys
	Thornbury	XXXX	Thornbury Castle
Cumbria	Pooley Bridge	★★★	Sharrow Bay
	Windermere	★★	Miller Howe (Dinner only)
London, Greater	W1	XXXXX	Mirabelle
	EC2	XXX	Le Poulbot
	SW3	XX	Tante Claire
	SW3	X	Ma Cuisine
Oxfordshire	Oxford	XX	Elizabeth
	Oxford	XX	La Sorbonne
	Oxford	X	Les Quat' Saisons
Suffolk	Hintlesham	XXX	Hintlesham Hall

One rosette ❀
England

County	Town	Classification	Establishment
Avon	Bath	★★★	Priory (Dinner only)
		✕✕✕	Hole in the Wall
		✕	Laden Table
	Marksbury	★★★ ⌂	Hunstrete House (Dinner only)
Bedfordshire	Turvey	★	Laws
Berkshire	Hurley	★★	Ye Olde Bell
Buckinghamshire	Aston Clinton	★★★	Bell Inn
Cambridgeshire	Cambridge	★★★★	Garden House
	Ely	✕	Old Fire Engine House
	St Ives	★★★	Slepe Hall
Cheshire	Handforth	★★★★	Belfry
Cornwall	Helford	✕✕	Riverside
	Polkerris	✕	Rashleigh (Dinner only)
	Polperro	✕✕	House on Props
	St Mawes	★★	Rising Sun
Cumbria	Brampton	★★ ⌂	Farlam Hall (Dinner only)
		★★	Tarn End
	Grasmere	★	White Moss House (Dinner only)
	Windermere	✕	Porthole (Dinner only)
Devon	Chagford	✕✕	Gidleigh Park (Dinner only)
	Dartmouth	✕✕	Carved Angel
	Gulworthy	✕✕✕	Horn of Plenty
	Ottery St Mary	✕✕	Lodge
	Salcombe	★★★	Tides Reach (Dinner only)
	Teignmouth	★★ ⌂	Venn Farm Country House (Dinner only)
	Tiverton	✕✕	Lowman
	Wrafton	✕✕	Poyers Farm
	Yarcombe	★	Belfry (Dinner only)
Dorset	Christchurch	✕	Splinters
	Sturminster Newton	✕✕	Plumber Manor
Co Durham	Durham	✕	Travellers' Rest (Dinner only)
Essex	Dedham	✕✕✕	Le Talbooth (restaurant for ★★★ for Maison Talbooth
Gloucestershire	Bishop's Cleeve	✕✕✕	Cleeveway House
	Blockley	★★	Lower Brook House
	Chipping Campden	★★	King's Arms (Dinner only)
	Cleeve Hill	✕✕✕	Malvern View
	Moreton in Marsh	✕✕	Lambs (Dinner only)
	Tetbury	★★	Close (Dinner only)
Hampshire	Alresford	✕	O'Rorkes
	Lymington	✕	Limpets
	New Milton	★★★★ ⌂	Chewton Glen
	Rake	✕✕	Les Gourmets
	Southampton	✕	Golden Palace
	Wickham	★★	Old House
Hereford & Worcester	Corse Lawn	✕✕✕	Corse Lawn
	Malvern, Great	★	Walmer Lodge (Dinner only)
	Malvern Wells	★★★ ⌂	Cottage in the Wood
	Witley, Great	✕✕	Hundred House (Dinner only)
Isle of Wight	St Helens	✕	Hayloft
	Ventnor	★★ ⌂	Peacock Vane
Kent	Biddenden	✕	Ye Maydes
	Burham	✕	Toastmaster's Inn
	Whitstable	✕	Le Pousse Bedaine (Dinner only)
	Wye	✕✕	Wife of Bath
Leicestershire	Leicester	✕✕✕	Manor Restaurant, Glen Parva Manor

London, Greater	SW8	XX	Alonso's
	SW19	X	Les Amoureaux
	NW11	X	L'Aubergade
	W1	XXXXX	Berkeley Hotel
	W8	XXX	Le Bressan
	EC1	X	Bubbs
	SW3	XXX	Capital Hotel
	SW1	XXXXX	Carlton Tower Hotel (*Chelsea Room*)
	N1	XXX	Carriers
	W11	XX	Chez Moi
	SE22	X	Chez Nico
	SW3	XX	Daphne's
	W1	XX	Gay Hussar
	W1	XXXXX	Grosvenor House Hotel (*La Fontaine*)
	WC2	XXXX	Inigo Jones
	NW3	XX	Keats
	W1	XXX	Lacy's
	W11	XXX	Leiths
	W1	XX	Odins
	SW1	XX	Pomegranates
	WC2	XX	Poons (King Street)
	WC2	X	Poons (Lisle Street)
	WC2	XXXXX	Savoy Hotel Grill
	SW7	XX	Shezan
	W1	X	Soho Rendezvous
	WC2	XX	Thomas de Quincey
	SW3	XXXX	Waltons
	NW1	XXX	White House
	W1	XXX	White Tower
Manchester	Manchester	★★★★	Midland (French Restaurant)
		XX	Isola Bella
Merseyside	Liverpool	XXX	Oriel
	Southport	X	Le Coq Hardi (Dinner only)
Norfolk	Brockdish	XX	Sheriff House
	Burnham Market	X	Fishes
	West Runton	XX	Mirabelle
Northamptonshire	Horton	XX	French Partridge
Oxfordshire	Chesterton	X	Kinch's (Dinner only)
Salop	Shrewsbury	X	Penny Farthing
Somerset	Montacute	XX	Milk House (Dinner only)
	South Petherton	XX	Oaklands
Staffordshire	Cauldon Lowe	X	Jean Pierre
Suffolk	Fressingfield	X	Fox and Goose
	Southwold	XX	Dutch Barn
Surrey	Alfold	XX	Chez Jean
	East Molesey	X	Lantern
Sussex, East	Bodiam	X	Curlew
	Eastbourne	XX	Summer Palace
	Hastings	X	Mitre
	Lewes	X	Trumps (Dinner only)
Sussex, West	Chilgrove	XX	White Horse Inn
	East Grinstead	★★★	Gravetye Manor
	Findon	XX	Findon Manor
	Storrington	XX	Manleys
Tyne & Wear	Newcastle-upon-Tyne	★★★★	Gosforth Park
Warwickshire	Henley in Arden	XXX	Beaudesert
	Kenilworth	X	Restaurant Bosquet
		X	Romano's
	Leamington Spa (Royal)	★★	Mallory Court
	Warwick	XXX	Westgate Arms
West Midlands	Birmingham	XX	Rajdoot
	Oldbury	X	Jonathans'
	Stourbridge	X	Gallery (Dinner only)

County	Town	Rating	Establishment
Wiltshire	Odstock	×	Yew Tree Inn
	Salisbury	×	Cranes
Yorkshire, North	Brompton by Sawdon	×	Brompton Forge
	Harrogate	××	Number Six
	Walshford	×××	Bridge Inn (*Byron Room*)
Yorkshire, West	Pool in Wharfedale	×××	Pool Court

Channel Islands

County	Town	Rating	Establishment
Guernsey	St Peter Port	★★★	La Frégate
		×××	Le Français
Jersey	St Helier	××	La Capannina
		××	Mauro's

Wales

County	Town	Rating	Establishment
Dyfed	Castlemorris	×	Y Gwesty Bach
Glamorgan, South	Cardiff	×	Gibsons
	Penarth	×××	Caprice
Gwent	Llandewi Skirrid	×	Walnut Tree
Gwynedd	Rhydymain	××	Rossi Ristorante (Dinner only)

Scotland

County	Town	Rating	Establishment
Dumfries & Galloway	Kirkcudbright	×	Ingle (Dinner only)
Fife	St Andrews	××	Grange Inn
Highland	Aviemore	×	Bumbles (Dinner only)
	Dulnain Bridge	★★	Muckrach Lodge (Dinner only)
	Glenborrodale	★★	Clan Morrison (Dinner only)
	Inverness	★★ 🌲	Dunain Park (Dinner only)
Lothian	Edinburgh	××	Howtowdie
		×	Flappers
	Gullane	×	La Potinière
	Linlithgow	×××	Champany
	Queensferry (South)	★★	Hawes Inn
Strathclyde	Bearsden	××	La Bavarde
	Clachan Seil	★	Willowburn (Dinner only)
	Glasgow	★★★★	Central (*Malmaison Restaurant*)
		××	Colonial
	Kilmartin	×	Cairn (Dinner only)
	Kilwinning	××	High Smithstown Farm (Dinner only)
	Lamlash	×	Carraig Mhor (Dinner only)
	Troon	××	L'Auberge de Provence (Dinner only)
Tayside	Bridge of Cally	★	Bridge of Cally (Dinner only)
	Cleish	××	Nivingston House
	Glencarse	★★	Newton House

Country-house hotels

Quiet, often secluded hotels are listed below. At an AA country-house hotel you should be assured of a restful night, together with a relaxed, informal atmosphere and personal welcome. On the other hand, some of the facilities may differ from those to be found in purpose-built, urban hotels of the same star rating.

It should be noted that not all rurally situated hotels are AA country-house hotels, neither are AA country-house hotels always located in an isolated situation.

England

Avon

Bath	★★	Combe Grove
Marksbury	❀★★★	Hunstrete House
Petty France	★★	Petty France
Rangeworthy	Ⓟ	Rangeworthy Court

Cambridgeshire

Six Mile Bottom	★★★	Swynford Paddocks

Cleveland

Loftus	★★★	Grinkle Park

Cornwall

Bodmin	★★	Castle Hill House
Falmouth	★★	Penmere Manor
Lamorna Cove	★★★	Lamorna Cove
	★	Menwinnion
Mawnan Smith	★★★	Meudon
Portscatho	★★★	Rosevine
	★★	Roseland House
Ruan High Lanes	★★	Pendower
	★★	Polsue Manor
St Agnes	★★	Rose-in-Vale
St Wenn	★	Wenn Manor
Talland Bay	★★★	Talland Bay
Trelights	★	Long Cross

Cumbria

Appleby	★★★	Appleby Manor
Bassenthwaite	★★★	Armathwaite Hall
	★★	Overwater
Brampton	❀★★	Farlam Hall
Grange-over-Sands	★★	Graythwaite Manor
Hawkshead	★★★	Tarn Hows
Keswick	★★	Red House
Levens	★★	Heaves
Longtown	★	March Bank
Pooley Bridge	❀❀★★★	Sharrow Bay
Thornthwaite	★★	Thwaite Howe
Whitehaven	★★	Roseneath
Windermere	★★★	Langdale Chase
	★★	Linthwaite

Derbyshire

Matlock	★★	Riber Hall

Devon

Ashburton	★★	Holne Chase
Axminster	★★	Woodbury Park
Barnstaple	❀★★	Downrew House
	★★	Roborough House
Belstone	★★	Skaigh House
Berry Pomeroy	★	Loventor Manor
Bideford	★★	Yeoldon House
	★	Rosskery
Bovey Tracey	★★	Edgemoor
	★★	Prestbury
Buckland in the Moor	★★	Buckland Hall
Burrington	★★★	Northcote Manor
Chagford	★★★	Great Tree
	★★★	Mill End
Clawton	★★	Court Barn
Coleford	★	Coombe House Country
Combeinteignhead	★★	Netherton House

Devon continued

Combe Martin	★★	Higher Leigh
Exeter	★★	Trood
Fairy Cross	★★★	Portledge
Gittisham	★★	Combe House
Haytor	★★	Bel Alp
Heddon's Mouth	★★	Heddon's Gate
Honiton	★★★	Deer Park
Horns Cross	★★	Foxdown Manor
Ilsington	★★	Haytor
Kingsbridge	★★	Buckland-Tout-Saints
Kingswear	★★	Redoubt
Lydford	★	Lydford House
Lynmouth	★★	Beacon
Lynton	★	Combe Park
Membury	★	Lee Hill Farm Hotel
Moreton-hampstead	★★★★	Manor House
Newton Ferrers	★★	Court House
Plymouth	★★	Elfordleigh
Sidmouth	★★	Brownlands
South Brent	★	Glazebrook House
South Tawton	★★	Wood Country
Stoke Gabriel	★★	Gabriel Court
Teignmouth	❀★★	Venn Farm
Wembury	★★	Langdon Court
Widecombe-in-the-Moor	★★	Wooder Manor

Dorset

Bridport	★	Little Wych
Fleet	★★	Moonfleet Manor
Milton-on-Stour	★★★	Milton Lodge
Studland	★★	Manor House

Essex

Dedham	❀★★★	Maison Talbooth
	★★	Dedham Vale

Gloucestershire

Cheltenham	★★	Greenway
Coleford	★	Lambsquay
Stinchcombe	★	Stinchcombe Manor
Stroud	★★	Burleigh Court
Upper Slaughter	★★★	Lords of the Manor

Hampshire

Bramshaw	★★	Bramble Hill
Burley	★★★	Burley Manor
	★★	Moorhill House
Lymington	★★★	Passford House
Lyndhurst	★★★	Parkhill
New Milton	❀★★★★	Chewton Glen

Hereford & Worcester

Abberley	★★★	Elms
Broadway	★★	Collin House
Brockhampton	★★	Brockhampton Court
Malvern Wells	❀★★★	Cottage-in-the-Wood
Pencraig	★★	Pencraig Court
Ross-on-Wye	★★	Chasedale
Symonds Yat (West)	★★	Wye Rapids
Walford	★	Walford House

Hertfordshire

Bishop's Stortford	★★	Thorley Place

Humberside

Little Weighton	★★★	Rowley Manor

Isle of Wight

Bembridge	★★	Elm Country
Ventnor	★★	Winterbourne
	❀★★	Peacock Vane
	★	Madeira Hall
Whippingham	★★	Padmore House

Kent

Cranbrook	★★	Kennel Holt
Ramsgate	★★	Court Stairs Hotel and Country Club

Manchester, Greater

Egerton	★★★	Egerton House

Midlands West

Knowle	★★★	Chadwick Manor

Norfolk

Bunwell	★★	Bunwell Manor
Caistor St Edmund	(ap)	Caistor Hall
Lenwade	★★	Lenwade House

Northamptonshire

Wicken	★★	Wicken Country

Northumberland

Allendale	★★	Ashleigh
	★★	Riding
Cornhill-on-Tweed	★★★	Tillmouth Park
Otterburn	★★	Otterburn Tower

Oxfordshire

Horton-Cum-Studley	★★★	Studley Priory

Salop

Telford	★★★	Buckatree Hall

Somerset

Dulverton	★★★	Carnarvon Arms
	★★	Three Acres
Evercreech	★★	Glen
Holford	★★	Alfoxton Park
	★★	Combe House
Horsington	★★	Horsington House
Watchet	★	Downfield
Wincanton	★★	Holbrook House
Withypool	★	Wester Close

Suffolk

Wetheringsett	★★	Wetheringsett Manor
Woodbridge	★★★	Seckford Hall

Surrey

Bagshot	★★★★	Pennyhill Park

Sussex, East

Hastings	★★★	Beauport Park
Stone Cross	★★★	Glyndley Manor

Sussex, West

Climping	★★★	Bailiffscourt
Cuckfield	★★	Hilton Park
East Grinstead	❀★★★	Gravetye Manor
Thakeham	★★	Abingworth Hall
Trotton	★★★	Southdowns

Warwickshire

Billesley	★★★	Billesley Manor Country Club
Ettington	★★	Chase
Leamington Spa (Royal)	❀★★	Mallory Court
Rugby	★★★	Clifton Court
Stratford upon Avon	★★	Haytor

Wiltshire

Castle Combe	★★★	Manor House
Limpley Stoke	★★★	Cliffe
Warminster	★★★	Bishopstrow House

Yorkshire, North

Lastingham	★★	Lastingham Grange
Monk Fryston	★★★	Monk Fryston Hall
Whitwell-on-the-Hill	★★	Whitwell Hall

Yorkshire, West

Marsden	★★	Hey Green
Wentbridge	★★★	Wentbridge House

Channel Islands

Jersey

St Saviour	★★★★	Longueville Manor

Wales

Clwyd

Churchstoke	★★	Mellington Hall
Corwen	★★	Glan Deva
Llangollen	★★★	Bryn Howel

Dyfed

Aberystwyth	★★★	Conrah
Broadhaven	★	Rosehill Country
Crugybar	★★	Glanrannell Park
Eglwysfach	★★★	Ynyshir Hall
Llandovery	★★	Llanfair Grange
	★	Picton Court
Llangadog	★★	Plas Glansevin
St Davids	★★★	Warpool Court
	★★★	Whitesands Bay
	★	Twr-y-Felin

Gwynedd

Abersoch	★★★	Porth Tocyn
Barmouth	★★	Plas Mynach
Beddgelert	★	Bryn Eglwys
Criccieth	★★★	Bron Eifion
	★★	Parciau Mawr
Llanbedr	★	Cae Nest Hall
Llanrwst	★★★	Gwesty-Plas Maenan
Pennal	★★	Llugwy
Talsarnau	★★	Maes-y-Neuadd

Powys

Caersws	★★	Maesmawr Hall
Crickhowell	★★	Gliffaes
Llanfyllin	★★	Bodfach Hall
Llangammarch Wells	★★★	Lake

Scotland

Borders

Chirnside	★★	Chirnside
Dryburgh	★★★	Dryburgh Abbey
Ettrick Bridge	★★	Ettrick Shaws Lodge
Peebles	★★	Cringletie House
Peebles	★★	Venlaw Castle

Central

Callander	★★★	Roman Camp

Dumfries & Galloway

Auchencairn	★★★	Balcary Bay
Borgue	★★	Senwick House
Corsock	★★	Glaisters Lodge
Crossmichael	★★	Culgruff House
Dalry	★★	Milton Park
Kirkcolm	★★	Knocknassie House
Moffat	★★	Beechwood
Portpatrick	★★★	Knockinaam Lodge
Rockcliffe	★★★	Barons Craig

Fife		
Glenrothes	★★★	Balgeddie
Kingskettle	★★★	Annfield House
Letham	★★★	Fernie Castle
Grampian		
Banchory	★★★	Banchory Lodge
	★★★	Raemoir
Huntly	★★	Castle
Rothes	★★★	Rothes Glen
Highland		
Achnasheen	★★	Ledgowan
Drumnadrochit	★★	Polmaily House
Dulnain Bridge	❀★★	Muckrach Lodge
Fort William	❀❀❀★★★★	Inverlochy Castle
Garve	★★★	Strathgarve Lodge
Glenborrodale	★★	Glenborrodale Castle
Invergarry	★★	Glengarry Castle
Inverness	★★★★	Culloden House
	❀★★	Dunain Park
Invershin	★★	Aultnagar Lodge
Isle Ornsay, Isle of Skye	★★	Kinloch Lodge
Leckmelm	⊕	Tir Aluinn
Nairn	★★★★	Newton
Skeabost Bridge,		
Highland continued		
Isle of Skye	★★★	Skeabost House
Strontian	★★	Kilcamb Lodge
Lothian		
Gullane	★★★	Greywalls
Uphall	★★★	Houstoun House
Strathclyde		
Easdale	★★	Dunmor House
Hollybush	★★★	Hollybush House
Kilchrenan	★★	Taychreggan
Langbank	★★★	Cleddoch House
Ledaig	★★★	Isle of Eriska
Skelmorlie	★★★	Manor Park
Stewarton	★★★	Chapeltoun House
Symington	★★	Wyndales House
Tarbert, Loch Fyne	★★★	Stonefield Castle
Tayside		
Almondbank	★★	Huntingtower
Alyth	★★★	Lands of Loyal
Crieff	★★	Cultoquhey
Dunkeld	★★★	Dunkeld House
Kinclaven	★★★	Ballathie House
Meigle	★★	Kings of Kinloch
Pitlochry	★★★	Pine Trees
	★	Dunfallandy House
Scone	★★★	Murrayshall House
Strathtummel	★★	Port-An-Eilean

Hotels with conference facilities

For those planning business seminars or conferences the list below gives hotels able to accommodate at least 40 guests in rooms with private bath. Each hotel has one or more conference rooms seating a minimum of 40 people at tables, a dining room, a conference office with telephones and syndicate rooms. Amplifying equipment and a speakers rostrum are available or can be supplied. The abbreviation **T** indicates that the hotel has telex, **MLT** means that it can arrange multi-language translation systems.

England

Avon		
Bath	☆☆☆☆	Beaufort **T MLT**
Blagdon	★★★	Mendip
Bristol	☆☆☆☆	Bristol EuroCrest **T**
	☆☆☆☆	Ladbroke Dragonara **T MLT**
	☆☆☆☆	Holiday Inn **T MLT**
	☆☆☆☆	Unicorn **T MLT**
	★★	Avon Gorge **T MLT**
Weston-Super-Mare	★★★	Grand Atlantic
Bedfordshire		
Bedford	★★★	Bedford Moat House **T MLT**
	★★★	Woodlands Manor **MLT**
Luton	☆☆☆☆	Luton EuroCrest **T**
	☆☆☆☆	Strathmore **T**
Berkshire		
Ascot	★★★	Berystede **T MLT**
Maidenhead	☆☆☆☆	Maidenhead EuroCrest **T MLT**
Slough	☆☆☆☆	Holiday Inn **T MLT**
Windsor	★★★	Castle **T**
Buckinghamshire		
Beaconsfield	☆☆☆☆	Bell House **MLT**
Marlow	★★★★	Compleat Angler **T**
Cambridgeshire		
Cambridge	❀★★★★	Garden House **T MLT**
	★★★★	University Arms **T**
	★★★	Gonville
Cheshire		
Backford Cross	☆☆☆	Wirral Ladbroke Mercury Motor Inn
Bollington	★★★	Belgrade Motel **T MLT**
Chester	★★★★	Grosvenor
	★★★	Abbots Well Motor Inn **T MLT**
	★★★	Blossoms **T MLT**
	☆☆☆	Post House **T**
	★★★	Mollington Banastre **MLT**
Daresbury	★★★	Lord Daresbury **T**
Handforth	❀★★★★	Belfry **T**
Mottram St Andrew	★★★	Mottram Hall **T MLT**
Runcorn	☆☆☆	Runcorn EuroCrest **T MLT**
Sandbach	☆☆☆	Saxon Cross Motel
Cleveland		
Middlesbrough	☆☆☆☆	Ladbroke Dragonara **T MLT**
	☆☆☆	Middlesbrough Crest **MLT**
Redcar	☆☆☆	Royal York **T MLT**
Stockton-on-Tees	☆☆☆☆	Swallow

Cornwall

Bude	★★★	Grenville **MLT**
Fowey	★★★	Fowey **T**
Looe	★★★	Hannafore Point
Newquay	★★★	Bristol **T MLT**
St Ives	★★★★	Tregenna Castle **T**

Cumbria

Carlisle	★★★	Crown & Mitre **T MLT**
	★★★	Hilltop Motor **T**
Kendal	★★★	Woolpack Inn
Windermere	★★★★	Old England **T MLT**
	★★★	Beech Hill
	★★★	Belsfield **T MLT**
	★★★	Hydro

Derbyshire

Derby	★★★	Pennine **MLT**
	★★	Derby Crest Motel
Long Eaton	☆☆☆	Novotel Nottingham **T MLT**
Matlock	★★★	New Bath

Devon

Bideford	★★★	Durrant House
Dawlish	★★★	Langstone Cliff **MLT**
Exeter	☆☆☆	Countess Wear Lodge
Kennford	☆☆☆	Exeter Ladbroke Mercury Motor Inn
Lewdown	☆☆	Coach House **T**
Paignton	★★★	Palace **MLT**
Plymouth	☆☆☆☆	Holiday Inn **T MLT**
	★★★	Duke of Cornwall **T MLT**
Sidmouth	★★★★	Victoria
Thurlestone	★★★	Thurlestone **MLT**
Torquay	★★★★★	Imperial **T MLT**
	★★★★	New Grand **T**
	★★★★	Osborne **MLT**
	★★★★	Palace **T MLT**
	★★★	Kistor **MLT**
	★★★	Livermead Cliff **T MLT**
	★★★	Livermead House **T MLT**
	★★★	Palm Court **T**
	★★★	Rainbow House **T MLT**
	★★★	Toorak
Woolacombe	★★★	Narracott Grand

Dorset

Bournemouth	★★★★★	Carlton **T MLT**
	★★★★	Eastcliff Court **T MLT**
	★★★★	Highcliff **T MLT**
	★★★★	Marsham Court **MLT**
	★★★★	Palace Court **MLT**
	☆☆☆	Crest Motor **T MLT**
	★★★	Heathlands **T MLT**
	★★★	Normandie International **MLT**
	★★★	Queens
Ferndown	★★★★	Dormy
Poole	★★★	Sandbanks

Durham

Darlington	★★★★	Europa Lodge **T**
Durham	★★★★	Royal County **MLT**
Tees-side Airport	★★★	St George

Essex

Basildon	★★★	Essex Centre **T MLT**
Brentwood	☆☆☆	Post House **T**
Harlow	★★★	Saxon Motor Inn **T MLT**
Marks Tey	☆☆☆	Marks Tey **T**
North Stifford	☆☆☆	Europa Lodge
Southend-on-Sea	☆☆☆	Airport Moat House **MLT**

Gloucestershire

Cheltenham	☆☆☆☆	Golden Valley **T**
	★★★★	Queens **T**
	★★★	Carlton **MLT**
Cirencester	★★★★	Kings Head **T MLT**
Newport	☆☆	Newport Towers

Hampshire

Ampfield	☆☆☆	Potters Heron
Basingstoke	★★★	Hampshire Moat House **MLT**
	☆☆☆	Ladbroke Mercury Motor Inn **T**
Brockenhurst	★★★	Balmer Lawn
Bursledon	☆☆☆	Solent
Farnborough	★★★	Queens
Hayling Island	☆☆☆☆	Post House **T**
Lyndhurst	★★★	Crown **MLT**
	★★★	Lyndhurst Park **T**
New Milton	❀★★★★★	Chewton Glen
Ower	☆☆☆	New Forest Lodge
Portsmouth	★★★	Portsmouth Centre **T MLT**
	★★★	Royal Beach
Southampton	★★★★	Polygon **T MLT**
	★★★	Dolphin **T**
	☆☆☆	Post House **T**
	★★★	Royal **T**
Winchester	★★★★	Wessex **T**

Hereford & Worcester

Broadway	★★★★	Lygon Arms **T MLT**
Bromsgrove	★★★	Perry Hall **MLT**
Droitwich	★★★★	Chateau Impney **T MLT**
	★★★	Worcestershire **T**
Hereford	★★★	Green Dragon **T MLT**
Malvern, Great	★★★	Abbey
Worcester	★★★	Giffard **T**

Hertfordshire

Boreham Wood	☆☆☆	Thatched Barn **MLT**
Hemel Hempstead	☆☆☆	Watermill **MLT**
Hitchin	★★★	Blakemore **T MLT**
Markyate	☆☆☆	Hertfordshire Moat House
Redbourn	☆☆☆	Aubrey Park
South Mimms	☆☆☆	South Mimms Crest Motel **T MLT**
Stevenage	☆☆☆	Grampian **T**
Ware	☆☆☆	Cannons Moat House **MLT**
Watford	☆☆☆	Caledonian

Humberside

Grimsby	☆☆☆☆	Humber Royal
Hull	★★★★	Royal Station
	★★★	Hull Centre **T MLT**

Kent

Canterbury	★★★	County **T**
Dunton Green	☆☆	Emma
Hollingbourne	★★★	Great Danes **T MLT**
Hythe	★★★★	Hotel Imperial **MLT**
Shorne	☆☆☆	Inn on the Lake
Tunbridge Wells	★★★	Spa **T MLT**

Lancashire

Blackburn	★★★	Saxon Inn **T MLT**
Blackpool	★★★	Savoy
	★★	Claremont
Burnley	☆☆☆	Burnley Crest Motel
Lytham St Annes	★★★★	Clifton Arms
	★★	Chadwick
	★★	Fernlea **T**
Preston	☆☆☆	Preston EuroCrest **T MLT**
	☆☆☆	Tickled Trout

Leicestershire

Location	Classification	Hotel
Leicester	☆☆☆☆	Holiday Inn **T**
	★★★	Leicester Centre **T MLT**
Loughborough	★★★	Kings Head

London Postal District

Location	Classification	Hotel
W1	★★★★★	Dorchester **T**
WC2	❁★★★★★	Savoy **T MLT**
SW1	❁★★★★★	Carlton Tower **T MLT**
W1	★★★★★	Churchill **T MLT**
W1	★★★★★	Grosvenor House **T MLT**
W1	★★★★★	Hilton **T MLT**
SW1	★★★★★	Hyde Park **T**
W1	★★★★★	Inn on the Park **T MLT**
W1	★★★★★	Inter-Continental **T MLT**
W1	★★★★★	May Fair **T MLT**
W8	★★★★★	Royal Garden **T MLT**
W1	★★★★	Selfridge **T MLT**
W1	★★★★	Athenaeum **T MLT**
W1	★★★★	Britannia **T MLT**
W1	★★★★	Browns **T MLT**
SW1	★★★★	Cavendish **T MLT**
WC2	★★★★	Charing Cross **T MLT**
W1	★★★★	Cumberland **T MLT**
W1	★★★★	Europa **T MLT**
SW7	★★★★	Gloucester **T MLT**
W2	★★★★	Great Western Royal **T MLT**
NW3	☆☆☆☆	Holiday Inn **T MLT**
SW1	☆☆☆☆	Holiday Inn Chelsea **T MLT**
WC1	☆☆☆☆	Imperial **T**
W8	★★★★	Kensington Close **T MLT**
W8	☆☆☆☆	Kensington Palace **T**
SW5	☆☆☆☆	London International **T MLT**
SW7	☆☆☆☆	London Penta **T MLT**
W1	★★★★	Park Lane **T MLT**
W1	★★★★	Piccadilly **T MLT**
W1	★★★★	Portman Inter-Continental
SW1	★★★★	Quaglino's
W1	☆☆☆☆	Regent Centre **T MLT**
W2	★★★★	Royal Lancaster **T MLT**
WC1	☆☆☆☆	Royal National **T MLT**
SW1	☆☆☆☆	Royal Westminster **T MLT**
WC1	★★★★	Russell **T MLT**
SW1	★★★★	St Ermins **T MLT**
E1	★★★★	Tower **T MLT**
WC2	★★★★	Waldorf **T MLT**
W1	★★★★	Westbury **T MLT**
SW3	★★★	Basil Street **T MLT**
SW5	★★★	Barkston **T MLT**
WC1	★★★	Bloomsbury Centre **T MLT**
W5	☆☆☆	Carnarvon **T**
EC1	☆☆☆	Central City
W2	☆☆☆	Central Park **T**
W9	★★★	Clarendon Court **T MLT**
W1	★★★	Clifton-Ford **T MLT**
W2	★★★	Coburg **T**
SW1	★★★	Eccleston
EC2	★★★	Great Eastern **T MLT**
WC1	★★★	Kingsley **T**
W8	☆☆☆	London Tara **T MLT**
W1	★★★	Mount Royal **T MLT**
W2	★★★	Park Court **T MLT**
SW7	★★★	Rembrandt **T MLT**
SW1	★★★	Royal Horseguards **T MLT**
W14	★★★	Royal Kensington **T MLT**
WC1	★★★	Royal Scot **T**

London Postal District continued

Location	Classification	Hotel
SW1	★★★	Rubens **T**
SW1	★★★	St James **T MLT**
WC2	★★★	Strand Palace **T**
WC1	★★★	Tavistock **T MLT**
W1	★★★	Washington **T MLT**
SW6	★★★	West Centre **T MLT**
NW1	❁★★★	White House **T MLT**
WC1	★★	Cora **T MLT**
SW7	★★	Eden **T MLT**
WC1	★★	Kenilworth **T MLT**
W1	★★	Mandeville **T MLT**
W1	★★	Mostyn **T MLT**

London, Greater

Location	Classification	Hotel
Bromley	★★★	Bromley Court **T MLT**
Enfield	★★★	Royal Chace **MLT**
Heathrow Airport	☆☆☆☆	Ariel **T**
	☆☆☆☆	Excelsior **T MLT**
	★★★★	Heathrow **T MLT**
	☆☆☆☆	Sheraton **T**
	★★★	Centre Airport **T MLT**
	★★★	Skyway **T MLT**
	☆☆	Arlington **MLT**
Hillingdon	☆☆☆	Master Brewer Motel
Hornchurch	☆☆☆	Ladbroke Mercury Motor Inn **T**
Sanderstead	★★★★	Selsdon Park **T**

Manchester, Greater

Location	Classification	Hotel
Altrincham	☆☆☆	Ashley **T MLT**
	☆☆☆	Cresta Court **T MLT**
Bolton	★★★	Pack Horse **MLT**
Bramhall	★★★	Pownall Arms **T MLT**
Bromley Cross	★★★	Last Drop **T MLT**
Manchester	★★★★★	Hotel Piccadilly **T MLT**
	★★★★	Grand **T MLT**
	❁★★★★	Midland **T**
	★★★★	Portland **T**
Manchester Airport	☆☆☆☆	Excelsior **T MLT**
	★★★	Valley Lodge **T**
Stockport	★★★	Alma Lodge **MLT**
	★★★	Belgrade **T MLT**

Merseyside

Location	Classification	Hotel
Kirkby	★★★	Golden Eagle **MLT**
Knowsley	☆☆☆	Liverpool Crest Motel
Liverpool	★★★★	Adelphi **T MLT**
	★★★★	Atlantic Tower **MLT**
Liverpool	☆☆☆☆	Holiday Inn **T MLT**
	★★★★	St George's **T MLT**
	★★★	Liverpool Centre **T MLT**
St Helens	★★★	Fleece
Southport	★★★★	Prince of Wales **T MLT**
	★★★	Royal Clifton **T MLT**

Midlands West

Location	Classification	Hotel
Barr, Great	☆☆☆	Post House **T**
Birmingham	★★★★	Albany **T MLT**
	★★★★	Grand **T MLT**
	☆☆☆☆	Holiday Inn **T MLT**
	★★★★	Midland **T MLT**
	★★★★	Plough & Harrow **T**
	☆☆☆☆	Strathallan **T**
	★★★	Birmingham Centre **T MLT**
	★★★	Royal Angus **T MLT**
Birmingham Airport	★★★★	Excelsior **T MLT**
Coventry	☆☆☆☆	Coventry EuroCrest **T MLT**
	★★★★	De Vere **T MLT**
	★★★★	Hotel Leofric **T MLT**
	☆☆☆	Novotel Coventry **T**
Solihull	★★★	George **MLT**
	★★★	St John's **T MLT**
Sutton Coldfield	★★★★	Penns Hall **MLT**
	★★★	Moor Hall **MLT**
Wolverhampton	★★★	Mount **MLT**
	★★★	Park Hall **MLT**

Norfolk		
Kings Lynn	★★★	Duke's Head **T**
Norwich	★★★	Maids Head **T**
	☆☆☆	Hotel Norwich **T MLT**
Yarmouth, Great	★★★	Carlton **T MLT**

Northamptonshire		
Crick	☆☆☆☆	Rugby Post House **T MLT**
Northampton	★★★	Saxon Inn **T MLT**
	★★★	Westone **MLT**
Sywell	☆	Sywell Airport Motel

Nottinghamshire		
Barnby Moor	★★★	Ye Olde Bell **T**
Nottingham	★★★★	Albany **T MLT**
	★★★★	Victoria **T MLT**

Oxfordshire		
Banbury	★★★★	Whately Hall **T MLT**
Oxford	★★★★	Randolph **T**
	★★★	Linton Lodge **MLT**
	☆☆☆	Oxford Europa Lodge **MLT**

Somerset		
Frome	☆☆☆	Mendip Lodge **MLT**
Street	☆☆☆	Wessex **MLT**

Staffordshire		
Haywood, Great	☆☆	Coach & Horses Motel **MLT**
Newcastle-under-Lyme	★★★	Clayton Lodge **MLT**
Stafford	☆☆☆	Tillington Hall **T MLT**
Stoke-on-Trent	★★★★	North Stafford **T MLT**

Suffolk		
Felixstowe	★★★★	Orwell Moat House

Surrey		
Cobham	☆☆☆	Seven Hills Motel **T**
Egham	☆☆☆☆	Runnymede **T MLT**
Weybridge	★★★	Oatlands Park **MLT**

Sussex, East		
Brighton	★★★★	Grand **T MLT**
	★★★	Old Ship **T MLT**
Eastbourne	★★★★★	Grand **T MLT**
	★★★★	Cavendish **T MLT**
	★★★★	Queen's **MLT**
	★★★	Burlington **T MLT**
	★★★	Lansdowne
	★★★	Mansion **T**
Hove	★★★★	Dudley **T**
Seaford	☆☆	Newhaven Ladbroke Mercury Motor **MLT**

Sussex, West		
Chichester	★★★	Dolphin & Anchor
East Grinstead	★★★	Ye Olde Felbridge **MLT**
Gatwick Airport	☆☆☆☆	Copthorne **T MLT**
	☆☆☆☆	Gatwick Park **T MLT**
	☆☆☆	Gatwick Hickmet **T MLT**
	★★★	George **T MLT**
Walberton	★★★	Avisford Park **MLT**
Worthing	★★★	Beach **MLT**
	★★★	Chatsworth
	★★★	Eardley
	★★★	Warnes

Tyne & Wear		
Gateshead	☆☆☆☆	Five Bridges **T MLT**
Newcastle-upon-Tyne		
	❋★★★★	Gosforth Park **T MLT**
	★★★★	Royal Station **T MLT**

Tyne & Wear continued		
	★★★	County **T MLT**
	★★★	Imperial
	☆☆☆	Swallow
Newcastle-upon-Tyne Airport	☆☆☆	Airport **MLT**
Seaton Burn	☆☆☆☆	Holiday Inn **T MLT**
Washington	☆☆☆	Post House **T MLT**

Warwickshire		
Brandon	★★★	Brandon Hall **T MLT**
Kenilworth	★★★★	De Montfort **MLT**
	★★★	Avonside **MLT**
Leamington Spa (Royal)	★★★★	Manor House **MLT**
Stratford upon Avon		
	★★★★	Hilton **T MLT**
	★★★★	Welcombe **T MLT**
	★★★	Alveston Manor **T**
	★★★	Falcon
Wishaw	★★★★	Belfry **MLT**

Wiltshire		
Swindon	☆☆☆	Wiltshire **T MLT**

Yorkshire, North		
Harrogate	★★★★	Majestic
	★★★★	Old Swan **T MLT**
	★★★	Cairn **T**
Leeming Bar	☆☆☆	Motel Leeming
Lumby	☆☆☆☆	Selby Fork Motor
York	★★★★	Royal Station **T**
	★★★★	Viking **T MLT**
	★★★	Chase
	☆☆☆	Post House **T MLT**

Yorkshire, South		
Doncaster	★★★	Earl of Doncaster **T**
Sheffield	★★★★	Grosvenor House **T MLT**
	★★★★	Hallam Tower **T MLT**

Yorkshire, West		
Bingley	★★★	Bankfield **MLT**
Bradford	☆☆☆☆	Norfolk Gardens **T**
	☆☆☆	Novotel Bradford **T MLT**
	★★★	Victoria **T MLT**
Bramhope	☆☆☆	Post House **T**
Huddersfield	★★★	Pennine President **T MLT**
Leeds	☆☆☆☆	Ladbroke Dragonara **T MLT**
	★★★★	Queens **T MLT**
	★★★	Merrion **T MLT**
	★★★	Metropole **T**
	☆☆☆	Windmill **MLT**
Wakefield	☆☆☆☆	Post House **T MLT**
Wetherby	☆☆☆	Wetherby Turnpike Motor Inn

Channel Islands

Guernsey		
St Martin	★★★	Ronnie Ronalde's St Martin's Hotel
	★★★	St Margarets Lodge **T MLT**
St Peter Port	★★★★	Duke of Richmond **T MLT**
	★★★★	Old Government House **T MLT**
	★★★	Royal **T MLT**

Jersey

Archirondel	★★	Les Arches **T**
St Brelade	★★★★	Atlantic **T**
	★★★★	Hotel l'Horizon **T**
St Helier	★★★	Ommaroo **T MLT**
	★★	Pomme d'Or **T MLT**
St Peter	★★★★	Mermaid **T**

Wales

Dyfed

Carmarthen	★★★	Ivy Bush Royal **T**
Gwbert-on-Sea	★★★	Cliff **T**
Llandissilio	★★	Nantyffin Motel **MLT**
Llanelli	★★★	Stradey Park **T**

Glamorgan, South

Cardiff	★★★★	Angel **T MLT**
	★★★	Cardiff Centre **T MLT**

Glamorgan, West

Port Talbot	☆☆☆	Executive
Swansea	☆☆☆☆	Dragon **T MLT**
	★★★	Dolphin

Gwynedd

Caernarfon	★★★	Royal
Llandudno	★★★	Imperial **MLT**
	★★★	Marine **T**

Scotland

Borders

Peebles	★★★	Peebles Hydro **MLT**

Central

Falkirk	☆☆☆	Park

Dumfries & Galloway

Stranraer	★★★	North West Castle

Fife

St Andrews	★★★★	Old Course **T MLT**

Grampian

Aberdeen	☆☆☆☆	Holiday Inn **T MLT**
	☆☆☆	Royal Darroch **T MLT**
Dyce	☆☆☆	Skean Dhu **T**
Elgin	☆☆☆	Eight Acres
Ellon	☆☆☆	Ellon Ladbroke Mercury Motor Inn **T**

Grampian continued

Westhill	☆☆☆	Westhill Inn

Highland

Aviemore	☆☆☆☆	Coylumbridge **T MLT**
	☆☆☆☆	Strathspey **T**
	☆☆☆	Freedom Inn
	☆☆☆	Post House **MLT**
Inverness	☆☆☆	Caledonian **T MLT**
	☆☆☆	Ladbroke Mercury Motor Inn **T**
	★★	Drumossie
Ullapool	☆☆☆	Ladbroke Mercury Motor Inn
Wick	★★	Ladbroke Mercury Motor Inn

Lothian

Bathgate	☆☆☆	Golden Circle **T**
Dunbar	★★★	Roxburghe **MLT**
Edinburgh	★★★★	Caledonian **T MLT**
	★★★★	George **T MLT**
	★★★★	North British **T MLT**
	☆☆☆☆	Royal Scot **T MLT**
	★★★	Carlton **MLT**
	☆☆☆	Edinburgh EuroCrest **T**
	☆☆☆	King James **T**
	☆☆☆	Post House **T MLT**
	☆☆	Commodore
Queensferry (South)	☆☆☆	Forth Bridges Lodge

Strathclyde

Ayr	☆☆☆	Caledonian **T MLT**
	★★★	Station **MLT**
East Kilbride	☆☆☆☆	Bruce **T MLT**
Erskine	☆☆☆☆	Glasgow EuroCrest **T MLT**
Glasgow	★★★	Bellahouston **T**
	☆☆☆	Glasgow Centre **T MLT**
	☆☆☆	Ingram **MLT**
	★★★	North British **T**
	★★★	Royal Stuart **T MLT**
Glasgow Airport	★★★★	Excelsior **T**
	☆☆☆☆	Normandy **T**
	★★★	Glynhill
Gourock	☆☆☆	Gantock **MLT**
Kilmarnock	☆☆☆	Howard Park
Oban	★★★	Great Western **MLT**
Turnberry	★★★★	Turnberry **T**

Tayside

Auchterarder	★★★★★	Gleneagles **T MLT**
Perth	☆☆☆	City Mills
Pitlochry	★★★	Atholl Palace **T**

Hotels with four-poster beds

England

Avon

Bath	★★★★	Royal Crescent 2 rooms
	★★★	Priory 2 rooms
	★★★	Royal York 1 room
Marksbury	⊛★★★ 🏠	Hunstrete House 1 room
Petty France	★★ 🏠	Petty France 1 room
Rangeworthy	⊕ 🏠	Rangeworthy Court 1 room

Bedfordshire

Dunstable	★★★	Old Palace Lodge 2 rooms

Berkshire

Elcot	★★	Elcot Park 2 rooms
Hungerford	★★	Bear 2 rooms

Buckinghamshire

Aston Clinton	⊛★★★	Bell 1 room
Gerrards Cross	★★★	Bull 1 room

Cambridgeshire

Six Mile Bottom	★★★ 🏠	Swynford Paddocks 1 room
Wansford	★★	Haycock 3 rooms

Cheshire

Bucklow Hill	☆☆☆	Swan Arms 4 rooms
Chester	★★★	Mollington Banastre 3 rooms

ornwall

odinnick	★	Old Ferry Inn 1 room
odmin	★★	Castle Hill House 1 room
lmouth	★★★	Gyllyndune 3 rooms
owey	★★★	Fowey 1 room
	★★	Penlee 1 room
amorna Cove	★★★⌂	Lamorna Cove 1 room
anreath	★★	Punch Bowl Inn 5 rooms
aunceston	★★	Eagle House 1 room
skeard	★★	Webbs 1 room
lousehole	★	Old Coastguard 1 room
ntagel	★	Atlantic View 1 room

umbria

arbon	★★	Barbon Inn 1 room
arlisle	★★★	Cumbrian 2 rooms
ockermouth	★★	Wordsworth 2 rooms
augh	★★	String of Horses 2 rooms
rasmere	★★★	Prince of Wales 1 room
Vatermillock	★★★	Leeming House 1 room
Vigton	★★	Greenhill Mansion 2 rooms
Vindermere	★★★	Wild Boar 1 room
	❀❀★★	Miller Howe 1 room
	★★	Royal 1 room

erbyshire

irk Langley	★★	Meynell House 1 room
Matlock	★★★⌂	Riber Hall 8 rooms
	★	High Tor 4 rooms

evon

shburton	☆☆	Dartmoor Motel 5 rooms
radworthy	★★	Lake Villa 3 rooms
rixham	★★	Quayside 1 room
hagford	★★	Three Crowns 2 rooms
artmouth	★★	Royal Castle 2 rooms
xeter	★★⌂	Trood 1 room
latherleigh	★	George 3 rooms
leddon's Mouth	★★⌂	Heddon's Gate 1 room
lorns Cross	★★⌂	Foxdown Manor 1 room
	★★	Hoops Inn 1 room
Kingsbridge	★★	Kings Arms 11 rooms
ynton	★★	Crown 4 rooms
	★	Rockvale 1 room
	★	Seawood 4 rooms
Mortehoe	★	Glenhaven 3 rooms
Voody Bay	★★	Woody Bay 2 rooms

Dorset

yme Regis	★★	Royal Lion 1 room
Piddletrenthide	★★	Old Bakehouse 3 rooms
Shaftesbury	★★★	Royal Chase 1 room

County Durham

Chester-le-Street	★★★	Lumley Castle 4 rooms
Greta Bridge	★★	Morritt Arms 2 rooms

Essex

Brentwood	★★★★	Brentwood Moat House 2 rooms
Brightlingsea	★★	Brightlingsea Hall 1 room
Colchester	★★	Kings Ford Park 1 room
	★★	Rose & Crown 1 room

Gloucestershire

Cheltenham	★★★	De la Bere 5 rooms
	★★⌂	Greenway 1 room
Chipping Campden	★★	Noel Arms 2 rooms
Cirencester	★★★★	Kings Head 2 rooms
Coleford	★★	Speech House 3 rooms
	★⌂	Lambsquay 1 room
Moreton-in-Marsh	★★★	Manor House 1 room
Stow-on-the-Wold	★★	Royalist 1 room
Tetbury	❀★★	Close 2 rooms
Tewkesbury	★★	Bell 2 rooms
Upper Slaughter	★★★⌂	Lords of the Manor 1 room

Hampshire

Alresford	★★	Bell 2 rooms
Beaulieu	★★★	Montague Arms 6 rooms
Burley	★★★⌂	Burley Manor 1 room
Lyndhurst	★★★	Lyndhurst Park 4 rooms
	★★★	Crown 1 room
Selborne	★	Queens 1 room
Southampton	★★	Star 1 room
Winchester	★★★	Royal 1 room

Hereford & Worcester

Abberley	★★★⌂	Elms 1 room
Broadway	★★★★	Lygon Arms 3 rooms
	★★★	Dormy House 1 room
Hereford	★★	Litchfield Lodge 1 room
Malvern Wells	❀★★★⌂	Cottage in the Wood 1 room
Pencraig	★★⌂	Pencraig Court 1 room
Ross-on-Wye	★★★	Chase 3 rooms
	★	Rosswyn 3 rooms

Hertfordshire

Harpenden	★★★★	Harpenden Moat House 1 room
Hitchin	★★	Sun 1 room
St Albans	★★★	St Michael's Manor 1 room

Humberside

Laceby	★★	Oaklands Hotel & Country Club 1 room
Little Weighton	★★★⌂	Rowley Manor 2 rooms

Isle of Wight

St Lawrence	❀	Rocklands 1 room
Ventnor	❀★★⌂	Peacock Vane 2 rooms

Kent

Canterbury	★★	Falstaff 1 room
Hythe	★★★★	Hotel Imperial 1 room
Maidstone	★★	Boxley 4 rooms
Tunbridge Wells (Royal)	★★	Royal Wells Inn 2 rooms
	★★	Wellington 1 room

Lancashire

Lytham St Annes	★★	Chadwick 1 room

Leicestershire

Castle Donington	★★	Donington Manor 2 rooms
Uppingham	★★★	Falcon 1 room

Lincolnshire

Stamford	★★★	George 1 room

London Postal District

W9	★★★	Clarendon Court 2 rooms
WC1	★★★	Royal Scot 8 rooms

London, Greater

Croydon	(ap)	Briarley 1 room
Enfield	★★★	Royal Chace 6 rooms
Hadley Wood	★★★★	West Lodge Park 2 rooms
Harrow Weald	★★★	Grims Dyke Country 1 room

Manchester, Greater

Bromley Cross	★★★	Last Drop 2 rooms

Midlands, West

Knowle	★★★⌂	Chadwick Manor 1 room
Walsall	★★★	Barons Court 11 rooms

Norfolk

Norwich	★★★	Maids Head 1 room

Northamptonshire

Northampton	★★	Angel 1 room

Northumberland

Cornhill-on-Tweed	★★★⌂	Tillmouth Park 1 room
Rochester	★	Redesdale Arms 3 rooms
Seahouses	★	Beach House 1 room

Nottinghamshire

Nottingham	★★★	George 1 room

Oxfordshire

Burford	★★	Bull 4 rooms
	★★	Golden Ball 2 rooms
Chadlington	★	Chadlington House 1 room
Chipping Norton	★★	White Hart 1 room
Clanfield	★★	Plough 1 room
Dorchester-on-Thames	★★	White Hart 2 rooms
Henley-on-Thames	★★★	Red Lion 1 room
Horton-cum-Studley	★★★⌂	Studley Priory 2 rooms
Milton Common	★★	Belfry 1 room
Moulsford	★	Beetle & Wedge 1 room
Wallingford	★★	Shillingford Bridge 1 room
Weston-on-the-Green	★★★	Weston Manor 2 rooms

Salop

Bridgnorth	★★	Parlors Hall 1 room
Ludlow	★★★	Feathers 6 rooms

Somerset

Castle Cary	★★	George 1 room
Dunster	★★★	Luttrell Arms 1 room
Holford	★★⌂	Alfoxton Park 5 rooms
Somerton	★★★	Red Lion 1 room
Taunton	★★★	Castle 5 rooms
Wells	★★★	Crown 4 rooms
	★★★	Swan 4 rooms
Withypool	★⌂	Wester Close 1 room

Staffordshire

Tutbury	★★	Ye Olde Dog & Partridge 2 rooms

Suffolk

Beccles	★★	Waveney House 1 room
Bury St Edmunds	★★★	Angel 4 rooms
Clare	★★	Bell 4 rooms
Harlesdon	★★	Swan 1 room
Ipswich	★★	Great White Horse 1 room
Woodbridge	★★★⌂	Seckford Hall 3 rooms

Surrey

Egham	★★★★	Great Fosters 3 room
Haslemere	★★★	Lythe Hill 1 room
Weybridge	★★★	Oatlands Park 1 room

Sussex, East

Brighton	★★★★	Grand 1 room
	★★★	Old Ship 1 room
Horsham	★★	Ye Olde King's Head 1 room
Lewes	★★★	Shelleys 2 rooms
Northiam	★	Hayes 1 room
Rottingdean	★★	White Horse 1 room

Sussex, West

East Grinstead	❁★★★⌂	Gravetye Manor 1 room
Midhurst	★★★	Spread Eagle 2 rooms
	★★	Angel 2 rooms
West Chillington	★★	Roundabout 2 rooms

Tyne & Wear

Newcastle-upon-Tyne	❁★★★★	Gosforth Park 1 room

Warwickshire

Billesley	★★★⌂	Billesley Manor 4 rooms
Kenilworth	★★	Clarendon House 2 rooms
Leamington Spa (Royal)	❁★★⌂	Mallory Court 1 room
	★★	Falstaff 1 room
Stratford-upon-Avon	★★	Grosvenor House 1 room
	★★⌂	Haytor 1 room
Wishaw	★★★★	Belfry 3 rooms

Wiltshire

Castle Combe	★★★⌂	Manor House 2 rooms
Hindon	★	Lamb at Hindon 1 room
Mere	★★	Old Ship 1 room
Salisbury	★★★	Rose and Crown 1 room
	★★	Kings Arms 1 room
	★★	Red Lion 2 rooms
Warminster	★★★⌂	Bishopstrow House 3 rooms

Yorkshire, North

Hovingham	★★	Worsley Arms 1 room
Whitwell-on-the-Hill	★★⌂	Whitwell Hall 1 room

Yorkshire, South

Rossington	★★	Mount Pleasant 1 room
Sheffield	★★★	Mosborough Hall 4 rooms

Yorkshire, West

Wentbridge	★★★⌂	Wentbridge House 1 room

Wales

Clwyd

Chirk	★★	Hand 1 room
Redbrook	★★	Redbrook Hunting Lodge 1 room
St Asaph	★★	Oriel House 1 room

Dyfed

Gwbert-on-Sea	★★★	Cliff 2 rooms
Haverfordwest	★★	Pembroke House 5 rooms
Llandeilo	★★	Cawdor Arms 2 rooms
Llandovery	★⌂	Picton Court 1 room

Gwent

Monmouth	★★	Kings Head 1 room
Usk	★★	Three Salmons 2 rooms

Gwynedd

Beaumaris	★★	Henllys Hall 8 rooms
Betws-y-Coed	★★	Royal Oak 8 rooms
Dolgellau	★★★	Golden Lion Royal 2 rooms
Deganwy	★★	Bryn Cregin 1 room
Dolwyddelen	★★	Elen's Castle 1 room
Llandudno	★★★	Empire 3 rooms

Powys

Brecon	★	Lansdowne 2 rooms

Scotland

Borders

Chirnside	★★	Chirnside 1 room
Dryburgh	★★★	Dryburgh Abbey 3 rooms
Ettrick Bridge	★★	Ettrick Shaws Lodge 1 room
St Boswells	★★	Buccleuch Arms 1 room

Central

Callander	★★★	Roman Camp 1 room
Killin	★	Tignabruaich 1 room
Strathblane	★★	Kirkhouse Inn 1 room

Dumfries & Galloway

Auchencairn	★★★	Balcary Bay 2 rooms
Gretna Green	★★	Gretna Hall 1 room

Fife

Letham	★★★	Fernie Castle 1 room

Grampian

Aberdeen	★★★	Caledonian 1 room
Banchory	★★★	Banchory Lodge 3 rooms
Banff	★★	County 2 rooms
Huntly	★★	Castle 1 room
Rothes	★★★	Rothes Glen 1 room

Highland

Drumnadrochit	★★	Polmaily House 1 room
Fort Augustus	★★	Inchnacardoch Lodge 1 room
Grantown-on-Spey	★★★	Grant Arms 1 room
Inverness	❀ ★★	Dunian Park 1 room
Isle Ornsay, Isle of Skye	★	Tigh-Osda Eilean Iarmain 2 rooms
Kincraig	Ⓟ	Suie 3 rooms
Nairn	★★	Clifton 1 room

Lothian

Ratho	★★	Craigpark House 1 room
Uphall	★★★	Houstoun House 7 rooms

Strathclyde

Ayr	★★★	Belleisle 1 room
Langbank	★★★★	Gleddoch House 1 room
Largs	★★★	Marine & Curlinghall 1 room
Rosebank	★★★	Popinjay 1 room
Symington	★★	Wyndales House 1 room

Tayside

Comrie	★★	Royal 1 room
Dundee	☆☆☆	Swallow 2 rooms
Edzell	★★	Panmure Arms 1 room

Hotels with special facilities for children

(For details of the specific facilities required see 'About this Guide' page 23)

England

Bedfordshire

Woburn	★★★	Bedford Arms

Berkshire

Elcot	★★	Elcot Park

Cheshire

Backford Cross	☆☆☆	Wirral Ladbroke Mercury Motor Inn
Chester	★★★	Mollington Banastre

Cornwall

Boscastle	★	Valency House
Bude	★★★	Grenville
Camelford	★★	Lanteglos Farmhouse
Crafthole	Ⓟ	Whitstand
Downderry	★★	Wide Sea
Falmouth	★★★	Bay
	★★★	St Michael's
	★	Somerdale
Fowey	★★★	Fowey
Lizard	★★	Lizard Polbrean
	★★	Polbrean
Looe	★★★	Hannafore Point
	★★	Klymiarven
Mullion	★★★	Poldhu
	★★★	Polurrian
	★★	Mullion Cove
Newquay	★★★	Atlantic
	★★★	Bay
	★★★	Edgcumbe
	★★★	Hotel Riviera
	★★★	St Rumon's
	★★★	Trebarwith
	★★★	Windsor
	★★	Barrowfield
	★★	Beachcroft
	★★	Great Western
	★	Sandy Lodge
Perranarworthal	★★	Goonrea
Port Isaac	★★	St Andrews
Praa Sands	★★★	Lesceave Cliff
	★★	Prah Sands
Rock	★★	Roscarnon House
St Austell	★★★	Porth Avallen
St Ives	★★★★	Tregenna Castle
	★★★	Garrack
	★★★	Porthminster

Cornwall continued

Town	Rating	Hotel
St Ives	★★	Carbis Bay
	★★	Hendra's
	★★	Karenzo
Tintagel	★	Atlantic View
	★	El Condado
Trebetherwick	★★	St Moritz
Trevone	★	Trevone Bay
Treyarnon Bay	★★	Waterbeach
Watergate Bay	★	Clevelands

Cumbria

Town	Rating	Hotel
Ambleside	★★★	Waterhead
Bassenthwaite	★★	Overwater
Borrowdale	★★★★	Lodore Swiss
	★★★	Mary Mount
Faugh	★★	String of Horses Inn
Grange-over-Sands	★★	Netherwood
Keswick	★	Lairbeck
Langdale, Great	★★★	Langdales
Penrith	★★	Round Thorn
Ravenstonedale	★★	Black Swan
Silloth	★★★	Skinburness
Whitehaven	★★	Chase
Wigton	★★★	Burn How Motel
	★★	Greenhill Mansions
Windermere	★	Ravensworth

Derbyshire

Town	Rating	Hotel
Long Eaton	☆☆☆	Novotel Nottingham
Buxton	★★	Lee Wood
Hartington	★	Charles Cotton
Newhaven	★	Newhaven

Devon

Town	Rating	Hotel
Beer	★★	Dolphin
Berry Pomeroy	★	Loventor Manor
Bovey Tracey	★★	Prestbury
	★	Redacre
Buckfastleigh	★	Bossell House
Chagford	★★★	Mill End
Combe Martin	★★★	Higher Leigh
Crockernford	★	Bay Tree Motel
Dawlish	★★★	Langstone Cliff
	★★	Charlton House
Exmouth	★★★	Royal Beacon
Hawkchurch	★★★	Fairwater Head
Hope Cove	★★	Cottage
	★★	Graystone
Ilfracombe	★★	Mount
	★★	St Helier
Lynmouth	★★	Bath
Moretonhampstead	★★★★	Manor House
Mortehoe	★★★	Rockham Bay
Newton Ferrers	★★	Court House
Ottery St Mary	★★★	Salston
Paignton	★★★	Redcliffe
Salcombe	★★★	Salcombe
	★★	Grafton Towers
	★★	South Sands
	★	Knowle
	★	Sunny Cliff
Saunton	★★★	Saunton Sands
Sidcot	★	Sidcot
Sidmouth	★★★★	Victoria
Stoke Gabriel	★★★	Gabriel Court
Teignmouth	★★	London
Torcross	★★	Torcross
Torquay	★★★★	New Grand
	★★★★	Osborne
	★★★★	Palace
	★★★	Corbyn Head
	★★★	Gleneagles
	★★★	Homes
	★★★	Kistor
	★★★	Lincombe Hall
	★★★	Livermead Cliff
	★★★	Livermead House
	★★★	Rainbow House

Devon continued

Town	Rating	Hotel
Torquay	★★★	Toorak
	★★	Coppice
	★★	Nethway
	★	Rock Walk
Woolacombe	★★★	Narracott Grand
	★★★	Woolacombe Bay
	★★	Rathleigh
	★	Headlands

Dorset

Town	Rating	Hotel
Bournemouth	★★★★★	Royal Bath
	★★★★	Highcliff
	★★★★	Marsham Court
	★★★	Anglo-Swiss
	★★★	Broughty Ferry Children's
	★★★	Burley Court
	★★★	Chesterwood
	★★★	Chine
	★★★	Cliff End
	★★★	Durlston Court
	★★★	Heathlands
	★★★	Miramar
	★★★	Pavilion
	★★★	Savoy
	★★★	Wessex
	★★	Durley Hall
	★★	Hinton Firs
	★★	Tralee
	★	Tree Tops
Charmouth	★★	Fern Hill
	★	Sea Horse
Ferndown	★★★★	Dormy
Fleet	★★	Moonfleet Manor
Lyme Regis	★	Tudor House
Milton-on-Stour	★★★	Milton Lodge
Poole	★★★	Sandbanks
Portland	★★	Portland Heights
Sherborne	★★	Eastbury
Swanage	★★★	Corrie
	★★★	Grosvenor
	(ap)	York
Weymouth	★★★	Ingleton
	★★	Streamside

Durham

Town	Rating	Hotel
Durham	★★★	Bowburn Hall

Essex

Town	Rating	Hotel
Brentwood	★★★★	Brentwood Moat House
Frinton-on-Sea	★	Rock
Southend-on-Sea	★	Roslin

Gloucestershire

Town	Rating	Hotel
Cheltenham	★★★	De la Bere
	★★★	Wyastone
Gloucester	★★★	Tara
Moreton-in-Marsh	★★★	Manor House
Stinchcombe	★★	Stinchcombe Manor
Stow-on-the-Wold	★★	Fosse Manor
Tewkesbury	★★	Bell
Westonbirt	★★★	Hare and Hounds

Hampshire

Town	Rating	Hotel
Brockenhurst	★★★	Balmer Lawn
	★★★	Carey's Manor Motor
	★★	Watersplash
Burley	★★	Moorhill House
Fleet	★★★	Lismoyne
Fordingbridge	★★	Ashburn
Lymington	★★★	Passford House
Stratfield Turgis	★★	Wellington Arms
Woodlands	★★	Busketts Lawn

Hereford & Worcester

Town	Rating	Hotel
Brockhampton	★★	Brockhampton Court
How Caple	★★	How Caple Grange
Ross-on-Wye	★★★	Pengethley
	★★★	Wye

ertfordshire
oreham Wood ☆☆☆ Thatched Barn

umberside
riffield, Great ★★ Wold House
illerby ☆☆☆ Willerby Manor

le of Wight
eshwater ★★★ Farringford
entnor ★★ Metropole
armouth ★★ George

ent
olkestone ★★★★ Burlington
ythe ★★★★ Hotel Imperial
★ Swan
largate ★★ Walpole Bay
ew Romney ★★★ Dormy House
Broadacre
amsgate ★★ Court Stairs & Country Club
unbridge Wells
Royal) ★★★ Spa
Vestgate-on-Sea ★★ Ivyside

ancashire
ytham St Annes ★★ Chadwick
★★ St Ives
★ Lindum

incolnshire
kegness ★★ County
tamford ★★★ George
etford ★ White Hart

ondon, Greater
Bickley ★★ Bickley Manor
Heathrow Airport ☆☆☆☆ Holiday Inn
Hornchurch ☆☆☆ Ladbroke Mercury Motor Inn

Manchester, Greater
Altrincham ★★★ Woodlands
Bramhall ★★★ Pownall Arms
Bromley Cross ★★ Last Drop
Stockport ★ Acton Court

Midlands, West
Coventry ☆☆☆ Novotel Coventry
Wolverhampton ★★★ Mount
★★★ Park Hall

Norfolk
Cromer ★★★ Colne House
King's Lynn ★ Stuart House
Mundesley-on-Sea ★★★ Continental
Overstrand ★ Overstrand Court
Yarmouth, Great ★★ Cliff
★★ Imperial

Northamptonshire
Marston Trussell ★★ Sun Inn
Rushton ★ Westward

Northumberland
Cornhill-on-Tweed ★★★★ Tilmouth Park
Rothbury ★★ Coquet Vale
Seahouses ★ Olde Ship
Wooler ★★ Tancarville Arms

Oxfordshire
Aston Rowfant ★★ Lambert Arms

Salop
Church Stretton ★★ Stretton Hall
Shifnal ★★★ Park House
Weston ★★ Hawkestone Park

Scilly (Isles of)
Old Grimsby ★★★ The Island

Somerset
Wellington ★★ Beam Bridge
Yeovil ★ Preston

Staffordshire
Haywood, Great ☆☆ Coach & Horses

Suffolk
Felixstowe ★★★★ Orwell Moat house
Ipswich ★★★ Belstead Brook
Walberswick ★★ Anchor

Surrey
Bagshot ★★★★ Pennyhill Park
Weybridge ★★★ Oatlands Park

Sussex, East
Cooden Beach ★★★ Cooden Beach
Cuckfield ★★ Hilton Park
Eastbourne ★★★★★ Grand
★★★★ Cavendish
★★★★ Queen's
★★★ Burlington
Forest Row ★★★ Roebuck
Hove ★★★ Courtlands
★★ St Catherine's Lodge
Mayfield ★★ Middle House

Sussex, West
Arundel ★★★ Norfolk Arms
Bognor Regis ★★ Clarehaven
★ Black Mill House
Climping ★★★ Baliffscourt
East Grinstead ★★★ Ye Olde Felbridge
Littlehampton ★★★ Beach
Worthing ★★★ Warnes

Tyne & Wear
Newcastle-upon-Tyne ★★★★ Gosforth Park

Warwickshire
Kenilworth ★★★ Avonside
Nuneaton ★★ Griff House
Southam ★★ Stoneythorpe

Wiltshire
Swindon ★★★ Blunsdon House

Yorkshire, North
Lastingham ★★ Lastingham Grange
Lumby ☆☆☆☆ Selby Fork Motor
Ravenscar ★★ Raven Hall
Robin Hood's Bay ★ Victoria
Scarborough ★★ Esplanade
★★ Southlands
York ★ Town Hills

Yorkshire, South
Sheffield ★★ Roslyn Court
★★ Rutland

Yorkshire, West
Wakefield ★★ Stoneleigh

Channel Islands

Guernsey
Câtel ★★ Hotel de Beauvoir
St Martin ★★★ Green Acres
★★★ Ronnie Ronalde's St Martin's Hotel
St Peter Port ★★★ Royal

Jersey

Archirondel	★★	Les Arches
Grouville Bay	★★	Beausite
St Helier	★★★	Ommaroo

Wales

Clwyd

Llangollen	★★★	Hand
Llanrhaedr	★★★	Bryn Morfydd

Dyfed

Fishguard	★	Manor House
Gwbert-on-Sea	★★★	Cliff
Milton	★	Milton Manor
Newcastle Emlyn	★★	Emlyn Arms
Pembroke Dock	★★	Commodore
St Davids	★★★	Warpool Court
	★★★	Whitesands Bay
Tenby	★★	Fourcroft

Glamorgan, West

Langland Bay	★★	Langland Court
Neath	★★	Cimla Court Motel
Port Talbot	☆☆☆	Executive

Gwent

Newport	☆☆☆	Gateway Motor

Gwynedd

Beaumaris	★★	Henllys Hall
Betws-y-Coed	★★	Craig-y-Dderwen Country House
	☆☆	Waterloo House
Llanbedrog	★★	Bryn Derwen
Llanberis	★★	Galt-y-Glyn
Llandudno	★★★	Imperial
	★★	Ormescliffe
Nefyn	⊕	Caeau Capel
Tywyn	★★	Corbett Arms

Powys

Libanus	☆☆	Mountains
Llandrindod Wells	★★	Hotel Commodore
Rhayader	★★	Elan Valley

Scotland

Borders

Dryburgh	★★★	Dryburgh Abbey
Kelso	★	Queens Head
Peebles	★★★	Peebles Hydro
	★	Kingsmuir

Central

Killin	★	Tignabruaich
Strathyre	★	Ben Sheann

Dumfries & Galloway

Beattock	★★	Auchen Castle
Crocketford	★★	Galloway Arms
Gatehouse of Fleet	★★★	Murray Arms
Johnstone Bridge	★★	Dinwoodie Lodge
Kirkcolm	★★	Knocknassie House
Moniaive	★	Craigdarroch Arms
Portpatrick	★★	Fernhill
	★★	Portpatrick
Rockcliffe	★★★	Barons Craig

Fife

Lundin Links	★	Beach
St Andrews	★★★★	Old Court

Grampian

Aberlour	★★	Dowans
Aboyne	★★	Huntley Arms
Ballater	★★	Craigard
Banchory	★★★	Raemoir
Cullen	★★	Cullen Bay
Elgin	★★	Laichmoray
	★	St Leonards
Monymusk	★★	Grant Arms
Stonehaven	☆☆☆	Commodore

Highland

Aviemore	☆☆☆☆	Strathspey
Boat of Garten	★★	Craigard
Brora	★★	Royal Marine
Dornoch	★★	Burghfield House
Dunnet	★★	Northern Sands
Glenborrodale	★★	Clan Morrison
Isle of Ornsay	★★	Kinloch Lodge
Letterfinlay	★★	Letterfinlay Lodge
Morar	★★	Morar
Muir of Ord	★★	Ord Arms
Nairn	★★★★	Golf View
Nethy Bridge	★★★	Nethy Bridge
Newtonmore	★★	Macdonald Lodge
	★★	Mains
Ullapool	★★★	Royal

Lothian

Aberlady	★★	Kispindle House
East Linton	★★★	Harvesters
Gullane	★★	Bissets

Strathclyde

Arduaine	★★★	Loch Melfort
Ayr	★★★	Savoy Park
Barrhead	★★	Dalmeny Park
Brodick, Isle of Arran	★★★	Douglas
Connel	★★	Lochnell Arms
Hollybush	★★★	Hollybush House
Kilcreggan	★★	Kilcreggan
Kirkmichael	★★	Log Cabin
Rothesay, Isle of Bute	★★★	Glenburn
Tarbet, Loch Fyne	★★★	Stonefield Castle
Tobermory, Isle of Mull	★★★	Western Isles
Troon	★★★	Sun Court
Whiting Bay, Isle of Arran	★★	Whiting Bay

Tayside

Almondbank	★★★	Huntingtower
Fearnan	★	Tigh-an-Loan
Killiecrankie	★★	Killiecrankie
Kinross	★★★	Green
	★	Kirklands
St Fillans	★★★	Four Seasons

Western Isles

Sheildinish, Isle of Lewis	★	Claitair